VISUAL BASIC
Programmer's Library

By Christopher J. Bockmann,
Lars Klander, and Lingyan Tang

JAMSA
P·R·E·S·S
...a computer user's best friend®

VISUAL BASIC PROGRAMMER'S LIBRARY

Published by

Jamsa Press
2975 S. Rainbow Blvd., Suite I
Las Vegas, NV 89102
U.S.A.

http://www.jamsa.com

For information about the translation or distribution of any Jamsa Press book, please write to Jamsa Press at the address listed above.

Visual Basic Programmer's Library

Copyright © 1998 by Jamsa Press. All rights reserved. Except as permitted under the Copyright Act of 1976, no part of this publication may be reproduced or distributed in any format or by any means, or stored in a database or retrieval system, without the prior written permission of Jamsa Press.

Printed in the United States of America.
98765432

ISBN 1-884133-57-6

Publisher	**Technical Advisor**	**Director of Publishing Operations**
Debbie Jamsa	Phil Schmauder	Janet Lawrie
Content Manager	**Cover Photograph**	**Cover Design**
Dorothy Oppenheimer	O'Gara/Bissell	Marianne Helm
		James Rehrauer
Composition	**Illustrators**	**Copy Editors**
Eugene Marks	Eugene Marks	Ann Edwards
James Rehrauer	James Rehrauer	Dorothy Oppenheimer
Nelson Yee	Nelson Yee	Renée Wesberry
Proofers	**Technical Editor**	**Indexer**
Rosemary Pasco	Kris Jamsa, Ph.D.	John Bianchi
Jeanne K. Smith		

This book identifies product names and services known to be trademarks or registered trademarks of their respective companies. They are used throughout this book in an editorial fashion only. In addition, terms suspected of being trademarks or service marks have been appropriately capitalized. Jamsa Press cannot attest to the accuracy of this information. Use of a term in this book should not be regarded as affecting the validity of any trademark or service mark.

The information and material contained in this book are provided "as is," without warranty of any kind, express or implied, including, without limitation, any warranty concerning the accuracy, adequacy, or completeness of such information or material or the results to be obtained from using such information or material. Neither Jamsa Press nor the author shall be responsible for any claims attributable to errors, omissions, or other inaccuracies in the information or material contained in this book, and in no event shall Jamsa Press or the author be liable for direct, indirect, special, incidental, or consequential damages arising out of the use of such information or material.

This publication is designed to provide accurate and authoritative information in regard to the subject matter covered. It is sold with the understanding that the publisher is not engaged in rendering professional service or endorsing particular products or services. If legal advice or other expert assistance is required, the services of a competent professional should be sought.

Jamsa Press is a wholly-owned subsidiary of Gulf Publishing Company:

Gulf Publishing Company
Book Division
P.O. Box 2608
Houston, TX 77252-2608
U.S.A.

http://www.gulfpub.com

III

To Brett: No matter how many times I say it, the fact remains: I could not do anything without you. Thank you for bringing real meaning into my life.

—Lars Klander

To my husband, Mao, my son, William, my daughter, Sharon, and my mom and dad. Thank you for your encouragement and love.

—Lingyan Tang

IV

CONTENTS AT A GLANCE

Table of Contents

VIII

X

Chapter 1

Introduction to Visual Basic

Many programmers began to program using the Beginner's All-Symbolic Instruction Code (BASIC) programming language. Visual Basic is a derivation of and an expansion of early BASIC. Microsoft calls it "Visual" because you can design programs with *forms* that include visual elements, such as buttons and display boxes, and other visual components, called *controls*. Visual Basic includes numerous *controls* (objects that you use to create an easy way for users to interact with your projects) that let the user get data, print data, write data, display pictures, and so on. Controls provide you, the programmer, with various properties (control characteristics), methods (control actions), and events (procedures where you can place responses to control actions).

This chapter introduces and explains the Visual Basic Interactive Development Environment (IDE), object-oriented programming basics, and how you can use Visual Basic classes within your projects. By the time you finish this chapter, you will understand the following key concepts:

- Visual Basic includes *controls*, which you will use to design an interface that lets the user interact with a project.

- A control is an object you will use within your programs to make them more accessible to users and to make it easier for your programs to respond to user input. A control is its own program that you will use within your Visual Basic programs to simplify the program's program code.

- Visual Basic includes *forms*, which you will use to contain controls.

- Visual Basic includes *user controls* and *user documents*, which you can use to design custom ActiveX components for your projects and Visual Basic programs that run on the World Wide Web.

- Visual Basic includes *modules*, which you will use to organize code, separate code from a specific visual component, and, potentially, make the code available to one or more forms.

- Visual Basic lets you design projects in *groups*, which let you include custom-designed controls, multiple executable files, and dynamic-link libraries within a single Visual Basic project file.

- *Object-oriented programming* is a programming style in which programmers divide programs into component objects and then design the programs to manage the component objects and their interactions.

- Programmers generally consider three characteristics—*inheritance*, *polymorphism*, and *encapsulation*—when determining whether a program language is object-oriented.

- *Event-oriented programming* is programming that focuses on the program's response to user input or activities.

- Visual Basic combines elements of object-oriented and event-oriented programming.

- An *Application Programming Interface* (API) lets other programs access features of the API's program. For example, the Windows API lets your programs directly access features of the Windows operating system and use those features within your programs' own processing. An API generally consists of functions, procedures, user-defined types, and symbolic constants that your programs can access.

- Windows exposes (makes available) several different APIs that you can use from within Visual Basic to create more powerful programs.

UNDERSTANDING A VISUAL BASIC PROJECT

When you first start Visual Basic, you begin a project. A project may consist of one or more forms, modules, class modules, user controls, or user documents. However, a project must consist of at least one form, module, class module, user control, or user document. You can use forms, user controls, or user documents to design the interface for your projects. Most interfaces will also include one or more controls, which you will use to make your programs interface better able to respond to user input and actions.

A Visual Basic project can also include one or more *modules*. Within your projects, you will use modules to contain code. You can determine whether your program can access the code you place within a module only within the module itself or whether the program can access the code from any other part of the program. A module will contain only program code. You can also add more than one module to a project. When you add an additional module to a project, you will organize your project because you can make the code within multiple modules available to any form in your project, or you can protect some code within each module so that it is available to other functions or procedures only within that module.

As you will learn later in this chapter, Visual Basic projects can also include one or more *class modules*. When you create classes, you will use a different class module for each class. A class is a set of similar objects. When you create an object, it is a single instance of a class. For example, you might think of Happy (the Jamsa Press mascot) as an object of class *Dog*. The class *Dog*, in turn, might have many objects—that is, there are many individual dogs. As your programs become more complex and you perform more object-oriented programming, you will use classes with increasing frequency.

As you will learn in Chapter 6, "Creating and Using ActiveX Controls," your projects can include *user controls*. A user control is an object that appears similar to a form during design, but you will use user controls to design the interface for a custom ActiveX control. As you will learn in Chapter 20, "Creating ActiveX Documents for the Web," you can use *user documents* to transport your applications to the Internet. User documents let you create Web-ready applications, which you can later call from within a Web page, with relative simplicity. You can also create *group projects*, which let you associate several programs together into a group. You will most commonly use group projects when you design custom ActiveX controls, a process that you will learn more about in Chapter 6. Figure 1.1 shows the relationship between the components you will use to design Visual Basic programs.

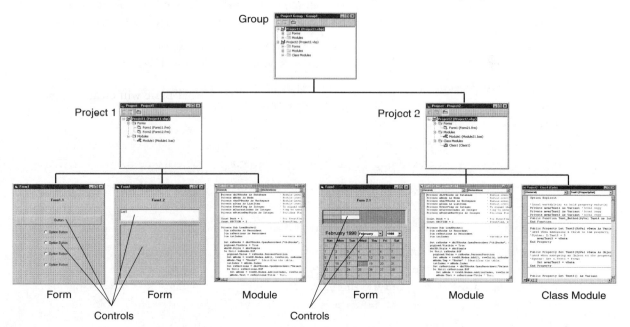

Figure 1.1 *The relationship among a Visual Basic program's components.*

As you can see in Figure 1.1, a group project will contain one or more component projects. Each component project may contain one or more forms, modules, or class modules, and a form may contain one or more controls.

UNDERSTANDING THE POWER OF VISUAL BASIC

If you have ever written a program in DOS, you know that DOS programs share many characteristics. For example, DOS programs generally provide only the simplest of user interfaces, such as a text menu that the user would select from with a single keystroke. Additionally, a DOS program is generally the only program that runs at any given time—the DOS environment is a single-tasking environment.

When you create a program in Windows, there are many different issues (from the DOS environment) that you must consider. The Graphical User Interface (GUI) that Windows provides makes it easier for users to interact with programs but harder for programmers to write those programs. Additionally, the Windows multi-tasking environment (which lets users run multiple programs simultaneously) forces programmers to consider a completely different set of issues than they would if they were not writing for Windows (or another multi-tasking environment).

3

In addition to the difficulties you encounter when writing programs for Windows that can handle multi-tasking, user actions, communication with other programs, and so on, your programs must also create each individual object, menu, icon, button, or other user interface within program code. When you put together all the possibilities that your programs must respond to, writing programs for Windows becomes a very complex task. Visual Basic provides many built-in structures and tools that simplify your programs and, therefore, let you avoid many issues that arise when you try to write programs for Windows.

For example, to draw a button control on a window within C/C++, you must first create a resource file (a text file which sets out the button's characteristics). The resource file will generally contain information about the button's size, color, caption, internal program identifier, and so on. After you create the resource file, the program must read the information in from the resource file and call a Windows Application Programming Interface (API) function to draw both the button and the window on which the button appears. The program must then use the button's internal program identifier to capture user actions (such as a mouse click) on that button within a procedure that receives all the other actions either the user or the system performs that affect the program. Similarly, to create a simple window within which you can display your program, you must define all the window's characteristics, check the current operating system type, determine the appropriate function name to create the window (which may vary between Windows 3.1, Windows 95, and Windows NT), and call the correct Windows API function to create the window.

Within Visual Basic, you can add a form to a project to create a window and add a *CommandButton* control to that form to add a button to the window. Both the form and the control have their own *events*, which your Visual Basic program will use to respond to user actions. Visual Basic will create the objects automatically when you compile the program, rather than forcing you to write all the program code to create the objects. When you write a program in C/C++ for Windows, you will generally have to write a minimum of 125 lines in every program simply to create the display and to add the functions that respond to user actions. Conversely, you can create a program in Visual Basic that creates the display and includes the procedures that respond to user events without ever writing a single line of code.

For most programmers who use Visual Basic, the program language's power lies within the program design. Letting the programmer create the program's visual presentation with forms and controls in the space of minutes or hours rather than days or weeks, lets the programmer spend more time focusing on writing the code that makes the program work, rather than focusing on writing the code that creates the program's display.

BETTER UNDERSTANDING A VISUAL BASIC FORM

As you have learned, Visual Basic projects, even simple ones, will contain at least one form. A form is a rectangular shape, similar to a window, that may hold controls. As you have learned, a Visual Basic form is a control itself, which also contains controls if you add them. A control, separate from a form, is a self-contained object a programmer can add to a form, which usually has a visual component. Within your programs, you will use controls to make the program's user interface more meaningful and useable. After the form contains a control, you can write code that lets a user interact with the control. Figure 1.2, for example, shows a standard form with several controls.

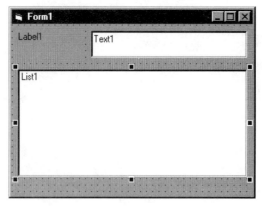

4   *Figure 1.2* *A Visual Basic form.*

UNDERSTANDING THE TOOLBOX

As you have learned, Visual Basic includes numerous controls that you can place onto a form. A control is an object that a user will interact with in your projects. Before you can place a control onto a form, you must access the control from within the *Toolbox*. Visual Basic includes the Toolbox, which displays *icons*. An icon is a small graphical item that represents another object. For example, Windows uses icons to represent, among other things, files and directories. Within the Toolbox, the icons represent controls you may want to use in your project. The Toolbox itself is simply a window that displays the control-representing icons, as Figure 1.3 shows.

Figure 1.3 *The Toolbox displays control icons.*

Before you or a user can interact with a control, you must add the control to a form. To add a control to a form, double-click your mouse on the control's icon in the Toolbox. Visual Basic will add the control to the form. You can add only one control to one form at a time. If your project contains multiple forms, you must click your mouse on the form to which you want to add the control before you try to add the control to the form.

After you select a form, Visual Basic will change the form's title bar's color to highlight the form. If you double-click your mouse on a control's icon in the Toolbox, Visual Basic will draw the control within the form you select. Alternately, you can click your mouse once on a control's icon in the Toolbox, and then click your mouse on a form and hold the mouse button down to draw the control within the form. After you size the control correctly within the form, you can release the mouse button.

CREATING A SAMPLE PROJECT

Visual Basic is a development environment that extensively uses visual icons and other cues to tell the programmer what comprises the program under development. Therefore, it is useful to create a simple project to visualize as you work through the remaining sections in this chapter. You can create simple projects with the Visual Basic New Project Wizard. Although you can create an executable program entirely with the Visual Basic (VB) Application Wizard, Visual Basic provides the Wizard only to speed up the process of creating frameworks, not to do the majority of your programming for you. To start the Visual Basic Application Wizard, perform the following steps:

1.   Within Visual Basic, select the File menu New Project option. Visual Basic will display the New Project dialog box.

2. Within the New Project dialog box, click your mouse once on the VB Application Wizard icon to select the icon. Figure 1.4 shows the New Project dialog box with the VB Application Wizard icon selected.

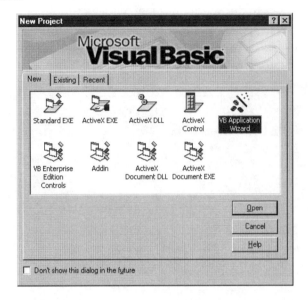

Figure 1.4 *The New Project dialog box with the VB Application Wizard icon selected.*

After you select the VB Application Wizard icon, click your mouse on the Open button to launch the Visual Basic Application Wizard.

Understanding Windows Interface Types

When you create a Windows-based program, you must select one of the two basic Windows interface types: Multiple-Document Interface or Single-Document Interface. Multiple-Document Interface (MDI) enabled applications are the Windows standard. The majority of Windows applications—from Microsoft *Word*® to Intuit *Quicken*®—use a Multiple-Document Interface. The words *Multiple-Document* refer to the program's ability to maintain several different presentations or files within a single overriding window. Figure 1.5 shows an example of the Multiple-Document Interface that has three separate documents open within the Microsoft *Word* window and one document minimized in the bottom left corner.

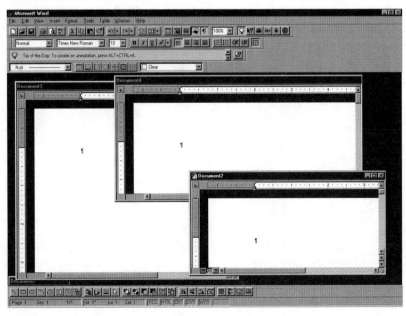

Figure 1.5 *The Multiple-Document Interface in Microsoft* **Word**.

Single-Document Interface (SDI) enabled applications are reminiscent of DOS-based applications, in that all views are at the same level. When you leave one view within a Single-Document Interface application for another, the program will typically hide or close the first view. Single-Document Interfaces are the simplest programs, and you will use them in subsequent chapters to discover more about Visual Basic. To begin creating a new project, which you can refer to for the next several sections, double-click your mouse on the VB Application Wizard icon that appears in the New Project dialog box, as previously shown in Figure 1.4. Visual Basic will display a dialog box that explains the Application Wizard's purpose. Figure 1.6 shows the Application Wizard–Introduction dialog box.

6

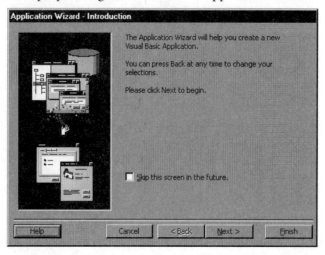

Figure 1.6 *The VB Application Wizard–Introduction dialog box.*

To move to the next dialog box, click your mouse on the Next button. Visual Basic, in turn, will display the Application Wizard–Interface Type dialog box. There are three options within the Application Wizard–Interface Type dialog box: Multiple Document Interface (MDI), Single-Document Interface (SDI), and Explorer Style interface. You can locate the text that explains interface types next to the options and under the graphic image with the *Hint!* header.

The Visual Basic Application Wizard also provides a third type of interface, the Explorer-style interface. The Explorer-style interface is a type of Single-Document Interface with the initial form divided into two frames. (The Explorer Style got its name because it is so similar to the Windows *Explorer.*) Programmers designed both frames to handle a *treeview*, which is a display composed of "branches" (directories), where each branch can have more branches (directories) and leaves (files). Treeviews most commonly occur within the Windows operating system in the Windows *Explorer*®—which you can use to view your computer's files and directories within a hierarchical tree. Your computer's root directory has subdirectories and files, many of which may also have additional subdirectories. Figure 1.7 shows the Windows *Explorer* with an expanded treeview.

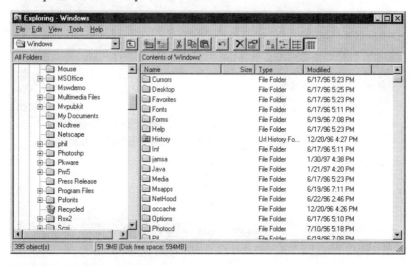

Figure 1.7 *The Windows Explorer with an expanded treeview.*

For the project framework you are creating, you will design a Single-Document Interface application. Select the Single-Document Interface radio button. Figure 1.8 shows the Application Wizard–Interface Type dialog box with the Single-Document Interface application radio button selected.

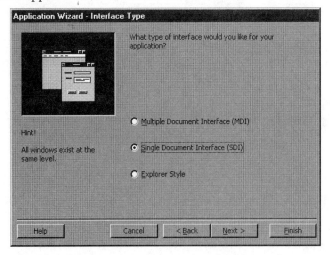

Figure 1.8 *Selecting a Single Document Interface.*

To continue creating your project framework, click your mouse on the Next button at the bottom of the Application Wizard–Interface Type dialog box. Visual Basic will respond with the Application Wizard–Menus dialog box.

UNDERSTANDING RADIO BUTTONS

Old-fashioned car radios had buttons that the listener pushed to select stations. Each button corresponded to a single station and the listener found the correct station without having to use the tuner dial. Radio buttons in Visual Basic are similar to those old-fashioned radio buttons. In later chapters, you will use radio buttons when you want the user to select only one option from among several possibilities, like the old-fashioned radio. In the particular example of the program you are creating with the Application Wizard, your program can consist of only one type of interface.

SELECTING MENUS IN THE APPLICATION WIZARD

The Application Wizard–Menus dialog box, which Visual Basic will display after you click the Next button in the Application Wizard–Interface dialog box, is another way the Visual Basic Application Wizard can simplify the process of writing program code. The Visual Basic Application Wizard can create starter menus for you. The Visual Basic Application Wizard's starter menus contain basic items, but no code.

In other words, the Wizard will provide the code to display the menus. You, in turn, must write the code the application will perform when the user selects a menu option. Again, Visual Basic tries to speed up your development process's initial stages by omitting some of the design issues—namely menus, resource files, and database connectivity. If you choose not to add menus within the Visual Basic Application Wizard, you can use the Menu Editor to add them to your project at any time during its development.

For the *VBPLExam1* project, that you are creating, you will not create any menus. Instead, click your mouse on the Clear All button. Visual Basic will clear the check marks next to all the menu names. Figure 1.9 shows the Application Wizard–Menus dialog box.

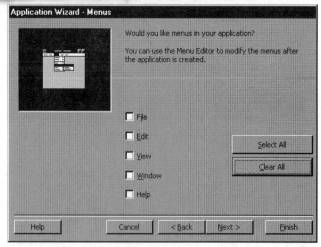

Figure 1.9 *The Application Wizard–Menus dialog box with the check boxes cleared.*

To continue with the Application Wizard, click your mouse on the Next button of the Application Wizard–Menus dialog box. Visual Basic will display the Application Wizard–Resources dialog box. You will not use resources within the sample project, so click your mouse on the Next button on the Application Wizard–Resources dialog box. Visual Basic will display the Application Wizard–Internet Connectivity dialog box.

USING THE APPLICATION WIZARD TO ADD AN INTERNET CONNECTION

The Application Wizard–Internet Connectivity dialog box lets you add a custom Web browser to your project framework. Included in the Visual Basic 5.0 set of Common Controls are a set of controls that provide you with an easy way to create programs that access the Internet. These controls include a simple browser control. If you develop an application to distribute to your customers or other third party users, or you develop shareware and want people to register the program online, the browser inclusion feature is helpful. These are only two suggested uses for the browser feature—there are infinite ways to use a browser within a program. In later chapters, you will learn how to create Internet-aware programs and controls.

Select the No radio button on the Application Wizard–Internet Connectivity dialog box. Click your mouse on the Next button within the Application Wizard–Internet Connectivity dialog box. The Visual Basic Application Wizard will respond with the Application Wizard–Standard Forms dialog box.

INCLUDING STANDARD FORMS IN YOUR WIZARD-GENERATED PROJECTS

The Application Wizard–Standard Forms dialog box asks if you would like to include any, some, or all four of the following forms: a splash screen, a login dialog, an options dialog, and an about box. These forms are common to many commercial and enterprise products. The *splash screen* is a screen that paints while the program is loading. Typically, a splash screen will contain some type of corporate graphic, a version number, and the program's registered user. You may include any information you want on the splash screen, but remember, it loads only briefly.

You can use the *login dialog* form to protect access to your application or to protect data accessible through the application. The *options dialog* form is another standard Windows item. Also known as a *preferences dialog* form, it offers users options for customizing a program to fit their specific needs. The *about box* form is similar to the splash screen. Most commonly a Help menu option, the about box typically states the product name, shows a graphic, and provides registration information.

The Visual Basic Application Wizard also displays an option to include other form templates (generic forms you can add to programs that contain controls and code that you often reuse). To add your own form template, you can click your mouse on the Other Templates command button. You can design your own form templates, similar to the standard forms listed in the dialog box, and add them to other projects you create. You will not, however, add any form templates to the current project. If you or another user previously selected any of these forms, you can click your left mouse button on each check mark until it disappears to deselect them. Figure 1.10 shows the Application Wizard–Standard Forms dialog box.

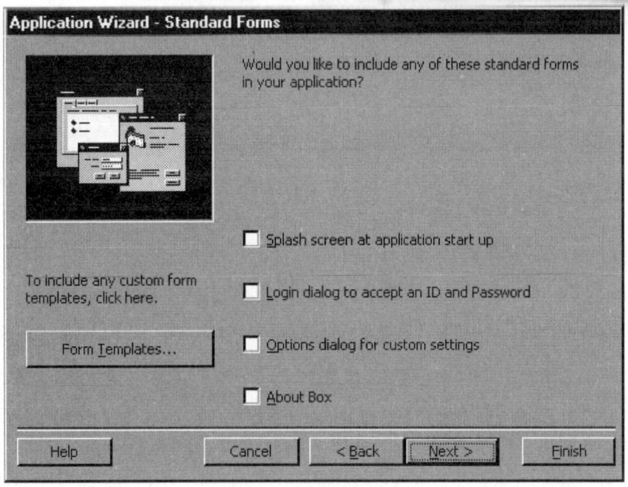

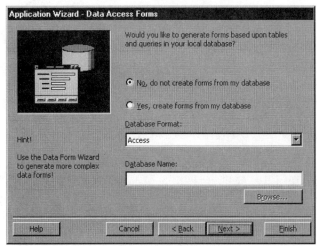

Figure 1.10 *The Application Wizard–Standard Forms dialog box with no forms selected.*

Click your mouse on the Next button on the Application Wizard–Standard Forms dialog box. Visual Basic will respond with the Application Wizard–Data Access Forms dialog box.

USING THE APPLICATION WIZARD TO CONNECT TO DATABASES

The Application Wizard–Data Access Forms dialog box helps you generate basic forms from a database for use within your applications. As your Visual Basic applications become more complex, your applications must sometimes interact with a database or databases. In later chapters, you will learn how to associate your applications with databases. You can create simple database access forms within the VB Application Wizard.

While the VB Application Wizard is helpful for creating database forms, you will eventually discover that the majority of your database applications require custom form design. However, the Wizard-designed forms are useful both for you to understand how your programs will use Visual Basic commands to perform database access and to help you understand the structure you must use to do so. The Wizard-designed forms are also useful when you create the base form for such database access within your application. For example, if you create a simple phone book application, the Wizard-generated data access form will be sufficient to return the phone number data. If you create a program you intend to use to manage clients, vendors, personal phone numbers, and order information, the Wizard-generated data access form will not be sufficient for your entire program—but it might provide a valuable template to use when you create that program.

Select the radio button with the caption "No, do not create forms from my database" on the Application Wizard–Data Access Forms dialog box. Figure 1.11 shows the Application Wizard–Data Access Forms dialog box.

Figure 1.11 *The Application Wizard–Data Access Forms dialog box with No selected.*

Click your mouse on the Next button on the Application Wizard–Data Access Forms dialog box. Visual Basic, in turn, will display the Application Wizard–Finished! dialog box.

FINISHING THE CREATION OF YOUR NEW WIZARD-GENERATED PROJECT

The Application Wizard–Finished! dialog box is the last dialog box that the VB Application Wizard presents to you when you create a new project with the Wizard. This dialog box gives you information about the steps the Wizard performed, provides a text box within which you can enter the new project's name, and presents the option to display further information about the Wizard's activities when the Wizard finishes creating the project. In the text box at the top of the dialog box, delete the project's default name (probably *PROJECT1*) and enter the project's name as *VBPLExam1*, which is short for Visual Basic Programmer's Library Example 1.

The Application Wizard–Finished! dialog box also asks if it should display a summary of what steps it has performed in designing your project framework. Click your mouse on the Yes radio button. The Save Current Settings As default check box lets you save all the steps you have previously completed as the project creation default for all future projects.

Make sure that the Save Current Settings As default box is not checked (because in the future you will probably want to specialize your settings for your own use). Click your mouse on the Finish button within this dialog box. Figure 1.12 shows the Application Wizard–Finished! dialog box.

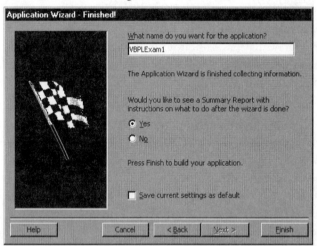

Figure 1.12 The Application Wizard–Finished! dialog box with the correct project name entered.

The VB Application Wizard will create a project file, a module file, and a form file, and will alert you that it has created the application. Click your mouse on the OK button in the Application Created dialog box. The VB Application Wizard will then display a brief summary of what it has created (including any menus, data control objects, Internet controls, standard forms, and more) and what steps it suggests you perform next.

Now that you have created a simple sample project, you will be better able to understand the concepts the following sections detail. In the following sections, you will learn more about controls, modules, and other important parts of Visual Basic program development.

BETTER UNDERSTANDING VISUAL BASIC CONTROLS

As you have learned, Visual Basic displays control icons in the Toolbox. When you double-click your mouse on a control's icon in the Toolbox, Visual Basic will draw the actual control within your project's form. The control is an object you can see on a form and which has shape, size, color, and usually text or a caption. In addition, a control contains properties, methods, and events. Figure 1.13 shows a form and some common controls that you will use with forms in your programs.

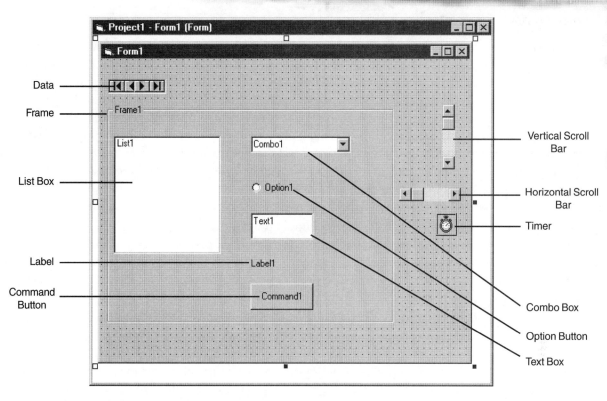

Figure 1.13 *A form and some common controls you will use with it.*

As you will learn, each Visual Basic control has a specific purpose. As a programmer, you will want your users to easily access a project you design. You can design a project with controls that let users click their mouse on a button, select a single option, select many items, enter text, read text, list thousands of lines of text, display pictures, watch television, and more. Visual Basic lets you write code for a control's properties, methods, and events. This means that you can change the manner in which a control behaves from within your programs. A control's properties will describe the control, such as its size and color. A control's methods let you perform actions on the control, such as positioning and resizing. A control's events let you write code to respond to an action, such as when you click the mouse or press a key.

When you design a Visual Basic project that uses forms, user controls, or user documents, you can place one or more controls onto one or more forms, user controls, or user documents. As you have learned, to place a control onto a form, you will double-click your mouse on the control's icon within the Toolbox. After you double-click your mouse on a control's icon, Visual Basic will draw the control within the currently selected form within the Visual Basic Interactive Development Environment. After you place a control on a form, you can change its properties, use its methods, and write code for its events. For example, in the *VBPLExam1* project, the main form includes four controls: a *Toolbar* control, a *StatusBar* control, an *ImageList* control, and a *CommonDialog* control. Figure 1.14 shows the main form, *frmMain,* and indicates its component controls.

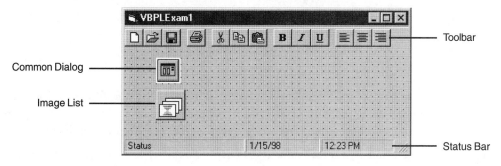

Figure 1.14 *The **frmMain** form and its component controls.*

UNDERSTANDING PROPERTIES

As you have learned, each Visual Basic control has properties, methods, and events. You can change a control's properties at both *design time* and *run time*. Some controls have properties that are available only at run time; others have properties that are available only at design time. Design time refers to a project's development, and most changes you make to a control at design time will be relatively static. In other words, the properties will not change significantly during program execution. During run time, the program is executing and the program will immediately display changes you make to control properties in the executing project, depending on the changed property's nature. Each control has one or more properties. A control's properties will describe the control, such as its size, color, and position. For example, the *Toolbar* control in your sample project has alignment properties, icon appearance properties, number of icon properties, and so on. You might design the control with thirteen icons (as shown in Figure 1.14) and change it at run time to include additional icons if the user makes certain selections during the installation process.

In Visual Basic you have the flexibility to change a control's properties in code or in the *Properties Window*. Visual Basic includes the Properties Window, which will display a control's properties. When you change a control's properties in the Properties Window, you change its properties at design time. First, Visual Basic will load a control's properties from the Properties Window's values. Second, Visual Basic will process the code if you have written any code to change a control's properties.

One of Visual Basic's most common controls is the *CommandButton* control, which appears as a rectangular button on a form. Some of the *CommandButton* control's properties include *BackColor, Caption, Enabled, Font, Height, Left, Top,* and *Width*. When you first add a *CommandButton* control to a form, Visual Basic will draw it with default settings. When you change the control's *BackColor* property, Visual Basic will change the control's color. Therefore, if Visual Basic painted the control with the default gray color and you change the *BackColor* property to red, Visual Basic will paint the control red.

When you change the *CommandButton* control's *Caption* property, Visual Basic will write the new caption on the control's face. When you change the control's *Enabled* property, Visual Basic will either let you use the control at run time (*Enabled* equals *True*), or color the control gray and disable it (*Enabled* equals *False*). When you change the control's *Font* property, Visual Basic will paint the current *Caption* value with the *Font* value you select. To better understand the Properties Window, see Figure 1.15, which shows the common *CommandButton* control's properties.

Figure 1.15 *The Properties Window listing the **CommandButton** control's properties.*

To change a control's properties in the Properties Window, click your mouse on the *Name* field in the Properties Window and enter the new value for the property. Visual Basic will display the control with the new properties you assign. In addition, Visual Basic will write a short description of each property at the bottom of the Properties Window.

For example, in Figure 1.15, the *Caption* property value is *Command Button*. If you change the *Caption* property to *VBPL First Command Button*, Visual Basic will display the *CommandButton* control with the new caption on the form, as Figure 1.16 shows.

*Figure 1.16 A **CommandButton** control after you change its **Caption** property.*

BETTER UNDERSTANDING METHODS

As you have learned, each control has properties and you can describe a control by its properties. In addition to properties, most controls have at least one method. You can think of a method as an action that the program performs with the control (as opposed to an event, which is the control's response to a user's action or a program action). For example, imagine the *Toolbar* control has a *Move* method (which it does). The *Toolbar* control's *Move* method lets you move the *Toolbar* control from its original position to a new position. Within your program code, you can write a procedure that uses the *Toolbar* control's *Move* method to shift the control from the top of the form to the bottom of the form. Then, you could write another procedure that uses the *Toolbar* control's *Move* method to shift the control from the right side of the form to the left side of the form.

Almost every Visual Basic control has at least one method. Before you use a method for a control, it is always helpful to understand what the method does. Visual Basic includes a large help file that you can use to find information on most controls. When you have a question about a control and Visual Basic displays a help file on the control, you can study each method the control includes. In addition to studying control methods from the Visual Basic *Help* file, you can view descriptions about control methods in the Visual Basic *Object Browser*. The Object Browser consists of a window that Visual Basic uses to display a control's properties, methods, and events. The Object Browser will display controls, as well as other items that you will learn about later in this book.

As you have learned, one of Visual Basic's most common controls is the *CommandButton* control. One of the *CommandButton* control's methods is *Move*. The *Move* method lets you move a control which supports the method (such as the *CommandButton* control) from one position to another on a form. The *Move* method consists of the keyword *Move* and four parameters, *Left*, *Top*, *Width*, and *Height*. You can assign a value to each parameter. You will use the *Left* and *Top* parameters to determine the control's position, such as it's distance from the top of a form to the top of the control, and the left side of a form to theleft side of the control. You will use the *Width* and *Height* parameters to determine the control's size. You can use the Object Browser to view the *CommandButton* control's properties, methods, and events. To display the Object Browser, select the View menu Object Browser option. Visual Basic will display the Object Browser. Select the *CommandButton* control's *Move* method, which Visual Basic will display, as Figure 1.17 shows.

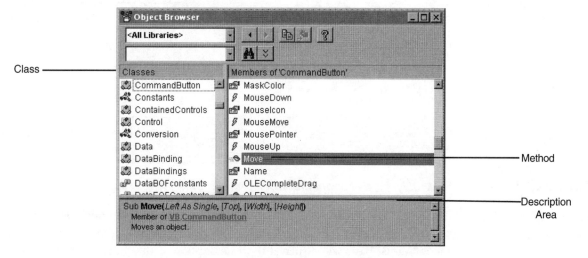

*Figure 1.17 The Object Browser showing the **CommandButton** control's **Move** method.*

13

As you can see in Figure 1.17, after you select a control's property, method, or event, Visual Basic will display a short description at the bottom of the Object Browser. In addition, the Object Browser's left hand window lists the available *Classes* for the currently selected library. Classes are often controls, although the *Classes* list may also describe custom classes that you create. In Chapter 12, "Using ActiveX Automation to Create a Database Server," for example, you will design a class that functions as a server across a network. In Chapter 12, you will also learn how to view information about a custom-designed class.

UNDERSTANDING EVENTS

As you have learned, most Visual Basic controls have properties and methods. You can describe a control by its properties and use a control's methods to take action on a control. In addition to properties and methods, most controls support at least one event. An event is something that may or may not occur to the control when the program executes. When you or Visual Basic perform an action on a control, Windows responds to that action. The action may cause an event, or the event may be a subsequent result of the action. For example, when you click your mouse on a *CommandButton* control during run time (that is, when the program is actually running), your program will invoke the control's *Click* event. On the other hand, when you click your mouse on a form's Close button, the form will invoke two events (*Unload* and *QueryUnload*), which are the result of the mouse click action, even though the action itself does not actually invoke the event (the form does).

You can write code for an event. For example, after you click your mouse on a *CommandButton* control and your program invokes its *Click* event, your program will also process any code you have already written in its *Click* event's code listing. The ability to extend processing after an event means you can cause Visual Basic to respond to an action in more complex ways, without having to create a new control. For example, a single button click might create a new form, populate that form's fields with information, update a record within a program-associated database, and display a message for the user. Visual Basic includes a large help file that you can use to find information on most controls. When you have a question about a control and Visual Basic displays a help file on the control, you can use the information the help file contains to study each event that the control includes. As you have learned, in addition to studying controls in the Visual Basic Help file, you can view descriptions about controls and their properties, methods, and events within the Visual Basic Object Browser. To view information about the *CommandButton* control's events, you can use the Object Browser. To display the Object Browser, select the View menu Object Browser option. Visual Basic will display the Object Browser. Select the *CommandButton* control's *Click* event, which Visual Basic will display, as Figure 1.18 shows.

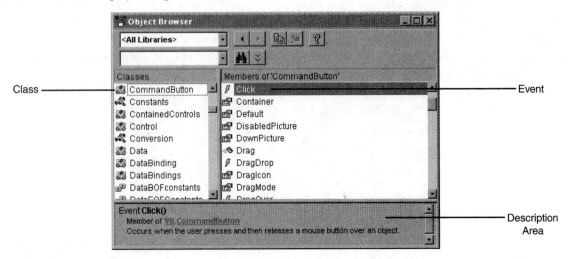

Figure 1.18 *The Object Browser showing the **CommandButton** control's **Click** event.*

As you can see in Figure 1.18, the Object Browser lets you view a control's properties, methods, and events when you click your mouse on the control's name below the *Classes* heading. Select a property, method, or event from the list on the right side of the window. Visual Basic will display a short description of the control's property, method, or event at the bottom of the Object Browser.

In Chapter 6, you will design your own ActiveX control. After you finish designing a custom ActiveX control, you can manipulate its properties, methods, and events. In addition, you can view each property, method, and event in the Object Browser. However, the Visual Basic Help file will not contain information about your new control (because you have not placed information into the Help file about your new control).

USING CONTROLS

As you have learned, a Visual Basic project usually consists of one or more forms with one or more controls. Because a form is a control, you do not have to add a control to a form to create a project. However, you will find that when you add a control to a form the result will be more useful than using a blank form alone. As you have learned, each Visual Basic control has a specific purpose. You can design a project with many controls. For instance, a user can click the mouse on a *CommandButton* control to interrupt a program, select a single option from two or more *OptionButton* controls, list thousands of data items in a *ListBox* control, and so on. Table 1.1 lists some common controls that you will use within your Visual Basic programs.

Visual Basic Controls

CheckBox	*ComboBox*	*CommandButton*	*CommonDialog*
Data Control	*Data-Bound Grid*	*DriveListBox*	*DirListBox*
FileListBox	*FlexGrid*	*Label*	*ListBox*
Listview	*OptionButton*	*ProgressBar*	*RichTextBox*
StatusBar	*TextBox*	*Toolbar*	*Web Browser*

Table 1.1 *Some common Visual Basic controls.*

Because a form is also a control and, at its foundation, an object class's visual representation, it will be helpful for you to understand *objects*. You can think of a control as an object. For example, when you start your computer, you usually flip a switch on the physical computer box. The switch is an object. However, because your computer will follow a set of instructions to start itself after you flip the switch, the switch is also a control. You can think of a control as an object that does something only after you perform some action on it. In comparison, a pencil is also an object, yet it does nothing until you pick it up and write with it.

As you will learn, Visual Basic programs define objects (controls) in terms of a *class*. A class is a listing of code that all applies to similar objects or a common purpose you relate to a similar purpose. For example, there are many breeds of horses throughout the world. You can think of each horse as belonging to the *Horse* class. The *Horse* class consists of functions, such as *Gallop* and *Eat*. All horses in the world share those characteristics. When you work with a galloping horse, however, you are working only with a single object, or *instance*, of that *Horse* class. If you were to create a *Horse* class, it would include code to perform the *Gallop, Whinny,* and *Eat* actions.

In the same way, Visual Basic uses a class to describe each of its controls. For example, the *CommandButton* control belongs to the *CommandButton* class. The *CommandButton* class consists of properties, methods, and events, such as *BackColor, Move,* and *Click,* that help describe the *CommandButton* control. When you use controls within your programs (which you will, and often), you should be sure to understand all the properties, methods, and events of the controls you use, because doing so will improve your program's presentation and usability, and can decrease your programming time significantly.

BETTER UNDERSTANDING MODULES

As you have learned, Visual Basic projects will generally contain at least one form or other visual object. As your projects grow, you will find you must use a *module*. A module is not a form, but rather a simple container for program code. Within a module's Code window, you can declare variables, write functions and procedures, and declare *structures*. You will learn more about structures in Chapter 5, "Creating and Using Fractals."

When you declare a variable in a module, you can control access to that variable within your program—you can make it accessible to any form in the project, or make it accessible only to that module. In other words, when you declare a *Private* variable within a module, you cannot access the variable directly from any form—just as when you declare a *Private* variable within a procedure, you cannot access that variable from other procedures. On the other hand, when you declare a *Public* variable within a module, your program code can access that variable from any location within the project. By default, variables that you define within a module are public.

When you protect private data within a module and access it only through a *Public* function, you can use the private data anywhere in your project. This means that when you design multiple forms, you can pass information from form to form and protect the original data. In Chapter 12, you will use classes to protect private data and *Public* functions (which programmers often refer to as *interface functions*) to access the data.

UNDERSTANDING THE CODE WINDOW

 As you have learned, a Visual Basic project may consist of forms, modules, class modules, user controls, and user documents. As you design your projects, you will eventually add program code for most objects that you add to a project. When you write program code that you associate with each object in a project, you will use the Visual Basic *Code window*. The Code window consists of a single window with two drop-down menus at the top.

The two drop-down combo boxes at the top of the Code window will let you select which procedure or function you want to view. How the Code window will organize procedures and functions will vary, depending on the object within which you are working. The combo box on the left, for example, will let you select controls on a form, user control, or user document, and the class within a class module. The combo box on the right will let you select procedures, functions, and control events. The blank area below the two fields will let you enter Visual Basic program code. Each Code window includes a General–Declarations section. This section will let you declare variables that any function, event, or procedure can use. Any variables that you declare in the General–Declarations section will be available throughout the form, meaning that any event or procedure you write for the form can access the variable.

Any time you write a procedure, event, or function in the Code window, the code will be outside of the General–Declarations section. The following sample code listing shows a form's *QueryUnload* event procedure, as shown in Figure 1.19.

```
prjCreateDatabase - frmAddFields (Code)

Form                              Load

    Private Sub Form_QueryUnload(Cancel As Integer, UnloadMode As Integer)
        Dim Response As Integer

        If lstFields.ListCount > 1 And Not Saved Then
            Response = MsgBox("Exit without saving?", vbYesNo, "Database Creator")
            If Response = vbNo Then
                Cancel = True
                Exit Sub
            Else
                frmCreateDatabase.Tag = "False"
            End If
        End If
    End Sub
```

Figure 1.19 *The Code window showing a procedure.*

As you can see, the Code window displays the procedure's name (in the case of Figure 1.19, *QueryUnload*) in the right field at the window's top. When you move through the Code window, Visual Basic will display each procedure, event, and function in the currently opened program object (for example, *CommandButton* control or *TextBox* control) within the combo boxes at the Code window's top as your cursor moves through that procedure, event, or function.

More on Objects and Classes

As you have learned, Visual Basic has aspects of object-oriented programming (support for objects and classes) and aspects of event-oriented programming. You have also learned some basics of classes and objects. However, the concept of classes and objects is so important to the programming you will do through the remainder of this book that it is worthwhile for you to revisit it here. In the next sections, you will learn more about classes and objects, how to create your own classes and objects in Visual Basic, and whether you can truly consider Visual Basic an object-oriented language.

Understanding Objects

In the simplest sense, an *object* is a thing or a real-world entity. When programmers create programs, they write instructions that work with different objects (things), like variables or files. Different objects have different *operations* that your programs perform on them. For example, given a *file* object, your program might perform such operations as reading, writing, or printing the file. As you will learn, Visual Basic programs can define objects in terms of a class. An *object class* defines the data the object will store and the functions that operate on the data. Visual Basic programs often refer to the functions that manipulate the class data as *methods*. Some of your Visual Basic programs, for example, might include the *Debug* and *RichTextBox* objects. In the case of these objects, functions, such as *Debug.Print* and *RichTextBox.SelRTF,* are the *operations* your program will perform on the objects. When you perform an operation on a control, you generally use a method. Within Visual Basic, every form and control your program uses is an object. You will more clearly understand what you learn in this and the following sections if you think about what you are learning in the context of forms and controls.

Understanding Object-Oriented Programming

To programmers, an object is a collection of data and a set of operations, called *methods*, that manipulate data. *Object-oriented programming* is a way of looking at programs in terms of the objects (things) that make up a system. After you have identified the objects, you can determine the operations you or the user will usually perform on the object. If you have a *document* object, for example, common operations might include printing, spell-checking, faxing, or even discarding. Object-oriented programming does not require a special programming language. You can write object-oriented programs in such languages as C++, Java, COBOL, and FORTRAN.

However, as you will learn, languages described as object-oriented usually provide class data structures that let your programs group the data and methods into one variable. As you will also learn, object-oriented programming has many advantages. The two main advantages of object-oriented programming are that you can reuse objects and they are easy to understand. Fortunately, the objects that you write for one program you can often use in another program—which means that you can reuse the objects easily. Rather than building a collection of function libraries, object-oriented programmers build *class libraries*. Likewise, by grouping an object's data and methods, object-oriented programs are often more readily understood than their non-object-based counterparts (at least after you learn the syntax the programming language uses). The best known object-oriented languages are C++ and Java. In Visual Basic 4.0, however, Microsoft started migrating Visual Basic toward an object-oriented language. Now, Visual Basic 5.0 is much more object-capable than Visual Basic 4.0, because of Visual Basic 5.0's expanded class support, its ability to design custom controls within Visual Basic, and more.

Understanding Why Visual Basic Is Not Truly Object-Oriented

As you have learned, you can write object-oriented programs in almost any language, including Visual Basic. However, you also learned that programmers generally do not consider Visual Basic a true object-oriented language because of its roots in BASIC and because most programmers use a number of predefined objects when they use Visual Basic. As you have already learned, the original BASIC language was a procedure-based language. In other words, every program started at some point A and finished at some point B, and the sequence of execution was in a relatively straight line. Later, BASIC gained the ability to call subroutines to perform branching activities. With the introduction of Visual Basic, BASIC became an event-driven language.

Nevertheless, even with all the advances that Microsoft has made in the BASIC language with the introduction of the new versions of Visual Basic, BASIC is still fundamentally a language that manages program flow with subroutines. Therefore, you cannot refer to it solely as an object-oriented language. The second argument that supports the conclusion that Visual Basic is not an object-oriented language is that someone else (usually Microsoft or a third-party developer) defines and encapsulates most of the objects that people use when they program in Visual Basic. Finally, as you will learn in later sections, one of the primary benefits of classes is the ability to inherit other classes' characteristics. Because you cannot inherit characteristics from the controls the majority of Visual Basic programmers use, the object-oriented nature of the controls is not sufficient to qualify Visual Basic as an object-oriented language.

UNDERSTANDING VISUAL BASIC STRUCTURES

In many of the programs that you will create in later chapters of this book, you will use *structures* to group related data. Within your programs, you will often use Visual Basic's simple types, such as *Integer, Double*, and *String* to store simple values—in this case, whole numbers, real numbers, and character sequences, respectively. A structure is a program-defined type you can use to store multiple values in a common location, rather than a single value, as you will with most of Visual Basic's simple types. Structures are important data constructs.

For example, assume you want to design a program that maintains information about employees. You determine that there are seven separate pieces of information you want to track for each employee—name, age, social-security number, pay grade, salary, last date paid, and the employee's employee number. You can either track the information about each employee within seven different variables, or you can define a structure that contains all seven pieces of information. The following code fragment declares a sample structure to maintain the employee information:

```
Type Employee
   Name As String * 64
   Age As Integer
   SSN As String * 11
   Pay_Grade As Integer
   Salary As Single
   LastPayDay As Date
   Employee_Number As String * 11
End Type
```

The *Employee* structure lets you store three *String* values, two *Integer* values, a *Single* value, and a *Date* value, all within a single location. Within your programs, you can then access all the information that relates to that particular variable from within the *Employee* structure—rather than using seven different variables to maintain that information. A structure, then, lets you store related data within a single construct that lets your programs easily access, maintain, and update the data.

When you access the data that you store within a structure within your programs, you must use the *dot operator* to reference the structure's members. For example, if you wanted to create a new variable of type *Employee* and set the employee's name to *Happy*, you would use code similar to that shown in the following fragment:

```
Dim NewEmployee As Employee
NewEmployee.Name = "Happy"
```

As you can see, the code fragment creates a new variable, *NewEmployee*, of the *Employee* type, and then uses the *dot* operator to assign the name *Happy* to the employee.

UNDERSTANDING VISUAL BASIC CLASSES

In the previous section, you learned that within your programs you can define a special kind of type called a structure. While structures are a very important data construct, they do have limitations. The biggest limitation of a structure is that it can only store data—a variable of a structure's type cannot, by itself, perform processing on the data it contains. To create data objects which can both store data and perform processing on the data the object stores, you must define a Visual Basic *class*.

You can best view a Visual Basic *class* as a structure which also has the ability to perform actions on the data the structure maintains. A class stores data, manipulates data, and can return values to the program code that uses an object of the class' type. If you use a class instead of a structure, you can process a *Last_Date_Paid* function within the class and automatically return the *LastPayDay* value whenever the user views an instance of an *Employee* object—for example, if the user were viewing payroll records in a report. The *Last_Date_Paid* function will be a *method* of the class. A class, like a structure, describes a template for future variable declarations, but it does not allocate memory for a variable. A class has a name (tag) and member fields. When you create classes within Visual Basic, you will do so within a specific module for that class, which Visual Basic calls a *class module*. If you create an *Employee* class module, you can then define the members within the class module much as you would the members within a structure. The following definition illustrates the member declarations for a simple class named *Employee* (remember, the class module's name is the class name):

```
Public Name As String
Public Age As Integer
Public SSN As String
Public Pay_Grade As Integer
Public Salary As Single
Public Employee_Number As String
Public Function Last_Date_Paid(Name As String) As String
```

As you can see, the class definition is similar to a structure. The first six lines in the definition correspond directly to the definitions within the *Employee* structure you viewed previously. The last line defines the *Last_Date_Paid* function that you learned about in the previous paragraph. The only new items in the definition are the *Public* labels and the *Public* function's definition. A later section in this chapter, "Understanding the *Public* Label," explains the *Public* label in detail.

CONCEPTUALIZING CLASSES

Classes and objects are some of the most difficult programming constructs for both beginning and advanced programmers to master. As you have learned, the best way to visualize classes and objects is to think about real-world objects. For example, Happy is a Dalmatian. In this case, *Dalmatian* is the class and *Happy* is the object. *Dalmatians* share many characteristics—they have eyes, legs, a tail, a nose, and spots. However, each Dalmatian also has unique characteristics, such as name, sex, eye color, tail length, and number of spots. The shared characteristics are items that are consistent throughout the class. In Visual Basic, the different *Button* classes share many common characteristics. For example, they all have the *Click* event, the *MouseDown* event, the *MouseUp* event, just as Dalmatians all have eyes, legs, and spots. The unique characteristics, on the other hand, would be properties: the object's name, the object's size, the object's color, the object's caption, and other properties that make the object unique.

The goal with any object-oriented program is to make generalizations about every object you use within your program, whether it is a visual object, a data object, or a mathematical object, to name a few, and group those generalized objects together in their own classes. Making generalizations makes the objects more reusable. If you define an object too closely, it will be correct only for a very specific purpose, while an object that you define only generally will be reusable in many different situations. In true object-oriented languages, you will derive many classes from other, more general classes. For example, you might derive the class *Dalmatian* from *Dog*. Similarly, within C/C++ programming for Windows, you will derive every visible object from the Windows-defined *CWin* class. In Visual Basic, because it does not fully support inheritance, your classes will probably not separate as efficiently as you might prefer (because you cannot derive classes from other classes, you will generally be unable to avoid the use of duplicate program code within your complex projects), but the classes that you can create support much of the power of object-oriented programming.

UNDERSTANDING POLYMORPHISM

As you read other books and articles on object-oriented programming, you will often encounter the term *polymorphism*. In general, polymorphism is an object's ability to change forms. If you break apart the term, you will find that *poly* means many and *morphism* refers to changing forms. A polymorphic object, therefore, is an object that can take on many forms. For example, you might create a *telephone* object. You might discover later, however, that your program must handle different telephone types—touch-tone, rotary, pay-phones, and so on. If you create your *telephone* object correctly, you should be able to easily change the *telephone* object from one phone type to another.

In C++, for example, *virtual functions* provide access to polymorphism. In the simplest sense, a virtual function is a pointer to a function that the compiler resolves at run time. Depending on the function to which a virtual function points, the operation the program performs will differ. As a result, a single interface (the virtual function) can provide access to different operations. Unfortunately, Visual Basic does not support true polymorphism—you can simulate polymorphism with variant and optional parameters, but it is an awkward and often difficult process.

CREATING CLASSES USING THE CLASS BUILDER UTILITY

As you begin to create classes within Visual Basic, you can use either the *Class Builder utility*, or you can write classes from scratch. The Class Builder utility is a dialog box that, like the Menu Editor, helps you create a structure in which you can create your class. To build your first class using the Class Builder utility, perform the following steps:

1. Select the File menu New Project option to create a new project. Visual Basic will display the New Project dialog box. Select the Standard EXE icon within the New Project dialog box. Visual Basic will create a new project and display the blank *Form1* within an object window.

2. Select the Project menu Add Class Module option. Visual Basic will display the Add Class Module dialog box. The Add Class Module dialog box will contain three icons: Class Module, VB Class Builder, and Addin. Double-click your mouse on the VB Class Builder icon. Visual Basic will open the VB Class Builder.

3. Select the File menu New option Class sub-option. Visual Basic will display the Class Module Builder dialog box.

4. Change the *Name* field to *Employees*. Click your mouse on the OK button. Visual Basic will add the *Employees* class to the *Class* tree below *Project1*.

5. Select the Properties tab on the right side of the Class Builder window. Select the File menu New option Property sub-option. Visual Basic will display the Property Builder dialog box.

6. Within the Property Builder dialog box, enter *Age* into the *Name* field. Press the TAB key to move to the *Data Type* field and select the *Integer* type. Click your mouse on the OK button. Visual Basic will add the *Age* property to the *Employees* class.

7. Select the Properties tab within the right side of the Class Builder window. Select the File menu New option Property sub-option. Visual Basic will display the Property Builder dialog box.

8. Within the Property Builder dialog box, enter *SSN* into the *Name* field. Press the TAB key to move to the *Data Type* field and select the *String* type. Click your mouse on the OK button. Visual Basic will add the *SSN* property to the *Employees* class.

9. Select the Properties tab within the right side of the Class Builder window. Select the File menu New option Property sub-option. Visual Basic will display the Property Builder dialog box.

10. Within the Property Builder dialog box, enter *Pay_Grade* into the *Name* field. Press the TAB key to move to the *Data Type* field and select the *Integer* type. Click your mouse on the OK button. Visual Basic will add the *Pay_Grade* property to the *Employees* class.

11. Select the Properties tab within the right side of the Class Builder window, then select the File menu New option Property sub-option. Visual Basic will display the Property Builder dialog box.

12. Within the Property Builder dialog box, enter *Name* into the *Name* field. Press the TAB key to move to the *Data Type* field and select the *String* type. Click your mouse on the OK button. Visual Basic will add the *Name* property to the *Employees* class.

13. Select the Properties tab on the right side of the Class Builder window. Select the File menu New option Property sub-option. Visual Basic will display the Property Builder dialog box.

14. Within the Property Builder dialog box, enter *Salary* into the *Name* field. Press the TAB key to move to the *Data Type* field and select the *Single* type. Click your mouse on the OK button. Visual Basic will add the *Salary* property to the *Employees* class.

15. Select the Properties tab within the right side of the Class Builder window. Select the File menu New option Property sub-option. Visual Basic will display the Property Builder dialog box.

16. Within the Property Builder dialog box, enter *Employee_Number* into the *Name* field. Press the TAB key to move to the *Data Type* field and select the *String* type. Click your mouse on the OK button. Visual Basic will add the *Employee_Number* property to the *Employees* class and display the new property within the *Properties* tab. Figure 1.20 shows the Class Builder window after you add properties to the *Employees* class.

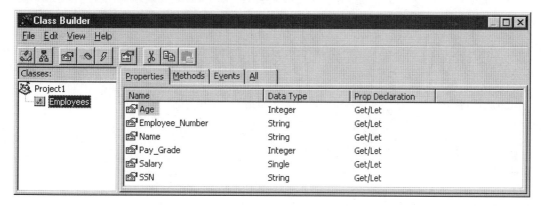

Figure 1.20 *The **Employees** class and its properties.*

17. Click your mouse on the Methods tab within the Class Builder window. Select the File menu New option Method sub-option. Visual Basic will display the Method Builder dialog box.

18. Within the *Name* field, enter *Last_Date_Paid*. Click your mouse on the + sign to the right of the *Arguments* field. Visual Basic will display the Add Argument dialog box.

19. Enter the name of the argument as *Name*. Select *String* from within the *Data Type* dialog box. Click your mouse on OK. Visual Basic will return to the Method Builder dialog box. Notice that Visual Basic added the *Name As String* argument to the *Arguments* field.

20. Within the *Return Type* combo box, select *String*. Click your mouse on the OK button to exit the Method Builder dialog box. Visual Basic will add the *Last_Date_Paid* method to the list of methods the *Employees* class recognizes.

21. Select the File menu Update Project option to add the new class descriptors to your project. Next, select the File menu Exit option to exit the VB Class Builder utility. Note that Visual Basic has added the *Employees* class file to your project.

If you open the *Employees* class file, you will notice the declarations within the listing that appeared earlier in this section. As you proceed through this book, you will learn what the definitions mean and how you will use them within your programs.

UNDERSTANDING THE PUBLIC LABEL

In the "Understanding Visual Basic Classes" section, you created a simple class, *Employees*, that contained the *Public* label, as shown in the following code:

```
Public Name As String
Public Age As Integer
Public SSN As String
Public Pay_Grade As Integer
Public Salary As Single
Public Employee_Number As String
Public Function Last_Date_Paid(Name As String) As String
```

As you can see, you have declared every variable or other object within your simple class with the *Public* keyword. When you created the *Employees* class in the previous section with the Class Builder utility, the declarations were slightly different from your first simple class. The following code implements the declarations for the Class Builder-generated *Employees* class:

```
Private mvarName As String                              ' local copy
Private mvarAge As Integer                              ' local copy
Private mvarSSN As String                               ' local copy
Private mvarPay_Grade As Integer                        ' local copy
Private mvarSalary As Single                            ' local copy
Private mvarEmployee_Number As String                   ' local copy
Public Function Last_Date_Paid(Name As String) As String
```

Unlike a structure that has members that are all accessible to a program, a class can have members that the program can directly access using the *dot* operator, and other members (called *private members*) that the program cannot access directly. The *Public* label identifies the class members the program can access from outside the class using the *dot* operator (.). If you want the program to access a member directly, you must declare the member using the *Public* keyword. For example, in the *Employees* class with the declarations you saw in the previous code listing, the first line of code in the following code listing will work, but the second line will cause an error:

```
Dim NewEmployee As Employee

Debug.Print NewEmployee.Last_Date_Paid("Happy")
Debug.Print NewEmployee.mvarName
```

The *mvarName* member variable is *private* to the class, and therefore your program code outside the class cannot access the variable. Instead, the Class Builder created *Property Get* and *Property Let* statements to let your programs access the internal variables as external properties. For the *mvarName* variable, the Class Builder created a *Property Get Name* and a *Property Let Name* procedure. In other words, if you have an object you name *Happy*, which is an instance of the class *Employees*, and you want to assign the *Name* property, you will assign the *Name* property using the *dot* operator, as shown in the following code fragment:

```
Happy.Name = "Triggerhill's I'm so Happy, CDX"
```

The Class Builder uses the *Property Let Name* procedure to determine that you are actually setting the *mvarName* variable within the class. However, your program cannot access the *mvarName* variable directly—only through the *Property Get Name* and *Property Let Name* procedures. Protecting the data in such a manner—forcing the program to access member variables only indirectly—is known as *information hiding*. You will learn more about information hiding in the next section.

UNDERSTANDING INTERFACE FUNCTIONS

As you have learned, your programs should try to declare most of an object's data as *Private*. When your programs declare object data as *Private*, other programs can access the data only by calling the class public methods. In this way, the public methods provide your program's *interface* to the object data. Using such interface functions, your programs can verify that the value the program wants to assign to a member is valid. For example, assume that you create a *NuclearReactor* class to maintain information about your nuclear reactor. You determine that the member *Melt_Down* in the *NuclearReactor* class should only contain the values 1 through 5. If the member is public, your programs can use the dot operator to assign an invalid value, as shown here:

```
Nuke.Melt_Down = 99
```

By restricting access to the *Melt_Down* member to the public *Property Let Melt_Down* procedure, the object can verify the value, as shown here:

```
Public Property Let Melt_Down(ByVal vData As Integer)
   If ((vData >= 1) And (vData <=5)) Then mvarMelt_Down = vData
End Property
```

By restricting access to object data to the public methods, the only operations your programs can perform on the data within the object are those operations the object itself defines.

Understanding Information Hiding

Information hiding is the process of hiding underlying implementation details about a function, a program, or even a class. Information hiding lets programmers treat functions and classes as *black boxes*. In other words, if a programmer passes a value to a function, the programmer knows a specific result will occur. The programmer does not have to know how a function calculates a result, but instead that the function works. For example, most programmers do not know the mathematics behind the *Atn* function, which returns an angle's arctangent. However, the programmers know that if they pass a specific value to the function, a known result will occur. To use the function, the programmers must know only the input parameters and the values the *Atn* function returns.

In object-oriented programming, an object may have underlying implementation details. For example, a program may store a document's data in *Word, Excel®*, or some other format. To use the *document* object, however, the program should not have to know the format. Instead, the program should be able to perform read, write, print, and fax operations without knowing the object's details. To help programmers hide an object's underlying details, Visual Basic lets you use the *Public* and *Private* keywords to divide class definitions. The program can directly access public data and methods, while it cannot access private data and methods.

23

Understanding Encapsulation

As you read articles and books about object-oriented programming, you might encounter the term *encapsulation*. In the simplest sense, encapsulation is the combination of data and methods into a single data structure. Encapsulation groups together all the components of an object. In the "object-oriented" sense, encapsulation also defines how both the object itself and the rest of the program can reference the object's data. As you have learned, Visual Basic classes let you divide your data into public and private sections. Programs can access an object's private data only by using defined public methods. Grouping together an object's data and dividing your data into public and private sections protects the data from program misuses (for example, the direct modification of an *Integer* variable with a *String* value, which may cause a program-stopping error). In Visual Basic, the class is the fundamental tool for encapsulation.

Using the Private Keyword within a Class

As you have learned, Visual Basic lets you divide a class definition into public and private parts. The program can directly access the public data and methods with the *dot* operator. The program cannot access the private data and methods. The following class definition again shows the *Employees* class, with private and public parts:

```
Private mvarName As String                    ' local copy
Private mvarAge As Integer                     ' local copy
Private mvarSSN As String                      ' local copy
Private mvarPay_Grade As Integer               ' local copy
Private mvarSalary As Single                   ' local copy
Private mvarEmployee_Number As String          ' local copy
Public Function Last_Date_Paid(Name As String) As String
```

The program can directly access the data and methods that reside in the public section with the *dot* operator. The only way the program can access the private data and methods, however, is through public methods. The next section presents an example program that manipulates both the public and private data.

Using Public and Private Data

As you have learned, Visual Basic lets you divide a class definition into public and private data and methods. Programs can access the public data and methods using the *dot* operator. To access the private data and methods, however, the program must call the public methods. The program cannot directly manipulate or invoke private data and methods. Before you create the program, however, you must add code to the *Last_Date_Paid* method, which you created in the section "Creating Classes Using the Class Builder Utility." Double-click your mouse on the *Employees* class' icon within the Project Explorer. Visual Basic will open a Code window. Locate the *Last_Date_Paid* method and enter the following code:

```
Public Function Last_Date_Paid(Name As String) As String
   If UCase(Left(Name, 1)) < "L" Then
      Last_Date_Paid = ReturnDate(1)
   Else
      Last_Date_Paid = ReturnDate(2)
   End If
End Function
```

The *Last_Date_Paid* method uses the *ReturnDate* function, which you have not defined yet. To define the *ReturnDate* function, perform the following steps:

1. Within Visual Basic, select the Add-Ins menu Class Builder option. Visual Basic will display the Class Builder dialog box. If the Class Builder option does not appear on your Add-Ins menu, select the Add-Ins menu Add-In Manager option. Visual Basic will display the Add-In Manager. Click your mouse one time on the space next to Class Builder to add the Class Builder option to your Add-Ins menu. Click your mouse on OK. Visual Basic will add the Class Builder to the Add-Ins menu.

2. Within the Class Builder, make sure that you have selected the *Employees* class. If you have not selected the *Employees* class, click your mouse once on the Employees icon to select the *Employees* class.

3. Select the File menu New option Method sub-option. Visual Basic will display the Method Builder dialog box.

4. Within the *Name* field, name the new function *ReturnDate*. Click your mouse one time on the + symbol to the right of the *Argument* field. Visual Basic will display the Add Argument dialog box.

5. Within the Add Argument dialog box's *Name* field, type "WhichDate." Select the *Data Type* as *Integer*. Click your mouse on OK. Visual Basic will add the *WhichDate As Integer* argument to the Method Builder dialog box.

6. Within the Method Builder dialog box, select the *Return Type* as *String*. Click your mouse on the OK button. Visual Basic will add the *ReturnDate* function to the *Employees* class.

7. Select the File menu Update Project option. Visual Basic will update the *Employees* class. Click your mouse on the X in the top right hand corner of the Class Builder window to exit the Class Builder.

8. If the *Employees* class Code window is not open, double-click your mouse on the Employees icon within the Class Modules sub-tree of the Project Explorer. Visual Basic will display the *Employees* class code within the Code window. Click your mouse within the Code window and change the *Public* keyword preceding the *ReturnDate* header to *Private*. Add the following code to the *ReturnDate* function:

```
Private Function ReturnDate(WhichDate As Integer) As String
   Dim DateValue As Integer

   DateValue = CInt(Format(Date, "d"))
   Select Case WhichDate
      Case 1
         If DateValue < 15 Then
            ReturnDate = "First of the month"
         Else
            ReturnDate = "Fifteenth of the month."
         End If
```

```
      Case 2
        If DateValue > 7 And DateValue < 22 Then
          ReturnDate = "Seventh of the month."
        Else
          ReturnDate = "Twenty-second of the month."
        End If
    End Select
End Function
```

The *ReturnDate* function returns a string that indicates the last date paid to the *Last_Paid_Date* calling method. However, because *ReturnDate* is a *Private* function, your programs cannot access *ReturnDate* from anywhere outside the class. To create a program to access the *Employees* class, perform the following steps:

1. Double-click your mouse on the Form1 icon within the Project Explorer to open the *Form1* form in an object window.

2. Select the Project menu Remove Form1 option. Visual Basic will prompt you to save changes to *Form1*. Click your mouse on the No button. Visual Basic will remove the *Form1* form from the project.

3. Select the Project menu Add Module option. Within the Add Module dialog box, select the Module icon. Visual Basic will add the blank *Module1* to your project. Within the Project Explorer, double-click your mouse on the Module1 icon to open the *Module1* Code window. Within the Code window, enter the following code:

```
Public Sub Main()
  Dim ThisEmployee As New Employees

  ThisEmployee.Name = "Happy"
  ThisEmployee.Age = "35"
  ThisEmployee.SSN = "999-99-9999"
  ThisEmployee.Pay_Grade = 100
  ThisEmployee.Salary = ThisEmployee.Pay_Grade * 100
  ThisEmployee.Employee_Number = "1"
  Debug.Print ThisEmployee.Last_Date_Paid(ThisEmployee.Name)
  Debug.Print ThisEmployee.ReturnDate
End Sub
```

After you enter the code, perform the following steps to save the project:

1. Within Visual Basic, select the File menu Save Project As option. Visual Basic will open the Save File As dialog box and fill the *File name* field with *Module1*.

2. Within the Save File As dialog box, change the value within the *File name* field to *mdlEmployee*. Next, click your mouse on the Save button. Visual Basic will save the *mdlEmployee* module and fill the *File name* field with *Employee*.

3. Within the Save File As dialog box, change the value within the *File name* field to *clsEmployee*. Next, click your mouse on the Save button. Visual Basic will save the *clsEmployee* module and fill the *File name* field with the *Project1* project name.

4. Within the *File name* field, replace the *Project1* project name with the new *prjUse_Public_and_Private* project name. Next, click your mouse on the Save button. Visual Basic will save the *prjUse_Public_and_Private* project and close the Save Project As dialog box.

After you save your project, select the Run menu Run option to execute the program. When you try to execute the program, Visual Basic will display a "Method or data member not found" error message.Visual Basic will not execute the private function *ReturnDate* if you try to invoke it from within the program. Delete the line that caused the error (the last line in the *Sub Main* procedure) and press the F5 function key to continue execution. When you execute the program, Visual Basic will display a message within the Immediate window, depending on what day of the month it is when you execute the program. The *Last_Date_Paid* function can easily execute the *ReturnDate* function because *ReturnDate* is inaccessible only from the main program.

One of the most difficult tasks programmers new to object-oriented programming face is determining what to hide and what to make public. As a general rule, the less a program's code outside the class knows about the internals of a class, the better. Therefore, you should use private data and methods as often as possible. In this way, programs will have to use the object's public methods to access the object data. As you will learn, if you force programs to manipulate object data with only public methods, you can decrease programming errors. In other words, you do not usually want a program to directly manipulate an object's data using only the *dot* operator. Forcing users to use public methods to access private data will improve information hiding and make your class objects more stable.

DEFINING CLASS FUNCTIONS

You have created several simple classes that defined public and private function members. As the number and complexity of the methods you create increases, so too will the number of functions you will eventually define as public and private to handle the class's processing.

Remember that when you define methods (functions) within a class, you should use the *Public* keyword to declare only those methods that the class must *expose* (that is, make available to procedures outside the class). You should use the *Private* keyword to declare all other functions internal to the class.

USING THE PROPERTY GET AND PROPERTY LET FUNCTIONS

As you have learned, you can use the Visual Basic Class Builder to design a series of *Property Get* and *Property Let* functions within the *Employees* class module. You also learned that the *Property Get* and *Property Let* functions are *interface functions*, which you will use to control the values that the program tries to set for properties, among other things. You will implement the *Property Get* and *Property Let* functions within your class modules, as shown in the following prototype (keywords and statements within brackets are optional, meaning the declaration does not require the object):

```
[Public | Private | Friend] [Static] Property Let name ([arglist,] value)
    [statements]
End Property

[Public | Private | Friend] [Static] Property Get name [(arglist)] _
    [As type]
    [statements]
    [name = expression]
End Property
```

As you can see, the *Property Get* and *Property Let* functions perform similar processing. However, the *Property Let* function only accepts a value—it does not let you return one. The *Property Get* function, on the other hand, will accept parameters and return the property's value. The *Property Get* and *Property Let* statements have the components Table 1.2 describes.

Component	Description
Public	An optional keyword that indicates the *Property Get* or *Property Let* procedure is accessible to all other procedures in all modules. If you do not use it in a module that contains an *Option Private* statement, the procedure is not available outside the project.
Private	An optional keyword that indicates the *Property Get* or *Property Let* procedure is accessible only to other procedures in the class.
Friend	An optional keyword that indicates that the *Property Get* or *Property Let* procedure is visible throughout the project, but not visible to a controller of an instance of an object. As you will learn in later chapters, you can create class modules that other projects can access. Declaring a procedure as a *Friend* lets the project in which you design the class access the procedure, but not other projects.

*Table 1.2 The **Property Get** and **Property Let** procedures' components. (continued on following page)*

Component	Description
Static	An optional keyword that indicates Visual Basic preserves the *Property Get* or *Property Let* procedure's local variables between calls. If you do not use the *Static* keyword, your programs will not preserve the value of local variables between calls.
name	The name of the *Property Get* or *Property Let* procedure. It follows standard variable naming conventions, except that the name can be the same as a corresponding *Property Get* or *Property Let* procedure in the same module.
arglist	A required list of variables that represent arguments the program must pass to the *Property Get* or *Property Let* procedure when the program calls it. The name and data type of each argument in a *Property Let* procedure must be the same as the corresponding argument in a *Property Get* procedure, and vice versa.
value	A variable that contains the value the *Property Get* or *Property Let* procedure is to assign to the property. When your program calls the procedure, the *value* argument must appear on the right side of the calling expression. The data type of *value* must be the same as the return type of the corresponding *Property Get* procedure. Visual Basic requires the *value* argument for the *Property Let* procedure only. Attempts to set a *value* argument in a *Property Get* procedure will cause a run-time error.
statements	Any group of statements for Visual Basic to execute within the *Property Get* or *Property Let* procedure. The *statements* typically check the incoming value or the value the procedure returns for validity.
type	An optional argument that determines the data type of the value the *Property Get* procedure returns. *Type* may be *Byte, Boolean, Integer, Long, Currency, Single, Double, Date, String* (except fixed length), *Object, Variant,* or user-defined type. The procedure cannot return arrays of any type, but a *Variant* that contains an array can. A *Property Get* procedure's return type must be the same data type as the last (or sometimes the only) argument in a corresponding *Property Let* procedure (if one exists) that defines the value the class assigns to the property on the right side of an expression.

27

*Table 1.2 The **Property Get** and **Property Let** procedures' components. (continued from previous page)*

Note: *Every **Property Let** statement must define at least one argument for the procedure it defines. That argument (or the last argument if there is more than one) contains the actual value for you to assign to the property when the program invokes the procedure the **Property Let** statement defines. Table 1.2 refers to that argument as a **value**.*

If you do not explicitly specify the *scope* of a *Property* procedure using either the *Public (*accessible from any project which creates an object instance)*, Private* (accessible only within the object itself), or *Friend* (accessible only within the project where the class resides) keyword, *Property* procedures are public. Scope refers to the accessibility of a variable, procedure, or object. The two basic types of scope are local (private) and global (public). Therefore, *Property* procedures are globally accessible within your programs unless you specifically define them otherwise. You can use the *Friend* keyword only in class modules. However, procedures in any module of a project can access *Friend* procedures. A *Friend* procedure does not appear in the type library of its parent class.

Like *Function* and *Property Get* procedures, a *Property Let* procedure is a separate procedure that takes arguments, performs a series of statements, and changes the value of its arguments. However, unlike *Function* and *Property Get* procedures, both of which return a value, you can only use a *Property Let* procedure on the left side of a property assignment expression or a *Let* statement. Conversely, you can only use a *Property Get* procedure on an expression's right side in the same way you use a *Function* or a property name when you want to return a property's value. As a general rule, you should design your class modules using *Property* procedures to ensure that bad input does not corrupt the data within the class module.

UNDERSTANDING OBJECT INSTANCES

Many books and articles about object-oriented programming refer to *object instances.* In short, an object instance is an object variable. As you have learned, a class defines a template for future variable declarations. When you declare an object, you create an object instance. In other words, when Visual Basic allocates memory for a variable, it creates an object instance. All instances of the same class have the same characteristics. For this book's purposes, an instance is a variable of a specific class.

CREATING OBJECT INSTANCES

As you have learned, Visual Basic does not allocate memory for classes until you create an instance of a class. You have also learned that Visual Basic creates an instance, or object instance, when you create a variable of the *Class* type. Within Visual Basic, you will create variables that have *Class* type using one of the following two declaration methods:

28

```
Dim VariableName As New ClassName

Dim VariableName As Object
 ' Statements
Set VariableName = New ClassName
```

Either method is valid. However, if you assign the *VariableName* to a specific type (as the first line of code does), the assignment forces Visual Basic to perform early binding. If you instead create an *Object* variable and later assign the *Class* type to that *Object* variable, Visual Basic will perform late binding. In other words, if you use the *Dim* statement to create the variable of type *Class*, Visual Basic will reserve that variable space at the beginning of the program (or whenever you declare *VariableName*). If you use the *Set* statement, Visual Basic will not reserve the variable space for that class variable until the program reaches the assignment statement.

Using early binding versus late binding has several implications in Visual Basic. The biggest implication is error-checking and program design. If you early bind your variables, the Visual Basic Interactive Development Environment will alert you if you try to perform a bad assignment with the variables, misuse a method, or any other similar incorrect processing. On the other hand, if you late bind your variables, the Visual Basic Interactive Development Environment will be unable to warn you if you try to perform an invalid activity on an object within your program (because it will be impossible to know it is invalid until the program executes). As a rule, you should try to use early binding within your programs whenever possible.

Early binding will also speed (even if only slightly) the program's execution, because the program can allocate space for the variable at the beginning of the program's execution, rather than having to allocate space for the variable during execution. Because of how the Windows memory model works, it is possible that allocating additional space for a late-binding variable can cause the operating system to access a hard disk as Windows reallocates other memory based on the program's memory use.

UNDERSTANDING INHERITANCE

As you visualize how you might derive classes using inheritance, drawing pictures might help you to understand the relationships between classes. You will find that one class you derive from one or more base classes might well become the base class for other classes. As you begin to define your classes, start with general characteristics and work toward specifics as you derive new classes.

For example, if you are deriving classes for types of dogs, your first base class might be *Dogs. Dogs* would contain characteristics common to all dog breeds, such as name, origin, height, weight, and color. Your next level might become more refined when you create the classes. The second level of class types, *DogsWithSpots* and *SpotlessDogs,* for example, would inherit the common characteristics that you defined in the *Dogs* base class.

As you further refine pedigrees (for example, between Dalmatians and Labradors), you can use these second level classes as base classes for other class definitions. Your base class levels will grow, conceptually similar to a family tree's growth, as shown in Figure 1.21.

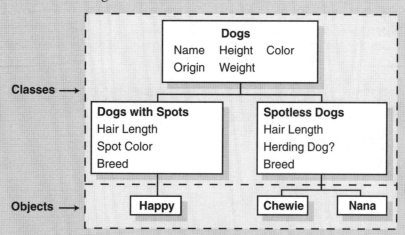

Figure 1.21 The **Dogs** *inheritance tree.*

Unfortunately, Visual Basic does not support true inheritance. While there are some methods that you can use to avoid Visual Basic's built-in constraints on inheritance, in general you cannot fully inherit classes, nor can you control how you inherit classes, as you can in C++. The programs in this book will design classes that do not use inheritance.

Understanding the Windows API

As you have learned, writing programs for Windows can be a difficult task, although Visual Basic makes that task simpler. When Microsoft's programmers wrote Windows, they also added many useful procedures and functions to the operating system that let your programs more easily access and manipulate the operating system. Generally, programmers group together all the functions and procedures that Windows lets your programs use to control the operating system into a catch-all category called the Windows API or the Win32 API.

API is an acronym that stands for *Application Programming Interface*. Almost every program, operating system, and language has an Application Programming Interface. The *Windows API* is a series of functions that let you access Windows programming constructs at the system level. Microsoft wrote most of the Windows API functions in the C/C++ and assembly languages, but your programs can use the *Declare* statement to access most of the functions within the Windows API from Visual Basic. You will implement the *Declare* statement as shown in the following prototype (keywords and statement within brackets are optional, meaning the declaration does not require the object):

```
[Public | Private] Declare Function name Lib "libname" [Alias _
    "aliasname"] [([arglist])] [As type]
```

The *Lib* keyword indicates within which library Visual Basic will find the function. Libraries always have a file extension of *.dll*, although you will not use the *.dll* extension within the *libname* string. You can find the majority of the API functions that you will use within this book in the *kernel32* library. The Windows API lets you do two things: perform certain tasks that your programs can perform only at the system level, and have faster access to some actions because you are performing those actions at the system level.

Note: Visual Basic 5.0 only works on 32–bit Windows platforms. The 32–bit Windows API differs significantly from the 16–bit Windows API. In this book, references to the Windows API and the Win32 API both refer to the 32–bit Windows API. If you use Windows 95 or Windows NT, you use the Win32 API.

USING THE API TEXT VIEWER

When you installed Visual Basic 5.0, Visual Basic installed a program called the *API Text Viewer* into the same program group. To execute the *API Text Viewer*, click your mouse on the Windows Start button and select the Programs group Microsoft Visual Basic 5.0 submenu. Within the Microsoft Visual Basic 5.0 group, select the API Text Viewer option. The API Text Viewer's opening screen appears in Figure 1.22.

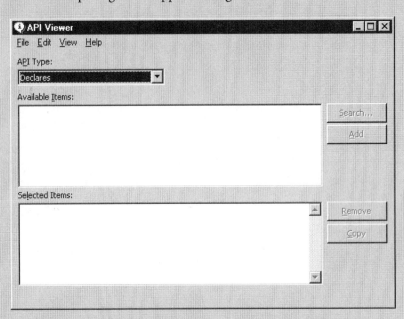

*Figure 1.22 The **API Text Viewer's** opening dialog box.*

Next, select the File menu Load Text File option. The *API Text Viewer* will respond with a list of text files. Double-click your mouse on the *win32api.txt* file to select the file. The *API Text Viewer* now has a long list of *Declares* (functions) inside the Available Items window. If you scroll through this list briefly, you will notice that it is extremely long. In fact, the Win32 API contains some 6,300 constants, 1,575 declarations, and 400 types (structures). As you will learn in later chapters, Windows also includes additional APIs the Win32 API does not provide, such as the Windows Telephony Application Programming Interface (TAPI), Speech Application Programming Interface (SAPI), and Mail Application Programming Interface (MAPI).

The *API Text Viewer* will simplify the process of adding API calls to your Visual Basic programs. After you locate the declares, constants, and structures that you must have for your program, you can then use the Copy button to copy all the code you selected to the Windows Clipboard. Next, you can switch into your Visual Basic project and select the Edit menu Paste option to paste the code directly into your project. This is especially useful because the majority of the API functions have long parameter lists, making it very easy to make entry mistakes.

Protecting against entry mistakes when you work with API calls is especially important because Visual Basic *will not return run-time errors from most API calls*. As you will learn, you must *wrap* (surround) all calls to the Win32 API, which returns a *String* value. However, you should wrap all your Win32 API function calls to ensure that the return values fall within the parameters the program expects. When you wrap your API function calls within another function whose sole purpose is to ensure that the API function returns the expected values, you create what is called a *wrapper function*.

A Visual Basic program must *wrap* (surround) the *GetCurrentDirectory* API function with a Visual Basic function or procedure because the API function returns a C-style string (as you will learn in the next section). To return the current directory using the Win32 API, for example, you would write a *GetCurrentDir* wrapper function similar to the following:

```
Private Function GetCurrentDir() As String
   Dim lBuffer As String, BufferLength As Long
   Dim ReturnVal As Long

   lBuffer = Space$(255)
   BufferLength = 255
   ReturnVal = GetCurrentDirectory(BufferLength, lBuffer)
   If ReturnVal = 0 Then
     MsgBox "Error"
   Else
     GetCurrentDir = StripTerminator(lBuffer)
   End If
End Function
```

Note how the code initializes the *lBuffer* variable with 255 spaces. Because the manner in which C/C++ handles strings differs from how Visual Basic handles strings, your program should fill every string it passes into a Win32 API function with some fixed number of spaces before it calls the API function. Filling the string with spaces simulates a fixed-length string to the API function. When the *GetCurrentDirectory* function returns *lBuffer*, *lBuffer* will actually contain the current directory and the *Chr(0)* value (a *NULL* character) to terminate the string. However, the remaining spaces beyond the length of the current directory up through 255 will still contain spaces. In the next section, you will learn how to write a *string–wrapper* function, which you can use to trim the extra spaces and the *Chr(0)* value.

WRITING THE STRIPTERMINATOR FUNCTION

As you learned in the previous section, Visual Basic does not use *Chr(0)*-terminated strings—unfortunately, C/C++ does, and to access the Windows API, you must you use C-style strings. Therefore, when you call a Win32 API function that returns a string value (such as *GetCurrentDirectory*), you must strip the string of its *NULL–terminator* so that Visual Basic will recognize the string correctly. The following function, *StripTerminator*, strips the *NULL–*terminator from the end of any C++ string:

```
Public Function StripTerminator(ByVal strString As String) As String
   Dim intZeroPos As Integer

   intZeroPos = InStr(strString, Chr$(0))
   If intZeroPos > 0 Then
     StripTerminator = Left$(strString, intZeroPos - 1)
   Else
     StripTerminator = strString
   End If
End Function
```

Note that the program code declares the *StripTerminator* function using the *Public* keyword. You will use the *StripTerminator* function so frequently when your programs use API functions that you should usually make it public in scope. Within this book, you will use the StripTerminator function within several programs that use Windows API calls to get information from the operating system.

PUTTING IT ALL TOGETHER

This chapter has introduced you to Visual Basic projects, forms, controls, and modules, as well as the basic concepts behind object-oriented programming with Visual Basic. In addition, you have learned about the Toolbox and the Code window, the Class Builder utility, and the *API Text Viewer* program that you can use to easily add API function declarations to your programs.

Future chapters in this book will go into detail on many of the more advanced controls that Visual Basic provides. Also, throughout each chapter, you will use the standard controls this chapter introduced. In Chapter 2, "Using the Multimedia MCI Control to Create a CD-ROM Player," you will use the multimedia control that Visual Basic provides to write a program that lets you play music CD-ROMs from within your computer's CD-ROM drive. Before you continue with Chapter 2, however, make sure you understand the following key concepts:

✓ Visual Basic includes forms, which you will use to contain controls and the program code that you assign to and associate with those controls.

✓ You will use controls, forms, modules, class modules, and more to design the interface for your Visual Basic program that lets the user interact with the program.

✓ Visual Basic includes user controls and user documents, which you will use to design custom ActiveX components for your Visual Basic programs, Web pages, and more.

✓ You can organize code that you do not directly associate with a form or other visual component into modules. You can make code within modules available only within the module itself or available to all the forms within a project.

✓ You can use Visual Basic group projects to include custom-designed controls, and more, within a Visual Basic program.

✓ Visual Basic and its Interactive Development Environment (IDE) make the process of quickly developing powerful software applications relatively easy.

✓ When you write an object-oriented program, you divide the program into its component objects and manage those components through public and private functions and procedures.

✓ Programmers generally evaluate whether a programming language supports inheritance, polymorphism, and encapsulation when determining whether the language is object-oriented.

✓ When you write programs that focus on the programs' response to user input or activities, you write event-oriented programs.

✓ Visual Basic combines elements of object-oriented and event-oriented programming.

✓ Windows exposes (makes available) several different APIs that you can use from within Visual Basic to create more powerful programs.

✓ You can easily access and use the *API Text Viewer* to place Windows API calls within your Visual Basic program code.

Chapter 2

Using the Multimedia MCI Control to Create a CD-ROM Player

As the CD-ROM became a popular standard in personal computers, creating programs that let users play their audio CDs through their computer speakers became an important task for many computer sellers. In fact, nearly every computer for sale in retail stores today includes a CD-ROM player that can play audio CDs back through the speakers. To create a program that plays audio CDs is a complex task. You must manage the audio tracks' special format, convert the incoming data from the CD-ROM into sound data that you can play through the speakers, and send the converted data to the speakers—all in real time (that is, as the CD plays). Writing a program that uses the Windows Application Programming Interface (API) to read the CD-ROM and play back the music files can be time consuming and difficult.

33

However, in Chapter 1, "Introduction to Visual Basic," you learned Visual Basic provides many controls that you can use to simplify the design of complex programs. One control you can add to your Visual Basic projects to simplify program development is the *Multimedia MCI* control. The *Multimedia MCI* control lets you play a variety of audio and video files on your computer—video on the computer's display, and audio through the computer's speakers. In this chapter's *prjCD-ROM* project, you will use the *Multimedia MCI* control to design your own audio CD player. By the time you finish this chapter, you will understand the following key concepts:

- Within your Visual Basic programs, you can use custom controls—either those that come with Visual Basic, controls that you buy from a third-party vendor, or controls that you design yourself—to simplify complex programming tasks.

- Visual Basic's *PictureBox* control lets you easily display bitmaps, Windows metafiles, and other graphics file types within your programs.

- Within your programs, you can use the Visual Basic *PictureBox* control to provide users with a convenient, easy-to-use interface to your programs. Within the *prjCD-ROM* project, you will use *PictureBox* controls to simulate the buttons on an audio CD player.

- Within your Visual Basic programs, you can use the *Timer* control to perform certain activities at regular intervals. In the *prjCD-ROM* project, you will use the *Timer* control to update the program's display once each second.

- Your programs can use *control arrays* (groups of controls sharing a common name and, often, common characteristics) to simplify and clarify your program's processing and structure.

USING THE PRJCD-ROM PROJECT

Before you design the *prjCD-ROM* project, you may find it helpful to run the program. The companion CD-ROM that accompanies this book contains the *prjCD-ROM.exe* program within the *Chapter02* directory. As with every other program on the CD-ROM, you should run the Jamsa Press *setup.exe* program to install the *prjCD-ROM.exe* program to your computer's hard drive before you run it. After you install the *prjCD-ROM.exe* program to your computer's hard drive, you can run it from the Start menu. To run the program, select the Windows Start menu Run option. Windows will display the Run dialog box. Within the Run dialog box, enter *x:\vbp\Chapter02\prjCD-ROM.exe*, where *x* corresponds to the drive letter of the hard drive on which you installed the *prjCD-ROM.exe* program, and click your mouse on OK. Windows will display the *prjCD-ROM.exe* program, as shown in Figure 2.1.

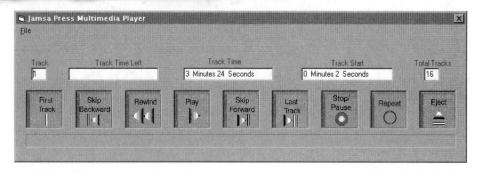

Figure 2.1 The *prjCD-ROM.exe* program's start-up screen.

Running prjCD-ROM from the CD-ROM

34

Because you will use the *prjCD-ROM.exe* program to play audio CDs, it is generally a good idea to install the program to your computer's hard drive before you try to run the program. If you try to run the *prjCD-ROM.exe* program from this book's companion CD-ROM, you may encounter errors during the program's processing after you remove the companion CD-ROM from the drive and replace it with the audio CD that you want to play.

To learn more about the Jamsa Press *setup.exe* program, see the "What's on the *Visual Basic Programmer's Library* Companion CD-ROM" section at the back of this book.

Before you use the *prjCD-ROM.exe* program, take a moment to familiarize yourself with the controls on the program's display. As you have learned, the *prjCD-ROM* project will let you play audio CDs from your computer's CD-ROM drive. When the program starts, you will see a medium-sized window with nine graphical buttons across the form and several text boxes above the buttons. You will use the graphical buttons to navigate and play an audio CD. From left to right, the buttons are First Track, Skip Backward, Rewind, Play, Skip Forward, Last Track, Stop/Pause, Repeat, and Eject. Labels on the text boxes above the buttons indicate that they represent the Track, Track Time Left, Track Time, Track Start, and Total Tracks. To play an audio CD that is currently in the CD-ROM drive, click your mouse on the Play button. Figure 2.2 shows the *prjCD-ROM* project after you click your mouse on the Play button.

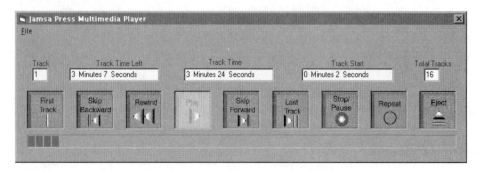

Figure 2.2 The *prjCD-ROM* project playing an audio CD.

You can also use the navigation buttons to change the current track. For example, if you click your mouse on the Skip Forward button, the CD player will advance to the next track and start to play the track. Figure 2.3 shows the *prjCD-ROM* project playing track 2 on an audio CD.

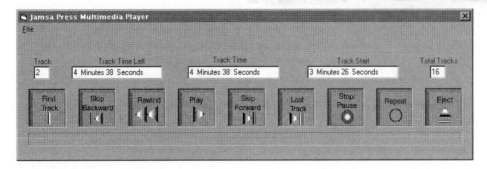

*Figure 2.3 The **prjCD-ROM** project playing track 2 on an audio CD.*

The majority of the *prjCD-ROM* program's buttons are self-explanatory. For example, to go back a track, click your mouse on the Skip Backward button. To move to the last track on the CD, click your mouse on the Last Track button. To pause the CD-ROM, click your mouse on the Stop/Pause button. The *prjCD-ROM* program will change the Stop/Pause button's appearance to sunken, change the button's caption to Stop, and the Track Time Left box will indicate that you have paused the CD playback. Figure 2.4 shows the *prjCD-ROM* project after you click the mouse on the Stop/Pause button.

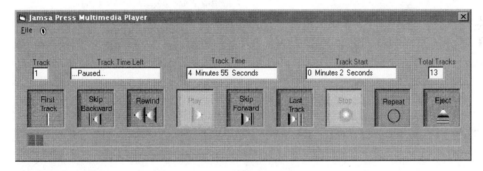

*Figure 2.4 The **prjCD-ROM** project after you pause a CD playback.*

If you click your mouse again on the Stop/Pause button (which now displays the caption Stop), the program will begin to play the CD from the point where you paused the CD's playback. On the other hand, if you double-click your mouse on the Stop/Pause button, the program will stop playing the audio CD and reset itself to the first track.

If you click your mouse on the Load/Eject Button, the program will eject the CD from the drive. If you insert a new disk into the drive, you can then click your mouse on the Load/Eject Button again to load the new CD.

UNDERSTANDING THE MULTIMEDIA *MCI* CONTROL'S LIMITATIONS

As you have learned, you can eject the audio CD from the drive and insert a new CD into the drive. However, the *Multimedia MCI* control cannot sense what type of CD-ROM is in the drive. It may actually let you try to play a data CD—which will return no sound, because it is not in a form that your computer can translate to sound. As you will learn with many other controls that you will use within your Visual Basic programs, the *Multimedia MCI* control helps you perform significant processing quickly and easily. However, it does lack certain features that may be necessary for your project. If you find that a control is insufficient for your needs, you may want to research other controls that perform similar processing, or you may want to design your own controls or program code to perform the same processing. In later chapters, you will write programs that include their own custom controls or libraries. You will design the custom controls or libraries so that your programs can perform processing with them, much as your programs do with Visual Basic's standard controls.

CREATING A BLANK FORM

Now that you have a better idea how to use the finished *prjCD-ROM* project, you can begin to design it. First, you will create an empty form that will contain all the controls the "Using the *prjCD-ROM* Project" section introduced. After you design the form, you will learn more about the *Multimedia MCI* control that you will use to play audio CDs.

To begin the *prjCD-ROM* project and create a blank form, perform the following steps:

1. Within Visual Basic, select the File menu New Project option. Visual Basic will open the New Project dialog box.

2. Within the New Project dialog box, click your mouse on the Standard EXE icon. Next, click your mouse on the OK button. Visual Basic will close the dialog box and open the *Form1* form window.

3. Select the View menu Properties Window option. Visual Basic will open the Properties Window listing the *Form1* properties.

4. Within the Properties Window, change the *Form1* properties to the values Table 2.1 lists.

Object	Property	Set As
Form1	*Caption*	*Jamsa Press Multimedia Player*
Form1	*Height*	3555
Form1	*Left*	0
Form1	*StartUpPosition*	2 - Center Screen
Form1	*Top*	0
Form1	*Width*	11055
Form1	*Name*	*frmMMedia*

Table 2.1 *The newly named* **frmMMedia** *form's properties.*

5. Select the File menu Save Project As option. Visual Basic will open the Save File As dialog box and fill the *File name* field with *frmMMedia*.

6. Within the Save File As dialog box, click your mouse on the Save button. Visual Basic will save the *frmMMedia* form and fill the *File name* field with the *Project1* project name.

7. Within the *File name* field, replace the *Project1* project name with the new *prjCD-ROM* project name. Next, click your mouse on the Save button. Visual Basic will save the *prjCD-ROM* project and close the Save Project As dialog box.

ADDING THE MICROSOFT PROGRESSBAR CONTROL TO THE PROJECT

As you can see from the *prjCD-ROM* project's interface, the program displays a progress bar across the bottom that indicates how far along the program is in the current track. The *Microsoft ProgressBar* control is one of the *Microsoft Windows Common Controls* that comes with Visual Basic. Before you can use the *Microsoft ProgressBar* control in the *prjCD-ROM* project, you must add it to the project as a component. After you add the *Microsoft ProgressBar* control to the *prjCD-ROM* project, Visual Basic will display the control's icon in the Toolbox. As you know, the Toolbox displays Visual Basic control icons. If you double-click your mouse on any icon in the Toolbox, Visual Basic will draw the control that the icon corresponds to within the active form.

To add the *Microsoft ProgressBar* control to the *prjCD-ROM* project, perform the following steps:

1. Select the Project menu Components option. Visual Basic will open the Components dialog box.

2. Within the Components dialog box, select the *Microsoft Windows Common Controls 5.0* listing. Next, click your mouse on the box to the left of the listing. Visual Basic will display a check mark in the box, as Figure 2.5 shows.

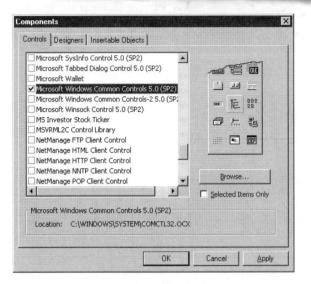

Figure 2.5 *The Components dialog box after you select the* **Microsoft Windows Common Controls 5.0** *component.*

3. Within the Components dialog box, click your mouse on OK. Visual Basic will add the *Microsoft Windows Common Controls* control components to the *prjCD-ROM* project.

ADDING THE MICROSOFT MULTIMEDIA CONTROL TO THE PROJECT

As you have learned, the *prjCD-ROM* project uses the *Multimedia MCI* control to play back audio CDs. Like the *Microsoft Windows Common Controls* that you added to the project in the previous section, the *Multimedia MCI* control comes with Visual Basic. Before you can use the *Multimedia MCI* control in the *prjCD-ROM* project, you must add it to the project as a component. After you add the *Multimedia MCI* control to the *prjCD-ROM* project, Visual Basic will display the control's icon in the Toolbox. As you know, the Toolbox displays Visual Basic control icons. If you double-click your mouse on any icon in the Toolbox, Visual Basic will draw the control that the icon corresponds to within the active form.

To add the *Microsoft Multimedia MCI* control to the *prjCD-ROM* project, perform the following steps:

1. Select the Project menu Components option. Visual Basic will open the Components dialog box.

2. Within the Components dialog box, select the *Microsoft Multimedia MCI Control 5.0* listing. Next, click your mouse on the box to the left of the listing. Visual Basic will display a check mark in the box.

3. Within the Components dialog box, click your mouse on OK. Visual Basic will add the *Microsoft Multimedia MCI* control component to the *prjCD-ROM* project.

ADDING CONTROLS TO THE FORM

In the *prjCD-ROM* project, you will use the *Multimedia MCI* control and the *ProgressBar* control you added to the project in the previous sections, five *TextBox* controls, five *Label* controls, nine *PictureBox* controls, and a *Timer* control. To begin, you will add each control to the *frmMMedia* form and assign properties to position each control on the form and provide a unique name for each control.

ADDING THE TIMER CONTROL TO THE FRMMMEDIA FORM

As you have learned, the *prjCD-ROM* project updates the display at regular intervals while you play an audio CD. To start the code that performs the update processing at regular intervals, you will use a *Timer* control. To add the *Timer* control to the *frmMMedia* form, perform the following steps:

1. If Visual Basic is not displaying the *frmMMedia* form within an object window, double-click your mouse on the *frmMMedia* form listing within the Project Explorer. Visual Basic will open the *frmMMedia* form.

2. Within Visual Basic, select the View menu Toolbox option. Visual Basic will open the Toolbox.

3. Within the Toolbox, double-click your mouse on the Timer icon. Visual Basic will draw a *Timer* control, *Timer1*, within the *frmMMedia* form.

4. Within the *frmMMedia* form, click your mouse on the *Timer1* control to highlight it. Visual Basic will draw a small frame around the control.

5. Select the View menu Properties Window option. Visual Basic will open the Properties Window listing the *Timer1* properties.

6. Within the Properties Window, change the *Timer1* properties to the values Table 2.2 lists.

38

Object	Property	Set As
Timer1	*Interval*	0
Timer1	*Left*	0
Timer1	*Top*	0

Table 2.2 *The* **Timer1** *control's properties.*

ADDING THE PROGRESSBAR CONTROL TO THE FRMMMEDIA FORM

As the previous section details, the *Timer1* control starts the interval processing that the program will use to update the display. The *prjCD-ROM* project uses the *ProgressBar* control to graphically display the project's progress in the current track's play. To add the *ProgressBar* control to the *prjCD-ROM* project, perform the following steps:

1. If Visual Basic is not displaying the *frmMMedia* form within an object window, double-click your mouse on the *frmMMedia* form listing within the Project Explorer. Visual Basic will open the *frmMMedia* form.

2. Within Visual Basic, select the View menu Toolbox option. Visual Basic will open the Toolbox.

3. Within the Toolbox, double-click your mouse on the ProgressBar icon. Visual Basic will draw a *ProgressBar* control, *ProgressBar1*, within the *frmMMedia* form. Figure 2.6 shows the ProgressBar icon within the Toolbox.

Figure 2.6 *The ProgressBar icon within the Toolbox.*

4. Within the *frmMMedia* form, click your mouse on the *ProgressBar1* control to highlight it. Visual Basic will draw a small frame around the control.

5. Select the View menu Properties Window option. Visual Basic will open the Properties Window listing the *ProgressBar1* properties.

6. Within the Properties Window, change the *ProgressBar1* properties to the values Table 2.3 lists.

Object	Property	Set As
ProgressBar1	Height	315
ProgressBar1	Left	240
ProgressBar1	Max	100
ProgressBar1	Min	0
ProgressBar1	Top	2280
ProgressBar1	Width	10515

Table 2.3 *The ProgressBar1 control's properties.*

ADDING THE MULTIMEDIA MCI CONTROL TO THE FRMMMEDIA FORM

As you learned at the beginning of this chapter, the *prjCD-ROM* project uses the *Multimedia MCI* control to play back audio CDs. Before the program can use the *Multimedia MCI* control, however, you must add it to the form. To add the *Multimedia MCI* control to the *prjCD-ROM* project, perform the following steps:

1. If Visual Basic is not displaying the *frmMMedia* form within an object window, double-click your mouse on the *frmMMedia* form listing within the Project Explorer. Visual Basic will open the *frmMMedia* form.

2. Within Visual Basic, select the View menu Toolbox option. Visual Basic will open the Toolbox.

3. Within the Toolbox, double-click your mouse on the MMControl icon. Visual Basic will draw a *Multimedia MCI* control, *MMControl1*, within the *frmMMedia* form. Figure 2.7 shows the *Multimedia MCI* control's icon within the Toolbox.

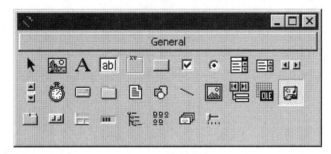

Figure 2.7 *The Multimedia MCI control's icon within the Toolbox.*

4. Within the *frmMMedia* form, click your mouse on the *MMControl1* control to highlight it. Visual Basic will draw a small frame around the control.

5. Select the View menu Properties Window option. Visual Basic will open the Properties Window listing the *MMControl1* properties.

6. Within the Properties Window, change the *MMControl1* properties to the values Table 2.4 lists.

Object	Property	Set As
MMControl1	AutoEnable	True
MMControl1	Height	540
MMControl1	Left	6525
MMControl1	Shareable	False
MMControl1	Top	0
MMControl1	UpdateInterval	1000
MMControl1	Width	10515

Table 2.4 *The MMControl1 control's properties.*

39

ADDING PICTUREBOX CONTROLS TO THE frmMMEDIA FORM

When you used the *prjCD-ROM* project in the "Using the *prjCD-ROM* Project" section of this chapter, you used the graphical buttons on the program to manipulate the audio CD. For the *prjCD-ROM* project, those buttons are actually *PictureBox* controls designed to respond when a user clicks the mouse. To add the nine *PictureBox* controls that let the user control the CD's playback, perform the following steps:

1. If Visual Basic is not displaying the *frmMMedia* form within an object window, double-click your mouse on the *frmMMedia* form listing within the Project Explorer. Visual Basic will open the *frmMMedia* form.

2. Within Visual Basic, select the View menu Toolbox option. Visual Basic will open the Toolbox.

3. Within the Toolbox, double-click your mouse on the PictureBox icon. Visual Basic will draw a *PictureBox* control, *Picture1*, within the *frmMMedia* form.

4. Within the *frmMMedia* form, click your mouse on the *Picture1* control to highlight it. Visual Basic will draw a small frame around the control.

5. Select the View menu Properties Window option. Visual Basic will open the Properties Window listing the *Picture1* control properties.

6. Within the Properties Window, click your mouse on the *Name* property and change the value from *PictureBox* to *ControlPanel*.

7. Select the Edit menu Copy option. Visual Basic will store a copy of the *ControlPanel* control in the Clipboard.

8. Select the Edit menu Paste option. Visual Basic will open a dialog box that asks, "You already have a control named '*ControlPanel*.' Do you want to create a control array?" Click your mouse on the Yes button. Visual Basic will draw a copy of the *ControlPanel* control within the *frmMMedia* form. Figure 2.8 shows the Create Control Array dialog box.

Figure 2.8 *The Create Control Array dialog box.*

9. Repeat Step 8 seven more times until you have added a total of nine *PictureBox* controls to the *ControlPanel* control array.

10. Within the *frmMMedia* form, click your mouse on a *ControlPanel* control to highlight it. Visual Basic will draw a small frame around the control.

11. Within the Properties Window, change the highlighted *ControlPanel* control's properties to the values Table 2.5 lists.

12. Repeat Steps 10 and 11 until you have changed each highlighted *ControlPanel* control's properties to the values Table 2.5 lists.

Object	Property	Set As
ControlPanel(0)	*Height*	915
ControlPanel(0)	*Left*	240
ControlPanel(0)	*ToolTipText*	*First Track*
ControlPanel(0)	*Top*	1245

Table 2.5 *The frmMMedia form's ControlPanel control array's properties. (continued on following page)*

Object	Property	Set As
ControlPanel(0)	Width	915
ControlPanel(1)	Height	915
ControlPanel(1)	Left	1440
ControlPanel(1)	ToolTipText	Previous Track
ControlPanel(1)	Top	1245
ControlPanel(1)	Width	915
ControlPanel(2)	Height	915
ControlPanel(2)	Left	2640
ControlPanel(2)	ToolTipText	Beginning of Current Track
ControlPanel(2)	Top	1245
ControlPanel(2)	Width	915
ControlPanel(3)	Height	915
ControlPanel(3)	Left	3840
ControlPanel(3)	ToolTipText	Play
ControlPanel(3)	Top	1245
ControlPanel(3)	Width	915
ControlPanel(4)	Height	915
ControlPanel(4)	Left	5040
ControlPanel(4)	ToolTipText	Next Track
ControlPanel(4)	Top	1245
ControlPanel(4)	Width	915
ControlPanel(5)	Height	915
ControlPanel(5)	Left	6240
ControlPanel(5)	ToolTipText	Last Track
ControlPanel(5)	Top	1245
ControlPanel(5)	Width	915
ControlPanel(6)	Height	915
ControlPanel(6)	Left	7440
ControlPanel(6)	ToolTipText	Stop or Pause
ControlPanel(6)	Top	1245
ControlPanel(6)	Width	915
ControlPanel(7)	Height	915
ControlPanel(7)	Left	8640
ControlPanel(7)	ToolTipText	Repeat
ControlPanel(7)	Top	1245
ControlPanel(7)	Width	915
ControlPanel(8)	Height	915
ControlPanel(8)	Left	9840
ControlPanel(8)	ToolTipText	Load or Eject
ControlPanel(8)	Top	1245
ControlPanel(8)	Width	915

Table 2.5 The *frmMMedia* form's **ControlPanel** control array's properties. *(continued from previous page)*

ADDING TextBox CONTROLS TO THE frmMMedia FORM

Now that you have the *ProgressBar* control to display the program's progress, and the *PictureBox* array that you will use to let the user control the player, you will add *TextBox* controls to the *frmMMedia* form. The *TextBox* controls will display information about the CD the player is playing. To add *TextBox* controls to the *frmMMedia* form, perform the following steps:

1. If Visual Basic is not displaying the *frmMMedia* form within an object window, double-click your mouse on the *frmMMedia* form listing within the Project Explorer. Visual Basic will open the *frmMMedia* form.

2. Within Visual Basic, select the View menu Toolbox option. Visual Basic will open the Toolbox.

3. Within the Toolbox, double-click your mouse on the TextBox icon. Visual Basic will draw a *TextBox* control, *Text1*, within the *frmMMedia* form.

4. Repeat Step 3 four more times. Visual Basic will draw four more *TextBox* controls within the *frmMMedia* form.

5. Within the *frmMMedia* form window, click your mouse on a *TextBox* control to highlight it. Visual Basic will draw a small frame around the control.

6. Select the View menu Properties Window option. Visual Basic will open the Properties Window listing the highlighted *TextBox* control's properties.

7. Within the Properties Window, change the highlighted *TextBox* control's properties to the values Table 2.6 lists.

8. Repeat Steps 5, 6, and 7 until you have changed each *TextBox* control's properties to the values Table 2.6 lists.

Object	Property	Set As
Text1	*Height*	315
Text1	*Index*	0
Text1	*Left*	375
Text1	*Text*	[blank]
Text1	*Top*	720
Text1	*Width*	390
Text1	*Name*	*Text1*
Text2	*Height*	315
Text2	*Index*	1
Text2	*Left*	1275
Text2	*Text*	[blank]
Text2	*Top*	720
Text2	*Width*	2205
Text2	*Name*	*Text1*
Text3	*Height*	315
Text3	*Index*	2
Text3	*Left*	4080
Text3	*Text*	[blank]
Text3	*Top*	720
Text3	*Width*	2205
Text3	*Name*	*Text1*
Text4	*Height*	315

Table 2.6 The TextBox controls' properties. (continued on following page)

Object	Property	Set As
Text4	Index	3
Text4	Left	6960
Text4	Text	[blank]
Text4	Top	720
Text4	Width	2250
Text4	Name	Text1
Text5	Height	315
Text5	Index	4
Text5	Left	9960
Text5	Text	[blank]
Text5	Top	720
Text5	Width	390
Text5	Name	Text1

Table 2.6 *The **TextBox** controls' properties. (continued from previous page)*

After you finish changing the *TextBox* controls' properties, you can add the labels for each text box to the *frmMMedia* form, which you will do in the next section.

ADDING THE LABEL CONTROLS TO THE FORM

As you have learned, within the *prjCD-ROM* project, you will use *Label* controls to place captions on the *TextBox* controls that display information to the user about the program's audio CD playback. Now that you have added to the form the *TextBox* controls that will display the actual information, you should add the *Label* controls to the form.

To add the *Label* controls to the *frmMMedia* form, perform the following steps:

1. If Visual Basic is not displaying the *frmMMedia* form within an object window, double-click your mouse on the *frmMMedia* form listing within the Project Explorer. Visual Basic will open the *frmMMedia* form.

2. Within Visual Basic, select the View menu Toolbox option. Visual Basic will open the Toolbox.

3. Within the Toolbox, double-click your mouse on the Label icon. Visual Basic will draw a *Label* control, *Label1*, within the *frmMMedia* form.

4. Repeat Step 3 four more times to add the *Label2, Label3, Label4,* and *Label5* controls to the *frmMMedia* form.

5. Within the *frmMMedia* form, click your mouse on the *Label1* control to highlight it. Visual Basic will draw a small frame around the control.

6. Select the View menu Properties Window option. Visual Basic will open the Properties Window listing the *Label1* properties.

7. Within the Properties Window, change the *Label1* properties to the values Table 2.7 lists.

8. Repeat Steps 5, 6, and 7 to change the properties for the other *Label* controls to the values Table 2.7 lists.

Object	Property	Set As
Label1	Caption	Track
Label1	ForeColor	&H00FF0000& (Royal Blue)
Label1	Height	195
Label1	Left	375
Label1	Top	510

Table 2.7 *The newly named **Label** controls' properties. (continued on following page)*

43

Object	Property	Set As
Label1	Width	420
Label1	Name	lblTrack
Label2	Caption	Track Time Left
Label2	ForeColor	&H00FF0000& (Royal Blue)
Label2	Height	195
Label2	Left	1920
Label2	Top	510
Label2	Width	1125
Label2	Name	lblTimeLeft
Label3	Caption	Track Time
Label3	ForeColor	&H00FF0000& (Royal Blue)
Label3	Height	195
Label3	Left	4680
Label3	Top	510
Label3	Width	810
Label3	Name	lblTrackTime
Label4	Caption	Track Start
Label4	ForeColor	&H00FF0000& (Royal Blue)
Label4	Height	195
Label4	Left	7680
Label4	Top	510
Label4	Width	795
Label4	Name	lblTrackStart
Label5	Caption	Total Tracks
Label5	ForeColor	&H00FF0000& (Royal Blue)
Label5	Height	195
Label5	Left	9720
Label5	Top	510
Label5	Width	900
Label5	Name	lblTotalTracks

Table 2.7 *The newly named* **Label** *controls' properties. (continued from previous page)*

When you finish changing the *Label* controls' properties, the *frmMMedia* form will look like Figure 2.9.

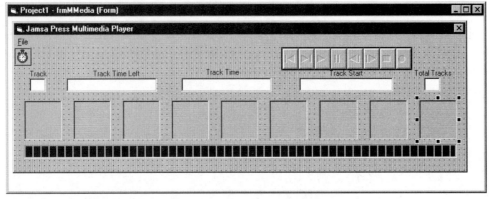

Figure 2.9 *The* **frmMMedia** *form after you finish its visual design.*

Writing the Code for the frmMMedia Form

Now that you have finished adding the controls to the *frmMMedia* form, you must write the program code that will react to the user's selections and perform the user-requested actions. The *frmMMedia* form uses several variables throughout the form to help it handle its processing. You must declare these variables within the form's General–Declarations section. The following code implements the variable declarations within the General–Declarations section:

```
Option Explicit

Dim Pause As Boolean, Playing As Boolean
Dim EjectButton As Boolean, RepeatButton As Boolean
Dim NumMinutes As Long
Dim NumSeconds As Long
Dim TrackNumber As Integer
Dim TrackTime As Integer
Dim numTracks As Integer
Dim NewTrack As Integer
Dim I As Integer                              ' counting variable
```

The first four variables are *flag* variables, meaning they contain either a *True* or *False* value depending on current conditions in the program. For example, if the *RepeatButton* variable contains a *True* value, the program knows that the user has selected the Repeat button and will replay the CD. The next series of variables, beginning at *NumMinutes* and ending at *NewTrack*, all maintain information about the CD that the user is currently playing. The last variable, *I*, is a counting variable that you will use in loops throughout the program.

Writing the Form's Startup Program Code

As you learned in Chapter 1, when you load a form, it first invokes its *Form_Load* event, even before the computer displays the form on the screen. When you run a program that uses only one form, unless you separately declare a *Sub Main* procedure, the program's execution will begin within the form's *Load* event. The following code implements the *Form_Load* event for the *frmMMedia* form:

```
Private Sub Form_Load()
  LoadButtons
  MMControl1.Command = "Close"
  MMControl1.Visible = False
  MMControl1.Enabled = True
  MMControl1.DeviceType = "CDAudio"
  MMControl1.Shareable = False
  MMControl1.AutoEnable = False
  MMControl1.Command = "Open"
  CheckCDRom
  FirstTrack
End Sub
```

The *Load* event's program code first invokes the *LoadButtons* procedure, which loads the button graphics for the form. The program code then initializes the *MMControl1* control, setting it to *CDAudio* and connecting the control to the CD-ROM drive. The program code then calls the *CheckCDRom* procedure, which initializes the program variables with information about the currently loaded CD-ROM. Finally, the program code in the *Load* event calls the *FirstTrack* procedure, which sets the *Multimedia MCI* control to point to the first track on the CD-ROM.

Writing the Procedures the Form_Load Event Calls

As you learned in the previous section, the *Form_Load* event calls several helper procedures that the program uses to initialize the display and the connection to the audio CD. The first procedure that the *Form_Load* event calls is the *LoadButtons* procedure, which loads the graphics into the form. The following code implements the *LoadButtons* procedure:

```
Private Sub LoadButtons()
   ControlPanel(0).Picture = LoadPicture(App.Path & "\FirstTrack.bmp")
   ControlPanel(1).Picture = LoadPicture(App.Path & "\PreviousTrack.bmp")
   ControlPanel(2).Picture = LoadPicture(App.Path & "\BeginningTrack.bmp")
   ControlPanel(3).Picture = LoadPicture(App.Path & "\NotPlaying.bmp")
   ControlPanel(4).Picture = LoadPicture(App.Path & "\NextTrack.bmp")
   ControlPanel(5).Picture = LoadPicture(App.Path & "\LastTrack.bmp")
   ControlPanel(6).Picture = LoadPicture(App.Path & "\NotPaused.bmp")
   ControlPanel(7).Picture = LoadPicture(App.Path & "\RepeatButton.bmp")
   ControlPanel(8).Picture = LoadPicture(App.Path & "\EjectButton.bmp")
End Sub
```

The *LoadButtons* procedure uses the *Picture* property of each *PictureBox* in the *ControlPanel* control array to add the graphical icon to each button in the control panel. The program uses the *LoadPicture* function to load the image into the *PictureBox*. The companion CD-ROM that accompanies this book contains all the icons that the program loads into the *PictureBox* control, and the Jamsa Press *setup.exe* program places these icons within the *x:\vbpl\Chapter02* directory with the *prjCD-ROM* executable program file.

As you learned in the previous section, the *Form_Load* event also calls the *CheckCDRom* procedure. The *CheckCDRom* procedure uses the *MMControl1* control and several of its own "helper" procedures—procedures that perform simple processing and either return a single value or update the display. The following code implements the *CheckCDRom* procedure:

```
Private Sub CheckCDRom()
   MMControl1.TimeFormat = mciFormatMilliseconds
   MMControl1.Command = "Stop"
   FirstTrack
   TotalNumberTracks
   Pause = False
End Sub
```

As you can see, after setting the *TimeFormat* property, the *CheckCDRom* procedure calls the *FirstTrack* procedure, which sets the current playback track to the first track on the audio CD and updates the display information within the form's fields. After the *FirstTrack* procedure completes its processing, the *CheckCDRom* procedure calls the *TotalNumberTracks* procedure, which uses the *Multimedia MCI* control to determine the total number of tracks the audio CD contains. The following code implements the *FirstTrack* procedure:

```
Private Sub FirstTrack()
   Dim I As Integer

   Me.MousePointer = vbHourglass
   If MMControl1.Track <> 1 Then
     MMControl1.Command = "Stop"
     For I = TrackNumber To 1 Step -1
       MMControl1.Command = "Prev"
     Next I
     getTrackPosition
     getTrackNumber
     getTrackLength
     If Playing And Not Pause Then
       MMControl1.Command = "Play"
       ControlPanel(3).Picture = LoadPicture(App.Path & "\PlayButton.bmp")
       ControlPanel(6).Picture = LoadPicture(App.Path & "\notpaused.bmp")
       Playing = True
     End If
   Else
     getTrackPosition
     getTrackNumber
```

```
        getTrackLength
        MMControl1.Command = "Prev"
    End If
    Me.MousePointer = vbNormal
End Sub
```

The *FirstTrack* procedure changes the mouse ~~pointer~~ to an hourglass, so that the user cannot make another selection within the ~~...~~ ~~proce~~dure completes its processing. The program code in the procedure ~~...~~ly at the first track. If so, the procedure simply updates the display ~~...~~ the user is not currently playing the first track, the procedure uses ~~...~~ntrol to stop the CD's playback, after which the code starts a *For*-~~...~~k, each time instructing the *Multimedia MCI* control to decrease ~~...~~rrent track on the CD will be the first track. The procedure then ~~...~~ength, *getTrackPosition*, and *getTrackNumber*, which update the ~~...~~ information procedures in the next section.

47

~~...~~ ~~c~~hanges and updates the display, the procedure checks to deter-~~...~~en the user clicked the mouse on the First Track button. If the ~~...~~aying the CD again at the first track. If the user was not, the

This belongs to

computerliteracy.com
Resources for technical minds℠
800.789.8590

~~...~~ *PROCEDURES*

~~...~~res to get information about the current track, *getTrackLength*, ~~...~~e, *getTrackLength,* uses information the *Multimedia MCI* con-~~...~~ ~~f~~ollowing code implements the *getTrackLength* procedure:

```
  ...cKLen = ...MControl1.TrackLength
    NumSeconds = TrackLen / 1000
    NumMinutes = NumSeconds \ 60
    NumSeconds = NumSeconds Mod 60
    Text1(1).Text = NumMinutes & "  Minutes " & NumSeconds & "  Seconds"
    TrackTime = Trim(CStr(NumMinutes) + CStr(NumSeconds))
End Sub
```

The *getTrackLength* procedure gets the track length in milliseconds from the *Multimedia MCI* control. The procedure then uses the real division operator (/) to convert the milliseconds into seconds. Next, the procedure uses the integer division operator (\) to determine the number of whole minutes in the total seconds, and the *Mod* operator to determine the number of seconds in the remaining fractional minute. Finally, the procedure's code displays the minutes and seconds within the Track Length text box.

The *getTrackPosition* procedure gets the current track's starting position from the *Multimedia MCI* control, then displays that information in the *Track Start* field on the *frmMMedia* form. The following code implements the *getTrackPosition* procedure:

```
  Private Sub getTrackPosition()
    Dim TrackPos As Long

    TrackPos = MMControl1.TrackPosition
    NumSeconds = TrackPos / 1000
    NumMinutes = NumSeconds \ 60
    NumSeconds = NumSeconds Mod 60
    Text1(2).Text = NumMinutes & "  Minutes " & NumSeconds & "  Seconds"
End Sub
```

The *getTrackPosition* procedure uses the *TrackPosition* property to determine the current track's start position in milliseconds. It then uses processing similar to *getTrackLength* to convert the milliseconds into minutes and seconds, which the procedure displays within the Track Position text box.

The *getRemainingTime* procedure determines the number of minutes and seconds that remain on the CD from the current playing position, and displays that information in the *Track Time Left* field on the *frmMMedia* form. The following code implements the *getRemainingTime* procedure:

```
Private Sub getRemainingTime(SecondsRemaining As Long)
  Dim StartingPosition As Long
  Dim PresentPosition As Long
  Dim SecondsIntoCurrentTrack As Long
  Dim TrackLengthSeconds As Long
  Dim I As Integer

  If Pause = False Then
    StartingPosition = MMControl1.TrackPosition
    StartingPosition = StartingPosition / 1000
    PresentPosition = MMControl1.Position
    PresentPosition = PresentPosition / 1000
    If StartingPosition = 0 And PresentPosition = 0 And _
        MMControl1.TrackLength = 0 Then
      SecondsRemaining = 0
      Exit Sub
    End If
    SecondsIntoCurrentTrack = PresentPosition - StartingPosition
    TrackLengthSeconds = MMControl1.TrackLength
    TrackLengthSeconds = TrackLengthSeconds / 1000
    ProgressBar1.Min = 0
    If TrackLengthSeconds = 0 Then TrackLengthSeconds = 1
    ProgressBar1.Max = TrackLengthSeconds / 5
    If Playing Then
      ProgressBar1.Value = Int(SecondsIntoCurrentTrack / 5)
    Else
      ProgressBar1.Value = 0
    End If
    SecondsRemaining = TrackLengthSeconds - SecondsIntoCurrentTrack
    NumMinutes = SecondsRemaining \ 60
    NumSeconds = SecondsRemaining Mod 60
    If NumMinutes = 0 And NumSeconds <= 2 Then
      MMControl1.Command = "Stop"
      getTrackPosition
      getTrackNumber
      getTrackLength
      ProgressBar1.Value = 0
      If TrackNumber <= numTracks Then
        MMControl1.Command = "Play"
        Playing = True
        ControlPanel(3).Picture = LoadPicture(App.Path & "\PlayButton.bmp")
      Else
        If RepeatButton = False Then
          MMControl1.Command = "Stop"
          FirstTrack
          Playing = False
          ControlPanel(3).Picture = LoadPicture(App.Path & "\notplaying.bmp")
        Else
          FirstTrack
          MMControl1.Command = "Play"
        End If
      End If
```

```
        End If
        Text1(4).Text = NumMinutes & "  Minutes " & NumSeconds & "  Seconds"
      Else
        Text1(4).Text = "...Paused..."
      End If
    End Sub
```

The *getRemainingTime* procedure uses an *If-Then* statement to determine whether the user has paused the program. If the user has paused it, the procedure displays *Paused* in the Time Remaining text box. Otherwise, the procedure uses the *Multimedia MCI* control's properties and a series of computations to determine how much time remains to play on the current track. The procedure first gets the track's starting position (that is, where it begins on the CD), and then the current position in the playback. The program code converts both values from milliseconds to seconds, then determines how many seconds the program is into the playback of the current track by subtracting the starting position from the current position.

Next, the procedure determines the total track length for the track (with the *Multimedia MCI* control's *TrackLength* property), which it also converts from milliseconds to seconds. The program code uses the track length to update the progress bar at the CD player's bottom. After the procedure updates the progress bar, it subtracts the number of seconds already played in the current track from the track's total number of seconds, which yields the number of remaining seconds on the track. If the number of seconds remaining is less than two, the procedure switches to the next track. If the number of seconds is more than two, the procedure exits.

When the procedure determines it is time to play the next track, it first checks that the program is not already playing the last track on the CD. If the program is playing the last track and the user has not selected the Repeat button, the procedure stops playing the CD and returns the counter to the first track. If the program is playing the last track and the user has selected the Repeat button, the procedure returns the counter to the first track and starts to play again from that track. If the program is not already playing the last track, the procedure uses the *Next* command to move to the next track.

The *TotalNumberTracks* procedure uses the *Multimedia MCI* control's *Tracks* property to determine and display the total number of tracks the CD contains. The *prjCD-ROM* project only calls the *TotalNumberTracks* procedure in two events—when the program begins, and when the user clicks the mouse on the First Track button. The following code implements the *TotalNumberTracks* procedure:

```
    Private Sub TotalNumberTracks()
      Text1(0).Text = Format(1, "##")
      numTracks = MMControl1.Tracks
      Text1(3).Text = Format(numTracks, "##")
    End Sub
```

The *TotalNumberTracks* procedure displays the current track as 1 (because the program only calls the procedure when it initializes a new CD or the user starts the CD over) within the *Current Track* field. The procedure then uses the *Tracks* property to determine the total tracks on the CD, which the procedure then displays within the Total Tracks text box.

The final information procedure, *getTrackNumber*, checks the *Multimedia MCI* control's current track location and returns the current track number. The following code implements the *getTrackNumber* procedure:

```
    Private Sub getTrackNumber()
      DoEvents
      Text1(0).Text = MMControl1.Track
      TrackNumber = MMControl1.Track
    End Sub
```

The *getTrackNumber* procedure updates the *Current Track* field to reflect the currently selected track. It also updates the *TrackNumber* variable to reflect the currently selected track.

49

WRITING THE TIMER EVENT

As you have learned, the *prjCD-ROM* project uses a *Timer* control to periodically update information in the player's display. The following code implements the *Timer1* control's *Timer* event:

```
Private Sub Timer1_Timer()
  Dim Seconds As Long

  getRemainingTime Seconds
End Sub
```

The *Timer* event calls the *getRemainingTime* procedure which, as you have learned, uses the information the *Multimedia MCI* control returns to update the program's display.

WRITING THE EVENTS THAT RESPOND TO USER INPUT AT THE CONTROL PANEL

As you learned in this chapter's "Using the *prjCD-ROM* Project" section, to control the CD player the user will click the mouse on the graphical buttons within the *ControlPanel* array. The program uses code within four separate events that belong to the *ControlPanel* array to perform its processing. The first two events, *MouseDown* and *MouseUp*, change a button's appearance when the user clicks on the button. The following code implements the *MouseDown* and *MouseUp* events:

```
Private Sub ControlPanel_MouseDown(Index As Integer, Button As Integer, _
    Shift As Integer, X As Single, Y As Single)
  ControlPanel(Index).BorderStyle = 0
End Sub
Private Sub ControlPanel_MouseUp(Index As Integer, Button As Integer, _
    Shift As Integer, X As Single, Y As Single)
  ControlPanel(Index).BorderStyle = 1
End Sub
```

The *MouseDown* event changes the user-selected button's *BorderStyle* property to no border. The *MouseUp* event, in turn, will change the style back to its original border. When the user clicks the mouse on a button, the two events in sequence will display a rapid border change on the button. The border changes give the illusion that the user has actually depressed the button momentarily when he or she clicks the mouse on the button.

While the *MouseDown* and *MouseUp* events change the button's display, the majority of the operative processing occurs within the *ControlPanel_Click* event. The *ControlPanel* array's *Click* event accepts as its sole parameter the index of the button the user has clicked. The procedure's program code then uses that index to determine what processing to perform. The following code implements the *ControlPanel_Click* event:

```
Private Sub ControlPanel_Click(Index As Integer)
  Dim I As Integer, StillTime As Long, NewTrack As Integer

  Timer1.Interval = 500
  DoEvents
  Select Case Index
    Case 0 '******* the First Track button **********
      TotalNumberTracks
      FirstTrack

    Case 1 '***************** go back one track *********************
      BackTrack

    Case 2 '************** the Beginning Button ******************
      MMControl1.Command = "Prev"
      getTrackPosition
      getTrackNumber
      getTrackLength
      If Not Pause Then
```

```
      MMControl1.Command = "Play"
      ControlPanel(3).Picture = LoadPicture(App.Path & "\PlayButton.bmp")
      Playing = True
   End If
Case 3   '**************  the Play Button  ******************
   If Not Playing Then
      getRemainingTime StillTime
      MMControl1.Command = "play"
      ProgressBar1.Value = 0   'set the value of the progress bar to 0
      ControlPanel(3).Picture = LoadPicture(App.Path & "\PlayButton.bmp")
      Playing = True
      Pause = False
      getTrackPosition
      getTrackNumber
      getTrackLength
   ElseIf Playing Then
      ControlPanel(3).Picture = LoadPicture(App.Path & "\NotPlaying.bmp")
      ProgressBar1.Value = 0
      Playing = False
      If Pause Then
        Pause = Not Pause
        ControlPanel(6).Picture = LoadPicture(App.Path & "\NotPaused.bmp")
      End If
      MMControl1.Command = "Stop"
   Else
      MsgBox "Not a Valid CD-ROM in the drive."
   End If

Case 4   '****************  the Next Button  *************************
   If MMControl1.Track <> numTracks Then
      MMControl1.Command = "Next"
      getTrackPosition
      getTrackNumber
      getTrackLength
   End If

Case 5   '****************  the Last Button  *************************
   LastTrack

Case 6   '****************  the Pause Button  *********************
   If Not Pause Then
      MMControl1.Command = "Pause"
      ControlPanel(6).Picture = LoadPicture(App.Path & "\Paused.bmp")
      Pause = True
   Else
      MMControl1.Command = "Play"
      ControlPanel(6).Picture = LoadPicture(App.Path & "\NotPaused.bmp")
      Pause = False
   End If

Case 7   '****************  the Repeat Button  *********************
   RepeatButton = Not RepeatButton
   If RepeatButton Then
      ControlPanel(7).Picture = LoadPicture(App.Path & _
         "\RepeatButtonOn.bmp")
   Else
      ControlPanel(7).Picture = LoadPicture(App.Path & _
         "\RepeatButton.bmp")
   End If

Case 8   '******************  the Load/Eject Button  ******************
   EjectButton = Not EjectButton
```

51

```
            If EjectButton = True Then
              FirstTrack
              MMControl1.Command = "Stop"
              Pause = True
              MMControl1.Command = "Eject"
              ControlPanel(3).Picture = LoadPicture(App.Path & "\NotPlaying.bmp")
              ProgressBar1.Value = 0
              Playing = False
              If Pause Then
                Pause = Not Pause
                ControlPanel(6).Picture = LoadPicture(App.Path & "\NotPaused.bmp")
              End If
              For I = 0 To 4
                Text1(I).Text = ""
              Next
              MMControl1.Command = "Close"
            Else
              MMControl1.DeviceType = "CDAudio"
              MMControl1.Shareable = False
              MMControl1.AutoEnable = False
              MMControl1.Command = "Open"
              MMControl1.Command = "Eject"
              FirstTrack
              TotalNumberTracks
              CheckCDRom
            End If
        End Select
    End Sub
```

The *ControlPanel_Click* event's program code uses a *Select Case* statement to determine what button the user clicked the mouse on and what action it should therefore perform. If the user clicks the mouse on the First Track button, the program calls the *FirstTrack* procedure, which you learned about previously, and which resets the playback to the first track on the CD. If the user clicks the mouse on the Back Track button, the program calls the *BackTrack* procedure, which sets the playback to the last track on the CD. You will learn more about the *BackTrack* procedure in this chapter's "Writing the Code for the *BackTrack* Procedure" section.

If the user clicks the mouse on the Beginning button, the program sends the *Prev* command to the *Multimedia MCI* control, which will set the current track back to its beginning and resume playback from the track's beginning point. The program will then update the display items and, if the user is currently playing the CD, start playing the CD over at the track's beginning.

If the user clicks the mouse on the Play button, the program's processing will depend on whether or not the user is currently playing a CD. If the user is playing a CD, the program code will stop the CD from playing and will keep the track pointer at the current track. If the user is not playing a CD, the program code will begin to play the CD. Finally, if the user is pausing the CD, the program code will stop playing and will reset the Stop/Pause button.

If the user clicks the mouse on the Next button, the program code will send the *Next* command to the *Multimedia MCI* control, which will set the control to point to the next track. The program code will then update the display. If the user is currently playing a CD, the *Multimedia MCI* control will automatically continue playing at the next track.

If the user clicks the mouse on the Last Track button, the program will call the *LastTrack* procedure, which the next section explains in detail. The *LastTrack* procedure uses the *Multimedia MCI* control's *Next* command to advance the CD player to the last track on the CD.

If the user clicks the mouse on the Stop/Pause button only one time, the program will either pause the CD player's playback or, if the user has already paused the CD player, will resume the playback. If the user double-clicks the mouse on the Stop/Pause button, the program stops the CD's playback. To capture the double-click event, you must write different program code, which you will learn about later in this section.

52

If the user clicks the mouse on the Repeat button, the program code changes the Repeat button's graphic to show that the user has selected the Repeat button. Next, the program code sets the *RepeatButton* flag variable so that the program knows to continue playing when it reaches the end of the CD.

Finally, if the user clicks the mouse on the Load/Eject Button, the program code will either eject the currently loaded CD or load a new CD into the player. In either case, the program code updates the display values—disabling the display fields if the user ejects the CD, enabling the fields and putting the appropriate values into them if the user loads a new CD.

As you learned in the "Using the *prjCD-ROM* Project" section, to stop the CD player when it is playing, the user must double-click the mouse on the Stop/Pause button. To handle the processing difference between a double-click and a single-click, the program must capture the Stop/Pause button within the *DblClick* event. The following code implements the *ControlPanel_DblClick* event:

```
Private Sub ControlPanel_DblClick(Index As Integer)
  Select Case Index

    Case 6   '***************  the Stop Button  *********************
      MMControl1.Command = "Stop"
      ControlPanel(3).Picture = LoadPicture(App.Path & "\notplaying.bmp")
      ControlPanel(6).Picture = LoadPicture(App.Path & "\notpaused.bmp")
      Pause = False
      Playing = Not Playing
      ProgressBar1.Value = 0
  End Select
End Sub
```

The *DblClick* event uses a *Select Case* statement to determine on which button the user has double-clicked the mouse. If the user double-clicks the mouse on any button other than the Stop/Pause button, the event's program code performs no processing. Otherwise, the event's program code changes the image within the Stop/Pause button to the Stop/Pause button (from the paused image, if the program had loaded it previously), and turns off the Play button. The program code then turns off the CD player, stops the current song, and resets the *ProgressBar1* control's value to 0.

Writing the Code for the LastTrack Procedure

As you learned in the previous section, if the user clicks the mouse on the Last Track button, the *ControlPanel_Click* event's program code calls the *LastTrack* procedure. The *LastTrack* procedure resets the CD player to the last track on the CD. The following code implements the *LastTrack* procedure:

```
Private Sub LastTrack()
  Me.MousePointer = vbHourglass
  If MMControl1.Track <> numTracks Then
    MMControl1.Command = "Stop"
    getTrackNumber
    For I = TrackNumber To numTracks
      MMControl1.Command = "Next"
    Next I
    getTrackPosition
    getTrackNumber
    getTrackLength
    If Playing And Not Pause Then
      MMControl1.Command = "Play"
      ControlPanel(3).Picture = LoadPicture(App.Path & "\PlayButton.bmp")
      ControlPanel(6).Picture = LoadPicture(App.Path & "\notpaused.bmp")
      Playing = True
    End If
  End If
  Me.MousePointer = vbNormal
End Sub
```

As you can see, the procedure's program code first checks to make sure that the program is not already at the last track on the CD. If the program is already at the last track, the procedure exits. If the program is not at the last track, the procedure steps through each individual track on the CD until it reaches the last track. If the user was playing the CD before he or she clicked the mouse on the *LastTrack* button, the program resumes the CD's playback at the last track. If the user was not playing the CD, the program waits for him or her to make an additional selection.

WRITING THE CODE FOR THE BACKTRACK PROCEDURE

As you learned in the "Writing the Events That Respond to User Input at the Control Panel" section, if the user clicks the mouse on the Back Track button, the *ControlPanel_Click* event's program code calls the *BackTrack* procedure. The *BackTrack* procedure moves the track counter back a single track and, if the CD player is already playing the CD, starts to play the new track. The following code implements the *BackTrack* procedure:

```
Private Sub BackTrack()
  Me.MousePointer = vbHourglass
  If MMControl1.Track <> 1 Then
    MMControl1.Command = "Stop"
    MMControl1.Command = "Prev"
    MMControl1.Command = "Prev"
    getTrackPosition
    getTrackNumber
    getTrackLength
    If Not Pause And Playing Then
      MMControl1.Command = "Play"
      ControlPanel(3).Picture = LoadPicture(App.Path & "\PlayButton.bmp")
    End If
  End If
  Me.MousePointer = vbNormal
End Sub
```

The *BackTrack* procedure uses the *Multimedia MCI* control's *Stop* and *Prev* commands to go to the previous track. The procedure calls the *Prev* command twice because on the first *Prev* command the *Multimedia MCI* control will move to the beginning of the current track. The *Multimedia MCI* control will only move to the previous track the second time you send the *Prev* command. The procedure then updates the display for the new track. If the user is playing the CD when he or she clicks the mouse on the Back Track button, the program will begin to play the new track. Otherwise, the program will wait for the user to make another selection.

WRITING THE EXIT CODE

Just as the first event to execute within the *prjCD-ROM* project is the *Form_Load* event, the last event to execute is the *Form_Unload* event. The following code implements the *Form_Unload* event:

```
Private Sub Form_Unload(Cancel As Integer)
  MMControl1.Command = "Stop"
  MMControl1.Command = "Close"
  DoEvents
  Unload Me
End Sub
```

The program code within the *Form_Unload* event stops the CD player, closes the *Multimedia MCI* control, and then exits the program. It is important to stop the CD player and close the control, because otherwise the CD will continue to play even after you stop the program's execution.

There are two ways to exit the program: the user can either click the mouse on the Close button or select the File menu Exit option. The following code implements the *mnuExit_Click* event, which occurs when the user selects the File menu Exit option:

```
Private Sub mnuExit_Click(Index As Integer)
   Unload Me
End Sub
```

The *mnuExit_Click* event unloads the form, which forces the program to execute the program code within the *Form_Unload* event. The program provides the File menu Exit option as an alternative to the user when the user closes the program.

Enhancements You Can Make to the prjCD-ROM Project

The *Multimedia MCI* control provides you with a simple and useful way to play back audio CDs from your computer. In addition to audio CDs, the *Multimedia MCI* control lets you play back audio (.wav) files, movie (.avi) files, animations, and more. With little extra programming time, you can easily expand the *prjCD-ROM* project into a full-fledged multimedia player capable of playing not only audio CDs but also any other sound, video, or animation file.

Putting It All Together

This chapter's project, *prjCD-ROM*, introduced you to how your programs can use the *Multimedia MCI* control to play back multimedia materials—CD-ROMs, movies, and so on. You have also learned that your programs can use Visual Basic's built-in controls to simplify their program code and efficiently manage complex tasks. In Chapter 3, "Writing a Screen Saver in Visual Basic," you will use simple forms and drawing methods, together with some complex processing that uses the Windows Application Programming Interface (API) functions, to create a simple screen saver that you can run on your computer. Before you continue with Chapter 3, however, make sure you understand the following key concepts:

✓ You will use custom controls—either those that come with Visual Basic, controls that you buy from a third-party vendor, or controls that you design yourself—to simplify complex programming tasks within most programs that you write in Visual Basic.

✓ Although controls are powerful tools for writing programs, most controls have limitations. Therefore, the drawback of using controls to perform tasks is that most controls will not perform all the tasks you may want, or may not perform them exactly as you want them to. You can solve such problems by creating your own custom controls.

✓ Although you will often use *CommandButton* controls within your programs to provide the user with a convenient, easy-to-use interface to your programs, you can also use *PictureBox* controls to perform similar processing. The advantage of using *PictureBox* controls is that they let you display text and graphics, rather than only text, as *CommandButton* controls do.

✓ You will often use the *Timer* control within your Visual Basic programs to provide you with a convenient way to perform certain activities at regular intervals.

✓ When your programs have groups of controls sharing common characteristics, you can group those controls into a *control array* to simplify and clarify your program's processing and structure.

55

Chapter 3

Writing a Screen Saver in Visual Basic

When personal computers became popular in the early 1980s, most of them used a monochrome (one color) screen. One significant problem early computer users had with their computer monitors was if a single image remained on the display for too long, the monitor would *etch* that image onto the display. After the monitor etched the image onto the display, remnants of the image were always visible. To alleviate the problem, programmers designed programs that ran when the computer was idle for some fixed period of time. Such programs came to be known as *screen savers*. In those early personal computers, a screen saver was typically a block outline that redrew itself every ten to fifteen seconds in a different position on the display. The block often contained text such as "Press Any Key to Wake Up." Programmers designed the earliest screen savers for function only, not for appearance.

The introduction of the Windows operating system gave programmers the ability to create graphical screen savers. As a result, users began to expect more from their screen savers than a simple message, and screen savers changed from purely functional to more decorative. Today, nearly every personal computer has a screen saver and the variety of screen savers that users can load is almost as vast as the number of computer users.

Within this chapter, you will learn how to create a simple screen saver in Visual Basic. The *prjVBPLSaver* project will simply draw small circles in different colors onto the user's screen. However, you can use the screen saver design principles that you learn in this chapter to create your own, more complex, screen savers. By the time you finish this chapter, you will understand the following key concepts:

- Within Windows, a screen saver is a special type of executable program that the operating system will run based on the user's display preferences and that you can create from within Visual Basic.

- When you write a screen saver, you must ensure that it contains three separate forms: one form for the settings screen, one form for the configuration screen, and one form that actually displays the screen saver.

- Within your Visual Basic programs, you can use the *Sub Main* procedure to perform processing without loading a form.

- You can use Windows Application Programming Interface (API) functions within your Visual Basic programs to capture screen images and convert them to bitmaps that you can display.

- Within your Visual Basic programs, you can use the Windows API *GetVersionEx* function to determine what operating system a computer is running.

- You can use the *GetSetting* and *SaveSetting* functions that Visual Basic provides to read information from the Windows system registry, but only if you save that information within your program's registry entry.

- You will use the *RegOpenKeyEx* and *RegQueryKeyEx* Windows API functions to retrieve information from the Windows system registry into your Visual Basic program that is not saved within the program's registry entry.

- Within your Visual Basic programs, you can use the Windows API *ShowCursor* function to hide or display the mouse cursor.

- The Windows operating system uses *messages* to send information to programs. A message is generally an integer value that your program must recognize and respond to appropriately.

- The Visual Basic Interactive Development Environment (IDE) intercepts most messages for your program and converts them into events.

♦ There may be times within your Visual Basic programs when you want to intercept your own messages or process messages that you cannot normally receive. In such cases, you can use *subclassing*—a technique that lets you intercept the Windows messages.

USING THE prjVBPLSAVER PROJECT

Before you design the *prjVBPLSaver* project, you may find it helpful to run the program. The companion CD-ROM that accompanies this book contains the *prjVBPLSaver.scr* program within the *Chapter03* directory. As with every other program on the CD-ROM, you should run the Jamsa Press *setup.exe* program to install the *prjVBPLSaver.scr* program to your computer's hard drive before you run it. After you install the *prjVBPLSaver.scr* program to your computer's hard drive, you can run it from within the Control Panel. Unlike the *prjCD-ROM* project that you created in Chapter 2, "Using the Multimedia MCI Control to Create a CD-ROM Player," you must run the screen saver program from within the Screen Saver tab of the Display Properties dialog box. To run the *prjVBPLSaver.scr* program's *VBPLSaver.scr* screen saver, perform the following steps:

1. Select the Windows Start menu Settings option Control Panel group. Windows will display the Control Panel group window.

2. Within the Control Panel group window, double-click your mouse on the Display icon. Windows will open the Display Properties dialog box.

3. Within the Display Properties dialog box, select the Screen Saver tab. Windows will display the Screen Saver properties.

4. Within the Screen Saver combo box, select the *Vbplsaver* screen saver. Windows will change to the *Vbplsaver* screen saver and begin to draw circles within the monitor on the dialog box. Figure 3.1 shows the Display Properties dialog box after you select the *Vbplsaver* screen saver.

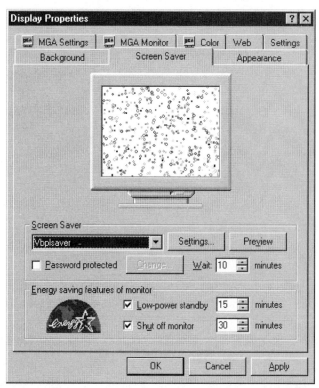

Figure 3.1 *The **Vbplsaver** screen saver.*

As you can see, the Display Properties dialog box lets you change your computer's settings for the screen saver. To change the settings for the *Vbplsaver* screen saver, click your mouse on the Settings button. Windows will display the VBPL Saver dialog box, as shown in Figure 3.2.

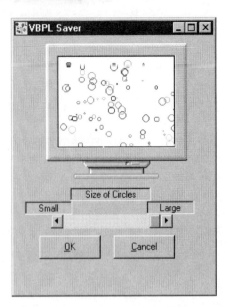

Figure 3.2 *The VBPL Saver dialog box.*

As you can see in Figure 3.2, the only setting that you can change within the *VBPLSaver* screen saver is the size of the circles the screen saver will draw. In Figure 3.2, the screen saver is set to draw the largest circles. If you click your mouse on the arrow on the scroll bar's left-hand side, you can decrease the circle size. Each time you change the circle size, the screen saver will clear the display and start drawing circles of the new size. If you set the size to its smallest setting, the screen saver will draw very small circles onto the screen. Figure 3.3 shows the VBPL Saver dialog box after you set the circle size to its smallest possible value.

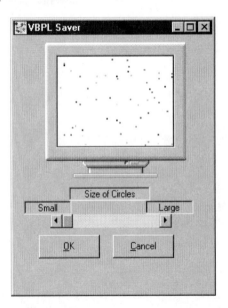

Figure 3.3 *The VBPL Saver dialog box after you set the circle size to its smallest possible value.*

After you determine what size circles you want the screen saver to draw, click your mouse on OK to exit the VBPL Saver dialog box. Windows will display the Display Properties dialog box. Within the Display Properties dialog box, click your mouse on the Preview button. Windows will run the *VBPLSaver.scr* program and start to draw circles on the screen. Figure 3.4 shows what your display might look like after you click your mouse on the Preview button.

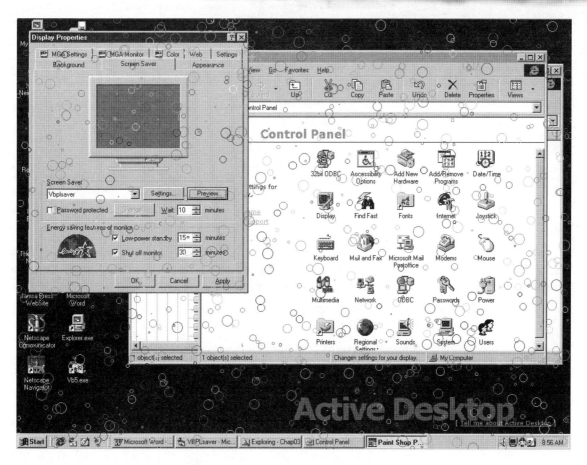

Figure 3.4 *A sample display after the* **VBPLSaver.scr** *program begins to execute.*

As you can see, the *VBPLSaver* screen saver draws circles all over the screen. To stop the screen saver, you can press a key, click your mouse, or even move your mouse. After you stop the screen saver, the operating system will return to the Display Properties dialog box.

CREATING THE BLANK FORMS

Now that you have a better idea how to use the finished *prjVBPLSaver* project, you can begin to design it. First, you will design three empty forms—one form for the actual screen saver, one form for the VBPL Saver dialog box, and one form for the display within the Display Properties dialog box. After you design the forms, you will add a module to the project and then add and place the controls the program will use to perform the program's processing.

CREATING THE FIRST FORM

As you learned in the previous section, the *prjVBPLSaver* project will use three different forms for its display. The first form you will design is the *frmMain* form, which the project will use to display the actual screen saver. To begin the *prjVBPLSaver* project and design an empty form, perform the following steps:

1. Within Visual Basic, select the File menu New Project option. Visual Basic will open the New Project dialog box.

2. Within the New Project dialog box, double-click your mouse on the Standard EXE icon. Visual Basic will close the New Project dialog box, start a new project, *Project1*, and add a form to it, *Form1*.

3. Select the View menu Properties Window option. Visual Basic will open the Properties Window listing the *Form1* properties.

4. Within the Properties Window, change the *Form1* property values to the values Table 3.1 lists.

Object	Property	Set As
Form1	BorderStyle	0 - None
Form1	Caption	Screen Saver Main Form
Form1	Height	3420
Form1	Left	0
Form1	Top	0
Form1	Width	4065
Form1	Name	frmMain

Table 3.1 *The newly named* **frmMain** *form's properties.*

CREATING THE SECOND FORM

Now that you have created the first form the *prjVBPLSaver* project will use, you can add the second form to the project. The *VBPLSaver* screen saver will display the second form when the user clicks the mouse on the Settings button within the Display Properties dialog box. To add the second form to the *prjVBPLSaver* project, perform the following steps:

1. Within Visual Basic, select the Project menu Add Form option. Visual Basic will display the Add Form dialog box.

2. Within the Add Form dialog box, click your mouse on the New tab and select the Form icon. Next, click your mouse on the Open button. Visual Basic will close the Add Form dialog box, and add a new form, *Form1*, to the *prjVBPLSaver* project.

3. Select the View menu Properties Window option. Visual Basic will open the Properties Window listing the *Form1* properties.

4. Within the Properties Window, change the *Form1* property values to those Table 3.2 lists.

Object	Property	Set As
Form1	BorderStyle	2 - Sizable
Form1	Caption	VBPL Saver
Form1	Height	4740
Form1	Left	0
Form1	StartUpPosition	2 - Center Screen
Form1	Top	0
Form1	Width	4020
Form1	Name	frmConfiguration

Table 3.2 *The newly named* **frmConfiguration** *form's properties.*

CREATING THE THIRD FORM

Now that you have created the second form, you can add the third form to the project. The *VBPLSaver* screen saver will use the third form to create its display within the Display Properties dialog box. To add the third form to the *prjVBPLSaver* project, perform the following steps:

1. Within Visual Basic, select the Project menu Add Form option. Visual Basic will display the Add Form dialog box.

2. Within the Add Form dialog box, click your mouse on the New tab and select the Form icon. Next, click your mouse on the Open button. Visual Basic will close the Add Form dialog box and add a new form, *Form1*, to the *prjVBPLSaver* project.

3. Select the View menu Properties Window option. Visual Basic will open the Properties Window listing the *Form1* properties.

4. Within the Properties Window, change the *Form1* property values to the values Table 3.3 lists.

Object	Property	Set As
Form1	*BorderStyle*	*0 - None*
Form1	*Height*	1800
Form1	*Left*	1470
Form1	*Top*	4710
Form1	*Width*	4155
Form1	*Name*	*frmControl*

*Table 3.3 The newly named **frmControl** form's properties.*

ADDING A MODULE TO THE PROJECT

After you design the *prjVBPLSaver* project's blank forms, you will create a module to store program code. Within the *prjVBPLSaver* project, the program code you will place within the module will declare several global variables and constants, several Windows API functions, and several new types you must use to call those Windows API functions. The *prjVBPLSaver* project's module, *mdlSaver*, will also contain several "helper" procedures the three program forms will use during their processing to perform tasks such as drawing the circles and checking the registry for a password. To add a module to the *prjVBPLSaver* project and save your work on the *prjVBPLSaver* project, perform the following steps:

1. Within Visual Basic, select the Project menu Add Module option. Visual Basic will open the Add Module dialog box.

2. Within the Add Module dialog box, select the Module option. Next, click your mouse on the Open button. Visual Basic will open a new Code window, *Module1*.

3. Select the View menu Properties Window option. Visual Basic will open the Properties Window listing the *Module1* properties.

4. Within the Properties Window, change the *Module1* module's name to *mdlSaver*.

5. Select the File menu Save Project As option. Visual Basic will open the Save File As dialog box and fill the *File name* field with *mdlSaver*.

6. Within the Save File As dialog box, click your mouse on the Save button. Visual Basic will save the *mdlSaver* module and fill the *File name* field with *frmControl*.

7. Within the Save File As dialog box, click your mouse on the Save button. Visual Basic will save the *frmControl* form and fill the *File name* field with *frmConfiguration*.

8. Within the Save File As dialog box, click your mouse on the Save button. Visual Basic will save the *frmConfiguration* form and fill the *File name* field with *frmMain*.

9. Within the Save File As dialog box, click your mouse on the Save button. Visual Basic will save the *frmMain* form and fill the *File name* field with *Project1*.

10. Within the *File name* field, replace the *Project1* project name with the new *prjVBPLSaver* project name. Next, click your mouse on the Save button. Visual Basic will save the *prjVBPLSaver* project and close the Save Project As dialog box.

DESIGNING THE PROJECT'S FORMS

As you have learned, the *prjVBPLSaver* project will use three different forms to perform its display activities. Each form will display a graphical image and update that image regularly. Both the *frmMain* and the *frmControl* forms contain little else beside the controls that display the graphics. The *frmConfiguration* form is slightly more complex, and includes a horizontal scroll bar and some command buttons.

ADDING THE TIMER CONTROL TO THE FRMMAIN FORM

As you learned in this chapter's "Using the *prjVBPLSaver* Project" section, the project will use the *frmMain* form as its primary display form when the user runs the screen saver. Because you can display graphics right onto a form, the *frmMain* form does not include a *PictureBox* control to contain the images you will draw. Instead, the *frmMain* form contains only a *Timer* control, which the program will use to draw circles on the screen at the correct intervals. To add a *Timer* control to the *frmMain* form, perform the following steps:

1. If Visual Basic is not displaying the *frmMain* form within an object window, double-click your mouse on the *frmMain* form listing within Project Explorer. Visual Basic will open the *frmMain* form.

2. Within Visual Basic, select the View menu Toolbox option. Visual Basic will open the Toolbox.

3. Within the Toolbox, double-click your mouse on the Timer icon. Visual Basic will draw a *Timer* control, *Timer1*, within the *frmMain* form.

4. Within the *frmMain* form, click your mouse on the *Timer1* control to highlight it. Visual Basic will draw a small frame around the control.

5. Select the View menu Properties Window option. Visual Basic will open the Properties Window listing the *Timer1* properties.

6. Within the Properties Window, change the *Timer1* properties to the values Table 3.4 lists.

Object	Property	Set As
Timer1	*Interval*	400
Timer1	*Left*	0
Timer1	*Top*	0
Timer1	*Name*	*tmrDrawCircles*

Table 3.4 The newly named **tmrDrawCircles** control's properties.

DESIGNING THE FRMCONTROL FORM

As the previous section details, the *prjVBPLSaver* project will use the *frmMain* form as its primary display form when the user runs the screen saver. Because you can display graphics directly on a form, the *frmMain* form does not include a *PictureBox* control to contain the images you will draw. However, the *frmControl* form does use a *PictureBox* control, because the *frmControl* form constrains (limits) both the image and what the user can do to the image. Additionally, the *frmControl* form contains a *Timer* control, which the program will use to draw circles on the *PictureBox* at the correct interval. To add a *PictureBox* and *Timer* control to the *frmControl* form, perform the following steps:

1. If Visual Basic is not displaying the *frmControl* form within an object window, double-click your mouse on the *frmControl* form listing within Project Explorer. Visual Basic will open the *frmControl* form.

2. Within Visual Basic, select the View menu Toolbox option. Visual Basic will open the Toolbox.

3. Within the Toolbox, double-click your mouse on the Timer icon. Visual Basic will draw a *Timer* control, *Timer1*, within the *frmControl* form.

4. Within the Toolbox, double-click your mouse on the PictureBox icon. Visual Basic will draw a *PictureBox* control, *Picture1*, within the *frmControl* form.

5. Within the *frmControl* form, click your mouse on the *Timer1* control to highlight it. Visual Basic will draw a small frame around the control.

6. Select the View menu Properties Window option. Visual Basic will open the Properties Window listing the *Timer1* properties.

7. Within the Properties Window, change the *Timer1* control's properties to the values Table 3.5 lists.

8. Repcat Steps 5, 6, and 7 to change the properties for the *Picture1* control to the values Table 3.5 lists.

Object	Property	Set As
Timer1	*Interval*	400
Timer1	*Left*	0
Timer1	*Top*	1320
Timer1	*Name*	*tmrControlDrawCircles*
Picture1	*Appearance*	*0 - Flat*
Picture1	*BackColor*	*&H00FFFFFF& (White)*
Picture1	*Height*	1080
Picture1	*Left*	0
Picture1	*Top*	0
Picture1	*Width*	1932
Picture1	*Name*	*picControl*

Table 3.5 *The newly named* **tmrControlDrawCircles** *and* **picControl** *controls' properties.*

Designing the frmConfiguration Form's Appearance

As you have learned, the *frmConfiguration* form contains more controls than the *frmMain* and *frmControl* forms. When you design the *frmConfiguration* form, you will add an *Image* control, a *PictureBox* control, three *Label* controls, two *CommandButton* controls, a *Timer* control, and an *HScrollBar* control to the form. To add the *Image, PictureBox,* and *Timer* controls to the *frmConfiguration* form, perform the following steps:

1. If Visual Basic is not displaying the *frmConfiguration* form within an object window, double-click your mouse on the *frmConfiguration* form listing within Project Explorer. Visual Basic will open the *frmConfiguration* form.

2. Within Visual Basic, select the View menu Toolbox option. Visual Basic will open the Toolbox.

3. Within the Toolbox, double-click your mouse on the Timer icon. Visual Basic will draw a *Timer* control, *Timer1*, within the *frmConfiguration* form.

4. Within the Toolbox, double-click your mouse on the PictureBox icon. Visual Basic will draw a *PictureBox* control, *Picture1*, within the *frmConfiguration* form.

5. Within the Toolbox, double-click your mouse on the Image icon. Visual Basic will draw an *Image* control, *Image1*, within the *frmConfiguration* form.

6. Within the *frmConfiguration* form, click your mouse on the *Timer1* control to highlight it. Visual Basic will draw a small frame around the control.

7. Select the View menu Properties Window option. Visual Basic will open the Properties Window listing the *Timer1* properties.

8. Within the Properties Window, change the *Timer1* control's properties to the values Table 3.6 lists.

9. Repeat Steps 6, 7, and 8 to change the properties for the *Picture1* and *Image1* controls to the values Table 3.6 lists.

Object	Property	Set As
Timer1	*Interval*	400
Timer1	*Left*	0
Timer1	*Top*	0
Timer1	*Name*	*tmrConfiguration*

Table 3.6 *The newly named* **Image**, **PictureBox**, *and* **Timer** *controls' properties. (continued on following page)*

Object	Property	Set As
Picture1	*Appearance*	0 - *Flat*
Picture1	*Height*	1356
Picture1	*Left*	900
Picture1	*Top*	240
Picture1	*Width*	1848
Picture1	*Name*	*picConfiguration*
Image1	*Height*	2175
Image1	*Left*	675
Image1	*Top*	120
Image1	*Width*	2385
Image1	*Name*	*imgConfiguration*

Table 3.6 *The newly named* **Image, PictureBox,** *and* **Timer** *controls' properties. (continued from previous page)*

ADDING THE HSCROLLBAR CONTROL TO THE FRMCONFIGURATION FORM

As you learned in this chapter's "Using the *prjVBPLSaver* Project" section, the *frmConfiguration* form lets the user set the size of the circles the form draws. To provide the user with an easy way to set the circle size, the *frmConfiguration* form uses a horizontal scroll bar. To add the *HScrollBar* control to the *frmConfiguration* form, perform the following steps:

1. If Visual Basic is not displaying the *frmConfiguration* form within an object window, double-click your mouse on the *frmConfiguration* form listing within Project Explorer. Visual Basic will open the *frmConfiguration* form.

2. Within Visual Basic, select the View menu Toolbox option. Visual Basic will open the Toolbox.

3. Within the Toolbox, double-click your mouse on the HScrollBar icon. Visual Basic will draw an *HScrollBar* control, *HScroll1*, within the *frmConfiguration* form. Figure 3.5 shows the HScrollBar icon in the Toolbox.

Figure 3.5 *The HScrollBar icon in the Toolbox.*

4. Within the *frmConfiguration* form, click your mouse on the *HScroll1* control to highlight it. Visual Basic will draw a small frame around the control.

5. Select the View menu Properties Window option. Visual Basic will open the Properties Window listing the *HScroll1* properties.

6. Within the Properties Window, change the *HScroll1* properties to the values Table 3.7 lists.

Object	Property	Set As
HScroll1	*Height*	252
HScroll1	*LargeChange*	1
HScroll1	*Left*	720
HScroll1	*Max*	9
HScroll1	*Min*	1

Table 3.7 *The newly named* **hscCircleSize** *control's properties. (continued on following page)*

Object	Property	Set As
HScroll1	*SmallChange*	1
HScroll1	*Top*	3000
HScroll1	*Width*	2385
HScroll1	*Name*	*hscCircleSize*

Table 3.7 *The newly named* **hscCircleSize** *control's properties. (continued from previous page)*

ADDING THE LABELS AND COMMAND BUTTONS TO THE FRMCONFIGURATION FORM

After you add the other controls to the *frmConfiguration* form, you can add the three *Label* controls and the *CommandButton* controls to the form. To add the *Label* and *CommandButton* controls to the *frmConfiguration* form, perform the following steps:

1. If Visual Basic is not displaying the *frmConfiguration* form within an object window, double-click your mouse on the *frmConfiguration* form listing within Project Explorer. Visual Basic will open the *frmConfiguration* form.

2. Within Visual Basic, select the View menu Toolbox option. Visual Basic will open the Toolbox.

3. Within the Toolbox, double-click your mouse on the Label icon. Visual Basic will draw a *Label* control, *Label1*, within the *frmConfiguration* form.

4. Repeat Step 3 two more times. Visual Basic will draw two more *Label* controls within the *frmConfiguration* form.

5. Within the Toolbox, double-click your mouse on the CommandButton icon. Visual Basic will draw a *CommandButton* control, *Command1*, within the *frmConfiguration* form.

6. Repeat Step 5 one more time. Visual Basic will draw a second *CommandButton* control within the *frmConfiguration* form.

7. Within the *frmConfiguration* form, click your mouse on a *Label* control to highlight it. Visual Basic will draw a small frame around the control.

8. Select the View menu Properties Window option. Visual Basic will open the Properties Window listing the *Label* control's properties.

9. Within the Properties Window, change the *Label* control's properties to the values Table 3.8 lists.

10. Repeat Steps 7, 8, and 9 to change the properties for all the *Label* and *CommandButton* controls to the values Table 3.8 lists.

Object	Property	Set As
Label1	*Alignment*	2 - Center
Label1	*BorderStyle*	1 - Fixed Single
Label1	*Caption*	Size of Circles
Label1	*Height*	252
Label1	*Left*	1092
Label1	*Top*	2424
Label1	*Width*	1596
Label1	*Name*	lblSize
Label2	*Alignment*	2 - Center
Label2	*BorderStyle*	1 - Fixed Single
Label2	*Caption*	Small
Label2	*Height*	252
Label2	*Left*	216

Table 3.8 *The newly named* **Label** *and* **CommandButton** *controls' properties. (continued on following page)*

Object	Property	Set As
Label2	Top	2760
Label2	Width	930
Label2	Name	lblSmall
Label3	Alignment	2 - Center
Label3	BorderStyle	1 - Fixed Single
Label3	Caption	Large
Label3	Height	252
Label3	Left	2595
Label3	Top	2760
Label3	Width	930
Label3	Name	lblLarge
Command1	Caption	&OK
Command1	Height	432
Command1	Left	600
Command1	Top	3480
Command1	Width	1200
Command1	Name	cmdOK
Command2	Caption	&Cancel
Command2	Height	432
Command2	Left	1920
Command2	Top	3480
Command2	Width	1200
Command2	Name	cmdCancel

Table 3.8 *The newly named* **Label** *and* **CommandButton** *controls' properties. (continued from previous page)*

When you finish designing the *frmConfiguration* form, it will look similar to Figure 3.6.

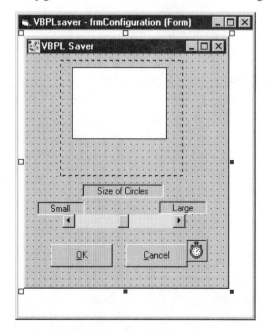

Figure 3.6 *The* **frmConfiguration** *form after you complete its design.*

Writing the Code for the prjVBPLSaver Project

As you have learned, the *prjVBPLSaver* project includes three forms and a module. The program code within the module performs the program's primary processing. In fact, the *prjVBPLSaver* program will start its execution within the *Sub Main* procedure the *mdlSaver* module contains. To write the program code for the *prjVBPLSaver* project, you will first write the program code within the *mdlSaver* module and then write the program code within the three forms.

Writing the mdlSaver Module's Program Code

As you learned in the previous paragraph, the *prjVBPLSaver* program performs much of its processing within the *mdlSaver* module. The types, API functions, and many of the constants the program will use are within the *mdlSaver* module's General–Declarations section. Because of the number of declarations you will make within the *mdlSaver* module's General–Declarations section, it is worthwhile to consider the section in pieces. The first piece is the declaration of two user-defined types:

```
Option Explicit

Type RECT                        ' Used by GetClientRect and GetWindowRect
  Left As Long
  Top As Long
  Right As Long
  Bottom As Long
End Type
Type OsVersionInfo               ' Used by GetVersionEx
  dwVersionInfoSize As Long
  dwMajorVersion As Long
  dwMinorVersion As Long
  dwBuildNumber As Long
  dwPlatform As Long
  szCSDVersion As String * 128
End Type
```

As you will learn, the *prjVBPLSaver* program uses Windows API functions to perform much of the program's processing. The first piece of the General–Declarations section declares two types; you will use both types when you make API function calls from within the *prjVBPLSaver* program. The first type, *RECT*, contains four *Long* values that correspond to a rectangle's four corner points. You will use the *RECT* type when you invoke the *GetClientRect* and *GetWindowRect* functions, as the next section details.

The second type, *OSVersionInfo*, contains five long members and a fixed-length string member. Variables of type *OSVersionInfo* will contain information about the version number of the computer's operating system, together with the operating system name and build number. You will use the *OSVersionInfo* type when you invoke the *GetVersionEx* function, as the next section details.

Writing the Windows API Function Declarations

As you have learned, the *prjVBPLSaver* program will use Windows API functions to perform much of its processing. The Windows API functions will perform activities ranging from reading keys from the Windows registry to copying bitmaps to the display. The following code implements the Windows API function declarations within the *mdlSaver* module:

```
Declare Function BitBlt Lib "gdi32" (ByVal hDestDC As Long, _
    ByVal x As Long, ByVal Y As Long, ByVal nWidth As Long, _
    ByVal nHeight As Long, ByVal hSrcDC As Long, ByVal XSrc As Long, _
    ByVal YSrc As Long, ByVal dwRop As Long) As Long
Private Declare Function CallWindowProc Lib "user32" Alias _
    "CallWindowProcA" (ByVal wndrpcPrev As Long, ByVal hwnd As Long, _
    ByVal uMsg As Long, ByVal wParam As Long, lParam As Any) As Long
```

```
Private Declare Function CreateDC Lib "gdi32" Alias "CreateDCA" _
    (ByVal lpDriverName$, ByVal lpDeviceName$, ByVal lpOutput$, _
    ByVal lpInitData As Long) As Long
Private Declare Function DeleteDC Lib "gdi32" (ByVal hDC As Long) As Long
Private Declare Function FindWindow Lib "user32" Alias "FindWindowA" _
    (ByVal lpClassName$, ByVal lpWindowName$) As Long
Public Declare Function GetClientRect Lib "user32" _
    (ByVal hwnd As Long, lpRect As RECT) As Long
Private Declare Function GetVersionEx Lib "kernel32" Alias "GetVersionExA" _
    (lpStruct As OsVersionInfo) As Long
Public Declare Function GetWindowRect Lib "user32" _
    (ByVal hwnd As Long, lpRect As RECT) As Long
Public Declare Function IsWindow Lib "user32" (ByVal hwnd As Long) As Long
Private Declare Function PwdChangePassword Lib "mpr" Alias _
    "PwdChangePasswordA" (ByVal lpcRegkeyname$, ByVal hwnd As Long, _
    ByVal uiReserved1 As Long, ByVal uiReserved2 As Long) As Long
Private Declare Function RegCloseKey Lib "advapi32.dll" _
    (ByVal HKey As Long) As Long
Private Declare Function RegOpenKeyExA Lib "advapi32.dll" _
    (ByVal HKey As Long, ByVal lpszSubKey$, dwOptions As Long, _
    ByVal samDesired As Long, lpHKey As Long) As Long
Private Declare Function RegQueryValueExA Lib "advapi32.dll" _
    (ByVal HKey As Long, ByVal lpszValueName$, lpdwRes As Long, _
    lpdwType As Long, ByVal lpDataBuff$, nSize As Long) As Long
Public Declare Function SetParent Lib "user32" _
    (ByVal hWndChild As Long, ByVal hWndNewParent As Long) As Long
Public Declare Function SetWindowLong Lib "user32" Alias "SetWindowLongA" _
    (ByVal hwnd As Long, ByVal nIndex As Long, _
    ByVal dwNewLong As Long) As Long
Public Declare Function SetWindowPos Lib "user32" (ByVal h As Long, _
    ByVal hb As Long, ByVal x As Long, ByVal Y As Long, ByVal cx As Long, _
    ByVal cy As Long, ByVal f As Long) As Integer
Public Declare Function ShowCursor Lib "user32" _
    (ByVal bShow As Long) As Long
Private Declare Function StretchBlt Lib "gdi32" (ByVal hDestDC As Long, _
    ByVal x As Long, ByVal Y As Long, ByVal nWidth As Long, _
    ByVal nHeight As Long, ByVal hSrcDC As Long, ByVal XSrc As Long, _
    ByVal YSrc As Long, ByVal nSrcWidth As Long, ByVal nSrcHeight As Long, _
    ByVal dwRop As Long) As Long
Public Declare Function SystemParametersInfo Lib "user32" Alias _
    "SystemParametersInfoA" (ByVal uAction As Long, ByVal uParam As Long, _
    lpvParam As Any, ByVal fuWinIni As Long) As Long
Public Declare Function VerifyScreenSavePwd Lib "password.cpl" _
    (ByVal hwnd As Long) As Boolean
```

As you can see, the program includes several API functions. Table 3.9 lists the API functions the *prjVBPLSaver* program will use and a brief description of each function's purpose.

Function	Description
BitBlt	Converts graphical information from a device context into a device-independent bitmap.
CallWindowProc	Invokes the Windows default message handler. You will use this to pass messages your sub classed message handler does not process.
CreateDC	Creates a *device context*, an internal structure that Windows uses to maintain information about a device.
DeleteDC	Deletes a device context previously created with *CreateDC*.
FindWindow	Lets you search all the currently open windows on the desktop for a window that matches a specific window class or caption.

Table 3.9 *The API Functions the **prjVBPLSaver** program uses. (continued on following page)*

Function	Description
GetClientRect	Retrieves a window's client-area dimensions. The return value is of type *RECT*, a Windows-defined type that contains four long values that correspond to the rectangle's corners.
GetVersionEx	Retrieves the current operating system version, both its name and its identification number.
GetWindowRect	Like *GetClientRect*, *GetWindowRect* returns a window's dimensions. However, *GetWindowRect* returns the window's outside dimensions.
IsWindow	Lets your programs determine whether a window handle points to a valid window. In the *prjVBPLSaver* program, you will use this function to ensure the user has not closed the screen saver before performing processing on the window.
PwdChangePassword	Displays the system-standard password change dialog box. In the *prjVBPLSaver* program, you will use this function to let the user change the screen saver password.
RegCloseKey	Closes a registry key that the program has previously opened with *RegOpenKeyEx*.
RegOpenKeyEx	Lets your programs open a registry key anywhere in the Windows registry.
RegQueryValueEx	Lets your programs retrieve a value from anywhere in the Windows registry.
SetParent	Lets your programs change the parent window of a specific child window. In the *prjVBPLSaver* program, you will use this function to place the configuration window within the Display Properties dialog box.
SetWindowLong	Lets your programs change values associated with a window. In the *prjVBPLSaver* program, you will use this function to subclass the window and to assign your own message-handling procedure to the window.
SetWindowPos	Lets your programs change the size, position, and order of a child, pop-up, or top-level window. In the *prjVBPLSaver* program, you will use this function to put the screen saver display on top of every other window on the desktop.
ShowCursor	Shows or hides the mouse pointer on the screen. In the *prjVBPLSaver* program, you will use this function to hide the mouse pointer while the screen saver is running.
StretchBlt	The *StretchBlt* function copies the data from a device context into a device-independent bitmap. Unlike *BitBlt*, *StretchBlt* lets you expand or contract the image from the device context to dimensions you specify.
SystemParametersInfo	Lets the calling program query or set system-wide parameters. In the *prjVBPLSaver* program, you will use this function to instruct the operating system the screen saver is running (or is complete).
VerifyScreenSavePwd	Part of the Windows 95 built-in screen saver library, the *VerifyScreenSavePwd* function will display the Windows 95 standard password dialog box.

Table 3.9 *The API Functions the **prjVBPLSaver** program uses. (continued from previous page)*

USING THE API TEXT VIEWER TO ADD API DECLARATIONS TO YOUR PROJECTS

As you learned in Chapter 1, "Introduction to Visual Basic," you can use the *API Text Viewer* easily to place API function declarations, constants, and types into your Visual Basic programs. For example, to add the *GetDriveType* function to your project, as well as the constants your program will use to evaluate *GetDriveType's* return value, perform the following steps:

1. Select the Start menu Programs option Microsoft Visual Basic 5.0 group. Within the Microsoft Visual Basic 5.0 group, select the API Text Viewer option. Windows will open the *API Text Viewer*, as shown in Figure 3.7.

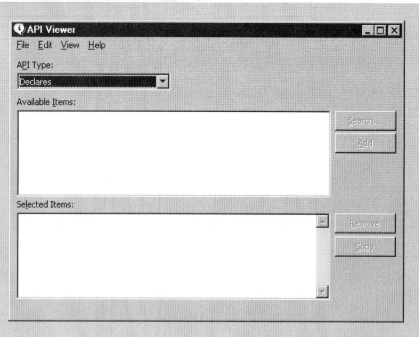

*Figure 3.7 The **API Text Viewer** at startup.*

2. Within the *API Text Viewer*, select the File menu Load Text File option. The *API Text Viewer* will display the Select a Text API File dialog box.

3. Within the Select a Text API File dialog box, select the *Win32API.txt* file. Click your mouse on OK to load the file. The *API Text Viewer* will take several moments to load the file.

4. After the *API Text Viewer* finishes loading the file, it may ask you whether you want to convert the text file to a database, as shown in Figure 3.8.

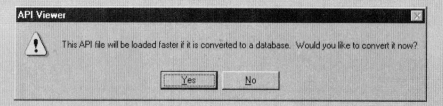

*Figure 3.8 The **API Text Viewer** "convert text to database" message box.*

5. If the program prompts you to save the text file as a database file, do so. Otherwise, select the File menu Convert Text to Database option. The *API Text Viewer* will display the Select a Name for the New Database dialog box.

6. Within the dialog box, save the file as *Win32API.mdb*. Click your mouse on OK to save the file. After you save the file, you can locate the API function and constants you want to add to your program.

7. Within the Available Items list box, click your mouse on any item. The *API Text Viewer* will select the item on which you click.

8. Within the Available Items list box, type *GetClientRect*. The list box will automatically select the *GetClientRect* API function. Click your mouse on the Add button to add the function to the copy list.

9. Click your mouse on the API Type combo box's drop-down arrow and select the Types option. The *API Text Viewer* will load the possible Type declarations you might use with API functions and refresh the list box.

10. Within the Available Items list box, click your mouse on any item. The *API Text Viewer* will select the item on which you click.

11. Type *Rect* in the Available Items list box. The Available Items list box will automatically change to the *RECT* type declaration. Click your mouse on the Add button to add the new type to the copy list. When you finish, the *API Text Viewer* will look similar to Figure 3.9.

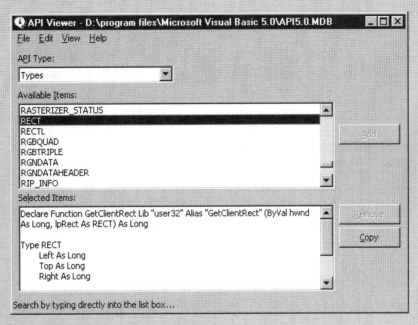

Figure 3.9 *The **API Text Viewer** after you add the **GetClientRect** function and its associated **RECT** type.*

12. Click your mouse on the Copy button to copy the constant declarations to the Clipboard. The *API Text Viewer* will copy the declarations to the Clipboard.

13. Use the ALT+TAB keyboard combination to switch back to Visual Basic and open the *mdlSaver* module Code window. Within the General–Declarations section, select the Edit menu Paste option. Visual Basic will paste the declarations (both the function declaration and the type declaration) into the module.

WRITING THE CONSTANT AND VARIABLE DECLARATIONS

After you have written the type and function declarations, you should add the constant and variable declarations to the project. The following code implements the constant and variable declarations within the *mdlSaver* module:

```
Private Const GWL_WNDPROC = -4                    ' Message procedure id
Public Const WM_CLOSE = &H10                       ' Message constant
Private Const WM_USER = &H400                       ' Message constant
Public Const SWP_NOMOVE = &H2                       ' Window position constant
Public Const SWP_NOSIZE = 1                         ' Window position constant
Public Const FLAGS = SWP_NOMOVE Or SWP_NOSIZE
Public Const HWND_TOPMOST = -1                      ' Window position constant
Public Const SRCCOPY = &HCC0020                     ' Bitmap copy constant
Public Const SRCAND = &H8800C6                      ' Bitmap copy constant
Public Const SRCINVERT = &H660046                   ' Bitmap copy constant
Public Const HKEY_CURRENT_USER = &H80000001         ' Registry constant
Private Const KEY_QUERY_VALUE = &H1&                ' Registry constant
Private Const KEY_ENUMERATE_SUB_KEYS = &H8&         ' Registry constant
Private Const KEY_NOTIFY = &H10&                    ' Registry constant
Private Const READ_CONTROL = &H20000                ' Registry constant
Private Const STANDARD_RIGHTS_READ = READ_CONTROL   ' Registry constant
```

```
Private Const Key_Read = STANDARD_RIGHTS_READ Or KEY_QUERY_VALUE Or _
    KEY_ENUMERATE_SUB_KEYS Or KEY_NOTIFY
Private Const REG_DWORD = 4&                      ' 32-bit number
Public Const SPI_SCREENSAVERRUNNING = 97&        ' System parameters constant
Public Const Win95 = 1&                          ' Version number
Public Const WinNT = 2&                          ' Version number
Private m_wndprcNext As Long                      ' Holds address of CtlProc
Public tempLong As Long
Public tempString As String
Public tempInt As Integer
Public PWProtect As Integer                       ' Sets password variable
Public MouseMoves As Integer                      ' Number of mouse moves
Public PictureLoaded As Integer                   ' Program flag
Public CPWindow As Long                           ' Window handle
Public CPRect As RECT                             ' Holds GetClientRect value
Public xPixel As Integer                          ' Pixel X position
Public yPixel As Integer                          ' Pixel Y position
Public Size As Integer                            ' Circle size
Public ScreenWidth As Integer                     ' Screen width, pixels
Public ScreenHeight As Integer                    ' Screen height, pixels
Private OsVers As OsVersionInfo                    ' Operating system info
Public winOS As Long                              ' OS version number
```

As with the Windows API function declarations, the following sections will detail the use of the constants and variables that you declare within the *mdlSaver* module.

WRITING THE CODE FOR THE SUB MAIN PROCEDURE

As you have learned, the *prjVBPLSaver* program will begin its execution within the *Sub Main* procedure, rather than in a *Form_Load* procedure. Because the *VBPLSaver* program will display only one of the forms it contains in any given execution, the program must first determine what form it should display before it displays anything. The *VBPLSaver* program uses the *Sub Main* procedure to determine the correct form. The following code implements the *Main* procedure:

```
Private Sub Main()
  Dim StartType As String

  xPixel = Screen.TwipsPerPixelX
  yPixel = Screen.TwipsPerPixelY
  Size = Val(GetSetting("Samples", "VBPL Screen Saver", "Size", "5"))
  If Size < 1 Then Size = 1
  If Size > 9 Then Size = 9
  StartType = UCase(Left$(Command, 2))
  If StartType = "" Then StartType = "/C"
  Select Case StartType
    Case "/C"
      frmConfiguration.Show
    Case "/S"
      If CheckUnique("Screen Saver Main Form") = False Then Exit Sub
      frmMain.Show
    Case "/P"
      CPWindow = Val(Right$(Command, Len(Command) - 2))
      Load frmControl
    Case "/A"
      CPWindow = Val(Right$(Command, Len(Command) - 2))
      tempLong = PwdChangePassword("SCRSAVE", CPWindow, 0, 0)
  End Select
End Sub
```

The *Sub Main* procedure begins by initializing the *xPixel* and *yPixel* values to the system values that determine how many *twips* (Visual Basic units of screen measurement) per pixel (operating system units of screen measurement) the program will use. After setting the twip-to-pixel ratios, the *Sub Main* program code uses the *GetSetting* Visual Basic function to load the current circle size from the system registry. The last parameter within the *GetSetting* function sets the default size to 5 units. If the registry contains no setting, the program code will set the *Size* variable to 5; otherwise, it will set the *Size* variable to the program's previously-saved registry setting. After setting the *Size* variable, the program code checks the variable's boundaries and, if the variable is outside its size limits, changes the variable's value to a value inside its size limits.

The program code then sets the *StartType* variable equal to the left two digits of the *Command* value. Within your Visual Basic programs, the *Command* value will contain any command-line parameters the operating system passes to the program when you execute it. For screen savers, the operating system will always pass in one of four command-line parameters. If, for some reason, the invocation passes in no parameters, the program code then sets the parameter to the default—the configuration screen.

The *Select Case* statement checks the command-line parameter that the program receives. As you have learned, the command-line parameter will be one of four values. If the parameter is */C*, the program will display the *frmConfiguration* form. If the parameter is */S,* the program code will call the *CheckUnique* function to determine that the computer is not already displaying the screen saver. If the computer is displaying the screen saver, the program will exit. Otherwise, the program will display the screen saver. If the command-line parameter is */P*, the program code will display the *frmControl* form within the Display Properties dialog box. Finally, if the command-line parameter is */A*, the program code will display the operating system-provided Password dialog box.

73

TELLING VISUAL BASIC TO START THE PROJECT'S EXECUTION WITHIN SUB MAIN

By default, Visual Basic will start the project's execution within the *Load* event of the first form that you add to the project. You must specifically instruct Visual Basic to start the program's execution from another location. In the case of the *prjVBPLSaver* project, the program should begin to execute within the *Sub Main* procedure. To instruct Visual Basic to start the program's execution within the *Sub Main* procedure, perform the following steps:

1. Within Visual Basic, select the Project menu VBPLSaver Properties option. Visual Basic will display the VBPLSaver – Project Properties dialog box.

2. Within the VBPLSaver – Project Properties dialog box's General tab, change the Startup Object combo box's selection to Sub Main. Figure 3.10 shows the VBPLSaver – Project Properties dialog box.

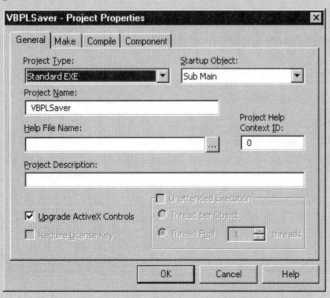

Figure 3.10 *The VBPLSaver – Project Properties dialog box.*

3. Click your mouse on OK. Visual Basic will close the VBPLSaver – Project Properties dialog box.

WRITING THE CODE FOR THE CHECKUNIQUE FUNCTION

As you learned in the previous section, if the user tries to run the actual screen saver within the *prjVBPLSaver* program, the program will first use the *CheckUnique* function to determine whether or not the screen saver is already running. The following code implements the *CheckUnique* function:

```
Public Function CheckUnique(ByVal FormCaption As String) As Boolean
  Dim HandleWin As Long

  HandleWin = FindWindow(vbNullString, FormCaption)
  If HandleWin = 0 Then
    CheckUnique = True
  Else
    CheckUnique = False
  End If
End Function
```

Within the *CheckUnique* function, the program code uses the *FindWindow* function to determine whether another window is already open with the same caption as that the calling procedure passes within the *FormCaption* parameter. If another window is already open, *CheckUnique* will return *False*. Otherwise, *CheckUnique* will return *True*.

WRITING THE CODE FOR THE GETVERSION32 PROCEDURE

As you will learn later in this chapter, if the *prjVBPLSaver* program is running on a Windows 95 machine, the program will perform different processing when it checks for password validity than it will if it is running on a Windows NT machine. To determine what type of operating system is running on the computer, the program will use the *GetVersion32* procedure. The following code implements the *GetVersion32* procedure:

```
Public Sub GetVersion32()
  OsVers.dwVersionInfoSize = 148&
  tempLong = GetVersionEx(OsVers)
  winOS = OsVers.dwPlatform
End Sub
```

As you just learned, the *GetVersion32* procedure uses the Windows API *GetVersionEx* function to determine what operating system is running on the computer. The procedure then sets the *winOS* variable equal to the *dwPlatform* member of the *OsVers* variable. The resulting value should be either 1 or 2, with 1 indicating Windows 95 and 2 indicating Windows NT. (Other values indicate an error.)

WRITING THE CODE FOR THE CENTERFORM PROCEDURE

Often, when you load a form onto the screen, you will want to ensure that you load that form at the display's exact center (for appearance). To move a form to the exact center of the screen, you will use the *Centerform* procedure. The following code implements the *Centerform* procedure:

```
Public Sub Centerform(FrmName As Form)
  FrmName.Top = Screen.Height / 2 - FrmName.Height / 2
  FrmName.Left = Screen.Width / 2 - FrmName.Width / 2
End Sub
```

The *Centerform* procedure accepts the form it is to center as its sole parameter, then uses the Visual Basic-defined *Screen* object to determine where to place the form. It is important to note that the *Screen* object represents the entire screen, including the task bar—which means the form may look slightly off center after you place it because the task bar takes up some space on the screen.

WRITING THE CODE FOR THE COPYSCREEN PROCEDURE

Each time you load a form within the *prjVBPLSaver* program, you will copy an image of the display to the form. The screen saver itself does not draw over other objects on screen—it simply copies an image of those objects to the form or *PictureBox* and then draws onto the form or picture. The *prjVBPLSaver* program uses the *CopyScreen* procedure to copy the screen image to the object the calling procedure specifies. The following code implements the *CopyScreen* procedure:

```
Public Sub CopyScreen(canvas As Object)
   Dim screendc As Long
   canvas.AutoRedraw = True
   screendc = CreateDC("DISPLAY", "", "", 0&)
   tempLong = StretchBlt(canvas.hDC, 0, 0, canvas.Width, canvas.Height, _
      screendc, 0, 0, Screen.Width, Screen.Height, SRCCOPY)
   tempLong = DeleteDC(screendc)
   canvas.AutoRedraw = False
End Sub
```

The *CopyScreen* procedure uses the *CreateDC* API function to create a device context (a Windows system object) for the entire display. The *StretchBlt* function copies the image from the screen into the *canvas* object (which either corresponds to a form or a *PictureBox*). As it copies the image, *StretchBlt* will expand or reduce the image's size to fit within the *canvas* object's space. Additionally, *StretchBlt* will convert the device context's contents into a bitmap as it draws. After the *CopyScreen* procedure finishes placing the screen image within the *canvas* object, the program code deletes the device context and returns to the calling procedure.

WRITING THE DRAW PROCEDURE

As you will learn in later sections in this chapter, each form in the *prjVBPLSaver* project includes a *Timer* control, which the form uses to draw circles at regular intervals onto either the form itself or onto a *PictureBox* within the form. All the *Timer* controls will call the *Draw* procedure to draw the circles. The following code implements the *Draw* procedure:

```
Public Sub Draw(canvas As Object)
   Dim X As Double, X2 As Double
   Dim Y As Double, Y2 As Double
   Dim Radius As Integer
   Dim Colr As Long
   Dim i As Integer

   ScreenWidth = canvas.Width
   ScreenHeight = canvas.Height
   For i = 1 To 1200 / Size / Size     'Many small or fewer large circles
      X = Rnd * ScreenWidth
      Y = Rnd * ScreenHeight
      canvas.FillColor = RGB(Rnd * 255, Rnd * 255, Rnd * 255)
      Radius = Rnd * ScreenWidth / 2600 * Size * Size   ' small circles
      canvas.Circle (X, Y), Radius, canvas.FillColor
   Next i
End Sub
```

The *Draw* procedure sets the *ScreenWidth* and *ScreenHeight* variables equal to the width of the canvas on which the procedure will draw. Do not confuse the *ScreenWidth* and *ScreenHeight* variables with the *Screen* object's *Width* and *Height* properties. The program code then enters a *For-Next* loop, which draws between 15 large circles and 1200 small circles onto the screen (depending on the size the user has chosen).

Within the *For-Next* loop, the program code uses the *Rnd* function to determine a random *x* and *y* coordinate at which the program should draw the circle, and then determines a random color that it should use to draw the circle. Finally, the program code determines a random radius (which may be as large as the maximum size) to draw the circle. The program code then uses the *Circle* method to draw the circle onto the *canvas* object. You will learn more about the *Circle* method in Chapter 5, "Creating and Using Fractals."

WRITING THE REGGETVALUE FUNCTION

As you have learned, you can protect against someone turning off your screen saver by setting a password for the screen saver. Windows will store the screen saver password within the Control Panel section of the Windows system registry. Unfortunately, the Visual Basic *GetSetting* function will let you retrieve information about settings only within the application's registry entries, so you must use Windows API functions to access the information within the Control Panel section of the registry. The following code implements the *RegGetValue* function, which you will use within the *prjVBPLSaver* program to retrieve password information from the registry:

```
Public Function RegGetValue(MainKey As Long, SubKey As String, _
    value As String) As String
  Dim sKeyType As Long
  Dim ret As Long
  Dim lpHKey As Long
  Dim lpcbData As Long
  Dim ReturnedString As String
  Dim fTempDbl As Double

  If MainKey >= &H80000000 And MainKey <= &H80000006 Then
    ret = RegOpenKeyExA(MainKey, SubKey, 0&, Key_Read, lpHKey)
    If ret <> 0 Then
      RegGetValue = ""
      Exit Function
    End If
    lpcbData = 255
    ReturnedString = Space$(lpcbData)
    ret& = RegQueryValueExA(lpHKey, value, ByVal 0&, sKeyType, _
        ReturnedString, lpcbData)
    If ret <> 0 Then
      RegGetValue = ""
    Else
      If sKeyType = REG_DWORD Then
        fTempDbl = Asc(Mid$(ReturnedString, 1, 1)) + &H100& * _
            Asc(Mid$(ReturnedString, 2, 1)) + &H10000 * _
            Asc(Mid$(ReturnedString, 3, 1)) + &H1000000 * _
            CDbl(Asc(Mid$(ReturnedString, 4, 1)))
        ReturnedString = Format$(fTempDbl, "000")
      End If
      RegGetValue = Left$(ReturnedString, lpcbData - 1)
    End If
    ret = RegCloseKey(lpHKey)
  End If
End Function
```

The first *If-Then* statement within the function ensures the *MainKey* value is a valid value. If the *MainKey* value is not valid, the *RegGetValue* function will immediately exit and perform no processing. If the program code ensures that the *MainKey* value is valid, the program will use the *RegOpenKeyExA* function to open the specified key within the registry. If the program does not successfully open the key its parameters specify, it will exit.

After opening the key, the program code must request the key's value from the registry. To request the value, the program code uses the *RegQueryValueExA* function, which will return the key within the *value* parameter. If the program is unable to retrieve a usable value from the registry key (that is, one that is either a string or an integer convertible to a string), it will close the key and exit.

If the program is able to retrieve a usable value from the registry key, it checks that value to determine whether it is an actual string or if it is a numeric indicator to the string. If the key value is a string, the program code returns the string (which now contains the password) to the calling procedure. If the key value is a numeric indicator to a string, the program code uses the *Asc* and *Mid$* functions to convert that numeric value to a string the program can use. After it gets the string, the *RegGetValue* function closes the key and exits.

BEGINNING TO UNDERSTAND FORM SUBCLASSING

Programmers find one of the most useful new keywords in Visual Basic 5.0 is the *AddressOf* keyword, which opens up a previously unavailable (from Visual Basic) set of callback functions and subclassing techniques to all Visual Basic programmers who work on 32-bit Windows platforms. *Subclassing* lets you change the default behavior and appearance of Visual Basic forms and controls, and accomplish tasks that would otherwise require you to purchase a third-party ActiveX control.

After you understand how to subclass forms, you can add icons to menus, gradients to window captions, and new items to *TextBox* control context menus, to name a few possibilities. Essentially, you have almost no limit to how you manipulate Windows and Visual Basic objects. However, it is fundamental to understand the importance of messages within the Windows operating system in order to understand how subclassing works.

Microsoft's programming team built the Windows operating system on messages. When you click your mouse on a window or a control, Windows sends the clicked item a *WM_LBUTTONDOWN* message with additional information about where the mouse cursor is and which control keys you have currently pressed. Similarly, Windows sends a *WM_SIZE* message when you resize a window and a *WM_PAINT* message when the window needs refreshing. Messages are not the operating system's exclusive domain, and you can send a message to a window or a control yourself using the *SendMessage* or the *PostMessage* API functions. Sending your own message often offers you new capabilities Visual Basic's controls and forms do not directly support. For instance, to set the internal left margin of a multi-line *TextBox* control to 20 pixels, you can use the following API function call:

```
SendMessage Text1.Hwnd,EM_SETMARGINS, EC_LEFTMARGIN, 20
```

The first argument is the handle of the window to which you address the message. The second argument, usually a symbolic constant, is the message's numeric value. The third and fourth arguments, traditionally named *wParam* and *lParam*, carry any additional information the message needs—in this case, which margin the program should set and the margin's new width, respectively. When you must send more than two values with the *SendMessage* function, you will usually gather the values in a structure and send the structure's address in the *lParam* argument. In addition to setting a value and sending a message to a form or a control, you can also use *SendMessage* to retrieve a value, such as the number of the first visible line in a multi-line text box, as shown here:

```
lineIndex = SendMessage(Text1.hWnd, EM_GETFIRSTVISIBLELINE, 0, 0)
```

Although sending messages is a relatively simple process, Visual Basic applications have never had the capability to detect when another application is sending a message to them. If Windows sends a *WM_SIZE* message, the Visual Basic run-time platform intercepts the message and exposes it to your program in the form of a *Form_Resize* event. Visual Basic handles many other Windows messages similarly. For instance, the *WM_ACTIVATE* message invokes a *Form_Activate* event, and *WM_PAINT* invokes a *Form_Paint* event. Unfortunately, Visual Basic does not transform all messages into events and may sometimes convert messages into events you do not want to invoke. For example, when a window moves, Windows sends the Window a *WM_MOVE* message. Visual Basic, however, does not offer any *Form_Move* event. Therefore, without subclassing, you cannot process the *WM_MOVE* message. Visual Basic internally processes many useful Windows messages or exposes them as events. Unfortunately, there are many other Windows messages that Visual Basic does not handle. The Windows messages that Visual Basic does not handle prevent Visual Basic programmers from responding to several important system messages and from intercepting messages and manipulating those messages in non-standard ways.

You will learn about form subclassing in detail in Chapter 14, "Using the Windows API to Intercept Windows Messages." For now, simply understand that the *prjVBPLSaver* program uses subclassing to capture one Windows message and perform processing on it different from the default processing Visual Basic would perform.

WRITING THE SUBCLASSING FUNCTIONS

As you have learned, the *prjVBPLSaver* program uses subclassing to intercept Windows messages. Before you can intercept messages the operating system sends to a given form, you must first subclass that form. Within the *prjVBPLSaver* program, you will use the *subclass* procedure to subclass forms. The following code implements the *subclass* procedure:

```
Public Sub subclass(hwnd As Long)
  m_wndprcNext = SetWindowLong(hwnd, GWL_WNDPROC, AddressOf CtlProc)
End Sub
```

The *subclass* procedure accepts as its sole parameter the handle of the window to subclass. The procedure then calls the *SetWindowLong* API function and uses the *AddressOf* keyword to pass to the *SetWindowLong* function the

CtlProc function's address. The *CtlProc* function performs the actual message interception and custom processing. The following code implements the *CtlProc* function:

```
Public Function CtlProc(ByVal hwnd As Long, ByVal MsgVal As Long, _
    ByVal wParam As Long, ByVal lParam As Long) As Long
  If m_wndprcNext = 0 Then Exit Function
  Select Case MsgVal
    Case WM_CLOSE
      tempLong = SetParent(frmControl.picControl.hwnd, frmControl.hwnd)
      PictureLoaded = False
      CtlProc = 0
      Exit Function
  End Select
  CtlProc = CallWindowProc(m_wndprcNext, hwnd, MsgVal, wParam, _
      ByVal lParam)
End Function
```

As you can see, the *CtlProc* function accepts the handle of the window receiving the message, the message, the *wParam* value, and the *lParam* value, just as the previous section details. The function then makes sure the window is still subclassed. If the window is subclassed, the function uses a *Select Case* statement to determine if the message is a *WM_CLOSE* message. If the message is a *WM_CLOSE* message, the function will use the *SetParent* API function to set the *picControl PictureBox* control's parent window to the *frmControl* form, and set the *PictureLoaded* value to *False*. As you will learn in the "Writing the Code for the *frmControl* Form" section later in this chapter, setting the *PictureLoaded* value to *False* will cause the *frmControl* form to unload itself the next time it invokes its timer event.

If the message is not a *WM_CLOSE* message, the function calls the *CallWindowProc* function and passes to the function the values the *CtlProc* function received. The *CallWindowProc* function ensures that the program processes the message correctly by passing the message to the default window procedure, even if it is not a message the program traps.

Because subclassing intercepts messages the system sends to your programs, it is generally a good idea to remove subclassing whenever you unload a form. Within the *prjVBPLSaver* program, you will use the *UnSubClass* procedure to remove the subclassing. The following code implements the *UnSubClass* procedure:

```
Public Sub UnSubClass(hWndCur&)
  If m_wndprcNext Then
    SetWindowLong hWndCur, GWL_WNDPROC, m_wndprcNext
    m_wndprcNext = 0
  End If
End Sub
```

The *UnSubClass* procedure again uses the *SetWindowLong* API function. In the *UnSubClass* procedure, the *SetWindowLong* function's invocation returns the message path to the Windows default handler for the form.

WRITING THE frmCONFIGURATION FORM'S CODE

As you have learned, when the user clicks the mouse on the Settings button within the Display Properties dialog box, the program will display the *frmConfiguration* form. The *frmConfiguration* form will display an image, similar to that on the Display Properties dialog box, within which it will draw circles. The form will also display a scroll bar that lets the user set the size of the circles that the program will draw. The program code for the *frmConfiguration* form is within six events, which you will write in the following sections. The *frmConfiguration* form also declares two local variables within its General–Declarations section. The following code shows the variable declarations for the *frmConfiguration* form:

```
Option Explicit
Dim xx As Integer, yy As Integer
```

The *frmConfiguration* form will use the *xx* and *yy* variables when it determines how many circles it should draw and how frequently to draw them. The *Option Explicit* statement, as you have learned, forces you to define all the variables that you will use within the form.

Writing the Code for the Form_Load Event

When the user clicks the mouse on the Settings button within the Display Properties dialog box, the *prjVBPLSaver* project will display the *frmConfiguration* form. As you have learned, the first program code that a form executes when it loads is the code within the *Form_Load* event for that form. The following code implements the *Form_Load* event for the *frmConfiguration* form:

```
Private Sub Form_Load()
  Dim nRet As Long

  Height = Picture2(0).Height * 2
  Picture2(2).Move Picture2(0).Left, Picture2(0).Top, _
      Picture2(0).Width, Picture2(0).Height
  nRet = BitBlt(Picture2(2).hDC, 0&, 0&, Picture2(2).ScaleWidth, _
      Picture2(2).ScaleHeight, Picture2(1).hDC, 0&, 0&, SRCAND)
  nRet = BitBlt(Picture2(2).hDC, 0&, 0&, Picture2(2).ScaleWidth, _
      Picture2(2).ScaleHeight, Picture2(0).hDC, 0&, 0&, SRCINVERT)
  imgConfiguration.Picture = Picture2(2).Image
  imgConfiguration.Move (Width - imgConfiguration.Width) / 2, _
      imgConfiguration.Top, imgConfiguration.Width, Picture2(0).Height
  tmrConfiguration.Move imgConfiguration.Left + 18 * xPixel, _
      imgConfiguration.Top + 18 * yPixel, 153 * xPixel, 114 * yPixel
  lblSize.Top = imgConfiguration.Top + imgConfiguration.Height + _
      8 * yPixel
  lblSmall.Top = lblSize.Top + lblSize.Height
  lblLarge.Top = lblSmall.Top
  hscCircleSize.Top = lblSmall.Top + lblSmall.Height
  cmdOK.Top = hscCircleSize.Top + hscCircleSize.Height + 10 * yPixel
  cmdCancel.Top = cmdOK.Top
  CopyScreen picConfiguration
  Centerform Me
  hscCircleSize.value = Size
End Sub
```

All the program code within the event that occurs before the *CopyScreen picConfiguration* statement performs alignment and design of the images that form the computer monitor display in the VBPL Saver dialog box when the program executes. The program code will place the monitor images within the *imgConfiguration* control and then align the other controls on the form based on the *imgConfiguration* control's resulting size. After the program code aligns all the controls, it calls the *CopyScreen* procedure and passes in the *picConfiguration* control to the procedure as the *canvas* object. As you have learned, the *CopyScreen* procedure will, in turn, copy an image of the entire display into the *picConfiguration* control. The last line of code sets the horizontal scroll bar's value to the *Size* value that the program retrieved from the system registry during the program's startup.

Writing the Code for the tmrConfiguration_Timer Event

All three forms that you designed for the *prjVBPLSaver* project include *Timer* controls and they all use the *Timer* controls to perform similar processing. Within each form, the program will invoke the *Timer* event every second and draw a circle onto the program-defined display. Within the *frmConfiguration* form, you named the *Timer* control *tmrConfiguration*. The following code implements the *tmrConfiguration_Timer* event:

```
Private Sub tmrConfiguration_Timer()
  yy = yy + 1
  Draw picConfiguration
  tmrConfiguration.Enabled = True
  tmrConfiguration.Interval = 1000
  If yy >= 30 Then
    picConfiguration.Cls
    yy = 1
    tmrConfiguration.Interval = 2000
  End If
End Sub
```

The *tmrConfiguration* event first increments the *yy* variable by one and then calls the *Draw* procedure. The *Draw* procedure will draw a circle onto the *picConfiguration* control. The program code then sets the *tmrConfiguration* control's *Interval* property to ensure that the *tmrConfiguration* control invokes the *Timer* event every second. Next, the program code checks the *yy* variable's value. If the *yy* variable is greater than 30 (which means that the user has not changed anything on the form in thirty seconds), the procedure will clear the screen, reset the *yy* variable to 1, and wait for another thirty seconds.

WRITING THE CODE FOR THE HSCCONFIGURATION_CHANGE EVENT

As you learned in this chapter's "Using the *prjVBPLSaver* Project" section, the user can set the size of the circles that the program draws. To change the circle size, the user must set the size with the scroll bar on the *frmConfiguration* form. Each time the user changes the size with the scroll bar, the program code will invoke the *hscConfiguration_Change* event. The following code implements the *hscConfiguration_Change* event:

```
Private Sub hscCircleSize_Change()
   Size = hscCircleSize.value
   picConfiguration.Cls
End Sub
```

WRITING THE CODE FOR THE CMDCANCEL AND CMDOK CLICK EVENTS

When the user finishes setting the size value for the circles, he or she can exit the *frmConfiguration* form either by clicking the mouse on the *cmdOK* button or by clicking the mouse on the *cmdCancel* button. The *cmdOK* button will save the current size selection before it exits the form. However, the *cmdCancel* button will not save the current size. The following code implements the *cmdOK_Click* event:

```
Private Sub cmdOK_Click()
   SaveSetting "Samples", "VBPL Screen Saver", "Size", Size
   Unload Me
End Sub
```

The *cmdOK_Click* event's program code uses the Visual Basic *SaveSetting* statement to save the user's currently selected circle size to the Windows system registry. The event then unloads the configuration form. The *cmdCancel_Click* event, on the other hand, simply closes the form without updating the registry. The following code implements the *cmdCancel_Click* event:

```
Private Sub cmdCancel_Click()
   Unload Me
End Sub
```

WRITING THE CODE FOR THE FRMCONTROL FORM

When you select the *Vbplsaver* screen saver from within the Display Properties dialog box, the Display Properties dialog box will display a small window and draw circles onto that window, just as the full-screen screen saver will. Although the screen appears when you select the Display Properties dialog box, the dialog box does not perform the processing. The *prjVBPLSaver* program has actually loaded the *frmControl* form into the space inside the monitor graphic within the Display Properties dialog box. The *frmControl* form includes only three events—the form's *Load* event, the *Unload* event, and the *Timer* event for the form's *Timer* control.

WRITING THE CODE FOR THE FORM_LOAD AND FORM_UNLOAD EVENTS

As you have learned, when the user selects the *Vbplsaver* screen saver within the Display Properties dialog box, the *prjVBPLSaver* program will load the *frmControl* form and display it within the dialog box. As with other forms, the first program code that the form will invoke is within its *Form_Load* event. The following code implements the *Form_Load* event for the *frmControl* form:

```
Private Sub Form_Load()
   subclass picControl.hwnd
   tempLong = GetClientRect(CPWindow, CPRect)
```

```
      picControl.Move 0, 0, (CPRect.Right - CPRect.Left) * xPixel, _
          (CPRect.Bottom - CPRect.Top) * yPixel
      CopyScreen picControl
      tempLong = SetParent(picControl.hwnd, CPWindow)
      PictureLoaded = True
   End Sub
```

The first statement within the event calls the *subclass* procedure and passes it the window handle of the *PictureBox* control on the form. As you have learned, the *subclass* procedure assigns a different message-handling routine to the object the program passes to it. Next, the program code determines the space inside the computer monitor image on the Display Properties dialog box and sets the *picControl PictureBox* control's size equal to that amount of space. After setting up the *picControl* control's size, the event's program code calls the *CopyScreen* function, which copies an image of the screen display into the *picControl* control and displays it as a bitmap. Finally, the program code sets the *picControl* control's parent window to the monitor image on the Display Properties dialog box. When the user exits the Display Properties dialog box, the program will invoke the *Form_Unload* event, as shown here:

```
   Private Sub Form_Unload(Cancel As Integer)
     UnSubClass Me.hwnd
   End Sub
```

As you learned earlier in this chapter, you must remove the subclass from windows after you subclass them. You will generally remove subclassing from a form when you unload the form, although you may also do so at any time after you subclass the form. The *Form_Unload* event calls the *mdlSaver* module's *UnSubClass* function to remove the subclass from the window.

WRITING THE TMRCONTROLDRAWCIRCLES_TIMER EVENT

As with the *frmConfiguration* form, the *frmControl* form will invoke its *Timer* event every 400 milliseconds and draw another circle onto the *PictureBox* control. The following code implements the *tmrControlDrawCircles_Timer* event:

```
   Private Sub tmrControlDrawCircles_Timer()
     If IsWindow(CPWindow) = 0 Or Not PictureLoaded Then
       Unload Me
     Else
       Draw picControl
     End If
   End Sub
```

The program code first checks to make sure that the program loads the image and that the window that the form is within is valid (that is, that the user has not closed the Display Properties dialog box). Then the program code calls the *Draw* procedure and passes the *picControl* control to it as the *canvas* object. As you learned, the *Draw* procedure will draw a circle onto whatever control you pass to it, provided that control supports the *Circle* method.

WRITING THE CODE FOR THE FRMMAIN FORM

As you have learned, the *prjVBPLSaver* program will use the *frmMain* form to display the screen saver during normal execution (as opposed to when the user is configuring the screen saver). The primary processing within the *frmMain* form occurs within the *Form_Load*, *Form_QueryUnload*, and *tmrDrawCircles_Timer* events. Program code within other form events will unload the form in the event the user presses a key or moves the mouse.

WRITING THE CODE FOR THE FORM_LOAD EVENT

As you have learned, the *prjVBPLSaver* program will invoke the *Sub Main* procedure when the program begins. *Sub Main* will check the command-line parameter the program receives and load the appropriate form based on that parameter. When the operating system runs the screen saver, it will pass the command-line parameter */S*, which will tell the *prjVBPLSaver* program to load the *frmMain* form. As you have learned, when a program loads a form, the first event to execute within that form is the form's *Form_Load* event, which executes even before the program displays the form. The following code implements the *Form_Load* event for the *frmMain* form:

```
Private Sub Form_Load()
   tempLong = SetWindowPos(hwnd, HWND_TOPMOST, 0, 0, 0, 0, FLAGS)
   Move 0, 0, Screen.Width, Screen.Height
   PWProtect = Val(RegGetValue(HKEY_CURRENT_USER, "Control Panel\Desktop", _
      "ScreenSaveUsePassword"))
   GetVersion32
   If PWProtect And winOS <> WinNT Then _
      tempLong = SystemParametersInfo(SPI_SCREENSAVERRUNNING, 1&, 0&, 0&)
   CopyScreen Me
   Do
   Loop Until ShowCursor(False) < -5
End Sub
```

The first statement within the *Form_Load* event invokes the *SetWindowPos* API function and passes the *frmMain* form's window handle to the function, together with the *HWND_TOPMOST* constant. The *HWND_TOPMOST* constant tells the operating system to place the *frmMain* form in front of every other window on the desktop. The second statement uses the *Move* method to size the *frmMain* form to the same size as the entire display.

After sizing the form, the program code sets the *PWProtect* variable equal to the password that the program saved previously in the registry. If there is no password, the program sets the *PWProtect* value to "". After retrieving the password, the event's program code calls the *GetVersion32* procedure, which you previously learned returns the computer's operating system type within the *winOS* variable. After it determines the operating system, the program code uses an *If-Then* statement to check the password value and operating system name. If the user sets a password, and if the operating system is not Windows NT, the program code calls the *SystemParametersInfo* function to let the operating system know that the screen saver is running. Next, the *CopyScreen Me* statement uses the *CopyScreen* procedure to copy the screen's graphical image onto the form. You learned about the *CopyScreen* procedure in this chapter's "Writing the *mdlSaver* Module's Program Code" section. The last code in the event calls the *ShowCursor* function repeatedly, until the operating system hides the mouse pointer.

WRITING THE CODE FOR THE TMRDRAWCIRCLES_TIMER EVENT

As you have learned, the *prjVBPLSaver* project uses *Timer* controls to ensure that the program draws circles every 400 milliseconds—and the *frmMain* form is no exception. The following code implements the *tmrDrawCircles_Timer* event for the *frmMain* form:

```
Private Sub tmrDrawCircles_Timer()
   Draw Me
End Sub
```

The *tmrDrawCircles_Timer* event calls the *Draw* procedure within the *mdlSaver* module and passes to the procedure the *frmMain* form. The *Draw* procedure, in turn, will draw circles on the *frmMain* form.

WRITING THE CODE FOR MOUSE OR KEYBOARD ACTIVITY

As with most screen savers, the *prjVBPLSaver* program will try to unload itself whenever you move the mouse, click the mouse, or press a key on the keyboard. Responding to a keypress or mouse click is relatively simple. The *KeyDown* event will respond to a keypress. The following code implements the *KeyDown* event:

```
Private Sub Form_KeyDown(KeyCode As Integer, Shift As Integer)
   Unload Me
End Sub
```

As you can see, the *KeyDown* event tries to unload the form. Similarly, you can use the *MouseDown* event to respond to a mouse click. The following code implements the *MouseDown* event:

```
Private Sub Form_MouseDown(Button As Integer, Shift As Integer, _
      X As Single, Y As Single)
   Unload Me
End Sub
```

Much as the *KeyDown* event does, the *MouseDown* event tries to unload the *frmMain* form. Processing mouse moves within the screen saver is only slightly more complex. Because a mouse tends to "creep" even when the user is not actively moving the mouse, the *MouseMove* event should make sure that the user has moved the mouse and that the program is not invoking the *MouseMove* event unnecessarily. The *MouseMove* event uses a static variable to keep track of the time expired since the *MouseMove* event's last invocation and requires at least ten moves per millisecond to qualify the move as an unload action. The following code implements the *MouseMove* event:

```
Private Sub Form_MouseMove(Button As Integer, Shift As Integer, _
    X As Single, Y As Single)
  Static TimeDelay As Long

  MouseMoves = MouseMoves + 1
  If MouseMoves = 4 Then Unload Me
  If TimeDelay = 0 Then
    TimeDelay = Timer
  ElseIf Timer - TimeDelay > 10 Then
    TimeDelay = 0
    MouseMoves = 0
  End If
End Sub
```

The *MouseMove* event creates the *TimeDelay* static value. It also uses the global *MouseMoves* value that you declared within the *mdlSaver* module. Each time the program invokes the *MouseMove* event, the program code within the event increases the *MouseMoves* variable by one. If the total number of mouse moves equals four, the program code tries to unload the form. Otherwise, the program code checks the current amount of elapsed time between moves. If the elapsed time exceeds 10 milliseconds, the program code resets the number of mouse moves and the time delay.

Writing the Form_QueryUnload Event's Code

In the previous section, you learned that each event the section discusses will try to unload the form when the program meets certain criteria (such as a keypress or a mouse click). The events will only try to unload the form because the form contains program code within the *Form_QueryUnload* event to verify that the program should unload the form. Every form that you create within Visual Basic will invoke the *Form_QueryUnload* event before it unloads, which gives you the chance to verify that the program should let the form unload. The following code implements the *Form_QueryUnload* event:

```
Private Sub Form_QueryUnload(Cancel As Integer, UnloadMode As Integer)
  If PWProtect And winOS <> WinNT Then
    Dim PassChck As Boolean

    Do
    Loop Until ShowCursor(True) > 5
    PassChck = VerifyScreenSavePwd(Me.hwnd)
    If PassChck = False Then
      Do
      Loop Until ShowCursor(False) < -5
      Cancel = True
    End If
  End If
End Sub
```

In the *frmMain* form, the *Form_QueryUnload* event first checks to determine whether the user has set a password and is not running Windows NT. If the user has not set a password or if the user is running Windows NT, the program code will exit the event, which will then call the *Form_Unload* event. The following section discusses the *Form_Unload* event in detail.

If the user has set a password and the user is not running Windows NT, the program code will show the cursor and then prompt the user to enter the password for the screen saver. If the user enters the correct password, the program code will then call the *Form_Unload* event. If the user does not enter the correct password, the program code will hide the cursor and resume the screen saver.

WRITING THE FORM_UNLOAD EVENT'S CODE

As you have learned, the *frmMain* form will first call the *Form_QueryUnload* event before it will unload the *frmMain* form. If the user has not set a password or if the user enters the correct password, the program code will invoke the *Unload* event as it unloads the form. The following code implements the *Unload* event:

```
Private Sub Form_Unload(Cancel As Integer)
   Do
   Loop Until ShowCursor(True) > 5
   If PWProtect And winOS <> WinNT Then _
      tempLong = SystemParametersInfo(SPI_SCREENSAVERRUNNING, 0&, 0&, 0&)
End Sub
```

The *Unload* event will use the *ShowCursor* function to display the cursor and then reset the *SystemParametersInfo* in the event that the program set the parameters when the form loaded.

84 ENHANCEMENTS YOU CAN MAKE TO THE prjVBPLSaver PROJECT

The *prjVBPLSaver* program is a fully operational and fully usable screen saver. The most likely enhancement you can make to this project is to change the graphics that the screen saver draws. In Chapter 5, "Creating and Using Fractals," for example, you will learn how to use the Visual Basic *Line* and *Circle* methods to create complex graphical images. You can combine the drawing routines from the *prjFractal* project that Chapter 5 details with the *prjVBPLSaver* project to create a more complex and interesting screen saver.

PUTTING IT ALL TOGETHER

This chapter's project, *prjVBPLSaver*, introduced you to how to use Windows API functions to perform low-level control activities over the computer's display. You have learned how to copy an image of the screen into a form and draw onto that image. You have learned how to use the *KeyPress* and *MouseMove* events, together with form and *PictureBox* events, to determine if the user is performing activities at the keyboard. In addition, you have learned how to subclass messages from the operating system, although Chapter 14 will cover the theory of subclassing in more detail. In Chapter 4, "Using Multiple Forms to Load Different File Types," you will learn how to use the multiple-document interface style to create a program that can read text, Rich Text, and image files, and display them all within a single user interface. Before you continue with Chapter 4, however, make sure that you understand the following key concepts:

- ✓ When you write a screen saver, you must ensure that the screen saver contains three separate forms: one form for the settings screen, one form for the configuration screen, and one form that actually displays the screen saver.

- ✓ Within your Visual Basic programs, you can use the *Sub Main* procedure to perform processing without loading a form. In programs that use no forms, you must include the *Sub Main* procedure as a place for the program to begin its processing.

- ✓ When you capture screen images, you must convert them to bitmaps before you can display them in Visual Basic. To convert screen captures, you can use Windows API functions within your Visual Basic programs, including *StretchBlt* and *BitBlt*.

- ✓ To determine what operating system a computer is running from within your Visual Basic programs, you can use the Windows API *GetVersionEx* function.

- ✓ If you save information within a program's registry entry, you can use the Visual Basic-provided *GetSetting* function and *SaveSetting* statement to read information from the system registry.

- ✓ If you did not save information within a program's registry entry, but must retrieve it from the system registry into your Visual Basic program, you can use the *RegOpenKeyEx* and *RegQueryKeyEx* Windows API functions.

- ✓ To hide or display the mouse cursor during program execution, you can use the Windows API *ShowCursor* function.

Chapter 4

Using Multiple Forms to Load Different File Types

When Microsoft first introduced the Windows operating system, the new operating system signaled a fundamental shift in the way people use computers. Before Windows, most home and desktop computers ran the Microsoft Disk Operating System (MS-DOS)—an operating system that, among other limitations, generally let users run only one program at a time. With the release of Windows, users became able to run several programs at the same time, look at information within a certain program in several different "views," and so on. *Views* let the user, for example, view a spreadsheet, a graph of the information the spreadsheet contains, and the information within a supporting spreadsheet, all at the same time.

Microsoft named the new operating system Windows because the operating system uses the window metaphor for much of its processing. For example, the operating system encloses the views that it shows the user within a frame; the user can open or close windows; and each window can show a different view. Within Visual Basic, you can easily create programs that display multiple views within a single "parent" window. As you learned in Chapter 1, "Introduction to Visual Basic," programs that display multiple views within a single parent window are *Multiple-Document Interface (MDI)* applications (programs). As your Visual Basic programs become more powerful and perform a wider range of activities, using the Multiple-Document Interface program style will become more important.

In this chapter, you will create a Multiple-Document Interface program that will let the user load, display, and, in some cases, edit and save files of several different types. The *prjFileViewer* project that you will create will load and display text (TXT), Rich Text (RTF), Tagged-Image Format (TIF), Windows bitmap (BMP), JPEG-JFIF compliant (JPG) files, and CompuServe® Graphics Image Format (GIF) files. The program will also let you edit and save text (TXT), Rich Text (RTF), and Tagged-Image Format (TIF) files. By the time you finish this chapter, you will understand the following key concepts:

   ◆ When you create a Multiple-Document Interface program, you will use an MDI parent form as a container for the program's other forms.

   ◆ To limit a form within a Visual Basic project so that the user cannot view the form after the user closes the project's MDI parent form, or before the project opens the MDI parent form, you must specify that the form is an MDI child form.

   ◆ To display forms within an MDI project that always remain on top, or that you otherwise use to perform specific processing (such as a Find dialog box), you must specify that the form is not an MDI child form.

   ◆ When you work with MDI-style programs, you will often use a *form array* to maintain information about the child windows the program currently has open. A form array, much like a control array, lets your programs use a unique numeric identifier (an index) to refer to each form within a set of forms. Additionally, as with a control array, you can add new form instances to the array at run time.

   ◆ Within your Visual Basic programs, you can use the *Microsoft Rich TextBox* control to display and store large amounts of text (up to about 2Mb) and to format the text.

   ◆ The *Microsoft Rich TextBox* control lets you format text, save the formats and the text together, and later recover the format and text when you reload the file.

   ◆ Within your Visual Basic programs, you can use the *Microsoft PictureBox* control to display images without providing the user with edit capabilities.

- Within your Visual Basic programs, you can use the *Eastman Software Imaging* controls, which come with Windows 95 and Windows NT 4.0, to open and display image files.

- The *Eastman Software Imaging* controls include the *Image Edit* control, which you will use to display, annotate, manipulate, and manage image files.

- The *Image Edit* control includes the *Annotation Palette* tool, which you will use to apply annotation to an image file.

USING THE prjFILEVIEWER PROJECT

Before you design the *prjFileViewer* project, you may find it helpful to run the program. The companion CD-ROM that accompanies this book contains the *prjFileViewer.exe* program within the *Chapter04* directory. As with every other program on the CD-ROM, you should run the Jamsa Press *setup.exe* program to install the *prjFileViewer.exe* program to your computer's hard drive before you run it. After you install the *prjFileViewer.exe* program to your computer's hard drive, you can run it from the Start menu. To run the program, select the Windows Start menu Run option. Windows will display the Run dialog box. Within the Run dialog box, enter *x:\vbpl\Chapter04\prjFileViewer.exe*, where *x* corresponds to the letter of the hard drive on which you installed the *prjFileViewer.exe* program, and click your mouse on OK. Windows will display the *prjFileViewer.exe* program, as shown in Figure 4.1.

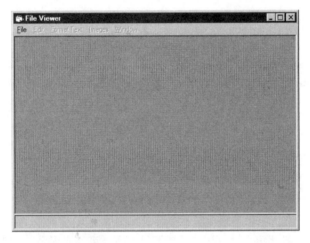

Figure 4.1 *The prjFileViewer.exe program's* **File Viewer** *window at startup.*

RUNNING prjFILEVIEWER FROM THE CD-ROM

As you have learned, you must first install many programs that you will use in this book to your computer's hard drive before you use the programs. The *prjFileViewer.exe* program, however, does not use any custom controls or references, other than those that Visual Basic installs onto your system. Because the *prjFileViewer.exe* uses no custom controls or references, you can run the program from the CD-ROM.

To run the program from the CD-ROM, perform the following steps:

1. Select the Windows Start menu Run option. Windows will display the Run dialog box.

2. Within the Run dialog box, enter *x:\Chapter04\prjFileViewer.exe*, where *x* corresponds to the letter of your computer's CD-ROM drive (usually D: or E:), and click your mouse on OK. Windows will run the *prjFileViewer.exe* program.

To learn more about the Jamsa Press *setup.exe* program, see the "What's on the *Visual Basic Programmer's Library* Companion CD-ROM" section at the back of this book.

UNDERSTANDING THE EASTMAN SOFTWARE IMAGING CONTROLS

As you will learn, the *prjFileViewer.exe* program uses the *Eastman Software Imaging* controls that come with most versions of Windows 95 and Windows NT 4.0. If you are using Windows NT 3.51 or an older version of Windows 95, you may be unable to run the *prjFileViewer.exe* program because you do not have the supporting controls on your computer.

However, you can download the controls for free and install them on your computer from the Eastman Software Web site at *http://www.eastmansoftware.com/imaging*, as shown in Figure 4.2. After you download and install the *Eastman Software Imaging* controls, you can run the *prjFileViewer.exe* program and design the *prjFileViewer* project without difficulty.

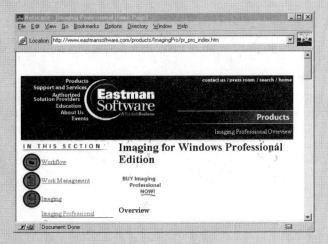

Figure 4.2 *The Eastman Software Web site at* **http://www.eastmansoftware.com/imaging**.

Before you use the *prjFileViewer.exe* program, take a moment to familiarize yourself with the program's appearance. After you start the program, your computer will display a form that fills the entire screen. Near the top of the File Viewer window, you will see the File menu option. To the right of the File menu option, you will see the Edit, Format Text, Images, and Window menu options. Because you have not opened a file, the program will disable these menu options. After you open a file, your program will enable some menu options and leave others disabled, depending on the type of file you open.

Below the File menu option, you will see a large blank area, called the window's *client area*. Your program will use the client area to display the files that you open within the program. The program will let you open three different general file types: text files, Rich Text files, and image files. The program will expect each file you load to include as its extension one of the six designations Table 4.1 lists.

Designation	File Type
TXT	Text file (Unformatted)
RTF	Rich Text Format file (Possibly formatted text)
BMP	Windows bitmap file
GIF	CompuServe Graphics Image Format file
JPG	JPEG-JFIF Format image file
TIF	Tagged-Image Format image file

Table 4.1 *The file types that you can load with the* **prjFileViewer** *project.*

In addition to using the File menu Open option to open the three file types, you can also create a new text file into which you can enter text, format the text, and then save or print the file. To create new text files, you will use the File menu New option.

Now that you have seen the *prjFileViewer.exe* program's layout, you can use the program to open one of the three file types. To open a text file and edit and format the text, perform the following steps:

1. Within the File Viewer window, select the File menu Open option. The program will open a submenu.

2. Within the submenu, select the Text option. The program will display an Open Text Files dialog box.

3. Within the Open Text Files dialog box, select the *C:\Bootlog.txt* file on your computer's *C:* drive (which contains information about programs and devices drivers that Windows loads when it begins). Next, click your mouse on the Open button. The program will open a separate window within the File Viewer window and display the selected text file. After the program opens the selected text file, it will enable the Edit menu and Format Text menu options. Figure 4.3 shows the File Viewer window after you open the *C:\Bootlog.txt* file.

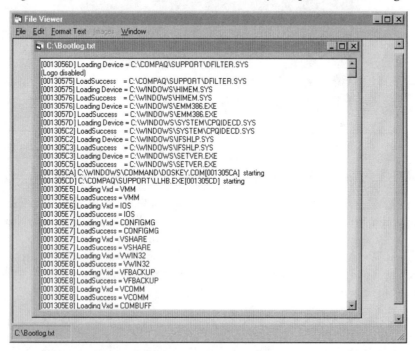

Figure 4.3 *The File Viewer window after you open the* **C:\Bootlog.txt** *file.*

As you have learned, you can also use the *prjFileViewer.exe* program to open, view, and edit Rich Text files. To open a Rich Text file, perform the following steps:

1. Within the File Viewer window, select the File menu Open option. The program will open a submenu.

2. Within the submenu, select the Rich Text option. The program will display an Open Rich Text Files dialog box.

3. Within the *x:\vbpl\Chapter04* directory (where *x* corresponds to the letter of the drive on which you installed the *Visual Basic Programmer's Library* companion CD-ROM), click your mouse on the *TwasTheNight2.rtf* file. Next, click your mouse on the Open button. The program will open a separate window with the caption *x:\vbpl\Chapter04\TwasTheNight2.rtf* within the File Viewer window and display the selected Rich Text file. After the program opens the selected Rich Text file, it will enable the Edit menu and Format Text menu options.

4. Within the opened Rich Text file window, click your mouse on the "J" in *Jamsa Press*, hold the mouse button down, and drag the mouse to the right to select both words in *Jamsa Press*. The program will highlight the selected text with a black background color.

5. Within the File Viewer window, select the Format Text menu Bold option. The program will set the selected portion of text to bold. Figure 4.4 shows the File Viewer after you format the text within the *x:\vbpl\Chapter04\TwasTheNight2.rtf* document.

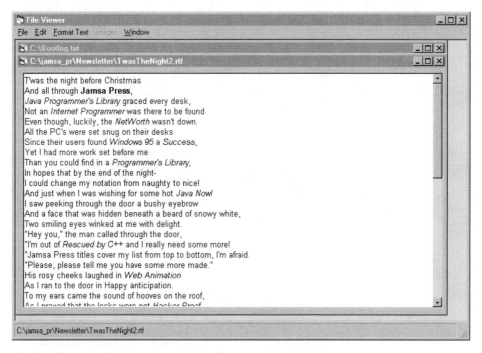

Figure 4.4 *The **TwasTheNight2.rtf** file after you bold the Jamsa Press text.*

6. Within the File Viewer window, click your mouse on the File menu Save As option. The program will open the Save File As dialog box.

7. Within the Save File As dialog box, change the original filename to *TwasTheNight3.rtf* within the *File name* field. Next, click your mouse on the Save button. The program will save the *TwasTheNight3.rtf* file on your computer, and close the Save File As dialog box.

Now that you have worked with both text and Rich Text files, you should also work with image files. As you learned earlier in this chapter, the *prjFileViewer.exe* program lets you view bitmaps (BMP), JPEG-JFIF compliant files (JPG), and Tagged-Image Format (TIF) files. In fact, the *prjFileViewer.exe* program will load bitmaps and JPEG-JFIF compliant files into one form, and Tagged-Image Format files into another. As you will learn later in this chapter, you can edit Tagged-Image Format files, but you cannot edit bitmaps or JPEG-JFIF compliant files. To load two image files, perform the following steps:

1. Within the File Viewer window, select the File menu Open option. The program will open a submenu.

2. Within the submenu, select the Image option. The program will display an Open Image Files dialog box.

3. Within the *x:\vbpl\Chapter04* directory (where *x* corresponds to the letter of the hard drive on which you installed the *Visual Basic Programmer's Library* companion CD-ROM), click your mouse on the *Image1.bmp* file. Next, click your mouse on the Open button. The program will open a separate window with the caption *x:\vbpl\Chapter04\Image1.bmp* within the File Viewer window and display the selected bitmap.

89

4. Within the File Viewer window, select the File menu Open option. The program will open a submenu.

5. Within the submenu, select the Image option. The program will display an Open Image Files dialog box.

6. Within the *x:\vbpl\Chapter04* directory (where *x* corresponds to the letter of the hard drive on which you installed the *Visual Basic Programmer's Library* companion CD-ROM), click your mouse on the *hacker.gif* file. Next, click your mouse on the Open button. The program will open a separate window with the caption *x:\vbpl\Chapter04\hacker.gif* within the File Viewer window and display the selected image file. Figure 4.5 shows the File Viewer window after you open two image files.

Figure 4.5 *The File Viewer window after you open two image files.*

In addition to bitmap and JPEG-JFIF compliant image files, you can also load Tagged-Image Format files into the File Viewer program. The File Viewer program will also let you edit and annotate Tagged-Image Format files—which it will not let you do with bitmap and JPEG-JFIF compliant image files. To open a Tagged-Image Format file and add annotation to the file, perform the following steps:

1. Within the File Viewer window, select the File menu Open option. The program will open a second submenu.

2. Within the second submenu, select the Image option. The program will open the Open Image Files dialog box.

3. Within the *x:\vbpl\Chapter04* directory (where *x* corresponds to the letter of the hard drive on which you installed the *Visual Basic Programmer's Library* companion CD-ROM), click your mouse on the *sci010_l.tif* file. Next, click your mouse on the Open button. The program will open a separate window with the caption *x:\vbpl\Chapter04\sci010_l.tif* within the File Viewer window and display the selected image file.

4. Within the File Viewer window, select the Images menu Rotate Right option. The program will rotate the image to the right.

5. Select the Images menu Rotate Left option. The program will rotate the image to the left, back to its original alignment.

6. Select the Images menu Flip option. The program will flip the image 180 degrees (upside down). Select the Images menu Flip option again. The program will flip the image 180 degrees again (right side up).

7. Select the Images menu Zoom Up option. The program will expand the image 150 percent, or 1.5 times its original size, on your display.

8. Select the Images menu Zoom Down option. The program will shrink the image to 50 percent, or 0.5 times its original size, on your display.

9. Select the Images menu Show Annotation Palette option. The program will display the Annotation dialog box, as shown in Figure 4.6.

Figure 4.6 *The Annotation dialog box.*

10. Within the Annotation dialog box, right-click your mouse on the Text icon. The program will display the Properties option. Click your mouse on the Properties option. The program will open the Text Properties dialog box.

11. Within the Text Properties dialog box, change the font size to 14 point and the font color to red. Click your mouse on OK to exit the Text Properties dialog box.

12. Within the *x:\vbpl\Chapter04\vbpsamp.tif* window, double-click your mouse anywhere on the image. The program will display the Text Edit dialog box.

13. Within the Text Edit dialog box, enter *VBPL Chapter 4 Test Annotation*. The dialog box will display the text you entered in 14 point, red characters, as shown in Figure 4.7.

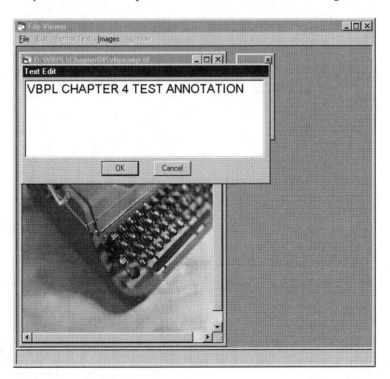

Figure 4.7 *The text you entered in the Text Edit dialog box.*

14. Within the Text Edit dialog box, click your mouse on OK to close the dialog box. The *prjFileViewer.exe* program will place the text you entered onto the *vbpsamp.tif* file, as shown in Figure 4.8.

Figure 4.8 *An image with text you appended using the Annotation Palette.*

15. Within the Annotation dialog box, right-click your mouse on any icon. The program will display the selected icon's Properties option. Click your mouse on the Properties option. The program will open the selected icon's Properties dialog box. Table 4.2 lists the name and description for each Annotation option's icon in the Annotation dialog box.

Annotation Icon	Description
Annotation Selection	Turns off any annotation and return focus to the cursor.
Freehand Line	Draws freehand lines of varying widths and colors.
Highlighter	Highlights blocks of an image in different colors.
Straight Line	Draws straight lines of varying widths and colors.
Hollow Rectangle	Draws hollow rectangles of varying widths and colors.
Filled Rectangle	Draws filled rectangles of various sizes and colors.
Text	Displays text of various fonts, colors, and styles, onto the image.
Attach-a-Note	Displays text of various fonts, colors, and styles in a solid colored rectangle and size the rectangle on the image.
Text From File	Displays text from a separate text file on your computer, in various fonts, colors, and styles, onto the image.
Rubber Stamp	Displays dated or word messages from default options, such as Approved or Received. Create your own stamp by adding a saved image from your computer or typing in a descriptive word.

Table 4.2 *The Annotation options for an image file.*

CREATING THE BLANK FORMS

Now that you have a better idea how to use the finished *prjFileViewer* project, you can begin to design it. First, you will design empty forms. After you design and implement the forms, you will learn more about the *Image Edit* control, *Image Admin* control, MDI parent forms, and child forms. The *prjFileViewer* project includes one MDI parent form and three child forms.

CREATING THE MDI PARENT FORM

To begin the *prjFileViewer* project and design an empty MDI Parent form, perform the following steps:

1. Within Visual Basic, select the File menu New Project option. Visual Basic will open the New Project dialog box.

2. Within the New Project dialog box, double-click your mouse on the Standard EXE icon. Visual Basic will close the New Project dialog box, start a new project, *Project1*, and add a form to it, *Form1*.

3. Within the new *Project1* project, select the Project menu Add MDI Form option. Visual Basic will open the Add MDI Form dialog box.

4. Within the Add MDI Form dialog box, double-click your mouse on the *MDI Form* icon. Visual Basic will add an MDI form, *MDIForm1*, to the new *Project1* project and display the *MDIForm1* form window.

5. Select the View menu Properties Window option. Visual Basic will open the Properties Window listing the *MDIForm1* properties.

6. Within the Properties Window, change the *MDIForm1* property values to the values Table 4.3 lists.

Object	Property	Set As
MDIForm1	Caption	File Viewer
MDIForm1	Height	5460
MDIForm1	Left	105
MDIForm1	Top	105
MDIForm1	Width	7000
MDIForm1	Name	frmMDIParent

*Table 4.3 The newly named **frmMDIParent** MDI form's properties.*

CREATING THE FIRST CHILD FORM

As you learned in the previous section, to design a Multiple-Document Interface project, you must first add an MDI form to the project. After you add the MDI form (the parent form) to the project, you can change the default *Form1* form you created with the project to the first child form in the project. To change the *Form1* form's properties and set it as the first child form, perform the following steps:

1. If Visual Basic is not displaying the *Form1* form within an object window, double-click your mouse on the Form1 icon within the Project Explorer. Visual Basic will open the *Form1* form.

2. Select the View menu Properties Window option. Visual Basic will open the Properties Window listing the *Form1* properties.

3. Within the Properties Window, change the *Form1* property values to those Table 4.4 lists.

Object	Property	Set As
Form1	*Caption*	*Image Edit Control Form*
Form1	*Height*	6945
Form1	*Left*	0
Form1	*Top*	0
Form1	*Width*	5760
Form1	*MDIChild*	*True*
Form1	*Name*	*frmChildImageEdit*

*Table 4.4 The newly named **frmChildImageEdit** child form's properties.*

CREATING THE SECOND CHILD FORM

Now that you have created the first child form, *frmChildImageEdit*, you can add a second child form to the project. To add a second child form to the *prjFileViewer* project, perform the following steps:

1. Within the *prjFileViewer* project, select the Project menu Add Form option. Visual Basic will display the Add Form dialog box.

2. Within the Add Form dialog box, click your mouse on the New tab and select the Form icon. Next, click your mouse on the Open button. Visual Basic will close the Add Form dialog box and add a new form, *Form1*, to the *prjFileViewer* project.

3. Select the View menu Properties Window option. Visual Basic will open the Properties Window listing the *Form1* properties.

4. Within the Properties Window, change the *Form1* property values to those Table 4.5 lists.

Object	Property	Set As
Form1	*Caption*	*Child Form*
Form1	*Height*	4170
Form1	*Left*	0
Form1	*Top*	0
Form1	*Width*	4965
Form1	*MDIChild*	*True*
Form1	*Name*	*frmChildRTB*

*Table 4.5 The newly named **frmChildRTB** child form's properties.*

CREATING THE THIRD CHILD FORM

Now that you have created a second child form, you can add a third child form to the project. To add a third child form to the *prjFileViewer* project, perform the following steps:

1. Within the *prjFileViewer* project, select the Project menu Add Form option. Visual Basic will display the Add Form dialog box.

2. Within the Add Form dialog box, click your mouse on the New tab and select the Form icon. Next, click your mouse on the Open button. Visual Basic will close the Add Form dialog box and add a new form, *Form1*, to the *prjFileViewer* project.

3. Select the View menu Properties Window option. Visual Basic will open the Properties Window listing the *Form1* properties.

4. Within the Properties Window, change the *Form1* property values to those Table 4.6 lists.

Object	Property	Set As
Form1	*Height*	4500
Form1	*Left*	0
Form1	*Top*	0
Form1	*Width*	4245
Form1	*MDIChild*	*True*
Form1	*Name*	*frmGraphicType*

Table 4.6 *The newly named **frmGraphicType** child form's properties.*

CREATING THE STANDARD FORM

Now that you have created one MDI parent form and three child forms, you can create the standard form that the *prjFileViewer* project will use. In the "Creating the MDI Parent Form" section, you created the *prjFileViewer* project and added an MDI parent form, *frmMDIParent*, to the project. To create a blank standard form in the *prjFileViewer* project, perform the following steps:

1. Within the *prjFileViewer* project, select the Project menu Add Form option. Visual Basic will display the Add Form dialog box.

2. Within the Add Form dialog box, click your mouse on the New tab and select the Form icon. Next, click your mouse on the Open button. Visual Basic will close the Add Form dialog box and add a new form, *Form1*, to the *prjFileViewer* project.

3. Select the View menu Properties Window option. Visual Basic will open the Properties Window listing the *Form1* properties.

4. Within the Properties Window, change the *Form1* property values to those Table 4.7 lists.

Object	Property	Set As
Form1	*Caption*	*Find Match*
Form1	*Height*	3720
Form1	*Left*	1080
Form1	*MDIChild*	*False*
Form1	*Top*	1170
Form1	*Width*	3465
Form1	*Name*	*frmFind*

Table 4.7 *The newly named **frmFind** standard form's properties.*

ADDING A MODULE TO THE PROJECT

After you design the *prjFileViewer* project's blank forms, you will create a module in which to store program code. Within the *prjFileViewer* project, the program code that you will place within the module will declare several global variables and constants, and will contain several "helper" procedures that forms will use during their processing. To add a module to the *prjFileViewer* project, perform the following steps:

1. Within Visual Basic, select the Project menu Add Module option. Visual Basic will open the Add Module dialog box.

2. Within the Add Module dialog box, select the Module option. Next, click your mouse on the Open button. Visual Basic will open a new Code window, *Module1*.

3. Select the View menu Properties Window option. Visual Basic will open the Properties Window listing the *Module1* properties.

4. Within the Properties Window, change the *Module1* module's name to *mdlFileViewer*.

5. Select the File menu Save Project As option. Visual Basic will open the Save File As dialog box and fill the *File name* field with *mdlFileViewer*.

6. Within the Save File As dialog box, click your mouse on the Save button. Visual Basic will save the *mdlFileViewer* module and fill the *File name* field with *frmFind*.

7. Within the Save File As dialog box, click your mouse on the Save button. Visual Basic will save the *frmFind* form and fill the *File name* field with *frmGraphicType*.

8. Within the Save File As dialog box, click your mouse on the Save button. Visual Basic will save the *frmGraphicType* form and fill the *File name* field with *frmChildRTB*.

9. Within the Save File As dialog box, click your mouse on the Save button. Visual Basic will save the *frmChildRTB* form and fill the *File name* field with *frmChildImageEdit*.

10. Within the Save File As dialog box, click your mouse on the Save button. Visual Basic will save the *frmChildImageEdit* form and fill the *File name* field with *frmMDIParent*.

11. Within the Save File As dialog box, click your mouse on the Save button. Visual Basic will save the *frmMDIParent* MDI form and fill the *File name* field with *Project1*.

12. Within the *File name* field, replace the *Project1* project name with the new *prjFileViewer* project name. Next, click your mouse on the Save button. Visual Basic will save the *prjFileViewer* project and close the Save Project As dialog box.

MORE ON THE IMAGING CONTROLS

As you have learned, the *prjFileViewer* project will let you open text files, Rich Text files, and image files. Your computer loads a text file into the project differently from the way it loads an image file. In the *prjFileViewer* project, you will use two separate controls, on two separate forms, to load image files. You learned about the first control, the *PictureBox* control, in Chapter 2, "Using the Multimedia MCI Control to Create a CD-ROM Player." The other control you will use, the *ImageEdit* control, is part of a suite of third-party controls—*Imaging* controls—that the Kodak Business Eastman Software, Inc. (formerly Wang software) developed.

The *Imaging* controls suite consists of four main controls: the *Image Edit* control, the *Image Admin* control, the *Image Annotation Tool Button* control, and the *Image Scan* control. The *Image Edit* control is the main *Imaging* control, and you will use it extensively in the *prjFileViewer* project. Eastman Software provides extensive documentation for each control, and you will find the documents that pertain to the *Imaging* controls within each control's help file on your computer. The following sections briefly discuss each control in the *Imaging* controls suite.

MORE ON THE IMAGE EDIT CONTROL

In the *prjFileViewer* project, you will use only the main control from the *Imaging* controls suite, the *Image Edit* control. The *Image Edit* control lets you add imaging and image annotation functions to your Visual Basic projects. In addition, the *Image Edit* control lets end users display, annotate, manipulate, and manage image files. The end user can display image files of many types within the *Image Edit* control. Specifically, the *Image Edit* control supports the file types Table 4.8 lists.

Supported File Type	Description
AWD	Microsoft *Fax*
BMP	Windows bitmap
JPG	JPEG-JFIF Compliant
PCX	Windows *Paintbrush*
TIF	Tagged-Image Format

Table 4.8 *The image file types that the* **Image Edit** *control supports.*

The *Image Edit* control includes properties, methods, and events that will help you add annotation functions to your Visual Basic projects. The annotation functions will let end users annotate images the *Image Edit* control displays. In addition, the *Image Edit* control includes an *Annotation Palette* tool that your programs can invoke. The user can use the Annotation Palette to make notes on, add text to, or otherwise change an image file. In addition, the *Image Edit* control has properties, methods, and events that you can use to add image manipulation functions to your Visual Basic projects. The manipulation functions will let end users change an image loaded into an *Image Edit* control. Table 4.9 lists the *Image Edit* control's image manipulation functions.

Image manipulation functions	Description
Copy and Cut to the Clipboard	Lets you copy into other controls or programs.
Paste from the Clipboard	Lets you paste into other controls or programs.
Flip	Rotates image 180 degrees.
Rotate	Rotates image 90 degrees, in either direction.
Scale	Sets the image's relative view size.
Scroll	Moves the viewing window over the image.
Zoom	Expands or contracts the image's display size.

Table 4.9 The **Image Edit** *control's image manipulation functions.*

The *Image Edit* control includes methods that will also let you add image and annotation file management functions to your Visual Basic programs. These functions will let end users retrieve, save, print, and delete image and annotation data.

As you have learned, you will use the *Image Edit* control in the *prjFileViewer* project to display, annotate, manipulate, and manage image files (such as Tagged-Image Format files). You will also use some of the *Image Edit* control's properties, methods, and events. Table 4.10 lists and describes each property and method you will use in the *prjFileViewer* project.

Name	Type	Description
Height	Property	Returns or sets the *Image Edit* control's height.
Image	Property	Returns or sets the image file the control is displaying or will display.
ImageHeight	Property	Returns the image height's read-only value.
ImageModified	Property	Returns a read-only value indicating whether the program or a user has modified the image.
ImageWidth	Property	Returns the image width's read-only value.
Width	Property	Returns or sets the *Image Edit* control's width.
Zoom	Property	Returns or sets the zoom factor for an image. The valid range is from 2 to 6500 percent.
ClearDisplay	Method	Clears the current displayed image in the *Image Edit* control.
Display	Method	Displays the image specified in the *Image* property.
Flip	Method	Rotates the displayed image 180 degrees.
Refresh	Method	Repaints the contents in the *Image Edit* control.
RotateLeft	Method	Rotates the displayed image 90 degrees counter-clockwise.
RotateRight	Method	Rotates the displayed image 90 degrees clockwise.

Table 4.10 Some of the **Image Edit** *control's properties and methods.(continued on following page)*

Name	Type	Description
Save	Method	Saves the displayed image to the original path and filename.
SaveAs	Method	Saves the displayed image using the path and filename specified.
ShowAnnotationToolPalette	Method	Shows the *Annotation Palette* tool, which lets end users edit images the *Image Edit* control displays.

Table 4.10 *Some of the **Image Edit** control's properties and methods.(continued from previous page)*

MORE ON THE IMAGE ADMIN CONTROL

The *Image Admin* control provides a method your programs will use to administer image files that reside on your computer or on a local area network (LAN). The *Image Admin* control will let you use File and Print dialog boxes to support image-specific methods, including general directory and file methods. The image-specific methods will let you insert, append, and replace images in a multi-page image file. The general methods will let you create, delete, rename, and move directories and files. In addition, the general methods will let you retrieve and set image file attributes.

MORE ON THE IMAGE SCAN CONTROL

The *Image Scan* control will add scanning capabilities to your Visual Basic projects that support 32-bit Object Linking and Embedding (OLE) or ActiveX controls (as you have learned, ActiveX is an expansion of OLE). The *Image Scan* control is invisible and you can use it independently of other controls in the *Imaging* controls group. The *Image Scan* control supports scanners that use Twain drivers. Each scanner will supply TWAIN DLL files that will provide dialog boxes and setup options that the scanner will use. To display an image as you scan it, you can link the *Image Scan* control to the *Image Edit* control.

MORE ON THE IMAGE ANNOTATION TOOL BUTTON CONTROL

The *Image Annotation Tool Button* control will add image annotation functions to your Visual Basic projects that support 32-bit OLE controls. It will let end users add text and graphical annotations to image files your programs display within the *Image Edit* control. You can then use the *Image Edit* control to save the image files after users alter them.

The *Image Annotation Tool Button* control will link to the *Image Edit* control and, therefore, let you annotate displayed images. The *Image Annotation Tool Button* control will send messages to the *Image Edit* control to set annotation attributes (such as adding text to an image). Additionally, users can use the *Image Annotation Tool Button* control to change all the *Image Edit* control's annotation attributes to the values the user sets within the control's display. Then, using the *Image Edit* control's *Draw* method, the user can draw the image with the newly added annotation.

MORE ON RICHTEXTBOX CONTROLS

As you have learned, the *prjFileViewer* project will let you open and save text files, Rich Text files, and image files. Text files are different from Rich Text files in that Rich Text files include advanced formatting, such as different font size, color, and type within the same document.

To display, edit, and save text in Visual Basic, you can use either a *TextBox* or a *RichTextBox* control. To format text, you must use a *RichTextBox* control. The *RichTextBox* control also provides you with a more advanced way to enter text, edit text, and format text than does the *TextBox* control. In the *prjFileViewer* project, you will use a *RichTextBox* control to display small and large (up to about 2Mb) text files, and to edit, format, save, and print the text.

The *RichTextBox* control supports almost all the *TextBox* control's properties, methods, and events, such as *MaxLength*, *ScrollBars*, *SelLength*, *SelStart*, and *SelText*.

UNDERSTANDING THE *RICHTEXTBOX* CONTROL'S PROPERTIES

The *RichTextBox* control will provide properties that let you apply formatting to any portion of text within the control. To format text, you must first select the text (in turn, the control will highlight the text). Using the *RichTextBox* control's properties, you can make the text bold or italic, change the text color, create superscripts and subscripts, and so on. In addition, you can set left, right, and hanging indents to adjust a paragraph's formatting. Table 4.11 lists some of the *RichTextBox* control's properties.

Property	Description
ScrollBars	Returns or sets a value indicating whether a *RichTextBox* control contains vertical or horizontal scrollbars.
SelAlignment	Returns or sets a value that controls a paragraph's alignment in a *RichTextBox* control.
SelBol	Returns or sets a bold format for the currently selected text.
SelBullet	Returns or sets a value that determines if a paragraph in a *RichTextBox* control has a bullet style.
SelCharOffset	Returns or sets a value that determines whether text in a *RichTextBox* control appears on the baseline (normal), as a superscript above the baseline, or as a subscript below the baseline.
SelColor	Returns or sets a value that determines the text color in a *RichTextBox* control.
SelFontName	Returns or sets the font that the program will use to display the currently selected (highlighted) text in a *RichTextBox* control.
SelFontSize	Returns or sets a value that specifies the font size used to display text in a *RichTextBox* control.
SelIndent	Returns or sets the distance between a *RichTextBox* control's left edge and the selected or added text's left edge at the current insertion point.
SelItalic	Returns or sets the currently selected text's italic format.
SelLength	Returns or sets the number of characters selected.
SelUnderline	Returns or sets the currently selected text's underline format.

*Table 4.11 Some of the **RichTextBox** control's properties.*

UNDERSTANDING THE *RICHTEXTBOX* CONTROL'S METHODS

The *RichTextBox* control provides methods that let you display and save files in both Rich Text File (RTF) format and regular ASCII text format. Using the *RichTextBox* control's methods, you can use the *LoadFile* method to load files, the *SaveFile* method to save files, and so on. Table 4.12 lists some of the *RichTextBox* control's methods and their descriptions.

Method	Description
Find	Searches the text in a *RichTextBox* control for a given string.
GetLineFromChar	Uses the *Find* method to return a line number in the *RichTextBox* control that contains a specified character position.
LoadFile	Loads a *.TXT file or *.RTF file into a *RichTextBox* control.
SaveFile	Saves the contents of a *RichTextBox* control to a *.TXT or *.RTF file.
SelPrint	Sends formatted text in a *RichTextBox* control to a printer device for printing.
Span	Selects text in a *RichTextBox* control based on a set of characters the calling program specifies within the method call.

*Table 4.12 Some of the **RichTextBox** control's methods.*

ADDING THE COMPONENT CONTROLS TO THE PROJECT

As you have learned, the *prjFileViewer* project has four component forms, each of which performs special processing. The *frmChildImageEdit* form, the *frmChildRTB* form, and the *frmMDIParent* form all use controls that you
must add to the project as components. As you have learned, the project will use the *Image Edit* control to let the
user view Tagged-Image Format files, and the *RichTextBox* control to let the user view text files. The project will
also use the *Microsoft Common Dialog* control, which will display the Open File and Save As dialog boxes. Finally,
the project will use the *Microsoft StatusBar* control, one of the *Microsoft Windows Common Controls* control suite,
to display information about the program's processing. To add the controls to the *prjFileViewer* project, perform
the following steps:

1. Within Visual Basic, select the Project menu Components option. Visual Basic will open
   the Components dialog box.

2. Within the Components dialog box, select the *Microsoft Common Dialog Control 5.0* listing.
   Next, click your mouse on the box to the left of the listing. Visual Basic will display a check
   mark in the box.

3. Within the Components dialog box, select the *Microsoft Rich Textbox Control 5.0* listing.
   Next, click your mouse on the box to the left of the listing. Visual Basic will display a check
   mark in the box.

4. Within the Components dialog box, select the *Microsoft Windows Common Controls 5.0*
   listing (which includes the *Microsoft StatusBar* control). Next, click your mouse on the box
   to the left of the listing. Visual Basic will display a check mark in the box.

5. Within the Components dialog box, select the *Wang Image Edit Control* listing. Next, click
   your mouse on the box to the left of the listing. Visual Basic will display a check mark in the
   box, as shown in Figure 4.9.

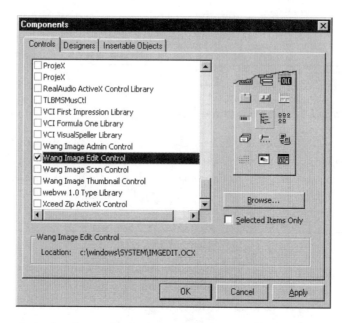

Figure 4.9 *The Components dialog box listing the **Wang Image Edit Control** listing.*

6. Within the Components dialog box, click your mouse on the OK button. Visual Basic will
   close the Components dialog box and add the controls to the *prjFileViewer* project.

DESIGNING THE frmMDIPARENT FORM'S APPEARANCE

As you learned in the "Using the *prjFileViewer* Project" section earlier in this chapter, the *frmMDIParent* form is essentially a container for the child forms that the program will display. You will add two controls to the *frmMDIParent* form, the *StatusBar* control and the *CommonDialog* control. In addition to the two controls, you will use the Menu Editor to add a menu to the *frmMDIParent* form. To add the *StatusBar* control to the *frmMDIParent* form, perform the following steps:

1. If Visual Basic is not displaying the *frmMDIParent* form within an object window, double-click your mouse on the *frmMDIParent* form listing within the Project Explorer. Visual Basic will open the *frmMDIParent* form.

2. Within Visual Basic, select the View menu Toolbox option. Visual Basic will open the Toolbox.

3. Within the Toolbox, double-click your mouse on the StatusBar icon. Visual Basic will draw a *StatusBar* control, *Status1*, within the *frmMDIParent* form. Figure 4.10 shows the StatusBar icon within the Toolbox.

Figure 4.10 *The StatusBar icon within the Toolbox.*

4. Within the *frmMDIParent* form, click your mouse on the *Status1* control to highlight it. Visual Basic will draw a small frame around the control.

5. Select the View menu Properties Window option. Visual Basic will open the Properties Window listing the *Status1* properties.

6. Within the Properties Window, change the *Status1* properties to the values Table 4.13 lists.

Object	Property	Set As
Status1	*Align*	2 - *vbAlignBottom*
Status1	*Name*	*stsFileViewer*

Table 4.13 *The newly named* **stsFileViewer** *control's properties.*

ADDING THE COMMONDIALOG CONTROL TO THE frmMDIPARENT FORM

In this chapter's "Using the *prjFileViewer* Project" section, you opened several different files and file types within the *prjFileViewer* program. To display the Open File dialog box, the Save As dialog box, the Print dialog box, and the Font dialog boxes, the *prjFileViewer* project uses the *CommonDialog* control. To add the *CommonDialog* control to the *frmMDIParent* form, perform the following steps:

1. If Visual Basic is not displaying the *frmMDIParent* form within an object window, double-click your mouse on the *frmMDIParent* form listing within the Project Explorer. Visual Basic will open the *frmMDIParent* form.

2. Within Visual Basic, select the View menu Toolbox option. Visual Basic will open the Toolbox.

3. Within the Toolbox, double-click your mouse on the CommonDialog icon. Visual Basic will draw a *CommonDialog* control, *CommonDialog1*, within the *frmMDIParent* form. Figure 4.11 shows the CommonDialog icon within the Toolbox.

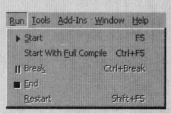

Figure 4.11 *The CommonDialog icon within the Toolbox.*

4. Within the *frmMDIParent* form, click your mouse on the *CommonDialog1* control to highlight it. Visual Basic will draw a small frame around the control.

5. Select the View menu Properties Window option. Visual Basic will open the Properties Window listing the *CommonDialog1* properties.

6. Within the Properties Window, change the *CommonDialog1* properties to the values Table 4.14 lists.

102

Object	Property	Set As
CommonDialog1	*Left*	0
CommonDialog1	*Top*	0
CommonDialog1	*Name*	*cdgParent*

Table 4.14 *The newly named **cdgParent** control's properties.*

UNDERSTANDING MENUS

Because you have designed forms for both Single Document Interface (SDI) and Multiple-Document Interface (MDI) applications, you have probably noticed one thing that is common to almost every Windows program has been conspicuously missing from each of them—a *menu*. Within your Visual Basic programs, *menus* provide a way to group consistent sets of commands under a single header for easy user access. To better understand this, consider the Visual Basic Run menu shown in Figure 4.12.

Run	Tools Add-Ins Window Help	
▶ Start		F5
Start With Full Compile		Ctrl+F5
‖ Break		Ctrl+Break
■ End		
Restart		Shift+F5

Figure 4.12 *The Visual Basic Run menu.*

The Run menu has five options: Start, Start with Full Compile, Break, End, and Restart. All these options have common functionality—all are primarily concerned with processing user requests that relate to the program's execution. Each menu that you design should have a consistent purpose as well.

Within Visual Basic, you will create menus using the *Menu* custom control. The *Menu* control will display custom-designed menus for your applications. Menus can include commands, submenus, and separator bars (lines across menus that separate menu options). Each menu you create can have up to four submenu levels. To create a *Menu* control, you should use the Menu Editor.

Just as Visual Basic provided the Application Setup Wizard to help you create applications, the Visual Basic Menu Editor is a dialog box Microsoft designed to expedite menu creation within your applications. To use the Visual Basic Menu Editor, make sure that a form is active within the Editing Window and select the Tools menu Menu Editor option (or use the CTRL+E keyboard shortcut). Visual Basic will display the Menu Editor, as shown in Figure 4.13.

Figure 4.13 *The Menu Editor window.*

Note that the Menu Editor is a modal dialog box—that is, you cannot work within your Visual Basic project until you have exited the Menu Editor. Table 4.15 lists the Menu Editor options.

Option	Effect
Caption	Lets you enter the menu or command name that you want to appear on your menu bar or in a menu. If you want to create a separator bar in your menu, type a single hyphen (-) in the Caption box. To give the user keyboard access to a menu item, insert an ampersand (&) before a letter. At run time, the program will underline this letter (the ampersand is not visible) and the user can press the ALT key and the letter to access the menu or command. If you want an ampersand to show in the menu, put two consecutive ampersands in the caption.
Name	Lets you enter a control name for the menu item. A control name is an identifier your programs will use only to access the menu item in code—the identifier does not appear within the menu itself.
Index	Lets you assign a numeric value that determines the control's position within a control array. This position does not necessarily correspond to the screen position (in other words, the numeric value has nothing to do with the item's placement within the menu).
Shortcut	Lets you select a shortcut key for each command.
HelpContextID	Lets you assign a unique numeric value for the context ID. Visual Basic uses this value to find the appropriate help topic in the Help file the *HelpFile* property identifies.
NegotiatePosition	Lets you select the menu's *NegotiatePosition* property. This property determines whether and how the menu appears in a container form.
Checked	Lets you select whether you want a check mark to appear to the left of a selected menu item. Programs generally use this option to indicate whether the user has turned a toggle option on or off.
Enabled	Lets you select whether you want the menu item to respond to events, or if you want the item to be unavailable and appear dimmed.

Table 4.15 *The options available within the Menu Editor dialog box. (continued on following page)*

Option	Effect
Visible	Lets you have the menu item appear on the menu.
WindowList	Determines if the menu control contains a list of open *MDI Child* forms in an MDI application.

Table 4.15 *The options available within the Menu Editor dialog box. (continued from previous page)*

In addition, the following navigational commands are available within the Menu Editor, as shown in Table 4.16.

Navigational Command	Effect
Right Arrow	Moves the selected menu down one level each time you click your mouse on it. You can create up to four submenu levels.
Left Arrow	Moves the selected menu up one level each time you click your mouse on it.
Up Arrow	Moves the selected menu item up one position within the same menu level each time you click your mouse on it.
Down Arrow	Moves the selected menu item down one position within the same menu level each time you click your mouse on it.
Menu List	A *ListBox* control that displays a hierarchical list of menu items. The Menu Editor will indent submenu items within the *Menu List* to indicate their hierarchical position or level within the menu.
Next	Moves selection to the next line.
Insert	Inserts a line in the *ListBox* control above the currently selected line.
Delete	Deletes the currently selected line.
OK	Closes the Menu Editor and applies all changes to the last form you selected. The menu is available at design time, but selecting a menu at design time opens the Code window for that menu's *Click* event, rather than executing any event code.
Cancel	Closes the Menu Editor and cancels all changes.

Table 4.16 *The navigational commands available within the Menu Editor dialog box.*

Although you can use the Menu Editor to set some *Menu* control properties, the Properties Window will display all *Menu* control properties, even those the Menu Editor does not display. To display a *Menu* control's properties, select the menu name in the Objects list at the top of the Properties Window.

Note: *When you create an MDI application, the menu bar on the MDI child form will replace the menu bar on the* **MDIForm** *object when the child form is active.*

ADDING THE MENUS TO THE FRM**MDIP**ARENT FORM

As you saw earlier in this chapter, the *prjFileViewer* project includes many menu items. To create the menu items for the *frmMDIParent* form, you will use the Visual Basic Menu Editor. To use the Menu Editor to create the project's menus, perform the following steps:

1. If Visual Basic is not displaying the *frmMDIParent* form within an object window, double-click your mouse on the *frmMDIParent* form listing within the Project Explorer. Visual Basic will open the *frmMDIParent* form.

2. Within Visual Basic, select the Tools menu Menu Editor option. Visual Basic will display the Menu Editor dialog box.

3. Enter *&File* in the *Caption* field. (Remember, the ampersand symbol (&) alerts Visual Basic to accept the letter immediately following the ampersand as a keyboard shortcut for the item.) Visual Basic will display the caption in the Menu Viewer at the bottom of the Menu Editor as you type.

4. Press the Tab key to move to the *Name* field. Enter the name as *mnuFile*.

5. Click your mouse on the Next button. Visual Basic will clear the *Caption* and *Name* fields, move the block cursor within the Menu Viewer down one line, and return the input cursor to the *Caption* field.

6. Click your mouse on the right arrow just above the Menu Viewer and to the left of the Next button. Visual Basic will display three dots on the current line in the Menu Viewer.

7. Within the *Caption* field, enter the next item's caption as *&New*. Visual Basic will display *&New*, preceded by three dots (which indicate the item is a submenu of the File menu), in the Menu Viewer as you type.

8. Press the Tab key to move the input cursor to the *Name* field. Enter the name as *mnuFile_New*.

9. Within the Menu Editor, select the Ctrl+N option within the Shortcut combo box. Visual Basic will add the shortcut to the Menu Viewer.

10. Click your mouse on the Next button. Visual Basic will clear the *Caption* and *Name* fields, move the block cursor within the Menu Viewer down one line, and return the input cursor to the *Caption* field.

11. Within the *Caption* field, enter the next item's caption as *Open*. Visual Basic will display *Open*, preceded by three dots, in the Menu Viewer as you type.

12. Press the Tab key to move the input cursor to the *Name* field. Enter the name as *mnuOpen*.

13. Click your mouse on the Next button. Visual Basic will clear the *Caption* and *Name* fields, move the block cursor within the Menu Viewer down one line, and return the input cursor to the *Caption* field.

14. Click your mouse on the right arrow just above the Menu Viewer and to the left of the Next button. Visual Basic will display three additional dots (for a total of six dots) on the current line in the Menu Viewer.

15. Within the *Caption* field, enter the next item's caption as *Text*. Visual Basic will display *Text*, preceded by six dots, in the Menu Viewer as you type.

16. Press the Tab key to move the input cursor to the *Name* field. Enter the name as *mnuFileOpen*.

17. Press the Tab key to move the input cursor to the *Index* field. Enter the index as 0.

18. Click your mouse on the Next button. Visual Basic will clear the *Caption* and *Name* fields, move the block cursor within the Menu Viewer down one line, and return the input cursor to the *Caption* field.

19. Within the *Caption* field, enter the next item's caption as *Rich Text*. Visual Basic will display *Rich Text*, preceded by six dots, in the Menu Viewer as you type.

20. Press the Tab key to move the input cursor to the *Name* field. Enter the name as *mnuFileOpen*.

21. Press the Tab key to move the input cursor to the *Index* field. Enter the index as 1.

22. Click your mouse on the Next button. Visual Basic will clear the *Caption* and *Name* fields, move the block cursor within the Menu Viewer down one line, and return the input cursor to the *Caption* field.

23. Within the *Caption* field, enter the next item's caption as *Image*. Visual Basic will display *Image*, preceded by six dots, in the Menu Viewer as you type.

24. Press the Tab key to move the input cursor to the *Name* field. Enter the name as *mnuFileOpen*.

25. Press the Tab key to move the input cursor to the *Index* field. Enter the index as 2.

26. Click your mouse on the Next button. Visual Basic will clear the *Caption* and *Name* fields, move the block cursor within the Menu Viewer down one line, and return the input cursor to the *Caption* field.

27. Click your mouse on the left arrow just above the Menu Viewer and to the left of the Next button. Visual Basic will remove three of the six dots on the current line in the Menu Viewer.

28. Within the *Caption* field, enter the next item's caption as *&Save*. Visual Basic will display *&Save*, preceded by three dots, in the Menu Viewer as you type.

29. Press the TAB key to move the input cursor to the *Name* field. Enter the name as *mnuFile_Save*.

30. Within the Menu Editor, select the CTRL+S option within the Shortcut combo box. Visual Basic will add the shortcut to the Menu Viewer.

31. Click your mouse on the Next button. Visual Basic will clear the *Caption* and *Name* fields, move the block cursor within the Menu Viewer down one line, and return the input cursor to the *Caption* field.

32. Within the *Caption* field, enter the next item's caption as *Save As*. Visual Basic will display *Save As*, preceded by three dots, in the Menu Viewer as you type.

33. Press the TAB key to move the input cursor to the *Name* field. Enter the name as *mnuFile_SaveAs*.

34. Within the Menu Editor, select the CTRL+A option within the Shortcut combo box. Visual Basic will add the shortcut to the Menu Viewer.

35. Click your mouse on the Next button. Visual Basic will clear the *Caption* and *Name* fields, move the block cursor within the Menu Viewer down one line, and return the input cursor to the *Caption* field.

36. Enter the caption as "-". Remember, a menu item you caption with the hyphen (-) results in Visual Basic displaying a separator bar at that position within the menu. The Menu Viewer will display three dots followed by a hyphen.

37. Press the TAB key to move the input cursor to the *Name* field. Enter the name as *mnuFile_Hyphen0*.

38. Click your mouse on the Next button. Visual Basic will clear the *Caption* and *Name* fields, move the block cursor within the Menu Viewer down one line, and return the input cursor to the *Caption* field.

39. Within the *Caption* field, enter the next item's caption as *&Print*. Visual Basic will display *Print*, preceded by three dots, in the Menu Viewer as you type.

40. Press the TAB key to move the input cursor to the *Name* field. Enter the name as *mnuFile_Print*.

41. Click your mouse on the Next button. Visual Basic will clear the *Caption* and *Name* fields, move the block cursor within the Menu Viewer down one line, and return the input cursor to the *Caption* field.

42. Within the *Caption* field, enter the next item's caption as *Close Document*. Visual Basic will display *Close Document*, preceded by three dots, in the Menu Viewer as you type.

43. Press the TAB key to move the input cursor to the *Name* field. Enter the name as *mnuFile_ExitDoc*.

44. Click your mouse on the Next button. Visual Basic will clear the *Caption* and *Name* fields, move the block cursor within the Menu Viewer down one line, and return the input cursor to the *Caption* field.

45. Within the *Caption* field, enter the next item's caption as *E&xit*. Visual Basic will display *E&xit*, preceded by three dots, in the Menu Viewer as you type.

46. Press the TAB key to move the input cursor to the *Name* field. Enter the name as *mnuFile_Exit*.

47. Click your mouse on the Next button. Visual Basic will clear the *Caption* and *Name* fields, move the block cursor within the Menu Viewer down one line, and return the input cursor to the *Caption* field.

48. Use these standard steps (such as Steps 45, 46, and 47) to add the menu items Table 4.17 lists to the Menu Editor. (For each indent value in the table, three dots should appear before the item.)

Indent Level	Caption	Name	Shortcut Key
0	*&Edit*	*mnuEdit*	n/a
1	*Cut*	*mnuCut*	C<small>TRL</small>+X
1	*Copy*	*mnuEdit_Copy*	C<small>TRL</small>+C
1	*Paste*	*mnuEdit_Paste*	C<small>TRL</small>+V
1	*-*	*mnuEdit_Hyphen0*	n/a
1	*Find*	*mnuEdit_Find*	F3
0	*&Format Text*	*mnuFormat_Text*	n/a
1	*&Bold*	*mnuText_Bold*	C<small>TRL</small>+B
1	*&Italics*	*mnuText_Italics*	C<small>TRL</small>+I
1	*&Underline*	*mnuText_Underline*	C<small>TRL</small>+U
1	*&Strikethru*	*mnuText_Strikethru*	C<small>TRL</small>+K
1	*-*	*mnuText_Hyphen0*	n/a
1	*&Font*	*mnuText_Font*	n/a
1	*&Color*	*mnuText_Color*	n/a
0	*&Images*	*mnuImages*	n/a
1	*Rotate Right*	*mnuRotateRight*	n/a
1	*Rotate Left*	*mnuRotateLeft*	n/a
1	*Flip*	*mnuFlip*	n/a
1	*-*	*mnuImages_Hyphen0*	n/a
1	*Zoom Up*	*mnuZoomUp*	n/a
1	*Zoom Down*	*mnuZoomDown*	n/a
1	*Zoom 100%*	*mnuZoom100*	n/a
1	*-*	*mnuImages_Hyphen1*	n/a
1	*Show Annotation Palette*	*mnuShowPalette*	n/a
1	*-*	*mnuImages_Hyphen2*	n/a
1	*Clear Image*	*mnuClearImage*	n/a
0	*&Window*	*mnuWindow*	n/a
1	*Cascade*	*mnuWindow_Cascade*	n/a
1	*Tile*	*mnuWindow_Tile*	n/a

Table 4.17 *The remaining items you must enter within the Menu Editor.*

Note: *When you add the **mnuWindow** item to the Menu Editor, click your mouse on the box next to the Windowlist option to have the menu display a list of open child windows during the program's execution.*

After you finish adding the items in Table 4.17, the Menu Editor dialog box will look similar to Figure 4.14.

Figure 4.14 *The Menu Editor dialog box after you complete the menu design for the* ***frmMDIParent*** *form.*

After you add the menu and format the *StatusBar* and *CommonDialog* controls, the *frmMDIParent* form will look similar to Figure 4.15.

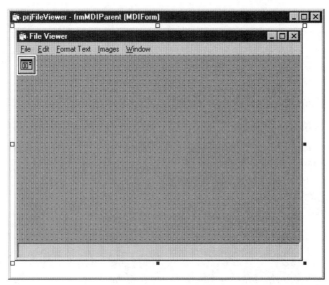

Figure 4.15 *The* ***frmMDIParent*** *form after you finish adding and formatting the controls.*

DESIGNING THE FRMCHILDRTB FORM'S APPEARANCE

As you learned in this chapter's "Using the *prjFileViewer* Project" section, you will display text files and Rich Text files within a *RichTextBox* control. The *RichTextBox* control is the only control that you will place onto the *frmChildRTB* form. To add a *RichTextBox* control to the *frmChildRTB* form, perform the following steps:

1. If Visual Basic is not displaying the *frmChildRTB* form within an object window, double-click your mouse on the *frmChildRTB* form listing within the Project Explorer. Visual Basic will open the *frmChildRTB* form.

2. Within Visual Basic, select the View menu Toolbox option. Visual Basic will open the Toolbox.

3. Within the Toolbox, double-click your mouse on the RichTextBox icon. Visual Basic will draw a *RichTextBox* control, *RichTextBox1*, within the *frmChildRTB* form. Figure 4.16 shows the RichTextBox icon within the Toolbox.

Figure 4.16 *The RichTextBox icon within the Toolbox.*

4. Within the *frmChildRTB* form, click your mouse on the *RichTextBox1* control to highlight it. Visual Basic will draw a small frame around the control.

5. Select the View menu Properties Window option. Visual Basic will open the Properties Window listing the *RichTextBox1* properties.

6. Within the Properties Window, change the *RichTextBox1* properties to the values Table 4.18 lists.

Object	Property	Set As
RichTextBox1	*Height*	2775
RichTextBox1	*Left*	0
RichTextBox1	*Top*	0
RichTextBox1	*Width*	3495
RichTextBox1	*Name*	*rtbFileViewer*

Table 4.18 *The newly named* **rtbFileViewer** *control's properties.*

Designing the frmChildImageEdit Form's Appearance

As you learned earlier in this chapter, the *prjFileViewer* project will use two different forms to display different types of graphic images. The first form that you will design is the *frmChildImageEdit* form, which uses the *Eastman Software Imaging* control suite to display Tagged-Image Format (TIF) files, and lets the user edit and annotate such files. The *frmChildImageEdit* form uses the *Image Edit* control to display images. To add an *Image Edit* control to the *frmChildImageEdit* form, perform the following steps:

1. If Visual Basic is not displaying the *frmChildImageEdit* form within an object window, double-click your mouse on the form's listing within the Project Explorer. Visual Basic will open the *frmChildImageEdit* form.

2. Within Visual Basic, select the View menu Toolbox option. Visual Basic will open the Toolbox.

3. Within the Toolbox, double-click your mouse on the ImageEdit icon. Visual Basic will draw an *Image Edit* control, *ImgEdit1*, within the *frmChildImageEdit* form. Figure 4.17 shows the ImageEdit icon within the Toolbox.

Figure 4.17 *The ImageEdit icon within the Toolbox.*

4. Within the *frmChildImageEdit* form, click your mouse on the *ImgEdit1* control to highlight it. Visual Basic will draw a small frame around the control.

5. Select the View menu Properties Window option. Visual Basic will open the Properties Window listing the *ImgEdit1* properties.

6.   Within the Properties Window, change the *ImgEdit1* properties to the values Table 4.19 lists.

Object	Property	Set As
ImgEdit1	Height	433
ImgEdit1	Left	0
ImgEdit1	Top	0
ImgEdit1	Width	369
ImgEdit1	Name	iecFileViewer

Table 4.19 *The newly named* **iecFileViewer** *control's properties.*

DESIGNING THE FRMGRAPHICTYPE FORM'S APPEARANCE

The last child form that you must design for the *prjFileViewer* project is the *frmGraphicType* form. Much like the other child forms, the *frmGraphicType* form contains only a single control, a *PictureBox* control. The *prjFileViewer* program will use the *PictureBox* control to display bitmaps and other non-TIF images. To add a *PictureBox* control to the *frmGraphicType* form, perform the following steps:

1.   If Visual Basic is not displaying the *frmGraphicType* form within an object window, double-click your mouse on the *frmGraphicType* form listing within the Project Explorer. Visual Basic will open the *frmGraphicType* form.

2.   Within Visual Basic, select the View menu Toolbox option. Visual Basic will open the Toolbox.

3.   Within the Toolbox, double-click your mouse on the PictureBox icon. Visual Basic will draw a *PictureBox* control, *Picture1*, within the *frmGraphicType* form.

4.   Within the *frmGraphicType* form, click your mouse on the *Picture1* control to highlight it. Visual Basic will draw a small frame around the control.

5.   Select the View menu Properties Window option. Visual Basic will open the Properties Window listing the *Picture1* properties.

6.   Within the Properties Window, change the *Picture1* properties to the values Table 4.20 lists.

Object	Property	Set As
Picture1	Height	4095
Picture1	Left	0
Picture1	Top	0
Picture1	Width	4095
Picture1	Name	picFileViewer

Table 4.20 *The newly named* **picFileViewer** *control's properties.*

DESIGNING THE FRMFIND FORM'S APPEARANCE

The *frmFind* form has by far the most complex appearance of all the forms within the *prjFileViewer* program. The program will display the *frmFind* form when the user tries to search a text file or Rich Text file's contents. The *frmFind* form contains fields for the text to search for, the text to replace the search text with, several search options, command buttons that instruct the program to begin the search, and so on. To design the *frmFind* form, you will first add a frame to the form, and then add the fields to the frame. After you complete the frame, you will add the *CheckBox* controls in the form's center, and add three command buttons at the form's bottom to finish the form's design.

ADDING THE FRAME TO THE FRMFIND FORM

When you place controls for a form within a *Frame* control, you must first place the *Frame* control onto the form, and then paste the controls onto the frame. Within the *prjFileViewer* project, the *frmFind* form will contain the *fraFindReplace* frame control. To place the *fraFindReplace* frame control onto the form, perform the following steps:

1. If Visual Basic is not displaying the *frmFind* form within an object window, double-click your mouse on the *frmFind* form listing within the Project Explorer. Visual Basic will open the *frmFind* form.

2. Within Visual Basic, select the View menu Toolbox option. Visual Basic will open the Toolbox.

3. Within the Toolbox, double-click your mouse on the Frame icon. Visual Basic will add a new *Frame* control, *Frame1*, to the *frmFind* form.

4. Within the *frmFind* form, click your mouse on the *Frame1* control to highlight it. Visual Basic will draw a small frame around the control.

5. Select the View menu Properties Window option. Visual Basic will open the Properties Window that lists the *Frame1* control's properties.

6. Within the Properties Window, change the *Frame1* control's properties to the values Table 4.21 lists.

Object	Property	Set As
Frame1	*Caption*	*Find and Replace*
Frame1	*Height*	1455
Frame1	*Left*	240
Frame1	*Top*	120
Frame1	*Width*	2895
Frame1	*Name*	*fraFindReplace*

Table 4.21 *The newly named **fraFindReplace** control's properties.*

Adding the TextBox and Label Controls to the fraFindReplace Frame

Now that you have added the *fraFindReplace* control to the *frmFind* form, you must place the two *Label* controls and the two *TextBox* controls that the form uses onto the form, cut them from the form, and paste them to the frame. To add *TextBox* and *Label* controls to the *frmFind* form, perform the following steps:

1. If Visual Basic is not displaying the *frmFind* form within an object window, double-click your mouse on the *frmFind* form listing within the Project Explorer. Visual Basic will open the *frmFind* form.

2. Within Visual Basic, select the View menu Toolbox option. Visual Basic will open the Toolbox.

3. Within the Toolbox, double-click your mouse on the TextBox icon. Visual Basic will draw a *TextBox* control, *Text1*, within the *frmFind* form.

4. Repeat Step 3 one time. Visual Basic will draw another *TextBox* control within the *frmFind* form.

5. Within the Toolbox, double-click your mouse on the Label icon. Visual Basic will draw a *Label* control, *Label1*, within the *frmFind* form.

6. Repeat Step 5 one time. Visual Basic will draw another *Label* control within the *frmFind* form.

7. Within the *frmFind* form window, click your mouse on a *Label* control to highlight it. Visual Basic will draw a small frame around the control.

8. Select the Edit menu Cut option. Visual Basic will remove the *Label* control from the *frmFind* form.

9. Within the *frmFind* form window, click your mouse on the *fraFindReplace* control to highlight it. Visual Basic will draw a small frame around the control.

10. Select the Edit menu Paste option. Visual Basic will paste the *Label* control within the *fraFindReplace* frame.

11. Repeat Steps 7, 8, 9, and 10 three more times until you have placed all the *Label* and *TextBox* controls within the *fraFindReplace* frame.

12. Within the *fraFindReplace* frame, click your mouse on a *Label* or *TextBox* control to highlight it. Visual Basic will draw a small frame around the control.

13. Select the View menu Properties Window option. Visual Basic will open the Properties Window listing the highlighted control's properties.

14. Within the Properties Window, change the highlighted control's properties to the values Table 4.22 lists.

15. Repeat Steps 12, 13, and 14 until you have changed each *Label* and *TextBox* control's properties to the values Table 4.22 lists.

Object	Property	Set As
Text1	*Height*	375
Text1	*Left*	840
Text1	*Text*	[blank]
Text1	*Top*	360
Text1	*Width*	1815
Text1	*Name*	*txtFind*
Text2	*Height*	375
Text2	*Left*	840
Text2	*Text*	[blank]
Text2	*Top*	840
Text2	*Width*	1815
Text2	*Name*	*txtReplace*
Label1	*Caption*	*Find:*
Label1	*Height*	375
Label1	*Left*	120
Label1	*Top*	360
Label1	*Width*	615
Label1	*Name*	*lblFind*
Label2	*Caption*	*Replace:*
Label2	*Height*	375
Label2	*Left*	120
Label2	*Top*	840
Label2	*Width*	615
Label2	*Name*	*lblReplace*

*Table 4.22 The **TextBox** and **Label** controls' properties for the **frmFind** form.*

ADDING CHECKBOX CONTROLS TO THE FRMFIND FORM

The *frmFind* form lets the user determine whether the find operation should match only whole words, and whether the find operation should enforce case matching between the search text and any text the search finds. To provide the user with an easy way to make choices about the two search options, the *frmFind* form uses two *CheckBox* controls, one for each option. When the user checks a box, the find operation will enforce the rule the user selects. Otherwise, the find operation will not enforce the rule. To add the two *CheckBox* controls to the *frmFind* form, perform the following steps:

1. If Visual Basic is not displaying the *frmFind* form within an object window, double-click your mouse on the *frmFind* form listing within the Project Explorer. Visual Basic will open the *frmFind* form.

2. Within Visual Basic, select the View menu Toolbox option. Visual Basic will open the Toolbox.

3. Within the Toolbox, double-click your mouse on the CheckBox icon. Visual Basic will draw a *CheckBox* control, *Check1*, within the *frmFind* form.

4. Repeat Step 3 one time. Visual Basic will draw another *CheckBox* control within the *frmFind* form.

5. Within the *frmFind* frame, click your mouse on a *CheckBox* control to highlight it. Visual Basic will draw a small frame around the control.

6. Select the View menu Properties Window option. Visual Basic will open the Properties Window listing the highlighted control's properties.

7. Within the Properties Window, change the highlighted control's properties to the values Table 4.23 lists.

8. Repeat Steps 5, 6, and 7 until you have changed both *CheckBox* controls' properties to the values Table 4.23 lists.

Object	Property	Set As
Check1	*Caption*	*Match Whole Word*
Check1	*Height*	375
Check1	*Left*	360
Check1	*Top*	1680
Check1	*Width*	2055
Check1	*Name*	*chkMatchWhole*
Check2	*Caption*	*Match Case*
Check2	*Height*	375
Check2	*Left*	360
Check2	*Top*	2160
Check2	*Width*	2055
Check2	*Name*	*chkMatchCase*

*Table 4.23 The newly named **CheckBox** controls' properties.*

ADDING COMMAND BUTTONS TO THE FRMFIND FORM

As you have learned, the *prjFileViewer* project will let the user perform find operations on text and Rich Text files. To start a search or replace operation, or to cancel the current operation, the user can use the buttons at the bottom of the *frmFind* form. The three *CommandButton* controls will let you search, replace, and cancel the current operation. To add three *CommandButton* controls and their enclosing frame to the *frmFind* form, perform the following steps:

1. If Visual Basic is not displaying the *frmFind* form within an object window, double-click your mouse on the *frmFind* form listing within the Project Explorer. Visual Basic will open the *frmFind* form.

2. Within Visual Basic, select the View menu Toolbox option. Visual Basic will open the Toolbox.

3. Within the Toolbox, double-click your mouse on the CommandButton icon. Visual Basic will draw a *CommandButton* control, *Command1*, within the *frmFind* form.

4. Repeat Step 3 two more times. Visual Basic will display a total of three command buttons within the *frmFind* form.

5. Within the *frmFind* form, click your mouse on a *CommandButton* control to highlight it. Visual Basic will draw a small frame around the control.

6. Select the View menu Properties Window option. Visual Basic will open the Properties Window that lists the highlighted *CommandButton* control's properties.

7. Within the Properties Window, change the highlighted *CommandButton* control's properties to the values Table 4.24 lists.

8. Repeat Steps 5, 6, and 7 until you have changed each *CommandButton* control's properties to the values Table 4.24 lists.

Object	Property	Set As
Command1	*Caption*	*Search*
Command1	*Height*	495
Command1	*Left*	120
Command1	*Top*	2640
Command1	*Width*	1095
Command1	*Name*	*cmdSearch*
Command2	*Caption*	*Replace*
Command2	*Height*	495
Command2	*Left*	1200
Command2	*Top*	2640
Command2	*Width*	1095
Command2	*Name*	*cmdReplace*
Command3	*Caption*	*Cancel*
Command3	*Height*	495
Command3	*Left*	2280
Command3	*Top*	2640
Command3	*Width*	975
Command3	*Name*	*cmdCancel*

Table 4.24 *The **frmFind** form's **CommandButton** control properties.*

When you finish adding and formatting the *frmFind* form's controls, the form will look similar to Figure 4.18.

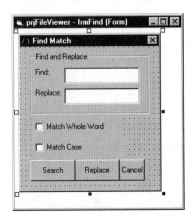

Figure 4.18 *The **frmFind** form after you complete its design.*

WRITING THE PROGRAM CODE FOR THE PRJFILEVIEWER PROJECT

Because of the number of different file types the *prjFileViewer* program will handle, it uses significant amounts of program code to process all the potential situations that can arise. As you will see in the following sections, much of the program code is within the menu items, because the user will use the menu items primarily to interact with the program. Within the next sections, you will first write the program code within the *mdlFileViewer* module, which declares the global variables and public functions and subroutines, and then write the code within the *frmMDIParent* form, which responds to the user's menu selections. Finally, you will write the code within the other forms that compose the project, most of which handles the program's appearance.

WRITING THE *MDLFILEVIEWER* MODULE'S PROGRAM CODE

As you have learned in previous chapters, you will generally use a module within your programs to contain code that you must share between two or more forms, and to contain code that does not have a specific application to a specific form. Additionally, you will place your global variable declarations within the *mdlFileViewer* module. The following code implements the General–Declarations section for the *mdlFileViewer* module:

```
Option Explicit
Option Base 1
Option Compare Text

Public gTextForms() As New frmChildRTB          ' Text Form Array
Public gImageForms() As New frmChildImageEdit   ' Image Form Array
Public gGraphicForms() As New frmGraphicType    ' PictureBox Form Array
Public gFileName() As String                    ' Filenames
Public Loading As Boolean
Public gNewestInstance As Integer               ' Points to Newest Form
Public gCurrentInstance As Integer              ' Points to Current
                                                ' Active Form
```

The first three statements within the section instruct the compiler that it should not let the program use any undeclared variables, that it should set the base element for arrays as 1 (not 0), and that it should perform text comparisons between strings, not between binary comparisons. In other words, the program will perform case insensitive comparisons unless you specifically instruct the program to do otherwise for a specific comparison.

The remainder of the variables within the General-Declarations section are global form arrays, pointers to the current forms, and a flag variable. The *gTextForms* array contains all the open *frmChildRTB* forms. When you create a new *frmChildRTB* form within the program, you will increase the array's size by one element. Similarly, the *gImageForms* array contains the open *frmChildImageEdit* forms, and the *gGraphicForms* array contains the open *frmGraphicType* forms. The *gFileName* array will contain the file name of all open files. The *Loading* variable is a flag variable the program uses when it loads new forms. The *gNewestInstance* variable and the *gCurrentInstance* variable contain integer values that correspond to the program's most recently created form instance and the user's currently selected form instance.

WRITING THE *CHANGEPANELSTATUS* PROCEDURE

As you learned when you designed the *frmMDIParent* form, the *prjFileViewer* program will display information about the program's processing within the *StatusBar* control at the form's bottom. *StatusBar* controls consist of one or more *panels*, within which your programs can display text, numbers, or other information (such as icons). When you want to display text within a panel in the *StatusBar* control, you must update the panel's contents to contain the text. The *ChangePanelStatus* procedure is the procedure you will generally use whenever you create a *StatusBar* control. The procedure accepts the number of the panel it is to change, and the text it is to display, and changes the panel. The following code implements the *ChangePanelStatus* procedure:

```
Public Sub ChangePanelStatus(ByVal PanelNumber As Integer, _
    ByVal NewText As String)
  Dim tmpPanel As Panel

  Set tmpPanel = frmMDIParent.stsFileViewer.Panels(PanelNumber)
  tmpPanel.Text = NewText
  DoEvents
  frmMDIParent.stsFileViewer.Refresh
End Sub
```

The *ChangePanelStatus* procedure creates a temporary panel object, and then sets that panel object equal to the panel that the procedure receives as its first parameter. Next, the procedure's code sets the text within the panel to the new text, and invokes the *DoEvents* statement, which yields execution so that the operating system can process other events. Finally, the program code calls the *StatusBar's Refresh* method to update the text display within the panel on the screen.

WRITING THE CHECKPANEL FUNCTION

Just as there are times when you must change the value within a panel in the *StatusBar*, there are also times when you must check the value within a panel in the *StatusBar*. The *CheckPanel* function checks the current value of the text within a panel. The following code implements the *CheckPanel* function:

```
Public Function CheckPanel(ByVal PanelNum As Integer, _
    ByVal CurrentCap As String) As Boolean
  Dim tmpPanel As Panel

  Set tmpPanel = frmMDIParent.stsFileViewer.Panels(PanelNum)
  If tmpPanel.Text = CurrentCap Then
    CheckPanel = True
  Else
    CheckPanel = False
  End If
End Function
```

Just as the *ChangeStatusPanel* procedure did, the *CheckPanel* function accepts a panel number and a text value. However, the *CheckPanel* function then checks the value against the panel's current text value. If the two values match, *CheckPanel* will return *True*. If the values do not match, *CheckPanel* will return *False*.

WRITING THE CHECKCLIPBOARD FUNCTION

When you created the menu for the *frmMDIParent* form, you included options within the form's Edit menu to let the user cut, copy, and paste information from and to a *RichTextBox* control within a child form. The *CheckClipboard* function verifies that whatever data is currently on the Clipboard is either text or rich text. Within the program, you will use the *CheckClipboard* function to update the Edit menu Paste option's display. The following code implements the *CheckClipboard* function:

```
Public Function CheckClipboard() As Boolean
  If Clipboard.GetFormat(vbCFText) Or Clipboard.GetFormat(vbCFRTF) Then
    CheckClipboard = True
  Else
    CheckClipboard = False
  End If
End Function
```

The *CheckClipboard* function uses the Visual Basic *Clipboard* object. The *If-Then* statement uses the Visual Basic *vbCFText* and *vbCFRTF* constants within the function to check the format of the data currently on the Clipboard. If the data is text or rich text, the function returns *True*. If the data on the Clipboard is some other data type (such as a file or a picture), the function returns *False*.

WRITING THE TURNONMENUS PROCEDURE

Within the *prjFileViewer* project, you will often enable and disable certain menus, depending on what type of child form is currently active. To simplify enabling and disabling menus, the *mdlFileViewer* module includes the *TurnOnMenus* procedure. The following code implements the *TurnOnMenus* procedure:

```
Public Sub TurnOnMenus(ByVal TurnOn As Boolean)
  frmMDIParent.mnuEdit.Enabled = TurnOn
  frmMDIParent.mnuFormatText.Enabled = TurnOn
  frmMDIParent.mnuWindow.Enabled = TurnOn
End Sub
```

As you can see, the *TurnOnMenus* procedure accepts a single, *Boolean* parameter. The procedure then sets the *Enabled* property for the Edit, Format Text, and Window menus to that parameter's value. To turn the menus off, the program code will invoke the *TurnOnMenus* procedure with a *False* parameter. On the other hand, to turn the menus on, the program code will invoke the *TurnOnMenus* procedure with a *True* parameter.

WRITING THE SIZEFORMBYPIXELS PROCEDURE

As you have learned, you can load different graphic sizes into the *prjFileViewer* program. To keep the forms within the program from being too small or too large, you must size the forms from the size of the image the program loads into the form. You will size both the *frmChildImageEdit* and *frmGraphicType* forms to be slightly larger than the size of the image within each form's control (so that the forms still maintain their borders, as the next paragraph explains). Both the *Image Edit* and *PictureBox* controls will let you determine the image size within the control in pixels. Therefore, the simplest way to size the form is by pixels. The following code implements the *SizeFormByPixels* procedure:

```
Public Sub SizeFormByPixels(frm As Form, nWidth As Integer, _
    nHeight As Integer)
  Dim OffsetX As Integer, OffsetY As Integer
  Dim NewSizeX As Integer, NewSizeY As Integer
  Dim OldScaleMode As Integer

  On Error Resume Next
  With frm
    OldScaleMode = .ScaleMode
    .ScaleMode = vbPixels
    OffsetX = .ScaleWidth - nWidth - 2
    OffsetY = .ScaleHeight - nHeight - 2
    NewSizeX = .Width - (Screen.TwipsPerPixelX * OffsetX)
    NewSizeY = .Height - (Screen.TwipsPerPixelY * OffsetY)
    .Move .Left, .Top, NewSizeX, NewSizeY
    .ScaleMode = OldScaleMode
  End With
End Sub
```

The *SizeFormByPixels* procedure receives as its parameters the form to size and the width and height of the control to size the form around. The program code within the procedure then sets the form's *ScaleMode* property to pixels. After setting the *ScaleMode* property to pixels, the program code determines how much it must shrink (or expand) the form and places those values into the *OffsetX* and *OffsetY* values. After it computes the *OffsetX* and *OffsetY* values, the program code multiplies those values by the *Screen.TwipsPerPixel* value, which yields the amount it is to adjust the form's size in twips (the Visual Basic screen measurement unit). The program code sets the form to the newly computed size, returns the form's *ScaleMode* property to what it was when the procedure began to execute, and returns to the calling procedure. The effect of the procedure's processing is that the form's inside area is only slightly larger than the image within the form—enough that the form's edge is visible to the user, but not enough to be distracting.

WRITING THE frmMDIParent FORM'S PROGRAM CODE

As you have learned, the *prjFileViewer* program will perform the majority of its processing within the *frmMDIParent* form's event procedures. The *frmMDIParent* form contains all the menu items that you created earlier in this chapter, and includes program code for each menu item. Within the following sections, you will write the program code for each of the events within the *frmMDIParent* form to which the program must respond.

WRITING THE MDIFORM_LOAD EVENT'S PROGRAM CODE

In Chapter 2, you learned that the first event to execute when a form loads into memory is that form's *Form_Load* event. In the *prjFileViewer* project, the first form to load into memory is the *frmMDIParent* form. Just as with the form you created in Chapter 2, the *frmMDIParent* form will first invoke its *Load* event. The following code implements the *MDIForm_Load* event:

```
Private Sub MDIForm_Load()
  Me.WindowState = vbMaximized
  mnuFile_Save.Enabled = False
  mnuFile_SaveAs.Enabled = False
  mnuFile_Print.Enabled = False
  mnuFile_ExitDoc.Enabled = False
  mnuEdit.Enabled = False
  mnuFormatText.Enabled = False
  mnuImages.Enabled = False
  mnuWindow.Enabled = False
  Clipboard.Clear
End Sub
```

The *MDIForm_Load* event's program code first maximizes the *frmMDIParent* form. Next, it disables all the menus except the File menu, and disables the options within the File menu, except for the Open and Exit options. Finally, the program code clears the *Clipboard* object of any current entries.

WRITING THE PROGRAM CODE FOR THE MNUFILE_NEW_CLICK EVENT

When you created the File menu for the *prjFileViewer* project, the first option you added to the menu was the New option. When the user selects the File menu New option, the program will invoke the *mnuFile_New_Click* event. The following code implements the *mnuFile_New_Click* event:

```
Private Sub mnuFile_New_Click()
  mnuEdit.Enabled = True
  mnuFormatText.Enabled = True
  gNewestInstance = gNewestInstance + 1
  gCurrentInstance = gNewestInstance
  Screen.MousePointer = vbHourglass
  ReDim gTextForms(gNewestInstance)
  ReDim Preserve gFileName(gNewestInstance)
  With gTextForms(gNewestInstance)
    .Caption = "Document: " & gCurrentInstance
    gFileName(gNewestInstance) = .Caption
    .Show
  End With
  Screen.MousePointer = vbNormal
End Sub
```

The *mnuFile_New_Click* event creates a new *frmRTBChild* form and sets the form's caption to a blank document. The program code first enables the Edit and Format Text menus. Next, the program code increases the number of instances of a child form by one and sets the current instance to the newly created instance.

The program code within the event next sets the mouse pointer to an hourglass. Then, the program code redimensions the *gTextForms* array, which creates a new *frmRTBChild* form. The program code also increases the *gFileName* array's size by one, so that the program has a place to store the name of the file within the form after the user saves the file. The program code then sets the form's caption and displays the form. The last line of code within the event sets the mouse pointer back to the normal mouse pointer.

WRITING THE PROGRAM CODE FOR THE MNUOPENFILE_CLICK EVENT

In the previous section, you wrote the program code to create a new, blank *frmRTBChild* form within which the user can create a new document. However, users will more commonly open files within the *prjFileViewer* program. As you learned in the "Using the *prjFileViewer* Project" section of this chapter, the user can use the File menu Open option to open different file types within the program. When the user selects the File menu Open option, the program will invoke the *mnuOpenFile_Click* event. The following code implements the *mnuOpenFile_Click* event:

```
Private Sub mnuOpenFile_Click(Index As Integer)
   cdgParent.FileName = ""
   cdgParent.InitDir = CurDir
   cdgParent.CancelError = True
   cdgParent.Flags = cdlOFNHideReadOnly
   Select Case Index
      Case 0                         ' TEXT files
         LoadText

      Case 1                         ' RICH TEXT files
         LoadRichText

      Case 2                         ' IMAGE files
         LoadImageFile
   End Select
End Sub
```

The *mnuOpenFile_Click* event first initializes the *cdgParent* common dialog control, setting its initial directory, clearing the *FileName* property, and hiding the *Read-Only* box at the bottom of the dialog box the control will display. The program code then uses a *Select Case* statement to determine what item the user selected. Depending on the user-selected item, the program code then calls a procedure specific to the file type the user wants to load and then loads the actual file. The following sections detail the three load procedures, *LoadText*, *LoadRichText*, and *LoadImageFile*.

WRITING THE CODE FOR THE LOADTEXT PROCEDURE

As the previous section explains, the user can select from three submenu items to load the file. If the user decides to load a text file, the *mnuOpenFile_Click* event will call the *LoadText* procedure. The following code implements the *LoadText* procedure:

```
Private Sub LoadText
   Dim FileName As String

   mnuImages.Enabled = False
   cdgParent.DialogTitle = "Open Text Files"
   cdgParent.Filter = "Text Files (*.TXT)|*.TXT|All Files (*.*)| *.*"
   On Error Resume Next
   cdgParent.ShowOpen
   DoEvents
   If Err.Number <> 0 Then
      TurnOnMenus False
      Exit Sub
   End If
   FileName = cdgParent.FileName
   HoldExtension = UCase(Right(FileName, 3))

   If HoldExtension = "TXT" Then
      gNewestInstance = gNewestInstance + 1
      gCurrentInstance = gNewestInstance
      Screen.MousePointer = vbHourglass
      ReDim gTextForms(gNewestInstance)
      ReDim Preserve gFileName(gNewestInstance)
      Loading = True
      With gTextForms(gNewestInstance)
         .rtbFileViewer.LoadFile FileName, rtfText
         .Caption = FileName
         gFileName(gNewestInstance) = FileName
         .Show
      End With
      mnuFile_Save.Enabled = True
      mnuFile_SaveAs.Enabled = True
      mnuFile_Print.Enabled = True
```

```
         mnuFile_ExitDoc.Enabled = True
         mnuEdit.Enabled = True
         mnuFormatText.Enabled = True
         mnuWindow.Enabled = True
         Loading = False
         Screen.MousePointer = vbNormal
    Else
         MsgText = "Not a TEXT file type. "
         Captn = "File Type Warning"
         MsgBox MsgText, 0, Captn
         DoEvents
         TurnOnMenus False
    End If
End Sub
```

120   The *LoadText* procedure disables the Images menu first (because it is not applicable to text files). Next, the procedure initializes the *cdgParent* common dialog control's title and its filter for text files. After initializing the title and filter, the program code displays the Open File dialog box. If the user clicks the mouse within the dialog box on the Cancel button, the procedure will exit. Otherwise, the procedure places the user-selected filename within the *FileName* variable. After assigning the filename to the variable, the program code checks the filename's extension. If the extension is not TXT (a valid text file extension), the program code will display a message that the filename's extension is invalid, and will exit without trying to load the file.

On the other hand, if the extension is valid, the program code will increment the number of instances, set the current instance to the number of instances, and redimension the *gTextForms* form array, which will then create a new form. After creating the new form, the program code will load the file into the form's *rtbFileViewer RichTextBox* control, set the form's caption, and display the form.

Next, the program code will enable the Save, Save As, Print, and Exit Document items on the File menu. The code will also enable the Edit, Format Text, and Window menus. After the program code loads the file and enables the menu items, it will exit, and the newly created child form will contain the file the user wanted to load.

WRITING THE CODE FOR THE LOADRICHTEXT PROCEDURE

As you have learned, the user can select from three submenu items to load a file. If the user decides to load a Rich Text file, the *mnuOpenFile_Click* event will call the *LoadRichText* procedure. The following code implements the *LoadRichText* procedure:

```
Private Sub LoadRichText
   Dim FileName As String

   mnuImages.Enabled = False
   cdgParent.DialogTitle = "Open Rich Text Files"
   cdgParent.Filter = "Rich Text Files (*.RTF)|*.RTF|All Files (*.*)| *.*"
   On Error Resume Next
   cdgParent.ShowOpen
   If Err.Number <> 0 Then Exit Sub
   FileName = cdgParent.FileName
   HoldExtension = UCase(Right(FileName, 3))
   If HoldExtension = "RTF" Then
      gNewestInstance = gNewestInstance + 1
      gCurrentInstance = gNewestInstance
      Screen.MousePointer = vbHourglass
      ReDim gTextForms(gNewestInstance)
      ReDim Preserve gFileName(gNewestInstance)
      Loading = True
      With gTextForms(gNewestInstance)
         .rtbFileViewer.LoadFile FileName, rtfRTF
         .Caption = FileName
         gFileName(gNewestInstance) = FileName
```

```
        .Show
     End With
     Screen.MousePointer = vbNormal
     mnuFile_Save.Enabled = True
     mnuFile_SaveAs.Enabled = True
     mnuFile_Print.Enabled = True
     mnuFile_ExitDoc.Enabled = True
     mnuEdit.Enabled = True
     mnuFormatText.Enabled = True
     mnuWindow.Enabled = True
     Loading = False
   Else
     MsgText = "Not a RICH TEXT file type. "
     Captn = "File Type Warning"
     MsgBox MsgText, 0, Captn
   End Select
End Sub
```

As you can see, the *LoadRichText* procedure performs processing similar to the *LoadText* procedure. However, the *LoadRichText* procedure displays a slightly different dialog box (prompting for RTF files, rather than TXT files), and uses the *rtRTF* constant to load the file into the form. The *rtRTF* constant tells the *rtbFileViewer* control that the incoming file includes rich text formatting codes and that the control should interpret those controls as formatting codes, not as plain text. After the program code loads the Rich Text file, it enables the menus as the *LoadText* procedure did, and exits.

WRITING THE CODE FOR THE LOADIMAGEFILE PROCEDURE

In the previous sections, you have written the program code to load text and Rich Text files into their correct forms. The program code that loads image files is slightly different from that which loads Rich Text files, primarily because the program code must decide into which form to load the user-requested file—either the *frmGraphicType* or the *frmChildImageEdit* form. The following code implements the *LoadImageFile* procedure:

```
Private Sub LoadImageFile(FileName As String)
   mnuImages.Enabled = True
   cdgParent.DialogTitle = "Open Image Files"
   cdgParent.Filter = "All Image Files(*.tif, *.bmp, *.jpg, *.gif) | " & _
      "*.tif; *.bmp; *.jpg; *.gif; | All files (*.*)|*.*|"
   On Error Resume Next
   cdgParent.ShowOpen
   If Err.Number <> 0 Then Exit Sub
   FileName = cdgParent.FileName
   HoldExtension = UCase(Right(FileName, 3))

   Select Case HoldExtension
     Case "BMP", "JPG", "GIF"                              ' Non-TIF files
        gNewestInstance = gNewestInstance + 1
        gCurrentInstance = gNewestInstance
        Screen.MousePointer = vbHourglass
        ReDim gGraphicForms(gNewestInstance)
        ReDim gFileName(gNewestInstance)
        With gGraphicForms(gNewestInstance)
          .Caption = FileName
          gFileName(gNewestInstance) = FileName
          .PictureContainer.Picture = LoadPicture(FileName)
          .Width = 600 + .PictureContainer.Width + 600
          .Height = 480 + .PictureContainer.Height + 480
          .Show
        End With
        Screen.MousePointer = vbNormal
     Case "TIF"                                            ' TIF files
```

```
            gNewestInstance = gNewestInstance + 1
            gCurrentInstance = gNewestInstance
            Screen.MousePointer = vbHourglass
            ReDim gImageForms(gNewestInstance)
            ReDim gFileName(gNewestInstance)
            With gImageForms(gNewestInstance)
               .Caption = FileName
               gFileName(gNewestInstance) = FileName
               .iecFileViewer.Image = FileName
               .iecFileViewer.Width = .iecFileViewer.ImageWidth + 6
               .iecFileViewer.Height = .iecFileViewer.Height + 6
               .Width = 600 + (.iecFileViewer.Width * 15) + 700
               .ScaleHeight = 480 + (.iecFileViewer.Height * 16) + 680
               .iecFileViewer.Display
               .Show
            End With
            Screen.MousePointer = vbNormal
         Case Else
            MsgText = "Not an IMAGE file type. "
            Captn = "File Type Warning"
            MsgBox MsgText, 0, Captn
      End Select
   End Sub
```

Much as the *LoadText* and *LoadRichText* procedures do, the *LoadImageFile* procedure first initializes and then displays the Open Image Files dialog box. You should note within the code that the *LoadImageFile* procedure, however, lets the user select from any of four file types—TIF, BMP, JPG, and GIF. Because the user has a choice of file types, using a *Select Case* statement in the *LoadImageFile* procedure is a more efficent way to determine whether the user selected a valid file or not.

The *Select Case* statement processes three possibilities: that the file is a BMP, GIF, or JPG; that the file is a TIF; or that the file is none of these types. In the first case, the program code will display a *frmGraphicType* child form with the graphic file in it. In the second case, the program code will display a *frmChildImageEdit* form with the graphic file in it. In the third case, the program code will display a message that lets the user know the file type is not valid, and exits.

To display the new *frmGraphicType* form, the program code will redimension the *gGraphicForms* form array, assign the file to the *PictureBox* control's *Picture* property for that form, and display the form. The program code will not enable any menu items because it does not let the user edit, save, or otherwise manipulate the image. To display the new *frmChildImageEdit* form, the program code will redimension the *gImageForms* form array, assign the file to the *iecFileViewer* control's *Image* property, and display the image within the control. After the program code displays the image within the control, the program code will display the form itself.

WRITING THE CODE FOR THE MNUFILE_SAVE_CLICK EVENT

As you have learned, the user can use the *prjFileViewer* program to edit and save text files, and to annotate and save image files. The file menu presents two options, Save and Save As, that the user can use to save files. The first option, Save, will save the currently displayed file over the file's existing copy. The following code implements the *mnuFile_Save_Click* event:

```
   Private Sub mnuFile_Save_Click()
      If Me.ActiveForm.Name = "frmChildRTB" Then
         If UCase(Right(gFileName(gCurrentInstance), 3)) = "TXT" Then
            MsgText = "This file may have formatting which will be lost if"
            MsgText = MsgText & NewLine & " you save it as type text."
            MsgText = MsgText & NewLine & "Continue anyway?"
            Captn = "Format Loss Warning"
            Response = MsgBox(MsgText, vbQuestion + vbYesNo, Captn)
            If Response = vbNo Then Exit Sub
         End If
```

```
      If Left(gFileName(gCurrentInstance), 8) = "Document" Then
        mnuFile_SaveAs_Click
      Else
        If UCase(Right(gFileName(gCurrentInstance), 3)) = "TXT" Then
          Me.ActiveForm.rtbFileViewer.SaveFile gFileName(gCurrentInstance), _
         rtfText
        Else
          Me.ActiveForm.rtbFileViewer.SaveFile gFileName(gCurrentInstance), _
        rtfRTF
        End If
        Me.ActiveForm.SetFileFlag False
      End If
    Else
      Me.ActiveForm.SetFocus
      Me.ActiveForm.iecFileViewer.Save
    End If
  End Sub
```

The first line of code within the event uses an *If-Then* statement to determine whether the currently displayed form is a *frmChildRTB* form or a *frmImageEdit* form. If the form is a *frmChildRTB* form, the program code will check to see if the file's extension indicates that the file is a text file. If so, the program code will display a message to the user that the file may contain formatting that the user will lose if the user saves the file as a text file. The user can then choose whether or not to exit the event.

The program code then checks whether the file is one that the user loaded from the disk, or a file that the user created with the File menu New option. If the user created the file within the program, the event will invoke the *mnuFile_SaveAs_Click* event, which will force the user to give the file a name before the user can save the file to the disk. If the user previously loaded the file from the disk, the program code checks the file's extension, and either saves the file as a text file or as a Rich Text file, depending on the file's current extension. If the form is a *frmChildImageEdit* form, the program code will save the file using the *ImageEdit* control's *Save* method. You learned about the *Save* method earlier in this chapter.

WRITING THE CODE FOR THE MNUFILE_SAVEAS_CLICK EVENT

As the previous section details, the user can save files using either the File menu's Save option or Save As option. If the user chooses the Save As option, the program will prompt the user to assign a new name to the file before saving the file. The following code implements the *mnuFile_SaveAs_Click* event:

```
  Private Sub mnuFile_SaveAs_Click()
    If Me.ActiveForm.Name = "frmChildRTB" Then
      SaveTxtRTF
    Else
      SaveTIF
    End If
    Me.ActiveForm.Caption = gFileName(gCurrentInstance)
  End Sub
```

As with the *mnuFile_Save_Click* event, the program code first checks to determine what form the user is displaying. If the form contains text, the event calls the *SaveTxtRTF* procedure. If the form contains an image, the event calls the *SaveTIF* procedure. You will learn more about the *SaveTxtRTF* and *SaveTIF* procedures in the following sections.

WRITING THE CODE FOR THE SAVETXTRTF PROCEDURE

As you learned in the previous section, when the user selects the File menu Save As option, the program will determine whether the user is currently viewing a text file or an image file. If the user is currently viewing a text file or a Rich Text file, the program code calls the *SaveTxtRTF* procedure. The following code implements the *SaveTxtRTF* procedure:

```
Private Sub SaveTxtRTF()
  Dim FileName As String

  cdgParent.DialogTitle = "Save File"
  cdgParent.InitDir = CurDir
  If Left(Me.ActiveForm.Caption, 8) <> "Document" Then
    cdgParent.FileName = Me.ActiveForm.Caption
  Else
    cdgParent.FileName = ""
  End If
  cdgParent.CancelError = True
  cdgParent.Filter = "Text Files (*.TXT)|*.TXT|Rich Text Files (*.RTF)" & _
    "|*.RTF|All Files (*.*)|*.*"
  cdgParent.Flags = cdlOFNHideReadOnly
  On Error Resume Next
  cdgParent.ShowSave
  If Err.Number <> 0 Then Exit Sub
  If cdgParent.FileName = "" Then Exit Sub
  On Error Resume Next
  If UCase(Right(cdgParent.FileName, 3)) = "TXT" Then
    MsgText = "This file may have formatting which will be lost if"
    MsgText = MsgText & NewLine & " you save it as type text."
    MsgText = MsgText & NewLine & "Continue anyway?"
    Captn = "Format Loss Warning"
    Response = MsgBox(MsgText, vbQuestion + vbYesNo, Captn)
    If Response = vbNo Then Exit Sub
    Me.ActiveForm.rtbFileViewer.SaveFile gFileName(gCurrentInstance), _
      rtfText
    If Err.Number <> 0 Then
      MsgBox "Error!"
      Exit Sub
    End If
  Else
    gFileName(gCurrentInstance) = cdgParent.FileName
    Me.ActiveForm.rtbFileViewer.SaveFile gFileName(gCurrentInstance), _
      rtfRTF
    If Err.Number <> 0 Then
      MsgBox "Error!"
      Exit Sub
    End If
  End If
  Me.ActiveForm.SetFileFlag False
End Sub
```

As the *Load* procedures did, the *SaveTxtRTF* procedure first initializes the *CommonDialog* control to display existing TXT and RTF files. Next, the procedure calls the Common Dialog box with the *ShowSave* method, which will display the Save As dialog box. If the user tries to save the file as a text file, the program will warn the user that doing so will lose all the formatting the user may have placed on the document. The program code uses the *RichTextBox* control's *SaveFile* method to save the file. If you use the *rtfText* flag, the method will save the code as ASCII text and remove all formatting. If you use the *rtfRTF* flag, the method will save the code as a Rich Text file and preserve all the file's formatting.

WRITING THE CODE FOR THE SAVETIF PROCEDURE

As you have learned, if the user selects the File menu Save As option when displaying an image file, the *mnuFile_SaveAs_Click* event will call the *SaveTIF* procedure. The following code implements the *SaveTIF* procedure:

```
Private Sub SaveTIF()
  cdgParent.DialogTitle = "Save File"
  cdgParent.InitDir = CurDir
  cdgParent.FileName = Me.ActiveForm.Caption
```

124

```
      cdgParent.CancelError = True
      cdgParent.Filter = "TIF Files (*.TIF)|*.TIF|All Files (*.*)| *.*"
      On Error Resume Next
      cdgParent.ShowSave
      If Err.Number <> 0 Then Exit Sub
      If cdgParent.FileName = "" Then Exit Sub
      gFileName(gCurrentInstance) = cdgParent.FileName
      Me.ActiveForm.iecFileViewer.SaveAs gFileName(gCurrentInstance)
      Me.ActiveForm.iecFileViewer.Save
   End Sub
```

Just as the *Load* procedures did, the *SaveTIF* procedure first initializes the *cdgParent* common dialog control to display existing TIF files. Next, the procedure calls the Common Dialog box with the *ShowSave* method, which will display the Save As dialog box. Finally, the program code uses the *SaveAs* method to save the file with its new name (as the user selects).

125

Writing the Code for the mnuFile_Print_Click Event

After the user generates a text file, the user will often want to print that file to a hard copy. The *prjFileViewer* program lets the user send both text files and formatted Rich Text files to a printer the user selects. The user can select a printer and send the file to that printer. The printer, in turn, prints the file to a hard copy. To send a text document to the printer, the user selects the File menu Print option. The following code implements the *mnuFile_Print_Click* event:

```
Private Sub mnuFile_Print_Click()
   Dim prtViewer As Printer

   cdgParent.Flags = cdlPDReturnDC + cdlPDNoPageNums
   cdgParent.PrinterDefault = True
   cdgParent.CancelError = True
   If Me.ActiveForm.rtbFileViewer.SelLength = 0 Then
     cdgParent.Flags = cdgParent.Flags + cdlPDAllPages + cdlPDNoSelection
   Else
     cdgParent.Flags = cdgParent.Flags + cdlPDSelection
   End If
   On Error Resume Next
   cdgParent.ShowPrinter
   If Err.Number <> 0 Then Exit Sub
   For Each prtViewer In Printers
     If prtViewer.DeviceName = Printer.DeviceName Then
       Set Printer = prtViewer
       Exit For
     End If
   Next
   Me.MousePointer = vbHourglass
   Me.ActiveForm.rtbFileViewer.SetFocus
   Printer.Print ""
   Me.ActiveForm.rtbFileViewer.SelPrint Printer.hDC
   Printer.EndDoc
   Me.MousePointer = vbNormal
End Sub
```

The *mnuFile_Print_Click* event code uses the *Printer* object, a Visual Basic-defined object type. After declaring a local variable (*prtViewer*) of the *Printer* object, the program code uses the *cdgParent* common dialog control to display the Print dialog box. Within the Print dialog box, the user can select the printer, format, page size, and other characteristics of the print job.

After the user selects a printer within the Print dialog box, the program code uses a *For-Each* loop to step through each printer in the *Printers* collection. After it finds the printer the user selected in the printer collection, it sets that printer to receive output. The program code then uses the *RichTextBox* control's *SelPrint* method to send the file to the printer. After the *SelPrint* method completes, the program code calls the *Printer* object's *EndDoc* method to let the object know that the print job has completed and then exits the event.

WRITING THE MNUFILE_EXITDOC_CLICK EVENT

As you have learned, the File menu includes options for creating, opening, saving, and printing files. The File menu also includes options to close files or to close the program. The user has two exit options within the File menu. The first option, Exit Document, lets the user close the current document or image. The following code implements the *mnuFile_ExitDoc_Click* event:

```
Private Sub mnuFile_ExitDoc_Click()
  Unload Me.ActiveForm
  ChangePanelStatus 1, ""
End Sub
```

The *mnuFile_ExitDoc_Click* event's code first tries to unload the active form (which it may or may not be able to do, depending on the current status of the objects within that form). The event's code then clears the status bar's panel of text.

WRITING THE MNUFILE_EXIT_CLICK EVENT

As you learned in the previous section, the user has two exit options within the File menu. The second option, Exit, lets the user shut down and exit the entire *prjFileViewer* program. The following code implements the *mnuFile_Exit_Click* event:

```
Private Sub mnuFile_Exit_Click()
  Unload Me
End Sub
```

The *mnuFile_Exit_Click* event's program code tries to unload the *frmMDIParent* form. When you write programs that use the Multiple-Document Interface, unloading the parent form will also unload each child form. Within the *prjFileViewer* project, each child form will intercept the event's *unload* message to ensure that the user has saved a copy of the document or image the form contains. When the user tries to unload the *frmMDIParent* form, it will unload each child form. In turn, each child form will prompt the user to save changes to the form, if appropriate.

WRITING THE MNUEDIT_CUT_CLICK EVENT

As this chapter's "Using the *prjFileViewer* Project" section details, the user can perform different activities on the text within a child form. One activity that the user can perform is to cut text from the child form and paste it onto the Clipboard. To cut text, the user must select the Edit menu Cut option. The following code implements the *mnuEdit_Cut_Click* event:

```
Private Sub mnuEdit_Cut_Click()
  Clipboard.Clear
  Clipboard.SetText Me.ActiveForm.rtbFileViewer.SelRTF, vbCFRTF
  Me.ActiveForm.rtbFileViewer.SelRTF = ""
  mnuEdit_Paste.Enabled = True
  Me.ActiveForm.rtbFileViewer.SetFocus
End Sub
```

The *mnuEdit_Cut_Click* event's program code will first clear the Clipboard of other items. The *Clipboard* object's *SetText* method will set the Clipboard's text equal to the user's currently selected text within the document. After placing the text into the *Clipboard* object, the program code sets the text equal to a *NULL* string—which effectively deletes the text from the document. After the program places the text onto the Clipboard, it must enable the Paste option so that the user can paste that text back into the document elsewhere, if the user chooses to do so. The *mnuEdit_Cut_Click* event's last command (the *SetFocus* method) sets the focus back to the form that contains the document, so that the user's input cursor remains present.

Writing the *mnuEdit_Copy_Click* Event

In the previous section, you learned that the *prjFileViewer* program uses the *Clipboard* object to store text the user cuts from a document. Similarly, the program will place text that the user copies from a document into the *Clipboard* object. To copy text, the user must select the Edit menu Copy option. The following code implements the *mnuEdit_Copy_Click* event:

```
Private Sub mnuEdit_Copy_Click()
    Clipboard.Clear
    Clipboard.SetText Me.ActiveForm.rtbFileViewer.SelRTF, vbCFRTF
    Me.ActiveForm.rtbFileViewer.SetFocus
    mnuEdit_Paste.Enabled = True
End Sub
```

The *mnuEdit_Copy_Click* event's program code will first clear the Clipboard of other items. The next command will set the Clipboard's text equal to the user's currently selected text within the document. After placing the text into the *Clipboard* object, the program code sets the focus back to the current child form so that the user's selection remains present and highlighted. Finally, the program code will enable the Paste option so that the user can later paste the text from the Clipboard back into the document.

Writing the *mnuEdit_Paste_Click* Event

As you have learned, after cutting or copying text from a document, the user can paste that text elsewhere within the document. To paste text, the user must select the Edit menu Paste option. The following code implements the *mnuEdit_Paste_Click* event:

```
Public Sub mnuEdit_Paste_Click()
  If CheckClipboard Then
    DoEvents
    Me.ActiveForm.rtbFileViewer.SetFocus
    DoEvents
    Me.ActiveForm.rtbFileViewer.SelRTF = Clipboard.GetText(vbCFRTF)
    Me.ActiveForm.rtbFileViewer.SetFocus
  Else
    MsgBox "Can't paste non-text objects."
  End If
End Sub
```

The *mnuEdit_Paste_Click* event's program code first calls the *CheckClipboard* function. The *CheckClipboard* function verifies that the Clipboard contains a valid text object. If the Clipboard contains text, the program code will use the *Clipboard* object's *GetText* method to retrieve the text from the Clipboard and place it at the user-selected location in the document. If the user selects a body of text, the pasted text will replace that text. If the user selects a single location, the program will insert the pasted text into the document from that location forward. If the *Clipboard* object does not contain text, the program code will display a message box to let the user know that the program does not paste non-textual objects.

Writing the *mnuEdit_Find_Click* Event

The last option that the user can select from within the Edit menu is the Find option. The user can use the Find option to open the Find dialog box and search the text within a child form. The following code implements the *mnuEdit_Find_Click* event:

```
Private Sub mnuEdit_Find_Click()
    frmFind.Show
    frmFind.ZOrder 0
End Sub
```

Setting the *frmFind* form's *ZOrder* property to 0 ensures that the form will remain on top of the display, even after a successful find operation. If you do not set the *ZOrder* property, the program will hide the *frmFind* form after each find operation.

WRITING THE MNUTEXT_BOLD_CLICK EVENT

As you learned in this chapter's "Using the *prjFileViewer* Project" section, users can use the menus that you created within the *frmMDIParent* form to format text within a *frmChildRTB* form. One of the most common formatting activities users will perform is to make the text they select bold. To make text bold, the user will select the Format Text menu Bold option, which will invoke the *mnuText_Bold_Click* event. The following code implements the *mnuText_Bold_Click* event:

```
Private Sub mnuText_Bold_Click()
  mnuText_Bold.Checked = Not mnuText_Bold.Checked
  Me.ActiveForm.rtbFileViewer.SelBold = mnuText_Bold.Checked
  Me.ActiveForm.SetFileFlag True
  Me.ActiveForm.rtbFileViewer.SetFocus
End Sub
```

The *mnuText_Bold_Click* event will use the *Checked* property of the *mnuText_Bold* menu item to set the text to bold. If the user selects the Bold option and the user has not marked the option with a check, the program will place a check next to the option and set the text to bold. If the user has already marked the option with a check, the program will remove the check and remove the bold from the user-selected text.

The program will then use the *SetFileFlag* method that the *frmChildRTB* form exposes (which you will learn about later in this chapter) to set a flag within that form. Setting the flag will tell the program to prompt the user to save changes before exiting the form. The code then sets the focus back to the *frmChildRTB* form so that the user's cursor remains in its original location.

WRITING THE MNUTEXT_ITALIC_CLICK EVENT

In the previous section, you learned that the user can select the Format Text menu Bold option to set a text selection to bold. In a similar way, the user can select the Format Text menu Italic option to set a text selection to italic. The following code implements the *mnuText_Italic_Click* event:

```
Private Sub mnuText_Italic_Click()
  mnuText_Italic.Checked = Not mnuText_Italic.Checked
  Me.ActiveForm.rtbFileViewer.SelItalic = mnuText_Italic.Checked
  Me.ActiveForm.rtbFileViewer.SetFileFlag = True
  Me.ActiveForm.rtbFileViewer.SetFocus
End Sub
```

Much as the *mnuText_Bold_Click* event does, the *mnuText_Italic_Click* event uses the *Checked* property of the *mnuText_Italic* menu item to determine whether it should add italics to or remove italics from the current text selection. The event will also set the file's flag to *True* and return the focus to the child form.

WRITING THE MNUTEXT_UNDERLINE_CLICK EVENT

As you have learned, the FormatText menu lets the user format text within a child form. Just as the user formats a selection to bold or italic, the user can select the Format Text menu Underline option to format a text selection to underlined. The following code implements the *mnuText_Underline_Click* event:

```
Private Sub mnuText_Underline_Click()
  mnuText_Underline.Checked = Not mnuText_Underline.Checked
  Me.ActiveForm.rtbFileViewer.SelUnderline = mnuText_Underline.Checked
  Me.ActiveForm.SetFileFlag True
  Me.ActiveForm.rtbFileViewer.SetFocus
End Sub
```

As with the events in the two previous sections, the *mnuText_Underline_Click* event uses the *Checked* property of the *mnuText_Underline* menu item to determine whether it should add underlining to or remove underlining from the current text selection. The event will also set the file's flag to *True* and return the focus to the child form.

Writing the mnuText_Strikethru_Click Event

The last of the standard text formatting options on the Format Text menu is the Strikethru option. As with the other formatting options, the user can select the Format Text menu Strikethru option to strike through a text selection. The following code implements the *mnuText_Strikethru_Click* event:

```
Private Sub mnuText_Strikethru_Click()
  mnuText_Strikethru.Checked = Not mnuText_Strikethru.Checked
  Me.ActiveForm.rtbFileViewer.SelStrikeThru = mnuText_Strikethru.Checked
  Me.ActiveForm.SetFileFlag True
  Me.ActiveForm.rtbFileViewer.SetFocus
End Sub
```

As with the previous three events, the *mnuText_Strikethru_Click* event uses the *Checked* property of the *mnuText_Strikethru* menu item to determine whether it should strike through or remove the strike through from the current text selection. The event will also set the file's flag to *True* and return the focus to the child form.

Writing the mnuText_Font_Click Event

As you have learned, the user can perform simple formatting operations on text within a child form with the options on the Format Text menu. However, the user can also use the Format Text menu to change the text's font and size. To perform such operations on the text within a child form, the user can select the Format Text menu Font option. The following code implements the *mnuText_Font_Click* event:

```
Private Sub mnuText_Font_Click()
  cdgParent.Flags = cdlCFBoth + cdlCFEffects
  On Error GoTo WrapUp
  cdgParent.ShowFont
  With Me.ActiveForm.rtbFileViewer
    .SelFontName = cdgParent.FontName
    .SelFontSize = cdgParent.FontSize
    .SelBold = cdgParent.FontBold
    .SelItalic = cdgParent.FontItalic
    .SelStrikeThru = cdgParent.FontStrikethru
    .SelUnderline = cdgParent.FontUnderline
  End With
  Me.ActiveForm.SetFileFlag True
  Exit Sub

WrapUp:
    MsgBox ("No Fonts!")
    Exit Sub
End Sub
```

The code within the event uses the *CommonDialog* control's *ShowFont* method to display the Fonts dialog box. After the user finishes with the Fonts dialog box, the program code sets each value within the menu to the values the user selects within the dialog box—which will change the selected text's formatting to match. As usual, the event finishes its processing by calling the *SetFileFlag* procedure.

Writing the mnuText_Color_Click Event

In addition to the other properties that the user can set for text within a document, the user can also set the text's color. To set the text's color, the user can select the Format Text menu Color option. The following code implements the *mnuText_Color_Click* event:

```
Private Sub mnuText_Color_Click()
  cdgParent.Flags = cdlCCPreventFullOpen
  On Error Resume Next
  cdgParent.ShowColor
  If Err.Number <> 0 Then Exit Sub
```

```
      Me.ActiveForm.rtbFileViewer.SelColor = cdgParent.Color
      Me.ActiveForm.SetFileFlag True
   End Sub
```

The event's program code will use the *cdgParent* common dialog control to display the Color dialog box. The user can then select any color from the dialog box's color palette, or create his or her own custom color. After the user selects a color within the Color dialog box, the program code will set the user-selected text within the document to the color the user selects.

WRITING THE CODE FOR THE IMAGE ROTATION EVENTS

In the previous sections, you have written code to handle many of the formatting and editing needs that a user will have when working with text documents. However, as the "Using the *prjFileViewer* Project" section of this chapter details, the *prjFileViewer* program will also let the user perform actions on TIF images the user displays within the *frmChildImageEdit* form. The *prjFileViewer* program supports three image rotation events: *Flip*, *Rotate Left*, and *Rotate Right*. The following code implements the menu events that the user can use to rotate a displayed image:

```
   Private Sub mnuFlip_Click()
      Me.ActiveForm.iecFileViewer.Flip
   End Sub

   Private Sub mnuRotateLeft_Click()
      Me.ActiveForm.iecFileViewer.RotateLeft
   End Sub

   Private Sub mnuRotateRight_Click()
      Me.ActiveForm.iecFileViewer.RotateRight
   End Sub
```

As you can see, each event calls its corresponding *ImageEdit* control method to rotate or flip the image within the control.

WRITING THE IMAGE ZOOM EVENTS

As the previous section details, the user can rotate images the user loads into the *prjFileViewer* program in any direction. The user can also zoom in and zoom out of an image with methods the *ImageEdit* control provides. The following code implements the *mnuZoom100_Click* event, which resets the image's size to its original base size:

```
   Private Sub mnuZoom100_Click()
      Me.ActiveForm.iecFileViewer.Zoom = 100
      Me.ActiveForm.iecFileViewer.Refresh
      mnuZoomDown.Enabled = True
      mnuZoom100.Enabled = False
      mnuZoomUp.Enabled = True
   End Sub
```

The *mnuZoom100_Click* event uses the *ImageEdit* control's *Zoom* property to change the image's size. After setting the zoom level, the event code enables the other two zoom events, *mnuZoomDown* and *mnuZoomUp,* and disables itself. The following code implements the *mnuZoomDown* and *mnuZoomUp* zoom events:

```
   Private Sub mnuZoomDown_Click()
      Me.ActiveForm.iecFileViewer.Zoom = 50
      Me.ActiveForm.iecFileViewer.Refresh
      mnuZoomDown.Enabled = False
      mnuZoom100.Enabled = True
      mnuZoomUp.Enabled = True
   End Sub

   Private Sub mnuZoomUp_Click()
      Me.ActiveForm.iecFileViewer.Zoom = 150
      Me.ActiveForm.iecFileViewer.Refresh
      mnuZoomDown.Enabled = True
```

```
    mnuZoom100.Enabled = True
    mnuZoomUp.Enabled = False
End Sub
```

Much as the *mnuZoom100_Click* event did, both the *mnuZoomDown* and the *mnuZoomUp* events set the file's *Zoom* property. Each event also disables itself and enables the other two Zoom events after the event performs its zoom action.

WRITING THE OTHER IMAGES MENU EVENTS

As you have learned, the *prjFileViewer* program lets the user rotate images and zoom in and out of images. The Images menu also contains two additional options, one to clear the image from the display and the other to display the Annotation Palette. The following code implements the *mnuClearImage_Click* event:

```
Private Sub mnuClearImage_Click()
    Me.ActiveForm.iecFileViewer.ClearDisplay
End Sub
```

As you can see, the event uses the *ImageEdit* control's *ClearDisplay* method to clear the image from the display. Similarly, the *mnuShowPalette_Click* event, shown in the following code fragment, displays the Annotation Palette for the user:

```
Private Sub mnuShowPalette_Click()
    Me.ActiveForm.iecFileViewer.ShowAnnotationToolPalette (True)
End Sub
```

The *ImageEdit* control handles all the processing for the Annotation Palette internally—all the *prjFileViewer* program must do is display the palette so that the user can access the annotation commands.

WRITING THE WINDOW MENU EVENTS

When you designed the Window menu earlier in this chapter, in the "Adding the Menus to the *frmMDIParent* Form" section, you set the Window menu's *Windowlist* property to *True*—which means that the Window menu will always display a list of open child windows within the *prjFileViewer* program. You also added a Cascade and a Tile option to the menu. Both the Cascade and Tile options let the user organize the display of child windows within the *frmMDIParent* window. The Cascade option arranges windows from the top left corner of the *frmMDIParent* window to the bottom right corner. The following code implements the *mnuWindow_Cascade_Click* event:

```
Private Sub mnuWindow_Cascade_Click()
    Me.Arrange vbCascade
End Sub
```

The event uses the *MDIForm* object's *Arrange* method to arrange the windows. The *vbCascade* constant is a Visual Basic-defined constant. Similarly, the Tile option arranges windows (which look like floor tiles), within the parent window. The program determines the tiles' size by the number of open child windows. The following code implements the *mnuWindow_Tile_Click* event:

```
Private Sub mnuWindow_Tile_Click()
    Me.Arrange vbTileVertical
End Sub
```

WRITING THE FRMCHILDIMAGEEDIT FORM'S PROGRAM CODE

As you have learned, most of the program code within the *prjFileViewer* program is within the *frmMDIParent* form. However, each child form in the project performs its own specific processing. All the child forms include within the General–Declarations section the following variable declaration:

```
Dim ThisIsOccurrenceNumber As Integer
```

When the program loads the form, it will set that form's *ThisIsOccurenceNumber* variable equal to the value of the *gCurrentInstance* global variable at the time of the form's creation. When the user performs an activity, such as saving the file, the program will use the *ThisIsOccurenceNumber* value to determine what file name to use to save the form's contents.

WRITING THE *FORM_LOAD* AND *FORM_ACTIVATE* EVENTS' PROGRAM CODE

As you learned earlier in this chapter, when the user loads a new image file into the program, the *LoadImageFile* procedure will load the form, place the file within the form's *ImageEdit* control, and display the form. When the program loads a new *frmChildImageEdit* form, the event will initialize the *ThisIsOccurenceNumber* variable to the *gCurrentInstance* variable's value. The following code implements the *Form_Load* event:

```
Private Sub Form_Load()
   ThisIsOccurrenceNumber = gCurrentInstance
End Sub
```

When the user activates (selects) the form, the program code within the *Form_Activate* event will perform processing to enable menus, change the *StatusBar* control, and update the *gCurrentInstance* pointer. The following code implements the *Form_Activate* event:

```
Private Sub Form_Activate()
   gCurrentInstance = ThisIsOccurrenceNumber
   ChangePanelStatus 1, Me.Caption
   TurnOnMenus False
   frmMDIParent.mnuImages.Enabled = True
   frmMDIParent.mnuFile_Save.Enabled = True
   frmMDIParent.mnuFile_SaveAs.Enabled = True
   frmMDIParent.mnuFile_Print.Enabled = False
   frmMDIParent.mnuFile_ExitDoc.Enabled = True
End Sub
```

As you can see, the first step the *Activate* event's program code performs is to set the *gCurrentInstance* global variable equal to the *frmChildImageEdit* form's instance. Next, the program code calls the *ChangePanelStatus* procedure to change the text within the *StatusBar* control. The *Activate* event then disables some menus, and enables the Image menu and Save, Save As, and Exit Document options within the File menu.

WRITING THE *FORM_DEACTIVATE* AND *FORM_UNLOAD* EVENTS' PROGRAM CODE

As you have learned, the program code within the form's *Activate* event will change menus, the status bar, and the *gCurrentInstance* variable. Similarly, both the *Form_Deactivate* and *Form_Unload* events will undo the changes the *Activate* event made to the parent form. The following code implements the *Form_Deactivate* event:

```
Private Sub Form_Deactivate()
   TurnOnMenus False
   frmMDIParent.mnuImages.Enabled = False
   frmMDIParent.mnuFile_Save.Enabled = False
   frmMDIParent.mnuFile_SaveAs.Enabled = False
   frmMDIParent.mnuFile_Print.Enabled = False
   frmMDIParent.mnuFile_ExitDoc.Enabled = False
   ChangePanelStatus 1, ""
End Sub
```

When the user exits the current form, the *Form_Deactivate* event's program code will disable all the menus that it enabled within the *Activate* event. In turn, the *Activate* event for the other form the user selects will enable the correct menus for its processing.

When you unload the *frmChildImageEdit* form, the *Form_Unload* event's program code performs processing identical to the *Form_Deactivate* event. There is a separate copy of the program code within the *Unload* event because it is possible to unload a form without activating the form (that is, giving the form the focus). The following code implements the *Form_Unload* event:

```
Private Sub Form_Unload(Cancel As Integer)
  TurnOnMenus False
  frmMDIParent.mnuImages.Enabled = False
  frmMDIParent.mnuFile_Save.Enabled = False
  frmMDIParent.mnuFile_SaveAs.Enabled = False
  frmMDIParent.mnuFile_Print.Enabled = False
  frmMDIParent.mnuFile_ExitDoc.Enabled = False
  ChangePanelStatus 1, ""
End Sub
```

The *Form_Unload* event performs no error checking before it unloads the form because the *QueryUnload* event handles that processing. You will learn about the *QueryUnload* event in the next section.

WRITING THE QUERYUNLOAD EVENT'S PROGRAM CODE

As you have learned in previous sections, the *frmChildImageEdit* form will check to determine whether a user has changed the image the program loads within its *ImageEdit* control before it unloads the form. The following code implements the *QueryUnload* event:

```
Private Sub Form_QueryUnload(Cancel As Integer, UnloadMode As Integer)
  If iecFileViewer.ImageModified Then
    If MsgBox("You have changed this image. Exit without saving anyway?", _
      vbYesNo) = vbNo Then _
        Cancel = True
  End If
End Sub
```

The *QueryUnload* event's program code checks the *iecFileViewer* control's *ImageModified* property to determine whether the user changed the image. If the user did change the image, the program code will display a message box to alert the user that unloading the form will close the file without saving the user's changes. The program code will display a dialog box to ask if the user wants to save or lose the changes. If the user wants to save the changes, the program will exit the event without unloading the form. If the user does not want to save the changes, the event will finish executing and call the *Form_Unload* event.

WRITING THE *FRMCHILDRTB* FORM'S PROGRAM CODE

As you learned in the "Writing the *frmChildImageEdit* Form's Program Code" section of this chapter, every child form within the *prjFileViewer* program includes its own instance of the *ThisIsOccurenceNumber* variable. In addition, the *frmChildRTB* form contains two *Boolean* variables, *FileChanged* and *Resizing*. The following code implements the variable declarations within the General–Declarations section for the *frmChildRTB* form:

```
Dim ThisIsOccurrenceNumber As Integer
Dim FileChanged As Boolean, Resizing As Boolean
```

The *frmChildRTB* form will use the *FileChanged* variable to maintain information about whether the user has changed the currently loaded file or not. The program code within the form will use the *Resizing* variable within the form's *Resize* event to keep the program from encountering errors during the form's loading process.

WRITING THE FORM_LOAD AND FORM_ACTIVATE EVENTS' PROGRAM CODE

Unlike the *frmChildImageEdit* form (which performs all initialization within the *Form_Activate* event), the *frmChildRTB* form performs initialization within the *Form_Load* event. Most of the initialization within the *Form_Load* event focuses on placing the form within the parent form and making sure the control has room to display a scroll bar on the form's bottom. The following code implements the *Form_Load* event:

```
Private Sub Form_Load()
  ThisIsOccurrenceNumber = gCurrentInstance
  Me.Top = ((ThisIsOccurrenceNumber - 1) Mod 10) * 300
  Me.Left = 0
```

133

```
    Me.Height = frmMDIParent.Height - 1250 - _
        (((ThisIsOccurrenceNumber - 1) Mod 10) * 300)
    Me.Width = frmMDIParent.Width - Me.Left - 650
    SetTextMenus False
    If rtbFileViewer.RightMargin > rtbFileViewer.Width Then _
        rtbFileViewer.Height = rtbFileViewer.Height - 200
    SetFileFlag False
End Sub
```

The *Form_Load* event begins its processing by setting the *ThisIsOccurenceNumber* variable equal to the *gCurrentInstance* variable. Next, the event places the form at the parent's inside left edge, and sets the form's height at just below the height of the previously opened form. Finally, the program code within the event checks the right margin for the *rtbFileViewer* control. If the right margin is greater than the form's width, the program code will shorten the *rtbFileViewer* control enough to display the horizontal scroll bar at the control's bottom.

Within the *Form_Activate* event, the program code will change the enabled menus and set the *StatusBar* control to show the file name for the file the form contains. The following code implements the *Form_Activate* event:

```
Private Sub Form_Activate()
    gCurrentInstance = ThisIsOccurrenceNumber
    ChangePanelStatus 1, Me.Caption
    TurnOnMenus True
    frmMDIParent.mnuImages.Enabled = False
    frmMDIParent.mnuFile_Save.Enabled = True
    frmMDIParent.mnuFile_SaveAs.Enabled = True
    frmMDIParent.mnuFile_Print.Enabled = True
    frmMDIParent.mnuFile_ExitDoc.Enabled = True
    SetTextMenus False
End Sub
```

As you can see, the *Form_Activate* event activates menus, just as the *frmChildImageEdit* form did. However, the event also calls the *SetTextMenus* procedure, which you will learn about later in this chapter. The *SetTextMenus* procedure enables and disables individual items within the Edit and Format Text menus, depending on the value it receives and whether the user has currently selected text within the form.

WRITING THE FORM_DEACTIVATE AND FORM_UNLOAD EVENTS' PROGRAM CODE

As you have learned, the program code within the form's *Activate* event will change menus, the status bar, and the *gCurrentInstance* variable. Similarly, both the *Form_Deactivate* and *Form_Unload* event will undo the changes the *Activate* event made to the parent form's menu items. The following code implements the *Form_Deactivate* event:

```
Private Sub Form_Deactivate()
    TurnOnMenus False
    frmMDIParent.mnuImages.Enabled = False
    frmMDIParent.mnuFile_Save.Enabled = False
    frmMDIParent.mnuFile_SaveAs.Enabled = False
    frmMDIParent.mnuFile_Print.Enabled = False
End Sub
```

When the user exits the current form, the program code will disable all the menus that it enabled within the *Activate* event. In turn, the *Activate* event for the other form the user selects will enable the correct menus the form must use for its processing. When you unload the *frmChildRTB* form, the program code performs identical processing to that of the *Deactivate* event. The program code is separate within the *Unload* event because it is possible to unload a form without activating the form (that is, giving the form the focus). The following code implements the *Form_Unload* event:

```
Private Sub Form_Unload(Cancel As Integer)
    TurnOnMenus False
    frmMDIParent.mnuImages.Enabled = False
    frmMDIParent.mnuFile_Save.Enabled = False
    frmMDIParent.mnuFile_SaveAs.Enabled = False
    frmMDIParent.mnuFile_Print.Enabled = False
```

```
      frmMDIParent.mnuFile_ExitDoc.Enabled = False
      ChangePanelStatus 1, ""
   End Sub
```

The *Form_Unload* event performs no error checking before it unloads the form because the *QueryUnload* event handles that processing. You will learn about the *QueryUnload* event in the next section.

WRITING THE FORM'S QUERYUNLOAD EVENT

As you have learned in previous sections, the *frmChildRTB* form will check to determine whether a user has changed the text the program previously loaded into the form's *RichTextBox* control before the program will unload the form. The following code implements the *QueryUnload* event:

```
Private Sub Form_QueryUnload(Cancel As Integer, UnloadMode As Integer)
   If FileChanged Then
      If MsgBox("You have changed this file. Are you sure you want to exit?", _
          vbYesNo) = vbNo Then _
         Cancel = True
   End If
End Sub
```

The *QueryUnload* event will first check the *FileChanged* variable's value. If it is *True*, which indicates that the user has changed the file, the program will display a message box to alert the user that unloading the form will close the file without saving the user's changes. If the user wants to save the changes, the program will exit the event without unloading the form. If the user does not want to save the changes, the event finishes its execution and calls the *Form_Unload* event.

WRITING THE CODE FOR THE FORM_RESIZE EVENT

The *frmChildRTB* form contains code within the *Form_Resize* event so that the user can change the *frmChildRTB* form's size. When the user does so, the form must change the size of the *RichTextBox* control within the form. The following code implements the *Form_Resize* event:

```
Private Sub Form_Resize()
   Resizing = True
   If Me.WindowState = vbMinimized Then Exit Sub
   Dim tmpHeight As Integer, tmpWidth As Integer

   If Me.WindowState = vbMaximized Then
     tmpHeight = frmMDIParent.Height - 700
     tmpWidth = frmMDIParent.Width - 250
   Else
     If Me.Width < 1100 Then Me.Width = 1100
     If Me.Height < 1000 Then Me.Height = 1000
     If Me.Width > frmMDIParent.Width Then _
         Me.Width = frmMDIParent.Width - 250
     If frmMDIParent.Height > 750 And _
         frmMDIParent.Height < 7000 Then _
             If Me.Height > (frmMDIParent.Height - 750) Then _
                 Me.Width = frmMDIParent.Height - 750
     tmpHeight = Me.Height - rtbFileViewer.Top - 500
     tmpWidth = Me.Width - 250
   End If
   rtbFileViewer.Top = 100
   rtbFileViewer.Left = 100
   rtbFileViewer.Width = tmpWidth
   rtbFileViewer.Height = tmpHeight
   Resizing = False
End Sub
```

The *Resize* event will first set the *Resizing* variable to *True* to protect against multiple, simultaneous invocations of the event. Next, the program code will check to see if the form is resizing because the user minimized the form. If so, the program code will exit the event and not perform additional processing. If the user has not minimized the *frmChildRTB* form, the user has either maximized the *frmChildRTB* form or manually resized the *frmChildRTB* form. If the user has maximized the form, the program code will set the height and width for the control to the size of the *frmMDIParent* form's approximate inner window. If the user has manually resized the *frmChildRTB* form, the program code will set the height and width for the control to just less than the actual height and width to which the user resized the *frmChildRTB* form. The program code also uses a series of *If-Then* statements to ensure the user has not sized the form below a certain level, because the control will become unsizable if the user does. Finally, the program code sets the internal *rtbFileViewer* control's size equal to slightly less than the *frmChildRTB* form's size.

WRITING THE CODE FOR THE SETTEXTMENUS PROCEDURE

As you have learned, when you load the *frmChildRTB* form, the program code within the *Form_Load* event will call the *SetTextMenus* procedure (to turn on and off the text formatting and editing menus). Other program code within the *frmChildRTB* form will also call the *SetTextMenus* procedure when the user performs actions within the document. The following code implements the *SetTextMenus* procedure:

136

```
Private Sub SetTextMenus(ByVal OnOff As Boolean)
   With frmMDIParent
      .mnuText_Font.Enabled = OnOff
      .mnuText_Bold.Enabled = OnOff
      .mnuText_Italic.Enabled = OnOff
      .mnuText_Underline.Enabled = OnOff
      .mnuText_Strikethru.Enabled = OnOff
      .mnuText_Color.Enabled = OnOff
      .mnuEdit_Cut.Enabled = OnOff
      .mnuEdit_Copy.Enabled = OnOff
      .mnuEdit_Paste.Enabled = CheckClipboard
   End With
   If OnOff Then
      If Not IsNull(rtbFileViewer.SelBold) Then
        frmMDIParent.mnuText_Bold.Checked = rtbFileViewer.SelBold
      Else
        frmMDIParent.mnuText_Bold.Checked = False
      End If
      If Not IsNull(rtbFileViewer.SelItalic) Then
        frmMDIParent.mnuText_Italic.Checked = rtbFileViewer.SelItalic
      Else
        frmMDIParent.mnuText_Italic.Checked = False
      End If
      If Not IsNull(rtbFileViewer.SelUnderline) Then
        frmMDIParent.mnuText_Underline.Checked = rtbFileViewer.SelUnderline
      Else
        frmMDIParent.mnuText_Underline.Checked = False
      End If
      If Not IsNull(rtbFileViewer.SelStrikeThru) Then
        frmMDIParent.mnuText_Strikethru.Checked = _
            rtbFileViewer.SelStrikeThru
      Else
        frmMDIParent.mnuText_Strikethru.Checked = False
      End If
   Else
      With frmMDIParent
         .mnuText_Bold.Checked = False
         .mnuText_Italic.Checked = False
         .mnuText_Underline.Checked = False
         .mnuText_Strikethru.Checked = False
      End With
   End If
End Sub
```

The program code uses the *OnOff* parameter that it receives from the calling function to perform most of its processing. If the *OnOff* parameter is *False*, the program code will disable all the menu items within the Edit and Format Text menus, except the Paste option. The program code uses the *Clipboard* object to determine the Paste option's state. If the *CheckClipboard* function finds text on the Clipboard, the program code will enable the Paste option. If there is no text on the Clipboard, the program code will disable the Paste option.

On the other hand, if the *OnOff* parameter is *True*, the program will enable all the menu items. Additionally, the program code will use a series of *If-Then* statements to determine whether or not to place check marks next to the Bold, Italic, Underline, and StrikeThru options. The *If-Then* statements use the Visual Basic *IsNull* function together with the *RichTextBox* control's *SelBold*, *SelItalic*, *SelUnderline*, and *SetlStrikeThru* properties to determine whether the program should place check marks next to the menu options. For example, if the currently selected text is bold, the *Not IsNull* construct will return *True* and the program code will place a check mark next to the Bold option.

Writing the Code for the rtbFileViewer Control's Events

With the exception of the *SetFileFlag* procedure, the remainder of the program code within the *frmChildRTB* form **137** is within the events for the *rtbFileViewer* control. The *prjFileViewer* program must respond to several different actions the user may perform within the *rtbFileViewer* control, and so the program uses the *frmChildRTB* control's event to respond to those user actions. For example, if the user makes a change to a file within the *rtbFileViewer* control (inserts a space, turns on some formatting, deletes some text, and so on), the control will invoke the *rtbFileViewer_Change* event. The following code implements the *rtbFileViewer_Change* event:

```
Private Sub rtbFileViewer_Change()
   If Not Resizing And Not Loading Then SetFileFlag True
End Sub
```

The program code within the *rtbFileViewer_Change* event makes sure that the program is not resizing or loading the *frmChildRTB* form, because the control will invoke the *Change* event in either situation. If the change is valid, the program code calls the *SetFileFlag* procedure, which sets the *FileChanged* variable to *True*. The following code implements the *SetFileFlag* procedure:

```
Public Sub SetFileFlag(ByVal SetVal As Boolean)
   FileChanged = SetVal
End Sub
```

If the user clicks within the *rtbFileViewer* control, particularly while viewing another form, the program must update the menus as it does when the user activates the *frmChildRTB* form. The following code implements the *rtbFileViewer_Click* event:

```
Private Sub rtbFileViewer_Click()
   gCurrentInstance = ThisIsOccurrenceNumber
   ChangePanelStatus 1, Me.Caption
   TurnOnMenus True
   frmMDIParent.mnuImages.Enabled = False
   frmMDIParent.mnuFile_Save.Enabled = True
   frmMDIParent.mnuFile_SaveAs.Enabled = True
   frmMDIParent.mnuFile_Print.Enabled = True
End Sub
```

As you can see, the program code within the *rtbFileViewer_Click* event is identical to that within the *Form_Activate* event—it enables the menus, changes the *StatusBar* control's display, and so on. If the user presses a key within the *rtbFileViewer* control, such a keypress qualifies as a change. The program code includes a capture within the *KeyPress* event to call the *SetFileFlag* procedure, as shown here:

```
Private Sub rtbFileViewer_KeyPress(KeyAscii As Integer)
   SetFileFlag True
End Sub
```

Finally, if the user selects text within the *rtbFileViewer* control, the program must enable the text menus so that the user can cut, copy, or format the text the user selects. The following code implements the *SelChange* event:

```
Private Sub rtbFileViewer_SelChange()
   If rtbFileViewer.SelLength > 0 Then
      SetTextMenus True
   Else
      SetTextMenus False
   End If
End Sub
```

Note that the *SelChange* event makes sure the user selects some text before it enables the menus. If the user changes the selection from selected text to the input cursor (in other words, the user clicks the mouse within the text without selecting any text), the program will actually disable the text menus.

WRITING THE *frmFind* FORM'S PROGRAM CODE

As you learned when you created the forms for the *prjFileViewer* project, the *frmFind* form is the only non-MDI child form that the project will use. Therefore, the user can create only a single instance of the *frmFind* form, and it does not include a *ThisIsOccurenceNumber* variable within its declarations. Instead, the *frmFind* form includes three variables within its General–Declarations section, which you will implement as shown here:

```
Dim MatchWhole As Integer, MatchCase As Integer
Dim FoundPos As Integer
```

The two variables correspond to the values within the *chkMatchWhole* and *chkMatchCase* check box controls that you placed onto the *frmFind* form when you designed the form. The *FoundPos* variable maintains information about the current search position within a file.

WRITING THE FORM_LOAD EVENT'S PROGRAM CODE

When you load the *frmFind* form, it will perform some initialization, place itself within the *frmMDIParent* form, and check to see whether the user has a current selection in the active form. The following code implements the *Form_Load* event:

```
Private Sub Form_Load()
   txtReplace.Text = ""
   cmdReplace.Enabled = False
   Me.Left = 0
   Me.Top = 100
   Me.Height = 4305
   Me.Width = 3450
   If gTextForms(gCurrentInstance).rtbFileViewer.SelLength > 0 Then
      txtFind.Text = gTextForms(gCurrentInstance).rtbFileViewer.SelText
      cmdSearch.Enabled = True
      cmdSearch.Caption = "&Search"
   Else
      txtFind.Text = ""
      cmdSearch.Caption = "&Search"
      cmdSearch.Enabled = False
   End If
End Sub
```

The *Form_Load* event will clear the replacement text field and disable the Replace button. Next, it will place the *frmFind* form on the screen. After placing the *frmFind* form on the screen, the program code checks to see whether the user has currently selected text in a child form. If a child form contains selected text, the program code places the text within the *txtFind* text box and enables the Search button. If a child form does not contain selected text, the program code clears the text and disables the Search button. As you will learn, the *txtFind* control includes program code to enable the Search button if the user changes the value within the *txtSearch* control.

WRITING THE *chkMatchWhole* AND *chkMatchCase* CLICK EVENTS' PROGRAM CODE

As you have learned, the *frmFind* form will determine how it should perform its text searches based on what the user enters within two check boxes on the form. When the user clicks the mouse on one of the check boxes, the program will invoke the check box's *Click* event. Within the *Click* event, the program code will set the *MatchWhole* variable's value. The following code implements the *chkMatchWhole_Click* event:

```
Private Sub chkMatchWhole_Click()
  If chkMatchWhole.Value = 0 Then
    MatchWhole = 0
  Else
    MatchWhole = rtfWholeWord
  End If
End Sub
```

If the user selects the Match Whole Word option, the program code will set the *MatchWhole* variable equal to the Visual Basic *rtfWholeWord* constant, which the program code will later use when it actually searches the document. Similarly, the *chkMatchCase_Click* event will set the *MatchCase* variable equal to a Visual Basic constant when the user selects the control. The following code implements the *chkMatchCase_Click* event:

```
Private Sub chkMatchCase_Click()
  If chkMatchCase.Value = 0 Then
    MatchCase = 0
  Else
    MatchCase = rtfMatchCase
  End If
End Sub
```

139

If the user selects the Match Case option, the program code will set the *MatchCase* variable equal to the Visual Basic *rtfMatchCase* constant, which the program code will later use when it actually searches the document.

Writing the Code for the Text Box Change Events

When the user enters text within the *Search* and *Replace* fields on the *frmFind* form, the program must change the state (from enabled to disabled and back again) of the *cmdSearch* and *cmdReplace* buttons to respond. When the user enters or deletes text, the program will invoke the *TextBox* control's *Change* event. The following code implements the *txtFind_Change* event:

```
Private Sub txtFind_Change()
  cmdSearch.Caption = "&Search"
  FoundPos = 0
  If Len(Trim(txtFind.Text)) > 0 Then
    cmdSearch.Enabled = True
  Else
    cmdSearch.Enabled = False
  End If
End Sub
```

For any change to the *txtFind* control's contents, the program code changes the *cmdSearch* button's caption back to Search and resets the search point's beginning to the file's beginning. Next, the program code verifies that the *txtFind* text box control actually contains text. If the control contains text, the program code will enable the *cmdSearch* button. If it does not contain text, the program code will disable the *cmdSearch* button.

The program code within the *txtReplace_Change* event performs similar processing. The following code implements the *txtReplace_Change* event:

```
Private Sub txtReplace_Change()
  cmdReplace.Caption = "&Replace"
  If Len(Trim(txtReplace.Text)) > 0 Then
    cmdReplace.Enabled = True
  Else
    cmdReplace.Enabled = False
  End If
End Sub
```

WRITING THE CODE FOR THE CMDSEARCH_CLICK EVENT

After the user enters the text to find and selects the search options, the user will click the mouse on the *cmdSearch* button to actually search the file for the text. The following code implements the *cmdSearch_Click* event:

```
Private Sub cmdSearch_Click()
  gTextForms(gCurrentInstance).rtbFileViewer.SetFocus
  If cmdSearch.Caption <> "&Search" Then
    FoundPos = _
        gTextForms(gCurrentInstance).rtbFileViewer.Find(txtFind.Text, _
        FoundPos + Len(txtFind.Text), , MatchCase + MatchWhole)
  Else
    FoundPos = _
        gTextForms(gCurrentInstance).rtbFileViewer.Find(txtFind.Text, _
        FoundPos, , MatchCase + MatchWhole)
  End If
  If FoundPos <> -1 Then
    gTextForms(gCurrentInstance).rtbFileViewer.SelStart = FoundPos
    gTextForms(gCurrentInstance).rtbFileViewer.UpTo txtFind.Text, _
        True, False
    cmdSearch.Caption = "Find Ne&xt"
    Me.ZOrder 0
    gTextForms(gCurrentInstance).rtbFileViewer.SetFocus
  Else
    MsgBox "Word not found.", vbExclamation + vbOKOnly, "Search Warning"
    cmdSearch.Caption = "&Search"
    Unload Me
    gTextForms(gCurrentInstance).Show
    frmMDIParent.ActiveForm.rtbFileViewer.SetFocus
  End If
End Sub
```

The program code within the event will first set the focus back to the current *frmChildRTB* form. Next, the program checks the *cmdSearch* button's caption. As you will learn, after a successful search, the program code will change the *cmdSearch* button's caption to *Find Next*. When searching for the next instance of a word or phrase, the program code must perform slightly different processing than it does when it searches for the first instance. If the program is not looking for the first instance, it uses the *FoundPos* variable plus the search text's length as its starting point for the *Find* method. If the program is looking for the first instance, it uses the *Find* method, and starts the search at the file's beginning. The *Find* method will return the first character's number in a match within the *FoundPos* variable, or -1 if the program found no matches.

If the *Find* method finds a match, the program code selects the text that matches, displays it in inverse text (within the *rtbFileViewer* control), changes the *cmdSearch* button's caption to *Find Next*, and resumes the program's execution. If the *Find* method does not find a match, the program will display a message box to let the user know, and unload the *frmFind* form.

WRITING THE CODE FOR THE CMDREPLACE_CLICK EVENT

After the program successfully finds a match for the search text, the user can click the mouse on the *cmdReplace* button to replace the search text, provided the user has entered replacement text within the *txtReplace* text box. The following code implements the *cmdReplace_Click* event:

```
Private Sub cmdReplace_Click()
  If UCase(gTextForms(gCurrentInstance).rtbFileViewer.SelText) = _
      UCase(txtFind.Text) Then
    gTextForms(gCurrentInstance).rtbFileViewer.SelText = _
        Trim(txtReplace.Text)
    gTextForms(gCurrentInstance).rtbFileViewer.SetFocus
  Else
    MsgText = "Selected text does not match search text."
```

```
         MsgText = MsgText & NewLine & "Cannot do replace."
         Captn = "Replace Warning"
         MsgBox MsgText, vbExclamation + vbOKOnly, Captn
         cmdReplace.Enabled = False
      End If
   End Sub
```

The program code within the event first verifies that the selection within the *RichTextBox* matches the *Find* text. If the selection does not match the *Find* text, the program will not perform the replace action and will display a message box to the user to let the user know why. If the text matches, the program code sets the selected text equal to the text in the *txtReplace* text box.

WRITING THE CODE FOR THE CMDCANCEL_CLICK EVENT

After the user finishes searching a document, the user can click the mouse on the *cmdCancel* button to unload the *frmFind* form. The following code implements the *cmdCancel_Click* event:

```
   Private Sub cmdCancel_Click()
      Unload Me
      gTextForms(gCurrentInstance).ZOrder 0
   End Sub
```

After the event unloads the *frmFind* form, it sets the form containing the file's *ZOrder* property to 0, which will place that form on top of the other forms.

WRITING THE FRMGRAPHICTYPE FORM'S PROGRAM CODE

As you have learned, most of the program code within the *prjFileViewer* program is within the *frmMDIParent* form. However, each child form in the project does perform its own specific processing. As you have seen, all the child forms include within the General–Declarations section the following variable declaration:

```
   Dim ThisIsOccurenceNumber As Integer
```

When the program loads the *frmGraphicType* form, it will set that form's *ThisIsOccurenceNumber* variable equal to the value of the *gCurrentInstance* global variable at the time of the form's creation. When the user performs activities, such as saving the file, the program will use the *ThisIsOccurenceNumber* value to determine what file name to use to save the form's contents.

WRITING THE FORM_LOAD AND FORM_ACTIVATE EVENTS' PROGRAM CODE

As you learned earlier in this chapter, when the user loads a new image file into the program, the *LoadImageFile* procedure will load the *frmGraphicType* form, place the file within the form's *PictureBox* control, and display the form. When the program loads a new *frmGraphicType* form, the *Form_Load* event will simply initialize the *ThisIsOccurenceNumber* variable to the *gCurrentInstance* variable's value. The following code implements the *Form_Load* event:

```
   Private Sub Form_Load()
      ThisIsOccurenceNumber = gCurrentInstance
   End Sub
```

When the user activates (selects) the *frmGraphicType* form, the program code within the *Form_Activate* event will will change the enabled menus and set the *StatusBar* control to show the file name for the file the form contains. The following code implements the *Form_Activate* event:

```
   Private Sub Form_Activate()
      gCurrentInstance = ThisIsOccurenceNumber
      ChangePanelStatus 1, Me.Caption
      TurnOnMenus False
      frmMDIParent.mnuImages.Enabled = False
      frmMDIParent.mnuFile_Save.Enabled = False
      frmMDIParent.mnuFile_SaveAs.Enabled = False
```

```
      frmMDIParent.mnuFile_Print.Enabled = False
      frmMDIParent.mnuFile_ExitDoc.Enabled = True
   End Sub
```

As you can see, the first step the program code performs is to set the *gCurrentInstance* global variable equal to this *frmGraphicType* form's instance. Next, the program code calls the *ChangePanelStatus* procedure to change the text within the *StatusBar* control. The *Activate* event then disables some menus, and enables the Image menu and the Save, Save As, and Exit Document options within the File menu.

Writing the Form_Deactivate and Form_Unload Events' Program Code

As you have learned, the program code within the form's *Activate* event will change menus, the status bar, and the *gCurrentInstance* variable. Similarly, both the *Form_Deactivate* and *Form_Unload* event will undo the changes the *Activate* event made to the parent form's menus. The following code implements the *Form_Deactivate* event:

142

```
   Private Sub Form_Deactivate()
      TurnOnMenus True
      frmMDIParent.mnuImages.Enabled = False
      frmMDIParent.mnuFile_Save.Enabled = False
      frmMDIParent.mnuFile_SaveAs.Enabled = False
      frmMDIParent.mnuFile_Print.Enabled = False
      frmMDIParent.mnuFile_ExitDoc.Enabled = False
   End Sub
```

When the user exits the current form, the program code will disable all the menus that it enabled within the *Activate* event. In turn, the *Activate* event for the other form the user selects will enable the correct menus the form must use for its processing.

When you unload the *frmGraphicType* form, the program code performs identical processing to that of the *frmGraphicType* form's *Deactivate* event. The program code is separate within the *Unload* event because it is possible to unload a form without activating the form (that is, giving the form the focus). The following code implements the *Form_Unload* event:

```
   Private Sub Form_Unload(Cancel As Integer)
      TurnOnMenus False
      frmMDIParent.mnuImages.Enabled = False
      frmMDIParent.mnuFile_Save.Enabled = False
      frmMDIParent.mnuFile_SaveAs.Enabled = False
      frmMDIParent.mnuFile_Print.Enabled = False
      frmMDIParent.mnuFile_ExitDoc.Enabled = False
   End Sub
```

The *Form_Unload* event performs no error checking before it unloads the form because the user cannot make changes to images that the program displays within a *frmGraphicType* form.

Enhancements You Can Make to the prjFileViewer Project

The *prjFileViewer* project provides you with many different choices for making your own enhancements. For example, you can modify the pasting routine within the program code to let users place bitmaps and other graphic files into their Rich Text documents.

You can also add support for more drawing and figure manipulation activities, scanning support (so that users can scan images directly into the *Image Edit* control and save them to a file), and more. In later chapters, you will learn how to use databases to maintain important information (such as information about documents you scan into the computer). You could then use the *Image Edit* control together with a custom database to maintain information about documents that the user scans into the program.

Putting It All Together

This chapter's project, *prjFileViewer*, introduced you to how to manage Multiple-Document Interfaces, create menus, and handle different file types within the program's code. You also learned how to use the *Microsoft StatusBar* control, the *Microsoft RichTextBox* control, the *Eastman Software Imaging* control suite, and the *Microsoft Common Dialog* control. You worked again within *PictureBox* controls and other simple Visual Basic controls, such as text boxes, labels, and buttons, to design programs that are easy for the user to manipulate.

Many of the principles you used during the design of the *prjFileViewer* program are principles you will use in later chapters when you develop other programs. In Chapter 5, "Creating and Using Fractals," you will use Visual Basic's *Line* and *Circle* methods, together with a class module and several program-defined types, to create complex graphical images that you will base on mathematical equations. Before you continue with Chapter 5, however, make sure you understand the following key concepts:

✓ Within Visual Basic, you will use an MDI parent form as a container for the program's other forms when you create Multiple-Document Interface programs.

✓ To create child forms that your programs can display within an MDI parent form, you must specify that the forms are MDI child forms.

✓ When your programs display forms within an MDI application that are not truly child windows, and that must always remain on top (or that you otherwise use to perform specific processing, such as a Find dialog box), you must specify that the form is not an MDI child form and manipulate it differently than child forms.

✓ When you work with MDI-style programs, you will often use a form array to maintain information about the currently opened child windows within the program. Form arrays let your programs use a unique numeric identifier (an index) to refer to each form within a set of forms and create copies of the base form within the array at run time.

✓ Within your Visual Basic programs, you will often use the *Microsoft RichTextBox* control when you must display and store large amounts of text (up to about 2Mb) or when the program lets the user format text the program displays.

✓ The *Microsoft RichTextBox* control lets you format text, save the text as Rich Text-format files, and later recover the formats when you reload the file. You can save both text files and Rich Text files from the control.

✓ To display images without providing the user with edit capabilities within your Visual Basic programs, you can use the *Microsoft PictureBox* control.

✓ To open and display image files, and to let the user edit the images you display, you can use the *Eastman Software Imaging* controls, which come with Windows 95 and Windows NT 4.0, within your Visual Basic programs. You can also download the controls.

✓ The *Eastman Software Imaging* controls include the *Image Edit* control, which you can use to display, annotate, manipulate, and manage image files.

✓ The *Image Edit* control includes the *Annotation Palette* tool, which you will use to apply annotation to an image file. Annotations may include graphics, text, notes, and more.

143

Chapter 5

Creating and Using Fractals

Many programmers and computer users find complex computer graphics exciting and intriguing because they recognize that such complex images are actually reflections of underlying complex equations. While end users may find computer graphics interesting, graphic images often fascinate programmers because they appreciate the complex programming that creates the image. Within the graphics programming field, fractal images, such as Figure 5.1 shows, combine sophisticated mathematical equations with equally sophisticated programming.

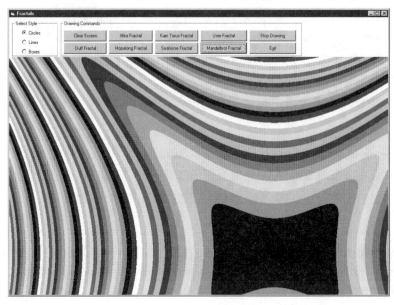

Figure 5.1 *Complex fractal graphic image.*

In this chapter, you will create the *prjFractal.exe* program, that draws colorful images from mathematical equations, which can be simple or complex. The images you will see in this chapter will be abstract images. Abstract images are images that are similar to scenes in nature, but that only approximate those scenes, rather than replicate them. On the other hand, a realistic image is a recognizable image (such as a photograph) that you can clearly associate with a scene in nature. The fractal images you will create in this chapter use abstract objects to create images the user can visualize as a "real" object.

No matter what the style, most fractal images consist of small circles or lines. Similarly, a painting will generally consist of many small, short lines (which the artist generally creates with brush strokes). This chapter introduces the Visual Basic *Line* and *Circle* methods, which your program will use to draw lines, boxes, and circles on your computer screen. In this chapter, you will use the *Line* and *Circle* methods to draw tiny colored circles, lines, or boxes, at a series of points on the screen that an equation within the program describes. While each circle, line, or box in an image may not be recognizable as part of the larger whole, when you see all the component shapes together within the complete image, rather than as distinct circles and lines, you will see the *fractal* image—an image that you compose from many smaller, component images, which appears as the larger image when you consider it as a whole.

In the *prjFractal* project, you will calculate values from a math equation, store the values in a *structure* (a structure can hold multiple values), and draw fractal images consisting of many lines and circles. Within a math equation, the values will change as you alter the input. For example, in the sample equation $Y=X^2$, when X equals 2, Y equals 4; similarly, when X equals 10, Y equals 100. To draw an image from a math equation, you will calculate many X and Y values, and then draw a circle or line on the computer screen where each X and Y value is located.

In the *prjFractal* project, you will store the *X* and *Y* coordinate values, together with other values that describe each component object (circle, line, or box) that the program will draw, such as color, radius, and density, within a *structure*. Within the structure, you will store the *X* and *Y* value results from a complex math equation. Each time the equation returns a different result, you will use a Visual Basic *Circle* or *Line* method to draw fractal images using the structure's coordinate values. This chapter examines in detail the Visual Basic structure, the *Circle* and the *Line* methods, and the *CommandButton*, *TextBox*, *Label*, and *OptionButton* controls—which you will use to store values and draw fractal images. By the time you finish this chapter, you will understand the following key concepts:

- ◆ Visual Basic includes the *Circle* method, which you will use to draw circles. Within the *prjFractal* project, your drawings may include many circles.

- ◆ Visual Basic includes the *Line* method, which you will use to draw lines and boxes. Within the *prjFractal* project, your drawings may include many lines or boxes, depending on your drawing style selection.

- ◆ Within your Visual Basic projects, you can use the *Circle* method to draw circles on objects that support the method, such as forms, user controls, and picture boxes.

- ◆ Within your Visual Basic projects, you can use the *Line* method to draw lines and boxes on objects that support the method, such as forms, user controls, and picture boxes.

- ◆ Within the *prjFractal* project, you will use the *Circle* and *Line* methods to draw the component pieces of fractal images.

- ◆ Visual Basic lets you define custom *structures*, which you will use to store one or more related values in a single location your programs can easily access.

- ◆ After you define a Visual Basic structure within your programs, you can declare variables of that structure's type within any procedure or function in the program.

- ◆ Visual Basic supports classes, which let you encapsulate information and protect it from other sections of a program.

- ◆ Within the *prjFractal* project, you will use a class module as a singular location in the program within which you will maintain complex mathematical information about the Mandelbrot fractal.

BETTER UNDERSTANDING THE HISTORY OF FRACTALS

Before you design the *prjFractal* project, some background information on fractals will help familiarize you with them.

Gaston Julia first recorded fractals in the early twentieth century. Julia knew he could calculate one or more values from a math equation, such as $Y=X^2$. He calculated a large number of X and Y values by hand from a complex math equation and then drew dots onto paper at the different positions representing each value. As he drew more dots, an image took shape. The images intrigued Julia and he recorded his work, now known as the *Julia Set*.

Benoit Mandelbrot discovered the Julia Set in the middle twentieth century. Mandelbrot thought of using a computer to draw the images. After Mandelbrot drew the images, he named them fractals, saying, "I coined fractal from the Latin adjective *fractus*." *Fractus* means "fragmented" and "irregular." As an example, if you broke a wine glass you would see "fragmented" and "irregular" glass pieces. Mandelbrot also recorded his work, now known as the *Mandelbrot Set*. Over time, the Mandelbrot Set has become one of the cornerstones of fractal graphics imaging.

Today, computer graphics professionals use fractals for many purposes. For example, meterologists use fractal images to model clouds, and learn more about how clouds form, what causes rain, and how two separate cloud masses will interact with each other.

USING THE prjFractal PROJECT

Before you design the *prjFractal* project, you may find it helpful to run the program. The companion CD-ROM that accompanies this book contains the *prjFractal.exe* program within the *Chapter05* directory. As with every other program on the CD-ROM, you should run the Jamsa Press *setup.exe* program to install the *prjFractal.exe* program to your computer's hard drive before you run it. After you install the *prjFractal.exe* program to your computer's hard drive, you can run it from the Start menu. To run the program, select the Windows Start menu Run option. Windows will display the Run dialog box. Within the Run dialog box, enter *x:\vbpl\Chapter05\prjFractal.exe*, where *x* corresponds to the letter of the hard drive on which you installed the *prjFractal.exe* program, and click your mouse on OK. Windows will display the *prjFractal.exe* program, as shown in Figure 5.2.

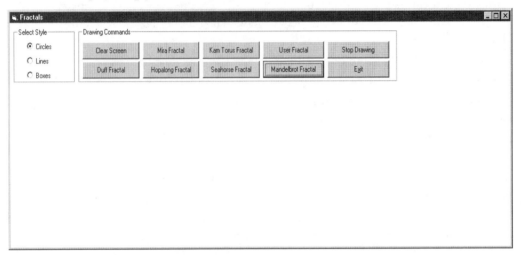

*Figure 5.2 The **prjFractal.exe** program's start-up screen.*

RUNNING prjFractal FROM THE CD-ROM

As you have learned, you must first install many programs that you will use within this book to your computer's hard drive before you try to use the programs. The *prjFractal.exe* program, however, does not use any custom controls or references, other than those that Visual Basic installs onto your system. Because the *prjFractal.exe* uses no custom controls or references, you can run the program from the CD-ROM.

To run the program from the CD-ROM, perform the following steps:

1. Select the Windows Start menu Run option. Windows will display the Run dialog box.

2. Within the Run dialog box, enter *x:\Chapter05\prjFractal.exe*, where *x* corresponds to the letter of your computer's CD-ROM drive (usually D: or E:), and click your mouse on OK. Windows will run the *prjFractal.exe* program.

Before you use the *prjFractal.exe* program, you should familiarize yourself with the controls on the *Fractals* form. You will see the *Select Style* frame on the form's left, which contains three option buttons (Circles, Lines, and Boxes) that you will use to select a shape when the program draws the fractal. You will also see ten buttons on the form. When you click your mouse on the Clear Screen button, the program will erase any images from the form. If you click your mouse on any one of the six Fractal buttons, the program will draw a fractal image on the form. In turn, if you click your mouse on the Stop Drawing button, the program will stop drawing the currently selected fractal. Finally, if you click your mouse on the Exit button, the program will unload itself. Finally, when you click your mouse on the User Fractal button, the program will display the *User Equation* form that you can use to plot functions and better understand how fractals work. Figure 5.3 shows the *prjFractal* project's *User Equation* form.

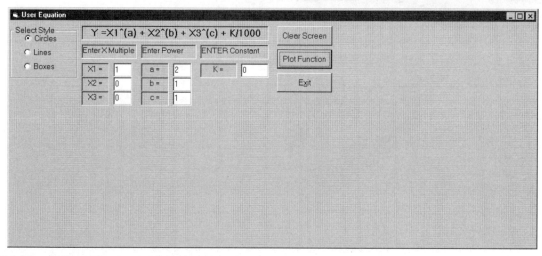

Figure 5.3 *The prjFractal project's **User Equation** form.*

Now that you have seen the *prjFractal.exe* program's layout, you can use the program to select a drawing style and draw a fractal image. To select a circle drawing style and draw a fractal image, perform the following steps:

1. Within the *Fractals* form, click your mouse on the Circles option in the *Select Style* frame. The program will display a dot within the *Circles* option field.

2. Within the *Fractals* form, click your mouse on the Kam Torus Fractal button. The program will use circles to draw a Kam Torus fractal image, as shown in Figure 5.4.

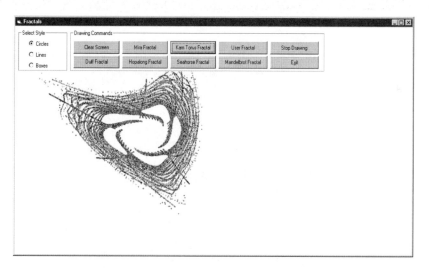

Figure 5.4 *The Kam Torus fractal image drawn with circles.*

Now that you have seen an image of the Kam Torus fractal drawn with circles, it is worthwhile to better understand the difference drawing the fractal with boxes will make in the fractal's appearance. To draw another image of the Kam Torus fractal, using boxes instead of circles, perform the following steps:

1. Within the *Fractals* form, click your mouse on the Clear Screen button to clear the *prjFractal* project's drawing area. The program will clear the drawing area.

2. Click your mouse on the Boxes option in the *Select Style* frame. The program will draw a dot in the *Boxes* option field.

3. Within the *Fractals* form, click your mouse on the Kam Torus Fractal button. The program will use many small boxes to draw a Kam Torus fractal image, as shown in Figure 5.5.

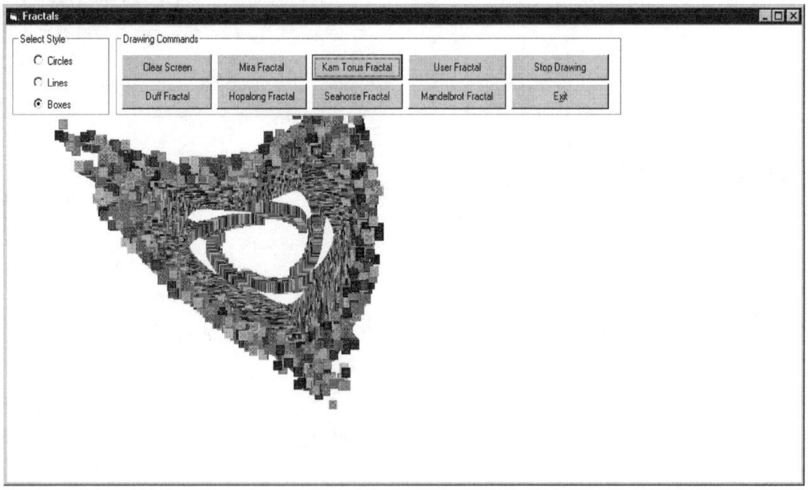

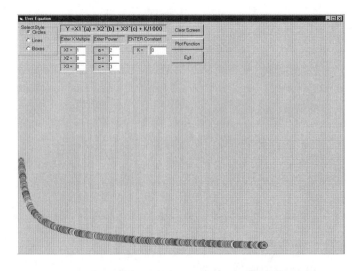

Figure 5.5 *The Kam Torus fractal image drawn with boxes.*

In addition to drawing predefined fractals, you can create your own math equation and the program will draw an image of it on the *UserEquation* form. To create your own user-defined math equation, perform the following steps:

1. Within the *Fractals* form, click your mouse on the UserFractal button. The program will close the *Fractals* form and open the *UserEquation* form.

2. Within the *UserEquation* form, enter 3 in the *b=* field, then enter 3 in the *c=* field.

3. Within the *UserEquation* form, click your mouse on the Plot Function button. The program will use the equation you enter to draw an image on the *UserEquation* form, as shown in Figure 5.6.

Figure 5.6 *The user-defined equation fractal image in the* **User Equation** *form.*

CREATING THE BLANK FORMS, MODULES, AND THE CLASS MODULE

Now that you have a better idea how to use the *prjFractal* project, you can begin to design it. You will design two blank forms that will contain all the controls introduced in the "Using the *prjFractal* Project" section. After you design and implement the forms, you will learn more about Visual Basic structures and the six predefined fractal equations. To begin the *prjFractal* project and design two blank forms, the modules, and the class module, perform the following steps:

1. Within Visual Basic, select the File menu New Project option. Visual Basic will open the New Project dialog box.

2. Within the New Project dialog box, click your mouse on the Standard EXE icon. Next, click your mouse on OK. Visual Basic will open the *Form1* form window.

3. Within Visual Basic, select the Project menu Add Form option. Visual Basic will open the Add Form dialog box.

4. Within the Add Form dialog box, select the Form option. Next, click your mouse on the Open button. Visual Basic will open a new form window, *Form2*.

5. Select the View menu Properties Window option. Visual Basic will open the Properties Window with the *Form1* properties listed.

6. Within the Properties Window, change the *Form1* properties to the values Table 5.1 lists.

7. Repeat Steps 5 and 6 to change the *Form2* properties to the values Table 5.1 lists.

Object	Property	Set As
Form1	*Caption*	*Fractals*
Form1	*Height*	10980
Form1	*Left*	0
Form1	*StartUpPosition*	2 - Center Screen
Form1	*Top*	0
Form1	*Width*	15090
Form1	*Name*	*frmFractal*
Form2	*Caption*	*User Equation*
Form2	*Height*	10935
Form2	*Left*	0
Form2	*Top*	0
Form2	*Width*	15090
Form2	*StartUpPosition*	2 - Center Screen
Form2	*Name*	*frmUserEquation*

Table 5.1 *The newly named **frmFractal** and **frmUserEquation** forms' properties.*

8. Within Visual Basic, select the Project menu Add Module option. Visual Basic will open the Add Module dialog box.

9. Within the Add Module dialog box, select the Module option. Next, click your mouse on the Open button. Visual Basic will open a new Code window, *Module1*.

10. Select the View menu Properties Window option. Visual Basic will open the Properties Window listing the *Module1* properties.

11. Within the Properties Window, change *Module1's* name to *mdlComplex*.

12. Within Visual Basic, select the Project menu Add Module option. Visual Basic will open the Add Module dialog box.

13. Within the Add Module dialog box, select the Module option. Next, click your mouse on the Open button. Visual Basic will open a new Code window, *Module1*.

14. Select the View menu Properties Window option. Visual Basic will open the Properties Window listing the *Module1* properties.

15. Within the Properties Window, change *Module1's* name to *mdlFractal*.

16. Within Visual Basic, select the Project menu Add Module option. Visual Basic will open the Add Module dialog box.

17. Within the Add Module dialog box, select the Module option. Next, click your mouse on the Open button. Visual Basic will open a new Code window, *Module1*.

18. Select the View menu Properties Window option. Visual Basic will open the Properties Window listing the *Module1* properties.

19. Within the Properties Window, change *Module1's* name to *mdlPoint*.

20. Within Visual Basic, select the Project menu Add Class Module option. Visual Basic will open the Add Class Module dialog box.

21. Within the Add Class Module dialog box, select the Class option. Next, click your mouse on the Open button. Visual Basic will open a new Code window, *Class1*.

22. Select the View menu Properties Window option. Visual Basic will open the Properties Window listing the *Class1* properties.

23. Within the Properties Window, change *Class1's* name to *Mandelbrot*.

24. Select the File menu Save Project As option. Visual Basic will open the Save File As dialog box and fill the *File name* field with *Mandelbrot*.

25. Within the Save Project As dialog box, click your mouse on the Save button. Visual Basic will save the *Mandelbrot* class and fill the *File name* field with *mdlPoint*.

26. Within the Save Project As dialog box, click your mouse on the Save button. Visual Basic will save the *mdlPoint* module and fill the *File name* field with *mdlFractal*.

27. Within the Save Project As dialog box, click your mouse on the Save button. Visual Basic will save the *mdlFractal* module and fill the *File name* field with *mdlComplex*.

28. Within the Save Project As dialog box, click your mouse on the Save button. Visual Basic will save the *mdlComplex* module and fill the *File name* field with *mdlFractal*.

29. Within the Save Project As dialog box, click your mouse on the Save button. Visual Basic will save the *mdlFractal* module and fill the *File name* field with *frmFractals*.

30. Within the Save Project As dialog box, click your mouse on the Save button. Visual Basic will save the *frmFractals* form and fill the *File name* field with *frmUserEquation*.

31. Within the Save Project As dialog box, click your mouse on the Save button. Visual Basic will save the *frmUserEquation* form and fill the *File name* field with *Project1*.

32. Within the *File name* field, replace the *Project1* project name with the new *prjFractal* project name. Next, click your mouse on the Save button. Visual Basic will save the *prjFractal* project and close the Save Project As dialog box.

UNDERSTANDING GRAPHS

In the *prjFractal* project, you will use a *graph* to determine each fractal image's position. When your program uses the *Circle* or *Line* method to draw a circle or line, Windows will interpret the method call and draw each circle or line at a specific position on a graph in the computer screen. A graph represents a position with two values, called the *x*-coordinate and the *y*-coordinate.

Your computer screen is two-dimensional and if you place your finger on a point on the screen, Windows has an X and Y value that marks the spot. The graph represents the top left corner of your computer screen as an X and Y coordinate value of (0, 0). As Windows moves down the left side of your screen, the Y value increases. Likewise, as Windows moves to the right across the top of your screen, the X value increases. Figure 5.7 shows a logical model of an X and Y coordinate system mapped against the Windows display.

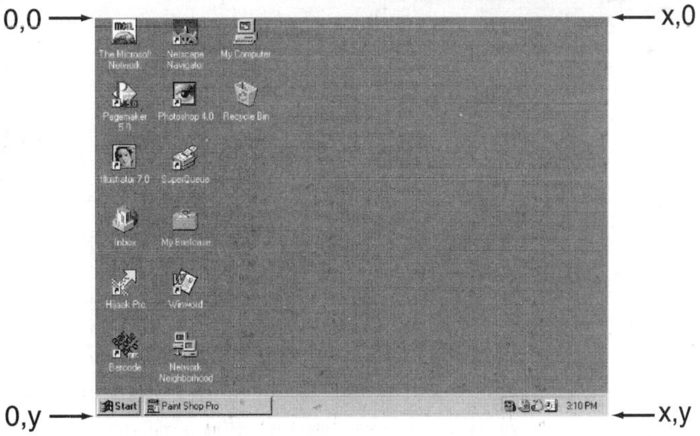

0,0 → [desktop screenshot] ← x,0

0,y → ← x,y

Figure 5.7 *Windows uses a graphing coordinate system.*

Depending on your screen's size, the bottom right corner might be (1024,768) or (800,600), or some other custom number. In the *prjFractal* project, the *Circle* and *Line* methods will draw many circles, lines, or boxes at different points on the graph. Because your program must calculate many different X and Y values for each equation, and will plot many of those values in close proximity to each other, it is worthwhile to plot those values in *pixels* (the individual dots the screen displays that make up the entire screen image), rather than *twips* (a Visual Basic unit of measurement which will vary depending on your screen's current size). Setting the screen measurement to pixels lets your program more closely control how it draws the fractal image.

In the *prjFractal* project, you will draw circles or lines as small as a single pixel on your computer screen. The *prjFractal* project uses many single pixel-sized images to compose the larger image, which will consist of hundreds of pixel-sized images. The program will position each pixel-sized image at a specific X and Y position on the screen graph that the particular equation for each fractal specifies.

UNDERSTANDING PIXELS

Pixels are circular areas on your computer screen that can be any combination of red, green, and blue colors. As you may know, computer screens (and other displays, such as television sets) determine the color of each point that you plot on the screen as some combination of red, green, and blue. A color value between 0 and 255 determined the amount of each color within the final pixel. If you plot a pixel with the highest color value (255) for each color, the resulting pixel will be white. Similarly, if you plot a pixel with the lowest color value (0) for each color, the resulting pixel will be black.

In general, a pixel is about the size of a pin head. Most computer screens are capable of displaying different levels of resolution, which represents the number of pixels the screen displays. For example, when your computer screen is set to display at 640 by 480, it will display 640 pixels across and 480 pixels from top to bottom. Similarly, when you set your computer screen to display at 1024 by 800, it will display 1024 pixels across and 800 pixels from top to bottom. Because many pixels compose each screen, the more pixels a screen display has, the clearer the screen's image will be—which means that a image you display at 1024 pixels by 800 pixels will have a higher *resolution*, or clarity, than an image you display at 640 pixels by 480 pixels.

MORE ON THE CIRCLE METHOD

In the *prjFractal* project, you will use the *Circle* method to draw images on the *frmFractal* and *frmUserEquation* forms. You will use the *Circle* method to draw thousands of small, thin, multi-colored circles. A combination of many small circles will appear as an image on your screen.

If you have ever studied geometry, you might remember that a circle has what is called a *radius*. The radius is the distance from the circle's center to the circle's outside edge. The *Circle* method will draw circles when you give it a radius, a color, and a position. For example, the following code fragment draws a red circle at the position (100, 100), with a radius of 50 units (because you do not know the program code previous to this fragment, it is impossible to say whether the units are twips, pixels, or some other drawing unit), on the current form:

```
Me.Circle (100, 100), 50, RGB(255, 0, 0)
```

The first and second parameters specify the circle center's *X* and *Y* positions, respectively. The third parameter specifies the radius of 50, and the fourth parameter uses the *RGB* function to set the color to red. As you learned in the previous section, computers determine the color of each pixel by setting the pixel to some combination of red, green, and blue. The *RGB(255,0,0)* function specifies that the pixel's color should contain all the possible red color and no green or blue color. The following section explains the *RGB* function in detail.

USING THE RGB FUNCTION

In the previous code fragment, you used the *RGB* function to select a screen color of red (which the *Circle* method then used to draw the circle's outline). The *Circle* method actually accepts a *Long* value, which corresponds to a Visual Basic color value, as the method's fourth parameter. Using the *RGB* function lets you specify that *Long* value as an RGB value.

RGB values (so named because you will compose them from a red value from 0 to 255, a green value from 0 to 255, and a blue value from 0 to 255) let you specify colors as a combination of primary colors. Many programming languages control colors with RGB color values. Visual Basic, on the other hand, expects your programs to specify colors as numeric values that represent the colors' positions within the Visual Basic color table—a single, *Long* value, rather than three separate *Integer* values. To convert from an RGB color value to a Visual Basic color value, your programs can use the *RGB* function. The *RGB* function returns a *Long* number that represents an RGB color value. You will use the *RGB* function as shown in the following prototype:

```
RGB(red, green, blue)
```

The *RGB* function syntax accepts three parameters, as Table 5.2 details.

Parameter	Description
red	*Variant (Integer)* number in the range 0 to 255, inclusive, that represents the color's red component.
green	*Variant (Integer)* number in the range 0 to 255, inclusive, that represents the color's green component.
blue	*Variant (Integer)* number in the range 0 to 255, inclusive, that represents the color's blue component.

*Table 5.2 The parameters for the **RGB** function.*

Application methods and properties that let you specify a color (whether drawing methods or object properties, such as the *Form* object's *BackColor* property) expect your programs to specify a number within the Visual Basic color table for that property. However, it is generally easier to specify colors as an RGB color value. (Because the color table includes all the possible RGB color values—or 256 * 256 * 256 = 16,77,216—it is unlikely that you will remember the integer in the color table that corresponds to the color value you want.) An RGB color value specifies the relative intensity of red, green, and blue that causes the computer to display a specific color. Table 5.3 lists some standard colors and the red, green, and blue values they include.

Color	Red Value	Green Value	Blue Value
Black	0	0	0
Blue	0	0	255
Green	0	255	0
Cyan	0	255	255
Red	255	0	0
Magenta	255	0	255
Yellow	255	255	0
White	255	255	255

Table 5.3 Some standard colors and their corresponding RGB color codes.

Note: Visual Basic assumes that the value of any parameter to the RGB function that exceeds 255 is 255.

To use the *Circle* method on your computer, perform the following steps:

1. Within Visual Basic, select the File menu New Project option. Visual Basic will open the New Project dialog box.

2. Within the New Project dialog box, select the Standard EXE option. Next, click your mouse on the OK button. Visual Basic will open the *Form1* form window.

3. Within Visual Basic, select the View menu Code option. Visual Basic will open the Code window.

4. Within the Code window, enter the following code within the *Form_Load* event:

```
Private Sub Form_Load()
  Me.Circle (100, 100), 50, RGB(255, 0, 0)
End Sub
```

5. After you enter the program code within the Code window, select the Run menu Start option. Visual Basic will run the project, and display a red circle on the form, as shown in Figure 5.8.

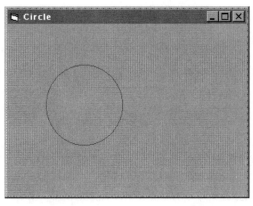

Figure 5.8 The image of a circle from the sample code.

The Visual Basic *Circle* method has seven parameters. In the *prjFractal* project, you will use the *Circle* method according to the following prototype (parameters in brackets are optional):

```
object.Circle [Step] (x, y), radius, [color, start, end, aspect]
```

Table 5.4 lists each parameter for the *Circle* method and describes the parameter's use.

Parameter	Description
object	An optional parameter that refers to the object on which the program is to draw the circle. If you omit the *object* parameter, Visual Basic will use the form with the current focus. Other valid objects that expose the *Circle* method include *PictureBox* controls, *UserControl* objects, and *UserDocument* objects.
step	Specifies that the center of the circle, ellipse, or arc is relative to the current coordinates the *object* parameter's *x* and *y* properties state.
x	The x-coordinate of the center point of the circle, ellipse, or arc.
y	The y-coordinate of the center point of the circle, ellipse, or arc.
radius	A required *Single* value that specifies the radius of the circle, ellipse, or arc.
color	An optional *Long Integer* value that indicates the circle outline's red, green, and blue color. If the method call omits the color parameter, Visual Basic will use the current form's *ForeColor* property.
start	An optional *Single* value. When your program instructs the *Circle* method to draw a circle, ellipse, or arc, the *start* value specifies the arc's beginning position, in radians. The range for the *start* parameter is -2.0 times pi radians to +2.0 times pi radians. The default value for *start* is 0 radians.
end	An optional *Single* value. When your program instructs the *Circle* method to draw a circle, ellipse, or arc, the *end* value specifies the arc's end position, in radians. The range for the *end* parameter is -2.0 times pi radians to +2.0 times pi radians. The default value for *end* is 2 times pi radians.
aspect	An optional *Single* value that indicates the aspect ratio of the circle. The default value is 1.0, which yields a perfect (non-elliptical) circle on your screen. *Aspect ratio* refers to the width-to-height ratio of a television image. When you set the aspect ratio to 1, it means that the width and height of the image are identical.

154

Table 5.4 *The **Circle** method's parameters and descriptions.*

MORE ON THE LINE METHOD

In the *prjFractal* project, you will use the *Line* method to draw images on the *frmFractal* and *frmUserEquation* forms. You will use the *Line* method to draw thousands of small, wide or thin, multi-colored or solid-colored, lines or boxes. The combination of many small lines and boxes will appear as an image on your screen.

Within your Visual Basic programs, you can use the *Line* method to draw a line, rectangle, or filled rectangle. To draw a line, you must specify the line's starting point, length, ending point, and color, as shown in the following code fragment:

```
Me.Line (1, 1)-(200, 200), RGB(255, 0, 0)
```

The previous code fragment draws a line beginning at the (1,1) coordinate—the upper left-hand corner—of the current form, and draws the line from the (1,1) coordinate to the (200, 200) coordinate. The line will be at a 45 degree angle to both the top and the left side of the form, and will slope down and to the right of its starting coordinate. The second parameter, *RGB(255,0,0)*, specifies that the program will draw the line in red, as you learned in the "More on the Circle Method" section of this chapter.

Within your programs, you can also use the *Line* method to draw rectangles and filled rectangles. As you know, a rectangle has *top*, *left*, *right* and *bottom* sides. The top, left, right, and bottom sides of the rectangle are four distinct line segments. In a rectangle, the top and bottom line segments are equal lengths, and the left and right line segments are equal lengths. When you draw a rectangle, you can describe the rectangle in terms of the coordinates of its four corners. The *Line* method will draw rectangles around an invisible diagonal line that runs from the top left to the bottom right of a rectangle. The *Line* method will draw a rectangle when you give it a starting point and ending point for the invisible diagonal line, and give the line's length and color.

To better understand the *Line* method, consider the following sample code:

```
Private Sub Form_Load()
   Me.ScaleMode = 3
   Me.Line (1, 1)-(200, 200), RGB(255, 0, 0)
   Me.Line (1, 1)-(150, 150), RGB(255, 255, 0), B
   Me.Line (1, 1)-(100, 100), RGB(0, 0, 255), BF
End Sub
```

As you can see, the previous code fragment uses the *Line* method three times. The first time the program invokes the *Line* method, the method will draw a red line that starts at (1,1) and ends at (200,200). The second time the program invokes the *Line* method, the method will draw a yellow rectangle with its top left corner at (1,1) and its bottom right corner at (150,150). The third time the program invokes the *Line* method, the method will draw a blue-filled rectangle with its top left corner at (1,1) and its bottom right corner at (100,100).

To try the *Line* method, perform the following steps:

155

1. Within Visual Basic, select the File menu New Project option. Visual Basic will open the New Project dialog box.

2. Within the New Project dialog box, double-click your mouse on the Standard EXE icon. Visual Basic will open the *Form1* form window.

3. Within Visual Basic, select the View menu Code option. Visual Basic will open the Code window.

4. Within the Code window, type the previous sample code. Next, select the Run menu Start option. Visual Basic will run the project and display lines and rectangles on the form, as Figure 5.9 shows.

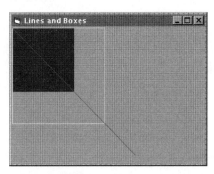

Figure 5.9 *The sample code uses the **Line** method to draw a line, a box, and a filled box.*

The Visual Basic *Line* method has nine parameters. In the *prjFractal* project, you will use the *Line* method as shown in the following basic format (parameters within brackets are optional):

```
object.Line [Step] (x1, y1) [Step] (x2, y2), [color], [B][F]
```

Table 5.5 lists each parameter in the *Line* method and describes its use.

Parameter	Description
object	An optional parameter that evaluates to the name of the object on which the method will draw. If the method call omits the *object* parameter, Visual Basic will use the form with the current focus. Other valid objects that expose the *Line* method include *UserControl* objects and *UserDocument* objects.
step	An optional keyword specifying that the starting point coordinates are relative to the line starting point.

Table 5.5 *The parameters and descriptions for the **Line** method. (continued on following page)*

Parameter	Description
x1	An optional *Single* value that specifies the x-coordinate of the starting point for the line or box. If you omit the *x1* parameter, Visual Basic will draw the line from the *object* parameter's current x-coordinate.
y1	An optional *Single* value that specifies the y-coordinate of the starting point for the line or box. If you omit the *y1* parameter, Visual Basic will draw the line from the *object* parameter's current y-coordinate.
step	An optional keyword that specifies that the end point coordinates are relative to the line's starting point.
x2	A required *Single* value that specifies the end point's x-coordinate for the line or box the program is to draw.
y2	A required *Single* value that specifies the end point's y-coordinate for the line or box the program is to draw.
color	An optional *Long* value that specifies the RGB color Visual Basic will use to draw the line. If the method call omits the *color* parameter, Visual Basic will use the *object's ForeColor* property.
B	An optional flag that, if you include it in the method call, causes Visual Basic to draw a box using the *(x1, y1)* and *(x2, y2)* coordinates to specify opposite corners of the box.
F	An optional flag that, if you include it in the method call, instructs Visual Basic to fill the box with the same color it used to draw the box. You cannot use *F* without *B*.

156

Table 5.5 *The parameters and descriptions for the* **Line** *method. (continued from previous page)*

MORE ON STRUCTURES

Now that you know more about the *Circle* and *Line* methods, you can learn about the structure that stores data within the *prjFractal* project. A Visual Basic *structure* is similar to a Visual Basic predefined type. In each chapter of this book, you will use variables of specific types, such as *Integers*, *Strings*, and *Long* integers. As you have learned, within your programs you will use variables to store data. When you access the variable, you access the data in that variable. With most simple types (such as *Integers*), you can store only a single value within the variable. When you create a structure, you can group together common values into a single location. With a structure, you can store multiple values (which may or may not be of the same type) within a single, common location. After you define a structure, the program that you define the structure within can define variables of that structure just as it would variables of any other type.

For example, assume you would like to represent certain information about a pencil within your Visual Basic program. Because a pencil has properties and dimensions (such as color and weight), you can declare a variable for each. For example, you can declare variables that you name *Length*, *Weight*, *Color*, and *Lead* for the *Pencil* structure. When you want to define information for a new pencil, you must again define four variables (such as *Length_Pencil2*, *Weight_Pencil2*, *Color_Pencil2*, and *Lead_Pencil2*) to manage information about the second pencil. As you can see, defining a different set of variables for each pencil will quickly become cumbersome and confusing. A better solution is to store the four pencil characteristics within a structure. Then, when you must define information for the second pencil, you simply create a new variable of the structure's type. When you define the structure, you will define each property of the pencil (such a length) as an element of the structure. Each variable in a structure is an *element* of that structure. The following code implements the *Pencil* structure example with four elements:

```
Type Pencil
   Length As Integer
   Color As String
   Weight As Single
   Lead As String
End Type
```

After you create a structure, Visual Basic will add it to the list of data types (*Integer, Long, String*, and so on) for the current program, and you can then declare a variable of the structure's type in the program code. For example, to declare a variable of the *Pencil* type, you would use program code similar to the following:

```
Dim MyPencil as Pencil
```

In the *prjFractal* project, you will use a structure to get rid of lengthy function parameters. For example, if you wanted to pass the *Pencil* structure's elements through function parameters, you would have to declare a function with four parameters. To do so, you would write a function and name it *HoldPencil* and add four parameters, which the following code shows:

```
HoldPencil(Length as Integer, Color As String, Weight As Single, _
    Lead As String)
```

On the other hand, if you declare the *Pencil* structure, you can pass the information about the pencil in with only a single parameter, as shown here:

```
Call HoldPencil(MyPencil)
```

In the *prjFractal* project, you will create a structure in which to store all the *Circle* and *Line* method parameters, which you will then pass as a single parameter into the procedures that perform the actual drawing of the fractal's component objecs.

Because a structure declaration is a new type definition, Visual Basic requires that you define each structure you create within a Visual Basic code module, rather than a form or other object. As you have learned, after you declare a structure within a module, the structure's type definition is available throughout the project.

The following code is the generalized format you will use to design a structure in Visual Basic. As you can see, the structure's name is *varname*, and each element in the structure is *element#*:

```
[Private | Public] Type varname
   element1[([subscripts])] As type1
   element2[([subscripts])] As type2
   element3[([subscripts])] As type3
. . .
   elementN[([subscripts])] As typeN
End Type
```

Table 5.6 describes the structure definition's components.

Parameter	Description
Public	An optional keyword you can use to declare your structure available to all procedures and functions in all form and code modules of the current project group. Structure definitions are public by default.
Private	An optional keyword you can use to declare your structure available only within the module where the program makes the structure declaration.
varname	The structure's name, which your programs will later use as a type name when you define variables of the structure's type.
element#	The name of the member within the structure. Each element is a structure member. Element names must be unique within a structure declaration.
subscripts	An optional parameter you will use when an element is an array (a special type of variable that lets you reference multiple values of the same type). The parameter contains the array's dimensions.

Table 5.6 The Visual Basic structure definition's components. (continued on following page)

Parameter	Description
type	Specifies the *element#'s* data type, and may be any of the Visual Basic predefined types, a user-defined type (such as another structure or class), or an object type (such as a *TextBox* or *ComboBox*). If the *type* is a user-defined type, you must define the user-defined type before you can use it in another structure definition. For example, if you wanted to use the *Pencil* type as an element type within another structure, you must define the *Pencil* type within the module before you define the second structure.

Table 5.6 The Visual Basic structure definition's components. (continued from previous page)

ADDING CONTROLS TO THE FRMFRACTAL FORM

Now that you have created the forms, modules, and class module that you will use within the *prjFractal* project, and you have learned about the drawing methods that you will use to create fractals, you will add controls to the *frmFractal* form. As you have learned, you will use the *frmFractal* form to select a fractal image to draw. First, you will add *CommandButton* controls. Second, you will add a *Label* control and place three *OptionButton* controls within the *Label* control in a control array. Third, you will change each control's properties. Finally, you will add controls to the *frmUserEquation* form.

ADDING COMMAND BUTTONS AND A FRAME TO THE FRMFRACTAL FORM

As you have learned, the *prjFractal* project will let the user draw six fractal images on the *frmFractal* form. To select a single fractal image, you will use *CommandButton* controls that will list each fractal by name. The ten *CommandButton* controls will let you clear the *frmFractal* form, select a fractal to draw, open the *frmUserEquation* form, and exit the *prjFractal* project.

To add ten *CommandButton* controls and their enclosing frame to the *frmFractal* form, perform the following steps:

1. If Visual Basic is not displaying the *frmFractal* form within an object window, double-click your mouse on the *frmFractal* form listing within the Project Explorer. Visual Basic will open the *frmFractal* form.

2. Within Visual Basic, select the View menu Toolbox option. Visual Basic will open the Toolbox.

3. Within the Toolbox, double-click your mouse on the CommandButton icon. Visual Basic will draw a *CommandButton* control, *Command1*, within the *frmFractal* form.

4. Repeat Step 3 nine more times until you have a total of ten command buttons within the *frmFractal* form.

5. Within the Toolbox, double-click your mouse on the Frame icon. Visual Basic will draw a frame control, *Frame1,* within the *frmFractal* form.

6. Within the *frmFractal* form, click your mouse on the *Frame1* control to highlight it. Visual Basic will draw a small frame around the control.

7. Select the View menu Properties Window option. Visual Basic will open the Properties Window that lists the *Frame1* control's properties.

8. Within the Properties Window, change the *Frame1* control's properties to the values Table 5.7 lists.

Object	Property	Set As
Frame1	*BackColor*	*&H00FFFFFF& (White)*
Frame1	*Caption*	*Drawing Commands*
Frame1	*Height*	13665

*Table 5.7 The newly named **fraFractals** control's properties. (continued on following page)*

Object	Property	Set As
Frame1	*Left*	2040
Frame1	*Top*	120
Frame1	*Width*	9495
Frame1	*Name*	*fraFractals*

*Table 5.7 The newly named **fraFractals** control's properties. (continued from previous page)*

9. Within the *frmFractal* form, click your mouse on a *CommandButton* control to highlight it. Visual Basic will draw a small frame around the control.

10. Press the SHIFT key, hold it down, and click on each of the remaining *CommandButton* controls in turn. Visual Basic will draw a small frame around each control.

11. Select the Edit menu Cut option to cut all the *CommandButton* controls and place them onto the Clipboard. Visual Basic will remove all the controls from the display.

12. Within the *frmFractal* form, click your mouse on the *fraFractals* control to highlight it. Visual Basic will draw a small frame around the control.

13. Select the Edit menu Paste option to paste all ten *CommandButton* controls onto the *fraFractals* frame control.

14. Within the *fraFractals* frame, click your mouse on a *CommandButton* control to highlight it. Visual Basic will draw a small frame around the control.

15. Select the View menu Properties Window option. Visual Basic will open the Properties Window that lists the *CommandButton* control's properties you selected.

16. Within the Properties Window, change the *CommandButton* control's properties you highlighted to the values Table 5.8 lists.

17. Repeat Steps 14, 15, and 16 until you have changed each *CommandButton* control's properties to the values Table 5.8 lists.

Object	Property	Set As
Command1	*Caption*	*Clear Screen*
Command1	*Height*	420
Command1	*Left*	120
Command1	*Top*	360
Command1	*Width*	1695
Command1	*Name*	*cmdCLS*
Command2	*Caption*	*Duff Fractal*
Command2	*Height*	420
Command2	*Left*	120
Command2	*Top*	840
Command2	*Width*	1695
Command2	*Name*	*cmdDuff*
Command3	*Caption*	*Mira Fractal*
Command3	*Height*	420
Command3	*Left*	1920
Command3	*Top*	360
Command3	*Width*	1695
Command3	*Name*	*cmdMira*

*Table 5.8 The **fraFractals** frame's **CommandButton** control properties.(continued on following page)*

Object	Property	Set As
Command4	Caption	Hopalong Fractal
Command4	Height	420
Command4	Left	1920
Command4	Top	840
Command4	Width	1695
Command4	Name	cmdHopalong
Command5	Caption	Kam Torus Fractal
Command5	Height	420
Command5	Left	3720
Command5	Top	360
Command5	Width	1695
Command5	Name	cmdKamTorus
Command6	Caption	Seahorse Fractal
Command6	Height	420
Command6	Left	3720
Command6	Top	840
Command6	Width	1695
Command6	Name	cmdSeahorse
Command7	Caption	User Fractal
Command7	Height	420
Command7	Left	5520
Command7	Top	360
Command7	Width	1815
Command7	Name	cmdUser
Command8	Caption	Mandelbrot Fractal
Command8	Height	420
Command8	Left	5520
Command8	Top	840
Command8	Width	1815
Command8	Name	cmdMandelbrot
Command9	Caption	Stop Drawing
Command9	Height	420
Command9	Left	7440
Command9	Top	360
Command9	Width	1815
Command9	Name	cmdStopDrawing
Command10	Caption	E&xit
Command10	Height	420
Command10	Left	7440
Command10	Top	840
Command10	Width	1815
Command10	Name	cmdExit

Table 5.8 *The* **fraFractals** *frame's* **CommandButton** *control properties. (continued from previous page)*

Adding a Second Frame Control to the frmFractal Form

Within the *prjFractal* project, you will use *OptionButton* controls to select a drawing style such as circles, lines, or boxes. In the *prjFracal* project, you will use a *Frame* control to contain the three *OptionButton* controls.

To add a second *Frame* control to the *frmFractal* form, perform the following steps:

1. If Visual Basic is not displaying the *frmFractal* form within an object window, double-click your mouse on the *frmFractal* form listing within the Project Explorer. Visual Basic will open the *frmFractal* form.

2. Within Visual Basic, select the View menu Toolbox option. Visual Basic will open the Toolbox.

3. Within the Toolbox, double-click your mouse on the Frame icon. Visual Basic will draw a *Frame* control, *Frame1*, within the *frmFractal* form.

4. Within the *frmFractal* form, click your mouse on the *Frame1* control to highlight it. Visual Basic will draw a small frame around the control.

5. Select the View menu Properties Window option. Visual Basic will open the Properties Window that lists the *Frame1* control's properties.

6. Within the Properties Window, change the *Frame1* control's properties to the values Table 5.9 lists.

Object	Property	Set As
Frame1	*BackColor*	*&H00FFFFFF& (White)*
Frame1	*Caption*	*Select Style*
Frame1	*Height*	1365
Frame1	*Left*	120
Frame1	*Top*	120
Frame1	*Width*	1815
Frame1	*Name*	*fraStyle*

*Table 5.9 The newly named **fraStyle** control's properties.*

Adding an OptionButton Control Array to the frmFractal Form

As you have learned, your programs can use the *Circle* and *Line* methods to draw circles, lines, and boxes. In the *prjFractal* project, you will use three *OptionButton* controls in a control array to list a drawing choice. When you click your mouse on an *OptionButton* control, the *prjFractal.exe* program will know what type of image to draw—a circle, a line, or a box. Remember, Visual Basic will assign a unique index value to each *OptionButton* control in a control array. In the *prjFractal* project, Visual Basic will assign three index values: 0, 1, and 2 to the three *OptionButton* controls.

To add three *OptionButton* controls to the *fraStyle* frame, perform the following steps:

1. If Visual Basic is not displaying the *frmFractal* form within an object window, double-click your mouse on the *frmFractal* form listing within the Project Explorer. Visual Basic will open the *frmFractal* form.

2. Within Visual Basic, select the View menu Toolbox option. Visual Basic will open the Toolbox.

3. Within the Toolbox, double-click your mouse on the OptionButton icon. Visual Basic will draw an *OptionButton* control, *Option1*, within the *frmFractal* form.

4. Within the form window, click your mouse on the *Option1* control. Visual Basic will draw a small frame around the control.

5. Select the Edit menu Cut option. Visual Basic will remove the control from the display.

6. Click your mouse on the *fraStyle* control. Visual Basic will draw a small frame around the control.

7. Select the Edit menu Paste option. Visual Basic will paste the *Option1* control within the *fraStyle* frame.

8. Select the View menu Properties Window option. Visual Basic will open the Properties Window and display the *Option1* control's properties.

9. Within the Properties Window, change the control's *Name* property from *Option1* to *optDrawStyle*.

10. Within the *fraStyle* control, click your mouse on the newly named *optDrawStyle* control. Next, select the Edit menu Copy option. Visual Basic will highlight the *optDrawStyle* control and copy it to the Clipboard.

11. Select the Edit menu Paste option. Visual Basic will display a dialog box that asks, "You already have a control named *optDrawStyle*. Do you want to create a control array?" Click your mouse on the Yes button. Visual Basic will add a copy of the *optDrawStyle* control to the *fraStyle* frame.

12. Select the Edit menu Paste option. Visual Basic will draw another copy of the *optDrawStyle* control within the *fraStyle* frame.

13. Within the *fraStyle* control, click your mouse on an *optDrawStyle* control to highlight it. Visual Basic will draw a small frame around the control.

14. Select the View menu Properties Window option. Visual Basic will open the Properties Window.

15. Within the Properties Window, change the highlighted control's properties to the values Table 5.10 lists.

16. Repeat Steps 13, 14, and 15 until you have changed each *optDrawStyle* control to the values Table 5.10 lists.

Object	Property	Set As
optDrawStyle(0)	*BackColor*	*&H00FFFFFF& (White)*
optDrawStyle(0)	*Caption*	*Circles*
optDrawStyle(0)	*Height*	195
optDrawStyle(0)	*Left*	375
optDrawStyle(0)	*Top*	360
optDrawStyle(0)	*Width*	975
optDrawStyle(1)	*BackColor*	*&H00FFFFFF& (White)*
optDrawStyle(1)	*Caption*	*Lines*
optDrawStyle(1)	*Height*	195
optDrawStyle(1)	*Left*	375
optDrawStyle(1)	*Top*	720
optDrawStyle(1)	*Width*	975
optDrawStyle(1)	*BackColor*	*&H00FFFFFF& (White)*
optDrawStyle(2)	*Caption*	*Boxes*
optDrawStyle(2)	*Height*	195
optDrawStyle(2)	*Left*	375
optDrawStyle(2)	*Top*	1080
optDrawStyle(2)	*Width*	975

Table 5.10 *The* **optDrawStyle** *control array's properties.*

After you finish changing the properties of the *frmFractal* form's controls, the *frmFractal* form will look similar to Figure 5.10.

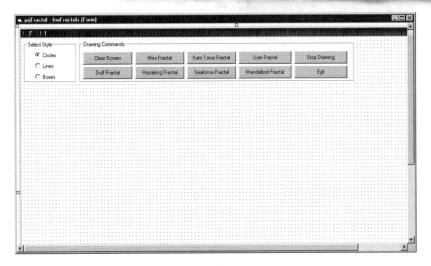

Figure 5.10 *The **frmFractal** form after you change its controls' properties.*

163

ADDING CONTROLS TO THE FRMUSEREQUATION FORM

As you learned in the "Using the *prjFractal* Project" section of this chapter, you will use the *frmUserEquation* form to enter a user-defined equation. To design the *frmUserEquation* form, you will add *Label* controls, which will display each section of a user-defined mathematical equation, *TextBox* controls, which will let you enter a user-defined mathematical equation, and *CommandButton* controls, which will let you clear the *frmUserEquation* form and draw an image of a user-defined equation within the *frmUserEquation* form. Finally, you will add *OptionButton* controls to the form, which will let the user select different shapes for the program to use when it draws your user-defined equation.

ADDING LABEL CONTROLS TO THE FRMUSEREQUATION FORM

As you learned, you will use the *frmUserEquation* form to enter a user-defined equation. The user-defined equation will plot the values for the equation $Y=X1^{\wedge}(a) + X2^{\wedge}(b) + X3^{\wedge}(c) + K/1000$. The user will be able to enter all the values within the equation (except the *Y* value). The program code will evaluate the equation to determine the equation's Y value. Within the *frmUserEquation* form, you will use *Label* controls to display the headings that correspond to each section of the user-defined equation.

To add *Label* controls to the *frmUserEquation* form, perform the following steps:

1. If Visual Basic is not displaying the *frmUserEquation* form within an object window, double-click your mouse on the *frmUserEquation* form listing within the Project Explorer. Visual Basic will open the *frmUserEquation* form.

2. Within Visual Basic, select the View menu Toolbox option. Visual Basic will open the Toolbox.

3. Within the Toolbox, double-click your mouse on the Label icon. Visual Basic will draw a *Label* control, *Label1*, within the *frmUserEquaton* form.

4. Repeat Step 3 ten more times until you have eleven *Label* controls within the *frmUserEquation* form.

5. Within the *frmUserEquation* window, click your mouse on a *Label* control to highlight it. Visual Basic will draw a small frame around the control.

6. Select the View menu Properties Window option. Visual Basic will open the Properties Window that lists the *Label* control's properties.

7. Within the Properties Window, change the highlighted control's properties to the values Table 5.11 lists.

8. Repeat Steps 5, 6, and 7 until you have changed each *Label* control's properties to the values Table 5.11 lists.

Object	Property	Set As
Label1	Caption	$Y=X1^{\wedge}(a) + X2^{\wedge}(b) + X3^{\wedge}(c) + K/1000$
Label1	Height	375
Label1	Left	1920
Label1	Top	120
Label1	Width	4935
Label1	Name	lblEquation
Label2	Caption	Enter X Multiple
Label2	Height	375
Label2	Left	1920
Label2	Top	600
Label2	Width	1455
Label2	Name	lblXMultiple
Label3	Caption	Enter Power
Label3	Height	375
Label3	Left	3480
Label3	Top	600
Label3	Width	1455
Label3	Name	lblPower
Label4	Caption	Enter Constant
Label4	Height	375
Label4	Left	5040
Label4	Top	600
Label4	Width	1815
Label4	Name	lblConstant
Label5	Caption	$X1 =$
Label5	Height	375
Label5	Left	1920
Label5	Top	1080
Label5	Width	735
Label5	Name	lblX1
Label6	Caption	$X2 =$
Label6	Height	375
Label6	Left	1920
Label6	Top	1440
Label6	Width	735
Label6	Name	lblX2
Label7	Caption	$X3 =$
Label7	Height	375
Label7	Left	1920
Label7	Top	1800
Label7	Width	735
Label7	Name	lblX3

Table 5.11 The **frmUserEquation** form's **Label** controls' properties. *(continued on following page)*

Object	Property	Set As
Label10	Caption	=
Label8	Height	375
Label8	Left	3480
Label8	Top	1080
Label8	Width	735
Label8	Name	lblA
Label9	Caption	b =
Label9	Height	375
Label9	Left	3480
Label9	Top	1440
Label9	Width	735
Label9	Name	lblB
Label10	Caption	c =
Label10	Height	375
Label10	Left	3480
Label10	Top	1800
Label10	Width	735
Label10	Name	lblC
Label11	Caption	K =
Label11	Height	375
Label11	Left	5040
Label11	Top	1080
Label11	Width	975
Label11	Name	lblK

Table 5.11 *The* **frmUserEquation** *form's* **Label** *controls' properties. (continued from previous page)*

ADDING TEXTBOX CONTROLS TO THE FRMUSEREQUATION FORM

As you have learned, you will use the *frmUserEquation* form to enter a user-defined equation. Within the *frmUserEquation* form, you will add *TextBox* controls that will store each section of the user-defined mathematical equation.

To add *TextBox* controls to the *frmUserEquation* form, perform the following steps:

1. If Visual Basic is not displaying the *frmUserEquation* form within an object window, double-click your mouse on the *frmUserEquation* form listing within the Project Explorer. Visual Basic will open the *frmUserEquation* form.

2. Within Visual Basic, select the View menu Toolbox option. Visual Basic will open the Toolbox.

3. Within the Toolbox, double-click your mouse on the TextBox icon. Visual Basic will draw a *TextBox* control, *Text1*, within the *frmUserEquaton* form.

4. Repeat Step 3 six more times until Visual Basic displays seven *TextBox* controls within the *frmUserEquation* form.

5. Within the *frmUserEquation* window, click your mouse on a *TextBox* control to highlight it. Visual Basic will draw a small frame around the control.

6. Select the View menu Properties Window option. Visual Basic will open the Properties Window that lists the *TextBox* control's properties.

7. Within the Properties Window, change the highlighted *TextBox* control's properties to the values Table 5.12 lists.

8. Repeat Steps 5, 6, and 7 until you have changed each *TextBox* control's properties to the values Table 5.12 lists.

Object	Property	Set As
Text1	Text	1
Text1	Height	360
Text1	Left	2760
Text1	Top	1080
Text1	Width	495
Text 1	Name	txtX1
Text2	Text	0
Text2	Height	360
Text2	Left	2760
Text2	Top	1440
Text2	Width	495
Text2	Name	txtX2
Text3	Text	0
Text3	Height	360
Text3	Left	2760
Text3	Top	1800
Text3	Width	495
Text3	Name	txtX3
Text4	Text	2
Text4	Height	360
Text4	Left	4320
Text4	Top	1080
Text4	Width	495
Text4	Name	txtA
Text5	Text	1
Text5	Height	360
Text5	Left	4320
Text5	Top	1440
Text5	Width	495
Text5	Name	txtB
Text6	Text	1
Text6	Height	360
Text6	Left	4320
Text6	Top	1800
Text6	Width	495
Text6	Name	txtC
Text7	Text	0
Text7	Height	360
Text7	Left	6120
Text7	Top	1080

Table 5.12 *The **frmUserEquation** form's **TextBox** controls' properties. (continued on following page)*

Object	Property	Set As
Text)	Width	735
Text7	Name	txtK

Table 5.12 The *frmUserEquation* form's **TextBox** controls' properties.(continued from previous page)

ADDING COMMAND BUTTONS TO THE FRMUSEREQUATION FORM

As you have learned, you will use the *frmUserEquation* form to enter a user-defined equation. Within the *frmUserEquation*, you will add *CommandButton* controls that will let you clear the form and draw a fractal image based on the user-defined equation. To add *CommandButton* controls to the *frmUserEquation*, perform the following steps:

1. If Visual Basic is not displaying the *frmUserEquation* form within an object window, double-click your mouse on the *frmUserEquation* form listing within the Project Explorer. Visual Basic will open the *frmUserEquation* form.

2. Within Visual Basic, select the View menu Toolbox option. Visual Basic will open the Toolbox.

3. Within the Toolbox, double-click your mouse on the CommandButton icon. Visual Basic will draw a *CommandButton* control, *Command1*, within the *frmUserEquation* form.

4. Repeat Step 3 two more times until Visual Basic displays three *CommandButton* controls within the *frmUserEquation* form.

5. Within the *frmUserEquation* window, click your mouse on a *CommandButton* control to highlight it. Visual Basic will draw a small frame around the control.

6. Select the View menu Properties Window option. Visual Basic will open the Properties Window that lists the *CommandButton* control's properties.

7. Within the Properties Window, change the highlighted *CommandButton* control's properties to the values Table 5.13 lists.

8. Repeat Steps 5, 6, and 7 until you have changed each *CommandButton* control's properties to the values Table 5.13 lists.

Object	Property	Set As
Command1	Caption	Clear Screen
Command1	Height	495
Command1	Left	7080
Command1	Top	120
Command1	Width	1455
Command1	Name	cmdClearPlot
Command2	Caption	Plot Function
Command2	Height	495
Command2	Left	7080
Command2	Top	720
Command2	Width	1455
Command2	Name	cmdPlotUser
Command2	Caption	E&xit
Command2	Height	495
Command2	Left	7080
Command2	Top	1320

Table 5.13 The *frmUserEquation* form's **CommandButton** control properties. (continued on following page)

Object	Property	Set As
Command2	Width	1455
Command2	Name	cmdExit

*Table 5.13 The **frmUserEquation** form's **CommandButton** control properties. (continued from previous page)*

ADDING A FRAME CONTROL TO THE FRMUSEREQUATION FORM

Within the *prjFractal* project, you will use *OptionButton* controls to select a drawing style such as circles, lines, or boxes. In the *prjFractal* project, you will use a *Frame* control to contain the three *OptionButton* controls.

To add a *Frame* control to the *frmUserEquation* form, perform the following steps:

1. If Visual Basic is not displaying the *frmUserEquation* form within an object window, double-click your mouse on the *frmUserEquation* form listing within the Project Explorer. Visual Basic will open the *frmUserEquation* form.

2. Within Visual Basic, select the View menu Toolbox option. Visual Basic will open the Toolbox.

3. Within the Toolbox, double-click your mouse on the Frame icon. Visual Basic will draw a *Frame* control, *Frame1*, within the *frmUserEquation* form.

4. Within the *frmUserEquation* form, click your mouse on the *Frame1* control to highlight it. Visual Basic will draw a small frame around the control.

5. Select the View menu Properties Window option. Visual Basic will open the Properties Window that lists the *Frame1* control's properties.

6. Within the Properties Window, change the *Frame1* control's properties to the values Table 5.14 lists.

Object	Property	Set As
Frame1	Caption	Select Style
Frame1	Height	1365
Frame1	Left	0
Frame1	Top	0
Frame1	Width	1815
Frame1	Name	fraStyle

*Table 5.14 The newly named **fraStyle** control's properties.*

ADDING AN OPTIONBUTTON CONTROL ARRAY TO THE FRMUSEREQUATION FORM

As you have learned, your programs can use the *Circle* and *Line* methods to draw circles, lines, and boxes. In the *prjFractal* project, you will use three *OptionButton* controls in a control array to list drawing choices. When you click your mouse on an *OptionButton* control, the *prjFractal.exe* program will know what type of image to draw—a circle, a line, or a box. Remember, Visual Basic will assign a unique index value to each *OptionButton* control in a control array. In the *prjFractal* project, Visual Basic will assign three index values: 0, 1, and 2 to the three *OptionButton* controls.

To add three *OptionButton* controls to the *fraStyle* frame, perform the following steps:

1. If Visual Basic is not displaying the *frmUserEquation* form within an object window, double-click your mouse on the *frmUserEquation* form listing within the Project Explorer. Visual Basic will open the *frmUserEquation* form.

2. Within Visual Basic, select the View menu Toolbox option. Visual Basic will open the Toolbox.

3. Within the Toolbox, double-click your mouse on the OptionButton icon. Visual Basic will draw an *OptionButton* control, *Option1*, within the *frmUserEquation* form.

4. Within the *frmUserEquation* form, click your mouse on the *Option1* control. Visual Basic will draw a small frame around the control.

5. Select the Edit menu Cut option. Visual Basic will remove the control from the display.

6. Click your mouse on the *fraStyle* control. Visual Basic will draw a small frame around the control.

7. Select the Edit menu Paste option. Visual Basic will paste the *Option1* control within the *fraStyle* control.

8. Select the View menu Properties Window option. Visual Basic will open the Properties Window and display the *Option1* control's properties.

9. Within the Properties Window, change the control's *Name* property from *Option1* to *optDrawStyle*.

10. Within the *fraStyle* control, click your mouse on the newly named *optDrawStyle* control. Within Visual Basic, select the Edit menu Copy option. Visual Basic will highlight the *optDrawStyle* control and copy it to the Clipboard.

11. Select the Edit menu Paste option. Visual Basic will display a dialog box that asks, "You already have a control named *optDrawStyle*. Do you want to create a control array?" Click your mouse on the Yes button. Visual Basic will add a copy of the *optDrawStyle* control to the *fraStyle* frame.

12. Select the Edit menu Paste option. Visual Basic will draw another copy of the *optDrawStyle* control within the *fraStyle* frame.

13. Within the *fraStyle* control, click your mouse on an *optDrawStyle* control to highlight it. Visual Basic will draw a small frame around the control.

14. Select the View menu Properties Window option. Visual Basic will open the Properties Window.

15. Within the Properties Window, change the highlighted control's properties to the values Table 5.15 lists.

16. Repeat Steps 13, 14, and 15 until you have changed each *optDrawStyle* control to the values Table 5.15 lists.

Object	Property	Set As
optDrawStyle(0)	*Caption*	*Circles*
optDrawStyle(0)	*Height*	195
optDrawStyle(0)	*Left*	375
optDrawStyle(0)	*Top*	240
optDrawStyle(0)	*Width*	975
optDrawStyle(1)	*Caption*	*Lines*
optDrawStyle(1)	*Height*	195
optDrawStyle(1)	*Left*	360
optDrawStyle(1)	*Top*	600
optDrawStyle(1)	*Width*	975
optDrawStyle(2)	*Caption*	*Boxes*
optDrawStyle(2)	*Height*	195
optDrawStyle(2)	*Left*	360
optDrawStyle(2)	*Top*	960
optDrawStyle(2)	*Width*	975

Table 5.15 *The **optDrawStyle** control array's properties.*

After you change the *frmUserEquation* form's controls, the *frmUserEquation* form will look similar to Figure 5.11.

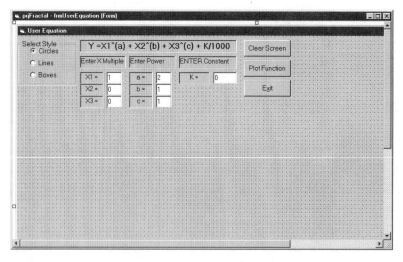

Figure 5.11 *The* **frmUserEquation** *form after you change all its controls' properties.*

WRITING THE CODE FOR THE PRJFRACTAL PROJECT

In the *prjFractal* project, you will write code for each control on the *frmFractal* and *frmUserEquation* forms, and you will write procedures and functions to communicate with each control. First, you will create a structure within the *mdlFractal* module. Second, you will declare local and global variables that the procedures and functions within the program will use to perform the program's processing. Finally, you will write code for each procedure and function.

DECLARING THE STRUCTURE AND THE GLOBAL VARIABLES

As you have learned, your programs can use Visual Basic structures to maintain groups of information within a single location. In the *prjFractal* project, you will use the *ImageData* structure to maintain information that the program code will use to draw the *Line* and *Circle* component objects for the fractals. The *ImageData* structure will include information that describes where the drawing method should draw the current circle, line, or box, the object's size and color, and other important member values. As you have learned, you must define structures within modules. In the *prjFractal* project, you will define the *ImageData* structure within the *mdlFractal* module. The following code implements the *ImageData* structure's definition in the *mdlFractal* module's General–Declarations section:

```
Type ImageData
   X As Double
   Y As Double
   Xaxis as Double
   Yaxis as Double
   X2axis as Double
   Y2axis as Double
   Radius As Double
   Density As Double
   Red As Integer
   Green As Integer
   Blue As Integer
   Shape As Integer
   Filled As Boolean
End Type

Public StopPainting As Boolean
Public Colors(13) As Long
```

As you can see, the *ImageData* structure contains thirteen members. Table 5.16 describes each member in detail.

Member	Purpose
X	Contains the value of the x-coordinate of the specified fractal the user chose to plot in your program.
Y	Contains the value of the y-coordinate of the specified fractal the user chose to plot in your program.
Xaxis	Contains the new value of the x-coordinate after the *Draw* procedure alters the original x-coordinate. (You will learn more about the *Draw* procedure in later sections.)
Yaxis	Contains the new value of the y-coordinate after the *Draw* procedure alters the original y-coordinate.
X2axis	Contains the second x-coordinate for the end position of a line.
Y2axis	Contains the second y-coordinate for the end position of a line.
Radius	Contains the numeric size of the radius for the *Circle* method to draw a user-selected fractal.
Density	Contains a value that specifies how many times the *Draw* procedure will redraw a circle, line, or box associated with a user-selected fractal.
Red	Contains the *Integer* value, from 0 to 255, that specifies how dense the color red will be in the finished fractal image.
Green	Contains the *Integer* value, from 0 to 255, that specifies how dense the color green will be in the finished fractal image.
Blue	Contains the *Integer* value, from 0 to 255, that specifies how dense the color blue will be in the finished fractal image.
Shape	Contains an *Integer* value that corresponds to the shape the user chooses, such as a circle, a line, or a box, from the *optDrawStyle* control.
Filled	Contains a *Boolean* value, *True* or *False*, that specifies whether the program should fill the image the procedure will draw, or draw only the image's outline.

Table 5.16 The **ImageData** *structure's variable descriptions.*

In addition to the *ImageData* structure declaration, the *mdlFractal* module contains the declarations for the *StopPainting* global variable, a flag variable that the program will use to stop drawing, and the declaration for the *Colors* array, which the program will use when it draws the Mandelbrot fractal, as you will learn in later sections. The *mdlFractal* module also includes the *InitColorArray* procedure, which the next section explains.

MORE ON THE PIXEL MEASUREMENT

As you learned in this chapter's "Understanding Graphs" section, the *prjFractal* project will draw circles and lines as small as a pixel. For the program to draw circles and lines in pixels, rather than Visual Basic twips, you must set the screen measurement to pixels, as shown here:

```
Me.ScaleMode = 3
```

Visual Basic uses the *ScaleMode* property to set screen measurements. In the *prjFractal* project, you will set the *ScaleMode* property to 3. Visual Basic supports eight scale modes; the default, 1, corresponds to twips. Setting the *ScaleMode* property to the constant 3 tells Visual Basic to use pixels as the scale mode. To ensure that you receive accurate values when you try to determine an object's size in pixels, you must read the object's *ScaleWidth*, *ScaleHeight*, *ScaleTop*, and *ScaleLeft* properties. Within the *prjFractal* project, you will assign the pixel measurement scale mode to the *frmFractals* form within the *Draw* procedure.

Note: You must set the **ScaleMode** *property for each object you define. You cannot set a project-wide* **ScaleMode** *property.*

171

WRITING THE CODE FOR THE INITCOLORARRAY PROCEDURE

As you have learned, the *prjFractal.exe* program uses a custom color array to draw the Mandelbrot fractal. When the program begins, *frmFractal's Form_Load* event calls the *InitColorArray* procedure, which assigns values to the array. The following code implements the *InitColorArray* procedure:

```
Public Sub InitColorArray()
  Colors(0) = RGB(0, 0, 0)          ' black
  Colors(1) = RGB(64, 64, 64)       ' dark gray
  Colors(2) = RGB(128, 128, 128)    ' gray
  Colors(3) = RGB(192, 192, 192)    ' light gray
  Colors(4) = RGB(255, 255, 0)      ' yellow
  Colors(5) = RGB(0, 255, 0)        ' green
  Colors(6) = RGB(255, 0, 255)      ' magenta
  Colors(7) = RGB(0, 0, 255)        ' blue
  Colors(8) = RGB(0, 255, 255)      ' cyan
  Colors(9) = RGB(255, 0, 0)        ' red
  Colors(10) = RGB(255, 200, 0)     ' orange
  Colors(11) = RGB(255, 175, 175)   ' pink
  Colors(12) = RGB(255, 255, 255)   ' white
  Colors(13) = RGB(128, 0, 0)       ' dark red
End Sub
```

As you will learn, the *Mandelbrot* class will use the values within the array to determine the color of each pixel within the fractal. You will learn more about the *Mandelbrot* class in later sections.

WRITING THE CODE FOR THE FRMFRACTAL FORM

The *frmFractal* form uses three variables throughout its processing. One variable contains the plot data for the fractals the program draws, one contains a range limiter (a value that specifies the upper-size boundary of the range in which the *Mandelbrot* equation will draw), and one is an object instance of the custom *Mandelbrot* class that you will create later in this chapter. The following code implements the variable declarations for the *frmFractal* form:

```
Option Explicit

Dim Plot As ImageData
Dim pRange As Integer
Dim mb As New Mandelbrot
```

The *Plot* variable is of the *ImageData* type, which you declared when you wrote the program code for the *mdlFractal* project. The *mb* variable is of the *Mandelbrot* type. The *Mandelbrot* type is a class that you will define later in this chapter. The *Mandelbrot* class is the primary container for the information the *prjFractal* program uses to draw the Mandelbrot fractal.

As you learned, the *prjFractal* project begins with the display of the *frmFractal* form. When you run the project, the *frmFractal* form loads, which results in the program's invoking the *Form_Load* event. The following code implements the *frmFractal* form's *Form_Load* event:

```
Private Sub Form_Load()
  InitColorArray
  Plot.Shape = 0
End Sub
```

The *Form_Load* event calls the *InitColorArray* procedure. As you have learned, the *InitColorArray* procedure initializes the color array that the program will use to draw the Mandelbrot fractal. After the *InitColorArray* procedure finishes its processing, the *Form_Load* event then initializes the drawing mode to circles (which corresponds to the initial selection in the *optDrawStyle* array).

WRITING THE CODE FOR THE DRAW PROCEDURE

As you have learned, the *prjFractal* program will calculate many values of a math equation and draw an image on your computer screen at the series of calculated X and Y values that the math equation describes. The *Draw* procedure will receive the calculated values and all the values in the *ImageData* structure, alter the values, and send them to the *DrawShape* procedure. The following code implements the *Draw* procedure:

```
Private Sub Draw(Plot As ImageData)
  Dim Xplus As Double, Yplus As Double, Constant As Double
  Dim Count As Integer

  Xplus = 150# * Plot.x + 320#
  Yplus = -88# * Plot.y + 240#
  DoEvents
  For Count = 1 To Plot.Density
    Constant = 0.099 * Count
    Plot.Xaxis = Xplus + Constant
    Plot.Yaxis = Yplus + Constant
    Plot.X2axis = Plot.Xaxis + 10
    Plot.Y2axis = Plot.Yaxis + 10
    If Plot.Filled Then
      For Plot.radius = 0 To 1
        Call DrawShape(Rnd * 255, Rnd * 255, Rnd * 255)
      Next Plot.radius
    ElseIf Plot.Density < 20 Then
      Call DrawShape(0, Rnd * Plot.Green, Rnd * Plot.Blue)
    Else
      If Count > (Plot.Density / 2) Then
        Call DrawShape(0, 0, Rnd * Plot.Blue)
      ElseIf Count > (Plot.Density / 6) Then
        Call DrawShape(Rnd * Plot.Red, Rnd * Plot.Green, Rnd * Plot.Blue)
      End If
    End If
  Next Count
End Sub
```

The *Draw* procedure declares several local variables that it initializes each time the program calls the procedure. The *Xplus* and *Yplus* variables store new values that the procedures offset by a constant multiplier to generate the actual drawing points on the screen that the program will use. The *Count* variable is a looping variable that stores an offset value.

After the procedure declares the local variables, the *Draw* procedure will alter the *ImageData* structure's *Plot* object *X* and *Y* elements, and assign the result to the *Xplus* and *Yplus* variables. Then, a *For-Next* loop will start at the value 1 and continue to loop until the loop counter reaches the value of the *Plot* object's *Density* element. Within the startup code for each fractal equation, the program code will set the *Density* element for the *Plot* object, which determines how many times the program draws an image. If the program draws an image many times, the image has a high density. On the other hand, if the program draws an image only a few times, the image has a low density. You will learn more about image densities in later sections of this chapter.

The *For-Next* loop will then multiply the *Count* variable's current value by a constant value and assign it to the *Constant* variable. After that, the code will add the *Constant* value to the *Xplus* value and assign it to the *Plot* object's *Xaxis* and *Yaxis* elements. Next, the code will add an arbitrary value of 10 to the *Plot* object's *Xaxis* and *Yaxis* elements, and assign the result to the *Plot* object's *X2axis* and *Y2axis* elements. Remember, the *ImageData* structure contains the *X2axis* and *Y2axis* variables to store the bottom right corner of a box if you select a box style.

Within the *For-Next* loop, an *If-Then* statement will check the *Plot* object's *Filled* and *Density* elements. If the *Filled* element is *True*, a *For-Next* loop will alter the *Plot* object's *Radius* element from 0 to 1 and pass random red, green, and blue colors to the *DrawShape* procedure. If the *Filled* element is *False*, the *ElseIf* statement will check the *Plot* object's *Density* element. If the *Density* element is less than 20, the *ElseIf* statement will pass green and blue colors to the *DrawShape* procedure. If the *Density* element is greater than 20, the *ElseIf* statement will use an *If-Then* statement to check the *Count* variable's value. If the *Count* variable's value is greater than the *Plot* object's *Density* element divided by 2, the code will pass a random blue color to the *DrawShape* procedure. If the *Count* variable's value is greater than the *Plot* object's *Density* value divided by 6, the code will pass random red, green, and blue colors to the *DrawShape* procedure.

Note: *The **DrawShape** procedure will receive three color values from the **Draw** procedure. Each color value will range from 0 to 255. 0 means no color and 255 means full color. In other words, if the red color value is 0, the resulting color will have no red in it. Within the **Draw** procedure, the three incoming color parameters will specify the RGB color values for red, green, and blue with three **Integer** values from 0 to 255.*

WRITING THE CODE FOR THE DRAWSHAPE PROCEDURE

Now that you have written the code for the *Draw* procedure, which will pass values to the *DrawShape* procedure, you can write the code for the *DrawShape* procedure. The *DrawShape* procedure will receive three color values from the *Draw* procedure, check the *Plot* object's *Shape* element to determine whether to draw a circle, line, or box shape, and then use the *Circle* or *Line* method to draw images on the *frmFractal* form. The following code implements the *DrawShape* procedure:

```
Private Sub DrawShape(RedFill As Integer, GreenFill As Integer, BlueFill _
    As Integer)
  If Plot.Shape = 0 Then
    Circle (Plot.Xaxis, Plot.Yaxis), Plot.Radius, RGB(RedFill, GreenFill, _
        BlueFill)
  ElseIf Plot.Shape = 1 Then
    Line (Plot.Xaxis, Plot.Yaxis)-(Plot.X2axis, Plot.Y2axis), _
        RGB(RedFill, GreenFill, BlueFill)
  ElseIf Plot.Shape = 2 Then
    Line (Plot.Xaxis, Plot.Yaxis)-(Plot.X2axis, Plot.Y2axis), _
        RGB(RedFill, GreenFill, BlueFill),BF
  End If
End Sub
```

Within the *frmFractal* form, if you choose the *optDrawStyle* control's Circles option, the *Plot* object's *Shape* element will equal 0. If you choose the Lines option, the *Plot* object's *Shape* element will equal 1. If you choose the Boxes option, the *Shape* element will equal 2.

Within the *DrawShape* procedure, an *If-Then* statement will check the *Plot* object's *Shape* value. If the *Shape* value is 0, the code will use the *Circle* method to draw circles on the *frmFractal* form. If the *Shape* value is 1, the code will use the *Line* method to draw lines on the *frmFractal* form. If the *Shape* value is 2, the code will use the *Line* method, including the *B* and *F* parameters, to draw filled boxes on the *frmFractal* form.

WRITING THE CODE FOR THE OPTDRAWSTYLE_CLICK EVENT

After you declare the *ImageData* structure in the *mdlFractal* module, you can set the *ImageData* structure's elements. Remember, you declared the *Plot* object as an *ImageData* structure type in the General–Declarations section of the Code window. The *Plot* object contains the *ImageData* structure's elements.

The *optDrawStyle* control's *Click* event will set the *Plot* object's *Shape* element to an integer value that represents a circle, a line, or a box. Remember, Visual Basic references each *optDrawStyle* control in the control array with an index value from 0 to 2. When you click your mouse on the *optDrawStyle* control, Visual Basic will store the underlying index value in memory. The following code implements the *optDrawStyle_Click* event:

```
Private Sub optDrawStyle_Click(Index As Integer)
  Plot.Shape = Index
End Sub
```

The *optDrawStyle* control's *Click* event assigns the *Index* value to the *Plot.Shape* member variable. As you learned in the previous section, the *DrawShape* function will use the *Plot.Shape* value to determine what shape to use to draw the fractal.

Writing the Code for the cmdCLS_Click Event

As you have learned, the *prjFractal* project uses the form's display area as its drawing area. When you run the *prjFractal* project, you will note that you can draw several fractals on top of each other. To avoid clutter and confusion, you will often want to clear the drawing area. As you know, you added the Clear Screen command button to the form for just that purpose. The following code implements the *cmdCLS_Click* event:

```
Private Sub cmdCls_Click()
    Me.Refresh
End Sub
```

The procedure calls the *Refresh* method, which clears the form's area. If you instead set the form's *AutoRedraw* property to *True*, clearing the form would be somewhat more complex. Opening another program in front of the *frmFractal* form will also clear the form.

175

Writing the Code for the cmdStopDrawing_Click Event

Because the fractal images the *prjFractal* program draws are, in some cases, quite large, it is useful to let you stop drawing a fractal image during its processing, if you want. The Stop Drawing button sets the global *StopPainting* flag, which the program code monitors, and stops drawing a fractal if the flag is *True*. The following code implements the *cmdStopDrawing_Click* event:

```
Private Sub cmdStopDrawing_Click()
   StopPainting = True
End Sub
```

Writing the Code for the cmdExit_Click Event

The last event to write before you begin to write the program code that will draw the fractal images is the *cmdExit_Click* event, which unloads the form and ends the program. The following code implements the *cmdExit_Click* event:

```
Private Sub cmdExit_Click()
   End
End Sub
```

More on the Six Predefined Fractal Images

Now that you have set up the two *frmFractal* and *frmUserEquation* forms, declared and written the code for the *ImageData* structure, and written the code for the *Draw* and *DrawShape* procedures, you will learn more about the six fractal equations. The *prjFractal* project will draw six images from six predefined fractal equations and one image from one user-defined fractal equation. The following sections explain each fractal equation and detail the program code that computes and draws each fractal.

Understanding the Hopalong Fractal

As you have learned, the *prjFractal* project will draw images from math equations. One of the equations will produce an image called the *Hopalong Fractal*. Although programmers based the Hopalong Fractal's algorithm design on a complex mathematical equation, the fractal looks similar to a snowflake when the program draws it on the screen. Snowflakes are fractals because each snowflake is constructed from many small, frozen water molecules. Similarly, the *prjFractal.exe* program constructs fractal images from many small circles, squares, or lines. Snowflakes form when water cools and crystallizes while falling through freezing air. The crystal form of a snowflake is based on a complex scientific principle, and water will crystallize the same way every time. As you will see, the Hopalong Fractal will repeatedly form the same image, as Figure 5.12 shows.

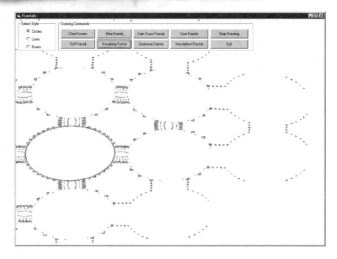

Figure 5.12 *The Hopalong Fractal image.*

WRITING THE CMDHOPALONG_CLICK EVENT

Now that you have seen an image of the Hopalong Fractal, you can code the math equation in Visual Basic. When you click your mouse on the Hopalong Fractal button on the *frmFractal* form, your program will invoke its *Click* event. The *Click* event will declare some variables, fill the *Plot* object's elements, and calculate *X* and *Y* values. Remember, the *Plot* object will store the *ImageData* structure elements, and will be available to all procedures and functions within the *frmFractal* form. The following code implements the *cmdHopalong_Click* event:

```
Private Sub cmdHopalong_Click()
   Dim Angle As Integer
   Dim B As Double, C As Double
   Dim A1 As Double, A2 As Double
   Dim Sign As Integer, Count As Integer
   Dim Xplus As Double, Yplus As Double

   StopPainting = False
   ScaleMode = 3
   Plot.Red = 255
   Plot.Green = 255
   Plot.Blue = 255
   Plot.Filled = True
   Plot.radius = 2
   Plot.Density = 8
   Angle = -3#
   B = Sin(Angle)
   C = Cos(Angle)
   Plot.x = 0
   Plot.y = 0
   Do While (Count < 5000)
     If Plot.x >= 0 Then
       Sign = 1
     Else
       Sign = -1
     End If
     Xplus = Plot.y - Sign * (Abs(B * Plot.x - C) ^ 0.5)
     Yplus = Angle - Plot.x
     Plot.x = Xplus
     Plot.y = Yplus
     Call Draw(Plot)
     Count = Count + 1
```

```
        If StopPainting Then Exit Sub
    Loop
End Sub
```

The procedure first declares the *Angle*, *B*, and *C* variables, which store an angle and its Sine and Cosine for the equation. Next, the procedure declares the *Sign* variable, which stores a negative or positive sign (depending on the fractal's current value), and the *Count* variable, which keeps count for a *Do-While* loop.

After finishing its declarations, the procedure sets the global *StopPainting* variable to *False*. If the user clicks the mouse on the Stop Drawing button, the program will set the *StopPainting* variable to *True*. As you can see, the last statement in the *Do-While* loop checks *StopPainting's* value and stops looping if it is *True*. The program code will assign the value 255 (the most dense color value) to the *Plot* object's *Red, Green,* and *Blue* elements, and will assign the *Plot* object's *Filled, Radius,* and *Density* elements.

The procedure uses the *Angle* value's *Sine* and *Cosine* to set some initial values, and then simply modifies the possible values for *X* and *Y* with the *Angle* value and the derived *Sine* and *Cosine* values. The program code then assigns the *Xplus* and *Yplus* values to the *Plot* object's *X* and *Y* elements. This ensures that the *If-Then-Else* statement at the beginning of the *Do-While* loop can check for a negative or positive value. After that, the code will call the *Draw* procedure, and the *Draw* procedure will call the *DrawShape* procedure, which will draw each point in the Hopalong Fractal image. The *Do-While* loop will continue until it reaches 5000. After the *cmdHopalong_Click* event finishes, you will see an image of the Hopalong Fractal on the *frmFractal* form.

177

MORE ON THE KAM TORUS FRACTAL

As you have learned, the *prjFractal* project will draw images from math equations. One of the equations will produce an image called the Kam Torus Fractal. The Kam Torus Fractal that you will draw with Visual Basic program code within this chapter derives from a complex math equation.

The Kam Torus Fractal looks similar to a spider web. Spider webs form when spiders emit a glue-like substance from their body, and weave it into a pattern. Depending on their environment and their type, spiders will form a web the same way each time. The Kam Torus Fractal will form the same image each time, as Figure 5.13 shows.

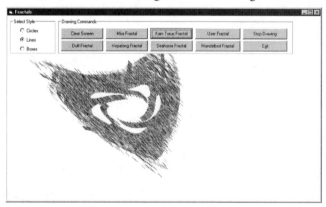

Figure 5.13 The Kam Torus Fractal image.

WRITING THE CMDKAMTORUS_CLICK EVENT

Now that you have seen another image of the Kam Torus Fractal, you can write the code for its math equation in Visual Basic. When you click your mouse on the Kam Torus Fractal button on the *frmFractal* form, your program will invoke its *Click* event. The *Click* event will declare some useful variables, fill the *Plot* object's elements, and calculate *X* and *Y* values. Remember, the *Plot* object will store the *ImageData* structure elements, and will be available to all procedures and functions within the *frmFractal* form. The following code implements the *cmdKamTorus_Click* event:

```
Private Sub cmdKamTorus_Click()
    Dim i As Integer
    Dim A As Single
```

```
Dim F As Double , Count As Double, maxcount As Double
Dim xNew As Double, yNew As Double

StopPainting = False
ScaleMode = 3
Plot.Red = 255
Plot.Green = 255
Plot.Blue = 255
Plot.radius = 1.025
Plot.Density = 1#
A = 10
F = 0.987
Count = 1.1
maxcount = 2.9

Do Until (Count > maxcount)
  Count = Count + 0.005
  Plot.x = Count / 3
  Plot.y = Count / 3
  For i = 0 To 50
    xNew = Plot.x * Cos(A) + (Plot.x * Plot.x - Plot.y) * Sin(A)
    yNew = Plot.x * Sin(A) - (Plot.x * Plot.x - F * Plot.y) * Cos(A)
    Plot.x = xNew
    Plot.y = yNew
    Call Draw(Plot)
    If StopPainting Then Exit Sub
  Next i
Loop
End Sub
```

As with the Hopalong Fractal, the crucial processing for the Kam Torus Fractal occurs within a pair of drawing loops. The outer loop, a *Do-Until* loop, loops from 1.1 to 2.9 in steps of 0.005. On each iteration, the loop sets the X and Y members' values for the *Plot* structure to a value between approximately 0.35 and approximately 0.96 (*Count / 3*). Each time it sets the outer value, the procedure then calls an internal loop, which uses the Sine and Cosine of the A variable to adjust the *Plot* value. After each adjustment, the procedure plots the value, then checks to make sure the user did not click the mouse on the Stop Drawing button. If not, the program code loops again, and again changes the *Plot* value.

UNDERSTANDING THE DUFF FRACTAL

As you have learned, the *prjFractal* project will draw images from math equations. One of the equations will produce an image called the *Duff Fractal*. The Duff Fractal is based on a complex math equation that you will use the Visual Basic language to write. The Duff Fractal looks similar to a spiral. Spirals form when you surround a small circle with a continuous circular line until the image grows larger. To draw a spiral, you must continuously surround a small image with a larger copy of the image. The Duff Fractal will continue to form the same image, as Figure 5.14 shows.

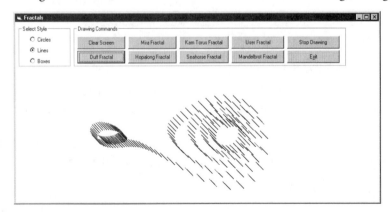

Figure 5.14 The Duff Fractal image.

WRITING THE CMDDUFF_CLICK EVENT

Now that you have seen an image of the Duff Fractal, you can write the code for the math equation in Visual Basic. When you click your mouse on the Duff Fractal button on the *frmFractal* form, your program will invoke its *Click* event. The *Click* event will declare some useful variables, fill the *Plot* object's elements, and calculate *X* and *Y* values. Remember, the *Plot* object will store the *ImageData* structure elements, and will be available to all procedures and functions within the *frmFractal* form. The following code implements the *cmdDuff_Click* event:

```
Private Sub cmdDuff_Click()
   Dim A As Double, C As Double
   Dim Xplus As Double, Yplus As Double
   Dim PIE As Double, PIE2 As Double
   Dim Count As Integer

   StopPainting = False
   ScaleMode = 3
   Plot.radius = 10
   Plot.Density = 100
   Plot.Red = 255
   Plot.Green = 0
   Plot.Blue = 255
   Plot.Filled = False
   Plot.x = 1#
   Plot.y = 0.2222222
   Status = True
   Count = 0
   PIE = 3.14159265358979
   PIE2 = 2# * PIE
   A = 0#
   C = 0.3
   Do While (Count < 201)
      Xplus = Plot.x + (Plot.y / PIE2)
      Yplus = Plot.y + (-(Plot.x * Plot.x * Plot.x) + Plot.x - (0.25 * _
          Plot.y) + C * Cos(A)) / PIE2
      Plot.x = Xplus
      Plot.y = Yplus
      Call Draw(Plot)
      Count = Count + 1
      If StopPainting Then Exit Sub
   Loop
End Sub
```

After the procedure code declares the variables, the program code will assign the *Plot* object's *Radius*, *Density*, *Red*, *Green*, *Blue*, and *Filled* elements. After that, the code will assign values to the *Plot* object's *X* and *Y* elements, initialize the count, and assign a 15-digit value (a constant representation of the complex mathematical number Pi) to *PIE*. The program code also doubles *PIE's* value and assigns the result to *PIE2*. The program code additionally initializes the *Angle* and *Constant* variables the program will use in the Duff Fractal equation.

A *Do-While* loop will then start at 0 and continue to 200. Within the *Do-While* loop, the code will calculate the Duff Fractal equation and assign the results to the *Xplus*, *Yplus*, and *Plot* objects' *X* and *Y* elements. Then, the code will call the *Draw* procedure, and the *Draw* procedure will call the *DrawShape* procedure, which will draw the Duff Fractal image on the *frmFractal* form. The *Do-While* loop will continue until it reaches 200, provided the user does not click the mouse on the Stop Drawing button. After the *Click* event finishes, you will see the Duff Fractal image on the *frmFractal* form.

UNDERSTANDING THE MIRA FRACTAL

As you have learned, the *prjFractal* project will draw images from math equations. One equation will produce an image called the *Mira Fractal*. The Mira Fractal is based on a complex math equation that you will use the Visual

Basic language to write. The Mira Fractal looks similar to a sky star field. Within the Mira Fractal, you will see what appears to be a black hole. The Mira Fractal will continue to form the same image, as Figure 5.15 shows.

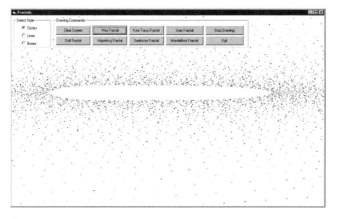

Figure 5.15 *The Mira Fractal image.*

WRITING THE CODE FOR THE CMDMIRA_CLICK EVENT

Now that you have seen an image of the Mira Fractal, you can write the code for the math equation in Visual Basic. When you click your mouse on the Mira Fractal button on the *frmFractal* form, your program will invoke its *Click* event. The *Click* event will declare some useful variables, fill the *Plot* object's elements, and calculate *X* and *Y* values. Remember, the *Plot* object will store the *ImageData* structure elements, and will be available to all procedures and functions within the *frmFractal* form. The following code implements the *cmdMira_Click* event:

```
Private Sub cmdMira_Click()
  Dim A As Double, B As Double, C As Double, z As Double
  Dim u As Double, w As Double
  Dim Count As Integer

  StopPainting = False
  ScaleMode = 3
  Plot.Filled = True
  Plot.Red = 0
  Plot.Green = 0
  Plot.Blue = 255
  Status = True
  Count = 0
  Plot.radius = 5
  Plot.Density = 3
  A = 0.98888888888
  B = 0.999444
  C = 2 - (2 * A)
  Plot.x = 3.5
  Plot.y = 4.5
  w = (A * Plot.x) + (C * Plot.x * Plot.x / (1 + (Plot.x * Plot.x)))
  Do While (Count < 9501)
    z = Plot.x
    Plot.x = (B * Plot.y) + w
    u = Plot.x * Plot.x
    w = (A * Plot.x) + (C * u / (1 + u))
    Plot.y = w - z
    Call Draw(Plot)
    Count = Count + 1
    If StopPainting Then Exit Sub
  Loop
End Sub
```

After declaring the procedure's local variables, the program code will assign the *Plot* object's *Filled, Red, Green, Blue, Radius,* and *Density* elements. Next, the program code will initialize the angle values for the *A* and *B* variables, calculate the *ConstantC* variable, and initialize *Plot.x* and *Plot.y*. Then, the code will do the first of three calculations of the Mira Fractal equation, and assign the result to the *W* variable.

As with the other fractals, a *Do-While* loop will start at 0 and continue to a pre-set value (in this case, 9500) and draw each point in the fractal during the loop. Within the *Do-While* loop, the code will assign the *Plot* object's *X* element to the *Z* variable, calculate the second of three calculations of the Mira Fractal equation, and assign the result to the *X* element. Next, the program code will calculate the *U* variable, perform the third of three calculations of the Mira Fractal equation, and assign the result to *Plot.y*. The procedure code will then call the *Draw* procedure, plotting each point in the fractal. The *Do-While* loop will continue until the *Count* value equals 9500, or until the user clicks the mouse on the Stop Drawing button.

UNDERSTANDING THE SEAHORSE FRACTAL

As you have learned, the *prjFractal* project will draw images from math equations. One equation will produce an image called the *Seahorse Fractal.* The Seahorse Fractal is based on a complex math equation that you will use the Visual Basic language to write. The Seahorse Fractal looks similar to the bones of a manta ray. The Seahorse Fractal will form the same image continuously, as Figure 5.16 shows.

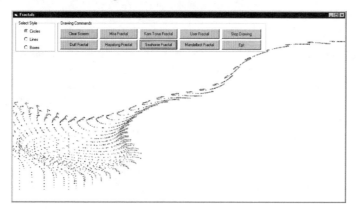

Figure 5.16 The Seahorse Fractal image.

WRITING THE CODE FOR THE CMDSEAHORSE_CLICK EVENT

Now that you have seen an image of the Seahorse Fractal, you can code the math equation in Visual Basic. When you click your mouse on the Seahorse Fractal button on the *frmFractal* form, your program will invoke its *Click* event. The *Click* event will declare some useful variables, fill the *Plot* object's elements, and calculate *X* and *Y* values. Remember, the *Plot* object will store the *ImageData* structure elements, and will be available to all procedures and functions within the *frmFractal* form. The following code implements the *cmdSeahorse_Click* event:

```
Private Sub cmdSeahorse_Click()
   Dim A As Double, B As Double, C As Double, d As Double, E As Double
   Dim Angle1 As Double, Angle2 As Double
   Dim x As Double, y As Double
   Dim Xplus As Double, Yplus As Double, Xold As Double, Yold As Double
   Dim i As Double, j As Double, K As Double
   Dim FuncX As Double, FuncY As Double

   StopPainting = False
   ScaleMode = 3
   Plot.Red = 0
   Plot.Green = 255
   Plot.Blue = 255
   A = 0.9
```

```
      B = 0.8
      C = 0.7
      d = 0.6
      E = 0.05
      Angle2 = 0.2
      Plot.radius = 2
      Plot.Density = 4
      For i = -1 To 1 Step 0.5
        For j = -1 To 1 Step 0.1
          x = i
          Xplus = x + 3
          y = j
          Yplus = y - 2
          Angle1 = Angle2
            For K = 1 To 60 Step 0.5
              Yplus = y - 2
              Xplus = x - 2
              Plot.x = Xplus
              Plot.y = Yplus
              Call Draw(Plot)
              Xold = x
              Yold = y
              FuncY = C * Yold
              FuncX = d * Xold
              x = E * K + (A * Xold - Angle1 * Sin(FuncY + Sin(3 * FuncY)))
              y = E * K + (B * Yold - Angle1 * Sin(FuncX + Sin(3 * FuncX)))
              If StopPainting Then Exit Sub
            Next K
        Next j
      Next i
    End Sub
```

Much like the other fractals, the process that draws the fractal falls almost entirely within a set of loops. For the Seahorse Fractal, there are three loops: *i, j,* and *K.* The Seahorse Fractal also uses a set of constants to manipulate the drawing equation, which uses the *Sine* function to obtain radian values on the increasing sequence of values. Each time the program completes an inner loop, it checks to ensure that the user has not clicked the Stop Drawing button.

Within the innermost *For-Next (K)* loop, the code will alter the *X* and *Y* values, and assign the results to the *Yplus, Xplus,* and *Plot* object's *X* and *Y* elements. Then, the code will call the *Draw* procedure, and the *Draw* procedure will call the *DrawShape* procedure, which will draw the Seahorse Fractal image on the *frmFractal* form. After the *Draw* procedure completes its cycle, still within the *K-For-Next* loop, the code will assign the *X* and *Y* values to *Xold* and *Yold,* alter the *Xold* and *Yold* values, and assign the results to the *FuncY* and *FuncX* variables. At this point, the code will calculate the Seahorse Fractal equation and assign the result to *X* and *Y.* The three *For-Next* loops will continue until *i =1* or the user clicks the mouse on the Stop Drawing button.

WRITING THE CMDUSERFUNCTION_CLICK EVENT

As you have learned, the *prjFractal* project lets you draw an image from your own user-defined equation. When you click your mouse on the User Fractal button, your program will invoke its *Click* event. First, the *Click* event will use the Visual Basic *Unload* method to remove the *frmFractal* form from the computer screen. Second, the *Click* event will use the Visual Basic *Show* method to open the *frmUserEquation* form. After Visual Basic displays the *frmUserEquation* form, you can enter your own user-defined equation and draw an image of it. The following code implements the *cmdUserFunction_Click* event:

```
    Private Sub cmdUserFunction_Click()
      Unload Me
      frmUserEquation.Show
    End Sub
```

MORE ON THE MANDELBROT FRACTAL

As you have learned, the *prjFractal* project will draw images from math equations. One of the equations will produce an image called the *Mandelbrot Fractal*. The Mandelbrot Fractals are some of the most commonly seen and drawn fractals. Because minor variations you make within the equation can have far-reaching consequences in the final image, Mandelbrot Fractals can look radically different, depending on the variation of the equation you use to draw the fractal. Within the *prjFractal* project, the Mandelbrot Fractal will form the same image continuously, as Figure 5.17 shows.

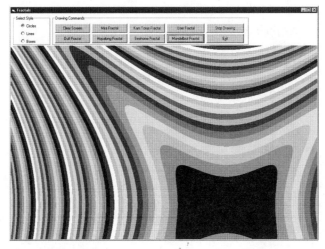

Figure 5.17 *The Mandelbrot Fractal image.*

WRITING THE CMDMANDELBROT_CLICK EVENT

The *cmdMandelbrot_Click* event is deceptively simple. Although the Mandelbrot Fractal clearly appears to be the most complex fractal this chapter explains, the *cmdMandelbrot_Click* event contains only five lines. The following code implements the *cmdMandelbrot_Click* event:

```
Private Sub cmdMandelbrot_Click()
   StopPainting = False
   Me.Refresh
   Me.ScaleMode = 3
   mb.Fractal
End Sub
```

The *Click* event sets the flag variable, refreshes the form (clearing the drawing area), sets the *ScaleMode* to pixels, and invokes two methods against the *mb* object. If you remember, the *mb* object is a variable of type *Mandelbrot*, the custom class module that you added to the project earlier in this chapter. In fact, the *mb.fractal* method invokes the *Mandelbrot* class's drawing routine, which performs extensive processing. In the next several sections, you will design the *Mandelbrot* class, as well as the component structures that support it.

WRITING THE CODE FOR THE MDLPOINT MODULE

The *Mandelbrot* class uses an object of type *POINT*, which represents an *x*-coordinate and a *y*-coordinate, to determine where it will draw next. The *prjFractal* project declares both the *POINT* structure and the only function that returns any *POINT* information, *ConstructPoint*, within the *mdlPoint* module. The following code implements the *POINT* declaration and the *ConstructPoint* function:

```
Type POINT
   x As Double
   y As Double
End Type
```

```
Function ConstructPoint(inX As Double, inY As Double) As POINT
  Dim ptLocal As POINT

  ptLocal.x = inX
  ptLocal.y = inY
  ConstructPoint = ptLocal
End Function
```

As you can see, the *POINT* type contains *x* and *y* members. The *ConstructPoint* function accepts an *x*-coordinate value and a *y*-coordinate value and returns those values as members within a *POINT* structure.

WRITING THE CODE FOR THE mdlComplex MODULE

184

If you have worked with advanced mathematics at all, you are probably familiar with the concept of a complex number. A *complex number* is a number that has both a real and an imaginary component. The *Mandelbrot* class uses complex numbers extensively when determining what color to draw a given point. The Visual Basic functions you use to manipulate complex numbers might be something you can reuse in other programs, so the function and the type definition are all within the *mdlComplex* module. The following code implements the *COMPLEX* type and the two variables of the type that functions throughout the module will use:

```
Type COMPLEX
  xReal As Double
  yImaginary As Double
End Type

Dim cmpLocal As COMPLEX
Dim absLocal As COMPLEX
```

BETTER UNDERSTANDING COMPLEX NUMBERS

As you have learned, a complex number is a number that has both a real and an imaginary component. In fact, a complex number is any number in the form $a + bi$, where both a and b are real numbers, and i is an imaginary number whose square is -1. Because squaring a number always yields a positive value (for example $(-5)*(-5)=25$), a number whose square is a negative number must be an imaginary number. By mathematical rules, a real number multiplied by an imaginary number must yield an imaginary number. Therefore, a complex number consists of a real number (a) and an imaginary number (bi).

WRITING THE CODE FOR THE COMPLEX NUMBER ADD AND SUBTRACT FUNCTIONS

As you have learned, the *Mandelbrot* class uses complex numbers extensively to determine what color to draw the fractal at a given point. Visual Basic, unlike C/C++ and Java, does not include built-in support for complex numbers, so you must write several functions to perform standard mathematical operations against the *COMPLEX* parameters the *Mandelbrot* class will pass in. Much like real numbers or integers, you will often perform simple arithmetic with complex numbers, such as addition, subtraction, multiplication, and division. Within the *prjFractal* project, you can use the *Add* function to perform mathematical addition of complex numbers. The following code implements the *Add* function:

```
Function Add(in1 As COMPLEX, in2 As COMPLEX) As COMPLEX
  cmpLocal.xReal = in1.xReal + in1.xReal
  cmpLocal.yImaginary = in2.yImaginary + in2.yImaginary
  Add = cmpLocal
End Function
```

The *Add* function first adds the real components of the two complex numbers, and then adds the imaginary components of the two complex numbers. Finally, the function returns the results as the real and imaginary components of a new *COMPLEX* number. As you can see, the add operation is relatively simple. The *Subtract* function performs similar processing. The following code implements the *Subtract* function:

```
Function Subtract(in1 As COMPLEX, in2 As COMPLEX) As COMPLEX
   cmpLocal.xReal = in1.xReal - in2.xReal
   cmpLocal.yImaginary = in1.yImaginary - in2.yImaginary
   Subtract = cmpLocal
End Function
```

The *Subtract* function first subtracts the real components of the two complex numbers, and then subtracts the imaginary components of the two complex numbers. Finally, the function returns the results as the real and imaginary components of a new *COMPLEX* number. As you can see, the subtract operation is also relatively simple. However, the multiply operation is significantly more complex, as you will find in the next section.

WRITING THE CODE FOR THE COMPLEX NUMBER MULTIPLY AND GETABSOLUTE FUNCTIONS

As you learned in the previous section, the code for the *Multiply* function is significantly more complex than the code for the *Add* and *Subtract* functions. In fact, when you multiply a complex number by a complex number, the real component contains elements of both the real and the imaginary numbers. The following code implements the *Multiply* function:

```
Function Multiply(in1 As COMPLEX, in2 As COMPLEX) As COMPLEX
   cmpLocal.xReal = in1.xReal * in2.xReal - in1.yImaginary * in2.yImaginary
   cmpLocal.yImaginary = in1.xReal * in2.yImaginary + in1.yImaginary * _
        in2.xReal
   Multiply = cmpLocal
End Function
```

As you can see, the resulting real number *(xReal)* is equal to *((Real1 * Real2) - (Imaginary1 * Imaginary2))*. The resulting imaginary number *(yImaginary)* is equal to *((Real1 * Imaginary2) + (Real2 * Imaginary1))*. The program uses similar processing to find the absolute value of a complex number. However, the program returns the absolute value as type *Double*, rather than as type *COMPLEX*. To find a complex number's absolute value, you can use the *getAbsolute* function. The following code implements the *getAbsolute* function:

```
Function getAbsolute(ResultIn As COMPLEX) As Double
   getAbsolute = Sqr(getSquare(ResultIn))
End Function
```

The *getAbsolute* function returns the square root of the square of the incoming complex number. The *getAbsolute* function calls the *getSquare* function to square the incoming complex number. The following code implements the *getSquare* function:

```
Function getSquare(ResultIn2 As COMPLEX) As Double
   getSquare = ResultIn2.xReal * ResultIn2.xReal + _
        ResultIn2.yImaginary * ResultIn2.yImaginary
End Function
```

The *getSquare* function returns the square of a complex number as the square of its real component plus the square of its imaginary component. As you will see, the *Mandelbrot* class uses all the complex number values and functions to determine the color to draw the current pixel.

WRITING THE CODE FOR THE MANDELBROT CLASS

As you have learned, the *prjFractal* project uses the *Mandelbrot* class to draw the *Mandelbrot* fractal. The *Mandelbrot* class contains member functions to determine the current point in the fractal, determine the color for the point, and paint the point. The class's only public method is the *Fractal* function, which in turn calls the *Paint* function.

DECLARING THE CLASS VARIABLES

As you have learned, the *Mandelbrot* class performs the drawing actions for the Mandelbrot Fractal within the *prjFractal* project. The *Mandelbrot* class uses five class-wide variables: three are points, one is the color to draw, and the last variable is the size of the drawing palette. The following code implements the variable declarations for the *Mandelbrot* class:

```
Option Explicit
Public pRange As Integer
Dim mbPoint1 As POINT
Dim mbPoint1Result As POINT
Dim mbPoint2Result As POINT
Dim ColorToDraw As Long
```

INITIALIZING THE MANDELBROT CLASS

186 As you learned in Chapter 1, "Introduction to Visual Basic," each time you create a class object, the class will invoke its *Initialize* event. The following code implements the *Class_Initialize* event for the *Mandelbrot* class:

```
Private Sub Class_Initialize()
   pRange = frmFractals.ScaleWidth
End Sub
```

The *Initialize* event sets the number of pixels the fractal will draw to the *ScaleWidth* of the *frmFractal* form. The class then performs no other processing until the user clicks the mouse on the *cmdMandelbrot* command button, which will invoke the *Mandelbrot* class's *Fractal* method. The next section explains the *Mandelbrot* class's *Fractal* method.

WRITING THE MANDELBROT DRAWING ROUTINES

As you have learned, when the user clicks the mouse on the *cmdMandelbrot* command button, the program code invokes the *Mandelbrot* class method *Fractal*. The *Fractal* method is the class's only public member. The following code implements the *Fractal* method:

```
Public Function Fractal()
   Call Paint
End Function
```

The *Fractal* method, in turn, calls the *Paint* method. The *Paint* method performs processing similar to that all the other fractals in this chapter perform—that is, it progresses through a series of loops, drawing points each time through the loop. The *Mandelbrot Paint* method differs from the fractal code you have seen previously in that it actually draws *every point on the screen*. The computations for the *Mandelbrot* fractal center around determining each point's color, rather than its location. The following code implements the *Paint* method:

```
Function Paint()
   Dim ix As Double, iy As Double
   Dim radius As Long

   For iy = 1 To pRange - 2
     For ix = 1 To pRange - 2
       Dim mbpoint2 As POINT
       mbPoint2Result = ConstructPoint(ix, iy)
       mbPoint1 = mbPoint2Result
       Call calcPoint
       frmFractals.Circle (mbPoint1.x, 100 + mbPoint1.y), 1, ColorToDraw
       DoEvents
       If StopPainting Then Exit Function
     Next ix
   Next iy
End Function
```

The *Paint* method loops through every pixel on the drawing area (unless the user clicks the mouse on the Stop Drawing button). The *Paint* method creates a point based on the current value of the loops, and calls the *calcPoint* function, which uses the point to determine the color to draw the point. The *Paint* method then draws a circle, one pixel wide, with the color that *calcPoint* sets. After drawing the pixel, the program checks the *StopPainting* flag. If it is *False*, the program loops again.

WRITING THE calcPoint FUNCTION

As you have learned, the *calcPoint* function accepts a point from the *Paint* function, and uses a series of mathematical equations to determine the correct color to draw that point. The *calcPoint* function uses the *COMPLEX* number definitions that you wrote earlier in this chapter. The following code implements the *calcPoint* function:

```
Function calcPoint()
  Dim i As Integer
  Dim x As Double, y As Double, abs1 As Double
  Dim iteration As Integer
  Dim r As Double
  Dim zLocal As COMPLEX, zLocal_OLD As COMPLEX, cLocal As COMPLEX
  Dim multResult As COMPLEX, addResult As COMPLEX

  iteration = 80
  r = 1.6
  x = 2# * r * (mbPoint1.x / pRange) - 1.25 * r
  y = r - 2# * r * (mbPoint1.y / pRange)
  cLocal.xReal = x
  cLocal.yImaginary = y
  zLocal.xReal = cLocal.xReal
  zLocal.yImaginary = cLocal.yImaginary
  zLocal_OLD = zLocal
  multResult = Multiply(zLocal, zLocal)
  addResult = Add(multResult, cLocal)
  abs1 = getAbsolute(Subtract(addResult, zLocal_OLD))
  ColorToDraw = selectColor(abs1)
End Function
```

As you can see, the *calcPoint* function initializes its local variables, sets the real and imaginary components of two *COMPLEX* numbers, and performs some processing on those numbers, which yields a *Double* value. The *calcPoint* function then calls the *selectColor* function with the *abs1* value (the absolute value of the complex number series), which returns the color value from the *Colors* array that you defined in the *mdlFractal* module. The following code implements the *selectColor* function:

```
Function selectColor(ColorIn As Double) As Long
  Dim i As Double, threshold As Double
  Dim nColor As Integer

  i = 0
  threshold = 0.2
  nColor = 12
  Do While (ColorIn > threshold)
    threshold = threshold + 0.2
    If i > nColor Then i = 0
    i = i + 1
  Loop
  selectColor = Colors(i)
End Function
```

As you can see, the function accepts the *ColorIn* parameter (a double value the *COMPLEX getAbsolute* function returns). The function then loops until it encounters the incoming color value. If *i* gets larger than the number of colors, the loop sets *i* back to 0. When the loop exits, the color that the point will draw is the array value to which *i* points.

CLOSING ON THE MANDELBROT FRACTAL

The Mandelbrot fractal is one of the more difficult fractals to start writing, but also one of the more interesting fractals to customize after you finish the initial design. You can add more colors to the color array, perform further processing on the incoming complex numbers, and more, to vary the program's results. For example, if you add the following code to the *calcPoint* function, you will double the number of color bands within the Mandelbrot fractal:

```
addResult = Add(multResult, cLocal)                    ' Existing
addResult = Add(addResult, cLocal)                     ' NEW
abs1 = getAbsolute(Subtract(addResult, zLocal_OLD))    ' Existing
```

If you have an interest in math or graphics, you should try to manipulate the various values within the Mandelbrot class to draw interesting designs.

WRITING THE PRJFRACTAL PROJECT'S FRMUSEREQUATION FORM

188

As you have learned, the *prjFractal* project will let you draw an image of your own user-defined equation. After you click your mouse on the User Fractal button on the *frmFractal* form, Visual Basic will open the *frmUserEquation* form. As you know, you have added *Label*, *TextBox*, and *CommandButton* controls to the *frmUserEquation* form, which will let you enter a user-defined mathematical equation. The *frmUserEquation* form code will use a procedure similar to the *frmFractal* form's *Draw* procedure, called *DrawUser*, to plot your user-defined function.

DECLARING THE FRMUSEREQUATION FORM'S VARIABLES

Just as the *frmFractal's* form did, the *frmUserEquation* form uses a *Plot* structure to manage the image drawing on the form. Additionally, the *frmUserEquation* form uses a flag value to ensure the program does not try to plot functions with out-of-range values (too large or too small to plot on the form). The following code implements the *frmUserEquation* form's variable declarations:

```
Dim Plot As ImageData
Dim OutofRange As Boolean
```

WRITING THE FRMUSEREQUATION'S FORM_LOAD EVENT

As you have learned, you will invoke the *frmUserEquation* form from within the *frmFractal* form. When you click your mouse on the *cmdUserEquation* button, the program code will load the *frmUserEquation* form. As with other forms, the first event the program will invoke is the *Form_Load* event. The following code implements the *frmUserEquation's Form_Load* event:

```
Private Sub Form_Load()
   Me.ScaleMode = 3
End Sub
```

The *Form_Load* event sets the *ScaleMode* for the form to 3. As you learned earlier in this chapter, *ScaleMode* 3 tells the program to use pixels as its drawing unit, rather than the default twip. The program code throughout the *frmUserEquation* form uses pixels to draw its images on the screen.

WRITING THE CMDCLEARPLOT_CLICK EVENT

As you learned with the *frmFractal* form, you can click your mouse on the Clear Screen button to clear the drawing area of the form. The following code implements the *cmdClearPlot_Click* event:

```
Private Sub cmdClearPlot_Click()
   Me.Refresh
End Sub
```

Just as with the *frmFractal* form's *cmdCLS_Click* event, refreshing the form erases any existing drawing, clearing the palette for other drawings. If the form's *AutoRedraw* property was set to *True*, clearing the form would be somewhat more complex. Opening another program in front of the *frmUserEquation* form will also clear the form.

WRITING THE CMDEXIT_CLICK EVENT

When you finish drawing your own equations on the *frmUserEquation* form, you can return to the *frmFractal* form. To return to the *frmFractal* form, click your mouse on the Exit button. The following code implements the *cmdExit_Click* event:

```
Private Sub cmdExit_Click()
   Unload Me
End Sub
```

The *cmdExit_Click* event unloads the *frmUserEquation* form and returns the focus to the *frmFractal* form.

WRITING THE CMDPLOTUSER_CLICK EVENT

After you enter a user-defined equation on the *frmUserEquation* form, you can write code that will calculate values from the equation. When you click your mouse on the Plot Function button on the *frmUserEquation* form, your program will invoke its *Click* event. The *Click* event will declare some useful variables, fill the *Plot* object's elements, and calculate X and Y values. Remember, the *Plot* object will store the *ImageData* structure elements, and will be available to all procedures and functions within the form. The following code implements the *cmdPlotUser_Click* event:

189

```
Private Sub cmdPlotUser_Click()
   Dim X1 As Double, X2 As Double, X3 As Double
   Dim A As Double, B As Double, C As Double
   Dim K As Double
   Dim Start As Double, Finish As Double

   Me.MousePointer = vbHourglass
   cmdPlotUser.Enabled = False
   OutofRange = False
   ScaleMode = 3
   Plot.radius = 10
   Plot.Density = 1
   Plot.Red = 255
   Plot.Green = 255
   Plot.Blue = 255
   Plot.Filled = True

   X1 = Val(txtX1.Text)
   X2 = Val(txtX2.Text)
   X3 = Val(txtX3.Text)
   A = Val(txtA.Text)
   B = Val(txtB.Text)
   C = Val(txtC.Text)
   K = Val(txtK.Text)
   If X1 < 0 Or X2 < 0 Or X3 < 0 Then
      varib = MsgBox("ENTER [x1] or [x2] or [x3] that is greater than 0.....", _
         vbCritical, "ENTER VALUES")
      cmdPlotUser.Enabled = True
      Me.MousePointer = vbNormal
      Exit Sub
   End If
   If (A) > 3 Or (B) > 3 Or (C) > 3 Then
      varib = MsgBox("ENTER [a] or [b] or [c] that is 3 or less.....", _
         vbCritical, "ENTER VALUES")
      cmdPlotUser.Enabled = True
      Me.MousePointer = vbNormal
      Exit Sub
   End If
   If K < -1000 Or K > 5000 Then
      MsgBox "K must be more than -1000 and less than 5000.", vbOKOnly
```

```
      cmdPlotUser.Enabled = True
      Me.MousePointer = vbNormal
      Exit Sub
   End If
   Start = 0.5
   Finish = 50
   If X1 = 0 Then X1 = 0.01
   Do Until (Start > Finish) Or OutofRange
      Start = Start + 0.05
      Plot.x = Start / 10
      Plot.y = (X1 * Plot.x) ^ (Cos(A)) + (X2 * Plot.x) ^ (B) + _
         (X3 * Plot.x) ^ (C) + K / 1000
      DrawUser
   Loop
   cmdPlotUser.Enabled = True
   Me.MousePointer = vbNormal
End Sub
```

The *cmdPlotUser_Click* event first initializes some internal values and sets certain defaults for the *Plot* object. The program code then performs error checking to protect against values that will not draw or that will cause the drawing function to crash the program. If all the values are acceptable, the program code will loop 100 times, or until the plot is out of plotting range. Each time the program iterates through the loop, the program code will compute *x* and *y* based on the loop value and values the user entered. The program will then draw the next point in the plot. The *Do-Until* loop will continue until the *Start* value equals the *Finish* value. After the *Click* event finishes, you will see an image of the user-defined equation on the *frmUserEquation* form.

Note: *Unlike the program code in the **frmFractal** form, the program code in the **frmUserEquation** form will disable the Plot Function button until the code finishes plotting a given function.*

WRITING THE CODE FOR THE DRAWUSER PROCEDURE

After you enter an equation on the *frmUserEquation* form, you can draw an image. As you learned, the *cmdPlotUser_Click* event calls the *DrawUser* procedure to draw the equation. The *DrawUser* procedure will use the *Circle* method to draw an image. The following code implements the *DrawUser* procedure:

```
Private Sub DrawUser()
   Dim XX As Double, YY As Double, C As Double
   Dim Count As Integer, i As Integer
   Dim Xaxis As Double, Yaxis As Double
   Dim RedFill As Double, GreenFill As Double, BlueFill As Double

   XX = 150# * Plot.x '+ 320#
   YY = -88# * Plot.y + 700#
   For Count = 1 To Plot.Density
      C = 0.099 * Count
      OutofRange = checkvals(XX, YY, C)
      If OutofRange Then Exit Sub
      If Plot.Shape = 0 Then
         Plot.Xaxis = XX + C
         Plot.Yaxis = YY + C
         Plot.X2axis = XX - C
         Plot.Y2axis = YY - C
      Else
         Plot.Xaxis = XX + 10
         Plot.Yaxis = YY + 10
         Plot.X2axis = XX - 10
         Plot.Y2axis = YY - 10
      End If
```

```
   If Plot.Filled Then
      For Plot.radius = 0 To 10
         Call DrawShape(Rnd * 255, Rnd * 255, Rnd * 255)
      Next Plot.radius
   ElseIf Plot.Density < 20 Then
      Call DrawShape(0, Rnd * Plot.Green, Rnd * Plot.Blue)
   Else
      If Count > (Plot.Density / 2) Then
         Call DrawShape(0, 0, Rnd * Plot.Blue)
      ElseIf Count > (Plot.Density / 6) Then
         Call DrawShape(Rnd * Plot.Red, Rnd * Plot.Green, Rnd * Plot.Blue)
      End If
   End If
   Next Count
End Sub
```

The *DrawUser* procedure performs processing nearly identical to the *Draw* procedure that you used in the *frmFractal* form. The only two significant differences are that if you set the drawing tool to circles, the *DrawUser* function draws concentric circles of random shades, unlike the small, filled circles the *frmFractal* form uses, and the *DrawUser* function uses the *CheckVals* function to check the values *DrawUser* will use to plot before it uses them. If the values are too small or too large, the *DrawUser* function does not draw the point. The *CheckVals* function checks the current set of drawing points to ensure that it is not out of the possible range of values for drawing. The following code implements the *CheckVals* function that the *frmUserEquation* form uses to check the values of plotting points:

```
Private Function CheckVals(xcoord As Double, ycoord As Double, _
    addition As Double) As Boolean
  CheckVals = False
  If xcoord > 32768 Or xcoord < -32767 Then CheckVals = True
  If ycoord > 32768 Or ycoord < -32767 Then CheckVals = True
End Function
```

WRITING THE CODE FOR THE DRAWSHAPE PROCEDURE

Now that you have written the code for the *DrawUser* procedure, which will pass values to the *DrawShape* procedure, you can write the code for the *DrawShape* procedure. Just as with *frmFractal*, the *DrawShape* procedure will receive three color values from the *DrawUser* procedure, check the *Plot* object's *Shape* element to determine whether to draw a circle, line, or box shape, and then use the *Circle* or *Line* method to draw images on the *frmUserEquation* form. The following code implements the *DrawShape* procedure:

```
Private Sub DrawShape(RedFill As Integer, GreenFill As Integer, _
    BlueFill As Integer)
  If Plot.Shape = 0 Then
    Circle (Plot.Xaxis, Plot.Yaxis), Plot.Radius, _
        RGB(RedFill, GreenFill, BlueFill)
  ElseIf Plot.Shape = 1 Then
    Line (Plot.Xaxis, Plot.Yaxis)-(Plot.X2axis, Plot.Y2axis), _
        RGB(RedFill, GreenFill, BlueFill)
  ElseIf Plot.Shape = 2 Then
    Line (Plot.Xaxis, Plot.Yaxis)-(Plot.X2axis, Plot.Y2axis), _
        RGB(RedFill, GreenFill, BlueFill), BF
  End If
End Sub
```

Within the *frmUserEquation* form, if you choose the *optDrawStyle* control's Circles option, the *Plot* object's *Shape* element will equal 0. If you choose the Lines option, the *Plot* object's *Shape* element will equal 1. If you choose the Boxes option, the *Shape* element will equal 2.

WRITING THE CODE FOR THE optDRAWSTYLE_CLICK EVENT

As you have learned, the *frmUserEquation* form uses the *optDrawStyle* option buttons to determine the shape of the user-defined equation. Just as with the *frmFractal* form, the *optDrawStyle_Click* event sets the shape to the currently selected option button's index value. The following code implements the *optDrawStyle_Click* event:

```
Private Sub optDrawStyle_Click(Index As Integer)
   Plot.Shape = Index
End Sub
```

ENHANCEMENTS YOU CAN MAKE TO THE prjFRACTAL PROJECT

Now that you have a better understanding of a Visual Basic structure and have used *TextBox*, *Label*, *OptionButton*, and *CommandButton* controls, you can make some adjustments to the *prjFractal* project. First, you can let the user change the colors for each fractal image on the *frmFractal* form. Second, you can mix up three fractal images to draw in thirds on the screen. Third, you can draw an image within a Visual Basic *PictureBox* control instead of a form. Fourth, you can modify the computations the *frmUserEquation* form uses to let the user draw more complex images. Finally, you can create fractal image screen savers. To create a screen saver, you must look at how to program Windows screen savers, then create an executable program that instantly draws the fractal you choose. Chapter 3, "Writing a Screen Saver in Visual Basic," discusses in detail how you can create a screen saver.

PUTTING IT ALL TOGETHER

This chapter's project, *prjFractal,* introduced you to Visual Basic structures and the *Circle* and *Line* methods. In this chapter you have used *CommandButton*, *OptionButton*, *Label*, and *TextBox* controls to draw and design fractal images. As you have learned, your Visual Basic programs can use a Visual Basic structure to store one or more variables that describe one or more objects. Instead of passing one or more variables to a function or procedure, your programs will instead fill the structure with values and pass the structure instance to the function or procedure. In addition, you can use the *Circle* and *Line* methods to draw circles, lines, or boxes on a Visual Basic form.

The *prjFractal* project shows you how to draw images from complex equations onto your computer screen. In addition, the project shows you how to use structures that contain data that you can pass from form to form. In Chapter 6, "Creating and Using ActiveX Controls," you will learn how to use ActiveX technology to design a user-defined control that many different programs can access and use. Before you continue with Chapter 6, however, make sure you understand the following key concepts:

✓ Within your Visual Basic programs, you can use structures to group and store multiple, related values in a single location.

✓ Within your Visual Basic programs, you can use a Visual Basic structure, you can assign values to one or more structure members, and then pass the entire structure into a function or procedure, rather than passing the members individually.

✓ Within your Visual Basic programs, you can use the *Draw* procedure, the *DrawShape* procedure, the *Circle* method, and the *Line* method, to paint multiple-colored images onto your computer screen.

✓ Visual Basic supports classes, which your programs can use to encapsulate information and protect the information from other sections of a program.

✓ Within Visual Basic, you can use a class module to maintain and process complex mathematical information.

Chapter 6

Creating and Using ActiveX Controls

Think back to the "good old days" when Apple introduced the Clipboard with the first Macintosh computers to let you cut and paste information between applications. Later, Microsoft realized that the ability for programs to exchange information was essential. Like the Macintosh, Windows let applications exchange information via the Clipboard.

The exchange of information that began with the Clipboard has since expanded to include many different types of inter-application communications. To support inter-application communications, Microsoft has, over time, supported three powerful technologies: Dynamic Data Exchange (DDE), Object Linking and Embedding (OLE), and ActiveX. In this chapter, you will learn about ActiveX technology and lay your ActiveX programming foundation for the chapters that follow. By the time you finish this chapter, you will understand the following key concepts:

◆ ActiveX is Object Linking and Embedding (OLE) that Microsoft has redefined for use on the Internet.

◆ The computing model that most software developers use is evolving from the traditional host-based model to the modern ActiveX client–server model.

◆ You can create ActiveX controls using tools such as Visual Basic, Visual C++, Borland C++, and Borland Delphi.

◆ Microsoft based ActiveX on the Component Object Model (COM), a specification for the creation of multiple objects within multiple files that combine to create applications, much like building blocks.

◆ The Component Object Model lets you create and manage entire programs as component objects for other programs.

◆ Visual Basic includes the ActiveX control option within the New Project dialog box, which lets you create an ActiveX control.

◆ Within this chapter, you will use the ActiveX control option to create two custom ActiveX controls.

◆ You can create custom ActiveX controls that you can later reuse in several projects, or that you can update individually without rewriting the code for an entire project.

◆ You can use a Visual Basic group project to create and use multiple custom ActiveX controls within a separate executable project.

◆ In this chapter, you will use a group project to create two custom ActiveX controls and include them within a third executable file.

◆ When you build an ActiveX control, you build a single, stand-alone object control file (OCX), which you can later transfer across a local network or the Internet, or easily distribute with your programs.

◆ Because each ActiveX control is a stand-alone component, you can use a custom ActiveX control as part of another custom ActiveX control.

BETTER UNDERSTANDING THE FOUNDATIONS OF ACTIVEX

As you have learned, Microsoft introduced Clipboard-style technology with the Windows operating system. Soon after the Clipboard's introduction, however, Microsoft determined that applications required a way to communicate that did not require the user's "hands on" cutting and pasting. To meet new communication requirements, Microsoft introduced the Dynamic Data Exchange (DDE) protocol to the technology market. Using DDE, programmers could write code that let two applications communicate behind the scenes. Although DDE provided a powerful communication protocol, many programmers found writing and debugging DDE-based programs difficult. As Figure 6.1 shows, when two programs use DDE to communicate, one application is the client (information receiver) and the other is the server (information provider).

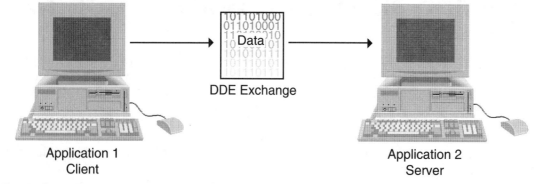

Figure 6.1 *Applications using Dynamic Data Exchange (DDE) to communicate.*

As the requirements for applications to exchange information continued to evolve, Microsoft developed Object Linking and Embedding (OLE). OLE uses *document-centric* computing to let one application use the functionality of another. Document-centric computing is a computing model that focuses on the *document's* type, as opposed to focusing on the *application* type that created the document. For example, you can use OLE to insert a *Paintbrush*™ picture into a *Word* document and have all the *Paintbrush* functions available to you inside your *Word* document. In other words, if you must change the *Paintbrush* image as you edit your *Word* document, you simply double-click your mouse on the image and Windows will start the *Paintbrush* program, loading the image. After you make your changes to the image, you can exit *Paintbrush* and return to your *Word* document.

Today, when you embed an object, such as a *Paintbrush* image, into a document, other users who receive your document must have *Paintbrush* or a compatible drawing program on their system before they can double-click their mouse on the object to edit it. In the future, document-centric objects will come with their own functionality, eliminating the need for the receiver to have the software that created the object.

When you use OLE, you can either *embed* or *link* the object into a document. When you embed the object, Windows places a copy of the object's file within the document. Changes that you may later make to the object outside the document will not affect the document's copy of the object. When you link an object within a document, Windows places a link (reference) to the object's file on disk. Each time you open the document, Windows loads the object from the corresponding file. Therefore, if you modify the object, your document will always contain the object's latest contents.

An *OLE container* (or client) is the application that contains the embedded or linked object. An *OLE server* is the application that creates the embedded or linked object. In Figure 6.2, Microsoft *Word* is the client and *Paintbrush* is the server.

Figure 6.2 *A* **Paintbrush** *picture inside a Microsoft* **Word** *document.*

Your decision to embed or link an object impacts the container size. Because the container stores an embedded object, the container size increases (in the previous example, the *Word* document becomes larger). In contrast, because a linked object resides outside the container, the container size decreases. However, if the linked object's location changes, you must update your documents to point (link) to the new location.

OLE has several implementations, which include the following:

- **OLE controls:** An OLE control is a container that holds an OCX (a control so named because of the control's *.ocx* file extension). For example, if you want to use an OCX with a *PowerBuilder®* application, you would insert the OCX into an OLE control within the *PowerBuilder* window or data window.

- **OCX:** An OCX is simply a control. You can choose from a variety of shareware and commercial third-party OCXs.

- **OLE automation:** Microsoft intends that Object Linking and Embedding (OLE) automation will replace Dynamic Data Exchange (DDE). Your Windows application can use, for example, Microsoft *Excel®* as a financial calculation engine using OLE automation. In such a case, your application will call *Excel* to perform the financial calculation by passing the data as parameters. In this case, your application is the client and Microsoft *Excel* is the server.

Today, the Internet's tremendous growth and popularity are forcing developers to migrate their applications to the "Net." Because OCXs are traditionally large files, potentially containing more functionality than an application requires, Microsoft developed a streamlined object technology. Microsoft's *ActiveX®*, which is OLE technology Microsoft redefined for use on the Internet, is emerging as a leading technology. The ActiveX technology facilitates easy and fast downloads across the Internet. Figure 6.3 illustrates the technology progression from the Clipboard to DDE to OLE to ActiveX.

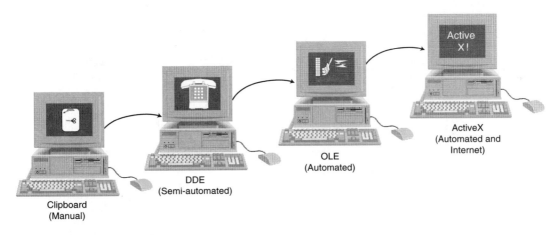

Figure 6.3 *The evolution from the Clipboard to ActiveX.*

Now that you better understand the evolution of Windows-based data communication, you will examine the different computing models. Understanding the different computing models will help you gain a better sense of how computing technology has evolved and the benefits each evolution provided to users and programmers.

THE ACTIVEX INTERNET MODEL

In the mainframe era, the computing model began as a host-based model within which users working at terminals ran programs that resided on the mainframe computer. With the advent of PC workstations and computer networks, the client–server model emerged. In the client–server model, users run programs that reside on their own PCs. These client-side programs, in turn, request information across the network from a server computer. In two-tier client–server architecture, the client program handles the user interface and user-input validation while the server program processes client requests. The client and server communicate over a network, as Figure 6.4 shows.

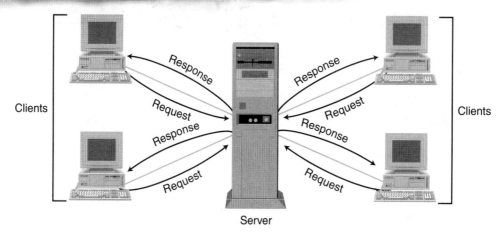

Figure 6.4 *The traditional two-tier client–server architecture.*

One of the best ways to understand the traditional two-tier client–server model is to consider *Hypertext Transport Protocol (HTTP)* transactions over the Internet between a client and a server. Because of widespread Internet use, the HTTP model has continued to evolve client–server processing. Within the HTTP-based model, a client (usually a browser) interacts with a server. Typically, the client–server interaction involves client requests to the server to provide specific Web pages. Because Web pages consist of HTML documents, the model is sometimes called the HTTP–HTML client–server model. As you know, the World Wide Web is based on this HTTP-based model, as Figure 6.5 shows.

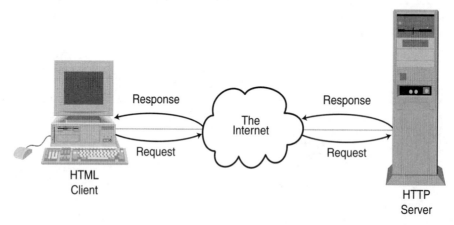

Figure 6.5 *The HTTP-based Web model.*

From the user's perspective, the HTTP model is inactive, offering little or no interaction. In short, the user could simply view a Web page's contents without interacting with elements on the page. Therefore, an interactive model was the next natural step for the Web's evolution. The Web gained such interactivity through the use of interactive forms programmers created with the Common Gateway Interface (CGI), Perl, and other programming languages. Using HTML entries, a Web designer can create a form with which users (via their browsers) can interact with the server. When users click their mouse on a form's Submit button, the browser sends the form to the server that, in turn, runs a program (normally written in Perl) that processes the form's entries. Depending on the server program's purpose, the program may generate an HTML-based response that the server sends back to the browser.

The drawback to CGI-based forms processing is that the server must spawn (create) a new process every time the browser invokes a CGI script. As the number of server processes increases, the server's processing power decreases. Figure 6.6 shows a client–server model that uses CGI.

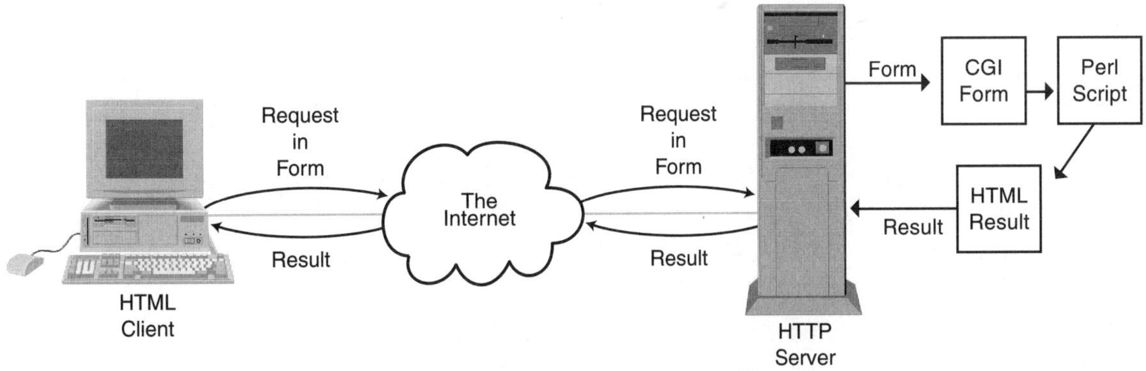

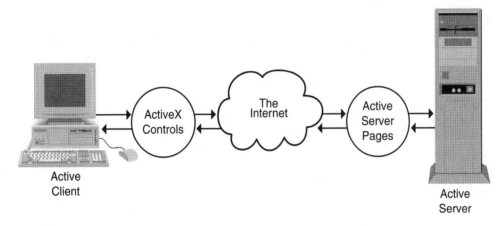

Figure 6.6 *A client–server model that uses the Common Gateway Interface (CGI).*

Recently, Microsoft introduced the Active Platform—a revolutionary computing model Microsoft designed specifically for the Internet. The Active Desktop and Active Server are functionally symmetric, which means you can use ActiveX controls and scripting on both. In other words, both the client and the server can take advantage of ActiveX controls. As Figure 6.7 shows, the Active Platform includes the Active Desktop (the client) and Active Server (the server).

Figure 6.7 *The Microsoft ActiveX Internet model.*

Currently, only Windows 95 and Windows NT support ActiveX technology. However, Microsoft is working toward implementing ActiveX technology for the Unix and Macintosh platforms.

ActiveX Technologies

The ActiveX model consists of several different technologies: ActiveX controls, ActiveX scripting, Active documents, Active Server, and ActiveX conferencing. The following sections, together with later chapters, will examine these technologies in detail. As you examine these technologies, you will become familiar with Microsoft's Component Object Model (COM) and Distributed Component Object Model (DCOM), and you will learn how these models relate to ActiveX. In addition, you will learn how ActiveX is an important part of Visual Basic development.

ActiveX Controls

An ActiveX control is a binary object that provides specific functionality, much like a computer program. You can integrate ActiveX controls within your client–server and Web applications, within Java applets, within Web pages using JavaScript™ or VBScript™, and within your Visual Basic programs. For example, the programs you designed in Chapter 2, "Using the Multimedia MCI Control to Create a CD-ROM Player," and Chapter 4, "Using Multiple Forms to Load Different File Types," used Microsoft-designed ActiveX controls. The advantage of ActiveX under

Visual Basic 5.0, however, is that for the first time you can create your own custom ActiveX controls from within Visual Basic.

You can use tools such as Visual Basic Control Creation Edition, Visual Basic 5.0, Visual C++, Visual J++, Borland C++, and Borland Delphi to create ActiveX controls. One example of an ActiveX control is Microsoft's *Chart* control. Using the *Chart* control, you can draw various charts, each with different styles. If your application requires charting, you simply integrate the *Chart* control into your application. You can also integrate the *Chart* control within Web-based applications that you write in JavaScript or VBScript. In other words, you can use the *Chart* control within a number of applications. You will use the *Chart* control in Chapter 11, "Using ActiveX to Create a Stock Analysis Program."

Visual Basic and Visual Basic Control Creation Edition both include many ActiveX controls. Additionally, you can download many more ActiveX controls from various locations on the World Wide Web. For example, Table 6.1 shows several Microsoft ActiveX controls that you can download from Microsoft's Web site at *http://www.microsoft.com/activex*.

198

Control	Description
AnimatedButton	Displays different frame video sequences previously stored within a video clip file (AVI format only).
Chart	Draws various types of charts with different styles.
Gradient	Shades an area with a range of colors or displays a transition from one color you specify to another.
Label	Displays given text at an angle you specify and renders text along user-defined curves.
Marquee	Scrolls, slides, or bounces text within a user-defined window.
Menu	Displays a menu button or a pull-down menu.
PopUpMenu	Displays a pop-up menu. The control fires a *Click* event when you select a menu item.
PopUpWindow	Displays an HTML document you specify in a pop-up window. You can use this control to provide tool tips or link previews.
Preloader	Downloads a URL you specify and places the document within the browser's cache. The control is invisible at run time and starts downloading when the HTML page that contains the control loads into the user's browser.
StockTicker	Continuously displays changing data. The control downloads the Uniform Resource Locator (URL) you specify at regular intervals and displays that data. The data can be in text or Extensible Markup Language (XML) format.
Timer	Invokes an event periodically. The control is invisible at run time.
ViewTracker	Generates *OnShow* and *OnHide* events whenever the control falls inside or outside the viewable area.

Table 6.1 ActiveX controls in Microsoft's ActiveX homepage at **http://www.microsoft.com/activex**.

The concepts of creating and using an ActiveX control adhere to the theories of object-oriented programming, which you learned about in Chapter 1, "Introduction to Visual Basic." Concepts applicable to ActiveX include the following:

- You create objects that are the building blocks for your applications.

- You can develop applications from existing objects and controls more quickly and easily than programming from scratch.

- You can share and reuse ActiveX objects across different applications.

- Using existing ActiveX controls, you do not have to "reinvent the wheel."

Microsoft's ActiveX technology continues to gain industry-wide support. Numerous vendors have adopted the ActiveX technology and introduced new and exciting ActiveX controls. When you develop client–server and Web applications, you should first use existing controls. As you create applications, you should build and maintain a library of ActiveX controls. If you cannot find a control that meets your needs, you can write your own.

IMPLICATIONS OF ACTIVEX

As you have learned, ActiveX controls provide you with powerful components that you can include within your Visual Basic programs—components that let you write interactive programs without greatly extended design times. In the past, to design a program (whether in Visual Basic or any other language), you used to write all the program code within one large code window. If you needed to change the program later, you had to rewrite the new parts, recompile the project, and ship out the entirely new program to your clients. Today, you can design a project in pieces and "plug" the pieces into each other—which lets you upgrade a single piece at a time without sending your customers entirely new programs. Programmers refer to such program design as *component programming*. When you must upgrade the project, you upgrade only the pertinent pieces (components). Instead of shipping out a new program to your client, you ship out only the pertinent pieces. Component programming is an extension of the object-oriented programming style you learned about in Chapter 1.

In addition, you can give the "a" component to the "a" department and the "b" component to the "b" department, and a separate person or group will work on each component. Separating the program into components lets you organize software development from one huge project into small manageable pieces that make up one large project. When you must later upgrade the program, you can work on the small manageable pieces, rather than the huge project. Because you can design a project with one or more ActiveX controls, it makes sense that you can also upgrade the project in pieces. When you change a piece of the project and want to ship it to distributors or clients, you can send the improved program only instead of the complete project.

USING THE grpACTIVEX GROUP PROJECT

Before you design the *grpActiveX* project, you may find it helpful to run the *grpActiveX.exe* program, which is within the *Chapter06* directory on the companion CD-ROM that accompanies this book. As with every other program on the CD-ROM, you should use the Jamsa Press *setup.exe* program on the CD-ROM to copy the *grpActiveX.exe* program to your computer's hard drive before you run it. After you copy the program to your computer's hard drive, you can run it from the Start menu. To run the program, select the Windows Start menu Run option. Windows will display the Run dialog box. Within the Run dialog box, enter *x:\vbp\Chapter06\ grpActiveX.exe*, where *x* corresponds to the drive letter of the hard drive on which you placed the program, and click your mouse on the OK button. Windows will run the *grpActiveX.exe* program, as shown in Figure 6.8.

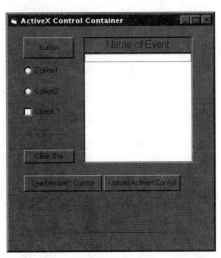

Figure 6.8 The *grpActiveX* project at run time.

Before you use the *grpActiveX.exe* program, familiarize yourself with the controls that appear on the form. Although it is not evident from viewing the program, when you design the project you will learn that all the controls the form contains are within a single ActiveX control, which you will design separately from the form itself. One of the strengths of ActiveX is that it is difficult to determine where the project stops and the ActiveX control begins. Within the custom ActiveX control on the form, you will see an empty Name of Event box on the right side of the *ActiveX Control Container* form. Near the bottom of the *ActiveX Control Container* form, you will see two buttons, which you will use to load and unload another ActiveX control. Although the program does not perform significant processing beyond loading the ActiveX control and responding to events you cause on or near the control, the loading of the ActiveX control is significant because it is a programming action that you could not perform in an earlier version of Visual Basic. By the end of this chapter, you will learn how to design and include a custom ActiveX control within your own Visual Basic projects.

200

In addition to the two ActiveX control command buttons, there are several other important buttons that the program displays during its execution. To the left of the *Name of Event* box, you will see the Button button. When you click your mouse on it, the program will display information in the *Name of Event* box. Below the Button button, you will see the Option1, Option2, and Check1 buttons. When you click your mouse on these buttons, the program will display information in the *Name of Event* box. Below the Check1 button, you will see the Clear Box button, which you will use to clear the *Name of Event* box.

UNDERSTANDING WHY YOU MUST RUN SETUP.EXE BEFORE YOU RUN GRPACTIVEX

As you have learned, the *grpActiveX.exe* program includes two custom ActiveX controls that you will design later in this Chapter. Each time you design or install a new ActiveX control on your computer, the installation program must *register* the control in the Windows Registry. If the installation program does not register the control, Windows will not know where to look for the control and will be unable to execute programs that use the control.

Although you could run the *grpActiveX.exe* program from the companion CD-ROM that accompanies this book, if you have not installed the custom ActiveX controls, Windows will be unable to execute the program and the program will stop with an unexpected run time. Instead, you must first use the Jamsa Press *setup.exe* program the CD-ROM contains to install the program, register the custom controls, and alert Windows to those controls' presence. To learn more about the *setup.exe* program, see the "What's On the *Visual Basic Programmer's Library* Companion CD-ROM" section at the back of this book.

Now that you have seen the *grpActiveX* program's layout, you can use the program to interact with a custom-designed ActiveX control. To interact with one of the program's ActiveX controls, perform the following steps:

1. Click your mouse on the Button button near the top left of the form. The program will display "Mouse Down, Click, Mouse Up" in the *Name of Event* box. The program responded to the three events, *Mouse Down,* the actual *Click* event, and *Mouse Up,* that the operating system sends to your program window when you click your mouse on an enabled object.

2. Click your mouse on the Option1 button, which is below the Button button. As with Step 1, the program will respond to the mouse click and will display "Click, optEvents(0) = True" in the *Name of Event* box in response to the messages the operating system sends to the Option1 button. Note, however, that the program responds only to the *Click* event, but not to the *Mouse Down* or *Mouse Up* events. (Even though Windows sent the messages for all three events, the program code responds only to the *Click* message.)

3. Click your mouse on the Option2 button. As with Step 1 and Step 2, the program will respond to the mouse click and will display "Click, optEvents(1) = True" in the *Name of Event* box.

4. Click your mouse on the Check 1 button. The program will display "Click, chkEvents = True" in the *Name of Event* box, in response to the message the operating system sent to the Check1 button.

5. Below the Check 1 button, move your mouse over the blank area. The program will alternately display "Mouse Move Event" and "Jamsa Press" in the area in response to the blank area's *Mouse Move* event.

6. Below the Check1 button and former blank area, click your mouse on the Clear Box button. The program will erase any text in the *Name of Event* box.

Figure 6.9 shows the *ActiveX Control Container* form displaying some of the button responses in the *Name of Event* box.

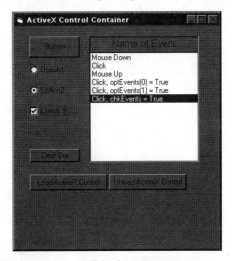

Figure 6.9 *The **Name of Event** box displaying some of the button responses.*

After you have used a few buttons on the *ActiveX Control Container* form, you can display a second ActiveX control on the first control (that is, the control that contains all the buttons). To display a second ActiveX control, click your mouse on the Load ActiveX Control button. The program will display an ActiveX control below the button. Figure 6.10 shows the newly displayed ActiveX control within the *ActiveX Control Container* form.

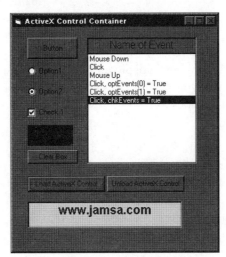

Figure 6.10 *The newly displayed ActiveX control within the **ActiveX Control Container** form.*

CREATING A BLANK FORM FOR THE GROUP PROJECT

Now that you have a better idea how to use the finished *grpActiveX* project, you can begin to design it. First, you will design a blank form that will contain the two ActiveX controls the "Using the grpActiveX Group Project" section introduced. After you design and implement the form, you will learn more about ActiveX controls.

When you design two or more ActiveX controls in the same project, Visual Basic will make two or more projects and then combine them into what Visual Basic calls a *group project*. A group project means that two or more projects make up the entire project.

To start the *grpActiveX* project and design an empty form, perform the following steps:

1. Within Visual Basic, select the File menu New Project option. Visual Basic will open the New Project dialog box.

2. Within the New Project dialog box, click your mouse on the Standard EXE icon. Next, click your mouse on OK. Visual Basic will open the *Form1* form window.

3. Select the View menu Properties Window option. Visual Basic will open the Properties Window listing the *Form1* properties.

4. Within the Properties Window, change the *Form1* properties to those values Table 6.2 lists.

Object	Property	Set As
Form1	*Caption*	*ActiveX Control Container*
Form1	*Height*	5625
Form1	*Left*	0
Form1	*Top*	0
Form1	*Width*	5070
Form1	*Name*	*frmActiveX*

Table 6.2 *The properties of the **frmActiveX** form.*

5. Select the File menu Save Project As option. Visual Basic will open the Save File As dialog box and fill the *File Name* field with *frmActiveX*.

6. Within the Save Project As dialog box, click your mouse on the Save button. Visual Basic will save the *frmActiveX* form and fill the *File Name* field with *Project1*.

7. Within the *File Name* field, replace the *Project1* project name with the new *prjActiveXContainer* project name. Visual Basic will save the *prjActiveXContainer* project and close the Save Project As dialog box.

MORE ON OBJECT-ORIENTED PROGRAMMING

As you have learned, in the *grpActiveX* project you will program with ActiveX controls, which programmers consider objects because they meet most of the definitions of object-oriented programming, which you learned about in Chapter 1. Remember, programmers consider three concepts, *inheritance*, *polymorphism*, and *encapsulation*, when determining whether a program is an object-oriented program.

It is important that you understand the difference between a control and an object. A *control* is a specific type of object that performs specific processing and generally has a visual component. An *object*, on the other hand, is an instance of a class, which generally performs specific processing, but will often also include extended data, and which may or may not have a visual component. In Visual Basic, you can use a control without necessarily knowing much information about the class from which the control derives. To learn more about object-oriented programming and inheritance, polymorphism, and encapsulation, refer to Chapter 1.

COM, DCOM, AND ACTIVEX

Microsoft Corporation and Digital Equipment Corporation first proposed the Component Object Model (COM) and Distributed Component Object Model (DCOM) in 1995. The COM model proposes to create, use, and integrate reusable component objects in a heterogeneous (diversified) system of networks and operating systems. In theory, these component objects should be able to communicate and interact with each other irrespective of their language, location, or platform of origin. In other words, the COM model promotes and encourages an open-system solution. The COM specification includes a set of standard APIs, a standard suite of interfaces, and network protocols COM uses to support distributed computing. While you will not specifically work with the COM model in this book, it is important to understand that ActiveX uses the underlying principles of COM. Therefore, your

ActiveX components should be component objects, which are easily accessible by other programs and provide a consistent interface.

If you have ever developed any software applications, you know that writing software is an intense task that takes time and effort. To minimize the time it takes to build an application, you can connect component objects. These component objects make up the building blocks of your application.

The COM specification defines a component as a reusable piece of software in binary form. You can use a component that meets the COM specification within your applications without worrying about the component's original programming language or original platform. You must know only the component's set of interfaces or methods and the manner in which you can call them. You must also know the component's external behavior and how it interacts with its environment.

The DCOM model is a set of COM objects in a distributed environment. In a DCOM environment, a COM object on one network can communicate with other COM objects on another network, as Figure 6.11 shows.

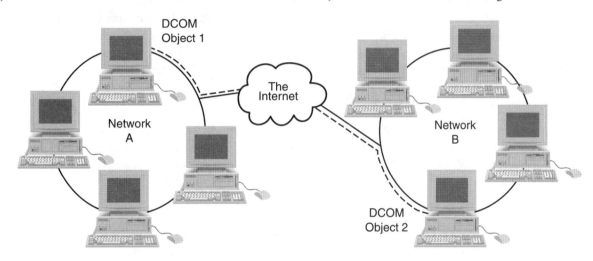

Figure 6.11 *An overview of the Distributed Component Object Model (DCOM).*

Microsoft modeled ActiveX technology after the COM specification. In other words, Microsoft built ActiveX technology around the presumption that components should be reusable with a minimum amount of additional programming. Microsoft has integrated COM and DCOM objects into its other programming tools, such as Visual J++ and Visual C++. In later chapters, you will work closely with ActiveX control design and implementation, and you will design DCOM objects in Chapter 22, "Writing DCOM Objects for Networks."

MORE ON ACTIVEX CONTROLS

Now that you know more about object-oriented programming and COM (the most common application of object-oriented programming in the Windows environment), you will learn more about ActiveX controls. Remember, an ActiveX control is only one component of COM. In this chapter, you will design two ActiveX controls, which will help you better organize the components of the chapter's project. In later chapters, you will design ActiveX servers, data-link libraries, and documents.

ActiveX controls use *containment*. Containment describes the relationship between one object and another object or objects when the first object contains one or more controls (or objects). For example, containment will occur when you fill a box with books; the box (object) contains the books (other objects). In the *grpActiveX* group project, you will design two custom ActiveX controls that contain one or more Visual Basic predefined controls. In addition, one of the custom ActiveX controls will contain both Visual Basic predefined controls and another custom ActiveX control (object).

As you have learned, an ActiveX control is actually an expanded OLE control that you can edit, upgrade, and change quickly and easily. Because of the Internet's increased growth, Microsoft redefined OLE controls to perform across *Local Area Networks (LAN)* and *Wide Area Networks (WAN)*, and called the new OLE control an *ActiveX control*.

In the *grpActiveX* group project, you will design each ActiveX control using the Visual Basic New Project dialog box ActiveX Control option. Visual Basic offers you five ActiveX New Project options—ActiveX EXE, ActiveX DLL, ActiveX Control, ActiveX Document DLL, and ActiveX Document EXE. In Chapter 12, "Using ActiveX Automation to Create a Database Server," you will use the ActiveX EXE New Project option to create a database server available across a network. In later chapters, you will use the other ActiveX project options to create ActiveX DLLs and ActiveX documents.

When you want to design an ActiveX control, select the ActiveX Control New Project option. Visual Basic will open a separate project and form that you will use to design each ActiveX control. In the *grpActiveX* project, you will design two ActiveX controls in two separate projects. Visual Basic will consider two or more projects as a group, which is why you will name the project *grpActiveX*.

After you design an ActiveX control, you must build the control in Visual Basic before you can transfer it across a network. Visual Basic will build the ActiveX control for you and assign an *OCX* extension to the file name, such as *HappysActiveXcontrol.OCX*. To transfer the control, use your network software to send it to another user or network server. (Depending on your network software and how you transfer the control, the receiving computer might have to register the control.) After transfer (and registration, if necessary), another user can use the entire ActiveX control. Because of this simplified transfer process, you can easily upgrade any software project that you used ActiveX controls to design.

CREATING A BLANK ACTIVEX CONTROL FORM

Now that you have learned about ActiveX controls, created a blank *frmActiveX* group project form, and saved the *prjActiveXContainer* project, you will create an ActiveX control project and name it *prjActiveXTimer*. Later in this chapter, you will add controls to the *prjActiveXTimer* project, which will create the actual ActiveX control. After you set up the first ActiveX control form, you will create another ActiveX control form.

To design an empty ActiveX control form, perform the following steps:

1. Within Visual Basic, select the File menu Add Project option. Visual Basic will open the Add Project dialog box.

2. Within the Add Project dialog box, select the ActiveX Control option and click your mouse on the Open button. Visual Basic will open the *Project1* project's *UserControl1* form window.

3. Select the View menu Properties Window option. Visual Basic will open the Properties Window listing the *UserControl1* properties.

4. Within the Properties Window, change the *UserControl1* properties to the values Table 6.3 lists.

Object	Property	Set As
UserControl1	Height	615
UserControl1	Width	3975
UserControl1	Name	ctlTimer

Table 6.3 The newly named **ctlTimer** ActiveX control's properties.

5. Select the File menu Save Project As option. Visual Basic will open the Save File As dialog box and fill the *File name* field with *ctlTimer*.

6. Within the Save File As dialog box, click your mouse on the Save button. Visual Basic will save the *ctlTimer* ActiveX control and fill the *File name* field with *Project1*.

7. Within the *File Name* field, replace the *Project1* project name with the *prjActiveXTimer* project name. Next, click your mouse on the Save button. Visual Basic will save the *prjActiveXTimer* project and fill the *File name* field with *Group1*.

8. Within the *File name* field, replace the *Group1* group project name with the *grpActiveX* group project name. Next, click your mouse on the Save button. Visual Basic will save the *grpActiveX* project, close the Save Group Project As dialog box, and display the ctlTimer icon in the Toolbox, as shown in Figure 6.12.

Figure 6.12 *The **ctlTimer** ActiveX control's ctlTimer icon within the Toolbox.*

CREATING ANOTHER BLANK ACTIVEX CONTROL FORM

Now that you have created the *ctlTimer* ActiveX control, saved the *prjActiveXTimer* project, and saved the *grpActiveX* project, you will create another ActiveX control project and name it *prjActiveXEvents*. Later in this chapter, you will add controls to the *prjActiveXEvents* project that will create the actual ActiveX control.

To design another empty ActiveX control form, perform the following steps:

1. Within Visual Basic, select the File menu Add Project option. Visual Basic will open the Add Project dialog box.

2. Within the Add Project dialog box, select the ActiveX Control option and click your mouse on the Open button. Visual Basic will open the *Project1* project's *UserControl1* form window.

3. Select the View menu Properties Window option. Visual Basic will open the Properties Window listing the *UserControl1* properties.

4. Within the Properties Window, change the *UserControl1* properties to the values Table 6.4 lists.

Object	Property	Set As
UserControl1	*Height*	5025
UserControl1	*Width*	4590
UserControl1	*Name*	*ctlEvents*

Table 6.4 *The newly named **ctlEvents** ActiveX control's properties.*

5. Select the File menu Save Project As option. Visual Basic will open the Save File As dialog box and fill the *File name* field with *ctlEvents*.

6. Within the Save Project As dialog box, click your mouse on the Save button. Visual Basic will save the *ctlEvents* ActiveX control and fill the *File name* field with *Project1*.

7. Within the *File name* field, replace the *Project1* project name with the *prjActiveXEvents* project name. Next, click your mouse on the Save button. Visual Basic will save the *prjActiveXEvents* project, close the Save Project As dialog box, and display the ctlEvents icon in the Toolbox, as Figure 6.13 shows.

Figure 6.13 *The **ctlEvents** ActiveX control's ctlEvents icon within the Toolbox.*

ADDING CONTROLS TO THE ctlTimer ACTIVEX CONTROL

Now that you have added two ActiveX control projects to the *grpActiveX* project, you can add controls to each ActiveX control. Remember, an ActiveX control consists of one or more Visual Basic controls or ActiveX controls. After you add the ActiveX control projects, the *ctlTimer* control is still blank, even though Visual Basic will display its icon in the Toolbox. If you were to add the *ctlTimer* control to the *frmActiveX* form, it would do nothing. You must add controls to an ActiveX control before you can use it in the *frmActiveX* form.

To add controls to the *ctlTimer* control, perform the following steps:

1. If Visual Basic is not displaying the *ctlTimer* form within an object window, double-click your mouse on the *ctlTimer* user control listing within Project Explorer. Visual Basic will open the *ctlTimer* form.

2. Within Visual Basic, select the View menu Toolbox option. Visual Basic will open the Toolbox.

3. Within the Toolbox, double-click your mouse on the Label icon. Visual Basic will draw a *Label* control, *Label1*, within the *ctlTimer* control form.

4. Within the Control Form window, click your mouse on the *Label1* control to highlight it. Visual Basic will draw a small frame around the control.

5. Select the View menu Properties Window option. Visual Basic will open the Properties Window listing the *Label1* properties.

6. Within the Properties Window, change the *Label1* properties to the values Table 6.5 lists.

Object	Property	Set As
Label1	*Caption*	*Jamsa Press*
Label1	*Height*	615
Label1	*Left*	120
Label1	*Top*	0
Label1	*Width*	3735
Label1	*Alignment*	2 - Center
Label1	*Backcolor*	*&H00FF8080&*
Label1	*Name*	lblTimer

*Table 6.5 The newly named **lblTimer** control's properties.*

7. Within the Toolbox, double-click your mouse on the Timer icon. Visual Basic will draw a *Timer* control, *Timer1*, within the *ctlTimer* control form.

8. Within the Control Form window, click your mouse on the *Timer1* control to highlight it. Visual Basic will draw a small frame around the control.

9. If Visual Basic is not displaying the Properties Window, select the View menu Properties Window option. Visual Basic will open the Properties Window listing the *Timer1* properties.

10. Within the Properties Window, change the *Timer1* properties to the values Table 6.6 lists.

Object	Property	Set As
Timer1	*Left*	480
Timer1	*Top*	120
Timer1	*Name*	tmrClock

*Table 6.6 The newly named **tmr**Timer control's properties.*

After you finish changing the properties of the *ctlTimer* control's component controls' properties, the *ctlTimer* control will look similar to Figure 6.14.

Figure 6.14 *The **ctlTimer** control after you change its controls' properties.*

WRITING THE CODE FOR THE PRJACTIVEXTIMER PROJECT

As you have learned, the *prjActiveXTimer* project is one of three projects within the *grpActiveX* project. The *prjActiveXTimer* project consists of one ActiveX control, *ctlTimer*. Now that you have added controls to the *ctlTimer* control, you can write procedures and functions that the custom ActiveX control will use to communicate with each of its component controls. First, you will declare variables that the procedures and functions will use. Then, you will write code for each procedure, function, and control event.

DECLARING THE VARIABLES

You will declare most variables in the General–Declarations section in the *ctlTimer* Code window. Remember, when you declare variables in the General–Declarations section of the *ctlTimer* control form, all procedures and functions in the form code can use them. You will declare the *Random* variable, which will store a color value, in the General–Declarations section. The following code implements the *Random* variable in the *ctlTimer* Code window's General–Declarations section:

```
Option Explicit
Dim Random As Integer
```

Note: *You must declare the **Random** variable outside of the **Timer** event that will use it. As you will learn, the **Timer** event will occur over an interval of time (in milliseconds). If you declare the **Random** variable within the **Timer** event, Visual Basic will initialize it to zero every time the event occurs.*

WRITING THE USERCONTROL_INITIALIZE EVENT

As you have learned, the *tmrClock* control's *Timer* event will occur over an interval in milliseconds. You will set an interval of milliseconds in the *Initialize* event. An ActiveX control's *Initialize* event is similar to a Visual Basic form's *Load* event because Visual Basic will invoke it first when an ActiveX control starts. Visual Basic does not precede the *Initialize* event with the ActiveX control name (in this case, *ctlTimer*). Instead, Visual Basic will precede the event with the generic *UserControl* name.

In the *prjActiveXTimer* project, the program code in the *Initialize* event will assign the *tmrClock* control's *Interval* property to 1000 milliseconds (one second), which instructs the *ctlTimer* control to fire its *Timer* event every second until you exit the *grpActiveX* program. The following code implements the *UserControl_Initialize* event:

```
Private Sub UserControl_Initialize()
  tmrClock.Interval = 1000
End Sub
```

Note: *When you look at listings in the **grpActiveX** project's Project Explorer window, you will see three projects: **prjActiveXContainer**, **prjActiveXEvents**, and **prjActiveXTimer**. The **prjActiveXEvents** and **prjActiveXTimer** project listings each contain a separate folder named **User Controls**. Visual Basic will list the **ctlEvents** and **ctlTimer** ActiveX controls within these **User Controls** headings—thus the generic **UserControl** name.*

WRITING THE TMRCLOCK_TIMER EVENT

As you will see, the *ctlTimer* control has a *Timer* event. After the *Initialize* event sets the *tmrClock* control's *Interval* property to one second, your program will invoke the *Timer* event. The *Timer* event will repeat every second until you exit the *grpActiveX* program. The following code implements the *tmrClock_Timer* event:

```
Private Sub tmrClock_Timer()
  lblTimer.FontName = "Arial"
  lblTimer.FontSize = 14
  lblTimer.FontBold = True
  lblTimer.BorderStyle = 1

  If Random = 1 Then
    lblTimer.BackColor = QBColor(11)
    lblTimer.Caption = "Visual Basic"
    Random = 2
  ElseIf Random = 2 Then
    lblTimer.BackColor = QBColor(10)
    lblTimer.Caption = "Programmer's Library"
    Random = 3
  Else
    lblTimer.BackColor = QBColor(14)
    lblTimer.Caption = "www.jamsa.com"
    Random = 1
  End If
End Sub
```

The *tmrClock* control's *Timer* event will change the *lblTimer* control's *BackColor* and *Caption* properties three times. In the first four lines of program code within the *tmrClock* event, the *Timer* event will assign values to the *lblTimer* control's *FontName*, *FontSize*, *FontBold*, and *BorderStyle* properties. The values will instruct the custom control to display text in the *lblTimer* control as Arial, bold, 14 point, inside a sunken label.

After the program assigns the initial property values, an *If-Then* statement will check the *Random* value. If *Random* equals 1, the program code will assign *QBColor(11)* (a light blue color), to the *lblTimer* control's *BackColor* property. Then the program code will assign "Visual Basic" to the *lblTimer* control's *Caption* property, and will assign the value 2 to *Random* at its conclusion. The program code performs similar processing for other *Random* values, changing the color and the caption text with each change in *Random's* value. The *tmrClock* control will continue to invoke its *Timer* event every second (unless you change the pre-set time interval) until you exit the *grpActiveX* project.

ADDING CONTROLS TO THE CTLEVENTS ACTIVEX CONTROL

Now that you have designed the *ctlTimer* ActiveX control, you will add it to the *ctlEvents* ActiveX control. Remember, an ActiveX control consists of one or more Visual Basic controls or ActiveX controls. After you have written the *Timer* event, the *ctlEvents* control is blank, even though Visual Basic will display its icon in the Toolbox. If you were to add the *ctlEvents* control to the *frmActiveX* form, it would do nothing. You must add controls to an ActiveX control before you can use it in the *frmActiveX* form.

To add controls to the *ctlEvents* control, perform the following steps:

1. If Visual Basic is not displaying the *ctlEvents* form within an object window, double-click your mouse on the *ctlEvents* user control listing within Project Explorer. Visual Basic will open the *ctlEvents* form.

2. Within Visual Basic, select the View menu Toolbox option. Visual Basic will open the Toolbox.

3. Within the Toolbox, double-click your mouse on the CommandButton icon. Visual Basic will draw a *CommandButton* control, *Command1*, within the *ctlEvents* control form.

4. Repeat Step 3 three more times until you have a total of four *CommandButton* controls within the *ctlEvents* control form.

5. Within the *ctlEvents* control form, click your mouse on a *CommandButton* control to highlight it. Visual Basic will draw a small frame around the control.

6. Select the View menu Properties Window option. Visual Basic will open the Properties Window listing the highlighted *CommandButton* control's properties.

7. Within the Properties Window, change the highlighted *CommandButton* control's properties to the values Table 6.7 lists.

8. Repeat Steps 5, 6, and 7 until you have changed each control's properties to the values Table 6.7 lists.

Object	Property	Set As
Command1	*Caption*	*Button*
Command1	*Height*	495
Command1	*Left*	240
Command1	*Top*	120
Command1	*Width*	1215
Command1	*Name*	*cmdEvents*
Command2	*Caption*	*Clear Box*
Command2	*Height*	315
Command2	*Left*	240
Command2	*Top*	2760
Command2	*Width*	1215
Command2	*Name*	*cmdClear*
Command3	*Caption*	*Load ActiveX Control*
Command3	*Height*	375
Command3	*Left*	240
Command3	*Top*	3360
Command3	*Width*	1875
Command3	*Name*	*cmdLoadControl*
Command4	*Caption*	*Unload ActiveX Control*
Command4	*Height*	375
Command4	*Left*	2160
Command4	*Top*	3360
Command4	*Width*	1875
Command4	*Name*	*cmdUnloadControl*

*Table 6.7 The **ctlEvents** control's **CommandButton** controls' properties.*

After you finish changing the properties of the *ctlEvents* control's *CommandButton* controls, the *ctlEvents* control will look similar to Figure 6.15.

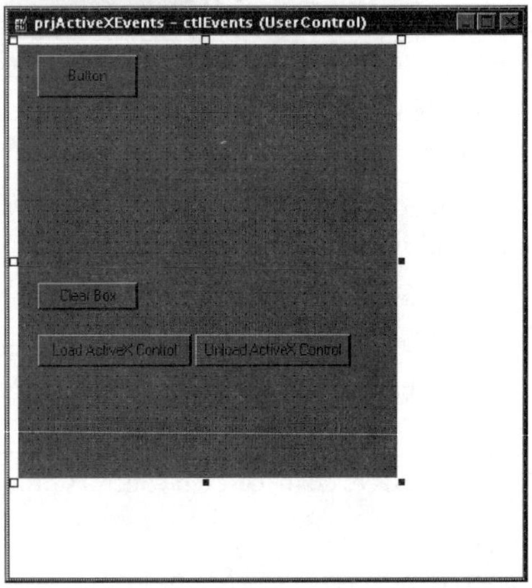

Figure 6.15 *The* **ctlEvents** *control after you modify its* **CommandButton** *controls.*

9. Within the Toolbox, double-click your mouse on the OptionButton icon. Visual Basic will draw an *OptionButton* control, *Option1*, within the *ctlEvents* control form.

10. Within the *ctlEvents* form, click your mouse on the *Option1* control to highlight it. Visual Basic will draw a small frame around the control.

11. If Visual Basic is not displaying the Properties Window, select the View menu Properties Window option. Visual Basic will open the Properties Window listing the *Option1* control properties.

12. Within the Properties Window, click your mouse on the *Name* property and change the value from *Option1* to *optEvents*.

13. Select the Edit menu Copy option. Visual Basic will store a copy of the *optEvents* control in the Clipboard.

14. Select the Edit menu Paste option. Visual Basic will open a dialog box that asks, "You already have a control named optEvents. Do you want to create a control array?" Click your mouse on the Yes button. Visual Basic will draw a copy of the *optEvents* control within the *ctlEvents* form.

15. Within the *ctlEvents* form, click your mouse on an *optEvents* control to highlight it. Visual Basic will draw a small frame around the control.

16. Within the Properties Window, change the highlighted *optEvents* control's properties to the values Table 6.8 lists.

17. Repeat Steps 14, 15, and 16 until you have changed each highlighted *optEvents* control's properties to the values Table 6.8 lists.

Object	Property	Set As
optEvents(0)	*Caption*	*Option 1*
optEvents(0)	*Height*	375
optEvents(0)	*Left*	240
optEvents(0)	*Top*	720
optEvents(0)	*Width*	1095
optEvents(1)	*Caption*	*Option 2*

Table 6.8 *The* **ctlEvents** *control's* **OptionButton** *controls' properties. (continued on following page)*

Object	Property	Set As
optEvents(1)	*Height*	375
optEvents(1)	*Left*	240
optEvents(1)	*Top*	1200
optEvents(1)	*Width*	1095

Table 6.8 *The **ctlEvents** control's **OptionButton** controls' properties. (continued from previous page)*

After you finish changing the properties of the *ctlEvents* control's *OptionButton* controls, the *ctlEvents* control will look similar to Figure 6.16.

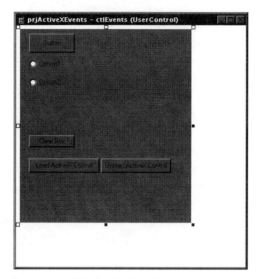

Figure 6.16 *The **ctlEvents** control after you modify its **OptionButton** controls.*

18. Within the Toolbox, double-click your mouse on the CheckBox icon. Visual Basic will draw a *CheckBox* control, *Check1*, within the *ctlEvents* form.

19. Within the Toolbox, double-click your mouse on the Label icon. Visual Basic will draw a *Label* control, *Label1*, within the *ctlEvents* form.

20. Repeat Step 18 one more time until you have two *Label* controls within the *ctlEvents* form.

21. Within the Toolbox, double-click your mouse on the ListBox icon. Visual Basic will draw a *ListBox* control, *List1*, within the *ctlEvents* form.

22. Within the *ctlEvents* form, click your mouse on a *CheckBox*, *Label*, or *ListBox* control to highlight it. Visual Basic will draw a small frame around the control.

23. If Visual Basic is not displaying the Properties Window, select the View menu Properties Window option. Visual Basic will open the Properties Window listing the highlighted control's properties.

24. Within the Properties Window, change the highlighted control's properties to the values Table 6.9 lists.

25. Repeat Steps 22, 23, and 24 until you have changed each *CheckBox*, *Label*, and *ListBox* control's properties to the values Table 6.9 lists.

Object	Property	Set As
Check1	*Caption*	*Check 1*
Check1	*Height*	375
Check1	*Left*	240

Table 6.9 *The **ctlEvents** control's **CheckBox**, **Label**, and **ListBox** controls' properties. (continued on following page)*

Object	Property	Set As
Check1	Top	1680
Check1	Width	1095
Check1	Name	chkEvents
Label1	Caption	Name of Event
Label1	Height	375
Label1	Left	1680
Label1	Top	120
Label1	Width	2655
Label1	Name	lblName
Label2	Caption	[blank]
Label2	Height	375
Label2	Left	240
Label2	Top	2160
Label2	Width	1095
Label2	Name	lblChangeColor
List1	Height	2595
List1	Left	1680
List1	Top	480
List1	Width	2655
List1	Name	listEvents

Table 6.9 The *ctlEvents* control's **CheckBox, Label,** and **ListBox** controls' properties. (continued from previous page)

26. Within the Toolbox, select the ctlTimer control icon.

27. Within the Toolbox, double-click your mouse on the ctlTimer icon. Visual Basic will draw an ActiveX control, *ctlTimer1*, within the *ctlEvents* control form.

28. Within the *ctlEvents* control form, click your mouse on the *ctlTimer1* control to highlight it. Visual Basic will draw a small frame around the control.

29. If Visual Basic is not displaying the Properties Window, select the View menu Properties Window option. Visual Basic will open the Properties Window listing the *ctlTimer1* control's properties.

30. Within the Properties Window, change the *ctlTimer1* control's properties to the values Table 6.10 lists.

Object	Property	Set As
ctlTimer1	Height	735
ctlTimer1	Left	120
ctlTimer1	Top	3960
ctlTimer1	Width	3975
ctlTimer1	Name	ctlTimerAdded

Table 6.10 The newly named **ctlTimerAdded** control's properties.

After you finish changing the *ctlTimerAdded* control's properties, the *ctlEvents* control will look similar to Figure 6.17.

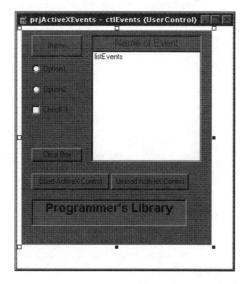

Figure 6.17 *The* **ctlEvents** *control after you modify its* **ctlTimerAdded** *control.*

WRITING THE PRJACTIVEXEVENTS PROJECT CODE

As you have learned, the *prjActiveXEvents* project is one of three projects within the *grpActiveX* project that contains an ActiveX control. Now that you have added controls to the *ctlEvents* ActiveX control, you can write procedures and functions to communicate with each control. First, you will declare variables that the procedures and functions will use. Then, you will write code for each procedure, function, and control event.

DECLARING THE VARIABLES

You will declare most variables in the General–Declarations section of the *ctlEvents* code window. Remember, when you declare variables in the General–Declarations section of the *ctlEvents* control form, all procedures and functions in the form code can use them. You will declare the *Random* variable, which will store a color value, in the General–Declarations section. The following code implements the *Random* variable in the *ctlEvents* code window's General–Declarations section:

```
Option Explicit
Dim Random As Integer
```

Note: *You must declare the* **Random** *variable outside of the* **MouseMove** *event that will use it. As you will learn, the* **MouseMove** *event will occur again and again when you move your mouse over a control. If you declare the* **Random** *variable within the* **MouseMove** *event, Visual Basic will initialize it to zero every time the event occurs.*

WRITING THE USERCONTROL_INITIALIZE EVENT

As you have learned, an ActiveX control's *Initialize* event is similar to a Visual Basic form's *Load* event because Visual Basic will invoke it first when an ActiveX control starts. Visual Basic does not precede the *Initialize* event with the ActiveX control name (in this case, *ctlEvents*). Instead, Visual Basic will precede it with the generic *UserControl* name. In the *prjActiveXEvents* project, the *Initialize* event will assign *False* to the *ctlTimerAdded* control's *Visible* property. When the program starts the *ctlEvents* control, it will hide the *ctlTimerAdded* ActiveX control on the form. The following code implements the *UserControl_Initialize* event:

```
Private Sub UserControl_Initialize()
   ctlTimerAdded.Visible = False
End Sub
```

WRITING THE cmdEVENTS CONTROL'S CLICK EVENT

As you have learned, in addition to containing the *ctlTimer* ActiveX control, the *ctlEvents* ActiveX control will display events in the *listEvents* control. When you click your mouse on the *cmdEvents* control, your program will invoke its *Click* event. Each time you click on the *cmdEvents* control, its *Click* event will display a reference to itself within the *listEvents* control. The program code will use the *listEvents* control's *AddItem* method to add "Click" to the *listEvents* control's box, and will increment the *listEvents* control's *ListIndex* value, which will force the cursor inside the list box to highlight the newly added item. The following code implements the *cmdEvents_Click* event:

```
Private Sub cmdEvents_Click()
   listEvents.AddItem "Click"
   listEvents.ListIndex = listEvents.ListIndex + 1
End Sub
```

WRITING THE cmdEVENTS CONTROL'S MOUSEDOWN EVENT

As you have learned, the *ctlEvents* ActiveX control will display events in the *listEvents* control. When you click your mouse on the *cmdEvents* control and hold down the mouse button, your program will invoke its *MouseDown* event. The *cmdEvents* control's *MouseDown* event will display a reference to itself within the *listEvents* control, just as it did with the *Click* event. The following code implements the *cmdEvents_MouseDown* event:

```
Private Sub cmdEvents_MouseDown(Button As Integer, Shift As Integer, _
   X As Single, Y As Single)
   listEvents.AddItem "Mouse Down"
   listEvents.ListIndex = listEvents.ListIndex + 1
End Sub
```

WRITING THE cmdEVENTS CONTROL'S MOUSEUP EVENT

As you have learned, the *ctlEvents* ActiveX control will display events in the *listEvents* control. When you click your mouse on the *cmdEvents* control and release the mouse button, your program will invoke its *MouseUp* event. The *cmdEvents* control's *MouseUp* event will display a reference to itself within the *listEvents* control, just as with the *Click* and *MouseDown* events. The following code implements the *cmdEvents_MouseUp* event:

```
Private Sub cmdEvents_MouseUp(Button As Integer, Shift As Integer, _
   X As Single, Y As Single)
   listEvents.AddItem "Mouse Up"
   listEvents.ListIndex = listEvents.ListIndex + 1
End Sub
```

WRITING THE optEVENTS CONTROL'S CLICK EVENT

As you have learned, the *ctlEvents* control's purpose is to show you that it can contain other controls, and that you can write code for each control. When you click your mouse on one of the *optEvents* controls, your program will invoke its *Click* event. The *optEvents* control's *Click* event will display a reference to itself within the *listEvents* control. The following code implements the *optEvents_Click* event:

```
Private Sub optEvents_Click(Index As Integer)
   If Index = 0 Then
      listEvents.AddItem "Click, optEvents(0) = True"
   Else
      listEvents.AddItem "Click, optEvents(1) = True"
   End If
   listEvents.ListIndex = listEvents.ListIndex + 1
End Sub
```

The program code for the *optEvents_Click* event differs slightly from that in the previous three *Click* events because the code must check the *optEvents* index property before it makes its addition for the event to the *lstEvents* box. The program code uses an *If-Then* statement to determine which button is currently checked, and then adds a notification to the list box, depending on the result.

WRITING THE chkEVENTS CONTROL'S CLICK EVENT

As you have learned, the *ctlEvents* control will display events within the *listEvents* control. When you click your mouse on the *chkEvents* control, your program will invoke its *Click* event. The *chkEvents* control's *Click* event will display a reference to itself in the *listEvents* control. The following code implements the *chkEvents_Click* event:

```
Private Sub chkEvents_Click()
   If chkEvents.Value = 1 Then
      listEvents.AddItem "Click, chkEvents = True"
   Else
      listEvents.AddItem "Click, chkEvents = False"
   End If
   listEvents.ListIndex = listEvents.ListIndex + 1
End Sub
```

Just as with the *optEvents* array, you must verify the *chkEvents* control's value before making the addition to the list box. The *chkEvents* control's *Click* event also uses an *If-Then* statement to change its response, depending on the current value of the control. Remember, a *CheckBox* control is either checked or not checked. The *Value* property will contain either 1 or 0, with 1 meaning the *CheckBox* control is checked, and 0 meaning the *CheckBox* control is not checked.

WRITING THE lblChangeColor CONTROL'S MouseMove EVENT

As you have learned, the *ctlEvents* ActiveX control contains other Visual Basic controls and one ActiveX control. You can write code that communicates with each control's properties, methods, and events. When you move your mouse over the *lblChangeColor* control, Windows will invoke the *lblChangeColors* control's *MouseMove* event. The *lblChangeColor* control's *MouseMove* event will rapidly change the control's color and text as you move your mouse over the control. The following code implements the *lblChangeColor_MouseMove* event:

```
Private Sub lblChangeColor_MouseMove(Button As Integer, Shift As Integer, _
   X As Single, Y As Single)
   lblChangeColor.FontName = "Arial"
   lblChangeColor.FontSize = 8
   lblChangeColor.Alignment = 2

   If Random = 1 Then
      lblChangeColor.BackColor = QBColor(9)
      lblChangeColor.Caption = "Move Move Event"
      Random = 2
   Else
      lblChangeColor.BackColor = QBColor(12)
      lblChangeColor.Caption = "Jamsa Press"
      Random = 1
   End If
End Sub
```

The *MouseMove* event first assigns font information to the *lblChangeColor* control's *FontName*, *FontSize*, and *Alignment* properties. Next, an *If-Then* statement will check the *Random* value, which the code will use to determine the current color of the control. Windows will continue to invoke the *lblChangeColor* control's *MouseMove* event as long as you move your mouse over the *lblChangeColor* control.

WRITING THE cmdCLEAR CONTROL'S CLICK EVENT

As you have learned, the *Click* events of the *cmdEvents*, *chkEvents*, and *optEvents* controls will list messages in the *listEvents* control. As the different *Click* events continue to add messages to the *listEvents* control, the amount of information within the list box may become congested, and you may want to clear the information within the

listEvents control. The *cmdClear* control's *Click* event will use the *listEvents* control's *Clear* method to erase all messages in the *listEvents* control. The following code implements the *cmdClear_Click* event:

```
Private Sub cmdClear_Click()
  listEvents.Clear
End Sub
```

WRITING THE CMDLOADCONTROL CONTROL'S CLICK EVENT

As you have learned, an ActiveX control can contain one or more other ActiveX controls. The *ctlEvents* ActiveX control contains the *ctlTimer* ActiveX control that you designed earlier in this chapter. When you click your mouse on the *cmdLoadControl* control, your program will assign *True* to the *ctlTimerAdded* control's *Visible* property (which the *ctlEvents* control initialized to *False* in the *UserControl_Initialize* event). The following code implements the *cmdLoadControl_Click* event:

```
Private Sub cmdLoadControl_Click()
  ctlTimerAdded.Visible = True
End Sub
```

WRITING THE CMDUNLOADCONTROL CONTROL'S CLICK EVENT

As you know, an ActiveX control can contain one or more other ActiveX controls. The *ctlEvents* ActiveX control contains the *ctlTimer* ActiveX control. When you click your mouse on the *cmdUnloadControl* control, the program code will assign *False* to the *ctlTimerAdded* control's *Visible* property. The following code implements the *cmdUnloadControl_Click* event:

```
Private Sub cmdUnloadControl_Click()
  ctlTimerAdded.Visible = False
End Sub
```

ADDING THE CTLEVENTS CONTROL TO THE FRMACTIVEX FORM

Now that you have created two ActiveX controls, *ctlTimer* and *ctlEvents*, you can design the *frmActiveX* form. As you have learned, the *ctlEvents* control contains Visual Basic controls and the *ctlTimer* control. This is one way of using an ActiveX control. As you know, to run a Visual Basic program that includes any kind of control, you must add one or more controls to a form. In the *grpActiveX* project, you will add the *ctlEvents* control to the *frmActiveX* form. After you do this, when you run the *grpActiveX* program, Visual Basic will display the *ctlEvents* control on the *frmActiveX* form and you can interact with its controls. To add the *ctlEvents* control to the *frmActiveX* form, perform the following steps:

1. If Visual Basic is not displaying the *ctlEvents* form within an object window, double-click your mouse on the *ctlEvents* user control listing within Project Explorer. Visual Basic will open the *ctlEvents* form.

2. Within Visual Basic, select the View menu Toolbox option. Visual Basic will open the Toolbox.

3. Within the Toolbox, select the ctlEvents icon.

4. Within the Toolbox, double-click your mouse on the ctlEvents icon. Visual Basic will draw an ActiveX control, *ctlEvents1*, within the *frmActiveX* form.

5. Within the *frmActiveX* form, click your mouse on the *ctlEvents1* control to highlight it. Visual Basic will draw a small frame around the control.

6. Select the View menu Properties Window option. Visual Basic will open the Properties Window listing the *ctlEvents1* properties.

7. Within the Properties Window, change the *ctlEvents1* control properties to the values Table 6.11 lists.

Object	Property	Set As
ctlEvents1	*Height*	4935
ctlEvents1	*Left*	120
ctlEvents1	*Top*	120
ctlEvents1	*Width*	4695
ctlEvents1	*Name*	*ctlEventsAdded*

Table 6.11 *The newly named* **ctlEventsAdded** *control's properties.*

After you finish changing the properties of the *ctlEventsAdded* control, the *frmActiveX* form will look similar to Figure 6.18.

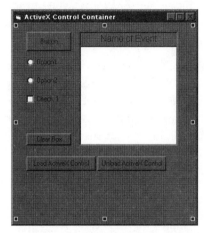

Figure 6.18 *The* **frmActiveX** *form that includes the* **ctlEventsAdded** *control.*

MORE ON BUILDING OCX FILES

As you have learned, when you compile an ActiveX control within Visual Basic, each control will have an *OCX* extension. After you compile an ActiveX control, you can use it in another project or in another development environment (such as Visual C++), locally or across a network. Whether you use the ActiveX control locally or on a network, you must access it by its *OCX* extension. In the *grpActiveX* project, you have designed the two ActiveX controls already, so you do not need to access either by *OCX* extension. To compile each ActiveX control in the *grpActiveX* project, perform the following steps:

1. Select the File menu Make Project Group option. Visual Basic will open the Build window listing three projects, *prjActiveXContainer*, *prjActiveXEvents*, and *prjActiveXTimer*, as shown in Figure 6.19.

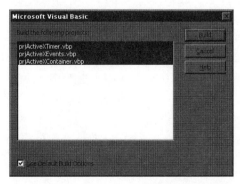

Figure 6.19 *The Build window listing the three projects of the* **grpActiveX** *group project.*

2. Within the Build window, click your mouse on the Build button. Visual Basic will build each project and add an *OCX* extension to *prjActiveXEvents* and *prjActiveXTimer*.

ENHANCEMENTS YOU CAN MAKE TO THE GRPACTIVEX PROJECT

Now that you have a better understanding of ActiveX controls and have added an ActiveX control within another ActiveX control, you can make some adjustments to the *grpActiveX* project. First, you can create an ActiveX control with more controls, functions, and procedures—perhaps an ActiveX control that performs one purpose, such as balancing your checkbook. Second, you can design an ActiveX control that a network browser can load from an HTML page on a Web site. For instance, a user can click an HTML button and the user's computer will download or use an ActiveX control.

PUTTING IT ALL TOGETHER

This chapter's project, grpActiveX, introduced you to ActiveX controls and *OptionButton*, *CommandButton*, *Label*, *CheckBox*, *Timer*, and *ListBox* controls. Using an ActiveX control, you can add one or more controls to it, and then you can add code variables, functions, and procedures that communicate with its controls, properties, methods, and events.

An important advantage of using an ActiveX control is that you can transfer it over a network. In addition, a client can benefit from a program designed with ActiveX controls because when you must upgrade the program, you will change only the pertinent sections that the ActiveX controls represent. As all programming languages progress, the future for Windows programmers will almost certainly involve the Component Object Module (COM), and ActiveX controls are an important part of that future. In Chapter 7, "Creating a Database Viewer and Designer," you will use the *DAO Object Library* objects to create and use a Microsoft *Access* database entirely from within program code. Before you continue with Chapter 7, however, make sure you understand the following key concepts:

✓ ActiveX is the descendant of both Dynamic Data Exchange (DDE) and Object Linking and Embedding (OLE), but Microsoft has redefined it from previous models for easier use on the Internet.

✓ The computing model that most software developers use is evolving from the traditional host-based model to the modern client–server model, and ActiveX provides effective means for you to take advantage of the new model.

✓ You can create ActiveX controls using a wide variety of development environments, including Visual Basic, Visual C++, Borland C++, and Borland Delphi.

✓ Microsoft based ActiveX on the Component Object Model (COM), a specification for the creation of multiple object files (components) that you can later use and reuse within your programs.

✓ After you create an ActiveX control in Visual Basic, you can reuse it in many different projects.

✓ Using an ActiveX control, you can design a software project in multiple components to simplify both the original design and software upgrading at a later date.

✓ When you use ActiveX controls, you can change the ActiveX controls within a project to update an existing project without changing the project itself, provided that you maintain the properties, methods, and events that the original controls used.

✓ Using ActiveX controls, you can save time and expense both in a program's original design and when you upgrade an existing program.

✓ You can transfer ActiveX controls across a network so that users or other programmers can use them.

Chapter 7

Creating a Database Viewer and Designer

As computers became more common in business in the 1970s and 1980s, one of the most significant benefits that they brought to worker productivity was to give each worker the ability to directly access important company information— about customers, transactions, new developments—from his or her desktop. Today, most companies maintain multiple databases of information, from customer and job information to internal performance information. Virtually any type of data that you can place into a sequence or other order, you can store on and retrieve from a computer.

To store data in ways that makes the data more useful and more accessible to users, many companies will use *databases*. A database is a logical construct that provides a program with a single location from which the program and therefore, its user, can access specific information about a particular transaction or customer without searching through the entire transaction or customer list. A database is conceptually similar to a filing cabinet. Just as with a filing cabinet, you store information in records—similar to a file folder. A database, however, lets you immediately access the record, rather than searching through cabinets to access the information the record contains. Moreover, databases let you combine the information from multiple records quickly and easily.

Visual Basic provides three different object libraries that your programs can use to access databases and the information within the databases: the Active Data Objects (ADO) Object Library, the Data Access Objects (DAO) Object Library, and the Remote Data Objects (RDO) Object Library. Within this book, you will work only with the Data Access Objects (DAO) Object Library. Each library provides types, such as the DAO *Database* type, that you can use within your programs to manage databases. Within this chapter, you will use the DAO Object Library to design, create, and access databases. The *prjCreateDatabase* project that you will create will help you learn the fundamentals of working with many objects the DAO Object Library provides and you will also learn about some of the data-based controls that Visual Basic provides. By the time you finish this chapter, you will understand the following key concepts:

219

- When you create a database, you will construct it from one or more data tables. In turn, you will construct the data tables from records, and you will construct the records from fields.

- To work with data objects, you must add to your project a reference to the Data Object Library that contains those objects. In this chapter's *prjCreateDatabase* project, you will add a reference to the DAO Object Library.

- When you create databases in Visual Basic, you will generally create databases that use the Microsoft Jet database engine, which Visual Basic shares with Microsoft *Access*®.

- The three base objects in the DAO Object Library are the *Workspace, Database*, and *Recordset* objects.

- Within your Visual Basic programs, you can use the *Workspace* object to connect to multiple databases.

- After you connect to a *Workspace* object within your programs, you will use the *Workspace* object's *OpenDatabase* method to open a database.

- After you open a database, you can use the *Database* object's *OpenRecordset* method to open a recordset.

- Visual Basic will let you work with most objects in the DAO Object Library as members of a *collection*. For example, a single *Database* object is also a member of the *Databases* collection for a given *Workspace* object.

- In addition to the base objects, the DAO Object Library supports *definition* objects, such as the *TableDef, QueryDef*, and *FieldDef* objects.

◆ To access the data within a database, you will generally use a Structured Query Language (SQL) *query*. A query is request for the database to perform an activity—generally, to return data to the calling program.

◆ A *Select* query is a request for records that match certain criteria, which you will specify within your *Select* queries using the *Where* keyword.

◆ Within your Visual Basic programs, you can also use controls, such as the *Data* control and the *Data-Bound Grid* control, to access database information.

◆ To create a database with the DAO Object Library objects, you must create the database file, add one or more *tables* to the file, and add one or more *fields* to the records that comprise the table.

◆ A field is a location within which you will store simple data (such as a number, a text string, or a date value). To create records, you will generally use multiple fields.

USING THE *prj*CREATEDATABASE PROJECT

Before you design the *prjCreateDatabase* project, you may find it helpful to run the *prjCreateDatabase.exe* program. The companion CD-ROM that accompanies this book contains the *prjCreateDatabase.exe* program within the *Chapter07* directory. As with every other program on the CD-ROM, you should run the Jamsa Press *setup.exe* program to install the *prjCreateDatabase.exe* program to your computer's hard drive before you run it. After you install the *prjCreateDatabase.exe* program to your computer's hard drive, you can run it from the Start menu. To run the program, select the Windows Start menu Run option. Windows will display the Run dialog box. Within the Run dialog box, enter *x:\vbpl\Chapter07\prjCreateDatabase.exe*, where *x* corresponds to the drive letter of the hard drive on which you installed the *prjCreateDatabase.exe* program, and click your mouse on OK. Windows will display the *prjCreateDatabase.exe* program, as shown in Figure 7.1.

Figure 7.1 *The* **prjCreateDatabase.exe** *program's startup screen.*

Much like the *prjFileViewer.exe* program that you created in Chapter 4, "Using Multiple Forms to Load Different File Types," the *prjCreateDatabase.exe* program uses a Multiple-Document Interface. The *prjCreateDatabase.exe* program, however, will let you create multiple copies of the database viewing window only. If you try to create multiple windows of the database creation window, the program will not process your request.

RUNNING *prj*CREATEDATABASE FROM THE CD-ROM

As you have learned, you must first install many programs that you will use in this book to your computer's hard drive before you use the programs. Because the *prjCreateDatabase.exe* program lets you create databases, you should install the *prjCreateDatabase.exe* program to a drive before you try to use it. If you try to run the *prjCreateDatabase.exe* program from the CD-ROM, however, it will not let you create databases in other directories, because it creates a temporary database file within the directory from which you execute the program. However, to run the *prjCreateDatabase.exe* program from the CD-ROM, and not create any new database, perform the following steps:

1. Select the Windows Start menu Run option. Windows will display the Run dialog box.

2. Within the Run dialog box, enter *x:\Chapter07\prjCreateDatabase.exe*, where *x* corresponds to the drive letter of your CD-ROM drive. Click your mouse on OK. Windows will run the *prjCreateDatabase.exe* program.

To learn more about the Jamsa Press *setup.exe* program, see the "What's on the *Visual Basic Programmer's Library* Companion CD-ROM" section at the back of this book.

The *prjCreateDatabase.exe* program will let you view existing databases and create new databases. To view an existing database, perform the following steps:

1. Within the Database Creation Program window, select the File menu Display Database option. The *prjCreateDatabase.exe* program will display an Open File dialog box.

2. Within the Open File dialog box, navigate to *x:\Program Files\DevStudio\VB*, where *x* corresponds to the drive letter of the hard drive on which you installed Visual Basic.

3. Within the Open File dialog box, double-click your mouse on the *Nwind.mdb* file. The *Nwind.mdb* file contains the *Northwind* database, which Microsoft ships with Visual Basic. The *prjCreateDatabase.exe* program will open the seven tables within the *Northwind* database, each within its own window, as shown in Figure 7.2.

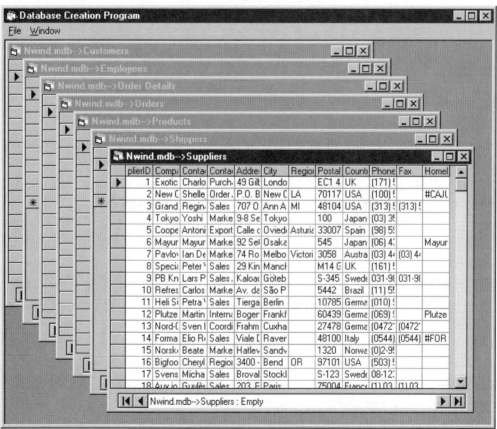

Figure 7.2 *The tables within the **Northwind** database.*

As you can see, the *prjCreateDatabase.exe* program opens each table within its own window and cascades the windows from the display's top left to the bottom right. You can, in fact, add additional records to any table within the database. You will learn how to add records to a database later in this section. For now, click your mouse on each child window's Close box to clear the child windows from the *prjCreateDatabase.exe* program.

Now that you have viewed the tables from a sample database, you can create your own database. To create your first database, perform the following steps:

1. Within the Database Creation Program window, select the File menu Create Database option. The *prjCreateDatabase.exe* program, in turn, will display the *frmCreateDatabase* window.

2. Within the *Table Name* field, enter *Sample*. Figure 7.3 shows the *frmCreateDatabase* window after you enter the table name.

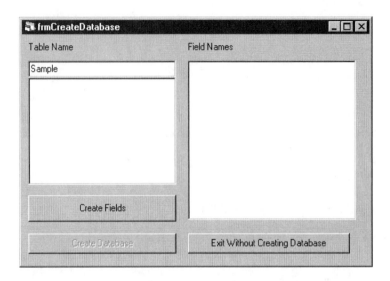

Figure 7.3 *The **frmCreateDatabase** window.*

3. Within the *frmCreateDatabase* window, click your mouse on the Create Fields button. The *prjCreateDatabase.exe* program will display the Sample window.

4. Within the Sample window, enter *Sample1* in the *Field Name* field and press the TAB key. The *prjCreateDatabase.exe* program will highlight the Field Type combo box.

5. Within the Field Type combo box, select the Text option and press the TAB key. The *prjCreateDatabase.exe* program will move the cursor to the *Field Size* field.

6. Within the *Field Size* field, enter 25. After you enter 25, click your mouse on the Add Field button. The *prjCreateDatabase.exe* program will add the *Sample1* field to the Fields list box on the Sample window's left-hand side, and clear the fields in the window of the values you entered in the previous Steps.

7. Within the Sample window, enter *Sample2* in the *Field Name* field and press the TAB key. The *prjCreateDatabase.exe* program will highlight the Field Type combo box.

8. Within the Field Type combo box, select the Integer option and press the TAB key. The *prjCreateDatabase.exe* program will move the cursor to the Add Field button.

9. Click your mouse on the Add Field button. The *prjCreateDatabase.exe* program will add the *Sample2* field to the Fields list box on the Sample window's left-hand side and clear the fields in the window of the values you entered in Steps 7 and 8. After you finish, your screen will look similar to Figure 7.4.

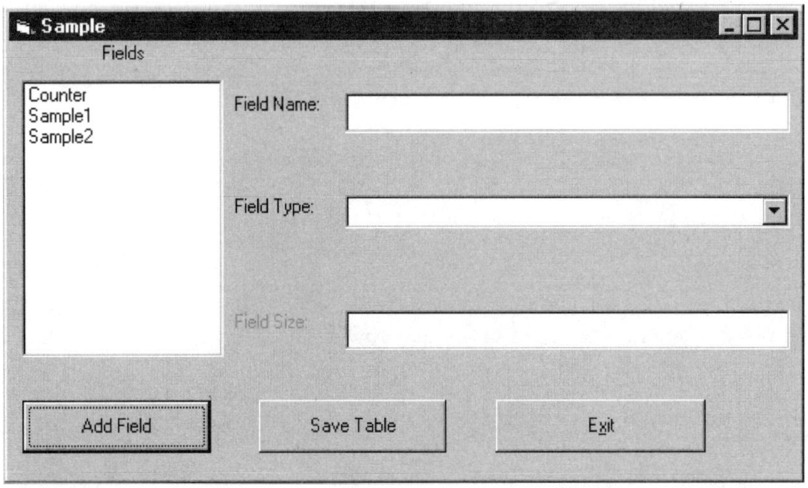

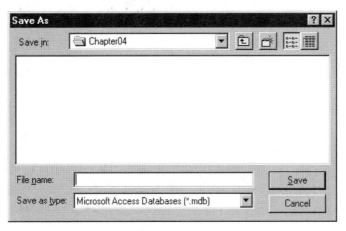

223

Figure 7.4 *The Sample window after you add the **Sample1** and **Sample2** fields.*

10. To exit the Sample window, click your mouse on the Save Table button. The *prjCreateDatabase.exe* program will close the Sample window and return to the *frmCreateDatabase* window.

11. Within the *frmCreateDatabase* window, click your mouse on the Create Database button. The *prjCreateDatabase.exe* program will display the Save As dialog box, as shown in Figure 7.5.

Figure 7.5 *The **prjCreateDatabase.exe** program's Save As dialog box.*

12. Within the Save As dialog box, enter the file name as *vbpl.mdb* within the *File name* field and click your mouse on the Save button to save the database. The *prjCreateDatabase.exe* program will save the *vbpl.mdb* database and close the *frmCreateDatabase* window.

After you create the *vbpl.mdb* database, you can use the *prjCreateDatabase.exe* program to add records to the *Sample* table within the database. To add records to the *Sample* table within the *vbpl.mdb* database, perform the following steps:

1. Within the Database Creation Program window, select the File menu Display Database option. The *prjCreateDatabase.exe* program will display an Open File dialog box.

2. Within the Open File dialog box, double-click your mouse on the *vbpl.mdb* database file, which contains the new *Sample* table you just created. The *prjCreateDatabase.exe* program will open the table within the *vbpl.mdb* database, within its own window.

3. In the *Sample1* field, enter *Test* and press the RIGHT ARROW key. The *prjCreateDatabase.exe* program will move the input cursor to the *Sample2* field.

4. Within the *Sample2* field, enter 2 and press the DOWN ARROW key. The program will insert a new row in the grid, place the number 1 within the *Counter* field, and display the input cursor within the *Sample2* field in the new row.

5. In the *Sample2* field, enter 3 and press the SHIFT+TAB keyboard combination (to leave the field). The *prjCreateDatabase.exe* program will move the input cursor to the *Sample1* field.

6. Within the *Sample1* field, enter *Test2* and press the DOWN ARROW key. The program will insert a new row in the grid, place the number 2 within the *Counter* field, and display the input cursor within the *Sample1* field in the new row. Figure 7.6 shows the *vbpl.mdb* database's *Sample* table.

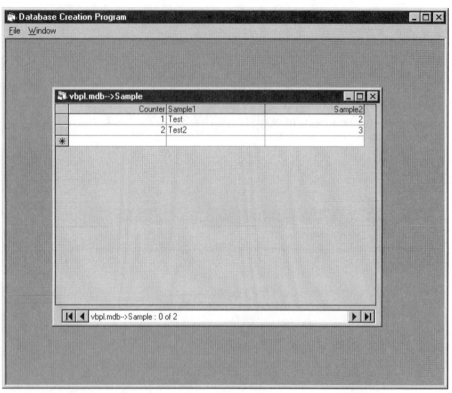

Figure 7.6 *The* **vbpl.mdb** *database window after you enter two new records in the* **Sample** *table.*

UNDERSTANDING WORKSPACE, DATABASE, AND RECORDSET OBJECTS

Within a Microsoft *Access* database or other database you create with the Jet database engine, a table contains records and fields of values. Microsoft *Access* uses the Jet database engine to handle its underlying database processing. The Data Access Objects (DAO) Object Library also uses the Jet database engine to handle its database processing. When you work with DAO Object Library objects in your Visual Basic programs, you will use three types of objects within your programs to manage and organize the database information: *Workspace*, *Database*, and *Recordset*.

A *Workspace* object can hold one or more *Database* objects. Each *Database* object can hold one or more *Recordset* objects. Each *Recordset* object can hold one or more records. Each record can hold one or more fields. Each field can hold one value. You can visualize a database as building blocks. A field is the simplest building block. You can put together one or more fields to create a record, as shown in Figure 7.7.

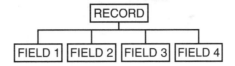

Figure 7.7 One or more fields composing a record.

Similarly, you can view a database recordset as a group of records. Each recordset can hold one or more records and will generally apply an order to the records that compose it. Figure 7.8 shows how adding a recordset to the record from Figure 7.7 will organize the information.

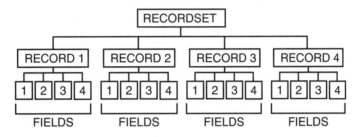

225

Figure 7.8 Using a recordset to organize one or more records.

A database can contain one or more recordsets. Large databases may have dozens of different recordsets. Figure 7.9 shows how recordsets, records, and fields combine to compose a database.

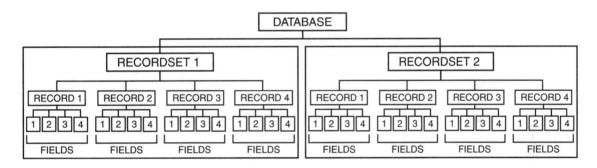

Figure 7.9 Creating a database by combining one or more recordsets and storing them within a single location.

Finally, you can use a single *Workspace* object within a program to maintain information about one or more databases. As you will learn, *Workspace* objects provide your programs with several different means to access databases. In fact, you can access multiple databases of different types (such as an *Access*® database, an *SQL Server*® database, and an *Oracle*® database) all from within a *Workspace* object. Figure 7.10 extends the hierarchical tree of database formation to its top level, the *Workspace* object.

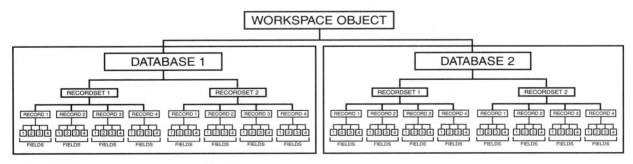

Figure 7.10 The complete hierarchical tree of database management objects in Visual Basic.

As you move down through the database objects in the hierarchical tree, you will find the types of information each level holds become more detailed and the uses more limited. As you move up the hierarchical tree, the reverse is true. For example, at the field level, you can only access a single datum—whatever is in that field. However, at the database level, you can use the value of that datum to search for records that contain similar values, to sort records, and so on.

BETTER UNDERSTANDING THE WORKSPACE OBJECT

A *Workspace* object is a non-persistent object that defines how your programs interact with data. A *non-persistent object* is one which does not save a copy of itself onto a disk drive or other permanent media. A non-persistent object will cease to exist either when you unload the program that creates the object or when you clear the computer's memory, depending on the object's definition. On the other hand, a persistent object is one that you can access from the drive, and which continues to exist even after its current instance finishes. An actual database, such as the *Northwind* database, that you save to the computer's hard drive is a persistent object. The *Workspace* object contains open databases and provides mechanisms for simultaneous transactions and secure workgroup support (that is, database security, with different users having different access levels). You can use a *Workspace* object to manage the current session, which begins when you open a workspace and ends when you close the workspace, or start an additional session. In a session, you can open multiple databases or database connections (for remote databases) and manage transactions. You will learn more about transactions later in this chapter.

Within your Visual Basic programs, the *Workspace* object is the object that holds all *Database* objects. That is, it is a *container object* for database and recordset information. A *Workspace* object defines a named session for a user. A *named session* is a session that includes the user's name, password (if required), and other access information. In non-secure environments (that is, in situations where users have unlimited access to databases), you can use a single *Workspace* object within your programs to access all available databases. In secure environments (that is, in situations where users must enter a password or otherwise identify themselves to have access to databases), you can use the *Workspace* object to communicate with a database to ensure that the communicating user has access privileges and to determine the type of access privileges the user has before your program opens the database.

For example, you can use the *Workspace* object's methods in a session to do the following:

- Use the *Name*, *UserName*, and *Type* properties to establish a named session. The named session creates a scope in which you can open multiple databases and conduct transactions.

- Use the *Close* method to terminate a session.

- Use the *OpenDatabase* method to open one or more existing databases within a *Workspace* object. In addition, you can use the *CreateDatabase* method to create a new database within the *Workspace* object.

- Use the *BeginTrans*, *CommitTrans*, and *Rollback* methods to manage nested transaction processing within a *Workspace*. You can also use several *Workspace* objects to conduct multiple, simultaneous, or overlapping transactions.

When you first refer to or use a *Workspace* object, you automatically create the default *Workspace*, which corresponds to *Workspaces(0)* (the first *Workspace* in the *Workspaces* collection). The default *Workspace* object's *Name* and *UserName* properties settings are *#Default Workspace#* and *Admin*, respectively. If security is enabled, the *UserName* property setting is the name of the user who logged on to the database.

When you use transactions to interact with a database, each transaction affects all databases in the specified *Workspace*, even if the *Workspace* currently contains multiple open *Database* objects. For example, assume you invoke the *BeginTrans* method, update several records in a database, and then delete records in another database. Because each transaction affects all the databases, you can then use the *Rollback* method to cancel and "roll back" both the update and delete operations you performed on two different databases. You can create additional *Workspace* objects to manage transactions independently across *Database* objects. You will learn more about transactions in the "Better Understanding Transactions" section of this chapter.

In addition, you can create *Workspace* objects with the *CreateWorkspace* method. After you create a new *Workspace* object, you must append it to the *Workspaces* collection, if you want to refer to the new *Workspace* from the collection. You must append named-session *Workspace* objects to the *Workspaces* collection. Alternatively, you can use a newly created *Workspace* object without appending it to the *Workspaces* collection. However, you must refer to the new *Workspace* object by the object variable to which you have assigned it.

BETTER UNDERSTANDING TRANSACTIONS

A *transaction* is a series of changes a program or a program's user makes to a database's data which the program and database engine do not save to the database until the program has completed all the changes. Often, when you are working with recordsets, you will use transaction processing to process additions, edits, and deletions to the recordset. Using transaction processing lets you (and your users) have more control over the way you place data within the database. For example, the following loop goes through a recordset and changes the *UpdateDate* field to the current date:

```
TempRs.MoveFirst
For I = 1 to TempRs.RecordCount
  TempRs.Edit
    TempRs.UpdateDate = Date
  TempRs.Update
  TempRs.MoveNext
Next I
```

When you perform a repeated process like the one the example shows, you will often not want to make changes to the database until the loop concludes successfully. As written, the program updates the database after each transaction. Alternatively, you could use transaction processing to handle the updates all at a single time, as shown here:

```
TempRs.MoveFirst
wkSpace.BeginTrans
  For I = 1 to TempRs.RecordCount
    TempRs.Edit
      TempRs.UpdateDate = Date
    TempRs.Update
    TempRs.MoveNext
  Next I
wkSpace.CommitTrans
```

The second example's program code will send the updates to the database only when execution reaches the *CommitTrans* method—which lets you stop the update at any point, and also reduces the number of interactions the program has with the database. Additionally, if you are, for example, deleting records that match a given criteria, you will typically want to prompt the user to confirm the deletion after your program has marked all the records. You can use both the *BeginTrans* and *CommitTrans* methods for transaction processing, and the *Rollback* method to return a database to its original state. When working with transactions, consider the following:

- You can often improve your application's performance by breaking operations that require the database to access the disk into transaction blocks. Such transaction blocks will buffer your operations and may significantly reduce the number of times the program and the database access the disk.

- In a Jet workspace, the Jet database engine logs transactions in a file the engine keeps in the directory the *TEMP* environment variable on the workstation specifies. If the transaction log file exhausts the available storage on your *TEMP* drive, the database engine triggers a run-time error. If you then try to use the *CommitTrans* method, the database engine will commit

227

all the operations for which there is storage available, but the remaining uncommitted operations are lost, and you must then restart the operation. Using the *Rollback* method releases the transaction log and rolls back all operations in the transaction.

As you have learned, you can use transaction processing to handle the addition, deletion, or batch editing of records within a recordset. You will use the *BeginsTrans* method to start a transaction. When you have completed the transaction and you want to save it to the *Recordset*, you will invoke the *CommitTrans* method. You will invoke these methods as shown here (remember that arguments within brackets are optional):

```
Workspace.BeginTrans
Workspace.CommitTrans [dbFlushOSCacheWrites]
```

The *Workspace* placeholder is an object variable that represents the *Workspace* containing the databases that will use transactions. You will use the *BeginTrans* and *CommitTrans* methods with a Workspace object when you want to treat a series of changes you have made to the databases in a session as one unit. Typically, you use transactions to maintain your data's integrity when you must update records in two or more tables and ensure that the database engine either completes all the changes in all the tables (after which, you use *CommitTrans* to commit them all) or that the engine completes none of the changes at all (after which, you use *RollBack* to reverse the successfully completed transactions). For example, if you transfer money from one account to another, you might subtract an amount from one and add the amount to the other. If either update fails, neither account will balance. Use the *BeginTrans* method before updating the first record, and use the *CommitTrans* method after you successfully update the last record.

In a Jet workspace, you can include the *dbFlushOSCacheWrites* constant with the *CommitTrans* method to force the database engine to flush all updates to disk immediately instead of caching them temporarily (that is, storing them within memory). If your program does not use the *dbFlushOSCacheWrites* constant when the program works with transactions, a user could immediately regain control after the application program calls *CommitTrans*, turn the computer off, and not have the database engine write the data to the disk. Although using the *dbFlushOSCacheWrites* constant may affect your application's performance, it is useful in situations where the user could turn off the computer before cached updates are saved to disk.

Note: *Within one **Workspace** object, transactions are always global to the Workspace and are not limited to only one **Connection** or **Database** object—meaning that a single transaction applies to all **Connection** or **Database** objects within a given workspace. If you perform operations on more than one connection or database within a **Workspace** transaction, resolving the transaction (that is, using the **CommitTrans** or **Rollback** method) affects all operations on all **Connections** and **Databases** within that **Workspace**. If you want to use single transaction processing on a database and extended transaction processing on another, open the databases within separate **Workspaces**.*

After you use the *CommitTrans* method, you cannot undo changes you made during that transaction unless you nest the transaction within another transaction that your program later rolls back. If you nest transactions, you must resolve the current transaction before you can resolve a transaction at a higher level of nesting. If you want to have simultaneous transactions with overlapping, non-nested scopes, you can create additional *Workspace* objects to contain the concurrent transactions. If you use the *CommitTrans* method without first using the *BeginTrans* method, an error will occur.

Some databases you access from within a Jet workspace may not support transactions, in which case the *Transactions* property of the *Database* object or *Recordset* object is *False*. To make sure a database supports transactions, check the *Database* object's *Transactions* property value before you use the *BeginTrans* method. If you are using a *Recordset* object that you have created from more than one database, check the *Transactions* property of the *Recordset* object. If a *Recordset* is based entirely on Jet tables, you can always use transactions. *Recordset* objects based on tables that other database products create, however, may not support transactions. For example, you cannot use transactions in a *Recordset* based on a *Paradox*® database table. In this case, the *Transactions* property is *False*. If the *Database* or *Recordset* does not support transactions, the object ignores the methods and no error occurs. You cannot nest transactions if you are accessing Open Database Connectivity (ODBC) standard data sources through the Microsoft Jet database engine.

One of the major benefits of transaction processing is the ability to erase all transactions within a transaction group if some event occurs (or does not occur). You can use the *Rollback* method to end the current transaction group and restore the databases in the *Workspace* object to the state the databases were in when the current transaction began—for example, if you were transferring funds between two bank accounts, and you had to log that change within two databases. Using transaction processing, you can remove the funds from the first account and place them in the second account. If an error occurred at any point within the process, you could use the *Rollbox* method to erase the transactions and return the databases to the state they were in before to the program's invocation of the *BeginTrans* method. You will implement the *Rollback* method as shown here:

```
Workspace.Rollback
```

Remember, if your program uses transaction processing, all databases within the workspace using transaction processing will save their changes within the temporary cache until either the *CommitTrans* or the *Rollback* method is invoked. To simultaneously process transactions and individual updates, open the databases within different workspaces.

If you close a *Workspace* object without resolving any pending transactions, the database engine will automatically roll back the transactions. Further, if you use the *Rollback* method without first using the *BeginTrans* method, an error will occur.

Understanding the Database Object

As you have learned, the *Workspace* object maintains session information for all open databases the program assigns to the *Workspace* object. In addition, the *Workspace* object's *OpenDatabase* and *CreateDatabase* methods add existing *Database* objects to a *Workspace* or create new *Database* objects within the *Workspace*. The *Database* object maintains a reference to a single database that may contain tables, indexes, queries, recordsets, and more. Each *Database* object represents a single, open database. In the *prjCreateDatabase* project, you will use the *Database* object and its methods and properties to manipulate an open database. In any type of database, you can perform the following activities:

- Use the *Execute* method to run an *action query*, a special type of request to a database that performs action on the database, rather than just returning information. For example, your programs can use a *Delete* query to delete large numbers of records that match criteria you specify.

- Set the *Connect* property to establish a connection to an Open Database Connectivity (ODBC) data source—that is, any data source that is not a Microsoft *Access* database.

- Set the *QueryTimeout* property to limit the length of time to wait for a query to execute at an ODBC data source. If the query does not return values before the time expires, the program will continue to execute, rather than waiting indefinitely.

- Use the *RecordsAffected* property to determine how many records an action query will change.

- Use the *OpenRecordset* method to execute a *Select* query and create a *Recordset* object. The section, "Understanding the Recordset Object," explains *Select* queries and *Recordset* objects in detail.

- Use the *Version* property to determine which database engine version created the database.

Note: *This is by no means a complete list of all methods, properties, and collections available for a **Database** object. For more information about the actions you can perform on or with the **Database** object, see the Visual Basic online Help file.*

When a procedure that declares a *Database* object completes execution, the program will close local *Database* objects along with any open *Recordset* objects. The database will lose any pending updates and "roll back" (reverse) any pending transactions, but no error that your program can trap will occur (that is, your program will be unable to respond to the data loss). You should explicitly complete any pending transactions or edits and close *Recordset* and *Database* objects before you exit procedures that declare such object variables locally.

When you use one of the transaction methods (*BeginTrans*, *CommitTrans*, or *Rollback*) on the *Workspace* object, these transactions apply to all databases currently open within the *Workspace* object from which you opened the *Database* object. If you want to use independent transactions, you must first open an additional *Workspace* object and then open another *Database* object in that *Workspace* object.

Note: *You can open the same data source or database more than once, which will create duplicate names in the* **Databases** *collection (the set of databases open within a given* **Workspace***). You should assign* **Database** *objects to object variables and refer to them by variable name.*

UNDERSTANDING THE RECORDSET OBJECT

As you have learned, a *Database* object is essentially a pointer to a database file. To manipulate the information the database contains, you must use additional objects. The object type your programs will most frequently use when you work with the information that databases contain is the *Recordset* object. A *dynaset-type Recordset* object is a dynamic set of records that can contain fields from one or more tables or queries in a database, which you may be able to update (depending on the fields within the *Recordset* object). A dynaset-type *Recordset* object is a type of *Recordset* object you use to manipulate data in an underlying database table or tables. Visual Basic also lets you create *snapshot-type Recordset* objects. *Snapshot-type Recordset* objects hold a copy of the database's contents at the moment the program created the *Recordset* objects—hence the name *snapshot.* In addition, Visual Basic lets you create *table-type Recordset* objects that your programs will access as though the recordsets were tables (which means your programs cannot sort, select, or perform any other type of Structured Query Language (SQL) query activity with table-type *Recordset* objects). In the *prjCreateDatabase* project, you will work exclusively with dynaset-type *Recordset* objects.

The dynaset-type *Recordset* object (which programmers often refer to simply as a *dynaset*) differs from a snapshot-type *Recordset* object because the dynaset stores only the primary key for each record, instead of actual data. As a result, the database engine will update a dynaset with changes the program or the user makes to the source data, but it will not do so with a snapshot-type *Recordset* object. Like the table-type *Recordset* object, a dynaset-type retrieves the full record only when the calling program needs the record for editing or display purposes. To create a dynaset-type *Recordset* object, you will use the *OpenRecordset* method on an open database against another dynaset- or snapshot-type *Recordset* object, on a *QueryDef* object, or on a *TableDef* object. To open recordsets with the *OpenRecordset* method, you will use program code similar to the following:

```
Set Rs = DB.OpenRecordset(dbOpenTable)      ' Table-type Recordset
Set Rs = DB.OpenRecordset(dbOpenDynaset)    ' Dynaset-type Recordset
Set Rs = DB.OpenRecordset(dbOpenSnapshot)   ' Snapshot-type Recordset
Set Rs = DB.OpenRecordset(dbOpenForwardOnly) ' Forward-only-type Recordset
```

If your program tries to create a dynaset-type *Recordset* object and the database engine cannot gain read or write access to the records, the database engine may create a read-only, dynaset-type *Recordset* object. As users update data, the base tables will reflect the users' updates. Therefore, current data is available to your application when you reposition the current record. In a multi-user database, more than one user can open a dynaset-type *Recordset* object and refer to the same records. Because a dynaset-type *Recordset* object is dynamic, when one user changes a record, other users have immediate access to the changed data. However, if one user adds a record, other users will not see the new record until the program uses the *Requery* method on the *Recordset* object. If a user deletes a record, the database engine will notify the program (which should then notify other users when they try to access the deleted record).

Records you add to the database do not become components of your dynaset-type *Recordset* object unless you use the *AddNew* and *Update* methods to add the records. For example, if you use an action query to add records, Visual Basic does not include the new records in your dynaset-type *Recordset* object until you either use the *Requery* method or you rebuild your *Recordset* object using the *OpenRecordset* method.

The order of the data within a dynaset-type *Recordset* object does not follow any specific sequence. If you must put your data in a specific order, use an SQL statement with an *Order By* clause to create the *Recordset* object. You can also use a *Where* clause to filter the records so that the database returns only certain records, which Visual Basic will add to the *Recordset* object. A later section, "The Structured Query Language (SQL) Where Keyword," explains the

Where keyword in detail. Using the SQL statements to select and order a subset of records will usually result in faster access to your data than using the *Filter* and *Sort* properties of the *Recordset* object. The following section, "Understanding Structured Query Language (SQL)," explains SQL statements in detail.

UNDERSTANDING STRUCTURED QUERY LANGUAGE (SQL)

As databases became more popular, database designers found it necessary to design a set of rules that users and programmers could use to design queries that managed and accessed databases. A *query* is a way to retrieve information from a single database table or a group of database tables. Typically, the information a query returns from a database meets some criteria the query's designer (such as a user or another programmer) specified.

In most Visual Basic programs, you will retrieve records from a database using one or more *queries*. You will write queries using the *Structured Query Language (SQL)*. After you design the *prjCreateDatabase* project's *vbpl.mdb* database, you will use SQL queries to access all the information the program or the user stores within the database. The SQL language contains clauses (sets of instructions that you must group together) that begin with keywords such as *Select*, *From*, *Where*, and *Order By*. The *prjCreateDatabase* program uses the keywords, generally in combination, to tell the Microsoft *Access* database what records the program wants. In the *prjCreateDatabase* project, you will display retrieved records in the *Microsoft Data-Bound Grid* control.

231

In addition to the keywords and clauses you will use to retrieve information from databases, the SQL language supports many other commands that you can use to create databases, delete records. update records in groups, and more. For example, you can create a new table using the SQL *CreateTable* keyword. Also, if you want to create a new index within a database table, you can use the *CreateIndex* keyword. For more information about the SQL language, see Kris Jamsa and Lars Klander's *1001 Visual Basic Programmer's Tips*, Jamsa Press, 1997.

In the *prjCreateDatabase* project, you will use the *Database* object's *OpenRecordset* method to open a recordset. The *OpenRecordset* method includes an SQL statement. To retrieve records from the *vbpl.mdb* database, you will write an SQL statement that contains *Select*, *From*, *Where*, and *Order By* keywords.

THE STRUCTURED QUERY LANGUAGE (SQL) SELECT AND FROM KEYWORDS

As you have learned, you will construct SQL queries to retrieve information from a database. Within an SQL query, the most commonly used keywords are *Select* and *From*. A SQL query that contains the *Select* keyword is a *Select* statement. In general, the *Select* statement directs the database to select (choose) records from the database that meet the criteria that follows the *Select* keyword. The *Select* statement contains four components: the *Select* keyword, the name of the fields to select, the *From* keyword, and the name of the table or tables from which to select.

As an example of how to use keywords within your SQL queries, imagine that you have designed a database with one table, *Tree*, and that you want to store different tree types. To start, you add two fields, *TreeType* and *Decoration*. After you define the fields, each record within the database table will contain the two fields you define. In the first record, you enter *Douglas Fir* in the *TreeType* field and *Holiday* in the *Decoration* field. Next, you make a second record and enter *Old Oak Tree* in the *TreeType* field and *Yellow Ribbon* in the *Decoration* field. Finally, you make a third record and enter *Cedar* in the *TreeType* field and *Squirrel House* in the *Decoration* field. (You will refer to this example in this section and the following SQL keyword sections.)

If you want to select all the records in the *Tree* table, but only retrieve the *TreeType* field from each record, you would write your SQL query as "Select [TreeType] From Tree." When you include this *Select* statement within an *OpenRecordset* method, the database will return three records containing the values *Douglas Fir, Old Oak Tree,* and *Cedar* as the recordset.

If you instead want to return all fields from the *Tree* table, you would use an asterisk (*). When a *Select* statement has an asterisk, the database will return all fields in the table or tables you specify. To select both fields, *TreeType* and *Description*, you would write "Select * From Tree." When you include this *Select* statement within an *OpenRecordset* method, the database will return all values in the *TreeType* and *Decoration* fields within the three records that comprise the recordset.

THE STRUCTURED QUERY LANGUAGE (SQL) WHERE KEYWORD

As you have learned, the most commonly used SQL keywords are *Select* and *From*. The *Select* statement returns specified fields *From* a table or tables. However, when you specify a field in a *Select* statement, the program returns all the values in that field. To return records that contain specific values, you will use a *Where* keyword. The *Where* keyword isolates specific records from a database table.

If you refer to the example in the "The Structured Query Language (SQL) Select and From Keywords" section, but instead you want to return all records where the *TreeType* field contains the value *Old Oak Tree*, you would write "Select * From Tree Where [TreeType] = 'Old Oak Tree'." When you include this *Select* statement within an *OpenRecordset* method, the program will return one record that contains *Old Oak Tree* for the *TreeType* field and *Yellow Ribbon* for the *Decoration* field.

A *Where* clause consists of the *Where* keyword and statements. A *Where* clause can contain up to 40 expressions that logical operators, such as *And* and *Or,* link. When you enter a field name that contains a space or punctuation in the *Where* clause, surround the field name with brackets [ ].

If you want to return all records where the *TreeType* field contains the value *Douglas Fir* or the *Description* field contains the value *Yellow Ribbon*, you would write "Select * From Tree Where [TreeType] = 'Douglas Fir' OR [Decoration] = 'Yellow Ribbon'." When you include this *Select* statement within an *OpenRecordset* method, the program will return two records. The first record will contain *Old Oak Tree* in the *TreeType* field and *Yellow Ribbon* in the *Decoration* field. The second record will contain *Douglas Fir* in the *TreeType* field and *Holiday* in the *Decoration* field.

THE STRUCTURED QUERY LANGUAGE (SQL) ORDER BY KEYWORD

As you have learned, the *Select* statement returns specified fields from a table or tables. However, when you include a *Select* statement within an *OpenRecordset* method, the program will open a recordset of records in order from the first record to the last record. (The order in which the database engine originally added the records to the table determines the order in which the program opens the recordset.) To return a *Recordset* object of records in an order that you specify (for example, alphabetically by a given field), you will use an ordering phrase that begins with the *Order By* keyword. The *Order By* keyword sorts a query's resulting records on a field or fields you specify in ascending or descending order.

If you refer to the database example that you used in the "The Structured Query Language (SQL) Select and From Keywords" section, but want to instead return all records in ascending alphabetical order by the *Decoration* field, you would write an SQL query in the following form:

```
Select * From Tree Order By [Decoration]
```

When you include the *Select* statement within an *OpenRecordset* method, the program will return three records in ascending order by the *Decoration* field's values. The first record will contain *Holiday*, then *Squirrel House* and, finally, *Yellow Ribbon* in the *Decoration* field. The sort order is ascending (alphabetical) order and the record with *Holiday* in the *Decoration* field is first because "H" comes first alphabetically in the *Decoration* field values.

The default sort value in an *Order By* clause is an ascending sort order. To specify a descending alphabetical sort order, you will write "Select * From Tree Order By [Decoration] DESC." When you include this *Select* statement within an *OpenRecordset* method, the program will return three records in descending order by the *Decoration* field values. The first record will contain *Yellow Ribbon*, then *Squirrel House* and, finally, *Holiday* in the *Evergreen* field. The sort order is descending and the first record contains *Yellow Ribbon* in the *Decoration* field because "Y" comes last alphabetically in the *Decoration* field values.

CREATING THE BLANK FORMS

Now that you have a better idea how to use the finished *prjCreateDatabase* project and how to compose a database, you can begin to design the *prjCreateDatabase* project. First, you will design empty forms. After you design and implement the forms, you will add controls to the forms to design them and maintain the database information. The *prjCreateDatabase* project includes one MDI parent form, two child forms, a standard form, and a module. You learned about MDI parent forms and child forms in Chapter 4.

CREATING THE MDI PARENT FORM

As you have learned, you will use an MDI parent form within the *prjCreateDatabase* project. The MDI parent form will serve as a container for the other forms within the program. To begin the *prjCreateDatabase* project and design an empty MDI form, perform the following steps:

1. Within Visual Basic, select the File menu New Project option. Visual Basic will open the New Project dialog box.

2. Within the New Project dialog box, select the Standard EXE icon. Then click your mouse on the OK button. Visual Basic will close the New Project dialog box, start a new project, *Project1*, and add a form to it, *Form1*.

3. Within the new *Project1* project, select the Project menu Add MDI Form option. Visual Basic will open the Add MDI Form dialog box.

4. Within the Add MDI Form dialog box, select the MDI Form icon. Then click your mouse on the Open button. Visual Basic will add an MDI form, *MDIForm1*, to the new *Project1* project and display the *MDIForm1* form window.

5. Select the View menu Properties Window option. Visual Basic will open the Properties Window listing the *MDIForm1* properties.

6. Within the Properties Window, change the *MDIForm1* property values to the values Table 7.1 lists.

Object	Property	Set As
MDIForm1	*Caption*	*Database Creation Program*
MDIForm1	*Height*	7935
MDIForm1	*Left*	0
MDIForm1	*StartupPosition*	2 - *CenterScreen*
MDIForm1	*Top*	0
MDIForm1	*Width*	9630
MDIForm1	*Name*	*frmMDIParent*

Table 7.1 *The newly named* **frmMDIParent** *MDI form's properties.*

CREATING THE FIRST CHILD FORM

As you have learned, the *prjCreateDatabase* project includes one MDI parent form, two child forms, one standard form, and a module. To continue the *prjCreateDatabase* project and add the first child form to it, perform the following steps:

1. If Visual Basic is not displaying the *Form1* form within an object window, double-click your mouse on the Form1 icon within the Project Explorer. Visual Basic will open the *Form1* form within an object window.

2. Select the View menu Properties Window option. Visual Basic will open the Properties Window listing the *Form1* properties.

3. Within the Properties Window, change the *Form1* property values to the values Table 7.2 lists.

Object	Property	Set As
Form1	*Caption*	*Create Database*
Form1	*Height*	4725

Table 7.2 *The newly named* **frmCreateDatabase** *child form's properties. (continued on following page)*

Object	Property	Set As
Form1	Left	0
Form1	Top	0
Form1	Width	6810
Form1	MDIChild	True
Form1	Name	frmCreateDatabase

Table 7.2 *The newly named **frmCreateDatabase** child form's properties. (continued from previous page)*

CREATING THE SECOND CHILD FORM

Now that you have created the first child form, *frmCreateDatabase*, you can add the second child form to the project. To add a second child form to the *prjCreateDatabase* project, perform the following steps:

1. Within the *prjCreateDatabase* project, select the Project menu Add Form option. Visual Basic will display the Add Form dialog box.

2. Within the Add Form dialog box, click your mouse on the New tab and select the Form icon. Next, click your mouse on the Open button. Visual Basic will close the Add Form dialog box and add a new form, *Form1*, to the *prjCreateDatabase* project.

3. Select the View menu Properties Window option. Visual Basic will open the Properties Window listing the *Form1* properties.

4. Within the Properties Window, change the *Form1* property values to the values Table 7.3 lists.

Object	Property	Set As
Form1	Caption	[blank]
Form1	Height	4085
Form1	Left	0
Form1	Top	0
Form1	Width	4800
Form1	MDIChild	True
Form1	Name	frmDatabaseChild

Table 7.3 *The newly named **frmDatabaseChild** child form's properties.*

CREATING THE STANDARD FORM

Now that you have created one MDI parent form and two child forms, you can create a standard form. In the "Creating the MDI Parent Form" section, you created the *prjCreateDatabase* project and added an MDI parent form, *frmMDIParent*, to the project. When you first created the *prjCreateDatabase* project, Visual Basic automatically added a standard form, *Form1*, to it. You will use the *Form1* form and change its properties to create a blank standard form. To create a blank standard form in the *prjCreateDatabase* project, perform the following steps:

1. Within the *prjCreateDatabase* project, select the Project menu Add Form option. Visual Basic will display the Add Form dialog box.

2. Within the Add Form dialog box, click your mouse on the New tab and select the Form icon. Next, click your mouse on the Open button. Visual Basic will close the Add Form dialog box and add a new form, *Form1*, to the *prjCreateDatabase* project.

3. Select the View menu Properties Window option. Visual Basic will open the Properties Window listing the *Form1* properties.

4. Within the Properties Window, change the *Form1* property values to the values Table 7.4 lists.

Object	Property	Set As
Form1	Caption	Add Fields
Form1	Height	4485
Form1	Left	0
Form1	StartupPosition	2 - CenterScreen
Form1	Top	0
Form1	Width	7770
Form1	Name	frmAddFields

Table 7.4 *The newly named **frmAddFields** standard form's properties.*

ADDING A MODULE TO THE PROJECT

After you design the *prjCreateDatabase* project's blank forms, you will create a module to store program code. Within the *prjCreateDatabase* project, the program code that you will place within the module will declare several global variables and constants and will contain several "helper" procedures that the forms will use during their processing. To add a module to the *prjCreateDatabase* project, perform the following steps:

1. Within Visual Basic, select the Project menu Add Module option. Visual Basic will open the Add Module dialog box.

2. Within the Add Module dialog box, select the Module option. Next, click your mouse on the Open button. Visual Basic will open a new Code window, *Module1*.

3. Select the View menu Properties Window option. Visual Basic will open the Properties Window listing the *Module1* properties.

4. Within the Properties Window, change *Module1* module's name to *mdlDeclarations*.

5. Select the File menu Save Project As option. Visual Basic will open the Save File As dialog box and fill the *File name* field with *mdlDeclarations*.

6. Within the Save File As dialog box, click your mouse on the Save button. Visual Basic will save the *mdlDeclarations* module and fill the *File name* field with *frmAddFields*.

7. Within the Save File As dialog box, click your mouse on the Save button. Visual Basic will save the *frmAddFields* form and fill the *File name* field with *frmDatabaseChild*.

8. Within the Save File As dialog box, click your mouse on the Save button. Visual Basic will save the *frmDatabaseChild* form and fill the *File name* field with *frmCreateDatabase*.

9. Within the Save File As dialog box, click your mouse on the Save button. Visual Basic will save the *frmCreateDatabase* form and fill the *File name* field with *frmMDIParent*.

10. Within the Save File As dialog box, click your mouse on the Save button. Visual Basic will save the *frmMDIParent* MDI form and fill the *File name* field with *Project1*.

11. Within the *File name* field, replace the *Project1* project name with the new *prjCreateDatabase* project name. Next, click your mouse on the Save button. Visual Basic will save the *prjCreateDatabase* project and close the Save Project As dialog box.

ADDING THE DATA ACCESS OBJECTS (DAO) OBJECT LIBRARY TO THE PROJECT

As you have learned, you will use the Data Access Objects (DAO) Object Library within the *prjCreateDatabase* project to create and manage databases. To manage database information from within Visual Basic, you must add a set of data objects to the project. Within the *prjCreateDatabase* project, you will use the Data Access Objects (DAO) Object Library to manage database information.

When you retrieve data from or save data to a database, you will manage that data within a *Recordset* object. As you know, before you can store records in a *Recordset* object, you must have a *Workspace* and a *Database* object in your project. To use the *Workspace*, *Database*, and *Recordset* objects within Visual Basic, you must make a reference to them. The Data Access Objects (DAO) Object Library contains each object. You must add a *DAO Object Library* reference to the *prjCreateDatabase* project before you can create and use the temporary database. After you add a *DAO Object Library* reference to the *prjCreateDatabase* project, you will declare and assign variables of each *Data Access Object* type. To add a *DAO Object Library* reference to the *prjCreateDatabase* project, perform the following steps:

1. Within Visual Basic, select the Project menu References option. Visual Basic will open the References dialog box.

2. Within the References dialog box, select the *Microsoft DAO 3.5 Object Library* listing from the *Available References* field. Next, click your mouse on the box to the left of the selection. Visual Basic will draw a check mark in the box, as shown in Figure 7.11.

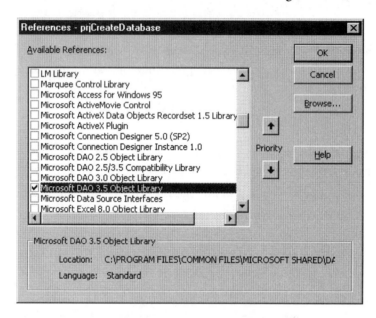

Figure 7.11 *The References dialog box after you select the **Microsoft DAO 3.5 Object Library** listing.*

3. Within the References dialog box, click your mouse on the OK button. Visual Basic will add the *DAO Object Library* reference to the *prjCreateDatabase* project.

ADDING THE COMPONENT CONTROLS TO THE PROJECT

As you have learned, the *prjCreateDatabase* project has four component forms that each perform special processing. The *frmMDIParent* form and the *frmDatabaseChild* form both use controls that you must add to the project as components. As you have learned, the project will display dialog boxes to let the user load and save database files, for which it will use the *CommonDialog* control. The project will also use the *Data-Bound Grid* control to let the user view the database tables. To add the *Data-Bound Grid* control and the *CommonDialog* control to the *prjCreateDatabase* project, perform the following steps:

1. Within Visual Basic, select the Project menu Components option. Visual Basic will open the Components dialog box.

2. Within the Components dialog box, select the *Microsoft Common Dialog Control 5.0* listing. Next, click your mouse on the box to the left of the listing. Visual Basic will display a check mark in the box.

3. Within the Components dialog box, select the *Microsoft Data Bound Grid Control 5.0* listing.

Next, click your mouse on the box to the left of the listing. Visual Basic will display a check mark in the box. Figure 7.12 shows the Components dialog box after you select the control components.

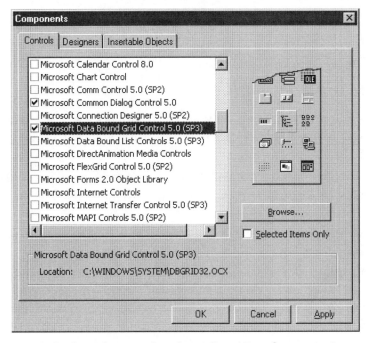

Figure 7.12 *The Components dialog box after you select the **prjCreateDatabase** project's control components.*

4. Within the Components dialog box, click your mouse on the OK button. Visual Basic will close the Components dialog box and add the controls to the *prjCreateDatabase* project.

Designing the frmMDIParent Form

As you learned in this chapter's "Creating the MDI Parent Form" section, the *frmMDIParent* form is essentially a container for the child forms that the program will display. You will add one control to the *frmMDIParent* form, the *CommonDialog* control. In addition to the control, you will use the Menu Editor to add a menu to the *frmMDIParent* form.

Adding the CommonDialog Control to the frmMDIParent Form

In the "Using the *prjCreateDatabase* Project" section of this chapter, you opened several different files and file types within the *prjCreateDatabase* program. To display the Open File dialog box (and the Save As dialog box), the *prjCreateDatabase* project uses the *CommonDialog* control. To add the *CommonDialog* control to the *frmMDIParent* form, perform the following steps:

1. If Visual Basic is not displaying the *frmMDIParent* form within an object window, double-click your mouse on the *frmMDIParent* form listing within Project Explorer. Visual Basic will open the *frmMDIParent* form.

2. Within Visual Basic, select the View menu Toolbox option. Visual Basic will open the Toolbox.

3. Within the Toolbox, double-click your mouse on the CommonDialog icon. Visual Basic will draw a *CommonDialog* control, *CommonDialog1*, within the *frmMDIParent* form.

4. Within the *frmMDIParent* form, click your mouse on the *CommonDialog1* control to highlight it. Visual Basic will draw a small frame around the control.

5. Select the View menu Properties Window option. Visual Basic will open the Properties Window listing the *CommonDialog1* properties.

6. Within the Properties Window, change the *CommonDialog1* properties to the values Table 7.5 lists.

Object	Property	Set As
CommonDialog1	*Left*	0
CommonDialog1	*Top*	0
CommonDialog1	*Name*	cdgDatabase

Table 7.5 *The newly named* **cdgDatabase** *control's properties.*

ADDING THE MENUS TO FRMMDIPARENT FORM

As you saw earlier in this chapter, the *prjCreateDatabase* project includes several menu items. To create the menu items for the *frmMDIParent* form, you will use the Visual Basic Menu Editor. To use the Menu Editor to create the form's menus, perform the following steps:

1. If Visual Basic is not displaying the *frmMDIParent* form within an object window, double-click your mouse on the *frmMDIParent* form listing within Project Explorer. Visual Basic will open the *frmMDIParent* form.

2. Within Visual Basic, select the Tools menu Menu Editor option. Visual Basic will display the Menu Editor dialog box.

3. Within the *Caption* field, enter the caption as *&File*. (Remember, the ampersand symbol (&) alerts Visual Basic to accept the letter immediately following the ampersand as a keyboard shortcut for the item.) Visual Basic will display the *&File* caption in the Menu Viewer at the bottom of the Menu Editor as you type.

4. Press the TAB key to move to the *Name* field. Enter the menu's name as *mnuFile*.

5. Click your mouse on the Next button. Visual Basic will clear the *Caption* and *Name* fields, move the block cursor within the Menu Viewer down one line, and return the input cursor to the *Caption* field.

6. Click your mouse on the right arrow just above the Menu Viewer and to the left of the Next button. Visual Basic will display three dots on the current line in the Menu Viewer.

7. Within the *Caption* field, enter the next item's caption as *&Create Database*. Visual Basic will display *&Create Database*, preceded by three dots (which indicate the item is a submenu), in the Menu Viewer as you type.

8. Press the TAB key to move the input cursor to the *Name* field. Enter the menu's name as *mnuFileCreateDatabase*.

9. Click your mouse on the Next button. Visual Basic will clear the *Caption* and *Name* fields, move the block cursor within the Menu Viewer down one line, and return the input cursor to the *Caption* field.

10. Within the *Caption* field, enter the next item's caption as *&Display Database*. Visual Basic will display *&Display Database*, preceded by three dots, in the Menu Viewer as you type.

11. Press the TAB key to move the input cursor to the *Name* field. Enter the menu's name as *mnuFileDisplayDatabase*.

12. Click your mouse on the Next button. Visual Basic will clear the *Caption* and *Name* fields, move the block cursor within the Menu Viewer down one line, and return the input cursor to the *Caption* field.

13. Within the *Caption* field, enter the next item's caption as *E&xit*. Visual Basic will display *E&xit*, preceded by three dots, in the Menu Viewer as you type.

14. Press the TAB key to move the input cursor to the *Name* field. Enter the menu's name as *mnuFileExit*.

15. Click your mouse on the Next button. Visual Basic will clear the *Caption* and *Name* fields, move the block cursor within the Menu Viewer down one line, and return the input cursor to the *Caption* field.

16. Click your mouse on the left arrow just above the Menu Viewer and to the left of the Next button. Visual Basic will remove the three dots (leaving no dots) on the current line in the Menu Viewer.

17. Within the *Caption* field, enter the next item's caption as *&Window*. Visual Basic will display *&Window* in the Menu Viewer as you type.

18. Press the TAB key to move the input cursor to the *Name* field. Enter the menu's name as *mnuWindow*.

19. Click your mouse on the check box next to the *Windowlist* item. Visual Basic will place a check mark in the box.

20. Click your mouse on the Next button. Visual Basic will clear the *Caption* and *Name* fields, move the block cursor within the Menu Viewer down one line, and return the input cursor to the *Caption* field.

21. Click your mouse on the right arrow just above the Menu Viewer and to the left of the Next button. Visual Basic will display three dots on the current line in the Menu Viewer.

22. Within the *Caption* field, enter the next item's caption as *&Tile*. Visual Basic will display *&Tile*, preceded by three dots, in the Menu Viewer as you type.

23. Press the TAB key to move the input cursor to the *Name* field. Enter the menu's name as *mnuWindow_Tile*.

24. Click your mouse on the Next button. Visual Basic will clear the *Caption* and *Name* fields, move the block cursor within the Menu Viewer down one line, and return the input cursor to the *Caption* field.

25. Within the *Caption* field, enter the next item's caption as *&Cascade*. Visual Basic will display *&Cascade*, preceded by three dots, in the Menu Viewer as you type.

26. Press the TAB key to move the input cursor to the *Name* field. Enter the menu's name as *mnuWindow_Cascade*. When you finish creating the menu, the Menu Editor will look similar to Figure 7.13.

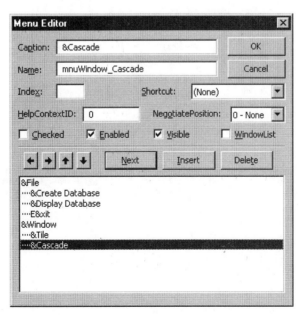

Figure 7.13 The Menu Editor after you finish creating the frmMDIParent form's menus.

27. Click your mouse on the OK button to exit the Menu Editor.

After you add the menu and format the *CommonDialog* control, the *frmMDIParent* form will look similar to Figure 7.14.

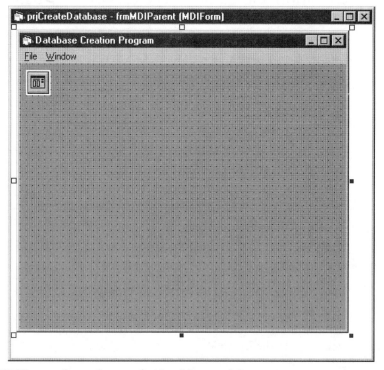

*Figure 7.14 The **frmMDIParent** form after you finish adding and formatting its controls.*

DESIGNING THE FRMDATABASECHILD FORM'S APPEARANCE

As you learned in the "Using the *prjCreateDatabase* Project" section of this chapter, you will display database tables that you load into the *prjCreateDatabase* program within a grid in the *frmDatabaseChild* form. You will add two controls to the *frmDatabaseChild* form—a *Data* control and a *Data-Bound Grid* control. To add a *Data* control to the *frmDatabaseChild* form, perform the following steps:

1. If Visual Basic is not displaying the *frmDatabaseChild* form within an object window, double-click your mouse on the *frmDatabaseChild* form listing within Project Explorer. Visual Basic will open the *frmDatabaseChild* form.

2. Within Visual Basic, select the View menu Toolbox option. Visual Basic will open the Toolbox.

3. Within the Toolbox, double-click your mouse on the Data icon. Visual Basic will draw a *Data* control, *Data1*, within the *frmDatabaseChild* form. Figure 7.15 shows the Data icon within the Toolbox.

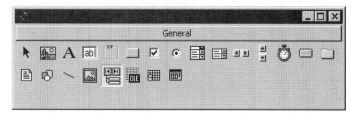

Figure 7.15 The Data icon within the Toolbox.

4. Within the *frmDatabaseChild* form, click your mouse on the *Data1* control to highlight it. Visual Basic will draw a small frame around the control.

5. Select the View menu Properties Window option. Visual Basic will open the Properties Window listing the *Data1* properties.

6. Within the Properties Window, change the *Data1* properties to the values Table 7.6 lists.

Object	Property	Set As
Data1	*EOFAction*	*2 - Add New*
Data1	*Height*	345
Data1	*Left*	120
Data1	*Top*	3240
Data1	*Width*	4455
Data1	*Name*	*dtaChild*

Table 7.6 *The newly named* **dtaChild** *control's properties.*

Now that you have added the *Data* control to the form, you must add the *Data-Bound Grid* control to the form and bind the control to the newly added *Data* control. To add the *Data-Bound Grid* control to the form, perform the following steps:

241

1. If Visual Basic is not displaying the *frmDatabaseChild* form within an object window, double-click your mouse on the *frmDatabaseChild* form listing within Project Explorer. Visual Basic will open the *frmDatabaseChild* form.

2. Within Visual Basic, select the View menu Toolbox option. Visual Basic will open the Toolbox.

3. Within the Toolbox, double-click your mouse on the DBGrid icon. Visual Basic will draw a *Data-Bound Grid* control, *DBGrid1*, within the *frmDatabaseChild* form. Figure 7.16 shows the DBGrid icon within the Toolbox.

Figure 7.16 *The DBGrid icon within the Toolbox.*

4. Within the *frmDatabaseChild* form, click your mouse on the *DBGrid1* control to highlight it. Visual Basic will draw a small frame around the control.

5. Select the View menu Properties Window option. Visual Basic will open the Properties Window listing the *DBGrid1* properties.

6. Within the Properties Window, change the *DBGrid1* properties to the values Table 7.7 lists.

Object	Property	Set As
DBGrid1	*DataSource*	*dtaChild*
DBGrid1	*Height*	3180
DBGrid1	*Left*	0
DBGrid1	*Top*	0
DBGrid1	*Width*	4575
DBGrid1	*Name*	*grdChildForm*

Table 7.7 *The newly named* **grdChildForm** *control's properties.*

After you finish designing the *frmDatabaseChild* form, the object window will look similar to Figure 7.17.

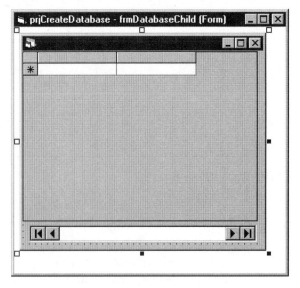

Figure 7.17 *The **frmDatabaseChild** form after you finish its design.*

DESIGNING THE FRMCREATEDATABASE FORM

As you saw in this chapter's "Using the *prjCreateDatabase* Project" section, the *frmCreateDatabase* form lets the user create multiple tables, view the record definitions within those tables, and add the tables to a new database. The *frmCreateDatabase* form includes a combo box, a list box, labels, and command buttons to help the user manage database information.

ADDING THE COMBO BOX TO THE FRMCREATEDATABASE FORM

As you have learned, the *prjCreateDatabase* project will use a *ComboBox* control to display the tables that you add to a database you want to create. To add a *ComboBox* control to the *frmCreateDatabase* form, perform the following steps:

1. If Visual Basic is not displaying the *frmCreateDatabase* form within an object window, double-click your mouse on the *frmCreateDatabase* form listing within the Project Explorer. Visual Basic will open the *frmCreateDatabase* form.

2. Within Visual Basic, select the View menu Toolbox option. Visual Basic will open the Toolbox.

3. Within the Toolbox, double-click your mouse on the ListBox icon. Visual Basic will draw a *ComboBox* control, *Combo1*, within the *frmCreateDatabase* form.

4. Within the *frmCreateDatabase* form window, click your mouse on the *Combo1* control to highlight it. Visual Basic will draw a small frame around the control.

5. Select the View menu Properties Window option. Visual Basic will open the Properties Window listing the *Combo1* properties.

6. Within the Properties Window, change the *Combo1* properties to those Table 7.8 lists.

Object	Property	Set As
Combo1	*Height*	2325
Combo1	*Left*	120
Combo1	*Style*	1 - *Simple Combo*
Combo1	*Top*	480
Combo1	*Width*	2895
Combo1	*Name*	*cmbTables*

Table 7.8 *The newly named **cmbTables** control's properties.*

ADDING THE LIST BOX TO THE *frmCreateDatabase* FORM

As you have learned, the *prjCreateDatabase* project will use a *ListBox* control to display the fields within a table that you want to add to a database. To add a *ListBox* control to the *frmCreateDatabase* form, perform the following steps:

1. If Visual Basic is not displaying the *frmCreateDatabase* form within an object window, double-click your mouse on the *frmCreateDatabase* form listing within the Project Explorer. Visual Basic will open the *frmCreateDatabase* form.

2. Within Visual Basic, select the View menu Toolbox option. Visual Basic will open the Toolbox.

3. Within the Toolbox, double-click your mouse on the ListBox icon. Visual Basic will draw a *ListBox* control, *List1*, within the *frmCreateDatabase* form.

4. Within the *frmCreateDatabase* form window, click your mouse on the *List1* control to highlight it. Visual Basic will draw a small frame around the control.

5. Select the View menu Properties Window option. Visual Basic will open the Properties Window listing the *List1* properties.

6. Within the Properties Window, change the *List1* properties to those Table 7.9 lists.

Object	Property	Set As
List1	*Height*	2985
List1	*Left*	3240
List1	*Top*	480
List1	*Width*	3255
List1	*Name*	*lstFields*

Table 7.9 *The newly named* **lstFields** *control's properties.*

ADDING THE LABEL CONTROLS TO THE *prjCreateDatabase* FORM

As you have learned, you will display database information in a *ComboBox* and *ListBox* control on the *frmCreateDatabase* form. You will add a *Label* control to the form above each control as a heading. To add the *Label* controls to the *frmCreateDatabase* form, perform the following steps:

1. If Visual Basic is not displaying the *frmCreateDatabase* form within an object window, double-click your mouse on the *frmCreateDatabase* form listing within the Project Explorer. Visual Basic will open the *frmCreateDatabase* form.

2. Select the View menu Toolbox option. Visual Basic will open the Toolbox.

3. Within the Toolbox, double-click your mouse on the Label icon. Visual Basic will draw a *Label* control, *Label1*, within the *frmCreateDatabase* form.

4. Repeat Step 3 one time. Visual Basic will add the *Label2* control to the form.

5. Within the *frmCreateDatabase* form, click your mouse on the *Label1* control to highlight it. Visual Basic will draw a small frame around the control.

6. Select the View menu Properties Window option. Visual Basic will open the Properties Window listing the *Label1* properties.

7. Within the Properties Window, change the *Label1* properties to the values Table 7.10 lists.

8. Repeat Steps 5, 6, and 7 to set the *Label2* properties to the values Table 7.10 lists.

Object	Property	Set As
Label1	*Caption*	*Table Name*
Label1	*Height*	255
Label1	*Left*	120

Table 7.10 *The newly named* **Label** *controls' properties. (continued on following page)*

Object	Property	Set As
Label1	*Top*	120
Label1	*Width*	2895
Label1	*Name*	*lblTableName*
Label2	*Caption*	*Field Names*
Label2	*Height*	255
Label2	*Left*	3240
Label2	*Top*	120
Label2	*Width*	3135
Label2	*Name*	*lblFieldNames*

*Table 7.10 The newly named **Label** controls' properties. (continued from previous page)*

244 ADDING THE COMMANDBUTTON CONTROLS TO THE prJCREATEDATABASE FORM

As you have learned, you will use the Create Field button to create fields for the database, the Create Database button to create the database itself, and the Exit Without Creating Database button to exit the form without creating the database. To add the *CommandButton* controls to the *frmCreateDatabase* form, perform the following steps:

1. If Visual Basic is not displaying the *frmCreateDatabase* form within an object window, double-click your mouse on the *frmCreateDatabase* form listing within the Project Explorer. Visual Basic will open the *frmCreateDatabase* form.

2. Within Visual Basic, select the View menu Toolbox option. Visual Basic will open the Toolbox.

3. Within the Toolbox, double-click your mouse on the CommandButton icon. Visual Basic will draw a *CommandButton* control, *Command1*, within the *frmCreateDatabase* form.

4. Repeat Step 3 two more times. Visual Basic will add the *Command2* and *Command3* buttons to the *frmCreateDatabase* form.

5. Within the *frmCreateDatabase* form, click your mouse on a *CommandButton* control to highlight it. Visual Basic will draw a small frame around the control.

6. Select the View menu Properties Window option. Visual Basic will open the Properties Window listing the selected control's properties.

7. Within the Properties Window, change the highlighted control's properties to the values Table 7.11 lists.

8. Repeat Steps 5, 6, and 7 to change the properties for all three *CommandButton* controls to the values Table 7.11 lists.

Object	Property	Set As
Command1	*Caption*	*Create Fields*
Command1	*Height*	495
Command1	*Left*	120
Command1	*Top*	3000
Command1	*Width*	2895
Command1	*Name*	*cmdCreateFields*
Command2	*Caption*	*Create Database*
Command2	*Height*	375
Command2	*Left*	120
Command2	*Top*	3720
Command2	*Width*	2895
Command2	*Name*	*cmdCreateDatabase*

*Table 7.11 The newly named **CommandButton** controls' properties. (continued on following page)*

Object	Property	Set As
Command3	*Caption*	*Exit without Creating Database*
Command3	*Height*	375
Command3	*Left*	3240
Command3	*Top*	3720
Command3	*Width*	3135
Command3	*Name*	*cmdExit*

Table 7.11 *The newly named **CommandButton** controls' properties.(continued from previous page)*

When you finish setting the properties for the command buttons, the *frmCreateDatabase* form will look similar to Figure 7.18.

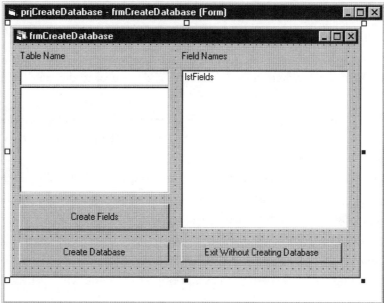

Figure 7.18 *The **frmCreateDatabase** form after you finish adding and formatting the controls.*

DESIGNING THE FRMADDFIELDS FORM'S APPEARANCE

As you have learned, when you use the *prjCreateDatabase* program to create new database tables, you will define the name and characteristics of each field in the tables within the *frmAddFields* form. To create the *frmAddFields* form, you will add a list box, a combo box, two text boxes, four labels, and three command buttons. After you complete the *frmAddFields* form's design, you will write the program code for the *prjCreateDatabase* program.

ADDING THE COMBO BOX TO THE FRMADDFIELDS FORM

As you have learned, the *prjCreateDatabase* project will use a *ComboBox* control within the *frmAddFields* form. The *ComboBox* control will display the possible field types you can use to design databases. To add a *ComboBox* control to the *frmAddFields* form, perform the following steps:

1. If Visual Basic is not displaying the *frmAddFields* form within an object window, double-click your mouse on the form's icon within the Project Explorer. Visual Basic will open the *frmAddFields* form.

2. Within Visual Basic, select the View menu Toolbox option. Visual Basic will open the Toolbox.

3. Within the Toolbox, double-click your mouse on the ComboBox icon. Visual Basic will draw a *ComboBox* control, *Combo1*, within the *frmAddFields* form.

4. Within the *frmAddFields* form window, click your mouse on the *Combo1* control to highlight it. Visual Basic will draw a small frame around the control.

5. Select the View menu Properties Window option. Visual Basic will open the Properties Window listing the *Combo1* properties.

6. Within the Properties Window, change the *Combo1* properties to the values Table 7.12 lists.

Object	Property	Set As
Combo1	*Height*	315
Combo1	*Left*	3240
Combo1	*Top*	1440
Combo1	*Width*	4335
Combo1	*Name*	*cmbFieldTypes*

Table 7.12 *The newly named* **cmbFieldTypes** *control's properties.*

ADDING THE LIST BOX TO THE FRMADDFIELDS FORM

As you have learned, the *prjCreateDatabase* project will use a *ListBox* control to display the field names for each field that the user has added to a new table definition. To add a *ListBox* control to the *frmAddFields* form, perform the following steps:

1. If Visual Basic is not displaying the *frmAddFields* form within an object window, double-click your mouse on the *frmAddFields* form listing within the Project Explorer. Visual Basic will open the *frmAddFields* form.

2. Within Visual Basic, select the View menu Toolbox option. Visual Basic will open the Toolbox.

3. Within the Toolbox, double-click your mouse on the ListBox icon. Visual Basic will draw a *ListBox* control, *List1*, within the *frmAddFields* form.

4. Within the *frmAddFields* form window, click your mouse on the *List1* control to highlight it. Visual Basic will draw a small frame around the control.

5. Select the View menu Properties Window option. Visual Basic will open the Properties Window listing the *List1* properties.

6. Within the Properties Window, change the *List1* properties to the values Table 7.13 lists.

Object	Property	Set As
List1	*Height*	2595
List1	*Left*	120
List1	*Top*	360
List1	*Width*	1935
List1	*Name*	*lstFields*

Table 7.13 *The newly named* **lstFields** *control's properties.*

ADDING THE LABEL CONTROLS TO THE FRMADDFIELDS FORM

As you have learned, you will display database field definitions in a *ListBox* control on the left-hand side of the *frmAddFields* form, and information about the field the user is currently creating within controls on the form's right-hand side. You will add four *Label* controls to the form as captions for the other controls. To add the *Label* controls to the *frmAddFields* form, perform the following steps:

1. If Visual Basic is not displaying the *frmAddFields* form within an object window, double-click your mouse on the *frmAddFields* form listing within the Project Explorer. Visual Basic will open the *frmAddFields* form.

2. Within Visual Basic, select the View menu Toolbox option. Visual Basic will open the Toolbox.

3. Within the Toolbox, double-click your mouse on the Label icon. Visual Basic will draw a *Label* control, *Label1*, within the *frmAddFields* form.

4. Repeat Step 3 three more times. Visual Basic will add three more *Label* controls to the *frmAddFields* form.

5. Within the *frmAddFields* form, click your mouse on a *Label* control to highlight it. Visual Basic will draw a small frame around the control.

6. Select the View menu Properties Window option. Visual Basic will open the Properties Window listing the *Label* control's properties.

7. Within the Properties Window, change the *Label* control's properties to the values Table 7.14 lists.

8. Repeat Steps 5, 6, and 7 until you have changed each *Label* control's properties to the values Table 7.14 lists.

Object	Property	Set As
Label1	*Caption*	*Fields*
Label1	*Height*	255
Label1	*Left*	120
Label1	*Top*	0
Label1	*Width*	1935
Label1	*Name*	*lblFields*
Label2	*Caption*	*Field Name:*
Label2	*Height*	375
Label2	*Left*	2160
Label2	*Top*	480
Label2	*Width*	975
Label2	*Name*	*lblFieldName*
Label3	*Caption*	*Field Type:*
Label3	*Height*	375
Label3	*Left*	2160
Label3	*Top*	1440
Label3	*Width*	975
Label3	*Name*	*lblType*
Label4	*Caption*	*Field Size:*
Label4	*Height*	375
Label4	*Left*	2160
Label4	*Top*	2525
Label4	*Width*	975
Label4	*Name*	*lblSize*

Table 7.14 *The newly named **Label** controls' properties.*

ADDING THE TEXTBOX CONTROLS TO THE FRMADDFIELDS FORM

Within the *frmAddFields* form, you will use two *TextBox* controls. One *TextBox* control will let the user enter the field name for the current field. The other *TextBox* control will let the user enter a field length for those fields (such as *Text* fields) that require a field length. To add the *TextBox* controls to the *frmAddFields* form, perform the following steps:

1. If Visual Basic is not displaying the *frmAddFields* form within an object window, double-click your mouse on the *frmAddFields* form listing within the Project Explorer. Visual Basic will open the *frmAddFields* form.

2. Within Visual Basic, select the View menu Toolbox option. Visual Basic will open the Toolbox.

3. Within the Toolbox, double-click your mouse on the TextBox icon. Visual Basic will draw a *TextBox* control, *Text1*, within the *frmAddFields* form.

4. Repeat Step 3 one time. Visual Basic will draw another *TextBox* control within the *frmAddFields* form.

5. Within the *frmAddFields* form window, click your mouse on a *TextBox* control to highlight it. Visual Basic will draw a small frame around the control.

6. Select the View menu Properties Window option. Visual Basic will open the Properties Window listing the highlighted control's properties.

7. Within the Properties Window, change the highlighted control's properties to the values Table 7.15 lists.

8. Repeat Steps 5, 6, and 7 until you have changed each *TextBox* control's properties to the values Table 7.15 lists.

Object	Property	Set As
Text1	*Height*	375
Text1	*Left*	3240
Text1	*Text*	[blank]
Text1	*Top*	480
Text1	*Width*	4335
Text1	*Name*	txtFieldName
Text2	*Height*	375
Text2	*Left*	3240
Text2	*Text*	[blank]
Text2	*Top*	2520
Text2	*Width*	4335
Text2	*Name*	txtFieldSize

*Table 7.15 The newly named **TextBox** controls' properties.*

ADDING THE COMMANDBUTTON CONTROLS TO THE FRMADDFIELDS FORM

Within the *frmAddFields* form, you will display three command buttons for users to use when they design database tables. The first button, Add Field, will add the currently entered field to the table. The second button, Save Table, will save the table and return the user to the Create Database window. The third button, Exit, will let the user exit the *frmAddFields* form without creating the database table. The *Click* events for each of these buttons will perform processing that corresponds to the button's caption.

To add the *CommandButton* controls to the *frmAddFields* form, perform the following steps:

1. If Visual Basic is not displaying the *frmAddFields* form within an object window, double-click your mouse on the *frmAddFields* form listing within the Project Explorer. Visual Basic will open the *frmAddFields* form.

2. Within Visual Basic, select the View menu Toolbox option. Visual Basic will open the Toolbox.

3. Within the Toolbox, double-click your mouse on the CommandButton icon. Visual Basic will draw a *CommandButton* control, *Command1*, within the *frmAddFields* form.

4. Repeat Step 3 two more times. Visual Basic will draw the *Command2* and *Command3* buttons within the *frmAddFields* form.

5. Within the *frmAddFields* form, click your mouse on a *CommandButton* control to highlight it. Visual Basic will draw a small frame around the control.

6. Select the View menu Properties Window option. Visual Basic will open the Properties Window listing the highlighted control's properties.

7. Within the Properties Window, change the highlighted control's properties to the values Table 7.16 lists.

8. Repeat Steps 5, 6, and 7 to change the properties for all three *CommandButton* controls to the values Table 7.16 lists.

Object	Property	Set As
Command1	*Caption*	*Add Field*
Command1	*Height*	495
Command1	*Left*	120
Command1	*Top*	3360
Command1	*Width*	1815
Command1	*Name*	*cmdAddField*
Command2	*Caption*	*Save Table*
Command2	*Height*	495
Command2	*Left*	2400
Command2	*Top*	3360
Command2	*Width*	1815
Command2	*Name*	*cmdSaveTable*
Command3	*Caption*	*E&xit*
Command3	*Height*	495
Command3	*Left*	4860
Command3	*Top*	3360
Command3	*Width*	1815
Command3	*Name*	*cmdExit*

Table 7.16 *The newly named **CommandButton** controls' properties.*

When you finish formatting the component controls for the *frmAddFields* form, the form will look similar to Figure 7.19.

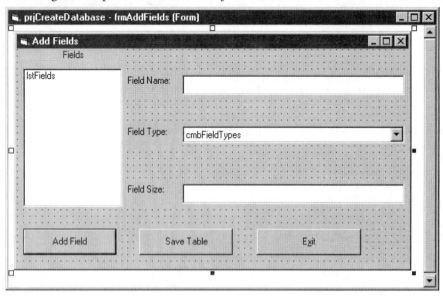

Figure 7.19 The **frmAddFields** *form after you finish its design.*

WRITING THE PROGRAM CODE

Within the program code for the *prjCreateDatabase* project, you must handle both the processing for the Multiple-Document Interface and the processing for working with the DAO Object Library. As you learned in Chapter 4, handling the Multiple-Document Interface, while not particularly difficult, does require that the program use extra code to respond to events in different forms. Handling database information is also not particularly difficult, but it will require that you create instances of objects from the DAO Object Library and work with those objects. All the forms in the program include their own code, as does the single module that you created earlier. In the following sections, you will write the program code for the module first, and then for the MDI parent form. After you write the code for the parent form, you will write the program code for each child form.

WRITING THE mdlDeclarations MODULE'S PROGRAM CODE

As you have learned, you must work with both the issues of Multiple-Document Interface (MDI) programming and database programming in the *prjCreateDatabase* program. You will use a form array to handle many of the MDI programming issues, and database objects and custom structures to handle the database issues. The following code implements the *mdlDeclarations* module's General–Declarations section, which includes global variable declarations and type definitions for the *prjCreateDatabase* program:

```
Type FieldConvert
  FieldConstant As Integer
  FieldDescription As String
End Type
Type FieldStruct
  FieldType As Integer
  FieldName As String
  FieldSize As String
End Type
Public gTableForms() As New frmDatabaseChild
Public gCurrentForm As Integer
Public IncomingDBName As String
Public IncomingTableName As Recordset
Public wkSpace As Workspace
Public defaultDB As Database, CreateDB As Database
Public defaultRS As Recordset
Public FieldTypes(11) As FieldConvert
```

As you can see, the program code defines two types and several global variables. The program uses the first type, *FieldConvert*, to hold the information the program will use to convert the user's text entries of field type in the *frmAddFields* form to the actual, numeric types you must use to create those fields. The second type, *FieldStruct*, uses the *FieldConvert* type, together with two string members, to hold information about each field you add to a table within the *frmAddFields* form.

The *gTableForms* array is a form array, which you learned about in Chapter 4. The *gCurrentForm* variable holds an index to the currently active form in the form array. The *IncomingDBName* variable holds the name of a database the user wants to load, and the *IncomingTableName* variable holds a recordset object that points to the incoming table the program is loading into an instance of the *frmDatabaseChild* form.

The program will assign the default *Workspace* object to the *wkSpace* variable. As you learned earlier in this chapter, your programs must perform all DAO operations within a workspace. In the *prjCreateDatabase* program, the *wkSpace* variable will hold the *Workspace* object the program will use. The *defaultDB* and *CreateDB* objects both hold database information, and the *defaultRS* object holds recordset information. Like the *Workspace* object, you learned about *Database* and *Recordset* objects earlier in this chapter.

Finally, the *FieldTypes* array will hold the twelve different field types that the DAO objects will let you define when you create a database. The program will initialize the array within the *InitFieldTypes* procedure. The following code implements the *InitFieldTypes* procedure:

```
Public Sub InitFieldTypes()
   FieldTypes(0).FieldConstant = dbBinary
   FieldTypes(0).FieldDescription = "Binary"
   FieldTypes(1).FieldConstant = dbBoolean
   FieldTypes(1).FieldDescription = "Boolean"
   FieldTypes(2).FieldConstant = dbByte
   FieldTypes(2).FieldDescription = "Byte"
   FieldTypes(3).FieldConstant = dbCurrency
   FieldTypes(3).FieldDescription = "Currency"
   FieldTypes(4).FieldConstant = dbDate
   FieldTypes(4).FieldDescription = "Date/Time"
   FieldTypes(5).FieldConstant = dbDouble
   FieldTypes(5).FieldDescription = "Double"
   FieldTypes(6).FieldConstant = dbGUID
   FieldTypes(6).FieldDescription = "GUID"
   FieldTypes(7).FieldConstant = dbInteger
   FieldTypes(7).FieldDescription = "Integer"
   FieldTypes(8).FieldConstant = dbLong
   FieldTypes(8).FieldDescription = "Long"
   FieldTypes(9).FieldConstant = dbMemo
   FieldTypes(9).FieldDescription = "Memo"
   FieldTypes(10).FieldConstant = dbSingle
   FieldTypes(10).FieldDescription = "Single"
   FieldTypes(11).FieldConstant = dbText
   FieldTypes(11).FieldDescription = "Text"
End Sub
```

As you can see, the *InitFieldTypes* procedure initializes the *FieldConstant* and *FieldDescription* members for each element in the *FieldTypes* array.

WRITING THE FRMMDIPARENT FORM'S PROGRAM CODE

As you learned in Chapter 4, when you work with a Multiple-Document Interface project, the first object to load in the program will be the *MDIParent* form (unless you use the *Sub Main* procedure, which Chapter 3, "Writing a Screen Saver in Visual Basic," explains in detail). When the program loads the *MDIParent* form, it will invoke the *MDIForm_Load* event, as shown here:

```
Private Sub MDIForm_Load()
   Set wkSpace = Workspaces(0)
   gCurrentForm = 0
   Me.Width = 9630
   Me.Height = 7935
   Me.Top = 200
   Me.Left = 200
   InitFieldTypes
End Sub
```

The *MDIForm_Load* event first declares the *wkSpace* variable as equal to the default *Workspace* object. As you have learned, you will use the *wkSpace* variable as a container within which you will open databases. The program code then sets the form's startup position and calls the *InitFieldTypes* procedure. As you learned in the previous section, the *InitFieldTypes* procedure fills the *FieldTypes* array with values.

252 WRITING THE CODE FOR THE MNUFILECREATEDATABASE MENU ITEM

When you created the menus for the *prjCreateDatabase* program, you created two menus—a File menu and a Window menu. Within the File menu, you created three options: Create Database, Display Database, and Exit. You named the Create Database option *mnuFileCreateDatabase*. The following code implements the *mnuFileCreateDatabase_Click* event, which the program will invoke when the user selects the File menu Create Database option:

```
Private Sub mnuFileCreateDatabase_Click()
   frmCreateDatabase.Show
End Sub
```

As you can see, the *Click* event's program code displays the *frmCreateDatabase* form. Because the program does not define an array of *frmCreateDatabase* forms, the program code will display only a single instance of the form—no matter how many times the user selects the Create Database option.

WRITING THE CODE FOR THE MNUDISPLAYDATABASE MENU ITEM

As you have learned, users will use the File menu Display Database option to display the tables within a database. The Display Database option lets the user select the database to load, performs initialization processing, and displays each table in the database within its own instance of the *frmDatabaseChild* form. The following code implements the *mnuDisplayDatabase_Click* event:

```
Private Sub mnuDisplayDatabase_Click()
   Dim SQLStatement As String

   cdgDatabase.Filter = "Microsoft Access Databases (*.mdb)|*.mdb"
   cdgDatabase.InitDir = CurDir$
   cdgDatabase.CancelError = True
   cdgDatabase.FileName = ""
   On Error Resume Next
   cdgDatabase.ShowOpen
   If Err.Number <> 0 Then Exit Sub
   IncomingDBName = cdgDatabase.FileName
   On Error Resume Next
   Set defaultDB = wkSpace.OpenDatabase(IncomingDBName)
   If Err.Number <> 0 Then
      MsgBox "Bad database."
      Exit Sub
   End If
   For I = 0 To defaultDB.TableDefs.Count - 1
      If defaultDB.TableDefs(I).Attributes = 0 Then
         SQLStatement = "Select * From [" & defaultDB.TableDefs(I).Name & "]"
```

```
            On Error GoTo 0
            Set IncomingTableName = defaultDB.OpenRecordset(SQLStatement)
            If CheckFieldTypes(I) Then
              gCurrentForm = gCurrentForm + 1
              ReDim Preserve gTableForms(gCurrentForm)
              gTableForms(gCurrentForm).Caption = FileOnly(IncomingDBName) & "->" _
                  & defaultDB.TableDefs(I).Name
              gTableForms(gCurrentForm).Show
              gTableForms(gCurrentForm).Tag = Me.Tag
            End If
          End If
      Next
End Sub
```

The first four statements within the *Click* event initialize the *CommonDialog* control to the current directory and display only Microsoft *Access* databases. The event's program code then invokes the control's *ShowOpen* method, which displays the Open File dialog box. After the user selects a filename within the dialog box, the program code assigns the filename to the *IncomingDBName* variable and uses the *Workspace* object's *OpenDatabase* method to try to open the database. If the method does not complete successfully, the program code displays a message to the user indicating the program's failure and exits the event.

On the other hand, if the *OpenDatabase* method is successful, the program code uses the newly opened database object's *TableDefs* member to iterate (count through, one by one) each table in the database. The *TableDefs* collection will include each table in the database, and the *TableDefs* collection's *Count* member corresponds to the one-based number of tables in the database—which means that if there are seven tables in the database, the *Count* member's value is seven (as opposed to a zero-based number, in which case the *Count* member's value would be six).

Each time through the loop, the program code checks the *TableDef* object's *Attributes* property to ensure that the table is not a system-defined table, a hidden table, or some other non-standard object. Zero is the default value for standard table definitions. Table 7.17 lists the other possible *Attributes* values for a table and their Visual Basic-defined constants.

Constant	Description
dbAttachExclusive	For databases that use the Microsoft Jet database engine (the underlying engine for Microsoft *Access* databases), the table is a linked table that the program or a user opened for exclusive use. You can set this constant on an appended *TableDef* object for a local table, but not on a remote table.
dbAttachSavePWD	For databases that use the Microsoft Jet database engine, the engine has saved the user ID and password for the remotely linked table with the connection information. You can set this constant on an appended *TableDef* object for a remote table, but not on a local table.
dbSystemObject	The Microsoft Jet database engine provides the table as a system table. You can set this constant on an appended *TableDef* object.
dbHiddenObject	The Microsoft Jet database engine created the table as a hidden table. You can set this constant on an appended *TableDef* object.
dbAttachedTable	The table is a linked table from a non-Open Database Connectivity (ODBC) data source, such as a Microsoft Jet database or a *Paradox* database. Only the database engine can set the *dbAttachedTable* attribute.
dbAttachedODBC	The table is a linked table from an Open Database Connectivity (ODBC) data source, such as a Microsoft *SQL Server*®. Only the database engine can set the *dbAttachedODBC* attribute.

*Table 7.17 The non-default constant values for the **TableDef** object's **Attributes** property.*

After the program code verifies that the table is not a non-standard table, it creates an SQL query statement from the table's name. The SQL query, *Select * From [TableName]*, will return every record in the table. The program code then opens a recordset with the query. If the table is a non-standard table type, the program code will not try to display the table.

After the recordset is open, the program code calls the *CheckFieldTypes* function to check the fields within the recordset. As you will learn, the *CheckFieldTypes* function ensures that the *Data-Bound Grid* control can display all the fields within the database. The function alerts the user if the program cannot display the fields and lets the user decide whether or not to load the table anyway. If the program can display all the fields in the table or if the user tells the program to display the visible fields and ignore the others, the program code will redimension the *gTableForms* form array and create a new form instance. The program code then sets the new form's caption and displays the form. Finally, the program code passes in the value of the *MDIParent* form's *Tag* property to the new *frmDatabaseChild* form's *Tag* property. The *Tag* property lets you easily pass values between forms without making those values public.

254 WRITING THE OTHER MENU EVENTS

As you have learned, the user can use the Exit option within the File menu to end the *prjCreateDatabase* program's execution. The following code implements the *mnuFileExit_Click* event:

```
Private Sub mnuFileExit_Click()
  Unload Me
End Sub
```

The event's program code simply tries to unload the *frmMDIParent* form. When you write programs that use the Multiple-Document Interface, unloading the parent form will also unload each of the child forms. Within the *prjCreateDatabase* project, each child form will intercept its *unload* message and ensure that the user has saved the copy of the document or image the form contains. When the user tries to unload the *frmMDIParent* form, it will unload each child form. In turn, each child form will prompt the user to save changes to the form, if the user has made changes to the child form's contents.

When you designed the Window menu earlier in this chapter, you set the Window menu's *Windowlist* property to *True*—which means that the Window menu will always display a list of open child windows within the *prjCreateDatabase* program. You also added a Cascade and a Tile option to the menu. Both the Cascade and Tile options let the user organize the display of child windows within the *frmMDIParent* window. The Cascade option arranges windows from the *frmMDIParent* window's top left corner to the bottom right corner. The following code implements the *mnuWindow_Cascade_Click* event:

```
Private Sub mnuWindow_Cascade_Click()
  Me.Arrange vbCascade
End Sub
```

The *mnuWindow_Cascade_Click* event uses the *MDIForm* object's *Arrange* method to arrange the windows. The *vbCascade* constant is a Visual Basic-defined constant. Correspondingly, the Tile option arranges child windows, similar to floor tiles, within the parent window. The program uses the number of open child windows to determine the size of the tiles. The following code implements the *mnuWindow_Tile_Click* event:

```
Private Sub mnuWindow_Tile_Click()
  Me.Arrange vbTileHorizontal
End Sub
```

WRITING THE CODE FOR THE CHECKFIELDTYPES FUNCTION

As you have learned, the Display Database option's program code checks the fields within each table. The program code within the *CheckFieldTypes* function actually checks to determine whether any of the fields within the table are of the *Binary* type. Within a Data Access Objects (DAO) *Recordset* object, *Binary* field types include graphics, files, and so on. The following code implements the *CheckFieldTypes* function:

```
Private Function CheckFieldTypes(ByVal WhichTable As Integer) As Boolean
   Dim I As Integer, MsgText As String, Response As Integer

   CheckFieldTypes = True
   Me.Tag = "No Binary"
   With IncomingTableName
      For I = 0 To .Fields.Count
         If .Fields(I).Type = dbBinary Then
            MsgText = "The Microsoft DBGrid Control Cannot Display Binary data, " _
                  & Chr(13) & Chr(10)
            MsgText = MsgText & "Which this database contains in table: " _
                  & Chr(13) & Chr(10)
            MsgText = MsgText & defaultDB.TableDefs(WhichTable).Name _
                  & Chr(13) & Chr(10)
            MsgText = MsgText & _
                  " Continue anyway (program will automatically disable grid)?"
            Response = MsgBox(MsgText, vbYesNo, "Unrecognized Data Type")
            If Response = vbNo Then
               CheckFieldTypes = False
               Exit Function
            Else
               Me.Tag = "Binary"
               Exit For
            End If
         End If
      Next
   End With
End Function
```

The *CheckFieldTypes* function uses the *TableDef* object's *Fields* collection. Just as the *TableDefs* collection's *Count* member corresponds to the number of tables in the database, the *Fields* collection's *Count* member corresponds to the number of fields there are within the table. The program code uses a *For-Next* loop to check each field in the table. If the field's type is *Binary*, the program code alerts the user that the *Data-Bound Grid* control cannot display binary fields and lets the user know the program can display the table anyway, but that the grid will not permit entries. If the user instructs the program to continue, the program will display the other fields in the table and disable the grid. If the user does not instruct the program to continue, the program will not display the table at all.

WRITING THE CODE FOR THE FILEONLY FUNCTION

As you learned previously, when the user selects the Display Database option, the *prjCreateDatabase* program will display every table within the database in its own child form. The program code sets the caption for the child form in the format *DatabaseName —> TableName*. To separate the database name from the path name, the *prjCreateDatabase* program uses the *FileOnly* function. The following code implements the *FileOnly* function:

```
Private Function FileOnly(FileName As String) As String
   Dim I As Integer

   For I = Len(FileName) To 1 Step -1
      If Mid(FileName, I, 1) = "\" Then
         FileOnly = Right(FileName, Len(FileName) - I)
         Exit Function
      End If
   Next
End Function
```

As you can see, the *FileOnly* function uses a *For-Next* loop to start at the last digit in the filename and step backward until it encounters the backslash symbol (\). The program then returns the string to the right of the backslash as the filename.

WRITING THE FORM'S RESIZE EVENT

As you learned in Chapter 4, when you work with sizable forms, you must be sure that the controls within the forms resize themselves when the user resizes the form. To perform resize processing, you must include program code within the form's *Resize* event. The following code implements the *Form_Resize* event for the *frmDatabaseChild* form:

```
Private Sub Form_Resize()
  Dim TmpWidth As Integer, TmpHeight As Integer

  If Me.WindowState = vbMinimized Then Exit Sub
  If Me.WindowState = vbMaximized Then
    TmpWidth = frmMDIParent.Width - 200
    TmpHeight = frmMDIParent.Height - 500
  Else
    If Me.Width < 5000 Then Me.Width = 5000
    If Me.Height < 5000 Then Me.Height = 5000
    TmpWidth = Me.Width
    TmpHeight = Me.Height
  End If
  grdChildForm.Width = TmpWidth - 200
  grdChildForm.Height = TmpHeight - 800
  dtaChild.Top = TmpHeight - 740
  dtaChild.Width = TmpWidth - 300
  ResizeGridContents
End Sub
```

As you can see, the program code first checks to determine whether the user minimized the form and then checks to determine whether the user maximized the form. If the user minimized the form, the procedure exits—because you cannot size controls on a minimized form (it only has a title bar). If the user maximized the form, the program code sets the temporary width and temporary height variables equal to slightly less than the size of the parent form container.

If the user neither minimized nor maximized the form, the user must have resized the form manually for the form to invoke the *Resize* event. The program code checks to make sure the user did not resize the form below a certain size, then sets the temporary width and temporary height variables equal to the child form's size. After it determines the temporary width and temporary height variables, the program code uses those variables to set both the *grdChildForm* and *dtaChild* controls' size.

WRITING THE CODE FOR THE CHANGEDTACAPTION PROCEDURE

As you have learned, the *Form_Activate* event will call the *ChangeDtaCaption* procedure to change the *Data* control's caption whenever the user activates the form. The following code implements the *ChangeDtaCaption* procedure:

```
Private Sub ChangeDtaCaption()
  If dtaChild.Recordset.RecordCount < 1 Then
    dtaChild.Caption = Me.Caption & " : " & _
        (dtaChild.Recordset.AbsolutePosition + 1) & " of " & _
        dtaChild.Recordset.RecordCount
  Else
    dtaChild.Caption = Me.Caption & " : Empty"
  End If
End Sub
```

The *ChangeDtaCaption* procedure first checks if there are records in the recordset and, if there are, how many. If there are records, the program code then fills the *Data* control's caption with the program's current position in the recordset, in the following form: *TableName : 1 of 5*. If there are no records in the recordset, the program code will display *Empty* within the *Data* control's caption.

Writing the Code for the *ResizeGridContents* Procedure

As you have learned, the *prjCreateDatabase* program lets you display tables within instances of the *frmDatabaseChild* form. However, there is no way to know in advance how many fields a given table will have. To adjust the grid size correctly for the number of fields in a table, the *prjCreateDatabase* program uses the *ResizeGridContents* procedure. The following code implements the *ResizeGridContents* procedure:

```
Private Sub ResizeGridContents()
  Dim I As Integer

  colsize = ((grdChildForm.Width - 500) / (grdChildForm.Columns.Count)) - 15
  For I = 0 To grdChildForm.Columns.Count - 1
    grdChildForm.Columns(I).Width = colsize
  Next
  grdChildForm.Col = 0
End Sub
```

The *ResizeGridContents* procedure determines how many columns the control contains (which the control determines based on how many fields the table contains) and sets the same width for each column—the form's size, minus a small offset value, divided by the number of fields within the database.

Writing the Code for the *Data Control's Reposition* Event

When a user works with the *Data-Bound Grid* control the *frmDatabaseChild* form displays, the user will move back and forth through the recordset. Each time the user exits a single record and goes to another record, the *dtaChild* control invokes its *Reposition* event. The following code implements the *dtaChild_Reposition* event:

```
Private Sub dtaChild_Reposition()
   ChangeDtaCaption
End Sub
```

The *Reposition* event calls the *ChangeDtaCaption* procedure, which updates the display within the *Data* control.

Writing the Code for the *Validate* Event

As you work with databases, you will find that the most consistent causes of errors with databases is bad data entry—that is, trying to assign a value to a field that is incorrect for that field. To help your programs avoid such problems, you should place code in the *Data* control's *Validate* event that checks user entries for validity. The following code implements the *dtaChild_Validate* event:

```
Private Sub dtaChild_Validate(Action As Integer, Save As Integer)
   If Action = vbDataActionUpdate Then
     With dtaChild.Recordset
       For I = 0 To .Fields.Count - 1
         If (.Fields(I).Attributes And dbAutoIncrField) <> dbAutoIncrField Then
           Select Case .Fields(I).Type
             Case dbBinary
               If Val(grdChildForm.Columns(I).Text) < 0 Or _
                   Val(grdChildForm.Columns(I).Text) > 1 Then
                 MsgBox "Data in Column " & I & " is not of correct form.", _
                     vbOKOnly
                 Save = vbDataActionCancel
                 Exit Sub
               End If
             Case dbBoolean
               If Not IsNumeric(grdChildForm.Columns(I).Text) Or _
                   CInt(grdChildForm.Columns(I).Text) < 0 Or _
                   CInt(grdChildForm.Columns(I).Text) < 1 Then
                 MsgBox "Data in Column " & I & " is not of correct form.", _
                   vbOKOnly
                 Save = vbDataActionCancel
```

```
                    Exit Sub
                End If
            Case dbByte, dbChar
                If Len(grdChildForm.Columns(I).Text) <> 1 Then
                  MsgBox "Data in Column " & I & " is not of correct form.", _
                      vbOKOnly
                  Save = vbDataActionCancel
                  Exit Sub
                End If
            Case dbCurrency, dbDouble, dbFloat, dbInteger, _
                    dbLong, dbNumeric, dbSingle
                If Not IsNumeric(grdChildForm.Columns(I).Text) Then
                  MsgBox "Data in Column " & I & " is not of correct form.", _
                      vbOKOnly
                  Save = vbDataActionCancel
                  Exit Sub
                End If
            Case dbDate
                If Not IsDate(grdChildForm.Columns(I).Text) Then
                  MsgBox "Data in Column " & I & " is not of correct form.", _
                      vbOKOnly
                  Save = vbDataActionCancel
                  Exit Sub
                End If
            Case dbText
                If Len(grdChildForm.Columns(I).Text) > .Fields(I).Size Then
                  MsgBox "Data in Column " & I & " is too long.", vbOKOnly
                  Save = vbDataActionCancel
                  Exit Sub
                End If
                If Len(grdChildForm.Columns(I).Text) < 1 Then
                  MsgBox "Data in Column " & I & " is too short.", vbOKOnly
                  Save = vbDataActionCancel
                  Exit Sub
                End If
            End Select
          End If
        Next I
      End With
    End If
End Sub
```

The *Validate* event lets you check user entries within a *Data* control after many different actions. In the *prjCreateDatabase* program's case, the *Validate* event checks the values that users have entered whenever a user indicates that the program should update the values within a given record in the recordset.

The *Validate* event uses a *For-Next* loop and a series of *If-Then* statements to check the entries in each field of the *Data-Bound Grid* control against the acceptable values for those fields. For example, the last *If-Then* statement checks to see if the field is a *Text* field. If it is a *Text* field, the program code makes sure the user entered at least one character. If the user did not enter one character, the program code displays a message box indicating the user's entry is invalid. If all the entries are valid, the program will update the entries in the database.

WRITING THE CODE FOR THE DATA-BOUND GRID CONTROL'S UPDATE CODE

When the user makes a change to the data the *Data-Bound Grid* control displays, or when the user adds new records to the *Data-Bound Grid* control, the control will invoke its *BeforeUpdate* event even before the *dtaChild* control invokes its *Validate* event. Within the *prjCreateDatabase* project, the *BeforeUpdate* event will call the *ValidateFieldRowChange* function to determine whether the user's entry is a valid value. The following code implements the *Data-Bound Grid* control's *BeforeUpdate* event:

```
Private Sub grdChildForm_BeforeUpdate(Cancel As Integer)
   If Not ValidateFieldRowChange Then
      MsgBox "Invalid entry!", vbCritical
      grdChildForm.SetFocus
   End If
End Sub
```

As you can see, the program code within the *BeforeUpdate* event calls the *ValidateFieldRowChange* function, which checks the user's entered value and verifies it matches the type the database expects before it lets the user change the field. If the *ValidateFieldRowChange* function indicates the value is not of the correct type, the program code will display an *Invalid Entry!* warning and maintain the focus within the current cell, rather than changing the cells. The following code implements the *ValidateFieldRowChange* function:

```
Private Function ValidateFieldRowChange() As Boolean
   ValidateFieldRowChange = False
   With dtaChild.Recordset
      If (.Fields(grdChildForm.Col).Attributes And dbAutoIncrField) <> _
         dbAutoIncrField Then
        Select Case .Fields(grdChildForm.Col).Type
          Case dbBinary
            If Val(grdChildForm.Columns(grdChildForm.Col).Text) < 0 Or _
               Val(grdChildForm.Columns(grdChildForm.Col).Text) > 1 Then _
               Exit Function
          Case dbBoolean
            If Not IsNumeric(grdChildForm.Columns(grdChildForm.Col).Text) Or _
               CInt(grdChildForm.Columns(grdChildForm.Col).Text) < 0 Or _
               CInt(grdChildForm.Columns(grdChildForm.Col).Text) < 1 Then _
               Exit Function
          Case dbByte, dbChar
            If Len(grdChildForm.Columns(grdChildForm.Col).Text) <> 1 Then _
               Exit Function
          Case dbCurrency, dbDouble, dbFloat, dbInteger, dbLong, dbNumeric, _
             dbSingle
            If Not IsNumeric(grdChildForm.Columns(grdChildForm.Col).Text) Then _
               Exit Function
          Case dbDate
            If Not IsDate(grdChildForm.Columns(grdChildForm.Col).Text) Then _
               Exit Function
          Case dbText
            If Len(grdChildForm.Columns(grdChildForm.Col).Text) > _
               .Fields(grdChildForm.Col).Size Then Exit Function
            If Len(grdChildForm.Columns(grdChildForm.Col).Text) < 1 Then _
               Exit Function
        End Select
      End If
   End With
   DoEvents
   ValidateFieldRowChange = True
End Function
```

Much as the *dtaChild_Validate* event does, the *ValidateFieldRowChange* function's program code will check the field type of the current cell the user is editing. After it determines the field's type, the program code makes sure that the entry is the right type and within the correct ranges. If the entry is valid, the *ValidateFieldRowChange* function will return *True*; otherwise, the *ValidateFieldRowChange* function will return *False*.

WRITING THE CODE FOR ROW CHANGES WITHIN THE GRID

The *Data-Bound Grid* control provides many events that you can use within your programs to ensure that you verify entries whenever the user makes a change to a value. In the event the user only changes to a different cell within the same row, the program code must still check to ensure that the entry to the field the user is changing from is valid.

To perform such processing, the program includes code within the *RowColChange* event. The following code implements the *RowColChange* event:

```
Private Sub grdChildForm_RowColChange(LastRow As Variant, ByVal LastCol As _
    Integer)
    If LastCol = -1 Or Not grdChildForm.AllowAddNew Then Exit Sub
    DoEvents
    If grdChildForm.Bookmark = LastRow Then
        If Not ValidateField(LastCol) Then
            grdChildForm.Col = LastCol
            MsgBox "Invalid entry!", vbCritical
            grdChildForm.SetFocus
        End If
    End If
End Sub
```

260   The *RowColChange* event first verifies that another event or function within the program is not handling the change. For example, if the user's change is within the row the control reserves for adding new records, the event will execute without further processing, because the *dtaChild_Validate* event will handle the entry. However, if the program code determines that the user is changing fields within the same record, the program code calls the *ValidateField* function to check the value of the entry within the cell. The following code implements the *ValidateField* function:

```
Private Function ValidateField(PreviousCol As Integer) As Boolean
    ValidateField = False
    With dtaChild.Recordset
        If (.Fields(PreviousCol).Attributes And _
            dbAutoIncrField) <> dbAutoIncrField Then
            Select Case .Fields(PreviousCol).Type
                Case dbBinary
                    If Val(grdChildForm.Columns(PreviousCol).Text) < 0 Or _
                        Val(grdChildForm.Columns(PreviousCol).Text) > 1 Then Exit Function

                Case dbBoolean
                    If Not IsNumeric(grdChildForm.Columns(PreviousCol).Text) Or _
                        CInt(grdChildForm.Columns(PreviousCol).Text) < 0 Or _
                        CInt(grdChildForm.Columns(PreviousCol).Text) < 1 Then _
                        Exit Function
                Case dbByte, dbChar
                    If Len(grdChildForm.Columns(PreviousCol).Text) <> 1 Then Exit Function
                Case dbCurrency, dbDouble, dbFloat, dbInteger, dbLong, _
                        dbNumeric, dbSingle
                    If Not IsNumeric(grdChildForm.Columns(PreviousCol).Text) Then _
                        Exit Function
                Case dbDate
                    If Not IsDate(grdChildForm.Columns(PreviousCol).Text) Then _
                        Exit Function
                Case dbText
                    If Len(grdChildForm.Columns(PreviousCol).Text) > _
                        .Fields(PreviousCol).Size Then Exit Function
                DoEvents
            End Select
        End If
    End With
    ValidateField = True
End Function
```

Much like the *dtaChild_Validate* event's and the *ValidateFieldRowChange* function's processing, the *ValidateField* function's program code will check the field type of the current cell the user is editing. After it determines the field's type, the program code makes sure that the entry is the right type and within the correct ranges. If the entry is valid, the *ValidateField* function will return *True*; otherwise, the *ValidateField* function will return *False*.

Writing the frmCreateDatabase Form's Program Code

As you have learned, when the user wants to create a new database, the user will use two forms. The first form, *frmCreateDatabase*, holds information about the tables within the database. The second form, *frmAddFields*, lets the user add fields to a new table definition. The *frmCreateDatabase* form will maintain the list of tables, use a temporary database to hold those tables and, finally, save the temporary database as a permanent database with the name the user specifies.

Writing the FrmCreateDatabase Form's Form_Load Event

When the user loads the *frmCreateDatabase* form within the *prjCreateDatabase* program, the form will first invoke its *Form_Load* event. The following code implements the *Form_Load* event for the *frmCreateDatabase* form:

```
Private Sub Form_Load()
   cmdCreateFields.Enabled = False
   cmdCreateDatabase.Enabled = False
End Sub
```

261

Within the *Form_Load* event, the program code disables the Create Fields and Create Database buttons. When the user enters text within the *cmbTables* combo box to add a new table to the database, the program code will reactivate the Create Fields button. After the user finishes a table's design, the program code will activate the Create Database button.

Writing the cmbTables_Change Event

As you learned in the previous section, after the user enters a table name into the *cmbTables* combo box, the program code will activate the *cmdCreateFields* button. Whenever the user enters text into the *cmbTables* combo box, the program will invoke the *cmbTables_Change* event. The following code implements the *cmbTables_Change* event:

```
Private Sub cmbTables_Change()
   If Len(cmbTables.Text) > 0 And cmbTables.ListIndex < 0 Then
      cmdCreateFields.Enabled = True
   Else
      cmdCreateFields.Enabled = False
   End If
End Sub
```

The *cmbTables_Change* event code uses an *If-Then* statement to determine whether or not there is an actual table name entry in the field, and to ensure that the table name entry is not from the user clicking the mouse on an item within the list of existing tables.

Writing the cmbTables_Click Event

As you have learned, the *prjCreateDatabase* program will respond differently if the user enters a table name into the *cmbTables* combo box than it will if the user selects an existing item from the combo box list. The following program code implements the *cmbTables_Click* event:

```
Private Sub cmbTables_Click()
   If cmbTables.ListIndex > -1 Then
      FillFieldList
      cmdCreateFields.Enabled = False
   Else
      lstFields.Clear
      cmdCreateFields.Enabled = True
   End If
End Sub
```

If the user selects an item within the list, the program code fills the list box on the form's right-hand side with the names of the fields within the table and disables the Create Fields button. If the *Click* event occurs while the user is adding text to the item in the combo box, the program code will clear the field list from the list box and enable the Create Fields button.

WRITING THE CODE FOR THE FILLFIELDLIST PROCEDURE

As you learned in the previous section, the program will fill the list box on the *frmCreateDatabase* form's right-hand side with the field names within the table the user selects whenever the user selects a table from within the *cmbTables* combo box. The program code uses the *FillFieldList* procedure to fill the list box. The following code implements the *FillFieldList* procedure:

```
Private Sub FillFieldList()
  Dim SqlText As String
  Dim TempRs As Recordset

  SqlText = "Select * From [" & cmbTables.Text & "]"
  Set TempRs = CreateDB.OpenRecordset(SqlText)
  lstFields.Clear
  For I = 0 To TempRs.Fields.Count - 1
    lstFields.AddItem TempRs.Fields(I).Name
  Next
End Sub
```

The *FillFieldList* procedure uses the SQL *Select* statement to open a recordset from the user's selected table. The program code then counts through the fields in the recordset, one by one, and adds the field name for each field to the list box on the *frmCreateDatabase* form's right-hand side.

WRITING THE CODE FOR THE CMDCREATEFIELDS_CLICK EVENT

As you have learned, when the user wants to create a new table within the *prjCreateDatabase* program, the user must first enter the table's name within the combo box on the *frmCreateDatabase* form's left-hand side, and then click the mouse on the *cmdCreateFields* button. When the user clicks the mouse on the *cmdCreateFields* button, the program code will open the *frmAddFields* form, and let the user add field definitions to the table. The following code implements the *cmdCreateFields_Click* event:

```
Private Sub cmdCreateFields_Click()
  If Len(Trim(cmbTables.Text)) = 0 Then
    MsgBox "Invalid table name!", vbCritical
    Exit Sub
  End If
  For I = 0 To cmbTables.ListCount - 1
    If cmbTables.List(I) = cmbTables.Text Then Exit Sub
  Next
  If cmbTables.ListCount = 0 Then OpenTempDatabase
  frmAddFields.Caption = cmbTables.Text
  frmAddFields.Show vbShowModal
  If Me.Tag = "True" Then
    cmbTables.AddItem cmbTables.Text
    cmdCreateFields.Enabled = False
    cmdCreateDatabase.Enabled = True
  End If
End Sub
```

The program code within the event first checks to ensure that the table name is valid. If the table name contains nothing but spaces, the program code will display a message box to alert the user and exit the event without letting the user create the table. Additionally, if the table name already exists within the database definition, the program code will display a message about the duplication and exit the event. Next, the program code checks to determine whether or not the user has already created table definitions for the current database. If the user has not created the definitions, the program code will use the *OpenTempDatabase* function to open the temporary database the program uses to hold the field definitions. The following section explains the *OpenTempDatabase* function.

After it ensures there is an open database to which the program can add new table definitions, the program code displays the *frmAddFields* form. Note that the program code uses the *vbShowModal* constant to ensure the *frmAddFields* form completes its processing before the *cmdCreateFields_Click* event does. The *frmAddFields* form will pass a *True* or *False* string value back to the *frmCreateDatabase* form within the *frmCreateDatabase* form's *Tag* property. If the value is *True*, the *frmAddFields* form successfully created the new table and the program code will add the table to the list of existing tables, disable the Create Fields button, and enable the Create Database button. If the value is *False*, the program code will exit without further processing—which returns the user to the position the user was in immediately before clicking the mouse on the Create Fields button.

WRITING THE CODE FOR THE OPENTEMPDATABASE FUNCTION

As you have learned, the *prjCreateDatabase* program actually creates a temporary database, which it uses to hold the table and field definitions the user enters until the user decides to save the database. To open the temporary database, the program calls the *OpenTempDatabase* function. The following code implements the *OpenTempDatabase* function:

```
Private Function OpenTempDatabase() As Boolean
  OpenTempDatabase = True
  If Dir(App.Path & "\tempfile.mdb") <> "" Then
    On Error Resume Next
    CreateDB.Close
    On Error GoTo 0
    Kill App.Path & "\tempfile.mdb"
  End If
  On Error Resume Next
  Set CreateDB = wkSpace.CreateDatabase(App.Path & "\tempfile.mdb", _
      dbLangGeneral)
  If Err.Number <> 0 Then OpenTempDatabase = False
End Function
```

The *OpenTempDatabase* function first checks to determine whether there is an existing temporary database within the application's directory. If there is a temporary database, the program code deletes the temporary database. Next, the program code uses the *Workspace* object's *CreateDatabase* method to create the temporary database. If the method succeeds, the function will return *True*. If the method fails, the function will return *False*. If the function returns *False*, the program code will let the user know that it cannot create the database and will return to the *frmCreateDatabase* form.

WRITING THE CODE FOR THE CMDCREATEDATABASE BUTTON

After the user finishes adding table and field definitions to the database, the user can click the mouse on the Create Database button to save the database with a filename and in a location the user can choose. The following code implements the *cmdCreateDatabase_Click* event:

```
Private Sub cmdCreateDatabase_Click()
  With frmMDIParent
    .cdgDatabase.Filter = "Microsoft Access Databases (*.mdb)|*.mdb"
    .cdgDatabase.InitDir = CurDir$
    .cdgDatabase.CancelError = True
    .cdgDatabase.FileName = ""
    .cdgDatabase.Flags = cdlOFNHideReadOnly
    On Error Resume Next
    .cdgDatabase.ShowSave
    If Err.Number <> 0 Then Exit Sub
    On Error GoTo 0
    If Dir(.cdgDatabase.FileName) <> "" Then
      MsgBox "Can't write over an existing database!", vbCritical
      Exit Sub
    End If
    CreateDB.Close
    FileCopy App.Path & "\tempfile.mdb", .cdgDatabase.FileName
  End With
  Unload Me
End Sub
```

The *cmdCreateDatabase_Click* event uses the *CommonDialog* control to open a Save As dialog box. The user can then navigate to the directory where the program should save the new database, save the database with whatever name the user wants, and exit the *frmCreateDatabase* form. If the user tries to save over an existing database, the program lets the user know it cannot do that, and exits the procedure. If the user does not try to save over an existing database, the program code copies the *tempfile.mdb* temporary database to the location the user selects, renames the database with the name the user selects, and unloads the *frmCreateDatabase* form.

WRITING THE CODE FOR THE CMDEXIT_CLICK EVENT

As you have learned, the user can exit the *frmCreateDatabase* form without creating a new database. If the user clicks the mouse on the *cmdExit* button, the *prjCreateDatabase* project will unload the *frmCreateDatabase* form and delete the temporary file. The following code implements the *cmdExit_Click* event:

```
Private Sub cmdExit_Click()
   On Error Resume Next
   CreateDB.Close
   Kill App.Path & "\tempfile.mdb"
   Unload Me
End Sub
```

The program code within the *cmdExit_Click* event first closes the temporary database and then deletes it. After the event's code deletes the temporary database, it unloads the *frmCreateDatabase* form.

WRITING THE FRMADDFIELDS FORM'S PROGRAM CODE

As you have learned, you will design fields and add them to table definitions within the *frmAddFields* form. The *frmAddFields* form uses Data Access Object (DAO) object methods and controls to make the addition of fields to the database table efficient and relatively painless to both the programmer and the user. The *frmAddFields* form uses four variables throughout its processing that you must define within the General–Declarations section. The following code implements the General–Declarations section for the *frmAddFields* form:

```
Option Explicit
Dim I As Integer
Dim TableFields() As FieldStruct
Dim TotalFields As Integer
Dim Saved As Boolean
```

The *I* variable is a counting variable that you will use in several loops throughout the form. The *TableFields* array will contain elements of type *FieldStruct* that specify the definition for each field in the table you are creating, the *TotalFields* variable contains the total number of fields within the array, and the Boolean variable *Saved* is a flag variable that you will use throughout the form's processing. In the following sections, you will write the code to load and unload the form, check the user's entries, and append the actual fields to the current table definition.

WRITING THE CODE FOR THE FORM'S STARTUP

When the user clicks the mouse on the Create Fields button within the *frmCreateDatabase* form, the program code will load the *frmAddFields* form. When the program loads the *frmAddFields* form, it will invoke its *Form_Load* event before it performs any other processing. The following code implements the *frmAddFields* form's *Form_Load* event:

```
Private Sub Form_Load()
   AddCounter
   AddFieldsToComboBox
   DisableFields False, False
End Sub
```

The program code for the *Form_Load* event first invokes the *AddCounter* procedure. The *AddCounter* procedure defines the default field for every table—an auto-numbered field that programs can use as an index. The program code then invokes the *AddFieldsToComboBox* procedure, which will add the possible field types to the combo box on the form's right-hand side. Finally, the program code will invoke the *DisableFields* procedure, which will disable all the entry fields except the *Field name* field.

Writing the Code for the *AddCounter* Procedure

As you have learned, the *Form_Load* event uses three "helper" procedures. The first helper procedure the event calls is the *AddCounter* procedure, which adds a single, default field to every table that you create within the *prjCreateDatabase* program. The following code implements the *AddCounter* procedure:

```
Private Sub AddCounter()
  ReDim TableFields(0)

  With TableFields(0)
    .FieldName = "Counter"
    .FieldType = dbLong
    .FieldSize = ""
  End With
  lstFields.AddItem TableFields(0).FieldName
  TotalFields = 0
  Saved = True
End Sub
```

The program code within the procedure first redimensions the *TableFields* array with only a single element and then adds the values for the element into the array. Next, the program code adds the newly defined field to the list box on the form's left-hand side. Finally, the program code initializes the *TotalFields* variable to 0 (because the user has not yet added any fields to the table definition) and sets the *Saved* flag to *True*.

Writing the Code for the *AddFieldsToComboBox* Procedure

As you have learned, the *Form_Load* event calls three "helper" procedures that help it to perform its processing. The second procedure is the *AddFieldsToComboBox* procedure, which adds all the possible field types to the combo box on the form's right-hand side. The following code implements the *AddFieldsToComboBox* procedure:

```
Private Sub AddFieldsToComboBox()
  For I = 0 To 11
    cmbFieldTypes.AddItem FieldTypes(I).FieldDescription
  Next
End Sub
```

As you can see, the *AddFieldsToComboBox* procedure uses a *For-Next* loop to step through the *FieldTypes* array a single element at a time and add the element's description to the combo box. When the loop exits, all 12 field types will be in the combo box's drop-down list.

Writing the Code for the *DisableFields* Procedure

The third "helper" procedure the *Form_Load* event uses is the *DisableFields* procedure, which many other events and procedures within the *frmAddFields* form also use. The *DisableFields* procedure accepts two *Boolean* values. The following code implements the *DisableFields* procedure:

```
Private Sub DisableFields(FirstSet As Boolean, SecondSet As Boolean)
  lblType.Enabled = FirstSet
  cmbFieldTypes.Enabled = FirstSet
  txtFieldSize.Enabled = SecondSet
  lblSize.Enabled = SecondSet
End Sub
```

Whenever the program calls the *DisableFields* procedure, it will either enable or disable each of the fields except the *Name* field, depending on the incoming values for *FirstSet* and *SecondSet*. When the *Form_Load* procedure calls *DisableFields,* the procedure will disable both fields (and their adjoining labels).

Writing the Program Code for the *txtFieldName_Change* Event

As you have learned, the user must enter a field name into the *frmAddFields* form for the program code to work properly. The program code within the *Change* event makes sure the user enters a field name, or it disables buttons and fields on the form. The following code implements the *txtFieldName_Change* event:

```
Private Sub txtFieldName_Change()
  If Len(txtFieldName.Text) = 0 Then DisableFields False, False
  If Len(txtFieldName.Text) > 0 Then DisableFields True, True
  If cmbFieldTypes.ListIndex <> 0 And cmbFieldTypes.ListIndex <> 11 Then _
      DisableFields True, False
End Sub
```

If the *txtFieldName* control contains less than a single character, the program code will disable the other two fields on the form (*cmbFieldTypes* and *txtFieldSize*). If the *txtFieldName* control contains one or more characters, the program code will enable the other two fields. However, the third field is necessary only to handle *Text* and *Byte* type fields— so if the user enters another field type, the program code will not enable the third field in the form, which corresponds to the field's size entry in the database.

WRITING THE CODE FOR THE *CMBFIELDTYPES* CONTROL

266   As you learned in the previous section, the program will let the user dictate field sizes only when the size is a variable—either *Text* or *Byte*. Otherwise, the database engine will determine the field size automatically. To ensure that the program captures the user's field type selection and disables the other field accordingly, you must place code within the *cmbFieldTypes* object's *Click* event. The following code implements the *cmbFieldTypes_Click* event:

```
Private Sub cmbFieldTypes_Click()
  If cmbFieldTypes.ListIndex = 11 Or cmbFieldTypes.ListIndex = 0 Then
    DisableFields True, True
  Else
    txtFieldSize.Text = ""
    DisableFields True, False
  End If
End Sub
```

As with the previous section, the program code enables the last field if the field type is *Text* or *Byte* and disables the field if it is neither type.

WRITING THE CODE FOR THE *CMDADDFIELD* BUTTON

After the user finishes defining the new field type, the user must click the mouse on the Add Field button to add the new field to the table's definition. The following code implements the *cmdAddField_Click* event:

```
Private Sub cmdAddField_Click()
  If Not CheckFields Then Exit Sub
  TotalFields = TotalFields + 1
  ReDim Preserve TableFields(TotalFields)
  FillStructure TableFields(TotalFields)
  lstFields.AddItem TableFields(TotalFields).FieldName
  ClearFields
  DisableFields False, False
  Saved = False
  cmbFieldTypes.ListIndex = -1
End Sub
```

The event's first line invokes the *CheckFields* function to determine whether the field entries are valid or not. You will learn about the *CheckFields* function in the following section. Next, the program code increases the total number of fields by one, redimensions the *TableFields* array, and calls the *FillStructure* procedure. The *FillStructure* procedure will fill the new element in the *TableFields* array with the information from the fields on the *frmAddFields* form.

After it adds the information to the array, the program code adds the new field name to the list box on the form's left-hand side and calls the *ClearFields* procedure, which clears all the fields on the form's display. The program code then disables the last two fields on the display, changes the *Saved* flag's value to *False*, and sets the combo box control back to the first item in its list.

WRITING THE CODE FOR THE CHECKFIELDS FUNCTION

As you have learned, when the user tries to add a field to the database table definition, the program code first checks the field for validity. The program uses the *CheckFields* function to check fields for validity. The following code implements the *CheckFields* function:

```
Private Function CheckFields() As Boolean
  CheckFields = False
  If txtFieldName.Text = "" Then
    MsgBox "You must enter a name for the field.", vbCritical
    Exit Function
  End If
  If Len(txtFieldName.Text) > 255 Then
    MsgBox "You must enter a shorter name for the field.", vbCritical
    Exit Function
  End If
  If Not IsChar(Left(txtFieldName.Text, 1)) Then
    MsgBox "The first character of the name must be a letter.", vbCritical
    Exit Function
  End If
  If Not NoPunct(txtFieldName.Text) Then
    MsgBox "The field name cannot contain punctuation or spaces.", vbCritical
    Exit Function
  End If
  If cmbFieldTypes.ListIndex < 0 Then
    MsgBox "Please choose a valid field type.", vbOKOnly
    Exit Function
  End If
  For I = 0 To lstFields.ListCount - 1
    If lstFields.List(I) = txtFieldName Then
      MsgBox "Field already exists!", vbCritical
      Exit Function
    End If
  Next
  If cmbFieldTypes.ListIndex = 11 Or cmbFieldTypes.ListIndex = 0 Then
    If Len(txtFieldSize.Text) = 0 Then
      MsgBox "Please enter a size value."
      Exit Function
    End If
    If CInt(Val(txtFieldSize.Text)) < 1 Or CInt(Val(txtFieldSize.Text)) > 254 Then
      MsgBox "Please enter a valid field size (between 1-254).", vbOKOnly
      Exit Function
    End If
  End If
  CheckFields = True
End Function
```

Much as the data-validation routines you wrote for the *frmDatabaseChild* do, the program code within the *CheckFields* function uses a series of *If-Then* statements to ensure that the user entered the correct values for the new field. The first two *If-Then* statements merely ensure that the user has entered a name, and that the name is not longer than 255 characters. Next, the program code calls the *IsChar* function to determine whether the first character in the new field is a valid character or not. The *IsChar* function checks the ASCII value of the character it receives and makes sure it is a valid letter (which the Jet database engine requires all field names begin with). Next, the program code calls the *NoPunct* function, to ensure the user used only valid characters to create the rest of the field name.

After it thoroughly checks the field name, the program code checks the field type to make sure it is a valid type. If the field type is valid, the program code checks the other field names the user has already assigned to the table to make sure the field name is not the same as another field name. Finally, if the field is a *Text* or *Byte* field, the program code makes sure the user entered a valid size for the field (greater than 0 and less than 255). If the user correctly performed all the steps the *CheckFields* function checks for, the function will return *True*. If the user did not perform everything correctly, the function will return *False*.

WRITING THE CODE FOR THE CHECKFIELDS FUNCTION'S HELPER FUNCTIONS

As you have learned, the *CheckFields* function uses two helper functions, the *IsChar* function and the *NoPunct* function, to check the user's entries within the field name. The *IsChar* function checks the field name's first digit to ensure it is a valid alphabetical character. The following code implements the *IsChar* function:

```
Private Function IsChar(Char As String) As Boolean
   IsChar = False
   If Len(Char) > 1 Then Exit Function
   If Asc(UCase(Char)) < 65 Or Asc(UCase(Char)) > 90 Then Exit Function
   IsChar = True
End Function
```

The *IsChar* function checks the ASCII value of the character to ensure that it is an alphabetical character. The function uses the Visual Basic *UCase* function to force each character to uppercase, then checks the ASCII value of the upper-case character. If it is an alphabetical character, the function will return *True*. If the character is not alphabetical, the function will return *False*.

The *NoPunct* function, on the other hand, checks all the characters in the field name. It uses a series of *For-Next* loops and *InStr* commands to determine whether or not the field name contains any invalid characters. The following code implements the *NoPunct* function:

```
Private Function NoPunct(CheckString As String) As Boolean
   NoPunct = False
   For I = 0 To 47
     If InStr(CheckString, Chr(I)) Then Exit Function
   Next I
   For I = 58 To 64
     If InStr(CheckString, Chr(I)) Then Exit Function
   Next I
   For I = 91 To 96
     If I <> 95 Then If InStr(CheckString, Chr(I)) Then Exit Function
   Next I
   For I = 123 To 254
     If InStr(CheckString, Chr(I)) Then Exit Function
   Next I
   NoPunct = True
End Function
```

The *NoPunct* function uses four *For-Next* loops to check and ensure the user did not enter any non-alphanumeric or non-printing characters within the field name. If all the characters are valid, the function will return *True*. If the field name contains invalid characters, the function will return *False*.

WRITING THE CODE FOR THE CLEARFIELDS PROCEDURE

Each time the user adds a new field to the table, the program code must clear the existing entries for that field from the form's right-hand side. The *prjCreateDatabase* program uses the *ClearFields* procedure to clear the entries. The following code implements the *ClearFields* procedure:

```
Private Sub ClearFields()
   cmbFieldTypes.ListIndex = 0
   txtFieldName.Text = ""
   txtFieldSize.Text = ""
End Sub
```

As you can see, the program code within the *ClearFields* procedure sets the combo box's *ListIndex* property back to 0 (the first item) and clears any text from the *Field name* and *Field Size* fields.

WRITING THE CODE FOR THE FILLSTRUCTURE PROCEDURE

As you have learned, the *FillStructure* procedure will assign values to the new elements in the *TableFields* array. The *FillStructure* procedure accepts a single *FieldStruct* parameter, to which it assigns values. The following code implements the *FillStructure* procedure:

```
Private Sub FillStructure(ByRef InStruct As FieldStruct)
   InStruct.FieldName = txtFieldName
   InStruct.FieldType = FieldTypes(cmbFieldTypes.ListIndex).FieldConstant
   InStruct.FieldSize = txtFieldSize.Text
End Sub
```

The program code assigns the two text fields' values and the database creation constant for the user-selected field type to the incoming *FieldStruct* parameter.

WRITING THE CODE FOR THE SAVE TABLE BUTTON

After the user adds all the fields he or she wants to add to a table, the user can save the table and return to the *frmCreateDatabase* form. To save the table, the user must click the mouse on the *cmdSaveTable* button. The following code implements the *cmdSaveTable_Click* event:

```
Private Sub cmdSaveTable_Click()
   If Not CreateTable Then
      MsgBox "Creation Error!", vbCritical
      Exit Sub
   Else
      Saved = True
      frmCreateDatabase.Tag = "True"
      Unload Me
   End If
End Sub
```

The *cmdSaveTable_Click* event calls the *CreateTable* function, which actually tries to create the table. If the *CreateTable* function fails to create the table, it will return *False*, and the *If-Then* statement will display a message box alerting the user to the creation error. The user can then either try to create the table again or exit the *frmAddFields* form.

If the *CreateTable* function successfully creates the table, the program code places the *True* value in the *frmCreateDatabase* form's *Tag* property and unloads the *frmAddFields* form.

WRITING THE CODE FOR THE CREATETABLE FUNCTION

As you learned in the previous section, when the user clicks the mouse on the *cmdSaveTable* button, the program code within the event calls the *CreateTable* function. The *CreateTable* function will create the table and return a *True* or *False* value that indicates its success or failure. The following code implements the *CreateTable* function:

```
Private Function CreateTable() As Boolean
   Dim NewField As Field, tdf As TableDef

   Set tdf = CreateDB.CreateTableDef(Me.Caption)
   For I = 0 To TotalFields
      With TableFields(I)
         If .FieldType = dbText Or .FieldType = dbBinary Then
            Set NewField = tdf.CreateField(.FieldName, .FieldType, .FieldSize)
         Else
            Set NewField = tdf.CreateField(.FieldName, .FieldType)
         End If
      End With
      If I = 0 Then NewField.Attributes = dbAutoIncrField
      NewField.OrdinalPosition = I + 1
      tdf.Fields.Append NewField
```

```
      Next
      CreateDB.TableDefs.Append tdf
      CreateTable = True
   End Function
```

The first line of code within the event uses the *Database* object's *CreateTableDef* method to create a new table definition. Next, the program code loops through all the fields the user added to the *TableFields* array. The program code checks each field type to determine if it is either *Text* or *Byte*. If it is either type, the program code uses the *TableDef* object's *CreateField* method with three arguments—the field name, the type, and the size.

If the field is of another type, the program code uses the *CreateField* method with two arguments—the field name and type. After adding the field to the table, the program code checks to see whether the field is the first field in the table. If it is the first field in the table, the program code sets the field's attribute to increment automatically, so that the number will be unique for every record.

270 After it adds all the fields to the table, the program code uses the *TableDefs* collection's *Append* method to add the newly defined table to the database.

WRITING THE CODE TO EXIT THE FORM

As you have learned, the user can either click the mouse on the Close box or click the mouse on the *cmdExit* button to exit the *frmAddFields* form. The following code implements the *cmdExit_Click* event:

```
Private Sub cmdExit_Click()
   frmCreateDatabase.Tag = "False"
   Unload Me
End Sub
```

The program code sets the *frmCreateDatabase* form's *Tag* property to *False*, so the *frmCreateDatabase* form knows that the *frmAddFields* form did not create a new table. The program code then tries to unload the form. Whether the user tries to unload the form with the Close box or the Exit button, the program will invoke the *QueryUnload* event, which will check to see if the user is currently designing a table and wants to lose all the changes before it lets the form unload. The following code implements the *QueryUnload* event:

```
Private Sub Form_QueryUnload(Cancel As Integer, UnloadMode As Integer)
   Dim Response As Integer

   If lstFields.ListCount > 1 And Not Saved Then
      Response = MsgBox("Exit without saving?", vbYesNo, "Database Creator")
      If Response = vbNo Then
         Cancel = True
         Exit Sub
      Else
         frmCreateDatabase.Tag = "False"
      End If
   End If
End Sub
```

If the *frmAddFields* form contains more than the single default field, and the user did not create and save the database, the program code within the *QueryUnload* event will let the user know that unloading the form now will cause the user to lose all the work he or she performed on this table. If the user wants to cancel the unload operation, the user can choose to cancel it. If the user does not want to cancel the operation, the form unloads and places *False* in the *frmCreateDatabase* form's *Tag* property, so the *frmCreateDatabase* form knows that the *frmAddFields* form did not create a new table.

Enhancements You Can Make to the prjCreateDatabase Project

The *prjCreateDatabase* project is a project that will support many enhancements. For example, you can make the program capable of creating *indexes*, which are database structures that you can use to speed up searches. In addition, you can let users define permanent queries that programs can use to retrieve information from the database.

Alternatively, you can add controls and program code to let users delete fields from the list of fields within the *frmAddFields* form, and to let users delete an entire table definition without losing a database they have already created. Finally, you can add program code to the project to let users add additional fields to table definitions, delete fields from table definitions, and so on, even after a user creates the original definition.

Putting It All Together

This chapter's project, *prjCreateDatabase*, introduced you to how you can use the Data Access Objects (DAO) Object Library, as well as many basics about working with databases. You have learned how to use Microsoft's *Data* control and *Data-Bound Grid* control together with the more powerful DAO Object Library to quickly and easily create powerful and useful database applications. In Chapter 8, "Creating a Schedule Planner," you will use the database design basics that you learned in this chapter to create a schedule or day planner that you can run on your computer. Before you continue with Chapter 8, however, make sure you understand the following key concepts:

- ✓ When you construct your databases, you will construct them from data tables, construct the data tables from records, and then construct the records themselves from fields.

- ✓ A field is a location within which you will store simple data, such as a number, a text string, or a date value. To create records, you will generally use multiple fields.

- ✓ When you work with data objects, you must add to your project a reference to the Data Object Library that contains those objects. Visual Basic provides three sets of Data Object Libraries, the Active Data Objects (ADO) Object Library, the Data Access Objects (DAO) Object Library, and the Remote Data Objects (RDO) Object Library.

- ✓ The three base objects in the DAO Object Library are the *Workspace, Database*, and *Recordset* objects. In addition to the base objects, the DAO Object Library supports *definition* objects, such as the *TableDef, QueryDef*, and *FieldDef* objects.

- ✓ Within your Visual Basic programs, you can use the *Workspace* object to connect to multiple databases and provide secure access to secure databases.

- ✓ Within your programs, you can use the *Workspace* object's *OpenDatabase* method to open a database.

- ✓ After you open a database, you can use the *Database* object's *OpenRecordset* method to open a recordset.

- ✓ Visual Basic will let you work with most objects in the DAO Object Library as members of a *collection*. For example, a single *TableDef* object is also a member of the *TableDefs* collection for a given *Database* object.

- ✓ When you work with databases and your programs must access information within a database, you will generally use a Structured Query Language (SQL) query to retrieve and manipulate information. SQL queries generally include the keywords *Select, From, Where,* and *Order By*.

- ✓ A *Select* query is a request for records that match certain criteria.

- ✓ In addition to the Data Access Objects that Visual Basic provides, your programs can also use controls, such as the *Data* control, the *Data-Bound Grid* control, and the *Data-Bound ComboBox* control to access database and recordset information.

Chapter 8

Creating a Schedule Planner

In our electronic world, organizing your day is no longer limited to the hand-held binder planner. Instead, you can now plan your day's schedule on a computer, save it to disk, and print out your schedule to use when you are away from your computer. Moreover, you can set alarms within an electronic planner to alert you to important appointments. If you are on a network, you can share your schedule with others. Most binder-based planners contain a section for schedules, addresses, and things to do. In this chapter you will design a computer-based planner, *prjPlanner*, that includes a Schedule and a Things to Do section. You can also add an address database, a relatively simple task that you will easily be able to do after you complete this chapter. As with a hand-held binder planner, you can use *prjPlanner* to select a specific time and day and schedule individual entries in different time blocks for that day.

This chapter introduces the *Microsoft Calendar* control, which you can use within your programs to display dates in a calendar format. The *Microsoft Calendar* control looks similar to a wall calendar. When you click your mouse on the *Microsoft Calendar* control, Visual Basic will store the selected day, month, and year in a structure the program can access. As you schedule appointments, you can add them to a database on the disk so you can recover the scheduled information later. In this chapter, you will use date values with schedule entries and add them to a database.

There are many good database products available, and any of them would be excellent for maintaining your schedule information. However, Visual Basic includes the *Visual Data Manager*, which lets you create, and later communicate with, a Microsoft *Access*® database in Visual Basic. In this chapter, you will use the *Visual Data Manager* to create a Microsoft *Access* database to store time, date, and schedule information.

Within a database, you can store large amounts of related information. In addition, you must present that information to the user in a manner that lets the user quickly and easily understand the information. One of the best ways to present database-style information to users is within a grid, such as the rows and columns you would find in a spreadsheet. This chapter introduces the *Microsoft Flex Grid* control, which lets your Visual Basic programs include a grid within the program's display. The *Microsoft Flex Grid* control will display rows and columns of information you use the program's code to set or retrieve. Within the *prjPlanner* program, you will use the *Microsoft Flex Grid* control to display the time, date, and schedule information that the program previously stored within its Microsoft *Access* database.

In this chapter, you will combine a *Microsoft Calendar* control, a Microsoft *Access* database, and a *Microsoft Flex Grid* control to design a computer planner. After you complete the computer planner, you can select a date from the *Microsoft Calendar* control and add a schedule entry to the *Microsoft Flex Grid* control. The program, in turn, will store the entered information in a Microsoft *Access* database. When you want to view the schedule entry later, you can select the date from the *Microsoft Calendar* control and the program will display the schedule entry within the *Microsoft Flex Grid* control.

This chapter examines in detail a *Microsoft Calendar* control, the *Visual Data Manager*, a Microsoft *Access* database, and a *Microsoft Flex Grid* control. By the time you finish this chapter, you will understand the following key concepts:

- Visual Basic includes the *Microsoft Calendar* control, which you will use in the *prjPlanner* project to display dates.

- Visual Basic includes the *Visual Data Manager*, which you will use in the *prjPlanner* project to create a Microsoft *Access* database in Visual Basic.

- The *Visual Data Manager* lets you create database tables, fields, queries, and reports.

- You can use *Structured Query Language (SQL)* to communicate with a Microsoft *Access* database in Visual Basic.

- Visual Basic includes the *Microsoft Flex Grid* control, which you will use in the *prjPlanner* project to input and display information in rows and columns.

USING THE PRJPLANNER PROJECT

Before you design the *prjPlanner* project, which lets the program's user schedule appointments and things to do, you may find it helpful to run the *prjPlanner.exe* program. The companion CD-ROM that accompanies this book contains the *prjPlanner.exe* program and a sample database within the *Chapter08* directory. As with every other program on the CD-ROM, you should use the Jamsa Press *setup.exe* program the CD-ROM contains to install the *prjPlanner.exe* program to your computer's hard drive before you run it. After you install the *prjPlanner.exe* program to your computer's hard drive, you can run the program from the Start menu. To run the program, select the Windows Start menu Run option. Windows will display the Run dialog box. Within the Run dialog box, enter *x:\vbpl\Chapter08\prjPlanner.exe*, where *x* corresponds to the drive letter of the hard drive on which you installed the program, and click your mouse on OK. Windows will display the *prjPlanner.exe* program, as shown in Figure 8.1.

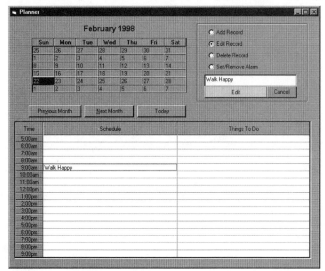

*Figure 8.1 The **prjPlanner** project at run time.*

Before you use the *prjPlanner.exe* program, take a moment to familiarize yourself with the controls on the form. First, the program will display the current date in the *Microsoft Calendar* control at the upper left corner of the form. When you click your mouse on a date in the *Microsoft Calendar* control, the program will access the data for that date within the Microsoft *Access* database and display the selected date's schedule, if any, in the *Microsoft Flex Grid* control at the bottom of the form.

UNDERSTANDING WHY YOU MUST RUN SETUP.EXE BEFORE YOU RUN PRJPLANNER

As you have learned, the *prjPlanner.exe* program uses the *Planner.mdb* database to maintain information about appointments and things to do. Although you could run the *prjPlanner.exe* program from the companion CD-ROM that accompanies this book, the database engine will be unable to save modifications to the *Planner.mdb* database, because it is a read-only file on the CD-ROM. Instead, you must first use the Jamsa Press *setup.exe* program the CD-ROM contains to install the program and enable the read–write properties for the database so that the *prjPlanner* program can update the information within the database.

To learn more about the *setup.exe* program, see the "What's on the *Visual Basic Programmer's Library* Companion CD-ROM" section at the back of this book.

To add a schedule or "things to do" entry, click your mouse on the *Microsoft Calendar* control to select a date. Next, click your mouse on a time that does not currently have a schedule or things to do entry in the *Microsoft Flex Grid* control. The program will display a *Frame* control in the upper right corner of the form. Inside the *Frame* control, you will see *OptionButton*, *TextBox*, and *CommandButton* controls, which will let you add, edit, delete, and set an alarm for individual schedule entries.

Now that you have a better view of the *prjPlanner.exe* program's layout, you can use the program to display, add, edit, and delete schedule entries. Before you can display a new schedule entry, however, you must first add it to a Microsoft *Access* database. After that, the program will display the new entry in the *Microsoft Flex Grid* control. To add a new schedule entry to a database and display it, perform the following steps:

1. Click your mouse on the *Microsoft Calendar* control to select a date, such as February 22, 1998. The program will store the selected date in memory, open the Microsoft *Access* database, and display any schedule entries in the *Microsoft Flex Grid* control.

2. Within the *Microsoft Flex Grid* control, click your mouse on the 2:00 p.m. time of day schedule entry. The program will display a *Frame* control in the upper right corner of the form.

3. Within the *Frame* control, click your mouse on the *Add Record* option button control. The program will change the selected time of day row to blue and change the previously blank *CommandButton* control within the *Frame* control to blue.

4. Within the *Frame* control's *TextBox* control, type a schedule entry, such as *Read This Chapter Today*. Figure 8.2 shows the new schedule entry before the program adds it to the Microsoft *Access* database.

274

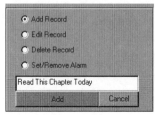

Figure 8.2 *The* **Frame** *control showing the new schedule entry before the program adds it to the database.*

5. Next, click your mouse on the Add button. The program will add the new schedule entry to the Microsoft *Access* database and display it in the *Microsoft Flex Grid* control at the time of day you selected.

6. Within the *Microsoft Calendar* control, click your mouse on another date. Then click back to the previous date. The program will display the new schedule entry in the *Microsoft Flex Grid* control.

USING THE CONTROLS WITHIN THE PRJPLANNER PROGRAM

When you install Visual Basic, it should automatically install all the controls this chapter uses. However, if you chose a custom or minimum setup, it is possible that you may not have installed all the controls in this chapter. If you encounter run-time errors such as "Unable to Create Reference" or "Unable to Find OLE Automation Object," it probably means that you do not have a complete Visual Basic installation on your computer. To fix the problem, re-install Visual Basic, and ensure that you install the standard set of controls and references, at a minimum.

After the program adds a new schedule entry to the Microsoft *Access* database, you can edit the schedule. To edit an already existing schedule entry, perform the following steps:

1. Within the *Microsoft Calendar* control, select a date, such as February 22, 1998. The program will display the schedule entry at 2:00 p.m. in the *Microsoft Flex Grid* control that you added to the schedule in the last section.

2. Within the *Microsoft Flex Grid* control, click your mouse on the 2:00 p.m. time of day schedule entry. The program will display the *Frame* control in the upper right corner and the scheduled entry in the *TextBox* control within the *Frame* control.

3. Within the *Frame* control, click your mouse on the *Edit Record* option button control. The program will change the entire *CommandButton* control to yellow.

4. Within the *Frame* control's *TextBox* control, change the entry to *Read This Chapter By Tomorrow*. Next, click your mouse on the *Edit* button. The program will replace the original entry in the database with the new one in the *TextBox* control and display the new entry in the *Microsoft Flex Grid* control.

Figure 8.3 shows the edited schedule entry before the program changes the original entry in the database.

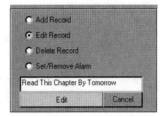

Figure 8.3 *The edited schedule entry before the program changes the Microsoft **Access** database.*

275

After the *prjPlanner.exe* program adds or edits a schedule entry, you can delete an entry. To delete an entry from the Microsoft *Access* database, perform the following steps:

1. Within the *Microsoft Calendar* control, select a date, such as February 22, 1998. The program will display the previously edited schedule entry at 2:00 p.m. in the *Microsoft Flex Grid* control.

2. Within the *Microsoft Flex Grid* control, click your mouse on the 2:00 p.m. time of day schedule entry. The program will display the *Frame* control in the upper right corner and the scheduled entry in the *TextBox* control within the *Frame* control.

3. Within the *Frame* control, click your mouse on the *Delete Record* option button control. The program will change the entire *CommandButton* control to red.

4. Within the *Frame* control, click your mouse on the *Delete* button. The program will open a message box that asks "Delete this Entry?" Within the message box, click your mouse on the Yes button. The program will delete the entry from the database and clear it from the *Microsoft Flex Grid* control.

After the program adds or edits a schedule entry, you can set an alarm for the entry. You might want to set alarms on your appointments any time you want to remind yourself of an appointment. Because the *prjPlanner* project does not incorporate the program code to control an extended-capability sound card, you will not add sound as an alarm component. Instead, the alarm will simply beep. To set an alarm, perform the following steps:

1. Within the *Microsoft Calendar* control, select a date, such as February 22, 1998. The program will display the schedule entry at 2:00 p.m. that you entered and modified in the previous sections within the *Microsoft Flex Grid* control.

2. Within the *Microsoft Flex Grid* control, click your mouse on the 2:00 p.m. time of day schedule entry. The program will display the *Frame* control in the upper right corner and the schedule entry in the *TextBox* control within the *Frame* control.

3. Within the *Frame* control, click your mouse on the *Set/Remove Alarm* option button control. The program will change the entry's background color to green and the entire *CommandButton* control to green.

4. Within the *Frame* control, click your mouse on the *Set Alarm* button. The program will add an alarm notification flag to the Microsoft *Access* database and display the schedule entry with a green background color in the *Microsoft Flex Grid* control.

Figure 8.4 shows the *Microsoft Flex Grid* control after the *prjPlanner.exe* program adds a green alarm highlight to the selected schedule entry.

Time	Schedule	Things To Do
5:00am		
6:00am		
7:00am		
8:00am		
9:00am		
10:00am		
11:00am		
12:00pm		
1:00pm		
2:00pm	Read This Chapter By Tomorrow	
3:00pm		
4:00pm		
5:00pm		
6:00pm		
7:00pm		
8:00pm		
9:00pm		

Figure 8.4 *The green alarm highlight on a schedule entry within the **Microsoft Flex Grid** control.*

276 CREATING A BLANK FORM

Now that you have seen a sample of the *prjPlanner* project (as shown in Figure 8.1), you will begin the *prjPlanner* project's design, design an empty form, and name the empty form *frmPlanner*. The *frmPlanner* form will contain all the controls the "Using the *prjPlanner* Project" section introduced. After you set up the form, you will learn more about the *Microsoft Calendar* and *Microsoft Flex Grid* controls and Microsoft *Access* databases.

To begin designing the *prjPlanner* project, you must first create an empty form. To create an empty form, perform the following steps:

1. Within Visual Basic, select the File menu New Project option. Visual Basic will open the New Project dialog box.

2. Within the New Project dialog box, select the Standard EXE icon. Next, click your mouse on the OK button. Visual Basic will start a new Standard EXE project and open the *Form1* form window.

3. Select the View menu Properties Window option. Visual Basic will open the Properties Window listing the *Form1* properties.

4. Within the Properties Window, change the *Form1* property values to those Table 8.1 lists.

Object	Property	Set As
Form1	*Caption*	*Planner*
Form1	*Height*	8100
Form1	*Left*	0
Form1	*Top*	0
Form1	*Width*	10230
Form1	*Name*	*frmPlanner*

Table 8.1 *The newly named **frmPlanner** form's properties.*

5. Select the File menu Save Project As option. Visual Basic will open the Save File As dialog box.

6. Within the Save File As dialog box, Visual Basic will fill the *File name* field with *frmPlanner*. Next, click your mouse on the Save button. Visual Basic will save the *frmPlanner* form and fill the *File name* field with the project name, *Project1*.

7. Within the *File name* field, replace the *Project1* project name with the new *prjPlanner* project name. Next, click your mouse on the Save button. Visual Basic will save the *prjPlanner* project and close the Save Project As dialog box.

More on the Microsoft Calendar Control

Within the *prjPlanner* project, you will use a *Microsoft Calendar* control to display and store day, month, and year values. The *Microsoft Calendar* control looks similar to a regular, printed calendar. Like Visual Basic standard controls, the *Microsoft Calendar* control has properties, methods, and events. When you click your mouse on the *Microsoft Calendar* control, the operating system will store the day, month, and year you select in three properties of the *Calendar* control, called *Day, Month*, and *Year*. The *Day, Month*, and *Year* properties store values from January 1, 1900, to February 28, 2100.

Table 8.2 lists some of the *Microsoft Calendar* control's properties, methods, and events. For a complete listing, use the Visual Basic Help file and search for *MSCalendar control*.

Type	Name	Purpose
Property	*Day*	Stores the selected day.
Property	*Month*	Stores the selected month.
Property	*Year*	Stores the selected year.
Property	*FirstDay*	Starts the displayed week at the day you specify.
Property	*DayLength*	Displays the day's name in short, medium, or long format (for example, S, Sun, or Sunday).
Property	*Value*	Stores a date value in the month/day/year format (for example, 2/22/98).
Method	*PreviousMonth*	Changes the calendar's display to the previous month.
Method	*NextMonth*	Changes the calendar's display to the next month.
Event	*Click*	Occurs when you click your mouse on the *Microsoft Calendar* control.
Event	*NewMonth*	Occurs when the *Month* property changes to a different month.
Event	*NewYear*	Occurs when the *Year* property changes to a different year.

*Table 8.2 Some of the **Microsoft Calendar** control's properties, methods, and events.*

Adding a Microsoft Calendar Control to the Project

As you have learned, you will use a *Microsoft Calendar* control to display day, month, and year values. Before you can use the *Microsoft Calendar* control in the *prjPlanner* project, you must add the control to the project as a component. After you add the *Microsoft Calendar* control to the *prjPlanner* project, Visual Basic will display the control's icon in the Toolbox. As you know, the Toolbox displays Visual Basic control icons. If you double-click your mouse on any icon in the Toolbox, Visual Basic will draw the control that the icon corresponds to within the active form.

To add a *Microsoft Calendar* control to the *prjPlanner* project, perform the following steps:

1. Within Visual Basic, select the Project menu Components option. Visual Basic will open the Components dialog box.

2. Within the Components dialog box, select the *Microsoft Calendar Control 8.0* listing. Next, click your mouse on the box to the left of the listing. Visual Basic will display a check mark in the box, as shown in Figure 8.5.

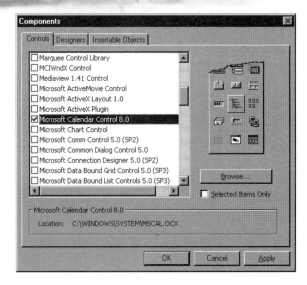

Figure 8.5 *The Components dialog box's list box showing the* **Microsoft Calendar Control 8.0** *listing.*

3. Within the Components dialog box, click your mouse on the OK button. Visual Basic will close the Components dialog box and add the *Microsoft Calendar* control component to the *prjPlanner* project.

MORE ON THE MICROSOFT FLEX GRID CONTROL

As you have learned, the *Microsoft Calendar* control lets you display and store day, month, and year values. Within the *prjPlanner* project, you will use a *Microsoft Flex Grid* control to display day, month, and year schedule entries for a computer planner. Like Visual Basic standard controls, the *Microsoft Flex Grid* control has properties, methods, and events. The *Microsoft Flex Grid* control will display schedule entries in rows and columns which are either fixed or standard. Fixed columns and rows do not move when you scroll the other columns or rows. The *Microsoft Flex Grid* control, by default, displays one fixed row and one fixed column. The *Microsoft Flex Grid* control limits the number of rows and columns that you can display based on the available virtual memory for the project.

You can alter the color, font, and text style for the fixed columns and rows. Programs typically use fixed columns and rows in spreadsheet applications to display row numbers and column names or letters. After you fix a row or column, you can add standard rows and columns. Standard rows and columns can store numbers or text, and move when you scroll. In the *prjPlanner* project, you will display schedule entries in standard rows and columns, and the time of day in fixed rows and columns.

Figure 8.6 shows a sample of a *Microsoft Flex Grid* control with one fixed row, one fixed column, two standard columns, and three standard rows.

Col: 0 Row: 0	Col: 1 Row: 0	Col: 2 Row: 0
Col: 0 Row: 1	Col: 1 Row: 1	Col: 2 Row: 1
Col: 0 Row: 2	Col: 1 Row: 2	Col: 2 Row: 2
Col: 0 Row: 3	Col: 1 Row: 3	Col: 2 Row: 3

Figure 8.6 *A sample of rows and columns within a* **Microsoft Flex Grid** *control.*

You reference each row and column in the *Microsoft Flex Grid* control with an integer value. The control represents the first row with the integer value 0, the second row with the integer value 1, and so on. Similarly, the *Microsoft Flex Grid* control represents the first column with the integer value 0, the second column with the integer value 1, and so on. When you click your mouse on the *Microsoft Flex Grid* control, Visual Basic will fill two properties, *Row* and *Col*. The *Row* and *Col* properties store the selected row and column values from the *Microsoft Flex Grid* control. The combination of a *Row* and a *Col* property results in a specific location within the *Microsoft Flex Grid* control, called a *cell*. For example, the position within the *Microsoft Flex Grid* control at *Row* = 1 and *Col* = 2 is also called the cell at *Row* = 1 and *Col* = 2.

In addition, you can set the total number of rows and columns that the *Microsoft Flex Grid* control has within program code in either a procedure or a function, or in the Properties Window. The virtual memory available on your computer determines the limit on the maximum number of rows and columns. To use a *Microsoft Flex Grid* control within the *prjPlanner* project, you must add the control to the project. You will add a *Microsoft Flex Grid* control to the project in the next section, "Adding a *Microsoft Flex Grid* Control to the Project." After you connect the control, Visual Basic will draw an icon representing the control in the Toolbox. Table 8.3 lists some of the *Microsoft Flex Grid* control's properties, methods, and events.

Type	Name	Purpose
Property	*Row*	Stores the row value.
Property	*Col*	Stores the column value.
Property	*Rows*	Sets or returns the number of rows in the grid.
Property	*Cols*	Sets or returns the number of columns in the grid.
Property	*RowHeight*	Sets or returns the height of each row.
Property	*ColWidth*	Sets or returns the width of each column.
Method	*Clear*	Erases all data in the grid.
Event	*Click*	Occurs when you click your mouse on the grid.

Table 8.3 *Some properties, methods, and events of the **Microsoft Flex Grid** control.*

ADDING A MICROSOFT FLEX GRID CONTROL TO THE PROJECT

As you have learned, within the *prjPlanner* program, you will use a *Microsoft Flex Grid* control to display schedule entries at specific times of day. Before you can use the *Microsoft Flex Grid* control in the *prjPlanner* project, you must add it to the project as a component. After you add the *Microsoft Flex Grid* control to the *prjPlanner* project, Visual Basic will display the control's icon in the Toolbox. As you know, the Toolbox displays Visual Basic control icons. If you double-click your mouse on any icon in the Toolbox, Visual Basic will draw the control that the icon corresponds to within the active form. To add a *Microsoft Flex Grid* control to the *prjPlanner* project, perform the following steps:

1. Select the Project menu Components option. Visual Basic will open the Components dialog box.

2. Within the Components dialog box, select the *Microsoft Flex Grid Control 5.0* listing. Next, click your mouse on the box to the left of the listing. Visual Basic will display a check mark in the box.

3. Within the Components dialog box, click your mouse on OK. Visual Basic will add the *Microsoft Flex Grid* control component to the *prjPlanner* project.

UNDERSTANDING A MICROSOFT ACCESS DATABASE

As you have learned, when you enter text into a cell of the *Microsoft Flex Grid* control, you can store that text in a database. In the *prjPlanner* project, text will reside in a Microsoft *Access* database *table*. A database consists of one or more tables, and you can visualize each table as storing data in *rows* and *columns*. In a table, each row is a *record* and each column is a *field*. A record can contain one or more fields. Each field can contain one *value*. The value can be a number, text, symbol, or other defined type. For example, a record for Santa Claus could contain a *Name* field, a *Weight* field, and a *Clothing* field. You can fill each field with values, such as *Name = Santa Claus, Weight = 300*, and *Clothing = Red Suit*. You can identify the record by name, weight, or clothing.

After you store text in a table (that is, within a database record), you can later retrieve the text, and display the database records within a Visual Basic program. Visual Basic includes three basic database objects that let programs communicate with a database table. The three objects are the *Workspace*, *Database*, and *Recordset* objects, as you learned in Chapter 7, "Creating a Database Viewer and Designer."

279

To retrieve records from a database table, you will write a *query*. A query is a statement that your program uses to tell the Microsoft *Access* database what it wants. You must write query statements in a special language called *Structured Query Language (SQL)*. You can use SQL to search a database table for specific field values in each record. The "Understanding SQL" section in Chapter 7 explains SQL in detail.

In the *prjPlanner* project, you will design a database table to emulate a schedule planner. After you write text in the *Microsoft Flex Grid* control, that text will have a specific location, time, and date. As you have learned, when you click your mouse on the *Microsoft Calendar* control, the control fills three of its properties with date information. Also, when you click your mouse on the *Microsoft Flex Grid* control, the control fills two properties with location information within the grid. To create the schedule planner, you will design a database table with fields called *TimeOfDay, Schedule, Row, Column, Day, Month*, and *Year*. Each field will contain a value that corresponds to the text you enter. When you want to find a specific record in the database table, you can look for specific time, day, month, year, or schedule text in the table records. After you find the information, the *Microsoft Flex Grid* control will display the record.

280   USING THE VISUAL DATA MANAGER TO CREATE A DATABASE

The Visual Basic Interactive Development Environment (IDE) includes the *Visual Data Manager*, an add-in utility that you can use to design databases. As you have learned, a database contains one or more tables, and you can conceptually organize a table into rows and columns of data. The Visual Data Manager lets you create one or more tables of data and saves the tables in the database. In the *prjPlanner* project, you will create a database table called *Planner*. You will then design a table for the *Planner.mdb* database that stores data from the *Microsoft Flex Grid* control. To create a database and a table to store the *Microsoft Flex Grid* control cell information, perform the following steps:

1. Select the Add-Ins menu Visual Data Manager option. Visual Basic will display the VisData window.

2. Within the VisData window, select the File menu New Microsoft Access Version 7.0 MDB option. Visual Basic will open the Select Microsoft Access Database To Create dialog box.

3. Within the Select Microsoft Access Database To Create dialog box, type the name of your database in the *File Name* field as *Planner*. Next, click your mouse on the Save button. Visual Data Manager will open the Database window.

4. Within the Database window, right-click your mouse on the *Properties* listing. Visual Data Manager will open the Table Structure dialog box.

5. Within the Table Structure dialog box, type the name of your table in the *Table Name* field as *DayMonthYear*. Next, click your mouse on the Add Field button. Visual Data Manager will open the Add Field dialog box.

6. Within the Add Field dialog box, enter in the *Name* and *Type* fields the field names and types Table 8.4 lists. After you enter the field names and types, click your mouse on the Close button. Visual Basic will close the Add Field dialog box and display the Table Structure dialog box.

Field Name	Type	Size
Day	Integer	n/a
Month	Integer	n/a
Year	Integer	n/a
Row	Integer	n/a
Column	Integer	n/a
Schedule	Text	70
Alarm	Boolean	n/a

Table 8.4 The field names and types for the **DayMonthYear** table in the **Planner.mdb** database.

7. Within the Table Structure dialog box, click your mouse on the Build the Table button. Visual Data Manager will build the *DayMonthYear* table, close the Table Structure dialog box, and display the *DayMonthYear* table in the Database window.

8. Within the Database window, double-click your mouse on the *DayMonthYear* table listing. Visual Data Manager will open the Dynaset: DayMonthYear dialog box.

9. Within the Dynaset: DayMonthYear dialog box, click your mouse on the Add button. Visual Data Manager will open the Update/Cancel dialog box.

10. Within the Update/Cancel dialog box, enter the values beside each field as *Day* = 1, *Month* = 12, *Year* = 1998, *Row* = 3, *Column* = 2, *Schedule* = *Almost Christmas*, *Alarm* = *True*.

11. Within the Update/Cancel dialog box, click your mouse on the Update button. Visual Data Manager will close the Update/Cancel dialog box and display the Dynaset: DayMonthYear dialog box.

12. Within the Dynaset: DayMonthYear dialog box, click your mouse on the Close button. Visual Data Manager will close the Dynaset: DayMonthYear dialog box and display the *Planner.mdb* database with the *DayMonthYear* table's fields in the Database window, as shown in Figure 8.7.

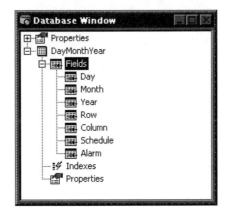

Figure 8.7 *The **Planner.mdb** database's **DayMonthYear** table fields.*

ADDING CONTROLS TO THE FORM

As you have learned, in the *prjPlanner* project you will use a *Microsoft Calendar* control, a *Microsoft Flex Grid* control, and a *Frame* control containing option buttons, a text box, and command buttons. To begin, you will add each control to the *frmPlanner* form and assign properties for each control.

ADDING A MICROSOFT CALENDAR CONTROL TO THE FORM

As you have learned, the *prjPlanner* project will use a *Microsoft Calendar* control to display day, month, and year values. To add a *Microsoft Calendar* control to the *frmPlanner* form, perform the following steps:

1. If Visual Basic is not displaying the *frmPlanner* form within an object window, double-click your mouse on the *frmPlanner* form listing within the Project Explorer. Visual Basic will open the *frmPlanner* form.

2. Within Visual Basic, select the View menu Toolbox option. Visual Basic will open the Toolbox.

3. Within the Toolbox, select the new *Microsoft Calendar* control Calendar icon, as shown in Figure 8.8.

Figure 8.8 *The Toolbox showing the **Microsoft Calendar** control's Calendar icon.*

4. Within the Toolbox, double-click your mouse on the Calendar icon. Visual Basic will draw a *Microsoft Calendar* control, *Calendar1*, within the *frmPlanner* form, as shown in Figure 8.9.

*Figure 8.9 The **Microsoft Calendar** control, **Calendar1**, on the **frmPlanner** form.*

5. Within the *frmPlanner* form window, click your mouse on the *Calendar1* control to highlight it. Visual Basic will draw a small frame around the control.

6. Select the View menu Properties Window option. Visual Basic will open the Properties Window listing the *Calendar1* properties.

7. Within the Properties Window, change the *Calendar1* properties to those Table 8.5 lists.

Object	Property	Set As
Calendar1	*Height*	2415
Calendar1	*Left*	600
Calendar1	*ShowDateSelectors*	*False*
Calendar1	*Top*	120
Calendar1	*Width*	5175
Calendar1	*Name*	*calPlanner*

*Table 8.5 The newly named **calPlanner** control's properties.*

ADDING A MICROSOFT FLEX GRID CONTROL TO THE FORM

As you have learned, the *prjPlanner* project will use a *Microsoft Flex Grid* control to display schedule entries. To add a *Microsoft Flex Grid* control to the *frmPlanner* form, perform the following steps:

1. If Visual Basic is not displaying the *frmPlanner* form within an object window, double-click your mouse on the *frmPlanner* form listing within the Project Explorer. Visual Basic will open the *frmPlanner* form.

2. Within Visual Basic, select the View menu Toolbox option. Visual Basic will open the Toolbox.

3. Within the Toolbox, select the new *Microsoft Flex Grid* control MSFlexGrid icon, as shown in Figure 8.10.

*Figure 8.10 The Toolbox showing the **Microsoft Flex Grid** control MSFlexGrid icon.*

4. Within the Toolbox, double-click your mouse on the MSFlexGrid icon. Visual Basic will draw a *Microsoft Flex Grid* control, *MSFlexGrid1*, within the *frmPlanner* form, as shown in Figure 8.11.

Figure 8.11 *The **Microsoft Flex Grid** control **MSFlexGrid1** on the **frmPlanner** form.*

5. Within the *frmPlanner* form window, click your mouse on the *MSFlexGrid1* control to highlight it. Visual Basic will draw a small frame around the control.

6. Select the View menu Properties Window option. Visual Basic will open the Properties Window listing the *MSFlexGrid1* properties.

7. Within the Properties Window, change the *MSFlexGrid1* property values to those Table 8.6 lists.

Object	Properties	Set As
MSFlexGrid1	Cols	3
MSFlexGrid1	Fixed Cols	1
MSFlexGrid1	Fixed Rows	1
MSFlexGrid1	Height	4335
MSFlexGrid1	Left	120
MSFlexGrid1	Rows	18
MSFlexGrid1	Top	3240
MSFlexGrid1	Width	9615
MSFlexGrid1	Name	flxPlanner

Table 8.6 *The newly named **flxPlanner** control's properties.*

ADDING A FRAME CONTROL TO THE FORM

As you have learned, the *prjPlanner* project will use a *Frame* control to hold *OptionButton*, *TextBox*, and *CommandButton* controls. To add a *Frame* control to the *frmPlanner* form, perform the following steps:

1. If Visual Basic is not displaying the *frmPlanner* form within an object window, double-click your mouse on the *frmPlanner* form listing within the Project Explorer. Visual Basic will open the *frmPlanner* form.

2. Within Visual Basic, select the View menu Toolbox option. Visual Basic will open the Toolbox.

3. Within the Toolbox, double-click your mouse on the Frame icon. Visual Basic will draw a *Frame* control, *Frame1*, within the *frmPlanner* form.

4. Within the *frmPlanner* form window, click your mouse on the *Frame1* control to highlight it. Visual Basic will draw a small frame around the control.

5. Select the View menu Properties Window option. Visual Basic will open the Properties Window listing the *Frame1* properties.

6. Within the Properties Window, change the *Frame1* properties to those Table 8.7 lists.

Object	Property	Set As
Frame1	Caption	[blank]
Frame1	Height	2535

Table 8.7 *The newly named **fraDatabase** control's properties. (continued on following page)*

Object	Property •	Set As
Frame1	Left	5280
Frame1	Top	120
Frame1	Width	3615
Frame1	Name	fraDatabase

Table 8.7 The newly named **fraDatabase** control's properties. (continued from previous page)

ADDING CONTROLS TO THE FRADATABASE FRAME CONTROL

As you have learned, a *Frame* control can hold one or more Visual Basic controls. In the *prjPlanner* project, you will add *OptionButton*, *TextBox*, and *CommandButton* controls to the *fraDatabase* control.

Remember, the *OptionButton* controls let you add, edit, delete, or set alarms for a schedule entry. The *TextBox* control will let you type in a new message or edit a message retrieved from the *flxPlanner* control. After you click your mouse on an *OptionButton* control, the program will display your choice on the left *CommandButton* control. When you click your mouse on the *CommandButton* control, the program will respond by adding, editing, deleting, or setting an alarm for a schedule entry in the *Planner.mdb* database.

To add *OptionButton*, *TextBox*, and *CommandButton* controls to the *fraDatabase* control, perform the following steps:

1. If Visual Basic is not displaying the *frmPlanner* form within an object window, double-click your mouse on the *frmPlanner* form listing within the Project Explorer. Visual Basic will open the *frmPlanner* form.

2. Within Visual Basic, select the View menu Toolbox option. Visual Basic will open the Toolbox.

3. Within the Toolbox, double-click your mouse on the OptionButton icon. Visual Basic will add an *OptionButton* control, *Option1*, to the *frmPlanner* form.

4. Within the form window, click your mouse on the *Option1* control and hold the mouse button down. Move the mouse cursor and drag the *Option1* control into the *fraDatabase* control. When you release the mouse button, Visual Basic will draw the *Option1* control inside the *fraDatabase* control.

5. Select the View menu Properties Window option. Visual Basic will open the Properties Window.

6. Within the *fraDatabase* control, click your mouse on the *Option1* control. Visual Basic will list the *Option1* control's properties in the Properties Window. Change the *Name* property from *Option1* to *optDatabase*.

7. Within the *fraDatabase* control, click your mouse on the *optDatabase* control and select the Edit menu Copy option. Visual Basic will highlight the *optDatabase* control and store a copy of it in the Clipboard.

8. Click your mouse on the *fraDatabase* control to highlight it. Next, select the Edit menu Paste option. Visual Basic will display a dialog box that asks, "You already have a control named *optDatabase*. Do you want to create a control array?" Click your mouse on the Yes button. Visual Basic will draw a copy of the *optDatabase* control within the *fraDatabase* control and display the first *optDatabase* control as *optDatabase(0)*, and the second as *optDatabase(1)*.

9. Click your mouse on the *fraDatabase* control to highlight it. Next, select the Edit menu Paste option. Visual Basic will draw another copy of the *optDatabase* control within the *fraDatabase* control and display it as *optDatabase(2)*.

10. Repeat Step 8 one more time until you have a total of four *OptionButton* controls in a control array within the *fraDatabase* control, as shown in Figure 8.12.

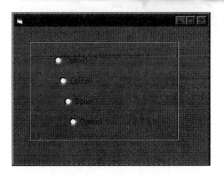

Figure 8.12 *The four **OptionButton** controls within the **fraDatabase** control.*

285

11. Within the Toolbox, double-click your mouse on the TextBox icon. Visual Basic will add a *TextBox* control, *Text1*, to the *frmPlanner* form.

12. Within the *frmPlanner* form, click your mouse on the *Text1* control and hold the mouse button down. Move the mouse cursor and drag the *Text1* control into the *fraDatabase* control. When you release the mouse button, Visual Basic will draw the *Text1* control inside the *fraDatabase* control.

13. Within the Toolbox, double-click your mouse on the CommandButton icon. Visual Basic will add a *CommandButton* control, *Command1*, to the *frmPlanner* form.

14. Repeat Step 12 one time until you have a total of two command buttons in the *frmPlanner* form.

15. Within the form window, click your mouse on the *Command1* control and hold the mouse button down. Move the mouse cursor and drag the *Command1* control into the *fraDatabase* control. When you release the mouse button, Visual Basic will draw the *Command1* control inside the *fraDatabase* control.

16. Repeat Step 14 one time to add the *Command2* control to the *fraDatabase* control. Visual Basic will draw the *Command2* control inside the *fraDatabase* control. Figure 8.13 shows the *fraDatabase* control after you add the *Textbox* and *CommandButton* controls.

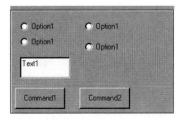

Figure 8.13 *The **TextBox** and **CommandButton** controls within the **fraDatabase** control.*

17. Select the View menu Properties Window option. Visual Basic will open the Properties Window.

18. Within the *fraDatabase* frame control, click your mouse on each control. Visual Basic will list the selected control's properties within the Properties Window. Change the selected control's properties to those Table 8.8 lists.

Object	Property	Set As
optDatabase(0)	*Caption*	*Add Record*
optDatabase(0)	*Height*	255
optDatabase(0)	*Left*	360
optDatabase(0)	*Top*	240

Table 8.8 *The **fraDatabase** control's component controls' properties. (continued on following page)*

Object	Property	Set As
optDatabase(0)	Width	2415
optDatabase(1)	Caption	Edit Record
optDatabase(1)	Height	255
optDatabase(1)	Left	360
optDatabase(1)	Top	600
optDatabase(1)	Width	2415
optDatabase(2)	Caption	Delete Record
optDatabase(2)	Height	255
optDatabase(2)	Left	360
optDatabase(2)	Top	960
optDatabase(2)	Width	2415
optDatabase(3)	Caption	Set Alarm
optDatabase(3)	Height	255
optDatabase(3)	Left	360
optDatabase(3)	Top	1320
optDatabase(3)	Width	2415
Text1	Text	[blank]
Text1	Height	385
Text1	Left	240
Text1	Top	1680
Text1	Width	3015
Text1	Name	txtAddEdit
Command1	Caption	[blank]
Command1	Height	385
Command1	Left	240
Command1	Top	2040
Command1	Width	2055
Command1	Name	cmdOption
Command2	Caption	Cancel
Command2	Height	385
Command2	Left	2280
Command2	Top	2040
Command2	Width	985
Command2	Name	cmdCancel

286

Table 8.8 The **fraDatabase** control's component controls' properties. (continued from previous page)

After you finish inputting the *fraDatabase* control's properties, the *fraDatabase* control will look similar to Figure 8.14.

Figure 8.14 The **fraDatabase** control after you change the properties for the controls it contains.

ADDING THE DATE SELECTION BUTTONS TO THE FORM

As you have learned, you can use buttons to change the *calPlanner* control's current date. In the *prjPlanner* project, you will use three command buttons, Previous Month, Next Month, and Today, to change the current date from within program code. To add the Date Selection buttons to the *frmPlanner* form, perform the following steps:

1. If Visual Basic is not displaying the *frmPlanner* form within an object window, double-click your mouse on the *frmPlanner* form listing within the Project Explorer. Visual Basic will open the *frmPlanner* form.

2. Within Visual Basic, select the View menu Toolbox option. Visual Basic will open the Toolbox.

3. Within the Toolbox, double-click your mouse on the CommandButton icon. Visual Basic will add a *CommandButton* control, *Command1*, to the *frmPlanner* form.

4. Repeat Step 2 two more times. Visual Basic will add two more *CommandButton* controls, *Command2* and *Command3,* to the form's center.

5. Within the *frmPlanner* form, click your mouse on the *Command3* control to highlight it. Visual Basic will draw a small frame around the control.

6. Select the View menu Properties Window option. Visual Basic will open the Properties Window listing the *Command3* control's properties.

7. Within the Properties Window, change the *Command3* control's properties to those Table 8.9 lists.

8. Repeat Steps 5, 6, and 7 to change the *Command1 and Command2* controls' properties to the values Table 8.9 lists.

287

Object	Property	Set As
Command1	*Caption*	*Pre&vious Month*
Command1	*Height*	*375*
Command1	*Left*	*600*
Command1	*Top*	*2760*
Command1	*Width*	*1695*
Command1	*Name*	*cmdPreviousMonth*
Command2	*Caption*	*&Next Month*
Command2	*Height*	*375*
Command2	*Left*	*2400*
Command2	*Top*	*2760*
Command2	*Width*	*1575*
Command2	*Name*	*cmdNextMonth*
Command3	*Caption*	*Today*
Command3	*Height*	*375*
Command3	*Left*	*4080*
Command3	*Top*	*2760*
Command3	*Width*	*1575*
Command3	*Name*	*cmdToday*

***Table 8.9** The properties for the Date Selection buttons.*

ADDING THE TIMER CONTROL TO THE PROJECT

As you have learned, the *prjPlanner* project lets the user set alarms on appointments, which the program will later alert the user to when the appointment time arrives. To periodically check whether an appointment time has arrived, the program uses a *Timer* control. To place the *Timer* control on your project form, perform the following steps:

1. If Visual Basic is not displaying the *frmPlanner* form within an object window, double-click your mouse on the *frmPlanner* form listing within the Project Explorer. Visual Basic will open the *frmPlanner* form.

2. Within Visual Basic, select the View menu Toolbox option. Visual Basic will open the Toolbox.

3. Within the Toolbox, double-click your mouse on the Timer icon, which looks similar to a stopwatch. Visual Basic will place the *Timer1* control in the center of the *frmPlanner* form.

4. Select the View menu Properties Window option to display the Properties Window. Within the Properties Window, change the properties for the *Timer1* control to the values Table 8.10 lists.

Object	Property	Setting
Timer1	*Interval*	30000
Timer1	*Left*	120
Timer1	*Top*	240
Timer1	*Name*	*tmrPlanner*

Table 8.10 *The newly named **tmrPlanner** control's properties.*

WRITING THE CODE FOR THE prjPLANNER PROJECT

In the *prjPlanner* project, you will write code for each control on the *frmPlanner* form, and you will write procedures to communicate with the controls and the *Planner.mdb* database. First, you will declare variables that the procedures will use. You will then write code for the program's procedures and control events.

DECLARING THE VARIABLES

You will declare most variables in the General–Declarations section in the *frmPlanner* Code Window. Remember, when you declare variables in the General–Declarations section of the *frmPlanner* form, all procedures and functions in the form code can use the variables. The General–Declarations section of the *frmPlanner* form declares several flag variables, such as *OpenRecordset* and *Initializing*, which the program uses to keep itself aware of certain ongoing conditions. It also declares variables to store information about the month, day, and year of the calendar selection, some counting variables, and variables to store and access the information from the *Planner.mdb* database. The following code implements the *prjPlanner* project variables in the *frmPlanner* form's General–Declarations section:

```
Option Explicit
Dim OpenRecordset As Boolean, Initializing As Boolean, NoRecord As Boolean
Dim OptionIndex As Integer
Dim tempMonth As Integer, tempYear As Integer, YesNo As Integer
Dim tempText As String, SelectString As String, DatabaseName As String
Dim FindString As String
Dim i As Integer, j As Integer, n As Integer
Dim r As Integer, s As Integer, t As Integer, v As Integer
Dim AmPm As String
Dim SelectedDate As PlannerDate
Dim PlannerWS As Workspace, PlannerDB As Database, PlannerRS As Recordset
```

WRITING THE CODE FOR THE FORM_LOAD EVENT

As you have learned, each form in a Visual Basic program invokes its *Load* event when the program loads the form into memory. In the case of the *frmPlanner* form, the *Load* event occurs when the project starts because the *frmPlanner* form is the startup form for the project. The following code implements the *Form_Load* event:

```
Private Sub Form_Load()
  Initializing = True
  SelectedDate = GetDate
  With calPlanner
    .Day = SelectedDate.Day
    .Month = SelectedDate.Month
    .Year = SelectedDate.Year
  End With
  fraDatabase.Visible = False
  OpenDatabase
  Initializing = False
  QueryTable
  InitializeGrid
  FillGrid
  ViewPlanner
End Sub
```

As you can see, the *frmPlanner* form's *Load* event calls the *GetDate* procedure, which will retrieve the system date and split it into three pieces. The *Load* event uses the values *GetDate* returns to initialize the *calPlanner* control's day, month, and year values. The program code calls the *OpenDatabase* procedure, which opens the database. The program code also calls the *QueryTable, FillGrid,* and *ViewPlanner* procedures, which respectively open the *DayMonthYear* table within the *Planner.mdb* database, initialize the legend for the *flxPlanner* control and, finally, display any appointments or things to do on the current day within the *flxPlanner* control.

WRITING THE CODE FOR THE GETDATE PROCEDURE

Now that you have written the code for the *Form_Load* event, you will write the first procedure, *GetDate,* which will retrieve the system date and split it into three component pieces. The three pieces will represent day, month, and year values. As you have learned, the *calPlanner* control has *Day, Month*, and *Year* properties. You can set or retrieve these properties in code. As you can see in the *Form_Load* event, you will use a *With* statement to set these *calPlanner* control properties. The *Day, Month,* and *Year* properties must be integer values. Because the system date returns a date in the month/day/year format, you must split the system date into three integer pieces. The program will store these integer pieces within a structure of type *PlannerDate,* as the next section explains.

You will use the *Format* function to generate a date string, and the *Left$, Mid$,* and *Right$* functions to return the components of the system date. After you have a month, day, and year value in the *Month, Day,* and *Year* member variables, the function will return those values to the calling procedure. The following code implements the *GetDate* function:

```
Private Function GetDate() As PlannerDate
  Dim DateString As String

  DateString = Format(Date, "mmddyyyy")
  With GetDate
    .Month = Left(DateString, 2)
    .Day = Mid(DateString, 3, 2)
    .Year = Right(DateString, 4)
  End With
End Function
```

LOOKING AT THE PLANNERDATE STRUCTURE DEFINITION

As you saw in the previous section, the *GetDate* function returns an integer-formatted date within a structure of type *PlannerDate.* To define the *PlannerDate* structure, you must first add a module to the project. To add the module to the project and define the *PlannerDate* structure, perform the following steps:

1. Within Visual Basic, select the Project menu Add Module option. Visual Basic will add a module named *Module1* to the project.

2. Double-click your mouse on the Module1 icon within the Project window. Visual Basic will open the *Module1* module.

3. Select the View menu Properties Window option to display the Properties Window. Change the *Module1* module name to *mdlPlanner*.

4. Select the File menu Save mdlPlanner As option to save the *mdlPlanner* module. Visual Basic will display the Save File As dialog box.

5. Within the Save File As dialog box, click your mouse on OK to save the module. Visual Basic will return to the Code window.

6. Within the *mdlPlanner* Code window, enter the following structure definition:

```
Type PlannerDate
   Day As String * 2
   Month As String * 2
   Year As String * 4
End Type
```

7. After you finish entering the structure definition, click your mouse on the Close button to close the *mdlPlanner* Code window.

As you can see, the *PlannerDate* structure uses fixed-length strings to maintain month, day, and year information for a given date value.

WRITING THE CODE FOR THE OPENDATABASE PROCEDURE

Earlier in this chapter, you used the Visual Data Manager to create the *Planner.mdb* database. The *OpenDatabase* procedure will open the *Planner.mdb* database for the *prjPlanner* project to access. The program code looks for the database in the application's current path, and then initializes a *Workspace* object and opens the database within the default workspace. The following code implements the *OpenDatabase* procedure:

```
Private Sub OpenDatabase()
   DatabaseName = App.Path & "\Planner.mdb"
   Set PlannerWS = Workspaces(0)
   Set PlannerDB = PlannerWS.OpenDatabase(DatabaseName)
End Sub
```

Note: *If the database is not within the same directory as the program, you must change the **DatabaseName** string's value.*

WRITING THE CODE FOR THE QUERYTABLE PROCEDURE

Now that you have an open database in the *PlannerDB* object, you can open one or more recordsets. The *QueryTable* procedure will use an SQL query to open the *DayMonthYear* table and assign some of its contents to the *PlannerRS* object. The *QueryTable* procedure opens a recordset that contains all the current month's records. The *QueryTable* procedure also sets certain flag variables, such as *NoRecord*, to indicate whether or not it was successful in opening the database and whether there are one or more records within the newly opened recordset. Finally, the code will assign the *calPlanner* control's current *Month* and *Year* properties to the *tempMonth* and *tempYear* variables to retain the current month and year values for later use. The following code implements the *QueryTable* procedure:

```
Private Sub QueryTable()
   If OpenRecordset Then
      PlannerRS.Close
   End If
   SelectString = "SELECT * FROM DayMonthYear WHERE Month = " & _
      calPlanner.Month
```

```
   Set PlannerRS = PlannerDB.OpenRecordset(SelectString)
   If PlannerRS.RecordCount > 0 Then
     OpenRecordset = True
     PlannerRS.MoveLast
     NoRecord = False
   Else
     NoRecord = True
   End If
   tempMonth = calPlanner.Month
   tempYear = calPlanner.Year
End Sub
```

Writing the Code for the *InitializeGrid* Procedure

As you have learned, you can set the size of the *flxPlanner* control in code. The *InitializeGrid* procedure will set up the *flxPlanner* control with a set size that avoids any gaps between columns (or rows). The *InitializeGrid* procedure uses a *With* statement with the *flxPlanner* object to make more clear to other programmers the operations it performs against the *flxPlanner* control. The *InitializeGrid* procedure first clears the entire grid of any text, then sets a few miscellaneous properties, including the default row height and the width of each column in the grid. The following code implements the *InitializeGrid* procedure:

```
Private Sub InitializeGrid()
  With flxPlanner
    .Clear
    .AllowUserResizing = flexResizeBoth
    .RowHeight(-1) = 230
    .RowHeight(0) = 400
    .ColWidth(0) = 900
    .ColWidth(1) = 4310
    .ColWidth(2) = 4310
  End With
End Sub
```

Writing the Code for the *FillGrid* Procedure

As you have learned, each time you select a different month in the *calPlanner* control, the program will fill the *PlannerRS* object with the new month's schedule entries. The *FillGrid* procedure sets the *flxPlanner* control's fixed row and column headings to display the schedule, which starts at 5:00 a.m. and ends a 9:00 p.m. The following code implements the *FillGrid* procedure:

```
Private Sub FillGrid()
  Dim CurrentHour as Integer

  AmPm = "am"
  CurrentHour = 5
  With flxPlanner
    .Clear
    .Row = 0
    For s = 0 To 2
      .Col = s
      .CellAlignment = 4
    Next s
    .Col = 0
    .Text = "Time"
    .Col = 1
    .Text = "Schedule"
    .Col = 2
    .Text = "Things To Do"
    .Col = 0
```

```
      For n = 1 To 17
         .Row = n
         .CellAlignment = 4
         .Text = CurrentHour & ":00" & AmPm
        If n >= 7 Then
          AmPm = "pm"
           If CurrentHour >= 12 Then
              CurrentHour = CurrentHour - 12
           End If
        End If
        CurrentHour = CurrentHour + 1
      Next n
   End With
End Sub
```

292 WRITING THE CODE FOR THE VIEWPLANNER PROCEDURE

As you have learned, the *InitializeGrid* and *FillGrid* procedures set up the *flxPlanner* control by initializing the size, row headings, and column headings. The *ViewPlanner* procedure will find the specific day selected on the *calPlanner* control and display that day's schedule entries. The *ViewPlanner* procedure uses the *PlannerRS* object's *FindFirst* method to find the day to display in the schedule. If there are no appointments or things to do that day, the procedure will exit without writing to the display.

On the other hand, if there are appointments, the remaining program code in the procedure will use the *MoveNext* method to count through each matching record in the database. The program will add the appointment or thing to do to the display and set the background color to green for any appointments on which the user has previously set an alarm. The following code implements the *ViewPlanner* procedure:

```
Private Sub ViewPlanner()
  Dim SqlText As String
    With calPlanner
    SqlText = "Select * From DayMonthYear WHERE Month = " & .Month
    SqlText = SqlText & " And Day = " & .Day
    SqlText = SqlText & " And Year = " & .Year
  End With
  Set PlannerRS = PlannerDB.OpenRecordset(SqlText)
  If PlannerRS.RecordCount = 0 Then Exit Sub
  PlannerRS.MoveLast
  PlannerRS.MoveFirst
  For i = 1 To PlannerRS.RecordCount
    flxPlanner.Row = PlannerRS("row")
    flxPlanner.Col = PlannerRS("column")
    If PlannerRS("alarm") Then flxPlanner.CellBackColor = RGB(0, 255, 128)
    flxPlanner.Text = PlannerRS("schedule")
    PlannerRS.MoveNext
  Next i
End Sub
```

WRITING THE CODE FOR THE CALPLANNER_AFTERUPDATE EVENT

As you have learned, the *prjPlanner* project will use the *calPlanner* control to display dates. The *calPlanner_AfterUpdate* event checks to be sure the program is not initializing, then calls the *DateChange* procedure if it is not. If the program is initializing, the *DateChange* procedure simply exits. The *DateChange* procedure, in turn, calls several other procedures. The following code implements the *calPlanner_AfterUpdate* event:

```
Private Sub calPlanner_AfterUpdate()
  If Not Initializing Then DateChange
End Sub
```

LOOKING AT THE DATECHANGE PROCEDURE

As you saw in the previous section, the *calPlanner_AfterUpdate* event calls the *DateChange* procedure. The *DateChange* procedure updates the recordset to reflect the currently selected month and day, and then updates the actual planner display. The following code implements the *DateChange* procedure:

```
Private Sub DateChange()
  txtSchedule.Text = ""
  fraDatabase.Visible = False
  If (calPlanner.Month = tempMonth) And _
    (calPlanner.Year = tempYear) Then _
    QueryTable
  FillGrid
  ViewPlanner
  calPlanner.Refresh
  flxPlanner.Refresh
End Sub
```

293

WRITING THE CODE FOR THE *FLXPLANNER* CONTROL'S EVENTS

As you have learned, the *prjPlanner* project will use the *flxPlanner* control to display schedule entries. The *flxPlanner_Click* event will display the *fraDatabase* control and assign the current cell contents to the *txtSchedule* control. The *flxPlanner_Click* event's code first checks to determine whether there are records in the recordset for the current day; if there are not, it does not enable the Edit or Set Alarm options in the frame. The code then checks for contents within the cell, and sets the focus to the Add or Edit options, depending on whether contents are present or not. Finally, the program code disables the alarm buttons if the user selects a Things To Do cell. The following code implements the *flxPlanner_Click* event:

```
Private Sub flxPlanner_Click()
  fraDatabase.Visible = True
  If PlannerRS.RecordCount = 0 Then
    optSchedule(3).Enabled = False
    optSchedule(2).Enabled = False
    optSchedule(1).Enabled = False
  Else
    optSchedule(3).Enabled = True
    optSchedule(2).Enabled = True
    optSchedule(1).Enabled = True
    If flxPlanner.Text = "" Then
      optSchedule(0).Value = True
      optSchedule_Click 0
    Else
      optSchedule(1).Value = True
      optSchedule_Click 1
    End If
    tempText = flxPlanner.Text
    txtSchedule.Text = tempText
    If flxPlanner.Col = 2 Then
      optSchedule(3).Enabled = False
    Else
      optSchedule(3).Enabled = True
    End If
  End If
End Sub
```

In addition to the *Click* event, the *prjPlanner* project includes program code in the *flxPlanner_GotFocus* event. The program code within the event simply sets the *txtSchedule* text box's text property equal to the text the currently selected cell within the grid contains. The following code implements the *flxPlanner_GotFocus* event:

```
Private Sub flxPlanner_GotFocus()
  txtSchedule.Text = flxPlanner.Text
End Sub
```

WRITING THE CODE FOR THE FINDRECORD PROCEDURE

As you have learned, the *fraDatabase* frame control lets you add, edit, delete, or set alarms for records in the *DayMonthYear* table and lets you add or edit text in the *flxPlanner* control. Before you can edit, delete, or set an alarm for a record, you must locate the correct record in the *PlannerRS* recordset. The *FindRecord* procedure uses the *FindFirst, FindNext,* and *MoveFirst* methods to locate the record whose entry it receives within the *RecordText* parameter. The following code implements the *FindRecord* procedure:

```
Private Sub FindRecord(ByVal RecordText As String)
  If NoRecord Then
    MsgBox "No Records", vbCritical
    Exit Sub
  End If
  FindString = "Day = " & calPlanner.Day
  PlannerRS.MoveFirst
  PlannerRS.FindFirst (FindString)
  For j = 1 To PlannerRS.RecordCount
    If PlannerRS.Fields("schedule") <> RecordText And _
        PlannerRS("row") <> flxPlanner.Row Then
      PlannerRS.FindNext (FindString)
    Else
      Exit For
    End If
  Next j
End Sub
```

WRITING THE CODE FOR THE ADDENTRY PROCEDURE

As you have learned, the *fraDatabase* control lets you add, edit, delete, or set alarms for records in the *DayMonthYear* table and lets you add or edit text in the *flxPlanner* control. Before you can add text to the *DayMonthYear* table, you must type the text in the *txtAddEdit* text box within the *fraDatabase* control. After you click on the Add Record button, the program code will call the *AddEntry* procedure, which adds the text. The *AddEntry* procedure adds a new appointment, requeries the recordset, and displays the schedule with the new appointment in the correct location. The following code implements the *AddEntry* procedure:

```
Private Sub AddEntry()
  If flxPlanner.Row < 1 Or flxPlanner.Col < 1 Then
    MsgBox "Must pick a valid cell!"
  Else
    PlannerRS.AddNew
      PlannerRS("day") = calPlanner.Day
      PlannerRS("month") = calPlanner.Month
      PlannerRS("year") = calPlanner.Year
      PlannerRS("row") = flxPlanner.Row
      PlannerRS("column") = flxPlanner.Col
      PlannerRS("schedule") = txtSchedule.Text
    PlannerRS.Update
    If NoRecord Then NoRecord = Not NoRecord
    PlannerRS.Requery
    PlannerRS.MoveLast
    ViewPlanner
  End If
  flxPlanner.SetFocus
End Sub
```

Writing the Code for the EditEntry Procedure

As you have learned, the *fraDatabase* frame control includes component controls that let you add, edit, delete, or set alarms for records in the *DayMonthYear* table and add or edit text in the *flxPlanner* control. The *EditEntry* procedure lets you edit the text in the *DayMonthYear* table. After you edit the text within the *txtAddEdit* text box, you can click on the Edit Record button which, in turn, will call the *EditEntry* procedure. The following code implements the *EditEntry* procedure:

```
Private Sub EditEntry()
  If flxPlanner.Text = "" Then
    MsgBox "Nothing To Edit"
    flxPlanner.CellBackColor = QBColor(15)
    Exit Sub
  End If
  FindRecord flxPlanner.Text
  PlannerRS.Edit
    PlannerRS("schedule") = txtAddEdit.Text
  PlannerRS.Update
  PlannerRS.Requery
  PlannerRs.MoveLast
  tempText = txtAddEdit.Text
  flxPlanner.CellForeColor = QBColor(0)
  flxPlanner.CellBackColor = QBColor(15)
  ViewPlanner
End Sub
```

To edit a record, you must use the *Edit* method to place the *PlannerRS* recordset in an edit mode. In the edit mode, the program will assign a word or number value to the changed field in the *Recordset*. After you assign a value to the updated field, the *Update* method closes the edit mode. The procedure then uses the *Requery* method to refresh the recordset and calls the *ViewPlanner* procedure to update the display.

Writing the Code for the DeleteEntry Procedure

As you have learned, the *fraDatabase* frame control lets you add, edit, delete, or set alarms for records in the *DayMonthYear* table. The *DeleteEntry* procedure lets you delete records from the *DayMonthYear* table. Before you can delete a record or message, you must click your mouse on the Delete Record option button in the *fraDatabase* control, and then click your mouse on the Delete button within the *fraDatabase* frame control. The following code implements the *DeleteEntry* procedure:

```
Private Sub DeleteEntry()
  If flxPlanner.Text = "" Then
    flxPlanner.CellBackColor = QBColor(15)
    MsgBox "No Record To Delete"
    Exit Sub
  End If
  YesNo = MsgBox("Delete this entry?? --> " & flxPlanner.Text, vbYesNo, _
    "DELETE")
  If YesNo = vbYes Then
    FindRecord flxPlanner.Text
    PlannerRS.Delete
    DoEvents
    PlannerRS.Requery
    FillGrid
    ViewPlanner
  Else
    flxPlanner.CellBackColor = QBColor(15)
  End If
  flxPlanner.SetFocus
End Sub
```

To delete a record from a recordset, you must use the *Delete* method, as the *DeleteEntry* procedure does after verifying the deletion. The *DeleteEntry* procedure also verifies a second time that you want to delete the record before it deletes the record. The *Delete* method instructs the database engine to delete the current record within the recordset which invoked the method. After you delete the entire record, the *Requery* method refreshes the recordset and the *ViewPlanner* procedure updates the program display.

WRITING THE CODE FOR THE SETALARM PROCEDURE

As you have learned, the *fraDatabase* frame control lets you add, edit, delete, or set alarms for records in the *DayMonthYear* table. The *SetAlarm* procedure sets the *Alarm* field in the *DayMonthYear* table to *True*. Before you can set an alarm for a record, you must click your mouse on the Set Alarm option in the *fraDatabase* control, and then click your mouse on the Set Alarm button. The following code implements the *SetAlarm* procedure:

```
Private Sub SetAlarm()
  Dim CurrentRow As Integer, CurrentCol As Integer
  If flxPlanner.Text = "" Then
    MsgBox "Nothing To Remind"
    Exit Sub
  End If
  If flxPlanner.Col = 1 Then
    CurrentRow = flxPlanner.Row
    CurrentCol = flxPlanner.Col
    FindRecord flxPlanner.Text
    flxPlanner.Row = CurrentRow
    flxPlanner.Col = CurrentCol
    flxPlanner.CellBackColor = RGB(0, 255, 128)
    PlannerRS.Edit
      PlannerRS("alarm") = True
    PlannerRS.Update
    PlannerRS.Requery
    PlannerRS.MoveLast
    OptionIndex = OptionIndex + 1
    cmdSchedule.Caption = "Remove Alarm"
    cmdSchedule.BackColor = QBColor(6)
    ViewPlanner
    flxPlanner.Row = CurrentRow
    flxPlanner.Col = CurrentCol
    flxPlanner.SetFocus
  Else
    MsgBox "Can't set an alarm on a 'Thing to do!'"
  End If
End Sub
```

The *SetAlarm* procedure first uses an *If-Then* statement to ensure that the current record contains an entry; if the record does not, the function exits with a message. The *SetAlarm* procedure uses a second *If-Then* statement to ensure that the user can set alarms only on appointments, not things to do. After it sets the alarm within the database, the *SetAlarm* procedure changes the cell's background color to a light green and changes the command button's caption to *Remove Alarm*.

WRITING THE ALARM CODE

As you have learned, the *prjPlanner* project lets you set an alarm on a scheduled appointment. The project uses the *tmrPlanner* control that you placed onto the form earlier in this chapter to regularly check appointments and determine if an alarm is due. The *tmrPlanner* control invokes its *Timer* event every 30 seconds, and checks the current time to determine whether the current time is the top of the hour (00 minutes). If so, the *Timer* event calls the *CheckAlarm* procedure. If not, the *tmrPlanner_Timer* event simply exits. The following code implements the *tmrPlanner_Timer* event:

```
Private Sub tmrPlanner_Timer()
   Dim DateString As String

   DateString = Format(Time, "Short Time")
   If Right(DateString, 2) = "00" Then CheckAlarm DateString
End Sub
```

As you have learned, the *CheckAlarm* procedure accepts the current time and date as its only parameters. The *CheckAlarm* procedure then compares that current time and date to the records in the database to determine if an alarmed appointment exists at the current date and time. The *CheckAlarm* procedure creates its own database rather than using the *PlannerRS* database, because you may actually be viewing or adding entries on another date when an alarmed appointment occurs, and the program should respond to that appointment without forcing you to return to the current date. Finally, if the *CheckAlarm* procedure finds an alarm entry, it displays a message box alerting you to the alarm and its nature. Otherwise, *CheckAlarm* exits without notice to the user. The following code implements the *CheckAlarm* procedure:

```
Private Sub CheckAlarm(ByVal Hour As String)
   Dim CurrentHour As Integer, TodaysDate As PlannerDate
   Dim CurrentRow As Integer, CurrentCol As Integer
   Dim TempSQL As String, TempRs As Recordset

   CurrentHour = Val(Hour) - 4
   If CurrentHour < 1 Or CurrentHour > 21 Then Exit Sub
   TodaysDate = GetDate
   With TodaysDate
      TempSQL = "Select * From DayMonthYear WHERE Month = " & Val(.Month) &" _
         And Day = " & Val(.Day) & " And Year = " & .Year & " _
         And Row = " & CurrentHour
   End With
   Set TempRs = PlannerDB.OpenRecordset(TempSQL)
   If TempRs.RecordCount = 0 Then Exit Sub
   TempRs.MoveLast
   TempRs.MoveFirst
   For i = 1 To TempRs.RecordCount
      MsgBox ("Alarm:: " & TempRs("Schedule") & " on " & Format(Date, _
         "Medium Date"))
      TempRs.Edit
         TempRs("Alarm") = False
      TempRs.Update
      TempRs.MoveNext
   Next
   ViewPlanner
End Sub
```

Writing the Code for the RemoveAlarm Procedure

As you have learned, the *fraDatabase* frame control lets you remove alarms from records that you have previously set. The *RemoveAlarm* procedure sets the *Alarm* field in the *DayMonthYear* table to *False*, removes the green background color from the cell, and changes the caption on the command button to *Set Alarm*. The following code implements the *RemoveAlarm* procedure:

```
Private Sub RemoveAlarm()
   flxPlanner.CellBackColor = QBColor(15)
   FindRecord flxPlanner.Text
   PlannerRS.Edit
      PlannerRS("alarm") = False
   PlannerRS.Update
   PlannerRS.Requery
```

```
      PlannerRS.MoveLast
      cmdSchedule.Caption = "Set Alarm"
      cmdSchedule.BackColor = QBColor(10)
      OptionIndex = OptionIndex - 1
      flxPlanner.SetFocus
   End Sub
```

WRITING THE CODE FOR THE OPTION BUTTON ARRAY

The name of your option button array is *optDatabase.* An option button array has more than one option button, and the program assigns an integer index value to each option button in an option button array, starting with zero. The *optDatabase* option button array has four option buttons and four integer *Index* values, which are 0, 1, 2, and 3, respectively. When you click on an option button during run time, the program automatically remembers which *Index* value you have selected. Therefore, the program can track what option you have chosen. The program will use the *Click* event to determine which option button you have selected.

When you click your mouse on an option button, the option button *Click* event assigns the current index value (that is, the index that appears after you clicked your mouse) to a parameter named *Index.* During the *Click* event, the program will assign the *Index* parameter value to the *OptionIndex* variable. Other procedures can use the *OptionIndex* variable out of the *Click* event's local scope. When you click your mouse on one of the *optSchedule* option buttons, the *Caption* and *Backcolor* properties of the *cmdSchedule* command button change values to reflect the option button you selected. Additionally, if the user selects the Add/Remove Alarm option, the program code will check the current entry's *Alarm* field to determine whether or not it should display the Add or Remove caption on the *cmdSchedule* button. The following code implements the *optSchedule_Click* event:

```
   Private Sub optSchedule_Click(Index As Integer)
     Dim CurrentRow As Integer, CurrentCol As Integer

     Select Case Index
       Case 0
         OptionIndex = Index
         cmdSchedule.Caption = "Add"
         cmdSchedule.BackColor = QBColor(11)
       Case 1
         OptionIndex = Index
         cmdSchedule.Caption = "Edit"
         cmdSchedule.BackColor = QBColor(14)
       Case 2
         OptionIndex = Index
         cmdSchedule.Caption = "Delete"
         cmdSchedule.BackColor = QBColor(12)
       Case 3
         CurrentRow = flxPlanner.Row
         CurrentCol = flxPlanner.Col
         If PlannerRS.RecordCount > 0 Then
           FindRecord flxPlanner.Text
         Else
           Exit Sub
         End If
         flxPlanner.Row = CurrentRow
         flxPlanner.Col = CurrentCol
         If PlannerRS("Alarm") = True Then
             OptionIndex = Index + 1
             cmdSchedule.Caption = "Remove Alarm"
             cmdSchedule.BackColor = QBColor(6)
         Else
             OptionIndex = Index
             cmdSchedule.Caption = "Set Alarm"
```

```
            cmdSchedule.BackColor = QBColor(10)
        End If
    End Select
    flxPlanner.Refresh
End Sub
```

WRITING THE CODE FOR THE SCHEDULING BUTTONS

As you have learned, the *Caption* and *Backcolor* properties of the *cmdSchedule* command button control will change when you choose an option from the option button array. When you click your mouse on the Add Record, Edit Record, Delete Record, Set Alarm, or Remove Alarm option buttons, the *cmdSchedule* command button's *Caption* property reflects your choice. After you click your mouse on the *cmdSchedule* command button, the *Click* event first makes sure that you have selected only a single cell. The program code then checks the *OptionIndex* variable to determine the currently selected option. The event then invokes the correct procedure for the activity. The following code implements the *cmdSchedule_Click* event:

```
Private Sub cmdSchedule_Click()
  With flxPlanner
    If (.RowSel - .Row) > 0 Or (.ColSel - .Col) > 0 Then
      MsgBox "Please select only a single cell for modification!"
      Exit Sub
    End If
  End With
  Select Case OptionIndex
    Case 0
      AddEntry
    Case 1
      EditEntry
    Case 2
      DeleteEntry
    Case 3
      SetAlarm
    Case 4
      RemoveAlarm
  End Select
End Sub
```

In addition to performing a scheduling operation, you have the choice to cancel the current operation. To do so, you must click your mouse on the Cancel button. The program code within the *cmdCancel_Click* event hides the frame until you click on another selection within the grid. The following code implements the *cmdCancel_Click* event:

```
Private Sub cmdCancel_Click()
  fraDatabase.Visible = False
End Sub
```

WRITING THE CODE FOR THE DATE CHANGE BUTTONS

When you created the form for the *prjPlanner* project, you included three buttons that the user could use to change the currently selected date within the *Calendar* control. These buttons, *cmdNextMonth*, *cmdPreviousMonth*, and *cmdToday*, all use similar code to change the current date. For example, the *Click* events for both the *cmdNextMonth* and *cmdPreviousMonth* buttons each invoke only a single *Calendar* control method, as shown here:

```
Private Sub cmdNextMonth_Click()
  calPlanner.NextMonth
End Sub

Private Sub cmdPreviousMonth_Click()
  calPlanner.PreviousMonth
End Sub
```

The *cmdToday* button's *Click* event, on the other hand, performs more extended processing. The program code first uses the *GetDate* function to obtain the current date, and then sets the *calPlanner* control's displayed date to the current date. Finally, the program code invokes the *DateChange* function to update the information the grid will display. The following code implements the *cmdToday_Click* event:

```
Private Sub cmdToday_Click()
   SelectedDate = GetDate
   With calPlanner
     .Day = SelectedDate.Day
     .Month = SelectedDate.Month
     .Year = SelectedDate.Year
   End With
   DateChange
End Sub
```

300 *ENHANCEMENTS YOU CAN MAKE TO THE prjPLANNER PROJECT*

Now that you know how to use a *Microsoft Calendar* control and a *Microsoft Flex Grid* control, you can make enhancements to your project. You can create a multiple document project and open separate windows for each day. You can expand the *Microsoft Flex Grid* control to include other planner items, such as a shopping list. You can also add more *Microsoft Flex Grid* controls and divide your organizer into sections. In addition, you can add printing capability to print your schedule on a day-to-day basis.

PUTTING IT ALL TOGETHER

This chapter's project, *prjPlanner*, introduced you to the *Microsoft Flex Grid* control, the *Microsoft Calendar* control, and a Microsoft *Access* database. With the *Microsoft Calendar* control, you can display and track day, month, and year data for hundreds of years. In addition, you can expand the *Microsoft Flex Grid* control to hold more than the three columns and 18 rows in the *prjPlanner* project. Only the amount of memory on your computer limits the number of rows and columns.

You have also learned that a Microsoft *Access* database file provides a storage place for data. The database organizes data into rows and columns. Within a Visual Basic program, you can communicate with a Microsoft *Access* database using *Workspace*, *Database*, and *Recordset* objects. In Chapter 9, "Using Databases and ActiveX to Manage Household Inventory," you will use a database to create a simple household inventory program. Before you continue with Chapter 9, however, make sure you understand the following key concepts:

✓ Using the *Microsoft Calendar* control, you can track a selected month, day, and year, from January 1, 1900 to February 28, 2100.

✓ Using the *Visual Data Manager*, you can create database tables, fields,quieries, and reports.

✓ Using the *Microsoft Flex Grid* control, you can organize data into rows and columns.

✓ Using a Microsoft *Access* database, you can store data in multiple tables of rows and columns.

✓ Within your Visual Basic programs, you can use Structured Query Language (SQL) to communicate with a Microsoft *Access* database.

✓ Using a *Frame* control, you can contain multiple controls and make them visible to the user or remove them from a form.

Chapter 9

Using Databases and ActiveX to Manage Household Inventory

As you have learned in previous chapters, two of Visual Basic's most powerful features are its ability to create custom ActiveX controls, and the ease with which you can write programs to access databases. You have also learned that Windows programmers use component-based program design to write their Windows programs. Within this chapter, you will use these features and the principles of component-based program design to create a custom ActiveX control. You will then use your custom-designed ActiveX control within another program as an interface to a database. The custom ActiveX control that you will create within this chapter will include properties and methods. You will use object-oriented design principles when you create the custom control. The custom control's methods and internal functions will include additions, deletions, and edits to the underlying database, as well as error-checking routines to handle a user's "bad" data entry.

301

As Chapter 8, "Creating a Schedule Planner," discusses, one of the most important steps in writing programs that use databases is to include error-checking code within the program's routines that manipulate the database. Such code will protect against the user's intentionally or inadvertently entering "bad" data (such as text for a numeric field), which may crash the database or the program, or both. Within this chapter's *prjActiveInventory* project (a component in the *prjHouseholdGroup* group project), you will handle the database error-checking the custom *Xhousehold.ocx* control that you will create requires. Over the course of this chapter, you will apply the techniques that you have learned in earlier chapters to create a program that combines two of Visual Basic's most common activities: creating custom controls and managing database information. By the time you finish this chapter, you will understand the following key concepts:

- Within your Visual Basic programs, you can use ActiveX controls to perform specific processing and to protect data from other parts of your programs.

- Your programs can use *Property Get* and *Property Let* procedures to perform error-checking and assignments for a public property of a control or class.

- You can create properties for your ActiveX controls in one of two ways: with public variables, or with private member variables that use *Property Get* and *Property Let* procedures. As a rule, you should use the second way to provide the best encapsulation for your control.

- Within your custom ActiveX controls, you can make a property read-only by not writing a *Property Let* procedure for that property.

- You can use ActiveX controls to maintain multiple, independent connections to the same database within a single program.

- Your custom ActiveX controls should use public methods to control the calling program's access to the protected data.

- You can create properties for your custom ActiveX controls that let the controls return meaningful, known error values to the calling programs.

USING THE *prjActiveHousehold* PROJECT

Before you design the *prjActiveHousehold* project and the *prjHouseholdGroup* group project, you may find it helpful to run the *prjActiveHousehold.exe* program. The companion CD-ROM that accompanies this book contains the *prjActiveHousehold.exe* program within the *Chapter09* directory. As with every other program on the CD-ROM, you should run the Jamsa Press *setup.exe* program to install the *prjActiveHousehold.exe* program to your computer's hard drive before you run it. After you install the *prjActiveHousehold.exe* program to your computer's hard drive, you can run it from the Start menu. To run the program, select the Windows Start menu Run option. Windows will display the Run dialog box. Within the Run dialog box, enter *x:\vbpl\Chapter09\prjActiveHousehold.exe*, where *x* corresponds to the drive letter of the hard drive on which you installed the *prjActiveHousehold.exe* program, and click your mouse on OK. Windows will display the *prjActiveHousehold.exe* program, as shown in Figure 9.1.

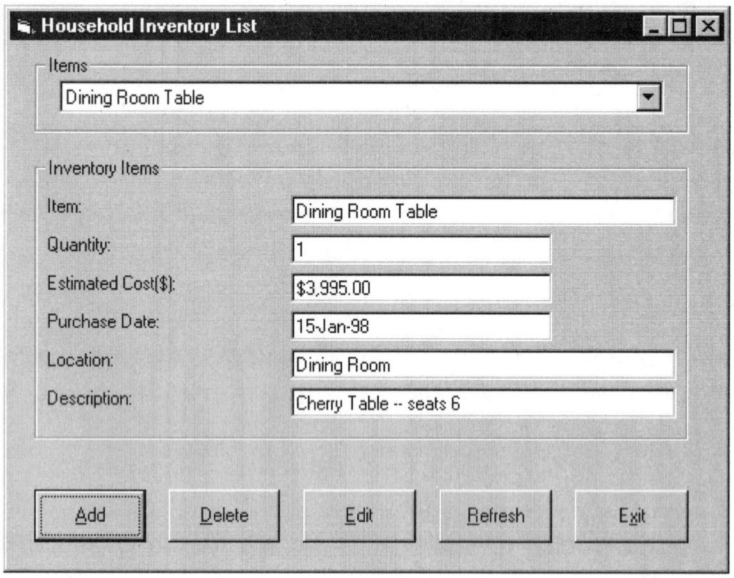

Figure 9.1 *The **prjActiveHousehold.exe** program's startup screen.*

Before you use the *prjActiveHousehold.exe* program, take a moment to familiarize yourself with the controls on the form. The *prjActiveHousehold* project will let you maintain an inventory of goods (such as furniture, art, equipment, and other household fixtures) within the *household.mdb* database. The program lets you maintain item names, descriptions, quantities, estimated costs, purchase dates, and locations. At the form's top, you will see a combo box that you can use to select what item you want to view. Below the combo box, within the frame labeled Inventory Items, you will see information about the currently selected item. While the Inventory Items frame is invisible to the user, the frame and all its contents are actually a single ActiveX control that the program uses to maintain the database. Across the form's bottom, you will see five command buttons, labeled Add, Delete, Edit, Refresh, and Exit, respectively. You will learn more about the buttons later in this section.

RUNNING PRJACTIVEHOUSEHOLD FROM THE CD-ROM

As you have learned, you must first install many of the programs that you will use in this book to your computer's hard drive before you can use the programs. Because the *prjActiveHousehold.exe* program creates a permanent database within its execution directory, which the program tries to maintain and update, you must install the *prjActiveHousehold.exe* program to a drive before you use it. If you try to run the *prjActiveHousehold.exe* program from the CD-ROM, the program will let you view the existing records, but it will not let you add new records or edit or delete the existing records.

To learn more about the Jamsa Press *setup.exe* program, see the "What's on the *Visual Basic Programmer's Library* Companion CD-ROM" section at the back of this book.

To view information about an item, select that item within the combo box at the form's top. For example, the sample database that *setup.exe* installed with the program includes an Entertainment Center entry. If you select the Entertainment Center entry within the combo box, your screen will display output similar to that shown in Figure 9.2.

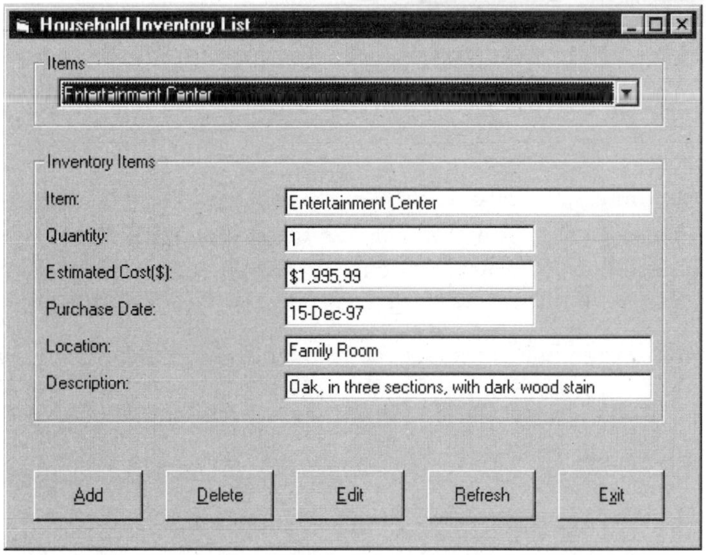

Figure 9.2 Information about the Entertainment Center item.

Now that you have learned a little about the *prjActiveHousehold* project's main form, it is useful to add a sample record of your own to the database. To add a sample record to the database, perform the following steps:

1. Within the Household Inventory List form, click your mouse on the Add button. The program will display the Add Items form.

2. Within the Add Items form, enter the values Table 9.1 lists into their corresponding fields in the form.

Field	Value
Item	Sample Entry
Quantity	1
Estimated Cost($)	100
Purchase Date	2/28/98
Location	Living Room
Description	Table

Table 9.1 The entries for the new record.

3. When you finish entering the values in Table 9.1, the Add Items form will look similar to Figure 9.3.

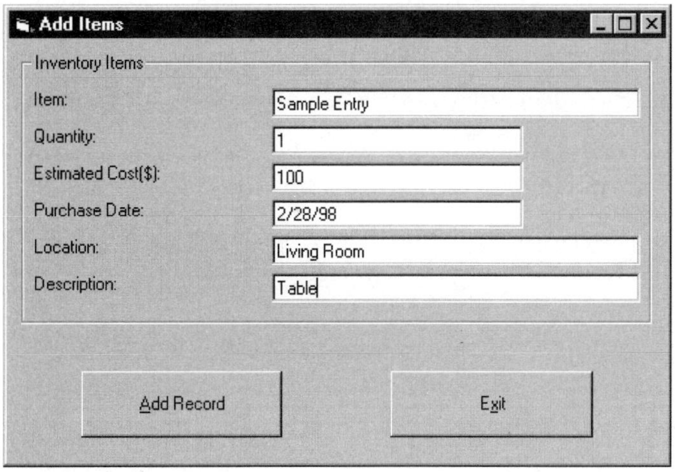

Figure 9.3 The Add Items form after you enter the new sample item.

4. To add the new item to the database, click your mouse on the Add Record button. The program will pause for a moment and then clear the entries from the Add Item form.

5. To exit the Add Item form, click your mouse on the Exit button. The program will return to the main form.

Within the main form, you can easily verify that the program added the new entry to the database. To verify the addition, click your mouse on the combo box at the form's top. Within the list, you will see the Sample Entry entry. Click your mouse on the Sample Entry entry to view it within the program's Household Inventory List form. To change the Sample Entry's item name to "Coffee Table," perform the following steps:

1. Click your mouse on the Edit button at the form's bottom. The program will disable the combo box at the form's top, disable the Add and Delete buttons, change the Edit button to Update, and change the Refresh button to Cancel. Figure 9.4 shows the Household Inventory List form in Edit mode.

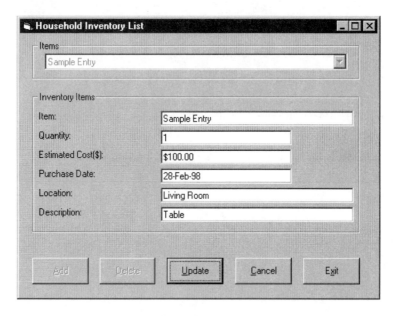

Figure 9.4 *The Household Inventory List form in Edit mode.*

2. Click your mouse within the *Item* field. The program will place the cursor at the field's end.

3. Delete the Sample Entry text from the *Item* field and type *Coffee Table* in its place.

4. After you finish the editing change, click your mouse on the Update button. The program will update the record and refresh the list.

To delete the record you have entered and edited in this section, perform the following steps:

1. Within the *Items* combo box, select the Coffee Table entry. The program will display the Coffee Table information within the Household Inventory List form.

2. Click your mouse on the Delete button. The program will display the "Are you sure you want to delete this record?" message box, as Figure 9.5 shows.

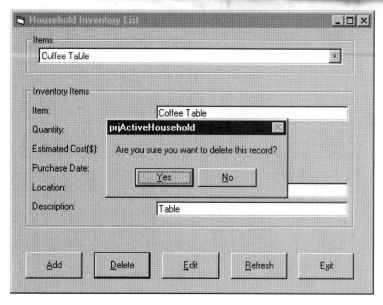

Figure 9.5 *The "Are you sure you want to delete this record?" message box.*

3. If you click your mouse on the Yes button, the program will delete the record and update the *Items* combo box at the form's top.

After you finish using the project, and you have a better understanding of the actions that the project will let the user perform, you can begin to design the *prjHouseholdGroup* group project, which you will do in the next section.

CREATING THE PRJHOUSEHOLDGROUP GROUP PROJECT

As you learned in Chapter 6, "Creating and Using ActiveX Controls," you can use group projects to create custom ActiveX controls. The *prjActiveHousehold* project uses a custom ActiveX control as its interface to the *household.mdb* database, which you will create in a later section in this chapter. To create the *prjHouseholdGroup* group project, you will create two component projects, *prjActiveHousehold* and *prjActiveInventory*. The *prjActiveInventory* project will contain the custom ActiveX control, *Xhousehold*, that you will use to access the database within the *prjActiveHousehold* project. The following sections detail how to create the two component projects and the project group.

CREATING THE PRJACTIVEHOUSEHOLD PROJECT

Now that you have a better idea of what the *prjActiveHousehold* project will look like, you can begin design the project's two empty forms, and add a code module to the project. You will name the two forms *frmViewInventory* and *frmAddItems*, and name the module *mdlRaiseErrors*. The *frmViewInventory* and *frmAddItems* forms will contain all the controls the "Using the *prjActiveHousehold* Project" section introduced. After you set up the *prjActiveHousehold* project, you will design the *prjActiveInventory* project and add the resulting control to the forms within the *prjActiveHousehold* project.

To begin designing the *prjActiveHousehold* project, you must first create an empty form. To create an empty form, perform the following steps:

1. Within Visual Basic, select the File menu New Project option. Visual Basic will open the New Project dialog box.

2. Within the New Project dialog box, double-click your mouse on the Standard EXE icon. Visual Basic will close the New Project dialog box, start a new project, *Project1*, and add a form to the project, *Form1*.

3. Select the Project menu Add Form option. Visual Basic will display the Add Form dialog box.

4. Within the Add Form dialog box, double-click your mouse on the Form icon. Visual Basic will add a new form, *Form2*, to the project.

5. Select the View menu Properties Window option. Visual Basic will open the Properties Window listing the *Form2* properties.

6. Within the Properties Window, change the *Form2* property values to those Table 9.2 lists.

7. Repeat Steps 5 and 6 to change the *Form1* property values to those Table 9.2 lists.

Object	Property	Set As
Form1	*Caption*	*Household Inventory List*
Form1	*Height*	5325
Form1	*Left*	0
Form1	*StartupPosition*	*2 - Center Screen*
Form1	*Top*	0
Form1	*Width*	7065
Form1	*Name*	*frmViewInventory*
Form2	*Caption*	*Add Item*
Form2	*Height*	4575
Form2	*Left*	0
Form2	*StartupPosition*	*1 - CenterOwner*
Form2	*Top*	0
Form2	*Width*	6765
Form2	*Name*	*frmAddItems*

*Table 9.2 The newly named **frmViewInventory** and **frmAddItems** forms' properties.*

ADDING A MODULE TO THE PROJECT

As you will learn, the *Xhousehold* ActiveX control returns error values to the calling program in case it is unable to perform its processing correctly. The *prjActiveHousehold* project processes those errors within the *DBError* procedure. To make the *DBError* procedure available to both forms, you must place it within a module. To add the module to the *prjActiveHousehold* project and save the project, perform the following steps:

1. Select the Project menu Add Module option. Visual Basic will display the Add Module dialog box.

2. Within the Add Module dialog box, double-click your mouse on the Module icon. Visual Basic will add the *Module1* module to the project and open it within a Code window.

3. Select the View menu Properties Window option. Visual Basic will display the Properties Window with the *Module1* properties visible.

4. Change the *Module1* module's *Name* property to *mdlRaiseErrors*.

5. Select the File menu Save Project As option. Visual Basic will open the Save File As dialog box and fill the *File name* field with *mdlRaiseErrors*.

6. Within the Save File As dialog box, click your mouse on the Save button. Visual Basic will save the *mdlRaiseErrors* module and fill the *File name* field with the *frmAddItems* form name.

7. Within the Save File As dialog box, click your mouse on the Save button. Visual Basic will save the *frmAddItems* form and fill the *File name* field with the *frmViewInventory* form name.

8. Within the Save File As dialog box, click your mouse on the Save button. Visual Basic will save the *frmViewInventory* form and fill the *File name* field with the *Project1* project name.

9. Within the *File name* field, replace the *Project1* project name with the new *prjActiveHousehold* project name. Next, click your mouse on the Save button. Visual Basic will save the *prjActiveHousehold* project and close the Save Project As dialog box.

UNDERSTANDING THE PROGRAM'S MICROSOFT ACCESS DATABASE

As you have learned, when you enter a new record into the *prjActiveHousehold* project, you can then store that record into a database. In the *prjActiveHousehold* project, records you enter will reside in a Microsoft *Access* database *table*. A database consists of one or more tables, and you can visualize each table as storing data in *rows* and *columns*. In a table, each row is a *record* and each column is a *field*. A record can contain one or more fields. Each field can contain one *value*. The value can be a number, text, symbol, or other defined type. For example, a record for a new piece of furniture would contain an *Item Name* field, a *Price* field, a *Quantity* field, a *Date Purchased* field, a *Description* field, and a *Location* field. You can fill each field with values, such as *Name = Table*, *Price = $795*, *Quantity = 1*, *Date Purchased = 2/28/98*, *Description = New Coffee Table*, and *Location = Living Room*. You can identify the record by name, price, quantity, purchase date, description, or location.

307

After you store text in a table (that is, within a database record), you can later retrieve the text, and display the database records within a Visual Basic program. Visual Basic includes three basic database objects that let programs communicate with a database table. The three objects are the *Workspace*, *Database*, and *Recordset* objects, as you learned in Chapter 7, "Creating a Database Viewer and Designer." To retrieve records from a database table, you will write a *query*. A query is a statement that your program uses to tell the Microsoft *Access* database what it wants. You must write query statements in a special language called *Structured Query Language (SQL)*. You can use SQL to search a database table for specific field values in each record. The "Understanding SQL" section in Chapter 7 explains SQL in detail.

In the *prjActiveHousehold* project, you will design a database table that will contain records which correspond to items in the house, and fields within the records that correspond to specific characteristics about household items—such as quantity and cost. After you enter text in the *Xhousehold* custom ActiveX control, that text will correspond to a specific item that you want to create or edit. To create the household inventory database, you will design a database table with fields called *Item, Qty, Est_Cost, Purchase Date, Location,* and *Description*. Each field will contain a value that corresponds to the text you enter.

When you want to find a specific record in the database table, you can look for a specific item, a price, a purchase data, and so on in the table records. After you find the information, you can then display it within the *Xhousehold* custom ActiveX control.

USING THE VISUAL DATA MANAGER TO CREATE A DATABASE

The Visual Basic Interactive Development Environment (IDE) includes the *Visual Data Manager*, an add-in utility that you can use to design databases. As you have learned, a database contains one or more tables, and you can organize a table into rows and columns of data. The Visual Data Manager lets you create one or more data tables and saves the tables in the database. In the *prjActiveHousehold* project, you will create the *Household* database table. You will then design a table for the *household.mdb* database that stores data that the database will receive from and send to the *Xhousehold* custom ActiveX control. To create a database and a table to store the *Xhousehold* control information, perform the following steps:

1. Select the Add-Ins menu Visual Data Manager option. Visual Basic will display the VisData window.

2. Within the VisData window, select the File menu New Microsoft Access Version 7.0 MDB option. Visual Basic will open the Select Microsoft Access Database To Create dialog box.

3. Within the Select Microsoft Access Database To Create dialog box, type the name of your database in the *File name* field as *household*. Next, click your mouse on the Save button. Visual Data Manager will open the Database window.

4. Within the Database window, right-click your mouse on the *Properties* listing. Visual Data Manager will open the Table Structure dialog box.

5. Within the Table Structure dialog box, type the name of your table in the *Table Name* field as *Household*. Next, click your mouse on the Add Field button. Visual Data Manager will open the Add Field dialog box.

6. Within the Add Field dialog box, enter the field names and types Table 9.3 lists in the *Name* and *Type* text boxes. After entering the field names and types, click your mouse on the Close button. Visual Basic will close the Add Field dialog box and display the Table Structure dialog box.

Field Name	Type	Size
Item	Text	25
Qty	Integer	n/a
Est_Cost	Currency	n/a
Purchase Date	Date	n/a
Location	Text	25
Description	Text	25

*Table 9.3 The field names and types for the **Household** table in the **household.mdb** database.*

7. Within the Table Structure dialog box, click your mouse on the Build the Table button. Visual Data Manager will build the *Household* table, close the Table Structure dialog box, and display the *Household* table in the Database window.

8. Within the Database window, double-click your mouse on the *Household* table listing. Visual Data Manager will open the Dynaset: Household dialog box.

9. Within the Dynaset: Household dialog box, click your mouse on the Add button. Visual Data Manager will open the Update/Cancel dialog box.

10. Within the Update/Cancel dialog box, enter the values beside each field as *Item = Table, Qty = 1, Est_Cost = $795, Purchase Date = 2/28/98, Location = Living Room, Description = New Coffee Table*.

11. Within the Update/Cancel dialog box, click your mouse on the Update button. Visual Data Manager will close the Update/Cancel dialog box and display the Dynaset: Household dialog box.

12. Within the Dynaset: Household dialog box, click your mouse on the Close button. Visual Data Manager will close the Dynaset: Household dialog box and display the *household.mdb* database with the *Household* table's fields in the Database window, as shown in Figure 9.6.

*Figure 9.6 The **household.mdb** database's **Household** table fields.*

Now that you have finished designing the *household.mdb* database, you must create the *Xhousehold* control that the *prjActiveHousehold* project uses to interact with the database.

CREATING THE PRJACTIVEINVENTORY PROJECT

As you have learned, the *prjActiveHousehold* project will use the *Xhousehold* ActiveX control to interact with the *household.mdb* database. As you learned in Chapter 6, the easiest way to design a custom ActiveX control is to use a group project. With the *prjActiveHousehold* project, you will add a second project, an ActiveX control project that you will name *prjActiveInventory*, to the *prjHouseholdGroup* group project. Then, you will save both projects together within the group project. To begin designing the *prjActiveInventory* project, you must first create an empty user control. To create an empty user control, perform the following steps:

1. Within Visual Basic, select the File menu Add Project option. Visual Basic will open the Add Project dialog box.

2. Within the Add Project dialog box, double-click your mouse on the ActiveX Control icon. Visual Basic will start a new ActiveX Control project and open *UserControl1* within an object window.

3. Select the View menu Properties Window option. Visual Basic will open the Properties Window listing the *UserControl1* properties.

4. Within the Properties Window, change the *UserControl1* property values to those Table 9.4 lists.

Object	Property	Set As
UserControl1	*Height*	300
UserControl1	*Width*	6705
UserControl1	*Name*	*Xhousehold*

Table 9.4 *The newly named **Xhousehold** user control's properties.*

ADDING THE DATA ACCESS OBJECTS (DAO) OBJECT LIBRARY TO THE PROJECT

As you have learned, you will use the *Xhousehold* control to interact with the *household.mdb* database. As you have learned in previous chapters, you must add a set of data objects to the project to manage database information from within Visual Basic. As you have learned in previous projects, you will use the Data Access Objects (DAO) Object Library to manage database information within the *prjActiveInventory* project.

When you retrieve data from or save data to the *household.mdb* database, you will manage that data within a *Recordset* object. As you know, before you can store records in a *Recordset* object, you must have a *Workspace* and a *Database* object in your project. To use the *Workspace*, *Database*, and *Recordset* objects within Visual Basic, you must add a reference to them within the current project. The Data Access Objects (DAO) Object Library contains each object. You must add a *DAO Object Library* reference to the *prjActiveInventory* project before you can create and use the temporary database. After you add a *DAO Object Library* reference to the *prjActiveInventory* project, you will declare and assign variables of each data access object type. To add a *DAO Object Library* reference to the *prjActiveInventory* project, perform the following steps:

1. Within Visual Basic, select the Project menu References option. Visual Basic will open the References dialog box.

2. Within the References dialog box, select the *Microsoft DAO 3.5 Object Library* listing from the *Available References* field. Next, click your mouse on the box to the left of the selection. Visual Basic will draw a check mark in the box.

3. Within the References dialog box, click your mouse on the OK button. Visual Basic will add the *DAO Object Library* reference to the *prjActiveInventory* project.

UNDERSTANDING REFERENCES IN GROUP PROJECTS

In the previous section, you added a *DAO Object Library* reference to the *prjActiveInventory* project. As you will learn in later sections in this chapter, the *prjActiveHousehold* project will also use the *DAO Object Library*. It might seem necessary, therefore, that you also add the *DAO Object Library* reference to the *prjActiveHousehold* project. However, the Visual Basic development environment does not require that you manually add references to the same object library to multiple projects within a group; instead, it automatically adds the references for you.

ADDING CONTROLS TO THE XHOUSEHOLD CONTROL

As you have learned, the *prjActiveHousehold* project will use the *Xhousehold* control to interact with the *household.mdb* database. As you saw in the "Using the *prjActiveHousehold* Project" section in this chapter, the *Xhousehold* control contains a *Frame* control, six *Label* controls, and six corresponding *TextBox* controls. You will add and place those controls onto the *Xhousehold* user control to complete the custom control's design.

ADDING THE CONTROLS TO THE XHOUSEHOLD USER CONTROL

As the previous section details, you will use thirteen controls in the *Xhousehold* user control. Because all the controls that you will place onto the *Xhousehold* user control will reside within the *fraControls* frame, you must add those controls to the user control first, cut them all from the user control, and then paste them onto the *Frame* control. After you place the other twelve controls onto the frame, you will set the properties for all thirteen controls. To place the controls within the *Xhousehold* user control, perform the following steps:

1. If Visual Basic is not displaying the *Xhousehold* user control within an object window, double-click your mouse on the *Xhousehold* user control listing within the Project Explorer. Visual Basic will open the *Xhousehold* user control.

2. Within Visual Basic, select the View menu Toolbox option. Visual Basic will open the Toolbox.

3. Within the Toolbox, double-click your mouse on the Frame icon. Visual Basic will draw a *Frame* control, *Frame1*, onto the *Xhousehold* user control.

4. Within the object window, click your mouse on the *Frame1* control to highlight it. Visual Basic will draw a small frame around the control.

5. Select the View menu Properties Window option. Visual Basic will open the Properties Window listing the *Frame1* properties.

6. Within the Properties Window, change the *Frame1* properties to the values Table 9.5 lists.

Object	Property	Set As
Frame1	*Caption*	*Inventory Items*
Frame1	*Height*	500
Frame1	*Left*	0
Frame1	*Top*	0
Frame1	*Width*	500
Frame1	*Name*	*fraControls*

Table 9.5 *The newly named fraControls frame control's properties.*

7. Within the Toolbox, double-click your mouse on the Label icon. Visual Basic will draw a *Label* control, *Label1*, onto the *Xhousehold* user control.

8. Repeat Step 7 five more times until Visual Basic displays a total of six *Label* controls on the *Xhousehold* user control.

9. Hold down the SHIFT key and click your mouse on each of the new *Label* controls. Visual Basic will draw a small frame around each of the six controls.

10. Select the Edit menu Cut option to cut the controls. Visual Basic will remove the controls from the object window.

11. Click your mouse on the *fraControls* control to highlight it. Visual Basic will draw a small frame around the control.

12. Select the Edit menu Paste option to paste the controls onto the *fraControls* frame. Visual Basic will draw all six controls within the *fraControls* frame.

13. Within the Toolbox, double-click your mouse on the TextBox icon. Visual Basic will draw a *TextBox* control, *Text1*, onto the *Xhousehold* user control.

14. Repeat Step 13 five more times until Visual Basic displays a total of six *TextBox* controls on the *Xhousehold* user control.

15. Hold down the SHIFT key and click your mouse on each of the new *TextBox* controls. Visual Basic will draw a small frame around each of the six controls.

16. Select the Edit menu Cut option to cut the controls. Visual Basic will remove the controls from the object window.

17. Click your mouse on the *fraControls* control to highlight it. Visual Basic will draw a small frame around the control.

18. Select the Edit menu Paste option to paste the controls onto the *fraControls* frame. Visual Basic will draw all six controls within the *fraControls* frame.

19. Within the *Xhousehold* user control, click your mouse on the *fraControls* control to highlight it. Visual Basic will draw a small frame around the control.

20. Select the View menu Properties Window option. Visual Basic will open the Properties Window listing the *fraControls* control's properties.

21. Within the Properties Window, change the *fraControls* control's property values to those Table 9.6 lists.

22. Repeat Steps 19, 20, and 21 until you have changed the property values for each control on the *Xhousehold* user control to those Table 9.6 lists.

311

Object	Property	Set As
fraControls	*Height*	2655
fraControls	*Left*	120
fraControls	*Top*	120
fraControls	*Width*	6375
Label1	*Caption*	*Item:*
Label1	*Height*	255
Label1	*Left*	120
Label1	*Top*	360
Label1	*Width*	2295
Label1	*Name*	*lblItem*
Label2	*Caption*	*Quantity:*
Label2	*Height*	255
Label2	*Left*	120
Label2	*Top*	720
Label2	*Width*	2295

Table 9.6 The properties for the **Xhousehold** user control's component controls. (continued on following page)

Object	Property	Set As
Label2	Name	lblQuantity
Label3	Caption	Estimated Cost ($):
Label3	Height	255
Label3	Left	120
Label3	Top	1080
Label3	Width	2295
Label3	Name	lblEstCost
Label4	Caption	Purchase Date:
Label4	Height	255
Label4	Left	120
Label4	Top	1440
Label4	Width	2295
Label4	Name	lblPurchaseDate
Label5	Caption	Location:
Label5	Height	255
Label5	Left	120
Label5	Top	1800
Label5	Width	2295
Label5	Name	lblLocation
Label6	Caption	Description:
Label6	Height	255
Label6	Left	120
Label6	Top	2160
Label6	Width	2295
Label6	Name	lblDescription
Text1	Height	285
Text1	Index	0
Text1	Left	2520
Text1	Top	360
Text1	Width	3735
Text1	Name	txtFields
Text2	Height	285
Text2	Index	1
Text2	Left	2520
Text2	Top	720
Text2	Width	3735
Text2	Name	txtFields
Text3	Height	285
Text3	Index	2
Text3	Left	2520
Text3	Top	1080
Text3	Width	3735
Text3	Name	txtFields
Text4	Height	285
Text4	Index	3

Table 9.6 *The properties for the* **Xhousehold** *user control's component controls. (continued on following page)*

Object	Property	Set As
Text4	Left	2520
Text4	Top	1440
Text4	Width	2535
Text4	Name	txtFields
Text5	Height	285
Text5	Index	4
Text5	Left	2520
Text5	Top	1800
Text5	Width	2535
Text5	Name	txtFields
Text6	Height	285
Text6	Index	5
Text6	Left	2520
Text6	Top	2160
Text6	Width	2535
Text6	Name	txtFields

Table 9.6 *The properties for the **Xhousehold** user control's component controls. (continued from previous page)*

When you finish designing the *Xhousehold* user control, the control's object window will look similar to Figure 9.7.

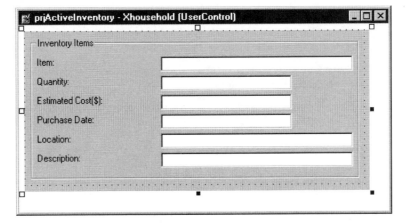

Figure 9.7 *The **Xhousehold** control after you complete its visual design.*

ADDING CONTROLS TO THE frmVIEWINVENTORY FORM

Now that you have completed the *Xhousehold* control's design, you will design the two forms that you will use within the *prjActiveHousehold* project. The first of the two forms is the *frmViewInventory* form. You will add a *Frame* control, a *ComboBox* control, and five *CommandButton* controls to the *frmViewInventory* form. After you add the standard controls, you will add the *Xhousehold* custom control to the form. To design the *frmViewInventory* form, perform the following steps:

1. If Visual Basic is not displaying the *frmViewInventory* form within an object window, double-click your mouse on the form's icon within the Project Explorer. Visual Basic will open the form.

2. Within Visual Basic, select the View menu Toolbox option. Visual Basic will open the Toolbox.

3. Within the Toolbox, double-click your mouse on the Frame icon. Visual Basic will draw a *Frame* control, *Frame1*, onto the *frmViewInventory* form.

4. Within the object window, click your mouse on the *Frame1* control to highlight it. Visual Basic will draw a small frame around the control.

313

5. Select the View menu Properties Window option. Visual Basic will open the Properties Window listing the *Frame1* properties.

6. Within the Properties Window, change the *Frame1* properties to the values Table 9.7 lists.

Object	Property	Set As
Frame1	*Caption*	*Items*
Frame1	*Height*	735
Frame1	*Left*	240
Frame1	*Top*	120
Frame1	*Width*	6375
Frame1	*Name*	*fraItems*

Table 9.7 *The newly named **fraItems** frame control's properties.*

7. Within the Toolbox, double-click your mouse on the ComboBox icon. Visual Basic will draw a *ComboBox* control, *Combo1*, onto the *frmViewInventory* form.

8. Click your mouse on the new *Combo1* control. Visual Basic will draw a small frame around the control.

9. Select the Edit menu Cut option to cut the control. Visual Basic will remove the control from the object window.

10. Click your mouse on the *fraItems* control to highlight it. Visual Basic will draw a small frame around the control.

11. Select the Edit menu Paste option to paste the *Combo1* control onto the *fraItems* frame. Visual Basic will draw the control within the *fraItems* frame.

12. Within the object window, click your mouse on the *Combo1* control to highlight it. Visual Basic will draw a small frame around the control.

13. Select the View menu Properties Window option. Visual Basic will open the Properties Window listing the *Combo1* properties.

14. Within the Properties Window, change the *Combo1* properties to the values Table 9.8 lists.

Object	Property	Set As
Combo1	*Height*	315
Combo1	*Left*	240
Combo1	*Text*	[blank]
Combo1	*Top*	240
Combo1	*Width*	5895
Combo1	*Name*	*cmbItemList*

Table 9.8 *The newly named **cmbItemList** control's properties.*

ADDING THE COMMANDBUTTON CONTROLS TO THE FORM

As you have learned, users will use the *CommandButton* controls at the *frmViewInventory* form's bottom to perform actions within the program. Within the *prjActiveHousehold* project, you will use five command buttons to add new records, edit records, delete records, refresh the list, and exit the program. The *Click* events for each of these buttons will perform processing that corresponds to the button's caption. To add the *CommandButton* controls to the *frmViewInventory* form, perform the following steps:

1. If Visual Basic is not displaying the *frmViewInventory* form within an object window, double-click your mouse on the *frmViewInventory* form listing within the Project Explorer. Visual Basic will open the *frmViewInventory* form.

2. Within Visual Basic, select the View menu Toolbox option. Visual Basic will open the Toolbox.

3. Within the Toolbox, double-click your mouse on the CommandButton icon. Visual Basic will draw a *CommandButton* control, *Command1*, within the *frmViewInventory* form.

4. Repeat Step 3 four more times until Visual Basic displays the *Command2*, *Command3*, *Command4*, and *Command5* buttons on the *frmViewInventory* form.

5. Within the *frmViewInventory* form, click your mouse on a *CommandButton* control to highlight it. Visual Basic will draw a small frame around the control.

6. Select the View menu Properties Window option. Visual Basic will open the Properties Window listing the selected control's properties.

7. Within the Properties Window, change the highlighted control's properties to the values Table 9.9 lists.

8. Repeat Steps 5, 6, and 7 to change the properties for all five *CommandButton* controls to the values Table 9.9 lists.

Object	Property	Set As
Command1	*Caption*	*&Add*
Command1	*Height*	495
Command1	*Left*	240
Command1	*Top*	4200
Command1	*Width*	1095
Command1	*Name*	*cmdAdd*
Command2	*Caption*	*&Delete*
Command2	*Height*	495
Command2	*Left*	1560
Command2	*Top*	4200
Command2	*Width*	1095
Command2	*Name*	*cmdDelete*
Command3	*Caption*	*&Edit*
Command3	*Height*	495
Command3	*Left*	2880
Command3	*Top*	4200
Command3	*Width*	1095
Command3	*Name*	*cmdEdit*
Command4	*Caption*	*&Refresh*
Command4	*Height*	495
Command4	*Left*	4200
Command4	*Top*	4200
Command4	*Width*	1095
Command4	*Name*	*cmdRefresh*
Command5	*Caption*	*E&xit*
Command5	*Height*	495
Command5	*Left*	5520
Command5	*Top*	4200
Command5	*Width*	1095
Command5	*Name*	*cmdExit*

*Table 9.9 The newly named **CommandButton** controls' properties.*

ADDING THE XHOUSEHOLD CONTROL TO THE FORM

After you add the other component controls to the *frmViewInventory* form, the last control to add is the custom *Xhousehold* control that you created previously in this chapter. You will display the database information within the *Xhousehold* control. To add the *Xhousehold* control to the *frmViewInventory* form, perform the following steps:

1. If Visual Basic is not displaying the *frmViewInventory* form within an object window, double-click your mouse on the *frmViewInventory* form listing within the Project Explorer. Visual Basic will open the *frmViewInventory* form.

2. Within Visual Basic, select the View menu Toolbox option. Visual Basic will open the Toolbox.

3. Within the Toolbox, double-click your mouse on the Xhousehold icon. Visual Basic will draw an *Xhousehold* control, *Xhousehold1*, within the *frmViewInventory* form. Figure 9.8 shows the Xhousehold icon within the Toolbox.

Figure 9.8 *The Xhousehold icon within the Toolbox.*

4. Within the *frmViewInventory* form, click your mouse on the *Xhousehold1* control to highlight it. Visual Basic will draw a small frame around the control.

5. Select the View menu Properties Window option. Visual Basic will open the Properties Window listing the selected control's properties.

6. Within the Properties Window, change the *Xhousehold1* control's properties to the values Table 9.10 lists.

Object	Property	Set As
Xhousehold1	*Height*	3015
Xhousehold1	*Left*	120
Xhousehold1	*Top*	960
Xhousehold1	*Width*	6615
Xhousehold1	*Name*	*ctlViewInventory*

Table 9.10 *The newly named **ctlViewInventory** control's properties.*

When you finish changing the properties for the *ctlViewInventory* control, the *frmViewInventory* form will look similar to Figure 9.9.

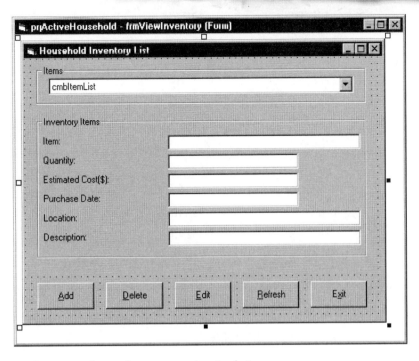

Figure 9.9 *The frmViewInventory form after you complete its design.*

ADDING CONTROLS TO THE FRMADDITEMS FORM

Now that you have completed the *frmViewInventory* form's design, you will design the *frmAddItems* form. To design the *frmAddItems* form, you will add two *CommandButton* controls to the form and one *Xhousehold* custom control to the form.

ADDING THE COMMANDBUTTON CONTROLS TO THE FORM

As you have learned, users will use the *CommandButton* controls at the *frmAddItems* form's bottom to perform actions within the program. Within the *frmAddItems* form, you will use two command buttons, one to add new records to the *household.mdb* database and one to exit the *frmAddItems* form. The *Click* events for each of these buttons will perform processing that corresponds to the button's caption. To add the *CommandButton* controls to the *frmAddItems* form, perform the following steps:

1. If Visual Basic is not displaying the *frmAddItems* form within an object window, double-click your mouse on the *frmAddItems* form listing within the Project Explorer. Visual Basic will open the *frmAddItems* form.

2. Within Visual Basic, select the View menu Toolbox option. Visual Basic will open the Toolbox.

3. Within the Toolbox, double-click your mouse on the CommandButton icon. Visual Basic will draw a *CommandButton* control, *Command1*, within the *frmAddItems* form.

4. Repeat Step 3. Visual Basic will draw the *Command2* button on the *frmAddItems* form.

5. Within the *frmAddItems* form, click your mouse on a *CommandButton* control to highlight it. Visual Basic will draw a small frame around the control.

6. Select the View menu Properties Window option. Visual Basic will open the Properties Window listing the selected control's properties.

7. Within the Properties Window, change the highlighted control's properties to the values Table 9.11 lists.

8. Repeat Steps 5, 6, and 7 to change the properties for the *Command2* control to the values Table 9.11 lists.

317

Object	Property	Set As
Command1	Caption	&Add Record
Command1	Height	645
Command1	Left	720
Command1	Top	3240
Command1	Width	2025
Command1	Name	cmdAddRecord
Command2	Caption	E&xit
Command2	Height	645
Command2	Left	3840
Command2	Top	3240
Command2	Width	2025
Command2	Name	cmdExit

*Table 9.11 The newly named **CommandButton** controls' properties.*

ADDING THE XHOUSEHOLD CONTROL TO THE FORM

After you add the *CommandButton* controls to the *frmAddItems* form, you must add the last control, the custom *Xhousehold* control, that you created previously in this chapter. You will use the *Xhousehold* control to enter new records for the *household.mdb* database. To add the *Xhousehold* control to the *frmAddItems* form, perform the following steps:

1. If Visual Basic is not displaying the *frmAddItems* form within an object window, double-click your mouse on the *frmAddItems* form listing within the Project Explorer. Visual Basic will open the *frmAddItems* form.

2. Within Visual Basic, select the View menu Toolbox option. Visual Basic will open the Toolbox.

3. Within the Toolbox, double-click your mouse on the Xhousehold icon. Visual Basic will draw an *Xhousehold* control, *Xhousehold1*, within the *frmAddItems* form.

4. Within the *frmAddItems* form, click your mouse on the *Xhousehold1* control to highlight it. Visual Basic will draw a small frame around the control.

5. Select the View menu Properties Window option. Visual Basic will open the Properties Window listing the *Xhousehold1* control's properties.

6. Within the Properties Window, change the *Xhousehold1* control's properties to the values Table 9.12 lists.

Object	Property	Set As
Xhousehold1	Height	3015
Xhousehold1	Left	0
Xhousehold1	Top	120
Xhousehold1	Width	6615
Xhousehold1	Name	ctlXHouseAdd

*Table 9.12 The newly named **ctlXHouseAdd** control's properties.*

When you finish changing the properties for the *ctlXHouseAdd* control, the *frmAddItems* form will look similar to Figure 9.10.

318

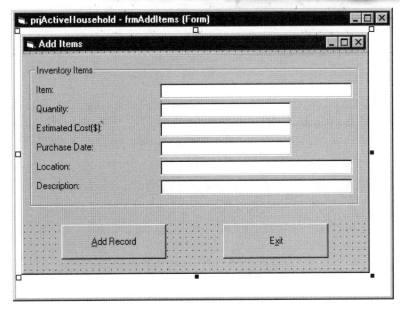

Figure 9.10 The *frmAddItems* form after you complete its design.

WRITING THE CODE FOR THE PRJGROUPHOUSEHOLD GROUP PROJECT

Now that you have completed the visual design of both the *prjActiveInventory* and *prjActiveHousehold* projects, you must add the program code to the projects. To write the program code for the component projects for the *prjGroupHousehold* group project, you will first write the program code for the *prjActiveInventory* project (and the resulting *Xhousehold* control), and then you will write the program code for the *prjActiveHousehold* project. You will first define the properties and methods for the *Xhousehold* control within the program code, and then add the *Form_Load* events and the various *Click* events for the two forms within the *prjActiveHousehold* project.

WRITING THE CODE FOR THE PRJACTIVEINVENTORY PROJECT

As you have learned, the *prjActiveInventory* project contains the *Xhousehold* custom ActiveX control. Within the *Xhousehold* custom ActiveX control, you will maintain information about the database connection, check entered values for validity, and display information within the control about a user-selected record. The methods within the *Xhousehold* control will also let the user add new records to the database, edit records within the database, and delete records from the database.

WRITING THE VARIABLE DECLARATIONS

The *Xhousehold* control uses several internal member variables, several database variables, and two public properties. The following code implements the variable declarations for the *Xhousehold* control:

```
Dim m_RecordNumber As Integer
Dim m_DirtyFields As Boolean
Dim InternalRS As Recordset
Dim InternalDB As Database
Dim InternalWS As Workspace
Public Adding As Boolean
Public Error As Integer
```

The *m_RecordNumber* and *m_DirtyFields* variables are internal member variables that correspond to control properties. The *Xhousehold* control will use only three DAO objects internally. The *Adding* and *Error* public variables also correspond to properties for the *Xhousehold* control that programs which use the control can access.

Note: *This project declares properties in two ways: using member variables and* **Property Get** *and* **Property Let** *procedures, and using public variables. Both ways are acceptable. However, using member variables and* **Property Get** *and* **Property Let** *procedures is generally better programming practice, and you should use member variables and* **Property**

319

*procedures in your own projects. Using **Property Get** and **Property Let** procedures lets your controls manage user entries, check the entries for validity, make properties read-only, and so on. In other words, using **Property Get** and **Property Let** procedures better encapsulates the control.*

WRITING THE *INITDB* METHOD'S CODE

As you will learn, the first action a program that uses the *Xhousehold* control must perform is to invoke the control's *InitDB* method with the directory name that contains the database. The *Xhousehold* control uses the *InitDB* method to open the database, and returns a *True* or *False* value that indicates the *InitDB* method's success or failure. The following code implements the *InitDB* method:

```
Public Function InitDB(ByVal DBDir As String) As Boolean
  On Error GoTo DBLoadError
  Set tmpWS = Workspaces(0)
  Set InternalDB = Workspaces(0).OpenDatabase(DBDir)
  Set InternalRS = _
       InternalDB.OpenRecordset("Select * From Household Order By Item")
  If InternalRS.RecordCount > 0 Then
    InternalRS.MoveLast
    RecordNumber = InternalRS.AbsolutePosition
  End If
  InitDB = True
  Exit Function

DBLoadError:
  InitDB = False
End Function
```

As you can see, the method tries to open the database within the directory the calling program specifies. It then tries to open the recordset against the database. If either step fails, the method will return a *False* value to the calling program and exit. Otherwise, the method will return a *True* value and the calling program can now use the control to manage the *household.mdb* database. Calling programs should always check the *InitDB* method's return value to ensure that the control was able to establish a connection to the database.

WRITING THE *PROPERTY GET* PROCEDURES

As you learned in the "Writing the Variable Declarations" section, the *Xhousehold* control maintains the *RecordNumber* and *DirtyFields* properties with internal member variables and *Property Get* and *Property Let* procedures. The following code implements the *Property Get* procedures for the *RecordNumber* and *DirtyFields* properties:

```
Public Property Get RecordNumber() As Integer
  RecordNumber = m_RecordNumber
End Property

Public Property Get DirtyFields() As Boolean
  Dim I As Integer

  m_DirtyFields = False
  For I = 0 To 5
    If Len(txtFields(I).Text) > 0 Then m_DirtyFields = True
  Next
  DirtyFields = m_DirtyFields
End Property
```

The *Property Get RecordNumber* procedure assigns the value of the *m_RecordNumber* member variable to the *RecordNumber* property. On the other hand, the *Property Get DirtyFields* procedure is slightly more complex. The procedure uses a *For-Next* loop to check each field in the currently displayed control. If the field contains an entry, the procedure sets *DirtyFields* to *True*. Otherwise, the procedure sets *DirtyFields* to *False*.

WRITING THE PROPERTY LET PROCEDURE

In the previous section, you wrote the *Property Get* procedures for the *Xhousehold* control's properties. The *DirtyFields* property is a read-only property, which means that the *Xhousehold* control has no *Property Let* procedure for that property. On the other hand, the *RecordNumber* property lets the user both retrieve the current record and set the current record. The following code implements the *Property Let RecordNumber* procedure:

```
Public Property Let RecordNumber(ByVal NewPosition As Integer)
    If NewPosition > -1 Then
        InternalRS.Requery
        InternalRS.MoveLast
        InternalRS.AbsolutePosition = NewPosition
        m_RecordNumber = InternalRS.AbsolutePosition
        Fill
    Else
        FillEmpty
    End If
End Property
```

The procedure first checks to make sure that there are records in the recordset and that the user is not adding a record. As you will learn, to add a record, you will set the *NewPosition* value to -1. If the user is trying to view an existing record, the procedure finds that record, sets the property to that record's *AbsolutePosition*, and calls the *Fill* procedure to display the information within the control. If the user is trying to add a record or if there are no records, the procedure calls the *FillEmpty* procedure, which clears the fields within the control.

WRITING THE CODE FOR THE FILL PROCEDURES

As you have learned, after you complete the *Xhousehold* control's design, programs which use the control will interact with the database through the control. When you design the *Xhousehold* control, there are two possible cases you must consider for the control's display. The control will either display a record, or it will display nothing. To change the control's display at various points through the program, you must have two procedures that fill the control's fields with information—one which handles the situations where the program wants to fill the control fields with actual values, and one which handles the situations where the program wants to fill the control with blank fields. The first procedure, *Fill*, fills the control's fields with information from a user-selected record. The following code implements the *Fill* procedure:

```
Private Sub Fill()
    txtFields(0).Text = InternalRS.Fields("item") & ""
    txtFields(1).Text = Format(InternalRS.Fields("qty"), "#,###")
    txtFields(2).Text = Format(InternalRS.Fields("est_cost"), "$#,##0.00")
    txtFields(3).Text = Format(InternalRS.Fields("purchase date"), _
        "Medium Date")
    txtFields(4).Text = InternalRS.Fields("location") & ""
    txtFields(5).Text = InternalRS.Fields("description") & ""
End Function
```

As you can see, the *Fill* procedure uses the *InternalRS* recordset object that you initialized when you initialized the control. The procedure fills the six fields in the control with the six corresponding fields within the *InternalRS* recordset's current record. The second case, where you must clear all text from the fields in the control, is similar. However, rather than filling the fields with values, the *FillEmpty* procedure sets all the fields to empty strings—which clears any values the fields might have contained. The following code implements the *FillEmpty* procedure:

```
Private Sub FillEmpty()
    txtFields(0).Text = ""
    txtFields(1).Text = ""
    txtFields(2).Text = ""
    txtFields(3).Text = ""
    txtFields(4).Text = ""
    txtFields(5).Text = ""
End Function
```

The *FillEmpty* procedure sets each field in the control to a *NULL*-string, which clears any entries that the field might have been displaying. In general, you will use the *FillEmpty* procedure only when you add a new record to the database or if the user has deleted all records from the database.

WRITING THE CODE FOR THE *ADDTODB* METHOD

As you have learned, the *Xhousehold* control exposes several methods. Programs that use the control can invoke the control's methods to perform actions on the database. One of these methods is the *AddToDB* method, which programs will call when they must add a new record to the *household.mdb* database. The following code implements the *AddToDB* method:

```
Public Function AddToDB() As Boolean
  If Not CheckFields Then
    AddToDB = False
  Else
    InternalRS.AddNew
      InternalRS.Fields("item") = txtFields(0).Text
      InternalRS.Fields("qty") = CInt(txtFields(1).Text)
      InternalRS.Fields("est_cost") = CCur(txtFields(2).Text)
      InternalRS.Fields("purchase date") = CDate(txtFields(3).Text)
      InternalRS.Fields("location") = txtFields(4).Text
      InternalRS.Fields("description") = txtFields(5).Text
    InternalRS.Update
    AddToDB = True
    InternalRS.Requery
  End If
End Function
```

The *AddToDB* method first checks the return value from the *CheckFields* function. If *CheckFields* returns a *True* value, the method adds the currently displayed fields to a new record in the database. If *CheckFields* returns a *False* value, the method exits with its own *False* return code, which lets the calling program know that the *AddToDB* method could not perform the add operation. If *CheckFields* determines that all field values are valid, the *AddToDB* method's program code adds the record to the database. Next, the program code requeries the database (which ensures that the data manager fully updates the *Recordset* object), and exits with a *True* return code, which lets the calling program know that the *AddToDB* method successfully performed the add operation.

The *CheckFields* function checks the fields within the control against the fields in the database to make sure that each field in the control is of the same type as its counterpart in the database. Checking the fields ensures that the program is not trying to assign an invalid value to a database record. The following code implements the *CheckFields* function:

```
Private Function CheckFields() As Integer
  Dim TmpCur As String

  CheckFields = False
  If Len(txtFields(0).Text) < 1 Then
    Error = 1
    Exit Function
  End If
  If Val(txtFields(1).Text) < 1 Or Val(txtFields(1).Text) > 32767 Then
    Error = 2
    Exit Function
  End If
  If Left$(txtFields(2).Text, 1) = "$" Then
    TmpCur = Right(txtFields(2).Text, Len(txtFields(2).Text) - 1)
  Else
    TmpCur = txtFields(2).Text
  End If
  If Len(TmpCur) > 15 Then
    Error = 3
    Exit Function
```

```
      End If
      If CCur(Val(TmpCur)) < 0.01 Or Val(TmpCur) > 1000000 Then
        Error = 3
        Exit Function
      End If
      If Not IsDate(txtFields(3).Text) Then
        Error = 4
        Exit Function
      End If
      If Len(txtFields(4).Text) < 1 Then
        Error = 5
        Exit Function
      End If
      If Len(txtFields(5).Text) < 1 Then
        Error = 6
        Exit Function
      End If
      If Len(txtFields(4).Text) > 255 Then
        Error = 7
        Exit Function
      End If
      If Len(txtFields(5).Text) > 255 Then
        Error = 8
        Exit Function
      End If
      If Len(txtFields(0).Text) > 255 Then
        Error = 9
        Exit Function
      End If
      CheckFields = True
    End Function
```

As you can see, the *CheckFields* function checks every field in the control, some fields more than once. If the field does not meet the correct criteria (it is the wrong type, it is too long, and so on), the function sets the *Xhousehold* control's *Error* property to a numeric value and exits. As you will learn, when you perform an action with the *Xhousehold* control, if the action is unsuccessful, the method will return a *False* value and place the error code within the control's *Error* property. As you will see in the *prjActiveHousehold* project, the program will then process that error code and return a meaningful message to the user (for example, "The entry in the *Item* field is too long," rather than "Error 9").

WRITING THE CODE FOR THE ENABLEFIELDS AND DISABLEFIELDS METHODS

As you have learned in previous sections, one of the *Xhousehold* control's purposes is to provide a single point which calling programs can use to access the *household.mdb* database. To force the user to use the *Xhousehold* control's methods when the user wants to add a new record or edit a record within the database, the *Xhousehold* control uses the *EnableFields* and the *DisableFields* methods. The following code implements the *EnableFields* and the *DisableFields* methods:

```
Public Function EnableFields() As Boolean
  Dim I As Integer

  For I = 0 To 5
    txtFields(I).Locked = False
  Next
End Function
Public Function DisableFields() As Boolean
  Dim I As Integer

  For I = 0 To 5
    txtFields(I).Locked = True
  Next
End Function
```

If the calling program invokes the *DisableFields* method, the control will lock all the text boxes in its display so that the user cannot enter values into the text boxes. When the calling program calls the *EnableFields* method, it will enable the fields so that the user can enter new values. You will generally only enable fields during an add or edit operation.

WRITING THE CODE FOR THE *EDITDB* METHOD

In previous sections, you have written the code for the *AddToDB* method and for the *InitDB* method, as well as the methods to enable and disable the control's entry fields. Another common activity that users will perform with the *Xhousehold* control is editing an existing record within the database. When the calling program must save an edited record, it will call the *EditDB* method. The following code implements the *EditDB* method:

```
Public Function EditDB() As Boolean
  Dim TmpCur As String
  On Error GoTo DBError
  If Not CheckFields Then
    EditDB = False
  Else
    Error = 0
    If Left$(txtFields(2).Text, 1) = "$" Then
      TmpCur = Right$(txtFields(2).Text, Len(txtFields(2).Text) - 1)
    Else
      TmpCur = txtFields(2).Text
    End If
    InternalRS.Edit
      InternalRS.Fields("item") = txtFields(0).Text
      InternalRS.Fields("qty") = CInt(txtFields(1).Text)
      InternalRS.Fields("est_cost") = CCur(Val(TmpCur))
      InternalRS.Fields("purchase date") = CDate(txtFields(3).Text)
      InternalRS.Fields("location") = txtFields(4).Text
      InternalRS.Fields("description") = txtFields(5).Text
    InternalRS.Update
    EditDB = True
    Exit Function
  End If

DBError:
  EditDB = False
End Function
```

As you learned in the "Writing the Code for the *AddToDB* Method" section, the *Xhousehold* control uses the *CheckFields* function to verify that the values the control currently displays are acceptable values to add to the database (that is, the values are of the same type as their corresponding fields within the database). Just as the *AddToDB* method did, the *EditDB* method invokes the *CheckFields* function before it performs any processing to ensure that the values are valid. If the currently entered values are all valid, the method performs some clean-up on the fields, if necessary, and then changes the current entry within the database to match the fields the control is displaying.

WRITING THE CODE FOR THE *CHECKUSERFIELDSAGAINSTDB* METHOD

As you will learn, the *prjActiveHousehold* program will let the user cancel an edit activity at any point before the user commits the edits to the database. To protect against losing changes that the user may have already entered when the user tries to cancel an edit activity, the calling program can invoke the *CheckUserFieldsAgainstDB* method, which returns a value that indicates whether or not the fields in the database differ from those in the control. The following code implements the *CheckUserFieldsAgainstDB* method:

```
Public Function CheckUserFieldsAgainstDB() As Integer
  If Not CheckFields Then
    CheckUserFieldsAgainstDB = 1
    Exit Function
  End If
  CheckUserFieldsAgainstDB = 0
```

```
      If InternalRS.Fields("item") <> txtFields(0).Text Then Exit Function
      If InternalRS.Fields("qty") <> CInt(txtFields(1).Text) Then Exit Function
      If InternalRS.Fields("est_cost") <> CCur(txtFields(2).Text) Then _
         Exit Function
      If InternalRS.Fields("purchase date") <> CDate(txtFields(3).Text) Then _
         Exit Function
      If InternalRS.Fields("location") <> txtFields(4).Text Then Exit Function
      If InternalRS.Fields("description") <> txtFields(5).Text Then _
         Exit Function
      CheckUserFieldsAgainstDB = 2
   End Function
```

The *CheckUserFieldsAgainstDB* method first calls the *CheckFields* function to determine that all entries are valid. If the edited entries are not valid, *CheckUserFieldsAgainstDB* will return a 1, which the calling procedure will process. If the entries are all valid entries, the procedure then checks the fields against the current record in the database. If any field is different in the control from the field it should match in the database record, the method will exit and return 0 to the calling procedure. Otherwise, the method will return 2 to the calling procedure. The calling procedure should check the method's return values and respond appropriately. For example, if *CheckUserFieldsAgainstDB* returns 1, the calling procedure should display a prompt that alerts the user that the program is about to discard the user's changes, and let the user cancel the action.

WRITING THE CODE FOR THE DELETE METHOD

The last method that you will create within the *Xhousehold* control is the *Delete* method. Programs that use the *Xhousehold* control should call the *Delete* method when the user wants to delete a previously entered record. The following code implements the *Delete* method:

```
   Public Function Delete() As Boolean
      Delete = True
      On Error Resume Next
      InternalRS.Delete
      If Err.Number <> 0 Then Delete = False
   End Function
```

The *Delete* method deletes the current record. If the method successfully deletes the record, it will return *True* to the calling procedure. If the method is unsuccessful, it will return *False* to the calling procedure.

WRITING THE CODE FOR THE PRJACTIVEHOUSEHOLD PROJECT

As you have learned, the *prjActiveHousehold* project contains two forms and a module, and is essentially a container for the *Xhousehold* control. The *prjActiveHousehold* project will use the *Xhousehold* control as its interface to all intrusive actions that the user performs on the database (for example, adding records and deleting records).

WRITING THE CODE FOR THE MDLRAISEERRORS MODULE

As you learned in the "Writing the Code for the *prjActiveInventory* Project" section of this chapter, the *Xhousehold* control will place error values within its *Error* property. The *prjActiveHousehold* project will process those error values within the *DbError* procedure, which you will place in the *mdlRaiseErrors* module and make public so that it is accessible from both forms. The following code implements the *DbError* procedure:

```
   Public Sub DbError(ErrorNumber As Integer)
      Dim MsgText As String

      Select Case ErrorNumber
        Case 1
          MsgText = "You must complete the 'Item' field."
        Case 2
          MsgText = "You must enter a quantity value between 1 and 32,767."
        Case 3
          MsgText = "You must enter a valid currency value."
```

```
    Case 4
      MsgText = "You must enter a valid date value."
    Case 5
      MsgText = "You must complete the 'Location' field."
    Case 6
      MsgText = "You must complete the 'Description' field."
    Case 7
      MsgText = "The 'Item' field name must be 255 characters or less."
    Case 8
      MsgText = "The 'Location' field name must be 255 characters or less."
    Case 9
      MsgText = "The 'Description' must be 255 characters or less."
  End Select
  MsgBox MsgText, vbCritical, "Database update/add error"
End Sub
```

As you can see, the program code within the procedure uses a *Select Case* statement to check the error values. The procedure then defines a string that corresponds to the error value and displays the error within a message box.

WRITING THE CODE FOR THE *FRMVIEWINVENTORY* FORM

The purpose of the *frmViewInventory* form's program code is mainly to provide the user with an easy way to access the *Xhousehold* control's methods. Additionally, the *frmViewInventory* form uses its own set of Data Access Objects (DAO) to create the list of items that it displays within the *cmbItemList* control. The following code implements the variable declarations that *frmViewInventory* uses:

```
Dim WS As Workspace
Dim HouseHoldDB As Database
Dim HouseHoldRS As Recordset
Dim I As Integer
Dim Editing As Boolean
```

The first three variables are the DAO objects that you must use to manage the form's local recordset. The *I* variable is a counting variable, and the *Editing* variable is a flag variable that you will use within the *cmdEdit_Click* and the *cmdRefresh_Click* events to perform specific processing if the user is currently editing a record.

WRITING THE FORM'S STARTUP CODE

As you know, when you develop a Single Document Interface (SDI) application, the *Form_Load* event for the opening form in the application is the first program code to execute, unless you define a separate *Sub Main* within a module. In the *prjActiveHousehold* project, the *frmViewInventory* form is the first to load. The following code implements the *Form_Load* event for the *frmViewInventory* form:

```
Private Sub Form_Load()
  Set WS = Workspaces(0)
  Set HouseHoldDB = WS.OpenDatabase(App.Path & "\household.mdb")
  If Not ctlViewInventory.InitDB(App.Path & "\household.mdb") Then
    MsgBox "Unable to open database", vbCritical
    End
  End If
  Set HouseHoldRS = _
      HouseHoldDB.OpenRecordset("Select * From Household ORDER BY Item")
  Refresh_Combo
End Sub
```

The *Form_Load* event's program code initializes the local database that the form uses and then calls the *InitDB* method to initialize the database within the *ctlViewInventory* control. If the program successfully opens both database objects, the program code opens the recordset that the *frmViewInventory* form's code uses to maintain the combo box and calls the *Refresh_Combo* procedure, which fills the combo box with item names. The following code implements the *Refresh_Combo* procedure:

```
Private Sub Refresh_Combo()
  HouseHoldRS.Requery
  If HouseHoldRS.RecordCount > 0 Then
    cmbItemList.Clear
    HouseHoldRS.MoveLast
    HouseHoldRS.MoveFirst
    For I = 0 To HouseHoldRS.RecordCount - 1
      cmbItemList.AddItem HouseHoldRS.Fields("item") & ""
      HouseHoldRS.MoveNext
    Next
    HouseHoldRS.MoveFirst
    cmbItemList.ListIndex = 0
    cmdDelete.Enabled = True
    cmdEdit.Enabled = True
  Else
    cmbItemList.Clear
    ctlViewInventory.RecordNumber = -1
    cmdDelete.Enabled = False
    cmdEdit.Enabled = False
  End If
End Sub
```

If there are no records in the recordset, the procedure clears the combo box, disables the Edit and Delete buttons, and displays blank fields in the control. If there are records in the recordset, the procedure loops through the recordset one record at a time, adding the *Item* entry from each record to the combo box. The procedure then sets the currently selected record to the first record in the combo box and enables the Edit and Delete buttons.

Setting the currently selected record to the first record will force the *ctlViewInventory* control to update the fields it displays. Similarly, setting the *ListIndex* value to 0 will force the *cmbItemList* control to update the values it displays. You must add the program code to perform the update to the *cmbItemList_Click* event. The following code implements the *cmbItemList_Click* event:

```
Private Sub cmbItemList_Click()
  ctlViewInventory.RecordNumber = cmbItemList.ListIndex
End Sub
```

As you can see, the code sets the *ctlViewInventory* control's current record number to the list index. As you learned earlier in this chapter, setting the *Xhousehold* control's *RecordNumber* property causes the *Xhousehold* control to change its displayed values to values that correspond to the new record's fields.

WRITING THE CODE FOR THE CMDADD_CLICK EVENT

As you learned in the "Using the *prjActiveHousehold* Project" section of this chapter, the user can click the mouse on the Add button to add new records to the database. The following code implements the Add button's *Click* event:

```
Private Sub cmdAdd_Click()
  frmAddItems.Show vbModal
  ctlViewInventory.RecordNumber = 0
  Refresh_Combo
End Sub
```

The *cmdAdd_Click* event shows the *frmAddItems* form modally (that is, the program will force the user to close the *frmAddItems* form before the user can return to the *frmViewInventory* form). When the user returns to the *frmViewInventory* form, the procedure resets the *RecordNumber* property to 0 and adds the new records to the *cmbItemList* control.

WRITING THE CODE FOR THE CMDDELETE_CLICK EVENT

When you designed the program code for the *Xhousehold* control, you included within the code a *Delete* method that the calling program can use to delete records from within the *household.mdb* database. To delete a record, the user must click the mouse on the Delete button. The following code implements the Delete button's *Click* event:

```
Private Sub cmdDelete_Click()
  Dim Response As Integer

  Response = MsgBox("Are you sure you want to delete this record?", vbYesNo)
  If Response = vbNo Then Exit Sub
  If ctlViewInventory.Delete Then
    Refresh_Combo
  Else
    MsgBox "Delete failed!", vbCritical
  End If
End Sub
```

The *cmdDelete_Click* event first displays a message box to verify that the user wants to delete the record. If the user verifies the deletion, the program code then calls the *Delete* method. If the *Delete* method is successful, the code refreshes the combo box and exits. If it is not, the program code lets the user know that the delete operation failed and exits.

WRITING THE CODE FOR THE CMDEDIT_CLICK EVENT

As you learned in the "Using the *prjActiveHousehold* Project" section of this chapter, when the user clicks the mouse on the Edit button, the program enters Edit mode. When the user finishes editing, the user clicks the mouse on the Update button (same button, just a different caption) to save the changes to the database. Both captions are still the *cmdEdit* control. The following code implements the *cmdEdit* control's *Click* event:

```
Private Sub cmdEdit_Click()
  If cmdEdit.Caption = "&Edit" Then
    cmbItemList.Enabled = False
    cmdAdd.Enabled = False
    cmdDelete.Enabled = False
    cmdRefresh.Caption = "&Cancel"
    cmdEdit.Caption = "&Update"
    ctlViewInventory.EnableFields
    Editing = True
  Else
    If ctlViewInventory.EditDB Then
      ctlViewInventory.DisableFields
      cmbItemList.Enabled = True
      cmdAdd.Enabled = True
      cmdDelete.Enabled = True
      cmdRefresh.Caption = "&Refresh"
      cmdEdit.Caption = "&Edit"
      Editing = False
    Else
      DbError ctlViewInventory.Error
    End If
  End If
End Sub
```

If the user is not currently editing, the program code places the control in Edit mode, changes the Edit button's caption and the *cmdRefresh* button's caption, and disables the Add and Delete buttons. If the user is currently editing, the program code tries to save the changes to the database. If it is successful, it returns the form to normal mode. If it is not successful, the control remains in Edit mode and the program code calls the *DbError* function to display the error message the control returns to the user.

WRITING THE CODE FOR THE CMDREFRESH_CLICK EVENT

As the previous section details, the *cmdRefresh* button performs different processing if the user is currently editing than it does if the user is not. The following code implements the *cmdRefresh* control's *Click* event:

```
Private Sub cmdRefresh_Click()
  If Editing Then
    Select Case ctlViewInventory.CheckUserFieldsAgainstDB
      Case 1
        Response = MsgBox("Invalid entries in one or more fields. " & _
            "Refresh and lose changes?", vbYesNo)
        If Response = vbNo Then Exit Sub
        Editing = False
      Case 0
        Response = MsgBox("Lose all changes?", vbYesNo)
        If Response = vbNo Then Exit Sub
        Editing = False
    End Select
  End If
  cmbItemList.Enabled = True
  Refresh_Combo
  cmdRefresh.Caption = "&Refresh"
  cmdEdit.Caption = "&Edit"
  cmdAdd.Enabled = True
End Sub
```

If the user is currently editing the record the *ctlViewInventory* control displays, the program code checks the edits with the *CheckUserFieldsAgainstDB* method. If any field within the control is different from the corresponding field in the current database record, the program code lets the user know that the program will lose all edits if the user continues, and gives the user the option to stop. If the user stops, the procedure exits, and the user can click the mouse on the Update button to save the changes. If the user does not stop, the procedure continues its processing and the user will lose all changes to that record. If there are no changes to the record, the procedure simply exits the edit mode without prompting the user. The button's remaining processing updates the combo box and the data within it and changes the button captions back to the default captions.

WRITING THE CODE FOR THE CMDEXIT_CLICK EVENT

To exit the program, the user can click the mouse on the *cmdExit* button. The following code implements the *cmdExit_Click* event:

```
Private Sub cmdExit_Click()
  Unload Me
End Sub
```

WRITING THE CODE FOR THE FRMADDITEMS FORM

The *frmAddItems* form performs similar processing to the *frmViewInventory* form. For example, when you load the *frmAddItems* form, it initializes its own instance of the *Xhousehold* control. The following code implements the *frmAddItems* form's *Form_Load* event:

```
Private Sub Form_Load()
  ctlXHouseAdd.InitDB App.Path & "\household.mdb"
  ctlXHouseAdd.RecordNumber = -1
  ctlXHouseAdd.EnableFields
End Sub
```

In addition to initializing the control, the *Form_Load* event sets the display so that it displays no records and enables the fields in the control so that the user can enter new values into the fields. The *Query_Unload* procedure, on the other hand, makes sure that the user has not made any changes to the control before it exits. The following code implements the *Query_Unload* procedure:

```
Private Sub Form_QueryUnload(Cancel As Integer, UnloadMode As Integer)
  Dim Response As Integer

  If ctlXHouseAdd.DirtyFields Then
    Response = MsgBox("Exit and lose unsaved changes?", vbYesNo)
    If Response = vbNo Then Cancel = True
  End If
End Sub
```

The *Query_Unload* procedure checks the fields in the control. If the user has already entered values in any field, the program code will display a message box that prompts the user to verify that the program should exit the form and lose the unsaved entries. Otherwise, the code lets the form unload.

330 *WRITING THE CODE FOR THE COMMAND BUTTON CLICK EVENTS*

As you learned when you designed the *frmAddItems* form, the form contains two command buttons. The command buttons either add a record to the database or exit the form, depending on which button the user clicks the mouse. The following code implements the *cmdAddRecord_Click* event:

```
Private Sub cmdAddRecord_Click()
  If ctlXHouseAdd.AddToDB Then
    ctlXHouseAdd.RecordNumber = -1
  Else
    DbError ctlXHouseAdd.Error
  End If
End Sub
```

The *cmdAddRecord_Click* event calls the *AddToDB* method. If the *AddToDB* method is successful, the procedure clears the display and waits for the user to enter another record. If the *AddToDB* method is not successful, the procedure calls the *DbError* procedure.

The other button the user can click the mouse on is the Exit button. When the user clicks the mouse on the Exit button, the program code will unload the *frmAddItems* form. The following code implements the *cmdExit_Click* event:

```
Private Sub cmdExit_Click()
  Unload Me
End Sub
```

ENHANCEMENTS YOU CAN MAKE TO THE prjACTIVEHOUSEHOLD PROJECT

To make the *prjActiveInventory* project more useful, you can add additional fields to the database and to the control to maintain more information. You can also create a separate ActiveX reporting control, which you can use to let the user create different reports from the information the database contains. The user could then place the printed permanent record in a safety deposit box or some other secure location.

Alternatively, you can make the *Xhousehold* control less specialized, not more, as the previous paragraph suggests. Because the *Xhousehold* control uses a control array for the fields, you can easily create an *Xhousehold* control that ties directly to a recordset and displays the same number of fields as the recordset. Such a control can use the field captions from the recordset to place the labels along the control's left hand side, and can include a new property, *FieldCount*, which the calling program can use to determine how tall it should make the control (because the control's height will change, depending upon the number of fields it displays).

PUTTING IT ALL TOGETHER

This chapter's project, *prjActiveInventory*, introduced you to how to create your own custom ActiveX control. Within the *prjHouseholdGroup* group project, you have used a Microsoft *Access* database and your own custom ActiveX control to create a household inventory program. You have further applied your understanding of ActiveX controls, and you have used principles of object-oriented programming to encapsulate data and protect it from program code outside of the control. In Chapter 10, "Extending Databases to Multiple Tables," you will work with your first multi-table database and use queries to join records from multiple tables into a single recordset. Before you continue with Chapter 10, however, make sure you understand the following key concepts:

✓ You can design custom ActiveX controls that you use within your Visual Basic programs to perform specific processing and protect data from other parts of your programs.

✓ Because an ActiveX control is a class with a visual component, you can add properties, methods, and events to ActiveX controls that you create.

✓ Within ActiveX controls or any other type of Visual Basic class, your programs can use *Property Get* and *Property Let* procedures to expose a public property to the remainder of the program (or other components). Using *Property Get* and *Property Let* procedures lets you perform error-checking and computations on properties before you actually assign the property values to the property itself.

✓ *Property Get* procedures let your program code retrieve a custom object's properties.

✓ *Property Let* procedures let your program code set a custom object's properties.

✓ To make a property for a custom ActiveX control read-only, you should write only a *Property Get* procedure for that property. Because member variables that you protect with the *Property Get* and *Property Let* procedures are private to the control, the user will be unable to modify the property.

✓ Within your ActiveX controls, you can create properties in two ways: with public variables, or with private member variables that use *Property Get* and *Property Let* procedures. As a rule, you should use *Property Get* and *Property Let* procedures because doing so lets you better encapsulate your control.

✓ Your Visual Basic programs can use a custom ActiveX control to maintain multiple, independent connections to the same database or recordset within a single program, or to create multiple, independent connections to the same database from multiple instances of the program that uses the ActiveX control.

✓ Your custom ActiveX controls should force the program that uses the controls to use the control's public methods (also known as *interface functions*) to access data the control protects.

✓ To return simple error information to a program that uses a custom control you design, you can define an error property that returns values to the program. Programs that use the control can then process the error value to display textual error messages to the program's user.

331

Chapter 10

Extending Databases to Multiple Tables

In previous chapters, you have designed several databases that contained only single tables. Each database you constructed maintained only a single information type. However, your programs will most commonly use databases with multiple tables. Within multiple tables, you will generally store information that relates to a single common object within a given record. In fact, good database design (known as *normalization*) specifies that you will *only* store information that relates to a single common object within a given record. For example, if you wanted to design a database to maintain customer information and customer sales, you would maintain the information about the customer (such as name, address, and telephone number) within one table, and information about the actual transactions (such as purchase date, purchase amount, and so on) within another table. Furthermore, if you maintained a permanent inventory of goods or services that the customer could purchase, you would maintain information about those goods and services within a third table. When you want to combine information and generate invoices, reports, and so on, you will use Structured Query Language (SQL) queries to combine the information from the tables into a form understandable to the user.

332

In this chapter's project, *prjBookList*, you will use two tables to maintain information about books. The first table will maintain information about book titles. The second table will maintain information about chapters within the books. You will use a query to determine what book the first table is currently referencing and what its corresponding chapters are within the second table. Within the *prjBookList* project, you will display records from the first table within a *TreeView* control and records from the second table within a *ListView* control. By the time you finish this chapter, you will understand the following key concepts:

- The *Microsoft Windows Common Controls* component is actually a suite of seven ActiveX controls, including the *TreeView* control, the *ListView* control, the *ProgressBar* control, the *StatusBar* control, and the *ImageList* control.

- Within your Visual Basic programs, you will use the *Microsoft Windows Common Dialog* control to display File and Print dialog boxes that conform to Microsoft's standard definitions.

- Within the *prjBookList* project, you will use the *TreeView* control to display book information in a Windows *Explorer*-style interface.

- Within your programs, you will work with the *Node* object and *Nodes* collection when your program code must modify or retrieve information from a *TreeView* control. Each *Node* object corresponds to a single item in the tree view. The *Nodes* collection corresponds to all the nodes within the tree view.

- Within the *prjBookList* project, you will use the *ListView* control to display chapter information, either in a list, as a series of icons, or as a report.

- Within your programs, you will work with the *ListItem* object and *ListItems* collection when your program code must modify or retrieve information from a *ListView* control. Each *ListItem* object corresponds to a single item in the list view. The *ListItems* collection corresponds to all the nodes within the tree view.

- Within your Visual Basic programs, you will use Structured Query Language (SQL) queries to retrieve information from multiple tables within a database and to format the data in the most useful way for the program.

- Within the *prjBookList* project, you will use the SQL *Join* statement to combine the data from multiple tables within the returned recordset from a single query.

USING THE PRJBOOKLIST PROJECT

Before you design the *prjBookList* project, you may find it helpful to run the *prjBookList.exe* program. The companion CD-ROM that accompanies this book contains the *prjBookList.exe* program within the *Chapter10* directory. As with every other program on the CD-ROM, you should run the Jamsa Press *setup.exe* program to install the *prjBookList.exe* program to your computer's hard drive before you run it. After you install the *prjBookList.exe* program to your computer's hard drive, you can run it from the Start menu. To run the program, select the Windows Start menu Run option. Windows will display the Run dialog box. Within the Run dialog box, enter *x:\vbpl\Chapter10\prjBookList.exe*, where *x* corresponds to the drive letter of the hard drive on which you installed the *prjBookList.exe* program, and click your mouse on OK. Windows will display the *prjBookList.exe* program, as shown in Figure 10.1.

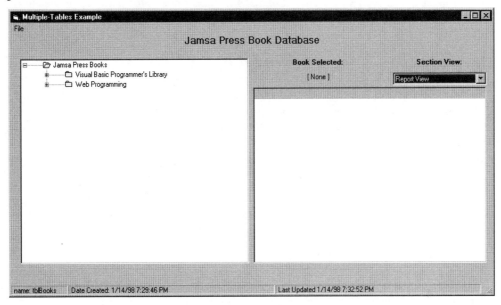

*Figure 10.1 The **prjBookList.exe** program's startup screen.*

The *prjBookList.exe* program uses a database, the *JPBook.mdb* database, to maintain information about the books the program displays. Depending on what directory your computer has currently selected, the program may be unable to locate the *JPBook.mdb* database. If it is unable to locate the database, the program will prompt you to locate the database on the program's behalf. Figure 10.2 shows the Can't Find JPBook.mdb dialog box that the program will display if it cannot find the database.

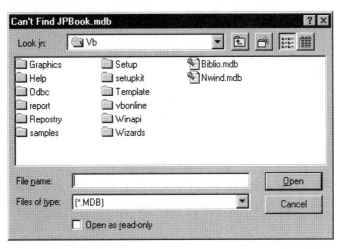

Figure 10.2 The Can't Find JPBook.mdb dialog box.

If the program displays the Can't Find JPBook.mdb dialog box, use the navigation controls within the dialog box to navigate to *x:\vbpl\Chapter10\prjBookList.exe*, where *x* corresponds to the drive letter of the hard drive on which you installed the *prjBookList.exe* program. The dialog box will display the *JPBook.mdb* database file. Double-click your mouse to load the file, and the program will continue its processing.

Before you use the *prjBookList.exe* program, take a moment to familiarize yourself with the controls on the Multiple-Tables Example form. The *prjBookList* project will let you view information about Jamsa Press books. In addition, you can view information about the chapters within the books, such as topic and number of pages. The program uses a *TreeView* control to display a Windows *Explorer*-type tree on the form's left hand side, and a *ReportView* control to let you view specific book information in different formats on the form's right hand side. In the *TreeView* control, you will see the Jamsa Press books list as a series of folders. At the form's bottom, you will see a blue *ProgressBar* control that the program will briefly display as it loads book information, and below the *ProgressBar* control, a *StatusBar* control, which displays information about the program's current processing.

334

RUNNING PRJBOOKLIST FROM THE CD-ROM

As you have learned, you must first install many programs that you will use in this book to your computer's hard drive before you use the programs. Because the *prjBookList.exe* program uses a permanent database within its execution directory, which the program maintains and updates, you must install the *prjBookList.exe* program to a drive before you use it. If you try to run the *prjBookList.exe* program from the CD-ROM, the program will let you view the existing book records, but will not let you add new records, or edit or delete the existing records.

To learn more about the Jamsa Press *setup.exe* program, see the "What's on the *Visual Basic Programmer's Library* Companion CD-ROM" section at the back of this book.

To view information about a book, click your mouse on that book's name within the tree view. The program, in turn, will display the book's chapters, page count, and so on, within the list view on the form's right side. To better understand the program's processing, click your mouse on the Web Programming icon within the list view. The *prjBookList* project will display information about chapters in Kris Jamsa, Sam Lalani, and Steve Weakley's book, *Web Programming*, Jamsa Press, 1996, as shown in Figure 10.3.

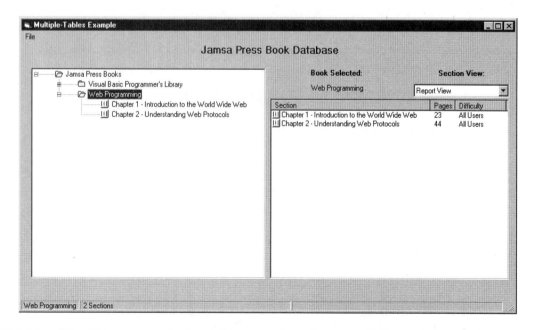

Figure 10.3 *The **prjBookList** program displays information about chapters in **Web Programming**.*

As you can see, the *prjBookList* program will display the chapter name, number of pages, and difficulty level in the *ListView* control. The program will also display the book name and the number of current chapter or section entries within the status bar at the form's bottom. If you then click your mouse on the *Chapter 2* listing within the list view, the program will change the *Web Programming* listing in the left-hand control to gray and select the *Chapter 2* listing, displaying it in blue. The status bar at the form's bottom will display additional information about the chapter, as shown in Figure 10.4.

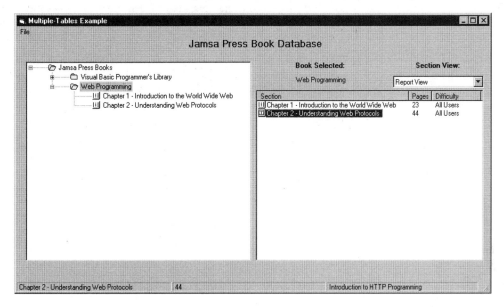

Figure 10.4 *The **prjBookList** program displays additional information about Chapter 2 in **Web Programming**.*

In addition to the report view that the program defaults to when you run the program, you can change the display appearance of the items on the form's right hand side. For example, to change the view from the report view to the icon view, perform the following steps:

1. Click your mouse on the drop-down arrow on the Section View combo box. The *prjBookList.exe* program, in turn, will display a list of four possible views.

2. Within the Section View drop-down list, select the Icon View option. The *prjBookList.exe* program will change the current view to the icon view. Figure 10.5 shows the *prjBookList.exe* program after you change the view to the icon view.

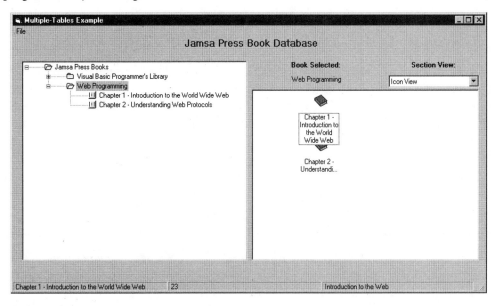

Figure 10.5 *The **prjBookList.exe** program in icon view.*

335

CREATING A BLANK FORM

Now that you have a better idea how to use the finished *prjBookList* project, you can begin to design it. First, you will create an empty form that will contain all the controls the "Using the *prjBookList* Project" section introduced. After you design the form, you will learn more about the Windows API calls that you will use to get the file information from the directory tree. To begin the *prjBookList* project and create a blank form, perform the following steps:

1. Within Visual Basic, select the File menu New Project option. Visual Basic will open the New Project dialog box.

2. Within the New Project dialog box, click your mouse on the Standard EXE icon. Next, click your mouse on the OK button. Visual Basic will close the dialog box and open the *Form1* form window.

3. Select the View menu Properties Window option. Visual Basic will open the Properties Window listing the *Form1* properties.

4. Within the Properties Window, change the *Form1* properties to the values Table 10.1 lists.

Object	Property	Set As
Form1	*Caption*	*Multiple-Tables Example*
Form1	*Height*	7245
Form1	*Left*	0
Form1	*StartUpPosition*	2 - Center Screen
Form1	*Top*	0
Form1	*Width*	11910
Form1	*Name*	*frmTreeView*

Table 10.1 *The newly named* **frmTreeView** *form's properties.*

5. Select the File menu Save Project As option. Visual Basic will open the Save File As dialog box and fill the *File name* field with the *frmTreeView* form name.

6. Within the Save File As dialog box, click your mouse on the Save button. Visual Basic will save the *frmTreeView* form and fill the *File name* field with the *Project1* project name.

7. Within the *File name* field, replace the *Project1* project name with the new *prjBookList* project name. Next, click your mouse on the Save button. Visual Basic will save the *prjBookList* project and close the Save Project As dialog box.

ADDING THE MICROSOFT COMMON CONTROLS TO THE PROJECT

As you can see from the interface the *prjBookList* project presents, you will add several extra controls to the project: *Microsoft ListView* control, *Microsoft TreeView* control, *Microsoft StatusBar* control, *Microsoft ImageList* control, *Microsoft ProgressBar* control, and *Microsoft CommonDialog* control. All the controls, except the Microsoft *CommonDialog* control, are *Microsoft Windows Common Controls* that come with Visual Basic. Before you can use the *Microsoft Windows Common Controls* in the *prjBookList* project, you must add them to the project as a component. After you add the *Microsoft Windows Common Controls* to the *prjBookList* project, Visual Basic will display the icons for all the controls in the Toolbox. As you know, the Toolbox displays Visual Basic control icons. If you double-click your mouse on any icon in the Toolbox, Visual Basic will draw the control that the icon corresponds to within the active form. To add the *Microsoft Windows Common Controls* to the *prjBookList* project, perform the following steps:

1. Select the Project menu Components option. Visual Basic will open the Components dialog box.

2. Within the Components dialog box, select the *Microsoft Windows Common Controls 5.0* listing. Next, click your mouse on the box to the left of the listing. Visual Basic will display a check mark in the box, as Figure 10.6 shows.

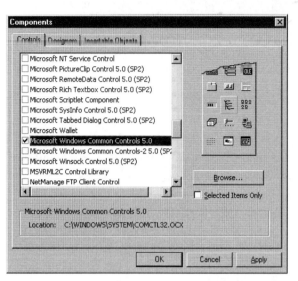

Figure 10.6 *The Components dialog box after you select the* **Microsoft Windows Common Controls 5.0** *listing.*

3. After you select the *Microsoft Windows Common Controls* within the Components dialog box, you can also add the *Microsoft CommonDialog* control to the project. To add the *Microsoft CommonDialog* control to the project, click your mouse on the *Microsoft CommonDialog Control 5.0* listing within the Components dialog box. Visual Basic will display a check mark in the box.

4. Within the Components dialog box, click your mouse on OK. Visual Basic will add the *Microsoft Windows Common Controls* control components and the *Microsoft CommonDialog Control 5.0* component to the *prjBookList* project.

ADDING THE DATA ACCESS OBJECTS (DAO) OBJECT LIBRARY TO THE PROJECT

As you have learned, you will use a temporary database within the *prjBookList* project to manage information about files within the search tree. As previous chapters have discussed in depth, to manage database information from within Visual Basic, you must add a set of data objects to the project. Within the *prjBookList* project, you will use the Data Access Objects (DAO) Object Library to manage database information.

When you retrieve data from or save data to the temporary database, you will manage that data within a *Recordset* object. As you know, before you can store records in a *Recordset* object, you must have a *Workspace* and a *Database* object in your project. To use the *Workspace*, *Database*, and *Recordset* objects within Visual Basic, you must make a reference to them. The Data Access Objects (DAO) Object Library contains each object. You must add a *DAO Object Library* reference to the *prjBookList* project before you can create and use the temporary database. After you add a *DAO Object Library* reference to the *prjBookList* project, you will declare and assign variables of each data access object type.

To add a *DAO Object Library* reference to the *prjBookList* project, perform the following steps:

1. Within Visual Basic, select the Project menu References option. Visual Basic will open the References dialog box.

2. Within the References dialog box, select the *Microsoft DAO 3.5 Object Library* from the *Available References* field. Next, click your mouse on the box to the left of the selection. Visual Basic will draw a check mark in the box.

3. Within the References dialog box, click your mouse on the OK button. Visual Basic will add the *DAO Object Library* reference to the *prjBookList* project.

UNDERSTANDING THE PROGRAM'S MICROSOFT ACCESS DATABASE

As you have learned, when you enter a new record into the *prjBookList* project, you can then store that record in a database. In the *prjBookList* project, records you enter will reside in a Microsoft *Access database table*. A database consists of one or more tables, and you can visualize each table as storing data in *rows* and *columns*. In a table, each row is a *record* and each column is a *field*. A record can contain one or more fields. Each field can contain one *value*. The value can be a number, text, symbol, or other defined type. For example, a record for a new car might contain a *Model Name* field, a *Price* field, a *Rebate* field, a *Date Purchased* field, and an *Options* field. You can fill each field with values, such as *Model Name = Indy Car, Price = $159,995, Rebate = $0, Date Purchased = 2/28/98,* and *Options = Air Conditioning, Spoiler.* You could then later identify the record by model name, price, purchase date, and options. After you store values in a table (that is, within a database record), you can later retrieve the values and display the database records within a Visual Basic program.

To retrieve records from a database table, you will write a *query*. A query is a statement that your program uses to tell the Microsoft *Access* database what it wants. You must write query statements in a special language called *Structured Query Language (SQL)*. You can use SQL to search a database table for specific field values in each record. The "Understanding SQL" section in Chapter 7 explains SQL in detail. In the *prjBookList* project, you will design a database table that will contain records that correspond to books within the Jamsa Press publication schedule (the *tblBooks* table). You will design a second table that will contain records that correspond to the chapters in those books (the *tblSections* table), and a third table that will contain difficulty ratings for the chapters (the *tblDifficulty* table). You will also design a query titled *qryAll*, which will combine the information from the three tables into records that provide all the information about each chapter in each book. When you want to find a specific record in the database tables, you can look for a specific book, a chapter, a difficulty level, and so on, in the table records. After you find the information, you can then display it within your program.

USING THE VISUAL DATA MANAGER TO CREATE THE DATABASE

The Visual Basic Interactive Development Environment (IDE) includes the *Visual Data Manager*, an add-in utility that you can use to design databases. As you have learned, a database contains one or more tables, and you can organize a table into rows and columns of data. The Visual Data Manager lets you create one or more data tables and lets you save the tables in a database. In the *prjBookList* project, you will create the *JPBook.mdb* database. You will then design three tables for the *JPBook.mdb* database that store data that the database will transmit to the *prjBookList* program. To create a database and three tables to store the book information, perform the following steps:

1. Within Visual Basic, select the Add-Ins menu Visual Data Manager option. Visual Basic will display the VisData window.

2. Within the VisData window, select the File menu New Microsoft Access Version 7.0 MDB option. Visual Basic will open the Select Microsoft Access Database To Create dialog box.

3. Within the Select Microsoft Access Database To Create dialog box, type the name of your database in the *File name* field as *JPBook*. Next, click your mouse on the Save button. Visual Data Manager will open the Database window.

4. Within the Database window, right-click your mouse on the *Properties* listing. Visual Data Manager will open the Table Structure dialog box.

5. Within the Table Structure dialog box, type the name of your table in the *Table name* field as *tblBooks*. Next, click your mouse on the Add Field button. Visual Data Manager will open the Add Field dialog box.

6. Within the Add Field dialog box, enter the field names and types Table 10.2 lists in the *Name* and *Type* text boxes.

Field Name	Type	Size
BookID	*Integer*	n/a
Book Name	*Text*	50

*Table 10.2 The field names and types for the **tblBooks** table in the **JPBook.mdb** database.*

7. After you enter the field names and types, click your mouse on the Close button. Visual Basic will close the Add Field dialog box and display the Table Structure dialog box.

8. Within the Table Structure dialog box, click your mouse on the Build the Table button. Visual Data Manager will build the *tblBooks* table, close the Table Structure dialog box, and display the *tblBooks* table in the Database window.

9. Within the Database window, double-click your mouse on the *tblBooks* table listing. Visual Data Manager will open the Dynaset: tblBooks dialog box.

10. Within the Dynaset: tblBooks dialog box, click your mouse on the Add button. Visual Data Manager will open the Update/Cancel dialog box.

11. Within the Update/Cancel dialog box, enter the values beside each field as *BookID = 1*, and *Book Name = Visual Basic Programmer's Library*. Next, click your mouse on the Update button. Visual Data Manager will close the Update/Cancel dialog box and display the Dynaset: tblBooks dialog box.

12. Within the Dynaset: tblBooks dialog box, click your mouse on the Add button. Visual Data Manager will open the Update/Cancel dialog box.

13. Within the Update/Cancel dialog box, enter the values beside each field as *BookID = 2*, and *Book Name = Web Programming*. Next, click your mouse on the Update button. Visual Data Manager will close the Update/Cancel dialog box and display the Dynaset: tblBooks dialog box.

14. Within the Dynaset: tblBooks dialog box, click your mouse on the Close button. Visual Data Manager will close the Dynaset: tblBooks dialog box and display the *JPBook.mdb* database with the *tblBooks* table's fields in the Database window.

15. Within the Database window, right-click your mouse on the *Properties* listing and select the New Table option within the drop-down menu. Visual Data Manager will open the Table Structure dialog box.

16. Within the Table Structure dialog box, type the name of your table in the *Table name* field as *tblDifficulty*. Next, click your mouse on the Add Field button. Visual Data Manager will open the Add Field dialog box.

17. Within the Add Field dialog box, enter the field names and types Table 10.3 lists in the *Name* and *Type* text boxes.

Field Name	Type	Size
Difficulty	*Integer*	n/a
Description	*Text*	50

Table 10.3 *The field names and types for the **tblDifficulty** table in the **JPBook.mdb** database.*

18. After you enter the field names and types, click your mouse on the Close button. Visual Basic will close the Add Field dialog box and display the Table Structure dialog box.

19. Within the Table Structure dialog box, click your mouse on the Build the Table button. Visual Data Manager will display the *tblDifficulty* table in the Database window.

20. Within the Database window, double-click your mouse on the *tblDifficulty* table listing. Visual Data Manager will open the Dynaset: tblDifficulty dialog box.

21. Within the Dynaset: tblDifficulty dialog box, click your mouse on the Add button. Visual Data Manager will open the Update/Cancel dialog box.

22. Within the Update/Cancel dialog box, enter the values beside each field as *Difficulty = 1*, and *Description = All Users*. Next, click your mouse on the Update button. Visual Data Manager will close the Update/Cancel box and display the Dynaset: tblDifficulty dialog box.

23. Within the Dynaset: tblDifficulty dialog box, click your mouse on the Add button. Visual Data Manager will open the Update/Cancel dialog box.

24. Within the Update/Cancel dialog box, enter the values beside each field as *Difficulty = 2*, and *Description = Beginner*. Next, click your mouse on the Update button. Visual Data Manager will close the Update/Cancel box and display the Dynaset: tblDifficulty dialog box.

25. Within the Dynaset: tblDifficulty dialog box, click your mouse on the Add button. Visual Data Manager will open the Update/Cancel dialog box.

26. Within the Update/Cancel dialog box, enter the values beside each field as *Difficulty = 3*, and *Description = Intermediate*. Next, click your mouse on the Update button. Visual Data Manager will close the Update/Cancel box and display the Dynaset: tblDifficulty dialog box.

27. Within the Dynaset: tblDifficulty dialog box, click your mouse on the Add button. Visual Data Manager will open the Update/Cancel dialog box.

28. Within the Update/Cancel dialog box, enter the values beside each field as *Difficulty = 4*, and *Description = Advanced*. Next, click your mouse on the Update button. Visual Data Manager will close the Update/Cancel box and display the Dynaset: tblDifficulty dialog box.

29. Within the Dynaset: tblDifficulty dialog box, click your mouse on the Add button. Visual Data Manager will open the Update/Cancel dialog box.

30. Within the Update/Cancel dialog box, enter the values beside each field as *Difficulty = 5*, and *Description = n/a*. Next, click your mouse on the Update button. Visual Data Manager will close the Update/Cancel box and display the Dynaset: tblDifficulty dialog box.

31. Within the Dynaset: tblDifficulty dialog box, click your mouse on the Close button. Visual Data Manager will close the Dynaset: tblDifficulty dialog box and display the *JPBook.mdb* database with the *tblDifficulty* table's fields in the Database window.

32. Within the Database window, right-click your mouse on the *Properties* listing and select the New Table option within the drop-down menu. Visual Data Manager will open the Table Structure dialog box.

33. Within the Table Structure dialog box, type the name of your table in the *Table name* field as *tblSections*. Next, click your mouse on the Add Field button. Visual Data Manager will open the Add Field dialog box.

34. Within the Add Field dialog box, enter the field names and types Table 10.4 lists in the *Name* and *Type* text boxes.

Field Name	Type	Size
SectionID	*Integer*	n/a
Title	*Text*	50
Pages	*Integer*	n/a
Difficulty	*Integer*	n/a
BookID	*Integer*	n/a
Description	*Text*	50

Table 10.4 *The field names and types for the* **tblSections** *table in the* **JPBook.mdb** *database.*

35. After entering the field names and types, click your mouse on the Close button. Visual Basic will close the Add Field dialog box and display the Table Structure dialog box.

36. Within the Table Structure dialog box, click your mouse on the Build the Table button. Visual Data Manager will build the *tblSections* table, close the Table Structure dialog box, and display the *tblSections* table in the Database window.

37. Within the Database window, double-click your mouse on the *tblSections* table listing. Visual Data Manager will open the Dynaset: tblSections dialog box.

38. Within the Dynaset: tblSections dialog box, click your mouse on the Add button. Visual Data Manager will open the Update/Cancel dialog box.

39. Within the Update/Cancel dialog box, enter the values beside each field as *SectionID = 1, Title = Chapter 1 - Introduction to Visual Basic, Pages = 28, Difficulty = 1, BookID = 1,* and *Description = Introduction to Visual Basic 5.0.* Next, click your mouse on the Update button. Visual Data Manager will close the Update/Cancel dialog box and display the Dynaset: tblSections dialog box.

40. Within the Dynaset: tblSections dialog box, click your mouse on the Add button. Visual Data Manager will open the Update/Cancel dialog box.

41. Within the Update/Cancel dialog box, enter the values beside each field as *SectionID = 2, Title = Chapter 2 - Using the Multimedia MCI Control, Pages = 32, Difficulty = 2, BookID = 1,* and *Description = Introduction to Controls.* Next, click your mouse on the Update button. Visual Data Manager will close the Update/Cancel dialog box and display the Dynaset: tblSections dialog box.

42. Within the Dynaset: tblSections dialog box, click your mouse on the Add button. Visual Data Manager will open the Update/Cancel dialog box.

43. Within the Update/Cancel dialog box, enter the values beside each field as *SectionID = 3, Title = Chapter 1 - Introduction to the World Wide Web, Pages = 23, Difficulty = 1, BookID = 2,* and *Description = Introduction to the Web.* Next, click your mouse on the Update button. Visual Data Manager will close the Update/Cancel dialog box and display the Dynaset: tblSections dialog box.

44. Within the Dynaset: tblSections dialog box, click your mouse on the Add button. Visual Data Manager will open the Update/Cancel dialog box.

45. Within the Update/Cancel dialog box, enter the values beside each field as *SectionID = 4, Title = Chapter 2 - Understanding Web Protocols, Pages = 44, Difficulty = 1, BookID = 2,* and *Description = Introduction to HTTP Programming.* Next, click your mouse on the Update button. Visual Data Manager will close the Update/Cancel dialog box and display the Dynaset: tblSections dialog box.

46. Within the Dynaset: tblSections dialog box, click your mouse on the Close button. Visual Data Manager will close the Dynaset: tblSections dialog box and display the *JPBook.mdb* database with the *tblSections* table's fields in the Database window, as shown in Figure 10.7.

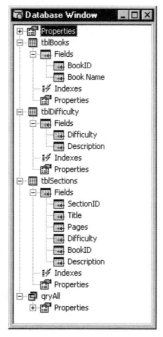

Figure 10.7 *The **JPBook.mdb** database after you complete the table and query designs.*

ADDING CONTROLS TO THE FORM

In the *prjBookList* project, you will use the *ListView* control you added to the project in the previous section, a *TextBox* control, three *Label* controls, and three *CommandButton* controls. To begin building the form, you will add each control to the *prjBookList* form and assign properties to each control.

ADDING A MICROSOFT LISTVIEW CONTROL TO THE FORM

As you have learned, the *prjBookList* project will use a *Microsoft ListView* control to display information about a user-selected drive. To add a *Microsoft ListView* control to the *frmTreeView* form, perform the following steps:

1. If Visual Basic is not displaying the *frmTreeView* form within an object window, double-click your mouse on the *frmTreeView* form listing within the Project Explorer. Visual Basic will open the *frmTreeView* form.

2. Within Visual Basic, select the View menu Toolbox option. Visual Basic will open the Toolbox.

3. Within the Toolbox, select the *Microsoft ListView* control icon, ListView, as shown in Figure 10.8.

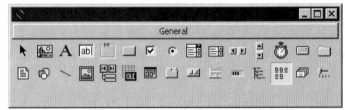

Figure 10.8 *The Toolbox showing the **Microsoft ListView** control icon, ListView.*

4. Within the Toolbox, double-click your mouse on the ListView icon. Visual Basic will draw a *Microsoft ListView* control, *ListView1*, within the *frmTreeView* form.

5. Within the *frmTreeView* form window, click your mouse on the *ListView1* control to highlight it. Visual Basic will draw a small frame around the control.

6. Select the View menu Properties Window option. Visual Basic will open the Properties Window listing the *ListView1* properties.

7. Within the Properties Window, change the *ListView1* property values to those Table 10.5 lists.

Object	Properties	Set As
ListView1	*Height*	4335
ListView1	*Left*	5760
ListView1	*SortOrder*	0 - *lvwAscending*
ListView1	*Top*	1320
ListView1	*View*	3 - *lvwReport*
ListView1	*Width*	6000
ListView1	*Name*	*lvwDB*

Table 10.5 *The newly named **lvwDB** control's properties.*

ADDING A MICROSOFT TREEVIEW CONTROL TO THE FORM

As you have learned, the *prjBookList* project will use a *Microsoft TreeView* control to display information about a user-selected drive. To add a *Microsoft TreeView* control to the *frmTreeView* form, perform the following steps:

1. If Visual Basic is not displaying the *frmTreeView* form within an object window, double-click your mouse on the *frmTreeView* form listing within the Project Explorer. Visual Basic will open the *frmTreeView* form.

2. Within Visual Basic, select the View menu Toolbox option. Visual Basic will open the Toolbox.

3. Within the Toolbox, select the *Microsoft TreeView* control icon, TreeView, as shown in Figure 10.9.

Figure 10.9 *The Toolbox showing the **Microsoft TreeView** control icon, TreeView.*

4. Within the Toolbox, double-click your mouse on the TreeView icon. Visual Basic will draw a *Microsoft TreeView* control, *TreeView1*, within the *frmTreeView* form.

343

5. Within the *frmTreeView* form window, click your mouse on the *TreeView1* control to highlight it. Visual Basic will draw a small frame around the control.

6. Select the View menu Properties Window option. Visual Basic will open the Properties Window listing the *TreeView1* properties.

7. Within the Properties Window, change the *TreeView1* property values to those Table 10.6 lists.

Object	Properties	Set As
TreeView1	Height	5055
TreeView1	HideSelection	False
TreeView1	Left	240
TreeView1	Style	7 - tvwTreelinesPlus
TreeView1	Top	600
TreeView1	Width	5400
TreeView1	Name	tvwDB

Table 10.6 *The newly named **tvwDB** control's properties.*

ADDING A MICROSOFT IMAGELIST CONTROL TO THE FORM

The *prjBookList* project will use a *Microsoft ImageList* control to store the icon files that the *prjBookList* project will use to draw the images within the *lvwDB* and *tvwDB* controls. To add a *Microsoft ImageList* control to the *frmTreeView* form, perform the following steps:

1. If Visual Basic is not displaying the *frmTreeView* form within an object window, double-click your mouse on the *frmTreeView* form listing within the Project Explorer. Visual Basic will open the *frmTreeView* form.

2. Within Visual Basic, select the View menu Toolbox option. Visual Basic will open the Toolbox.

3. Within the Toolbox, select the *Microsoft ImageList* control icon, ImageList, as shown in Figure 10.10.

Figure 10.10 *The Toolbox showing the **Microsoft ImageList** control icon, ImageList.*

4. Within the Toolbox, double-click your mouse on the ImageList icon. Visual Basic will draw a *Microsoft ImageList* control, *ImageList1*, within the *frmImageList* form

5. Within the *frmImageList* form window, click your mouse on the *ImageList1* control to highlight it. Visual Basic will draw a small frame around the control.

6. Select the View menu Properties Window option. Visual Basic will open the Properties Window listing the *ImageList1* properties.

7. Within the Properties Window, change the *ImageList1* property values to those Table 10.7 lists.

Object	Properties	Set As
ImageList1	Left	480
ImageList1	Top	0
ImageList1	Name	imlSmallIcons

*Table 10.7 The newly named **imlSmallIcons** control's properties.*

8. Click your mouse on the *Custom* field within the Properties Window. Visual Basic will display the Property Pages dialog box.

9. Within the Property Pages dialog box, select the Images tab. Visual Basic will change the dialog box's display to the Images tab.

10. Within the Property Pages dialog box, click your mouse on the Insert Picture button. Visual Basic will display the Select Picture dialog box.

11. Within the Select Picture dialog box, navigate to *x:\vbpl\Chapter10*, where *x* corresponds to the drive letter of the hard drive on which you installed the *prjBookList.exe* program. Double-click your mouse on the *closed.ico* file. Visual Basic will add the *closed.ico* file to the *imlSmallIcons* control's Property Pages dialog box.

12. Within the Property Pages dialog box, enter *Closed* within the *Key* field.

13. Within the Property Pages dialog box, click your mouse on the Insert Picture button. Visual Basic will display the Select Picture dialog box.

14. Within the Select Picture dialog box, navigate to *x:\vbpl\Chapter10*, where *x* corresponds to the drive letter of the hard drive on which you installed the *prjBookList.exe* program. Double-click your mouse on the *cylinder.ico* file. Visual Basic will add the *cylinder.ico* file to the *imlSmallIcons* control's Property Pages dialog box.

15. Within the Property Pages dialog box, enter *Cylinder* within the *Key* field.

16. Within the Property Pages dialog box, click your mouse on the Insert Picture button. Visual Basic will display the Select Picture dialog box.

17. Within the Select Picture dialog box, navigate to *x:\vbpl\Chapter10*, where *x* corresponds to the drive letter of the hard drive on which you installed the *prjBookList.exe* program. Double-click your mouse on the *leaf.ico* file. Visual Basic will add the *leaf.ico* file to the *imlSmallIcons* control's Property Pages dialog box.

18. Within the Property Pages dialog box, enter *Leaf* within the *Key* field.

19. Within the Property Pages dialog box, click your mouse on the Insert Picture button. Visual Basic will display the Select Picture dialog box.

20. Within the Select Picture dialog box, navigate to *x:\vbpl\Chapter10*, where *x* corresponds to the drive letter of the hard drive on which you installed the *prjBookList.exe* program. Double-click your mouse on the *open.ico* file. Visual Basic will add the *open.ico* file to the *imlSmallIcons* control's Property Pages dialog box.

21. Within the Property Pages dialog box, enter *Open* within the *Key* field.

22. Within the Property Pages dialog box, click your mouse on the Insert Picture button. Visual Basic will display the Select Picture dialog box.

23. Within the Select Picture dialog box, navigate to *x:\vbp\Chapter10*, where *x* corresponds to the drive letter of the hard drive on which you installed the *prjBookList.exe* program. Double-click your mouse on the *smlbook.ico* file. Visual Basic will add the *smlbook.ico* file to the *imlSmallIcons* control's Property Pages dialog box.

24. Within the Property Pages dialog box, enter *SmlBook* within the *Key* field. When you finish, the Property Pages dialog box will look similar to Figure 10.11.

345

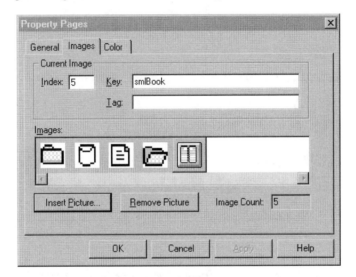

Figure 10.11 The Property Pages dialog box after you finish adding icons.

25. Within the Property Pages dialog box, click your mouse on the OK button to exit the dialog box.

ADDING A MICROSOFT COMMON DIALOG CONTROL TO THE FORM

As you have learned, the *prjBookList* project will use a *Microsoft CommonDialog* control with drive and directory information in the event the program is unable to locate the *JPBooks.mdb* file on its own. To add a *Microsoft CommonDialog* control to the *frmTreeView* form, perform the following steps:

1. If Visual Basic is not displaying the *frmTreeView* form within an object window, double-click your mouse on the *frmTreeView* form listing within the Project Explorer. Visual Basic will open the *frmTreeView* form.

2. Within Visual Basic, select the View menu Toolbox option. Visual Basic will open the Toolbox.

3. Within the Toolbox, select the *Microsoft CommonDialog* control icon, CommonDialog, as shown in Figure 10.12.

Figure 10.12 The Toolbox showing the **Microsoft CommonDialog** control icon, CommonDialog.

4. Within the Toolbox, double-click your mouse on the CommonDialog icon. Visual Basic will draw a *Microsoft CommonDialog* control, *CommonDialog1*, within the *frmTreeView* form.

5. Within the *frmTreeView* form window, click your mouse on the *CommonDialog1* control to highlight it. Visual Basic will draw a small frame around the control.

6. Select the View menu Properties Window option. Visual Basic will open the Properties Window listing the *CommonDialog1* properties.

7. Within the Properties Window, change the *CommonDialog1* property values to those Table 10.8 lists.

Object	Properties	Set As
CommonDialog1	*Left*	0
CommonDialog1	*Top*	0
CommonDialog1	*Name*	*dlgDialog*

Table 10.8 *The newly named **dlgDialog** control's properties.*

ADDING A MICROSOFT STATUSBAR CONTROL TO THE FORM

The *prjBookList* project will use a *Microsoft StatusBar* control to display additional information about the program's current state or about a user-selected object. To add a *Microsoft StatusBar* control to the *frmTreeView* form, perform the following steps:

1. If Visual Basic is not displaying the *frmTreeView* form within an object window, double-click your mouse on the *frmTreeView* form listing within the Project Explorer. Visual Basic will open the *frmTreeView* form.

2. Within Visual Basic, select the View menu Toolbox option. Visual Basic will open the Toolbox.

3. Within the Toolbox, select the *Microsoft StatusBar* control icon, StatusBar, as shown in Figure 10.13.

Figure 10.13 *The Toolbox showing the **Microsoft StatusBar** control icon, StatusBar.*

4. Within the Toolbox, double-click your mouse on the StatusBar icon. Visual Basic will draw a *Microsoft StatusBar* control, *StatusBar1*, within the *frmTreeView* form.

5. Within the *frmTreeView* form window, click your mouse on the *StatusBar1* control to highlight it. Visual Basic will draw a small frame around the control.

6. Select the View menu Properties Window option. Visual Basic will open the Properties Window listing the *StatusBar1* properties.

7. Within the Properties Window, change the *StatusBar1* property values to those Table 10.9 lists.

Object	Properties	Set As
StatusBar1	*Align*	*2 - vbAlignBottom*
StatusBar1	*Height*	255
StatusBar1	*Left*	0
StatusBar1	*Top*	6300
StatusBar1	*Width*	11790
StatusBar1	*Name*	*sbrDB*

Table 10.9 *The newly named **sbrDB** control's properties.*

ADDING A MICROSOFT PROGRESSBAR TO THE FORM

As you have learned, the *prjBookList* project will use a *Microsoft ProgressBar* control to display information about the program's current status while the program loads records from the *JPBook.mdb* database and places the records into the program's *ListView* and *TreeView* controls. To add a *Microsoft ProgressBar* control to the *frmTreeView* form, perform the following steps:

1. If Visual Basic is not displaying the *frmTreeView* form within an object window, double-click your mouse on the *frmTreeView* form listing within the Project Explorer. Visual Basic will open the *frmTreeView* form.

2. Within Visual Basic, select the View menu Toolbox option. Visual Basic will open the Toolbox.

3. Within the Toolbox, select the *ProgressBar* control icon, ProgressBar, as shown in Figure 10.14.

*Figure 10.14 The Toolbox showing the **Microsoft ProgressBar** control icon, ProgressBar.*

4. Within the Toolbox, double-click your mouse on the ProgressBar icon. Visual Basic will draw a *Microsoft ProgressBar* control, *ProgressBar1*, within the *frmTreeView* form.

5. Within the *frmTreeView* form window, click your mouse on the *ProgressBar1* control to highlight it. Visual Basic will draw a small frame around the control.

6. Select the View menu Properties Window option. Visual Basic will open the Properties Window listing the *ProgressBar1* properties.

7. Within the Properties Window, change the *ProgressBar1* property values to those Table 10.10 lists.

Object	Properties	Set As
ProgressBar1	*Height*	330
ProgressBar1	*Left*	240
ProgressBar1	*Top*	5760
ProgressBar1	*Visible*	*False*
ProgressBar1	*Width*	11490
ProgressBar1	*Name*	*prgLoad*

*Table 10.10 The newly named **prgLoad** control's properties.*

ADDING THE REMAINING CONTROLS TO THE FORM

As you have learned, within the *prjBookList* project you will use *Label* controls to name other controls in the project and to provide the user with the title of the currently selected book. You will also use a *ComboBox* control to let the user select the display type for the *lvwDB* control. Now that you have added all the other controls to the form, you should add the *Label* controls and the *ComboBox* control to the form. After you add the remaining controls, you will begin to write the program's code. To add the *Label* controls to the *frmTreeView* form, perform the following steps:

1. If Visual Basic is not displaying the *frmTreeView* form within an object window, double-click your mouse on the *frmTreeView* form listing within the Project Explorer. Visual Basic will open the *frmTreeView* form.

2. Within Visual Basic, select the View menu Toolbox option. Visual Basic will open the Toolbox.

3. Within the Toolbox, double-click your mouse on the Label icon. Visual Basic will draw a *Label* control, *Label1*, within the *frmTreeView* form.

4. Repeat Step 3 three more times. Visual Basic will add the *Label2, Label3,* and *Label4* controls to the *frmTreeView* form.

5. Within the Toolbox, double-click your mouse on the ComboBox icon. Visual Basic will draw a *ComboBox* control, *Combo1,* within the *frmTreeView* form.

6. Within the *frmTreeView* form, click your mouse on the *Label1* control to highlight it. Visual Basic will draw a small frame around the control.

7. Select the View menu Properties Window option. Visual Basic will open the Properties Window listing the *Label1* properties.

8. Within the Properties Window, change the *Label1* properties to the values Table 10.11 lists.

9. Repeat Steps 6, 7, and 8 to change the properties for the other *Label* controls and the *ComboBox* control to the values Table 10.11 lists.

Object	Property	Set As
Label1	Alignment	2 - Center
Label1	Caption	Jamsa Press Book Database
Label1	Font	MS San Serif, Bold, 12 Point
Label1	Height	495
Label1	Left	240
Label1	Top	0
Label1	Width	11535
Label1	Name	lblTopForm
Label2	Alignment	2 - Center
Label2	Caption	Book Selected:
Label2	Height	255
Label2	Left	5760
Label2	Top	600
Label2	Width	3375
Label2	Name	lblBookSelected
Label3	Alignment	2 - Center
Label3	Caption	[blank]
Label3	Height	375
Label3	Left	5760
Label3	Top	960
Label3	Width	3375
Label3	Name	lblCurrentSelection
Label4	Alignment	2 - Center
Label4	Caption	Section View
Label4	Height	255
Label4	Left	9240
Label4	Top	600
Label4	Width	2415
Label4	Name	lblSections
Combo1	Height	315
Combo1	Left	9240
Combo1	Top	960
Combo1	Width	2415
Combo1	Name	cmbViewTypes

*Table 10.11 The newly named **Label** and **ComboBox** controls' properties.*

Adding the File Menu to the Form

As you learned in Chapter 4, "Using Multiple Forms to Load Different File Types," Visual Basic lets you create menus for your programs with the Visual Basic Menu Editor. The *prjBookList* project uses a single menu and a single menu item, Exit, to simplify the form's design and still provide an easy way for the user to exit the program. To add a menu to the *frmTreeView* form, perform the following steps:

1. Select the Tools menu Menu Editor option. Visual Basic will open the Menu Editor dialog box.

2. Within the Menu Editor dialog box, enter *&File* within the *Caption* field. (As with command buttons, the ampersand symbol (&) within a menu alerts Visual Basic to accept the letter immediately following the ampersand as a keyboard shortcut for the item.) Visual Basic will display the *&File* caption in the Menu Viewer at the bottom of the Menu Editor as you type.

3. Press the TAB key to move to the *Name* field. Within the *Name* field, enter the menu item's name as *mnuFile*.

4. Click your mouse on the Next button. Visual Basic will clear the *Caption* and *Name* fields, move the block cursor (the solid blue block) within the Menu Viewer down one line, and return the input cursor (the flashing vertical bar) to the *Caption* field.

5. Within the Menu Editor dialog box, click your mouse on the right arrow just above the Menu Viewer and to the left of the Next button. Visual Basic will display three dots on the current line in the Menu Viewer.

6. Within the *Caption* field, enter the caption of the next item as *E&xit*. Visual Basic will display three dots and follow them with the *E&xit* caption in the Menu Viewer.

7. Press the TAB key to move the input cursor to the *Name* field. Within the *Name* field, enter the name of the menu item as *mnuFile_Exit*.

8. Click your mouse on the OK button. Visual Basic will close the Menu Editor dialog box and return to the Visual Basic editing window.

Figure 10.15 shows the *frmTreeView* form after you complete its design.

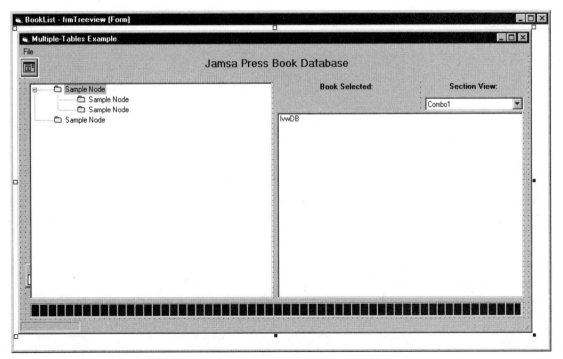

Figure 10.15 *The **frmTreeView** form after you complete its design.*

WRITING THE PROGRAM CODE FOR THE prjBOOKLIST PROJECT

As you have learned, the *prjBookList* project reads data from the *JPBook.mdb* database and displays records from that data within the *ListView* and *TreeView* controls that you have placed onto the *frmTreeView* form. The *prjBookList* project uses only a single form, *frmTreeView*, and you will place all the project's program code within the form. The *frmTreeView* form uses several variables throughout its component procedures and functions, as well as two constants. The following code implements the variable declarations for the *frmTreeView* form:

```
Dim EventFlag As Integer
Dim mCurrentIndex As Integer
Dim mStatusBarStyle As Integer
Dim JPBooksDB As Database
Dim JPBooksWS As Workspace
Dim mNode As Node
Dim mItem As ListItem

Const Book = 1
Const SECTION = 2
```

The variable declarations include three *Integer* variables, two *DAO Object* variables, a *Node* variable, and a *ListItem* variable. The program uses the *EventFlag* variable as a flag variable, the *mCurrentIndex* variable to keep track of the user's current selection, and the *mStatusBarStyle* variable to keep information about the status bar's style setting. The *JPBooksDB* variable will contain the *JPBook.mdb* database object within the program, and the *JPBooksWS* variable is simply a workspace variable.

The program uses the *mNode* variable to maintain a reference to items within the *tvwDB TreeView* control. Within your programs, you will work with the items in a *TreeView* control as individual *Node* objects within the *Nodes* collection. The *tvwDB TreeView* control is, essentially, a container for all the *Node* objects you assign to the *tvwDB TreeView's Nodes* collection.

Similarly, the program uses the *mItem* variable to maintain a reference to items within the *lvwDB ListView* control. Within your programs, you will work with the items in a *ListView* control as individual *ListItem* objects within the *ListItems* collection. The *lvwDB ListView* control is, essentially, a container for all the *ListItem* objects you assign to the *lvwDB ListView* control's *ListItems* collection.

WRITING THE CODE FOR THE FORM_LOAD EVENT

As you have learned in previous chapters, the first program code that will execute when you load a form is the form's *Form_Load* event. Because the *prjBookList* project is a Single Document Interface application, the program code within the *frmTreeView* form's *Load* event will be the first program code to execute when you run the *prjBookList* project. The following code implements the *frmTreeView* form's *Load* event:

```
Private Sub Form_Load()
  With cmbViewTypes
    .AddItem "Icon View"
    .AddItem "SmallIcon View"
    .AddItem "List View"
    .AddItem "Report View"
    .ListIndex = 3
  End With
  lvwDB.View = lvwReport
  prgLoad.Max = 100
  sbrDB.Panels.Add
  sbrDB.Panels.Add
  sbrDB.Panels(1).AutoSize = sbrContents
  sbrDB.Panels(2).AutoSize = sbrSpring
  sbrDB.Panels(3).AutoSize = sbrSpring
```

```
      With dlgDialog
         .DialogTitle = "Can't Find JPBook.mdb"
         .Filter = "(*.MDB)|*.mdb"
      End With
      On Error GoTo errFind
      Set JPBooksDB = DBEngine.OpenDatabase("JPBOOK.MDB")
      tvwDB.Sorted = True
      Set mNode = tvwDB.Nodes.Add()
      mNode.Text = "Jamsa Press Books"
      mNode.Tag = "Publisher"
      mNode.Image = "closed"
      tvwDB.LabelEdit = False

  errFind:
    If Err = 3024 Then
       dlgDialog.ShowOpen
       Set JPBooksDB =
  DBEngine.Workspaces(0).OpenDatabase(dlgDialog.filename)
       Resume Next
    ElseIf Err <> 0 Then
       MsgBox "Unexpected Error: " & Err.Description
       End
    ElseIf Err = 0 Then
       Exit Sub
    End If
  End Sub
```

The *Form_Load* event performs significant initialization processing for the *frmTreeView* form. Over the course of its execution, the program code initializes the *cmbViewTypes* combo box, the *lvwDB* list view, the program's status bar and progress bar, the *tvwDB* tree view, and the *JPBooksDB* database object.

The program code begins by assigning four possible values, Icon View, SmallIcon View, List View, and Report View, to the *cmbViewTypes* combo box. During the program's execution, the user will be able to change the view within the *lvwDB* list view based on the current selection in the *cmbViewTypes* combo box. Next, the program code sets the *lvwDB* control to the default setting (Report View), sets the progress bar's maximum value to 100, and initializes the *sbrDB* status bar control's appearance. The program code adds two additional panels (the spaces within the status bar that display information) to the status bar (which always has one panel by default), and then formats all three panels.

After it finishes initializing the status bar, the program code sets two properties for the *dlgDialog* dialog box and tries to open the database. If the program successfully opens the database, the *Form_Load* event goes on to initialize the *tvwDB* tree view control. If the program does not successfully open the database, the *Form_Load* event will execute the code within the *errFind* error handling routine. The *errFind* routine displays the *dlgDialog* dialog box and lets the user locate the *JPBook.mdb* database. The *errFind* routine then loads the *JPBook.mdb* database into the *JPBooksDB* object and resumes execution within the event's body.

After it opens the database successfully (with or without user assistance), the *Form_Load* event's program code will add the first node to the *tvwDB* control. After the program adds the first node to the *tvwDB* control, it sets the text within the node to *Jamsa Press Books*, sets other node properties that the program will use, sets the node's *Tag* and *Image* properties, and exits the event.

WRITING THE CODE FOR THE *FORM_ACTIVATE* EVENT AND THE *LOADBOOKS* PROCEDURE

As you learned in the previous section, the *Form_Load* event initializes many of the controls within the *frmTreeView* form. After the *Form_Load* event completes its processing, the program will automatically invoke the *Form_Activate* event, because the *frmTreeView* form will receive the focus from the operating system after the form completes the *Form_Load* event. *Focus* is the ability to receive user input through the mouse or keyboard. When an object has the focus, it can receive input from a user. The following code implements the *Form_Activate* event:

```
Private Sub Form_Activate()
  DoEvents
  Me.Show
  Me.MousePointer = vbHourglass
  LoadBooks
  Me.MousePointer = vbNormal
End Sub
```

As you can see, the *Form_Activate* event uses the *Me.Show* method to ensure that the program fully displays the form, and then calls the *LoadBooks* procedure to load the data from the *JPBook.mdb* database and add the books within the database to the *tvwDB* control. The following code implements the *LoadBooks* procedure:

```
Private Sub LoadBooks()
  Dim BooksRS As Recordset
  Dim SectionsRS As Recordset
  Dim intIndex As Integer

  Set BooksRS = JPBooksDB.OpenRecordset("tblBooks", dbOpenDynaset)
  prgLoad.Visible = True
  sbrDB.Style = sbrSimple
  Do Until BooksRS.EOF
    prgLoad.Value = BooksRS.PercentPosition
    Set mNode = tvwDB.Nodes.Add(1, tvwChild, BooksRS!BookID & " ID", _
        CStr(BooksRS.Fields("Book Name")), "closed")
    mNode.Tag = "Books"
    intIndex = mNode.Index
    Set SectionsRS = _
        JPBooksDB.OpenRecordset("Select * from tblSections Where " & _
        " BookID = " & BooksRS.Fields("BookID"))
    Do Until SectionsRS.EOF
      Set mNode = tvwDB.Nodes.Add(intIndex, tvwChild)
      mNode.Text = SectionsRS!Title
      mNode.Key = "BK" & CStr(BooksRS!BookID) & "Section" & _
          CStr(SectionsRS!SectionID)
      mNode.Tag = "Sections"
      mNode.Image = "smlBook"
      SectionsRS.MoveNext
    Loop
    BooksRS.MoveNext
  Loop
  prgLoad.Visible = False
  sbrDB.Style = sbrNormal
  tvwDB.Nodes(1).Sorted = True
  tvwDB.Nodes(1).Expanded = True
  PublishersStatusBar
End Sub
```

The *LoadBooks* procedure uses two local recordsets—the *BooksRS* recordset, in which it stores data about books, and the *SectionsRS* recordset, in which it stores data about chapters. The first line of code within the procedure opens and initializes the *BooksRS* recordset to include all the books in the *tblBooks* table. The code then makes the *prgLoad* progress bar visible while it processes the data within the *BooksRS* recordset. After it makes the progress bar visible, the program code enters a *Do-Until* loop to process all the records within the *BooksRS* recordset.

Within the loop, the program code sets the progress bar to the *BooksRS* recordset's *PercentPosition* property, which represents the percentage of the recordset the program has processed. The code then adds a new *Node* object to the *lvwDB* property, and labels the node with the book's name from the *BooksRS* recordset. Next, the program code uses the *BookID* field from the *BooksRS* recordset to open the *SectionsRS* recordset for that book. The program code then enters a second *Do-Until* loop to process the records within the *SectionsRS* recordset.

Within the second *Do-Until* loop, the program code adds additional child nodes (that is, nodes that are below the book node within the tree) until the loop processes all the chapters for the book within the database. The last statement within the loop moves to the next record in the *SectionsRS* recordset and the loop continues.

After the second *Do-Until* loop exits, the program code moves to the next record in the *BooksRS* recordset and the first loop continues. After the first *Do-Until* loop exits, the program code hides the progress bar, sorts the nodes within the *tvwDB* control alphabetically, and expands the first node. The program's expanding the first node results in the display of all the books within the *BooksRS* recordset. The last statement in the procedure calls the *PublishersStatusBar* procedure, which sets the status bar information to display when the program displays the first node in the tree view. The following section explains the *PublishersStatusBar* procedure.

WRITING THE CODE FOR THE PUBLISHERSSTATUSBAR PROCEDURE

As the previous section explains, the *PublishersStatusBar* procedure sets the values that the status bar control at the form's bottom will display whenever the user has not selected a book node. The following code implements the *PublishersStatusBar* procedure:

```
Private Sub PublishersStatusBar()
  Dim rs As Recordset

  Set rs = JPBooksDB.OpenRecordset("tblBooks", dbOpenTable)
  sbrDB.Panels(1).Text = "name: " & rs.Name
  sbrDB.Panels(2).Text = "Date Created: " & CStr(rs.DateCreated)
  sbrDB.Panels(3).Text = "Last Updated " & rs.LastUpdated
End Sub
```

The *PublishersStatusBar* procedure opens a temporary recordset from the *tblBooks* table and then fills the three panels in the *StatusBar* control with the recordset's name, creation date, and last update date. Other procedures within the *prjBookList* project will change the status bar's panel values.

WRITING CODE FOR THE TREEVIEW CONTROL'S EVENTS

As you learned in this chapter's "Using the *prjBookList* Project" section, the user can click the mouse on different nodes within the tree view control in order to move through them. There are three actions the user can perform with each node: Expand, Collapse, or Select. The *Expand* and *Collapse* events (which the control invokes in response to the user's Expand or Collapse action) will display or hide the child nodes beneath that node, respectively. The *NodeClick* event (which the control invokes in response to the user's Select action), within the *prjBookList* project, will fill the list view with the chapters for the book the user selects. Because the *Expand* and *Collapse* events are simpler than the *NodeSelect* event, it is worthwhile for you to create them first. The following code implements the *tvwDB_Expand* event:

```
Private Sub tvwDB_Expand(ByVal Node As Node)
  If Node.Tag = "Books" Or Node.Index = 1 Then
    Node.Image = "open"
    Node.Sorted = True
  End If
  If Node.Tag = "Publisher" Then
    lvwDB.ListItems.Clear
    LblCurrentSelection.Caption = "[ None ]"
  End If
End Sub
```

The *Expand* event receives as its sole parameter a reference to the node on which the user clicked the mouse. The event's code then checks on which node the user clicked. If the user clicked on a book node, the program code will change that node's icon to Open and then display the child nodes under that node. (In the *prjBookList* project, the chapters are the child nodes.) If the user clicked the mouse on the first node, the program code will clear the chapters from the *ListView* control and change the *lblCurrentSelection* label's caption to "[None]." Conversely, if the user collapses a node (to collapse a node, the user clicks on the plus (+) sign to the node's left), the control will invoke the *Collapse* event. The following code implements the *tvwDB_Collapse* event:

```
Private Sub tvwDB_Collapse(ByVal Node As Node)
   If Node.Tag = "Books" Or Node.Index = 1 Then Node.Image = "closed"
   If Node.Tag = "Publisher" Then
      lvwDB.ListItems.Clear
      LblCurrentSelection.Caption = "[ None ]"
   End If
End Sub
```

If the user clicks the mouse on any book node, the program code within the *Collapse* event will change that node's image and hide the chapters the node's child nodes are currently displaying. If the user clicks the mouse on the topmost node, the program will hide all the book nodes, clear the *ListView* control, and change the *lblCurrentSelection* label's caption to "[None]."

354

On the other hand, if the user clicks the mouse on a node (rather than on the expand or collapse icon to the node's left), the control will call its *NodeClick* event. Within the *NodeClick* event, the program code will update the *ListView* control and change the display within the status bar. The following code implements the *NodeClick* event:

```
Private Sub tvwDB_NodeClick(ByVal Node As Node)
   If Node.Tag = "Books" And EventFlag <> Book Then MakeColumns
   If Node.Tag = "Publisher" Then
      lvwDB.ListItems.Clear
      LblCurrentSelection.Caption = "[ None ]"
      PublishersStatusBar
      Exit Sub
   End If
   If Node.Tag = "Sections" Then Set Node = Node.Parent
   If Node.Tag = "Books" And mCurrentIndex <> Val(Node.Key) Then
      LblCurrentSelection.Caption = Node.Text
      GetTitles Val(Node.Key)
   End If
   If Node.Tag = "Books" Then
      sbrDB.Panels(1).Text = Node.Text
      sbrDB.Panels(2).Text = Node.Children & " Sections"
      sbrDB.Panels(3).Text = ""
      Node.Sorted = True
   End If
End Sub
```

Within the *NodeClick* event, the first line of program code checks to ensure that the program has already placed the headers onto the *ListView* control. If the program has not placed the headers, it calls the *MakeColumns* procedure, which adds column headers to the control. You will learn more about the *MakeColumns* procedure in the next section. If the program has already placed the headers, the event's execution simply continues.

After the event's code ensures that the program has correctly formatted the headers for the *ListView* control, the program code checks to see if the user clicked the mouse on the topmost node. If the user has clicked the mouse on the topmost node, the program code clears the *ListView* control and sets the *lblCurrentSelection* label's caption to "[None]," just as it does with the *Expand* and *Collapse* events, and then exits the event.

If the user has not clicked the mouse on the topmost node, the program code checks to see if the user clicked the mouse on a chapter within the list view. If the user clicked the mouse on a chapter, the program code sets the *Node* variable to point to the chapter's parent—that is, the book that contains the chapter.

Next, the program code checks to see whether the user clicked the mouse on a new node, or if the user clicked the mouse on the currently selected node. If the user clicked the mouse on a new node, the program code calls the *GetTitles* procedure, which retrieves the section titles from the *tblSection* database and places the titles into the *ListView* control. A later section will discuss the *GetTitles* procedure in detail. Finally, the program code within the procedure updates the *StatusBar* control with the book's name and number of sections, and leaves the third panel blank.

WRITING THE CODE FOR THE *MAKECOLUMNS* PROCEDURE

As the previous section explains, the first time the user clicks the mouse on a node within the tree view, the program code will set the headers for the *ListView* control. After the user clicks the mouse on a node one time, the program code will not set the headers again. The *MakeColumns* procedure sets the headers within the *lvwDB ListView* control. The following code implements the *MakeColumns* procedure:

```
Private Sub MakeColumns()
  lvwDB.ColumnHeaders.Clear
  lvwDB.ColumnHeaders.Add , , "Section", 3700
  lvwDB.ColumnHeaders.Add , , "Pages", 350
  lvwDB.ColumnHeaders.Add , , "Difficulty", 1000
  EventFlag = Book
End Sub
```

The *MakeColumns* procedure clears the current column headers (if any) within the list view, and then sets the control to three columns and three headers. As you can see, the three headers are *Section*, *Pages*, and *Difficulty*. The last value within each *Add* method call is the width, in twips (the Visual Basic unit of screen measurement, as you learned in Chapter 5, "Creating and Using Fractals"), of the column. When the procedure completes its processing, it sets the *EventFlag* variable's value to 1 to ensure that the program will not call the procedure again.

WRITING THE CODE FOR THE *GETTITLES* PROCEDURE

As you have learned, when the user clicks the mouse on a node that is different from the current node, the *tvwDB_NodeClick* event calls the *GetTitles* procedure with the newly selected node's key (which contains the node's unique identifier). In the *prjBookList* project, the node *key* values correspond to the book ID. The *GetTitles* procedure uses the book ID to retrieve the sections or chapters within that book, their difficulty level, and their number of pages. The following code implements the *GetTitles* procedure:

```
Private Sub GetTitles(BookID)
  Dim QueryText As String
  Dim SectionsRS As Recordset

  prgLoad.Visible = True
  lvwDB.ListItems.Clear
  QueryText = "SELECT tblSections.BookId, tblSections.SectionID, " & _
      "tblSections.Title, tblSections.Pages, tblSections.Description " & _
      "FROM (tblSections INNER JOIN tblSections ON " & _
      "tblSections.Difficulty = tblSections.Difficulty) INNER JOIN " & _
      "tblBooks ON tblSections.BookID = tblBooks.BookID "
  QueryText = QueryText & "Where tblSections.BookID = " & BookID & _
      " ORDER BY tblSections.Title"
  Set SectionsRS = JPBooksDB.OpenRecordset(QueryText)
  Do Until SectionsRS.EOF
    prgLoad.Value = SectionsRS.PercentPosition
    Set mItem = lvwDB.ListItems.Add(, CStr(SectionsRS!BookID) & " " & _
        CStr(SectionsRS!SectionID), SectionsRS!Title, "book", "smlBook")
    mItem.SubItems(1) = SectionsRS!Pages
    mItem.SubItems(2) = SectionsRS!Description
    SectionsRS.MoveNext
  Loop
  prgLoad.Visible = False
  mCurrentIndex = PubID
End Sub
```

The *GetTitles* procedure's code first makes the progress bar at the form's bottom visible, which provides the user with a visual cue to the program's progress. The code then clears the *ListView* control of all items within the control. Next, the program code sets the value for the *QueryText* variable. As you can see, the *QueryText* variable's value is an extended SQL string that returns all the sections for the given book ID, in order, together with their difficulty level.

The program code places the recordset that results from the *QueryText* query within the *SectionsRS* recordset. The program code within the procedure then loops through each record in the recordset. Each time the procedure passes through the loop, it adds the current record to the *lvwDB ListView* control, placing the chapter name in the first column, the chapter's number of pages in the second column, and the chapter's difficulty level in the third column. After the loop exits, the program hides the progress bar and exits the procedure.

UNDERSTANDING JOIN STATEMENTS AND CLAUSES

As you have learned in previous chapters, much of the power that your programs will take advantage of when working with relational databases comes from the database's ability to combine information from multiple tables into a single resulting recordset. When you join records from multiple tables, you will do so using a *Join* clause within your SQL *Select* statement. When you use a *Join* statement to combine records from multiple tables, the *Join* statement will use the values within the fields you specify in the two tables to combine the tables and yield the resulting recordset. For example, the following statement joins two tables on their respective *EmployeeID* fields:

```
FROM Table1 INNER JOIN Table2 ON Table1.EmployeeID = Table2.EmployeeID
```

The resulting recordset will display only the records from within both tables with the same value in the *EmployeeID* field. Typically, you will use a *Join* clause to yield a recordset containing some values from both the original tables, sorted and selected by shared values in the original tables.

The most commonly used *Join* clause is the *Inner Join* clause, which combines records from two tables whenever there are matching values in a common field. In other words, if Table1 has an Employee ID field, and you invoke the SQL *Select* statement with the clause *Table1.EmployeeID Inner Join Table2.EmployeeID*, the resulting *Recordset* will include all records in both tables that share the same EmployeeID value. You will implement the *Inner Join* statement within your *Select* statements immediately following the *From* statement, as shown here:

```
FROM Table1 INNER JOIN Table2 ON Table1.Field1 Comparison Table2.Field2
```

When you implement the *Inner Join* clause, you will use the arguments Table 10.12 details.

Argument	Description
Table1, Table2	The names of the tables from which the *Select* statement will combine the records.
Field1, Field2	The names of the fields that the *Select* statement will join. If the fields are not numeric, the fields must be of the same data type and contain the same kind of data, but it is not necessary for them to have the same name.
Comparison	Any relational comparison operator: "=," "<," ">," "<=," ">=," or "<>."

*Table 10.12 The arguments for the **Inner Join** clause.*

You can use an *Inner Join* operation in any *From* clause. *Inner Join* operations combine records from two tables whenever there are matching values in a field common to both tables. The following example shows how you can join two tables, *Categories* and *Products*, on the *CategoryID* field:

```
SELECT CategoryName, ProductName
FROM Categories INNER JOIN Products
ON Categories.CategoryID = Products.CategoryID
```

In this example, *CategoryID* is the joined field, but the query output does not include *CategoryID* because the *Select* statement does not include it. To include the joined field, include the field name in the *Select* statement—in this case, *Categories.CategoryID*. You can also link several *On* clauses in a *Join* clause using the following syntax (remember that items within brackets are optional):

```
SELECT fields
FROM table1 Inner Join table2
```

```
ON table1.field1 Comparison table2.field1 [ AND
(ON table1.field2 Comparison table2.field2) OR
(ON table1.field3 Comparison table2.field3)]
```

Finally, you can nest *Join* clauses using the following syntax (remember that items within brackets are optional):

```
SELECT fields
FROM table1 Inner Join
(table2 Inner Join [( ]table3
[Inner Join [( ]tablex [Inner Join ...)]
ON table3.field3 Comparison tablex.fieldx)]
ON table2.field2 Comparison table3.field3)
ON table1.field1 Comparison table2.field2
```

As you have learned, an *Inner Join* clause combines records from source tables when the same values appear in both tables the *Join* references. Sometimes, your programs will want to return all the records in a given table, and the matching records in another table. In this case, you can use either a *Left Join* or a *Right Join* clause. A *Left Join* clause returns all records in the table to the left of the *Join*, and matching records in the table to the right; a *Right Join* clause returns all records in the table to the right of the *Join,* and only matching records from the table to the left of the *Join*. You can nest a *Left Join* clause or a *Right Join* clause inside an *Inner Join* clause, but you cannot nest an *Inner Join* clause inside a *Left Join* clause or a *Right Join* clause. You will implement the *Left Join* and *Right Join* statments as shown here:

```
FROM table1 [ LEFT | RIGHT ] JOIN table2
ON table1.field1 Comparison table2.field2
```

The *Left Join* and *Right Join* clauses have the same syntax as the *Inner Join* clause Table 10.12 details. For example, you can use a *Left Join* with the *Departments* (left) and *Employees* (right) tables the previous examples use to select all departments, including those that have no employees. On the other hand, to select all employees without concern for their department, you can instead use the *Right Join* clause. The following example shows how you can join the *Clients* and *Orders* tables on the *ClientID* field. The query produces a list of all clients, including those that have placed no orders:

```
SELECT ClientName,
OrderDescription
FROM Clients LEFT JOIN Orders
ON Clients.ClientID = Orders.ClientID
```

In this example, *ClientID* is the joined field, but the query does not include *ClientID* in the query results because *ClientID* is not included in the *Select* statement. To include the joined field, enter the field name in the *Select* statement—in this case, *Clients.ClientID*. When working with *Joins* statements and clauses, consider the following basic rules:

- To create a query that includes only records in which the data in the joined fields is the same, use an *Inner Join* clause.

- You can link multiple *On* clauses with any type of *Join*.

- If you try to perform a *Join* operation on fields containing Memo or OLE Object data, an error occurs.

- You can join any two numeric fields of like types. For example, you can perform a *Join* operation on *AutoNumber* and *Long* fields because they are like types. However, you cannot perform a *Join* operation on *Single* and *Double* fields because they are not of like types.

Writing the Code for the ListView Control's Click Events

As the previous sections have detailed, when the user clicks the mouse within the *TreeView* control, the program code can respond to the user's click in many different ways, depending on whether the user chose the expand, collapse, or selection action. Similarly, the *lvwDB ListView* control will respond to the user's actions. If the user clicks the mouse on a column header, for example, the program will sort the data within the *ListView* control in ascending order of that column's values. The *ColumnClick* event handles the program's response to the user's mouse click on a column header. The following code implements the *ColumnClick* event:

```
Private Sub lvwDB_ColumnClick(ByVal ColumnHeader As ColumnHeader)
  lvwDB.SortKey = ColumnHeader.Index - 1
  lvwDB.Sorted = True
End Sub
```

The *ColumnClick* event's program code changes the *ListView* control's *SortKey* property to the column the user clicked the mouse on. Next, the program code sets the *Sorted* property to *True*, which will cause the control to re-sort the list based on the new *SortKey* value.

When the user clicks the mouse on an actual item within the *ListView* control, the program will change the status bar's values to reflect information about the item. The *ListView* control's *ItemClick* event responds to a user's mouse click on an item within a list. The following code implements the *ItemClick* event:

```
Private Sub lvwDB_ItemClick(ByVal Item As ListItem)
  GetData Item.Key
End Sub
```

The *ItemClick* event calls the *GetData* procedure, and passes to the procedure the *Key* value for the item. The *GetData* procedure uses the *Key* value to create its own recordset, which the *GetData* procedure then uses to fill the status bar control's panels. The following code implements the *GetData* procedure:

```
Private Sub GetData(SectionNode)
  Dim I As Integer, BookID As String, SectionID As String

  For I = 1 To Len(SectionNode)
    If Mid(SectionNode, I, 1) = " " Then
      BookID = Left(SectionNode, I - 1)
      SectionID = Right(SectionNode, Len(SectionNode) - I)
      Exit For
    End If
  Next
  If EventFlag <> Title Then
    sbrDB.Panels.Clear
    Dim pnlX As Panel
    Set pnlX = sbrDB.Panels.Add(, "Section")
    pnlX.AutoSize = sbrSpring
    Set pnlX = sbrDB.Panels.Add(, "Pages")
    pnlX.AutoSize = sbrSpring
    Set pnlX = sbrDB.Panels.Add(, "Description")
    pnlX.AutoSize = sbrSpring
  End If
  Dim SectionsRS As Recordset, qryText As String
  qryText = "Select * FROM tblSections Where [BookID] = " & BookID & _
      " And [SectionID] = " & SectionID
  Set SectionsRS = JPBooksDB.OpenRecordset(qryText, dbOpenDynaset)
  sbrDB.Panels("Section").Text = SectionsRS!Title
  sbrDB.Panels("Pages").Text = SectionsRS!Pages
  sbrDB.Panels("Description").Text = SectionsRS!Description
  EventFlag = Title
End Sub
```

As you have learned, the *GetData* procedure receives the user-selected item's *Key* value, which, in the case of the *prjBookList* project, is a unique string that contains the item's *BookID* field and *SectionID* field. The *GetData* procedure's code uses a *For-Next* loop, together with the *Right* and *Left* functions, to separate the *BookID* field from the *SectionID* field. After the loop exits, the program checks the *EventFlag* variable, which will indicate whether or not the user was already viewing a title or other information.

If the user was viewing other information, the *GetData* procedure clears the panels within the *StatusBar* control and adds three panels back to the control: the *Section* panel, the *Pages* panel, and the *Description* panel. After it initializes the panel settings, the procedure continues its execution.

If the user was not viewing other information, or after the *GetData* procedure initializes the status bar if the user was viewing other information, the program code defines a new SQL query string, which the program then uses to create a new recordset. In the *GetData* procedure, the SQL query retrieves only that single record from the *tblSections* table that has the same *BookID* and *SectionID* as the user-selected list item. The procedure then fills the three panels on the status bar with the section name, the number of pages, and the section's description.

WRITING THE PROGRAM'S REMAINING CODE

In addition to the other procedures and events that you have already written, the *prjBookList* project uses three other simple event routines. The first of the three, the *cmbViewTypes_Click* event, changes the *ListView* control's list style to the style the user selects. The following code implements the *cmbViewTypes_Click* event:

```
Private Sub cmbViewTypes_Click()
   lvwDB.View = cmbViewTypes.ListIndex
End Sub
```

As you learned earlier in this chapter, the *Form_Load* event adds four view types to the *cmbViewTypes* control. When the user selects a view type, the *Click* event sets the *ListView* control's *View* property to the view the user selected. As you learned in the "Adding the File Menu to the Form" section of this chapter, the *prjBookList* project contains a File menu Exit option. The File menu Exit option provides the user with a convenient alternative to the Close box. The *mnuExit_Click* event will respond when the user selects the File menu Exit option. The following code implements the *mnuExit_Click* event:

```
Private Sub mnuExit_Click()
   Unload Me
   End
End Sub
```

The *mnuExit_Click* event first unloads the form, then uses the *End* statement to ensure the program severs its connection with the database.

The final one-line event within the program is the *AfterLabelEdit* event of the *TreeView* control. As you may know, users can edit entries within a *TreeView* control by default. To edit entries within a *TreeView* control, you must click your mouse on the entry and press the F2 function key to enter edit mode. However, the *prjBookList* project uses a semi-fixed database—meaning you do not want the user to be able to edit the node entries. You can cancel a node edit within the *AfterLabelEdit* event. The following code implements the *tvwDB* control's *AfterLabelEdit* event:

```
Private Sub tvwDB_AfterLabelEdit(Cancel As Integer, NewString As String)
   Cancel = True
End Sub
```

Within the *AfterLabelEdit* event, you can cancel the edit, process the edit, or do error-checking actions on the user-edited node. The *prjBookList* project simply cancels the edit within the *AfterLabelEdit* event.

ENHANCEMENTS YOU CAN MAKE TO THE PRJBOOKLIST PROJECT

As you have learned, the *prjBookList* project uses three tables—one for books, one for chapters, and one simply as a reference—to display information about books. However, you can easily modify the *prjBookList* project to support any type of multiple-table information. For example, you can display customer names in the tree view, and each customer's invoice list sorted from the most recent to the oldest invoice.

You can also use the *TreeView* control within your programs to sort any type of hierarchical information, whether it is books, directories on a computer, or a corporate filing system. Now that you better understand how to use the tree view, it can be a valuable tool for your future program development.

PUTTING IT ALL TOGETHER

This chapter's project, *prjBookList*, introduced you to using the *Microsoft ListView* and *Microsoft TreeView* controls to display information from several tables within a single database. You have also used Structured Query Language (SQL) *Join* statements to create more complex queries. In Chapter 11, "Using ActiveX to Create a Stock Analysis Program," you will use a multiple-table database, together with the *Microsoft Chart* control, to create a program that tracks stock performance. Before you continue with Chapter 11, however, make sure you understand the following key concepts:

✓ The *Microsoft Windows Common Controls* component is actually a suite of seven ActiveX controls, including the *TreeView* control, the *ListView* control, the *ProgressBar* control, the *StatusBar* control, and the *ImageList* control.

✓ When your Visual Basic programs must display Windows-standard File and Print dialog boxes, you can use the *Microsoft Windows Common Dialog* control to create such dialog boxes.

✓ Within your programs, you can use the *TreeView* control to display hierarchical (ordered) information in a Windows *Explorer*-style interface.

✓ When your Visual Basic programs must modify or retrieve information from a *TreeView* control, your programs will work with the *Node* object and *Nodes* collection.

✓ Within your Visual Basic programs, you can use the *ListView* control to display any type of sequential information, such as that a database contains.

✓ When your Visual Basic programs must modify or retrieve information from a *ListView* control, your programs will work with the *ListItem* object and *ListItems* collection.

✓ You can define custom SQL Queries, both in advance and at run-time, to retrieve information from multiple tables within a database and format the data in the most useful way for your programs.

✓ Your programs can use the SQL *Join* statement to combine the data from multiple tables within the returned recordset from a single query. Your programs can use *Inner Joins* clauses, *Left Joins* clauses, and *Right Joins* clauses to create different record combinations.

Chapter 11

Using ActiveX to Create a Stock Analysis Program

Stock market trading is rapidly changing. In the past, to place an order for stock, you called your broker on the telephone. Your broker would call the market floor, the floor person would dispatch a runner, the runner would relay your order to the floor trader, and the floor trader would purchase the stock from another floor trader. Today, you can trade online, which means no more waiting, no more brokers trying to sell you their house favorite, and no more high commission fees. Now, your stock order goes directly to a computer, the computer contacts the market floor, the floor person dispatches a runner, the runner relays your message to a floor trader, and the floor trader buys the stock for you.

If you trade online, or dabble in the stock market at all, you most likely read the latest stock prices from a newspaper or Internet Web site. As you probably realize, your stock's price can change from day to day. It is easy to visualize the difference between, for example, Tuesday's price and Wednesday's price. However, it is difficult to easily see the difference between an entire week's or month's price changes. To clearly see a large number of price changes for your stock, you must draw a chart. When you look at a chart, you can clearly see day-to-day and week-to-week price changes for a selected stock.

To find out more about online trading, visit the New York Stock Exchange Web site at *http://www.nyse.com* and the NASDAQ Web site at *http://www.nasdaq.com*. You can also download ActiveX controls and Java applets from many sources that will let you have data automatically delivered directly to your desktop, often in the form of a stock ticker or similar control.

In this chapter's project, *prjStock*, you will use a *Microsoft Chart* control to display the high price, low price, and close price for a selected stock on a specific trading day. In addition, you will store stock names and prices in a Microsoft *Access*® database and select trading dates from a *Microsoft Calendar* control. This chapter examines in detail the *Microsoft Chart* control, the *Microsoft Calendar* control, the Microsoft *Access* database, *Frame* controls, and *ListBox* controls. By the time you finish this chapter, you will understand the following key concepts:

- ◆ Visual Basic includes a *Microsoft Chart* control, which you will use to draw charts.
- ◆ The *Microsoft Chart* control draws bar, pie, and line charts.
- ◆ Visual Basic includes a *Microsoft Calendar* control, which you will use to display dates.
- ◆ In the *prjStock* project, you will use a *Microsoft Calendar* control to help the user select specific trading dates.
- ◆ Visual Basic includes database management objects, such as the *Workspace, Database,* and *Recordset* objects, which your programs will use to access and manage databases.
- ◆ In the *prjStock* project, you will use a database to store stock names, prices, and trading dates.
- ◆ Visual Basic includes a *ListBox* control, which you will use within the *prjStock* project to list stock names.
- ◆ Visual Basic includes a *ComboBox* control, which you will use within the *prjStock* project to list stock prices.
- ◆ You will use a structure, a special kind of *type* that you define, within the *prjStock* project to store stock names, prices, and trading dates.

- Visual Basic includes an *OptionButton* control. Within the *prjStock* project, you will copy a single button to create an option button array.

- Within the *prjStock* project, you will use an *OptionButton* array to let the user select the type of chart to draw.

USING THE PRJSTOCK PROJECT

Before you design the *prjStock* project, you may find it helpful to run the program. The companion CD-ROM that accompanies this book includes the *prjStock.exe* program and a sample stock database within the *Chapter11* directory. As with every other program on the CD-ROM, you should use the Jamsa Press *setup.exe* program to install the program to your computer's hard drive before you run it. After you install the program to your computer's hard drive, you can run the program from the Start menu. To run the program, select the Windows Start menu Run option. Windows will display the Run dialog box. Within the Run dialog box, enter *x:\vbp\Chapter11\prjStock.exe*, where *x* corresponds to the hard drive on which you installed the program, and click your mouse on OK. Windows will run the *prjStock.exe* program, as shown in Figure 11.1.

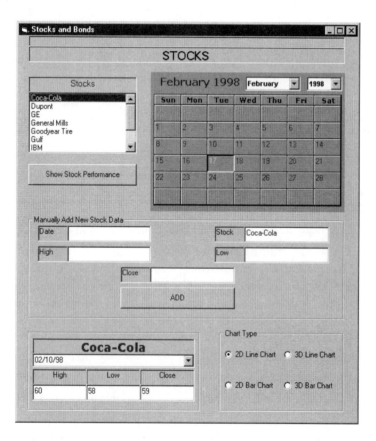

*Figure 11.1 The **prjStock.exe** program's startup screen.*

Before you use the *prjStock.exe* program, you should familiarize yourself with the controls on the form. When the program first starts to run, it will retrieve some stock names from the sample database and display them in a *ListBox* control in the form's upper left corner. When you click your mouse on a name, the program will retrieve the corresponding trading dates for that name from the database and then display the trading dates in a *ComboBox* control at the form's bottom. You will also see the high price, low price, and close price for each stock's trading date, which the program will display within three *TextBox* controls.

Running prjStock from the CD-ROM

As you have learned, you must first install many programs that you will use in this book to your computer's hard drive before you try to use the programs. Because the *prjStock.exe* program tries to create a temporary database within its execution directory, you must install the *prjStock.exe* program to a drive before you try to use it. If you try to run the *prjStock.exe* program from the CD-ROM, the program will not perform searches because it cannot create the temporary database it requires.

For more information about the Jamsa Press *setup.exe* program, see the "What's on the *Visual Basic Programmer's Library* Companion CD-ROM" section at the back of this book.

To the *ListBox* control's right, you will see a *Microsoft Calendar* control. When you click your mouse on a day, the program will display that day in the *TextBox* control within the *Manually Add New Stock Data* frame control below the calendar. You will also see *TextBox* controls for adding a high price, low price, and close price for each stock's trading date within the *Manually Add New Stock Data* frame control.

The last frame on the form, at the bottom right, lets you control the display within the stock chart. To display a stock chart, you must click your mouse on the Show Stock Performance button below the list box containing stock names and to the left of the calendar control. When you click your mouse on the Show Stock Performance button, the *prjStock.exe* program will display a second form with the caption Stock Performance. The Stock Performance form uses a *Microsoft Chart* control to display information about a stock's performance. Figure 11.2 shows the Stock Performance form drawing a default-style two-dimensional Line Chart.

363

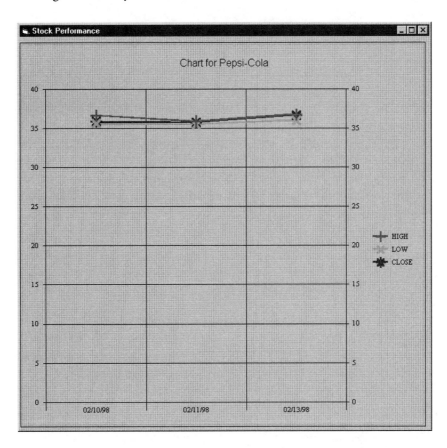

Figure 11.2 *The Stock Performance form with the Pepsi-Cola stock information displayed.*

VISUAL BASIC PROGRAMMER'S LIBRARY

You can click your mouse on the Stocks and Bonds form to switch back to it. Within the Stocks and Bonds form, you can change the chart's display type. For example, if you click your mouse on the 3D Bar Chart option, the form will display a three-dimensional bar chart, rather than the line chart it displayed originally. Figure 11.3 shows the Stock Performance form drawing the newly selected three-dimensional bar chart.

364

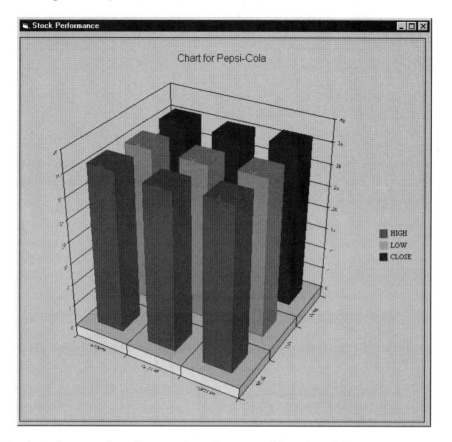

Figure 11.3 *The Stock Performance form drawing the 3-dimensional bar chart for Pepsi-Cola.*

Now that you have a better view of the *prjStock.exe* program's layout, and you have viewed some of the sample information within the *StockMarket.mdb* database, you can use the program to display, add, edit, and delete stocks, and to draw charts. Before you can display a new stock name, however, you must first add it to the database. To add a new stock name to the database, perform the following steps:

1. Within the *prjStock.exe* program's main display, click your mouse on a date within the *Microsoft Calendar* control. The program will display the date you select in the *TextBox* control within the *Manually Add New Stock Data* frame control below the *Microsoft Calendar* control.

2. Within the *Add New Stock Data* frame, click your mouse in the Stock text box to the right of the Date text box control. Next, enter the name of the stock as *Goodyear*. The program will display the stock name as *Goodyear*.

3. Within the *Manually Add New Stock Data* frame, click your mouse in the High text box. Next, enter the high price as 68.875. The program will display the high price as 68.875 dollars.

4. Within the *Manually Add New Stock Data* frame, click your mouse in the Low text box. Next, enter the low price as 67.875. The program will display the low price as 67.875 dollars.

5. Within the *Manually Add New Stock Data* frame, click your mouse on the Close text box. Next, enter the close price as 68.125. The program will display the close price as 68.125 dollars. Figure 11.4 shows the new entry for the Goodyear stock name with one trading date and prices.

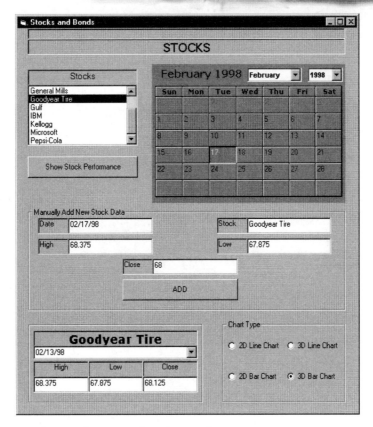

Figure 11.4 *The Goodyear stock entry for one trading date and prices.*

6. Within the *Manually Add New Stock Data* frame, click your mouse on the Add button. The program will add the new stock name, trading date, and prices to the database. Then, the program will display the new stock name in the Stocks list box in the form's upper left corner.

After you have added a stock name to the database, you can add additional trading dates and prices to it. To add a new trading date and prices to an already established stock name, perform the following steps:

1. Within the Stocks list box control in the form's upper left corner, select the stock name IBM. The program will display the IBM stock name in the *Frame* control at the form's bottom, listing its most recent trading date in the *ComboBox* control. In addition, the program will display IBM's most recent trading date's high, low, and close prices in the High, Low, and Close text boxes below the *ComboBox* control. Finally, the program will display the IBM stock name in the Stock text box within the *Manually Add New Stock Data* frame.

2. Within the *Microsoft Calendar* control, click your mouse on the date for which you want to add prices (in this case, Monday, February 17, 1998). The program will display the date you select in the Date text box within the *Manually Add New Stock Data* frame control.

3. Within the *Manually Add New Stock Data* frame, click your mouse in the High text box. Next, enter the high price as 103.6875. The program will display the high price as 103.6875 dollars.

4. Within the *Manually Add New Stock Data* frame, click your mouse in the Low text box. Next, enter the low price as 102.25. The program will display the low price as 102.25 dollars.

5. Within the *Manually Add New Stock Data* frame, click your mouse on the Close text box. Next, enter the close price as 102.4375. The program will display the close price as 102.4375 dollars.

6. Within the *Manually Add New Stock Data* frame control, click your mouse on the Add button. The program will check the database for the IBM stock listing. Because the stock

listing already exists in the database, Visual Basic will only add the new trading date and prices to the database.

7. Within the *Frame* control at the form's bottom, click your mouse on the *ComboBox* control. Next, select the newly added trading date, February 17, 1998. The program will display the newly added date and the high, low, and close prices in the three text boxes below the *ComboBox* control. Figure 11.5 shows the already present IBM stock name with the newly added trading date and prices.

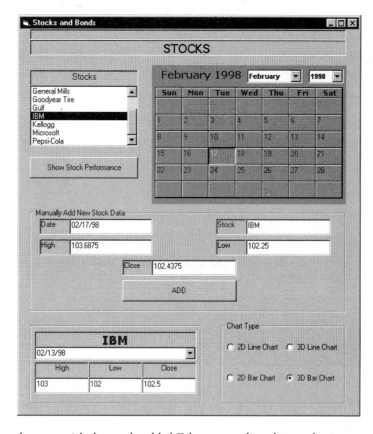

Figure 11.5 *The IBM stock name with the newly added February trading date and prices.*

After you have added one or more trading dates and prices to a stock name, you can draw a bar, pie, or line chart reflecting the high, low, and close prices. To draw a chart for any stock listing, perform the following steps:

1. Within the *ListBox* control in the upper right corner of the form, select a listed stock. The program will display the stock name, most recent trading date, and prices in the *Frame* control to the right.

2. Click your mouse on the Show Stock Performance button to display the Stock Performance form. The program will draw a default line chart for the stock name you select in the *Microsoft Chart* control. As you move through each selection in the *ListBox* control, the program will draw a chart for each selection.

3. Within the Chart Type frame on the form's bottom right side, select the *2D Bar Chart* option button. The program will draw a two-dimensional bar chart in the *Microsoft Chart* control on the Stock Performance form that represents the trading information for the program's currently selected stock name.

4. Within the Chart Type frame on the form's bottom right side, select the *3D Line Chart* option button. The program will draw a three-dimensional line chart in the *Microsoft Chart*

control on the Stock Performance form that represents the trading information for the program's currently selected stock name. Figure 11.6 shows a three-dimensional line chart for the IBM stock.

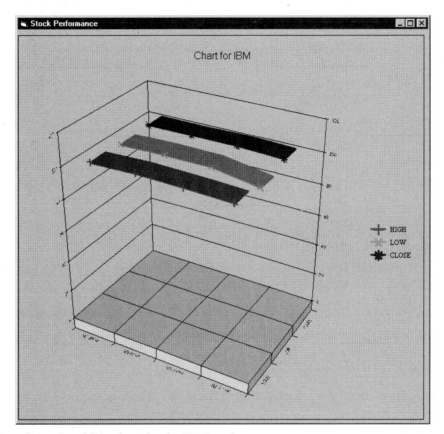

Figure 11.6 *A three-dimensional line chart for the IBM stock.*

5. Within the Chart Type frame on the form's bottom right side, select the *3D Line Chart* option button. The program will draw a three-dimensional bar chart in the *Microsoft Chart* control on the Stock Performance form that represents the trading information for the program's currently selected stock name.

CREATING THE BLANK FORMS

Now that you have a better idea how to use the *prjStock* project, you can begin to design it. First, you will design a pair of empty forms that will contain all the controls introduced in the "Using the *prjStock* Project" section. After you design and implement the forms, you will learn more about the *Microsoft Calendar* control, the *Microsoft Chart* control, and the Microsoft *Access* database. To begin the *prjStock* project and add the empty forms, perform the following steps:

1. Within Visual Basic, select the File menu New Project option. Visual Basic will open the New Project dialog box.

2. Within the New Project dialog box, click your mouse on the Standard EXE icon. Next, click your mouse on OK. Visual Basic will open the *Form1* form window.

3. Select the Project menu Add Form option. Visual Basic will display the Add Form dialog box.

4. Within the Add Form dialog box, double-click your mouse on the Form icon. Visual Basic will add the *Form2* object to the project.

5. Select the View menu Properties Window option. Visual Basic will open the Properties Window listing the *Form2* properties.

6. Within the Properties Window, change the *Form2* form's property values to the values Table 11.1 lists.

7. Repeat Step 6 to change the *Form1* form's property values to the values Table 11.1 lists.

Object	Property	Set As
Form1	*Caption*	*Stocks and Bonds*
Form1	*Height*	9405
Form1	*Left*	0
Form1	*StartupPosition*	2 - Center Screen
Form1	*Top*	0
Form1	*Width*	8355
Form1	*Name*	*frmStockList*
Form2	*Caption*	*Stock Performance*
Form2	*Height*	9585
Form2	*Left*	0
Form2	*StartupPosition*	1 - Center Owner
Form2	*Top*	0
Form2	*Width*	10065
Form2	*Name*	*frmStockPerformance*

Table 11.1 The newly named **frmStockList** and **frmStockPerformance** forms' properties.

ADDING A MODULE TO THE PRJSTOCK PROJECT

In the *prjStock* project, you will store stock names, trading dates, and prices in a database. For more information on databases, see Chapter 7, "Creating a Database Viewer and Designer." When you retrieve information from the database within the *prjStock* project, you will store the information in a *Recordset* object. To simplify using a *Recordset* object, you will store its data in a Visual Basic structure.

As you have learned in Chapter 5, "Creating and Using Fractals," you must define structures within a Visual Basic module. You will add a Visual Basic module to the *prjStock* project and then declare the structure within it. To use the structure definition within your program's code, you will declare a variable of the structure type. When you type the structure name, followed by a period in code, Visual Basic will open a small submenu that lists the structure's elements. To add a module that will contain the structure to the *prjStock* project, perform the following steps:

1. Select the Project menu Add Module option. Visual Basic will open the Add Module dialog box.

2. Within the Add Module dialog box, double-click your mouse on the Module icon. Visual Basic will add the module, *Module1*, to the *prjStock* project and open the *Module 1* Code window.

3. Select the View menu Properties Window option. Visual Basic will open the Properties Window listing the *Module1* properties.

4. Within the Properties Window, click your mouse on the *Name* property. Replace the *Module1* name with *mdlStockList* and press ENTER.

5. Select the File menu Save Project As option. Visual Basic will open the Save File As dialog box and fill the *File name* field with *mdlStockList*.

6. Within the Save File As dialog box, click your mouse on the Save button. Visual Basic will save the *mdlStockList* module and fill the *File name* field with *frmStockPerformance*.

7. Within the Save File As dialog box, click your mouse on the Save button. Visual Basic will save the *frmStockPerformance* form and fill the *File name* field with *frmStockList*.

8. Within the Save File As dialog box, click your mouse on the Save button. Visual Basic will save the *frmStockList* form and fill the *File name* field with the project name, *Project1*. Visual Basic will also change the dialog box's caption to Save Project As.

9. Within the Save Project As dialog box, replace the *Project1* project name within the *File name* field with the new *prjStock* project name and click your mouse on the Save button. Visual Basic will save the *prjStock* project and close the Save Project As dialog box.

MORE ON THE MICROSOFT CHART CONTROL

In the *prjStock* project, you will use the *Microsoft Chart* control, which will draw bar, pie, and line charts of stock prices. The *Microsoft Chart* control is helpful because it lets you view a stock's prices in a chart. For example, assume a stock price closes at two different values on Monday and Tuesday, respectively. Using a *Microsoft Chart* control, you can draw two bars that will represent the price on Monday and the price on Tuesday. When you look at such a chart, you will clearly see the price change.

The *prjStock* project will use the *Microsoft Chart* control to draw bar, pie, and line charts, and assign labels to each bar, pie, and line. For example, if you draw a bar chart, and the first bar is the closing price for a stock on Monday, you could label the bar *Monday*. If the next bar in the chart is the closing price for a stock on Tuesday, you could label the bar *Tuesday*. When you look at such a chart, you will clearly see the labels that display the days the price changed.

The *Microsoft Chart* control draws charts in rows and columns. These rows and columns look different from rows and columns in a database. Each row in the *Microsoft Chart* control can have one or more columns. For example, if you record a stock's high, low, and close prices on Monday, the row will be Monday and the columns will be the stock's high, low, and close prices. In the *prjStock* project, you will design five rows that contain three columns each. The five rows will represent the stock's most recent five trading days and the columns will represent the stock's high, low, and close prices on each trading day.

Before the *Microsoft Chart* control draws a chart, it must have numerical data. The *prjStock* project will use the *Microsoft Chart* control's *ChartData* property to supply data in code. The *ChartData* property receives input as a two-dimensional array. An array lets your programs store related values of the same type within a single variable. You can then reference the values within the array as array elements. You can visualize a one-dimensional array as a sequence of values, and you can visualize a two-dimensional array as being similar to pages in a spreadsheet. The following section explains arrays in detail. In the *prjStock* project, you will design a five row by three column two-dimensional array. Next, you will add stock data (trading dates and prices) to the two-dimensional array. Finally, you will assign the five row by three column two-dimensional array to the *Microsoft Chart* control's *ChartData* property. The *Microsoft Chart* control will use the data within the array to draw charts with five rows for trading dates that contain three columns to each row. The columns will contain the display information for the high, low, and close prices; the rows will contain the display information for each date.

Table 11.2 lists some important *Microsoft Chart* control properties you will use in the *prjStock* project. To obtain a complete list, see the Visual Basic Help file and search for *MSChart control*.

Property	Use
ChartData	Connects the values in a two-dimensional array to the *Microsoft Chart* control.
Row	Sets the row number.
RowLabel	Sets the label at the *Row* property number.
Column	Sets the column number.
ColumnLabel	Sets the label at the *Column* property number.
ChartType	Sets the chart type, such as a bar, pie, or line chart.
ShowLegend	Displays the *ColumnLabel* property values in a list, known as a *legend*.

*Table 11.2 The **Microsoft Chart** control's properties.*

VISUAL BASIC PROGRAMMER'S LIBRARY

ADDING THE MICROSOFT CHART CONTROL TO THE PRJSTOCK PROJECT

As you have learned, your Visual Basic programs can use the *Microsoft Chart* control to draw bar, pie, and line charts. Before you can use the *Microsoft Chart* control in the *prjStock* project, you must add it to the project as a component. To add a *Microsoft Chart* control to the *prjStock* project, perform the following steps:

1. Select the Project menu Components option. Visual Basic will open the Components dialog box.

2. Within the Components dialog box, select the *Microsoft Chart Control* listing. Next, click your mouse on the check box to the left of the listing. Visual Basic will draw a check mark in the box.

3. Within the Components dialog box, click your mouse on OK. Visual Basic will close the Components dialog box and add the control to the project.

370   After you add the *Microsoft Chart* control to the *prjStock* project, the control's icon will appear in the Toolbox. As you know, the Toolbox displays Visual Basic control icons. If you double-click your mouse on any icon in the Toolbox, Visual Basic will draw the control the icon corresponds to within the active form.

ADDING THE MICROSOFT CALENDAR CONTROL TO THE PRJSTOCK PROJECT

As you have learned, you will use the *Microsoft Calendar* control to display and store dates. Chapter 8, "Creating a Schedule Planner," explains the *Microsoft Calendar* control in detail. As with the *Microsoft Chart* control, before you can use the *Microsoft Calendar* control, you must add it to the *prjStock* project as a component. After you add the *Microsoft Calendar* control to the *prjStock* project, its icon will appear in the Toolbox. To add a *Microsoft Calendar* control to the *prjStock* project, perform the following steps:

1. Select the Project menu Components option. Visual Basic will open the Components dialog box.

2. Within the Components dialog box, locate the *Microsoft Calendar Control 8.0* listing within the list of available components. Next, click your mouse on the check box to the left of the listing. Visual Basic will draw a check mark in the box. Figure 11.7 shows the Components dialog box after you select the *Microsoft Calendar Control 8.0*.

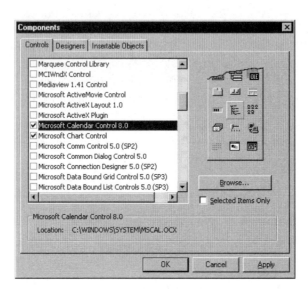

*Figure 11.7 The Components dialog box after you select the **Microsoft Calendar Control 8.0**.*

3. Within the Components dialog box, click your mouse on OK. Visual Basic will close the Components dialog box.

ADDING THE DATA ACCESS OBJECTS (DAO) LIBRARY TO THE *PRJSTOCK* PROJECT

As you have learned, you will use a database to store stock names, trading dates, and prices. When you retrieve data from a database, you will most often store it in a *Recordset* object. However, before you can fill the *Recordset* object with data, you must access a *Workspace* and a *Database* object. Before you can use the three objects, you must add them to your project by making a reference to the *Data Access Objects (DAO) Object Library* in Visual Basic. After you add the reference, you will declare and assign a variable name for each object. To place a reference to the *DAO Object Library* in the *prjStock* project, perform the following steps:

1. Select the Project menu References option. Visual Basic will open the References dialog box.

2. Within the References dialog box, select the *Microsoft DAO Object Library 3.5* listing. Next, click your mouse on the box to the left of the listing. Visual Basic will draw a check mark in the box.

3. Within the References dialog box, click your mouse on OK. Visual Basic will close the References window and add the *DAO Object Library* reference to the project.

371

REVIEWING THE *DAO* OBJECT LIBRARY'S USE

After you add a *DAO Object Library* reference to the *prjStock* project, you can design the database. You will name the database *StockMarket*. The *StockMarket* database will contain two tables, *StockName* and *StockPrices*. The *StockName* table will store the stock names and the *StockPrices* table will store the trading dates, high prices, low prices, close prices, and stock names (which it will use to interact with the *StockName* table).

Every day the stock trades, you can input the stock name, prices, and trading date. Because each company has one stock name and many trading dates, you will put the name into the *StockName* table and the prices and trading dates into the *StockPrices* table. This way you create a one-to-many relationship between the stock name and the stock's trading dates and prices, as Figure 11.8 shows.

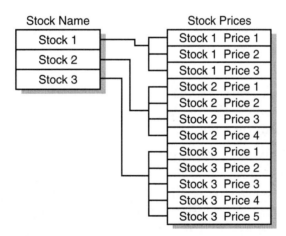

Figure 11.8 *The one-to-many relationship between the **StockName** table and the **StockPrices** table.*

After you design the *StockMarket* database, you will use the database objects in the DAO Object Library to access the database from within Visual Basic.

CREATING THE STOCKMARKET DATABASE

After adding a *DAO Object Library* reference to the *prjStock* project, you can create the *StockMarket* database. To create the *StockMarket* database, perform the following steps:

1. Select the Add-Ins menu Visual Data Manager option. Visual Basic will open the VisData window.

2. Within the VisData window, select the File menu New option. Within the New option, select the Microsoft Access 7.0 MDB submenu option. Visual Basic will open the Select Microsoft Access Database To Create dialog box.

3. Within the Select Microsoft Access Database To Create dialog box, type *StockMarket* in the *File name* field. Next, click your mouse on the Save button. Visual Basic will save the database, close the dialog box, and open the Database window with the new database listing, as shown in Figure 11.9.

Figure 11.9 *The **StockMarket** database in the Database window.*

CREATING THE STOCKNAME TABLE

After you create the *StockMarket* database, you can create database tables. As you have learned, in the *prjStock* project you will create two tables, the *StockName* and *StockPrices* tables. To create the *StockName* table, perform the following steps:

1. Select the Add-Ins menu Visual Data Manager option. Visual Basic will open the VisData window.

2. Within the VisData window, select the File menu Open Microsoft Access Database option. Visual Data Manager will open the Open Microsoft Access Database dialog box.

3. Within the Open Microsoft Access Database dialog box, double-click your mouse on the *StockMarket* listing. Visual Data Manager will open the Database window.

4. Within the Database window, right-click your mouse on the *Properties* listing. Visual Data Manager will open the Visual Data Manager pop-up menu. Within the pop-up menu, click your mouse on the New Table option. Visual Data Manager will open the Table Structure window.

5. Within the Table Structure window, type *StockName* in the *Table Name* field. Next, click your mouse on the Add Field button. Visual Data Manager will open the Add Field window.

6. Within the Add Field window, type *Stock* in the *Name* field. Click your mouse on the down arrow of the Type combo box and select the Text type. Next, click your mouse on the OK button. Visual Data Manager will add the new field and clear the Add Field window.

7. Within the Add Field window, click your mouse on the Close button. Visual Data Manager will close the Add Field window and display the Table Structure window.

8. Within the Table Structure window, click your mouse on the Build the Table button. Visual Data Manager will build the *StockName* table, close the Table Structure window, and open the Database window.

9. Within the Database window, click your mouse on *StockName*. Visual Data Manager will show the *Fields, Indexes,* and *Properties* listings within the Database window. Next, click your mouse on the *Fields* listing. Visual Data Manager will show the *StockName* fields, as Figure 11.10 shows.

Figure 11.10 *The **StockName** table's fields.*

CREATING THE STOCKPRICES TABLE

After you create the *StockName* table, you can create the *StockMarket* database's second component table. As you have learned, in the *prjStock* project you will create two tables, the *StockName* and *StockPrices* tables. To create the *StockPrices* table, perform the following steps:

1. Select the Add-Ins menu Visual Data Manager option. Visual Basic will open the VisData window.

2. Select the File menu Open Microsoft Access Database option. Visual Data Manager will open the Open Microsoft Access Database dialog box.

3. Within the Open Microsoft Access Database dialog box, double-click your mouse on the *StockMarket* listing. Visual Data Manager will open the Database window.

4. Within the Database window, right-click your mouse on the *Properties* listing. Visual Data Manager will open a pop-up menu.

5. Within the pop-up menu, select the New Table option. Visual Data Manager will open the Table Structure window.

6. Within the Table Structure window, type *StockPrices* in the *Table Name* field. Next, click your mouse on the Add Field button. Visual Data Manager will open the Add Field window.

7. Within the Add Field window, type *Date* in the *Name* field. Click your mouse on the down arrow of the Type combo box and select the *Long* type. Next, click your mouse on the OK button. Visual Data Manager will add the new field and clear the Add Field window.

8. Within the Add Field window, type *High* in the *Name* field. Click your mouse on the down arrow of the Type combo box and select the *Long* type. Next, click your mouse on the OK button. Visual Data Manager will add the new field and clear the Add Field window.

9. Within the Add Field window, type *Low* in the *Name* field. Click your mouse on the down arrow of the Type combo box and select the *Long* type. Next, click your mouse on the OK button. Visual Data Manager will add the new field and clear the Add Field window.

10. Within the Add Field window, type *Close* in the *Name* field. Click your mouse on the down arrow of the Type combo box and select the *Long* type. Next, click your mouse on the OK button. Visual Data Manager will add the new field and clear the Add Field window.

11. Within the Add Field window, type *Stock* in the *Name* field. Click your mouse on the down arrow of the Type combo box and select the *Text* type. Next, click your mouse on the OK button. Visual Data Manager will add the new field and clear the Add Field window.

12. Within the Add Field window, click your mouse on the Close button. Visual Data Manager will close the Add Field window and display the Table Structure window.

13. Within the Table Structure window, click your mouse on the Build the Table button. Visual Data Manager will build the table and show the Database window.

14. Within the Database window, click your mouse on *StockPrices*. Visual Data Manager will show the *Fields, Indexes,* and *Properties* listings. Next, click your mouse on the *Fields* listing. Visual Data Manager will show the *StockPrices* fields, as shown in Figure 11.11.

373

Figure 11.11 The **StockPrices** table's fields.

ADDING CONTROLS TO THE FRMSTOCKLIST FORM

374

Now that you have added the *Microsoft Chart* control, *Microsoft Calendar* control components, and a *DAO Object Library* reference to the *prjStock* project, you will add controls to the *frmStockList* form. After you add the controls, you will write code that links the controls to your project. First, you will add a *Microsoft Calendar* control to the *frmStockList* form. Second, you will add a *ListBox* control. Next, you will add three *Frame* controls. After that, you will fill the *Frame* controls with *TextBox*, *Label*, *OptionButton*, *ComboBox*, and *CommandButton* controls.

ADDING A MICROSOFT CALENDAR CONTROL TO THE FORM

As you have learned, in the *prjStock* project you will use a *Microsoft Calendar* control to display and select trading dates for stocks. To add a *Microsoft Calendar* control to the *frmStockList* form, perform the following steps:

1. If Visual Basic is not displaying the *frmStockList* form, double-click your mouse on the *frmStockList* form listing within Project Explorer. Visual Basic will open the *frmStockList* form within an object window.

2. Within Visual Basic, select the View menu Toolbox option. Visual Basic will open the Toolbox.

3. Within the Toolbox, select the new *Microsoft Calendar* control icon, Calendar, as Figure 11.12 shows.

Figure 11.12 The Toolbox showing the **Microsoft Calendar** control's Calendar icon.

4. Within the Toolbox, double-click your mouse on the Calendar icon. Visual Basic will draw a *Microsoft Calendar* control, *Calendar1*, onto the *frmStockList* form.

5. Within the object window, click your mouse on the *Calendar1* control to highlight it. Visual Basic will draw a small outline around the control.

6. Select the View menu Properties Window option. Visual Basic will open the Properties Window listing the *Calendar1* properties.

7. Within the Properties Window, change the *Calendar1* properties to the values Table 11.3 lists.

Object	Property	Set As
Calendar1	*Height*	3255
Calendar1	*Left*	3240
Calendar1	*Top*	840

Table 11.3 The newly named **calStocks** control's properties. *(continued on following page)*

Object	Property	Set As
Calendar1	Value	02/22/98
Calendar1	Width	4095
Calendar1	Name	calStocks

Table 11.3 *The newly named* **calStocks** *control's properties. (continued from previous page)*

ADDING THE LSTSTOCKS LIST BOX TO THE FORM

Now that you have designed the *StockMarket* database and added a *DAO Object Library* reference to the *prjStock* project, you can retrieve database records and view them within the program. The *StockMarket* database has two tables, *StockName* and *StockPrices*. The *StockName* table will hold companies' names that trade on one of the stock markets. The *StockPrices* table will store stock names, stock prices, and stock trading dates.

To list the records in the *StockName* table, you will add a *ListBox* control to the *frmStockList* form, which you will name *lstStocks*. In addition, to specify that the *lstStocks* control will contain stock names, you will add a *Label* control above the *lstStocks* control that will contain the word *Stock*.

To place a *ListBox* and a *Label* control onto the *frmStockList* form, perform the following steps:

1. If Visual Basic is not displaying the *frmStockList* form, double-click your mouse on the *frmStockList* listing within Project Explorer. Visual Basic will open the *frmStockList* form within an object window.

2. Within Visual Basic, select the View menu Toolbox option. Visual Basic will open the Toolbox.

3. Within the Toolbox, double-click your mouse on the ListBox icon. Visual Basic will draw a *ListBox* control, *List1*, within the *frmStockList* form.

4. Within the form window, click your mouse on the *List1* control to highlight it. Visual Basic will draw a small frame around the control.

5. Select the View menu Properties Window option. Visual Basic will open the Properties Window and display the *List1* control's properties.

6. Within the Properties Window, change the *List1* properties to the values Table 11.4 lists.

Object	Property	Set As
List1	Height	1425
List1	Left	240
List1	Top	1320
List1	Width	2655
List1	Name	lstStocks

Table 11.4 *The newly named* **lstStocks** *control's properties.*

7. Within the Toolbox, double-click your mouse on the Label icon. Visual Basic will draw a label control, *Label1*, within the *frmStockList* form.

8. Within the form window, click your mouse on the *Label1* control to highlight it. Visual Basic will draw a small frame around the control.

9. Select the View menu Properties Window option. Visual Basic will open the Properties Window and display the *Label1* control's properties.

10. Within the Properties Window, change the *Label1* control's properties to the values Table 11.5 lists.

Object	Property	Set As
Label1	Caption	Stocks
Label1	Height	375
Label1	Left	240
Label1	Top	960
Label1	Width	2655
Label1	Name	lblStocks

Table 11.5 The newly named **lblStocks** *control's properties.*

ADDING THE *fraShowStockDate* FRAME CONTROL TO THE FORM

Now that you have added the *lstStocks* and *lblStocks* controls to the *frmStockList* form, you will add a *Frame* control to show stock names, trading dates, and prices. You will name the *Frame* control *fraShowStockDate* and add *ComboBox*, *Label*, and *TextBox* controls to it.

As you learned in the previous section, titled "Adding the *lstStocks* List Box to the Form," the *lstStocks* control will display stock names. When you click your mouse on the *lstStocks* control, the program will fill a *Label* control within the *fraShowStockDate* with the *lstStocks* control stock name and a *ComboBox* control within the frame with any existing trading dates for the stock you select. If you select a trading date within the *ComboBox*, Visual Basic will fill three *TextBox* controls with high price, low price, and close price for that date.

To place the *fraShowStockDate* control within the *frmStockList* form, perform the following steps:

1. If Visual Basic is not displaying the *frmStockList* form, double-click your mouse on the *frmStockList* listing within Project Explorer. Visual Basic will open the *frmStockList* form within an object window.

2. Within Visual Basic, select the View menu Toolbox option. Visual Basic will open the Toolbox.

3. Within the Toolbox, double-click your mouse on the Frame icon. Visual Basic will draw a *Frame* control, *Frame1*, onto the *frmStockList* form.

4. Within the form window, click your mouse on the *Frame1* control to highlight it. Visual Basic will draw a small frame around the control.

5. Select the View menu Properties Window option. Visual Basic will open the Properties Window listing the *Frame1* properties.

6. Within the Properties Window, change the *Frame1* properties to the values Table 11.6 lists.

Object	Property	Set As
Frame1	Caption	[blank]
Frame1	Height	1935
Frame1	Left	240
Frame1	Top	6840
Frame1	Width	4215
Frame1	Name	fraShowStockDate

Table 11.6 The newly named **fraShowStockDate** *frame control's properties.*

ADDING THE CONTROLS TO THE *fraShowStockDate* FRAME CONTROL

As you have learned, in the *prjStock* project you will add controls to the *fraShowStockDate* control so that Visual Basic can display a selected stock name, trading date, and high, low, and close prices. To add *ComboBox*, *Label*, and *TextBox* controls to the *fraShowStockDate* frame control, perform the following steps:

1. If Visual Basic is not displaying the *frmStockList* form, double-click your mouse on the *frmStockList* form listing within Project Explorer. Visual Basic will open the *frmStockList* form within an object window.

2. Within Visual Basic, select the View menu Toolbox option. Visual Basic will open the Toolbox.

3. Within the Toolbox, double-click your mouse on the ComboBox icon. Visual Basic will draw a *ComboBox* control, *Combo1*, within the *frmStockList* form.

4. Within the form window, click your mouse on the *Combo1* control and hold the mouse button down. Move the mouse cursor to drag the *Combo1* control into the *fraShowStockDate* control. Release the mouse button. Visual Basic will draw the *Combo1* control inside the *fraShowStockDate* control.

5. Within the Toolbox, double-click your mouse on the Label icon. Visual Basic will draw a *Label* control, *Label1*, within the *frmStockList* form.

6. Within the form window, click your mouse on the *Label1* control and hold the mouse button down. Move the mouse cursor to drag the *Label1* control into the *fraShowStockDate* control. Release the mouse button. Visual Basic will draw the *Label1* control inside the *fraShowStockDate* control.

7. Repeat Steps 5 and 6 until you have a total of four *Label* controls inside the *fraShowStockDate* control.

8. Within the Toolbox window, double-click your mouse on the TextBox icon. Visual Basic will draw a *TextBox* control, *Text1*, within the *frmStockList* form.

9. Within the form window, click your mouse on the *Text1* control and hold the mouse button down. Move the mouse cursor to drag the *Text1* control into the *fraShowStockDate* control. Release the mouse button. Visual Basic will draw the *Text1* control inside the *fraShowStockDate* control.

10. Repeat Steps 8 and 9 until you have a total of three *TextBox* controls inside the *fraShowStockDate* control.

11. Within the *fraShowStockDate* control, click your mouse on a control to highlight it. Visual Basic will draw a small frame around the control.

12. Select the View menu Properties Window option. Visual Basic will open the Properties Window listing the selected control's properties.

13. Within the Properties Window, change the highlighted control's properties to the values Table 11.7 lists.

14. Repeat Steps 11, 12, and 13 until you have changed each control's properties in the *fraShowStockDate* control to the values Table 11.7 lists.

Object	Property	Set As
Combo1	*Height*	315
Combo1	*Left*	120
Combo1	*Top*	600
Combo1	*Width*	3975
Combo1	*Text*	[blank]
Combo1	*Name*	cmbStockDate
Label1	*Caption*	[blank]
Label1	*Font*	Verdana, Bold, 14 Point
Label1	*ForeColor*	&H00C00000& (Dark Blue)
Label1	*Height*	375

*Table 11.7 The **fraShowStockDate** controls' properties. (continued on following page)*

377

Object	Property	Set As
Label1	Left	120
Label1	Top	240
Label1	Width	3975
Label1	Name	lblStockName
Label2	Caption	High
Label2	Height	375
Label2	Left	120
Label2	Top	960
Label2	Width	1335
Label2	Name	lblHigh
Label3	Caption	Low
Label3	Height	375
Label3	Left	1440
Label3	Top	960
Label3	Width	1335
Label3	Name	lblLow
Label4	Caption	Close
Label4	Height	375
Label4	Left	2760
Label4	Top	960
Label4	Width	1335
Label4	Name	lblClose
Text1	Height	375
Text1	Left	120
Text1	Top	1320
Text1	Width	1335
Text1	Text	[blank]
Text1	Name	txtHigh
Text2	Height	375
Text2	Left	1440
Text2	Top	1320
Text2	Width	1335
Text2	Text	[blank]
Text2	Name	txtLow
Text3	Height	375
Text3	Left	2760
Text3	Top	1320
Text3	Width	1335
Text3	Text	[blank]
Text3	Name	txtClose

Table 11.7 The *fraShowStockDate* controls' properties. *(continued from previous page)*

After you finish changing the *fraShowStockDate* controls' properties, the *fraShowStockDate* control will look similar to Figure 11.13.

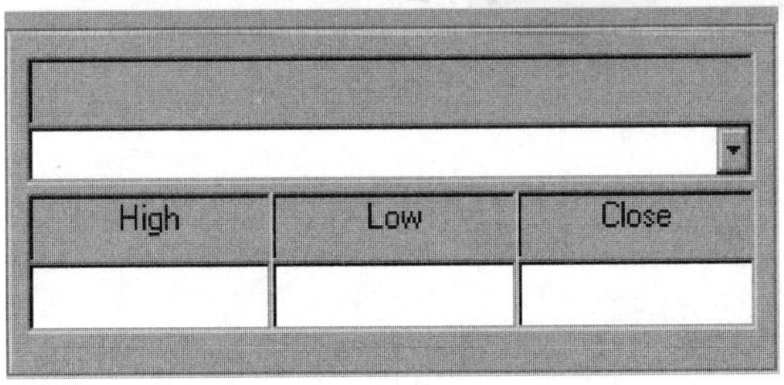

*Figure 11.13 The **fraShowStockDate** control after you change its controls' properties.*

ADDING THE FRAADDSTOCK FRAME CONTROL TO THE FORM

Now that you have added the *fraShowStockDate* frame control and finished changing its controls' properties, you will add another *Frame* control to the *frmStockList* form that lets you add a stock name, trading date, and prices to the *StockMarket* database. You will name the *Frame* control *fraAddStock*. After that, you will add *TextBox*, *Label*, and *CommandButton* controls to the *fraAddStock* control.

As you learned in the "Using the *prjStock* Project" section, the *Microsoft Calendar* control, *calStocks*, will display dates. When you click your mouse on the *calStocks* control, the *fraAddStock* control will respond. In a later section, you will add the code to the *calStocks* control's *Click* event to drive the response. The program will fill a *TextBox* control within the *fraAddStock* control with the date you select. If you click your mouse on the *lstStocks* control, Visual Basic will fill another *TextBox* control within the *fraAddStock* control with the stock name you select. After that, if you want to add high, low, and close prices for the selected trading date, you can enter the information within the three remaining empty *TextBox* controls.

To place the *fraAddStock* control within the *frmStockList* form, perform the following steps:

1. If Visual Basic is not displaying the *frmStockList* form, double-click your mouse on the *frmStockList* form listing within Project Explorer. Visual Basic will open the *frmStockList* form within an object window.

2. Within Visual Basic, select the View menu Toolbox option. Visual Basic will open the Toolbox.

3. Within the Toolbox window, double-click your mouse on the Frame icon. Visual Basic will draw a *Frame* control, *Frame1*, within the *frmStockList* form.

4. Within the form window, click your mouse on the *Frame1* control to highlight it. Visual Basic will draw a small frame around the control.

5. Select the View menu Properties Window option. Visual Basic will open the Properties Window listing the *Frame1* properties.

6. Within the Properties Window, change the *Frame1* properties to the values Table 11.8 lists.

Object	Property	Set As
Frame1	*Caption*	*Manually Add New Stock Date*
Frame1	*Height*	2415
Frame1	*Left*	240
Frame1	*Top*	4200
Frame1	*Width*	7695
Frame1	*Name*	*fraAddStock*

*Table 11.8 The newly named **fraAddStock** control's properties.*

ADDING THE CONTROLS TO THE FRAADDSTOCK CONTROL

Now that you have added the *fraAddStock* control to the form, you will add controls to it so that Visual Basic can display stock names and trading dates you select, and you can enter high, low, and close prices. You will add *TextBox*,

Label, and *CommandButton* controls to the *fraAddStock* control. Remember, you can add controls to the *fraAddStock* control only after you have added it to the *frmStockList* form. To add *TextBox, Label,* and *CommandButton* controls to the *fraAddStock* control, perform the following steps:

1. If Visual Basic is not displaying the *frmStockList* form, double-click your mouse on the *frmStockList* form listing within Project Explorer. Visual Basic will open the *frmStockList* form within an object window.

2. Within Visual Basic, select the View menu Toolbox option. Visual Basic will open the Toolbox.

3. Within the Toolbox, double-click your mouse on the TextBox icon. Visual Basic will draw a *TextBox* control, *Text1,* within the *frmStockList* form.

4. Within the form window, click your mouse on the *Text1* control and hold the mouse button down. Move the mouse cursor to drag the *Text1* control into the *fraAddStock* control. Release the mouse button. Visual Basic will draw the *Text1* control inside the *fraAddStock* control.

5. Repeat Steps 3 and 4 four more times until you have a total of five *TextBox* controls inside the *fraAddStock* control.

6. Within the Toolbox, double-click your mouse on the CommandButton icon. Visual Basic will draw a command button control, *Command1,* within the *frmStockList* form.

7. Within the form window, click your mouse on the *Command1* control and hold the mouse button down. Move the mouse cursor to drag the *Command1* control into the *fraAddStock* control. Release the mouse button. Visual Basic will draw the *Command1* control inside the *fraAddStock* control.

8. Within the Toolbox, double-click your mouse on the Label icon. Visual Basic will draw a label control, *Label1,* within the *frmStockList* form.

9. Within the form window, click your mouse on the *Label1* control and hold the mouse button down. Move the mouse cursor to drag the *Label1* control into the *fraAddStock* control. Release the mouse button. Visual Basic will draw the *Label1* control inside the *fraAddStock* control.

10. Repeat Steps 8 and 9 four more times until you have a total of five *Label* controls inside the *fraAddStock* control.

11. Within the *fraAddStock* control, click your mouse on a control to highlight it. Visual Basic will draw a small frame around the control.

12. Select the View menu Properties Window option. Visual Basic will open the Properties Window listing the highlighted control's properties.

13. Within the Properties Window, change the highlighted control's properties to the values Table 11.9 lists.

14. Repeat Steps 11, 12, and 13 until you have changed the properties of each control in the *fraAddStock* control to the values Table 11.9 lists.

Object	Property	Set As
Text1	*Height*	375
Text1	*Left*	960
Text1	*Top*	240
Text1	*Width*	2055
Text1	*Text*	[blank]
Text1	*Name*	*txtAddDate*
Text2	*Height*	375
Text2	*Left*	5280

*Table 11.9 The **fraAddStock** controls' properties. (continued on following page)*

Object	Property	Set As
Text2	Top	240
Text2	Width	2055
Text2	Text	[blank]
Text2	Name	txtAddStock
Text3	Height	375
Text3	Left	960
Text3	Top	720
Text3	Width	2055
Text3	Text	[blank]
Text3	Name	txtAddHigh
Text4	Height	375
Text4	Left	5280
Text4	Top	720
Text4	Width	2055
Text4	Text	[blank]
Text4	Name	txtAddLow
Text5	Height	375
Text5	Left	3000
Text5	Top	1200
Text5	Width	2055
Text5	Text	[blank]
Text5	Name	txtAddClose
Label1	Caption	Close
Label1	Height	375
Label1	Left	2280
Label1	Top	1200
Label1	Width	735
Label1	Name	lblAddClose
Label2	Caption	Date
Label2	Height	375
Label2	Left	240
Label2	Top	240
Label2	Width	735
Label2	Name	lblAddDate
Label3	Caption	Stock
Label3	Height	375
Label3	Left	4560
Label3	Top	240
Label3	Width	735
Label3	Name	lblAddStock
Label4	Caption	High
Label4	Height	375

Table 11.9 The **fraAddStock** controls' properties. *(continued on following page)*

Object	Property	Set As
Label4	Left	240
Label4	Top	720
Label4	Width	735
Label4	Name	lblAddHigh
Label5	Caption	Low
Label5	Height	375
Label5	Left	4560
Label5	Top	720
Label5	Width	735
Label5	Name	lblAddLow
Command1	Caption	ADD
Command1	Height	495
Command1	Left	2280
Command1	Top	1680
Command1	Width	2775
Command1	Name	cmdAdd

Table 11.9 *The **fraAddStock** controls' properties. (continued from previous page)*

After you finish changing the *fraAddStock* controls' properties, the *fraAddStock* control will look similar to Figure 11.14.

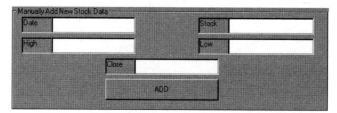

Figure 11.14 *The **fraAddStock** control after you change its controls' properties.*

ADDING THE FRACHOOSECHART FRAME CONTROL TO THE FORM

Now that you have added the controls to the *fraAddStock* control, you will add another *Frame* control that lets you choose the type of chart that the *Microsoft Chart* control will draw. You will name the *Frame* control *fraChooseChart*. To provide choices, you will add four *OptionButton* controls to the *fraChooseChart* control.

Remember, the *Microsoft Chart* control will draw bar, pie, and line charts in two or three dimensions. You will add *OptionButton* controls that let you select two- and three-dimensional chart types. To select a chart type, you will click your mouse on an *OptionButton* control within the *fraChooseChart* control. Next, Visual Basic will assign the chart type you select to the *Microsoft Chart* control's *ChartType* property. Then, the *Microsoft Chart* control will draw the chart type you select. In the *prjStock* project, you will use an *OptionButton* control array so that Visual Basic will know the chart type you select.

To place the *fraChooseChart* control within the *frmStockList* form, perform the following steps:

1. If Visual Basic is not displaying the *frmStockList* form, double-click your mouse on the *frmStockList* form listing within the Project Explorer. Visual Basic will open the *frmStockList* form within an object window.

2. Within Visual Basic, select the View menu Toolbox option. Visual Basic will open the Toolbox.

3. Within the Toolbox, double-click your mouse on the Frame icon. Visual Basic will draw a *Frame* control, *Frame1*, within the *frmStockList* form.

4. Within the form window, click your mouse on the *Frame1* control to highlight it. Visual Basic will draw a small frame around the control.

5. Select the View menu Properties Window option. Visual Basic will open the Properties Window listing the *Frame1* properties.

6. Within the Properties Window, change the *Frame1* properties to the values Table 11.10 lists.

Object	Property	Set As
Frame1	*Caption*	*Chart Type*
Frame1	*Height*	1935
Frame1	*Left*	4920
Frame1	*Top*	6840
Frame1	*Width*	3015
Frame1	*Name*	*fraChooseChart*

Table 11.10 *The newly named **fraChooseChart** control's properties.*

Adding the Controls to the fraChooseChart Control

Now that you have added the *fraChooseChart* control to the form, you will add controls to it. You will add four *OptionButton* controls to the control. Remember, you can add controls to a *Frame* control only after you have added the *Frame* control to a form. You will add the *OptionButton* controls to the *fraChooseChart* frame as a control array. Remember, Visual Basic will assign a unique index value to each control in a control array. For example, Visual Basic will assign the first *OptionButton* control the index value zero. When you click your mouse on an *OptionButton* control in a control array, Visual Basic will store the *OptionButton* control's unique index value in memory. In the *prjStock* project's Code window, you will write a *Select Case* statement that responds to each unique index value.

To add four *OptionButton* controls in a control array to the *fraChooseChart* control, perform the following steps:

1. If Visual Basic is not displaying the *frmStockList* form, double-click your mouse on the *frmStockList* form listing within Project Explorer. Visual Basic will open the *frmStockList* form within an object window.

2. Within Visual Basic, select the View menu Toolbox option. Visual Basic will open the Toolbox.

3. Within the Toolbox, double-click your mouse on the OptionButton icon. Visual Basic will draw an *OptionButton* control, *Option1*, within the *frmStockList* form.

4. Within the form window, click your mouse on the *Option1* control and hold the mouse button down. Move the mouse cursor to drag the *Option1* control into the *fraChooseChart* control. Release the mouse button. Visual Basic will draw the *Option1* control inside the *fraChooseChart* control.

5. Select the View menu Properties Window option. Visual Basic will open the Properties Window.

6. Within the *fraChooseChart* control, click your mouse on the *Option1* control. Visual Basic will fill the Properties Window with the *Option1* control properties. Next, click your mouse on the *Name* property and change the value from *Option1* to *optChart*.

7. Within the *fraChooseChart* control, click your mouse on the *optChart* control and select the Edit menu Copy option. Visual Basic will highlight the *optChart* control and store a copy of it in the Clipboard.

8. Click your mouse on the *fraChooseChart* control to highlight it. Next, select the Edit menu Paste option. Visual Basic will open a dialog box that asks, "You already have a control named 'optChart.' Do you want to create a control array?" Click your mouse on the Yes button. Visual Basic will draw a copy of the *optChart* control within the *fraChooseChart* control. Visual Basic will display the first *optChart* control as *optChart(0)*, and the second *optChart* control as *optChart(1)*.

9. Click your mouse on the *fraChooseChart* control to highlight it. Next, select the Edit menu Paste option. Visual Basic will draw another copy of the *optChart* control within the *fraChooseChart* control, and display it as *optChart(2)*.

10. Repeat Step 9 one more time so that you have a total of four *OptionButton* controls in a control array within the *fraChooseChart* control.

11. Within the *fraChooseChart* control, click your mouse on an *OptionButton* control. Next, select the View menu Properties Window option. Visual Basic will open the Properties Window listing the *optChart* properties. Each *optChart* control contains a parentheses. Each parentheses contains an integer value from 0 to 3.

12. Within the Properties Window, change the selected *optChart* control properties to the values Table 11.11 lists.

13. Repeat Steps 11 and 12 three more times until you have changed each indexed *optChart* control from index 0 to 3 to the values Table 11.11 lists.

Object	Property	Set As
optChart(0)	*Caption*	*2D Line Chart*
optChart(0)	*Height*	495
optChart(0)	*Left*	120
optChart(0)	*Top*	360
optChart(0)	*Width*	1335
optChart(1)	*Caption*	*2D Bar Chart*
optChart(1)	*Height*	495
optChart(1)	*Left*	120
optChart(1)	*Top*	1080
optChart(1)	*Width*	1335
optChart(2)	*Caption*	*3D Line Chart*
optChart(2)	*Height*	495
optChart(2)	*Left*	1560
optChart(2)	*Top*	360
optChart(2)	*Width*	1335
optChart(3)	*Caption*	*3D Bar Chart*
optChart(3)	*Height*	495
optChart(3)	*Left*	1560
optChart(3)	*Top*	1080
optChart(3)	*Width*	1335

*Table 11.11 Each **optChart** control's properties in the **fraChooseChart** control.*

After you finish changing the *fraChooseChart* controls' properties, the *frmStockLists* form will look similar to Figure 11.15.

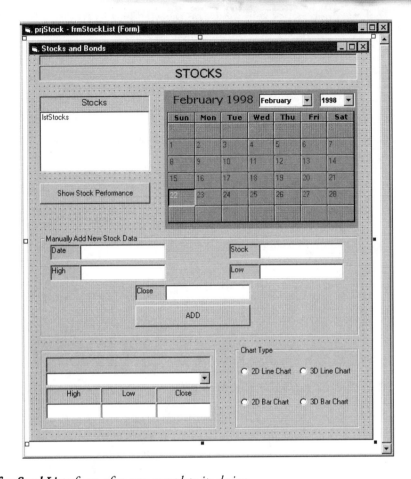

Figure 11.15 *The **frmStockLists** form after you complete its design.*

ADDING A MICROSOFT CHART CONTROL TO THE FRMSTOCKPERFORMANCE FORM

As you have learned, the *prjStock* project will use a *Microsoft Chart* control to draw bar, line, and pie charts of stock trading dates and prices to display to the user. The *prjStock* project will display the chart within the *frmStockPerformance* form. To add a *Microsoft Chart* control to the *frmStockPerformance* form, perform the following steps:

1. If Visual Basic is not displaying the *frmStockPerformance* form, double-click your mouse on the *frmStockPerformance* form listing within Project Explorer. Visual Basic will open the *frmStockPerformance* form within an object window.

2. Within Visual Basic, select the View menu Toolbox option. Visual Basic will open the Toolbox.

3. Within the Toolbox, select the new *Microsoft Chart* control icon, MSChart, as Figure 11.16 shows.

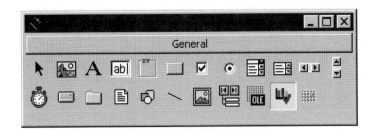

Figure 11.16 *The Toolbox showing the **Microsoft Chart** control's MSChart icon.*

4. Within the Toolbox, double-click your mouse on the MSChart icon. Visual Basic will draw a *Microsoft Chart* control, *MSChart1*, on the *frmStockPerformance* form.

5. Within the *frmStockPerformance* object window, click your mouse on the *MSChart1* control to highlight it. Visual Basic will draw a small frame around the control.

6. Select the View menu Properties Window option. Visual Basic will open the Properties Window with *MSChart1* properties.

7. Within the Properties Window, change the *MSChart1* properties to the values Table 11.12 lists.

Object	Property	Set As
MSChart1	*AllowDynamicRotation*	False
MSChart1	*AllowSelections*	False
MSChart1	*AllowSeriesSelections*	False
MSChart1	*Height*	9015
MSChart1	*Left*	0
MSChart1	*Top*	120
MSChart1	*Width*	9855
MSChart1	*Name*	chtStocks

*Table 11.12 The newly named **chtStocks** control's properties.*

WRITING THE CODE FOR THE prjStock PROJECT

In the *prjStock* project, you will write code for each control on the *frmStockList* form, and you will write procedures to communicate with the controls and the *StockMarket* database. First, you will declare variables that the procedures will use. Second, you will create a structure within the *mdlStockList* module. After that, you will write code for the procedures and control events within the *frmStockList* form. There is no code within the *frmStockPerformance* form.

WRITING THE CODE FOR THE VARIABLES

You will declare most variables that you will use in the *prjStock* project within the General–Declarations section in the *frmStockList* Code window. Remember, when you declare variables in the *frmStockList* form's General–Declarations section, all procedures and functions in the form code can use them. The following code implements the *prjStock* project variables in the *frmStockList* Code window's General–Declarations section:

```
Option Explicit
Dim StockDB As Database
Dim StockWS As Workspace
Dim StockNameRS As Recordset
Dim StockRS As Recordset
Dim DatabaseName As String
Dim SelectString As String
Dim NoRecord As Boolean
Dim i As Integer, j As Integer, k As Integer
Dim TradingDate As Variant
Dim TradingMonth As String, TradingDay As String, TradingYear As String
Dim DateString As String, DateLong As Long
Dim tempstring As String
Dim tempDate As String
Dim FoundRecord As Integer
Dim Market() As stcStocks, Chart() As stcStocks
Dim ChartArray(4, 2) As Variant
```

The *StockWS, StockDB, StockNameRS,* and *StockRS* variables will contain *Workspace, Database,* and *Recordset* objects, respectively. The *DatabaseName, SelectString, tempstring,* and *tempDate* variables will hold string values related to the database, stock name, and trading date. The *i, j,* and *k* variables will store counting values in *For-Next* loops. The *TradingDate, TradingDay, TradingMonth, TradingYear, DateString,* and *DateLong* variables will store values that pertain to a trading date. The *Chart* and *Market* variables will let you access an entire array of the *stcStocks* structure that you will define in the next section. You will dimension the number of elements within the program's code to reflect the number of records in the *StockRS* object. Finally, the *ChartArray* variable will let you assign numeric values to the *chtStock* control's *ChartData* property.

WRITING THE CODE FOR THE STRUCTURE

As you have learned, a structure holds related information about a specific object within a single location. In the *prjStock* project, the object is the stock. Each stock has a name, a high price, a low price, a closing price, and a trading date. You will store each piece of stock information about a given stock and trading date and price within the structure named *stcStocks*. The following code implements the *stcStocks* structure in the *mdlStockList* Code window's General–Declarations section:

```
Type stcStocks
   StockName As String
   StockDate As Long
   StockHigh As String
   StockLow As String
   StockClose As String
End Type
```

For example, to represent the stock name, you will refer to the *StockName* member within your program code. Remember, the *stcStocks* structure will contain a single record from the *StockRS* object, and your program will maintain two arrays of the *stcStocks* structure to handle all the records in the *StockRS* object.

WRITING THE CODE FOR THE FRMSTOCKLIST FORM_LOAD EVENT

As you learned in Chapter 1, "Introduction to Visual Basic," the *Form_Load* event occurs first when you load a form in Visual Basic, even before the form loads. The *prjStock* project loads the *frmStockList* form when the project starts. Therefore, the first code that the program executes is within the *frmStockList* form's *Form_Load* event. The following code implements the *frmStockList* form's *Form_Load* event:

```
Private Sub Form_Load()
   OpenDatabase
   OpenRecordsetStockName
   OpenRecordsetStockPrices
   ViewRecordsetStockName
   FillArray
   GetDate
   With calStocks
     .Month = TradingMonth
     .Day = TradingDay
     .Year = TradingYear
   End With
   With frmStockPerformance
     .chtStocks.ShowLegend = True
   End With
   lstStocks.ListIndex = 0
   optGraph(0).Value = True
End Sub
```

In the *prjStock* project, the *Load* event first calls the *OpenDatabase* procedure, which opens the *StockMarket* database. Then, the program calls the *OpenRecordsetStockName* procedure, which fills the *StockNameRS* object with records from the *StockMarket* database. Similarly, the *OpenRecordsetStockPrices* procedure fills the *StockRS* variable with stock price and date records. The event's program code then calls the *ViewRecordStockName* procedure to display the available stock names, and the *FillArray* procedure to fill the arrays you defined previously with stock information. Then, the *GetDate* procedure returns the current date and the program code assigns the current data to the *calStocks* control.

After it assigns the date, the *Load* event's program code will set the *chtStocks ShowLegend* property to *True*. When the *ShowLegend* property is *True*, the *chtStocks* control will display a legend (a series of captions that explain the chart's meaning) when it draws a chart. Finally, the *Load* event will set the *lstStocks* control's *ListIndex* property to zero. When the program code sets the *ListIndex* property to zero, the *lstStocks* control will invoke its own *Click* event, just as if the user had clicked the mouse on the control to change the selected item.

WRITING THE CODE FOR THE OPENDATABASE PROCEDURE

Now that you have written the code for the *Form_Load* event, you will write the first procedure, *OpenDatabase*, which will open the *StockMarket* database and assign it to the *Database* object *StockDB*. When you write the *OpenDatabase* procedure, you must specify the *StockMarket* database's location. The code uses the *App.Path* property to determine the database's location. If you have placed your copy of the *StockMarket* database in a different directory from the program's directory, you must change the *DatabaseName* variable's value to point to the correct location on your computer. The following code implements the *OpenDatabase* procedure:

```
Private Sub OpenDatabase()
  DatabaseName = App.Path & " \StockMarket.mdb"
  Set StockWS = Workspaces(0)
  Set StockDB = StockWS.OpenDatabase(DatabaseName)
End Sub
```

After the program code assigns the *DatabaseName* variable a value that corresponds to the *StockMarket* database's location, you will set the *Workspace* object, *StockWS,* to the default workspace, *Workspaces(0).* After that, the *StockWS* object's *OpenDatabase* method will open the *StockMarket* database, which the *DatabaseName* string variable contains, and assign its contents to the *Database* object *StockDB.*

WRITING THE CODE FOR THE OPENRECORDSETSTOCKNAME PROCEDURE

In the previous section, you initialized both the *Workspace* and *Database* objects. Now that the *StockDB* object contains an open database, your program can open a recordset in the *prjStock* project. The *OpenRecordsetStockName* procedure will open the *StockName* table and assign its contents to the *Recordset* object *StockNameRS*. You will write a Structured Query Language (SQL) statement that selects all records from the *StockName* table. The following code implements the *OpenRecordsetStockName* procedure:

```
Private Sub OpenRecordsetStockName()
  SelectString = "Select * from StockName Order By [Stock]"
  Set StockNameRS = StockDB.OpenRecordset(SelectString)
  StockNameRS.MoveLast
  If StockNameRS.RecordCount <= 0 Then
    NoRecord = True
  Else
    NoRecord = False
  End If
End Sub
```

As you can see, the *OpenRecordsetStockName* procedure opens the *StockNameRS* recordset, then checks to make sure it contains records. If it does not, the procedure assigns the flag variable *NoRecord* the value *True*. Otherwise, the procedure assigns the flag variable *NoRecord* the value *False*.

WRITING THE CODE FOR THE VIEWRECORDSETSTOCKNAME PROCEDURE

After the *OpenRecordsetStockName* procedure places all records from the *StockName* table into the *StockNameRS* object, you can view the records within Visual Basic. The *ViewRecordsetStockName* procedure will display each stock name in the *lstStocks* control. The following code implements the *prjStock* project's *ViewRecordsetStockName* procedure:

```
Private Sub ViewRecordsetStockName()
  StockNameRS.MoveFirst
  For i = 1 To StockNameRS.RecordCount
    lstStocks.AddItem (StockNameRS.Fields("Stock"))
    StockNameRS.MoveNext
  Next i
End Sub
```

As you can see, the *ViewRecordsetStockName* procedure uses a *For-Next* loop to step through each stock name in the *StockNameRS* recordset and add the name within the record to the *lstStocks* control. After the code finishes adding the available stocks to the list box, it returns execution to the calling procedure or function.

Writing the Code for the *OpenRecordsetStockPrices* Procedure

As you have learned, after the *OpenDatabase* procedure opens the *StockMarket* database, you can open one or more *Recordset* objects. The *OpenRecordsetStockName* procedure has already opened the *StockNameRS* object. Now, the *OpenRecordsetStockPrices* procedure will open the *StockPrices* table and assign its contents to the *Recordset* object *StockRS*. The following code implements the *prjStock* project's *OpenRecordsetStockPrices* procedure:

389

```
Private Sub OpenRecordsetStockPrices()
  SelectString = "SELECT * FROM StockPrices ORDER BY Date DESC"
  Set StockRS = StockDB.OpenRecordset(SelectString)
  StockRS.MoveLast
  If StockRS.RecordCount <= 0 Then
    NoRecord = True
  Else
    NoRecord = False
  End If
End Sub
```

Similar to the *OpenRecordsetStockName* procedure, the *OpenRecordsetStockPrices* procedure uses an SQL statement to open the *StockRS* recordset and fill it with records. Then, the program code checks to make sure that there are records. If there are not, the program code assigns the flag variable *NoRecord* the value *True*. Otherwise, the procedure assigns the flag variable *NoRecord* the value *False*.

Writing the Code for the *FillArray* Procedure

Now that you have an open recordset of stock prices in the *StockRS* object, you can view the records or store them in variable arrays. The *FillArray* procedure stores the *StockRS* object's records in the *Market* array. You will use the *StockRS* object's *RecordCount* value with the *ReDim* method to reset the *Market* array's dimensions. The following code implements the *prjStock* project's *FillArray* procedure:

```
Private Sub FillArray()
  ReDim Market(StockRS.RecordCount)

  StockNameRS.MoveLast
  StockNameRS.MoveFirst
  If StockNameRS.RecordCount = 0 Then Exit Sub
  StockRS.MoveFirst
  For J = 0 To StockRS.RecordCount - 1
    Market(J).StockName = StockRS.Fields("stock")
    Market(J).StockDate = StockRS.Fields("date")
    Market(J).StockHigh = StockRS.Fields("high")
    Market(J).StockLow = StockRS.Fields("low")
    Market(J).StockClose = StockRS.Fields("close")
    StockRS.MoveNext
  Next J
End Sub
```

The *FillArray* procedure first makes sure the *StockRS* object is filled with all available records, then sets the *Market* array's size as large enough to handle all the records. The procedure checks to make sure there are records to process and then initializes the array's values for every record in the recordset.

Note: *The first index value for each array in the* **stcStockArray** *begins with 0. The first record in the* **StockRS** *object begins with 1. To accommodate the difference in starting numbers, the* **For-Next** *loop starts at 0 and ends at the* **RecordCount** *property's value minus 1.*

WRITING THE CODE FOR THE GETDATE PROCEDURE

As you have learned, your programs can use the *Microsoft Calendar* control to display dates in a clear, concise format. Within the *prjStocks* project, there are several procedures that handle date display. The *GetDate* procedure will retrieve the computer system date and the *Load* event will assign it to the *calStocks* control. You will declare a local variable, *DateString*, to hold the formatted system date. Visual Basic stores the system date in the *Date* property. To retrieve the system date, you will assign the *Date* property to a variable. Visual Basic stores the *Date* property in a compressed 4-byte numeric format. In the *GetDate* procedure, the program code will assign the *Date* property to the *TradingDate Variant*-type variable and then convert the date to a string.

The following code implements the *prjStock* project's *GetDate* procedure:

```
Private Sub GetDate()
  Dim DateString As String

  TradingDate = Date
  DateString = Format(TradingDate, "mmddyy")
  TradingMonth = Left$(DateString, 2)
  TradingDay = Mid$(DateString, 2, 2)
  TradingYear = Right$(DateString, 2)
End Sub
```

After the program code determines the current date, it parses that date into a month value, a day value, and year value. The procedure uses the *Left$, Mid$,* and *Right$* functions because it knows that it will receive a string, not a *Variant,* for those functions to parse, because it declared the string within the procedure.

WRITING THE CODE FOR THE LSTSTOCKS_CLICK EVENT

As you have learned, your program will use the *ViewRecordsetStockName* procedure to add stocks to the *lstStocks* control. After the *ViewRecordsetStockName* procedure displays each stock name in the *lstStocks* control, you can then select a stock name from the *lstStocks* control. When you click your mouse on the *lstStocks* control, the *lstStocks_Click* event will occur. The following code implements the *prjStock* project's *lstStocks_Click* event:

```
Private Sub lstStocks_Click()
  tempstring = lstStocks.Text
  lblStockName.Caption = tempstring
  FindStockInArray
  If FoundRecord > 0 Then
    txtAddStock.Text = lstStocks.Text
    txtAddHigh.Text = ""
    txtAddLow.Text = ""
    txtAddClose.Text = ""
    cmbStockDate.ListIndex = 0
  Else
    txtAddStock.Text = lstStocks.Text
    txtHigh.Text = ""
    txtLow.Text = ""
    txtClose.Text = ""
    lblStockName.Caption = ""
    txtAddHigh.Text = ""
    txtAddLow.Text = ""
```

```
      txtAddClose.Text = ""
    End If
    QueryRecordsetForStocks
    SetChartData
    SetChartLabels
End Sub
```

The program code within the *Click* event initializes the display frame and places values within it. The program code uses the *lstStocks* control's currently selected value to set the caption for the frame. The *Click* event's program code then calls the *FindStockInArray* procedure, which will find the stock name the user selected within the list box in the *Market* array. If matching records exist in the array, the *If-Then-Else* statement will assign the *lstStocks* control's *Text* property to the *txtAddStock* control's *Text* property, clear the bottom three *TextBox* controls in the *fraAddStock* control, and set the *cmbStockDate* control's *ListIndex* property to zero (which will cause the *cmbStockDate* control to invoke its own *Click* event).

If matching records do not exist, the *If-Then-Else* statement will assign the *lstStocks* control's *Text* property to the *txtAddStock* control's *Text* property, clear the bottom three *TextBox* controls in the *fraAddStock* control, clear the bottom three *TextBox* controls in the *fraShowStockDate* control, and clear the *lblStockName* control's *Caption* property—which will make all the frame's controls blank.

WRITING THE CODE FOR THE *FINDSTOCKINARRAY* PROCEDURE

After you select a stock name from the *lstStocks* control, you can search for it in the recordset or in the structure. The *FindStockInArray* procedure will find the stock name you select in the *Market* array of *stcStocks* structures. Remember, the *Market* array contains the elements of the *stcStocks* structure, with the total elements equaling the number of records in the *StocksRS* recordset. The following code implements the *FindStockInArray* procedure:

```
Private Sub FindStockInArray()
  cmbStockDate.Clear
  FoundRecord = 0
  For I = 0 To StockRS.RecordCount
    If Market(I).StockName = tempstring Then
      DateString = Format(Market(I).StockDate, "####/##/##")
      DateString = Format(DateString, "mm/dd/yy")
      cmbStockDate.AddItem (DateString)
      cmbStockDate.ListIndex = 0
      FoundRecord = FoundRecord + 1
    End If
  Next I
End Sub
```

The *FindStockInArray* procedure first clears the *cmbStockDate* control of any listings. It then loops through the *Market* array, looking for stock records that match the currently selected stock. The procedure adds the date for each transaction record it finds to the *cmbStockDate* control.

WRITING THE CODE FOR THE *CMBSTOCKDATE_CLICK* EVENT

After you click your mouse on the *lstStocks* control, the *FindStockInArray* procedure will add the corresponding trading date to the *cmbStockDate* control. When you click your mouse on the *cmbStockDate* control, the *Click* event will also occur. The *cmbStockDate* control's *Click* event will assign values to the trading information fields that correspond to the user-selected trading date. The following code implements the *cmdStockDate_Click* event:

```
Private Sub cmbStockDate_Click()
  DateString = cmbStockDate.Text
  DateString = Format(DateString, "yyyymmdd")
  DateLong = DateString
  FindDateInArray
End Sub
```

As you can see, the *Click* event formats the date string within the *cmbStockDate* control and calls the *FindDateInArray* procedure. The following code implements the *FindDateInArray* procedure:

```
Private Sub FindDateInArray()
  For I = 0 To StockRS.RecordCount - 1
    If Market(I).StockName = tempstring Then
      If Market(I).StockDate = DateLong Then
        txtHigh.Text = Market(I).StockHigh
        txtLow.Text = Market(I).StockLow
        txtClose.Text = Market(I).StockClose
        Exit Sub
      Else
        txtHigh.Text = ""
        txtLow.Text = ""
        txtClose.Text = ""
      End If
    End If
  Next I
End Sub
```

The *FindDateInArray* procedure performs processing similar to the *FindStockInArray* procedure. The procedure loops through the *Market* array, looking for a match for the stock name and trading date. When it finds a match, it displays the high, low, and close information for that record within the form's display and then exits the procedure. If the program code does not find a match, it clears the fields out and continues searching the array.

WRITING THE CODE FOR THE *QueryRecordsetForStocks* PROCEDURE

After the *lstStocks_Click* event finds the stock the user selects in the *stcStockList* structure, the program can search for that stock's records in the *StockRS Recordset* object. The *QueryRecordsetForStocks* procedure will find the selected stock name, and assign the high, low, and close prices for the five most recent trading dates. After the program retrieves the five most recent trading dates, it will display the values in the *chtStocks* control. The following code implements the *QueryRecordsetForStocks* procedure:

```
Private Sub QueryRecordsetForStocks()
  Dim searchstring As String
  Dim k As Integer
  ReDim Chart(5)

StockRS.MoveFirst
  searchstring = "Stock = '" & tempstring & "'"
  StockRS.FindFirst (searchstring)
  If StockRS.NoMatch Then
    Exit Sub
  Else
    Chart(k).StockName = tempstring
    Chart(k).StockDate = StockRS.Fields("date")
    Chart(k).StockHigh = StockRS.Fields("high")
    Chart(k).StockLow = StockRS.Fields("low")
    Chart(k).StockClose = StockRS.Fields("close")
    k = k + 1
  End If
  Do Until (k = 5)
    StockRS.FindNext (searchstring)
    If StockRS.NoMatch = False Then
      Chart(k).StockName = tempstring
      Chart(k).StockDate = StockRS.Fields("date")
      Chart(k).StockHigh = StockRS.Fields("high")
      Chart(k).StockLow = StockRS.Fields("low")
      Chart(k).StockClose = StockRS.Fields("close")
```

```
         k = k + 1
      Else
         Exit Sub
      End If
   Loop
End Sub
```

The *QueryRecordsetForStocks* procedure performs straightforward processing. It clears the chart variable first and then checks the *StockRS* recordset for all the matches it can find, up to five, for the stock trade. For each match it finds, it assigns the values into the *Chart* array. If it finds only one match, it assigns values to the *Chart(0)* element only. If it finds five values, it assigns values to all five *Chart* elements. The program's code will later use the *Chart* array when it draws the *frmStockPerformance* form.

WRITING THE CODE FOR THE SETCHARTDATA PROCEDURE

After you fill the *Chart* object's elements with the five most recent trading dates, you can set the *chtStocks* control's chart data. The *SetChartData* procedure will assign the five most recent trading dates' high, low, and close prices to the *ChartArray* array. Remember, a *Microsoft Chart* control must have data from which to draw. The program must contain the data in a two-dimensional array, which it will present to the *Chart* control. Within a two-dimensional array, the first element corresponds to the row value and the second element corresponds to the column value. Because you designed the *chtStocks* control with five rows and three columns per row, you must assign a value to each row and column, even if the value is zero. The following code implements the *SetChartData* procedure:

```
Private Sub SetChartData()
   ChartArray(0, 0) = Chart(0).StockHigh
   ChartArray(0, 1) = Chart(0).StockLow
   ChartArray(0, 2) = Chart(0).StockClose
   ChartArray(1, 0) = Chart(1).StockHigh
   ChartArray(1, 1) = Chart(1).StockLow
   ChartArray(1, 2) = Chart(1).StockClose
   ChartArray(2, 0) = Chart(2).StockHigh
   ChartArray(2, 1) = Chart(2).StockLow
   ChartArray(2, 2) = Chart(2).StockClose
   ChartArray(3, 0) = Chart(3).StockHigh
   ChartArray(3, 1) = Chart(3).StockLow
   ChartArray(3, 2) = Chart(3).StockClose
   ChartArray(4, 0) = Chart(4).StockHigh
   ChartArray(4, 1) = Chart(4).StockLow
   ChartArray(4, 2) = Chart(4).StockClose
   frmStockPerformance.chtStocks.ChartData = ChartArray
End Sub
```

As you can see, the program code assigns the elements of the *Chart* array to their corresponding positions within the chart. The last line of the procedure sends the *ChartArray*'s data to the *chtStocks* control.

WRITING THE CODE FOR THE SETCHARTLABELS PROCEDURE

As you learned in the previous section, you must assign the array values that you wish to display within the array to the *ChartArray*'s elements. After the *ChartData* property contains the *ChartArray* array values, the program can set the *chtStocks* control's labels. The *SetChartLabels* procedure will assign labels to each row and column in the *chtStocks* control. Remember, the program can set values for the labels only after the *ChartData* property contains values. The code will assign the *chtStocks* control's *TitleText* property to the stock name you select. The *chtStocks* control contains five rows and fifteen columns. The following code implements the *SetChartLabels* procedure:

```
Private Sub SetChartLabels()
   chtStocks.TitleText = "Chart for " & tempstring
   chtStocks.Column = 1
```

```
    chtStocks.ColumnLabel = "HIGH"
    chtStocks.Column = 2
    chtStocks.ColumnLabel = "LOW"
    chtStocks.Column = 3
    chtStocks.ColumnLabel = "CLOSE"
    chtStocks.Row = 1
    DateString = Format(Chart.StockDate(0), "####/##/##")
    chtStocks.RowLabel = Format(DateString, "mm/dd/yy")
    If chtStocks.RowLabel = "//" Then chtStocks.RowLabel = ""
    chtStocks.Row = 2
    DateString = Format(Chart.StockDate(1), "####/##/##")
    chtStocks.RowLabel = Format(DateString, "mm/dd/yy")
    If chtStocks.RowLabel = "//" Then chtStocks.RowLabel = ""
    chtStocks.Row = 3
    DateString = Format(Chart.StockDate(2), "####/##/##")
    chtStocks.RowLabel = Format(DateString, "mm/dd/yy")
    If chtStocks.RowLabel = "//" Then chtStocks.RowLabel = ""
    chtStocks.Row = 4
    DateString = Format(Chart.StockDate(3), "####/##/##")
    chtStocks.RowLabel = Format(DateString, "mm/dd/yy")
    If chtStocks.RowLabel = "//" Then chtStocks.RowLabel = ""
    chtStocks.Row = 5
    DateString = Format(Chart.StockDate(4), "####/##/##")
    chtStocks.RowLabel = Format(DateString, "mm/dd/yy")
    If chtStocks.RowLabel = "//" Then chtStocks.RowLabel = ""
End Sub
```

Within each row, the *chtStocks* control contains three columns. When the *chtStocks* control's *Column* property sets the column to a value, the next *ColumnLabel* property value will correspond to the set column number. The *SetChartLabels* procedure assigns the *High, Low,* and *Close* captions to the three columns. Next, the procedure's program code labels the area below each plot with the date for the plot. If there is no date or data, the procedure leaves the area blank.

WRITING THE CODE FOR THE CALSTOCKS_CLICK EVENT

As you learned, the *Form_Load* event sets the *calStocks* control to the current date. However, the user can select any valid date to add stock information to the program. To select a new date, the user will click the mouse on the *calStocks* control. To respond correctly, your program must include program code within the *calStocks_Click* event. The following code implements the *calStocks_Click* event:

```
Private Sub calStocks_Click()
  DateString = calStocks.Year & "/" & calStocks.Month & "/" & calStocks.Day
  tempDate = Format(DateString, "yyyymmdd")
  txtAddDate.Text = Format(DateString, "dddd, mmmm d, yyyy")
End Sub
```

The *calStocks_Click* event's program code converts the user's selection into a year and date string, then assigns that value to the *tempDate* variable and a formatted version of the values to the *txtAddDate* control's *Text* property.

WRITING THE CODE FOR THE CMDADD_CLICK EVENT

After the *fraAddStock* control's *txtAddDate* control displays a selected date, the user can add a new stock name and the stock's high, low, and close prices to the *StockMarket* database. When the user clicks the mouse on the ADD button within the *fraAddStock* control, the *Click* event will occur. The following code implements the *cmdAdd_Click* event:

```
Private Sub cmdAdd_Click()
  Dim searchstring As String

  If Val(txtAddHigh.Text) < 0 Or Val(txtAddLow.Text) < 0 Or _
      Val(txtAddClose.Text) < 0 Or Val(txtAddHigh.Text) > 32767 Or _
```

```
          Val(txtAddLow.Text) > 32767  Or Val(txtAddClose.Text) > 32767 Then
        MsgBox "Enter Values for High, Low, and Close", vbCritical
        Exit Sub
     End If
     searchstring = ("Stock = '" & txtAddStock.Text & "'")
     StockNameRS.FindFirst (searchstring)
     If StockNameRS.NoMatch Then
        StockNameRS.AddNew
           StockNameRS.Fields("Stock") = txtAddStock.Text
        StockNameRS.Update
        StockNameRS.Requery
        StockRS.AddNew
          StockRS.Fields("Stock") = txtAddStock.Text
          StockRS.Fields("High") = txtAddHigh.Text
          StockRS.Fields("Low") = txtAddLow.Text
          StockRS.Fields("Close") = txtAddClose.Text
          StockRS.Fields("Date") = tempDate
        StockRS.Update
        StockRS.Requery
        StockRS.MoveLast
        FillArray
        lstStocks.ListIndex = 0
     Else
        StockRS.AddNew
          StockRS.Fields("Stock") = txtAddStock.Text
          StockRS.Fields("High") = txtAddHigh.Text
          StockRS.Fields("Low") = txtAddLow.Text
          StockRS.Fields("Close") = txtAddClose.Text
          StockRS.Fields("Date") = tempDate
        StockRS.Update
        StockRS.Requery
        StockRS.MoveLast
        FillArray
        lstStocks.ListIndex = 0
        End If
   End Sub
```

The *Click* event checks the entries to be sure that the user entered valid values for the *High, Low,* and *Close* numbers. If the user did not, the program code tells the user and exits the event. If the user did enter valid values, the program code then adds the new values to the database. It also checks that the name the user entered exists and, if it does not, adds the new stock name to the database.

Writing the Code for the optGraph_Click Event

After the *Microsoft Chart* control *chtStocks* draws a chart, you can select a different type of chart. When you click your mouse on one of the *optChart* controls in the *fraChooseChart* control, the *Click* event will occur. Remember, Visual Basic references each *optChart* control in the control array with an index value from 0 to 3. When you click your mouse on an *optChart* control, Visual Basic will store the underlying index value in memory. The following code implements the *optGraph_Click* event:

```
Private Sub optGraph_Click(Index As Integer)
   With frmStockPerformance
     .chtStocks.ShowLegend = True
     Select Case Index
       Case 0
         .chtStocks.chartType = VtChChartType2dLine
       Case 1
         .chtStocks.chartType = VtChChartType2dBar
```

```
      Case 2
         .chtStocks.chartType = VtChChartType3dLine
      Case 3
         .chtStocks.chartType = VtChChartType3dBar
    End Select
  End With
End Sub
```

The *Click* event assigns the *chtStocks* control's *ShowLegend* property to *True,* then uses a *Select-Case* statement to determine which *optChart* control the user selected. The program code within the procedure sets the chart type to correspond to the user's selection.

WRITING THE CODE FOR THE *CMDSHOWPERFORMANCE_CLICK* EVENT

As you learned earlier in this chapter, the user can view information about the currently selected stock in a chart-style display. To display the chart, the user must click the mouse on the *cmdShowPerformance* button. The following code implements the *cmdShowPerformance_Click* event:

```
Private Sub cmdShowPerformance_Click()
  Dim I As Integer
  SetChartData
  SetChartLabels
  With frmStockPerformance
    .chtStocks.ShowLegend = True
    For I = 0 To 3
      If optGraph(I).Value = True Then
        Select Case I
          Case 0
            .chtStocks.chartType = VtChChartType2dLine
          Case 1
            .chtStocks.chartType = VtChChartType2dBar
          Case 2
            .chtStocks.chartType = VtChChartType3dLine
          Case 3
            .chtStocks.chartType = VtChChartType3dBar
        End Select
      End If
    Next
  End With
  frmStockPerformance.Show
End Sub
```

The *cmdShowPerformance_Click* event initializes the chart, initializes the labels, and checks the *optGraph* control array's value to determine what chart type to show. It then calls the *Show* method for the *frmStockPerformance* form, which displays the form. When you run the *prjStock* project, you can minimize the *frmStockPerformance* form and keep it available all the time, or you can close it after you create each chart and re-open it later.

WRITING THE CODE FOR THE *FRMSTOCKLIST* FORM_UNLOAD EVENT

As you have learned, when you unload all the forms for a program that uses a single-document interface, the program itself will unload. The following code implements the *frmStockList's* *Form_Unload* event:

```
Private Sub Form_Unload(Cancel As Integer)
  On Error Resume Next
  Unload frmStockPerformance
  Unload Me
  End
End Sub
```

As you can see, the *frmStockList's Form_Unload* event will unload the *frmStockPerformance* form, unload the *frmStockList* form, and end the program's execution.

ENHANCEMENTS YOU CAN MAKE TO THE prjStock PROJECT

Now that you have a better understanding of the *Microsoft Chart* control, and have used a *Microsoft Calendar* control with *TextBox, ListBox,* and *CommandButton* controls, you can make some adjustments to the project. For instance, you can place the *Microsoft Chart* control onto a separate form and size it to the size of your computer screen. This size will be a better display than the smaller size of the *prjStock* project.

You can also write more error trapping code, especially when you retrieve records from the database, to protect against bad data entry or bad data returns. In addition, you can add the stock open price to the high, low, and close prices. Also, many investors like to view stock trading volume. You can add the trading volume and, because trading volume can be large, you can add another *Microsoft Chart* control to display the volume alone. With separate stock volume, you can display the five most recent volumes to match the five most recent open, high, low, and close prices of the stock you select. Moreover, you can design the project to display four or more stocks at the same time in four separate *Microsoft Chart* controls. Finally, you can insert a *Microsoft Excel* worksheet to do more extensive analysis than price displays.

PUTTING IT ALL TOGETHER

This chapter's project, *prjStock*, introduced you to the *Microsoft Chart* control, a *Microsoft Calendar* control, and an *OptionButton* control array. In addition, you have learned about *TextBox, ListBox, ComboBox,* and *Frame* controls. Using the *Microsoft Chart* control you can draw bar, line, and pie charts. The *Microsoft Calendar* control lets you select a day, month, and year, which you used in the *prjStock* project to add stock high, low, and close prices to a database.

In this chapter you also used a Microsoft *Access* database to provide a storage place for stock names, stock trading dates, and stock high, low, and close prices. Using *Workspace, Database,* and *Recordset* objects from the DAO Object Library, you accessed a Microsoft *Access* database from within Visual Basic. The next chapter, Chapter 12, "Using ActiveX Automation to Create a Database Server," uses a class module to create an out-of-process database server program. Before you continue with Chapter 12, however, make sure you understand the following key concepts:

✓ Within your Visual Basic programs, you can use the *Microsoft Chart* control to draw many different types of charts. Possible chart types include bar charts, line charts, and pie charts.

✓ Visual Basic includes the *Microsoft Calendar* control, which you will use within your Visual Basic programs to display dates.

✓ Within your programs, you can use the *Microsoft Calendar* control to provide the user with a simple, clear way to access date-based information.

✓ Visual Basic includes database management objects, such as the *Workspace, Database,* and *Recordset* objects, which your programs will use to access and manage databases.

✓ Your Visual Basic programs can use Microsoft *Access* databases to store related information and retrieve it later. Additionally, you can relate values in one table to values in other tables.

✓ Even the simplest Visual Basic programs may have good use for multiple forms, if the amount of data the program must display is too wide, too tall, or too confusing to place on a single form.

✓ Within your programs, you will often use a structure, a special kind of *type* that you define, to store related information in a single location.

✓ Visual Basic includes the *OptionButton* control, which you will generally use within an option button array.

397

Chapter 12

Using ActiveX Automation to Create a Database Server

As the use of networks becomes more central to most businesses, and as most users begin to access databases remotely, database storage methods are rapidly changing. As databases change, so too do the programs that programmers must create to access the valuable information databases store. Historically, users accessed a database on their local computers, or used dumb terminals to access information within a mainframe computer. Today, most companies are moving (or have already moved) to a database structure that lets users access complex databases from their desktop computers. As you learned in Chapter 8, "Creating a Schedule Planner," you can use a database to store, retrieve, and search for specific data. When you access a database over a network, you (and your software) are a *client*. The database that stores the information you retrieve, store, edit, and so on, plus the software that maintains the database, is the *server*. Information Services (IS) professionals generally refer to a database structure that combines the powerful local component with the powerful remote component as a *client–server* structure.

Throughout this book you have used the *Standard EXE* project type option to design projects, and in Chapter 6, "Creating and Using ActiveX Controls," you used the *ActiveX Control* option to design ActiveX controls. In Chapter 21, "Using Windows Sockets for Two-Way Internet Communications," you will create an ActiveX DLL (which is an *in-process server*). This chapter introduces the Visual Basic *ActiveX EXE* project option, another special type of Visual Basic project. The ActiveX EXE project differs from the ActiveX DLL in that it lets you create a complete stand-alone project that one or more client programs can access over a network, or even on a single location machine. Further, not only does the user not have to download a control to the user's machine, the ActiveX EXE runs within its own process and address space, so it is simultaneously available to many instances of the same program. This chapter's project, *prjServer*, will consist of a database plus the software to access the database. After you finish creating the server, you can use it over a network—only the information a client retrieves, stores, edits, and searches will transfer across the network. The rest of the server program, together with the database that contains the information, will stay on the server computer.

This chapter examines in detail the ActiveX EXE project option and a Microsoft *Access* database. However, this chapter's project is different from every other project in this book because an ActiveX EXE project does not have any Visual Basic controls or a Visual Basic form—in other words, it does not have a user interface. By the time you finish this chapter, you will understand the following key concepts:

♦ An ActiveX EXE project is a special type of Visual Basic project.

♦ An in-process server is one that runs in the same process space as the calling program.

♦ An out-of-process server is one that runs in its own process space so that many calling programs can access the same server.

♦ To create out-of-process servers, you must use the Visual Basic ActiveX EXE project option.

♦ Using Visual Basic, you can create an ActiveX EXE project to make information one or more users previously stored in a central database available to one or more users across a network.

♦ When you design out-of-process servers, you can use a single ActiveX EXE program as a server for each database, or you can construct the ActiveX EXE program so that each instance can access a different database.

♦ When you create an ActiveX EXE project within Visual Basic, you will create one or more class modules with private and public sections and one or more code modules, but you will not use any forms because an ActiveX EXE has no visual presence.

♦ When you create a server program, you can expose properties, methods, and events that the client program will use to access the information the server program maintains.

♦ When you create a client program to access your server, the client's visual interface will present the information the server program returns.

USING THE PRJSERVER PROJECT

The ActiveX EXE project in this chapter consists of only a *class module* which, as you have learned in previous chapters, is code stored within a class. You will name this chapter's project *prjServer*. Because *prjServer* contains only a class module and has no forms or controls, when you run *prjServer*, there is nothing to click your mouse on and nothing to see. In Chapter 13, "Creating a Network-Aware Client," you will design the client side, which will view the *prjServer* project's database. Figure 12.1 shows the relationship between the client program, the server program, and the database itself.

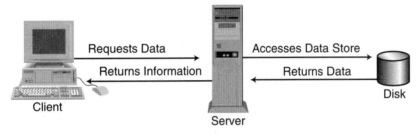

Figure 12.1 *The relationship between the client and server programs and the information within the database.*

Each chapter in this book has a *Using the Project* section that details how you can use that chapter's fully compiled program or programs. In this chapter, however, the *prjServer* project does not expose any controls, forms, or other controls that you can manipulate. In fact, the only access that you will have to the *prjServer* project is from another client program. In Chapter 13, you will design a form with controls, functions, and procedures. After you run Chapter 13's project, you will see the *prjServer* project's information.

RUNNING PRJSERVER FROM THE CD-ROM

As you have learned, you must first install many programs that you will use in this book to your computer's hard drive before you use the programs. Because you will only access the *prjServer.exe* program from the *prjClient.exe* program that you will create in Chapter 13, and because you must use ActiveX automation to access the *prjServer.exe* program, you must install the *prjServer.exe* program to a drive before you try to use it. If you try to run the *prjServer.exe* program from the CD-ROM, Windows will not recognize that the server component is loaded, and therefore will not run the *prjClient.exe* program.

Moreover, the *prjServer.exe* program is an interface between the *prjClient.exe* program and the *ClientServer.mdb* database. Even if you were able to get the *prjServer.exe* program to run and the *prjClient.exe* program to recognize it, you would be unable to use the programs to their full potential because you would not be able to make changes to the *ClientServer.mdb* database.

To learn more about the Jamsa Press *setup.exe* program, see the "What's on the *Visual Basic Programmer's Library* Companion CD-ROM" section at the back of this book.

As you have learned, the *prjServer* project will maintain information in a Microsoft *Access* database. First, you will design a database. Then, you will write procedures, functions, and variables to communicate with the database. The database will contain information similar to what a company might use to track its customers. The database will store a customer's name, address, phone number, and identification number (ID). Figure 12.2 shows the logical model of the information the database will store.

ID	Customer Name	Address	Telephone	Fax
1	Joe Smith	1234 Any Street	555-1213	555-1212
2	Bill Jones	1235 Any Street	555-1923	555-4412
3	Sam Snead	1236 Any Street	555-1666	555-1292
4	Matt Brown	1237 Any Street	555-1773	555-1316
5	Ann Jensen	1238 Any Street	555-4113	555-1333
n	Pat Smart	1299 Any Street	555-4222	555-1693

Figure 12.2 *The logical model of a database record for the* **prjServer** *project.*

As you develop the *prjServer* project, you will write functions that retrieve an ID number from the database and return the ID to the client program (which you will develop in Chapter 13). The client will ask the *prjServer* project (the server) to check the ID number and verify the number's uniqueness. If everything is okay (that is, if the ID number is acceptable and unique), the client can add a new customer to the database. In addition, the client can view all the records the server database contains. Multiple users can use Chapter 13's client project to simultaneously access the server from across a network. Figure 12.3 uses a hardware model to show an example of two clients connected to a single server.

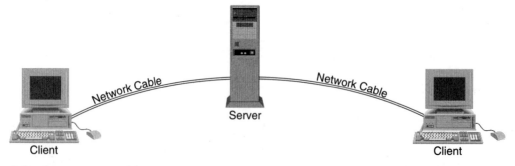

Client   Network Cable   Server   Network Cable   Client

Figure 12.3 *The client–server model.*

CREATING A BLANK CLASS MODULE

Now that you know an ActiveX EXE project has only class modules, you can begin to design the *prjServer* project. First, you will start an ActiveX EXE project and open a blank class module within the module. After you set up the *prjServer* project and its mandatory blank class module, you will learn more (in the following section) about ActiveX EXE projects. After you create the project and learn more about its general characteristics, you will write the code to implement the ActiveX server.

To begin the *prjServer* project and to create a blank class module, perform the following steps:

1. Within Visual Basic, select the File menu New Project option. Visual Basic will open the New Project dialog box.

2. Within the New Project dialog box, click your mouse on the ActiveX EXE icon. Next, click your mouse on the OK button. Visual Basic will open the *Class1* code window.

3. Select the View menu Properties Window option. Visual Basic will display the Properties Window.

4. Within the Properties Window, change the *Name* property to *clsServer*.

5. Select the Project menu Project1 Properties option. Visual Basic will display the Project Properties dialog box.

6. Within the Project Properties dialog box, change the Project Name field from *Project1* to *prjServer*.

7. Select the File menu Save Project As option. Visual Basic will open the Save File As dialog box and fill the *File name* field with *clsServer*. Click your mouse on the Save button. Visual Basic will save the *clsServer* module and fill the *File name* field with the *Project1* project name.

8. Within the *File name* field, replace the *Project1* project name with the new *prjServer* project name. Next, click your mouse on the Save button. Visual Basic will save the *prjServer* project and close the Save Project As dialog box. The Project Explorer will look similar to Figure 12.4.

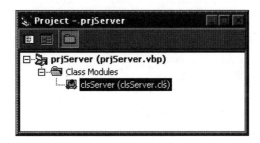

Figure 12.4 *Project Explorer after you add the* **clsServer** *class module to the project.*

More on ActiveX EXE Projects

As you have learned, an ActiveX EXE project consists of one or more class modules. A class module is similar to a standard module. In Chapter 5, "Creating and Using Fractals," you used a standard module to declare a structure. A class module can also contain structures, procedures, functions, and variables.

As you know, a Visual Basic form can contain controls, structures, variables, functions, and procedures. A form will process and display information in controls that you can see. A class module, on the other hand, will generally process information that you cannot see. To view a class module's results, you must access objects of that class from some exterior point. In the case of the *prjServer* project, you must actually design a separate project, which you will do in Chapter 13, "Creating a Network-Aware Client."

In the *prjServer* project, you will use the *clsServer* class module to write procedures, functions, and variables that will let another user (running a client program) access a Microsoft *Access* database. The *prjServer* project is a program and, like all other programs, it contains some combination of procedures, functions, and variables. However, because the program performs actions only in response to a request from a client program (known as providing *services*), programmers refer to programs such as the *prjServer* program as *servers*.

As you know, a client is software that uses the functions, procedures, and database information the server exposes. In the *prjServer* project, the *clsServer* server will maintain information in a Microsoft *Access* database, and the Chapter 13 client will view the information. When the Chapter 13 client uses the *prjServer* project's functions and procedures to maintain information, the client uses *automation*. Automation lets one project or object control another project or object. For more information on automation, see the "Understanding Automation" section.

In summary, an ActiveX EXE project will let you write procedures, functions, structures, and variables that manage all kinds of information. Other users with the correct software can access the information the project maintains through the project's public variables, functions, and procedures. As you have learned, such public components are known as *properties, methods,* and *events.* The properties and methods will be available locally or across a network to the client program, and the client program may also manipulate events the server raises. Although this chapter uses an ActiveX EXE project to maintain a database and much of the discussion in previous sections has been about data, you can use an ActiveX EXE project to provide many different types of services. For example, you can use an ActiveX EXE project to implement any type of information storage, management, and processing you want to accomplish.

MORE ON PRIVATE AND PUBLIC PROCEDURES AND FUNCTIONS

You will write public and private functions and procedures in the *prjServer* project. As you learned in Chapter 1, "Introduction to Visual Basic," a private procedure or function is one that has *limited scope*. In other words, programs can access a private procedure or function only from within the area where the program defines the procedure or function. For example, only procedures within the same form can access a procedure within a form you declare as *private*. Similarly, procedures or functions that you declare as private within an ActiveX EXE module are visible or accessible only to other procedures or functions within the module. To let other programs (clients) access procedures or functions, you must make those procedures and functions *public*. Programmers refer to the process of letting other programs outside the class module access public functions within the class module as *exposing* those functions.

Private functions or procedures let you protect data from outside sources. The only way to retrieve and manipulate data in a private function or procedure is to call the routine from another public or private function or procedure within the same class module. Such indirect access to private functions or procedures lets the class (in this case, the ActiveX EXE) protect sensitive data. For example, imagine you have a private library of rare books in your house. A friend wants to read two of the books. However, you do not want anyone physically touching the books, as they are simply too valuable. If you let the friend physically touch the books, he may spill water on one, or worse, lose one. You must find a way to let your friend read the books without touching them. So, you make a digital copy of each page and transfer the contents to a computer program. Now, your friend can read the books at his leisure without destroying anything. (Luckily, because the books are so old and rare, the copyright has expired, and you can make as many copies as you like.) In the same way, a private function would store the rare books. A public function would read the rare books on a computer screen without touching them.

In the *prjServer* project, you will write private functions that open, close, and search a Microsoft *Access* database. Then you will write public functions that retrieve information from the database and let other users view the information. In this way, the database information is read-only. However, for the *prjServer* project to better understand an ActiveX EXE project, you will provide full access to the Chapter 13 client. The client can then view, add, edit, and delete records from the database. As you will see, you can easily change the *prjServer* project's code so that the Chapter 13 client can only read the database information and not cause *client corruption*. Client corruption occurs when the client alters an original source of data and makes it inaccessible to other users.

Note: *The Chapter 13 client will not open or close the Microsoft **Access** database. Instead, it will ask the **prjServer** project to open or close the database. This indirect access will let you protect sensitive data from corruption.*

UNDERSTANDING AUTOMATION

As you have learned, when the Chapter 13 client uses the *prjServer* project's functions and procedures to maintain information, the client uses automation. ActiveX automation lets one project or object control another program or object. Microsoft used to call ActiveX automation "OLE Automation." In Chapter 6, you learned that ActiveX is a descendant of Object Linking and Embedding (OLE). You also learned that Microsoft designed OLE to let one program automatically run another program and use that program to access data (for example, an *Excel®* spreadsheet within a *Word®* document). Microsoft referred to the automatic execution of the embedded program as *automation*. Automation has since expanded to refer to any program that provides automated services to a client program—whether on the same computer or another computer on a network.

Automation will let any client that knows the *prjServer* project's "exposed" methods control the *prjServer* project's activities. An *exposed* method is a function or procedure that you define as public, which generally performs a specific task or series of tasks in the server and generally returns a result (which may be a number, a string, a recordset, and so on) on its completion. You will design the ActiveX EXE project with variables, procedures, and functions. After you design the ActiveX EXE project, another program can set and read its variables and invoke its procedures and functions.

Automation lets you access another program or object either *in-process* or *out-of-process*. You designed two ActiveX controls in Chapter 6 and will design an ActiveX Dynamic-Link Library (DLL) in Chapter 21, "Using Windows Sockets for Two-Way Internet Communications." When you use an ActiveX control or DLL in a project, the ActiveX object runs in-process. An in-process control or object will run within the project's address space—which means that the ActiveX control must be on the program's computer, and that only the program that loads the control or object can access its properties, methods, and events. You can also use controls on the Web with VBScript. However, even though some Web sites on the Internet contain ActiveX controls, you must download each control before you can use it—meaning that the control effectively runs within *Internet Explorer's* program space, rather than within its own space. When you use either ActiveX controls or ActiveX DLLs, your program must access the object as an in-process object, as shown in Figure 12.5.

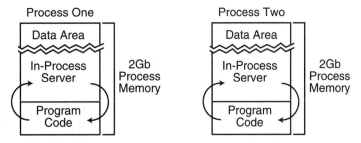

Figure 12.5 An in-process server or other component runs in the same address space.

Maintaining Server Compatibility

When you work with ActiveX and COM components, the operating system, together with the Visual Basic compiler, assigns each component a Globally Unique Identifier (GUID). When you add a reference to a component to another project, Visual Basic keys that reference off the GUID. If you later change the GUID, the project that accessed and used the original component may not be able to access the new component. You can protect against accidental changes to the GUID of your components. To do so, ensure that the project properties are set to Project Compatibility. To set the properties to Project Compatibility, perform the following steps:

1. Select the Project menu prjServer properties option. Visual Basic will display the Project Properties dialog box.

2. Select the Component tab within the dialog box. Visual Basic will change the display to the Components option.

3. At the dialog box's bottom, select the Project Compatibility option. Click your mouse on OK to save the changes.

It is important to note that, if you do not enforce Project Compatibility, it is possible to accidentally delete or change the parameters for interface functions of the class. You should work to ensure that your classes remain consistent after you register them, and that you later add only properties and methods to the class. Maintaining project compatibility helps protect against accidentally breaking component-use rules.

When you use an ActiveX EXE project, such as the *prjServer* project you will design in this chapter, the program runs *out-of-process* of the calling object or program. An out-of-process object or program will run within its own address space, with its own process, its own virtual memory, and its own threads. Because the ActiveX EXE runs in its own process, a copy of an ActiveX EXE program can be on your computer (the client), or on another computer (the host), and the process that requires access to the EXE can locate the server and execute it, regardless of its location. One of the most significant advantages of an ActiveX EXE program is that you can access it across a network and the program does not have to load onto your computer; rather, the program stays on the host computer.

As you have learned, when a separate project sets and reads an ActiveX EXE program's variables (the server), and invokes the server's procedures and functions, the second program is a client of the server. The client can tell the out-of-process server to do something (such as make an addition to the database) and then the client can go about its business (performing other user processing) while the server does the work. When you design the server properly, it can notify the client when a task is complete.

When you access an out-of-process object as a client, you use the technology of automation. Automation is the operating system mechanism that lets you access an ActiveX EXE program, whether on your local computer or on a distant computer. The server stays on the other computer and processes the tasks the clients request there, which leaves the client's computer processor free to do other tasks. The server sends the complete requested information back to the client, which results in fewer back-and-forth transmissions. While the network traffic may slow the client's access time, the ability of multiple clients to access the server simultaneously, and the freeing of the client computer to perform other tasks results in increased productivity. You will learn more about connecting to servers on remote systems in Chapter 22, "Writing DCOM Objects for Networks."

The ActiveX EXE can send you data or you can send it data. In effect, when you access an ActiveX EXE on another computer, you transmit a specific request to the other computer. While the other computer processes your request, you are free to perform other processing. When the other computer sends back the response, your computer can resume its processing with the information the other computer returned. Optimally, your ActiveX EXE should run on the fastest available computer on your network, because the server may ultimately process tens or even hundreds of requests in very close sequence. Figure 12.6 shows an out-of-process application.

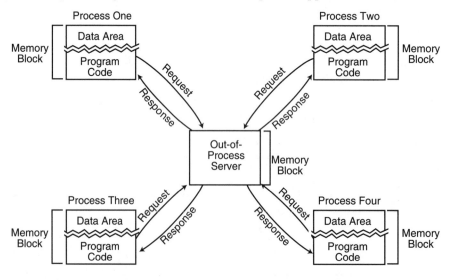

Figure 12.6 *An out-of-process server runs in its own application space.*

ADDING A DATA ACCESS OBJECTS (DAO) REFERENCE TO THE PROJECT

As you know, the *prjServer* project will use a Microsoft *Access* database to store information about a customer. Before you can use a Microsoft *Access* database within Visual Basic, you must add a *DAO Object Library* reference to the project. As you learned in Chapter 7, "Creating a Database Viewer and Designer," the *DAO Object Library* reference lets you open databases, recordsets, and workspaces from within your Visual Basic programs. In addition, the reference lets you add, edit, and delete records in a database table, among other tasks.

The *DAO Object Library* contains three objects that you will most often use to access a Microsoft *Access* database from within Visual Basic: *Workspace*, *Database*, and *Recordset* objects. After you add a *DAO Object Library* reference to the *prjServer* project, you can use all three objects to access the Microsoft *Access* database. Remember, to use each object within Visual Basic, you must declare one or more variables of each data access object type within your program's code. To add a *DAO Object Library* reference to the *prjServer* project, perform the following steps:

1. Within Visual Basic, select the Project menu References option. Visual Basic will open the References dialog box.

2. Within the References dialog box, select the *Microsoft DAO 3.5 Object Library* listing. Next, click your mouse on the box to the left of the listing. Visual Basic will place a check mark in the box.

3. Within the References dialog box, click your mouse on the OK button. Visual Basic will add a *DAO Object Library* reference to the *prjServer* project and close the References dialog box.

USING THE OBJECT BROWSER FOR THE DAO REFERENCE

As you have learned, the *DAO Object Library* contains the *Workspace*, *Database*, and *Recordset* objects. After you add a *DAO Object Library* reference to the *prjServer* project, you can view the variables, procedures, and functions that comprise each object's properties, methods, and events within the Visual Basic *Object Browser*. The Object Browser will show classes and class functions for each database object. Programmers generally refer to the objects as *classes*, and the class functions as *members*.

To view the members of the *Workspace*, *Database*, and *Recordset* objects (or classes), perform the following steps:

1. Within Visual Basic, select the View menu Object Browser option. Visual Basic will open the Object Browser window.

2. Within the Object Browser window, select the *Workspace* listing below the *Classes* heading. Visual Basic will list the members of the *Workspace* class within the area below the *Members of 'Workspace'* heading.

3. Within the Object Browser window, select the *Recordset* listing below the *Classes* heading. Visual Basic will list the members of the *Recordset* class within the area below the *Members of 'Recordset'* heading.

4. Within the Object Browser window, select the *Database* listing below the *Classes* heading. Visual Basic will list the members of the *Database* class within the area below the *Members of 'Database'* heading.

5. Within the Object Browser's *Members of 'Database'* heading, click your mouse on the *OpenRecordset* member. Visual Basic will display information about *OpenRecordset* at the bottom of the Object Browser window. Note that the *OpenRecordset* member is a member of *DAO Database*, as shown in Figure 12.7.

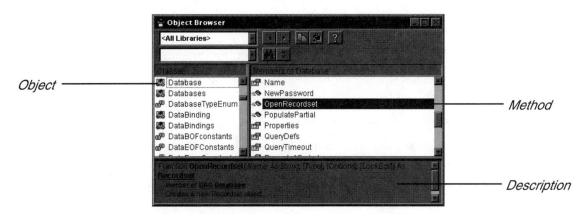

Figure 12.7 The Object Browser showing the **OpenRecordset** function of **Recordset**, a member of **DAO Database**.

MORE ON THE prjSERVER PROJECT'S DATABASE

As you have learned, the *prjServer* project is an ActiveX EXE project you will use to maintain a Microsoft *Access* database. You will design the database to include customer names, addresses, and phone numbers, and you will name it the *ClientServer* database. Within the *ClientServer* database, you will create three tables: *Customer*, *Address*, and *ID*.

The *Customer* table will store customer names. The *Address* table will store customer addresses and phone numbers. The *ID* table will store customer ID and customer address ID numbers. You will use the *ID* table to keep track of each customer name and address in the *Customer* and *Address* tables. To do this, you will assign a unique ID number to each customer and to each customer's address. After that, you can search for the unique number and retrieve the corresponding database record (which will include the customer information).

As your customer list grows, you can quickly find each customer name in the *Customer* table and each customer address and phone number in the *Address* table. When you add a new customer's name and address, Visual Basic will update the *ID* table and prepare a new unique ID number for that customer. As your project grows, you can add multiple tables and connect each one with a unique ID number.

In large databases, using a multiple table design similar to the *ClientServer* database is more efficient than using only one table, as you learned in Chapter 10, "Extending Databases to Multiple Tables." Although more advanced principles of database design are beyond the scope of this book, understanding the importance of using multiple tables to store related information is relatively easy if you visualize a database record as a set of related objects. Just as you have learned in earlier chapters how important it is to use component objects when you design programs and complex functions, you should use component objects (tables and records) to build database records. Using one table will result in disorganized information management (as well as significantly slowed access and an increased likelihood of data repetition). If you use multiple tables, you can better organize data, find it quickly, and maintain large amounts of data.

CREATING THE CLIENTSERVER DATABASE

As you know, you will design the *ClientServer* database and access it from the *prjServer* project. To design the database, you will use the Visual Basic Visual Data Manager. To create the *ClientServer* database, perform the following steps:

1. Within Visual Basic, select the Add-Ins menu Visual Data Manager option. Visual Basic will open the VisData window.

2. Within the VisData window, select the File menu New option, Microsoft Access submenu Version 7.0 MDB option. The Visual Data Manager will open the Select Microsoft Access Database To Create dialog box.

3. Within the *File name* field, type *ClientServer*, and click your mouse on the Save button. Visual Data Manager will save the *ClientServer* database and open the Database Window.

CREATING THE CUSTOMER TABLE

As you know, the *ClientServer* database will contain three tables. The *Customer* table will store customer first and last names. Within the *Customer* table, you will design three fields, *CustomerID*, *CustomerFirst*, and *CustomerLast*.

To design the *Customer* table, perform the following steps:

1. Within Visual Basic, select the Add-Ins menu Visual Data Manager option. Visual Basic will open the VisData window.

2. Select the File menu Open Database Microsoft Access option. Visual Basic will open the Open Microsoft Access Database dialog box.

3. Within the Open Microsoft Access Database dialog box, select the *ClientServer.mdb* database file. Click your mouse on the Open button. The Visual Data Manager will open the Database window.

4. Within the Database window, right-click your mouse on the *Properties* listing. The Visual Data Manager will open a submenu that lists the *ClientServer* database's properties.

5. Within the submenu, select the New Table option. Visual Data Manager will open the Table Structure window.

6. Within the *Table Name* field, type *Customer* and click your mouse on the Add Field button. Visual Data Manager will open the Add Field window.

7. Within the *Name* field, type *CustomerID*. Visual Data Manager will fill the *Name* field with *CustomerID*.

8. Within the *Type* field, click your mouse on the down arrow, select the *Long* type, and click your mouse on the OK button. Visual Data Manager will add the new field.

9. Within the *Name* field, type *CustomerFirst*. Visual Data Manager will fill the *Name* field with *CustomerFirst*.

10. Within the *Type* field, click your mouse on the down arrow, select the *Text* type, and click your mouse on the OK button. Visual Data Manager will add the new field.

11. Within the *Name* field, type *CustomerLast*. Visual Data Manager will fill the *Name* field with *CustomerLast*.

12. Within the *Type* field, click your mouse on the down arrow, select the *Text* type, and click your mouse on the OK button. Visual Data Manager will add the new field.

13. Within the Add Field window, click your mouse on the Close button. Visual Data Manager will close the Add Field window and display the Table Structure window.

14. Within the Table Structure window, click your mouse on the Build the Table button. Visual Data Manager will build the table and display the Database window.

15. Within the Database window, click your mouse on *Customer*. Visual Data Manager will list the Fields, Indexes, and Properties options.

16. Within the Database window, click your mouse on *Fields*. Visual Data Manager will display the *Customer* field listings, as shown in Figure 12.8.

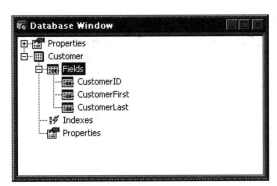

*Figure 12.8 The **Customer** table's fields.*

CREATING THE ADDRESS TABLE

As you know, the *ClientServer* database will contain three tables. The *Address* table will store customer addresses and phone numbers. Within the *Address* table, you will design seven fields: *CustomerID*, *Street*, *City*, *State*, *Zip*, *Phone*, and *Fax*.

To design the *Address* table, perform the following steps:

1. Within Visual Basic, select the Add-Ins menu Visual Data Manager option. Visual Basic will open the VisData window.

2. Select the File menu Open Database Microsoft Access option. Visual Data Manager will open the Open Microsoft Access Database dialog box.

3. Within the Open Microsoft Access Database dialog box, select the *ClientServer.mdb* database file. Click your mouse on the Open button. Visual Basic will open the Database Window.

4. Within the Database Window, right-click your mouse on the *Properties* listing. Visual Basic will open a submenu that lists the *ClientServer* database's properties.

5. Within the submenu, select the New Table option. Visual Data Manager will open the Table Structure window.

6. Within the Table Name field, type *Address* and click your mouse on the Add Field button. Visual Data Manager will open the Add Field window.

7. Within the *Name* field, type *CustomerID*. Visual Data Manager will fill the *Name* field with *CustomerID*.

8. Within the *Type* field, click your mouse on the down arrow, select the *Long* type, and click your mouse on the OK button. Visual Data Manager will clear the *Name* field.

9. Within the *Name* field, type *Street*. Visual Data Manager will fill the *Name* field with *Street*.

10. Within the *Type* field, click your mouse on the down arrow, select the *Text* type, and click your mouse on the OK button. Visual Data Manager will clear the *Name* field.

11. Within the *Name* field, type *City*. Visual Data Manager will fill the *Name* field with *City*.

12. Within the *Type* field, click your mouse on the down arrow, select the *Text* type, and click your mouse on the OK button. Visual Data Manager will clear the *Name* field.

13. Within the *Name* field, type *State*. Visual Data Manager will fill the *Name* field with *State*.

14. Within the *Type* field, click your mouse on the down arrow, select the *Text* type, and click your mouse on the OK button. Visual Data Manager will clear the *Name* field.

15. Within the *Name* field, type *Zip*. Visual Data Manager will fill the *Name* field with *Zip*.

16. Within the *Type* field, click your mouse on the down arrow, select the Text type, and click your mouse on the OK button. Visual Data Manager will clear the *Name* field.

17. Within the *Name* field, type *Phone*. Visual Data Manager will fill the *Name* field with *Phone*.

18. Within the *Type* field, click your mouse on the down arrow, select the *Text* type, and click your mouse on the OK button. Visual Data Manager will clear the *Name* field.

19. Within the *Name* field, type *Fax*. Visual Data Manager will fill the *Name* field with *Fax*.

20. Within the *Type* field, click your mouse on the down arrow, select the *Text* type, and click your mouse on the OK button. Visual Data Manager will clear the *Name* field.

21. Within the Add Field window, click your mouse on the Close button. Visual Data Manager will close the Add Field window and display the Table Structure window.

22. Within the Table Structure window, click your mouse on the Build the Table button. Visual Data Manager will build the *Address* table and display the Database Window.

23. Within the Database window, click your mouse on *Address*. Visual Basic will list the Fields, Indexes, and Properties options.

24. Within the Database window, click your mouse on *Fields*. Visual Basic will display the *Address* field listings, as shown in Figure 12.9.

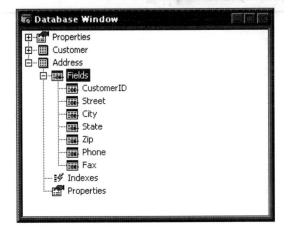

*Figure 12.9 The **Address** table's fields.*

CREATING THE ID TABLE

As you know, the *ClientServer* database will contain three tables. The *ID* table will store customer ID numbers. Within the *ID* table, you will design one field, *CustomerID*.

To design the *ID* table, perform the following steps:

1. Within Visual Basic, select the Add-Ins menu Visual Data Manager option. Visual Basic will open the VisData window.

2. Select the File menu Open Database Microsoft Access option. Visual Data Manager will open the Open Microsoft Access Database dialog box.

3. Within the Open Microsoft Access Database dialog box, select the *ClientServer.mdb* database file. Click your mouse on the Open button. Visual Data Manager will open the Database window.

4. Within the Database window, right-click your mouse on the *Properties* listing. Visual Data Manager will open a submenu listing the *ClientServer* database's properties.

5. Within the submenu, select the New Table option. Visual Data Manager will open the Table Structure window.

6. Within the *Table Name* field, type *ID* and click your mouse on the Add Field button. Visual Data Manager will open the Add Field window.

7. Within the *Name* field, type *CustomerID*. Visual Data Manager will fill the *Name* field with *CustomerID*.

8. Within the *Type* field, click your mouse on the down arrow, select the *Long* type, and click your mouse on the OK button. Visual Data Manager will clear the *Name* field.

9. Within the Add Field window, click your mouse on the Close button. Visual Data Manager will close the Add Field window and display the Table Structure window.

10. Within the Table Structure window, click your mouse on the Build the Table button. Visual Data Manager will build the *ID* table and display the Database window.

11. Within the Database window, click your mouse on *ID*. Visual Basic will list the Fields, Indexes, and Properties options.

12. Within the Database window, click your mouse on *Fields*. Visual Basic will display the *ID* field listings, as shown in Figure 12.10.

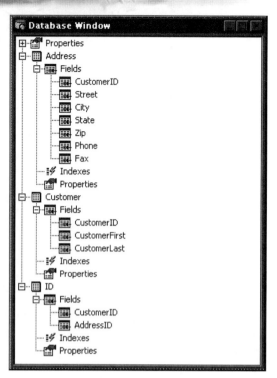

*Figure 12.10 The **Address, Customer**, and **ID** tables' fields.*

Because the Visual Data Manager is itself an out-of-process server, you can return to the Visual Basic development environment and leave the Visual Data Manager open—which is often useful when designing the relationships between a project and its database store. However, for now, because you will not require the Visual Data Manager through the remainder of this chapter, you can close the Visual Data Manager. To close the Visual Data Manager, select the File menu Exit option.

WRITING THE PROJECT CODE

In the *prjServer* project, you will write functions and procedures to open and maintain the *ClientServer* database. Unlike most programs in this book, the *prjServer* project has no controls and no forms. Therefore, you will not write code for any control properties, methods, or events. You will write code for private and public functions that open the *ClientServer* database, fill recordsets, retrieve customer ID numbers, check them, and send results to the Chapter 13 client program.

DECLARING VARIABLES

You will declare most variables that you use within the ActiveX EXE project in the General–Declarations section in the *clsServer* code window. Remember, when you declare variables in the General–Declarations section of the *clsServer* class module, all private or public functions and procedures in the module can use the variables. The following code implements the *prjServer* project variables in the *clsServer* code window's General–Declarations section:

```
Dim ServerWS As Workspace
Dim ServerDB As Database
Dim ServerRS As Recordset
Dim IDRS As Recordset
Private DBOpen As Boolean
```

To start, the program code declares the *ServerWS* variable, which will contain a *Workspace* object. Then, the code will declare the *ServerDB* variable, which will contain a *Database* object associated with the *ClientServer* database. Next, the code will declare the *ServerRS* variable, which will contain a *Recordset* object associated with the *Customer* and *Address* tables. Finally, the code will declare the *IDRS* variable, which will contain a *Recordset* object associated with the *ID* table.

WRITING THE INITIALIZE EVENT

As you have learned in previous chapters, every Visual Basic form has a *Load* event. The *Load* event will occur first when you run a project with a form. As you know, the *prjServer* project has no form, it only has the *clsServer* class module. A Visual Basic class module also has an *Initialize* event, which Visual Basic will automatically invoke first when the program initializes the class. When you run the *prjServer* project, the program will first invoke the *Initialize* event within the *clsServer* class. Any code within the *Initialize* event will occur before any other code in the entire project. Within a project that combines classes and other object types, the program will fire the *Class_Initialize* event for a given class the first time you declare a variable of that class within the program. The *prjServer* project's *Initialize* event will call the *OpenDatabase* function to open the *ClientServer* database. The following code implements the *Class_Initialize* event:

```
Private Sub Class_Initialize()
   OpenDatabase
End Sub
```

It is important to recognize that you can pass initializing values into the *Class_Initialize* event. For example, when you design your own database servers, you may want to make them multi-purpose programs, so you might actually pass the database name into the server when you initialize a server object. Then, you would call the database name from within the *Initialize* event in the *OpenDatabase* call, as shown in the following code:

```
Private Sub Class_Initialize(ByVal DatabaseName As String)
   OpenDatabase DatabaseName
End Sub
```

WRITING THE CODE FOR THE OPENDATABASE FUNCTION

Now that you have written the code for the *Initialize* event, you will write the first private function, *OpenDatabase*, which will open the *ClientServer* database. Before you write the *OpenDatabase* function, however, you must specify the location of the *ClientServer* database. By default, the program code presumes that the database is in the same directory as the executing server program. Because the *OpenDatabase* function is private, your program can access it from only within the *clsServer* class. The following code implements the *OpenDatabase* function:

```
Private Function OpenDatabase() As Boolean
  Dim DatabaseName As String

  DatabaseName = App.Path & "\ClientServer.mdb"
  Set ServerWS = Workspaces(0)
  On Error Resume Next
  Set ServerDB = ServerWS.OpenDatabase(DatabaseName)
  If Err.Number <> 0 Then
    OpenDatabase = False
  Else
    OpenDatabase = True
  End If
End Function
```

The *OpenDatabase* function simply sets a location for the database, creates a default workspace, and opens the database within the default workspace. Finally, the code will assign *True* to the *OpenDatabase* function to indicate to the program that the *ClientServer* database is open. You will use the *True* value in other functions to check whether the database is open or closed.

WRITING THE OPENRECORDSET FUNCTION

Now that you have written the *OpenDatabase* function that opens the *ClientServer* database, you can open a recordset, which you will comprise from records within a database. The *OpenRecordset* function will open a database table that you specify within the *TableName* parameter. In Chapter 13, you will learn how to use the *OpenRecordset* function to open recordsets. Because the *OpenRecordset* function is public, other programs can access it with a method call outside of the *prjServer* project. The following code implements the *OpenRecordset* function:

```
Public Function OpenRecordset(TableName As String) As Recordset
  Dim SQLstring As String

  SQLstring = "SELECT * FROM " & TableName
  If DBOpen Then
    Set ServerRS = ServerDB.OpenRecordset(SQLstring)
    If ServerRS.RecordCount = 0 Then
      Set OpenRecordset = ServerRS
      Exit Function
    Else
      If ServerRS.RecordCount > 0 Then
        ServerRS.MoveLast
        ServerRS.MoveFirst
      End If
      Set OpenRecordset = ServerRS
    End If
  Else
    MsgBox "Database closed.", vbCritical
    Exit Function
  End If
End Function
```

The *OpenRecordset* function declares a basic SQL string, checks to make sure the program has not closed the database, and then uses that string to open a recordset (provided the database is open—otherwise the function exits). (For more information on SQL statements, see Chapter 8.) After *OpenRecordset* opens the recordset, an *If-Then* statement will check the *ServerRS* object's *RecordCount* property. If *RecordCount* equals zero, the SQL query found no records, and Visual Basic will exit the *OpenRecordset* function. If *RecordCount* is greater than zero, the SQL query found one or more records and the *ServerRS* object's *MoveLast* method will move the *ServerRS* recordset to the last record, which will ensure the *ServerRS* object is full. Then, the *ServerRS* object's *MoveFirst* method will move the *ServerRS* to its first record and return the resulting recordset.

WRITING THE GETID FUNCTION

Now that you have written the *OpenRecordset* function that will open a table, you can get an ID number from a table. The *GetID* function will retrieve the latest ID number from the *ID* table. As you can see in the following code listing, the *GetID* function has one parameter, *FieldName*. When you call the *GetID* function from the client program, you will pass a field name into the function. In the *prjServer* project, the *ID* table has only one field, *CustomerID*. As your needs grow, you can expand the *ID* table to include product, inventory, and sales ID numbers. When you do so, you can pass the pertinent field to retrieve a recent ID number for your entire warehouse, for example. Because the *GetID* function is public, you can access it outside of the *prjServer* project. The following code implements the *GetID* function:

```
Public Function GetID(FieldName As String) As Integer
  Dim SQLstring As String

  SQLstring = "SELECT * FROM ID"
  Set IDRS = ServerDB.OpenRecordset(SQLstring)
  If IDRS.RecordCount = 0 Then
    GetID = 0
  Else
    IDRS.MoveLast
    IDRS.MoveFirst
    GetID = IDRS.Fields(FieldName)
  End If
End Function
```

Within the *GetID* function, the program code initializes an SQL query string, opens the recordset of possible ID values (which contains the next available ID), and returns either that value or zero in the event of an error. Because the *ID* table contains ID numbers, the return value is an integer.

WRITING THE CHECKID FUNCTION

Now that you have written the *GetID* function that will open the *ID* table and return an ID number, you can check an ID number. The *CheckID* function will compare the client's retrieved ID number to the *ID* table's current ID number. Because many users can simultaneously access the *ClientServer* database within the *prjServer* project, the *CheckID* function must compare ID numbers.

When many users access the *ClientServer,* the threat of ID number corruption (the result of *client data corruption,* which may occur because the client shuts the program down early, because of a bad network connection, and so on. When clients use the *GetID* function to retrieve an ID number, they will usually add a new customer name and address. When they finish, they will add the new customer to the *ClientServer* database. At this point, the *clsServer* class will increment the *ID* table with a new ID number. If the first client delays his or her transmission for any reason, it is possible that a second client could use the *GetID* function, enter a new customer, and add the new customer data to the *ClientServer* database, thereby forcing Visual Basic to increment the *ID* table with a new ID number. In such a case, the *CheckID* function is necessary to show the first client his ID number is invalid.

413

As you can see in the following code listing, the *CheckID* function has two parameters, *tempID* and *FieldName.* When you call the *CheckID* function from the client program, you will pass the initial ID number and the field name (in this case, *CustomerID*). The client project will call the *GetID* function and the *CheckID* function within a few lines of code from each other. With single-client use, the *CheckID* function is not necessary. However, it is necessary with multiple users. Because the *CheckID* function is public, you can access it from outside the *prjServer* project. The following code implements the *CheckID* function:

```
Public Function CheckID(tempID As Integer, FieldName As String) As Boolean
  IDRS.Requery
  If tempID = IDRS.Fields(FieldName) Then
    CheckID = True
  Else
    CheckID = False
  End If
End Function
```

The program code in the function uses the *IDRS* object's *Requery* method to refresh the *IDRS* recordset. Remember, the *Requery* method will use the original SQL statement. Next, the program code compares the *tempID* parameter to the *IDRS* object's *FieldName* field. The *tempID* parameter contains the initial ID number, before you add a new customer to the *ClientServer* database. If the *IDRS* object's *FieldName* equals the *tempID* function, the code will assign *True* to the *CheckID* function; otherwise, the code will assign *False* to the *CheckID* function's return value.

WRITING THE INCREMENTID FUNCTION

Now that you have written the *CheckID* function, which will check an initial ID value to the *ID* table's ID number, you can increment a customer ID number in the *ID* table. The *IncrementID* function will increase the ID number field by one. You can change the increment value as you want. For example, you may want to increment the ID number by 10, so that in the future you can add extra records related to the main one, and therefore ensure close numeric values for a customer. Because the *IncrementID* function is public, other programs can access it with a method call outside of the *prjServer* project. The following code implements the *IncrementID* function:

```
Public Function IncrementID(FieldName As String) As Integer
  Dim NewID As Integer

  NewID = IDRS.Fields(FieldName) + 1
  IDRS.Edit
    IDRS.Fields(FieldName) = NewID
  IDRS.Update
  IDRS.Requery
  IncrementID = NewID
End Function
```

The program code within the *IncrementID* function first declares the *NewID* variable, which will store a new ID number, which the program computes as the *IDRS* object's *FieldName* field's value plus one. The program code then uses the *IDRS* object's *Edit* method to open the *IDRS* recordset's edit mode and change the *FieldName* field's valuetothe *NewID* value. The function then saves the new ID and requeries the recordset.

WRITING THE CLOSEDATABASE FUNCTION

Now that you have written the *IncrementID* function, which will increase the ID number, you have written all the code that processes the client database. It is, if anything, even more important to clean up after yourself when you work with client–server connections, so you must write code to close the *ClientServer* database. The *CloseDatabase* function will close the *ClientServer* database. Because the *CloseDatabase* function is private, other programs cannot access it outside of the *prjServer* project. In fact, the only procedure that calls the function is the *Class_Terminate* procedure, which you will write in the next section. The following code implements the *CloseDatabase* function:

```
Private Function CloseDatabase() As Boolean
   ServerDB.Close
   CloseDatabase = True
End Function
```

WRITING THE TERMINATE EVENT

As you have learned, an ActiveX EXE class module has an *Initialize* event, similar to a Visual Basic form's *Load* event. Similarly, the ActiveX EXE class module has a *Terminate* event. When you exit the *prjServer* project from the client side and destroy all references to the *prjServer* project, the *clsServer* class will invoke the *Terminate* event. The *prjServer* program will execute any program code in the *Terminate* event last, just before it closes the ActiveX EXE class module. In the *prjServer* project, the *Terminate* event will do one thing—close the *ClientServer* database. The following code implements the *Class_Terminate* event:

```
Private Sub Class_Terminate()
   CloseDatabase
End Sub
```

ENHANCEMENTS YOU CAN MAKE TO THE prjSERVER PROJECT

Now that you have a better understanding of an ActiveX EXE class module, you can make enhancements to the *prjServer* project. You can expand the *ClientServer* database to model more than a customer's name, address, and phone numbers. You can also add tables that model product inventory, warehouse inventory, sales inventory, and customer sales information. In addition, you can expand the *ID* table to include multiple ID number fields, such as inventory ID numbers and sales ID numbers. You can also expand the *prjServer* project by writing more error-trapping code within the *clsServer* class module. For example, you can write code that will check whether another client has added, edited, or deleted a customer record during an interim period. After that, you can write code to display reports on all customers, products, inventory, and sales.

The *prjServer* project also has significant limitations on how it can return data. You can expand the server so that it returns more information to the client about existing table and query definition objects within the database. The client program can then use this information to make its access to the server program more useful to the user at the client's location. As previous sections of this chapter discuss, you can change the ActiveX EXE so that it can access many different databases; and you can change it so that you can vary the recordsets within a given database that you access. Without significant modifications, you can enable the server program to requery recordsets in mid-process and return more complete data about its activities.

Finally, as you will learn in Chapter 22, you could modify the ActiveX EXE so that it supports multiple asynchronous requests. Most client–server applications use asynchronous technology to make the servers more *scalable*, a term that refers to how well a server can handle small client numbers and large numbers of clients. As written, the *prjServer* project is not scalable—a limitation that you must address should you want to use the server as the backbone of a larger server project.

PUTTING IT ALL TOGETHER

This chapter's project, *prjServer*, introduced you to an ActiveX EXE class module, and you have written public and private functions. An ActiveX EXE class module lets you write public functions and procedures that a client program can access from outside the original project. It is important to understand that ActiveX EXEs are not only excellent programs for you to use when you create client–server database management programs, but they are also useful for performing any type of automated task that your programs may require, but which are not completely necessary for the program's execution. Using such automated servers not only lets you keep your programs smaller and easier for you to update, but it also lets the user access a more scalable piece of software, which they may be able to use over a network, if you create the ActiveX EXE program using the principles of the Distributed Component Object Model (DCOM), Microsoft's model for the creation of object components for use over networks of any size.

In Chapter 13, you will write the client side of the *prjServer* project. The client side will use a standard form to contain controls that let you display, add, edit, and delete records from the *ClientServer* database. Before you continue with Chapter 13, however, make sure you understand the following key concepts:

415

- ✓ An ActiveX EXE project, like an ActiveX control, is a special type of Visual Basic project.

- ✓ An in-process server is one that runs in the same process space as the calling program, while an out-of-process server is one that runs in its own process space.

- ✓ Only the calling process can access an in-process server, while many calling programs can simultaneously access an out-of-process server.

- ✓ To create out-of-process servers, you must use the Visual Basic ActiveX EXE project option.

- ✓ Using Visual Basic, you can create a stand-alone server that provides information across a network with an ActiveX EXE project.

- ✓ You can use a single ActiveX EXE program as a server for each database, or you can construct the ActiveX EXE program so that each instance can access a different database.

- ✓ When you create ActiveX EXE server programs, you can let multiple users access a single database or other service, and force them to access the database or other service only in certain ways.

- ✓ Just as with class modules in general, ActiveX EXEs let you use private functions or procedures to protect data within any ActiveX EXE from outside corruption.

- ✓ When you create an ActiveX EXE project within Visual Basic, you will create one or more class modules with private and public sections and one or more code modules. However, you will not use any forms because ActiveX EXEs have no visual component.

- ✓ When you create a client program to access your server, you should design the client's visual interface to best present the information the server program returns.

- ✓ When you create a server program, you can expose properties, methods, and events that the client program will then use to access the information the server program maintains and to respond to errors, changes, or other important database events.

Chapter 13

Creating a Network-Aware Client

As you learned in Chapter 12, "Using ActiveX Automation to Create a Database Server," Visual Basic lets you design programs that can communicate with each other across a network or other connection. With the power of ActiveX automation, you can now design a form with controls in Visual Basic that sends and receives data from a separate program across a network, and lets the other computer do all the processing. The other computer, the *server*, will manage the data and process any requests you make. Using the remote computer to process your requests will free your computer's processing time for other tasks. As you know, a network consists of two or more computers connected by a phone line, coaxial cables, or fiber optic line. The software that lets two or more computers communicate with each other is called *network-aware* software. Software that is network-aware can communicate from your computer with another computer across a network. After you design this chapter's project, the *prjClient* network-aware program will communicate with the *prjServer* program you designed previously, either locally or across a network.

Using a remote computer to store information will also provide a central location for large amounts of data and let multiple users access data from that single source. Although letting multiple users access a single data store will present additional risk to the original data's validity, you can protect all the data in the data store from damage if you design the remote server properly. You can visualize a server as an individual who stands between users and the data and checks each user's request to make sure that it is not damaging to the database. The server takes the user's request, checks it, and sends it on to the database. The server then receives the data back from the database, checks it, and then sends it back to the user. If you set up the server properly, users can access any data they may need from afar, without ever having access to the actual database or its structures.

This chapter teaches you how to use a Standard EXE project, *prjClient*, to reference and access the ActiveX EXE *prjServer* project in Chapter 12. As you learned in Chapter 12, the *prjServer* project will run out-of-process (though it may be on the same computer as the *prjClient* program or on another computer). In this chapter, you will design a project with a form and controls to display the *ClientServer* database information from the *prjServer* project at the client's location. To perform the client actions, *prjClient* will reference Chapter 12's *prjServer* project and use its public functions to operate the *ClientServer* database across a network. The *prjClient* program will perform the actual processing locally on your computer. As you learned in Chapter 5, "Creating and Using Fractals," a structure lets you group related information within a single reference location (a variable of the structure's type). Because this chapter's project is separate from Chapter 12's *prjServer* project, and any changes made to the *prjServer* project transmit across a network, the *prjClient* program uses an array of *stcCUSTOMER* structures to maintain the information locally and updates that information only during or after a request to the server. Maintaining the data locally will save the client processing time (because it does not have to get out and request new data every time the user performs even the simplest action).

This chapter examines in detail how to add an ActiveX EXE project reference and use its public functions to maintain and manage a Microsoft *Access* database. By the time you finish this chapter, you will understand the following key concepts:

♦ Using Visual Basic, you can write programs that include *References* to other programs outside the current project, a technique you will use to add a reference within the *prjClient* project to the ActiveX EXE *prjServer* project you designed in Chapter 12.

♦ Within Visual Basic, you can use a reference (which you add from within the References dialog box) to a server project (such as the ActiveX EXE *prjServer* project) to gain access to the server project's methods and manage the *ClientServer* database across a network.

♦ Your programs can use the Data Access Objects (DAO) Object Library and the Jet Database Engine to use a single set of information to create multiple sets of records with different inclusion criteria.

◆ With Windows 95 or Windows NT, you can use ActiveX automation (technology that lets a program access and manipulate another program) to combine a powerful, local front end (user interface) with a powerful, remote back end (server program).

◆ Within your Visual Basic programs, you can use the properties, methods, and events of an ActiveX EXE's class module as if it were a class module within the client project.

◆ Your Visual Basic programs can perform error checking at the client level, the server level, or both, and should generally perform specific error checking in both locations. For example, your respective components should check data both before the client transmits the data and after the server receives the data.

◆ The *prjClient* program cannot access the data the ActiveX EXE *prjServer* project manages, except through the server's interface functions—which protects against data corruption, intentional or unintentional.

USING THE PRJCLIENT PROJECT

Before you design the *prjClient* project, you may find it helpful to run the program. The companion CD-ROM that accompanies this book contains the *prjClient.exe* program within the *Chapter13* directory. As with every other program on the CD-ROM, you should run the Jamsa Press *setup.exe* program to install the *prjClient.exe* program to your computer's hard drive before you run it. After you install the *prjClient.exe* program to your computer's hard drive, you can run it from the Start menu. To run the program, select the Windows Start menu Run option. Windows will display the Run dialog box. Within the Run dialog box, enter *x:\vbpl\Chapter13\prjClient.exe*, where *x* corresponds to the drive letter of the hard drive on which you installed the *prjClient.exe* program, and click your mouse on OK. Windows will run the *prjClient.exe* program. Figure 13.1 shows the *prjClient* project with the *Client* form listing one customer's name, address, and phone numbers.

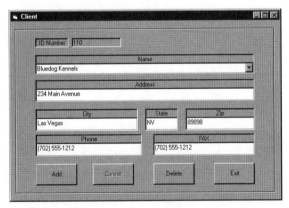

Figure 13.1 The prjClient project's Client form displaying customer information.

UNDERSTANDING WHY YOU SHOULD RUN SETUP.EXE BEFORE YOU RUN PRJCLIENT

As you have learned, the *prjClient.exe* program uses a *reference* to the *prjServer.exe* program that you designed in Chapter 12, "Using ActiveX Automation to Create a Database Server." Although you could run the *prjClient.exe* program from the CD-ROM, Windows will be unable to create the reference to the *prjServer.exe* program if you have not previously installed it onto your hard drive—a process that the *setup.exe* program performs for you. Additionally, because the *prjServer.exe* program uses a database, you must install the program and enable the read-write properties for the database so that the *prjClient* project can update the information within the database.

To learn more about the Jamsa Press *setup.exe* program, see the "What's on the *Visual Basic Programmer's Library* Companion CD-ROM" section at the back of this book.

417

Before you use the *prjClient.exe* program, take a moment to familiarize yourself with the controls on the form. When you run *prjClient.exe*, the first step the program will perform is to access Chapter 12's *clsServer* class module within the *prjServer* project. Then, the *prjClient* program will send table names to the *clsServer* class to open the *ClientServer* database and associated tables, *Customer*, *Address*, and *ID*. After the *prjClient* project has customer names, addresses, and phone numbers from the *ClientServer* database, it will display them in the *Client* form. At the top of the *Client* form, you can see the *ID Number* field. Each customer you view has a unique ID number. Below the *ID Number* field, you will see a drop-down *Name* field. When you click your mouse on this field, Visual Basic will display a scrollable box listing all customer names in the *ClientServer* database. Below the *Name* field, you will see six more fields, which display the customers' addresses and phone numbers.

Below the customer fields, you will see four buttons, *Add*, *Commit*, *Delete*, and *Exit*. When you click your mouse on these buttons, you can add, edit, or delete records from the *ClientServer* database, or you can exit the program, respectively. Now that you have seen the *prjClient.exe* program's layout, you can use the program to add, edit, and delete customer records from the *ClientServer* database. Remember, the *clsServer* class module within the *prjServer* ActiveX program (the automation server) maintains the *ClientServer* database. To add a record to the *ClientServer* database, perform the following steps:

418

1. Within the *Client* form, click your mouse on the *Name* field. The program will highlight the field.

2. Within the *Name* field, type in a new customer name, such as *Jamsa Press*. (Disregard any pre-existing *Name* field entry.) The program will enable the Commit button at the bottom of the form.

3. Click your mouse on the *Address* field below the *Name* field, and type in an address for the new customer, such as *2975 South Rainbow*.

4. Click your mouse on the *City* field below the *Address* field, and type in a city for the new customer, such as *Las Vegas*. Next, click your mouse on the *State* field, and type in a state for the new customer, such as *NV*. Finally, click your mouse on the *Zip* field, and type in a Zip code, such as *89102*.

5. Click your mouse on the *Phone* field below the *City* field, and type in a phone number for the new customer, such as *800-555-1212*. Next, click your mouse on the *FAX* field, and type in a fax number for the new customer, *800-555-1212*.

6. Click your mouse on the Add button. The program will add the new customer to the *ClientServer* database and display it in the *Client* form, as shown in Figure 13.2.

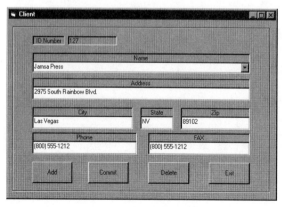

Figure 13.2 *The **Client** form displaying the newly added customer.*

Now that you have added a new customer to the *ClientServer* database, you can edit a customer record. To edit a customer record, perform the following steps:

1. Within the *Client* form, select the *Jamsa Press* listing from the *Name* field. The program will fill the *Name* field with *Jamsa Press*.

2. Click your mouse on the *Name* field, and re-enter the listing as *Jamsa Press Corporation*. The program will highlight the Edit button.

3. Click your mouse on the Edit button. The program will update the listing and display it in the *Name* field of the *Client* form, as shown in Figure 13.3.

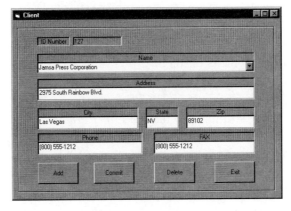

*Figure 13.3 The **Client** form displaying the newly edited customer record.*

Now that you have edited a customer record in the *ClientServer* database, you can delete a customer record. To delete a customer record from the *ClientServer* database, perform the following steps:

1. Within the *Client* form, select the "Jamsa Press Corporation" listing from the *Name* field. The program will fill the *Name* field with "Jamsa Press Corporation."

2. Click your mouse on the Delete button at the bottom of the *Client* form. The program will display a message box asking you to confirm the deletion of a record.

3. Within the message box, click your mouse on the Yes button. The *prjClient* program (together with the *prjServer* program) will delete the customer record from the *ClientServer* database and re-display the new customer listings in the *Client* form.

CREATING A BLANK FORM

Now that you have a better idea how to use the finished *prjClient* project, you can begin to design it. To do so, you will first design an empty form, which will contain all the controls the "Using the *prjClient* Project" section introduced. After you design and implement the form, you will learn more about adding the *clsServer* class module in Chapter 12 to the *prjClient* project. To begin the *prjClient* project and design an empty form, perform the following steps:

1. Within Visual Basic, select the File menu New Project option. Visual Basic will open the New Project dialog box.

2. Within the New Project dialog box, click your mouse on the Standard EXE icon. Next, click your mouse on the OK button. Visual Basic will open the *Form1* form window.

3. Select the View menu Properties Window option. Visual Basic will open the Properties Window listing the *Form1* properties.

4. Within the Properties Window, change the *Form1* properties to the values Table 13.1 lists.

Object	Property	Set As
Form1	*Caption*	*Client*
Form1	*Height*	5505
Form1	*Width*	8085
Form1	*Name*	*frmClient*

*Table 13.1 The newly named **frmClient** form's properties.*

5. Select the File menu Save Project As option. Visual Basic will open the Save File As dialog box, and list *frmClient* in the *File name* field.

6. Within the Save File As dialog box, click your mouse on the Save button. Visual Basic will save the *frmClient* form. After it saves the *frmClient* form, Visual Basic will re-display the Save File As dialog box with the new caption *SaveProject As,* and will fill the *File name* field with *Project1.*

7. Within the *File name* field, replace the *Project1* project name with the new *prjClient* project name. Next, click your mouse on the Save button. Visual Basic will save the *prjClient* project and close the Save File As dialog box.

ADDING A CLSSERVER REFERENCE TO THE PROJECT

In Chapter 12, you designed the *prjServer* project to maintain the *ClientServer* database, and you wrote private and public functions to open, close, and use the *ClientServer* database. In this chapter, you will use the *prjServer* project within the *prjClient* project. Remember, the *prjServer* project is an ActiveX EXE project type your programs can access over a network. In this chapter, you will only access the *prjServer* project locally on your machine, but in Chapter 22, "Writing DCOM Objects for Networks," you will learn how to access automation servers on remote machines.

The *ClientServer* database has three tables, *Customer, Address,* and *ID.* The three tables contain customer names, addresses, phone numbers, and ID numbers. After you add a reference to the *prjServer* project, you can use its public functions within the *prjClient* project, which means you can open the *ClientServer* database and view, add, edit, or delete its records from within the *prjClient* program. To add the *prjServer* project as a reference to the *prjClient* project, perform the following steps:

1. Within Visual Basic, select the Project menu References option. Visual Basic will open the References dialog box.

2. Within the References dialog box, select *prjServer* from the *Available References* field. Next, click your mouse on the box to the left of the selection. Visual Basic will draw a check mark in the box, as shown in Figure 13.4.

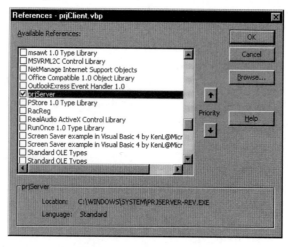

Figure 13.4 The References dialog box with the **prjServer** project selected.

3. Within the References dialog box, click your mouse on the OK button. Visual Basic will add the *prjServer* project reference to the *prjClient* project.

THE PRJSERVER PROJECT'S PUBLIC FUNCTIONS

Now that you have added the *prjServer* project to the *prjClient* project, you can use the *prjServer* project's public functions. In Chapter 12 you designed the *prjServer* project with private functions and four public functions, *OpenRecordset, GetID, CheckID,* and *IncrementID.* Each public function accesses one or more private functions within the *prjServer* project. Because your programs use the public functions to interface with the private functions, public functions are often known as *interface functions.*

The *clsServer* class module's public functions are now visible to the *prjClient* project. To better understand each public function, and to refresh your memory of Chapter 12, you can view each public function within the Visual Basic Object Browser. The Object Browser lists classes and class functions (*members*). To view the four public functions of the *prjServer* project within the Object Browser, perform the following steps:

1. Select the View menu Object Browser option. Visual Basic will open the Object Browser window and display the *Classes* and *Members of Class* headings.

2. Below the Object Browser *Classes* heading, click your mouse on *clsServer*. Visual Basic will list the members of *clsServer* below the *Members of clsServer* heading.

3. Below the *Members of clsServer* heading, click your mouse on the *OpenRecordset* member. Visual Basic will display the member at the bottom of the Object Browser, as shown in Figure 13.5.

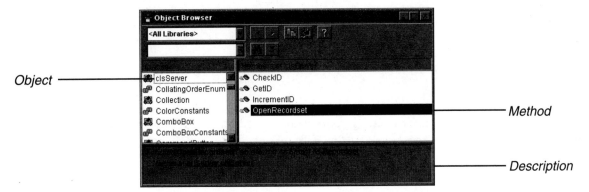

Figure 13.5 *The Object Browser showing the* **clsServer** *object reference's* **OpenRecordset** *member.*

ADDING A DATABASE REFERENCE TO THE PROJECT

As you have learned, you will use the *ClientServer* database of Chapter 12 within the *prjClient* project. The *ClientServer* database has three tables, *Customer*, *Address*, and *ID*. These three tables contain customer names, addresses, phone numbers, and ID numbers. Within the *prjClient* project, you will retrieve records from the *ClientServer* database. Although the *clsServer* class module of Chapter 12 will do most of the database work, you must still manipulate database objects within the *prjClient* project.

When you retrieve data from the *ClientServer* database, you will store it in a *Recordset* object. As you know, before you can store records in a *Recordset* object, you must have a *Workspace* and a *Database* object in your project. To use the *Workspace*, *Database*, and *Recordset* objects within Visual Basic, you must make a reference to them. The *Data Access Objects (DAO) Object Library* contains each object. You must add a *DAO Object Library* reference to the *prjClient* project before you can use the *ClientServer* database. After you add the reference to the *prjClient* project, you will declare and assign variables of each *Database* object. To add a *DAO Object Library* reference to the *prjClient* project, perform the following steps:

1. Within Visual Basic, select the Project menu References option. Visual Basic will open the References dialog box.

2. Within the References dialog box, select the *Microsoft DAO 3.5 Object Library* listing from the *Available References* field. Next, click your mouse on the box to the left of the selection. Visual Basic will draw a check mark in the box.

3. Within the References dialog box, click your mouse on the OK button. Visual Basic will add the *DAO Object Library* reference to the *prjClient* project.

THE DAO OBJECT LIBRARY'S MEMBERS

Now that you have added a *DAO Object Library* reference to the *prjClient* project, you can use the three database objects. The three objects, *Workspace*, *Database*, and *Recordset*, let you use a Microsoft *Access* database within Visual

Basic. You will use the *Recordset* object within the *prjClient* project to view the *ClientServer* database and to add, edit, or delete records.

To better understand each database object and to refresh your memory of Chapter 7, "Creating a Database Viewer and Designer," you can view each object's members within the Visual Basic Object Browser. As you have learned, the Object Browser lists classes and class functions (members). Visual Basic also calls each database object a class. In addition, Visual Basic calls each object's methods as class functions or members. To view the members for the *Database, Recordset,* and *Workspace* objects within the Object Browser, perform the following steps:

1. Select the View menu Object Browser option. Visual Basic will open the Object Browser window and display the *Classes* and *Members of Class* headings.

2. Below the Object Browser *Classes* heading, click your mouse on *Recordset*. Visual Basic will list the members of *Recordset* below the *Members of Recordset* heading.

3. Below the *Members of Recordset* heading, click your mouse on the *MoveLast* member. Visual Basic will display the member at the bottom of the Object Browser.

THE CLIENTSERVER DATABASE

As you know, the *ClientServer* database you designed in Chapter 12 has three tables. These three tables, *Customer, Address,* and *ID,* contain customer names, addresses, phone numbers, and ID numbers. Remember, the *Customer* and *Address* tables have a *CustomerID* field, which will store a customer's unique ID number. The *ID* table has a *CustomerID* field, which will store the latest ID number available when you add a new customer. To refresh your memory of the three tables in the *ClientServer* database, Table 13.2 lists each table's fields.

Table Name	Field
Customer	*CustomerID*
Customer	*CustomerFirst*
Customer	*CustomerLast*
Address	*CustomerID*
Address	*Street*
Address	*City*
Address	*State*
Address	*Zip*
Address	*Phone*
Address	*Fax*
ID	*CustomerID*

*Table 13.2 The **Customer, Address** and **ID** table fields.*

ADDING A MODULE TO THE PROJECT

As you have learned, the *Customer* and *Address* tables will store customer names, addresses, phone numbers, and ID numbers. Because the *prjClient* project will access the *ClientServer* database from the *prjServer* project, you will add a module to store all the customer information locally within the *prjClient* project (because the *prjServer* project maintains the actual database information separately from the *prjClient* project).

In the *prjClient* project, after you access customer information over a network from the *prjServer* project, you will add the information to a structure within a module. For more information on structures, see Chapter 5. The *prjClient* project's structure will store customer names, addresses, phone numbers, and ID numbers. When you want to search for a specific customer, you will do so from within the structure. When you want to add or edit a customer, you will transmit the data within the structure to the *prjServer* automation server, which will make the actual changes within the *ClientServer* database.

To add a module to the *prjClient* project, perform the following steps:

1. Select the Project menu Add Module option. Visual Basic will open the Add Module dialog box.

2. Within the Add Module dialog box, select the Module option. Next, click your mouse on the Open button. Visual Basic will add the module, *Module1*, to the *prjClient* project, and open the *Module1* Code window.

3. Select the View menu Properties Window option. Visual Basic will open the Properties Window listing the *Module1* properties.

4. Within the Properties Window, click your mouse on the *Name* property. Next, replace the *Module1* name with *mdlClient* and press ENTER. Visual Basic will rename the module.

5. Select the File menu Save Module As option. Visual Basic will open the Save File As dialog box, listing *mdlClient* in the *File name* field.

6. Within the Save File As dialog box, click your mouse on the Save button. Visual Basic will save the *mdlClient* module and close the Save File As dialog box.

7. Select the View menu Project Explorer option. Visual Basic will display the Project Explorer window, as shown in Figure 13.6.

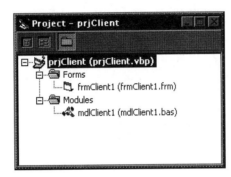

*Figure 13.6 The Project Explorer window showing the **prjClient** project's **frmClient** and **mdlClient** listings.*

ADDING CONTROLS TO THE FRMCLIENT FORM

Now that you have added a *DAO Object Library* reference and the *mdlClient* module to the *prjClient* project, you will add controls to the *frmClient* form. After you add the controls introduced in the "Using the *prjClient* Project" section to the *frmClient* form, you will write code that links the controls to the *prjClient* project. When you write code, you will first add a *ComboBox* control to list customer names. Then, you will add *TextBox* controls to list customer addresses and phone numbers. After that, you will add *Label* controls to display pertinent headings for a customer. Finally, you will add *CommandButton* controls that will let you add, edit, or delete records from the *ClientServer* database.

ADDING A COMBOBOX CONTROL TO THE FRMCLIENT FORM

As you have learned, the *prjClient* project will display customer information from the *ClientServer* database. You will add a *ComboBox* control to the *frmClient* form so that the *prjClient* project can display customer first and last names. To add a *ComboBox* control to the *frmClient* form, perform the following steps:

1. If Visual Basic is not displaying the *frmClient* form, double-click your mouse on the *frmClient* form listing within Project Explorer. Visual Basic will open the *frmClient* form.

2. Within Visual Basic, select the View menu Toolbox option. Visual Basic will open the Toolbox.

3. Within the Toolbox, double-click your mouse on the ComboBox icon. Visual Basic will draw a *ComboBox* control, *Combo1*, within the *frmClient* form.

4. Within the *frmClient* form, click your mouse on the *Combo1* control to highlight it. Visual Basic will draw a small frame around the control.

5. Select the View menu Properties Window option. Visual Basic will open the Properties Window listing the *Combo1* properties.

6. Within the Properties Window, change the *Combo1* properties to the values Table 13.3 lists.

Object	Property	Set As
Combo1	*Height*	315
Combo1	*Left*	600
Combo1	*Top*	1080
Combo1	*Width*	6495
Combo1	*Text*	[blank]
Combo1	*Name*	*cmbCustomer*

*Table 13.3 The newly named **cmbCustomer** control's properties.*

After you finish changing the *cmbCustomer* control's properties, you can add the other controls to the *frmClient* form.

ADDING TEXTBOX CONTROLS TO THE FRMCLIENT FORM

Now that you have a *ComboBox* control, *cmbCustomer*, to display customer names, you will add *TextBox* controls to the *frmClient* form. The *TextBox* controls will display customer addresses and phone numbers. To add *TextBox* controls to the *frmClient* form, perform the following steps:

1. If you have closed the *frmClient* form, double-click your mouse within the Project Explorer on the *frmClient* form listing to reopen the form. Visual Basic will open the *frmClient* form.

2. Select the View menu Toolbox option. Visual Basic will open the Toolbox.

3. Within the Toolbox, double-click your mouse on the TextBox icon. Visual Basic will draw a *TextBox* control, *Text1*, within the *frmClient* form.

4. Repeat Step 3 five more times. Visual Basic will draw five more *TextBox* controls within the *frmClient* form.

5. Within the *frmClient* form window, click your mouse on a *TextBox* control to highlight it. Visual Basic will draw a small frame around the control.

6. Select the View menu Properties Window option. Visual Basic will open the Properties Window listing the highlighted *TextBox* control's properties.

7. Within the Properties Window, change the highlighted *TextBox* control's properties to the values Table 13.4 lists.

8. Repeat Steps 5, 6, and 7 until you have changed each *TextBox* control's properties to the values Table 13.4 lists.

Object	Property	Set As
Text1	*Height*	375
Text1	*Left*	600
Text1	*Top*	1800
Text1	*Width*	6495
Text1	*Name*	*txtStreet*
Text2	*Height*	375

*Table 13.4 The **TextBox** controls' properties. (continued on following page)*

Object	Property	Set As
Text2	Left	600
Text2	Top	2640
Text2	Width	3015
Text2	Name	txtCity
Text3	Height	375
Text3	Left	3840
Text3	Top	2640
Text3	Width	975
Text3	Name	txtState
Text4	Height	375
Text4	Left	5040
Text4	Top	2640
Text4	Width	2055
Text4	Name	txtZip
Text5	Height	375
Text5	Left	600
Text5	Top	3360
Text5	Width	3135
Text5	Name	txtPhone
Text6	Height	375
Text6	Left	3720
Text6	Top	3360
Text6	Width	3015
Text6	Name	txtFax

Table 13.4 The **TextBox** *controls' properties. (continued from previous page)*

After you finish changing the *TextBox* controls' properties, you can add the labels for each text box to the *frmClient* form, as you will do in the next section.

ADDING LABEL CONTROLS TO THE FRMCLIENT FORM

Now that you have a *ComboBox* control and *TextBox* controls to display customer names, addresses, and phone numbers, you will add *Label* controls to the *frmClient* form. The *Label* controls will display headings for the customer information fields, and one *Label* control will display the customer's ID number. To add *Label* controls to the *frmClient* form, perform the following steps:

1. If you have closed the *frmClient* form, double-click your mouse within the Project Explorer on the *frmClient* form listing to reopen the form. Visual Basic will open the *frmClient* form.

2. Select the View menu Toolbox option. Visual Basic will open the Toolbox.

3. Within the Toolbox, double-click your mouse on the Label icon. Visual Basic will draw a *Label* control, *Label1*, within the *frmClient* form.

4. Repeat Step 3 eight more times. Visual Basic will draw eight more *Label* controls within the *frmClient* form.

5. Within the *frmClient* form window, click your mouse on a *Label* control to highlight it. Visual Basic will draw a small frame around the control.

6. Select the View menu Properties Window option. Visual Basic will open the Properties Window listing the highlighted *Label* control's properties.

7. Within the Properties Window, change the highlighted *Label* control's properties to the values Table 13.5 lists.

8. Repeat Steps 5, 6, and 7 until you have changed each *Label* control's properties to the values Table 13.5 lists.

426

Object	Property	Set As
Label1	Caption	ID Number
Label1	Height	255
Label1	Left	600
Label1	Top	360
Label1	Width	975
Label1	Name	lblIDHeader
Label2	Caption	Phone
Label2	Height	255
Label2	Left	600
Label2	Top	3120
Label2	Width	3135
Label2	Name	lblPhoneHeader
Label3	Caption	FAX
Label3	Height	255
Label3	Left	4080
Label3	Top	3120
Label3	Width	3015
Label3	Name	lblFaxHeader
Label4	Caption	[blank]
Label4	Height	255
Label4	Left	1680
Label4	Top	360
Label4	Width	1455
Label4	Name	lblID
Label5	Caption	Name
Label5	Height	255
Label5	Left	600
Label5	Top	840
Label5	Width	6495
Label5	Name	lblNameHeader
Label6	Caption	Address
Label6	Height	255
Label6	Left	600
Label6	Top	1560
Label6	Width	6495
Label6	Name	lblAddressHeader
Label7	Caption	City
Label7	Height	255
Label7	Left	4080

*Table 13.5 The **prjClient** project's **Label** controls' properties. (continued on following page)*

Object	Property	Set As
Label7	*Top*	600
Label7	*Width*	2400
Label7	*Name*	*lblCityHeader*
Label8	*Caption*	*State*
Label8	*Height*	255
Label8	*Left*	3840
Label8	*Top*	2400
Label8	*Width*	975
Label8	*Name*	*lblStateHeader*
Label9	*Caption*	*Zip*
Label9	*Height*	255
Label9	*Left*	5040
Label9	*Top*	2400
Label9	*Width*	2055
Label9	*Name*	*lblZipHeader*

Table 13.5 *The **prjClient** project's **Label** controls' properties. (continued from previous page)*

After you finish changing the *Label* controls' properties, you have almost completed the *prjClient* form's design. However, you must still add the command buttons to the form, which will instruct the program to perform certain actions.

ADDING COMMANDBUTTON CONTROLS TO THE FRMCLIENT FORM

Now that you have *ComboBox*, *TextBox*, and *Label* controls to display customer names, addresses, and phone numbers, you will add *CommandButton* controls to the *frmClient* form. The *CommandButton* controls will let you add, edit, or delete records, and exit the *prjClient* program. To add *CommandButton* controls to the *frmClient* form, perform the following steps:

1. If you have closed the *frmClient* form, double-click your mouse within the Project Explorer on the *frmClient* form listing to reopen the form. Visual Basic will open the *frmClient* form.

2. Select the View menu Toolbox option. Visual Basic will open the Toolbox.

3. Within the Toolbox, double-click your mouse on the CommandButton icon. Visual Basic will draw a *CommandButton* control, *Command1*, within the *frmClient* form.

4. Repeat Step 3 three more times. Visual Basic will draw three more *CommandButton* controls within the *frmClient* form.

5. Within the *frmClient* form window, click your mouse on a *CommandButton* control to highlight it. Visual Basic will draw a small frame around the control.

6. Select the View menu Properties Window option. Visual Basic will open the Properties Window listing the highlighted *CommandButton* control's properties.

7. Within the Properties Window, change the highlighted *CommandButton* control's properties to the values Table 13.6 lists.

8. Repeat Steps 5, 6, and 7 until you have changed each *CommandButton* control's properties to the values Table 13.6 lists.

Object	Property	Set As
Command1	*Caption*	*Add*
Command1	*Height*	615
Command1	*Left*	600

Table 13.6 *The **prjClient** project's **CommandButton** controls' properties. (continued on following page)*

Object	Property	Set As
Command1	Top	3960
Command1	Width	1215
Command1	Name	cmdAdd
Command2	Caption	Commit
Command2	Height	615
Command2	Left	2280
Command2	Top	3960
Command2	Width	1215
Command2	Name	cmdEdit
Command3	Caption	Delete
Command3	Height	615
Command3	Left	4080
Command3	Top	3960
Command3	Width	1215
Command3	Name	cmdDelete
Command4	Caption	E&xit
Command4	Height	615
Command4	Left	5880
Command4	Top	3960
Command4	Width	1215
Command4	Name	cmdExit

428

Table 13.6 The *prjClient* project's **CommandButton** controls' properties. *(continued from previous page)*

After you finish changing the *CommandButton* controls' properties, the *frmClient* form will look similar to Figure 13.7.

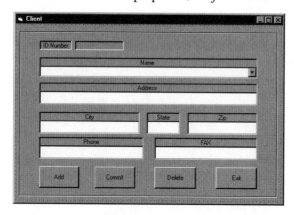

Figure 13.7 The *frmClient* form after you change its **CommandButton** controls' properties.

WRITING THE PROJECT CODE

Now that you have added controls to the *frmClient* form, you will write code for each one and then write procedures to communicate with each control and the *ClientServer* database. When you write code, you will first declare the variables that the procedures will use. Then you will create a structure within the *mdlClient* module to store customer information. After that, you will write code for functions, procedures, and control events.

DECLARING THE VARIABLES

As you have learned in previous chapters, you will declare most variables either within the procedure in which you use the variable, or within the General–Declarations section of the form or module within which you use the variable. In the *prjClient* project, you will declare most variables in the General–Declarations section in the *frmClient* Code window. Remember, when you declare variables in the General–Declarations section of the *frmClient* Code window, all procedures and functions in the form code can use them. The following code implements the *prjClient* project variable declarations in the *frmClient* Code window's General–Declarations section:

```
Dim tempIndex As Integer
Dim tempText As String
Dim tempID As Integer, tempAddressID As Integer
Dim tempFirst As String, tempLast As String
Dim CustomerRS As Recordset
Dim AddressRS As Recordset
Dim SelectedTable As String
Dim i As Integer, j As Integer
Dim Updated As Boolean
Dim FieldName As String
Dim Customer() As stcCUSTOMER
Private Server As clsServer
```

Many of the variables you will define within the General–Declarations section are temporary variables that the program will use to pass information back and forth between procedures. The *tempIndex* and *tempText* variables will store the *cmbCustomer* control's *ListIndex* and *Text* properties, while the *tempID* and *tempAddressID* variables will store a temporary ID value before the *prjClient* program sends the value to the *prjServer* program. Additionally, the *tempFirst* and *tempLast* variables will store a customer's first and last name before the *prjClient* project adds the names to the *ClientServer* database. The *i* and *j* variables will store counting values for *For-Next* loops.

The *CustomerRS* and *AddressRS* variables will store recordsets from the *ClientServer* database. The *SelectedTable* variable will store the table name—*Customer*, *Address*, or *ID*—and you will pass this variable to one of the *prjServer* project's public functions to query a table. The *Updated* variable will store a *True* or *False* value, which indicates whether or not the user has made changes to the current record. The *Customer* array is an unbounded array of the structure type *stcCUSTOMER*, which the next section explains in detail. The last variable the declarations section code declares is the *Server* variable as a type of the *prjServer* project's *clsServer* module. The *Server* variable lets the *prjClient* program access the public functions within the *prjServer* program.

Writing the stcCUSTOMER Structure's Code

As you have learned, a structure holds information about a specific conceptual object (such as a dog or a car). In the *prjClient* project, the object is the customer. Each customer has a name, address, phone number, fax number, and ID number. You will store each piece of customer information within a structure of type *stcCUSTOMER*. The *stcCUSTOMER* structure will contain ten member variables. The *prjClient* program will create and update an array (the *Customer* array) of *stcCUSTOMER* structures to maintain the information the *prjServer* program returns. The following code implements the *stcCUSTOMER* structure's definition in the *mdlClient* Code window's General–Declarations section:

```
Type stcCUSTOMER
  ID As Integer
  FirstName As String
  LastName As String
  AddressID As Integer
  Street As String
  City As String
  State As String
  Zip As String
  Phone As String
  Fax As String
End Type
```

The member variables of the *stcCUSTOMER* structure correspond to the fields in the client display; the ID number reflects the unique database-assigned number for the customer. You will use the *stcCUSTOMER* structure within the

Customer array, as the previous section explains. For example, to access the first customer in a list's first name, you will use program code similar to the following:

```
ReturnVal = Customer(0).FirstName
```

Because you are unsure of the number of customers the *ClientServer* database will return, the program will create the array as an undimensioned-size array and apply actual dimensions to the array during execution. You will make the dimension of the number of array elements in code reflect the number of records in a *Recordset* object. After you fill the *Customer* array, it will contain all records that the *prjServer* program returns from the *ClientServer* database.

WRITING THE LOAD EVENT

As you learned in Chapter 1, "Introduction to Visual Basic," a form's *Load* event will occur whenever a program loads the form; in fact, the *Form_Load* event occurs before the program actually displays the form. In the *prjClient* project, the *Form_Load* event is the first procedure to execute. The following code implements the *Form_Load* procedure:

```
Private Sub Form_Load()
   Set Server = New clsServer
   OpenCustomer
   If CustomerRS.RecordCount = 0 Then
     FillCustomerEmpty
     cmdDelete.Enabled = False
   Else
     FillCustomer
     ViewCustomer
   End If
   cmdEdit.Enabled = False
End Sub
```

The program code in the *Load* event will first set the *clsServer* module to the *Server* variable. After that, the *OpenCustomer* procedure will open two recordsets from the *ClientServer* database's *Customer* and *Address* tables. The program code uses an *If-Then* statement to determine whether the recordset opening was successful; if not, the program fills the client with blank fields and disables the Delete button. Otherwise, the program calls the *FillCustomer* procedure, which will fill the *Customer* array with customer information, and invokes the *ViewCustomer* procedure, which will display the customer's first and last name in the *cmbCustomer* control. The procedure also disables the *cmdEdit* control.

WRITING THE OPENCUSTOMER PROCEDURE

Now that you have written the *frmClient* form's *Load* event, you will write the first procedure it calls, the *OpenCustomer* procedure. The *OpenCustomer* procedure will open two recordsets and assign their contents to *Recordset* objects. The following code implements the *OpenCustomer* procedure:

```
Private Sub OpenCustomer()
   SelectedTable = "Customer"
   Set CustomerRS = Server.OpenRecordset(SelectedTable)
   SelectedTable = "Address"
   Set AddressRS = Server.OpenRecordset(SelectedTable)
End Sub
```

The *SelectedTable* variable stores a string that the *OpenRecordset* method uses to open the table. The procedure then passes the *SelectedTable* variable to the server, which uses the string to open the recordset remotely. The procedure assigns both "Customer" and "Address" to the variable, in turn, to open the two recordsets.

Note: *When you type the **Server** object name in code, Visual Basic will display a small submenu that lists the four public functions in the **clsServer** class module of the **prjServer** project.*

WRITING THE FILLCUSTOMER PROCEDURE

As you have learned, the *Form_Load* event calls procedures to open the recordset and to fill the *Customer* array with the records the recordset returns. After you have written the *OpenCustomer* procedure, you can use the two open *Recordset* objects, *CustomerRS* and *AddressRS*, to fill the *stcCUSTOMER* structure with information. The *FillCustomer* procedure will place records from the *Customer* and *Address* tables into the *Customer* object. As you know, the *Customer* array is an array of type *stcCUSTOMER*, and the *stcCUSTOMER* structure contains ten members. The following code implements the *FillCustomer* procedure:

```
Private Sub FillCustomer()
  Dim Count As Integer

  CustomerRS.MoveLast
  CustomerRS.MoveFirst
  AddressRS.MoveFirst
  Count = CustomerRS.RecordCount
  ReDim Customer(Count)
  For i = 1 To Count
    With Customer(i)
       .ID = CustomerRS.Fields("CustomerID")
       .FirstName = CustomerRS.Fields("CustomerFirst")
       .LastName = CustomerRS.Fields("CustomerLast")
       .AddressID = AddressRS.Fields("CustomerID")
       .Street = AddressRS.Fields("Street")
       .City = AddressRS.Fields("City")
       .State = AddressRS.Fields("State")
       .Zip = AddressRS.Fields("Zip")
       .Phone = AddressRS.Fields("Phone")
       .Fax = AddressRS.Fields("Fax")
    End With
    CustomerRS.MoveNext
    AddressRS.MoveNext
  Next i
End Sub
```

In the first line of code, the *FillCustomer* procedure will declare the *Count* variable, which will store the *CustomerRS* object's record count. The code then ensures that both recordsets are filled, and re-dimensions the *Customer* array's size to equal the total number of records. Finally, the program code uses a *For-Next* loop to step through each record in each recordset and fill the corresponding array member with the correct recordset values.

WRITING THE FILLCUSTOMEREMPTY PROCEDURE

As you have learned, the *prjClient* program will respond differently if the *CustomerRS* recordset has no records than it will if the *CustomerRS* recordset has records. The program will call the *FillCustomerEmpty* procedure to update the display whenever the *CustomerRS* recordset contains no records. The following code implements the *FillCustomerEmpty* procedure:

```
Private Sub FillCustomerEmpty()
  ReDim Customer(0)
  With Customer(0)
     .ID = 0
     .FirstName = ""
     .LastName = ""
     .AddressID = 0
     .Street = ""
     .City = ""
     .State = ""
     .Zip = ""
```

```
          .Phone = ""
          .Fax = ""
     End With
     lblID.Caption = ""
     txtStreet.Text = ""
     txtCity.Text = ""
     txtState.Text = ""
     txtZip.Text = ""
     txtPhone.Text = ""
     txtFax.Text = ""
     ViewCustomer
     cmdEdit.Enabled = False
End Sub
```

The *FillCustomerEmpty* procedure resets the *Customer* array to one record, then fills the record with empty information and null strings. The procedure then sets each field in the *frmClient* form to a null string to clear it of text. The *FillCustomerEmpty* procedure calls *ViewCustomer* to complete the display's update, which fills the *cmbCustomer* text field with the string "empty," and disables the *cmdEdit* button, because the user must first add a record to the database before the user can edit the record.

WRITING THE VIEWCUSTOMER PROCEDURE

After you fill the *Customer* array with customer information, you can view the information within the array, one record at a time. To view records within the *prjClient* project, you must first select a record from the *cmbCustomer* control at the form's top. The *ViewCustomer* procedure fills the *cmbCustomer* control with the customer's first and last name for each member in the *Customer* array. The following code implements the *ViewCustomer* procedure:

```
Private Sub ViewCustomer()
  cmbCustomer.Clear
  If CustomerRS.RecordCount > 0 Then
    For i = 1 To CustomerRS.RecordCount
      cmbCustomer.AddItem (Customer(i).FirstName & " " & _
            Customer(i).LastName)
    Next i
    cmbCustomer.ListIndex = 0
  Else
    cmbCustomer.Text = "Empty"
  End If
End Sub
```

The procedure first clears the combo box of entries, then checks to ensure that there are records within the *CustomerRS* recordset. If there are, it steps through the records in the *Customer* array one record at a time and adds the first and last name of each customer to the combo box. If there are no records in the *CustomerRS* recordset, the program code adds an "Empty" entry to the combo box and exits.

WRITING THE FORMATNAME FUNCTION

As you have learned, the *prjClient* project will let you add, edit, or delete records from the *ClientServer* database. You will change the *cmbCustomer* control's *Text* value when you edit a customer's name. As you know, the *cmbCustomer* control displays a customer's name. When you select a name within the *cmbCustomer* control, the *FormatName* function splits the customer's name into two pieces, first name and last name, which the program then uses to fill the remaining entries within the *frmClient* form. The following code implements the *FormatName* function:

```
Private Function FormatName(tempText As String) As Boolean
   Dim SearchString As String, SearchChar As String
   Dim FindCount As Integer, SearchPos As Integer
   Dim intLength As Integer
```

```
        FormatName = True
        SearchString = tempText
        SearchChar = " "
        SearchPos = InStr(1, SearchString, SearchChar, 1)
        If Len(tempText) < 3 Then
          FormatName = False
          Exit Function
        End If
        If SearchPos > 0 Then
          tempFirst = Left(tempText, SearchPos - 1)
          intLength = Len(tempText) - SearchPos
          tempLast = Right(tempText, intLength)
        ElseIf SearchPos = 0 Then
          FormatName = False
          Exit Function
        End If
        If tempFirst = "" Or tempLast = "" Then FormatName = False
      End Function
```

433

When you click your mouse on the *cmbCustomer* control, your program will invoke the control's *Click* event. Within the *Click* event, the code will assign the *cmbCustomer* control's *Text* property to the *tempText* variable (you declared the *tempText* variable in the Code window's General–Declarations section). When you want to edit a customer's name, you can click your mouse on the *cmdEdit* control. The *cmdEdit* control's *Click* event will call the *FormatName* function.

The *FormatName* function declares several local variables, which it then uses to perform the search for the value within the *cmbCustomer* control. The program code uses the *InStr* member function to search for a space within the *SearchString*. After searching, the program code checks the string length to ensure that the string is at least three characters long (two letters and a space between). If it is not, *FormatName* exits and returns *False*. Otherwise, *FormatName* changes the values of the *tempFirst* and *tempLast* string variables to the left and right halves of the string. Additionally, the *Len* method will calculate the length of *tempText* minus *SearchPos* and assign it to *intLength*. You will use the *Len* method to retrieve the *tempText* length minus the search position because the right side of *tempText* is the customer's last name. The *Right* method will return a string equal in length to the *intLength* value and assign it to *tempLast*.

To better understand how the *FormatName* function works, imagine you have a customer named *John's Bar*. When you click your mouse on the *cmbCustomer* control, the *tempText* variable's value will equal "John's Bar". The code in the *FormatName* procedure will use the *InStr* method against the *tempText* variable and will find a space at position 7 (the space is seven characters over from *J* in *John's*). Then, the *Left* method will return a string from *tempText* that is the length of *SearchPos* (7) minus one, which is *John's*. (*John's* is six characters long.) Next, the *Len* method will calculate the length of *tempText*, which is 10, then subtract *SearchPos* (7) and assign the value of 3 to *intLength*. After that, the *Right* method will return a string from *tempText* that is the *intLength* value (3), which is *Bar*. Therefore, you have *John's* in *tempFirst* and *Bar* in *tempLast*.

WRITING THE FINDINSTRUCTURE PROCEDURE

As the previous section discusses, the *FormatName* function splits the *tempText* variables into its first and last name components. After the *FormatName* function completes its processing, the *FindInStructure* procedure will use the values *FormatName* sets to find a customer in the *Customer* array. The following code implements the *FindInStructure* procedure:

```
Private Sub FindInStructure()
  Dim AddressFound As Boolean

  For i = 1 To CustomerRS.RecordCount
    If tempLast = Customer(i).LastName And tempFirst = _
       Customer(i).FirstName Then
```

```
          tempID = Customer(i).ID
          If AddressFound = False Then
            For j = 1 To CustomerRS.RecordCount
              If tempID = Customer(j).AddressID Then
                tempIndex = j
                AddressFound = True
              End If
            Next j
          End If
        End If
      Next i
End Sub
```

The *FindInStructure* procedure uses an *AddressFound* variable to reduce the number of loops it must perform. It uses both the *i* and *j* counting variables that you defined in the General–Declarations section to loop through the **434** *Customer* array. It first locates a match for the first and last name, then locates the correct address, and returns the customer's ID in the *tempID* variable and the index for the customer's address in the *tempIndex* variable.

You should compare the *Customer* array's *AddressID* to the *tempID* to ensure that you do not confuse customer names. The only way for you to tell whether you have two or more customers with the same name is to compare each customer's unique ID number.

WRITING THE CMBCUSTOMER CONTROL'S CLICK EVENT

As you have learned, the *cmbCustomer* control will display customer names. When you click your mouse on the *cmbCustomer* control, your program will invoke its *Click* event. The *cmbCustomer* control's *Click* event will call the *FormatName* and *FindInStructure* procedures and fill the customer *TextBox* controls with information. The following code implements the *cmbCustomer_Click* event:

```
Private Sub cmbCustomer_Click()
  If Updated = False Then
    cmdEdit.Enabled = False
  End If
  tempText = cmbCustomer.Text
  If FormatName(tempText) Then
    FindInStructure
    lblID.Caption = tempID
    With Customer(tempIndex)
      txtStreet.Text = .Street
      txtCity.Text = .City
      txtState.Text = .State
      txtZip.Text = .Zip
      txtPhone.Text = .Phone
      txtFax.Text = .Fax
    End With
  End If
End Sub
```

When a user clicks the mouse on the *cmbCustomer* control, the code in the *Click* event first uses an *If-Then* statement to check the *Updated* variable. If *Updated* equals *False*, the user is not editing the customer name, and the code will assign *False* to the *cmdEdit* control's *Enabled* property. This means that Visual Basic will temporarily disable the *cmdEdit* control. Next, the code will assign the *cmbCustomer* control's *Text* value to *tempText*. As you have learned, you assign the selected customer name to *tempText* so that the *FindInStructure* procedure can find the correct name after you make any changes before an edit. The program then passes the *tempText* value to the *FormatName* procedure, which splits the *tempText* string into two pieces.

The code will then call the *FindInStructure* procedure. As you know, *FindInStructure* will find the currently selected customer name within the *Customer* array. After *FindInStructure* returns, the selected customer is active and the code will assign the *tempID* value to the *lblID* control's *Caption* property. The program will display the customer's ID number in the *lblID* control. Finally, the code will assign the *Customer* array's *Street, City, State, Zip, Phone,* and *Fax* array variables to the *txtStreet, txtCity, txtState, txtZip, txtPhone,* and *txtFax* control's *Text* properties.

WRITING THE *CMBCUSTOMER* CONTROL'S *DROPDOWN* EVENT

As you have learned, the *cmbCustomer* control holds information about customers in the recordset. When the user clicks on the combo box, the program must update the combo box to be sure that the recordset the program displays is the most fully updated version of the recordset. The following code implements the *cmbCustomer_DropDown* event:

```
Private Sub cmbCustomer_DropDown()
  CustomerRS.Requery
  If CustomerRS.RecordCount = 0 Then
    cmdDelete.Enabled = False
    cmdEdit.Enabled = False
    FillCustomerEmpty
    Exit Sub
  End If
  CustomerRS.MoveLast
  DoEvents
  AddressRS.Requery
  FillCustomer
  ViewCustomer
  cmdEdit.Enabled = False
  If CustomerRS.RecordCount > 0 Then cmdDelete.Enabled = True
End Sub
```

435

The *cmbCustomer_DropDown* event re-queries the recordset and verifies that the recordset contains records. If the recordset is empty, the procedure disables the *cmdEdit* and *cmdDelete* buttons and fills the form with blank data. The procedure then fills the *Customer* array and displays the newly filled array in the combo box. The *If-Then* statement in the final line checks to be sure there is a least one record in the recordset and, if so, enables the *cmdDelete* button.

WRITING THE *FINDINCUSTOMERTABLE* AND *FINDINADDRESSTABLE* PROCEDURES

As you have learned, the *cmbCustomer* control's *Click* event will call the *FindInStructure* procedure, which will find a selected customer and assign its ID to *tempID*. The *FindInCustomerTable* procedure will use the *tempID* to find the specific customer in the *ClientServer* database's *Customer* table. Remember, the *Customer* table has three fields, *CustomerID, CustomerFirst,* and *CustomerLast.* You will use the *CustomerID* field to find the *tempID* value. The following code implements the *FindInCustomerTable* procedure:

```
Private Sub FindInCustomerTable(tempID As Integer)
  Dim FindString As String

  CustomerRS.MoveFirst
  FindString = "CustomerID = " & tempID
  CustomerRS.FindFirst FindString
End Sub
```

The *FindInCustomerTable* procedure uses the *FindFirst* method to find the value within the recordset that matches the known ID number. The procedure does not loop through the recordset looking for multiple matches because the *CustomerID* field is unique, and therefore the first match will be the only match. The program code uses similar processing to find the *AddressID* within the *FindInAddressTable* procedure, as shown in the following code:

```
Private Sub FindInAddressTable(tempAddressID As Integer)
  Dim FindString As String

  AddressRS.MoveFirst
  FindString = "CustomerID = " & tempAddressID
  AddressRS.FindFirst FindString
End Sub
```

Note: *When you want to find a string value in a database, you must enclose the string you are searching for with single quotes, for example, "**FieldName = '**" & **StringName** & "'". When you want to find a numeric value in a database, you do not need quotes around the numeric value you are searching for, for example, "**FieldName = **" & **NumericName**.*

WRITING THE CMBCUSTOMER CONTROL'S CHANGE EVENT

As you have learned, the *Form_Load* event will disable the *cmdEdit* control at startup, which means you cannot click your mouse on the *cmdEdit* control. When you change the text in the *cmbCustomer* control, your program will invoke the control's *Change* event. The following code implements the *cmbCustomer_Change* event:

```
Private Sub cmbCustomer_Change()
  If CustomerRS.RecordCount > 0 And cmbCustomer.Text <> "empty" Then
    cmdEdit.Enabled = True
  End If
End Sub
```

436

The *cmbCustomer* control's *Change* event will first make sure that there is a record in the recordset, and then make sure that the entry is not "empty." If both cases are true, the program code will enable the *cmdEdit* control. If one of the cases is not true, there are either no records in the database to edit, or the user is entering an invalid value, and the event procedure will exit without enabling the *cmdEdit* control.

WRITING THE CHANGE EVENTS FOR THE OTHER CONTROLS

Just as with changes to the *cmbCustomer* control, changes to the other controls in the user interface should enable the *cmdEdit* command button so that the user can save the changes to the database. To perform such processing, you must add an *If-Then* statement to the control's *Change* event. For example, the following code implements the *txtPhone_Change* event:

```
Private Sub txtPhone_Change()
  If CustomerRS.RecordCount > 0 Then
    cmdEdit.Enabled = True
  End If
End Sub
```

You should add identical *If-Then* statements to the change events for the *txtStreet*, *txtCity*, *txtState*, *txtZip*, and *txtFax* fields. When you complete the additions, the program will enable the *cmdEdit* button in response to any change to any field.

WRITING THE CMDADD CONTROL'S CLICK EVENT

As you have learned, the *prjClient* project will let you add, edit, or delete records from the *ClientServer* database. When you click your mouse on the *cmdAdd* control, your program will invoke the control's *Click* event. The *cmdAdd* control's *Click* event will perform some traps to identify bad data or other errors, and then call the *AddCustomer* procedure, which will add new customer data to the *ClientServer* database. The following code implements the *cmdAdd_Click* event:

```
Private Sub cmdAdd_Click()
  Dim IDconfirm As Boolean

  If Not CheckFields Then
    MsgBox "One or more fields is blank. Complete all fields."
    Exit Sub
  End If
  FieldName = "CustomerID"
  tempID = Server.GetID(FieldName)
  lblID.Caption = tempID
  tempText = cmbCustomer.Text
  If Not FormatName(tempText) Then
    MsgBox "Name must have space between First and Last names."
    Exit Sub
```

```
      End If
      IDconfirm = Server.CheckID(tempID, FieldName)
      If IDconfirm Then
        AddCustomer
        cmdDelete.Enabled = True
        cmdEdit.Enabled = False
      Else
        MsgBox "tempID value does not match database. Press OK for another " _
            "value.", vbOKCancel
        tempID = Server.GetID(FieldName)
        IDconfirm = Server.CheckID(tempID, FieldName)
        If IDconfirm Then
          AddCustomer
        Else
          MsgBox "No match. Start again.", vbCritical
        End If
      End If
End Sub
```

The program code declares the *IDconfirm* variable, which will store a *True* or *False* value that the *Click* event will check. The procedure then calls the *CheckFields* function, which verifies that all fields in the form contain valid values, and returns *True* if they do and *False* if they do not. If not all fields in the form contain valid entries, the program code displays a message and exits. After verifying the entries, the program code uses the public server *GetID* and *CheckID* methods to obtain an ID number and confirm its uniqueness. If all the fields contain values and the program is able to verify that all the ID numbers are correct, the procedure calls the *AddCustomer* procedure, which the next section details.

As you have learned, the *CheckFields* function checks all the fields for valid entries and returns a success or failure value. The following code implements the *CheckFields* function:

```
Private Function CheckFields() As Boolean
  CheckFields = True
  If cmbCustomer.Text = "" Then CheckFields = False
  If txtStreet.Text = "" Then CheckFields = False
  If txtCity.Text = "" Then CheckFields = False
  If txtState.Text = "" Then CheckFields = False
  If txtZip.Text = "" Then CheckFields = False
  If txtPhone.Text = "" Then CheckFields = False
  If txtFax.Text = "" Then CheckFields = False
End Function
```

As you can see, the code verifies that every field contains an entry. You can expand the code so that it checks each entry to make sure that it falls within a given set of parameters, should you want to do so.

WRITING THE ADDCUSTOMER PROCEDURE

As you know, after the *cmdAdd* control's *Click* event determines that *tempID* contains a unique value, it will call the *AddCustomer* procedure. The *AddCustomer* procedure will add a new customer's name, address, phone number, and ID number to the *Customer* and *Address* tables. The following code implements the *AddCustomer* procedure:

```
Private Sub AddCustomer()
  Dim tableID As Integer

  tableID = Server.IncrementID(FieldName)
  With CustomerRS
    .AddNew
      .Fields("CustomerID") = tempID
      .Fields("CustomerFirst") = tempFirst
      .Fields("CustomerLast") = tempLast
```

```
            .Update
            .Requery
            .MoveLast
            .MoveFirst
         End With
         With AddressRS
            .AddNew
               .Fields("CustomerID") = tempID
               .Fields("Street") = txtStreet.Text
               .Fields("City") = txtCity.Text
               .Fields("State") = txtState.Text
               .Fields("Zip") = txtZip.Text
               .Fields("Phone") = txtPhone.Text
               .Fields("Fax") = txtFax.Text
            .Update
            .Requery
            .MoveLast
            .MoveFirst
         End With
         FillCustomer
         ViewCustomer
      End Sub
```

The program code within the *AddCustomer* procedure updates the *CustomerRS* and *AddressRS* recordsets and uses the *AddNew* method and the *Update* method to add the current screen entries to the databases. After the *AddCustomer* procedure completes the add process, the procedure calls *FillCustomer* and *ViewCustomer* to refill the array with the records in the database and display the first customer in the database.

WRITING THE CODE TO EDIT RECORDS

As you have learned, the *prjClient* project will let you edit records from the *ClientServer* database. When you click your mouse on the *cmdEdit* control, your program will invoke its *Click* event. The *cmdEdit* control's *Click* event will call the *EditRecord* procedure, which will edit a selected customer record in the *ClientServer* database. The following code implements the *cmdEdit_Click* event:

```
Private Sub cmdEdit_Click()
   If CustomerRS.RecordCount = 0 Then
      MsgBox "No records to edit!"
      cmdEdit.Enabled = False
      Exit Sub
   End If
   If FormatName(tempText) Then
      FindInStructure
      FindInCustomerTable tempID
      FindInAddressTable tempID
      FormatName cmbCustomer.Text
      EditRecord
      cmdEdit.Enabled = False
      Updated = True
   End If
End Sub
```

The *Click* event checks the number of records in the recordset to be sure that there are actually records to edit. If there are no records in the recordset, the procedure will display a message and end. Otherwise, the procedure will call the *FormatName* procedure, which will split the *tempText* value into two pieces and assign them to *tempFirst* and *tempLast*. Remember, the *cmbCustomer* control's *Click* event will assign the *cmbCustomer* control's *Text* property to *tempText*. Next, the *FindInStructure* procedure will use the *tempFirst* and *tempLast* values to find the selected customer and assign the ID number to *tempID*. The *FindInCustomerTable* procedure will then use the *tempID* value to find the selected customer in the *Customer* table. After successfully locating the correct position in the *CustomerRS* and *AddressRS* recordsets, the code calls the *EditRecord* procedure, which edits the record. The following code implements the *EditRecord* procedure:

```
Private Sub EditRecord()
  CustomerRS.Edit
    CustomerRS.Fields("CustomerFirst") = tempFirst
    CustomerRS.Fields("CustomerLast") = tempLast
  CustomerRS.Update
  CustomerRS.Requery
  With AddressRS
    .Edit
      .Fields("Street") = txtStreet.Text
      .Fields("City") = txtCity.Text
      .Fields("State") = txtState.Text
      .Fields("Zip") = txtZip.Text
      .Fields("Phone") = txtPhone.Text
      .Fields("Fax") = txtFax.Text
    .Update
    .Requery
  End With
  tempString = cmbCustomer.Text
  CustomerRS.MoveLast
  AddressRS.MoveLast
  CustomerRS.MoveFirst
  AddressRS.MoveFirst
  FillCustomer
  ViewCustomer
End Sub
```

The *EditRecord* procedure's code invokes the *Edit* and *Update* methods against *CustomerRS* and *AddressRS* to change the fields in those recordsets. Next, just as with the *AddRecord* procedure, the *EditRecord* procedure refills the recordsets, refills the *Customer* array, and displays the first record in the array within the combo box. After the *EditRecord* procedure returns, the *cmdEdit_Click* event's program code will disable the *cmdEdit* control. Finally, the code will assign *True* to *Updated*, and you can check *Updated* to determine that the customer's information was successfully changed.

WRITING THE CMDDELETE CONTROL'S CLICK EVENT

As you have learned, the *prjClient* project will let you delete records from the *ClientServer* database. When you click your mouse on the *cmdDelete* control, your program will invoke its *Click* event. The *cmdDelete* control's *Click* event will call the *DeleteRecord* procedure, which will delete a customer record you select from the *ClientServer* database. The following code implements the *cmdDelete_Click* event:

```
Private Sub cmdDelete_Click()
  Dim YesNo As Integer

  If CustomerRS.RecordCount = 0 Then
    cmdDelete.Enabled = False
    cmdEdit.Enabled = False
    Exit Sub
  End If
  YesNo = MsgBox("Delete this record ? " & tempText, vbYesNoCancel)
  If YesNo = vbYes Then
    FormatName(tempText)
    FindInStructure
    FindInCustomerTable tempID
    FindInAddressTable tempID
    DeleteRecord
  Else
    Exit Sub
```

```
      End If
      If CustomerRS.RecordCount = 0 Then
        cmdDelete.Enabled = False
        cmdEdit.Enabled = False
        FillCustomerEmpty
      End If
  End Sub
```

The *cmdDelete_Click* event checks to ensure that there are records in the recordset. If there are not, it exits immediately. If there are, the event's program code displays a message box that will ask the user if the user really wants to delete the selected record and assign the user's response to *YesNo*. When the user clicks the mouse on the Yes or No button within a message box, Visual Basic will assign a system-defined constant to the *YesNo* variable. If the user selects the Yes button, the procedure will then call the *FormatName* function, format the data, find the correct records, and call the *DeleteRecord* procedure. The following code implements the *DeleteRecord* procedure:

440

```
  Private Sub DeleteRecord()
    CustomerRS.Delete
    CustomerRS.Requery
    AddressRS.Delete
    AddressRS.Requery
    If CustomerRS.RecordCount = 0 Or AddressRS.RecordCount = 0 Then
      FillCustomerEmpty
      Exit Sub
    End If
    CustomerRS.MoveLast
    CustomerRS.MoveFirst
    AddressRS.MoveLast
    AddressRS.MoveFirst
    FillCustomer
    ViewCustomer
  End Sub
```

The *DeleteRecord* subroutine first deletes the selected record, then updates the recordsets. If the recordsets are empty, the program will fill the screen with blank fields. Otherwise, the program will refill the recordsets, the *Customer* array, and display the first record in the *Customer* array within the *frmClient* form. After *DeleteRecord* returns, the *cmdDelete_Click* event also checks the number of records in the *CustomerRS* recordset, and disables certain command buttons in the event that the recordset is empty.

WRITING THE CODE TO END THE PROGRAM

After the user finishes with the *prjClient* program, you must provide the user with a convenient way to exit the program. This exit should also provide you with the opportunity to clean up some of the information the client maintains, which it may or may not have already pushed to the server. The *cmdExit_Click* event solves both problems—it gives the user a convenient way to close the program, and it gives you one last opportunity for data checking. The following code implements the *cmdExit_Click* event:

```
  Private Sub cmdExit_Click()
    Unload Me
  End Sub
```

As you have learned, when you work with Single Document Interface (SDI) applications, unloading all the program's open forms ends the program. Because the *prjClient* project uses only one form, unloading the form will terminate the program's execution. Unlike using the *End* statement, however, the *Unload Me* statement lets your program perform error or validation checking within the form's *Unload* and *QueryUnload* events. You should always try to unload all the forms within a program to end the program, because it gives you the opportunity to validate the information the program maintains.

ENHANCEMENTS YOU CAN MAKE TO THE *prjClient* PROJECT

Now that you have a better understanding of how to use the separate ActiveX EXE *prjServer* project within the *prjClient* project, and you have used *TextBox*, *ComboBox*, *Label*, and *CommandButton* controls to display customer information, you can make some adjustments to the project.

First, you can change the code so that you can update only one portion of the customer's information and then process only that section. This will cut down on processing time because the current code will update all fields in the *Customer* and *Address* tables, even though you may only change one of them. Second, you can also change the form to include product, inventory, and sales information, if you change the *ClientServer* database discussed in Chapter 12. Finally, you can test the project by sending either the *prjServer* or *prjClient* project to another user, and try to access the ActiveX EXE across a network. In addition, you can change the code to do less processing on the client side. For example, you could send new customer information to the *prjServer* project and have it add the information to the *Customer* and *Address* tables.

441

PUTTING IT ALL TOGETHER

This chapter's project, *prjClient*, introduced you to how you can use an executable at the client level in conjunction with an ActiveX executable, either on the same computer or on a networked computer, to provide your programs with more flexibility. Although you used the *prjServer* ActiveX EXE project locally on your computer, you can just as easily use it on a network, as you will learn in Chapter 22. In addition, you have used *TextBox*, *Label*, and *ComboBox* controls to display customer information, such as customer names, addresses, phone numbers, and ID numbers. You have also used *CommandButton* controls to add, edit, or delete records from the *ClientServer* database across a network.

This chapter has also introduced you to using public functions from the ActiveX EXE *prjServer* project. You can use public functions to make another computer do the processing for you, or you can save downloading time by using another project across a network.

In the next chapter, Chapter 14, "Using the Windows API to Intercept Windows Messages," you will create a Visual Basic program that lets you control a form's actions and intercept messages from the operating system and handle them within your program (which you could not do before Visual Basic 5.0). Before you continue with Chapter 14, however, make sure you understand the following key concepts:

- ✓ Using Visual Basic, you can reference an independent ActiveX EXE project across a network from within a different program.

- ✓ Using an ActiveX EXE project across a network, you can save download time.

- ✓ Using Visual Basic, you can access public functions in a separate ActiveX EXE project.

- ✓ Using public functions in a separate ActiveX EXE project, you have no access to any private functions and therefore you protect your private data.

- ✓ Using public functions in a separate ActiveX EXE project, you can pass and receive data across a network.

- ✓ Using the *DAO Object Library*, you can maintain a Microsoft *Access* database within Visual Basic.

Chapter 14

Using the Windows API to Intercept Windows Messages

Throughout much of this book, you have used Visual Basic's forms to design the user interfaces for your projects. As you have learned, forms (like most other Visual Basic controls and objects) expose *events*. As you learned in Chapter 1, "Introduction to Visual Basic," events let you write program code to respond to program occurrences. For example, if a user clicks the mouse on a form within your Visual Basic program, the program will execute any program code that you place within that form's *Click* event. Similar events let your program capture mouse movements, form load and unload activities, and more.

Events, however, are actually Visual Basic interpretations of messages the operating system (Windows) sent to the program. For example, when the user resizes a form, Windows sends a *WM_SIZING* message to the program. The Visual Basic run-time interpreter (which your Visual Basic programs will load each time you run a program) translates that message into a *Form_Resize* event. Unfortunately, Visual Basic interprets the messages and lets your program handle only certain messages within events. Visual Basic will handle other messages internally or, in some cases, ignore them altogether.

Historically, Visual Basic programmers have not been able to work around the limitation of Visual Basic-interpreted messages. However, Visual Basic 5.0 includes the new *AddressOf* operator, which lets you pass a function or procedure's address to a Windows Application Programming Interface (API) function. You can use the new *AddressOf* operator to *subclass* forms within your Visual Basic programs. When you subclass a form, you place your own program code to handle Windows messages within your Visual Basic programs—doing so lets you bypass the Visual Basic run-time interpreter to handle those messages yourself. Within this chapter's project, *prjFormEvents*, you will write a simple application that intercepts messages from the operating system and uses those intercepted messages to perform processing that you cannot normally perform with forms. By the time you finish this chapter, you will understand the following key concepts:

- When you subclass a form, you intercept the messages that Windows sends to that form.

- A message is a numeric value that Windows sends to a program as the result of a user or an operating system action. Common messages indicate the user has moved the mouse, clicked the mouse button, and so on.

- Windows maintains a separate message queue for each execution thread.

- When you subclass forms and controls, you must create custom functions or procedures that intercept and process the messages.

- A *callback function* is a function within your Visual Basic program to which you can pass the Windows API function's address so that the Windows API function can "call back" the function within your program. Visual Basic 5.0 uses the new *AddressOf* operator to let your programs support callback functions.

- Visual Basic's new *AddressOf* operator lets you pass function and procedure addresses within your Visual Basic programs to Windows API functions.

- Visual Basic's *WithEvents* and *Event* keywords let your program create classes that expose its own events, much like the controls and forms you have used in previous chapters.

- Subclassing forms lets you customize your program's interface to a degree not possible in previous Visual Basic versions.

- Whenever your program intercepts messages, your program code should use the *CallWindowProc* procedure to pass the message on to the window's default message processing procedure.

Using the prjFormEvents Project

Before you design the *prjFormEvents* project, you may find it helpful to run the program. The companion CD-ROM that accompanies this book contains the *prjFormEvents.exe* program within the *Chapter14* directory. As with every other program on the CD-ROM, you should run the Jamsa Press *setup.exe* program to install the *prjFormEvents.exe* program to your computer's hard drive before you run it. After you install the *prjFormEvents.exe* program to your computer's hard drive, you can run it from the Start menu. To run the program, select the Windows Start menu Run option. Windows will display the Run dialog box. Within the Run dialog box, enter *x:\vbpl\Chapter14\prjFormEvents.exe*, where *x* corresponds to the drive letter of the hard drive on which you installed the *prjFormEvents.exe* program, and click your mouse on OK. Windows will display the *prjFormEvents.exe* program, as shown in Figure 14.1.

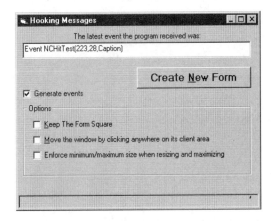

443

*Figure 14.1 The **prjFormEvents.exe** program's window at startup.*

Running prjFormEvents from the CD-ROM

As you have learned, you must first install many programs that you will use in this book to your computer's hard drive before you use them. The *prjFormEvents.exe* program, however, does not use any custom controls or references, other than those Visual Basic installs onto your system. Because the *prjFormEvents.exe* program uses no custom controls or references, you can run it from the CD-ROM. To run the program from the CD-ROM, perform the following steps:

1. Select the Windows Start menu Run option. Windows will display the Run dialog box.

2. Within the Run dialog box, enter *x:\Chapter14\prjFormEvents.exe*, where *x* corresponds to the letter of your computer's CD-ROM drive (usually D: or E:), and click your mouse on OK. Windows will run the *prjFormEvents.exe* program.

To learn more about the Jamsa Press *setup.exe* program, see the "What's on the *Visual Basic Programmer's Library* Companion CD-ROM" section at the back of this book.

Before you use the *prjFormEvents.exe* program, take a moment to familiarize yourself with the program's appearance. After you start the *prjFormEvents.exe* program, your computer will display a single window, Hooking Messages. Near the top of the Hooking Messages window, you will see a field with the caption "The latest event the program received was." If you move your mouse over the form, the field will change its contents to reflect the mouse movements. Below the field, you will see a button with the caption "Create New Form." Below the button, you will see a frame with the caption "Options." Within the frame, the program displays three check boxes: one that forces the form to always be square, one that lets the user click the mouse on the form's client area to move the form, and one that enforces minimum and maximum sizes when you resize the form.

Now that you have seen the *prjFormEvents.exe* program's layout, you can use the program to test the message interceptions. To test the message interceptions, perform the following steps:

1. Within the Hooking Messages window, click your mouse on the Keep the Form Square check box. The program will place a check mark in the box.

2. Move the mouse pointer to the window's bottom-right corner. The operating system will change the mouse pointer to a double arrow (the *sizing* pointer).

3. Click your mouse on the corner and hold the button down. If you drag the pointer to the right, you will see that the sizing block for the window keeps a square shape—and whenever you let the mouse button go, the program will display the Hooking Messages window as a square window.

4. Within the Hooking Messages window, click your mouse on the Keep the Form Square check box. The program will remove the check mark from the box.

5. Within the Hooking Messages window, click your mouse on the Move the window by clicking anywhere on its client area check box. The program will place a check mark in the box.

6. Click your mouse anywhere within the Hooking Messages window's client area and hold the button down. If you drag the mouse in any direction, you will see that the program moves the entire form with the mouse movements.

7. Within the Hooking Messages window, click your mouse on the Move the window by clicking anywhere on its client area check box. The program will remove the check mark from the box.

8. Within the Hooking Messages window, click your mouse on the Enforce minimum/maximum size when resizing and maximizing check box. The program will place a check mark in the box.

9. Click your mouse on the Maximize button in the form's top-right corner. The program will center the form on the screen and maximize it. However, as you can see, the program does not fill the screen with the maximized window—it limits the window's size to values set within the program. You can tell, however, that the program did maximize the form because the control box displays the Restore button, as shown in Figure 14.2.

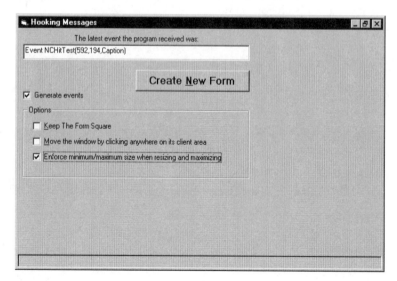

Figure 14.2 *The maximized window does not fill the screen, but it does display the Restore button.*

In addition to intercepting messages individually, the program will intercept and process groups of messages. For example, if you select both the Keep The Form Square and Enforce minimum/maximum size when resizing and maximizing check boxes, the program will force the form to be square and will not let the user size it larger or smaller than the program-specified sizes.

BETTER UNDERSTANDING MESSAGES

As you have learned, the *prjFormEvents* project intercepts Windows messages to perform specific processing on forms. To understand subclassing, it is important to understand Windows messages. The fundamental means of communication that Windows and programs written for Windows use is *messages*. Simply put, each time an operation occurs, Windows responds to that operation or action by sending a message to itself or another program. For example, when a user clicks the mouse within your program's window, Windows reads that mouse click and sends a message to your program that the user has clicked the mouse at a certain location within the program's window. Your program, on receiving that message, will begin its own processing as appropriate for the message. If the message is not relevant to the program (that is, if your program does not require specific processing to respond to the message), your program should ignore the message. To better understand the Windows message model, consider Figure 14.3, which shows the model in a simplified, linear form.

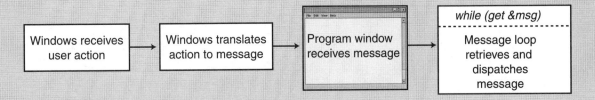

Figure 14.3 A linear diagram of the Windows message model.

As you learned earlier in this chapter, when you write programs in Visual Basic, the Visual Basic run-time interpreter intercepts most messages and converts them into the events your program processes. However, when you write programs that subclass forms and controls, you will actually process those messages yourself.

As you can see, the program must retrieve messages from the operating system and dispatch those messages. When you subclass a form, you must process the messages the program receives from the operating system within a function similar to what C/C++ programmers commonly call the *WndProc* function. In the *prjFormEvents.exe* program, for example, you will declare the *WndProc* function as shown here:

```
Function WndProc(ByVal ndx As Integer, ByVal hWnd As Long, _
    ByVal uMsg As Long, ByVal wParam As Long, _
    ByVal lParam As Long) As Long

  ' Other Code Here

  Select Case uMsg
  '   Other Code Here

  End Select
  ' Other Code Here

  ' call the standard window procedure
  retValue = CallWindowProc(wndInfo(ndx).wndProcAddr, hWnd, uMsg, _
    wParam, lParam)

  ' Other Code Here
End Function
```

As you can see, the *WndProc* function receives five parameters. The *ndx* parameter, which you will learn more about later, corresponds to the form instance. The *uMsg* value corresponds to the long message value the program receives from the operating system. Within the *WndProc* function, you will use a *Select Case* statement to process the *uMsg* value. Depending on the message that you receive from the operating system, you may then refer to the *wParam* or *lParam* values to determine additional information. For example, the *WM_DISPLAYCHANGE* message includes the new color depth (16, 256, or true color) within the *wParam* value, while the *lParam* value includes the new screen height within the value's *high word* and the new screen width within the value's *low word*. As you know, Visual Basic constructs *Long* integers from four consecutive bytes. When programmers refer to high and low words, each word represents a byte pair—the high word represents the first two bytes, and the low word represents the second two bytes. Figure 14.4 shows how you can visualize a *Long* integer as a high word and a low word.

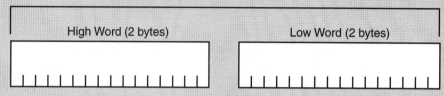

Figure 14.4 *You can divide* **Long** *integer values into high and low words.*

Table 14.1 lists the symbolic constants for some common Windows messages, their hexadecimal values, and their descriptions.

Message Symbolic Constant	Hex Value	Description
WM_ACTIVATEAPP	&H1C	The operating system sends this message to the active window when the operating system is activating (*wParam = True*) or deactivating (*wParam = False*) the application. The *lParam* value will contain the thread identifier of the application that has just lost or received the input focus. This message is useful when you must coordinate two or more applications, as is often the case with ActiveX EXE components.
WM_COMPACTING	&H41	The operating system sends this message to all top-level windows when it is low on memory. You should regard the *WM_COMPACTING* message as a request for your program to free some memory.
WM_DISPLAYCHANGE	&H7E	The operating system sends this message to all top-level windows after the display resolution changes. The *wParam* value holds the new value of bits-per-pixel (color depth), and the *lParam* value's low and high words hold the display area's new width and height, respectively.
WM_GETMINMAXINFO	&H24	The operating system sends this message just before a user operation that affects the window's size. When the operating system sends the message, *lParam* points to a *MINMAXINFO* structure that holds the window's size and position when the user maximizes it, and the window's minimum and maximum dimensions when the user resizes it with the mouse. You can modify these values after you receive them—which lets you set the actual minimum or maximum size for the window.

Table 14.1 *Windows messages the* **prjFormEvents.exe** *program intercepts. (continued on following page)*

Message Symbolic Constant	Hex Value	Description
WM_MOVE	*&H3*	The operating system sends this message to a window or a control that the user has moved. The *lParam* value's low word and high word hold the new *X* and *Y* coordinates, respectively. Windows expresses the *X* and *Y* coordinates as screen coordinates for windows and client coordinates for controls. The *clsSubclassedForm* class this chapter's *prjFormEvents* program includes uses the *WM_MOVE* message to simulate a *Form_Move* event.
WM_MOVING	*&H216*	The operating system sends this message to a window or control while the user is moving the window or control. When the window receives the message, the *wParam* value holds one *WMSZ_* constant, indicating which border or corner the user is moving, such as *WMSZ_BOTTOM* or *WMSZ_TOPRIGHT*. The *lParam* value points to a *RECT* structure with the drag rectangle's screen coordinates. When you modify these values within your programs, your program should return *True* to notify Windows of the changes.
WM_NCHITTEST	*&H84*	Windows sends this message to a window or control whenever a mouse event occurs, and expects the window to return a value that indicates the portion of the window on which the user clicked the mouse. The value is in the form of a constant, such as *HTCAPTION* or *HTCLIENT*. When the operating system sends the message, the *lParam* value's low and high words hold the mouse cursor's current *X* and *Y* coordinates in pixels. If you trap this message, you can disable the standard Minimize, Maximize, and Close buttons or draw your customized form buttons and title bars.
WM_PAINT	*&HF*	The operating system sends this message to a window or control to request that the window or control update its client area (similar to the *Form_Paint* event). There are two reasons to hook (that is, intercept) this message: you may want to receive a repaint notification, even when *AutoRedraw* is *True*, or you may want to optimize the repaint process by redrawing only the area that actually needs the window or control to update it. In the latter case, you must intercept this message before the program fires the regular *Form_Paint*, and then call the *GetUpdateRect* API function to retrieve the coordinates of the smallest area that the window or control actually must refresh.

447

Table 14.1 *Windows messages the **prjFormEvents.exe** program intercepts. (continued on following page)*

Message Symbolic Constant	Hex Value	Description
WM_SETCURSOR	*&H20*	The operating system sends this message to a window when the program performs a mouse action while the cursor is over a window or one of its child windows. When the program receives the message, *wParam* holds the handle of the window under the cursor. The *lParam* value's low word is a "hit-test" code, which you will define within your programs with symbolic constants that begin with *HT* (this is the value *WM_NCHITTEST* returns). A "hit-test" code corresponds to the control currently under the mouse cursor. The *lParam* value's high word is the mouse message. If a parent window processes this message, it should return zero (because there are no controls under the cursor). Hooking this message lets you know at any moment which control is under the cursor, and lets you provide a default action for mouse buttons that is valid for the entire form (such as showing a popup menu wherever the user has clicked the mouse).
WM_SIZING	*&H214*	The operating system sends this message to a window or control when the user (or program code) is resizing the window. When the program receives the message, *wParam* holds one *WMSZ_* constant, indicating which border or corner the window must resize (such as *WMSZ_BOTTOM* or *WMSZ_TOPRIGHT*). The *lParam* value points to a *RECT* structure that holds the drag rectangle's screen coordinates. You can modify these values within your programs, in which case your program should return *True* to notify Windows of the changes.

Table 14.1 *Windows messages the* **prjFormEvents.exe** *program intercepts. (continued from previous page)*

After you process the messages you specifically want to intercept, you must always pass the remaining messages to the operating system's default window procedure. The program's invocation of the *CallWindowProc* procedure ensures that the window procedure receives the message.

CREATING THE PROJECT

Now that you have a better idea how to use the finished *prjFormEvents* project, you can begin to design it. First, you will create the program's form, class module, and modules. After you create the project, you will then design the form's interface (with a frame, several check boxes, and more controls) and write the code for the form, class module, and modules.

CREATING THE FORM

To begin the *prjFormEvents* project and design a standard empty form to contain the controls, perform the following steps:

1. Within Visual Basic, select the File menu New Project option. Visual Basic will open the New Project dialog box.

2. Within the New Project dialog box, double-click your mouse on the Standard EXE icon. Visual Basic will close the New Project dialog box, start a new project, *Project1*, and add a form to it, *Form1*.

3. If Visual Basic is not displaying the *Form1* form within an object window, double-click your mouse on the Form1 icon within the Project Explorer to open the *Form1* form.

4. Select the View menu Properties Window option. Visual Basic will open the Properties Window listing the *Form1* properties.

5. Within the Properties Window, change the *Form1* property values to those Table 14.2 lists.

Object	Property	Set As
Form1	*Caption*	*Hooking Messages*
Form1	*Height*	4650
Form1	*Left*	270
Form1	*Top*	285
Form1	*Width*	5955
Form1	*Name*	*frmHookedForm*

*Table 14.2 The newly named **frmHookedForm** form's properties.*

ADDING THE CLASS MODULE TO THE PROJECT

Within the *prjFormEvents* project, you will use a class module, *clsSubclassedForm,* to derive the subclassed form, handle its incoming messages from the operating system, and raise events to respond to those messages. To create the *clsSubclassedForm* class module, perform the following steps:

1. Within Visual Basic, select the Project menu Add Class Module option. Visual Basic will open the Add Class Module dialog box.

2. Within the Add Class Module dialog box, double-click your mouse on the Class Module option. Visual Basic will open a new Code window, *Class1.*

3. Select the View menu Properties Window option. Visual Basic will open the Properties Window listing the *Class1* properties.

4. Within the Properties Window, change the *Class1* module's name to *clsSubclassedForm.*

ADDING THE MODULES TO THE PROJECT AND SAVING THE PROJECT

After you design the *prjFormEvents* project's blank form and class module, you will create two modules for storing program code. Within the *prjFormEvents* project, the program code that you will place within the first module will declare the program's global variables, constants, and API functions. The program code you will place within the second module will contain the functions and procedures that intercept the Windows messages. To add the modules to the *prjFormEvents* project and then save the project, perform the following steps:

1. Within Visual Basic, select the Project menu Add Module option. Visual Basic will open the Add Module dialog box.

2. Within the Add Module dialog box, select the Module option. Next, click your mouse on the Open button. Visual Basic will open a new Code window, *Module1.*

3. Select the View menu Properties Window option. Visual Basic will open the Properties Window listing the *Module1* properties.

4. Within the Properties Window, change the *Module1* module's name to *mdlHookEvents.*

5. Within Visual Basic, select the Project menu Add Module option. Visual Basic will open the Add Module dialog box.

6. Within the Add Module dialog box, select the Module option. Next, click your mouse on the Open button. Visual Basic will open a new Code window, *Module1.*

7. Select the View menu Properties Window option. Visual Basic will open the Properties Window listing the *Module1* properties.

8. Within the Properties Window, change the *Module1* module's name to *mdlAPIDeclares.*

9. Select the File menu Save Project As option. Visual Basic will open the Save File As dialog box and fill the *File name* field with *clsSubclassedForm*.

10. Within the Save File As dialog box, click your mouse on the Save button. Visual Basic will save the *clsSubclassedForm* class module and fill the *File name* field with *mdlAPIDeclares*.

11. Within the Save File As dialog box, click your mouse on the Save button. Visual Basic will save the *mdlAPIDeclares* module and fill the *File name* field with *mdlHookEvents*.

12. Within the Save File As dialog box, click your mouse on the Save button. Visual Basic will save the *mdlHookEvents* module and fill the *File name* field with *frmHookedForm*.

13. Within the Save File As dialog box, click your mouse on the Save button. Visual Basic will save the *frmHookedForm* form and fill the *File name* field with *Project1*.

14. Within the *File name* field, replace the *Project1* project name with the new *prjFormEvents* project name. Next, click your mouse on the Save button. Visual Basic will save the *prjFormEvents* project and close the Save Project As dialog box.

REVISITING MESSAGES

As you have learned, message handling is at the "heart" of what makes Windows applications work. Both the operating system and the applications that the operating system runs generate messages for every event that occurs in Windows. Messages are fundamentally important to the value of Windows as a multi-tasking operating system. As you have learned in previous chapters, including Chapter 12, "Using ActiveX Automation to Create a Database Server," each task (or program) uses one or more threads within the operating system. The 32-bit Windows platforms (Windows NT and Windows 95) maintain a separate set of messages (a *message queue*) for each thread executing on the operating system. Figure 14.5 shows how Windows processes messages throughout several message queues.

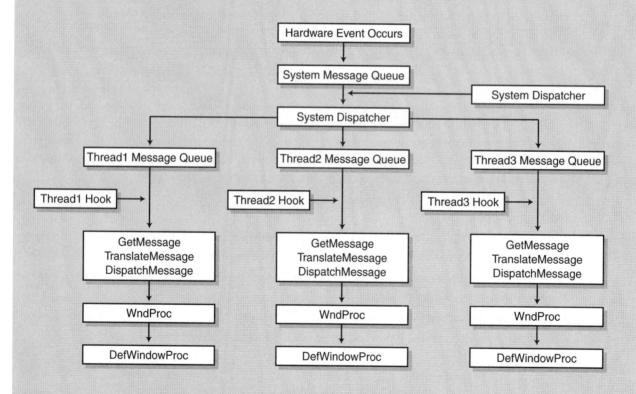

Figure 14.5 *Windows processes messages throughout several message queues.*

Windows generates messages for every hardware event that occurs, such as a key press on the keyboard or a user's mouse click. Windows then passes each message to the appropriate message queue. In other words, if the user clicks the mouse, but not within your application, your application will not know that the user clicked the mouse. Occasionally, the system will generate several copies of a message that it simultaneously places in multiple message queues.

Clearly, the Windows message structure is fundamental to the way that Windows manages multiple tasks in close sequence. You should understand the flow of messages, not just to the program's message queue, but also from the program's message queue into a program's message loop. When Windows accepts a message from the computer's hardware, it determines internally to which message queues it will pass that message. After Windows passes the message into the program's message queue, the program processes each message in the queue in turn. For example, sometimes when you are typing on a word processor you will type faster than the screen can display your keystrokes. However, the program is able to maintain your typing, even while the screen tries to catch up, because Windows is storing each keystroke you make into the program's message queue, as shown in Figure 14.6.

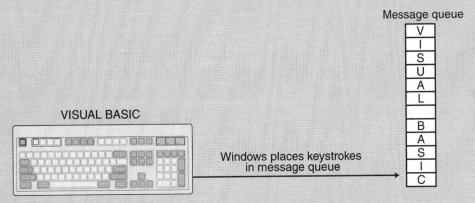

Figure 14.6 *Windows processes keystrokes and places them into the message queue.*

After Windows places the keystrokes within the message queue, the program pulls the messages one message at a time from the message queue, retrieving the earliest message first and continuing in order until it retrieves the last message in the queue. After it retrieves each message, the program then uses the message loop to call the program's message callback function (the window procedure), which processes each of the entries, as shown in Figure 14.7. You will learn more about callback functions in the "Understanding Callback Functions and Visual Basic's *AddressOf* Operator" section later in this chapter.

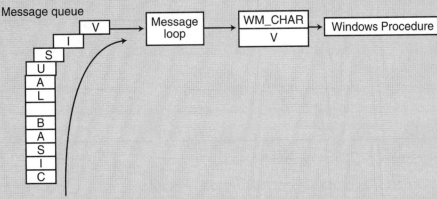

Figure 14.7 *The program's message loop calls its message callback function.*

As you have learned, your programs that support subclassing will then check the values within the messages to determine how to respond to them. If, for example, the command is a keystroke that the user wants to place within the word processor's actual document, the message loop will dispatch the character to the current window and add the character to the word processing document at its current location, as shown in Figure 14.8.

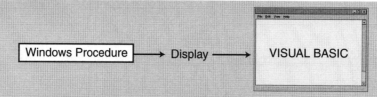

Figure 14.8 *The message callback function inserts each character into the word processing document in sequence.*

DESIGNING THE FRMHOOKEDFORM FORM

As you learned in this chapter's "Using the *prjFormEvents* Project" section, the *prjFormEvents* program will display only a single form. Although the program code to manage the subclassed form is extensive, the form that you will use for the interface is relatively simple. You will add a *Frame* control, four *CheckBox* controls, several *Label* controls, a *CommandButton* control, and a *TextBox* control to the form. After you finish the form's design, you will write the code to subclass the form within the *clsSubclassedForm* class.

452

ADDING A FRAME CONTROL TO THE FRMHOOKEDFORM FORM

Within the *prjFormEvents* project, you will use *CheckBox* controls to try different subclassing activities and you will use a *Frame* control as the container for three of the *CheckBox* controls. To add the *Frame* control to the *frmHookedForm* form, perform the following steps:

1. If Visual Basic is not displaying the *frmHookedForm* form within an object window, double-click your mouse on the *frmHookedForm* form listing within the Project Explorer. Visual Basic will open the *frmHookedForm* form.

2. Within Visual Basic, select the View menu Toolbox option. Visual Basic will open the Toolbox.

3. Within the Toolbox, double-click your mouse on the Frame icon. Visual Basic will draw a *Frame* control, *Frame1*, within the *frmHookedForm* form.

4. Within the *frmHookedForm* form, click your mouse on the *Frame1* control to highlight it. Visual Basic will draw a small frame around the control.

5. Select the View menu Properties Window option. Visual Basic will open the Properties Window and display the *Frame1* control's properties.

6. Within the Properties Window, change the *Frame1* control's properties to the values Table 14.3 lists.

Object	Property	Set As
Frame1	*Caption*	*Options*
Frame1	*Height*	1695
Frame1	*Left*	120
Frame1	*Top*	1800
Frame1	*Width*	5532
Frame1	*Name*	*fraOptions*

Table 14.3 *The newly named* **fraOptions** *control's properties.*

ADDING THE CHECKBOX CONTROLS TO THE FRAOPTIONS FRAME

As you have learned, within the *prjFormEvents* project, the program will display three *CheckBox* controls the user can use to test the form's subclassing. To add three *CheckBox* controls to the *fraOptions* frame, perform the following steps:

1. If Visual Basic is not displaying the *frmHookedForm* form within an object window, double-click your mouse on the *frmHookedForm* form listing within the Project Explorer. Visual Basic will open the *frmHookedForm* form.

2. Within Visual Basic, select the View menu Toolbox option. Visual Basic will open the Toolbox.

3. Within the Toolbox, double-click your mouse on the CheckBox icon. Visual Basic will draw a *CheckBox* control, *Check1*, within the *frmHookedForm* form.

4. Within the *frmHookedForm* object window, click your mouse on the *Check1* control. Visual Basic will draw a small frame around the control.

5. Select the Edit menu Cut option. Visual Basic will remove the control from the display and place it on the Clipboard.

6. Click your mouse on the *fraOptions* frame control. Visual Basic will draw a small frame around the control.

7. Select the Edit menu Paste option. Visual Basic will paste the *Check1* control within the *fraOptions* frame.

8. Repeat Steps 3 through 7 two more times. Visual Basic will paste the *Check2* and *Check3* controls within the *fraOptions* frame.

9. Within the *fraOptions* frame, click your mouse on the *Check1* control. Visual Basic will draw a small frame around the control.

10. Select the View menu Properties Window option. Visual Basic will open the Properties Window and display the *Check1* control's properties.

11. Within the Properties Window, change the highlighted control's properties to the values Table 14.4 lists.

12. Repeat Steps 9, 10, and 11 until you have changed each *CheckBox* control to the values Table 14.4 lists.

453

Object	Property	Set As
Check1	Caption	&Keep The Form Square
Check1	Height	252
Check1	Left	240
Check1	Top	360
Check1	Width	3972
Check1	Name	chkSquare
Check2	Caption	&Move the window by clicking anywhere on its client area
Check2	Height	252
Check2	Left	240
Check2	Top	720
Check2	Width	3972
Check2	Name	chkMove
Check3	Caption	Enforce minimum/maximum size when resizing and maximizing
Check3	Height	252
Check3	Left	240
Check3	Top	1080
Check3	Width	3972
Check3	Name	chkSize

*Table 14.4 The newly named **CheckBox** controls' properties.*

ADDING A CHECKBOX CONTROL TO THE FRMHOOKEDFORM FORM

As you have learned, within the *prjFormEvents* project, the program will display three *CheckBox* controls the user can use to test the form's subclassing. In addition to the three *CheckBox* controls within the *fraOptions* frame, you will also add a single *CheckBox* control to the *frmHookedForm* form. To add the *CheckBox* control to the *frmHookedForm* form, perform the following steps:

1. If Visual Basic is not displaying the *frmHookedForm* form within an object window, double-click your mouse on the *frmHookedForm* form listing within the Project Explorer. Visual Basic will open the *frmHookedForm* form.

2. Within Visual Basic, select the View menu Toolbox option. Visual Basic will open the Toolbox.

3. Within the Toolbox, double-click your mouse on the CheckBox icon. Visual Basic will draw a *CheckBox* control, *Check1*, within the *frmHookedForm* form.

4. Within the *frmHookedForm* object window, click your mouse on the *Check1* control. Visual Basic will draw a small frame around the control.

5. Select the View menu Properties Window option. Visual Basic will open the Properties Window and display the *Check1* control's properties.

6. Within the Properties Window, change the highlighted control's properties to the values Table 14.5 lists.

Object	Property	Set As
Check1	*Caption*	*Generate events*
Check1	*Height*	255
Check1	*Left*	120
Check1	*Top*	1440
Check1	*Value*	1 - *Checked*
Check1	*Width*	2535
Check1	*Name*	*chkEvents*

*Table 14.5 The newly named **chkEvents** control's properties.*

ADDING THE LABEL CONTROLS TO THE FRMHOOKEDFORM FORM

Within the *prjFormEvents* project, you will use two *Label* controls to display information about the form's current processing. You will add a *Label* control to the form above the *TextBox* control as that control's caption and to the form's bottom to display status information. To add the *Label* controls to the *frmHookedForm* form, perform the following steps:

1. If Visual Basic is not displaying the *frmHookedForm* form within an object window, double-click your mouse on the *frmHookedForm* form listing within the Project Explorer. Visual Basic will open the *frmHookedForm* form.

2. Within Visual Basic, select the View menu Toolbox option. Visual Basic will open the Toolbox.

3. Within the Toolbox, double-click your mouse on the Label icon. Visual Basic will draw a *Label* control, *Label1*, within the *frmHookedForm* form.

4. Repeat Step 3 one time. Visual Basic will add the *Label2* control to the form.

5. Within the *frmHookedForm* form, click your mouse on the *Label1* control to highlight it. Visual Basic will draw a small frame around the control.

6. Select the View menu Properties Window option. Visual Basic will open the Properties Window listing the *Label1* control's properties.

7. Within the Properties Window, change the *Label1* properties to the values Table 14.6 lists.

8. Repeat Steps 5, 6, and 7 to change the *Label2* properties to the values Table 14.6 lists.

Object	Property	Set As
Label1	Caption	The latest event the program received was:
Label1	Height	255
Label1	Left	120
Label1	Top	120
Label1	Width	5535
Label1	Name	lblEvents
Label2	BorderStyle	1 - Fixed Single
Label2	Caption	lblStatus
Label2	Height	375
Label2	Left	0
Label2	Top	3840
Label2	Width	5775
Label2	Name	lblStatus

455

*Table 14.6 The newly named **Label** controls' properties.*

ADDING A COMMAND BUTTON TO THE FRMHOOKEDFORM FORM

As you have learned, the user can click the mouse on the Create New Form command button to create new instances of the subclassed form. To add a *CommandButton* control to the *frmHookedForm* form, perform the following steps:

1. If Visual Basic is not displaying the *frmHookedForm* form within an object window, double-click your mouse on the *frmHookedForm* form listing within the Project Explorer. Visual Basic will open the *frmHookedForm* form.

2. Within Visual Basic, select the View menu Toolbox option. Visual Basic will open the Toolbox.

3. Within the Toolbox, double-click your mouse on the CommandButton icon. Visual Basic will draw a *CommandButton* control, *Command1*, within the *frmHookedForm* form.

4. Within the *frmHookedForm* object window, click your mouse on the *Command1* control to highlight it. Visual Basic will draw a small frame around the control.

5. Select the View menu Properties Window option. Visual Basic will open the Properties Window listing the *Command1* control's properties.

6. Within the Properties Window, change the *Command1* control's properties to the values Table 14.7 lists.

Object	Property	Set As
Command1	Caption	Create&New Form
Command1	Font	MS San Serif, Bold, 12 Point
Command1	Height	495
Command1	Left	2880
Command1	Top	960
Command1	Width	2775
Command1	Name	cmdNewForm

*Table 14.7 The newly named **cmdNewForm** control's properties.*

ADDING THE TEXTBOX CONTROL TO THE FRMHOOKEDFORM FORM

As you have learned, the *frmHookedForm* form will display information within a *TextBox* control about events the program is currently receiving from the operating system. To add the *TextBox* control to the *frmHookedForm* form, perform the following steps:

1. If Visual Basic is not displaying the *frmHookedForm* form within an object window, double-click your mouse on the *frmHookedForm* form listing within the Project Explorer. Visual Basic will open the *frmHookedForm* form.

2. Within Visual Basic, select the View menu Toolbox option. Visual Basic will open the Toolbox.

3. Within the Toolbox, double-click your mouse on the TextBox icon. Visual Basic will draw a *TextBox* control, *Text1*, within the *frmHookedForm* form.

4. Within the *frmHookedForm* window, click your mouse on the *Text1* control to highlight it. Visual Basic will draw a small frame around the control.

5. Select the View menu Properties Window option. Visual Basic will open the Properties Window listing the *Text1* control's properties.

6. Within the Properties Window, change the *Text1* control's properties to the values Table 14.8 lists.

Object	Property	Set As
Text1	Height	372
Text1	Left	120
Text1	Text	txtDisplayEvent
Text1	Top	360
Text1	Width	5532
Text1	Name	txtDisplayEvent

*Table 14.8 The newly named **txtDisplayEvent** control's properties.*

After you finish formatting the controls, the *frmHookedForm* will look similar to Figure 14.9.

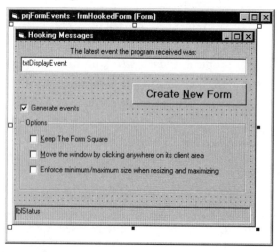

*Figure 14.9 The **frmHookedForm** form after you finish its design.*

UNDERSTANDING CALLBACK FUNCTIONS AND VISUAL BASIC'S ADDRESSOF OPERATOR

One of Visual Basic's biggest limitations in versions before 5.0 was its inability to support *callback functions*. Normally, your programs call Windows API functions. A callback function is a function within your program that you define so that the Windows API function can call your custom function directly. In other words, your program will call an API function, which, in turn, will "call back" your program's function. To call back a function, Windows must know the function's address—in other words, your program must specify the function within your program that the API function will call back. The callback function is critical to Windows processing. To understand how the callback function fits into a function call, consider the logical diagram shown in Figure 14.10.

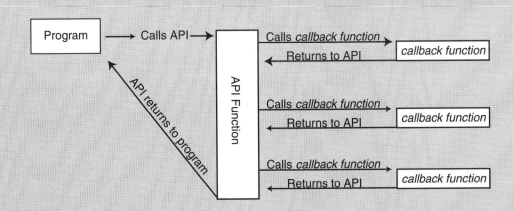

Figure 14.10 *The logical model of a callback function's processing.*

Your programs can use callback functions in many ways; however, as previously detailed, you will most frequently use callback functions together with API calls that generate an unknown number of return values. You will often encounter functions that perform callback activities whose names begin with *Enum* (for enumerate), including *EnumFontFamilies*, *EnumWindows*, and *EnumProps*.

When you work within Visual Basic programs, you must use the *AddressOf* operator to pass function addresses. The *AddressOf* operator is a unary operator that causes the program to pass the address of the procedure the operator precedes to an API procedure that expects a function pointer at that position in the argument list. You will use the *AddressOf* operator within your programs as shown in the following prototype:

```
AddressOf procedurename
```

The required *procedurename* placeholder specifies the procedure whose address the program is to pass. It must represent a procedure in a standard module in the project from which the program makes the call. When a procedure name appears in an argument list, the program usually evaluates the procedure and passes the procedure's return value address. The *AddressOf* operator lets your programs pass the procedure's address to a Windows API function, rather than passing the procedure's return value. The API function can then use the address to call the Visual Basic procedure, which, as you have learned, is known as a callback. The *AddressOf* operator appears only in the call to the API function. However, in the *Declare* statement that describes the API function to which the program passes the pointer, you must declare *As Any* as the procedure address argument's type.

Although you can use the *AddressOf* operator to pass pointers to custom procedures and functions among functions and procedures in your programs, you cannot call a function through such a pointer from within your Visual Basic programs. The limitation on pointers means, for example, that a class you write in Visual Basic cannot make a callback to its controller using a procedure pointer. When you use the *AddressOf* operator to pass a procedure pointer among functions and procedures within Visual Basic, you must type *As Long* as the called procedure's parameter.

Note: *Using the **AddressOf** operator may cause unpredictable results if you do not completely understand the concept of callback functions. You must understand how the Visual Basic procedure's portion of the callback works, and also the Dynamic-Link Library's (DLL) code into which you are passing your function address. Debugging callback function interactions is difficult because the Dynamic-Link Library runs in the same process as the development environment. In some cases, systematic debugging may not be possible.*

Because a callback's caller is not within your program, it is important that your program does not transmit an error in the callback procedure back to the caller. You can place the *On Error Resume Next* statement at the callback procedure's beginning to prevent your program from transmitting the error.

WRITING THE CODE FOR THE prjFORMEVENTS PROJECT

As you have learned, the *prjFormEvents* project uses subclassing to intercept messages from the Windows operating system. In addition to the form that you have designed for the project, the project uses two modules, a class module (which contains the subclassing for the form), and program code for the form itself. In the following sections, you will write the program code for the project. First, you will write the API declarations (functions, types, and constants). Next, you will write the code to process messages the program receives from the operating system and the code to perform the actual subclassing. Finally, you will write the code within the *frmHookedForm* form itself.

WRITING THE CODE FOR THE mdlAPIDECLARES MODULE

As with other programs that you have written in this book, the *prjFormEvents* project declares its API functions, constants, and types within a module the program uses specifically for that purpose. The declarations are long enough that it is worthwhile to consider them in sections. The first program code that you will write within the *mdlAPIDeclares* module's General–Declarations section defines the program's custom types. The following code implements the type definitions:

458

```
Type POINTAPI
  X As Long
  Y As Long
End Type

Type RECT
  Left As Long
  Top As Long
  Right As Long
  Bottom As Long
End Type

Type MINMAXINFO
  ptReserved As POINTAPI
  ptMaxSize As POINTAPI
  ptMaxPosition As POINTAPI
  ptMinTrackSize As POINTAPI
  ptMaxTrackSize As POINTAPI
End Type
```

As you learned in Chapter 3, "Writing a Screen Saver in Visual Basic," the *POINTAPI* type contains a long *X* and a long *Y* value. Together, the values correspond to a specific point's coordinates on the display. Within the *prjFormEvents* program, you will use the *POINTAPI* type within the *MINMAXINFO* type, which the program uses to control the maximized form's appearance when the user selects the Enforce minimize/maximum size when resizing and maximizing check box. As you also learned in Chapter 3, the *RECT* type contains four values that correspond to a rectangle's four corners on the screen. Within the *prjFormEvents* program, you will use the *RECT* type with the *GetUpdateRect* API function.

The *MINMAXINFO* type is a type the program uses to maintain information about a maximized window's system-defined size and its program-defined size (different variable instances). As you can see, the *MINMAXINFO* type consists of five *POINTAPI* members and each member contains size information.

DECLARING THE prjFORMEVENTS PROGRAM'S CONSTANTS

The *prjFormEvents* program uses more constants than any other program you have written in this book. Because the program intercepts Windows messages, the program must respond to them. However, as you have learned, a Windows message is merely a numeric value. Working directly with numeric values is much more confusing than working with symbolic constants. Therefore, the program defines symbolic constants for many messages Windows may send to the program. Moreover, because the *mdlAPIDeclares* module is a module that you can reuse in your own programs, the constant declarations include many constants the *prjFormEvents* program itself does not use. The following code implements the *mdlAPIDeclares* module's constant declarations that you will use within the *prjFormEvents* program (the actual *mdlAPIDeclares* module that the companion CD-ROM that accompanies this book contains includes the remaining constant declarations that you will often use):

```
Public Const WM_ACTIVATEAPP = &H1C
Public Const WM_COMPACTING = &H41
Public Const WM_DISPLAYCHANGE = &H7E
Public Const WM_GETMINMAXINFO = &H24
Public Const WM_MOVE = &H3
Public Const WM_MOVING = &H216
Public Const WM_NCHITTEST = &H84
Public Const WM_PAINT = &HF
Public Const WM_SETCURSOR = &H20
Public Const WM_SIZING = &H214

' these are the values that can be returned by a WM_NCHITTEST message
Public Const HTBORDER = 18
Public Const HTBOTTOM = 15
Public Const HTBOTTOMLEFT = 16
Public Const HTBOTTOMRIGHT = 17
Public Const HTCAPTION = 2
Public Const HTCLIENT = 1
Public Const HTCLOSE = 20
Public Const HTERROR = (-2)
Public Const HTGROWBOX = 4
Public Const HTHELP = 21
Public Const HTHSCROLL = 6
Public Const HTLEFT = 10
Public Const HTMAXBUTTON = 9
Public Const HTMENU = 5
Public Const HTMINBUTTON = 8
Public Const HTNOWHERE = 0
Public Const HTOBJECT = 19
Public Const HTRIGHT = 11
Public Const HTSYSMENU = 3
Public Const HTTOP = 12
Public Const HTTOPLEFT = 13
Public Const HTTOPRIGHT = 14
Public Const HTVSCROLL = 7
```

When the program receives a *WM_NCHITTEST* message, it must check the *lParam* value against the constants that begin with *HT*. When the mouse crosses over the client area of a window, for example, the operating system will pass the *HTCLIENT* value within the *lParam* parameter. The program code must then respond to the *HTCLIENT* constant and perform the appropriate processing.

WRITING THE CODE FOR THE API FUNCTION DECLARATIONS

Despite all the processing the *prjFormEvents* program performs, and all the low-level interactions it has with the operating system, the program declares only two API functions, *CopyMemory* and *GetUpdateRect*, within the *mdlAPIDeclares* module. (The program declares the *SetWindowLong* and *CallWindowProc* API functions elsewhere.) The following code implements the API function declarations:

```
Declare Sub CopyMemory Lib "kernel32" Alias "RtlMoveMemory" _
    (dest As Any, source As Any, ByVal numBytes As Long)
Declare Function GetUpdateRect Lib "user32" (ByVal hWnd As Long, _
    lpRect As RECT, ByVal bErase As Long) As Long
```

The *CopyMemory* function copies the values in memory from any memory location to any other memory location. You will specify the number of bytes for the function to copy within the *numBytes* parameter. The *GetUpdateRect* API function retrieves the smallest rectangle that completely contains the current update region of the window you specify within the *hWnd* parameter. In other words, the function returns a *RECT* value whose four corners correspond to the display area the operating system must update. For example, if you move a window partially over another, and then move it back, the operating system must update only the section of the second window that the first window covered.

WRITING THE CODE FOR THE MDLHOOKEVENTS MODULE

As you have learned, the program code for the *prjFormEvents* project uses custom functions to intercept messages from the operating system and process those messages. In the previous sections, you declared constants to represent messages and API functions to perform certain processing for you. Within the *mdlHookEvents* module, you will write the actual functions to handle the incoming messages, as well as the procedures to subclass and to remove the subclass from a given form instance. The *mdlHookEvents* module contains a single custom type, two constants, two API function declarations, and an array declaration. The following code implements the *mdlHookEvents* module's General–Declarations section:

```
Private Type TWndInfo
   hWnd As Long                  ' handle of subclassed window - zero if none
   wndProcAddr As Long           ' address of original window procedure
   localProcAddr As Long         ' address of custom window procedure
   obj_ptr As Long               ' pointer to clsSubclassedForm object to notify
End Type

Const GWL_WNDPROC = -4
Const MAX_WNDPROC = 10

Declare Function CallWindowProc Lib "user32" Alias "CallWindowProcA" _
    (ByVal lpPrevWndFunc As Long, ByVal hWnd As Long, ByVal Msg As Long, _
    ByVal wParam As Long, ByVal lParam As Long) As Long
Declare Function SetWindowLong Lib "user32" Alias _
    "SetWindowLongA" (ByVal hWnd As Long, ByVal nIndex As Long, _
    ByVal dwNewLong As Long) As Long

Dim wndInfo(1 To MAX_WNDPROC) As TWndInfo
```

The first segment of the General–Declarations section declares the type *TWndInfo*, which contains information about subclassed windows. The *hWnd* member corresponds to the subclassed window's handle. If the program has not subclassed a window, *hWnd's* value is zero. The *wndProcAddr* member contains the address of the subclassed window's original window procedure (which Visual Basic creates), and the *localProcAddr* member contains the custom window procedure's address that you define for the subclassed window within the program. The *obj_ptr* member is a pointer to the *clsSubclassedForm* object the window procedure should notify when the procedure receives messages.

The *GWL_WNDPROC* constant is a constant your programs will pass to the *SetWindowLong* function when you subclass forms. The *MAX_WNDPROC* function specifies the maximum number of subclassed forms the user can open at a given time. As you will learn in later sections, each subclassed form requires its own window procedure, so ten is a reasonable limit on the number of subclassed forms the user can create.

The *CallWindowProc* function calls the window's default window procedure (rather than the custom window procedure you will create). The *SetWindowLong* API function lets you change information about a window that the operating system maintains with the window. In the *prjFormEvents* project, you will use *SetWindowLong* to enable and disable subclassing.

Finally, the *wndInfo* array maintains ten instances of the *TWndInfo* type and each instance may correspond to a subclassed window (or may, depending on the program's current execution, not correspond to anything). The elements in the array will each hold a different *WndProc* function's address.

WRITING THE HOOKWINDOW FUNCTION

When you run the *prjFormEvents* program, the program code will begin its execution within the *frmHookedForm* form's *Form_Load* event, which you will write later in this chapter. After it performs some simple processing, the *frmHookedForm* form calls the *HookWindow* function, which subclasses the new window. The following code implements the *HookWindow* function:

```
Public Function HookWindow(obj As clsSubclassedForm, _
    ByVal hWnd As Long) As Integer
  Dim Index As Integer

  On Error Resume Next
  If wndInfo(1).localProcAddr = 0 Then InitLocalData
  Index = 1
  Do
    If wndInfo(Index).hWnd = 0 Then Exit Do
    Index = Index + 1
  Loop Until Index > MAX_WNDPROC
  If Index > MAX_WNDPROC Then
    HookWindow = 0
    Exit Function
  End If
  With wndInfo(Index)
    .obj_ptr = ObjPtr(obj)
    .hWnd = hWnd
    .wndProcAddr = SetWindowLong(hWnd, GWL_WNDPROC, .localProcAddr)
  End With
  HookWindow = Index
End Function
```

The *HookWindow* function accepts a *clsSubclassedForm* object and a window handle. The function also declares a local variable (*Index*) that it uses to hold the new window's index (the window's reference within the *wndInfo* array) until the function's completion, and then the function returns the *Index* value as its value. Within the function, the first line of program code checks to determine whether or not the program has already initialized the *wndInfo* array. If the program has not initialized the array, the code within the *HookWindow* function calls the *InitLocalData* procedure to initialize the array's members. You will learn more about the *InitLocalData* procedure in the next section.

After it ensures the program has initialized the *wndInfo* array, the program code searches the array for the first member that the program has not already associated with a window. If the program code does not find an available member, the *HookWindow* function returns 0 as the function's value—which lets the program code that called the function know that there are no available slots for additional subclassing. On the other hand, if the program code within the *HookWindow* function finds an available slot for subclassing, it assigns the window handle, a pointer to the *clsSubclassedForm* object, and the new *WndProc* address to the member. The function then returns the index value to the calling procedure.

WRITING THE CODE FOR THE INITLOCALDATA PROCEDURE AND THE PROCADDR FUNCTION

As you learned in the previous section, the *prjFormEvents* project uses the *InitLocalData* procedure to initialize the members within the *wndInfo* array. The *InitLocalData* procedure sets each member's *localProcAddr* value equal to the address of the member's corresponding window procedure. The following code implements the *InitLocalData* procedure:

```
Private Sub InitLocalData()
  On Error Resume Next
  wndInfo(1).localProcAddr = ProcAddr(AddressOf WndProc1)
  wndInfo(2).localProcAddr = ProcAddr(AddressOf WndProc2)
  wndInfo(3).localProcAddr = ProcAddr(AddressOf WndProc3)
  wndInfo(4).localProcAddr = ProcAddr(AddressOf WndProc4)
  wndInfo(5).localProcAddr = ProcAddr(AddressOf WndProc5)
```

```
      wndInfo(6).localProcAddr = ProcAddr(AddressOf WndProc6)
      wndInfo(7).localProcAddr = ProcAddr(AddressOf WndProc7)
      wndInfo(8).localProcAddr = ProcAddr(AddressOf WndProc8)
      wndInfo(9).localProcAddr = ProcAddr(AddressOf WndProc9)
      wndInfo(10).localProcAddr = ProcAddr(AddressOf WndProc10)
   End Sub
```

As you learned earlier in this chapter, the *AddressOf* operator evaluates the argument it receives (a function name) and returns the function's address. However, to assign the *AddressOf* operator's return value to a variable, you must actually pass the value into a function and return the address as the function's result. The *prjFormEvents* project uses the *ProcAddr* function to convert function addresses into values that a variable can maintain. The following code implements the *ProcAddr* function:

```
   Public Function ProcAddr(ByVal address As Long) As Long
      ProcAddr = address
   End Function
```

As you can see, the routine returns the incoming *address* value as its own *Long* value. When the *InitLocalData* function completes its processing, the elements within the *wndInfo* array will contain the addresses of the ten custom window procedures the *mdlHookEvents* module declares.

WRITING THE CODE FOR THE TEN CUSTOM WINDOW FUNCTIONS

As you have learned, the program code for the *prjFormEvents* project uses a different custom function for each of the ten subclassed forms the user may create. In fact, the program code for each custom function simply calls the custom *WndProc* function that you will create in the next section and passes the index for the current window (as the *HookWindow* function sets) to the *WndProc* function. You could, instead, place a separate *WndProc* function in each instance of the form—but doing so would make it more difficult to enforce the limitation on subclassed forms. The following code implements the first custom window function:

```
   Public Function WndProc1(ByVal hWnd As Long, ByVal uMsg As Long, _
      ByVal wParam As Long, ByVal lParam As Long) As Long
      WndProc1 = WndProc(1, hWnd, uMsg, wParam, lParam)
   End Function
```

Each of the ten custom functions accepts a window handle, a message, a *wParam* value, and an *lParam* value. The custom function then passes those values, together with the index for the window, to the *WndProc* function (which corresponds to the custom function's number). The following section implements and explains the *WndProc* function.

WRITING THE CODE FOR THE WNDPROC FUNCTION

As you learned in the previous section, each of the ten custom window functions calls the *WndProc* function. The only difference between the procedures, in fact, is that each procedure passes a different index value to the function. The *WndProc* function is, mostly, a generic window procedure that processes program-intercepted messages. The *WndProc* function should look very familiar to you if you have experience with programming C/C++ in Windows. The only difference between the *WndProc* function in the *prjFormEvents* project and a generic *WndProc* function is that the *WndProc* function within the *mdlHookEvents* module includes a single parameter for an index to the form instance transmitting the message. The following code implements the *WndProc* function:

```
   Public Function WndProc(ByVal ndx As Integer, ByVal hWnd As Long, _
      ByVal uMsg As Long, ByVal wParam As Long, ByVal lParam As Long) As Long
      Dim preProcess As Boolean, Cancel As Boolean
      Dim retValue As Long
      Dim obj As clsSubclassedForm

      On Error Resume Next
      If wndInfo(ndx).hWnd <> hWnd Then
         UnhookWindow ndx
```

```
            Exit Function
      End If
      Select Case uMsg
        Case WM_ACTIVATEAPP, WM_MOVE, WM_MOVING, WM_SIZING, _
            WM_GETMINMAXINFO, WM_NCHITTEST, WM_SETCURSOR, _
            WM_COMPACTING, WM_DISPLAYCHANGE
        Case WM_PAINT
          preProcess = True
        Case Else
          WndProc = CallWindowProc(wndInfo(ndx).wndProcAddr, hWnd, uMsg, _
              wParam, lParam)
          Exit Function
      End Select
      CopyMemory obj, wndInfo(ndx).obj_ptr, 4
      If obj.hWnd <> hWnd Then
        WndProc = CallWindowProc(wndInfo(ndx).wndProcAddr, hWnd, uMsg, _
              wParam, lParam)
        UnhookWindow ndx
        GoTo WndProc_Exit
      End If
      If preProcess Then
        WndProc = obj.BeforeMessage(hWnd, uMsg, wParam, lParam, Cancel)
        If Cancel Then GoTo WndProc_Exit
      End If
      retValue = CallWindowProc(wndInfo(ndx).wndProcAddr, hWnd, uMsg, _
            wParam, lParam)
      obj.AfterMessage hWnd, uMsg, wParam, lParam, retValue
      WndProc = retValue
    WndProc_Exit:
      CopyMemory obj, 0&, 4
    End Function
```

After it declares local variables, the *WndProc* function checks the window handle it received within the *hWnd* parameter against the *wndInfo(ndx)* member's *hWnd* member. If the two values are the same, the program continues its processing. If the two values are not the same, the operating system somehow destroyed the window without the program calling the *UnhookWindow* procedure. The program code within the *WndProc* function therefore calls the *UnhookWindow* procedure and exits.

After it checks the window handle, the program code checks the *uMsg* parameter's value. If the value does not correspond to one of the messages the program intercepts, the program passes on the information to the window's default message-handling procedure and exits the *WndProc* function. If, on the other hand, the program intercepts and processes the message, the program code will continue with the *WndProc* function's execution. The messages the program intercepts are: *WM_ACTIVATEAPP, WM_MOVE, WM_MOVING, WM_SIZING, WM_GETMINMAXINFO, WM_NCHITTEST, WM_SETCURSOR, WM_COMPACTING, WM_DISPLAYCHANGE,* and *WM_PAINT.*

The program code within the *WndProc* function next uses the *CopyMemory* API function to copy a reference to the current window into the *obj* variable. The program does this because, as you know, Visual Basic does not let you process points. The program use of the *CopyMemory* function lets the program simulate pointer management, and deal with the window's reference value, rather than the window directly. If the program successfully copies the reference, it will continue processing the messages. On the other hand, if the program is not successful, it will call the standard window procedure for the window, *unhook* the window, and call the *WndProc_Exit* label to exit the function. The program unhooks the window after a bad reference copy, because the bad copy generally indicates that the value the *HookWindow* function stored in memory (which should point to the window) is corrupt for some reason, generally because of an operating system error.

After determining it has successfully copied a reference to the window into the *obj* variable, the program code checks to determine whether the Windows message was a *WM_PAINT* message. If it was a *WM_PAINT* message, the program invokes the *clsSubclassedForm's BeforeMessage* method, which handles the message internally.

In any case, the program code next sends the subclassed message to the default window procedure. After it calls the default window procedure, the program code invokes the *obj* object's *AfterMessage* method, which will, in turn, raise events to the form itself. The program code then instructs the function to return the *retValue* parameter from the default window procedure call.

All the processing the *WndProc* function performs is to accomplish the goal of raising events into the object instance. Within your own programs, you might add additional event processing to the *BeforeMessage* method, and you will almost certainly add additional processing to the *AfterMessage* method. Remember, the program code must not only intercept the message, but then do something with the message that is meaningful within your Visual Basic program. Generally, you will raise events from a class module as your meaningful response to messages.

At the *WndProc* function's end, the program code again uses the *CopyMemory* API function. However, the program code uses the second *CopyMemory* occurrence to copy the 4 bytes of memory starting at 0 over the temporary object—without setting it to the *Nothing* keyword, as you might if you had initialized the object normally. However, because you used the *CopyMemory* function to initialize the object originally, trying to set the *obj* object to *Nothing* will cause a General Protection Fault (GPF), because the operating system's reference counter to the object is incorrect.

464

WRITING THE CODE FOR THE UNHOOKWINDOW PROCEDURE

As you learned in Chapter 3, "Writing a Screen Saver in Visual Basic," when you finish with a window that you have subclassed, you must, in turn, end the window's subclassing. Within the *prjFormEvents* program, you must also free the slot in the *wndInfo* array (whose sole purpose is to maintain window procedure addresses for subclassed forms) the subclassed form was using. The following code implements the *UnhookWindow* procedure, which performs both actions:

```
Public Sub UnhookWindow(Index As Integer)
  With wndInfo(Index)
    SetWindowLong .hWnd, GWL_WNDPROC, .wndProcAddr
    .hWnd = 0
    .wndProcAddr = 0
    .obj_ptr = 0
  End With
End Sub
```

The call to *SetWindowLong* turns off the subclassing. The next three statements within the procedure reset the other values (except the *WndProc* procedure's address for that element) to 0, which lets the program know the array element is empty and available for the program's use.

UNDERSTANDING THE WITHEVENTS PROPERTY IN A DIMENSION STATEMENT

As you learned in the "Writing the Code for the *WndProc* Function" section, the *clsSubclassedForm* class will raise its own, custom events. However, to use the custom events the *clsSubclassedForm* class raises, you must declare an instance of the *clsSubclassedForm* class and modify the declaration with the *WithEvents* keyword. You will implement the class variable's declaration within the *frmHookedForm* form as shown here:

```
Private WithEvents frmSubclassed As clsSubclassedForm
```

When you dimension a variable with the *WithEvents* keyword, you alert Visual Basic that the variable is an *Object* variable the program will use to respond to events the class, of which the variable is a type, raises. You will use the *WithEvents* keyword only when you declare variables that correspond to objects that are either ActiveX designers (custom controls you design in Visual Basic) or class modules. You can use *WithEvents* to declare as many individual variables as you like, but you cannot use *WithEvents* to create arrays. You cannot use the *New* keyword with the *WithEvents* keyword. When you use *WithEvents* to declare a variable, you must also have declared *Events* within the class module of which the variable represents an object instance.

Writing the Program Code for the *clsSubclassedForm* Class

As you have learned, you will write the code that performs the subclassing activities that you will define for the *frmHookedForm* form within the *clsSubclassedForm* class. The *clsSubclassedForm* class differs from the classes that you have created in many previous chapters because it raises events in addition to exposing properties and methods. The *prjWinsockDLL* project that you will create in Chapter 21, "Using Windows Sockets for Two-Way Internet Communications," and the asynchronous DCOM examples that you will create in Chapter 22, "Writing DCOM Objects for Networks," will both use events.

The *clsSubclassedForm* class raises twelve events. You must define each event and the parameters it exposes within the class's General–Declarations section. The following code implements the event declarations for the *clsSubclassedForm* class:

```
Event ActivateApp()
Event DeactivateApp()
Event Move()
Event GetMinMaxInfo(MaxSizeX As Long, MaxSizeY As Long, MaxPosX As Long, _
    MaxPosY As Long, MinTrackSizeX As Long, MinTrackSizeY As Long, _
    MaxTrackSizeX As Long, MaxTrackSizeY As Long)
Event Paint(X1 As Single, Y1 As Single, X2 As Single, Y2 As Single)
Event NCHitTest(ByVal X As Integer, ByVal Y As Integer, hitCode As Long)
Event MouseEnter(ByVal ctrl As Control)
Event MouseExit(ByVal ctrl As Control)
Event CompactingMemory()
Event DisplayChanged(ByVal newWidth As Integer, _
    ByVal newHeight As Integer, ByVal numberOfColors As Long)
Event Resizing(X1 As Long, Y1 As Long, X2 As Long, Y2 As Long, _
    ByVal draggedBorder As Integer)
Event Moving(X1 As Long, Y1 As Long, X2 As Long, Y2 As Long, _
    ByVal draggedBorder As Integer)
```

As you can see, the class defines some events the class raises (into each instance of the class) that do not pass parameters and some events that do pass parameters. For example, the *ActivateApp* event does not pass parameters. The *MouseEnter* event, however, passes a *Control* object as its parameter. You will learn more about the events the *clsSubclassedForm* class raises when you write the code within the *frmHookedForm* form that responds to the events. In addition to the events the *clsSubclassedForm* class raises, the class also defines four local variables that it uses within its processing. The following code implements the variable definitions:

```
Private wndInfoIndex As Integer
Private m_Form As Form
Private m_hWnd As Long
Private ctrlUnderCursor As Control
```

The *wndInfoIndex* value corresponds to the *Index* value that you used within the *mdlHookEvents* module to determine to which window the operating system sent a given message. The *m_Form* and *m_hWnd* variables are local variables that correspond to properties the class exposes with *Property Get* and *Property Set* procedures. The *ctrlUnderCursor* variable holds a reference to a control under the mouse pointer on the form.

Writing the Property Get Procedures

The *clsSubclassedForm* class exposes two properties that the program can access from within the class with the dot operator (.). The class lets the program retrieve both properties, but lets it set only one of them, as you will learn in the following section. The following code implements the *Property Get* procedures for the *clsSubclassedForm* class:

```
Property Get hWnd() As Long
   hWnd = m_hWnd
End Property
```

```
Property Get HookedForm() As Form
   Set HookedForm = m_Form
End Property
```

The *hWnd* property returns the handle of the hooked (that is, subclassed) window the class references. Similarly, the *HookedForm* property returns a *Form* object—a *Form*-based reference to the hooked window.

WRITING THE PROPERTY SET PROCEDURE

As you have learned in previous chapters, the operating system assigns a window's handle to the window when it creates the window—which makes the *hWnd* property (because it is a window handle) read-only. However, if the program does subclass a form, it does set the *HookedForm* property. The following code implements the *Property Set* procedure for the *HookedForm* property:

```
Property Set HookedForm(new_Form As Form)
   If new_Form Is Nothing Then
      If m_hWnd = 0 Then Exit Property
   Else
      If new_Form.hWnd = m_hWnd Then Exit Property
   End If
   If m_hWnd Then
      UnhookWindow wndInfoIndex
      wndInfoIndex = 0
   End If
   Set m_Form = new_Form
   If new_Form Is Nothing Then
      m_hWnd = 0
      Exit Property
   End If
   m_hWnd = new_Form.hWnd
   wndInfoIndex = HookWindow(Me, m_hWnd)
   If wndInfoIndex = 0 Then Err.Raise 999, _
       "clsSubclassedForm class", "Too many subclassed windows"
End Property
```

The *HookedForm Property Set* procedure accepts as its parameter the form the program should subclass. If the program does not pass in a new form, the program exits the procedure. If, on the other hand, the program passes in a form name that the program has already subclassed, the program will use the *UnhookWindow* procedure to remove the subclassing from that form. If the form is valid and the program has not already subclassed it, the program code sets the *m_Form* private variable equal to the form the calling procedure passes into the *Property Set* procedure. The program code checks to ensure the objects are valid; if they are not valid, the program code stops the subclassing and exits without subclassing the form. If the objects are valid, the program code assigns the *hWnd* handle for the form the program is about to subclass to the *m_hWnd* member variable. The program code then calls the *HookWindow* function, which you wrote previously. As you have learned, the *HookWindow* function will subclass the window it receives as its second parameter.

If there is an error, the program code uses the *Err.Raise* method to raise the error outside the class module and into the form itself. After the program successfully sets the *HookedForm* property and exits the *Property Let* procedure, the program will have fully subclassed the form it originally passed into the class as a parameter.

WRITING THE CLASS_TERMINATE EVENT

As you have learned in previous chapters, whenever a program terminates an object instance, the class will invoke its *Class_Terminate* event. Within the *clsSubclassedForm* class, the *Class_Terminate* event will unhook the hooked window whenever the program destroys the object. The following code implements the *Class_Terminate* event:

```
Private Sub Class_Terminate()
   If wndInfoIndex Then UnhookWindow wndInfoIndex
End Sub
```

Understanding the Friend Keyword

As you learned in Chapter 1, "Introduction to Visual Basic," the *Friend* keyword is an optional keyword that indicates that the procedure the keyword modifies is visible throughout the project, but not visible to a controller of a class's object instance. Declaring a procedure as a *Friend* lets the project in which you design the class access the procedure, but does not let other projects access the procedure. In other words, the *Friend* keyword modifies a procedure's definition in a class module to make the procedure callable from modules that are outside the class, but part of the project within which you defined the class.

Public procedures in a class can be called from anywhere, even from controllers of the class's instances. Declaring a procedure a *Private* procedure prevents the object's controllers from calling the procedure, but also prevents code within the project that defines the class itself from calling the procedure. The *Friend* keyword makes the procedure visible throughout the project, but not to a controller of an object's instance. The *Friend* keyword can appear only in class modules and can modify only procedure names, not variables or types. Procedures in a class can access the *Friend* procedures of all other classes in a project. *Friend* procedures do not appear in the type library of their class. You cannot late bind a *Friend* procedure.

467

Writing the BeforeMessage Method Function

As you learned in previous sections, the program code within the *WndProc* function may call the *BeforeMessage* method before the window's message procedure actually processes the message the operating system sends to the window's window procedure. Within your programs, you will perform processing on the values Windows passes with a message only when doing so will let you modify the message's default processing. The only message that the *clsSubclassedForm* class processes before the program sends the message is the *WM_PAINT* message. The following code implements the *BeforeMessage* method, which processes the *WM_PAINT* message before the operating system does:

```
Friend Function BeforeMessage(ByVal hWnd As Long, ByVal uMsg As Long, _
    ByVal wParam As Long, ByVal lParam As Long, Cancel As Boolean) As Long
  Select Case uMsg
    Case WM_PAINT
      ' Windows is requesting the window repaint itself
      Dim lp As RECT

      GetUpdateRect m_hWnd, lp, False
      RaiseEvent Paint(m_Form.ScaleX(lp.Left, vbPixels), _
          m_Form.ScaleY(lp.Top, vbPixels), _
          m_Form.ScaleX(lp.Right, vbPixels), _
          m_Form.ScaleY(lp.Bottom, vbPixels))
  End Select
End Function
```

As you can see, the *BeforeMessage* method double-checks to ensure the message it received is the *WM_PAINT* message. If the message is *WM_PAINT*, the operating system is requesting that the window repaint itself. The program code within the *Select Case* statement then uses the *GetUpdateRect* API function to determine the rectangle that the program must repaint, and raises the *Paint* event to the subclassed form. As you will learn, the event displays information only within the event's event procedure; however, in your own programs, you can perform any processing you want within the event procedure. The program code declares the method as a *Friend* method purely as a precautionary measure—to avoid inadvertently subclassing forms outside the project with the code in the class.

Writing the Code for the AfterMessage Event

As you have learned, the subclassing you performed on the *frmHookedForm* form directs messages into your custom *WndProc* function. The *WndProc* function, in turn, will call the *clsSubclassedForm* class's *AfterMessage* event to perform the program's specific processing (provided the message is not *WM_PAINT*). The following code implements the *AfterMessage* event:

```
Friend Sub AfterMessage(ByVal hWnd As Long, ByVal uMsg As Long, _
   ByVal wParam As Long, ByVal lParam As Long, retVal As Long)
  On Error Resume Next
  Select Case uMsg
    Case WM_ACTIVATEAPP
      If wParam Then
        RaiseEvent ActivateApp
      Else
        RaiseEvent DeactivateApp
      End If

    Case WM_MOVE
      RaiseEvent Move

    Case WM_SIZING, WM_MOVING
      Dim i As Integer
      ReDim coords(0 To 3) As Long, saveCoords(0 To 3) As Long

      CopyMemory coords(0), ByVal lParam, 16
      CopyMemory saveCoords(0), ByVal lParam, 16
      If uMsg = WM_SIZING Then
        RaiseEvent Resizing(coords(0), coords(1), coords(2), _
            coords(3), wParam)
      Else
        RaiseEvent Moving(coords(0), coords(1), coords(2), _
            coords(3), wParam)
      End If
      For i = 0 To 3
        If coords(i) <> saveCoords(i) Then retVal = True
      Next
      If retVal Then CopyMemory ByVal lParam, coords(0), 16
    Case WM_GETMINMAXINFO
      Dim mmInfo As MINMAXINFO

      CopyMemory mmInfo, ByVal lParam, Len(mmInfo)
      With mmInfo
        RaiseEvent GetMinMaxInfo(.ptMaxSize.X, .ptMaxSize.Y, _
            .ptMaxPosition.X, .ptMaxPosition.Y, _
            .ptMinTrackSize.X, .ptMinTrackSize.Y, _
            .ptMaxTrackSize.X, .ptMaxTrackSize.Y)
      End With
      CopyMemory ByVal lParam, mmInfo, Len(mmInfo)

    Case WM_NCHITTEST
      RaiseEvent NCHitTest(lParam And &HFFFF&, lParam \ &H10000, retVal)

    Case WM_SETCURSOR
      Dim ctrlHWnd As Long
      Dim mouseAction As Long
      Dim hitTest As Long
      Dim ctrl As Control

      ctrlHWnd = wParam
      mouseAction = (lParam \ &H10000)
      If mouseAction = WM_MOUSEMOVE Then
        If ctrlUnderCursor.hWnd <> ctrlHWnd Then
          If Not (ctrlUnderCursor Is Nothing) Then
            RaiseEvent MouseExit(ctrlUnderCursor)
            Set ctrlUnderCursor = Nothing
          End If
          For Each ctrl In m_Form.Controls
            If ctrl.hWnd = ctrlHWnd Then
```

```
                        Set ctrlUnderCursor = ctrl
                        RaiseEvent MouseEnter(ctrlUnderCursor)
                        Exit For
                    End If
                Next
            End If
        End If

    Case WM_COMPACTING
        RaiseEvent CompactingMemory

    Case WM_DISPLAYCHANGE
        RaiseEvent DisplayChanged(lParam And &HFFFF&, lParam \ &H10000, _
                2 ^ wParam)
    End Select
End Sub
```

The first Windows message that the method responds to is the *WM_ACTIVATEAPP* message, which Windows sends to the program whenever the operating system activates or deactivates it. The code within the case checks the *wParam* value to determine whether the *clsSubclassedForm* class should raise its *ActivateApp* or *DeactivateApp* events. If *wParam* contains a value greater than -1, the operating system is activating the program. If the value is less than -1, the operating system is deactivating the program.

The second message that the method responds to is the *WM_MOVE* message. If the method receives the *WM_MOVE* message, it raises the *clsSubclassedForm* class's *Move* event. The program code within the *frmHookedForm* form then responds to the raised event.

If the method receives either the *WM_SIZING* or *WM_MOVING* message, the operating system is indicating that the user is resizing or moving the form, respectively. The program code within the case will then dimension two arrays, *coords* and *saveCoords*, which the program code uses to maintain the window's coordinates before and after the proposed move. The program code uses arrays because using them makes comparisons simpler than using a *RECT* structure (with arrays, you can simply loop through the elements—with a structure, you must compare each element individually). When the program receives the *WM_SIZING* or *WM_MOVING* message, the *lParam* parameter will contain the address for sixteen bytes (four sets of four bytes), which specify the window's corner coordinates. The program then saves the values into both arrays.

Next, the program code raises the correct event, depending on whether the message from the operating system was *WM_SIZING* or *WM_MOVING*. After the event completes its processing, the program code checks the values within the *coords* array against the values within the *saveCoords* array. If the values differ, the program returns *True* to the operating system, and passes the modified coordinates back to the operating system within the *lParam* value. If the values do not differ, the program code exits the function after the events return.

If the method receives the *WM_GETMINMAXINFO* message, Windows is querying the window for its minimum and maximum size and position. As you have learned, within the *prjFormEvents* program, the user can limit the minimum and maximum values. To let the program set the values, the *clsSubclassedForm* class raises the *GetMinMaxInfo* event, and passes within the event's parameters the values Windows wants to use. The program code within the event, as you will learn, sets the values based on the user's selections and returns the values to the *AfterMessage* event. The program code then sends the program-specified values back to the window procedure within the *lParam* value.

If the method receives the *WM_NCHITTEST* message, Windows is querying the form about which component is currently under the mouse cursor. The program code within the method raises the *NCHitTest* event and passes in to the event the cursor's *X* and *Y* positions, together with the value that represents the component under the mouse cursor. The program will interpret the value and convert it to text.

The next message the method responds to is the *WM_SETCURSOR* message. Windows will send a set cursor message whenever the mouse pointer moves, when the user clicks the mouse, and so on—in short, any time the mouse pointer must change, the operating system sends the *WM_SETCURSOR* message. Within the *clsSubclassedForm* class, the program code first acquires the handle to the control under the mouse pointer (which the method receives in the *wParam* parameter), and then determines what action the mouse is undergoing (which the method receives in the *lParam* parameter's high word). If the action is not *WM_MOUSEMOVE*, the program code exits the method. If the action is *WM_MOUSEMOVE*, the program code checks the window handle of the control under the cursor. If the handle is different from the current handle the class retains in the *ctrlUnderCursor* variable, the program code checks to ensure that *ctrlUnderCursor* contained a valid handle. If *ctrlUnderCursor's* handle is valid, the program raises the *MouseExit* event.

Next, the program code uses a *For-Each* loop to check each control on the *frmHookedForm* form. For each control on the form, it checks the control's window handle against the window handle the method received from the operating system within the *wParam* parameter. If the program code finds a match, it sets the *ctrlUnderCursor* variable equal to the new control and raises the *MouseEnter* event.

If the method receives the *WM_COMPACTING* message, the operating system is low on memory. When your programs receive this message, you should immediately save all currently open files within a backup location. If you do not, it is highly likely that you will lose the files, either from a system "crash" or from memory corruption as Windows tries to make more memory available. For the *prjFormEvents* project, the *clsSubclassedForm* class raises the *CompactingMemory* event.

The last message the method tries to capture within the *Select Case* statement is the *WM_DISPLAYCHANGE* message. If the method receives the *WM_DISPLAYCHANGE* message, the program code will raise the *DisplayChanged* event to the *frmHookedForm* form. In your own programs, you might change the size of your windows and controls, split the display, or perform similar processing in response to the *WM_DISPLAYCHANGE* message.

WRITING THE CODE FOR THE FRMHOOKEDFORM FORM

As you have learned, the majority of the code that performs the actual subclassing and message response occurs within the *mdlHookEvents* module and the *clsSubclassedForm* class. However, the *frmHookedForm* does turn on the subclassing and does include code within the events the *clsSubclassedForm* class raises into the form. Before you can write the program code for the *frmHookedForm* form, you must declare an instance of the *clsSublassedForm* object. The following code implements the declaration, which you must place within the form's General–Declarations section:

```
Private WithEvents frmSubclassed As clsSubclassedForm
```

Notice that you declare the object with the *WithEvents* keyword. If you check the Object combo box at the Code window's top left side, you will see that the Visual Basic Editor has added the *frmSubclassed* object to the *Object* list. If you then select the *frmSubclassed* object, you will see that the Editor displays the events the *clsSubclassedForm* class raises within the event selector on the Code window's top right side. You will write the code for the events later in this chapter.

WRITING THE CODE FOR THE FORM_LOAD EVENT

As you have learned in previous chapters, the first program code to execute whenever you load a form instance is the form's *Load* event, which executes even before the program displays the form. Within the *frmHookedForm* form, the *Form_Load* event turns on the subclassing and sets the *chkEvents* check box control to checked. The following code implements the *Form_Load* event:

```
Private Sub Form_Load()
  Set frmSubclassed = New clsSubclassedForm
  chkEvents.Value = 0
  chkEvents.Value = 1
End Sub
```

As you learned earlier in this chapter, you cannot use both the *WithEvents* keyword and the *As New* modifier to declare a variable. Instead, you must create the object the variable references at run time. The first statement within the *Form_Load* event sets the *frmSubclassed* object equal to a new instance of the *clsSubclassedForm* class. The next two statements toggle the *chkEvents* check box off, and then on again, which ensures that the form hooks the class. You will write the code for the *chkEvents_Click* event in the following section.

Writing the Code for the chkEvents_Click Event

As you learned earlier in this chapter, the user can toggle the form's subclassing by turning the *chkEvents* check box on and off. Each time the user (or the program) changes the *chkEvents* check box's value, the program will invoke the *chkEvents_Click* event. The following code implements the *chkEvents_Click* event:

```
Private Sub chkEvents_Click()
  If chkEvents.Value = True Then
    Set frmSubclassed.HookedForm = Me
  Else
    Set frmSubclassed.HookedForm = Nothing
  End If
  fraOptions.Enabled = chkEvents.Value
End Sub
```

If the user toggles the check box on, the program subclasses the form. If the user toggles the check box off, the program removes the form's subclassing. The program code then enables or disables the *fraOptions* frame control, depending on whether the program enabled or disabled the subclassing.

Writing the Code for the cmdNewForm_Click Event

As you learned in this chapter's "Using the *prjFormEvents* Project" section, the user can click the mouse on the Create New Form command button to create new forms. When the user clicks the mouse on the Create New Form command button, the program code will invoke the *cmdNewForm_Click* event. The following code implements the *cmdNewForm_Click* event:

```
Private Sub cmdNewForm_Click()
  Dim f As New frmHookedForm

  f.Show
End Sub
```

As you can see, the program code creates a new instance of the *frmHookedForm* form. The program code then displays the new form (which effectively creates a newly subclassed form, as you learned in this chapter's "Writing the Code for the *Form_Load* Event" section).

Writing the Code for the frmSubclassed_ActivateApp Event

As you have learned, the *frmSubclassed* object exposes events to which the *frmHookedForm* program code must respond. For some events, the program code will simply display information within the *txtDisplayEvent* text box. For other events, the program code must check the options the user has selected and respond accordingly. One of the simplest events is the *ActivateApp* event. The following code implements the *frmSubclassed_ActivateApp* event:

```
Private Sub frmSubclassed_ActivateApp()
  txtDisplayEvent.Text = "Event ActivateApp"
End Sub
```

As you can see, the program code within the event updates the text box to show that the object raised the event.

Writing the Code for the Other Information-Only Events

As you learned in the previous sections, the *frmHookedForm* uses several of the events the *clsSubclassedForm* raises to generate informational displays. The code in this section implements the events, except for the *ActivateApp* event, that the *frmHookedForm's* program code uses to display information. The following code implements the *CompactingMemory*, *DeactivateApp,* and *Move* events:

```
Private Sub frmSubclassed_CompactingMemory()
  txtDisplayEvent.Text = "Event CompactingMemory"
End Sub
```

```
Private Sub frmSubclassed_DeactivateApp()
  txtDisplayEvent.Text = "Event DeactivateApp"
End Sub

Private Sub frmSubclassed_Move()
  txtDisplayEvent.Text = "Event Move"
End Sub
```

As the *ActivateApp* event did, both the *CompactingMemory* and *DeactivateApp* events simply display the information that the *clsSubclassedForm* raised the event. Some of the other informational events, however, are more complex. For example, the *DisplayChanged* event displays information about the change's effects, in addition to the notification to the user of the event itself. The following code implements the *DisplayChanged* event:

```
Private Sub frmSubclassed_DisplayChanged(ByVal newWidth As Integer, _
    ByVal newHeight As Integer, ByVal numberOfColors As Long)
  txtDisplayEvent.Text = "Event DisplayChanged(" & newWidth & "," & _
    newHeight & "," & numberOfColors & ")"
End Sub
```

As you can see, the *DisplayChanged* event receives the new screen width, the new screen height, and the new number of screen colors after the change. The code within the event displays that information within the *txtDisplayEvent* control. Similarly, both the *Paint* and *Moving* events display information about the area the user's action impacts. The following code implements the *Paint* event:

```
Private Sub frmSubclassed_Paint(X1 As Single, Y1 As Single, _
    X2 As Single, Y2 As Single)
  txtDisplayEvent.Text = "Event Paint - Update area is (" _
    & X1 & "," & Y1 & ")-(" & X2 & "," & Y2 & ")"
End Sub
```

The *Paint* event displays the four corners of the rectangle that the program retrieved from the operating system with the *GetUpdateRect* function. The *Moving* event similarly displays the new rectangle resulting from the user's moving action. The following code implements the *Moving* event:

```
Private Sub frmSubclassed_Moving(X1 As Long, Y1 As Long, X2 As Long, _
    Y2 As Long, ByVal draggedBorder As Integer)
  txtDisplayEvent.Text = "Event Moving(" & X1 & "," & Y1 & "," & X2 & "," _
    & Y2 & ")"
End Sub
```

As you can see, the *Moving* event also receives four values, which correspond to the points on the rectangle to which the user is moving the window.

WRITING THE CODE FOR THE MOUSEENTER AND MOUSEEXIT EVENTS

As you have learned, the program code will display information about controls as the user moves the mouse over the *frmHookedForm* form. To display mouse information, the program code defines two events, *MouseEnter* (when the mouse moves over a new control), and *MouseExit* (when the mouse moves off a control). The following code implements the *MouseEnter* and *MouseExit* events:

```
Private Sub frmSubclassed_MouseEnter(ByVal ctrl As Control)
  txtDisplayEvent.Text = "Event MouseEnter - control is " & ctrl.Name
  lblStatus.Caption = ctrl.Name
End Sub

Private Sub frmSubclassed_MouseExit(ByVal ctrl As Control)
  txtDisplayEvent.Text = "Event MouseExit - control is " & ctrl.Name
  lblStatus.Caption = ""
End Sub
```

The program code within both events displays the control's name within the events box. The *MouseEnter* event also displays the control's name within the *lblStatus* control. The *MouseExit* event clears the *lblStatus* control.

Writing the Code for the GetMinMaxInfo Event

As you learned in the "Using the *prjFormEvents* Project" section of this chapter, there are three events to which the program lets the user control its response. One of the options that the user can select is to enforce minimum and maximum sizes on forms. The *frmHookedForm* form implements that user option within the *GetMinMaxInfo* event. The following code implements the *GetMinMaxInfo* event:

```
Private Sub frmSubclassed_GetMinMaxInfo(MaxSizeX As Long, _
    MaxSizeY As Long, MaxPosX As Long, MaxPosY As Long, _
    MinTrackSizeX As Long, MinTrackSizeY As Long, _
    MaxTrackSizeX As Long, MaxTrackSizeY As Long)
  txtDisplayEvent.Text = "Event GetMinMaxInfo"
  If chkSize.Value = 0 Then Exit Sub
  If chkSquare.Value = 1 Then
    MaxSizeX = 400
    MaxSizeY = 400
  Else
    MaxSizeX = 600
    MaxSizeY = 400
  End If
  ' position of maximized form (center of screen)
  MaxPosX = (ScaleX(Screen.Width, vbTwips, vbPixels) - MaxSizeX) \ 2
  MaxPosY = (ScaleY(Screen.Height, vbTwips, vbPixels) - MaxSizeY) \ 2
  MinTrackSizeX = MaxSizeX / 2
  MinTrackSizeY = 200
  MaxTrackSizeX = MaxSizeX
  MaxTrackSizeY = 400
End Sub
```

The program code within the event first displays the event within the text box, and then checks to determine whether the user has selected the *chkSize* check box (to enforce minimum and maximum sizes). If the user has not selected the check box, the program code exits the event. If the user did select *chkSize,* the program code checks to determine if the user has also selected the Keep The Form Square check box. If the user wants to keep the form square, the program code sets square maximum dimensions; if the user does not want to keep the form square, the program code sets rectangular maximum dimensions. The program code then sets the position on the screen where the program will display maximized forms and returns the information to the class. The class then passes the new dimensions back into the operating system, which enforces the custom size limitations.

Writing the Code for the NCHitTest Event

As you have learned, the operating system will send the program *WM_NCHITTEST* messages regularly during its processing. The *clsSubclassedForm* class captures each message and exposes it within the *NCHitTest* event. The *NCHitTest* event then checks the *hitCode* parameter (which corresponds to the return value from the window procedure) within a *Select Case* statement. The code applies the correct string for the *txtDisplayEvent* control based on the mouse pointer's current position, and also lets the user click anywhere in its client area to move the form. The following code implements the *NCHitTest* event:

```
Private Sub frmSubclassed_NCHitTest(ByVal X As Integer, _
    ByVal Y As Integer, hitCode As Long)
  ' X and Y are in screen pixel coordinates
  Select Case hitCode
    Case HTBORDER: txtDisplayEvent.Text = "Border"
    Case HTBOTTOM: txtDisplayEvent.Text = "Bottom edge"
```

```
      Case HTBOTTOMLEFT: txtDisplayEvent.Text = "Bottom Left corner"
      Case HTBOTTOMRIGHT: txtDisplayEvent.Text = "Bottom Right corner"
      Case HTCAPTION: txtDisplayEvent.Text = "Caption"
      Case HTCLIENT: txtDisplayEvent.Text = "Client area"
      Case HTCLOSE: txtDisplayEvent.Text = "Close button"
      Case HTERROR: txtDisplayEvent.Text = "ERROR !"
      Case HTGROWBOX: txtDisplayEvent.Text = "Grow box"
      Case HTHELP: txtDisplayEvent.Text = "Help button"
      Case HTHSCROLL: txtDisplayEvent.Text = "Horizontal scrollbar"
      Case HTLEFT: txtDisplayEvent.Text = "Left edge"
      Case HTMAXBUTTON: txtDisplayEvent.Text = "Max Button"
      Case HTMENU: txtDisplayEvent.Text = "Menu bar"
      Case HTMINBUTTON: txtDisplayEvent.Text = "Min Button"
      Case HTNOWHERE: txtDisplayEvent.Text = "(nowhere)"
      Case HTOBJECT: txtDisplayEvent.Text = "Object"
      Case HTRIGHT: txtDisplayEvent.Text = "Right edge"
      Case HTSYSMENU: txtDisplayEvent.Text = "System menu"
      Case HTTOP: txtDisplayEvent.Text = "Top edge"
      Case HTTOPLEFT: txtDisplayEvent.Text = "Top left corner"
      Case HTTOPRIGHT: txtDisplayEvent.Text = "Top right corner"
      Case HTVSCROLL: txtDisplayEvent.Text = "Vertical scrollbar"
   End Select
   txtDisplayEvent.Text = "Event NCHitTest(" & X & "," & Y & "," _
      & txtDisplayEvent.Text & ")"
   If chkMove.Value = 0 Then Exit Sub
   If hitCode = HTCLIENT Then hitCode = HTCAPTION
End Sub
```

As you can see, the *Select Case* statement determines what text to display within the control. After the *Select Case* statement finishes processing, the program code checks to determine whether the user has selected the *chkMove* check box control. If the user has selected *chkMove*, the program code sets the *hitCode* parameter to *HTCAPTION*—which tells the operating system the user is clicking on the window's title bar, and therefore can move the window, even when the user is clicking on the form's client area.

WRITING THE CODE FOR THE RESIZING EVENT

As you learned earlier in this chapter, the user can enforce minimum and maximum sizes, drag the form from anywhere within its client area, and make the form remain square. The code to keep the form square must go within the *Resizing* event, because it applies whenever the user tries to resize the form. The following code implements the *Resizing* event:

```
Private Sub frmSubclassed_Resizing(oldWidth As Long, oldHeight As Long, _
   newWidth As Long, newHeight As Long, ByVal draggedBorder As Integer)
   txtDisplayEvent.Text = "Event Resizing(" & oldWidth & "," _
      & oldHeight & "," & newWidth & "," & newHeight & ")"
   If chkSquare.Value = 0 Then Exit Sub
   newHeight = oldHeight + (newWidth - oldWidth)
End Sub
```

The program code displays the simple information for the user (that the operating system is resizing the form, and that the form has new dimensions). The program code then checks to determine whether the user has selected the Keep The Form Square check box. If the user has not selected the check box, the program code exits the event. If the user has selected the check box, the program code forces the *newHeight* value to be equal to the old height plus the new width minus the old width.

474

Enhancements You Can Make to the prjFormEvents Project

Clearly, the *prjFormEvents* program by itself does not perform useful processing. However, the concepts that you have learned within this chapter will apply to a wide variety of programming tasks. For example, many current programs include a File Preview option and corresponding display within the File Open dialog box. Your programs can, in fact, subclass the *CommonDialog* control and create a File Preview option with the dialog box. Similarly, you can use the subclass to generate custom printing dialogs, and so on.

Subclassing windows and intercepting system messages, however, really provides you with significant control over the way users interact with your programs. The ability to see automatically (through raised events) when a user changes the display settings, for example, provides you with control over your programs' appearance that Visual Basic programmers have never had before. As you apply subclassing concepts within your programs, you will find that your programs have a more professional interface, are easier for users to control, and are generally more responsive to your specific programming needs.

Putting It All Together

This chapter's project, *prjFormEvents*, introduced you to Windows messages and their importance to all programs that run on the Windows operating system. You learned about the *AddressOf* operator and using classes to subclass forms. You revisited raising events, using the *WithEvents* keyword, and using the *Event* keyword, and also expanded your knowledge of programming with classes. Within Chapter 15, "Using the Windows API to Check Disk Devices," you will work with the Win32 API to determine what disks and drives a computer can access, as well as information about those disks and drives. Before you continue with Chapter 15, however, make sure you understand the following key concepts:

✓ When you subclass a form, you intercept the messages that Windows sends to that form. In general, to subclass a form, you must have a form, a class module, and a code module with a window procedure that performs the actual interception of the message from the operating system.

✓ A message is a *Long* numeric value that Windows sends to a program as the result of a user or an operating system action. When you work with messages within your programs, you will generally define symbolic constants (which most programmers begin with *WM*, for Windows Message) to refer to the messages. Common messages indicate the user has moved the mouse, clicked the mouse button, and so on.

✓ Windows maintains a separate message queue for each execution thread. Within your Visual Basic programs, each program will have its own message queue, unless you use Windows API functions to create additional threads. In the event you create additional threads from within your Visual Basic programs, each additional thread will have its own message queue.

✓ When you subclass forms and controls, you must create a custom function or procedure (which programmers refer to as a *window procedure*) that intercepts and processes the messages. In the event you subclass multiple instances of the same form, you must ensure that each instance uses its own custom window procedure. In the *prjFormEvents* program, you defined ten custom window procedures and a single overriding window procedure that each custom window procedure called in turn.

✓ A callback function is a function within your Visual Basic program to which you can pass the address of a Windows API function so that the Windows API function can "call back" the function within your program. Visual Basic 5.0 uses the new *AddressOf* operator to support callback functions. In the *prjFormEvents* program, you used the *AddressOf* operator to pass the address of the custom window procedure for a form into the operating system, so that the operating system knew where to send messages later .

✓ Visual Basic's new *AddressOf* operator lets you pass function addresses within your Visual Basic programs to Windows API functions. However, to store a function address within a variable (as you did in the *prjFormEvents* program), you must pass the function address into another function as a parameter and let that function return the variable's value.

✓ Visual Basic's *WithEvents* and *Event* keywords let your programs create classes that expose their own events, much like the controls and forms you have used in previous chapters. As you saw in this chapter, there is virtually no limit to the number of events a given class can raise. Additionally, the *WithEvents* keyword forces the Visual Basic Editor to display the information about an object's events within the Code window's selection boxes.

✓ Subclassing forms lets you customize your program's interface to a degree not possible in previous Visual Basic versions. Subclassing controls (such as the *CommonDialog* control) lets you provide custom interfaces at all levels within your programs, not just within the program's basic windows.

✓ When your programs receive a message from the operating system, the operating system will often send additional information to the program within the *wParam* and *lParam* values.

✓ Whenever your window procedure finishes its custom processing on the messages the program receives from the operating system, it should use the *CallWindowProc* procedure to pass the message on to the window's default message processing procedure.

Chapter 15

Using the Windows API to Check Disk Devices

As you have learned, the Windows Application Programming Interface (API) lets your programs access built-in operating system functions. While Visual Basic offers many built-in functions and statements that let you perform processing similar to Windows API functions, a Windows API function will often let you perform a specific task that a Visual Basic command may not. The Windows API also lets you access functions that you cannot access with a standard Visual Basic command. In many cases, the Windows API may also let you access functions in a different way then you would access them with a Visual Basic built-in function or statement—which means that you may have more control over how the function works or what it returns.

In Chapter 3, "Writing a Screen Saver in Visual Basic," you used the Windows API, together with form subclassing, to intercept Windows messages and control the screen saver's appearance. You can also use the Windows API to access many other operating-system functions. For example, in Chapter 23, "Using the CryptoAPI to Encrypt Documents," you will use the Microsoft Cryptography API to create a program that lets you encrypt and decrypt text files.

In this chapter's project, *prjDeviceAccess*, however, you will use the Windows API to retrieve information about disks and drives connected to a computer. The Windows API functions that you will use will return information about the disk's volume, the total space and the free space on the volume, and the drive type. By the time you finish this chapter, you will understand the following key concepts:

- ◆ While you can perform many disk activities with Visual Basic's built-in functions and statements, you will often require greater control over disk activities than the built-in function or statement provides. Your programs can use Windows API function calls to achieve that control.

- ◆ Using the *GetDiskFreeSpace* function, your programs can determine a drive's free space and its total space, as well as information about the number of clusters the drive contains, the number of sectors per cluster, and the number of bytes per sector.

- ◆ Using the *GetVolumeInformation* function, your programs can retrieve specific information about a disk or drive, including its volume number and label.

- ◆ Using the *GetDriveType* function, your programs can determine whether a drive is a fixed or removable drive, whether the drive is local or across a network, and so on.

- ◆ You should always "wrap" your API calls within a "wrapper function" to protect against return values you do not expect. A wrapper function processes an API function's return value and performs processing on the value before it returns the value to the calling procedure or function.

- ◆ Your programs should always remove the *NULL*-terminator from strings that your programs receive as a return value from a Windows API call. Because the Windows API works with C-style strings, every string that a Windows API call returns has a *NULL*-terminator, while Visual Basic strings do not.

- ◆ Your programs should always add the *NULL*-terminate to strings that your programs pass in as parameters to a Windows API call. Because the Windows API works with C-style strings, every string that your programs pass into a Windows API call must have a *NULL*-terminator, which Visual Basic strings do not, by default.

USING THE prjDeviceAccess PROJECT

Before you design the *prjDeviceAccess* project, you may find it helpful to run the program. The companion CD-ROM that accompanies this book contains the *prjDeviceAccess.exe* program within the *Chapter15* directory. As with every other program on the CD-ROM, you should run the Jamsa Press *setup.exe* program to install the *prjDeviceAccess.exe* program to your computer's hard drive before you run the *prjDeviceAccess.exe* program. After you install the *prjDeviceAccess.exe* program to your computer's hard drive, you can run it from the Start menu. To run the program, select the Windows Start menu Run option. Windows will display the Run dialog box. Within the Run dialog box, enter *x:\vbpl\Chapter15\prjDeviceAccess.exe*, where *x* corresponds to the drive letter of the hard drive on which you installed the *prjDeviceAccess.exe* program, and click your mouse on OK. Windows will display the *prjDeviceAccess.exe* program, as shown in Figure 15.1.

*Figure 15.1 The **prjDeviceAccess** project's startup screen.*

Before you use the *prjDeviceAccess.exe* program, take a moment to familiarize yourself with the controls on the form. As you have learned, the *prjDeviceAccess* project will let you check the available drives on your computer and obtain information about those drives. When the program starts, you will see the list of available drives on the left side of the Drive Management form. Next to the list of available drives, on the screen you will see a grid with the caption *Device Information*. When you execute the program, the grid is empty and no drive is highlighted within the drive list.

To view information about a drive, click your mouse on the drive letter in the drive letter list box. For example, if you click your mouse on "C:\," the program will display output similar to that shown in Figure 15.2.

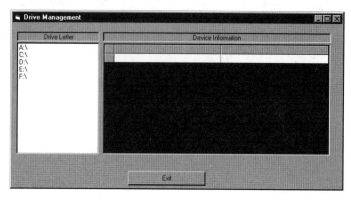

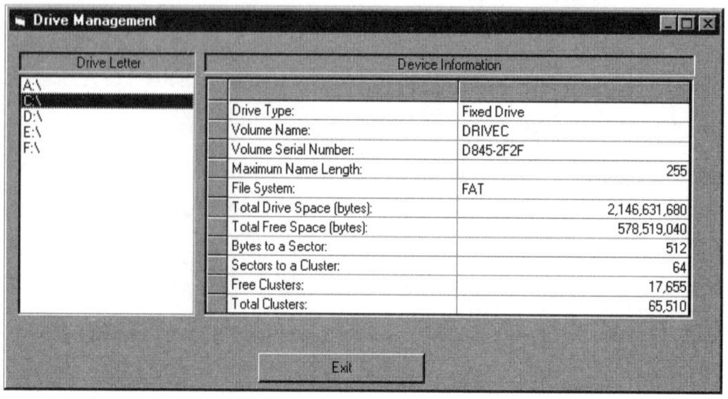

Figure 15.2 The information on the C:\ drive.

As you can see, the program displays the drive's type, volume name, and serial number, as well as the file system type. Below the file system type, the grid also displays the drive's total space, free space, and cluster and sector information. If the drive is an NTFS drive or a FAT32 drive, the program will display a message below the grid, which indicates that the information may not be accurate. Because NTFS and FAT32 have the ability to handle drives larger than 2.15Gb and the *GetDiskFreeSpace* function has limitations, you may have a drive that is larger than 2.15Gb that the program will treat as only 2.15Gb.

RUNNING PRJDEVICEACCESS FROM THE CD-ROM

As you have learned, you must first install many programs that you will use in this book to your computer's hard drive before you use them. The *prjDeviceAccess.exe* program, however, does not use any custom controls or references and, in fact, uses the Windows API almost exclusively. Because the *prjDeviceAccess.exe* program uses no custom controls or references, you can run the program from the CD-ROM if you want. To run the program from the CD-ROM, perform the following steps:

1. Select the Windows Start menu Run option. Windows will display the Run dialog box.

2. Within the Run dialog box, enter *x:\Chapter15\prjDeviceAccess.exe*, where *x* corresponds to the drive letter of your computer's CD-ROM drive (usually D: or E:), and click your mouse on OK. Windows will run the *prjDeviceAccess.exe* program.

To learn more about the Jamsa Press *setup.exe* program, see the "What's on the *Visual Basic Programmer's Library* Companion CD-ROM" section at the back of this book.

CREATING A BLANK FORM

Now that you have a better idea how to use the finished *prjDeviceAccess* project, you can begin to design it. First, you will create an empty form that will contain all the controls the "Using the *prjDeviceAccess* Project" section introduced. After you design the form, you will learn more about the *Microsoft Flex Grid* control and the Windows API functions you will use to get drive information.

To begin the *prjDeviceAccess* project and create a blank form, perform the following steps:

1. Within Visual Basic, select the File menu New Project option. Visual Basic will open the New Project dialog box.

2. Within the New Project dialog box, click your mouse on the Standard EXE icon. Next, click your mouse on the OK button. Visual Basic will close the dialog box and open the *Form1* form window.

3. Select the View menu Properties Window option. Visual Basic will open the Properties Window listing the *Form1* properties.

4. Within the Properties Window, change the *Form1* properties to the values Table 15.1 lists.

Object	Property	Set As
Form1	*Caption*	*Drive Management*
Form1	*Height*	4785
Form1	*Left*	0
Form1	*StartUpPosition*	*2 - Center Screen*
Form1	*Top*	0
Form1	*Width*	9330
Form1	*Name*	*frmDevice*

*Table 15.1 The newly named **frmDevice** form's properties.*

ADDING A MODULE TO THE PRJDEVICEACCESS PROJECT

As you have learned, in the *prjDeviceAccess* project, you will use a series of Windows API functions to determine information about a user-selected drive. You will declare the Windows API functions and their constants and data types within a separate module. To add a module that will contain the definitions and type to the *prjDeviceAccess* project, perform the following steps:

1. Select the Project menu Add Module option. Visual Basic will open the Add Module dialog box.

2. Within the Add Module dialog box, double-click your mouse on the Module icon. Visual Basic will add the module, *Module1*, to the *prjDeviceAccess* project and open the *Module1* Code window.

3. Select the View menu Properties Window option. Visual Basic will open the Properties Window listing the *Module1* properties.

4. Within the Properties Window, click your mouse on the *Name* property. Replace the *Module1* name with *mdlDriveInfo* and press ENTER.

5. Select the File menu Save Project As option. Visual Basic will open the Save File As dialog box and fill the *File name* field with *mdlDriveInfo*.

6. Click your mouse on the OK button. Visual Basic will save the module and fill the Save File As dialog box's *File name* field with *frmDevice*.

7. Within the Save Project As dialog box, click your mouse on the Save button. Visual Basic will save the *frmDevice* form and fill the *File name* field with the *Project1* project name.

8. Within the *File name* field, replace the *Project1* project name with the new *prjDeviceAccess* project name. Next, click your mouse on the Save button. Visual Basic will save the *prjDeviceAccess* project and close the Save Project As dialog box.

ADDING A MICROSOFT FLEX GRID CONTROL TO THE PROJECT

As you can see from the relatively simple interface the *prjDeviceAccess* project presents, you will only add one extra control reference to the project, the *Microsoft Flex Grid* control, which the program will use to display information about the currently selected drive. Before you can use the *Microsoft Flex Grid* control in the *prjDeviceAccess* project, you must add it to the project as a component. After you add the *Microsoft Flex Grid* control to the *prjDeviceAccess* project, Visual Basic will display the control's icon in the Toolbox. As you know, the Toolbox displays Visual Basic control icons. If you double-click your mouse on any icon in the Toolbox, Visual Basic will draw the control that the icon corresponds to within the active form.

To add a *Microsoft Flex Grid* control to the *prjDeviceAccess* project, perform the following steps:

1. Select the Project menu Components option. Visual Basic will open the Components dialog box.

2. Within the Components dialog box, select the *Microsoft Flex Grid Control 5.0* listing. Next, click your mouse on the box to the left of the listing. Visual Basic will display a check mark in the box.

3. Within the Components dialog box, click your mouse on OK. Visual Basic will add the *Microsoft Flex Grid* control component to the *prjDeviceAccess* project.

ADDING CONTROLS TO THE FORM

In the *prjDeviceAccess* project, you will use a *ListBox* control, a *CommandButton* control, and the *Microsoft Flex Grid* control you added to the project in the previous section. To begin the project's design, you will add each control to the *frmDevice* form and assign properties to each control on the form.

ADDING THE LISTBOX CONTROL TO THE FORM

As you have learned, the *prjDeviceAccess* project will use a *ListBox* control to display information about the disk drives currently connected to the computer. To add a *ListBox* control to the *frmDevice* form, perform the following steps:

1. If Visual Basic is not displaying the *frmDevice* form within an object window, double-click your mouse on the *frmDevice* form listing within the Project Explorer. Visual Basic will open the *frmDevice* form.

2. Within Visual Basic, select the View menu Toolbox option. Visual Basic will open the Toolbox.

3. Within the Toolbox, double-click your mouse on the ListBox icon. Visual Basic will draw a *ListBox* control, *List1*, within the *frmDevice* form.

4. Within the *frmDevice* form window, click your mouse on the *List1* control to highlight it. Visual Basic will draw a small frame around the control.

5. Select the View menu Properties Window option. Visual Basic will open the Properties Window listing the *List1* properties.

6. Within the Properties Window, change the *List1* properties to the values Table 15.2 lists.

Object	Property	Set As
List1	*Height*	2985
List1	*Left*	120
List1	*Top*	525
List1	*Width*	2295
List1	*Name*	lstDevices

Table 15.2 *The newly named **lstDevices** control's properties.*

ADDING A MICROSOFT FLEX GRID CONTROL TO THE FORM

As you have learned, the *prjDeviceAccess* project will use a *Microsoft Flex Grid* control to display information about a user-selected drive. To add a *Microsoft Flex Grid* control to the *frmDevice* form, perform the following steps:

1. If Visual Basic is not displaying the *frmDevice* form within an object window, double-click your mouse on the *frmDevice* form listing within the Project Explorer. Visual Basic will open the *frmDevice* form.

2. Within Visual Basic, select the View menu Toolbox option. Visual Basic will open the Toolbox.

3. Within the Toolbox, select the new *Microsoft Flex Grid* control icon, MSFlexGrid, as shown in Figure 15.3.

Figure 15.3 *The Toolbox showing the **Microsoft Flex Grid** control icon MSFlexGrid.*

4. Within the Toolbox, double-click your mouse on the MSFlexGrid icon. Visual Basic will draw a *Microsoft Flex Grid* control, *MSFlexGrid1*, within the *frmDevice* form, as shown in Figure 15.4.

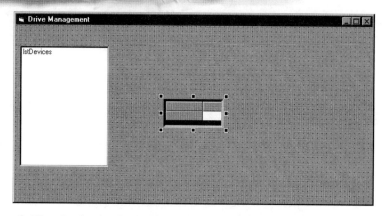

*Figure 15.4 The **Microsoft Flex Grid** control, **MSFlexGrid1**, on the **frmDevice** form.*

5. Within the *frmDevice* form window, click your mouse on the *MSFlexGrid1* control to highlight it. Visual Basic will draw a small frame around the control.

6. Select the View menu Properties Window option. Visual Basic will open the Properties Window listing the *MSFlexGrid1* properties.

7. Within the Properties Window, change the *MSFlexGrid1* property values to the values Table 15.3 lists.

Object	Properties	Set As
MSFlexGrid1	*Cols*	3
MSFlexGrid1	*Fixed Cols*	1
MSFlexGrid1	*Fixed Rows*	1
MSFlexGrid1	*Height*	3000
MSFlexGrid1	*Left*	2520
MSFlexGrid1	*Rows*	2
MSFlexGrid1	*Top*	525
MSFlexGrid1	*Width*	6375
MSFlexGrid1	*Name*	*flxDevices*

*Table 15.3 The newly named **flxDevices** control's properties.*

ADDING THE COMMANDBUTTON CONTROL TO THE FORM

As you have learned, you will use the *ListBox* control on the *frmDevice* form's left side to perform most of your processing within the *prjDeviceAccess* project. However, to provide the user with an easy way to exit the program, you will also add an Exit button (a *CommandButton* control), to the *frmDevice* form's bottom.

To add the *CommandButton* control to the *frmDevice* form, perform the following steps:

1. If Visual Basic is not displaying the *frmDevice* form within an object window, double-click your mouse on the *frmDevice* form listing within the Project Explorer. Visual Basic will open the *frmDevice* form.

2. Within Visual Basic, select the View menu Toolbox option. Visual Basic will open the Toolbox.

3. Within the Toolbox, double-click your mouse on the CommandButton icon. Visual Basic will draw a *CommandButton* control, *Command1*, within the *frmDevice* form.

4. Within the *frmDevice* form, click your mouse on the *CommandButton1* control to highlight it. Visual Basic will draw a small frame around the control.

5. Select the View menu Properties Window option. Visual Basic will open the Properties Window listing the *CommandButton1* control's properties.

6. Within the Properties Window, change the *CommandButton1* control's properties to the values Table 15.4 lists.

Object	Property	Set As
Command1	*Caption*	*E&xit*
Command1	*Height*	375
Command1	*Left*	3240
Command1	*Top*	3960
Command1	*Width*	2175
Command1	*Name*	*cmdOK*

Table 15.4 *The newly named* **cmdOK** *control's properties.*

When you finish setting the properties for the *cmdOK* control, the *frmDevice* form will look similar to Figure 15.5.

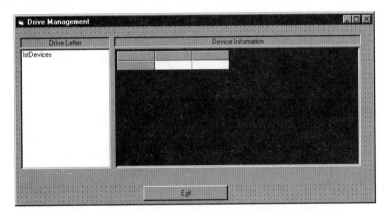

Figure 15.5 *The* **frmDevice** *form after you add and format its component controls.*

WRITING THE CODE FOR THE *MDLDEVICEINFO* MODULE

Within the *prjDeviceAccess* project, the majority of the program code that declares and invokes the Windows API is within the *mdlDeviceInfo* module. There are several excellent reasons for the code's location, but the simplest one is also the most compelling: most of the code in the *mdlDeviceInfo* module is code that you can reuse within several projects. Therefore, if you place the code within an easily reusable module, rather than enclosing it within a procedure in a form, you make reusing the program code easier. Additionally, placing the functions and procedures that use the API function calls in a module will let you make those functions and procedures available throughout your project when you create more complex projects. In the following sections, you will write and learn about the code for the *mdlDeviceInfo* module.

DECLARING THE *API* FUNCTIONS, CUSTOM TYPES, AND PROGRAM CONSTANTS

As you have learned, you will write most of the API-specific program code for the project within the *mdlDeviceInfo* module. You will also declare two custom structures and a series of Windows API-defined constants within the General–Declarations section. The *mdlDeviceInfo* module's General–Declarations section is long enough that it is valuable to consider it in segments, because each segment relates to a specific purpose. The following code implements the first segment, which declares the three API calls:

```
Option Explicit

Declare Function GetDriveType Lib "kernel32" Alias "GetDriveTypeA" _
    (ByVal nDrive As String) As Long
Declare Function GetDiskFreeSpace Lib "kernel32" Alias "GetDiskFreeSpaceA" _
    (ByVal lpRootPathName As String, lpSectorsPerCluster As Long, _
    lpBytesPerSector As Long, lpNumberOfFreeClusters As Long, _
    lpTotalNumberOfClusters As Long) As Long
Declare Function GetVolumeInformation Lib "kernel32" Alias _
    "GetVolumeInformationA" _
    (ByVal lpRootPathName As String, ByVal lpVolumeNameBuffer As String, _
    ByVal nVolumeNameSize As Long, lpVolumeSerialNumber As Long, _
    lpMaximumComponentLength As Long, lpFileSystemFlags As Long, _
    ByVal lpFileSystemNameBuffer As String, _
    ByVal nFileSystemNameSize As Long) As Long
```

484 The *GetDriveType* function accepts as its sole parameter a *NULL*-terminated string that corresponds to the drive letter for the drive whose type you want to know. It returns a *Long* value, which your program must then process to get a textual type for a drive. You will declare the constants that the program uses to process the *GetDriveType* function's return value later in this section, and in the third segment of the General–Declarations section.

The *GetDiskFreeSpace* function accepts as its sole parameter the fully qualified path name of the drive you want to get information about. It returns within the other parameters the number of bytes per sector, sectors per cluster, number of free clusters, and total number of clusters.

The *GetVolumeInformation* function accepts a *NULL*-terminated string that corresponds to the drive letter for the drive whose volume information you want to know. It returns the volume name, the volume serial number, the volume's file system type (for example, FAT, NTFS, FAT32, or CDFS), and several internal system flags that you will not use in this book.

As you have learned, whenever you call an API function that processes strings and, in general, whenever you call an API function that accesses drives, disks, or other media, you should "wrap" the function within a Visual Basic function. The Visual Basic "wrapper" should handle the *NULL*-termination of strings, the function's return value, and any system-level error checking that you want to do with the function. Within the *prjDeviceAccess* project, you will wrap the three API functions within their own functions. For the sake of program clarity, the wrapper functions for both the *GetDiskFreeSpace* and *GetVolumeInformation* functions accept custom structures, rather than the number of parameters the API functions accept. The following code implements the structure definitions:

```
Type DiskInfo
    lDiskFree As Long
    lSectorsToACluster As Long
    lBytesToASector As Long
    lFreeClusters As Long
    lTotalClusters As Long
End Type
Type VolInfo
    lpVolName As String
    lpVolSerNum As Long
    lpMaxLength As Long
    lpFileFlags As Long
    lpFileSystemName As String
End Type
```

As you can see, the *DiskInfo* structure contains five members, which correspond to the information the *GetDiskFreeSpace* API function returns. Similarly, the *VolInfo* structure also contains five members, which correspond to the information the *GetVolumeInformation* API function returns. As you will learn, the wrapper functions (*GetDiskSpaceFree* and *GetVolInfo*, respectively) for the two API functions return the system information within the structure members, which the program then uses to fill the display grid.

In addition to the API declarations and the structure type definitions, the General–Declarations section declares a global variable and a series of constants. The following code implements the remaining declarations within the *mdlDriveInfo* module's General–Declarations section:

```
Public CancelAccess As Boolean
Public Const gstrSEP_DRIVE = ":"
Public Const DRIVE_UNKNOWN = 0
Public Const DRIVE_NO_ROOT_DIR = 1
Public Const DRIVE_REMOVABLE = 2
Public Const DRIVE_FIXED = 3
Public Const DRIVE_REMOTE = 4
Public Const DRIVE_CDROM = 5
Public Const DRIVE_RAMDISK = 6
Public Const errDeviceUnavailable = 68
Public Const errDiskNotReady = 71
Public Const errDeviceIO = 2404&
Public Const errBadFileName = 64
Public Const errBadFileNameOrNumber = 52
Public Const errPathDoesNotExist = 76
Public Const errBadFileMode = 54
Public Const errFileAlreadyOpen = 55
Public Const errInputPastEndOfFile = 62
```

The *CancelAccess* variable holds a *True* or *False* value that indicates to the program code whether it should continue trying to process a user-requested drive. The program code sets the *CancelAccess* variable equal to the result of the *CheckDrive* function, which the following section explains in detail. The constants that begin with *DRIVE* are system constants that correspond to the return values from the *GetDriveType* function. The constants that begin with *err* correspond to system-returned error codes that the program must process when the program fails to access a file or drive.

USING THE API TEXT VIEWER TO ADD API DECLARATIONS TO YOUR PROJECTS

As you learned in Chapter 1, "Introduction to Visual Basic," you can use the *API Text Viewer* to easily place API function declarations, constants, and types into your Visual Basic programs. For example, to add the *GetDriveType* function to your project, as well as the constants your program will use to evaluate *GetDriveType's* return value, perform the following steps:

1. Select the Start menu Programs option Microsoft Visual Basic 5.0 group. Within the Microsoft Visual Basic 5.0 group, select the API Text Viewer option. Windows will open the *API Text Viewer*, as shown in Figure 15.6.

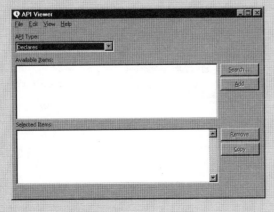

Figure 15.6 The API Text Viewer at startup.

2. Within the *API Text Viewer*, select the File menu Load Text File option. The *API Text Viewer* will display the Select a Text API File dialog box.

3. Within the Select a Text API File dialog box, select the *Win32API.txt* file. Click your mouse on OK to load the file. The *API Text Viewer* will take several moments to load the file.

4. After the *API Text Viewer* finishes loading the file, it may ask you whether you want to convert the text file to a database, as shown in Figure 15.7.

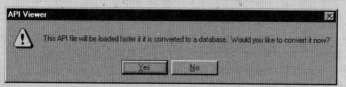

*Figure 15.7 The **API Text Viewer** convert text to database message box.*

5. If the program prompts you to save the text file as a database file, do so. Otherwise, select the File menu Convert Text to Database option. The *API Text Viewer* will display the Select a Name for the New Database dialog box.

6. Within the dialog box, save the file as *Win32API.mdb*. Click your mouse on OK to save the file.

7. After you save the file, you can locate the API function and constants you want to add to your program. Within the Available Items list box, click your mouse on any item. The *API Text Viewer* will select the item on which you click.

8. Type "GetDriveType" into your computer. The list box will automatically change to the *GetDriveType* API function. Click your mouse on the Add button to add the function to the copy list.

9. Click your mouse on the API Type combo box's drop-down arrow and select the Constants option. The *API Text Viewer* will load the constant declarations, and refresh the list box.

10. Within the Available Items list box, click your mouse on any item. The *API Text Viewer* will select the item on which you click.

11. Type "Drive" into your computer. The list box will automatically change to the *DRIVE_CDROM* constant declaration. Click your mouse on the Add button to add the constant to the copy list.

12. Repeat Step 10 four times to copy each of the four constants that immediately follow the *DRIVE_CDROM* constant in the list box to the copy list. When you finish, the *API Text Viewer* will look similar to Figure 15.8.

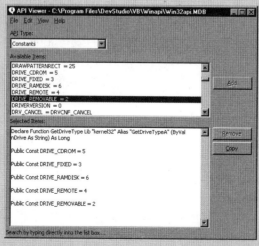

*Figure 15.8 The **API Text Viewer** after you add the **GetDriveType** function and its associated constants.*

13. Click your mouse on the Copy button to copy the constant declarations to the Clipboard. The *API Text Viewer* will copy the declarations to the Clipboard.

14. Use the ALT+TAB keyboard combination to switch back to Visual Basic and open the *mdlDeviceInfo* module Code window. Within the General–Declarations section, select the Edit menu Paste option. Visual Basic will paste the declarations into the module.

WRITING THE CHECKDRIVE FUNCTION

As you have learned, the *prjDeviceAccess* project tries to display information about drives and disks. While reading fixed disks and network drives is a relatively straightforward process (because the disk will always return information), trying to read information from a removable disk is not so simple. The *CheckDrive* function checks the drive to ensure that the user has inserted a disk before the API calls try to read from the disk. The following code implements the *CheckDrive* function:

```
Public Function CheckDrive(ByVal chkDriveName As String) As Boolean
   Dim Action As Integer
   Dim FirstFile As String

   On Error GoTo DriveError
   CancelAccess = False
   FirstFile = Dir(Left$(chkDriveName, 3), vbNormal)
   CheckDrive = True
   Exit Function
DriveError:
   CheckDrive = False
   Action = FileErrors(Err)
   Select Case Action
     Case 0
        Resume
     Case Else
        Exit Function
   End Select
   Exit Function
End Function
```

The *CheckDrive* function uses the Visual Basic *Dir* command to try to read the first file on the inserted disk. If successful, the function returns a *True* value to the calling procedure and exits. If it fails, the function calls the *FileErrors* function with the error number and exits. As you will learn in the next section, the *FileErrors* function accepts an error value and displays a text error message for the user. The *CheckDrive* function uses a *Select Case* statement to process the values that *FileErrors* returns so that you can add additional code to the project to respond to different errors.

WRITING THE FILEERRORS FUNCTION

As you have learned, the *prjDeviceAccess* program must process bad disk entries to ensure that it does not cease operation and that the user understands why *prjDeviceAccess* will not return information on the user-selected drive or disk. The *FileErrors* function accepts an error value and uses a *Select Case* statement to create the appropriate message to the user for the error. The following code implements the *FileErrors* function:

```
Public Function FileErrors(errVal As Integer) As Integer
   Dim MsgType As Integer
   Dim Response As Integer
   Dim Action As Integer
   Dim Msg As String

   MsgType = vbExclamation + vbRetryCancel
   Select Case errVal
```

```
      Case errDeviceUnavailable
        Msg = "That device appears to be unavailable."
        MsgType = vbExclamation + 5
      Case errDiskNotReady
        Msg = "The disk is not ready."
      Case errDeviceIO
        Msg = "The disk is full."
      Case errBadFileName, errBadFileNameOrNumber
        Msg = "That filename is illegal."
      Case errPathDoesNotExist
        Msg = "That path doesn't exist."
      Case errBadFileMode
        Msg = "Can't open your file for that type of access."
      Case errFileAlreadyOpen
        Msg = "That file is already open."
      Case errInputPastEndOfFile
        Msg = "This file has a nonstandard end-of-file marker,"
        Msg = Msg + "or an attempt was made to read beyond "
        Msg = Msg + "the end-of-file marker."
      Case Else
        FileErrors = 3
        Msg = "Other error - the Drive is Not Ready"
        MsgType = vbExclamation + vbRetryCancel
    End Select
    Response = MsgBox(Msg, MsgType, "File Error")
    Select Case Response
      Case vbRetry
        FileErrors = 0
      Case vbIgnore
        FileErrors = 1
      Case 1, 2, 3     vbOK, vbcancel
        FileErrors = 2
        CancelAccess = True
      Case Else
        FileErrors = 3
    End Select
  End Function
```

As you can see, the *FileErrors* function uses the constants that you defined in the General–Declarations section to evaluate the error value a failed disk-access returns. If the *Select Case* statement does not find an exact error match, the *prjDeviceAccess* program will display a generic error message. For all error messages, the user has the choice either to retry the operation or to cancel. If the user chooses to retry, the *CheckDrive* function will resume at the error-causing statement and try again to access the disk. If the user chooses to cancel, the code will set the *CancelAccess* flag to *True* and return to the *CheckDrive* function, which also exits, and the *prjDeviceAccess* program will stop trying to read the drive.

WRITING THE CODE FOR THE GETDRIVE FUNCTION

When the *prjDeviceAccess* project begins, it will step through each possible drive letter and try to determine whether the letter corresponds to a valid drive. The *CheckDrives* routine within the *frmDevice* form, which steps through the possible drive letters, calls the *GetDrive* function with each letter. The following code implements the *GetDrive* function:

```
Public Function GetDrive(ByVal DriveName As String, ReturnName As String) _
    As Boolean
  Dim ReturnVal As Long

  GetDrive = True
  On Error Resume Next
  ReturnVal = GetDriveType(DriveName)
  If ReturnVal < 0 Then MsgBox "Error"
```

```
        Select Case ReturnVal
          Case 0
            ReturnName = "Unknown"
          Case 1
            ReturnName = "Root directory doesn't exist"
            GetDrive = False
          Case 2
            ReturnName = "Removable drive"
          Case 3
            ReturnName = "Fixed Drive"
          Case 4
            ReturnName = "Remote (Network) Drive"
          Case 5
            ReturnName = "CD-ROM Drive"
          Case 6
            ReturnName = "RamDisk"
          Case Else
            ReturnName = "Unknown Return Value: " & CStr(ReturnVal)
        End Select
    End Function
```

The *GetDrive* function accepts the letter of the drive to get information about as its sole incoming parameter. It returns a string that corresponds to the drive type as its sole outgoing parameter, and also returns a *True* or *False* value that corresponds to the function's success or failure. Within the *GetDrive* function, the program code calls the *GetDriveType* API function and uses a *Select Case* statement to convert the numeric value the API function returns to a string value that represents the drive type.

WRITING THE CODE FOR THE GETVOLINFO FUNCTION

As you have learned, the *GetVolInfo* function is the wrapper for the *GetVolumeInformation* API function. The *GetVolInfo* function accepts as its sole incoming parameter the drive to get the information about, and returns as its sole outgoing parameter a structure of type *VolInfo* that contains the volume information that *GetVolumeInformation* returns. The following code implements the *GetVolInfo* function:

```
Public Function GetVolInfo(ByVal lRoot As String, _
     ByRef Volume As VolInfo) As Boolean
  Dim lVolumeBuffer As Long, lFileNameBuff As Long
  Dim ReturnVal As Long

  With Volume
    lVolumeBuffer = 255
    .lpVolName = Space$(lVolumeBuffer)
    lFileNameBuff = 255
    .lpFileSystemName = Space$(lFileNameBuff)
    On Error Resume Next
    ReturnVal = GetVolumeInformation(lRoot, .lpVolName, lVolumeBuffer, _
        .lpVolSerNum, .lpMaxLength, .lpFileFlags, .lpFileSystemName, _
        lFileNameBuff)
    If ReturnVal = 0 Then
      MsgBox "Error: Could not read from drive.", vbCritical
      GetVolInfo = False
      Exit Function
    Else
      .lpVolName = StripTerminator(.lpVolName)
      .lpFileSystemName = StripTerminator(.lpFileSystemName)
    End If
  End With
  GetVolInfo = True
End Function
```

As you learned in Chapter 1, C++ handles string values differently from Visual Basic. To ensure that the API call returns the correct values, the program code must first initialize some parameters for the API function call. The program code initializes the two string buffers and fills them with 255 spaces, and then sets the buffer values for those strings to 255, so the API function knows how many bytes it can return. The *GetVolInfo* function's program code then calls the *GetVolumeInformation* function, which returns either a zero value, which means it was unable to read from the drive, or a non-zero value, which means that the API function read the information from the drive and filled the members of the *VolInfo* structure with the information about the volume. Before returning to the calling procedure, the function invokes the *StripTerminator* function to strip the terminating zero from the API-returned string values. As you learned in Chapter 1, you should always call the *StripTerminator* function (or a function that performs similar processing) when your programs accept return strings from API function calls.

REMOVING AND ADDING THE ZERO TERMINATOR

As you learned in the previous section, the program code for the *GetVolInfo* function calls the *StripTerminator* function to remove the ASCII 0 (the *NULL* character) from the string's end. Other functions within the *prjDeviceAccess* project call the *StripTerminator* function as well. In fact, as you start to work with API calls more often, the *StripTerminator* function will likely become one of your most reused code fragments. The following code implements the *StripTerminator* function:

```
Public Function StripTerminator(ByVal strString As String) As String
  Dim intZeroPos As Integer

  intZeroPos = InStr(strString, Chr$(0))
  If intZeroPos > 0 Then
    StripTerminator = Left$(strString, intZeroPos - 1)
  Else
    StripTerminator = strString
  End If
End Function
```

The *StripTerminator* function looks for the *Chr(0)* terminator that the Windows API places on strings. If *StripTerminator* finds the terminator, it will return the string up to the terminator. If it does not find the terminator, it will return the entire string.

Just as the Windows API returns zero-terminated strings, it expects to receive zero-terminated strings. As you will see, the program code for the *prjDeviceAccess* project calls the *ZeroTerminate* function to zero terminate (*NULL*-terminate) drive names before the project calls any API functions. The following code implements the *ZeroTerminate* function:

```
Public Function ZeroTerminate(ByVal TerminateString As String) As String
   ZeroTerminate = TerminateString & Chr$(0)
End Function
```

As you can see, the *ZeroTerminate* function adds the ASCII 0 to the string's end and returns the result as the function's value.

WRITING THE CODE FOR THE GETDISKSPACEFREE FUNCTION

The final API wrapper function that you will write within the *mdlDriveInfo* module is the *GetDiskSpaceFree* function, which wraps the *GetDiskFreeSpace* API function. Just as the *GetVolInfo* function does, the *GetDiskSpaceFree* function accepts the drive letter as its incoming parameter and returns a structure of type *DiskInfo,* which returns the values from the *GetDiskFreeSpace* API function to the calling procedure. The following code implements the *GetDiskSpaceFree* function:

```
Function GetDiskSpaceFree(ByVal strDrive As String, _
    DiskInf As DiskInfo) As Boolean
  Dim strCurDrive As String
```

```
        GetDiskSpaceFree = False
        With DiskInf
          If Err <> 0 Then
            .lDiskFree = -1
            Exit Function
          Else
            .lDiskFree = GetDiskFreeSpace(strDrive, .lSectorsToACluster, _
                .lBytesToASector, .lFreeClusters, .lTotalClusters)
            If .lDiskFree <> 1 Then
              .lDiskFree = -1
              Exit Function
            Else
              .lDiskFree = .lSectorsToACluster * .lBytesToASector * .lFreeClusters
            End If
          End If
        End With
        GetDiskSpaceFree = True
      End Function
```

491

The *GetDiskSpaceFree* function uses the *strDrive* parameter to call the *GetDiskFreeSpace* function, which returns information about the disk in *DiskInfo's* members. The program code uses *lDiskFree* twice to save on declaration overhead—the first time, as a return value (to ensure the function was successful), and the second time to store the total bytes of the drive's free disk space. If the call to *GetDiskFreeSpace* fails, the *GetDiskSpaceFree* function returns *False* and the program will not display information. If the call to *GetDiskFreeSpace* succeeds, the *GetDiskSpaceFree* function returns *True* and the program will display the information about the drive's free space, total space, and so on.

WRITING THE CODE FOR THE FRMDEVICE FORM

As you have learned, you will declare most of the API functions, and write the wrapper functions that use the API functions to return meaningful values to the *prjDeviceAccess* program, within the *mdlDeviceInfo* module. However, the *frmDevice* form also performs significant processing, converting the return values from the functions into information the program will display, as well as placing the return values into the display. Most of the code within the *frmDevice* form handles the display's appearance and the program's response to user actions.

DECLARING THE FRMDEVICE FORM'S LOCAL VARIABLE

The *frmDevice* form uses only one variable, *DriveArray*, throughout its processing that you must declare within the form's General–Declarations section. The *DriveArray* string array maintains the drive type for each available drive. The program code initializes and fills the *DriveArray* array within the *CheckDrives* function, which you will write in the next section. The following code implements the declarations for the *frmDevice* form:

```
Option Explicit
Dim DriveArray() As String
```

WRITING THE FRMDEVICE FORM'S INITIALIZING CODE

As you have learned, the *prjDeviceAccess* project displays only a single form, which it initializes when the program loads. However, to ensure the *prjDeviceAccess* project updates the available drives whenever the *prjDeviceAccess* program becomes the active window, you will place the form's initializing code within the *Form_Activate* event, rather than within the *Form_Load* event. The following code implements the *Form_Activate* event:

```
Private Sub Form_Activate()
    flxDevices.ColWidth(0) = 275
    flxDevices.ColWidth(1) = 3000
    flxDevices.ColWidth(2) = 3000
    CheckDrives
End Sub
```

The *Form_Activate* event sets the correct widths for the columns within the *flxDevices* control, then invokes the *CheckDrives* procedure to fill the *DriveArray* array and the *lstDevices* list box with the names of the available drives. The following code implements the *CheckDrives* procedure:

```
Private Sub CheckDrives()
  Dim I As Integer, DriveString As String, DriveType As String

  lstDevices.Clear
  For I = 1 To 26
    DriveString = Chr(64 + I) & ":\"
    If GetDrive(DriveString, DriveType) Then
      lstDevices.AddItem DriveString
      ReDim Preserve DriveArray(lstDevices.ListCount)
      DriveArray(lstDevices.ListCount) = DriveType
    End If
  Next
End Function
```

The *CheckDrives* procedure clears the list box of current entries, then loops through the alphabet looking for valid drives. If the *GetDrive* function returns *True*, the program code adds the drive letter to the list box and the drive type to the *DriveArray* array. If the *GetDrive* function returns *False*, the program code loops and tries the next drive letter. After the procedure code finishes looping through the alphabet, the procedure exits.

FILLING THE GRID AFTER A USER SELECTION

As you have learned, after the program loads the valid drive letters into the *lstDevices* control, the user must click on a drive letter within the list box to display the information about the drive in the *flxDevices* control. To fill the grid after a user clicks the mouse, you must add a single line of code to the event procedure. The following code implements the *lstDevices_Click* event:

```
Private Sub lstDevices_Click()
  FillGrid lstDevices.List(lstDevices.ListIndex)
End Sub
```

As you can see, the code within the *Click* event invokes the *FillGrid* procedure and passes to the procedure the drive letter of the user-selected drive. The following code implements the *FillGrid* procedure:

```
Private Sub FillGrid(DriveName As String)
  Dim CurrentVol As VolInfo, LocalDriveName As String
  Dim DriveSp As DiskInfo, TotalSpace As Double

  flxDevices.Rows = 2
  flxDevices.RowHeight(0) = 275
  LocalDriveName = ZeroTerminate(DriveName)
  flxDevices.Row = 1
  flxDevices.Col = 1
  flxDevices.Text = "Drive Type:"
  flxDevices.Col = 2
  flxDevices.Text = DriveArray(lstDevices.ListIndex + 1)
  If Not GetVolInfo(LocalDriveName, CurrentVol) Then Exit Sub
  With CurrentVol
    flxDevices.Rows = flxDevices.Rows + 4
    flxDevices.Row = flxDevices.Row + 1
    flxDevices.Col = 1
    flxDevices.Text = "Volume Name:"
    flxDevices.Col = 2
    flxDevices.Text = .lpVolName
    flxDevices.Row = flxDevices.Row + 1
    flxDevices.Col = 1
```

```
      flxDevices.Text = "Volume Serial Number:"
      flxDevices.Col = 2
      If .lpVolSerNum = 0 Then
        flxDevices.Text = "Unknown"
      Else
        flxDevices.Text = Left$(Hex(.lpVolSerNum), 4) & "-" & _
            Right$(Hex(.lpVolSerNum), 4)
      End If
      flxDevices.Row = flxDevices.Row + 1
      flxDevices.Col = 1
      flxDevices.Text = "Maximum Name Length:"
      flxDevices.Col = 2
      flxDevices.Text = .lpMaxLength
      flxDevices.Row = flxDevices.Row + 1
      flxDevices.Col = 1
      flxDevices.Text = "File System:"
      flxDevices.Col = 2
      flxDevices.Text = .lpFileSystemName
  End With
  If Not GetDiskSpaceFree(LocalDriveName, DriveSp) Then Exit Sub
  With DriveSp
    On Error Resume Next
    TotalSpace = .lBytesToASector * .lSectorsToACluster * .lTotalClusters
    flxDevices.Rows = flxDevices.Rows + 6
    flxDevices.Row = flxDevices.Row + 1
    flxDevices.Col = 1
    flxDevices.Text = "Total Drive Space (bytes): "
    flxDevices.Col = 2
    flxDevices.Text = Format(TotalSpace, "#,###")
    flxDevices.Row = flxDevices.Row + 1
    flxDevices.Col = 1
    flxDevices.Text = "Total Free Space (bytes): "
    flxDevices.Col = 2
    flxDevices.Text = Format(.lDiskFree, "#,###")
    flxDevices.Row = flxDevices.Row + 1
    flxDevices.Col = 1
    flxDevices.Text = "Bytes to a Sector: "
    flxDevices.Col = 2
    flxDevices.Text = Format(.lBytesToASector, "#,###")
    flxDevices.Row = flxDevices.Row + 1
    flxDevices.Col = 1
    flxDevices.Text = "Sectors to a Cluster: "
    flxDevices.Col = 2
    flxDevices.Text = Format(.lSectorsToACluster, "#,###")
    flxDevices.Row = flxDevices.Row + 1
    flxDevices.Col = 1
    flxDevices.Text = "Free Clusters: "
    flxDevices.Col = 2
    flxDevices.Text = Format(.lFreeClusters, "#,###")
    flxDevices.Row = flxDevices.Row + 1
    flxDevices.Col = 1
    flxDevices.Text = "Total Clusters: "
    flxDevices.Col = 2
    flxDevices.Text = Format(.lTotalClusters, "#,###")
  End With
  If CurrentVol.lpFileSystemName <> "FAT32" And _
      CurrentVol.lpFileSystemName <> "NTFS" Then
    lblFat32.Visible = False
  Else
```

```
      lblFat32.Visible = True
      lblFat32.Caption = _
         "Note: Program may not correctly process sizes" & _
         " for FAT32 and NTFS Drives"
   End If
End Sub
```

While the code for the *FillGrid* procedure is long, in general it mostly handles the assignment of values to their correct cells within the *flxDevices* control. However, there are several important processing considerations that the program code within the procedure handles. The General–Declarations section contains declarations of both the *VolInfo* and *DiskInfo* types, which the procedure will use to handle return values from the *GetVolInfo* and *GetDiskSpaceFree* functions, respectively.

After filling the first two lines of the grid with the drive letter and type, the program calls the *GetVolInfo* function, which returns a *True* or *False* value. If the function returns *False*, the program code exits without displaying more information about the drive (generally, a *False* return indicates that a removable or CD-ROM drive does not currently contain a disk). If the function returns *True*, the program code adds the *CurrentVol* structure's members to the grid, together with their appropriate captions. Note that the program code converts the *Long* value within the *lpSerNum* member to its hexadecimal representation.

Next, the program code calls the *GetDiskSpaceFree* function, which also returns a *True* or *False* value. If *GetDiskSpaceFree* returns *False*, the procedure will exit without displaying further information. On the other hand, if *GetDiskSpaceFree* returns *True*, the procedure will display the values the function returns within the *DriveSp* structure. Finally, the procedure's program code checks the file system. If the file system is NTFS or FAT32, the program will display a message that lets the user know that the free space and total space values may be wrong for that drive. As you learned earlier in this chapter, the *GetDiskFreeSpace* function will not report correct total sizes for drives over 2.15Gb, and cannot report free space for drives with over 2.15Gb of free space.

WRITING THE CODE TO EXIT THE PROGRAM

As with other single-document interface programs that you have designed throughout this book, writing the code to exit the *prjDeviceAccess* program is a simple process. As with previous Single-Document Interface programs you have written, you must unload the form to exit the program. The user can either click the mouse on the *cmdOK* control to unload the form or click the mouse on the form's close box. The following code implements the *cmdOK_Click* event:

```
Private Sub cmdOK_Click()
   Unload Me
End Sub
```

ENHANCEMENTS YOU CAN MAKE TO THE PRJDEVICEACCESS PROJECT

The *prjDeviceAccess* project, because of the specific nature of its processing, is not particularly a program that you will enhance. In fact, the project primarily serves as a container for the excellent reusable API function calls and wrappers the *mdlDriveInfo* module contains. However, there are some enhancements you can make to the project that might help it provide more valuable information.

For example, you can add a call to the *GetVersionEx* function, which would let you determine not only the disk operating system for each drive, but also the operating system on the computer that is running the program. You can also use *GetVersionEx* to set a program flag that would force the program to use *GetDiskFreeSpaceEx* to get information about the drive, which would ensure that you received accurate size values from both NTFS and FAT32 drives.

In addition to information about disks and drives, you can get a large amount of information about the system from within the program and display the information within the grid. For example, you might call the *GetSystemMetrics* API function to obtain information about the current display settings. You might also use the *EnumPrinters* and *EnumPrinterDrivers* functions together with the Visual Basic *AddressOf* operator to display a list of available printers.

Finally, you can use an entire series of Windows API calls such as *GetFileSecurity*, *GetFileSize*, and *GetFileTitle* to get information about files on a given drive and display that information for the user. The Windows API provides functions that will let you return almost any combination of information about any file.

PUTTING IT ALL TOGETHER

This chapter's project, *prjDeviceAccess*, introduced you to how to use the Windows API, together with custom structures and error trapping, to display information about disks and drives. You learned how to check for a drive's readiness, and how to use the information the Windows API functions return as a foundation for meaningful communication with the user. In Chapter 16, "Accessing Local Drives to Find Duplicate Files," you will use the Windows API, together with a recursive search procedure, to locate duplicate files within different directories on your local computer. Before you continue with Chapter 16, however, make sure you understand the following key concepts:

- ✓ Visual Basic's built-in set of functions and statements lets your programs perform many useful disk activities. However, the Windows API provides you with the greatest control over disk activity.

- ✓ Your Windows programs can use the *GetDiskFreeSpace* function to determine a drive's free space and the drive's total space, provided the drive is not larger than 2.15Gb.

- ✓ Your Windows programs can use the *GetVolumeInformation* function to access specific information about a disk or drive, including its volume number and label.

- ✓ Your Windows programs can use the *GetDriveType* function to determine whether a drive is a fixed or removable drive, whether the drive is local or is a network drive, and more.

- ✓ When you call Windows API functions from within Visual Basic, you should always wrap your API calls within a wrapper function to protect against return values that you do not expect.

- ✓ When you call Windows API functions from within Visual Basic, you should ensure that you process the zero terminator with each string you send to or receive from a Windows API call.

495

Chapter 16

Accessing Local Drives to Find Duplicate Files

If you have studied computer history, you may know that the earliest computers received information from electrical switches and output information as light sequences. Because the earliest computers could store information only while turned on, engineers quickly realized that computers must have a way to store information for extended time periods for them to be useful. Since those early computing days, storage has come a long way: from tapes, to disk platters, to the small hard drives that most modern personal computers have inside. Storage remains one of the most important computer system features—in fact, as people continue to use computers, storage has become more important, for every computer from the smallest to the largest. The most common form of storage most people use is the *file*, a self-contained element conceptually similar to a file folder. A file stores data, which may be text information, a program you can execute, a picture you can view, even a song on a CD-ROM that you can listen to. Whenever you write programs, whether in Visual Basic or in any other language, understanding and using the computer's storage media is an essential task. Visual Basic provides several ways that you can access and manipulate the computer's storage—whether hard drive, disk drive, network drive, or other media. The two most common ways are with Visual Basic's built-in commands and with Windows Application Programming Interface (API) functions.

As you have learned, the Windows Application Programming Interface (API) lets your programs access built-in operating system functions. In Chapter 15, "Using the Windows API to Check Disk Devices," you used a series of Windows API calls to gather information about a user-selected drive and display that information to the user. In this chapter, you will use a combination of Visual Basic controls, Windows API functions, and a recursive procedure to read an entire directory tree and search the tree for duplicate files. Additionally, the *prjDuplicate* program that you will design in this chapter uses several custom structures and a temporary database that it creates each time you start a search to maintain information about the files the program locates. The program will then display any duplicate files it locates for the user to view, and delete them if the user so chooses.

Every file that you save onto a disk or drive has certain unique characteristics that identify the file to the operating system. In this chapter, you will use file characteristics, such as size and modification date, to determine whether a file is a duplicate of another file. In Chapter 17, "Using the Windows API to Manage File Types," you will use the attribute value that the operating system attaches to each file that you save to sort files based on other attributes. Because the operating system maintains valuable information about each file you save, managing and manipulating that information from within your Visual Basic programs can be extremely useful.

In the *prjDuplicate* project, you will use a combination of Windows API calls and Visual Basic built-in commands to process the files within the user-specified directory tree. By the time you finish this chapter, you will understand the following key concepts:

- ◆ Within your Visual Basic programs, you must use the Windows API directory functions to perform recursive searches because Visual Basic's *Dir* function does not support recursion.

- ◆ Your programs can use the *FindFirstFile* and *FindNextFile* functions to locate files that meet user- or program-specified characteristics.

- ◆ Because the *FindFirstFile* function returns a *handle* (a unique integer value), your programs can use the *FindFirstFile* and *FindNextFile* functions within recursive sub-routines without losing the handle from a previous search.

- ◆ Your programs can get information about files previously saved onto a drive or disk either with Visual Basic's built-in commands or with Windows API calls.

◆ Your programs should always close handles they create after they finish using the handles. When you work with the handle that *FindFirstFile* returns, your programs should use the *FindClose* call to close each handle.

◆ Within Visual Basic, your programs can nest structures for additional program clarity, which will help you and other programmers better manage the program code.

◆ Within your programs, you can create and delete temporary databases to store and process information.

◆ You can use information that you place with each item (for example, a duplicate file) in a *ListView* control to perform user-directed processing with that item.

◆ Within your programs, you can use the *Directory* attribute to determine whether a filename you return from a Windows API call is a directory or a file.

USING THE prjDUPLICATE PROJECT

497

Before you design the *prjDuplicate* project, you may find it helpful to run the program. The companion CD-ROM that accompanies this book contains the *prjDuplicate.exe* program within the *Chapter16* directory. As with every other program on the CD-ROM, you should run the Jamsa Press *setup.exe* program to install the *prjDuplicate.exe* program to your computer's hard drive before you run it. After you install the *prjDuplicate.exe* program to your computer's hard drive, you can run it from the Start menu. To run the program, select the Windows Start menu Run option. Windows will display the Run dialog box. Within the Run dialog box, enter *x:\vbpl\Chapter16\prjDuplicate.exe*, where *x* corresponds to the drive letter of the hard drive on which you installed the *prjDuplicate.exe* program, and click your mouse on OK. Windows will run the *prjDuplicate* program, as shown in Figure 16.1.

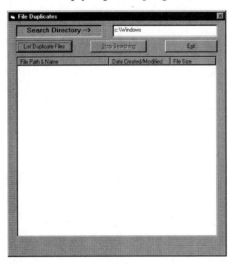

Figure 16.1 The prjDuplicate project's start-up screen.

RUNNING prjDUPLICATE FROM THE CD-ROM

As you have learned, you must first install many programs that you will use in this book to your computer's hard drive before you use the programs. Because the *prjDuplicate.exe* program tries to create a temporary database within its execution directory, you must install the *prjDuplicate.exe* program to a drive before you try to use it. If you try to run the *prjDuplicate.exe* program from the CD-ROM, the program will not perform searches because it cannot create the temporary database it requires.

To learn more about the Jamsa Press *setup.exe* program, see the "What's on the *Visual Basic Programmer's Library* Companion CD-ROM" section at the back of this book.

Before you use the *prjDuplicate.exe* program, take a moment to familiarize yourself with the controls on the form. As you have learned, the *prjDuplicate* project will let you check a directory tree on your computer and obtain information about the files within that directory and all its subdirectories. When the program starts, you will see a large empty box with three columns: File Path & Name, Date Created/Modified, and File Size. Above the box, you will see three command buttons: List Duplicate Files, Stop Searching, and Exit. Above the command buttons, you will see a text box labeled Search Directory. The program's default search directory is *C:\windows*. To see the processing the program performs, click your mouse on the List Duplicate Files button. The program will begin to search the *C:\windows* directory and all its subdirectories for duplicate files. The program will also disable the List Duplicate Files button and enable the Stop Searching button. While the program searches, you can observe the program's progress at the bottom of the program display. The program will display the message *Currently Scanning:* and the directory name as it searches each directory in turn. Figure 16.2 shows the *prjDuplicate* project during its search.

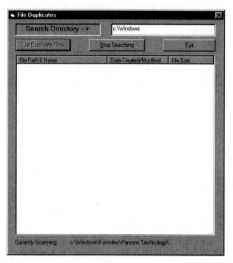

Figure 16.2 *The **prjDuplicate** project searching a directory.*

For each duplicate set of files the program finds, it will add those files to the list view. If there are more than two files with the same characteristics, the program will add all the duplicate files to the view. When the program completes its search, the cursor will return to the text box and the program will again enable the List Duplicate Files button and disable the Stop Searching button. For example, Figure 16.3 shows duplicate file listings within the *D:\sample* directory.

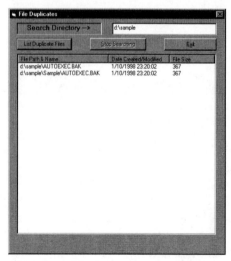

Figure 16.3 *The duplicate files within the **D:\sample** directory.*

As you can see, there are two identical copies of *AUTOEXEC.BAK* in the tree; one in the *D:\sample* directory, and one in the *D:\sample\Sample* directory. After you determine which duplicate file or files you want to keep and which ones you want to delete, you can click your mouse on the file or files you want to delete. When you click your mouse on a duplicate filename, the program will highlight the filename and display a message box, Delete Duplicate Message, that asks if you want to delete the file, as Figure 16.4 shows.

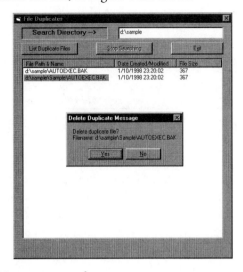

Figure 16.4 *The Delete Duplicate Message message box.*

If you click your mouse on the No button, the program will return to its normal display. If you click your mouse on the Yes button, the program will prompt you again, with a second message box, to ensure that you truly want to delete the file. Figure 16.5 shows the Delete Protection message box.

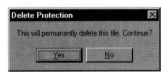

Figure 16.5 *The Delete Protection message box.*

If you click your mouse on the Yes button within the second dialog box, the program will delete the duplicate file and update the program display. If you click your mouse on the No button, the program will return to its normal display without deleting the file.

CREATING A BLANK FORM

Now that you have a better idea how to use the finished *prjDuplicate* project, you can begin to design it. First, you will create an empty form that will contain all the controls the "Using the *prjDuplicate* Project" section introduced. After you design the form, you will learn more about the Windows API calls that you will use to get the file information from the directory tree. To begin the *prjDuplicate* project and create a blank form, perform the following steps:

1. Within Visual Basic, select the File menu New Project option. Visual Basic will open the New Project dialog box.

2. Within the New Project dialog box, click your mouse on the Standard EXE icon. Next, click your mouse on the OK button. Visual Basic will close the dialog box and open the *Form1* form window.

3. Select the View menu Properties Window option. Visual Basic will open the Properties Window listing the *Form1* properties.

4. Within the Properties Window, change the *Form1* properties to the values Table 16.1 lists.

Object	Property	Set As
Form1	Caption	File Duplicates
Form1	Height	7680
Form1	Left	0
Form1	StartUpPosition	2 - Center Screen
Form1	Top	0
Form1	Width	7080
Form1	Name	frmDuplicate

Table 16.1 *The newly named* **frmDuplicate** *form's properties.*

ADDING A MODULE TO THE PROJECT

As you will learn, the *prjDuplicate* project declares its API functions, structures, and constants within a code module. As you learned in Chapter 5, "Creating and Using Fractals," Visual Basic requires that you declare structures within modules so that the type definitions are available throughout the project. As you have learned in other chapters, you should generally declare API functions within modules as well, so that they are also available throughout the project. To add a module to the *prjDuplicate* project, perform the following steps:

1. Select the Project menu Add Module option. Visual Basic will display the Add Module dialog box.

2. Within the Add Module dialog box, double-click your mouse on the Module icon. Visual Basic will add the *Module1* module to the project and open it within a Code window.

3. Select the View menu Properties Window option. Visual Basic will display the Properties Window with the *Module1* properties visible.

4. Change the *Module1* module's *Name* property to *mdlFileData*.

5. Select the File menu Save Project As option. Visual Basic will open the Save Project As dialog box and fill the *File name* field with *mdlFileData*.

6. Within the Save Project As dialog box, click your mouse on the Save button. Visual Basic will save the *mdlFileData* module and fill the *File name* field with the *frmDuplicate* form name.

7. Within the Save Project As dialog box, click your mouse on the Save button. Visual Basic will save the *frmDuplicate* form and fill the *File name* field with the *Project1* project name.

8. Within the *File name* field, replace the *Project1* project name with the new *prjDuplicate* project name. Next, click your mouse on the Save button. Visual Basic will save the *prjDuplicate* project and close the Save Project As dialog box.

ADDING A MICROSOFT LISTVIEW CONTROL TO THE PROJECT

As you can see from the relatively simple interface the *prjDuplicate* project presents, you will add only one extra control, *Microsoft ListView*, to the project, which the program will use to display information about duplicate file matches. The *Microsoft ListView* control is one of the *Microsoft Windows Common Controls* that comes with Visual Basic. Before you can use the *Microsoft ListView* control in the *prjDuplicate* project, you must add it to the project as a component. After you add the *Microsoft ListView* control to the *prjDuplicate* project, Visual Basic will display the control's icon in the Toolbox. As you know, the Toolbox displays Visual Basic control icons. If you double-click your mouse on any icon in the Toolbox, Visual Basic will draw the control that the icon corresponds to within the active form. To add the *Microsoft ListView* control to the *prjDuplicate* project, perform the following steps:

1. Select the Project menu Components option. Visual Basic will open the Components dialog box.

2. Within the Components dialog box, select the *Microsoft Windows Common Controls 5.0* listing. Next, click your mouse on the box to the left of the listing. Visual Basic will display a check mark in the box, as Figure 16.6 shows.

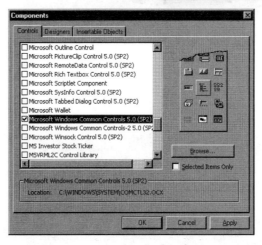

Figure 16.6 *The Components dialog box after you select the **Microsoft Windows Common Controls 5.0** component.*

3. Within the Components dialog box, click your mouse on OK. Visual Basic will add the *Microsoft Windows Common Controls* control components to the *prjDuplicate* project.

ADDING THE DATA ACCESS OBJECTS (DAO) OBJECT LIBRARY TO THE PROJECT

As you have learned, you will use a temporary database within the *prjDuplicate* project to manage information about files within the search tree. As you have learned in previous chapters, you must add a set of data objects to the project to manage database information from within Visual Basic. As you have in previous projects, you will use the Data Access Objects (DAO) Object Library to manage database information within the *prjDuplicate* project.

When you retrieve data from or save data to the temporary database, you will manage that data within a *Recordset* object. As you know, before you can store records in a *Recordset* object, you must have a *Workspace* and a *Database* object in your project. To use the *Workspace*, *Database*, and *Recordset* objects within Visual Basic, you must add a reference to them within the current project. The Data Access Objects (DAO) Object Library contains each object. You must add a *DAO Object Library* reference to the *prjDuplicate* project before you can create and use the temporary database. After you add a *DAO Object Library* reference to the *prjDuplicate* project, you will declare and assign variables of each data access object type. To add a *DAO Object Library* reference to the *prjDuplicate* project, perform the following steps:

1. Within Visual Basic, select the Project menu References option. Visual Basic will open the References dialog box.

2. Within the References dialog box, select the *Microsoft DAO 3.5 Object Library* listing from the *Available References* field. Next, click your mouse on the box to the left of the selection. Visual Basic will draw a check mark in the box.

3. Within the References dialog box, click your mouse on the OK button. Visual Basic will add the *DAO Object Library* reference to the *prjDuplicate* project.

ADDING CONTROLS TO THE FORM

In the *prjDuplicate* project, you will use the *ListView* control you added to the project in the "Adding a Micrososft *ListView* Control to the Project" section—a *TextBox* control, three *Label* controls, and three *CommandButton* controls. To begin, you will add each control to the *prjDuplicate* form and assign properties to position each control on the form and to provide a unique name for each control.

ADDING A MICROSOFT LISTVIEW CONTROL TO THE FORM

As you have learned, the *prjDuplicate* project will use a *Microsoft ListView* control to display information about a user-selected drive. To add a *Microsoft ListView* control to the *frmDuplicate* form, perform the following steps:

1. If Visual Basic is not displaying the *frmDuplicate* form within an object window, double-click your mouse on the *frmDuplicate* form listing within the Project Explorer. Visual Basic will open the *frmDuplicate* form.

2. Within Visual Basic, select the View menu Toolbox option. Visual Basic will open the Toolbox.

3. Within the Toolbox, select the new *Microsoft ListView* control icon, ListView, as shown in Figure 16.7.

Figure 16.7 *The Toolbox showing the **Microsoft ListView** control icon ListView.*

4. Within the Toolbox, double-click your mouse on the ListView icon. Visual Basic will draw a *Microsoft ListView* control, *ListView1*, within the *frmDuplicate* form.

5. Within the *frmDuplicate* form window, click your mouse on the *ListView1* control to highlight it. Visual Basic will draw a small frame around the control.

6. Select the View menu Properties Window option. Visual Basic will open the Properties Window listing the *ListView1* properties.

7. Within the Properties Window, change the *ListView1* property values to those Table 16.2 lists.

Object	Property	Set As
ListView1	*Height*	5655
ListView1	*Left*	240
ListView1	*SortOrder*	0 - *lvwAscending*
ListView1	*Top*	1080
ListView1	*View*	3 - *lvwReport*
ListView1	*Width*	6495
ListView1	*Name*	*lstDupFiles*

Table 16.2 *The newly named **lstDupFiles** control's properties.*

ADDING THE LABEL CONTROLS TO THE FORM

As you have learned, within the *prjDuplicate* project, you will use *Label* controls to place a caption on the *TextBox* control and to display information to the user on the search's progress at the form's bottom. Now that you have added the *lstDupFiles* control, you should add the *Label* controls to the form. After you add the *Label* controls, you will add a *TextBox* control and three *CommandButton* controls. To add the *Label* controls to the *frmDuplicate* form, perform the following steps:

1. If Visual Basic is not displaying the *frmDuplicate* form within an object window, double-click your mouse on the *frmDuplicate* form listing within the Project Explorer. Visual Basic will open the *frmDuplicate* form.

2. Within Visual Basic, select the View menu Toolbox option. Visual Basic will open the Toolbox.

3. Within the Toolbox, double-click your mouse on the Label icon. Visual Basic will draw a *Label* control, *Label1*, within the *frmDuplicate* form.

4. Repeat Step 3 two more times to add the *Label2* and *Label3* controls to the *frmDuplicate* form.

5. Within the *frmDuplicate* form, click your mouse on the *Label1* control to highlight it. Visual Basic will draw a small frame around the control.

6. Select the View menu Properties Window option. Visual Basic will open the Properties Window listing the *Label1* properties.

7. Within the Properties Window, change the *Label1* properties to the values Table 16.3 lists.

8. Repeat Steps 5, 6, and 7 to change the properties for the other *Label* controls to the values Table 16.3 lists.

Object	Property	Set As
Label1	*Alignment*	2 - Center
Label1	*Caption*	*Search Directory —>*
Label1	*Font*	*MS San Serif, Bold, 10 Point*
Label1	*Height*	375
Label1	*Left*	240
Label1	*Top*	120
Label1	*Width*	2775
Label1	*Name*	*lblSearchDir*
Label2	*Caption*	*Currently Scanning:*
Label2	*Height*	375
Label2	*Left*	240
Label2	*Top*	6840
Label2	*Visible*	*False*
Label2	*Width*	1575
Label2	*Name*	*lblScanning*
Label3	*Caption*	[blank]
Label3	*Height*	375
Label3	*Left*	2040
Label3	*Top*	6840
Label3	*Visible*	*False*
Label3	*Width*	4695
Label3	*Name*	*lblCurDir*

Table 16.3 *The newly named **Label** controls' properties.*

Adding a TextBox Control to the frmDuplicate Form

Now that you have the *frmDuplicate* form's general outline, you can add the *TextBox* control to the *frmDuplicate* form as a place for the user to enter the search directory. You will set a default value for the *TextBox* control in the properties, but the user will be able to alter the text value to search the directory of the user's choice. To add the *TextBox* control to the *frmDuplicate* form, perform the following steps:

1. If Visual Basic is not displaying the *frmDuplicate* form within an object window, double-click your mouse on the *frmDuplicate* form listing within the Project Explorer. Visual Basic will open the *frmDuplicate* form.

2. Within Visual Basic, select the View menu Toolbox option. Visual Basic will open the Toolbox.

3. Within the Toolbox, double-click your mouse on the TextBox icon. Visual Basic will draw a *TextBox* control, *Text1*, within the *frmDuplicate* form.

4. Within the *frmDuplicate* form window, click your mouse on the *Text1* control to highlight it. Visual Basic will draw a small frame around the control.

5. Select the View menu Properties Window option. Visual Basic will open the Properties Window listing the *Text1* control's properties.

6. Within the Properties Window, change the *Text1* control's properties to the values Table 16.4 lists.

Object	Property	Set As
Text1	Height	375
Text1	Left	3360
Text1	Top	120
Text1	Width	3375
Text1	Text	c:\Windows
Text1	Name	txtSearchDir

Table 16.4 *The* **Text1** *control's properties.*

After you change the *TextBox* control's properties, you can add the *CommandButton* controls to the *frmDuplicate* form, which you will do in the next section.

ADDING THE COMMANDBUTTON CONTROLS TO THE FORM

As you have learned, you will use the *ListView* control to display information on any duplicate files that the *prjDuplicate* project finds within the user-specified directory tree. Within the *prjDuplicate* project, you will use three command buttons to start the search, stop the search, and exit the program. The *Click* events for each command button will perform processing that corresponds to the button's caption.

To add the *CommandButton* controls to the *frmDuplicate* form, perform the following steps:

1. If Visual Basic is not displaying the *frmDuplicate* form within an object window, double-click your mouse on the *frmDuplicate* form listing within the Project Explorer. Visual Basic will open the *frmDuplicate* form.

2. Within Visual Basic, select the View menu Toolbox option. Visual Basic will open the Toolbox.

3. Within the Toolbox, double-click your mouse on the CommandButton icon. Visual Basic will draw a *CommandButton* control, *Command1*, within the *frmDuplicate* form.

4. Repeat Step 3 two more times to add the *Command2* and *Command3* buttons to the *frmDuplicate* form.

5. Within the *frmDuplicate* form, click your mouse on a *CommandButton* control to highlight it. Visual Basic will draw a small frame around the control.

6. Select the View menu Properties Window option. Visual Basic will open the Properties Window listing the selected control's properties.

7. Within the Properties Window, change the highlighted control's properties to the values Table 16.5 lists.

8. Repeat Steps 5, 6, and 7 to change the properties for all three *CommandButton* controls to the values Table 16.5 lists.

Object	Property	Set As
Command1	Caption	List Duplicate Files
Command1	Height	375

Table 16.5 *The* **CommandButton** *controls' properties. (continued on following page)*

Object	Property	Set As
Command1	*Left*	240
Command1	*Top*	600
Command1	*Width*	1815
Command1	*Name*	*cmdFiles*
Command2	*Caption*	*&Stop Searching*
Command2	*Height*	375
Command2	*Left*	2640
Command2	*Top*	600
Command2	*Width*	1815
Command2	*Name*	*cmdStop*
Command3	*Caption*	*E&xit*
Command3	*Height*	375
Command3	*Left*	5040
Command3	*Top*	600
Command3	*Width*	1815
Command3	*Name*	*cmdExit*

Table 16.5 The **CommandButton** *controls' properties. (continued from previous page)*

After you set the properties for the *CommandButton* controls, the *frmDuplicate* form will look similar to Figure 16.8.

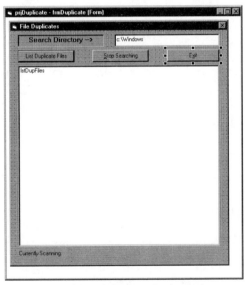

Figure 16.8 The **frmDuplicate** *form after you add and format the controls.*

WRITING THE PROGRAM CODE FOR THE PRJDUPLICATE PROJECT

As you have learned, the *prjDuplicate* project performs significant processing. The project searches an entire directory tree, examines every file, remembers certain characteristics from each file's total set of characteristics, and maintains that information about the file as the program continues to search the tree. The project uses a recursive procedure to search the directory tree and uses a temporary database to maintain information on the files the project examines.

WRITING THE MDLFILEDATA MODULE

As you have learned, the *prjDuplicate* project uses Windows API calls and a recursive procedure to search through all the subdirectories of a user-provided directory tree and to read the files from the subdirectories. The *mdlFileData* module declares the API functions, the constants you will use to check the API function return values, and the structures you will use within the *DirWalk* and *DirWalkRecurse* procedures. The *mdlFileData* module also includes the *StripTerminator* function.

Writing the Declarations for the mdlFileData Module

As you have learned, you will declare the constants, structures, and API functions for the *prjDuplicate* project in the *mdlFileData* module's General–Declarations section. As you have seen in other chapters, the General–Declarations section is long because of the number of different declarations within it. Just as with other long sections, it is worthwhile to consider each declaration set on its own. The declarations begin with the constant declarations, which the following program code implements:

```
Public Const MAX_PATH = 255
Public Const FILE_ATTRIBUTE_DIRECTORY = &H10
Public Const FILE_ATTRIBUTE_ARCHIVE = &H20
Public Const FILE_ATTRIBUTE_COMPRESSED = &H800
Public Const FILE_ATTRIBUTE_HIDDEN = &H2
Public Const FILE_ATTRIBUTE_NORMAL = &H80
Public Const FILE_ATTRIBUTE_READONLY = &H1
Public Const FILE_ATTRIBUTE_SYSTEM = &H4
Public Const FILE_ATTRIBUTE_TEMPORARY = &H100
Public Const INVALID_HANDLE_VALUE = -1
```

The first constant represents the maximum length the program believes the operating system supports for a path; depending on your installation (Windows NT 4.0, FAT32, and so on), the maximum path length may be longer. However, 260 characters is a reasonable number and ensures that the program will work on Windows 95, as well as on the newer operating systems. The next eight constants, which all begin with *FILE*, represent the file attribute constants that you will check each file against to determine its characteristics. The *prjDuplicate* program does not use all eight constants; however, it is useful to know the others for your own programs. Finally, the program uses the *INVALID_HANDLE_VALUE* constant to make sure the *FindFirstFile* function returns a valid search handle that the *FindNextFile* function can use to continue searching.

The next block in the General–Declarations section includes the declarations for the *FILETIME* structure, the *WIN32_FIND_DATA* structure, and the *DIRWALKDATA* structure. The following code implements the *FILETIME* structure's definition:

```
Type FILETIME
  dwLowDateTime As Long
  dwHighDateTime As Long
End Type
```

The *FILETIME* structure contains two *Long* members. Windows stores date and time values within a compressed time structure. When you work with the *FILETIME* structure, you must convert the *FILETIME* structure's *Long* values into a Visual Basic *Date* value to perform date-specific processing on a file.

The *WIN32_FIND_DATA* structure uses the *FILETIME* structure to define several of its members. The following code implements the *WIN32_FIND_DATA* structure's definition:

```
Type WIN32_FIND_DATA
  dwFileAttributes As Long
  ftCreationTime As FILETIME
  ftLastAccessTime As FILETIME
  ftLastWriteTime As FILETIME
  nFileSizeHigh As Long
  nFileSizeLow As Long
  dwReserved0 As Long
  dwReserved1 As Long
  cFileName As String * MAX_PATH
  cAlternate As String * 14
End Type
```

The *WIN32_FIND_DATA* structure contains several important members that the *prjDuplicate* project will manipulate. The most important members for the *prjDuplicate* project are the *ftCreationTime*, *nFileSizeLow*, and *cFileName* members. These three members contain the time and date of the file's creation, the file's size, and the file's name, respectively. The *dwFileAttributes* member, which you will use extensively in Chapter 17, contains a *Long* value that represents the currently set file attributes. The *ftLastAccessTime* and *ftLastWriteTime* members correspond to the file's last access time and last write time. The *nFileSizeHigh* and *nFileSizeLow* members represent the file's size, in bytes. If the file's size is less than 2.15Gb, the entire file size is within the *nFileSizeLow* member. If the file's size is larger than 2.15Gb, the *nFileSizeHigh* member will contain an offset value that, when you combine it with the *nFileSizeLow* member, yields the complete file size. The *prjDuplicate* project assumes that files are not larger than 2.15Gb in size.

The *dwReserved* members correspond to operating system-reserved values that may be available for program access in future Windows versions. The *cFileName* member contains the filename for the file. If the filename is a long filename (as opposed to an MS-DOS 8.3 name) and the operating system supports alternate filenames (as Windows 95 does), the *cAlternate* member will contain the 8.3 style name for the file. Both the *FindFirstFile* and *FindNextFile* functions return values within an instance of the *WIN32_FIND_DATA* structure.

The last structure definition for the project is the *DIRWALKDATA* structure. The following code implements the *DIRWALKDATA* structure:

507

```
Type DIRWALKDATA
    TreeLB As Long
    nDepth As Integer
    Recurse As Boolean
    szBuf As String * 1000
    nIndent As Integer
    OK As Boolean
    IsDir As Boolean
    FindData As WIN32_FIND_DATA
End Type
```

The *DIRWALKDATA* structure contains information that the program uses during the recursive procedure that performs the operative processing for the search routine. The *nDepth* member, for instance, contains the current directory tree level that the search routine is within. For example, if the search begins in *c:\sample* and the program is currently searching the *c:\sample\subdir1\subdir2\subdir3* directory, the *nDepth* member will contain the value 4, because the program is currently three levels below the starting directory. The *szBuf* member contains the full path to the program's current location. The *nIndent* member contains an indent value that corresponds to the *nDepth* member that you can use to create indented directory tree reports. The program sets the *IsDir* flag to *True* if the current filename is a directory, and sets the *IsDir* flag to *False* if it is not. The *FindData* member is a variable of type *WIN32_FIND_DATA*. The *FindData* member maintains information about the currently retrieved file within the current directory. The only procedures within the program that use the *DIRWALKDATA* structure are the *DirWalk* procedure and the *DirWalkRecurse* procedure.

As you have learned, the *prjDuplicate* project uses a series of Windows API function calls to perform its processing. The following code implements the declarations for the Windows API functions:

```
Declare Function SetCurrentDirectory Lib "kernel32" Alias _
    "SetCurrentDirectoryA" (ByVal lpPathName As String) As Long
Declare Function GetCurrentDirectory Lib "kernel32" Alias _
    "GetCurrentDirectoryA" (ByVal nBufferLength As Long, _
    ByVal lpBuffer As String) As Long
Declare Function FindFirstFile Lib "kernel32" Alias "FindFirstFileA" _
    (ByVal lpFileName As String, lpFindFileData As WIN32_FIND_DATA) As Long
Declare Function FindNextFile Lib "kernel32" Alias "FindNextFileA" _
    (ByVal hFindFile As Long, lpFindFileData As WIN32_FIND_DATA) As Long
Declare Function FindClose Lib "kernel32" (ByVal hFindFile As Long) As Long
```

The *prjDuplicate* program uses five Windows API functions. The *GetCurrentDirectory* and *SetCurrentDirectory* functions let you retrieve and set, respectively, the current directory on the current drive. The *FindFirstFile* and *FindNextFile* functions let you search a directory for all files that match a pattern you specify. If *FindFirstFile* is successful, it will return a search handle that you will use with the *FindNextFile* function to locate the next file within the search directory that matches the search pattern. If *FindFirstFile* is not successful, it will return -1 *(INVALID_HANDLE_VALUE)*. If *FindFirstFile* returns a valid handle value, you will use the *FindClose* function to close a handle after your program finishes using it.

WRITING THE CODE FOR THE STRIPTERMINATOR FUNCTION

As you have learned, you must always strip the *NULL*-terminator from the end of strings the Windows API returns to your Visual Basic programs. The string members within the *WIN32_FIND_DATA* structure are no exception. To strip the *NULL*-terminator from the strings within the *WIN32_FIND_DATA* structure, you will use the *StripTerminator* function. The following code implements the *StripTerminator* function:

```
Public Function StripTerminator(ByVal strString As String) As String
  Dim intZeroPos As Integer

  intZeroPos = InStr(strString, Chr$(0))
  If intZeroPos > 0 Then
    StripTerminator = Left$(strString, intZeroPos - 1)
  Else
    StripTerminator = strString
  End If
End Function
```

As Chapter 1, "Introduction to Visual Basic" detailed, the *StripTerminator* function checks an incoming string to determine whether or not it contains a *NULL*-terminator. If the string does contain the terminator, the function will return everything before the terminator as the string's value. If the string does not contain the terminator, the function will return the entire incoming string as the string's value.

WRITING THE CODE FOR THE TEXTONLY FUNCTION

In the previous two sections, you have defined the project's constants and types, declared the Windows API functions the program will use, and written the *StripTerminator* function. The second function that you will define within the *mdlFileData* module is the *TextOnly* function. The following code implements the *TextOnly* function:

```
Public Function TextOnly(ByVal Buffer As String) As String
  TextOnly = Trim(Buffer)
End Function
```

The *TextOnly* function accepts an incoming *String* value and returns the string value without leading or trailing spaces. Within the *prjDuplicate* project, you will use the *TextOnly* function to trim the trailing spaces from fixed-length strings and return the resulting string within a standard variable-length string.

WRITING THE CODE FOR THE FRMDUPLICATE FORM

As you have learned, the *mdlFileData* module contains the declarations for the program, the *StripTerminator* function you will use whenever you return a string from an API call to Visual Basic, and the *TextOnly* function, which returns a trimmed variable-length string from an incoming string. The primary processing for the *prjDuplicate* project occurs within the *frmDuplicate* form. The *frmDuplicate* form also declares several variables that the program uses or checks within multiple procedures. The following code implements the General–Declarations section for the *frmDuplicate* form:

```
Option Explicit
Dim Current As String
Dim StopSearching As Boolean
Dim wkSpace As Workspace, dbSearchTable As Database, idxNew As Index
Dim SearchRs As Recordset
```

The *Current* variable maintains the current directory at the time the user starts the program, and changes the current directory back to the original directory when the program completes its processing. The *StopSearching* flag variable maintains a *True* or *False* value that the program uses within the recursing search loop to stop the search if the user clicks the mouse on the Stop Searching button. The next four declarations are also data access objects that you will use to manipulate the temporary database the *prjDuplicate* program uses to manage the file information it retrieves from the directory tree.

WRITING THE CODE FOR THE FORM_LOAD EVENT

As you have learned, each time you load a form, the first event the form invokes is the *Form_Load* event—even before the program displays the form. In the *prjDuplicate* project, the *frmDuplicate* form loads when the project begins. The following code implements the *frmDuplicate* form's *Form_Load* event:

```
Private Sub Form_Load()
   Set wkSpace = Workspaces(0)
   Current = CurDir$
   RefreshList
   cmdStop.Enabled = False
   StopSearching = True
End Sub
```

The *Form_Load* event performs three important tasks. It initializes the *wkSpace* object to the default workspace and sets the *Current* variable to the current directory. The event's program code then calls the *RefreshList* procedure, which initializes the *lstDupFiles* control. When you close the project and unload the form, the program code will set the directory back to the starting directory. The following code implements the *Form_Unload* event:

```
Private Sub Form_Unload(Cancel As Integer)
   SetCurrentDirectory (Current)
End Sub
```

The *Form_Unload* event uses the *SetCurrentDirectory* API function to change the directory back to the original directory. Remember, you set the *Current* variable equal to the system's current directory at the time the program began. When the user tries to stop the program, however, the program will first check its status to determine whether or not it is currently searching. The following code implements the *Form_QueryUnload* event:

```
Private Sub Form_QueryUnload(Cancel As Integer, UnloadMode As Integer)
   Dim Response As Integer

   If Not StopSearching Then
     Response = MsgBox("Exiting now will cancel search. Continue?", _
         vbYesNo, "DupFiles")
     If Response = vbNo Then Cancel = True
   End If
End Sub
```

If the user clicks the mouse on the form's close box while the program is searching, the program will use a message box to let the user know that exiting will stop the current search, and will then verify that the user actually wants to exit. If the user does not want to cancel, the program continues its processing; otherwise, the program stops searching and unloads itself.

WRITING THE CODE FOR THE REFRESHLIST PROCEDURE

As you learned in the previous section, the *Form_Load* event calls the *RefreshList* procedure, which resets the *lstDupFiles* *ListView* control, clears its contents, and places the headers at the control's top. The following code implements the *RefreshList* procedure:

```
Private Sub RefreshList()
   Dim pdblWidth As Double
```

```
    Me.lstDupFiles.ListItems.Clear
    Me.lstDupFiles.ColumnHeaders.Clear
    pdblWidth = Me.lstDupFiles.Width
    Me.lstDupFiles.ColumnHeaders.Add , , "File Path & Name", _
        pdblWidth / 3 + 500
    Me.lstDupFiles.ColumnHeaders.Add , , "Date Created/Modified", _
        pdblWidth / 3 - 475
    Me.lstDupFiles.ColumnHeaders.Add , , "File Size", pdblWidth / 3 - 975
End Sub
```

The *RefreshList* procedure uses a single local variable, the *pdblWidth* variable, a *Double* value to which the program code assigns the *lstDupFiles* control's width. The program code within the procedure clears the items in the list, clears the headers in the list, and then adds the three headers to the *lstViewControl* that you saw in the "Using the *prjDuplicate* Project" section earlier in this chapter.

510 *WRITING THE CODE FOR THE CMDFILES_CLICK EVENT*

As you have learned, to begin the search process, the user must click the mouse on the *cmdFiles* command button. The *Click* event for the command button calls the actual search routine. The following code implements the *cmdFiles_Click* event:

```
Private Sub cmdFiles_Click()
  StopSearching = False
  cmdFiles.Enabled = False
  cmdStop.Enabled = True
  Me.MousePointer = vbArrowHourglass
  lblScanning.Visible = True
  CreateDB
  If Left$(txtSearchDir.Text, 1) = "\" Then _
      txtSearchDir.Text = Left$(CurDir$, 2) & txtSearchDir.Text
  DirWalk
  lblScanning.Visible = False
  lblCurDir.Caption = ""
  cmdStop.Enabled = False
  StopSearching = True
  cmdFiles.Enabled = True
  Me.MousePointer = vbNormal
  If lstDupFiles.ListItems.Count = 0 Then _
    MsgBox "Program detected no duplicate files!", vbOKOnly
End Sub
```

The program code within the event sets the *StopSearching* flag to *False*, enables the Stop Searching button, disables the List Duplicate Files button, makes the *lblScanning* label visible, and calls the *CreateDB* procedure. As you will learn in the next section, the *CreateDB* procedure creates the temporary database. The program code within the *cmdFiles_Click* event then checks the directory name to ensure it is a valid directory name, and calls the *DirWalk* procedure, which performs the actual drive search. You will learn about the *DirWalk* procedure in this chapter's "Writing the Search Program Code" section. After the search completes, the program code again enables the List Duplicate Files button and disables the Stop Searching button. If the search found no duplicate files, the last statement in the event's program code alerts the user that the program located no duplicates.

WRITING THE CREATEDB PROCEDURE'S CODE

When you begin a search, the program creates a new instance of the temporary database. The *cmdFiles_Click* event calls the *CreateDB* procedure to create the new database. The following code implements the *CreateDB* procedure:

```
Private Sub CreateDB()
  Dim NewField As Field, tdf As TableDef
```

```
      On Error Resume Next
      dbSearchTable.Close
      On Error GoTo 0
      If Dir(App.Path & "\tempfile.mdb") <> "" Then
        On Error Resume Next
        dbSearchTable.Close
        On Error GoTo 0
        Kill App.Path & "\tempfile.mdb"
      End If
      On Error Resume Next
      Set dbSearchTable = wkSpace.CreateDatabase(App.Path & "\tempfile.mdb", _
          dbLangGeneral)
      If Err.Number <> 0 Then
        MsgBox "Internal Data Creation Error", vbCritical
        Exit Sub
      End If
      On Error GoTo 0
      Set tdf = dbSearchTable.CreateTableDef("SearchTable")
      Set NewField = tdf.CreateField("Counter", dbLong)
      NewField.Attributes = dbAutoIncrField
      tdf.Fields.Append NewField
      Set NewField = tdf.CreateField("File Name", dbText, MAX_PATH)
      tdf.Fields.Append NewField
      Set NewField = tdf.CreateField("Path", dbText, MAX_PATH)
      tdf.Fields.Append NewField
      Set NewField = tdf.CreateField("Created/Modified", dbText, 100)
      tdf.Fields.Append NewField
      Set NewField = tdf.CreateField("File Size", dbLong)
      tdf.Fields.Append NewField
      dbSearchTable.TableDefs.Append tdf
      With tdf
        Set idxNew = .CreateIndex("NewIndex")
        With idxNew
          .Fields.Append .CreateField("File Name")
          .Fields.Append .CreateField("Created/Modified")
          .Fields.Append .CreateField("File Size")
          .Unique = True
        End With
        .Indexes.Append idxNew
        .Indexes.Refresh
      End With
      DoEvents
      Set SearchRs = dbSearchTable.OpenRecordset("Select * From SearchTable")
    End Sub
```

The *CreateDB* procedure uses several of the data access objects to create and structure the temporary database. In addition to the *dbSearchTable*, *idxNew*, and *SearchRs* variables that you declared previously, the procedure creates local instances of a *Field* object and a *TableDef* object, which it will use to create the table definition and append the fields the temporary database uses to the table.

The procedure's program code first tries to close the *dbSearchTable* object—which closes the temporary database that the program may have created on a previous search. After it closes the object, it then deletes the temporary database from the drive. After ensuring that there is not a *tempfile.mdb* database within the application's directory, it creates the new database within the application's directory. If the program is unable to create the database (for example, if the user tries to run the program from the CD-ROM), the *CreateDB* procedure will alert the user to the error, and exit.

After it successfully creates the *tempfile.mdb* database, the *CreateDB* procedure creates a new table within the database. As you have learned, you will store information within databases in tables, which you can visualize as being similar to spreadsheet pages. After it creates the new table, the procedure's program code appends five fields to the table definition: a counter field, a field to hold the file's name, a field to hold the file's paths, a field to hold the file's last modified data, and a field to hold the file's size. After the procedure code finishes appending fields to the table definition, it appends the table definition to the database.

The procedure's program code then uses the newly created table definition to create an index. The program code creates the index as a unique combination of file name, modification date, and file size. Because the index is unique, when the program code tries to add entries to the database for duplicate files, the database engine will return an error, which the program will then use as its cue to display the duplicate files within the *lstDupFiles* *ListView* control. You will learn more about the record-adding process in the next section.

After the procedure creates the index and appends it to the table definition, the program code initializes the *SearchRS* recordset with a Structured Query Language (SQL) query against the table. When the procedure finishes its execution, the program has created a new database and initialized the *Recordset* object that the program code will later use to add records to and retrieve records from the database.

WRITING THE SEARCH PROGRAM CODE

As you have learned, the *cmdFiles_Click* event creates the temporary database and then calls the *DirWalk* procedure, which begins the search process. As you will learn, *DirWalk* in turn calls *DirWalkRecurse*, the recursive procedure that performs the actual search of the entire tree. The following code implements the *DirWalk* procedure:

```
Private Sub DirWalk()
  Dim TreeLB As Long
  Dim DW As DIRWALKDATA
  Dim SearchDir As String
  Dim Result As Boolean

  RefreshList
  SearchDir = txtSearchDir
  If Mid(SearchDir, 2, 1) <> ":" Then _
    SearchDir = Left(CurDir$, 2) & "\" & SearchDir
  Result = SetCurrentDirectory(SearchDir)
  If Not Result Then
    MsgBox "Couldn't set directory!"
    Exit Sub
  End If
  DW.TreeLB = TreeLB
  DW.Recurse = True
  DirWalkRecurse DW
End Sub
```

The *DirWalk* procedure calls the *RefreshList* procedure to reset the *lstDupFiles* control, then tries to set the directory to the user-entered directory. If the procedure is unable to set the directory, the program will display a message box indicating the error to the user, and exit. If the procedure is able to set the directory, it initializes some elements of the *DW* variable (of type *DIRWALKDATA*) and calls the *DirWalkRecurse* procedure with the *DW* variable. The following code implements the *DirWalkRecurse* procedure:

```
Private Sub DirWalkRecurse(ByRef DW As DIRWALKDATA)
  Dim GetCurrentResult As Long
  Dim Result As Boolean
  Dim hFind As Long
  Dim PathName As String, AddFileName As String
  Dim testlong As Long
  Dim GetDir As String * MAX_PATH
  Dim ItemX As ListItem

  DW.nDepth = DW.nDepth + 1
  GetCurrentResult = GetCurrentDirectory(1000, DW.szBuf)
  DW.szBuf = StripTerminator(DW.szBuf)
```

```
        hFind = FindFirstFile("*.*", DW.FindData)
        testlong = GetCurrentDirectory(1000, GetDir)
        DW.OK = (hFind <> INVALID_HANDLE_VALUE)
        Do While DW.OK And Not StopSearching
           DW.IsDir = ((DW.FindData.dwFileAttributes And _
              FILE_ATTRIBUTE_DIRECTORY) = FILE_ATTRIBUTE_DIRECTORY)
           If DW.IsDir = False Then
              If Right(TextOnly(DW.szBuf), 1) = "\" Then
                 PathName = TextOnly(DW.szBuf)
              Else
                 PathName = TextOnly(DW.szBuf) & "\"
              End If
              AddFileName = StripTerminator(DW.FindData.cFileName)
              lblCurDir.Caption = PathName
              SearchRs.AddNew
                 SearchRs.Fields("Path") = PathName
                 SearchRs.Fields("File Name") = AddFileName
                 SearchRs.Fields("Created/Modified") = _
                    Format(FileDateTime(PathName & AddFileName), "m/d/yyyy h:mm:ss")
                 SearchRs.Fields("File Size") = DW.FindData.nFileSizeLow
              On Error Resume Next
              SearchRs.Update
              If Err.Number = 3022 Then
                 On Error GoTo 0
                 DisplayFiles PathName, AddFileName, DW.FindData.nFileSizeLow
                 DoEvents
              End If
           End If
           DW.OK = FindNextFile(hFind, DW.FindData)
           DoEvents
        Loop

        If Not (hFind = INVALID_HANDLE_VALUE) Then Result = FindClose(hFind)
        If DW.Recurse Then
           hFind = FindFirstChildDir("*.*", DW.FindData)
           DW.OK = hFind <> INVALID_HANDLE_VALUE
           Do While DW.OK And Not StopSearching
              If (SetCurrentDirectory( _
                 Trim(StripTerminator(DW.FindData.cFileName)))) _
                 Then DirWalkRecurse DW
                 Result = SetCurrentDirectory("..")
              End If
              DW.OK = FindNextChildDir(hFind, DW.FindData)
           Loop
           If (hFind <> INVALID_HANDLE_VALUE) Then Result = FindClose(hFind)
        End If
     End Sub
```

The *DirWalkRecurse* procedure manages the search within the *prjDuplicate* project and adds the files to the list boxes as it retrieves them. Each time the program finds a new subdirectory, it will call the *DirWalkRecurse* procedure to process the files within that subdirectory. The procedure begins with a call to *GetCurrentDirectory*, which returns the current directory into the *szBuf* member. After it sets the current directory, the procedure calls the *FindFirstFile* function to get a handle to the files within the directory. If *FindFirstFile* finds no files within the directory, the procedure will skip the search loop and move on to the end of the procedure. If *FindFirstFile* finds files within the directory, the procedure will loop through all the files in the directory within a *Do-While* loop.

Within the *Do-While* loop, the program code tries to add the file name, path name, last modification time, and file size of each file it finds within the directory. As you learned in the previous section, if a record with the same file name, last modification time, and file size already exists within the database, the database engine will return an error when the program tries to add the record. The program code within the *DirWalkRecurse* procedure checks for that error, and if the database engine returns the error, the program code calls the *DisplayFiles* procedure, which displays the duplicate files within the *lstDupFiles* control. The next section examines the *DisplayFiles* procedure in detail.

After the program finishes with the files in the current directory, it then searches the current directory to determine whether or not it contains any subdirectories. If the directory contains subdirectories, the procedure calls itself with each subdirectory in turn. The recursion continues until the procedure reaches the directory tree's bottom, then the program returns to the directory that is one directory above the current directory in the tree. If that directory contains additional subdirectories, the procedure will search them. If it does not, the procedure will go up another level in the tree until it processes every file and subdirectory in the tree the user specified as the search tree.

514

The *DirWalkRecurse* procedure uses a series of helper functions to process the possible subdirectories within the current directory. A later section in this chapter, "Writing the Code for the Subdirectory Helper Functions," explains the helper functions.

UNDERSTANDING RECURSION

As you have learned, Visual Basic lets you divide your program into smaller pieces called functions or procedures. Using functions and procedures, your program becomes easier to understand, program, and test. In addition, you can often use the functions and procedures you create for one program within another program. As your programs execute, one function may call another, which calls another, which may, in turn, call several other functions—each function to perform a specific operation. Visual Basic even lets a function call itself.

A *recursive function* is a function that calls itself to perform a specific operation. The process of a function calling itself is *recursion*. As the complexity of your programs and functions increases, you might find that you can easily define many operations in terms of themselves. For such cases, you might want to create a recursive function. Many programming books, for example, use the problem of how to reverse the characters within a string to illustrate how recursion works. For example, you can display the characters within a string in reverse using code similar to the following:

```
For I = Len(String) to 1 - 1
  Debug.Print Mid(String, I, 1)
Next
```

However, this code may not be clear to some readers and is also not reusable, although it is the quickest way to process the string. A function that more clearly shows how the process works might appear similar to the *Display_Backward* procedure, as shown in the following code fragment:

```
Private Sub Display_Backward(ByVal DisplayString As String)
  If Len(DisplayString) >1 Then _
    Display_Backward Right(DisplayString, Len(DisplayString) - 1)
  Debug.Print Left(DisplayString, 1);
End Sub
```

When the program's code first calls the *Display_Backward* procedure, the procedure will evaluate the *DisplayString* string's length. If it is longer than one, the procedure calls itself with the full string, except for the first digit. The *Display_Backward* procedure then evaluates the new string, and continues to call itself until the string is only a single digit in length. The procedure then prints that character and returns to the calling instance of the procedure, which prints its leftmost character, and so on. Figure 16.9 illustrates the chain of recursive function invocations and return values for the *Display_Backward("ABCD")* procedure call.

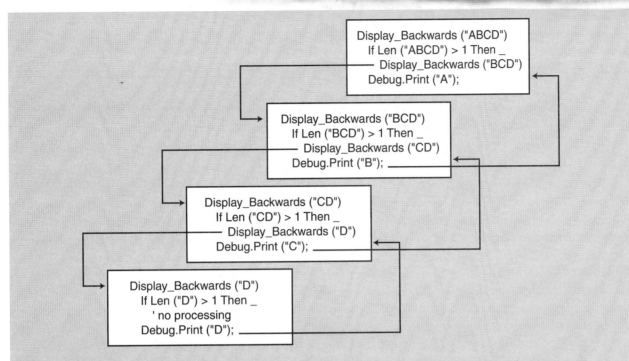

Figure 16.9 *The chain of procedure calls and output values for the recursive* **Display_Backward** *procedure.*

A recursive function or procedure is somewhat like a looping construct in that you must specify an ending condition. If you do not, the function will never end. In the case of the *Display_Backward* procedure, the ending condition is the string's length of 1.

WRITING THE CODE FOR THE DISPLAYFILES PROCEDURE

As you learned in the previous section, the *DirWalkRecurse* procedure calls the *DisplayFiles* procedure whenever it encounters a duplicate file. The *DisplayFiles* procedure, in turn, will add one or both duplicate files to the *lstDupFiles* control. The following code implements the *DisplayFiles* procedure:

```
Private Sub DisplayFiles(Path As String, FileName As String, _
   FileSize As Long)
 Dim TempRs As Recordset, SQLText As String, ItemX As ListItem
 Dim AlreadyShown As Boolean, I As Integer

 SQLText = "Select * From SearchTable Where [File Name] = """ & FileName
 SQLText = SQLText & """ And [File Size] = " & FileSize
 SQLText = SQLText & " And [Created/Modified] = """ & _
     Format(FileDateTime(Path & FileName), "m/d/yyyy h:mm:ss") & """"
 Set TempRs = dbSearchTable.OpenRecordset(SQLText)

 For I = 1 To lstDupFiles.ListItems.Count
   If lstDupFiles.ListItems(I).Tag = TempRs.Fields("Path") & _
      TempRs.Fields("File Name") Then
     AlreadyShown = True
     Exit For
   End If
 Next
 If Not AlreadyShown Then
   With TempRs
     Set ItemX = lstDupFiles.ListItems.Add(, , .Fields("Path") & _
       .Fields("File Name"))
     ItemX.SubItems(1) = .Fields("Created/Modified")
     ItemX.SubItems(2) = .Fields("File Size")
```

```
            ItemX.Tag = .Fields("Path") & .Fields("File Name")
        End With
    End If
    Set ItemX = lstDupFiles.ListItems.Add(, , Path & FileName)
    ItemX.SubItems(1) = Format(FileDateTime(Path & FileName), _
        "m/d/yyyy h:mm:ss")
    ItemX.SubItems(2) = FileSize
    ItemX.Tag = Path & FileName
End Sub
```

The *DisplayFiles* procedure declares a local *Recordset* object that it uses to get the duplicate file the database contains, a *ListItem* variable, which you will use to add items to the *lstDupFiles* control, and several other local variables. The first three program code lines construct an SQL query, which will return the record within the database of the duplicate file the program just encountered. The program code then loops through each element in the *lstDupFiles* control to determine whether or not the control is already displaying a duplicate occurrence for the file. If it is, the program code assigns the *AlreadyShown* variable a *True* value to protect against displaying that file multiple times. If the *lstDupFiles* control is not already displaying the duplicate file, the program code adds the information from the database to the list view. In any event, the procedure adds the new occurrence of the duplicate file in its last four lines. Note that the procedure sets the *Tag* property equal to the file's fully qualified path and filename, which the program will use when the user clicks the mouse on a duplicate file. You will learn more about the effect of a user's mouse click in the "Writing the Code for the *lstDupFiles_Click* Event" section later in this chapter.

WRITING THE CODE FOR THE SUBDIRECTORY HELPER FUNCTIONS

As you have learned, the *DirWalkRecurse* procedure calls a series of helper functions to help it determine the subdirectories within the current directory. The first helper function that *DirWalkRecurse* calls is the *FindFirstChildDir* function. The following code implements the *FindFirstChildDir* function:

```
Private Function FindFirstChildDir(szPath As String, _
        lclFindData As WIN32_FIND_DATA) As Long
    Dim hFindFile As Long
    Dim Found As Boolean
    Dim Result As Boolean

    hFindFile = FindFirstFile(szPath, lclFindData)
    If (hFindFile <> INVALID_HANDLE_VALUE) Then
        If Not IsChildDir(lclFindData) Then _
            Found = FindNextChildDir(hFindFile, lclFindData)
        If Not Found Then
            Result = FindClose(hFindFile)
            hFindFile = INVALID_HANDLE_VALUE
        End If
    End If
    FindFirstChildDir = hFindFile
End Function
```

The *FindFirstChildDir* function accepts as its incoming parameters the current path and a *WIN32_FIND_DATA* structure. The *FindFirstChildDir* function then searches that path for subdirectories. If the search finds any files, the function enters a series of search checks. The first search check calls the *IsChildDir* function. If the *IsChildDir* function returns *False*, the program will call the *FindNextChildDir* function. If the *FindNextChildDir* function is also unsuccessful in locating a subdirectory, the function sets the file handle to *INVALID_HANDLE_VALUE* and returns to the *DirWalkRecurse* function, which then climbs a level in the tree.

The *IsChildDir* function checks the found file's attribute byte and ensures that it is a directory name and not the system-generated "." or ".." subdirectory. If the file is actually a subdirectory, the function returns *True*; otherwise, the function returns *False*. The following code implements the *IsChildDir* function:

```
Private Function IsChildDir(FindData As WIN32_FIND_DATA) As Boolean
  If ((FindData.dwFileAttributes And FILE_ATTRIBUTE_DIRECTORY) = _
     FILE_ATTRIBUTE_DIRECTORY And Left(FindData.cFileName, 1) <> "." _
     And Left(FindData.cFileName, 2) <> "..") Then
    IsChildDir = True
  Else
    IsChildDir = False
  End If
End Function
```

The *FindNextChildDir* function accepts a search handle and a *WIN32_FIND_DATA* structure. It loops either until it finds a valid subdirectory or until there are no more files to search in the directory. The following code implements the *FindNextChildDir* function:

```
Private Function FindNextChildDir(hFindFile As Long, _
    FindData As WIN32_FIND_DATA) As Boolean
  Dim Found As Boolean

  Found = False
  Do
    FindData.cFileName = Space$(MAX_PATH)
    Found = FindNextFile(hFindFile, FindData)
    FindData.cFileName = StripTerminator(FindData.cFileName)
  Loop While (Found = True And (Not IsChildDir(FindData)))
  FindNextChildDir = Found
End Function
```

The *FindNextChildDir* function uses the *IsChildDir* function to verify that a filename is a subdirectory. If the filename is not a subdirectory, the loop continues. If the filename is a subdirectory, the loop exits, the function returns *True*, and the *WIN32_FIND_DATA* structure contains the name of the subdirectory.

WRITING THE CODE FOR THE LSTDUPFILES_CLICK EVENT

As you learned in the "Using the *prjDuplicate* Project" section of this chapter, a user can click the mouse on an entry within the *lstDupFiles* control after a successful search for duplicate files. The program will then give the user the option to delete the file. The following code implements the *lstDupFiles_Click* event:

```
Private Sub lstDupFiles_ItemClick(ByVal Item As ComctlLib.ListItem)
  Dim Response As Integer
  Static JustDeleted As Boolean

  If JustDeleted Then
    JustDeleted = False
    Exit Sub
  End If
  Response = MsgBox("Delete duplicate file? " & Chr(13) & Chr(10) & _
      "Filename: " & Item.Tag, vbYesNo, "Delete Duplicate Message")
  If Response = vbYes Then
    Response = MsgBox("This will permanently delete this file. Continue?", _
        vbYesNo, "Delete Protection")
    If Response = vbYes Then
      On Error Resume Next
      Kill Item.Tag
      If Err.Number <> 0 Then
        MsgBox "Access Error", vbCritical
      Else
        lstDupFiles.ListItems.Remove Item.Index
        JustDeleted = True
      End If
    Else
```

```
            JustDeleted = True
         End If
      Else
         JustDeleted = True
      End If
End Sub
```

When the user clicks the mouse on an item within the *lstDupFiles* control, the program will invoke the *Click* event. As you can see, the *Click* event receives the user-selected item as its sole parameter. Within the *Click* event, the program code declares the *Static JustDeleted* variable. Because of the way the control handles the *Click* event, you must use the *JustDeleted* flag variable to protect against the program prompting the user multiple times to delete the file after a single mouse click.

The event's program code first checks the *JustDeleted* variable. If the program has previously set the variable's value to *True*, the user has already clicked the mouse on the item and progressed through the options. The *If-Then* statement resets the variable's value and exits the subroutine. If the *JustDeleted* variable is *False*, the program code asks the user whether the user wants to delete the selected file. If the user clicks the mouse on the Yes button, the program displays a second message box that double-checks to be sure the user wants to delete the file, and deletes the file. The program code then updates the *lstDupFiles* control's display, and exits. If the user clicks the mouse on the No button for either the initial delete query or the follow-up delete query, the procedure exits without deleting the file.

WRITING THE CODE FOR THE OTHER COMMAND BUTTONS

When you created the *frmDuplicate* form, you added three command buttons to the form. As you learned, the *cmdFiles* command button starts the search and calls the *DirWalk* procedure. The other two command buttons perform much simpler processing. The *cmdStop* command button sets the *StopSearching* flag variable to *True*. When the program code next encounters the *StopSearching* test, it will stop searching. The following code implements the *cmdStop_Click* event:

```
Private Sub cmdStop_Click()
   StopSearching = True
End Sub
```

The *cmdExit* command button performs similarly simple processing. The following code implements the *cmdExit_Click* event:

```
Private Sub cmdExit_Click()
   Unload Me
End Sub
```

As you have learned, when the program unloads the form, it will reset the operating system's current directory to the operating system directory the program had set before it began to execute.

ENHANCEMENTS YOU CAN MAKE TO THE prjDuplicate PROJECT

As you have learned, the Windows API functions that you use within the *prjDuplicate* project are powerful and useful. For example, your own programs might use a procedure similar to the *DirWalkRecurse* procedure to search a user's drive for previously installed components, and then update or replace the components the user needs.

Alternatively, you can use the Windows API calls to *FindFirstFile* and *FindNextFile* to create useful tools that let you search a location based on certain criteria you specify. You can use the information the *WIN32_FIND_DATA* structure contains to perform significant pre-processing on files and determine if they match more specific criteria than a simple name match.

You can also use the information the *prjDuplicate* project returns about duplicate files to more effectively administer your own computer or a network. With some modifications, the *prjDuplicate* project can search all the drives on a network that a user had access to, and generate information about unnecessary duplications. On large networks, the potential to reduce storage space use and better optimize network drives is especially significant.

PUTTING IT ALL TOGETHER

This chapter's project, *prjDuplicate*, introduced you to how you can use Windows API functions, custom structures, and recursion to search an entire drive or directory tree and return valuable information about all the files within that drive or tree. You also learned how to create temporary databases and how to use the Data Access Objects (DAO) Object Library to create tables within databases and to create indexes within the tables. In addition, you worked with the *Microsoft ListView* control and used the extra information you can store within items in the control to perform additional processing.

This chapter also introduced you to using recursive functions and procedures to perform repetitive tasks. The recursive procedure discussed in this chapter travels up and down a directory tree and returns information about files located within each tree level. You can use recursive functions and procedures in other programs for many different programming tasks, but your recursive functions and procedures will generally follow the form of the *DirWalkRecurse* procedure in that they will call themselves repeatedly until the procedure reaches some end condition.

In the next chapter, Chapter 17, "Using the Windows API to Manage File Types," you will create a Visual Basic program similar to the *prjDuplicate* program that you can use to retrieve extended information about file attributes and locations. Before you continue with Chapter 17, however, make sure you understand the following key concepts:

✓ Within Visual Basic, your programs can nest structures for additional clarity. The *prjDuplicate* program nests three levels of structures to make the structures' purpose more evident.

✓ Within your programs, you can use either Visual Basic's built-in commands or Windows API function calls to get information about files previously saved onto a drive or disk.

✓ While Visual Basic's *Dir* function is generally sufficient for most directory tasks, it does not support recursion. To perform recursive directory searches within your Visual Basic programs, you must use the Windows API directory functions.

✓ Within your programs, you can use a file's *Directory* attribute bit (within the attribute byte) to determine whether the file is a directory or a file. You can check the attribute of any file, whether it is a file that a Windows API call returns or a file that Visual Basic's built-in commands return.

✓ When your Visual Basic programs must locate files that meet user- or program-specified characteristics, you can use the *FindFirstFile* and *FindNextFile* API functions to perform the searches.

✓ Within your Visual Basic programs, you can use the *FindFirstFile* and *FindNextFile* functions to perform searches within recursive subroutines because the *FindFirstFile* function returns a *handle* (a unique integer value) that you can maintain within different instances of the same recursive function.

✓ When you use *ListView* controls within your Visual Basic programs, you can use the information that you place with each item in a *ListView* control to perform user-directed processing with that item.

✓ When you work with handles within your programs, whether search handles, window handles, or other handles, your programs should always close handles they create after they finish using the handle. For example, your programs should use the *FindClose* call to close handles that *FindFirstFile* returns.

✓ Within your Visual Basic programs, you can use the Data Access Objects (DAO) Object Library to create and delete temporary databases, which your programs can use to store and process information that they do not have to retain after execution.

✓ Your Visual Basic programs can use the DAO Object Library to create database tables and indexes during the programs' processing.

Chapter 17

Using the Windows API to Manage File Types

In previous chapters, you have learned that your Visual Basic programs can use the Windows Application Programming Interface (API) to access built-in operating system functions. In Chapter 16, "Accessing Local Drives to Find Duplicate Files," you used a combination of Visual Basic controls, Windows API calls, and recursive functions to read an entire directory tree and search the tree for duplicate files. In this chapter, you will use the Windows API to perform similar processing. However, rather than searching for specific matches, the *prjFileAttributes* program will search the entire tree and return all files within that tree. The *prjFileAttributes* program will then sort those files based on their *file attributes* and place them into list boxes that reflect the files' characteristics.

520

Every file you save onto a disk or a drive has certain unique characteristics that identify the file to the operating system. In Chapter 16, you used file characteristics, such as size and modification date, to determine whether a file was a duplicate of another file. Your computer's operating system also attaches an *attribute value* to each file that you save. The attribute value represents four specific characteristics about the file: *Read-Only, Hidden, Archive,* or *System*. Files may have none, one, some, or all of these attributes. *Read-Only* files are files that users cannot write to or save over, although users may still have the right to delete the files. *Hidden* files are files that do not usually appear in a directory listing or in Windows *Explorer*. (You might use the *Hidden* attribute to protect important program files from casual examination.) The *Archive* attribute, when set, indicates that the user has not backed up a file since its most recent modification. *System* files are files that Windows or DOS uses to administer the operating system. Most Dynamic-Link Library (DLL) files are system files.

As in Chapter 16, in this chapter you will use a combination of Windows API calls and Visual Basic built-in commands to process the files within the user-specified directory tree. By the time you finish this chapter, you will understand the following key concepts:

- Your programs can use the *FindFirstFile* and *FindNextFile* API functions to locate files that meet user- or program-specified characteristics.

- When your programs perform searches of directories and their subdirectories, you must use a *recursive* procedure (a procedure that calls itself until it meets some end condition) within the program to perform the searches.

- Within your Visual Basic programs, you must use the Windows API directory functions to perform recursive searches, because Visual Basic's *Dir* function does not let you maintain information from one search to the next, and therefore is not useful within a recursive procedure.

- When your programs use the *FindFirstFile* API function, it will return a *handle* (a unique integer value that the operating system associates with the function's specified file characteristics) to the program. Your program can maintain that handle within recursive procedures without losing information about a previous search. Therefore, when you use recursive procedures to perform searches, your programs should use the *FindFirstFile* and *FindNextFile* API functions.

- Your programs can get information about files saved onto a drive or disk either with Visual Basic's built-in commands or with Windows API calls.

- Your programs should always close handles they create after they finish using the handles. With the handle that *FindFirstFile* returns, your programs should use the *FindClose* call to close each handle.

♦ Within Visual Basic, your programs define a structure and then use that structure's definition within the definition for another structure. Using such *nested structures* will result in additional program clarity, which will help you and other programmers better manage the program code.

♦ Within your programs, you can use the *Directory* attribute to determine whether a filename your program receives from a Windows API call is a directory or a file.

USING THE PRJFILEATTRIBUTES PROJECT

Before you design the *prjFileAttributes* project, you may find it helpful to run the program. The companion CD-ROM that accompanies this book contains the *prjFileAttributes.exe* program within the *Chapter17* directory. As with every other program on the CD-ROM, you should run the Jamsa Press *setup.exe* program to install the *prjFileAttributes.exe* program to your computer's hard drive before you run it. After you install the *prjFileAttributes.exe* program to your computer's hard drive, you can run it from the Start menu. To run the program, select the Windows Start menu Run option. Windows will display the Run dialog box. Within the Run dialog box, enter *x:\vbpl\Chapter17\prjFileAttributes.exe*, where *x* corresponds to the letter of the hard drive on which you installed the *prjFileAttributes.exe* program, and click your mouse on OK. Windows will run the *prjFileAttributes* project, as shown in Figure 17.1.

521

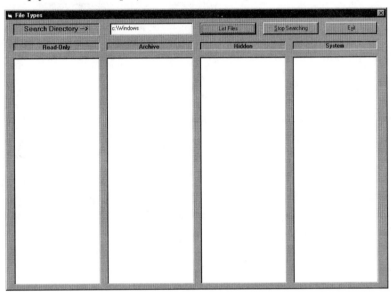

Figure 17.1 *The **prjFileAttributes** project's opening screen.*

RUNNING PRJFILEATTRIBUTES FROM THE CD-ROM

As you have learned, you must first use the Jamsa Press *setup.exe* program the companion CD-ROM that accompanies this book contains to install many of the programs that you will use within this book to your computer's hard drive before you try to use the programs. The *prjFileAttributes.exe* program, however, does not use any custom controls or references and, in fact, uses the Windows API almost exclusively. Because the *prjFileAttributes.exe* program does not use any custom controls or references, you can run the program from the CD-ROM. To run the program from the CD-ROM, perform the following steps:

1. Select the Windows Start menu Run option. Windows will display the Run dialog box.

2. Within the Run dialog box, enter *x:\vbpl\Chapter17\prjFileAttributes.exe*, where *x* corresponds to the drive letter of your computer's CD-ROM drive (usually D: or E:), and click your mouse on OK. Windows will run the *prjFileAttributes.exe* program.

To learn more about the Jamsa Press *setup.exe* program, see the "What's on the *Visual Basic Programmer's Library* CD-ROM" section at the back of this book.

Before you use the *prjFileAttributes.exe* program, take a moment to familiarize yourself with the controls on the form. As you have learned, the *prjFileAttributes* project will let you check a directory tree on your computer and obtain file information about the files within that directory and all its subdirectories. When the program starts, you will see four empty list boxes across the form's main area, labeled *Read-Only, Archive, Hidden,* and *System*. Above the list boxes, you will see a text box with the default search directory, *c:\Windows*, and three command buttons, List Files, Stop Searching, and Exit. To see the processing the program performs, click your mouse on the List Files button. The program will begin to fill the list boxes with file information about the files within the *Windows* directory and all its subdirectories. Figure 17.2 shows the *prjFileAttributes* project during its search.

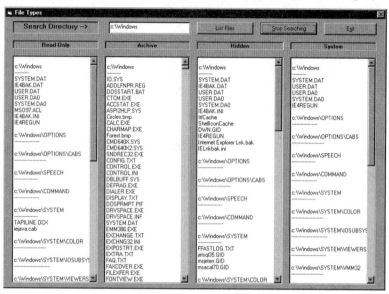

Figure 17.2 The prjFileAttributes project searching a directory.

As you can see, the program adds each directory to every list box to provide the user with regular feedback about what directory the program is currently searching. Under each directory, the program adds the names of the files with the appropriate attributes to each list box. When you search a directory, the Archive list box will probably contain the most files because it contains every file that you have modified since you last backed up the file. As you can see, the program might be most useful to you as a way to check the current status of files within your data directories. For example, Figure 17.3 shows a listing of the *C:\My Documents* directory that most Microsoft applications use as their default data storage location.

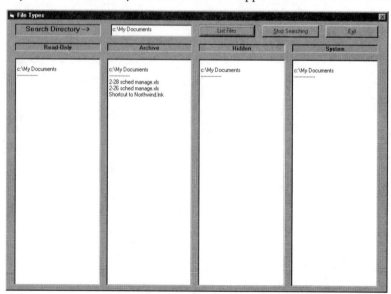

Figure 17.3 The information in the C:\My Documents directory.

As you can see, there are no files that contain other attributes, and three files that have their archive bit set (that is, files with the *archive* attribute). After you identify those files that you do not have back-up copies for, you can then use a back-up program to create the back-up copies and to reset (clear) the archive bit. For example, to view the contents of an entire hard drive, you could change the search directory to *c:* and click your mouse on the List Files button. Figure 17.4 shows what a search of an entire directory might return to the *prjFileAttributes* project.

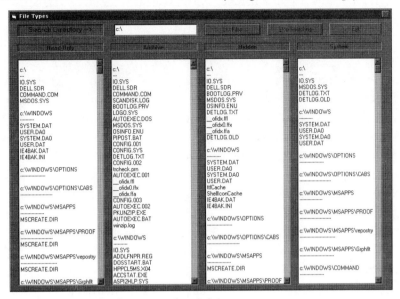

Figure 17.4 *Sample results from a search of an entire hard drive.*

CREATING A BLANK FORM

Now that you have a better idea how to use the finished *prjFileAttributes* project, you can begin to design it. First, you will create an empty form that will contain all the controls the "Using the *prjFileAttributes* Project" section introduced. After you design the form, you will learn more about the Windows API calls that you will use to get the file information from the directory tree. To begin the *prjFileAttributes* project and create a blank form, perform the following steps:

1. Within Visual Basic, select the File menu New Project option. Visual Basic will open the New Project dialog box.

2. Within the New Project dialog box, click your mouse on the Standard EXE icon. Next, click your mouse on the OK button. Visual Basic will close the dialog box and open the *Form1* form window.

3. Within Visual Basic, select the View menu Properties Window option. Visual Basic will open the Properties Window listing the *Form1* properties.

4. Within the Properties Window, change the *Form1* properties to the values Table 17.1 lists.

Object	Property	Set As
Form1	*Caption*	*File Types*
Form1	*Height*	8790
Form1	*Left*	0
Form1	*StartUpPosition*	2 - Center Screen
Form1	*Top*	0
Form1	*Width*	12390
Form1	*Name*	*frmFileTypes*

Table 17.1 *The newly named **frmFileTypes** form's properties.*

Adding a Module to the Project

As you will learn, the *prjFileAttributes* project declares its API functions, structures, and constants within a code module. As you learned in Chapter 5, "Creating and Using Fractals," Visual Basic requires that you declare structures within modules so that the type definitions are available throughout the project. As you have learned in other chapters, you should generally declare API functions within a module as well so that they are also available throughout the project. To add a module to the *prjFileAttributes* project, perform the following steps:

1. Select the Project menu Add Module option. Visual Basic will display the Add Module dialog box.

2. Within the Add Module dialog box, double-click your mouse on the Module icon. Visual Basic will add the *Module1* module to the project and open it within a Code window.

3. Select the View menu Properties Window option. Visual Basic will display the Properties Window with the *Module1* properties visible.

4. Change the *Module1* module's *Name* property to *mdlFileType*.

5. Select the File menu Save Project As option. Visual Basic will open the Save File As dialog box and fill the *File name* field with *mdlFileType*.

6. Within the Save Project As dialog box, click your mouse on the Save button. Visual Basic will save the *mdlFileType* module and fill the *File name* field with the *frmFileTypes* form name.

7. Within the Save Project As dialog box, click your mouse on the Save button. Visual Basic will save the *frmFileTypes* form and fill the *File name* field with the *Project1* project name.

8. Within the *File name* field, replace the *Project1* project name with the new *prjFileAttributes* project name. Next, click your mouse on the Save button. Visual Basic will save the *prjFileAttributes* project and close the Save Project As dialog box.

Adding Controls to the Form

In the *prjFileAttributes* project, you will use four *ListBox* controls, a *TextBox* control, several *Label* controls, and three *CommandButton* controls. To begin, you will add each control to the *prjFileAttributes* form and assign properties to position each control on the form and provide a unique name for each control.

Adding the ListBox Controls to the Form

As you have learned, the *prjFileAttributes* project will use four *ListBox* controls to display files whose attributes include that particular file attribute (for example, the program might add a file to the Read-Only, Archive, and Hidden list boxes). To add the *ListBox* controls to the *frmFileTypes* form, perform the following steps:

1. If Visual Basic is not displaying the *frmFileTypes* form within an object window, double-click your mouse on the *frmFileTypes* form listing within the Project Explorer. Visual Basic will open the *frmFileTypes* form.

2. Within Visual Basic, select the View menu Toolbox option. Visual Basic will open the Toolbox.

3. Within the Toolbox, double-click your mouse on the ListBox icon. Visual Basic will draw a *ListBox* control, *List1*, within the *frmFileTypes* form.

4. Repeat Step 3 three more times to add the *List2, List3,* and *List4 ListBox* controls to the *frmFileTypes* form.

5. Within the *frmFileTypes* form window, click your mouse on the *List1* control to highlight it. Visual Basic will draw a small frame around the control.

6. Select the View menu Properties Window option. Visual Basic will open the Properties Window listing the *List1* properties.

7. Within the Properties Window, change the *List1* properties to those Table 17.2 lists.

8. Repeat Steps 5, 6, and 7 for each of the other *ListBox* controls and change their properties to the values Table 17.2 lists.

Object	Property	Set As
List1	*Height*	7080
List1	*Left*	240
List1	*Top*	1200
List1	*Width*	2775
List1	*Name*	*lstReadOnly*
List2	*Height*	7080
List2	*Left*	3240
List2	*Top*	1200
List2	*Width*	2775
List2	*Name*	*lstArchive*
List3	*Height*	7080
List3	*Left*	6240
List3	*Top*	1200
List3	*Width*	2775
List3	*Name*	*lstHidden*
List4	*Height*	7080
List4	*Left*	9240
List4	*Top*	1200
List4	*Width*	2775
List4	*Name*	*lstSystem*

Table 17.2 *The newly named* **ListBox** *controls' properties.*

Adding the Label Controls to the Form

As you have learned, within the *prjFileAttributes* project, you will use *Label* controls to place captions on the four *ListBox* controls and to prompt the user to enter a search directory. Now that you have added the four *ListBox* controls, you should add the *Label* controls to the form. After you add the *Label* controls, you will add a *TextBox* control and three *CommandButton* controls. To add the *Label* controls to the *frmFileTypes* form, perform the following steps:

1. If Visual Basic is not displaying the *frmFileTypes* form within an object window, double-click your mouse on the *frmFileTypes* form listing within the Project Explorer. Visual Basic will open the *frmFileTypes* form.

2. Within Visual Basic, select the View menu Toolbox option. Visual Basic will open the Toolbox.

3. Within the Toolbox, double-click your mouse on the Label icon. Visual Basic will draw a *Label* control, *Label1*, within the *frmFileTypes* form.

4. Repeat Step 3 four more times to add the *Label2, Label3, Label4,* and *Label5* controls to the *frmFileTypes* form.

5. Within the *frmFileTypes* form, click your mouse on the *Label1* control to highlight it. Visual Basic will draw a small frame around the control.

6. Select the View menu Properties Window option. Visual Basic will open the Properties Window listing the *Label1* properties.

7. Within the Properties Window, change the *Label1* properties to the values Table 17.3 lists.

8. Repeat Steps 5, 6, and 7 to change the properties for the other *Label* controls to the values Table 17.3 lists.

Object	Property	Set As
Label1	Alignment	2 - Center
Label1	Caption	Search Directory —>
Label1	Font	MS San Serif, Bold, 10 Point
Label1	Height	375
Label1	Left	240
Label1	Top	120
Label1	Width	2775
Label1	Name	lblSearch
Label2	Alignment	2 - Center
Label2	Caption	Read-Only
Label2	Font	MS San Serif, Bold, 8 Point
Label2	Height	255
Label2	Left	240
Label2	Top	720
Label2	Width	2775
Label2	Name	lblReadOnly
Label3	Alignment	2 - Center
Label3	Caption	Archive
Label3	Font	MS San Serif, Bold, 8 Point
Label3	Height	255
Label3	Left	3240
Label3	Top	720
Label3	Width	2775
Label3	Name	lblArchive
Label4	Alignment	2 - Center
Label4	Caption	Hidden
Label4	Font	MS San Serif, Bold, 8 Point
Label4	Height	255
Label4	Left	6240
Label4	Top	720
Label4	Width	2775
Label4	Name	lblHidden
Label5	Alignment	2 - Center
Label5	Caption	System
Label5	Font	MS San Serif, Bold, 8 Point
Label5	Height	255
Label5	Left	240
Label5	Top	720
Label5	Width	2775
Label5	Name	lblSystem

Table 17.3 The newly named **Label** controls' properties.

ADDING A TEXTBOX CONTROL TO THE FRMFILETYPES FORM

Now that you have the *frmFileTypes* form's general outline, you can add the *TextBox* control to the *frmFileTypes* form as a place for the user to enter the search directory. You will set a default value for the *TextBox* in the properties, but the user will be able to alter the text value to search the directory of the user's choice. To add the *TextBox* control to the *frmFileTypes* form, perform the following steps:

1. If Visual Basic is not displaying the *frmFileTypes* form within an object window, double-click your mouse on the *frmFileTypes* form listing within the Project Explorer. Visual Basic will open the *frmFileTypes* form.

2. Within Visual Basic, select the View menu Toolbox option. Visual Basic will open the Toolbox.

3. Within the Toolbox, double-click your mouse on the TextBox icon. Visual Basic will draw a *TextBox* control, *Text1*, within the *frmFileTypes* form.

4. Within the *frmFileTypes* form window, click your mouse on the *Text1* control to highlight it. Visual Basic will draw a small frame around the control.

5. Select the View menu Properties Window option. Visual Basic will open the Properties Window listing the *Text1* control's properties.

6. Within the Properties Window, change the *Text1* control's properties to the values Table 17.4 lists.

Object	Property	Set As
Text1	*Height*	375
Text1	*Left*	3360
Text1	*Top*	120
Text1	*Width*	2665
Text1	*Text*	*c:\Windows*
Text1	*Name*	*txtSearchDir*

*Table 17.4 The **Text1** control's properties.*

After you change the *TextBox* control's properties, you can add the *CommandButton* controls to the *frmFileTypes* form, which you will do in the next section.

ADDING THE COMMANDBUTTON CONTROLS TO THE FORM

As you have learned, you will use the *ListBox* controls to display the information that the directory tree search returns. Within the *prjFileAttributes* project, you will use three command buttons to start the search, stop the search, and exit the program. The *Click* events for each command button will perform processing that corresponds to the button's caption. To add the *CommandButton* controls to the *frmFileTypes* form, perform the following steps:

1. If Visual Basic is not displaying the *frmFileTypes* form within an object window, double-click your mouse on the *frmFileTypes* form listing within the Project Explorer. Visual Basic will open the *frmFileTypes* form.

2. Within Visual Basic, select the View menu Toolbox option. Visual Basic will open the Toolbox.

3. Within the Toolbox, double-click your mouse on the CommandButton icon. Visual Basic will draw a *CommandButton* control, *Command1*, within the *frmFileTypes* form.

4. Repeat Step 3 two more times to add the *Command2* and *Command3* buttons to the *frmFileTypes* form.

5. Within the *frmFileTypes* form, click your mouse on a *CommandButton* control to highlight it. Visual Basic will draw a small frame around the control.

6. Select the View menu Properties Window option. Visual Basic will open the Properties Window listing the selected control's properties.

7. Within the Properties Window, change the highlighted control's properties to the values Table 17.5 lists.

8. Repeat Steps 5, 6, and 7 to change the properties for all three *CommandButton* controls to the values Table 17.5 lists.

Object	Property	Set As
Command1	Caption	List Files
Command1	Height	375
Command1	Left	6240
Command1	Top	120
Command1	Width	1815
Command1	Name	cmdFiles
Command2	Caption	&Stop Searching
Command2	Height	375
Command2	Left	8280
Command2	Top	120
Command2	Width	1815
Command2	Name	cmdStop
Command3	Caption	E&xit
Command3	Height	375
Command3	Left	10320
Command3	Top	120
Command3	Width	1815
Command3	Name	cmdExit

Table 17.5 *The* **CommandButton** *controls' properties.*

When you finish setting the properties for the *CommandButton* controls, the *frmFileTypes* form will look similar to Figure 17.5.

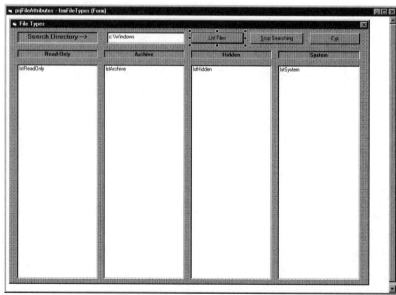

Figure 17.5 *The* **frmFileTypes** *form after you add and format the controls.*

WRITING THE PROGRAM CODE FOR THE *prjFileAttributes* PROJECT

As you have learned, the *prjFileAttributes* project performs processing similar to that of the project you designed in Chapter 16. There are significant differences in the way the program code for the *prjFileAttributes* project parses the information the operating system returns from the *prjDuplicate* project, however, so be careful that you do not confuse Chapter 16's program code with the *prjFileAttributes* project's program code.

WRITING THE *mdlFileType* MODULE

As you have learned, the *prjFileAttributes* project uses Windows API calls and a recursive procedure to search through all the subdirectories of a user-provided directory tree and to read the files from the subdirectories. The *mdlFileType* module declares the API functions, the constants you will use to check the API function return values, and the structures you will use within the *DirWalk* and *DirWalkRecurse* procedures. The *mdlFileType* module also includes the *StripTerminator* function.

WRITING THE DECLARATIONS FOR THE *mdlFileType* MODULE

As you have learned, you will declare the constants, structures, and API functions for the *prjFileAttributes* project within the *mdlFileType* module. As you have seen in other chapters, the General–Declarations section is long because of the number of different declarations within it. Just as with other long sections, it is worthwhile to consider each declaration set on its own. The declarations begin with the constant declarations, as the following program code implements:

```
Public Const MAX_PATH = 260
Public Const FILE_ATTRIBUTE_DIRECTORY = &H10
Public Const FILE_ATTRIBUTE_ARCHIVE = &H20
Public Const FILE_ATTRIBUTE_COMPRESSED = &H800
Public Const FILE_ATTRIBUTE_HIDDEN = &H2
Public Const FILE_ATTRIBUTE_NORMAL = &H80
Public Const FILE_ATTRIBUTE_READONLY = &H1
Public Const FILE_ATTRIBUTE_SYSTEM = &H4
Public Const FILE_ATTRIBUTE_TEMPORARY = &H100
Public Const INVALID_HANDLE_VALUE = -1
```

The first constant represents the maximum length the program believes the operating system supports for a path name; depending on your installation (Windows NT 4.0, FAT32, and so on), the actual maximum path name length may be longer. However, 260 characters is a reasonable number and ensures that the program will work on Windows 95, as well as the newer operating systems. The next eight constants, which all begin with *FILE*, represent the file attribute constants that you will check each file against to determine its characteristics. The *prjFileAttributes* program does not use all eight constants; however, it is useful to know the others for your own programs. Finally, the program uses the *INVALID_HANDLE_VALUE* to make sure the *FindFirstFile* function returns a valid search handle that the *FindNextFile* function can use to continue searching.

The next block in the General–Declarations section includes the declarations for the *FILETIME* structure, the *WIN32_FIND_DATA* structure, and the *DIRWALKDATA* structure. The following code implements the *FILETIME* structure's definition:

```
Type FILETIME
   dwLowDateTime As Long
   dwHighDateTime As Long
End Type
```

The *FILETIME* structure contains two *Long* members. Windows stores date and time values within a compressed time structure. As you learned in Chapter 16, you must convert the *FILETIME* structure's *Long* values into a Visual Basic *Date* value to perform date-specific processing on a file.

The *WIN32_FIND_DATA* structure uses the *FILETIME* structure to define several of its members. The following code implements the *WIN32_FIND_DATA* structure's definition:

```
Type WIN32_FIND_DATA
   dwFileAttributes As Long
   ftCreationTime As FILETIME
   ftLastAccessTime As FILETIME
   ftLastWriteTime As FILETIME
   nFileSizeHigh As Long
   nFileSizeLow As Long
   dwReserved0 As Long
   dwReserved1 As Long
   cFileName As String * MAX_PATH
   cAlternate As String * 14
End Type
```

530   The *WIN32_FIND_DATA* structure contains several important members that the *prjFileAttributes* project will manipulate. The most important member is the *dwFileAttributes* member, which contains a *Long* value that represents the currently set file attributes. Within the *prjFileAttributes* project, you will use the *dwFileAttributes* member to determine the list boxes to which you must add the current file. The next three members are *FILETIME* members, which correspond to the file's creation time and date, last access time, and last write time. The *nFileSizeHigh* and *nFileSizeLow* members represent the file's size, in bytes. If the file's size is less than 2.15Gb, the entire file size is within the *nFileSizeLow* member. If the file's size is larger than 2.15Gb, the *nFileSizeHigh* member will contain an offset value that, when you combine it with the *nFileSizeLow* member, yields the complete file size. The *dwReserved* members correspond to operating system-reserved values that may be available for program access in future Windows versions. The *cFileName* member contains the filename for the file. If the filename is a long filename (as opposed to an MS-DOS 8.3 name) and the operating system supports alternate filenames (as Windows 95 does), the *cAlternate* member will contain the 8.3 style name for the file. Both the *FindFirstFile* and *FindNextFile* functions return values within an instance of the *WIN32_FIND_DATA* structure.

The last structure definition for the project is the *DIRWALKDATA* structure. The following code implements the *DIRWALKDATA* structure:

```
Type DIRWALKDATA
   TreeLB As Long
   nDepth As Integer
   Recurse As Boolean
   szBuf As String * 1000
   nIndent As Integer
   OK As Boolean
   IsDir As Boolean
   FindData As WIN32_FIND_DATA
End Type
```

The *DIRWALKDATA* structure contains information that the program uses during the recursive procedure that performs the actual directory search routine. The *nDepth* member, for instance, contains the current level that the search routine is within in the directory tree. For example, if the search begins in *c:\temp* and the program is currently searching the *c:\temp\subdir1\subdir2\subdir3* directory, the *nDepth* member will contain the value 4, because the program is currently three levels below the starting directory. The *szBuf* member contains the full path to the program's current location. The *nIndent* member contains an indent value that corresponds to the *nDepth* member that you can use to create indented directory tree reports. The program sets the *IsDir* flag to *True* if the current filename is a directory, and sets the *IsDir* flag to *False* if it is not. The *FindData* member is a variable of type *WIN32_FIND_DATA*. The only procedures within the program that use the *DIRWALKDATA* structure are the *DirWalk* procedure and the *DirWalkRecurse* procedure.

As you have learned, the *prjFileAttributes* project uses a series of Windows API function calls to perform its processing. The following code implements the declarations for the Windows API functions:

```
Declare Function SetCurrentDirectory Lib "kernel32" Alias _
    "SetCurrentDirectoryA" (ByVal lpPathName As String) As Long
Declare Function GetCurrentDirectory Lib "kernel32" Alias _
    "GetCurrentDirectoryA" _
    (ByVal nBufferLength As Long, ByVal lpBuffer As String) As Long
Declare Function FindFirstFile Lib "kernel32" Alias "FindFirstFileA" _
    (ByVal lpFileName As String, lpFindFileData As WIN32_FIND_DATA) _
    As Long
Declare Function FindNextFile Lib "kernel32" Alias "FindNextFileA" _
    (ByVal hFindFile As Long, lpFindFileData As WIN32_FIND_DATA) As Long
Declare Function FindClose Lib "kernel32" (ByVal hFindFile As Long) _
    As Long
```

The *prjFileAttributes* program uses five Windows API functions. The *GetCurrentDirectory* and *SetCurrentDirectory* functions let you retrieve and set, respectively, the current directory on the current drive. The *FindFirstFile* and *FindNextFile* functions let you search a directory for all files that match a pattern you specify. If *FindFirstFile* is successful, it will return a search handle that you will use with the *FindNextFile* function to locate the next file within the search directory that matches the search pattern. If *FindFirstFile* is not successful, it will return -1 *(INVALID_ HANDLE_VALUE)*. If *FindFirstFile* returns a valid handle value, you will use the *FindClose* function to close a handle after your program finishes using it.

Writing the Code for the StripTerminator Function

As you have learned, you must always strip the *NULL*-terminator from the end of strings the Windows API returns to your Visual Basic programs. The string members within the *WIN32_FIND_DATA* structure are no exception. As you have learned in previous chapters, you will use the *StripTerminator* function to remove the *NULL*-terminator from the string's end. The following code implements the *StripTerminator* function:

```
Public Function StripTerminator(ByVal strString As String) As String
  Dim intZeroPos As Integer

  intZeroPos = InStr(strString, Chr$(0))
  If intZeroPos > 0 Then
    StripTerminator = Left$(strString, intZeroPos - 1)
  Else
    StripTerminator = strString
  End If
End Function
```

As Chapter 1, "Introduction to Visual Basic," detailed, the *StripTerminator* function checks an incoming string to determine whether or not it contains a *NULL*-terminator. If the string does contain the terminator, the function will return everything before the terminator as the string's value. If the string does not contain the terminator, the function will return the entire incoming string as the string's value.

Writing the Code for the frmFileTypes Form

As you have learned, the *mdlFileType* module contains only the declarations for the program and the *StripTerminator* function that you will use whenever you return a string from an API call to Visual Basic. The primary processing for the *prjFileAttributes* project occurs within the *frmFileTypes* form. The form also declares two local variables that the program uses or checks within multiple procedures. The following code implements the declarations for the *frmFileTypes* form:

```
Option Explicit
Dim Current As String
Dim StopSearching As Boolean
```

The *Current* variable maintains the current directory at the time the user starts the program, and changes the current directory back to the original directory when the program completes its processing. The *StopSearching* flag variable maintains a *True* or *False* value that the program uses within the recursing search loop to stop the search if the user clicks the mouse on the Stop Searching button.

WRITING THE CODE FOR THE FORM_LOAD EVENT

As you have learned, each time you load a form, the first event the form invokes is the *Form_Load* event—even before the program displays the form. In the *prjFileAttributes* project, the *frmFileTypes* form loads when the project begins. The following code implements the *frmFileTypes* form's *Form_Load* event:

```
Private Sub Form_Load()
   Current = CurDir$
End Sub
```

The *Form_Load* event sets the *Current* variable to the current directory. When you unload the form, the program code will set the directory back to the starting directory. The following code implements the *Form_Unload* event:

```
Private Sub Form_Unload(Cancel As Integer)
   SetCurrentDirectory (Current)
End Sub
```

The *Form_Unload* event uses the *SetCurrentDirectory* API function to change the directory back to the original directory. Remember, you set the *Current* variable equal to the system's current directory at the time the program began.

WRITING THE CODE FOR THE CMDFILES_CLICK EVENT

As you have learned, to begin the search process, the user must click the mouse on the *cmdFiles* command button. The *Click* event for the command button calls the actual search routine. The following code implements the *cmdFiles_Click* event:

```
Private Sub cmdFiles_Click()
   StopSearching = False
   If Left(txtSearchDir.Text, 1) = "\" Then _
       txtSearchDir.Text = Left(CurDir$, 2) & txtSearchDir.Text
   DirWalk
End Sub
```

The program code within the event sets the *StopSearching* flag to *False*, checks the directory name to ensure it is a valid directory name, and then calls the *DirWalk* procedure. You will learn about the *DirWalk* procedure in the next section.

WRITING THE SEARCH PROGRAM CODE

As you have learned, the *cmdFiles_Click* event calls the *DirWalk* procedure, which begins the search process. As you will learn, *DirWalk,* in turn, calls *DirWalkRecurse*, the recursive procedure that performs the actual search of the entire tree. The following code implements the *DirWalk* procedure:

```
Private Sub DirWalk()
   Dim TreeLB As Long
   Dim DW As DIRWALKDATA
   Dim SearchDir As String
   Dim Result As Boolean

   lstArchive.Clear
   lstHidden.Clear
   lstReadOnly.Clear
   lstSystem.Clear
   SearchDir = txtSearchDir
   If Mid(SearchDir, 2, 1) <> ":" Then _
       SearchDir = Left(CurDir$, 2) & "\" & SearchDir
   Result = SetCurrentDirectory(SearchDir)
```

```
     If Not Result Then
       MsgBox "Couldn't set directory!"
       Exit Sub
     End If
     DW.TreeLB = TreeLB
     DW.Recurse = True
     DirWalkRecurse DW
  End Sub
```

The *DirWalk* procedure clears the list boxes, then tries to set the directory to the user-entered directory. If the procedure is unable to set the directory, the program will display a message box indicating the error to the user, and exit. If the procedure is able to set the directory, it initializes some elements of the *DW* variable (of type *DIRWALKDATA*) and calls the *DirWalkRecurse* procedure with the *DW* variable. The following code implements the *DirWalkRecurse* procedure:

533

```
Private Sub DirWalkRecurse(ByRef DW As DIRWALKDATA)
  Dim GetCurrentResult As Long
  Dim Result As Boolean
  Dim hFind As Long
  Dim testlong As Long
  Dim GetDir As String * MAX_PATH

  DW.nDepth = DW.nDepth + 1
  GetCurrentResult = GetCurrentDirectory(1000, DW.szBuf)
  DW.szBuf = StripTerminator(DW.szBuf)
  lstArchive.AddItem (" ")
  lstArchive.AddItem (Trim(DW.szBuf))
  lstArchive.AddItem (String(Len(Trim(DW.szBuf)), "-"))
  lstReadOnly.AddItem (" ")
  lstReadOnly.AddItem (Trim(DW.szBuf))
  lstReadOnly.AddItem (String(Len(Trim(DW.szBuf)), "-"))
  lstHidden.AddItem (" ")
  lstHidden.AddItem (Trim(DW.szBuf))
  lstHidden.AddItem (String(Len(Trim(DW.szBuf)), "-"))
  lstSystem.AddItem (" ")
  lstSystem.AddItem (Trim(DW.szBuf))
  lstSystem.AddItem (String(Len(Trim(DW.szBuf)), "-"))
  hFind = FindFirstFile("*.*", DW.FindData)

  testlong = GetCurrentDirectory(1000, GetDir)
  DW.OK = (hFind <> INVALID_HANDLE_VALUE)
  Do While DW.OK And Not StopSearching
    With DW.FindData
      DW.IsDir = ((.dwFileAttributes And FILE_ATTRIBUTE_DIRECTORY) = _
          FILE_ATTRIBUTE_DIRECTORY)
      If DW.IsDir = False Then
        If ((.dwFileAttributes And FILE_ATTRIBUTE_ARCHIVE) = _
            FILE_ATTRIBUTE_ARCHIVE) Then
          lstArchive.AddItem (Trim(StripTerminator((.cFileName))))
        End If
        If ((.dwFileAttributes And FILE_ATTRIBUTE_READONLY) = _
            FILE_ATTRIBUTE_READONLY) Then
          lstReadOnly.AddItem (Trim(StripTerminator((.cFileName))))
        End If
        If ((.dwFileAttributes And FILE_ATTRIBUTE_HIDDEN) = _
            FILE_ATTRIBUTE_HIDDEN) Then
          lstHidden.AddItem (Trim(StripTerminator((.cFileName))))
        End If
        If ((.dwFileAttributes And FILE_ATTRIBUTE_SYSTEM) = _
            FILE_ATTRIBUTE_SYSTEM) Then
          lstSystem.AddItem (Trim(StripTerminator((.cFileName))))
```

```
            End If
         End If
      End With
      DW.OK = FindNextFile(hFind, DW.FindData)
      DoEvents
   Loop
   If Not (hFind = INVALID_HANDLE_VALUE) Then Result = FindClose(hFind)
   If DW.Recurse Then
      hFind = FindFirstChildDir("*.*", DW.FindData)
      DW.OK = hFind <> INVALID_HANDLE_VALUE
      Do While DW.OK And Not StopSearching
         If (SetCurrentDirectory(Trim(StripTerminator(DW.FindData.cFileName)))) _
            Then DirWalkRecurse DW
            Result = SetCurrentDirectory("..")
         End If
         DW.OK = FindNextChildDir(hFind, DW.FindData)
      Loop
      If (hFind <> INVALID_HANDLE_VALUE) Then Result = FindClose(hFind)
   End If
End Sub
```

The *DirWalkRecurse* procedure manages the search within the *prjFileAttributes* project and adds the files to the list boxes as it retrieves them. Each time the program finds a new subdirectory, it will call the *DirWalkRecurse* procedure to process the files within that subdirectory. The procedure begins with a call to *GetCurrentDirectory*, which returns the current directory into the *szBuf* member. The *DirWalkRecurse* procedure then adds the current directory to each list box. After it adds the current directory to the list boxes, the procedure calls the *FindFirstFile* function to get a handle to the files within the directory. If *FindFirstFile* finds no files within the directory, the procedure will skip the search loop and move on to the end of the procedure. If *FindFirstFile* finds files within the directory, the procedure will loop through all the files in the directory within a *Do-While* loop.

Within the *Do-While* loop, the program code checks the current file's attributes to determine which list box to add the file to. The program uses a series of *If-Then* statements and bitwise comparisons to determine which flags the operating system has previously set within the *dwFileAttributes* member. After the program finishes with the files in the current directory, it then searches the current directory to determine whether or not it contains any subdirectories. If the directory contains subdirectories, the procedure calls itself with each subdirectory in turn. The recursion continues until the procedure reaches the directory tree's bottom, then the program returns to the directory that is one directory above the current directory in the tree. If that directory contains additional subdirectories, the procedure will search them. If it does not, the procedure will go up another level in the tree until it processes every file and subdirectory in the tree the user specified as the search tree.

The *DirWalkRecurse* procedure uses a series of helper functions to process the possible subdirectories within the current directory. The following section, "Writing the Code for the Subdirectory Helper Functions," explains the helper functions.

UNDERSTANDING RECURSION

As you have learned, Visual Basic lets you divide your program into smaller pieces called functions or procedures. Using functions and procedures, your program becomes easier to understand, program, and test. In addition, you can often use the functions and procedures you create for one program within another program. As your programs execute, one function may call another, which calls another, which may, in turn, call several other functions—each function to perform a specific operation. Visual Basic even lets a function call itself.

A *recursive function* is a function that calls itself to perform a specific operation. The process of a function calling itself is *recursion*. As the complexity of your programs and functions increases, you might find that you can easily define many operations in terms of themselves. For such cases, you might want to create a recursive function. Many programming books, for example, use the factorial problem to illustrate how recursion works. The factorial of the value 1 is 1. The factorial of the value 2 is 2*1. The factorial of the value 3 is 3*2*1. Likewise, the factorial of the value 4 is 4*3*2*1. You can continue to increase the integers in the series; the factorial of the value 5 is 5*4*3*2*1, and so on. This process can essentially go on indefinitely. If you take a close look at the processing that the factorial performs, you will find that the factorial of 5, for example, is actually 5 times the factorial of 4 (4*3*2*1). Likewise, the factorial of 4 is actually 4 times the factorial of 3 (3*2*1). The factorial of 3 is 3 times the factorial of 2 (2*1). Finally, the factorial of 2 is 2 times the factorial of 1 (1). Table 17.6 illustrates the factorial processing.

Value	Calculation	Result	Factorial
1	1	1	1
2	2*1	2	2 * Factorial(1)
3	3*2*1	6	3 * Factorial(2)
4	4*3*2*1	24	4 * Factorial(3)
5	5*4*3*2*1	120	5 * Factorial(4)

Table 17.6 *Factorial processing.*

The following code fragment shows a sample recursive function, *Factorial*:

```
Private Function Factorial(ByVal Value As Integer) As Long
   If Value = 1 Then
      Factorial = 1
   Else
      Factorial = Value * Factorial(Value - 1)
   End If
End Function
```

As you can see, the *Factorial* function returns a result that is based on the result of the function itself. The *Factorial* function receives a specific parameter value. When the function begins, it first checks if the value is 1, which by factorial definition, is 1. If the value is 1, the function returns the value 1. If the value is not 1, the function returns the result of the value times the factorial of the value minus 1. Assume, for example, the program invokes the function with the value 3. The function will return the result of *3 * Factorial(3–1)*. When Visual Basic encounters the function call within the assignment, Visual Basic will invoke the function a second time—now with the value of 3–1 or 2. Again, because the value is not 1, the function returns the result of *2 * Factorial(2–1)*. On the final invocation of the function, the value is 1. As a result, the function returns the value 1 to the caller, which in turn returns the result of 2*1 to its caller, which in turn returns the result of 3*2*1 to its caller. Figure 17.6 illustrates the chain of recursive function invocations and return values for the *Factorial(3)* function call.

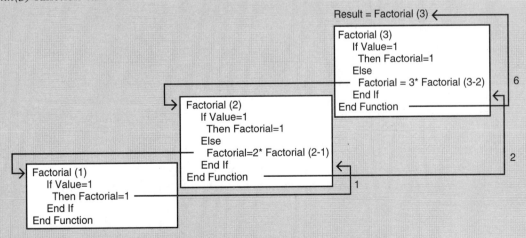

Figure 17.6 *The chain of function calls and value returns for the recursive **Factorial** function.*

535

A recursive function is somewhat like a looping construct in that you must specify an ending condition. If you do not, the function will never end. In the case of the factorial problem, the ending condition is the factorial of 1, which by definition, is 1.

WRITING THE CODE FOR THE SUBDIRECTORY HELPER FUNCTIONS

As you have learned, the *DirWalkRecurse* procedure calls a series of helper functions to help it determine the subdirectories within the current directory. The first helper function that *DirWalkRecurse* calls is the *FindFirstChildDir* function. The following code implements the *FindFirstChildDir* function:

```
Private Function FindFirstChildDir(szPath As String, _
    lclFindData As WIN32_FIND_DATA) As Long
  Dim hFindFile As Long
  Dim Found As Boolean
  Dim Result As Boolean

  hFindFile = FindFirstFile(szPath, lclFindData)
  If (hFindFile <> INVALID_HANDLE_VALUE) Then
    If Not IsChildDir(lclFindData) Then _
      Found = FindNextChildDir(hFindFile, lclFindData)
    If Not Found Then
      Result = FindClose(hFindFile)
      hFindFile = INVALID_HANDLE_VALUE
    End If
  End If
  FindFirstChildDir = hFindFile
End Function
```

The *FindFirstChildDir* function accepts as its incoming parameters the current path and a *WIN32_FIND_DATA* structure. The *FindFirstChildDir* function then searches that path for subdirectories. If the search finds any files, the function enters a series of search checks. The search check first calls the *IsChildDir* function. If the *IsChildDir* function returns *False*, the program will call the *FindNextChildDir* function. If the *FindNextChildDir* function is also unsuccessful in locating a subdirectory, the function sets the file handle to *INVALID_HANDLE_VALUE* and returns to the *DirWalkRecurse* function, which then climbs a level in the tree.

The *IsChildDir* function checks the attribute byte of the found file and ensures that it is a directory name, and that it is not the system-generated "." or ".." subdirectory. If the file is actually a subdirectory, the function returns *True*; otherwise, the function returns *False*. The following code implements the *IsChildDir* function:

```
Private Function IsChildDir(FindData As WIN32_FIND_DATA) As Boolean
  If ((FindData.dwFileAttributes And FILE_ATTRIBUTE_DIRECTORY) = _
    FILE_ATTRIBUTE_DIRECTORY _
    And Left(FindData.cFileName, 1) <> "." _
    And Left(FindData.cFileName, 2) <> "..") Then
    IsChildDir = True
  Else
    IsChildDir = False
  End If
End Function
```

The *FindNextChildDir* function accepts a search handle and a *WIN32_FIND_DATA* structure. It loops either until it finds a valid subdirectory or until there are no more files to search in the directory. The following code implements the *FindNextChildDir* function:

```
Private Function FindNextChildDir(hFindFile As Long, _
    FindData As WIN32_FIND_DATA) As Boolean
  Dim Found As Boolean
```

```
      Found = False
      Do
         FindData.cFileName = Space$(MAX_PATH)
         Found = FindNextFile(hFindFile, FindData)
         FindData.cFileName = StripTerminator(FindData.cFileName)
      Loop While (Found = True And (Not IsChildDir(FindData)))
      FindNextChildDir = Found
   End Function
```

The *FindNextChildDir* function uses the *IsChildDir* function to verify that a filename is a subdirectory. If the filename is not a subdirectory, the loop continues. If the filename is a subdirectory, the loop exits, the function returns *True*, and the *WIN32_FIND_DATA* structure contains the name of the subdirectory.

WRITING THE CODE FOR THE OTHER COMMAND BUTTONS

537

When you created the *frmFileTypes* form, you added three command buttons to the form. As you learned, the *cmdFiles* command button starts the search and calls the *DirWalk* procedure. The other two command buttons perform much simpler processing. The *cmdStop* command button sets the *StopSearching* flag variable to *True*. When the program code next encounters the *StopSearching* test, it will stop searching. The following code implements the *cmdStop_Click* event:

```
   Private Sub cmdStop_Click()
      StopSearching = True
   End Sub
```

The *cmdExit* command button performs similar processing. The following code implements the *cmdExit_Click* event:

```
   Private Sub cmdExit_Click()
      Unload Me
   End Sub
```

As you have learned, when the program unloads the form, it will reset the operating system's current directory to the directory before the program began.

ENHANCEMENTS YOU CAN MAKE TO THE *prjFileAttributes* PROJECT

As you have learned, the Windows API functions that you use within the *prjFileAttributes* project are powerful and useful. For example, your own programs might use a procedure similar to the *DirWalkRecurse* procedure to search a user's drive for previously installed components, and then update or replace the components the user needs.

Alternatively, you can use the Windows API calls to *FindFirstFile* and *FindNextFile* to create useful tools that let you search a location based on certain criteria you specify. You can use the information the *WIN32_FIND_DATA* structure contains to perform significant preprocessing on files and determine if they match more specific criteria than a simple name match.

Finally, you can use the information the *prjFileAttributes* program returns about files marked for archiving to create and implement your own back-up systems. You can write a program that searches the entire drive, and lets the user select which files to back up. You can then copy the files into a back-up location and set the *Archive* bit to *False* for each file you copy.

Putting It All Together

This chapter's project, *prjFileAttributes*, introduced you to how you can use the Windows API functions, custom structures, and recursion to search an entire drive or directory tree and return valuable information about all the files within that tree. If you combine what you learned in this chapter with what you learned during the design of the *prjDuplicateFiles* project that you created in Chapter 16, you have a strong foundation for manipulating and managing files within your Visual Basic programs.

This chapter has also introduced you to using recursive functions and procedures to perform repetitive tasks. The recursive procedure in this chapter travels up and a down a directory tree and returns information about files located within each level of the tree. You can use recursive functions and procedures in other programs for many different programming tasks, but your recursive functions and procedures will generally follow the form of the *DirWalkRecurse* procedure, in that they will call themselves repeatedly until the procedure reaches some end condition.

538   In the next chapter, Chapter 18, "Creating an Internet Research Program," you will create a Visual Basic program that you can use to retrieve Internet documents and search their contents. Before you continue with Chapter 18, however, make sure you understand the following key concepts:

✓ Within Visual Basic, your programs can declare a structure and use that structure declaration to declare other structures or classes. Such processing is known as *nesting structures*. You will generally use nested structures to make your program code more clear and readable. The *prjFileAttributes* program nests three levels of structures to make the structure's purpose more evident.

✓ Within your programs, you can use either Visual Basic's built-in commands or Windows API function calls to get information about files previously saved onto a drive or disk.

✓ Although Visual Basic's *Dir* function is generally sufficient for most directory tasks, it will not let your procedures maintain information about the directories it searches from one procedure call to the next—that is, you cannot use it to perform recursive searches. To perform recursive directory searches within your Visual Basic programs, you must use the Windows API directory functions.

✓ Within your programs, you can use a file's *Directory* attribute bit to determine whether the file is a directory or a file. You can check the attribute of any file, whether it is a file that a Windows API call returns or a file that Visual Basic's built-in commands returns.

✓ When your Visual Basic programs must locate files that meet user- or program-specified characteristics, you can use the *FindFirstFile* and *FindNextFile* API functions to perform the searches.

✓ Within your Visual Basic programs, you can use the *FindFirstFile* and *FindNextFile* functions to perform searches within recursive subroutines, because the *FindFirstFile* function returns a *handle* (a unique integer value) that your programs can maintain within different instances of the same recursive function or procedure.

✓ When you work with handles within your programs, whether search handles, window handles, or other handles, your programs should always close each handle the program creates after the program finishes using the handle. For example, your programs should use the *FindClose* call to close handles that *FindFirstFile* returns.

Chapter 18
Creating an Internet Research Program

If you have spent any time on the Internet recently, you know that the amount of Net-based electronic traffic is growing rapidly. Even though Internet designers are trying to increase the size of the Internet's "highway" or *bandwidth*, you will often experience significant slowdowns when you connect to the Internet. Bandwidth represents the size or amount of information your current Internet connection can handle at any given time, similar to a traffic highway with multiple lanes. There are several technologies available that let you search through the large amount of information on the Internet. For example, you can find information on the Internet on both *File Transfer Protocol* (FTP) sites and *Hypertext Transport Protocol* (HTTP) sites. Each FTP or HTTP site on the Internet includes an *Internet address*. For example, *http://www.jamsa.com* is the Jamsa Press Web address (HTTP site). When you visit a specific Internet address using a Web browser, such as Netscape or Microsoft Internet Explorer, you can view the document or documents at that address, which your browser will generally display as pages of information. Each Web document, or page, is actually a file that consists of text, program commands, and output formatting commands. In addition, each page has its own unique Internet address, called a *Uniform Resource Locator* (URL). When you navigate the Internet, you will generally use the Uniform Resource Locator for the sites you want to visit.

This chapter introduces the *Internet Transfer* control, which your programs can use to connect to a URL and retrieve the page at that URL. However, the *Internet Transfer* control will do much more than let your program connect to URLs and display documents on your computer screen. You can use an *Internet Transfer* control to track each portion of an Internet connection. For example, you can write Visual Basic code that will let you know what is happening during a connection, such as whether your program has connected to the Internet address or not, how fast a transmission will arrive at your computer, and whether errors occurred during transfer. The *Internet Transfer* control is similar to other Visual Basic controls in that it has properties, methods, and events. Using its properties, methods, and events, you can write code that lets you manage an Internet connection in all aspects.

In addition to opening URLs and tracking an Internet connection, in this chapter's project, *prjResearch*, you will use an *Internet Transfer* control to open FTP and HTTP sites. Remember, a URL is a document's Internet address, and an FTP or HTTP site means that your program will display and manage data as the FTP or HTTP protocol defines. Usually, an FTP site will contain a directory, similar to a directory or a directory tree on your computer. Using the *Internet Transfer* control, you can browse an FTP directory, get files from a remote computer, and place the files you want onto your computer. An HTTP site usually will not contain a directory and you will have to write extra code to view graphics the page may reference.

After you complete this chapter's project, you will have the means to access Internet documents, open FTP or HTTP sites, and search for a specific word or phrase. Also, after you open an FTP or HTTP site at a particular URL address, you can store the site address and search phrase within a Microsoft *Access* database. This chapter examines in detail the *Internet Transfer* control. By the time you finish this chapter, you will understand the following key concepts:

- Visual Basic includes the *Internet Transfer* control, which you will use to open File Transfer Protocol (FTP) and Hypertext Transport Protocol (HTTP) sites.
- Each FTP and HTTP site includes at least one document with its own URL, and your program can use the *Internet Transfer* control to connect to URLs.
- The *Internet Transfer* control will let your programs download or upload files to and from your computer across the Internet.
- The *Internet Transfer* control will let your programs regulate and monitor Internet connections because it will return response codes to your project.
- The *Internet Transfer* control lets you easily add additional Internet functionality to your programs.

539

USING THE prjRESEARCH PROJECT

Before you design the *prjResearch* project, you may find it helpful to run the program. The companion CD-ROM that accompanies this book contains the *prjResearch.exe* program and a sample database within the *Chapter18* directory. As with every other program on the CD-ROM, you should use the Jamsa Press *setup.exe* program the CD-ROM contains to copy the program to your computer's hard drive before you run it. After you copy the program to your computer's hard drive, you can run the program from the Start menu. To run the program, select the Windows Start menu Run option. Windows will display the Run dialog box. Within the Run dialog box, enter *x:\vbpl\Chapter18\prjResearch.exe*, where *x* corresponds to the drive letter of the hard drive on which you placed the program, and click your mouse on OK. Windows will display the *prjResearch.exe* program, as shown in Figure 18.1.

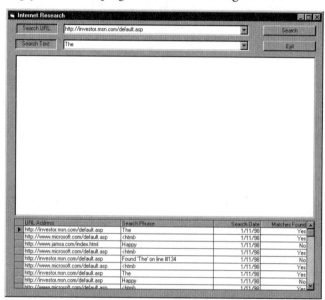

Figure 18.1 The **prjResearch.exe** *program at startup.*

Before you use the *prjResearch.exe* program, take a moment to familiarize yourself with the controls on the form. As you have learned, the *prjResearch* project will let you connect to an Internet Web site (HTTP site) or FTP site by the site's URL address. When the program starts, you will see the Search and Exit buttons near the top right corner of the *Internet Research* form. Next to the buttons, you will see two combo boxes labeled "Search URL" and "Search Text." The Search URL combo box will default to *http://www.jamsa.com/*, and the Search Text combo box will be blank.

RUNNING prjRESEARCH FROM THE CD-ROM

As you have learned, you must first install most programs that you will use within this book to your computer's hard drive before you try to use the programs. The *prjResearch.exe* program, however, does not use any custom controls or references, and in fact uses only Visual Basic's standard control set. Because the *prjResearch.exe* program does not use any custom controls or references, you can run the program from the CD-ROM. To run the program from the CD-ROM, perform the following steps:

1. Select the Windows Start menu Run option. Windows will display the Run dialog box.

2. Within the Run dialog box, enter *x:\Chapter18\prjResearch.exe*, where *x* corresponds to the drive letter of your computer's CD-ROM drive (usually D: or E:), and click your mouse on OK. Windows will run the *prjResearch.exe* program.

To learn more about the Jamsa Press *setup.exe* program, see the "What's on the *Visual Basic Programmer's Library* Companion CD-ROM" section at the back of this book.

Now that you have seen the *prjResearch.exe* program's layout, you can use the program to connect to a Web site address. After you connect to a Web site address, the program will ask you if you want to save the address in a database. To connect to a Web site address by name (URL) or number (IP address) and save the address in a database, perform the following steps:

1. Enter the address *http://www.jamsa.com/jamsa1.htm* into the Search URL combo box.

2. Click your mouse in the Search Text combo box. Enter *Hacker* within the combo box.

3. Click your mouse on the Search command button. The program will display the "Searching" message, as shown in Figure 18.2.

SEARCHING...

Figure 18.2 The program's Searching message.

4. After the program locates the Web site, it will open the site, search for the phrase *Hacker*, display the site in the large box below the Search and Display buttons, and display a message box asking, "Text found. Store site address in database?"

5. Click your mouse on the Yes button within the message box. The program will store the address in the database and display all available addresses at the bottom of the form, as shown in Figure 18.3.

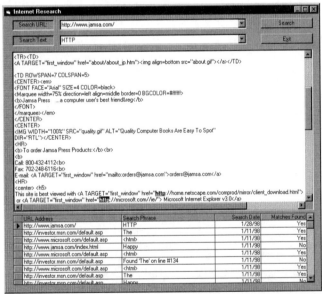

*Figure 18.3 The **Internet Research** form displaying the newly added **http://www.jamsa.com/jamsa1.htm** address.*

Before you can begin to search, you must make sure that you have entered both a location and the text to search for within the two combo boxes. When you click your mouse on the Search button, the program will let you connect to a Web or FTP site by URL address, and will let you search for a word or phrase inside the Web or FTP site's document. Whether or not the program finds the word or phrase in the connected Web or FTP site, you can add the site's address, as well as the search's success, to a Microsoft *Access* database file. The grid at the bottom of the page lists previous sites that you have visited and searched, the search word or phrase you used, and the search's success. As you will learn, you can click your mouse on an entry within the grid to search a previously searched page.

When you begin to search, the program will change the Exit button's caption to Stop. If you click your mouse on the Stop button, the program will stop searching whether it is successful or not. After you stop a search, the program will change the Exit button's caption back to Exit. If you click your mouse on the button again, the program will end. Below the buttons and the combo box and above the grid at the form's bottom, you will see a larger blank box. After you click your mouse on the Search button and connect to a Web site, the program will fill the blank box with the text that comprises the actual Web or FTP site document.

Near the bottom of the *Research* form, you will see a grid with four columns. Whenever you click your mouse on the Search button and connect to a Web site, the program will save the Web site address to the database, and display the address in the column labeled "URL Address." After the program saves any URL addresses into the database, you can click your mouse on any listing in the grid and click your mouse on Search and the program will reconnect to and again search the selected URL address. After you have entered a Web site address, connected to it, and added the address to the database, you can connect to a stored Web site address. To select a stored address and connect to it over the Internet, perform the following steps:

1. Within the *Internet Research* form, click your mouse on any entry in the grid at the form's bottom. The program will add the URL address and the search text to their respective combo boxes. Figure 18.4 shows what the grid might look like.

URL Address	Search Phrase	Search Date	Matches Found
http://investor.msn.com/default.asp	The	1/11/98	Yes
http://www.microsoft.com/default.asp	<html>	1/11/98	Yes
http://www.jamsa.com/index.html	Happy	1/11/98	No
http://www.microsoft.com/default.asp	<html>	1/11/98	Yes
http://investor.msn.com/default.asp	Found 'The' on line #134	1/11/98	No
http://www.microsoft.com/default.asp	<html>	1/11/98	Yes
http://investor.msn.com/default.asp	The	1/11/98	Yes
http://investor.msn.com/default.asp	Happy	1/11/98	No
http://www.microsoft.com/default.asp	<html>	1/11/98	Yes

Figure 18.4 *The search grid containing previously searched Web sites.*

2. Click your mouse on the Search button to begin the search. The program will try to connect to the URL and search the document at the URL's location.

CREATING A BLANK FORM

Now that you have a better idea how to use the finished *prjResearch* project, you can begin to design it. First, you will create an empty form that will contain all the controls introduced in the "Using the *prjResearch* Project" section. After you design the form, you will learn more about the *Internet Transfer* control and the Microsoft *Access* database. To begin the *prjResearch* project and create a blank form, perform the following steps:

1. Within Visual Basic, select the File menu New Project option. Visual Basic will open the New Project dialog box.

2. Within the New Project dialog box, double-click your mouse on the Standard EXE icon. Visual Basic will close the New Project dialog box, start a new project, *Project1*, and add a form to it, *Form1*.

3. If Visual Basic is not displaying the *Form1* form within an object window, double-click your mouse on the *Form1* listing within the Project Explorer. Visual Basic will open the *Form1* form.

4. Select the View menu Properties Window option. Visual Basic will open the Properties Window listing the *Form1* properties.

5. Within the Properties Window, change the *Form1* properties to the values Table 18.1 lists.

Object	Property	Set As
Form1	*Caption*	*Internet Research*
Form1	*Height*	9000
Form1	*Left*	0
Form1	*Top*	0
Form1	*Width*	10275
Form1	*Name*	*frmResearch*

Table 18.1 *The newly named* ***frmResearch*** *form's properties.*

6. Select the File menu Save Project As option. Visual Basic will open the Save File As dialog box and fill the *File name* field with *frmResearch*.

7. Within the Save File As dialog box, click your mouse on the Save button. Visual Basic will save the *frmResearch* form and fill the *File name* field with the *Project1* project name.

8. Within the *File name* field, replace the *Project1* project name with the new *prjResearch* project name. Next, click your mouse on the Save button. Visual Basic will save the *prjResearch* project and close the Save Project As dialog box.

MORE ON FTP AND HTTP

As you have learned, the Internet supports many protocols, including the FTP and HTTP protocols that this chapter uses. The FTP protocol will provide you with a continuous Internet connection until an error occurs or until you break the connection. Because the FTP connection is continuous, it is a *state-maintaining connection*. However, the HTTP protocol is *stateless*, which means that a browser and server combine to make a network connection and both later break the connection. For example, when you connect to a Web site, your browser and the server create a connection that lets the server download the site's HTML (Hypertext Markup Language) file to the browser.

543

After the browser receives the file, the server breaks the connection. As your browser parses the HTML file (that is, breaks the file down into its component parts), if it encounters HTML references to images, Java applets, or to other objects, it must then download them from the server. Each time the browser must download a file, it must establish a new connection to the server. A primary reason for developing some of the new HTML standards (such as dynamic HTML) is that stateless transmissions are, by their nature, very slow. On the one hand, because the server and your browser must establish a new connection for each file the Web server downloads to the browser (which causes delays in delivering content to users), much of the Web's promise remains unrealized. On the other hand, stateless HTML is much more efficient from the server perspective than the new proposed standards. To illustrate the differences, Figure 18.5 compares the way servers handle stateless HTML with the way servers might handle some of the proposed, state-maintaining HTML.

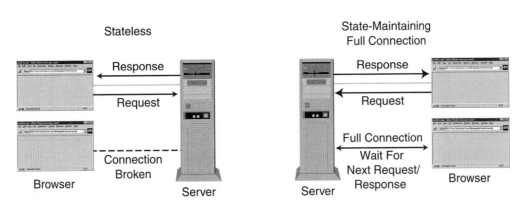

Figure 18.5 *Stateless HTML transmissions versus the proposed, state-maintaining HTML transmissions.*

Note: *Web authors generally name files they write in HTML as "FileName.HTML" or "FileName.HTM." Either way is acceptable to HTTP, which does not care about filenames, their length, or their format. However, you should name your files consistently throughout your Web site.*

BETTER UNDERSTANDING THE EFFICIENCY OF STATELESS COMMUNICATIONS

A single HTTP request-and-response pair is a *transaction*. HTTP uses a Transport Control Protocol/Internet Protocol (TCP/IP) connection that it maintains only for the time a single transaction takes. The Transport Control Protocol/ Internet Protocol is the set of protocols that determines what form communications over the Internet are and how the Internet transports those communications. Neither the client (which usually runs a Web browser program) nor the server remembers a connection's last state. If you think about how you browse a Web site, the HTTP transactions will make sense. As you know, when you click your mouse on a hypertext link, or *hyperlink*, your browser will move you from one site to another. Knowing that you may use a hyperlink to leave a Web site at any time, it is easier for the server to assume you are going to leave and break the connection first. If you stay, the server simply creates a new connection. If you leave, the server does not have to do anything else—it has already broken the connection. Releasing connections in this way lets a server respond to other clients, and thereby improves the server's efficiency.

Recently, however, server programmers have experimented with *connection caching*, in which a server does not immediately close a connection after providing a response. By caching the connection, the server can respond quickly to a client should the client "revisit" the site. As Web sites become more complex and offer users more local links, connection caching (for known local links) will improve performance.

Understanding the Four-Step HTTP Transaction

As you learned in Chapter 13, "Creating a Network-Aware Client," before a client and server can exchange data, they must first establish a connection. Clients and servers on the Internet must also establish connections before they can communicate. On the Internet, clients and servers use TCP/IP to establish the connection. You also know that clients request data from servers and that servers respond to client requests to provide the data the clients request. Clients and servers use HTTP for their requests and responses. In addition, you know that servers and clients maintain their TCP/IP connection for only one transaction (HTTP is stateless), and that servers usually close the connection after the transaction is complete. Therefore, when you put this information together, you have the four step HTTP transaction process, which the following sections describe in detail.

Step 1: Establish a Connection

Before a client and a server can exchange information, they must first establish a TCP/IP connection. As you know, the Internet uses the TCP/IP protocol suite to let computers communicate. To distinguish protocols, applications use a unique number, called a *port number*, for each protocol. Common protocols, such as FTP and HTTP, have *well-known* port numbers that client and server programs use. Developers refer to ports as well-known because programmers commonly use the ports for certain protocols, even though no standards body has specified them as the "correct" ports for those protocols. The usual port assignment for HTTP is port 80, but HTTP can use other ports—provided that the client and the server agree to use a different port number. Table 18.2 lists the well-known port assignments for commonly used Web and Internet protocol ports.

Protocol	Port Number
File Transfer Protocol	21
Telnet Protocol	23
Simple Mail Transfer Protocol	25
Trivial File Transfer Protocol	69
Gopher Protocol	70
Finger Protocol	79
Hypertext Transfer Protocol	80

Table 18.2 Well-known port assignments on the Internet.

Note: *TCP/IP treats all ports below 1024 as privileged ports (that is, TCP/IP reserves the ports for protocols), and all well-known port assignments fall under the privileged port category. You should never designate your own port numbers to be less than 1024.*

Step 2: Client Issues a Request

Each HTTP request a client issues to a Web server begins with a *request method*, followed by an object's URL. The client appends the HTTP protocol version the client uses to the method and the URL, followed by a carriage return linefeed (CRLF) character pair. The browser, depending on the request, may follow the carriage return linefeed with information the browser encodes in a particular header style. After it completes the preceding information, the browser appends a carriage return linefeed to the request. Again, depending on the request's nature, the browser may follow the entire request with an entity body (a Multi-Purpose Internet Mail Extensions (MIME)-encoded document).

An HTTP *method* is a command the client uses to specify the purpose of its server request. All HTTP methods correspond to a resource (which its URL identifies). The client also specifies the HTTP version it is using (such as HTTP 1.0). Together, the method, the URL, and the HTTP protocol version comprise the *Request-Line*. The Request-Line is a section within the *Request-Header* field. For example, a client may use the HTTP *GET* method to request a Web-page graphic from a server.

The client uses a *Request-Header* field to provide information to the server about the request itself, and about the client making the request. In a request, the entity body is supporting data for the request. The client generally uses the name of the data the server is to transfer to compose the entity body. Figure 18.6 shows the process the client and the server perform when they make a connection and the client sends a request.

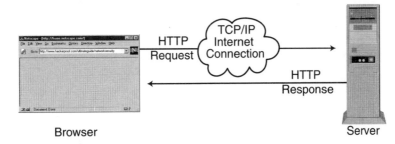

Figure 18.6 *The communication between the client (browser) and the server on a client request.*

STEP 3: SERVER ISSUES A RESPONSE

After a Web server receives and interprets a request message, the server responds to the client with an HTTP *response message*. The response message always begins with the HTTP protocol version, followed by a three-digit status code and a reason phrase (Response-Header). Next, the response message includes a carriage return linefeed, and then, depending on the client's request, information the client requested, which the server encodes in a particular header style. Finally, the server appends a carriage return linefeed to the preceding information, optionally following it with an entity body.

The *status code* is a three-digit number that describes the server's ability to understand and satisfy the client's request. The *reason phrase* is a short, text description of the status code. See *Web Programming*, by Kris Jamsa, Ph.D., Suleiman "Sam" Lalani, and Steve Weakley, Jamsa Press, 1996, for more information on understanding the HTTP Response-Code Classes and a list of the HTTP three-digit status codes and their corresponding reason phrases. The HTTP protocol version, status code, and reason phrase, when combined, comprise the *status line*.

A *Response-Header* may contain specific information relating to the requested resource, plus whichever MIME declarations the server may require to deliver the response. When a Web server sends a Response-Header to a client, the Web server usually includes the same information the client's Request-Header supplies. The entity body (which the server composes in bytes) within the response contains the data the server is transferring to the client. Figure 18.7 depicts the server's response to the client.

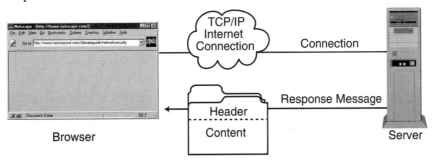

Figure 18.7 *The server's response to the client (browser).*

STEP 4: SERVER TERMINATES THE CONNECTION

The server is responsible for terminating a TCP/IP connection with a client after it performs the client's request. However, both the client and the server must manage a connection's unexpected closing. That is, if you click your mouse on your browser's Stop button, the browser must close the connection. Therefore, the remaining computer must recognize the previously connected computer's unexpected closing. The remaining computer, in turn, will close the connection. In any case, when either one or both parties close a connection, the current transaction always terminates, regardless of the transaction's status. Figure 18.8 shows a complete HTTP transaction.

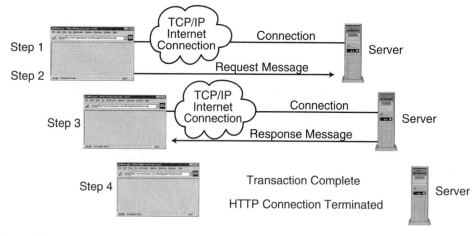

Figure 18.8 *A complete HTTP transaction.*

A CLOSER LOOK AT URIs

As you read Web literature, you may encounter the term Uniform Resource Identifier (URI). Most texts refer to URIs as Web addresses, Uniform Document Identifiers, Uniform Resource Locators (URLs), and Uniform Resource Names (URNs) combined. HTTP defines a URI as a formatted string that uses names, locations, or other characteristics to identify a network resource. In other words, a URI is a simple text string that addresses an object on the Web.

REVIEWING URLs

To locate a document on the Web, you must know the document's Internet address. A Web document's Internet address is called a Uniform Resource Locator (URL). You can compare the relationship between a URL and a resource to the relationship between a book and its index. To find information in a book, you look in the book's index. To find a Web resource, you must use its address (URL). Web browsers use URLs to locate Web resources. The basic syntax for a URL is simple. A URL contains two parts, as the following code fragment shows:

```
<scheme>:<scheme-specific-part>
```

The following code fragment shows the full syntax for an HTTP URL:

```
http://<host>:<port>/<path>?<search_part>
```

As you can see, the URL's *<scheme>* portion is *"http,"* and the *<scheme-specific-part>* identifies a *host*, an optional *port*, an optional *path*, and an optional *search_part*. If you omit the *port* element in the URL, the URL will default to the protocol port 80 (the well-known port for HTTP). Do not include the *search_part* within your URLs because HTTP does not currently implement the URL's *search_part*, though you will often see it in combination with scripted pages to pass queries.

You can locate a section inside a document by referring to a specific section of the document. For example, if you type the following URL into your browser's *location line* (the white box at the top that displays URLs) and press ENTER, you will access the author biography for Lars Klander at the Jamsa Press Web site:

```
http://www.jamsa.com/AUTHORS/bio.htm#lklander
```

In this example, the URL attaches an *anchor* named *#lklander* to the end of the file's pathname. This anchor directs your browser to open the resource located at the address the URL specifies, and positions the browser's view of the opened resource at the named anchor. Figure 18.9 shows the Web site at *http://www.jamsa.com/AUTHORS/bio.htm#lklander*.

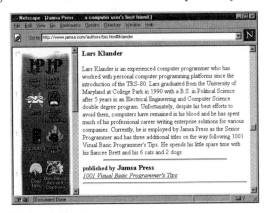

Figure 18.9 *The author biography for Lars Klander.*

Note: *URLs are not unique to the Web. In fact, several other protocols use URLs, such as FTP, GOPHER, and Telnet. However, all URLs have the same purpose: to identify an object's address on the Internet.*

RELATING URLS, PROTOCOLS, AND FILE TYPES

A URL not only provides an address for an Internet object, it also describes the protocol the application must use to access that object. For example, the HTTP URL scheme indicates a Web space (area), while a File Transfer Protocol (FTP) scheme indicates an FTP space. You can think of a space on the Internet as an area reserved for information of a particular type. For example, all Internet FTP documents reside in FTP space. Figure 18.10 shows the difference between an HTTP document within a Web space and a directory within an FTP space.

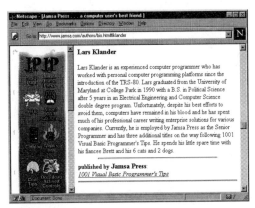 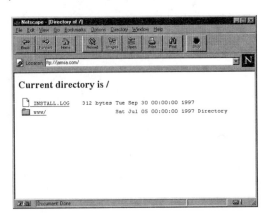

Figure 18.10 *The difference in the appearance of HTTP and FTP documents.*

A URL can also include a *document-resource identifier*. The document-resource identifier specifies the file's format—provided the file's creator followed the correct naming conventions for the resource. For example, filenames with an *html* file extension will contain text in the HTML format, and a file with an *au* extension will contain audio.

UNDERSTANDING URL PIECES

As you examine a URL, you may find it easier to identify the URL's exact reference if you break the URL into pieces. To better understand this, consider the following URL:

```
http://www.jamsa.com/catalog/vbpl/vbpl.htm
```

547

In the previous example, the URL's scheme specifies the HTTP protocol. The double slashes that follow the colon indicate that the object is an Internet object. Following the slashes, you will find the server's address which, in this case, is *www.jamsa.com*. Next, the slash separator specifies a directory path, *catalog/vbpl*. Finally, the last (rightmost) slash specifies the name (*vbpl*) and, optionally, the document-resource identifier extension that corresponds to the desired object (*htm*). Breaking a URL into pieces is important when you create *relative URLs*. You will learn about relative URLs later in this chapter, in the section "Defining Relative URLs."

LOOKING AT HTML AND URLs

Explaining Hypertext Markup Language (HTML) in detail is beyond this book's scope. (To learn more about HTML, refer to Jamsa, Lalani, and Weakley's book, *Web Programming*, Jamsa Press, 1996.) For this book's purposes, you can view HTML as a language designers use to structure Web documents. Hyperlinks are a significant portion of this structure. When a browser renders a Web document for display, the browser typically highlights the document's hyperlink portions to differentiate them from the normal text. When you create a Web document, HTML lets you control the creation of each hyperlink you add to the document.

As you have learned, you use a special HTML element, called an *anchor*, to represent a link in a Web document. An HTML anchor is a tag the designer inserts into a Web document to specify a link (a corresponding URL) that the browser should associate with specific text or a graphic image. Designers specify a URL within an anchor element to inform the browser of the linked resource's address. The following example contains a reference to the *jamsa2.htm* URL, which is up two levels in the directory tree from the current page (as the next section, "Introducing Absolute and Relative URLs," explains). The example also references a *gif* image file, as shown here:

```
<A target="main" href="../../jamsa2.htm">
<img align=bottom src="../../mainmnu2.gif"></a>
```

In other words, the anchor contains the URL of the resource attached to your hypertext or, as in this example, a graphic image. Figure 18.11 shows how an anchor within a Web page might point to another Web page.

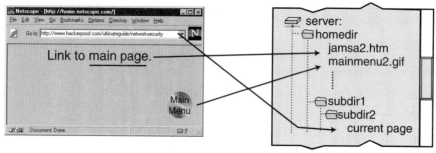

Figure 18.11 *An anchor points to another Web page.*

INTRODUCING ABSOLUTE AND RELATIVE URLs

A *hypertext* document is a document that contains many *links*, often known as *hyperlinks*. The Web is a maze of hyperlinked documents. When designers create a Web document, they typically link their document to other documents that they or someone else created, though they may also link it to video files, graphics, and other interactive content. Each link requires a URL address to identify the corresponding object. As you have learned, browsers use URLs to locate Web documents. As designers specify URLs, they can use two address types: *absolute URLs* and *relative URLs*.

DEFINING ABSOLUTE URLs

An absolute URL specifies an object's complete address and protocol. In other words, if the URL's scheme (such as *http*) is present, the URL is an absolute URL. The following is an example of an absolute URL:

```
http://www.jamsa.com/catalog/vbpl/vbpl.htm
```

Defining Relative URLs

A relative URL, on the other hand, uses the URL associated with the document currently open in your browser. Using the same scheme, server address, and directory tree (if present) as the open document, the browser reconstructs the URL by replacing the filename and extension with those of the relative URL. For example, consider the following absolute URL:

```
http://www.jamsa.com/catalog/catalog.htm
```

If a hyperlink within the HTML document specifies a reference to the relative URL *vbpl/vbpl.htm*, as shown in the following code, the browser will reconstruct the URL as *http://www.jamsa.com/catalog/vbpl/vbpl.htm*:

```
<A HREF="/vbpl/vbpl.htm"> Visual Basic Programming Information</A>
```

Note: *When you use the single dot (.) in front of the relative URL (for example, **.vbpl/vbpl.htm**), it has the same result as entering **vbpl/vbpl.htm**.*

549

Going Further with Relative URLs

As you work with relative URLs, there may be times when you want to move up one level (above the open document's directory location) within the directory tree. To move up the directory tree, you may precede the relative URL with a double dot (..) notation. For example, suppose you write the current document's absolute URL as shown here:

```
http://www.jamsa.com/dir1/dir2/file.ext
```

If a hyperlink within the HTML document specifies a reference to the relative URL *..dir3/newfile.ext*, as shown in the following code, the browser will reconstruct the URL as *http://www.jamsa.com/dir1/dir3/newfile.ext*:

```
<A HREF="..dir3/newfile.ext">New File Link</A>
```

Alternatively, you may want to move up multiple levels in the directory tree. You can make a relative URL move up several branches in the tree by separating multiple instances of the *double dot* operator with a slash. For example, suppose the current document's absolute URL is as shown in the following code:

```
http://www.jamsa.com/dir1/dir2/file.ext
```

If a hyperlink within the HTML document specifies a reference to the relative URL *../../dir3/newfile.ext*, as shown in the following code, the browser will reconstruct the URL as *http://www.jamsa.com/dir3/newfile.ext*:

```
<A HREF="../../dir3/newfile.ext">New File Link</A>
```

Finally, suppose you want to use relative URLs to append a directory path only to the server's address. In other words, you want to ignore the open file's directory path, but still use the file's scheme and server address. In such cases, you can use the forward slash (/) notation. For example, suppose the absolute URL of the current document open within the browser is as follows:

```
http://www.jamsa.com/dir1/dir2/file.ext
```

If a hyperlink within the HTML document specifies a reference to the relative URL */dir3/newfile.ext*, as shown in the following code, the browser will reconstruct the URL as *http://www.jamsa.com/dir3/newfile.ext*:

```
<A HREF="/dir3/newfile.ext">New File Link</A>
```

More on the Internet Transfer Control

As you have learned, the *prjResearch* project will let you connect to an Internet Web site across a network. Visual Basic includes the *Internet Transfer* control, which you will use to connect to a Web site. The *Internet Transfer* control has properties, methods, and events similar to other Visual Basic controls. In the *prjResearch* project, you will add the *Internet Transfer* control to the *frmResearch* form. After you add the control, you can use the control's components. The *prjResearch* project will use the *Internet Transfer* control to open a Web or FTP site address by name or number. Remember, the address is also called a URL and the URL will start with the letters HTTP or FTP. With the *prjResearch* project, you can connect to both HTTP and FTP addresses.

You will use the *Internet Transfer* control's URL property to assign a URL name or number to the control that it should access. After you assign a URL name or number, you can open the Web site. You will use the *Internet Transfer* control's *OpenURL* method to open the URL name or number. After you open the document at the target URL, you can dump the document into a storage container; in this case, a *RichTextBox* control. The *RichTextBox* control will receive any text and display it on your computer screen. Unfortunately, the *RichTextBox* control will not display graphics it receives as a binary stream; instead, you would have to convert the received stream from a byte series into a metafile or a bitmap and display it within the text box. Such conversions are beyond the scope of this book; should you need them, you must add them on your own.

The *Internet Transfer* control includes the *Execute* method. You will not use the *Execute* method in the *prjResearch* project. The *Execute* method will let you open a URL site in a way similar to the *OpenURL* method, except you cannot "dump" the URL site data into a *RichTextBox* control. You can use the *Execute* method to make an active connection to a URL site, similar to a Web browser. At that point, you must write additional software to view the site and that is a project beyond the scope of this book.

INCLUDING A WEB BROWSER WITHIN YOUR PROGRAMS

As you learned in Chapter 1, "Introduction to Visual Basic," you can add an ActiveX version of Microsoft's *Internet Explorer®* browser to your programs. In fact, you can add the browser to your programs by adding the component to your project.

To add a browser control to your programs, perform the following steps:

1. Select the Project menu Components option. Visual Basic will display the Components dialog box.

2. Within the Components dialog box, select the *Microsoft Internet Controls* option. Click your mouse on the check box next to the listing to add the component to your project.

3. Click your mouse on OK to exit the Components dialog box. Visual Basic will add the *Web Browser* control and the *ShellFolderView* control to the Toolbox.

As the text indicates, creating your own Web browser is not a simple process; however, if you want to add a Web browser to your programs so that clients can easily access your Web site, or for whatever other reason, using the ActiveX *Web Browser* control makes it easy to do so.

MORE ON THE INTERNET TRANSFER CONTROL'S OPENURL METHOD

In the *prjResearch* project, you will use the *OpenURL* method to open a URL site. The *OpenURL* method will open and retrieve a document at a specified URL address and the *Internet Transfer* control will return the document at the Web site as a Visual Basic *Variant* type. Remember, a *Variant* type can contain numbers, text, binary value sequences, object references, and more.

Using the *OpenURL* method, you will connect to an FTP or HTTP address. As you have learned, the client generally views an FTP site as a collection of directories and files, while the client generally sees the HTTP site as a series of HTML documents. As you have learned, most Web site designers use HTML to write the documents that compose their Web sites. When you use a Web browser to connect to a document written in HTML, the browser will interpret the file's contents and display interactive pages, which often contain colored graphics, videos, and other multimedia content. When you access an FTP site, you can access only the files themselves, not display them in an interactive manner as you can with HTML documents.

In the *prjResearch* project, you will use the *OpenURL* method to open a Web site. Then you will dump the information at each Web site into a *RichTextBox* control on the *frmResearch* form. The *RichTextBox* control can hold a large amount (up to about 64K, or 64,000 digits) of number and text data (but no graphics). Because the *RichTextBox* control does not interpret HTML tags, if you connect to a site written in HTML, the *OpenURL* method will display any HTML code in brackets (< >) within the *RichTextBox* control. You will use the *Internet Transfer* control's *OpenURL* method as shown in the following prototype:

```
object.OpenUrl url [,datatype]
```

Table 18.3 lists each parameter and description of the *OpenURL* method's syntax.

Parameter	Description
object	Your *Internet Transfer* control's name.
url	A control-required string value that contains the name of the URL address.
datatype	An optional *Integer* value that specifies the type of data to dump into a *RichTextBox* control.

*Table 18.3 The **OpenURL** method's parameters and descriptions.*

MORE ON THE DATATYPE PARAMETER

As you can see, the *OpenURL* method's syntax includes the *datatype* parameter. The *datatype* parameter can contain an *Integer* value. The *Integer* value will represent the type of data, string or binary, to dump into a control, such as a *RichTextBox* control or a *TextBox* control. Table 18.4 lists the two predefined system constants and their values for the *OpenURL* method's *datatype* parameter.

Constant	Value	Description
icString	0	The *datatype* parameter's default value. The *Internet Transfer* control receives data as a string.
icByteArray	1	The *datatype* parameter's alternate value. The *Internet Transfer* control receives data as a binary *Byte* array.

*Table 18.4 The **datatype** parameter's constant values.*

Most Web sites will contain string data, which means you will see numbers and text within the Web site. If you want to download a binary file, such as an executable program or a graphic, you must download it as binary data. This means that you cannot see numbers or text within the Web site; instead, you will see a file name, followed by the *EXE* extension.

As you have learned, the *OpenURL* method will return data of the type *Variant* if you do not use a datatype constant of *icByteArray* or 1. When you do assign the *datatype* parameter to 1, you can retrieve a binary file. To successfully retrieve a binary file, you must assign it to a *Byte* array. You create a *Byte* array just as you would any other array. To better understand *Byte* arrays, consider the following sample code, which uses the *itcByte* control (an *Internet Transfer* control), and implements a simple binary download:

```
Private Sub FillByteArray()
  Dim ByteArray() As Byte
  Dim URLstring As String

  URLstring = "FTP://ftp.Jamsa.com/SomeProgram.exe"
  ByteArray() = itcByte.OpenURL(URLstring, icByteArray)
End Sub
```

MORE ON THE INTERNET TRANSFER CONTROL'S EXECUTE METHOD

In the *prjResearch* project, you will not use the *Execute* method to open a URL site. However, you may want to use the *Execute* method in another project. The *Execute* method differs from the *OpenURL* method because you do not use it to view Web sites. You can use the *Execute* method to navigate through a remote server's directory and to download files onto your computer.

The *Execute* method will give you much more information about a file than will the *OpenURL* method. Each time you use the *Execute* method it will produce a *response code* to describe the transaction. A response code is an integer value that you can translate into words. The words will describe such things as connection status and connection completion. Each time your program invokes the *Execute* method it will simultaneously invoke the *StateChanged* event. You can use the *StateChanged* event to retrieve and process response codes for each *Execute* method transaction. The following prototype shows the *Execute* method's basic syntax:

```
object.Execute url, operation, data, requestHeaders
```

Table 18.5 lists the *Execute* method's parameters and descriptions.

Parameter	Description
object	The name of your *Internet Transfer* control on your project form.
url	An optional string value that specifies the name of the URL address the control is to open. You can also set the *url* parameter as an environment variable before you run the containing program. If you have not written a URL string, the *Execute* method will use the *url* environment variables.
operation	An optional parameter that specifies the type of operation for the *Execute* method to execute.
data	An optional string that specifies the data for the *operation* parameter.
requestHeaders	An optional string that specifies additional headers for the remote server to send to the program.

*Table 18.5 The **Execute** method's parameters.*

MORE ON THE STATECHANGED EVENT

As you have learned, when you invoke the *Internet Transfer* control's *Execute* or *OpenURL* method, the control will invoke its *StateChanged* event. The *StateChanged* event will supply response codes that the program can process. The *StateChanged* event has one parameter, *State*. The *State* parameter contains an integer value that is the control's response code, and you can translate the code into text. The resulting text will tell you the method's status. The following prototype shows the *StateChanged* event's basic syntax:

```
object_StateChanged(ByVal State As Integer)
```

As you can see, the *StateChanged* event's syntax includes the *State* parameter. The *State* parameter will contain an integer value that represents a response code. The response code will show an Internet connection's step-by-step processing following the invocation of the *Execute* method. After you have a response code, you can translate it into descriptive text. Visual Basic will store the text as a *constant*. Remember, a constant can contain numbers or text, and you cannot change its value in code. Table 18.6 lists each predefined constant that the *State* parameter associates with a response code.

Constant	Response Code	Description
icNone	0	No state to report.
icHostResolvingHost	1	The *Internet Transfer* control is looking up the specified host computer's Internet Protocol (IP) address.

*Table 18.6 The **State** parameter's constants and their corresponding integer values. (continued on following page)*

Constant	Response Code	Description
icHostResolved	2	The *Internet Transfer* control successfully found the specified host computer's IP address.
icConnecting	3	The *Internet Transfer* control is connecting to the host computer.
icConnected	4	The *Internet Transfer* control successfully connected to the host computer.
icRequesting	5	The *Internet Transfer* control is sending a request to the host computer.
icRequestSent	6	The *Internet Transfer* control successfully sent the request.
icReceivingResponse	7	The *Internet Transfer* control is receiving a response from the host computer.
icDisconnecting	9	The *Internet Transfer* control is disconnecting from the host computer.
icDisconnected	10	The *Internet Transfer* control successfully disconnected from the host computer.
icError	11	An error occurred in communicating with the host computer.
icResponseCompleted	12	The request has completed and Visual Basic has received all data.
icResponseReceived	20	The *Internet Transfer* control successfully received a response from the host computer.

Table 18.6 *The **State** parameter's constants and their corresponding integer values. (continued from previous page)*

Within the *prjResearch* project, you will use response codes to update information the program presents to the user, or to trap errors in the user-requested connection.

THE INTERNET TRANSFER CONTROL'S GETCHUNK METHOD

As you have learned, when you use the *Execute* method to open a URL site, you can navigate a remote computer's directories and download files onto your computer. Sometimes, the downloaded file's size is so large that retrieving it in bulk will cause your computer system to slow down or stall. You will use the *Internet Transfer* control's *GetChunk* method to manage system slowdowns. The *GetChunk* method will let you retrieve data in chunks (usually each chunk is 1024 bytes). In addition to managing system slowdowns, you can use the *GetChunk* method and associate it with a progress bar to show download flow status.

You can use the *GetChunk* method within the *StateChanged* event. As you have learned, within the *StateChanged* event, you can process response codes and translate them into descriptive text in the form of constants. Two of the constants you will most often use are *icResponseReceived* and *icResponseCompleted*. The moment the *Execute* or *OpenURL* method connects to a URL address, the *StateChanged* event will receive the *icResponseReceived* response. After the program receives the response code, the program can receive data from the remote server, usually in the form of a file. When the transaction completes, the *StateChanged* event will receive the *icResponseCompleted* response. Within the *StateChanged* event you will use a *Select-Case* statement to process each response, including the *icResponseReceived* and *icResponseCompleted* responses. After the *Select-Case* statement determines that the *icResponseReceived* response exists, you will use the *GetChunk* method to download any data you want in 1024 byte chunks. Using the *GetChunk* method will speed up any downloads you make with the *Execute* method. For example, the following sample code waits for an *icResponseReceived* status, then uses the *GetChunk* method to download the data encapsulated within the response:

```
Private Sub itcData_StateChanged(ByVal State As Integer)
   Select Case State
   Case icResponseReceived
     Dim vtData As Variant
     Dim strData As String
     strData = ""
     Dim FileDone As Boolean
     FileDone = False
     vtData = itcData.GetChunk(1024, icString)
     Do While Not FileDone
        strData = Data & vtData
        vtData = itcData.GetChunk(1024, icString)
        If Len(vtData) = 0 Then
           FileDone = True
        End If
     Loop
     txtData.Text = strData
   End Select
End Sub
```

As you can see, the code loops until the connection provides no more data, then exits. However, as you will notice, the program writes the data into a variable length *String*, rather than a *Byte* array. Because Visual Basic treats strings as byte sequences, you can manage incoming data with strings, rather than *Byte* arrays, if you choose to do so.

MORE ON THE EXECUTE METHOD'S operation PARAMETER

As you have learned, the *Internet Transfer* control will let you connect to FTP or HTTP Web sites. When you connect to FTP sites, you can download files from the site to your computer. After you use the *Internet Transfer* control to connect to an FTP site, you can use a keyword, called an *operation*, to look at files and transfer them to your computer. An operation keyword will specify what Visual Basic will do while connected to an FTP site. As you have learned, the *Execute* method includes the *operation* parameter. To learn more about an operation keyword, consider the following *operation* parameter syntax:

```
itcdata.execute OperationName file1 file2
```

The *OperationName* parameter specifies the operation to perform, and the *file1* and *file2* parameters specify the files on which to perform the operation. Table 18.7 lists the *OperationName* parameter's operation keywords and descriptions.

Keyword	Description
CD file1	Changes the directory pointer to the directory the statement specifies as *file1*.
CDUP	Changes the directory pointer to the parent directory.
CLOSE	Closes the current FTP connection.
DELETE file1	Deletes the file the statement specifies as *file1*.
DIR file1	Searches the directory the statement specifies as *file1* and lists the directory contents. FTP permits wildcards (either * for whole words or ? for single characters) and the remote server dictates the syntax. If the statement does not specify *file1*, the server returns a full directory of the current working directory.
GET file1 file2	Retrieves the remote file the statement specifies as *file1* and creates a new local file the statement specifies as *file2*.

Table 18.7 *The operation keywords of the **Execute** method's **operation** parameter. (continued on following page)*

Keyword	Description
LS file1	Searches the directory the statement specifies as *file1* and lists the directory contents. FTP permits wildcards and the remote host dictates the syntax.
MKDIR file1	Creates a directory as the statement specifies in *file1*. The remote server determines user privileges, such as whether the client can create a directory or not.
PUT file1 file2	Copies a local file the statement specifies as *file1* to the remote host and names the copy on the host as *file2*.
PWD	Returns the current directory name.
QUIT	Terminates the user's current session.
RECV file1 file2	Retrieves the remote file the statement specifies as *file1* and creates a new local file the statement specifies as *file2*. The *RECV* operation is equivalent to *GET*.
RENAME file1 file2	Renames the remote file the statement names in *file1* to the new name the statement specifies in *file2*. The remote server determines user privileges, such as whether the client can rename a file or not.
RMDIR file1	Removes the remote directory the statement specifies as *file1*. The remote server determines user privileges, such as whether the client can remove a directory or not.
SEND file1 file2	Copies a local file, which the statement specifies in *file1*, to the remote host, and names the copy on the remote host as *file2*. The *SEND* operation is equivalent to *PUT*.
SIZE file1	Returns the size of the directory the statement specifies as *file1*.

*Table 18.7 The operation keywords of the **Execute** method's **operation** parameter. (continued from previous page)*

Now that you better understand the *Execute* method's *operation* parameter, you can use it to send and copy files to and from a remote computer. For example, to copy a remote file onto your computer, write the *GET* operation followed by *file1* (the name of the file to get) and *file2* (the name of the file or folder to download to). For example, consider the following program code, in which *itcData* is the *Internet Transfer* control's name:

```
itcData.Execute "FTP://ftp.Jamsa.com", "GET Jamsa.doc
   C:\MyFolder\NewJamsa.doc"
```

The program code will download the *Jamsa.doc* file from the *ftp.jamsa.com* site and save it locally as *NewJamsa.doc*, provided that the *Jamsa.doc* file exists at the FTP site.

ADDING AN INTERNET TRANSFER CONTROL TO THE PROJECT

In the *prjResearch* project, you will use an *Internet Transfer* control to connect to both HTTP and FTP sites, though you will most commonly connect to HTTP (Web) sites. Before you can use an *Internet Transfer* control in your project, you must add it to the project as a component. After you add the *Internet Transfer* control to the *prjResearch* project, Visual Basic will draw its icon in the Toolbox. As you know, the Toolbox displays Visual Basic control icons. If you double-click your mouse on any icon in the Toolbox, Visual Basic will draw the corresponding control within the active form. To add an *Internet Transfer* control to the *prjResearch* project, perform the following steps:

1. Within Visual Basic, select the Project menu Components option. Visual Basic will open the Components dialog box.

2. Within the Components dialog box, select the *Microsoft Internet Transfer Control 5.0* listing. Next, click your mouse on the box to the left of the listing. Visual Basic will display a check mark in the box, as shown in Figure 18.12.

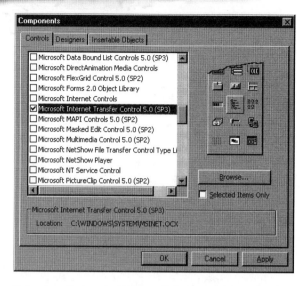

*Figure 18.12 The Components dialog box listing the **Microsoft Internet Transfer Control 5.0** option.*

3. While the Components dialog box is open, you can also add the *Microsoft Rich Text Box* control to the project. Select the *Microsoft Rich Textbox Control 5.0* listing. Next, click your mouse on the box to the left of the listing. Visual Basic will draw a check mark in the box, just as it did with the *Internet Transfer* control.

4. The third control you must add to the *prjResearch* project is the *Microsoft Data Bound Grid* control. To add the *Microsoft Data Bound Grid* control, select the *Microsoft Data Bound Grid Control 5.0* listing. Next, click your mouse on the box to the left of the listing. Visual Basic will draw a check mark in the box, just as it did with the *Internet Transfer* and *Microsoft Rich Text Box* controls.

5. Within the Components dialog box, click your mouse on the OK button. Visual Basic will close the Components dialog box and add the controls to the *prjResearch* project.

ADDING A DATA ACCESS OBJECTS (DAO) OBJECT LIBRARY REFERENCE TO THE PROJECT

As you have learned, the *prjResearch* project will let you store a Web site address in a Microsoft *Access* database. Visual Basic includes the DAO Object Library, which will let you manage and use a database from within Visual Basic. For more information on databases and the DAO Object Library, see Chapter 7, "Creating a Database Viewer and Designer."

As you have learned, before you can use a database from within Visual Basic, you must first add the DAO Object Library as a reference. After you add a DAO Object Library reference to the *prjResearch* project, you can use *Workspace*, *Database*, and *Recordset* objects within Visual Basic. To add a DAO Object Library reference to the *prjResearch* project, perform the following steps:

1. Within Visual Basic, select the Project menu References option. Visual Basic will open the References dialog box.

2. Within the References dialog box, select the *Microsoft DAO 3.5 Object Library* listing. Next, click your mouse on the box to the left of the listing. Visual Basic will draw a check mark in the box, as shown in Figure 18.13.

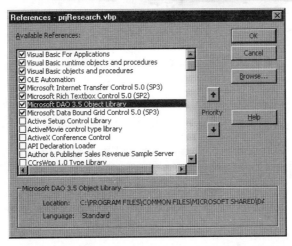

Figure 18.13 *The References dialog box listing the **Microsoft DAO 3.5 Object Library** option.*

3. Within the References dialog box, click your mouse on the OK button. Visual Basic will close the References dialog box and add the DAO Object Library reference to the *prjResearch* project.

CREATING THE DICTIONARY DATABASE

As you have learned, in the *prjResearch* project you will connect to Web sites using an *Internet Transfer* control. After you successfully connect to a Web site, you may want to save the Web site's address and use it later. You will design a Microsoft *Access* database to store the Web site addresses you want to keep. You will name the database *Dictionary.mdb*. The *Dictionary* database will consist of one table and five fields. As you have learned, database tables contain one or more fields which, in turn, contain one or more values. In the *prjResearch* project, you will store a Web site address and a search phrase that corresponds to that address in two fields within the *Research* table, while you will maintain dates, success values, and a counter variable in the other three fields.

To create the *Dictionary* database, perform the following steps:

1. Select the Add-Ins menu Visual Data Manager option. Visual Basic will open the VisData window.

2. Within the VisData window, select the File menu New option. Within the New option, select the Microsoft Access 7.0 MDB submenu option. Visual Basic will open the Select Microsoft Access Database To Create dialog box.

3. Within the Select Microsoft Access Database To Create dialog box, type "Dictionary" in the *File name* field. Next, click your mouse on the Save button. Visual Basic will save the database, close the dialog box, and open the Database window, as shown in Figure 18.14.

Figure 18.14 *The Database window listing the **Dictionary** database.*

CREATING THE DICTIONARY DATABASE'S RESEARCH TABLE

After you create the *Dictionary* database, you can design the *Research* table. As you have learned, the *Research* table will contain five fields, and you will use two of those fields to store Web site addresses and search phrases. You will use the other fields to maintain information on search dates and search success. To create the *Research* table with five fields, perform the following steps:

1. Select the Add-Ins menu Visual Data Manager option. Visual Basic will open the VisData window.

2. Within the VisData window, select the File menu Open Database option Microsoft Access sub-option. Visual Data Manager will open the Open Microsoft Access Database dialog box.

3. Within the Open Microsoft Access Database dialog box, select the *Database* listing. Next, click your mouse on the Open button. Visual Data Manager will open the Database window.

4. Within the Database window, right-click your mouse on the *Properties* listing. Visual Data Manager will open a submenu.

5. Within the submenu, click your mouse on the New Table option. Visual Data Manager will open the Table Structure dialog box.

6. Within the Table Structure dialog box, type *Research* in the *Table Name* field. Next, click your mouse on the Add Field button. Visual Data Manager will open the Add Field dialog box.

7. Within the Add Field dialog box, type *RecordNumber* in the *Name* field. Next, click your mouse on the *Type* field's down arrow and select the *Long* type. Then click your mouse on the OK button. Visual Data Manager will add the new field and clear the Add Field dialog box.

8. Within the Add Field dialog box, type *Search Phrase* in the *Name* field. Next, click your mouse on the *Type* field's down arrow and select the *Text* type. Then click your mouse on the OK button. Visual Data Manager will add the new field and clear the Add Field dialog box.

9. Within the Add Field dialog box, type *SearchDate* in the *Name* field. Next, click your mouse on the *Type* field's down arrow and select the *Date/Time* type. Then click your mouse on the OK button. Visual Data Manager will add the new field and clear the Add Field dialog box.

10. Within the Add Field dialog box, type *MatchesFound* in the *Name* field. Next, click your mouse on the *Type* field's down arrow and select the *Boolean* type. Then click your mouse on the OK button. Visual Data Manager will add the new field and clear the Add Field dialog box.

11. Within the Add Field dialog box, type *URL Address* in the *Name* field. Next, click your mouse on the *Type* field's down arrow and select the *Text* type. Then click your mouse on the OK button. Visual Data Manager will add the new field and clear the Add Field dialog box.

12. Within the Add Field dialog box, click your mouse on the Close button. Visual Data Manager will close the Add Field dialog box and display the Table Structure dialog box.

13. Within the Table Structure dialog box, click your mouse on the Build the Table button. Visual Data Manager will build the table and display the Database window.

14. Within the Database window, click your mouse on the Research icon (the icon for the *Research* table). Visual Data Manager will show the *Fields, Indexes,* and *Properties* listings. Next, click your mouse on *Fields*. Visual Data Manager will show the *Research* fields, as shown in Figure 18.15.

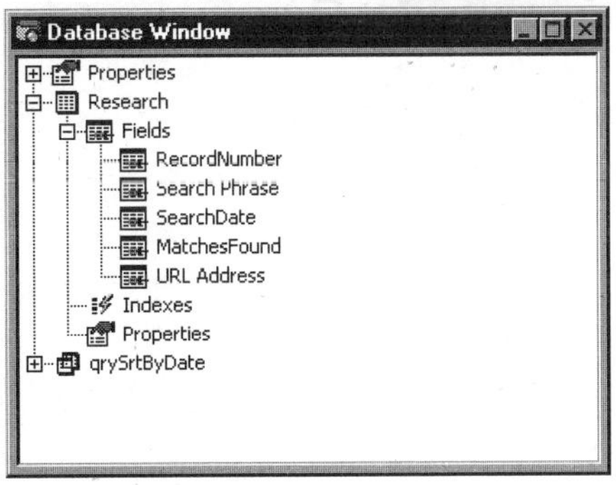

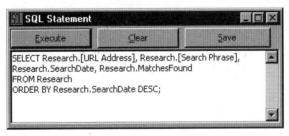

Figure 18.15 *The Database window listing the **Research** table's fields.*

DESIGNING THE QRYSRTBYDATE QUERY

As you have learned, the *Research* table that you designed in the previous section will store information about Web **559** sites that you search within the *prjResearch* project. However, when you display the information within the grid at the bottom of the *frmResearch* form, you will return the information in reverse date order—that is, the most recent search will appear in the grid's first row, and the oldest search will appear in the grid's last row. The program will return the data more quickly if you define a query as part of the database, rather than using a Structured Query Language (SQL) query within the program.

To add the *qrySrtByDate* query to the *Dictionary* database, perform the following steps:

1. Within the VisData window, click your mouse in the SQL Statement window.

2. Within the SQL Statement window, enter the following SQL statement:

```
SELECT Research.[URL Address], Research.[Search Phrase], Research.SearchDate,
    Research.MatchesFound FROM Research ORDER BY Research.SearchDate DESC;
```

Figure 18.16 shows the SQL Statement window with the query text.

Figure 18.16 *The query text within the SQL Statement window.*

3. Click your mouse on the Save button to save the new query. The VisData window will display the Enter QueryDef Name input box.

4. Within the Enter QueryDef Name input box, enter the name of the query as *qrySrtByDate*. Click your mouse on OK to add the query to the *Dictionary* database. *VisData* will add the query to the database tree after the *Research* table.

ADDING CONTROLS TO THE FRMRESEARCH FORM

Now that you have added an *Internet Transfer* control, a *RichTextBox* control, a *Data-Bound Grid* control, and a DAO Object Library reference and component to the *prjResearch* project, you will add controls to the *frmResearch* form. After you add the controls, you will write code that links the controls to your project. First, you will add an *Internet Transfer* control to the *frmResearch* form. Then you will add the *RichTextBox, Data, Data-Bound Grid, ComboBox, CommandButton,* and *Label* controls to the *frmResearch* form.

ADDING AN INTERNET TRANSFER CONTROL TO THE FORM

As you have learned, the *prjResearch* project will use an *Internet Transfer* control to open URL sites and download the information to a *RichTextBox* control. To use the *Internet Transfer* control in the *prjResearch* project, you will add it to the *frmResearch* form. To add an *Internet Transfer* control to the *frmResearch* form, perform the following steps:

1. If Visual Basic is not displaying the *frmResearch* form, double-click your mouse on the *frmResearch* form listing within Project Explorer. Visual Basic will open the *frmResearch* form.
2. Within Visual Basic, select the View menu Toolbox option. Visual Basic will open the Toolbox.
3. Within the Toolbox, select the new *Internet Transfer* control icon, Inet, as shown in Figure 18.17.

Figure 18.17 *The Toolbox showing the* **Internet Transfer** *control's Inet icon.*

4. Within the Toolbox, double-click your mouse on the Inet icon. Visual Basic will draw an *Internet Transfer* control, *Inet1*, within the *frmResearch* form.
5. Within the *frmResearch* form, click your mouse on the *Inet1* control to highlight it. Visual Basic will draw a small frame around the control.
6. Select the View menu Properties Window option. Visual Basic will open the Properties Window listing the *Inet1* properties.
7. Within the Properties Window, change the *Inet1* properties to the values Table 18.8 lists.

Object	Property	Set As
Inet1	Left	0
Inet1	Top	1250
Inet1	Name	itcSearch

Table 18.8 *The newly named* **itcSearch** *control's properties.*

ADDING THE RICHTEXTBOX CONTROL TO THE FORM

As you have learned, when you use the *Internet Transfer* control's *OpenURL* method to open a Web site, you can place data into a Visual Basic control that can receive the data. In the *prjResearch* project, you will use a *RichTextBox* control to receive data from a Web site. To add a *RichTextBox* control to the *frmResearch* form, perform the following steps:

1. If Visual Basic is not displaying the *frmResearch* form, double-click your mouse on the *frmResearch* form listing within Project Explorer. Visual Basic will open the *frmResearch* form.
2. Within Visual Basic, select the View menu Toolbox option. Visual Basic will open the Toolbox.
3. Within the Toolbox, double-click your mouse on the RichTextBox icon. Visual Basic will draw a *RichTextBox* control, *RichTextBox1*, within the *frmResearch* form.
4. Within the *frmResearch* form, click your mouse on the *RichTextBox1* control to highlight it. Visual Basic will draw a small frame around the control.
5. Select the View menu Properties Window option. Visual Basic will open the Properties Window listing the *RichTextBox1* properties.
6. Within the Properties Window, change the *RichTextBox1* properties to the values Table 18.9 lists.

Object	Property	Set As
RichTextBox1	*Height*	5055
RichTextBox1	*Left*	240
RichTextBox1	*Top*	1080
RichTextBox1	*Width*	9735
RichTextBox1	*Name*	*rtbURLSite*

Table 18.9 *The newly named* **rtbURLSite** *control's properties.*

ADDING THE DATA CONTROL TO THE FORM

As you have learned, you can use several different methods to maintain database information within your programs. In the *prjResearch* project, for the sake of simplicity, you will use a *Data* control to provide access to the *Dictionary* database (rather than using a grid control and a series of recordset objects). To add the *Data* control to the *frmResearch* form, perform the following steps:

1. If Visual Basic is not displaying the *frmResearch* form, double-click your mouse on the *frmResearch* form listing within Project Explorer. Visual Basic will open the *frmResearch* form.

2. Within the Toolbox, double-click your mouse on the Data icon. Visual Basic will draw a *Data* control, *Data1*, within the *frmResearch* form.

3. Within the *frmResearch* form, click your mouse on the *Data1* control to highlight it. Visual Basic will draw a small frame around the control.

4. Select the View menu Properties Window option. Visual Basic will open the Properties Window listing the *Data1* properties.

5. Within the Properties Window, change the *Data1* properties to the values Table 18.10 lists.

Object	Property	Set As
Data1	*DatabaseName*	*x:\Dictionary.mdb*, where *x* corresponds to the drive and directory letter where you previously saved the *Dictionary.mdb* database
Data1	*RecordSource*	*qrySrtByDate*
Data1	*Left*	0
Data1	*Top*	1500

Table 18.10 *The* **Data1** *control's properties.*

Note: *Be sure to change the* **DatabaseName** *property before you try to change the* **RecordSource** *property.*

ADDING THE DBGRID CONTROL TO THE FORM

As you have learned, the *prjResearch* project will display the history of user-accessed Web sites within a *Data-Bound Grid* control at the form's bottom. The *Data-Bound Grid* control will display the information the *Dictionary* database maintains. To add a *Data-Bound Grid* control to the *frmResearch* form, perform the following steps:

1. If Visual Basic is not displaying the *frmResearch* form, double-click your mouse on the *frmResearch* form listing within Project Explorer. Visual Basic will open the *frmResearch* form.

2. Within Visual Basic, select the View menu Toolbox option. Visual Basic will open the Toolbox.

3. Within the Toolbox, double-click your mouse on the DBGrid icon. Visual Basic will draw a *RichTextBox* control, *RichTextBox1*, within the *frmResearch* form.

4. Within the *frmResearch* form, click your mouse on the *DBGrid1* control to highlight it. Visual Basic will draw a small frame around the control.

5. Select the View menu Properties Window option. Visual Basic will open the Properties Window listing the *DBGrid1* properties.

6. Within the Properties Window, change the *DBGrid1* properties to the values Table 18.11 lists.

Object	Property	Set As
DBGrid1	*DataSource*	*Data1*
DBGrid1	*AllowAddNew*	*False*
DBGrid1	*AllowDelete*	*False*
DBGrid1	*Height*	2175
DBGrid1	*Left*	240
DBGrid1	*Top*	6210
DBGrid1	*Width*	9735
DBGrid1	*Name*	*grdSearchResults*

*Table 18.11 The newly named **grdSearchResults** control's properties.*

7. In addition to the settings within the Properties Window, you must also set custom settings for the *grdSearchResults* control. To enter the custom settings, double-click your mouse on the *Custom* block within the Properties Window. Visual Basic will display the Property Page dialog box for the *Data-Bound Grid* control.

8. Within the Property Page dialog box, set the appropriate properties on the appropriate page to the values Table 18.12 lists.

Property Page	Column	Property	Value
Columns	*Column0*	*Caption*	*URL Address*
Columns	*Column0*	*DataField*	*URL Address*
Columns	*Column1*	*Caption*	*Search Phrase*
Columns	*Column1*	*DataField*	*Search Phrase*
Columns	*Column2*	*Caption*	*SearchDate*
Columns	*Column2*	*DataField*	*Search Date*
Columns	*Column3*	*Caption*	*Matches Found*
Columns	*Column3*	*DataField*	*MatchesFound*
Columns	*Column3*	*NumberFormat*	*Yes/No*
Layout	*Column0*	*Width*	3195.213
Layout	*Column1*	*Width*	3195.213
Layout	*Column2*	*Width*	1500.095
Layout	*Column3*	*Width*	1500.095

*Table 18.12 The custom Property Page values for the **grdSearchResults** control.*

9. When you finish entering the custom properties, click your mouse on OK to close the Property Page dialog box. Visual Basic will return to the Properties Window.

ADDING THE COMBOBOX CONTROLS TO THE FORM

As you have learned, the *prjResearch* project will use an *Internet Transfer* control to open a URL address. However, before you can search for a URL address or search the URL for the text to match, you must enter the text into the program. As you have learned, the program uses a pair of combo boxes to accept the entries. To add the *ComboBox* controls to the *frmResearch* form, perform the following steps:

1. If Visual Basic is not displaying the *frmResearch* form, double-click your mouse on the *frmResearch* form listing within Project Explorer. Visual Basic will open the *frmResearch* form.

2. Within the Toolbox, double-click your mouse on the ComboBox icon. Visual Basic will draw a *ComboBox* control, *Combo1*, within the *frmResearch* form.

3. Repeat Step 2 to add the *Combo2* control to the *frmResearch* form.

4. Within the *frmResearch* form, click your mouse on the *Combo1* control to highlight it. Visual Basic will draw a small frame around the control.

5. Select the View menu Properties Window option. Visual Basic will open the Properties Window listing the *Combo1* properties.

6. Within the Properties Window, change the *Combo1* properties to the values Table 18.13 lists.

7. Repeat Steps 4, 5, and 6 to change the *Combo2* properties to the values Table 18.13 lists.

Object	Property	Set As
Combo1	*Height*	315
Combo1	*Left*	1800
Combo1	*Text*	*http://www.jamsa.com/*
Combo1	*Top*	120
Combo1	*Width*	6015
Combo1	*Name*	*cmbSearchURL*
Combo2	*Height*	315
Combo2	*Left*	1800
Combo2	*Text*	[blank]
Combo2	*Top*	600
Combo2	*Width*	6015
Combo2	*Name*	*cmbSearchText*

*Table 18.13 The newly named **cmbSearchURL** and **cmbSearchText** controls' properties.*

ADDING THE LABEL CONTROLS TO THE FORM

As you have learned, you will select sites to search and text for which to search within a pair of combo boxes at the top of the *frmResearch* form. You will add two *Label* controls, one to the left of each *ComboBox* control, to clarify the combo box's purpose. To add the *Label* controls to the *frmResearch* form, perform the following steps:

1. If Visual Basic is not displaying the *frmResearch* form, double-click your mouse on the *frmResearch* form listing within Project Explorer. Visual Basic will open the *frmResearch* form.

2. Within the Toolbox, double-click your mouse on the Label icon. Visual Basic will draw a *Label* control, *Label1*, within the *frmResearch* form.

3. Repeat Step 2 to add the *Label2* control to the *frmResearch* form.

4. Within the *frmResearch* form, click your mouse on the *Label1* control to highlight it. Visual Basic will draw a small frame around the control.

5. Select the View menu Properties Window option. Visual Basic will open the Properties Window listing the *Label1* properties.

6. Within the Properties Window, change the *Label1* properties to the values Table 18.14 lists.

7. Repeat Steps 4, 5, and 6 to change the *Label2* properties to the values Table 18.14 lists.

Object	Property	Set As
Label1	*Height*	315
Label1	*Left*	270
Label1	*Top*	120
Label1	*Width*	1335
Label1	*Name*	*lblSearchURL*

*Table 18.14 The newly named **lblSearchURL** and **lblSearchText** controls' properties. (continued on following page)*

Object	Property	Set As
Label2	Height	315
Label2	Left	270
Label2	Top	600
Label2	Width	1335
Label2	Name	lblSearchText

*Table 18.14 The newly named **lblSearchURL** and **lblSearchText** controls' properties. (continued from previous page)*

ADDING COMMANDBUTTON CONTROLS TO THE FORM

As you have learned, you will use an *Internet Transfer* control in the *prjReserach* project to open URL sites. In addition, you will save URL sites and search phrases within a database. To start a search for a site, display found sites, or stop a search and exit the program, you will use three *CommandButton* controls. To add three *CommandButton* controls to the *frmResearch* form, perform the following steps:

1. If Visual Basic is not displaying the *frmResearch* form, double-click your mouse on the *frmResearch* form listing within Project Explorer. Visual Basic will open the *frmResearch* form.

2. Within the Toolbox, double-click your mouse on the CommandButton icon. Visual Basic will draw a *CommandButton* control, *Command1*, within the *frmResearch* form.

3. Repeat Step 2 to add the *Command2* control to the *frmResearch* form.

4. Within the *frmResearch* form, click your mouse on a *CommandButton* control to highlight it. Visual Basic will draw a small frame around the control.

5. Select the View menu Properties Window option. Visual Basic will open the Properties Window listing the selected control's properties.

6. Within the Properties Window, change the highlighted control's properties to the values Table 18.15 lists.

7. Repeat Steps 4, 5, and 6 until you have changed the properties for both *CommandButton* controls to the values Table 18.15 lists.

Object	Property	Set As
Command1	Caption	Search
Command1	Height	315
Command1	Left	8280
Command1	Top	120
Command1	Width	1700
Command1	Name	cmdSearch
Command2	Caption	E&xit
Command2	Height	315
Command2	Left	8280
Command2	Top	600
Command2	Width	1700
Command2	Name	cmdStop

*Table 18.15 The newly named **cmdSearch** and **cmdStop** controls' properties.*

ADDING THE FRMSEARCHING FORM TO THE PRJRESEARCH PROJECT

As you have learned, the *prjResearch* project will display a *Searching* dialog box while it searches for the URL site that you specify. The *frmSearching* form displays the word "Searching" while the *Internet Transfer* control does its work. To add the *frmSearching* form to the *prjResearch* project, perform the following steps:

1. Select the Project menu Add Form option. Visual Basic will display the New Form dialog box.

2. Within the New Form dialog box, double-click your mouse on the Form icon. Visual Basic will add the blank *Form1* to the project.

3. Select the View menu Properties Window option. Visual Basic will display the Properties Window with the *Form1* object information.

4. Change the properties for *Form1* to the values Table 18.16 lists.

Object	Property	Value
Form1	*Border Style*	1 - *Fixed Single*
Form1	*Control Box*	False
Form1	*Height*	645
Form1	*MaxButton*	False
Form1	*MinButton*	False
Form1	*Start-Up Position*	2 - *Center Screen*
Form1	*Width*	2775
Form1	*Name*	*frmSearching*

Table 18.16 *The properties for the newly named **frmSearching** form.*

ADDING A LABEL CONTROL TO THE frmSEARCHING FORM

As you learned in the previous section, the *prjResearch* project will use the *frmSearching* form to inform the user that the program is currently searching for a site with which to connect. The *frmSearching* form contains only a single control—a label that fills the form. To add the *Label* control to the *frmSearching* form, perform the following steps:

1. If Visual Basic is not displaying the *frmSearching* form, double-click your mouse on the *frmSearching* form listing within Project Explorer. Visual Basic will open the *frmSearching* form.

2. Within the Toolbox, double-click your mouse on the Label icon. Visual Basic will draw a *Label* control, *Label1*, within the *frmSearching* form.

3. Within the *frmSearching* form, click your mouse on the *Label* control to highlight it. Visual Basic will draw a small frame around the control.

4. Select the View menu Properties Window option. Visual Basic will open the Properties Window listing the selected control's properties.

5. Within the Properties Window, change the *Label* control's properties to the values Table 18.17 lists.

Object	Property	Value
Label1	*Border Style*	0 - *None*
Label1	*Caption*	SEARCHING...
Label1	*Height*	420
Label1	*Left*	90
Label1	*Top*	90
Label1	*Width*	2535
Label1	*Name*	*lblSearching*

Table 18.17 *The values for the newly named **lblSearching** control's properties.*

WRITING THE prjRESEARCH PROJECT CODE

In the *prjResearch* project, you will write code for each control on the *frmResearch* form and you will write procedures to communicate with the controls. First, you will declare variables that the procedures will use. Then, you will write code for the procedures and control events.

DECLARING THE VARIABLES

You will declare most variables in the General–Declarations section in the *frmResearch* Code window. Remember, when you declare variables in the *frmResearch* form's General–Declarations section, all procedures and functions in the form can use them. The following code implements the *prjResearch* project's variables in the *frmResearch* Code window's General–Declarations section:

```
Option Explicit
Dim YesNo As Integer, I As Integer
Dim FoundCounter As Integer
Dim SearchPhrase As String
Dim ResearchWS As Workspace
Dim ResearchDB As Database
Dim ResearchRS As Recordset
Dim CancelSearch As Boolean, Refreshing As Boolean
Dim itcSearchError As Boolean, Connected As Boolean
```

The *YesNo* variable will contain a constant return value (either *vbYes* or *vbNo*) after you click your mouse on a Yes or No button within a *MessageBox*. Then, the *I* variable will store a counting number for *For-Next* loops. The *SearchPhrase* variable will contain any search words or phrases that you want to find in a URL address. Next, the *ResearchWS*, *ResearchDB*, and *ResearchRS* variables will contain a *Workspace, Database,* and *Recordset* object, respectively, which you will use to manage the *Dictionary* database. The remainder of the variables contain flag values that the program uses to perform the correct processing in different situations.

WRITING THE FORM_LOAD EVENT

As you have learned, your programs will invoke the *Form_Load* event for every form before displaying the form. Because the *Form_Load* event is the first action the program performs in a Single-Document Interface program, the *Form_Load* event is an excellent place to put the *prjResearch* project's startup code. The following code implements the *Form_Load* event:

```
Private Sub Form_Load()
   Data1.DatabaseName = App.Path & "\dictionary.mdb"
   cmbSearchURL.AddItem "http://www.jamsa.com/ "
   cmbSearchText.AddItem "Happy"
   OpenDatabase
   OpenRecordset
End Sub
```

The *Form_Load* event makes sure that the *Data1* control links to the proper version of the *Dictionary* database, initializes some screen values, and calls the *OpenDatabase* and *OpenRecordset* procedures to open the *Recordset* object the program will use when it adds new search entries to the database.

WRITING THE OPENDATABASE PROCEDURE

As you know, the *prjResearch* project will let you store URL sites and search phrases in a Microsoft *Access* database. When your project uses the *itcURL* control to open a URL site, Visual Basic will prompt you with a *MessageBox* that will ask you if you want to store the URL address. If you click your mouse on the Yes button, Visual Basic will invoke the *OpenDatabase* procedure. The *OpenDatabase* procedure will open the *Dictionary* database. The following code implements the *OpenDatabase* procedure:

```
Private Sub OpenDatabase()
   Dim DatabaseName As String
   DatabaseName = App.Path & "\Dictionary.mdb"
   Set ResearchWS = Workspaces(0)
   Set ResearchDB = ResearchWS.OpenDatabase(DatabaseName)
End Sub
```

The program code assigns the *Dictionary* database's location to the *DatabaseName* variable, creates a workspace from the default workspace, and opens the database.

Writing the OpenRecordset Procedure

Now that your *ResearchDB* object contains an open *Dictionary* database, you can open a recordset in the *prjResearch* project. The *OpenRecordset* procedure will open the *Research* table and assign its contents to the *Recordset* object, *ResearchRS*. The following code implements the *OpenRecordset* procedure:

```
Private Sub OpenRecordset()
   Set ResearchRS = ResearchDB.OpenRecordset("qrySrtByDate")
   If ResearchRS.RecordCount = 0 Then
      ' Do Nothing
   Else
      ResearchRS.MoveLast
   End If
End Sub
```

The *OpenRecordset* procedure uses the *qrySrtByDate* definition you created earlier in this chapter to open the *ResearchRS* recordset. If the recordset contains records, the program calls the *MoveLast* method to ensure that the recordset is full (so that other procedures process the correct number of records).

Writing the cmdSearch Control's Click Event

As you have learned, you can open URL sites in the *prjResearch* project. When you click your mouse on the *cmdSearch* control, your program will invoke its *Click* event. The *cmdSearch* control's *Click* event will use the *itcURL* control's *OpenURL* method to open a URL site. For more information on the *OpenURL* method, see the earlier section, "More on the Internet Transfer Control's *OpenURL* Method." The following code implements the *cmdSearch* control's *Click* event:

```
Private Sub cmdSearch_Click()
   Dim First As Boolean

   If cmbSearchURL.Text = "" Or cmbSearchText.Text = "" Then
      MsgBox "You must enter a search URL and search text."
      Exit Sub
   End If
   CancelSearch = False
   itcSearchError = False
   cmdStop.Caption = "Stop"
   If cmbSearchURL.ListIndex = -1 Then _
        cmbSearchURL.AddItem cmbSearchURL.Text, 0
   If cmbSearchText.ListIndex = -1 Then _
        cmbSearchText.AddItem cmbSearchText.Text, 0
   rtbURLsite.SelBold = False
   rtbURLsite.SelUnderline = False
   rtbURLsite.Font.Bold = False
   rtbURLsite.Font.Underline = False
   rtbURLsite.Text = ""
   itcSearch.URL = cmbSearchURL.Text
   SearchPhrase = cmbSearchText.Text
   Me.MousePointer = vbHourglass
   frmSearching.Show
   DoEvents
   itcSearch.RequestTimeout = 60
   itcSearch.AccessType = icUseDefault
   On Error Resume Next
   rtbURLsite.Text = itcSearch.OpenURL
   If Err.Number <> 0 And Not itcSearchError Then
      MsgBox "The request timed out or the site name was invalid.", vbOKOnly
```

```
        Me.MousePointer = vbNormal
        cmdStop.Caption = "E&xit"
        frmSearching.Hide
        Exit Sub
    ElseIf itcSearchError Then
        Me.MousePointer = vbNormal
        cmdStop.Caption = "E&xit"
        frmSearching.Hide
        Exit Sub
    End If
    frmSearching.Hide
    Me.MousePointer = vbNormal
    Me.Refresh
    If Not Connected Then
        MsgBox "Unable to connect to the server.", vbOKOnly
        Exit Sub
    End If
    First = True
    Do While SearchForPhrase(First) And Not CancelSearch
        DoEvents
    Loop
    cmdStop.Caption = "E&xit"
End Sub
```

As you can see, the *cmdSearch_Click* event performs the majority of the program's operative processing. In fact, the code within the event opens the connection, ensures that the control successfully established the connection, retrieves the data, and calls the routine to search the data for the search phrase. The event begins with an *If-Then* statement that checks to ensure the URL and Search Phrase are not zero-length strings.

After the *If-Then* statement verifies that both the URL and the Search Phrase are valid, the program code initializes some flag variables, changes the Exit button's caption to *Stop*, and adds the new URL to the combo box list if the URL does not already exist within the list. The code then performs similar processing with the Search Text combo box list. The program code also clears the *rtbURLSite* control of text and turns off the control's bold and underline flag settings. When the program code completes all the cleanup processing, the code assigns the URL to the *Internet Transfer* control's *URL* property.

*Note: You must set an **Internet Transfer** control's **URL** property before you do anything else with the control. In this case, you must set the **itcSearch** control's **URL** property to a valid URL address.*

After the program assigns the URL address, the code will display the *frmSearching* form, set the *Internet Transfer* control's *TimeOut* property to 60 seconds, and open an Internet connection across which it will search for the URL. As you can see, the program code includes an error-handling statement just before the *OpenURL* invocation and processes the result in an *If-Then* statement after the method returns.

If the *OpenURL* method returns an error, but the error is not internal to the control, the program code uses the *If-Then* statement to determine that the URL was invalid or the site timed out. The program code alerts the user to the error and returns to the main screen. If, on the other hand, the error is internal to the control, the program returns to the search screen. If the program sets neither error flag, the program continues its processing. As a final protection against a bad connection, the program checks the *Connected* variable, which the *Internet Transfer* control's *StateChanged* event sets to *True* after the control establishes the connection.

If everything works correctly and the *Internet Transfer* control connects, the returned value is within the *rtbURLSite* control. The *cmdSearch_Click* event's code then calls the *SearchForPhrase* function, which searches the text for a match to the search phrase. The *Do-While* loop repeats until the program finds no more matches or the user clicks the mouse on the *cmdStop* command button. The *SearchForPhrase* function performs the text search and prompts the user to add the site to the database. After it returns to the *cmdSearch_Click* event, the program code resets some flag variables to clean up after itself, and resets the *cmdStop* command button's caption to *Exit*.

Note: *Before you click your mouse on the Search button, you must have an active Internet connection. If you do not have an active Internet connection, your computer screen will display the Searching dialog box for 60 seconds. After that time elapses, it will display a message stating that your request has "timed out."*

Writing the frmSearching Form's Form_Load Event

As you learned in the previous section, the *cmdSearch_Click* event displays the *frmSearching* form while the *Internet Transfer* control tries to connect to the URL you specify. The *frmSearching* form performs no processing; it is simply a way to inform the user that the *Internet Transfer* control is currently trying to connect to the specified URL. However, you must include two lines of code within the *frmSearching* form's *Form_Load* event to ensure that the program displays the form while the program is searching. Otherwise, the *Internet Transfer* control will hold the program's processing and will only display the *frmSearching* form after the *Internet Transfer* control completes its processing—just in time for the program code to hide the form. The following code implements the *Form_Load* event:

```
Private Sub Form_Load()
   Me.Show
   DoEvents
End Sub
```

Writing the itcSearch_StateChanged Event

As you have learned, the *Internet Transfer* control calls the *StateChanged* event periodically, whenever a change in the control's connection status occurs. In the *prjResearch* project, you will use the connection states to set flags and respond to internal errors. The following code implements the *itcSearch_StateChanged* event:

```
Private Sub itcSearch_StateChanged(ByVal State As Integer)
   Dim strMess As String ' Message variable.

   DoEvents
   Select Case State
     Case icHostResolvingHost
       Connected = False

     Case icConnected
       Connected = True

     Case icError
       strMess = "ErrorCode: " & itcSearch.ResponseCode & " : " & _
         itcSearch.ResponseInfo
       MsgBox strMess, vbOKOnly
       itcSearchError = True
   End Select
End Sub
```

In a normal connection, the code will first set the variable *Connected* to *False*, then set it to *True* on a later pass, which will result in the *cmdSearch_Click* event continuing to process the data the control returns. On the other hand, if there is an error internal to the control, the *StateChanged* event will display the error message and exit.

Writing the SearchForPhrase Function

As you have learned, the *cmdSearch* control's *Click* event will store a search word or phrase in the *SearchPhrase* variable. Then the *Click* event will call the *SearchForPhrase* function. The *SearchForPhrase* function will try to find the text the *SearchPhrase* variable contains within the *rtbURLSite* RichTextBox control. If successful, the function will return a *True* value to the calling procedure. If unsuccessful, the function will return a *False* value to the calling procedure. The following code implements the *SearchForPhrase* function:

```
Private Function SearchForPhrase(FirstTime As Boolean) As Boolean
   Static FoundPos As Integer
   Dim FoundLine As Integer
```

```
     Dim YesNo As Integer

     If FirstTime Then FoundPos = 0
     FoundPos = rtbURLsite.Find(SearchPhrase, FoundPos)
     If FoundPos <> -1 Then
       FoundCounter = FoundCounter + 1
       FoundLine = rtbURLsite.GetLineFromChar(FoundPos) + 1
       rtbURLsite.SetFocus
       rtbURLsite.SelBold = True
       rtbURLsite.SelUnderline = True
       FoundPos = FoundPos + Len(SearchPhrase)
       If FirstTime Then
         YesNo = MsgBox("Text found. Store Site Address in Database ?", vbYesNo)
         If YesNo = vbYes Then
           AddURL True
           Data1.Refresh
         End If
       End If
       SearchForPhrase = True
     Else
       If FirstTime Then
         YesNo = MsgBox("Search Phrase Not Found. Store Site Address in _
             Database?", vbYesNo)
         If YesNo = vbYes Then
           AddURL False
           Data1.Refresh
         End If
       End If
       SearchForPhrase = False
     End If
     FirstTime = False
   End Function
```

Despite the function's length, the actions that the *SearchForPhrase* function performs are relatively simple. The program code uses the *RichTextBox* control's *Find* method to locate the text. If the program code finds the text, the code will display a message box that asks the user whether the user wants to save the address. If the user wants to save the address, the function calls the *AddURL* procedure with a *True* parameter, sets the *SearchForPhrase* function's return value to *True*, and exits. If the program code does not find the text on the first try, it still asks whether the user wants to save the address. If the user wants to save the address, the function instead calls the *AddURL* procedure with a *False* parameter.

The *cmdSearch_Click* event calls the *SearchForPhrase* function within a *Do-While* loop, and the function highlights every match within the document the program received from the user-specified address. However, the function only queries the user whether or not to save the address into the database on the function's first invocation for each location.

WRITING THE ADDURL PROCEDURE

As you learned in the previous section, each time the program searches a new address, whether the program finds at least one instance of the *SearchPhrase* value in the site text, or if the *SearchForPhrase* function finds no instances of the *SearchPhrase* value, the program will display a *MessageBox* that asks if the user wants to save the URL address in the database. When you click your mouse on the Yes button within the *MessageBox*, the *SearchForPhrase* function will call the *AddURL* procedure. The *AddURL* procedure will add the URL address, search phrase, search date, and search success values to the *Dictionary* database. The following code implements the *AddURL* procedure:

```
     Private Sub AddURL(Match As Boolean)
       ResearchRS.AddNew
```

```
        ResearchRS("URL address") = Left(itcSearch.URL, 50)
        ResearchRS("Search Phrase") = Left(SearchPhrase, 50)
        ResearchRS("SearchDate") = Format(Date, "Medium Date")
        ResearchRS("MatchesFound") = Match
    ResearchRS.Update
    ResearchRS.Requery
    Refreshing = True
    Data1.Refresh
    Refreshing = False
End Sub
```

The *AddURL* procedure adds the information about the search to the database, requeries the recordset, and refreshes the *Data1* control so that the new entry will display in the first line of the *grdSearchResults* control.

WRITING THE CMDSTOP_CLICK EVENT

As you have learned, the *cmdStop* command button serves double duty. If the program is currently performing a search, the *cmdStop* button sets the *CancelSearch* flag so that the program will cease the search the next time the program executes the *Do* loop within the *cmdSearch_Click* event. On the other hand, if the program is not currently performing a search, the *cmdStop* command button tells the program to exit. The following code implements the *cmdStop_Click* event:

```
Private Sub cmdStop_click()
    If cmdStop.Caption = "Stop" Then
        CancelSearch = True
    Else
        Unload Me
        End
    End If
End Sub
```

WRITING THE GRDSEARCHRESULTS_ROWCOLCHANGE EVENT

As you have learned, you can click your mouse within the *Data-Bound Grid* control at the bottom of the form to recover the address and search text from a previous search. To perform such processing, you must include code in the event that processes the user's mouse click. In fact, the only event that the program code must address is the user's changing of the currently selected row (because if the user clicks within the same row, the search URL and phrase will not change). Therefore, the best place to capture the click is within the *RowColChange* event. The following code implements the *grdSearchResults_RowColChange* event:

```
Private Sub grdSearchResults_RowColChange(LastRow As Variant, _
    ByVal LastCol As Integer)
    If Refreshing Then Exit Sub
    If Data1.Recordset.RecordCount > 7 Then _
        grdSearchResults.Columns(1).Width = 3000
    grdSearchResults.Col = 1
    cmbSearchText.Text = grdSearchResults.Text
    grdSearchResults.Col = 0
    cmbSearchURL.Text = grdSearchResults.Text
End Sub
```

The program code first checks to ensure that the program is not in the process of updating the grid contents; if it is, the event immediately exits. If not, the program checks the number of records in the database—because after seven records, the *Data-Bound Grid* control automatically adds a scroll bar to the grid's right side. The vertical scroll bar will have the cascading effect of adding a horizontal scroll bar at the control's bottom unless the code makes one of the grid columns narrower. The code then finishes by assigning the contents of the two search items in the grid to the appropriate combo boxes.

ENHANCEMENTS YOU CAN MAKE TO THE prjRESEARCH PROJECT

Now that you better understand the *Internet Transfer* control, FTP and HTTP sites, and URL addresses, you can make some enhancements to the *prjResearch* project. First, you can open an FTP or HTTP site using the *Internet Transfer* control's *Execute* method. Remember, the *Execute* method will let you download information from sites in chunks—meaning you can download entire files (such as Microsoft *Word*® documents, bitmaps, or any other non-text file) from Internet locations, and then search the resulting files.

Next, as you use the *prjResearch* project, the *Dictionary* database will grow in size. As you know, each record in the *Dictionary* database's *Research* table will contain a URL address and search phrase, together with other information. You can either change the *qrySrtByDate* query definition to include a *WHERE* statement or add additional query definitions that use *WHERE* statements. With the *WHERE* statement you can organize Web sites, search phrases in related groups, and display the phrases and sites in one or more *Data-Bound Grid* controls. You can also change the display within the *grdSearchResults* control to let the user have more control over the organization of Web sites within the control.

In addition, you can write code that opens an FTP site and searches its entire directory, pulling down document after document and checking them for your search content. Alternatively, you can open a Web site and use the hyperlinks the site contains to travel to other Web sites it references and search those sites. While such a search would likely take an impossibly long time if you tried to perform it manually, the resulting data might well be worth the wait; however, if you write program code to perform the acquisition and searching on your behalf, it would be much quicker and infinitely more useful.

PUTTING IT ALL TOGETHER

In the *prjResearch* project, you have learned about the *Internet Transfer* control and have revisited the DAO Object Library, Microsoft *Access* database, the *Data-Bound Grid* control, and the *RichTextBox* control. In addition, you have used *Label*, *TextBox*, *ComboBox*, and *CommandButton* controls to manage and display Internet information. As you have learned, you can use the *Internet Transfer* control to open an FTP site or HTTP site at a particular URL address. You can display the open site's contents within a *RichTextBox* control. Then, you can search the *RichTextBox* control's text for any words or phrases that you want.

Also, using a Microsoft *Access* database, you can store a URL address and a search phrase. Using a *Workspace*, *Database,* and *Recordset* object, you can access a Microsoft *Access* database from within Visual Basic. In Chapter 19, "Creating a Web Crawler," you will further examine the *Internet Transfer* control and create an automated program that uses the information Web documents contain to navigate itself from site to site (a program often called a Web *robot* or Web *crawler*.) Before you continue with Chapter 19, however, make sure you understand the following key concepts:

✓ Using the *Internet Transfer* control, you can open an FTP or HTTP site at a particular URL address.

✓ You can use a *RichTextBox* control to display the textual content of Web sites and search for specific words within the Web page.

✓ You can use the *Internet Transfer* control to regulate and monitor Internet connections because the *Internet Transfer* control will return response codes to your project.

✓ You can use the *Internet Transfer* control from within your Visual Basic programs to download or upload files to and from your computer across the Internet.

Chapter 19

Creating a Web Crawler

With the explosive growth of the Internet, one of the largest markets for new Visual Basic programs is the World Wide Web. With respect to programming for the Web, some of the most interesting applications and programs to emerge have been Web *robots* (sometimes called *spiders*), *agents*, and *wanderers*. In short, these programs automatically search the hypertext (HTML) documents that make up the Web, seemingly moving from one Web site to another. As you will learn in this chapter, however, these applications do not really travel the Web. Instead, the applications run on one computer and simply "visit" the remote systems by requesting HTML documents—that is, the applications retrieve the documents from the remote systems and perform processing on the documents locally.

573

Programmers create robot programs to build *Web indexes* (lists of the information specific sites contain), to create search engines, or to validate the links in an HTML document. In this chapter's project, *prjWanderer*, you will create a recursive wanderer that "wanders" from one site to another, collecting a list of site addresses from sites the wanderer visits. You will also learn how to protect your system from unethical or badly behaved robots and what steps your programs should perform to qualify as ethical or well-behaved robots. By the time you finish this chapter, you will understand the following key concepts:

- A *robot* is a client program that retrieves HTML documents that the program will then process from sites across the Web.

- An *agent* is a program that performs a task on behalf of another program or user.

- The names *wanderer*, *crawler*, and *spider* are simply alternate names for a robot program.

- Within your Visual Basic programs, you can use the *Microsoft Internet Transfer* control to establish Internet connections, retrieve files from the Internet, and save the files the programs retrieve on a local computer.

- Within an HTML file, tags indicate instructions to the browser about text formatting, Web page appearance, hyperlink definitions, and other Web constructions.

- A robot program must retrieve and pause HTML files, looking for tags.

- When a robot program looks for other addresses from which it can retrieve documents, it must search for the <A HREF> tag.

- Within Visual Basic, you can use the Internet Transfer Control to create a Web robot.

- To create a well-behaved robot that does not intrude on Web sites that do not want robots to visit, your robots should read the *robots.txt* server file that resides on a Web server's hard disk.

USING THE prjWANDERER PROJECT

Before you design the *prjWanderer* project, you may find it helpful to run the program. The companion CD-ROM that accompanies this book contains the *prjWanderer.exe* program within the *Chapter19* directory. As with every other program on the CD-ROM, you should run the Jamsa Press *setup.exe* program to install the *prjWanderer.exe* program to your computer's hard drive before you run it. After you install the *prjWanderer.exe* program to your computer's hard drive, you can run it from the Start menu. To run the program, select the Windows Start menu Run option. Windows will display the Run dialog box. Within the Run dialog box, enter *x:\vbpl\Chapter19\prjWanderer.exe*, where *x* corresponds to the drive letter of the hard drive on which you installed the *prjWanderer.exe* program, and click your mouse on OK. Windows will display the *prjWanderer.exe* program, as shown in Figure 19.1.

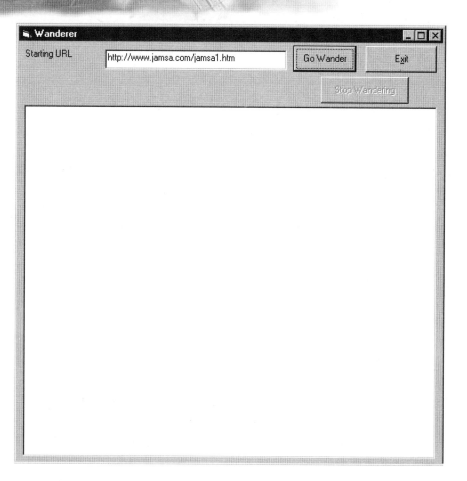

Figure 19.1 *The **prjWanderer.exe** program's start-up screen.*

RUNNING PRJWANDERER FROM THE CD-ROM

As you have learned, you must first install many of the programs that you will use in this book to your computer's hard drive before you use the programs. Because the *prjWanderer.exe* program tries to create a temporary text file within its execution directory, you must install the *prjWanderer.exe* program to a drive before you use it. If you try to run the *prjWanderer.exe* program from the CD-ROM, the program will not perform searches because it cannot create the temporary text file it requires.

To learn more about the Jamsa Press *setup.exe* program, see the "What's on the *Visual Basic Programmer's Library* Companion CD-ROM" section at the back of this book.

Before you use the *prjWanderer.exe* program, take a moment to familiarize yourself with the controls on the program's display. As you have learned, the *prjWanderer.exe* program will let you "wander" the Web, reading Uniform Resource Locators (URLs) from within HyperText Markup Language (HTML) documents and using those URLs to get other HTML documents on the Web. When the program starts, you will see a large window with a central text area, a single field at the top, and three command buttons on the top right hand side.

When you first run the *prjWanderer.exe* program, the *Starting URL* field contains the address *http://www.jamsa.com/ jamsa1.htm*. If you click your mouse on the Go Wander button, the program will begin its search at the *http:// www.jamsa.com/jamsa1.htm* Web document. Figure 19.2 shows the *prjWanderer.exe* program after you click your mouse on the Go Wander button.

Figure 19.2 *The* **prjWanderer.exe** *program after you click your mouse on the Go Wander button.*

As you can see, the program will display a dialog box that lets you know it is searching for the site. In fact, as you wander, the program will always display the dialog box when it tries to connect to a Web address. The dialog box informs you that the program is searching and displays the address for which the program is searching. After a few moments (depending on the speed of your Internet connection), the program will connect to the *jamsa1.htm* page, parse the page's contents, and add the addresses within the page to its reference list. After the program finishes parsing the page, it will go to the first address it finds within the *jamsa1.htm* document and repeat the process. Eventually, the program will fill the text box with addresses and will keep adding additional text to the file. Figure 19.3 shows the *prjWanderer.exe* program during the program's parsing of an HTML file.

575

Figure 19.3 *The* **prjWanderer.exe** *program during its parsing loop.*

Because the *prjWanderer.exe* program travels from Web site to Web site, it is possible that the program will continue its processing indefinitely or at least until it can no longer store all the addresses the program finds within the text box. However, to stop the program's processing, you can click your mouse on the Stop Wandering button. Figure 19.4 shows the *prjWanderer.exe* program after it has parsed several sites and you have clicked your mouse on the Stop Wandering button.

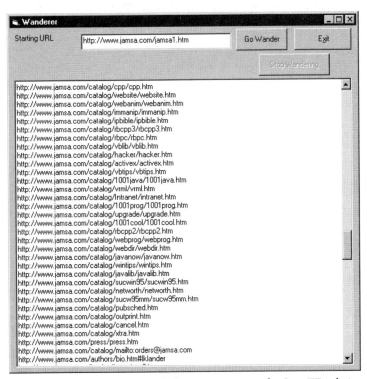

Figure 19.4 *The* **prjWanderer.exe** *program after you click your mouse on the Stop Wandering button.*

After you stop the *prjWanderer.exe* program from wandering, you can enter a new start address into the *Starting URL* field and start wandering from the new location. If you decide that you want to save the results of a given wander, you must copy the *taglist.txt* to another location because the program writes over the file each time you start to wander. The *taglist.txt* file is a file that contains the list of hyperlinks the *prjWanderer.exe* program will display within its output. You can find the *taglist.txt* file in the same directory as the *prjWanderer.exe* program.

UNDERSTANDING ROBOTS

A *robot* is a Web-based program that automatically "visits" Web sites by way of the site's HTML documents. When many programmers first think about robots, they imagine a program that makes its way across the World Wide Web by moving from one site to another. However, a robot program does not really travel anywhere, but instead stays at the computer from which the program began to search. To visit a site, the robot requests the site's HTML document (much like a browser would request a document). The site's server, in turn, returns the document to the robot, which then starts processing the document's contents.

The processing the robot performs is entirely up to the programmer who creates the robot program. For example, a robot might become a search engine, searching the document for a specific word or phrase, or the robot might simply make a list of other sites it wants to visit.

THE W3C MINI ROBOT

One of the best ways to learn about robot applications is to read about the *W3C Mini Robot*, a program that programmers at the Massachusetts Institute of Technology (MIT) created for the World Wide Web consortium (W3C), using the C programming language. By examining the robot's source code, you will learn a great deal about how to create your own robot. For more information on the W3C Mini Robot, visit the World Wide Web consortium's Web site at *http://www.w3.org/Robot/*, as shown in Figure 19.5.

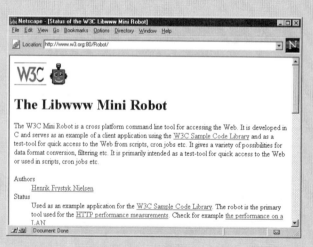

Figure 19.5 *Information on the MIT W3C Mini Robot at* **http://www.w3.org/Robot/**.

CREATING THE BLANK FORMS

Now that you have a better idea how to use the *prjWanderer* project, you can begin to design it. You will design a blank form that will contain all the controls the "Using the *prjWanderer* Project" section introduced, and two additional forms that the program will use as dialog boxes. After you design and implement the forms, you will add a Visual Basic module to the project, in which you will store additional program code. To begin the *prjWanderer* project and design three blank forms, perform the following steps:

1. Within Visual Basic, select the File menu New Project option. Visual Basic will open the New Project dialog box.

2. Within the New Project dialog box, double-click your mouse on the Standard EXE icon. Visual Basic will open *Form1* within an object window.

3. Within Visual Basic, select the Project menu Add Form option. Visual Basic will open the Add Form dialog box.

4. Within the Add Form dialog box, double-click your mouse on the Form option. Visual Basic will open a new object window containing *Form2*.

5. Repeat Step 4 one time. Visual Basic will open a third object window containing *Form3*.

6. Select the View menu Properties Window option. Visual Basic will open the Properties Window with the *Form3* properties listed.

7. Within the Properties Window, change the *Form3* properties to the values Table 19.1 lists.

8. Repeat Steps 6 and 7 twice to change the *Form1* and *Form2* properties to the values Table 19.1 lists.

Object	Property	Set As
Form1	Caption	Wanderer
Form1	Height	8250
Form1	Left	0
Form1	StartUpPosition	2 - Center Screen
Form1	Top	0
Form1	Width	8355
Form1	Name	frmWanderer
Form2	BorderStyle	3 - Fixed Dialog
Form2	Caption	Searching
Form2	Height	1665
Form2	Left	0
Form2	StartUpPosition	1 - Center Owner
Form2	Top	0
Form2	Width	3330
Form2	Name	frmSearching
Form3	BorderStyle	3-Fixed Dialog
Form3	Caption	Parsing
Form3	Height	1140
Form3	Left	0
Form3	Top	0
Form3	Width	4770
Form3	StartUpPosition	1 - Center Owner
Form3	Name	frmParsing

Table 19.1 The newly named frmWanderer, frmSearching, and frmParsing forms' properties.

ADDING A MODULE TO THE PROJECT

After you design the *prjWanderer* project's blank forms, you will create a module to store program code. Within the *prjWanderer* project, the program code that you will place within the module will perform the majority of the project's processing. To add a module to the *prjWanderer* project, perform the following steps:

1. Within Visual Basic, select the Project menu Add Module option. Visual Basic will open the Add Module dialog box.

2. Within the Add Module dialog box, select the Module option. Next, click your mouse on the Open button. Visual Basic will open a new Code window, *Module1*.

3. Select the View menu Properties Window option. Visual Basic will open the Properties Window listing the *Module1* properties.

4. Within the Properties Window, change *Module1's* name to *mdlWanderer*.

5. Select the File menu Save Project As option. Visual Basic will open the Save File As dialog box and fill the *File name* field with *mdlWanderer*.

6. Within the Save File As dialog box, click your mouse on the Save button. Visual Basic will save the *mdlWanderer* module and fill the *File name* field with *frmParsing*.

7. Within the Save File As dialog box, click your mouse on the Save button. Visual Basic will save the *frmParsing* form and fill the *File name* field with *frmSearching*.

8. Within the Save File As dialog box, click your mouse on the Save button. Visual Basic will save the *frmSearching* form and fill the *File name* field with *frmWanderer*.

9. Within the Save File As dialog box, click your mouse on the Save button. Visual Basic will save the *frmWanderer* form and fill the *File name* field with *Project1*.

10. Within the *File name* field, replace the *Project1* project name with the new *prjWanderer* project name. Next, click your mouse on the Save button. Visual Basic will save the *prjWanderer* project and close the Save Project As dialog box.

ADDING AN INTERNET TRANSFER CONTROL TO THE PROJECT

In the *prjWanderer* project, you will use an *Internet Transfer* control to connect to HTML documents, which you will then download and parse within the program. Before you can use an *Internet Transfer* control in your project, you must add it to the project as a component. After you add the *Internet Transfer* control to the *prjWanderer* project, Visual Basic will draw the control's icon in the Toolbox. As you know, the Toolbox displays Visual Basic control icons. If you double-click your mouse on any icon in the Toolbox, Visual Basic will draw the corresponding control within the active form.

To add an *Internet Transfer* control to the *prjWanderer* project, perform the following steps:

1. Within Visual Basic, select the Project menu Components option. Visual Basic will open the Components dialog box.

2. Within the Components dialog box, select the *Microsoft Internet Transfer Control 5.0* listing. Next, click your mouse on the box to the left of the listing. Visual Basic will display a check mark in the box.

3. While the Components dialog box is open, you can also add the *Microsoft Rich Text Box* control to the project. Select the *Microsoft Rich Textbox Control 5.0* listing. Next, click your mouse on the box to the left of the listing. Visual Basic will display a check mark in the box, just as it did with the *Internet Transfer* control.

4. Within the Components dialog box, click your mouse on the OK button. Visual Basic will close the Components dialog box and add the controls to the *prjWanderer* project.

ADDING THE INTERNET TRANSFER CONTROL TO THE FRMWANDERER FORM

As you have learned, the *prjWanderer* project will use an *Internet Transfer* control to open HTML documents at URL addresses and will download the information. After the program parses the information and removes other URLs from the document, it will add the new URLs to the listing within a *RichTextBox* control. To use the *Internet Transfer* control in the *prjWanderer* project, you will add it to the *frmWanderer* form. To add an *Internet Transfer* control to the *frmWanderer* form, perform the following steps:

1. If Visual Basic is not displaying the *frmWanderer* form, double-click your mouse on the *frmWanderer* form listing within Project Explorer. Visual Basic will open the *frmWanderer* form within an object window.

2. Within Visual Basic, select the View menu Toolbox option. Visual Basic will open the Toolbox.

3. Within the Toolbox, select the new *Internet Transfer* control icon, Inet, as shown in Figure 19.6.

Figure 19.6 *The Toolbox showing the* **Internet Transfer** *control's Inet icon.*

4. Within the Toolbox, double-click your mouse on the Inet icon. Visual Basic will draw an *Internet Transfer* control, *Inet1*, within the *frmWanderer* form.

5. Within the *frmWanderer* form, click your mouse on the *Inet1* control to highlight it. Visual Basic will draw a small frame around the control.

6. Select the View menu Properties Window option. Visual Basic will open the Properties Window listing the *Inet1* properties.

7. Within the Properties Window, change the *Inet1* properties to the values Table 19.2 lists.

Object	Property	Set As
Inet1	*Left*	0
Inet1	*Top*	810
Inet1	*Name*	*itcWander*

Table 19.2 *The newly named* **itcWander** *control's properties.*

ADDING COMMANDBUTTON, LABEL, AND TEXTBOX CONTROLS TO THE FRMWANDERER FORM

In the "Using the *prjWanderer* Project" section of this chapter, you learned that the *frmWanderer* form also contains three command buttons, a label, and a text box. To add these five controls to the *frmWanderer* form, perform the following steps:

1. If Visual Basic is not displaying the *frmWanderer* form within an object window, double-click your mouse on the *frmWanderer* form listing within Project Explorer. Visual Basic will open the *frmWanderer* form.

2. Within Visual Basic, select the View menu Toolbox option. Visual Basic will open the Toolbox.

3. Within the Toolbox, double-click your mouse on the CommandButton icon. Visual Basic will draw a *CommandButton* control, *Command1*, within the *frmWanderer* form.

4. Repeat Step 3 two more times. Visual Basic will draw the *Command2* and *Command3* buttons on the *frmWanderer* form.

5. Within the Toolbox, double-click your mouse on the Label icon. Visual Basic will draw a *Label* control, *Label1*, within the *frmWanderer* form.

6. Within the Toolbox, double-click your mouse on the TextBox icon. Visual Basic will draw a *TextBox* control, *Text1*, within the *frmWanderer* form.

7. Within the *frmWanderer* form, click your mouse on any of the controls you have just added to highlight the control. Visual Basic will draw a small frame around the control.

8. Select the View menu Properties Window option. Visual Basic will open the Properties Window listing the highlighted control's properties.

9. Within the Properties Window, change the highlighted control's properties to the values Table 19.3 lists.

10. Repeat Steps 7, 8, and 9 to change the properties for all the controls to the values Table 19.3 lists.

Object	Property	Set As
Label1	*Caption*	*Starting URL*
Label1	*Height*	375
Label1	*Left*	120
Label1	*Top*	120
Label1	*Width*	1335
Label1	*Name*	*lblStart*
Text1	*Height*	375
Text1	*Left*	1680
Text1	*Text*	[blank]
Text1	*Top*	135
Text1	*Width*	3555
Text1	*Name*	*txtSite*
Command1	*Caption*	*E&xit*
Command1	*Height*	495
Command1	*Left*	6840
Command1	*Top*	45
Command1	*Width*	1365
Command1	*Name*	*cmdExit*
Command2	*Caption*	*Go Wander*
Command2	*Height*	495
Command2	*Left*	5355
Command2	*Top*	45
Command2	*Width*	1365
Command2	*Name*	*cmdGoWander*
Command3	*Caption*	*Stop Wandering*
Command3	*Height*	495
Command3	*Left*	5895
Command3	*Top*	630
Command3	*Width*	1680
Command3	*Name*	*cmdStopWandering*

Table 19.3 *The **frmWanderer** form's component controls' properties.*

ADDING THE RICHTEXTBOX CONTROL TO THE FRMWANDERER FORM

The *prjWanderer* project will display the links (the URLs for other hypertext documents the program reads during its search) it extracts from within HTML documents within a *RichTextBox* control on the *frmWanderer* form. To add a *RichTextBox* control to the *frmWanderer* form, perform the following steps:

1. If Visual Basic is not displaying the *frmWanderer* form, double-click your mouse on the *frmWanderer* form listing within Project Explorer. Visual Basic will open the *frmWanderer* form.

2. Within Visual Basic, select the View menu Toolbox option. Visual Basic will open the Toolbox.

3. Within the Toolbox, double-click your mouse on the RichTextBox icon. Visual Basic will draw a *RichTextBox* control, *RichTextBox1*, within the *frmWanderer* form.

4. Within the *frmWanderer* form, click your mouse on the *RichTextBox1* control to highlight it. Visual Basic will draw a small frame around the control.

5. Select the View menu Properties Window option. Visual Basic will open the Properties Window listing the *RichTextBox1* properties.

6. Within the Properties Window, change the *RichTextBox1* properties to the values Table 19.4 lists.

Object	Property	Set As
RichTextBox1	*Height*	6615
RichTextBox1	*Left*	90
RichTextBox1	*Top*	1200
RichTextBox1	*Width*	8055
RichTextBox1	*Name*	*rtbLinkNames*

581

Table 19.4 *The newly named **rtbLinkNames** control's properties.*

After you finish setting the properties for the *rtbLinkNames* control, the *frmWanderer* form will look similar to Figure 19.7.

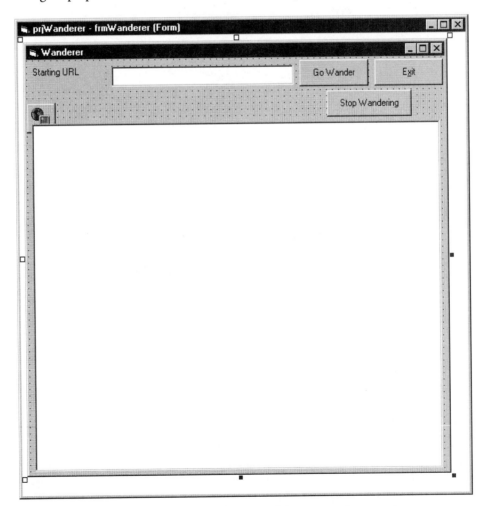

Figure 19.7 *The **frmWanderer** form after you finish adding and formatting the controls.*

ADDING THE LABEL CONTROL TO THE FRMPARSING FORM

When the *prjWanderer* project parses a large HTML file, the project may take some time to complete its processing. To provide the user with better information about the program's current activities, the *prjWanderer* project will display the *frmParsing* form while it parses data within an HTML file. The *frmParsing* form contains a single label control, which displays text to inform the user that the program is parsing the file. To add a *Label* control to the *frmParsing* form, perform the following steps:

1. If Visual Basic is not displaying the *frmParsing* form within an object window, double-click your mouse on the *frmParsing* form listing within Project Explorer. Visual Basic will open the *frmParsing* form.

2. Select the View menu Toolbox option. Visual Basic will display the Toolbox.

3. Within the Toolbox, double-click your mouse on the Label icon. Visual Basic will draw a *Label* control, *Label1*, within the *frmParsing* form.

4. Within the *frmParsing* form, click your mouse on the *Label1* control to highlight the control. Visual Basic will draw a small frame around the control.

5. Select the View menu Properties Window option. Visual Basic will open the Properties Window listing the *Label1* properties.

6. Within the Properties Window, change the *Label1* properties to the values Table 19.5 lists.

Object	Property	Set As
Label1	*Caption*	*Parsing Site Contents*
Label1	*Font*	*MS Sans Serif, Bold, 10 Point*
Label1	*Height*	510
Label1	*Left*	135
Label1	*Top*	135
Label1	*Width*	4335
Label1	*Name*	*lblParsing*

*Table 19.5 The newly named **lblParsing** control's properties.*

After you finish changing the properties for the *lblParsing* control, the *frmParsing* form will look similar to Figure 19.8.

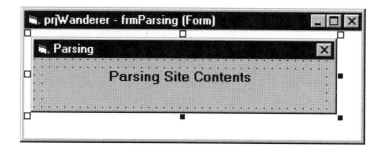

*Figure 19.8 The **frmParsing** form after you complete its design.*

ADDING THE LABEL CONTROLS TO THE FRMSEARCHING FORM

As you learned in Chapter 18, "Creating an Internet Research Program," your computer may take a significant amount of time to connect to a URL, depending on Internet traffic, the speed of your Internet connection, and other factors. To provide the user with better information about the program's current activities, the program will display the *frmSearching* form while it tries to connect to the next URL in the search list. The *frmSearching* form contains two *Label* controls: one that displays text that informs the user the program is searching for an address, and another that displays the name of the address for which the program is searching. To add the *Label* controls to the *frmSearching* form, perform the following steps:

1. If Visual Basic is not displaying the *frmSearching* form within an object window, double-click your mouse on the *frmSearching* form listing within Project Explorer. Visual Basic will open the *frmSearching* form.

2. Select the View menu Toolbox option. Visual Basic will display the Toolbox.

3. Within the Toolbox, double-click your mouse on the Label icon. Visual Basic will draw a *Label* control, *Label1*, within the *frmSearching* form.

4. Repeat Step 3 onetime. Visual Basic will draw a second *Label* control, *Label2*, within the *frmSearching* form.

5. Within the *frmSearching* form, click your mouse on the *Label1* control to highlight the control. Visual Basic will draw a small frame around the control.

6. Select the View menu Properties Window option. Visual Basic will open the Properties Window listing the *Label1* properties.

7. Within the Properties Window, change the *Label1* properties to the values Table 19.6 lists.

8. Repeat Steps 5, 6, and 7 to change the *Label2* properties to the values Table 19.6 lists.

Object	Property	Set As
Label1	*Caption*	*Searching for Site*
Label1	*Font*	*MS Sans Serif, Bold, 10 Point*
Label1	*Height*	330
Label1	*Left*	180
Label1	*Top*	180
Label1	*Width*	2805
Label1	*Name*	*lblCaption*
Label2	*Caption*	[blank]
Label2	*Height*	420
Label2	*Left*	135
Label2	*Top*	630
Label2	*Width*	2895
Label2	*Name*	*lblSite*

*Table 19.6 The newly named **lblCaption** and **lblSite** controls' properties.*

After you finish changing the properties for the *lblCaption* and *lblSite* controls, the *frmSearching* form will look similar to Figure 19.9.

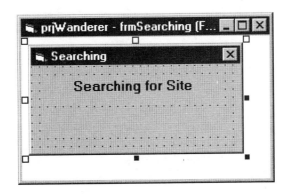

*Figure 19.9 The **frmSearching** form after you complete its design.*

BREAKING APART THE PRJWANDERER PROJECT

When you run the *prjWanderer* program, you must specify the address of the page from which you want to start wandering. The *prjWanderer* program, in turn, will parse the file, looking for the links specified in anchor *<A>* tags, which it prints to the *rtbLinkNames* control and appends to the *taglist.txt* file. After the *prjWanderer* program examines the current file, the program reads the next link in the *taglist.txt* file, fetches the corresponding document from the Internet, and then parses the document.

Although the *prjWanderer* program checks the list of Web sites to ensure the program is not duplicating a site name, it is possible that the *prjWanderer* program may (unintentionally) return to a site the program has previously visited. Should the *prjWanderer* program start to revisit sites, it is possible that the program will run forever. If you feel that the *prjWanderer* program is stuck in such an infinite loop, you can click your mouse on the Stop Wandering button to end the program.

584 WRITING THE PRJWANDERER PROJECT'S PROGRAM CODE

As you learned earlier in this chapter, the *prjWanderer* project consists of three forms and a code module. Neither the *frmParsing* nor the *frmSearching* form performs any processing. Therefore, only the *mdlWanderer* module and the *frmWanderer* form will contain any program code. To write the program code for the project, you will first write the program code for the *mdlWanderer* module, which performs the majority of the program's processing. Next, you will write the program code for the *frmWanderer* form.

DECLARING THE VARIABLES WITHIN THE MDLWANDERER MODULE

The *mdlWanderer* module declares two constants and several public variables that the program code will use to maintain information about the current address, the address's contents, and the *itcWander* control's status. The following code implements the variable declarations within the *mdlWanderer* module's General–Declarations section:

```
Option Explicit
Option Compare Text

Const TAG_LENGTH% = 1000
Const OUT_FILE = "\taglist.txt"
Public Current_Pos As Long
Public Tag As String
Public Real_File_Name As String
Public File_Name As String
Public Site As String
Public Location As String
Public Site_Length As Integer
Public NewLine As String
Public SiteContents As String
Public inetSearchError As Boolean, StopSearching As Boolean
```

As you have learned in previous chapters, the *Option Explicit* statement forces you to define every variable within your program. The *Option Compare Text* statement tells Visual Basic that your program should perform string comparisons based on the actual letters in the strings, not the ASCII values of the letters. In other words, the *Option Compare Text* statement forces your program to perform case-insensitive comparisons.

The *TAG_LENGTH* constant specifies the maximum number of characters between two HTML tags, which the parsing routine will use to protect against errors in the original HTML code. The *OUT_FILE* constant specifies the file to which the program will write the links it extracts from HTML pages. The *Current_Pos* variable corresponds to the program's current search point within the current document, and the *Tag* variable contains tags the program reads from the HTML document. The program uses the *Real_File_Name, File_Name, Site,* and *Location* values to maintain information about the page the program is reading. The *Site_Length* variable contains the length of the site's address, the *NewLine* variable contains the new line constant value *(Chr(10) & Chr(13))*, and the *SiteContents* variable contains the HTML document the program retrieves from the address.

The last two variables, *inetSearchError* and *StopSearching*, contain values that indicate, respectively, that an error occurred when the *Internet Transfer* control tried to connect to the site and that the user has clicked the mouse on the Stop Wandering button.

WRITING THE CODE FOR THE GET_FILE FUNCTION

As you may have determined, you can break down the processing the *prjWanderer* program performs into two components: retrieving the Internet file and parsing that file to get the addresses of other Internet files. The first step, therefore, is to retrieve the Internet file, which the *prjWanderer* program does within the *Get_File* function. The following code implements the *Get_File* function:

```
Public Function Get_File(ByVal txtURL As String) As Boolean
  frmSearching.Hide
  frmSearching.lblSite.Caption = txtURL
  If Len(txtURL) > 40 Then
    frmSearching.lblSite.Width = Len(txtURL) * 73
    frmSearching.lblCaption.Width = frmSearching.lblSite.Width
    frmSearching.Width = frmSearching.lblCaption.Width + 435
  End If
  frmSearching.Show
  DoEvents
  Real_File_Name = txtURL
  Site = Real_File_Name
  Site_Length = Len(Site)
  inetSearchError = False
  frmWanderer.itcWander.RequestTimeout = 60
  frmWanderer.itcWander.AccessType = icUseDefault
  On Error Resume Next
  SiteContents = frmWanderer.itcWander.OpenURL(txtURL, icString)
  Unload frmSearching
  DoEvents
  If Err.Number <> 0 And Not inetSearchError Then
    Get_File = False
    Exit Function
  End If
  Get_File = True
End Function
```

585

When the *Get_File* function begins its processing, it places the site's name the program is currently searching for onto the *frmSearching* form and then displays the *frmSearching* form. After the function displays the *frmSearching* form, the function's program code initializes the *Real_File_Name* and *Site* variables to the value within the *txtUrl* parameter that the calling procedure passes to the function. Next, the function uses the *itcWander* control to try to retrieve the file. If the function successfully retrieves the file, it places the file into the *SiteContents* variable, exits, and returns *True* to the calling procedure. If the function does not successfully retrieve the file, the function exits and returns *False* to the calling procedure.

In the *prjWanderer* program, if *Get_File* returns *True*, the calling procedure will then call the *Parse* function to parse the file, as the next section details.

BETTER UNDERSTANDING ABSOLUTE AND RELATIVE URLS

An absolute URL specifies an object's complete address and protocol. In other words, if the URL's scheme (such as *http*) is present, the URL is an absolute URL. The following is an example of an absolute URL:

```
http://www.jamsa.com/catalog/vbpl/vbpl.htm
```

A relative URL, on the other hand, uses the URL associated with the document currently open in your browser. Using the same scheme, server address, and directory tree (if present) as the open document, the browser reconstructs the URL by replacing the filename and extension with those of the relative URL. For example, consider the following absolute URL:

```
http://www.jamsa.com/catalog/catalog.htm
```

If a hyperlink within the HTML document specifies a reference to the relative URL *vbpl/vbpl.htm*, as shown in the following code, the browser will reconstruct the URL as *http://www.jamsa.com/catalog/vbpl/vbpl.htm*:

```
<A HREF="/vbpl/vbpl.htm"> Visual Basic Programming Information</A>
```

Note: *When you use the* **single dot** *operator (.) in front of a relative URL (for example, .vbpl/vbpl.htm), it has the same result as entering* **vbpl/vbpl.htm** *(the relative URL without the* **single dot** *operator).*

As you work with relative URLs, there may be times when you want to move up one level (above the open document's directory location) within the directory tree. To move up the directory tree, you may precede the relative URL with a double dot (..) notation. For example, suppose you write the current document's absolute URL as shown here:

```
http://www.jamsa.com/dir1/dir2/file.ext
```

If a hyperlink within the HTML document specifies a reference to the relative URL *..dir3/newfile.ext*, as shown in the following code, the browser will reconstruct the URL as *http://www.jamsa.com/dir1/dir3/newfile.ext*:

```
<A HREF="..dir3/newfile.ext">New File Link</A>
```

Alternatively, you may want to move up multiple levels in the directory tree. You can make a relative URL move up several branches in the tree by separating multiple instances of the *double dot* operator with a slash. For example, suppose the current document's absolute URL is as shown in the following code:

```
http://www.jamsa.com/dir1/dir2/file.ext
```

If a hyperlink within the HTML document specifies a reference to the relative URL *../../dir3/newfile.ext*, as shown in the following code, the browser will reconstruct the URL as *http://www.jamsa.com/dir3/newfile.ext*:

```
<A HREF="../../dir3/newfile.ext">New File Link</A>
```

Finally, suppose you want to use relative URLs to append a directory path to only the server's address. In other words, you want to ignore the open file's directory path, but still use the file's scheme and server address. In such a case, you can use the forward slash (/) notation. For example, suppose the absolute URL of the current document open within the browser is as follows:

```
http://www.jamsa.com/dir1/dir2/file.ext
```

If a hyperlink within the HTML document specifies a reference to the relative URL */dir3/newfile.ext*, as shown in the following code, the browser will reconstruct the URL as *http://www.jamsa.com/dir3/newfile.ext*:

```
<A HREF="/dir3/newfile.ext">New File Link</A>
```

WRITING THE CODE FOR THE PARSE FUNCTION

As you might expect, the *Parse* function is the heart of the *prjWanderer* program. The *Parse* function will identify tags within the document the *Get_File* function retrieves and add those tags to both the output file and the *rtbLinkNames* text box. The following code implements the *Parse* function:

```
Public Function Parse() As Boolean
   Dim PositionInString As Long, Response As Integer
   Dim ThisLinkLength As Integer, AddToFileString As String
   Dim End_Of_List As Boolean, NewFileName As String, GotFile As Boolean
   Dim Parent As String, Tag As String, lclTag As String
```

```
Dim Done As Boolean, RelativeAddress As Boolean
Dim lclTag_Length As Integer, I As Integer
Dim FirstQuote As Integer, SecondQuote As Integer

End_Of_List = False
PositionInString = 0
Done = False
Do While Not End_Of_List And Not StopSearching
 Current_Pos = 1
  Done = Get_Tag(Tag)
  Do While Not Done And Not StopSearching
    frmParsing.Show
    DoEvents
    lclTag = Tag
    lclTag_Length = Len(Tag)
    FirstQuote = 0
    SecondQuote = 0
    If InStr(lclTag, "href") Then
      Do While Left$(lclTag, 4) <> "href"
        lclTag = Right$(lclTag, Len(lclTag) - 1)
      Loop
      If Not InStr(lclTag, "::") Then
        RelativeAddress = True
      Else
        RelativeAddress = False
      End If
      For I = 1 To lclTag_Length
        If Mid$(lclTag, I, 1) = Chr(34) Then
          If FirstQuote <> 0 Then
            SecondQuote = I
            Exit For
          Else
            FirstQuote = I + 1
          End If
        End If
      Next
      AddToFileString = Mid$(lclTag, FirstQuote, _
        SecondQuote - FirstQuote)
      If InStr(AddToFileString, "://") Then
        AddLink (AddToFileString)
      Else
        If Not ResolvedSite(Site, Parent, AddToFileString) Then
          frmParsing.Hide
          MsgBox "Unable to resolve site!"
        Else
          AddLink (Parent & AddToFileString)
        End If
      End If
    End If
    Done = Get_Tag(Tag)
    DoEvents
  Loop
  frmParsing.Hide
  If Done Then
    If Len(frmWanderer.rtbLinkNames.Text) > 0 Then _
        frmWanderer.rtbLinkNames.SaveFile App.Path & OUT_FILE, rtfText
    GotFile = False
  Else
    Response = MsgBox("Are you sure you want to stop search?", vbYesNo)
    If Response = vbYes Then
      frmWanderer.rtbLinkNames.SaveFile App.Path & OUT_FILE, rtfText
```

```
            frmWanderer.itcWander.Cancel
            Parse = Not StopSearching
            Exit Function
         End If
      End If
      DoEvents
      Do Until GotFile Or StopSearching
         If PositionInString < Len(frmWanderer.rtbLinkNames.Text) Then
            ThisLinkLength = 0
            If PositionInString = 0 Then PositionInString = 1
            Do While Mid$(frmWanderer.rtbLinkNames.Text, PositionInString + _
               ThisLinkLength, 1) <> Chr(10)
               ThisLinkLength = ThisLinkLength + 1
               DoEvents
            Loop
            NewFileName = Mid$(frmWanderer.rtbLinkNames.Text, _
               PositionInString, ThisLinkLength - 1)
            If Left$(NewFileName, 6) <> "mailto" Then
               PositionInString = PositionInString + ThisLinkLength + 1
               ThisLinkLength = 0
               If Not Get_File(NewFileName) Then
                 MsgBox "Error opening page. Moving on to next page. Bad page = " _
                    & NewFileName
                 GotFile = False
               Else
                  GotFile = True
               End If
            Else
               GotFile = False
            End If
         Else
            GotFile = True
            End_Of_List = True
         End If
         DoEvents
      Loop
   Loop
   Parse = Not StopSearching
End Function
```

588

The *Parse* function first initializes the local variables the function will use during its processing. The function then initializes the *End_Of_List* variable to *False*. The function will later set the *End_Of_List* variable to *True* when it finishes processing the last tag within the file. The function also initializes the *PositionInString* variable to 0—the start of the string.

The *Parse* function then enters the first of several *Do-While* and *Do-Until* loops that the function uses to perform its processing. The first *Do-While* loop will continue to retrieve and parse files, either until there are no more files to parse or until the user clicks the mouse on the Stop Searching button.

Each time the *Parse* function starts to loop again, the program code sets the *Current_Pos* variable to 1 (which tells the program to start searching the newly retrieved file at the file's beginning), and then calls the *Get_Tag* function. The *Get_Tag* function searches the HTML file for the greater-than (<) and less-than (>) symbols that indicate an HTML tag. You will learn more about the *Get_Tag* function in the next section. The *Get_Tag* function returns *True* if it finds a tag, and *False* if it does not. If you look closely at the loop structure, you will see that the *Parse* function begins its second loop after the call to *Get_Tag*. If *Get_Tag* does not find a tag within the file, the program code exits the current loop and resumes processing at the first statement after the loop, which will hide the *frmParsing* form. If *Get_Tag* does find a tag within the file, the internal *Do-While* loop begins to execute, and will continue to execute until there are no more tags within the file for the loop to process.

Within the loop that processes tags, the program code shows the *frmParsing* form to alert the user that the program is currently parsing a file. The loop's program code then checks the tag to determine whether the tag contains *href*—which signifies a link to another file. If the tag is an *href* tag, the program code retrieves the link from within the tag and adds the link to the file. The loop uses two functions, *ResolvedSite* and *AddLink*, to verify the link's validity and to add it to the file. You will learn more about both functions in later sections.

After checking the tag, the program code tries to retrieve another tag from the file. If the program succeeds, it will evaluate the new tag. If the program does not find another tag within the file, the second loop will exit and the program code will resume its processing at the first statement that follows the loop.

After the loop's end, the program first checks to determine whether the loop ended because the program reached the end of the file or because the user clicked the mouse on the Stop Wandering button. If the loop ended because the program reached the end of the file, the program will save the updated text file. If the loop ended because the user clicked the mouse on the Stop Wandering button, the program will display a message box to verify that the user truly wants to stop the search. If the user verifies that the program should stop the search, the function will exit and return *False*, and the calling procedure will exit as well, stopping the search and letting the user access the list.

If the loop ended because the program reached the end of the file, the program will then enter the next loop, which searches for the next valid address within the list of addresses the program retrieved. When the program finds a valid address, it exits the loop and the program code loops back to the beginning of the *Parse* function and repeats its processing for the new address.

WRITING THE CODE FOR THE GET_TAG FUNCTION

As you learned in the previous section, the *Get_Tag* function searches the currently retrieved file for a valid HTML tag. The *Get_Tag* function searches through the string, one character at a time, looking for the less-than sign (<), followed by the letter "A," which symbolizes the beginning of another address. When the function finds the less-than sign, it enters an internal loop. Within the internal loop, the program code searches for the greater-than sign (>). After the program code finds the greater-than sign, the program code returns the entire text between the two signs to the calling function within the *ReturnTag* parameter and exits the *Get_Tag* function. The following code implements the *Get_Tag* function:

```
Public Function Get_Tag(ReturnTag As String) As Boolean
  ReturnTag = ""
  Get_Tag = False
  Do While Current_Pos < Len(SiteContents)
     If Mid(SiteContents, Current_Pos, 1) = "<" _
        And Mid(SiteContents, Current_Pos + 1, 1) = "A" Then
       Dim Local_I As Integer

       Local_I = 1
       Do While Mid(SiteContents, Current_Pos + Local_I, 1) <> ">"
         If Local_I < TAG_LENGTH Then
           ReturnTag = ReturnTag & Mid(SiteContents, _
               Current_Pos + Local_I, 1)
         End If
         Local_I = Local_I + 1
       Loop
       Current_Pos = Current_Pos + Local_I
       Exit Function
     End If
     Current_Pos = Current_Pos + 1
  Loop
  Get_Tag = True
End Function
```

As you can see, the program code uses the *Mid* function to check each character within the HTML file in turn. When the function finds an "<A" character pair, the function enters an internal loop. The internal loop places all the characters between the "A" and the greater-than (>) symbol into the *Return Tag* parameter, a single character at a time. When the function encounters the greater-than (>) symbol, it exits and returns a *False* value (which indicates to the calling procedure that it has not reached the end of the file, but is actually returning a tag value). The function maintains its current position inside the file within the *Current_Pos* variable. When the *Parse* function again calls *Get_Tag* for the current file, *Get_Tag* will begin to search for the next tag from its current position in the file and move forward.

If *Get_Tag* does not find a tag, it returns a *True* value, which indicates to the *Parse* function that *Get_Tag* has searched the entire file and that the *Parse* function should move on to the next file.

WRITING THE CODE FOR THE RESOLVEDSITE FUNCTION

When you create a Web robot, it should be able to process relative addresses, because many Web sites use relative addresses for documents internal to the Web site. The *prjWanderer* program uses the *ResolvedSite* function to resolve relative addresses. The following code implements the *ResolvedSite* function:

```
Private Function ResolvedSite(FileAddr As String, Parent As String, _
    NewTag As String) As Boolean
  On Error GoTo ResolveError
  ResolvedSite = True
  Parent = FileAddr
  If Right$(Parent, 1) <> "/" Then Parent = TrimPage(Parent)
  If Left$(NewTag, 3) <> "../" And Left$(NewTag, 5) <> "http:" Then _
      Exit Function
  If Left$(NewTag, 6) = "http:/" And Left$(NewTag, 7) <> "http://" Then _
      NewTag = Right$(NewTag, Len(NewTag) - 6)
  Do While Left$(NewTag, 3) = "../"
    NewTag = Right$(NewTag, Len(NewTag) - 3)
    Parent = Left(Parent, Len(Parent) - 1)
    Do While Right$(Parent, 1) <> "/"
      Parent = Left$(Parent, Len(Parent) - 1)
    Loop
  Loop
Exit Function

ResolveError:
  ResolvedSite = False
  MsgBox "Unable to resolve parent site!"
End Function
```

The *ResolvedSite* function uses a series of *If-Then* statements to check the incoming tag and to determine into which general category the tag falls. The *ResolvedSite* function uses two variables, *Parent* and *New Tag*, to process the site address. The *ResolvedSite* function begins its processing with three *If-Then* statements, which check the *Parent* tag and the *New Tag* tag to determine their contents and trim the contents so the remaining code in the function can resolve the site name correctly.

The first *If-Then* statement checks the *Parent* variable to determine whether or not it ends in a forward slash (/). If it does end in a forward slash (which indicates the parent tag contains a directory address and not a specific file address), the function calls the *TrimPage* function to trim the trailing slashes until *Parent* is a valid address within a directory tree. The next section explains the *TrimPage* function in detail.

Next, the function checks the *New Tag* string, which corresponds to the newly located tag in the HTML file. If the *New Tag* string does not begin with two dots and a forward slash (../), or *New Tag* does not begin with *http:*, the address is not a valid Web site address (it may be an FTP address, a mail address, or another type of URL). If the new tag is not a valid Web address, the function does not try to resolve the address. Instead, the function exits and returns the address to the calling procedure, which will, in turn, add the address to the *taglist.txt* file. If the new address is a valid relative address, the *ResolvedSite* function resolves the relative address.

If a tag contains the *http://* string, which indicates that the address is an absolute address, the *ResolvedSite* function reduces the parent tree by one level for each double dot operator and forward slash (*../*) the function encounters in the new tag. For example, if the parent address is *http://www.jamsa/com/catalog/vbpl/*, and the new tag is *../../jamsa1.htm*, the *ResolvedSite* function will resolve the address as *http://www.jamsa.com/jamsa1.htm*.

WRITING THE CODE FOR THE TRIMPAGE FUNCTION

As the previous section details, the *TrimPage* function removes trailing slashes from a parent address until the parent address no longer ends in a trailing slash. The following code implements the *TrimPage* function:

```
Public Function TrimPage(ByVal Address As String) As String
  Do While Right$(Address, 1) <> "/"
    Address = Left$(Address, Len(Address) - 1)
  Loop
  TrimPage = Address
End Function
```

591

As you can see, the *TrimPage* function checks the incoming address and shortens it one character at a time until the last character is no longer a forward slash.

WRITING THE CODE FOR THE ADDLINK PROCEDURE

One of the most significant problems you must avoid when you create a Web robot is multiple instances of the same address. Multiple instances of the same address are a problem because they can clutter your output and cause the program to repeatedly read the same page and the same address. To keep the program from adding the same address to the *taglist.txt* file multiple times, the *prjWanderer* program uses the *AddLink* procedure to add links to the *rtbLinkNames* control. The following code implements the *AddLink* procedure:

```
Public Sub AddLink(LinktoAdd As String)
  Dim FoundPos As Integer

  FoundPos = 0
  FoundPos = frmWanderer.rtbLinkNames.Find(LinktoAdd, FoundPos)
  If FoundPos <> -1 Then                              'the phrase was found.
    Exit Sub
  Else
    frmWanderer.rtbLinkNames.Text = frmWanderer.rtbLinkNames.Text & _
        LinktoAdd & NewLine
  End If
End Sub
```

The *AddLink* procedure uses the *RichTextBox* control's *Find* method to determine whether the link already exists in the *taglist.txt* file. If the link exists, the function ends without adding the link. If the link does not exist, the procedure adds the link to the *RichTextBox* control.

WRITING THE CODE FOR THE FRMWANDERER FORM

As you have learned, the *mdlWanderer* module performs the majority of the actual search processing within the *prjWanderer* program. However, the *frmWanderer* form also performs processing and must respond to events. In the following sections, you will write the code for the *frmWanderer* form. The *frmWanderer* form's program code will respond both to user-generated events and to the *itcWander* control's *State_Changed* event.

As you know, the first code to execute in a single-document interface project, such as the *prjWanderer* project, is the *Form_Load* event. The following code implements the *frmWanderer* form's *Form_Load* event:

```
Private Sub Form_Load()
  txtSite.Text = "http://www.jamsa.com/jamsa1.htm"
  NewLine = Chr(13) & Chr(10)
  StopSearching = True
  cmdStopWandering.Enabled = False
End Sub
```

The *Form_Load* event sets the initial value for the *txtSite* control's *Text* property, defines the *NewLine* variable, and disables the Stop Wandering button (which the program code will later enable after the user clicks the mouse on the Go Wander button). You can set the initial value for the *txtSite* control's *Text* property to any URL you want. Whatever value you assign to the control's *Text* property will be a default value that users can always use to begin their search.

WRITING THE CODE FOR THE CMDGOWANDER_CLICK EVENT

As this chapter's "Using the *prjWanderer* Project" section details, the user must click the mouse on the Go Wander button to start wandering at a specified address. The *cmdGoWander_Click* event's program code starts the robot wandering. The following code implements the *cmdGoWander_Click* event:

```
Private Sub cmdGoWander_Click()
   StopSearching = False
   rtbLinkNames.Text = ""
   Current_Pos = 1
   Me.MousePointer = vbArrowHourglass
   cmdGoWander.Enabled = False
   cmdStopWandering.Enabled = True
   If Get_File(txtSite.Text) Then
     If Not Parse Then Me.MousePointer = vbNormal
   Else
     Me.MousePointer = vbNormal
     MsgBox "Unable to find the desired site."
   End If
   cmdGoWander.Enabled = True
   cmdStopWandering.Enabled = False
   Me.MousePointer = vbNormal
   StopSearching = True
End Sub
```

The *cmdGoWander_Click* event clears the *rtbLinkNames* control (to remove the results of a previous wander), and sets the mouse pointer to an hourglass. The event's program code then calls the *Get_File* function with the user-entered URL. Calling *Get_File* from within the event, rather than letting the *Parse* function handle the first address, lets the program provide a meaningful response to the user in the event that the URL the user entered was not valid or was unavailable. If the *Get_File* function successfully locates the address, the *cmdGoWander_Click* event calls the *Parse* function and begins to wander. If the *Get_File* function does not successfully locate the user-entered URL, the *cmdGoWander_Click* event will display a message box explaining that it was unable to find the URL and will exit.

WRITING THE CODE FOR THE OTHER COMMAND BUTTONS

When the user is performing a search, the user can either click the mouse on the Stop Wandering button to stop the search or click the mouse on the Exit button to exit the program. The following code implements the *cmdStopWandering_Click* event:

```
Private Sub cmdStopWandering_Click()
   StopSearching = True
End Sub
```

The *cmdStopWandering_Click* event sets the *StopSearching* flag variable to *True* so that the program code will know to stop the search the next time the program code checks the *StopSearching* variable (which the program does often, as you saw when you wrote the *Parse* and *Get_Tag* functions). The *cmdExit_Click* event, on the other hand, tries to unload the *frmWanderer* form and exit the program. The following code implements the *cmdExit_Click* event:

```
Private Sub cmdExit_Click()
   Unload Me
End Sub
```

To exit a search, and the program, the user must simply click the mouse on the *cmdExit* button. However, to protect against the user inadvertently unloading the program during a search, you must place program code within the

QueryUnload event to stop unloading the form and to verify with the user that the user really wants to exit the program. The program code within the *QueryUnload* event must check whether or not the user is currently searching. If the user is searching, the code must let the user know that closing the program will end the search. Whether or not the user is searching, the program code within the *QueryUnload* event should let the user verify the choice to close the form and end the program. The following code implements the *QueryUnload* event:

```
Private Sub Form_QueryUnload(Cancel As Integer, UnloadMode As Integer)
   Dim Response As Integer

   If Not StopSearching Then
      Response = MsgBox("Stop search and lose updated file?", vbYesNo)
      If Response = vbNo Then
         Cancel = 1
         Exit Sub
      End If
   Else
      Response = MsgBox("Close program?", vbYesNo)
      If Response = vbNo Then
         Cancel = 1
         Exit Sub
      End If
   End If
   itcWander.Cancel
End Sub
```

The program code prompts the user to determine whether or not the user truly wants to exit—if so, the program code cancels the *itcWander* control's actions and lets the *Form_Unload* event unload the form. If not, the program code cancels the unload activity and returns to whatever processing it was performing when the user tried to close the form.

If the user does choose to close the form and end the program, the program code must also unload both the *frmParsing* and *frmSearching* forms. If the program code does not do so, the program will continue its execution, even though the *frmWanderer* form is no longer visible. You will place the program code to unload the *frmParsing* and *frmSearching* forms within the *Unload* event, which will execute only after the user verifies the unload activity and chooses to exit the program. The following code implements the *Unload* event:

```
Private Sub Form_Unload(Cancel As Integer)
   Unload frmSearching
   Unload frmParsing
End Sub
```

The *Form_Unload* event unloads the *frmSearching* and the *frmParsing* form. Because the *frmWanderer* form invokes the *Form_Unload* event only when the program fully unloads the form, the program also unloads the *frmWanderer* form. Unloading all three forms ensures that the program's processing stops.

WRITING THE CODE FOR THE *ITCWANDER_STATECHANGED* EVENT

As you learned in Chapter 18, the *Internet Transfer* control invokes its *StateChanged* event each time the control's current state changes. For example, when the control connects to the host address, the control will invoke the *StateChanged* event. Similarly, after the control finishes its processing on an address and disconnects from that address, the control will invoke the *StateChanged* event. The *itcWander_StateChanged* event returns information to the program about whether or not the *Internet Transfer* control connected successfully. The following code implements the *itcWander_StateChanged* event:

```
Private Sub itcWander_StateChanged(ByVal State As Integer)
   Dim strMess As String

   DoEvents
   Select Case State
      Case icHostResolvingHost
         Connected = False
      Case icConnected
```

```
            Connected = True
      Case State = icError
        strMess = "ErrorCode: " & itcWander.ResponseCode & " : " & _
            itcSearch.ResponseInfo
        MsgBox strMess, vbOKOnly
        itcWanderSearchError = True
    End Select
  End Sub
```

If the *Internet Transfer* control encounters an error, the program code will display the error within a message box to let the user know of the error.

UNDERSTANDING ETHICAL ROBOTS

As you examine books, articles, and Web-based documents that discuss robots, you will encounter terms such as *well-behaved robots* and *ethical robots*. In general, because a robot does not really "visit" a site, the robot can normally cause only a limited amount of damage to a site. If a site uses proper file protection, even a malicious robot can do little or no damage to the site's files. Normally, the only way a robot can impact a server is to consume the server's processing time. In other words, to respond to the robot's requests, the server must read files (HTML documents) from its own hard disk and then transmit the files to the robot. While the server is responding to the robot's requests, the server cannot respond to requests from other clients.

Depending on the contents of HTML documents that reside on a server's disk, the server may want to place some documents off limits to robots and agents. To do so, the server can request that the robot not process specific files or directories. To make such a request, the server's Webmaster must place entries within the file *robots.txt*, which resides on a hard disk at the server computer.

A well-behaved or ethical robot is a program that reads the contents of the *robots.txt* file and performs its processing accordingly. When you create your own robots, your robots should examine each system's *robot.txt* file before the robot performs any processing at the site. To simplify the program's code, the *prjWanderer.exe* program this chapter presents is not well behaved. Think of the *prjWanderer.exe* program as a perfect example of what you should not do when you write your robots, at least as far as being well-behaved is concerned. For more information on ethical robots, visit the Web site at *http://info.webcrawler.com/mak/projects/robots/guidelines.html*, as shown in Figure 19.10.

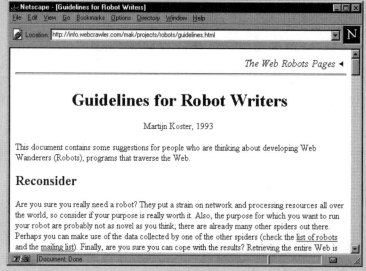

Figure 19.10 *Information for robot writers at **http://info.webcrawler.com/mak/projects/robots/guidelines.html**.*

Enhancements You Can Make to the *prjWanderer* Project

As Chapter 18 suggests, the best enhancement to make to the *prjWanderer* project is to expand the code to handle a true search, rather than simply retrieving new addresses. You can easily add a search routine to the program code that searches a found page for a given return value and then adds that information to a database. With only minimal additional program code, you can easily create your own custom search engine.

Putting It All Together

This chapter's project, *prjWanderer*, introduced you to robots, spiders, agents, and wanderers, which are Web-based programs that visit Web sites. The difference between these programs and a browser is that the user controls the sites a browser visits, whereas the robot itself determines the sites the robot visits. Also, you learned that although these programs give the illusion of "traveling" from one site to another, that is not really the case. Instead, the programs run on only one computer, and they "visit" the remote sites. In Chapter 20, "Creating ActiveX Documents for the Web," you will use the new *UserDocument* object to transport the *prjFractal* project that you created in Chapter 5, "Creating and Using Fractals," to the Web. Before you continue with Chapter 20, however, make sure you understand the following key concepts:

✓ Robot programs visit sites across the Web by retrieving HTML documents for processing. The *prjWanderer* project retrieves HTML documents and parses the documents, looking for tags that signify other Web addresses.

✓ Within your Visual Basic programs, you can use the *Microsoft Internet Transfer* control to establish Internet connections, retrieve files from the Internet, and save the files the programs retrieve onto a local computer.

✓ Within Visual Basic, you can use the *Internet Transfer* control to easily connect to multiple sites in sequence.

✓ *Wanderers*, *crawlers*, and *spiders* are alternate names for robot programs.

✓ An ethical robot is one that reads and abides by the guidelines the server file *robots.txt* specifies.

✓ When you design Web robots, you should follow the accepted guidelines for creating ethical robots. An ethical robot is a robot that will not intrude on a Web site if the server instructs the robot not to.

Chapter 20

Creating ActiveX Documents for the Web

As you have learned, the Internet is one of the fastest growing and most exciting new areas of computer programming. Over the past several years, the growth in Internet servers and customer use has been startling, and this growth is not showing any signs of slowing down. One of the biggest reasons for the Internet's growth is the World Wide Web, which lets users interact with the Internet through a graphical interface. The graphical interface that users access to interact with the Web is very similar to a Visual Basic program—users interact with a Web page, similar to a Visual Basic form, and use graphics, buttons, fields, and so on during their interaction. Unfortunately, programmers have historically been unable to transport Visual Basic programs to the Web. After the programmers designed the application for a local computer, they typically had to use HTML, Java™, JavaScript™, or some other language to create an interface consistent with the Visual Basic programs—and the Web page's interface was never identical to the original program.

In this chapter, you will create the *prjDocFractals.exe* program, which draws colorful images from mathematical equations. The program that you will design within this chapter will be very similar to the *prjFractal* project that you designed in Chapter 5, "Creating and Using Fractals." However, users will use the program that you will design within this chapter only on the Web. In fact, the program will run inside the Microsoft *Internet Explorer*® browser. Such a program is an *ActiveX document*. This chapter's project, *prjDocFractals*, examines in detail ActiveX documents, the *Circle* and the *Line* methods, and various program controls. By the time you finish this chapter, you will understand the following key concepts:

- ◆ Visual Basic lets you create custom ActiveX documents within which you can build programs that you can easily distribute on and execute from the World Wide Web.

- ◆ To use an ActiveX document, the browser must access an HTML page that uses VBScript to refer to, and load, the document. When you compile an ActiveX document project, you actually create an executable file, which the HTML page then uses VBScript to load into the browser.

- ◆ When you distribute compiled ActiveX documents, you will use a Microsoft Cabinet (CAB) file to hold the components for the document.

- ◆ To create both the CAB files that will contain your ActiveX documents and a simple HTML page or pages to access the CAB files, you can use the Visual Basic Application Setup Wizard.

USING THE PRJDOCFRACTALS PROJECT

Before you design the *prjDocFractals* project, you may find it helpful to run the program. The companion CD-ROM that accompanies this book contains the *prjDocFractals.exe* program and the *udcFractal.vbd* and *udcUserEquation.vbd* supporting files within the *Chapter20* directory. As with every other program on the CD-ROM, you should run the Jamsa Press *setup.exe* program to install the *prjDocFractals.exe* program and its supporting files to your computer's hard drive before you run the program. After you install the *prjDocFractals.exe* program and supporting files to your computer's hard drive, you can run the program—but not from the Start menu, as you have with most other programs. Instead, you must run the program from within Microsoft's *Internet Explorer*® browser. In fact, you must load an HTML page into the browser, which will, in turn, load the ActiveX documents. To load the *prjDocFractals.exe* program into Microsoft's *Internet Explorer*® browser, perform the following steps:

1. Select the Start menu Programs option. Within the Programs menu, select the Internet Explorer option. Windows will run *Internet Explorer*.

2. Within *Internet Explorer*, select the File menu Open option. *Internet Explorer* will display the Open dialog box.

3. Within the Open dialog box, click your mouse on the Browser button. *Internet Explorer* will display another Open dialog box with folder names and file names, as well as navigation buttons.

4. Within the newly displayed Open dialog box, navigate to *x:\vbpl\Chapter20\Fractals.htm*, where *x* corresponds to the letter of the hard drive on which you installed the *prjDocFractals.exe* program, and click your mouse on OK.

5. *Internet Explorer* will display the *udcFractals.vbd* document (part of the *prjDocFractals.exe* program) within its browser window, as shown in Figure 20.1.

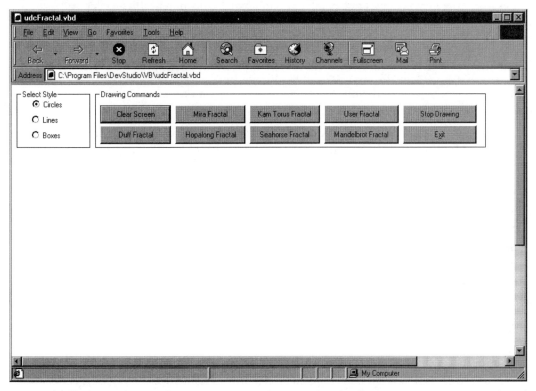

Figure 20.1 *The* **prjDocFractals.exe** *program running within* **Internet Explorer.**

RUNNING PRJDOCFRACTALS FROM THE CD-ROM

As you have learned, you must first install many programs that you will use within this book to your computer's hard drive before you try to use the programs. The *prjDocFractals.exe* program, however, does not use any custom controls or references, other than those that Visual Basic installs onto your system. Because the *prjDocFractals.exe* program uses no custom controls or references, you can run the program from the CD-ROM. To run the *prjDocFractals.exe* program from the CD-ROM, perform the following steps:

1. Select the Start menu Programs option. Within the Programs menu, select the Internet Explorer option. Windows will run *Internet Explorer*.

2. Within *Internet Explorer*, select the File menu Open option. *Internet Explorer* will display the Open dialog box.

3. Within the Open dialog box, click your mouse on the Browser button. *Internet Explorer* will display another Open dialog box with folder names and file names, as well as navigation buttons. Navigate to *x:\Chapter20\docFractals.htm*, where *x* corresponds to the drive letter of your CD-ROM drive, and click your mouse on OK.

4. *Internet Explorer* will display the *udcFractals.vbd* document (part of the *prjDocFractals.exe* program) within its browser window.

To learn more about the Jamsa Press *setup.exe* program, see the "What's on the *Visual Basic Programmer's Library* Companion CD-ROM" section at the back of this book.

Before you use the *prjDocFractals.exe* program, you should familiarize yourself with the controls the ActiveX document displays. You will see the *Select Style* frame on the ActiveX document's left, which contains three option buttons (Circles, Lines, and Boxes) that you will use to select the shape the program draws when the program draws the fractal. You will also see ten buttons on the ActiveX document. When you click your mouse on the Clear Screen button, the program will erase any images from the ActiveX document. If you click your mouse on any one of the six Fractal buttons, the program will draw a fractal image on the ActiveX document. If you click your mouse on the Stop Drawing button, the program will stop drawing the currently selected fractal. If you click your mouse on the Exit button, the program will unload itself and try to navigate the browser to *http://www.jamsa.com* (the Jamsa Press Web site). Finally, when you click your mouse on the User Fractal button, the *Internet Explorer* window will display the *udcUserDocument* ActiveX document, that you can use to plot functions. Now that you have seen the layout of the *prjDocFractals.exe* program, you can use the *prjDocFractals.exe* program to select a drawing style and draw a fractal image. To select a circle drawing style and draw a fractal image, perform the following steps:

1. Within the *udcFractals.vbd* ActiveX document, click your mouse on the Circles option in the *Select Style* label. The program will display a dot within the *Circles* option field.

2. Within the *udcFractals.vbd* document, click your mouse on the Duff Fractal button. The program will use circles to draw a Duff Fractal image.

Now that you have seen a Duff Fractal image drawn with circles, it is worthwhile to better understand the difference drawing a fractal with lines will make in the fractal's appearance. To draw a Kam Torus Fractal image using lines instead of circles, perform the following steps:

1. Within the *udcFractals.vbd* ActiveX document, click your mouse on the Clear Screen button to clear the *udcFractals.vbd* ActiveX document's drawing area. The program will clear the drawing area.

2. Click your mouse on the Lines option in the *Select Style* frame. The program will draw a dot in the *Lines* option field.

3. Within the *udcFractals.vbd* ActiveX document, click your mouse on the Kam Torus Fractal button. The program will use many small lines to draw a Kam Torus Fractal image, as shown in Figure 20.2.

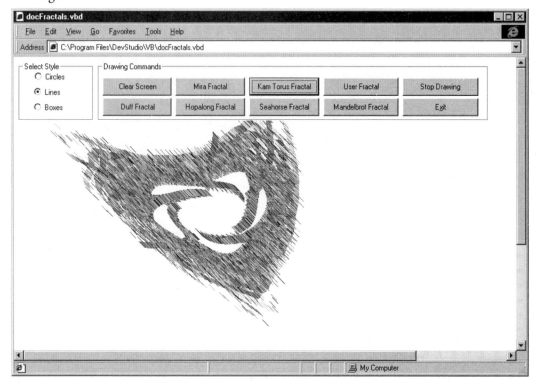

Figure 20.2 The Kam Torus Fractal image drawn with lines.

In addition to drawing predefined fractals, you can create your own math equation and the *prjDocFractals.exe* program will draw an image of it on the *udcUserEquation.vbd* ActiveX document. To create your own user-defined math equation, perform the following steps:

1. Within the *udcFractals.vbd* ActiveX document, click your mouse on the User Fractal button. *Internet Explorer* will close the *udcFractals.vbd* ActiveX document and open the *udcUserEquation* ActiveX document.

2. Within the *udcUserEquation* ActiveX document, enter 1 in the *X1=* field, then enter 1 in the *X2=* field, and then enter 1 in the *X3=* field. Next, enter 1.5 in the *a=* field, .5 in the *b=* field, and 0 in the *c=* field.

3. Within the *udcUserEquation* ActiveX document, click your mouse on the Lines option.

4. Within the *udcUserEquation* ActiveX document, click your mouse on the Plot Function button. The program will use the equation you entered to draw an image on the *udcUserEquation* ActiveX document.

5. Within the *udcUserEquation* ActiveX document, enter 2 in the *a=* field and click your mouse on the Plot Function button. The program will use the equation you entered to draw an image on the *udcUserEquation* ActiveX document.

6. Within the *udcUserEquation* ActiveX document, enter .75 in the *c=* field and click your mouse on the Plot Function button. The program will use the equation you entered to draw an image on the *udcUserEquation* ActiveX document. Figure 20.3 shows the *prjDocFractals* project's ActiveX document, *UserEquation,* after you draw the three equations.

599

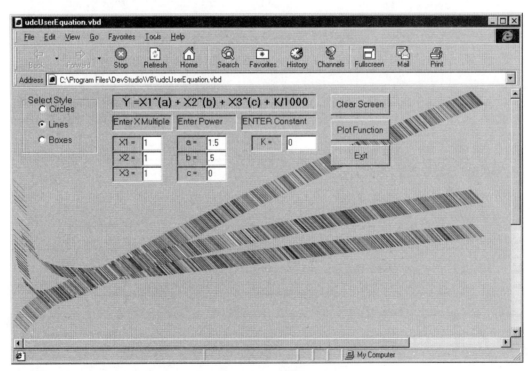

Figure 20.3 The *prjDocFractals* project's *udcUserEquation.vbd* document.

CREATING THE BLANK USER DOCUMENTS AND MODULES

Now that you have a better idea how to use the *prjDocFractals* project, you can begin to design the project. You will design two blank *user documents* that will contain all the controls the "Using the *prjDocFractals* Project" section introduced, as well as the project's modules. After you design and implement the user documents, you will learn more about Visual Basic structures and the six predefined fractal equations. To begin the *prjDocFractals* project and design the two blank user documents and the modules the project will use, perform the following steps:

1. Within Visual Basic, select the File menu New Project option. Visual Basic will open the New Project dialog box.

2. Within the New Project dialog box, click your mouse on the ActiveX Document EXE icon. Next, click your mouse on OK. Visual Basic will open the *UserDocument1* ActiveX document within an object window.

3. Select the View menu Properties Window option. Visual Basic will open the Properties Window with the *UserDocument1* properties listed.

4. Within the Properties Window, change the *UserDocument1* properties to the values Table 20.1 lists.

Object	Property	Set As
UserDocument1	*BackColor*	*&H00FFFFFF& (White)*
UserDocument1	*Height*	10575
UserDocument1	*Width*	14970
UserDocument1	*Name*	*udcFractal*

Table 20.1 *The newly named* **udcFractal** *user document's properties.*

5. Within Visual Basic, select the Project menu Add User Document option. Visual Basic will open the Add User Document dialog box.

6. Within the Add User Document dialog box, click your mouse on the User Document icon. Next, click your mouse on OK. Visual Basic will add the *UserDocument1* ActiveX document to the project and open it within an object window.

7. Select the View menu Properties Window option. Visual Basic will open the Properties Window with the *UserDocument1* properties listed.

8. Within the Properties Window, change the *UserDocument1* properties to the values Table 20.2 lists.

Object	Property	Set As
UserDocument1	*BackColor*	*&H00FFFFFF& (White)*
UserDocument1	*Height*	10530
UserDocument1	*Width*	14970
UserDocument1	*Name*	*udcUserEquation*

Table 20.2 *The newly named* **udcUserEquation** *user document's properties.*

9. Within Visual Basic, select the Project menu Add Module option. Visual Basic will open the Add Module dialog box.

10. Within the Add Module dialog box, select the Module option. Next, click your mouse on the Open button. Visual Basic will open a new Code window, *Module1*.

11. Select the View menu Properties Window option. Visual Basic will open the Properties Window listing the *Module1* properties.

12. Within the Properties Window, change the *Module1* module's name to *mdlComplex*.

13. Within Visual Basic, select the Project menu Add Module option. Visual Basic will open the Add Module dialog box.

14. Within the Add Module dialog box, select the Module option. Next, click your mouse on the Open button. Visual Basic will open a new Code window, *Module1*.

15. Select the View menu Properties Window option. Visual Basic will open the Properties Window listing the *Module1* properties.

16. Within the Properties Window, change the *Module1* module's name to *mdlFractal*.

17. Within Visual Basic, select the Project menu Add Module option. Visual Basic will open the Add Module dialog box.

18. Within the Add Module dialog box, select the Module option. Next, click your mouse on the Open button. Visual Basic will open a new Code window, *Module1*.

19. Select the View menu Properties Window option. Visual Basic will open the Properties Window listing the *Module1* properties.

20. Within the Properties Window, change the *Module1* module's name to *mdlPoint*.

21. Select the File menu Save Project As option. Visual Basic will open the Save File As dialog box and fill the *File name* field with *mdlPoint*.

22. Within the Save File As dialog box, click your mouse on the Save button. Visual Basic will save the *mdlPoint* module and fill the *File name* field with *mdlFractal*.

23. Within the Save File As dialog box, click your mouse on the Save button. Visual Basic will save the *mdlFractal* module and fill the *File name* field with *mdlComplex*.

24. Within the Save File As dialog box, click your mouse on the Save button. Visual Basic will save the *mdlComplex* module and fill the *File name* field with *mdlFractal*.

25. Within the Save File As dialog box, click your mouse on the Save button. Visual Basic will save the *mdlFractal* module and fill the *File name* field with *udcUserEquation*.

26. Within the Save File As dialog box, click your mouse on the Save button. Visual Basic will save the *udcUserEquation* user document and fill the *File name* field with *udcFractal*.

27. Within the Save File As dialog box, click your mouse on the Save button. Visual Basic will save the *udcFractal* user document and fill the *File name* field with *Project1*.

28. Within the *File name* field, replace the *Project1* project name with the new *prjDocFractals* project name. Next, click your mouse on the Save button. Visual Basic will save the *prjDocFractals* project and close the Save Project As dialog box.

UNDERSTANDING PIXELS

Pixels are circular areas on your computer screen that can be any combination of red, green, and blue colors. As you may know, computer screens (and other displays, such as television sets) determine the color of each point that you plot on the screen as some combination of red, green, and blue. A color value between 0 and 255 determines the amount of each color within the final pixel. If you plot a pixel with the highest color value (255) for each color, the resulting pixel will be white. Similarly, if you plot a pixel with the lowest color value (0) for each color, the resulting pixel will be black.

In general, a pixel is about the size of a pin head. Most computer screens have the capability to display different levels of *resolution*, which represents the number of pixels the screen displays. For example, when you set your computer screen to display a resolution of 640 by 480, it will display 640 pixels across and 480 pixels from top to bottom. Similarly, when you set your computer screen to display a resolution of 1024 by 800, it will display 1024 pixels across and 800 pixels from top to bottom. Because many pixels compose each screen, the more pixels a screen display has, the clearer the screen's image will be—which means that an image you display at 1024 pixels by 800 pixels will have a higher *resolution*, or clarity, than an image you display at 640 pixels by 480 pixels.

ADDING CONTROLS TO THE UDCFRACTAL USER DOCUMENT

Now that you have created the user documents and modules that you will use within the *prjDocFractals* project, and you have learned about the drawing methods that you will use to create fractals, you will add controls to the *udcFractal* user document. As you have learned, the user will use the *udcFractal* user document to select a fractal image to draw. First, you will add *CommandButton* controls and place them within a *Frame* control. Second, you will add another *Frame* control and place three *OptionButton* controls within the *Label* control in a control array. Third, you will change each control's properties. After you finish the *udcFractal* user document's design, you will add controls to the *udcUserEquation* user document.

ADDING COMMAND BUTTONS AND A FRAME TO THE UDCFRACTAL USER DOCUMENT

As you have learned, the *prjDocFractals* project will let the user draw six fractal images on the *udcFractal* user document. To select a single fractal image, you will use *CommandButton* controls that list each fractal by name. The ten *CommandButton* controls will let you clear the *udcFractal* user document, select a fractal to draw, open the *udcUserEquation* user document, and exit the *prjDocFractals* project. To add ten *CommandButton* controls and their enclosing frame to the *udcFractal* user document, perform the following steps:

1. If Visual Basic is not displaying the *udcFractal* user document within an object window, double-click your mouse on the user document's icon within the Project Explorer. Visual Basic will open the *udcFractal* user document.

2. Within Visual Basic, select the View menu Toolbox option. Visual Basic will open the Toolbox.

3. Within the Toolbox, double-click your mouse on the CommandButton icon. Visual Basic will draw a *CommandButton* control, *Command1*, within the *udcFractal* user document.

4. Repeat Step 3 nine more times until you have a total of ten command buttons within the *udcFractal* user document.

5. Within the Toolbox, double-click your mouse on the Frame icon. Visual Basic will draw a frame control, *Frame1*, within the *udcFractal* user document.

6. Within the *udcFractal* user document, click your mouse on the *Frame1* control to highlight it. Visual Basic will draw a small frame around the control.

7. Select the View menu Properties Window option. Visual Basic will open the Properties Window that lists the *Frame1* control's properties.

8. Within the Properties Window, change the *Frame1* control's properties to the values Table 20.3 lists.

Object	Property	Set As
Frame1	BackColor	&H00FFFFFF& (White)
Frame1	Caption	Drawing Commands
Frame1	Height	13665
Frame1	Left	2040
Frame1	Top	120
Frame1	Width	9495
Frame1	Name	fraFractals

*Table 20.3 The newly named **fraFractals** control's properties.*

9. Within the *udcFractal* user document, click your mouse on a *CommandButton* control to highlight it. Visual Basic will draw a small frame around the control.

10. Press the SHIFT key, hold it down, and click your mouse on each of the remaining *CommandButton* controls, in turn. Visual Basic will draw a small frame around each control.

11. Select the Edit menu Cut option to cut all the *CommandButton* controls and place them onto the Clipboard. Visual Basic will remove all the controls from the display.

12. Within the *udcFractal* user document, click your mouse on the *fraFractals* frame control to highlight it. Visual Basic will draw a small frame around the control.

13. Select the Edit menu Paste option to paste all ten *CommandButton* controls onto the *fraFractals* frame control.

14. Within the *fraFractals* frame control, click your mouse on a *CommandButton* control to highlight it. Visual Basic will draw a small frame around the control.

15. Select the View menu Properties Window option. Visual Basic will open the Properties Window that lists the selected *CommandButton* control's properties.

16. Within the Properties Window, change the highlighted *CommandButton* control's properties to the values Table 20.4 lists.

17. Repeat Steps 14, 15, and 16 until you have changed each *CommandButton* control's properties to the values Table 20.4 lists.

Object	Property	Set As
Command1	*Caption*	*Clear Screen*
Command1	*Height*	420
Command1	*Left*	120
Command1	*Top*	360
Command1	*Width*	1695
Command1	*Name*	*cmdCLS*
Command2	*Caption*	*Duff Fractal*
Command2	*Height*	420
Command2	*Left*	120
Command2	*Top*	840
Command2	*Width*	1695
Command2	*Name*	*cmdDuff*
Command3	*Caption*	*Mira Fractal*
Command3	*Height*	420
Command3	*Left*	1920
Command3	*Top*	360
Command3	*Width*	1695
Command3	*Name*	*cmdMira*
Command4	*Caption*	*Hopalong Fractal*
Command4	*Height*	420
Command4	*Left*	1920
Command4	*Top*	840
Command4	*Width*	1695
Command4	*Name*	*cmdHopalong*
Command5	*Caption*	*Kam Torus Fractal*
Command5	*Height*	420
Command5	*Left*	3720
Command5	*Top*	360
Command5	*Width*	1695

Table 20.4 *The **fraFractals** frame's **CommandButton** control properties. (continued on following page)*

Object	Property	Set As
Command5	Name	cmdKamTorus
Command6	Caption	Seahorse Fractal
Command6	Height	420
Command6	Left	3720
Command6	Top	840
Command6	Width	1695
Command6	Name	cmdSeahorse
Command7	Caption	User Fractal
Command7	Height	420
Command7	Left	5520
Command7	Top	360
Command7	Width	1815
Command7	Name	cmdUser
Command8	Caption	Mandelbrot Fractal
Command8	Height	420
Command8	Left	5520
Command8	Top	840
Command8	Width	1815
Command8	Name	cmdMandelbrot
Command9	Caption	Stop Drawing
Command9	Height	420
Command9	Left	7440
Command9	Top	360
Command9	Width	1815
Command9	Name	cmdStopDrawing
Command10	Caption	E&xit
Command10	Height	420
Command10	Left	7440
Command10	Top	840
Command10	Width	1815
Command10	Name	cmdExit

*Table 20.4 The **fraFractals** frame's **CommandButton** control properties. (continued from previous page)*

ADDING A SECOND FRAME CONTROL TO THE udcFRACTAL USER DOCUMENT

Within the *prjDocFractals* project, you will use *OptionButton* controls to select a drawing style, such as circles, lines, or boxes. In the *prjDocFractals* project, you will use a *Frame* control to contain the three *OptionButton* controls. To add a second *Frame* control to the *udcFractal* user document, perform the following steps:

1. If Visual Basic is not displaying the *udcFractal* user document within an object window, double-click your mouse on the user document's icon within the Project Explorer. Visual Basic will open the *udcFractal* user document.

2. Within Visual Basic, select the View menu Toolbox option. Visual Basic will open the Toolbox.

3. Within the Toolbox, double-click your mouse on the Frame icon. Visual Basic will draw a *Frame* control, *Frame1*, within the *udcFractal* user document.

4. Within the *udcFractal* user document, click your mouse on the *Frame1* control to highlight it. Visual Basic will draw a small frame around the control.

5. Select the View menu Properties Window option. Visual Basic will open the Properties Window that lists the *Frame1* control's properties.

6. Within the Properties Window, change the *Frame1* control's properties to the values Table 20.5 lists.

Object	Property	Set As
Frame1	*BackColor*	*&H00FFFFFF& (White)*
Frame1	*Caption*	*Select Style*
Frame1	*Height*	1365
Frame1	*Left*	120
Frame1	*Top*	120
Frame1	*Width*	1815
Frame1	*Name*	*fraStyle*

Table 20.5 *The newly named **fraStyle** control's properties.*

ADDING AN OPTIONBUTTON CONTROL ARRAY TO THE UDCFRACTAL USER DOCUMENT

As you have learned, your programs can use the *Circle* and *Line* methods to draw circles, lines, and boxes. In the *prjDocFractals* project, you will use three *OptionButton* controls in a control array to list a drawing choice. When you click your mouse on an *OptionButton* control, the *prjDocFractals* program will know what type of image to draw—a circle, a line, or a box. Remember, Visual Basic will assign a unique index value to each *OptionButton* control in a control array. In the *prjDocFractals* project, you will assign three index values: 0, 1, and 2 to the three *OptionButton* controls. To add three *OptionButton* controls to the *fraStyle* frame, perform the following steps:

1. If Visual Basic is not displaying the *udcFractal* user document within an object window, double-click your mouse on the *udcFractal* user document listing within the Project Explorer. Visual Basic will open the *udcFractal* user document.

2. Within Visual Basic, select the View menu Toolbox option. Visual Basic will open the Toolbox.

3. Within the Toolbox, double-click your mouse on the OptionButton icon. Visual Basic will draw an *OptionButton* control, *Option1*, within the *udcFractal* user document.

4. Within the *udcFractal* object window, click your mouse on the *Option1* control. Visual Basic will draw a small frame around the control.

5. Select the Edit menu Cut option. Visual Basic will remove the control from the display and place it on the Clipboard.

6. Click your mouse on the *fraStyle* frame control. Visual Basic will draw a small frame around the control.

7. Select the Edit menu Paste option. Visual Basic will paste the *Option1* control within the *fraStyle* frame.

8. Select the View menu Properties Window option. Visual Basic will open the Properties Window and display the *Option1* control's properties.

9. Within the Properties Window, change the control's *Name* property from *Option1* to *optDrawStyle*.

10. Within the *fraStyle* frame control, click your mouse on the newly named *optDrawStyle* control. Next, select the Edit menu Copy option. Visual Basic will highlight the *optDrawStyle* control and copy it to the Clipboard.

11. Select the Edit menu Paste option. Visual Basic will display a dialog box that asks, "You already have a control named *optDrawStyle*. Do you want to create a control array?" Click your mouse on the Yes button. Visual Basic will add a copy of the *optDrawStyle* control to the *fraStyle* frame.

605

12. Select the Edit menu Paste option. Visual Basic will draw another copy of the *optDrawStyle* control within the *fraStyle* frame.

13. Within the *fraStyle* frame control, click your mouse on an *optDrawStyle* control to highlight it. Visual Basic will draw a small frame around the control.

14. Select the View menu Properties Window option. Visual Basic will open the Properties Window and display the *optDrawStyle* control's properties.

15. Within the Properties Window, change the highlighted control's properties to the values Table 20.6 lists.

16. Repeat Steps 13, 14, and 15 until you have changed each *optDrawStyle* control to the values Table 20.6 lists.

Object	Property	Set As
optDrawStyle(0)	*BackColor*	*&H00FFFFFF& (White)*
optDrawStyle(0)	*Caption*	*Circles*
optDrawStyle(0)	*Height*	195
optDrawStyle(0)	*Left*	375
optDrawStyle(0)	*Top*	360
optDrawStyle(0)	*Width*	975
optDrawStyle(1)	*BackColor*	*&H00FFFFFF& (White)*
optDrawStyle(1)	*Caption*	*Lines*
optDrawStyle(1)	*Height*	195
optDrawStyle(1)	*Left*	375
optDrawStyle(1)	*Top*	720
optDrawStyle(1)	*Width*	975
optDrawStyle(1)	*BackColor*	*&H00FFFFFF& (White)*
optDrawStyle(2)	*Caption*	*Boxes*
optDrawStyle(2)	*Height*	195
optDrawStyle(2)	*Left*	375
optDrawStyle(2)	*Top*	1080
optDrawStyle(2)	*Width*	975

*Table 20.6 The **optDrawStyle** control array's properties.*

ADDING CONTROLS TO THE udcUSEREQUATION USER DOCUMENT

As you learned in this chapter's "Using the *prjDocFractals* Project" section, you will use the *udcUserEquation* user document to enter a user-defined equation. To design the *udcUserEquation* user document, you will add *Label* controls, which will display each section of a user-defined mathematical equation, and *TextBox* controls, which will let you enter a user-defined mathematical equation. You will also add *CommandButton* controls, which will let you clear the *udcUserEquation* user document and draw an image of a user-defined equation within the document. Finally, you will add *OptionButton* controls to the user document, which will let the user select different shapes for the program to use when it draws your user-defined equation.

ADDING LABEL CONTROLS TO THE udcUSEREQUATION USER DOCUMENT

As you have learned, you will use the *udcUserEquation* user document to enter a user-defined equation. The user-defined equation will consist of *X1*, *X2*, and *X3* values, together with varying powers and multipliers that the program will use to determine the points at which it will plot the equation. The program code will evaluate the equation to determine the equation's *Y* value. Within the *udcUserEquation* user document, you will use *Label* controls to display the headings that correspond to each section of the user-defined equation. To add *Label* controls to the *udcUserEquation* user document, perform the following steps:

1. If Visual Basic is not displaying the *udcUserEquation* user document within an object window, double-click your mouse on the *udcUserEquation* user document listing within the Project Explorer. Visual Basic will open the *udcUserEquation* user document.

2. Within Visual Basic, select the View menu Toolbox option. Visual Basic will open the Toolbox.

3. Within the Toolbox, double-click your mouse on the Label icon. Visual Basic will draw a *Label* control, *Label1*, within the *udcUserEquation* user document.

4. Repeat Step 3 ten more times until you have eleven *Label* controls within the *udcUserEquation* user document.

5. Within the *udcUserEquation* window, click your mouse on a *Label* control to highlight it. Visual Basic will draw a small frame around the control.

6. Select the View menu Properties Window option. Visual Basic will open the Properties Window that lists the *Label* control's properties.

7. Within the Properties Window, change the highlighted control's properties to the values Table 20.7 lists.

8. Repeat Steps 5, 6, and 7 until you have changed each *Label* control's properties to the values Table 20.7 lists.

607

Object	Property	Set As
Label1	*Caption*	*Y=X1^(a) + X2^(b) + X3^(c) + K/1000*
Label1	*Height*	375
Label1	*Left*	1920
Label1	*Top*	120
Label1	*Width*	4935
Label1	*Name*	*lblEquation*
Label2	*Caption*	*Enter X Multiple*
Label2	*Height*	375
Label2	*Left*	1920
Label2	*Top*	600
Label2	*Width*	1455
Label2	*Name*	*lblXMultiple*
Label3	*Caption*	*Enter Power*
Label3	*Height*	375
Label3	*Left*	3480
Label3	*Top*	600
Label3	*Width*	1455
Label3	*Name*	*lblPower*
Label4	*Caption*	*Enter Constant*
Label4	*Height*	375
Label4	*Left*	5040
Label4	*Top*	600
Label4	*Width*	1815
Label4	*Name*	*lblConstant*

Table 20.7 *The **udcUserEquation** user document's **Label** control properties. (continued on following page)*

Object	Property	Set As
Label5	Caption	X1 =
Label5	Height	375
Label5	Left	1920
Label5	Top	1080
Label5	Width	735
Label5	Name	lblX1
Label6	Caption	X2 =
Label6	Height	375
Label6	Left	1920
Label6	Top	1440
Label6	Width	735
Label6	Name	lblX2
Label7	Caption	X3 =
Label7	Height	375
Label7	Left	1920
Label7	Top	1800
Label7	Width	735
Label7	Name	lblX3
Label8	Caption	a =
Label8	Height	375
Label8	Left	3480
Label8	Top	1080
Label8	Width	735
Label8	Name	lblA
Label9	Caption	b =
Label9	Height	375
Label9	Left	3480
Label9	Top	1440
Label9	Width	735
Label9	Name	lblB
Label10	Caption	c =
Label10	Height	375
Label10	Left	3480
Label10	Top	1800
Label10	Width	735
Label10	Name	lblC
Label11	Caption	K =
Label11	Height	375
Label11	Left	5040
Label11	Top	1080
Label11	Width	735
Label11	Name	lblK

Table 20.7 The **udcUserEquation** user document's **Label** control properties. (continued from previous page)

ADDING TEXTBOX CONTROLS TO THE udcUserEquation USER DOCUMENT

As you have learned, you will use the *udcUserEquation* user document to enter a user-defined equation. Within the *udcUserEquation* user document, you will add *TextBox* controls that will store each section of the user-defined mathematical equation. To add *TextBox* controls to the *udcUserEquation* user document, perform the following steps:

1. If Visual Basic is not displaying the *udcUserEquation* user document within an object window, double-click your mouse on the *udcUserEquation* user document listing within the Project Explorer. Visual Basic will open the *udcUserEquation* user document.

2. Within Visual Basic, select the View menu Toolbox option. Visual Basic will open the Toolbox.

3. Within the Toolbox, double-click your mouse on the TextBox icon. Visual Basic will draw a *TextBox* control, *Text1*, within the *udcUserEquation* user document.

4. Repeat Step 3 six more times until Visual Basic displays seven *TextBox* controls within the *udcUserEquation* user document.

5. Within the *udcUserEquation* window, click your mouse on a *TextBox* control to highlight it. Visual Basic will draw a small frame around the control.

6. Select the View menu Properties Window option. Visual Basic will open the Properties Window that lists the *TextBox* control's properties.

7. Within the Properties Window, change the highlighted *TextBox* control's properties to the values Table 20.8 lists.

8. Repeat Steps 5, 6, and 7 until you have changed each *TextBox* control's properties to the values Table 20.8 lists.

Object	Property	Set As
Text1	Text	1
Text1	Height	360
Text1	Left	2760
Text1	Top	1080
Text1	Width	495
Text1	Name	txtX1
Text2	Text	0
Text2	Height	360
Text2	Left	2760
Text2	Top	1440
Text2	Width	495
Text2	Name	txtX2
Text3	Text	0
Text3	Height	360
Text3	Left	2760
Text3	Top	1800
Text3	Width	495
Text3	Name	txtX3
Text4	Text	0
Text4	Height	360
Text4	Left	4320
Text4	Top	1080

Table 20.8 The **udcUserEquation** user document's **TextBox** control properties. *(continued on following page)*

Object	Property	Set As
Text4	Width	495
Text4	Name	txtA
Text5	Text	0
Text5	Height	360
Text5	Left	4320
Text5	Top	1440
Text5	Width	495
Text5	Name	txtB
Text6	Text	0
Text6	Height	360
Text6	Left	4320
Text6	Top	1800
Text6	Width	495
Text6	Name	txtC
Text7	Text	0
Text7	Height	360
Text7	Left	6120
Text7	Top	1080
Text7	Width	735
Text7	Name	txtK

Table 20.8 The **udcUserEquation** user document's **TextBox** control properties. (continued from previous page)

ADDING COMMAND BUTTONS TO THE UDCUSEREQUATION USER DOCUMENT

As you have learned, you will use the *udcUserEquation* user document to enter a user-defined equation. Within the *udcUserEquation* user document, you will add *CommandButton* controls that will let you clear the user document and draw a fractal image based on the user-defined equation. To add *CommandButton* controls to the *udcUserEquation* user document, perform the following steps:

1. If Visual Basic is not displaying the *udcUserEquation* user document within an object window, double-click your mouse on the *udcUserEquation* user document listing within the Project Explorer. Visual Basic will open the *udcUserEquation* user document.

2. Within Visual Basic, select the View menu Toolbox option. Visual Basic will open the Toolbox.

3. Within the Toolbox, double-click your mouse on the CommandButton icon. Visual Basic will draw a *CommandButton* control, *Command1*, within the *udcUserEquation* user document.

4. Repeat Step 3 two more times until Visual Basic displays three *CommandButton* controls within the *udcUserEquation* user document.

5. Within the *udcUserEquation* window, click your mouse on a *CommandButton* control to highlight it. Visual Basic will draw a small frame around the control.

6. Select the View menu Properties Window option. Visual Basic will open the Properties Window that lists the *CommandButton* control's properties.

7. Within the Properties Window, change the highlighted *CommandButton* control's properties to the values Table 20.9 lists.

8. Repeat Steps 5, 6, and 7 until you have changed each *CommandButton* control's properties to the values Table 20.9 lists.

Object	Property	Set As
Command1	*Caption*	*Clear Screen*
Command1	*Height*	495
Command1	*Left*	7080
Command1	*Top*	120
Command1	*Width*	1455
Command1	*Name*	*cmdClearPlot*
Command2	*Caption*	*Plot Equation*
Command2	*Height*	495
Command2	*Left*	7080
Command2	*Top*	720
Command2	*Width*	1455
Command2	*Name*	*cmdPlotUser*
Command3	*Caption*	*E&xit*
Command3	*Height*	495
Command3	*Left*	7080
Command3	*Top*	1320
Command3	*Width*	1455
Command3	*Name*	*cmdExit*

*Table 20.9 The **udcUserEquation** user document's **CommandButton** control properties.*

Adding the Frame Control to the udcUserEquation User Document

Within the *udcUserEquation* user document, you will use *OptionButton* controls to select a drawing style, such as circles, lines, or boxes. In the *prjDocFractals* project, you will use a *Frame* control to contain the three *OptionButton* controls. To add the *Frame* control to the *udcUserEquation* user document, perform the following steps:

1. If Visual Basic is not displaying the *udcFractal* user document within an object window, double-click your mouse on the *udcFractal* user document listing within the Project Explorer. Visual Basic will open the *udcFractal* user document.

2. Within the *udcFractal* user document, click your mouse on the *fraStyle* control. Visual Basic will draw a small frame around the control.

3. Within Visual Basic, select the Edit menu Copy option.

4. If Visual Basic is not displaying the *udcUserEquation* user document within an object window, double-click your mouse on the *udcUserEquation* user document listing within the Project Explorer. Visual Basic will open the *udcUserEquation* user document.

5. Click your mouse anywhere on the *udcUserEquation* user document. Visual Basic will draw a frame around the document.

6. Select the Edit menu Paste option. Visual Basic will paste the copied *fraStyle* control onto the *udcUserEquation* user document.

7. Within the *udcUserEquation* user document, click your mouse on the *fraStyle* control to highlight it. Visual Basic will draw a small frame around the control.

8. Select the View menu Properties Window option. Visual Basic will open the Properties Window that lists the *fraStyle* control's properties.

9. Within the Properties Window, change the *fraStyle* control's properties to the values Table 20.10 lists.

VISUAL BASIC PROGRAMMER'S LIBRARY

Object	Property	Set As
fraStyle	*Height*	1365
fraStyle	*Left*	120
fraStyle	*Top*	120
fraStyle	*Width*	1815

Table 20.10 *The **fraStyle** control's properties.*

BETTER UNDERSTANDING CABINET (CAB) FILES

As you have learned, when you create ActiveX documents or other ActiveX components you wish to distribute over the Internet, you will package those files within a Microsoft Cabinet (or *CAB*) file. Later in this chapter, you will learn how to create an Internet distribution for your ActiveX components.

When you create ActiveX controls, ActiveX DLLs, ActiveX EXEs, and ActiveX documents from within Visual Basic that a user can then access within an Internet browser, you must refer to the ActiveX component in the underlying HTML code, perhaps using VBScript. In other words, you must host each control you create on one or more Web pages.

The Web pages, along with your component and any other dependent files, resides at a specific location on the World Wide Web. When the user accesses this Web page, the browser will activate your control. In other words, the user's browser will download the component (in the form of a compressed *CAB* file) along with the Web page to the user's computer. The user's browser then verifies the component for safety, decompresses the component, registers the component in the Windows registry, installs the component, and *then* activates the component.

When you create an Internet distribution, with the Visual Basic Application Setup Wizard, the Setup Wizard will create a *CAB* file, known as the primary *CAB* file, which contains the following files:

- The project components, such as the ActiveX control, ActiveX DLL, or ActiveX EXE.

- The *.inf* file, which contains links to other *CAB* files that contain Visual Basic support files and controls, as well as other information, such as whether the control is safe for scripting and safe for initialization and registry information as defined by the user. This file replaces the *Setup.lst* file that the Setup Wizard creates in the standard setup.

- Reserved space for digital signatures.

- All files that are not in other (secondary) *CAB* files.

For ActiveX control projects, ActiveX EXEs, and ActiveX DLLs, the Application Setup Wizard packages all run-time components—such as *msvbvm50.dll*, individual controls, Data Access Objects (DAO), and Remote Data Objects (RDO)— into separate *CAB* files. The Application Setup Wizard will then place the *CAB* files on the Microsoft Web site. You can choose to link your files to the *CAB* files on the Microsoft Web site, or you can download local copies of them (as you will learn later in this chapter). The benefit of using secondary *CAB* files from a Web site include the following:

- You do not need to distribute all the *CAB* files your application requires. The only file you need to distribute is the primary *CAB* file.

- The *.inf* file within the primary *CAB* file points to the Microsoft Web site and downloads the necessary *CAB* files based on the end user's needs.

- Secondary *CAB* files provide an efficient means of delivering updates to your product.

Note: *If you cannot or do not want your application setup to require a connection to the Internet, you may place the secondary **CAB** files on a server within your intranet. An intranet lets users download components more quickly and also keeps the users on a secure network.*

WRITING THE CODE FOR THE PRJDOCFRACTALS PROJECT

In the *prjDocFractals* project, you will write code for each control on the *udcFractal* and *udcUserEquation* user documents, and you will write procedures and functions to communicate with each control. First, you will create a structure within the *mdlFractal* module. Second, you will declare local and global variables that the procedures and functions within the program will use to perform the program's processing. Finally, you will write code for each procedure and function.

DECLARING THE STRUCTURE AND THE GLOBAL VARIABLES

As you have learned, your programs can use Visual Basic structures to maintain groups of information within a single location. In the *prjDocFractals* project, you will use a structure, *ImageData,* to maintain information that the program code will use to draw the *Line* and *Circle* component objects for the fractals. The *ImageData* structure will include information that describes where the drawing method should draw the current circle, line, or box, the object's size and color, and other important member values. As you have learned, you must define structures within modules. In the *prjDocFractals* project, you will define the *ImageData* structure within the *mdlFractal* module. The declarations for the *prjDocFractals* project are identical to those within Chapter 5's *mdlFractal* module. You can find the declarations in the *mdlFractal* module in the *Chapter20* directory on the companion CD-ROM that accompanies this book.

613

WRITING THE CODE FOR THE INITCOLORARRAY PROCEDURE

As you have learned, the *prjDocFractals* program uses a custom color array to draw the Mandelbrot fractal. When the program begins, the *udcFractal's User Document_Initialize* event calls the *InitColorArray* procedure, which assigns values to the array. The *InitColorArray* procedure within the *prjDocFractals* project is identical to the *InitColorArray* procedure within Chapter 5's *mdlFractal* module. You can find the procedure in the *mdlFractal* module in the *Chapter20* directory on the companion CD-ROM that accompanies this book.

WRITING THE CODE FOR THE UDCFRACTAL USER DOCUMENT

The *udcFractal* user document uses several variables throughout its processing. One variable (*Plot*) contains the plot data for the fractals the program draws and another variable (*pRange*) contains a range limiter (a value that specifies the upper-size boundary of the range in which the *Mandelbrot* equation will draw). The following code implements the variable declarations for the *udcFractal* user document:

```
Option Explicit

Dim Plot As ImageData
Public EVENT_FLAG As Boolean
Dim mbPoint1 As POINT
Dim mbPoint1Result As POINT
Dim mbPoint2Result As POINT
Dim ColorToDraw As Long
Dim pRange As Integer
Dim Circles As Boolean
```

The *Plot* variable is of the *ImageData* type, which you declared when you wrote the program code for the *mdlFractal* module. You will use the three variables of type *POINT* (which begin with the *mbPoint* identifier), the *EVENT_FLAG* variable, and the *ColorToDraw* variable to draw the Mandelbrot Fractal.

Note: *Unlike the **prjFractals** program code you wrote in Chapter 5, you must include the program code to draw the Mandelbrot Fractal within the user document itself because user document projects do not support classes.*

As you learned, the *prjDocFractals* project begins with the display of the *udcFractal* user document. When you run the project from within *Internet Explorer,* the *udcFractal* user document loads, which results in the program invoking the *User Document_Initialize* event. The following code implements the *udcFractal* user document's *User Document_Initialize* event:

```
Private Sub UserDocument_Initialize()
   Circles = True
   InitColorArray
   Plot.Shape = 0
End Sub
```

The *User Document_Initialize* event calls the *InitColorArray* procedure. As you have learned, the *InitColorArray* procedure initializes the color array that the program will use to draw the Mandelbrot Fractal. After the *InitColorArray* procedure finishes its processing, the *User Document_Initialize* event then initializes the drawing mode to circles (which mode corresponds to the first selection in the *optDrawStyle* array).

WRITING THE CODE FOR THE DRAW PROCEDURE

As you have learned, the *prjDocFractals* program will calculate many values of a math equation and draw an image on your computer screen at the series of calculated *X* and *Y* values that the math equation describes. The *Draw* procedure will receive the calculated values and all the values in the *ImageData* structure, alter the values, and send them to the *DrawShape* procedure. The *Draw* procedure within the *udcFractal* user document is identical to the *Draw* procedure within Chapter 5's *frmFractals* form. You can find the procedure in the *udcFractal* user document in the *Chapter20* directory on the companion CD-ROM that accompanies this book.

WRITING THE CODE FOR THE DRAWSHAPE PROCEDURE

Now that you have written the code for the *Draw* procedure, which will pass values to the *DrawShape* procedure, you can write the code for the *DrawShape* procedure. The *DrawShape* procedure will receive three color values from the *Draw* procedure, check the *Plot* object's *Shape* element to determine whether to draw a circle, line, or box shape, and then use the *Circle* or *Line* method to draw images on the *udcFractal* user document. The *DrawShape* procedure within the *udcFractal* user document is identical to the *DrawShape* procedure within Chapter 5's *frmFractals* form. You can find the procedure in the *udcFractal* user document in the *Chapter20* directory on the companion CD-ROM that accompanies this book.

WRITING THE CODE FOR THE OPTDRAWSTYLE_CLICK EVENT

After you declare the *ImageData* structure in the *mdlFractal* module, you can set the *ImageData* structure's elements. The *Plot* object contains the *ImageData* structure's elements. The *optDrawStyle* control's *Click* event will set the *Plot* object's *Shape* element to an integer value that represents a circle, a line, or a box. Remember, Visual Basic references each *optDrawStyle* control in the control array with an index value from 0 to 2. When you click your mouse on the *optDrawStyle* control, Visual Basic will store the underlying index value in memory. The following code implements the *optDrawStyle_Click* event:

```
Private Sub optDrawStyle_Click(Index As Integer)
   Plot.Shape = Index
End Sub
```

The *optDrawStyle* control's *Click* event assigns the *Index* value to the *Plot.Shape* member. As you learned in the previous section, the *DrawShape* function will use the *Plot* object's *Shape* member to determine what shape to use to draw the fractal.

WRITING THE CODE FOR THE CMDCLS_CLICK EVENT

As you have learned, the *prjDocFractals* project uses the user document's display area as its drawing area. When you run the *prjDocFractals* project, you will note that you can draw several fractals on top of each other. To avoid clutter and confusion, you will often want to clear the drawing area. As you know, you added the Clear Screen command button to the *udcFractal* user document for just that purpose. The following code implements the *cmdCLS_Click* event:

```
Private Sub cmdCls_Click()
   Me.Refresh
End Sub
```

The procedure calls the *Refresh* method, which clears the user document's area. If you instead set the user document's *AutoRedraw* property to *True* to clear the drawing area, clearing the user document would be somewhat more complex (because the program would actually draw over the existing fractal, rather than simply refreshing the form). Opening another program in front of the *udcFractal* user document will also clear the user document.

WRITING THE CODE FOR THE CMDSTOPDRAWING_CLICK EVENT

Because the fractal images the *prjDocFractals* program draws are, in some cases, quite large, it is useful to have the option to stop drawing a fractal image during its processing. To let the user stop drawing an image, the *udcFractal* user document includes the Stop Drawing button. The Stop Drawing button sets the global *StopPainting* flag, which the program code monitors. The program code will stop drawing a fractal if the flag becomes *True*. The following code implements the *cmdStopDrawing_Click* event:

```
Private Sub cmdStopDrawing_Click()
   StopPainting = True
End Sub
```

WRITING THE CODE FOR THE CMDEXIT_CLICK EVENT

The last event you must write before you begin to write the program code that will draw the fractal images is the *cmdExit_Click* event, which unloads the user document and ends the program. The following code implements the *cmdExit_Click* event:

```
Private Sub cmdExit_Click()
   End
End Sub
```

WRITING THE CMDHOPALONG_CLICK EVENT

When you click your mouse on the Hopalong Fractal button on the *udcFractal* user document, the user document will invoke the button's *Click* event. The *Click* event will declare some variables, fill the *Plot* object's elements, and calculate the *X* and *Y* values. Remember, the *Plot* object will store the *ImageData* structure elements and will be available to all procedures and functions within the *udcFractal* user document. The *cmdHopalong_Click* procedure within the *udcFractal* user document is identical to the *cmdHopalong_Click* procedure within Chapter 5's *frmFractals* form. You can find the procedure in the *udcFractal* user document in the *Chapter20* directory on the companion CD-ROM that accompanies this book.

WRITING THE CMDKAMTORUS_CLICK EVENT

When you click your mouse on the Kam Torus Fractal button on the *udcFractal* user document, your program will invoke its *Click* event. The *Click* event will declare some useful variables, fill the *Plot* object's elements, and calculate the *X* and *Y* values. Remember, the *Plot* object will store the *ImageData* structure elements and will be available to all procedures and functions within the *udcFractal* user document. The *cmdKamTorus_Click* procedure within the *udcFractal* user document is identical to the *cmdKamTorus_Click* procedure within Chapter 5's *frmFractals* form. You can find the procedure in the *udcFractal* user document in the *Chapter20* directory on the companion CD-ROM that accompanies this book.

WRITING THE CMDDUFF_CLICK EVENT

When you click your mouse on the Duff Fractal button on the *udcFractal* user document, your program will invoke its *Click* event. The *Click* event will declare some useful variables, fill the *Plot* object's elements, and calculate the *X* and *Y* values. Remember, the *Plot* object will store the *ImageData* structure elements and will be available to all procedures and functions within the *udcFractal* user document. The *cmdDuff_Click* procedure within the *udcFractal* user document is identical to the *cmdDuff_Click* procedure within Chapter 5's *frmFractals* form. You can find the procedure in the *udcFractal* user document in the *Chapter20* directory on the companion CD-ROM that accompanies this book.

WRITING THE CODE FOR THE CMDMIRA_CLICK EVENT

When you click your mouse on the Mira Fractal button on the *udcFractal* user document, the user document will invoke the button's *Click* event. The *Click* event will declare some useful variables, fill the *Plot* object's elements, and calculate the *X* and *Y* values. Remember, the *Plot* object will store the *ImageData* structure elements and will be available to all procedures and functions within the *udcFractal* user document. The *cmdMira_Click* procedure within the *udcFractal* user document is identical to the *cmdMira_Click* procedure within Chapter 5's *frmFractals* form. You can find the procedure in the *udcFractal* user document in the *Chapter20* directory on the companion CD-ROM that accompanies this book.

WRITING THE CODE FOR THE CMDSEAHORSE_CLICK EVENT

When you click your mouse on the Seahorse Fractal button on the *udcFractal* user document, your program will invoke its *Click* event. The *Click* event will declare some useful variables, fill the *Plot* object's elements, and calculate the *X* and *Y* values. Remember, the *Plot* object will store the *ImageData* structure elements and will be available to all procedures and functions within the *udcFractal* user document. The *cmdSeahorse_Click* procedure within the *udcFractal* user document is identical to the *cmdSeahorse_Click* procedure within Chapter 5's *frmFractals* form. You can find the procedure in the *udcFractal* user document in the *Chapter20* directory on the companion CD-ROM that accompanies this book.

WRITING THE CMDUSERFUNCTION_CLICK EVENT

As you have learned, the *prjDocFractals* project lets you draw an image from your own user-defined equation. When you click your mouse on the User Fractal button, the *udcFractal* user document will invoke the button's *Click* event. The *Click* event will use the *Internet Explorer* container's *Hyperlink.NavigateTo* method to open the *udcUserEquation* user document. After Visual Basic displays the *udcUserEquation* user document, you can enter your own user-defined equation and draw an image of it. The following code implements the *cmdUserFunction_Click* event:

```
Private Sub cmdUserFunction_Click()
  StopPainting = True
  UserDocument.Hyperlink.NavigateTo App.Path & _
      "\swsetup\udcUserEquation.vbd"
End Sub
```

The *cmdUserFunction_Click* event uses the *NavigateTo* method to open the *udcUserEquation* ActiveX document. The *Internet Explorer* container exposes the *Hyperlink* object and its *NavigateTo* method for your user documents to access.

MORE ON THE MANDELBROT FRACTAL

As you have learned, the *prjDocFractals* project will draw images from math equations. One equation will produce an image called the *Mandelbrot Fractal*. The Mandelbrot Fractals are some of the most commonly seen and drawn fractals. Because minor variations you make within the equation can have far-reaching consequences in the final image, Mandelbrot Fractals can look radically different, depending on the variation of the equation you use to draw the fractal.

WRITING THE CMDMANDELBROT_CLICK EVENT

The *cmdMandelbrot_Click* event is deceptively simple. Although the Mandelbrot Fractal clearly appears to be the most complex fractal this chapter explains, the *cmdMandelbrot_Click* event contains only five lines. The following code implements the *cmdMandelbrot_Click* event:

```
Private Sub cmdMandelbrot_Click()
  StopPainting = False
  UserDocument.Refresh
  UserDocument.ScaleMode = 3        ' Pixels
  pRange = UserDocument.ScaleWidth
  MBFractal
End Sub
```

The *cmdMandelbrot_Click* event sets the flag variable, refreshes the user document (clearing the drawing area), sets the *ScaleMode* to pixels, sets the drawing range to the user document's width in pixels, and calls the *MBFractal* procedure. In fact, the *MBFractal* procedure invokes the Mandelbrot figure's drawing routine, which performs extensive processing. In the next several sections, you will write the code to draw the Mandelbrot figure, as well as the component structures that support the Mandelbrot color's computations.

WRITING THE CODE FOR THE MDLPOINT MODULE

The *Mandelbrot* class uses an object of type *POINT*, which represents an *x*-coordinate and a *y*-coordinate, to determine where it will draw next. The *prjDocFractals* project declares both the *POINT* structure and the only function that returns any *POINT* information, *ConstructPoint*, within the *mdlPoint* module. The *mdlPoint* module within the *prjDocFractals* project is identical to the *mdlPoint* module within Chapter 5's *prjFractals* project. You can find the code for the *mdlPoint* module in the *Chapter20* directory on the companion CD-ROM that accompanies this book.

WRITING THE CODE FOR THE MDLCOMPLEX MODULE

617

If you have worked with advanced mathematics at all, you are probably familiar with the concept of a complex number. A *complex number* is a number that has both a real and an imaginary component. For example, the value $(3 + 3^{1/2})$ has a real component (3) and an imaginary component $(3^{1/2})$. The *Mandelbrot* class uses complex numbers extensively when determining what color to draw a given point. The Visual Basic functions you use to manipulate complex numbers might be something you can reuse in other programs, so the function and the type definition are all within the *mdlComplex* module. The *mdlComplex* module within the *prjDocFractals* project is identical to the *mdlComplex* module within Chapter 5's *prjFractals* project. You can find the code for the *mdlComplex* module in the *Chapter20* directory on the companion CD-ROM that accompanies this book.

BETTER UNDERSTANDING COMPLEX NUMBERS

As you have learned, a complex number is a number that has both a real and an imaginary component. In fact, a complex number is any number in the form $a + bi$, where both *a* and *b* are real numbers, and *i* is an imaginary number whose square is -1. Because squaring a number always yields a positive value (for example (-5)*(-5)=25), a number whose square is a negative number must be an imaginary number. By mathematical rules, a real number multiplied by an imaginary number must yield an imaginary number. Therefore, a complex number consists of a real number (*a*) and an imaginary number (*bi*).

WRITING THE MBFRACTAL FUNCTION

As you have learned, when the user clicks the mouse on the *cmdMandelbrot* command button, the program code invokes the *MBFractal* function. The *MBFractal* function performs processing similar to the processing that all the other fractals in this chapter perform—that is, it progresses through a series of loops, drawing points each time through the loop. The *MBFractal* function differs from the fractal code you have seen previously in that it actually draws *every point on the screen*. The computations for the Mandelbrot Fractal center around determining each point's color, rather than its location. The following code implements the *MBFractal* function:

```
Private Function MBFractal()
   Dim ix As Double, iy As Double
   Dim radius As Long

   For iy = 1 To pRange - 2
     For ix = 1 To pRange - 2
       Dim mbpoint2 As POINT
       mbPoint2Result = ConstructPoint(ix, iy)
       mbPoint1 = mbPoint2Result
```

```
            Call calcPoint
            udcFractals.Circle (mbPoint1.x, 100 + mbPoint1.y), 1, ColorToDraw
            DoEvents
            If StopPainting Then Exit Function
        Next ix
    Next iy
End Function
```

The *MBFractal* function loops through every pixel on the drawing area (unless the user clicks the mouse on the Stop Drawing button). The *MBFractal* function creates a point based on the loops' current value and calls the *calcPoint* function, which uses the point to determine what color to draw the point. The *MBFractal* function then draws a circle, one pixel wide, with the color that *calcPoint* sets. After drawing the pixel, the program checks the *StopPainting* flag. If the flag is *False*, the program loops again.

618

WRITING THE *CALCPOINT* FUNCTION

As you have learned, the *calcPoint* function accepts a point from the *Paint* function and uses a series of mathematical equations to determine the correct color to draw that point. The *calcPoint* function uses the *COMPLEX* number definitions that you wrote earlier in this chapter. The *calcPoint* function in the *prjDocFractals* project is identical to the function you created within the *prjFractals* project, except it is located within the user document, rather than in the *clsMandelbrot* class module.

WRITING THE CODE FOR THE *UDCUSEREQUATION* USER DOCUMENT

As you have learned, the *prjDocFractals* project will let you draw an image of your own user-defined equation. After you click your mouse on the User Fractal button on the *udcFractal* user document, Visual Basic will open the *udcUserEquation* user document. As you know, you have added *Label*, *TextBox*, and *CommandButton* controls to the *udcUserEquation* user document, which will let you enter a user-defined mathematical equation. The *udcUserEquation* user document code will use a procedure similar to the *udcFractal* user document's *Draw* procedure, called *DrawUser*, to plot your user-defined function.

DECLARING THE *UDCUSEREQUATION* USER DOCUMENT'S VARIABLES

Just as the *udcFractal's* user document did, the *udcUserEquation* user document uses a *Plot* structure to manage the image the program is drawing on the user document. Additionally, the *udcUserEquation* user document uses a flag value to ensure the program does not try to plot functions with out-of-range values (values too large or too small to plot on the user document). The following code implements the *udcUserEquation* user document's variable declarations:

```
Dim Plot As ImageData
Dim OutofRange As Boolean
```

WRITING THE *UDCUSEREQUATION'S* USER DOCUMENT_INITIALIZE EVENT

As you have learned, the user will invoke the *udcUserEquation* user document from within the *udcFractal* user document. When the user clicks the mouse on the User Equation button *(cmdUserEquation)*, the program code will load the *udcUserEquation* user document. As with other user documents, the first event the program will invoke is the *UserDocument_Initialize* event. The following code implements the *udcUserEquation's* *UserDocument_Initialize* event:

```
Private Sub UserDocument_Initialize()
    ScaleMode = 3
End Sub
```

The *UserDocument_Initialize* event sets the *ScaleMode* for the user document to pixels, which the program code then uses when it draws the images. The *UserDocument_Initialize* event performs identical processing to the *prjFractals* project's *frmUserEquation* form's *Load* event.

Writing the cmdClearPlot_Click Event

As you learned with the *udcFractal* user document, you can click your mouse on the Clear Screen button to clear a user document's drawing area. The following code implements the *udcUserEquation's cmdClearPlot_Click* event, which is identical to the *frmUserEquation* form's *cmdClearPlot_Click* event in the *prjFractals* project:

```
Private Sub cmdClearPlot_Click()
  Me.Refresh
End Sub
```

As with the *udcFractal* user document's *cmdCLS_Click* event, refreshing the *udcUserEquation* user document erases any existing drawing, clearing the palette for other drawings. If you set the *udcUserEquation* user document's *AutoRedraw* property to *True*, clearing the user document would be somewhat more complex (because you would have to draw over every point to erase the user document). Opening another program in front of the *udcUserEquation* user document will also clear it.

619

Writing the cmdExit_Click Event

When you finish drawing your own equations on the *udcUserEquation* user document, you can return to the *udcFractal* user document. To return to the *udcFractal* user document, click your mouse on the Exit button. The following code implements the *cmdExit_Click* event:

```
Private Sub cmdExit_Click()
  UserDocument.Hyperlink.NavigateTo App.Path & "\udcFractals.vbd"
End Sub
```

The *cmdExit_Click* event uses the *NavigateTo* method to return the *Internet Explorer* to the *udcFractal.vbd* file that references the *udcFractal* ActiveX document after compilation.

Writing the cmdPlotUser_Click Event

After you enter a user-defined equation on the *udcUserEquation* user document, you can write code that will calculate values from the equation. When you click your mouse on the Plot Function button on the *udcUserEquation* user document, your program will invoke its *Click* event. The *Click* event will declare some useful variables, fill the *Plot* object's elements, and calculate the *X* and *Y* values. Remember, the *Plot* object will store the *ImageData* structure elements and will be available to all procedures and functions within the user document. The *PlotUser_Click* procedure within the *udcUserEquation* user document is identical to the *PlotUser_Click* procedure within Chapter 5's *frmUserEquation* form. You can find the procedure in the *udcUserEquation* user document in the *Chapter20* directory on the companion CD-ROM that accompanies this book.

Writing the Code for the DrawUser Procedure

After you enter an equation into the *udcUserEquation* user document, you can draw an image. As you learned, the *cmdPlotUser_Click* event calls the *DrawUser* procedure to draw the equation. The *DrawUser* procedure will use the *Circle* method to draw an image. The *DrawUser* procedure within the *udcUserEquation* user document is identical to the *DrawUser* procedure within Chapter 5's *frmUserEquation* form. You can find the procedure in the *udcUserEquation* user document in the *Chapter20* directory on the companion CD-ROM that accompanies this book.

Writing the Code for the DrawShape Procedure

Now that you have written the code for the *DrawUser* procedure, which will pass values to the *DrawShape* procedure, you can write the code for the *DrawShape* procedure. As with *udcFractal*, the *DrawShape* procedure will receive three color values from the *DrawUser* procedure, check the *Plot* object's *Shape* element to determine whether to draw a circle, line, or box shape, and then use the *Circle* or *Line* method to draw images on the *udcUserEquation* user document. The *DrawUser* procedure within the *udcUserEquation* user document is identical to the *DrawUser* procedure within Chapter 5's *frmUserEquation* form. You can find the procedure in the *udcUserEquation* user document in the *Chapter20* directory on the companion CD-ROM that accompanies this book.

WRITING THE CODE FOR THE *optDRAWSTYLE_CLICK* EVENT

As you have learned, the *udcUserEquation* user document uses the *optDrawStyle* option buttons to determine the user-defined equation's shape. As with the *udcFractal* user document, the *optDrawStyle_Click* event sets the shape to the currently selected option button's index value. The *optDrawStyle_Click* event within the *udcUserEquation* user document is identical to the *optDrawStyle_Click* event within Chapter 5's *frmUserEquation* form. You can find the event in the *udcUserEquation* user document in the *Chapter20* directory on the companion CD-ROM that accompanies this book.

SETTING THE PROJECT'S COMPATIBILITY COMPONENT

After you finish designing and writing the program code for the *prjDocFractals* ActiveX document project, you must perform one additional step before you can build and distribute the ActiveX documents. Because the HTML file that references the ActiveX document will use the document's class ID (an internal, Windows-required number), you must ensure that Visual Basic creates a class ID for the ActiveX document when you compile the document. You will set the project's Version Compatibility option to instruct Visual Basic to assign class IDs to the documents. To make Visual Basic assign the Version Compatibility setting for the *prjDocFractals* project, perform the following steps:

620

1. Select the Project menu prjDocFractals Properties option. Visual Basic will display the Project Properties dialog box.

2. Within the Project Properties dialog box, select the Component tab. Visual Basic will change the dialog box's display to represent your selection.

3. Within the Component tab, select the Project Compatibility option. Figure 20.4 shows the Project Properties dialog box after you select the Project Compatibility option within the Version Compatibility frame.

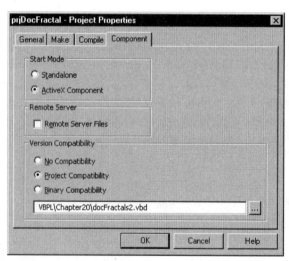

Figure 20.4 *The Project Properties dialog box after you select the correct Version Compatibility option.*

4. Within the Project Properties dialog box, click your mouse on OK to close the Project Properties dialog box.

As you will learn in the next section, when you compile the program, Visual Basic will generate a unique class identifier for the documents. Your programs will then use the identifier to design Web pages that download the documents for the user.

Note: *Visual Basic will automatically select the ActiveX component start mode for the program when you start the project as an **ActiveX Document** project.*

CREATING AN INTERNET DISTRIBUTION FOR THE PROJECT

As you learned earlier in this chapter, when you distribute ActiveX documents that users will view within a browser container (such as *Internet Explorer*), you must create an HTML document that references the user documents and loads them into the browser. The simplest way to create the document is to use the *Application Setup Wizard*, which you installed to your hard drive when you installed Visual Basic. To use the *Application Setup Wizard* to create an HTML document and distribute your ActiveX documents project, perform the following steps:

1. Select the Windows Start menu Programs option. Within the Programs menu, select the Microsoft Visual Basic 5.0 group Application Setup Wizard option. Windows will display the opening dialog box for the *Application Setup Wizard*.

2. Within the opening dialog box for the *Application Setup Wizard*, click your mouse on the Next button to move to the next dialog box. The *Application Setup Wizard* will display the Select Project and Options dialog box.

3. Within the Select Project and Options dialog box, click your mouse on the Browse button. The *Application Setup Wizard* will display the Locate VB Application's .VBP Project file dialog box.

4. Within the Locate VB Application's .VBP Project file dialog box, navigate to *x:\vbpl\Chapter20\ prjDocFractals.vbp,* where *x* corresponds to the drive letter of the drive where you installed the *Visual Basic Programmer's Library* companion CD-ROM. After you navigate to the file, double-click your mouse on the file name. The *Application Setup Wizard* will return to the Select Project and Options dialog box.

5. Within the Select Project and Options dialog box, click your mouse in the check box next to the Rebuild the Project option. The *Application Setup Wizard* will place a check mark in the box.

6. Within the Options frame, click your mouse next to the Create Internet Download Setup option. The *Application Setup Wizard* will select the radio button next to the option, and display What's New text on the dialog box's left-hand side. Figure 20.5 shows the Select Project and Options dialog box after you finish selecting the project name and the options.

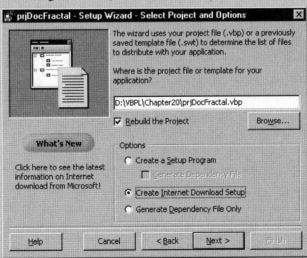

Figure 20.5 *The Setup Wizard's Select Project and Options dialog box.*

7. Within the Select Project and Options dialog box, click your mouse on the Next button. The *Application Setup Wizard* will display the Internet Distribution Location dialog box.

8. When you create your own Internet distributions, you will generally specify the directory on your Internet server where the documents will reside within this box. For this example, however,

you will specify a subdirectory of the project directory as the location where the files will reside. To specify the subdirectory, first select the drive within the Destination combo box.

9. Next, select the *x:\vbpl\Chapter20\swsetup* directory, where *x* corresponds to the drive letter of the hard drive on which you installed the program from the Visual Basic companion CD-ROM. When you finish, the Internet Distribution Location dialog box will look similar to Figure 20.6.

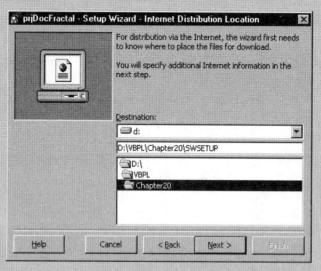

Figure 20.6 *The Setup Wizard's Internet Distribution Location dialog box.*

10. Within the Internet Distribution Location dialog box, click your mouse on the Next button. The *Application Setup Wizard* will display a Directory Does Not Exist dialog box and prompt you to specify whether the *Application Setup Wizard* should create the new directory. Click your mouse on the Yes button to create the new directory.

11. After you click your mouse on Yes, the *Application Setup Wizard* will pause while it reads directory information and performs other processing. The *Application Setup Wizard* will then display the Internet Package dialog box. The Internet Package dialog box lets you select the location your run-time cabinet files should link to—either on the Microsoft Web site or some other location. Generally, you will link to the Microsoft Web site, unless you are building components for a corporate intranet or other secure location, in which case you may specify a site within your secure location. Because the *prjDocFractals* program does not use any additional run-time cabinets, you can simply click your mouse on Next to move to the ActiveX Server Components dialog box.

12. When you create your own applications, your programs may occasionally have dependencies on out-of-process servers that the *Application Setup Wizard* cannot locate. If the *Application Setup Wizard* cannot locate an out-of-process server, you can specify it within the ActiveX Server Components dialog box. Because the *prjDocFractals.exe* program does not use any ActiveX Server components, click your mouse on Next to move to the File Summary dialog box.

13. After you click your mouse on Next, the *Application Setup Wizard* will display a Working dialog box as it continues to process the files necessary for your installation. After it completes processing the files, it will display the File Summary dialog box. Within the File Summary dialog box, you should see three files: *msvbm50.dll*, *AsycFilt.dll*, and *prjDocFractals.exe*. The first two files are Visual Basic dependencies; the third file is your *prjDocFractals.exe* program file. If, for some reason, all three files are not displayed, the *Application Setup Wizard* experienced an error of some type. You should exit the *Application Setup Wizard* and restart it. Figure 20.7 shows the File Summary dialog box.

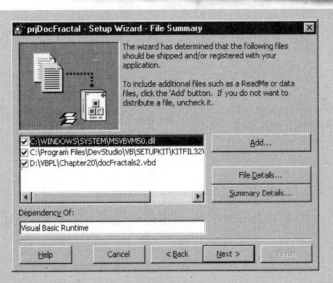

Figure 20.7 *The Application Setup Wizard's File Summary dialog box.*

14. Within the File Summary dialog box, click your mouse on the Next button. The *Application Setup Wizard* will display the Finished! dialog box.

15. Within the Finished! dialog box, click your mouse on the Finish button. The *Application Setup Wizard* will build the files necessary for an Internet distribution.

After you finish building the Internet distribution, the *Application Setup Wizard* will create the *prjDocFractals.exe* program file, the *udcFractals* and *udcUserDocument* supporting document files, and the *docFractals.htm* HTML file.

As you have learned, the *docFractals.htm* HTML file will load the *prjDocFractals.exe* program into *Internet Explorer*. To view the *docFractals.htm* file, perform the following steps:

1. Select the Windows Start menu Programs option. Within the Programs menu, select the Accessories group Notepad option. Windows will display the *Notepad*^{TM} program.

2. Within *Notepad*, select the File menu Open option. *Notepad* will display the File Open dialog box.

3. Within the File Open dialog box, navigate to *x:\vbpl\Chapter20\swsetup\docFractals.htm,*where *x* corresponds to the drive letter of the hard drive on which you installed the program from the Visual Basic companion CD-ROM. Click your mouse on the Open button to open the file. The *Notepad* will display the following:

```
<HTML>
<OBJECT ID="udcFractal"
CLASSID="CLSID:17376471-AF47-11D1-ABDD-0040054B3218"
CODEBASE="docFractals.CAB#version=1,0,0,1">
</OBJECT>

<SCRIPT LANGUAGE="VBScript">
Sub Window_OnLoad
  Document.Open
  Document.Write "<FRAMESET>"
  Document.Write "<FRAME SRC=""udcFractal.VBD"">"
  Document.Write "</FRAMESET>"
  Document.Close
End Sub
</SCRIPT>
</HTML>
```

When you use ActiveX documents, you will use HTML to provide a means for the browser to download, register, and navigate to the ActiveX document. The lines between the two *OBJECT* tags in the *docFractals.htm* file instruct *Internet Explorer* to download the ActiveX component and register the ActiveX document in the Windows registry. The *OBJECT* tag in this example includes:

- The ActiveX document's class ID so that the browser can include it with the document or find it in the Windows registry.
- A *CODEBASE* attribute to tell the browser where to find the component if the component is not already on the client machine (and a version number to check against for updating).

On the same page, the *Application Setup Wizard* placed VBScript that instructs *Internet Explorer* to navigate immediately to the ActiveX document through its *VBD* file. (Visual Basic created this file when it compiled the ActiveX document, and contains a pointer to the component that provides the ActiveX document's objects.)

This code fragment contains only the name of the *VBD* file itself, rather than a fully qualified path to the file. Using the relative path to the file, *Internet Explorer* will look for it in the same directory as the *HTML* file that contains the VBScript. If you want to place the *VBD* file in another directory, you must place the fully qualified path to the file within the *HTML* file.

ENHANCEMENTS YOU CAN MAKE TO THE prjDocFractals PROJECT

Now that you understand the basics behind creating ActiveX documents, you can integrate the documents from this chapter's project into your Web site, use the information about creating ActiveX documents to create front-end forms that users must complete, and even create on-line CD players. In fact, you can convert virtually any program that you have written in this book that does not support the Internet into an ActiveX document, which will give the user the ability to run the document from within *Internet Explorer*.

You may also want to develop a more complex HTML page to load the document. For example, if your site uses frames, or if you have a specific way you want the browser itself to appear every time you load the documents, you can use *VBScript*™ to change the browser's appearance before the browser loads the user document.

PUTTING IT ALL TOGETHER

This chapter's project, *prjDocFractals,* introduced you to Visual Basic ActiveX documents. You have also revisited the Visual Basic *Circle* and *Line* methods and have seen the impact of not using classes within your programs. The *prjDocFractals* project shows you how to draw images from complex equations onto your computer screen—within the user's browser. In addition, the project shows you how to use structures that contain data that you can pass from procedure to function within a user document. In Chapter 21, "Using Windows Sockets for Two-Way Internet Communications," you will learn how to use ActiveX technology and the Windows Sockets Library to design a user-defined library that your programs can use to communicate over the Internet. Before you continue with Chapter 21, however, make sure you understand the following key concepts:

- ✓ Visual Basic lets you create custom ActiveX documents, which let you create programs that you can easily distribute on and execute from the World Wide Web.
- ✓ To use a compiled ActiveX document, *Internet Explorer* must first access an HTML page that refers to the document's component. The HTML page provides the browser information that it will use to load the component.
- ✓ When you distribute compiled ActiveX documents, you will use a Microsoft Cabinet (CAB) file to hold the components for the document. When you use the *Application Setup Wizard,* the Wizard will create the cabinet file for you automatically.
- ✓ You can use the Visual Basic *Application Setup Wizard* to create Internet distributions of your ActiveX documents.

Chapter 21

Using Windows Sockets for Two-Way Internet Communications

In previous chapters, you have created programs that let you access information on the Internet and display your own programs within a Web browser. One of the most exciting features of the Internet, however, is how easy it is for you to create programs that let you communicate with programs on other computers in "real time." In the past, when you wanted to send an electronic file to someone in another city or some other distant point from your office, you had to mail the file to them on a floppy disk. Today, many users instead attach the file to an e-mail transmission and send it directly to the user in the remote location—meaning they receive the file more quickly, there is no risk of physical damage to the media that contains the file, and the remote user can quickly respond in the event of a transmission difficulty.

625

E-mail transmissions, however, are still not fully in real time. When you send an e-mail message to someone over the Internet, you must first save the e-mail message on your local server, which transmits the message (possibly through several other servers) to the user's remote server, which then forwards the e-mail to the user to whom you addressed it. Rather than sending the information over one or more intermediary servers, a better solution might be to transmit directly to the remote user.

In this chapter's projects, *prjSocketsDLL* and *prjInternetChat*, you will use *Windows Sockets* to create and maintain a direct Internet connection with another computer. The *prjInternetChat* program will let you send text messages, transmit files, and send pictures back and forth to another user who is running the program on a remote machine. All your transmissions and communications with the *prjInternetChat* program will be in real time, meaning that the user on the connection's opposite end will receive your transmissions as you send them.

This chapter's projects teach you about ActiveX Dynamic-Link Library (DLL) projects, using the *Winsock* control within your programs, raising events from a class module, and adding "drag-and-drop" support to your programs. By the time you finish this chapter, you will understand the following key concepts:

- You can use the ActiveX DLL project option to create in-process servers for your Visual Basic programs.

- You can use the *Winsock* control within your Visual Basic programs to provide easy access to Transport Control Protocol (TCP) and User Datagram Protocol (UDP) network services.

- You can raise events within an ActiveX DLL project so that projects that reference the DLL can use the events to perform processing in response to those events.

- With the *OLEDragDrop* and *OLEDragOver* events, your programs can easily respond to the user's mouse actions.

- When you communicate with another computer over the Internet, your programs must open a socket to that computer, which the programs will then use to communicate with that remote computer.

USING THE prjINTERNETCHAT PROGRAM

Before you design the *prjInternetChat* project, you may find it helpful to run the program. The companion CD-ROM that accompanies this book contains the *prjInternetChat.exe* program within the *Chapter21* directory. As with every other program on the CD-ROM, you should run the Jamsa Press *setup.exe* program to install the *prjInternetChat.exe* program to your computer's hard drive before you run it. After you install the *prjInternetChat.exe* program to your computer's hard drive, you can run it from the Start menu. To run the program, select the Windows Start menu Run option. Windows will display the Run dialog box. Within the Run dialog box, enter *x:\vbpl\Chapter21\prjInternetChat.exe*, where *x* corresponds to the drive letter of the hard drive on which you installed the *prjInternetChat.exe* program, and click your mouse on OK. Windows will display the *prjInternetChat.exe* program, as shown in Figure 21.1.

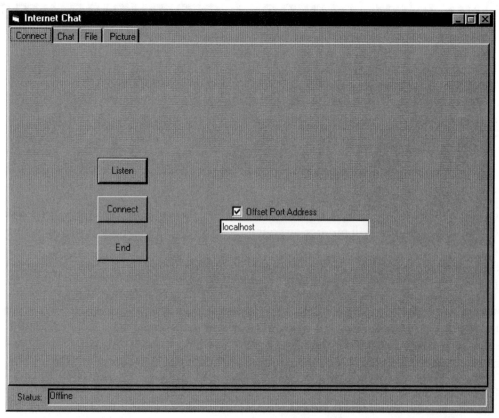

*Figure 21.1 The **prjInternetChat.exe** program's Internet Chat window at startup.*

RUNNING *prjINTERNETCHAT* FROM THE *CD-ROM*

As you have learned, you must first install many programs that you will use in this book to your computer's hard drive before you use the programs. Because the *prjInternetChat.exe* program uses a custom ActiveX DLL that you must register on your computer before the program will execute, you cannot run the *prjInternetChat.exe* program from the CD-ROM.

To learn more about the Jamsa Press *setup.exe* program, see the "What's on the *Visual Basic Programmer's Library* Companion CD-ROM" section at the back of this book.

Before you use the *prjInternetChat.exe* program, take a moment to familiarize yourself with the program's appearance. After you start the *prjInternetChat.exe* program, your computer will display a window (the Internet Chat window) in the display's center. Near the top of the Internet Chat window, you will see four tabs, each of which contains a caption. When the program begins, it displays the first tab, with the caption *Connect*. On the tab, you will see three buttons: Listen, Connect, and End. Next to the buttons, you will see a check box with the caption *Offset Local Port Address* and a field that contains the caption *localhost*. To connect to another computer running the program, you must enter the second computer's Internet Protocol (IP) address, turn off the Offset Local Port Address check box, and click your mouse on the Connect button.

In addition, the *prjInternetChat.exe* program will let you communicate with another instance of the program running on your local computer. To start a second instance of the *prjInternetChat.exe* program and begin to communicate between the two programs, perform the following steps:

1. Select the Windows Start menu Run option. Windows will display the Run dialog box.

2. Within the Run dialog box, enter *x:\vbpl\Chapter21\prjInternetChat.exe*, where *x* corresponds to the drive letter of the hard drive on which you installed the *prjInternetChat.exe* program, and click your mouse on OK. Windows will display a second instance of the *prjInternetChat.exe* program.

3. Within the second instance of the *prjInternetChat.exe* program, click your mouse on the check mark next to the Offset Local Port Address check box. The *prjInternetChat.exe* program will turn off the check mark.

4. Within the second instance of the *prjInternetChat.exe* program, click your mouse on the Listen button. The status line at the Internet Chat window's bottom will change to "Listening for remote connection request."

5. Click your mouse on the Minimize button in the top-right corner of the *prjInternetChat.exe* program's second instance. Windows will minimize the instance and place on the Start bar an icon that represents the instance.

6. Within the first instance of the *prjInternetChat.exe* program, click your mouse on the Connect button. The status bar at the Internet Chat window's bottom will change to *Connected to localhost.*

If you then change back to the second instance, you will see that it also indicates that it is connected to the local host—the other program instance. Now that you are connected, you can communicate between the two hosts. To try the Chat tab and communicate between the two hosts, perform the following steps:

1. If you have not minimized the second instance of the *prjInternetChat.exe* program, click your mouse on the Minimize button in the top-right corner of the *prjInternetChat.exe* program's second instance. Windows will minimize the instance and place on the Start bar an icon that represents the instance.

2. Within the first instance of the *prjInternetChat.exe* program, click your mouse on the Chat tab. The Internet Chat window will change its display to the Chat tab. Within the Chat tab is a large, gray area for recent transmissions and a field at the form's bottom where you can enter new transmissions. If you enter text into the field and click your mouse on the Send Text button, the program will send the message to the other local instance. Within the field, type *This is Instance1* and click your mouse on the Send Text button. The *prjInternetChat.exe* program will clear the text from the field, place it within the chat history area, and transmit the message to the second instance.

3. On the Windows Start bar, click your mouse on the icon for the second instance of the *prjInternetChat.exe* program. After the operating system restores the window to its original size, click your mouse on the Chat tab. Within the chat area, you will see that the program received the *This is Instance1* transmission. Within the field, type *This is Instance2* and click your mouse on the Send Text button. The *prjInternetChat.exe* program will clear the text from the field, place it within the chat history area, and transmit the message to the first instance of the program. Figure 21.2 shows the program after you transmit two messages.

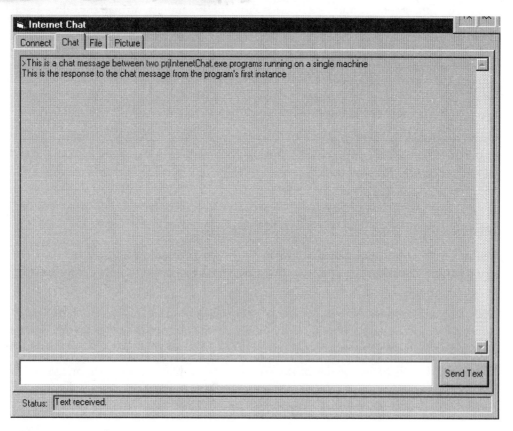

Figure 21.2 The **prjInternetChat.exe** *program after you transmit two messages.*

Sending a file from within the *prjInternetChat.exe* program is similarly as easy as chatting with a remote user. In fact, you can simply click your mouse on a program name within Microsoft *Explorer®*, hold down the mouse button, and drag the file into the field on the File tab.

The *prjInternetChat.exe* program, in turn, will place the filename within the tab. To transmit the file, click your mouse on the Send File button. The connected user will receive the transmission, which the receiving computer will save within the program's current directory.

UNDERSTANDING FILE TRANSMISSIONS

As you can see, the *prjInternetChat.exe* program will let you transmit both picture files and other file types. When you want to transmit a file of any type other than a picture type, you must use the File tab. However, you can also use the File tab to transmit pictures—if you do not want to view the picture before you send it. Additionally, when you send pictures, the program will automatically save the picture file within a temporary file in the application's directory—which may be a concern for you if you are transmitting picture files whose names it is important the recipient knows.

The last tab within the *prjInternetChat.exe* program lets you transmit picture files directly to the other copy of the program on the receiving end or view the files locally within your computer. Again, the program lets you drag-and-drop the picture files from anywhere, and will display them within the Picture tab. After you load a picture in the Picture tab, simply click your mouse on the Send Pic button to send the picture to the user on the connection's other end. Figure 21.3 shows the *prjInternetChat.exe* program after you drag-and-drop a picture into the program.

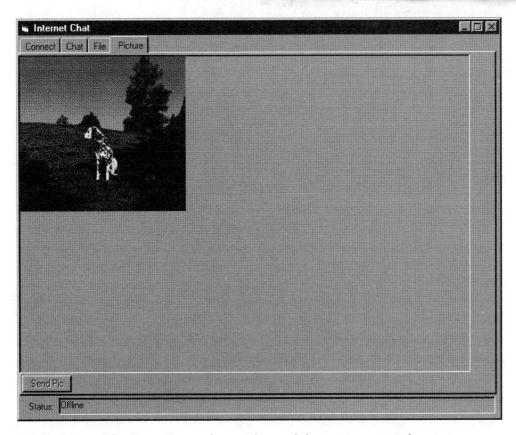

Figure 21.3 The **prjInternetChat.exe** *program after you drag-and-drop a picture into the program.*

CREATING THE PROJECTS

Now that you have a better idea about how to use the finished *prjInternetChat* program, you can begin to design the two projects, *prjInternetChat* and *prjSocketsDLL*, that comprise the program itself and the Dynamic-Link Library (DLL) that the program uses. First, you will design a single empty form for the *prjInternetChat* project. Next, you will add the second project, *prjSocketsDLL*, to the *prjInternetChat* project and add a form, a module, and a class module to that project. After you finish designing the projects, you will learn more about Visual Basic's *Winsock* and *Tabbed Dialog* controls.

CREATING THE FRMINTERNETCHAT FORM

As you have learned, the *prjInternetChat* project uses a single form, together with a set of tabs on the form, to let the user transfer information across the Internet. To begin the *prjInternetChat* project and design the empty *frmInternetChat* form, perform the following steps:

1. Within Visual Basic, select the File menu New Project option. Visual Basic will open the New Project dialog box.

2. Within the New Project dialog box, double-click your mouse on the Standard EXE icon. Visual Basic will close the New Project dialog box, start a new project, *Project1*, and add a form to it, *Form1*.

3. Select the View menu Properties Window option. Visual Basic will open the Properties Window listing the *Form1* form's properties.

4. Within the Properties Window, change the *Form1* form's property values to those Table 21.1 lists.

Object	Property	Set As
Form1	*Caption*	*Internet Chat*
Form1	*Height*	7545
Form1	*Left*	0
Form1	*StartUpPosition*	2 - Center Screen
Form1	*Top*	0
Form1	*Width*	9495
Form1	*Name*	*frmInternetChat*

Table 21.1 *The newly named **frmInternetChat** form's properties.*

5. Within Visual Basic, select the Project menu Project1 Properties option. Visual Basic will display the Project1 Properties dialog box.

6. Within the Project1 Properties dialog box, type *prjInternetChat* within the *Project Name* field. Next, click your mouse on OK. Visual Basic will close the Project1 Properties dialog box.

After you finish setting the properties for the *frmInternetChat* form and the *prjInternetChat* project, you must save the project before you design the *prjSocketsDLL* project. To save the *prjInternetChat* project, perform the following steps:

1. Select the File menu Save Project As option. Visual Basic will display the Save File As dialog box and fill the *File name* field with *frmInternetChat*.

2. Within the Save File As dialog box, click your mouse on the Save button. Visual Basic will save the *frmInternetChat* form and fill the *File name* field with *prjInternetChat*.

3. Within the Save Project As dialog box, click your mouse on the Save button. Visual Basic will save the *prjInternetChat* project and close the Save Project As dialog box.

ADDING THE PRJSOCKETSDLL PROJECT

Now that you have created the form for the *prjInternetChat* project, you can add the *prjSocketsDLL* project to the *prjInternetChat* project and add a form, module, and class module to the *prjSocketsDLL* project. The *prjSocketsDLL* project contains the program code that performs the actual transfer and reception of data across the open sockets. To add the new *prjSocketsDLL* project and its forms and modules to the *prjInternetChat* project, perform the following steps:

1. Within Visual Basic, select the File menu Add Project option. Visual Basic will display the Add Project dialog box.

2. Within the Add Project dialog box, double-click your mouse on the ActiveX DLL icon. Visual Basic will add a new ActiveX DLL project, *Project1*, to the *prjInternetChat* project, and open a class module, *Class1*.

3. Select the View menu Properties Window option. Visual Basic will open the Properties Window listing the *Class1* class module's properties.

4. Within the Properties Window, change the *Class1* class module's name to *clsSocketsDLL*.

5. Within Visual Basic, select the Project menu Add Module option. Visual Basic will add a new module, *Module1*, to the *Project1* project.

6. Select the View menu Properties Window option. Visual Basic will open the Properties Window listing the *Module1* module's properties.

7. Within the Properties Window, change the *Module1* module's name to *mdlSocketsDLL*.

8. Within Visual Basic, select the Project menu Add Form option. Visual Basic will add a new form, *Form1*, to the *Project1* project.

9. Select the View menu Properties Window option. Visual Basic will open the Properties Window listing the *Form1* form's properties.

10. Within the Properties Window, change the *Form1* form's property values to those Table 21.2 lists.

Object	Property	Set As
Form1	*Caption*	*Winsock Control Holder*
Form1	*Height*	1110
Form1	*Left*	0
Form1	*Top*	0
Form1	*Width*	2835
Form1	*Name*	*frmWinsockFrm*

Table 21.2 *The newly named* **frmWinsockFrm** *form's properties.*

11. Within Visual Basic, select the Project menu Project1 Properties option. Visual Basic will display the Project1 Properties dialog box.

12. Within the Project1 Properties dialog box, type *prjSocketsDLL* within the *Project Name* field. Next, click your mouse on OK. Visual Basic will close the Project1 Properties dialog box.

631

After you finish setting the properties for the form, module, and class module within the *prjSocketsDLL* project and the properties for the *prjSocketsDLL* project itself, you must save the project. To save the *prjSocketsDLL* project, perform the following steps:

1. Select the File menu Save Project Group As option. Visual Basic will display the Save File As dialog box and fill the *File name* field with *clsSocketsDLL*.

2. Within the Save File As dialog box, click your mouse on the Save button. Visual Basic will save the *clsSocketsDLL* class module and fill the *File name* field with *mdlSocketsDLL*.

3. Within the Save File As dialog box, click your mouse on the Save button. Visual Basic will save the *mdlSocketsDLL* module and fill the *File name* field with *frmWinsockFrm*.

4. Within the Save File As dialog box, click your mouse on the Save button. Visual Basic will save the *frmWinsockFrm* form and fill the *File name* field with *prjSocketsDLL*.

5. Within the Save Project As dialog box, click your mouse on the Save button. Visual Basic will save the *prjSocketsDLL* project and fill the *File name* field with *Group1*.

6. Within the Save Project Group As dialog box, change the group name to *prgInternetChat*. Next, click your mouse on the Save button. Visual Basic will save the *prgInternetChat* project group and close the Save Project Group As dialog box.

UNDERSTANDING THE WINSOCK CONTROL

The *Winsock* control, invisible to the user, provides easy access to Transport Control Protocol (TCP) and User Datagram Protocol (UDP) network services. Microsoft Access, Visual Basic, Visual C++, and Visual FoxPro developers can use the *Winsock* control—which lets programs open sockets to programs on other computers. A *socket* is a communications channel between two computers. *Winsock* is an abbreviation for *Windows sockets*. To write client or server applications, you do not need to understand the details of TCP or call low level Winsock APIs. By setting properties and invoking the control's methods, you can easily connect to a remote machine and exchange data in both directions.

The Transfer Control Protocol lets you create and maintain a connection to a remote computer. Using the connection, both computers can transfer data between themselves along the socket the program opens. If you are creating a client application, you must know the server computer's name or IP address (*RemoteHost* property), as well as the port (*RemotePort* property) on which it will be "listening"—that is, waiting for another computer to try to connect. You can then invoke the *Winsock* control's *Connect* method.

If you are creating a server application, you must set a port (*LocalPort* property) on which to listen and then invoke the *Listen* method. When the client computer requests a connection, the *ConnectionRequest* event will occur. To complete the connection, invoke the *Accept* method within the *ConnectionRequest* event.

After you successfully complete a connection, either computer can send and receive data. To send data, invoke the *SendData* method. Whenever the control receives data, it raises the *DataArrival* event. To retrieve the data, invoke the *GetData* method within the *DataArrival* event.

The User Datagram Protocol (UDP) is a connectionless protocol. In contrast to when a computer performs TCP operations, computers do not establish a connection when they perform UDP operations. Also, a UDP application can be either a client or a server. To transmit data, you must first set the client computer's *LocalPort* property. The server computer then must set the *RemoteHost* to the client computer's Internet address, set the *RemotePort* property to the same port as the client computer's *LocalPort* property, and invoke the *SendData* method to begin sending messages. The client computer then uses the *GetData* method within the *DataArrival* event to retrieve the sent messages.

632

ADDING THE WINSOCK CONTROL COMPONENT TO THE PRJSOCKETSDLL PROJECT

As you have learned, the *prjSocketsDLL* project uses the *Winsock* control to create Internet connections. Before you can use the *Winsock* control within the *prjSocketsDLL* project, you must add it to the project as a component. To add the *Winsock* control to the *prjSocketsDLL* project, perform the following steps:

1. If the *prjSocketsDLL* project is not currently selected within the Project Explorer, click your mouse on the *prjSocketsDLL* project listing within the Project Explorer.

2. Within Visual Basic, select the Project menu Components option. Visual Basic will open the Components dialog box.

3. Within the Components dialog box, select the *Microsoft Winsock Control 5.0* listing. Next, click your mouse on the box to the left of the listing. Visual Basic will display a check mark in the box, as shown in Figure 21.4.

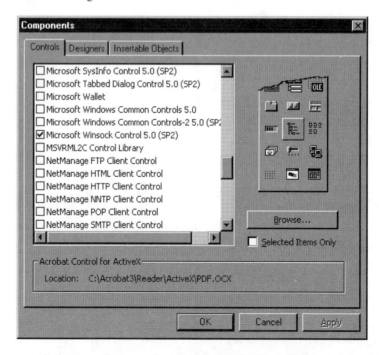

Figure 21.4 *The Components dialog box after you select the **Microsoft Winsock Control 5.0** listing.*

4. Within the Components dialog box, click your mouse on the OK button. Visual Basic will close the Components dialog box and add the control to the *prjSocketsDLL* project.

ADDING THE TABBED DIALOG CONTROL COMPONENT TO THE *PRJINTERNETCHAT* PROJECT

As you have learned, the *prjInternetChat* project will display information on several tabs within the *frmInternetChat* form. The *prjInternetChat* project uses the *Microsoft Tabbed Dialog* control to display separate tabs on the form. Before you can use the *Microsoft Tabbed Dialog* control within the *prjInternetChat* project, you must add it to the project as a component. To add the *Microsoft Tabbed Dialog* control to the *prjInternetChat* project, perform the following steps:

1. If the *prjInternetChat* project is not currently selected within the Project Explorer, click your mouse on the *prjInternetChat* project listing within the Project Explorer.

2. Within Visual Basic, select the Project menu Components option. Visual Basic will open the Components dialog box.

633

3. Within the Components dialog box, select the *Microsoft Tabbed Dialog Control 5.0* listing. Next, click your mouse on the box to the left of the listing. Visual Basic will display a check mark in the box.

4. Within the Components dialog box, click your mouse on the OK button. Visual Basic will close the Components dialog box and add the control to the *prjInternetChat* project.

DESIGNING THE *FRMWINSOCKFRM* FORM

As you have learned, the *prjSocketsDLL* project uses the *Microsoft Winsock* control to establish Internet communications. The *prjSocketsDLL* project also uses *Timer* controls, which the program uses to regularly check th status of a transmission or reception—that is, it causes the program to check at regular intervals and make sure the transmission or reception has not stopped working for some reason. In fact, the *prjSocketsDLL* project uses three *Microsoft Winsock* controls and two *Timer* controls. You will place all the controls onto the *frmWinsockFrm* form.

ADDING THE *TIMER* CONTROLS TO THE *FRMWINSOCKFRM* FORM

As the previous section details, the *frmWinsockFrm* form uses two *Timer* controls to maintain transmission and reception status information. To add the *Timer* controls to the *frmWinsockFrm* form, perform the following steps:

1. If Visual Basic is not displaying the *frmWinsockFrm* form within an object window, double-click your mouse on the *frmWinsockFrm* form listing within the Project Explorer. Visual Basic will open the *frmWinsockFrm* form.

2. Within Visual Basic, select the View menu Toolbox option. Visual Basic will open the Toolbox.

3. Within the Toolbox, double-click your mouse on the Timer icon. Visual Basic will draw a *Timer* control, *Timer1*, within the *frmWinsockFrm* form.

4. Repeat Step 3 one time. Visual Basic will draw a second *Timer* control, *Timer2*, within the *frmWinsockFrm* form.

5. Within the *frmWinsockFrm* form, click your mouse on the *Timer1* control to highlight it. Visual Basic will draw a small frame around the control.

6. Select the View menu Properties Window option. Visual Basic will open the Properties Window listing the *Timer1* properties.

7. Within the Properties Window, change the *Timer1* properties to the values Table 21.3 lists.

8. Repeat Steps 5, 6, and 7 to change the *Timer2* properties to the values Table 21.3 lists.

Object	Property	Set As
Timer1	*Interval*	60000
Timer1	*Left*	120
Timer1	*Top*	120
Timer1	*Name*	*tmrReceive*
Timer2	*Interval*	60000
Timer2	*Left*	600
Timer2	*Top*	120
Timer2	*Name*	*tmrSend*

Table 21.3 *The newly named* **Timer** *controls' properties.*

634 ADDING THE WINSOCK CONTROLS TO THE FRMWINSOCKFRM FORM

As the previous section details, the *frmWinsockFrm* form uses three *Winsock* controls to maintain transmission and reception status information. To add the *Winsock* controls to the *frmWinsockFrm* form, perform the following steps:

1. If Visual Basic is not displaying the *frmWinsockFrm* form within an object window, double-click your mouse on the *frmWinsockFrm* form listing within the Project Explorer. Visual Basic will open the *frmWinsockFrm* form.

2. Within Visual Basic, select the View menu Toolbox option. Visual Basic will open the Toolbox.

3. Within the Toolbox, double-click your mouse on the Winsock icon. Visual Basic will draw a *Winsock* control, *Winsock1*, within the *frmWinsockFrm* form. Figure 21.5 shows the Winsock icon within the Toolbox.

Figure 21.5 *The Winsock icon within the Toolbox.*

4. Repeat Step 3 two more times. Visual Basic will draw a second and a third *Winsock* control, *Winsock2* and *Winsock3*, within the *frmWinsockFrm* form.

5. Within the *frmWinsockFrm* form, click your mouse on the *Winsock1* control to highlight it. Visual Basic will draw a small frame around the control.

6. Select the View menu Properties Window option. Visual Basic will open the Properties Window listing the *Winsock1* properties.

7. Within the Properties Window, change the *Winsock1* properties to the values Table 21.4 lists.

8. Repeat Steps 5, 6, and 7 to change the *Winsock2* and *Winsock3* properties to the values Table 21.4 lists.

Object	Property	Set As
Winsock1	Left	1200
Winsock1	Top	120
Winsock1	Name	wskListen
Winsock2	Left	1680
Winsock2	Top	120
Winsock2	Name	wskSend
Winsock3	Left	2160
Winsock3	Top	120
Winsock3	Name	wskReceive

Table 21.4 *The newly named* **Winsock** *controls' properties.*

After you finish setting the properties for the *Winsock* and *Timer* controls, the *frmWinsockFrm* form will look similar to Figure 21.6.

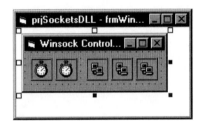

Figure 21.6 *The* **frmWinsockFrm** *form after you finish its design.*

DESIGNING THE FRMINTERNETCHAT FORM

Now that you have designed the *frmWinsockFrm* form and placed the form's component controls onto it, you can design the *frmInternetChat* form. As you have learned, the *frmInternetChat* form uses a *Microsoft Tabbed Dialog* control to let it display different information within a single form. After you add the *Microsoft Tabbed Dialog* control to the project, you will add additional tabs to the control and place controls onto each tab.

ADDING THE MICROSOFT TABBED DIALOG CONTROL TO THE FRMINTERNETCHAT FORM

As you have learned, the *frmInternetChat* form uses a *Microsoft Tabbed Dialog* control to maintain the display of four separate tabs within the single form. To add the *Microsoft Tabbed Dialog* control to the *frmInternetChat* form, perform the following steps:

1. If Visual Basic is not displaying the *frmInternetChat* form within an object window, double-click your mouse on the *frmInternetChat* form listing within the Project Explorer. Visual Basic will open the *frmInternetChat* form.

2. Within Visual Basic, select the View menu Toolbox option. Visual Basic will open the Toolbox.

3. Within the Toolbox, double-click your mouse on the SSTab icon. Visual Basic will draw a *Microsoft Tabbed Dialog* control, *SSTab1*, within the *frmInternetChat* form. Figure 21.7 shows the SSTab icon within the Toolbox.

Figure 21.7 The SSTab icon within the Toolbox.

4. Within the *frmInternetChat* form, click your mouse on the *SSTab1* control to highlight it. Visual Basic will draw a small frame around the control.

5. Select the View menu Properties Window option. Visual Basic will open the Properties Window listing the *SSTab1* properties.

6. Within the Properties Window, change the *SSTab1* properties to the values Table 21.5 lists.

Object	Property	Set As
SSTab1	Height	6735
SSTab1	Left	0
SSTab1	Tabs	4
SSTab1	Top	0
SSTab1	Width	9345
SSTab1	Name	tabIChatChoices

*Table 21.5 The newly named **tabIChatChoices** control's properties.*

7. Click your mouse on the Custom item within the Properties Window. Visual Basic will display the Property Pages dialog box.

8. Within the Property Pages dialog box, select the General tab. Visual Basic will change the dialog box's display to the General tab.

9. Within the Property Pages dialog box, use the arrow keys on the dialog box to set the *TabCaption* property for each tab in the *tabIChatChoices* control to the values Table 21.6 lists.

Tab Number	Property	Set As
0	TabCaption	Connect
1	TabCaption	Chat
2	TabCaption	File
3	TabCaption	Picture

*Table 21.6 The values for the caption on each tab within the **tabIChatChoices** control.*

ADDING THE CONTROLS TO THE *TABICHATCHOICES* CONTROL'S CONNECT TAB

As you have learned in previous sections, you will add controls individually to each tab on the *tabIChatChoices* control. Within the Connect tab, you will add three *CommandButton* controls, a *CheckBox* control, and a *TextBox* control. To add the controls to the Connect tab, perform the following steps:

1. If Visual Basic is not displaying the *frmInternetChat* form within an object window, double-click your mouse on the *frmInternetChat* form listing within the Project Explorer. Visual Basic will open the *frmInternetChat* form.

2. If Visual Basic is not displaying the Connect tab within the *tabIChatChoices* control, click your mouse on the Connect tab at the control's top.

3. Within Visual Basic, select the View menu Toolbox option. Visual Basic will open the Toolbox.

4. Within the Toolbox, double-click your mouse on the CommandButton icon. Visual Basic will draw a *CommandButton* control, *Command1*, within the *frmInternetChat* form.

5. Repeat Step 3 two more times. Visual Basic will add the *Command2* and *Command3* controls to the *frmInternetChat* form.

6. Within the Toolbox, double-click your mouse on the CheckBox icon. Visual Basic will draw a *CheckBox* control, *Check1*, within the *frmInternetChat* form.

7. Within the Toolbox, double-click your mouse on the TextBox icon. Visual Basic will draw a *TextBox* control, *Text1*, within the *frmInternetChat* form.

8. Within the *frmInternetChat* form, click your mouse on the *Text1* control to highlight it. Visual Basic will draw a small frame around the control.

9. Select the View menu Properties Window option. Visual Basic will open the Properties Window listing the *Text1* properties.

10. Within the Properties Window, change the *Text1* properties to the values Table 21.7 lists.

11. Repeat Steps 8, 9, and 10 to change the properties for the other controls to the values Table 21.7 lists.

637

Object	Property	Set As
Check1	*Caption*	*Offset Port Address*
Check1	*Height*	195
Check1	*Left*	4380
Check1	*Top*	3360
Check1	*Width*	1695
Check1	*Name*	*chkOffset*
Command1	*Caption*	*Listen*
Command1	*Height*	495
Command1	*Left*	1740
Command1	*Top*	2460
Command1	*Width*	975
Command1	*Name*	*cmdListen*
Command2	*Caption*	*Connect*
Command2	*Height*	495
Command2	*Left*	1740
Command2	*Top*	3180
Command2	*Width*	975
Command2	*Name*	*cmdConnect*
Command3	*Caption*	*End*
Command3	*Height*	495
Command3	*Left*	1740

Table 21.7 The newly named **CheckBox, CommandButton,** and **TextBox** controls' properties. (continued on following page)

Object	Property	Set As
Command3	Top	3900
Command3	Width	975
Command3	Name	cmdEnd
Text1	Height	285
Text1	Left	4140
Text1	Text	localhost
Text1	Top	3600
Text1	Width	2895
Text1	Name	txtHost

Table 21.7 *The newly named* **CheckBox**, **CommandButton**, *and* **TextBox** *controls' properties. (continued from previous page)*

ADDING THE CONTROLS TO THE *tabIChatChoices* CONTROL'S CHAT TAB

638

As you learned in the previous section, you will add controls to each tab individually on the *tabIChatChoices* control. Within the Chat tab, you will add two *TextBox* controls and a *CommandButton* control. To add the controls to the Chat tab, perform the following steps:

1. If Visual Basic is not displaying the *frmInternetChat* form within an object window, double-click your mouse on the *frmInternetChat* form listing within the Project Explorer. Visual Basic will open the *frmInternetChat* form.

2. If Visual Basic is not displaying the Chat tab within the *tabIChatChoices* control, click your mouse on the Chat tab at the control's top.

3. Within Visual Basic, select the View menu Toolbox option. Visual Basic will open the Toolbox.

4. Within the Toolbox, double-click your mouse on the CommandButton icon. Visual Basic will draw a *CommandButton* control, *Command1*, within the *frmInternetChat* form.

5. Within the Toolbox, double-click your mouse on the TextBox icon. Visual Basic will draw a *TextBox* control, *Text1*, within the *frmInternetChat* form.

6. Repeat Step 5 one time. Visual Basic will draw a second *TextBox* control, *Text2*, within the *frmInternetChat* form.

7. Within the *frmInternetChat* form, click your mouse on the *Text1* control to highlight it. Visual Basic will draw a small frame around the control.

8. Select the View menu Properties Window option. Visual Basic will open the Properties Window listing the *Text1* properties.

9. Within the Properties Window, change the *Text1* properties to the values Table 21.8 lists.

10. Repeat Steps 7, 8, and 9 to change the properties for the other controls to the values Table 21.8 lists.

Object	Property	Set As
Command1	Caption	Send Text
Command1	Height	495
Command1	Left	8280
Command1	Top	6120
Command1	Width	975
Command1	Name	cmdText

Table 21.8 *The newly named* **CommandButton** *and* **TextBox** *controls' properties. (continued on following page)*

Object	Property	Set As
Text1	BackColor	&H8000000F& (Gray)
Text1	Height	5595
Text1	Left	120
Text1	Locked	True
Text1	Multiline	True
Text1	Scrollbars	2 - Vertical
Text1	Text	[blank]
Text1	Top	420
Text1	Width	9135
Text1	Name	txtIn
Text2	Height	495
Text2	Left	120
Text2	Text	[blank]
Text2	Top	6120
Text2	Width	8055
Text2	Name	txtOut

Table 21.8 *The newly named* **CommandButton** *and* **TextBox** *controls' properties. (continued from previous page)*

ADDING THE CONTROLS TO THE tabIChatChoices CONTROL'S FILE TAB

As the previous sections detail, you will add controls individually to each tab on the *tabIChatChoices* control. Within the File tab, you will add two *Label* controls, a *TextBox* control, and a *CommandButton* control. To add the controls to the File tab, perform the following steps:

1. If Visual Basic is not displaying the *frmInternetChat* form within an object window, double-click your mouse on the *frmInternetChat* form listing within the Project Explorer. Visual Basic will open the *frmInternetChat* form.

2. If Visual Basic is not displaying the File tab within the *tabIChatChoices* control, click your mouse on the File tab at the control's top.

3. Within Visual Basic, select the View menu Toolbox option. Visual Basic will open the Toolbox.

4. Within the Toolbox, double-click your mouse on the CommandButton icon. Visual Basic will draw a *CommandButton* control, *Command1*, within the *frmInternetChat* form.

5. Within the Toolbox, double-click your mouse on the TextBox icon. Visual Basic will draw a *TextBox* control, *Text1*, within the *frmInternetChat* form.

6. Within the Toolbox, double-click your mouse on the Label icon. Visual Basic will draw a *Label* control, *Label1*, within the *frmInternetChat* form.

7. Repeat Step 6 one time. Visual Basic will draw a second *Label* control, *Label2*, within the *frmInternetChat* form.

8. Within the *frmInternetChat* form, click your mouse on the *Text1* control to highlight it. Visual Basic will draw a small frame around the control.

9. Select the View menu Properties Window option. Visual Basic will open the Properties Window listing the *Text1* properties.

10. Within the Properties Window, change the *Text1* properties to the values Table 21.9 lists.

11. Repeat Steps 8, 9, and 10 to change the properties for the other controls to the values Table 21.9 lists.

Object	Property	Set As
Command1	Caption	Send File
Command1	Height	495
Command1	Left	2920
Command1	Top	5280
Command1	Width	975
Command1	Name	cmdFile
Text1	Height	495
Text1	Left	240
Text1	Text	[blank]
Text1	Top	3960
Text1	Width	8835
Text1	Name	txtFile
Label1	Alignment	2 - Center
Label1	Caption	Enter File Name, or Drop From Folder
Label1	Font	MS San Serif, Bold, 10 Point
Label1	Height	375
Label1	Left	120
Label1	Top	3480
Label1	Width	8835
Label1	Name	lblFileName
Label2	BorderStyle	1 - Fixed Single
Label2	Caption	[blank]
Label2	Height	375
Label2	Left	240
Label2	Top	4680
Label2	Width	8835
Label2	Name	lblIncomingFile

*Table 21.9 The newly named **CommandButton**, **TextBox**, and **Label** controls' properties.*

ADDING THE CONTROLS TO THE *tabIChatChoices* CONTROL'S PICTURE TAB

As the previous sections detail, you will add controls individually to each tab on the *tabIChatChoices* control. Within the Picture tab, you will add two *PictureBox* controls, a *CommandButton* control, an *HScrollBar* control, and a *VScrollBar* control. The *PictureBox* controls will display a picture the user is about to send or has received, the *CommandButton* control will send the picture to the remote computer, and the scroll bar controls will let the user move the viewing area of a picture in the event the picture is larger than the form's display area. To add the controls to the Picture tab, perform the following steps:

1. If Visual Basic is not displaying the *frmInternetChat* form within an object window, double-click your mouse on the *frmInternetChat* form listing within the Project Explorer. Visual Basic will open the *frmInternetChat* form.

2. If Visual Basic is not displaying the Picture tab within the *tabIChatChoices* control, click your mouse on the File tab at the control's top.

3. Within Visual Basic, select the View menu Toolbox option. Visual Basic will open the Toolbox.

4. Within the Toolbox, double-click your mouse on the CommandButton icon. Visual Basic will draw a *CommandButton* control, *Command1*, within the *frmInternetChat* form.

5. Within the Toolbox, double-click your mouse on the PictureBox icon. Visual Basic will draw a *PictureBox* control, *Picture1*, within the *frmInternetChat* form.

6. Repeat Step 5 one time. Visual Basic will draw a second *PictureBox* control, *Picture2*, within the *frmInternetChat* form.

7. Within the Toolbox, double-click your mouse on the HScrollBar icon. Visual Basic will draw an *HScrollBar* control, *HScroll1*, within the *frmInternetChat* form.

8. Within the Toolbox, double-click your mouse on the VScrollBar icon. Visual Basic will draw a *VScrollBar* control, *VScroll1*, within the *frmInternetChat* form.

9. Within the *frmInternetChat* form, click your mouse on the *VScroll1* control to highlight it. Visual Basic will draw a small frame around the control.

10. Select the View menu Properties Window option. Visual Basic will open the Properties Window listing the *VScroll1* properties.

11. Within the Properties Window, change the *VScroll1* properties to the values Table 21.10 lists.

12. Repeat Steps 9, 10, and 11 to change the properties for the other controls to the values Table 21.10 lists.

641

Object	Property	Set As
Command1	Caption	*Send Pic*
Command1	Height	315
Command1	Left	60
Command1	Top	6360
Command1	Width	975
Command1	Name	cmdSendPic
Picture1	BorderStyle	0 - None
Picture1	Height	2055
Picture1	Left	0
Picture1	Top	0
Picture1	Width	2055
Picture1	Name	picTransfer
Picture2	Height	5955
Picture2	Left	60
Picture2	Top	360
Picture2	Width	8835
Picture2	Name	picHolder
HScrollBar1	Height	315
HScrollBar1	LargeChange	100
HScrollBar1	Left	1080
HScrollBar1	SmallChange	100
HScrollBar1	Top	6360

Table 21.10 *The newly named* **CommandButton**, **PictureBox**, *and* **ScrollBar** *controls' properties. (continued on following page)*

Object	Property	Set As
HScrollBar1	Width	7815
HScrollBar1	Name	hscPictures
VScrollBar1	Height	6015
VScrollBar1	LargeChange	100
VScrollBar1	Left	8340
VScrollBar1	SmallChange	100
VScrollBar1	Top	360
VScrollBar1	Width	315
VScrollBar1	Name	vscPictures

642

*Table 21.10 The newly named **CommandButton**, **PictureBox**, and **ScrollBar** controls' properties. (continued from previous page)*

After you finish designing the *frmInternetChat* form, it will look similar to Figure 21.8.

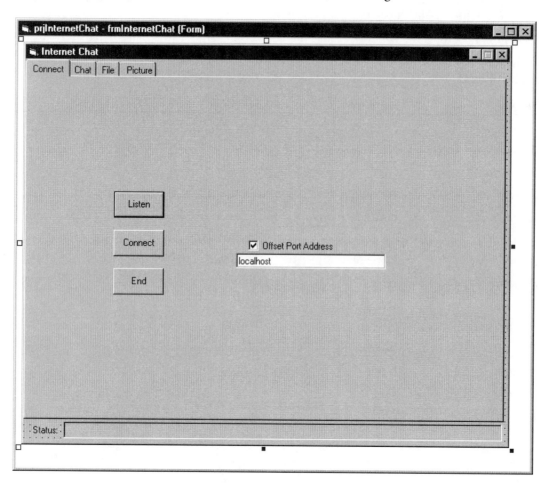

Figure 21.8 *The **frmInternetChat** form after you finish its design.*

WRITING THE CODE FOR THE PRJSOCKETSDLL PROJECT

As you have learned, the *prjSocketsDLL* project uses *Winsock* controls to connect to the Internet and control communications. The *prjInternetChat* program primarily calls methods in response to user actions and responds to events the *prjSocketsDLL* project raises. In addition, because you will declare the object that you use to access the *prjSocketsDLL* project with the *WithEvents* keyword, you will write the code for the *prjSocketsDLL* project first. After you write the code for the *prjSocketsDLL* project, you will write the program code for the *prjInternetChat* project. Within the *prjSocketsDLL* project, you will write the code for the *clsSocketsDLL* class first.

WRITING THE CODE FOR THE *clsSocketsDLL* CLASS

Within the *clsSocketsDLL* class, you will declare the local variables, the events the class raises, and the internal constants the class uses. The *clsSocketsDLL* class uses five variables, four of which are flag variables. The following code implements the declarations within the *clsSocketsDLL* class:

```
Private WithEvents frmHolder As frmWinsockFrm
Private Success As Boolean, bOffset As Boolean
Private bSending As Boolean, bReceiving As Boolean
```

The *frmHolder* object that the class defines with *WithEvents* lets the *clsSocketsDLL* class respond to the events the *Timer* and *Winsock* controls will raise. In turn, the *clsSocketsDLL* class will raise some of those events into the *frmInternetChat* form itself. All four *Boolean* variables indicate information about the DLL's current status—whether an action was successful, whether the program is currently sending or receiving, and whether the program should open the socket on an offset port from the port the program usually uses to open a socket. Using an offset port value lets the user open two instances of the program and communicate between the instances on a single machine, as you learned in this chapter's "Using the *prjInternetChat* Project" section.

The *frmHolder* object lets the *clsSocketsDLL* class respond to events that the *Timer* or *Winsock* controls on the *frmWinsockFrm* raise. The *clsSocketsDLL* class will, in turn, raise some events into programs that use the DLL. The following code implements the *Event* declarations that the *clsSocketsDLL* class will raise into programs that use the DLL:

```
Public Event PictureReceived(Filename As String)
Public Event TextReceived(TextContent As String)
Public Event FileReceived(Filename As String)
Public Event BinaryReceived(BinaryContent As Variant)
Public Event RemoteConnected(Remotehost As String)
Public Event WinsockError(ErrorCode As Integer, ErrorText As String, _
    ErrorProcedure As String)
Public Event Timeout(Direction As String)
Public Event SendBegin()
Public Event SendCompleted()
Public Event ReceiveBegin()
Public Event ReceiveCompleted()
```

Table 21.11 details the events the *clsSocketsDLL* class will raise and the occurrences that cause the class to raise the events.

Event	Description
PictureReceived	The *clsSocketsDLL* class raises the *PictureReceived* event when the DLL receives a picture file—which the *frmInternetChat* form will then display within the Picture tab.
TextReceived	The *clsSocketsDLL* class raises the *TextReceived* event when the DLL receives text—which the *frmInternetChat* form will then display within the Chat tab.
FileReceived	The *clsSocketsDLL* class raises the *FileReceived* event when the DLL receives a file—which the *frmInternetChat* form will then display within the File tab.
BinaryReceived	The *clsSocketsDLL* class raises the *BinaryReceived* event when the DLL receives binary content of an unknown type. The *frmInternetChat* form does not respond to the *BinaryReceived* event.

Table 21.11 *The events the **clsSocketsDLL** class raises. (continued on following page)*

Event	Description
RemoteConnected	The *clsSocketsDLL* class will raise the *RemoteConnected* event when a remote user successfully connects to the DLL.
WinsockError	The *clsSocketsDLL* class will raise the *WinsockError* event if a Winsock error of any type occurs (such as no available sockets).
Timeout	The *clsSocketsDLL* class will raise the *TimeOut* event if a Timeout error occurs within a transmitting or receiving *Winsock* control.
SendBegin	The *clsSocketsDLL* class will raise the *SendBegin* event when a *Winsock* control starts to transmit data to the remote user.
SendCompleted	The *clsSocketsDLL* class will raise the *SendCompleted* event when a *Winsock* control completes the transmission of data to the remote user.
ReceiveBegin	The *clsSocketsDLL* class will raise the *ReceiveBegin* event when a *Winsock* control starts to receive data from the remote user.
ReceiveCompleted	The *clsSocketsDLL* class will raise the *ReceiveCompleted* event when a *Winsock* control finishes receiving data from the remote user.

644

Table 21.11 *The events the* **clsSocketsDLL** *class raises. (continued from previous page)*

In addition to the events the *clsSocketsDLL* class raises and the internal variables it uses, the *clsSocketsDLL* class declares two constants, which you will implement as shown here:

```
Private Const SETON = 1
Private Const SETOFF = 2
```

The *clsSocketsDLL* class uses the *SETON* and *SETOFF* constants to enable *Timer* controls during transmissions and to disable the controls after the transmissions complete.

UNDERSTANDING EVENT RAISING

As you have learned, the *clsSocketsDLL* class raises events to the *frmInternetChat* form. You learned in Chapter 14, "Using the Windows API to Intercept Windows Messages," that you can raise events from your classes, modules, or forms in any other class, module, or form that uses the *WithEvents* keyword to declare an instance of the object. When you raise an event, variables of the object's type that you use the *WithEvents* keyword to declare will expose the event. In other words, if you create a class that you call *Class1*, which raises an event that you call *Event1*, and then declare an object of that class *Object1* with the *WithEvents* keyword, the *Object1* object will expose the event *Event1*. You can, in turn, write code within the *Object1_Event1* event procedure. The program code within the event will generally perform actions that the program must perform when it receives that event. For example, in the *prjInternetChat* program, the *frmInternetChat* form's *SocketsDLL* object raises the *ReceiveCompleted* event. The *clsSocketsDLL* class (of which the *SocketsDLL* object is an instance) raises that event.

The *clsSocketsDLL* class, in turn, raises that event from within its *frmHolder* object's *ReceiveCompleted* event. The *frmHolder* object raises its own *ReceiveCompleted* event to the *clsSocketsDLL* class. The *frmHolder* object (which is an instance of a *frmWinsockFrm* form) raises the *ReceiveCompleted* event when the *wskReceive Winsock* control indicates it has received all the data from the remote connection. Each of the objects raises another event, in turn, because you can raise an event only to an object instance. Figure 21.9 shows how programs raise events from forms, to classes, to other programs (the *frmWinsockFrm* form is within the *prjSocketsDLL* program, while the *frmInternetChat* form is within the *prjInternetChat* program).

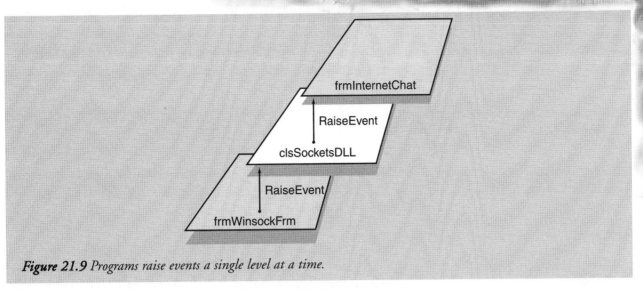

Figure 21.9 *Programs raise events a single level at a time.*

WRITING THE PROPERTY PROCEDURES FOR THE DLPATH PROPERTY

As you have learned, the *prjSocketsDLL* project will let the program that uses the DLL receive a file from a remote user. In the *prjInternetChat* project, the user can select the File tab on the *frmInternetChat* form to transmit or receive a file. After the *prjSocketsDLL* project receives the file from the remote computer, the *prjSocketsDLL* project will then save the received file locally onto a hard drive or other drive. The *clsSocketsDLL* class exposes the *DLPath* property, which programs that use the DLL can use to control the directory to which the programs should download the incoming file. The following code implements the *Property Get* and *Property Let* statements for the *DLPath* property:

```
Public Property Get DLPath() As String
   DLPath = sDLPath
End Property

Public Property Let DLPath(ByVal sNewValue As String)
   sDLPath = sNewValue
End Property
```

As you can see, the *Property Let* procedure sets the *DLPath* property equal to the path the calling program passes to the procedure. In the *prjInternetChat* project, the program code sets the *DLPath* to the application's path. Similarly, the *Property Get* procedure returns the current path to the calling program.

WRITING THE PROPERTY PROCEDURES FOR THE OFFSET PROPERTY

As you have learned, the user can set an offset value for the connection, which lets the user open a socket to another instance of the program that is running on the same computer. The *Offset* property either indicates that the offset is enabled, or sets the offset to be either enabled or disabled. The following code implements the *Property Get* and *Property Let* procedures for the *Offset* property:

```
Public Property Get Offset() As Boolean
   Offset = bOffset
End Property

Public Property Let Offset(ByVal bNewValue As Boolean)
   bOffset = bNewValue
   PortOffset = Abs(bOffset) * 10
End Property
```

In the event the calling program requests the property's current value, the program code will return the *bOffset* member variable's value. If the calling program sets the property's value, the program code will set the *bOffset* member variable equal to the value the calling program passes to the procedure within the *bNewValue* parameter, and set the offset to 10 (because *True* equals 1), an arbitrary socket offset.

WRITING THE CLASS_INITIALIZE PROCEDURE

As you have learned, whenever a program initializes a class object, the first program code within the class to execute is the code within the *Class_Initialize* event. The following code implements the *Class_Initialize* event for the *clsSocketsDLL* class:

```
Private Sub Class_Initialize()
   Set frmHolder = New frmWinsockFrm
End Sub
```

The program code within the event initializes the *frmHolder* object. As you learned in Chapter 14, you must initialize a variable that you use the *WithEvents* keyword to declare separate from the variable's declaration. The *clsSocketsDLL* class initializes the *frmHolder* variable within the *Class_Initialize* event.

WRITING THE CODE FOR THE CONNECT METHOD

As you have learned, a program has two options when it tries to establish a Winsock connection: the program can either listen (wait) for a connection from a remote computer, or the program can connect (start a connection) to the remote computer. In every Winsock connection, one computer connects (generally the remote client) and one computer listens (generally the server). To use the *prjSocketsDLL* project to connect to a listening computer, your programs should invoke the *Connect* method. The following code implements the *Connect* method:

```
Public Function Connect(Remotehost As String, RemotePort As Long) As Boolean
   On Error Resume Next
   Connected = False
   frmHolder.Waiting = True                          'Send out connect request
   frmHolder.wskSend.Close
   Do While frmHolder.wskSend.State
     DoEvents
   Loop
   frmHolder.wskSend.RemotePort = RemotePort
   frmHolder.wskSend.Remotehost = Remotehost
   frmHolder.wskSend.Connect
   If Err Then
     RaiseEvent WinsockError(Err.Number, Err.Description, _
         "Connect[send] method")
     Err = 0
     LockStep = frmHolder.CloseSockets
     Connect = False
     Exit Function
   End If
   Do While frmHolder.Waiting
     DoEvents
   Loop
   Connected = True
   frmHolder.wskListen.Close            'Listen for connection request from remote
   Do While frmHolder.wskListen.State
     DoEvents
   Loop
   frmHolder.wskListen.LocalPort = RemotePort + PortOffset
   frmHolder.wskListen.Listen
   If Err Then
     RaiseEvent WinsockError(Err.Number, Err.Description, _
         "Connect[listen] method")
     Err = 0
     LockStep = frmHolder.CloseSockets
     Connect = False
     Exit Function
   End If
```

```
      On Error GoTo 0
      Connect = True
   End Function
```

The program code within the *Connect* method first sets the *Connect* variable to *False*. If the program successfully connects, it will set the *Connect* variable to *True* at its processing end. Next, the program code makes sure that the *wskSend Winsock* control does not have an open connection (by closing the current connection, if a connection is open). The program code then sets the port on which to connect (which is either the port the remote computer is using, or an offset value from that port if the user is running two instances on the local computer) and the host address of the other computer to which the program wants to connect, and invokes the *wskSend* control's *Connect* method. The *Connect* method tries to establish a connection with the remote host.

If the *wskSend* control does not successfully establish a connection with the remote host, the *If–Then* statement will execute, and the program will raise a *WinsockError* event that contains information about the error. The program code will then close all sockets and exit the method.

647

If the *wskSend* control successfully establishes a connection with the remote host, the program code will perform similar processing with the *wskListen* control, except the *wskListen* control will wait for a connection response from the remote computer. If the *wskListen* control does not receive or successfully process the remote computer's connection request, the program will again raise a *WinsockError* event that contains information about the error. The program code will then close all sockets and exit the method. If both the *wskSend* and *wskListen* controls successfully connect, the method will exit successfully and set the *Connect* variable to *True*.

WRITING THE CODE FOR THE LISTEN METHOD

As you learned in the previous section, when you connect to a remote computer with the *Winsock* control, you must perform a two-step connection. However, for the first step (the connect step) to work, the remote computer must be listening on the correct port for the user to try to connect. To instruct a computer to listen for another computer trying to connect, your programs must invoke the *Listen* method the *clsSocketsDLL* class exposes. You will implement the *Listen* method as shown here:

```
Public Sub Listen(LocalPort As Long)
   On Error Resume Next
   If frmHolder.wskListen.State Then _
       frmHolder.wskListen.Close
   frmHolder.wskListen.LocalPort = LocalPort
   frmHolder.wskListen.Listen
   If Err And (Err <> 10037) Then
     LockStep = frmHolder.CloseSockets
     RaiseEvent WinsockError(Err.Number, Err.Description, "Listen method")
     Err = 0
     Exit Sub
   End If
   On Error GoTo 0
End Sub
```

The *Listen* method first closes any open sockets, and then invokes the *wskListen Winsock* control's *Listen* method. If the program invokes the control's *Listen* method successfully, it will wait until another computer tries to connect. If it does not successfully start to listen, the program code will raise the *WinsockError* event with information about the error that caused the *Winsock* control to fail. In either event, the method executes immediately thereafter.

WRITING THE CODE FOR THE SEND METHODS

As you have learned, the *prjSocketsDLL* project lets your programs send information across a socket to another computer. In fact, the *prjSocketsDLL* project includes methods for four transmission types: binary, file, picture, and text.

The *prjSocketsDLL* project implements four methods to support the four transmission types: *SendBinary, SendFile, SendPic,* and *SendText.* The following code implements the four *Send* methods that the *clsSocketsDLL* class exposes:

```
Public Function SendPic(PicFileName As String)
  Timer SETON
  Success = frmHolder.SendPic(PicFileName)
  Timer SETOFF
End Function

Public Function SendBinary(BinVar As Variant)
  Timer SETON
  Success = frmHolder.SendBinary(BinVar)
  Timer SETOFF
End Function

Public Function SendText(TextContent As String)
  Timer SETON
  Success = frmHolder.SendText(TextContent)
  Timer SETOFF
End Function

Public Function SendFile(Path As String, Filename As String)
  Timer SETON
  SendFile = frmHolder.SendFile(Path, Filename)
  Timer SETOFF
End Function
```

Each method invokes the *clsSocketsDLL* class's *Timer* procedure, which enables the *tmrSend* timer on the *frmWinsockFrm* form. Each method then calls the corresponding public function on the *frmWinsockFrm* form and calls the *Timer* procedure again to turn the *tmrSend Timer* off. You will learn more about the corresponding *Send* functions on the *frmWinsockFrm* form in later sections in this chapter.

WRITING THE CODE FOR THE TIMER PROCEDURE

As the previous section details, the *Timer* procedure either enables or disables the *tmrSend* timer on the *frmWinsockFrm* form. The following code implements the *Timer* procedure:

```
Private Sub Timer(Action As Byte)
  Select Case Action
    Case SETON
      frmHolder.tmrSend.Enabled = True
    Case SETOFF
      frmHolder.tmrSend.Enabled = False
  End Select
End Sub
```

WRITING THE CODE FOR THE FRMHOLDER OBJECT'S RAISED EVENTS

As you learned in this chapter's "Writing the Code for the *clsSocketsDLL* Class" section, the *frmHolder* object exposes events within the *clsSocketsDLL* class. The *clsSocketsDLL* class will, in turn, raise each of the events the *frmHolder* object raises into the class into the calling program. The following code implements the events for the *frmHolder* object:

```
Private Sub frmholder_BinaryReceived(BinaryContent As Variant)
  RaiseEvent BinaryReceived(BinaryContent)
End Sub

Private Sub frmholder_ReceiveCompleted()
  RaiseEvent ReceiveCompleted
End Sub
```

```
Private Sub frmholder_ReceiveBegin()
  RaiseEvent ReceiveBegin
End Sub

Private Sub frmholder_RemoteConnected(Remotehost As String)   '(State As
Boolean, RemotePort As Long)
  RaiseEvent RemoteConnected(Remotehost)      '(State, RemotePort)
End Sub

Private Sub frmholder_PictureReceived(Filename As String)
  RaiseEvent PictureReceived(Filename)
End Sub

Private Sub frmholder_SendBegin()
  RaiseEvent SendBegin
End Sub

Private Sub frmholder_SendCompleted()
  RaiseEvent SendCompleted
End Sub

Private Sub frmholder_SockError(ErrorCode As Integer, ErrorText As String,
ErrorProcedure As String)
  RaiseEvent WinsockError(ErrorCode, ErrorText, ErrorProcedure)
End Sub

Private Sub frmholder_TextReceived(TextContent As String)
  RaiseEvent TextReceived(TextContent)
End Sub

Private Sub frmholder_FileReceived(Filename As String)
  RaiseEvent FileReceived(Filename)
End Sub
```

As you can see, the code for each event invokes the *RaiseEvent* keyword and raises the corresponding event within the calling program. When you write the code for the *frmInternetChat* form later in this chapter, you will write code that responds to the events the *clsSocketsDLL* class raises.

Writing the Code for the mdlSocketsDLL Module

As you have learned, the *clsSocketsDLL* class is the interface class for the *prjSocketsDLL* project. The *clsSocketsDLL* class exposes the methods the client program can use and raises the events to which the client program will respond. In addition, the *prjSocketsDLL* project includes several public functions that the *frmWinsockFrm* form invokes during its processing. To declare these public functions, as well as several constants and two Win32 Application Programming Interface (API) functions that the *frmWinsockFrm* form uses, you will use the *mdlSocketsDLL* module. The following code implements the declarations for the *mdlSocketsDLL* module:

```
Public Const DATATEXT As Byte = 0        ' Text Data
Public Const DATABINARY As Byte = 1      ' Binary Data
Public Const DATAFILE As Byte = 2        ' File data
Public Const DATAPICTURE As Byte = 3     ' Picture Data
Public Const HEADERTYPE As Byte = 0      ' Header indicates Type Information
Public Const HEADERSIZE As Byte = 1      ' Header indicates Transfer Size
Public Const HEADERDONE As Byte = 2      ' Header indicates Transfer Finished

Public Connected As Boolean              ' Connection flag
Public PortOffset As Long                ' Offset value
Public sDLPath As String                 ' Path to storage location
Public LockStep As Boolean               ' forces function to complete before
                                         ' it continues execution
Declare Function GetTempPath Lib "kernel32" Alias "GetTempPathA" _
    (ByVal nBufferLength As Long, ByVal lpBuffer As String) As Long
Declare Function GetTempFileName Lib "kernel32" Alias "GetTempFileNameA" _
    (ByVal lpszPath As String, ByVal lpPrefixString As String, _
    ByVal wUnique As Long, ByVal lpTempFileName As String) As Long
```

All the constants define information about the transfer type and the current information the *Winsock* control is receiving. The public variables define two flag variables—the *Connected* variable, which indicates whether the program is connected across a socket, and the *LockStep* variable, which indicates whether a transfer is complete. The *PortOffset* variable indicates the offset value (which you set within the *clsSocketsDLL* class), and the *sDLPath* variable indicates the path to the location into which the *prjSocketsDLL* project will store any files it receives.

The *GetTempPath* API function lets the DLL retrieve the computer's current temporary path (as set within the Windows *TEMP* environment variable). The *GetTempFileName* API function retrieves an operating-system generated, temporary filename that the program can use to write temporary files into the temporary path.

WRITING THE CODE FOR THE *MAKEBA* PROCEDURE

When you transfer data across a socket, you will generally transfer the data as a *Byte* array. Within the *mdlSocketsDLL*, you will use the *MakeBA* procedure to convert numeric variants into *Byte* arrays before you transfer the numeric variants. The following code implements the *MakeBA* procedure:

```
Public Sub MakeBA(NumIn As Variant, NumArrOut() As Byte)
  Dim temString As String

  temString = NumIn          'Convert numeric variant to string
  NumArrOut = temString      'Convert string to byte array
End Sub
```

WRITING THE CODE FOR THE *UNMAKEBA* PROCEDURE

As you learned in the previous section, when you transfer data across a socket, you will generally transfer the data as a *Byte* array. Within the *mdlSocketsDLL*, you will convert numeric variants into *Byte* arrays before you transfer the numeric variants. Similarly, you must convert *Byte* arrays back into variants after you receive them. The *UnMakeBA* procedure converts *Byte* arrays back into variants. The following code implements the *UnMakeBA* procedure:

```
Public Function UnMakeBA(NumArrIn() As Byte) As Variant
  Dim temString As String

  temString = NumArrIn       'Convert byte array to string
  UnMakeBA = temString       'Convert string to variant
End Function
```

WRITING THE CODE FOR THE *TEMPFILE* FUNCTION

As you have learned, the *prjSocketsDLL* project will often save data from a transfer into a temporary file. For example, when the program receives a picture file from a remote computer, it will save the picture file to a temporary file and then load the temporary file into the program's display. To retrieve a temporary filename from the operating system, the *prjSocketsDLL* project uses the *TempFile* function. The following code implements the *TempFile* function:

```
Public Function TempFile() As Variant
  Dim Success As Long
  Dim TempPath As String
  Dim TempName As String

  TempPath = Space$(255)
  TempName = Space$(255)
  Success = GetTempPath(Len(TempPath), TempPath)
  TempPath = Left$(TempPath, InStr(TempPath, Chr$(0)) - 1)
  Success = GetTempFileName(TempPath, "bin", 0, TempName)
  TempName = Left$(TempName, InStr(TempName, Chr$(0)) - 1)
  TempFile = TempName
  TempPath = ""
  TempName = ""
End Function
```

The *TempFile* function invokes the *GetTempPath* API function to get the temporary directory (as set within the Windows *TEMP* environment variable) and then invokes the *GetTempFileName* API function to obtain a temporary filename within that directory. The function then returns the temporary file name as its value.

WRITING THE CODE FOR THE *FRMWINSOCKFRM* FORM

As you saw when you wrote the code for the *clsWinsockDLL* class, the *frmWinsockFrm* form raises several events. The program code for the *frmWinsockFrm* form declares each of these events within the form's General–Declarations section. In addition to the events the form raises, the program code within the General–Declarations section declares five local variables. You can find the events' declarations within the program code for the form on the companion CD-ROM that accompanies this book. The following code implements the variables' declarations for the *frmWinsockFrm* form:

```
Private bReceiving As Boolean
Private BufferBinary() As Byte
Private BufferText As String
Public Waiting As Boolean
Public Sending As Boolean
```

The *bReceiving* variable indicates whether or not the form is currently receiving data from the remote computer, and is actually a local member for the form's *ReceivingData* property, which the next section details. The *BufferBinary* variable is a *Byte* array, which the program uses for transfers. The *BufferText* variable holds a string of characters, either before it transmits data or after it receives data. The *Waiting* and *Sending* variables indicate information about the *Winsock* control's current status.

WRITING THE PROPERTY PROCEDURES FOR THE *RECEIVINGDATA* PROPERTY

As the previous section details, the *frmWinsockFrm* form exposes the *ReceivingData* property, which indicates whether or not the program is currently receiving data from the remote computer. The *clsSocketsDLL* class, in turn, will check the *ReceivingData* property before it commences new processing. The following code implements the *Property Get* and *Property Let* procedures for the *ReceivingData* property:

```
Private Property Get ReceivingData() As Boolean
   ReceivingData = bReceiving
End Property
Private Property Let ReceivingData(ByVal bNewValue As Boolean)
   If (bReceiving = False) And bNewValue = True Then
     RaiseEvent ReceiveBegin
   ElseIf (bReceiving = True) And bNewValue = False Then
     RaiseEvent ReceiveCompleted
   End If
   bReceiving = bNewValue
End Property
```

The *Property Get* procedure is relatively simple—it returns the *bReceiving* variable's value. However, the *Property Let* procedure is slightly more complex. If the program is not currently receiving data and the *Property Let* procedure receives the new *True* value (indicating the program is about to start receiving data) for the *bReceiving* variable, the procedure will raise the *ReceiveBegin* event. On the other hand, if the program is currently receiving data and the *Property Let* procedure receives the new *False* value (indicating the program is about to stop receiving data) for the *bReceiving* variable, the program code will raise the *ReceiveCompleted* event.

WRITING THE CODE FOR THE *CLOSESOCKETS* FUNCTION

As you have learned, the *prjSocketsDLL* project lets you open a socket to a remote computer. Just as with many other constructs that your programs create, you should make sure that you close any open sockets when the user disconnects from a connected remote computer or when the user shuts down the program. The *CloseSockets* function closes all open sockets. The following code implements the *CloseSockets* function:

```
Public Function CloseSockets()
  wskSend.Close
  wskSend.Remotehost = ""
  wskSend.RemotePort = 0
  wskReceive.Close
  wskReceive.Remotehost = ""
  wskReceive.RemotePort = 0
End Function
```

As you can see, the program code invokes the *Close* method for each *Winsock* control and then sets the *Remotehost* and *RemotePort* properties to a *NULL* string and 0, respectively. When you clear the properties, you ensure that the calling program will not inadvertently try to reconnect along a socket connection the program already closed.

WRITING THE TIMER EVENTS

Whenever you perform transmissions, you always risk losing a connection, encountering overly slow network traffic, or other, similar problems that can result in a *timeout* error. A timeout error generally occurs when the connection transmits no data for a program-specified duration—usually 30 or 60 seconds. The *prjSocketsDLL* project traps for timeouts within the two *Timer* controls' *Timer* events, which the program invokes every 60 seconds. The following code implements the *Timer* events for the two *Timer* controls:

```
Private Sub tmrReceive_Timer()
  RaiseEvent Timeout("receive")
End Sub

Private Sub tmrSend_Timer()
  RaiseEvent Timeout("send")
End Sub
```

As you can see, both events raise the *Timeout* event—the *tmrReceive* timer raises it with a *receive* string, while the *tmrSend* raises it with a *send* string.

WRITING THE EVENTS FOR THE WSKLISTEN WINSOCK CONTROL

As you learned when you designed the *frmWinsockFrm* form, the *prjSocketsDLL* project uses three *Winsock* controls—the *wskListen, wskReceive,* and *wskSend* controls. When the *prjSocketsDLL* project waits for a connection request from a remote computer, it will use the *wskListen Winsock* control. Within the *wskListen* control's events, you will write program code within the *ConnectionRequest* and *Connect* events. The following code implements the *ConnectionRequest* event:

```
Private Sub wskListen_ConnectionRequest(ByVal requestID As Long)
  On Error Resume Next                          'reject multiple requests
  wskReceive.Accept requestID
  If Err Then Exit Sub
  On Error GoTo 0
  If Connected = False Then
     wskSend.RemotePort = wskListen.LocalPort + PortOffset
     wskSend.Remotehost = wskReceive.RemoteHostIP
     wskSend.Close
     wskSend.Connect
  End If
End Sub
```

The *Winsock* control will raise the *ConnectionRequest* event whenever it receives an incoming request to connect from a remote computer. The program code within the event first tries to accept the incoming request. The *On Error Resume Next* statement protects against the control trying to open a socket to multiple incoming connection requests. After it successfully accepts an incoming connection request, the program code sends out its own connection request along the *wskSend* control, which lets the computer use two-way communications.

After the control successfully establishes a connection, the *wskListen* control will raise the *Connect* event. Within the *Connect* event, the program simply turns off the *Waiting* variable. The following code implements the *Connect* event:

```
Private Sub wskListen_Connect()
   Waiting = False
End Sub
```

WRITING THE CODE FOR THE WSKRECEIVE WINSOCK CONTROL

As you have learned, the *frmWinsockFrm* form uses three *Winsock* controls. The *wskSend* and *wskListen* controls establish two-way communications between two computers. However, when the program receives incoming data from a remote computer, it will do so on the *wskReceive Winsock* control. When a *Winsock* control receives incoming data, it raises its *DataArrival* event. The following code implements the *DataArrival* event:

```
Private Sub wskReceive_DataArrival(ByVal bytesTotal As Long)
   Static TransferType As Byte
   Static ContentSize As Long
   Static Filename As String
   Static Mode As Byte

   ReceivingData = True
   tmrReceive.Enabled = False   'reset timeout counter
   tmrReceive.Enabled = True
   Select Case Mode
     Case HEADERTYPE
       wskReceive.GetData TransferType, vbByte
       Mode = HEADERSIZE                         ' set to receive data size info
       wskReceive.SendData "ok"
     Case HEADERSIZE
       wskReceive.GetData ContentSize, vbLong
       Mode = HEADERDONE                         ' set to receive content
       wskReceive.SendData "ok"
     Case HEADERDONE
       Select Case TransferType
         Case DATATEXT
           GetText ContentSize, Mode
         Case DATABINARY
           GetBinary Mode
         Case DATAFILE
           If Filename = "" Then
             wskReceive.GetData Filename, vbString
             wskReceive.SendData "ok"
           Else
             GetFile Filename, ContentSize, Mode
           End If
         Case DATAPICTURE
             GetPic ContentSize, Mode
       End Select
   End Select
End Sub
```

653

Within the *DataArrival* event, the program code first resets the *tmrReceive* control each time it receives incoming data to protect against a *Timeout* event in the middle of a transmission. Next, the program code checks the *Mode* variable's value to determine how the program will respond. The *Mode* variable's value is always 0 at the beginning of a transmission, which equals the *HEADERTYPE* constant. If the program is receiving the file's header, which specifies the incoming file type and the file's length, it processes that data and places the file type information within the *TransferType* variable and the file's length within the *ContentSize* variable.

After the program code processes the incoming header, it will process the content within the file. The program code uses a second *Select Case* statement on the *TransferType* variable. If the *TransferType* variable indicates the incoming data is text, the program calls the *GetText* procedure. If the variable indicates the data is binary, the program calls the *GetBinary* procedure. For incoming files and pictures, the program code calls the *GetFile* and *GetBinary* procedures to perform similar processing.

WRITING THE CODE FOR THE GETTEXT PROCEDURE

As the previous section details, when the *wskReceive* control receives data whose header indicates the data is of type text, the *DataArrival* event will invoke the *GetText* procedure. The *GetText* procedure, in turn, will retrieve the incoming data from the *wskReceive* control, place it into a buffer, and raise the *TextReceived* event. The following code implements the *GetText* procedure:

```
Sub GetText(TextSize As Long, Mode As Byte)
   Dim TextComplete As Boolean
   Dim DataIn As String

   wskReceive.GetData DataIn, vbString          ' retrieve the data
   BufferText = BufferText & DataIn
   If InStr(DataIn, Chr$(0)) Then _
       DataIn = Left$(DataIn, EndPoint - 1)
   If Len(BufferText) = TextSize Then _
       TextComplete = True                      ' got the whole thing
   DoEvents
   If TextComplete Then
     tmrReceive.Enabled = False
     TextComplete = False
     Mode = HEADERTYPE
     wskReceive.SendData "ok"
     RaiseEvent TextReceived(BufferText)   ' let program know transfer over
     BufferText = ""
     ReceivingData = False
   End If
End Sub
```

The program code within the *GetText* procedure first uses the *wskReceive* control's *GetData* method to retrieve the data from the socket connection and place it into the *DataIn* string variable. The program code then adds the *DataIn* value to the *BufferText* variable. The program code then checks to determine whether the *DataIn* string contains the *Chr(0)* value (which, as you have learned, indicates the end of a string in C/C++ and, because Windows API calls handle the underlying Winsock transfers, a string that ends in *Chr(0)* should not be particularly surprising). If the string does contain the *Chr(0)* value, the program trims the value from the string. If the string's length equals the total string size, as the transfer's header indicated, the program code sets the *TextComplete* flag to *True*. If *TextComplete* is *True*, the program completes the reception, sends an *ok* message to the remote computer, and raises the *TextReceived* event, passing the *BufferText* value within the event.

WRITING THE CODE FOR THE GETBINARY PROCEDURE

As you have learned, when the *wskReceive* control receives data whose header indicates the data is of type binary, the *DataArrival* event will invoke the *GetBinary* procedure. The *GetBinary* procedure, in turn, will retrieve the incoming data from the *wskReceive* control and raise the *BinaryReceived* event. The following code implements the *GetBinary* procedure:

```
Sub GetBinary(Mode As Byte)
  Dim DataIn() As Byte

  tmrReceive.Enabled = False
  wskReceive.GetData DataIn, vbArray + vbByte
  Mode = HEADERTYPE
  wskReceive.SendData "ok"
```

```
RaiseEvent BinaryReceived(UnMakeBA(DataIn))
ReceivingData = False
End Sub
```

The program code within the *GetBinary* procedure retrieves the data from the *wskReceive* control within a *Byte* array. After it completes the retrieval, the program code sends an *ok* message to the remote computer and raises the *BinaryReceived* event, within which it passes the *Byte* array after the program converts the array to a *Variant* (within the *UnMakeBA* function you wrote earlier in this chapter).

Writing the Code for the GetFile Procedure

As this chapter's "Writing the Code for the *wskReceive Winsock* Control" section details, after the *wskReceive* control receives data whose header indicates the data is a file, the *DataArrival* event will invoke the *GetFile* procedure. The *GetFile* procedure, in turn, will retrieve the incoming data from the *wskReceive* control, write the file information to the download directory, and raise the *FileReceived* event after it finishes saving the file. The following code implements the *GetFile* procedure:

655

```
Private Sub GetFile(Filename As String, FileSize As Long, Mode As Byte)
    Static SoFarIn As Long
    Static ThisFile As Long
    Dim SaveComplete As Boolean
    Dim DataIn() As Byte

    wskReceive.GetData DataIn, vbArray + vbByte
    If SoFarIn = 0 Then
      ThisFile = FreeFile
      On Error Resume Next
      Open sDLPath & "\" & Filename For Output As ThisFile
      Close ThisFile
      If Err Then
        MsgBox "Invalid download directory!"
        SaveComplete = True
        GoTo CompleteProcessing
      End If
      Open sDLPath & "\" & Filename For Binary As ThisFile
    End If
    SoFarIn = LOF(ThisFile) + 1     'Set start point
    Put ThisFile, SoFarIn, DataIn()
    If LOF(ThisFile) = FileSize Then
      SaveComplete = True
      SoFarIn = 0
    End If

CompleteProcessing:
    If SaveComplete Then
      tmrReceive.Enabled = False
      SaveComplete = False
      Mode = HEADERTYPE
      Close ThisFile
      wskReceive.SendData "ok"
      RaiseEvent FileReceived(Filename)
      Filename = ""
      ReceivingData = False
    End If
End Sub
```

The *SoFarIn* variable maintains information about how much of the file the program has already written to the disk. If *SoFarIn* is 0, the program has not yet written information to the disk, and the program must create the file on the drive to which it will write the incoming file. The program opens the file for output and then closes the file. If the program cannot successfully open a file to write to, it will display an error message to the user, call the *CompleteProcessing* routine, and exit the *GetFile* procedure. If, on the other hand, the program successfully opens the file for output, it will reopen the file for binary output and begin to write the incoming data to the file.

The program code uses the *Put* method to write the *DataIn Byte* array to the file. The code then checks to determine whether the file's length equals the length the header indicates for the file. If it does, the program sets *SaveComplete* to *True* and calls the *CompleteProcessing* routine.

Within the *CompleteProcessing* routine, the program code determines whether or not the file is complete. If the file's download is not complete, the program code performs no processing. If the file's download is complete, the program code sends the *ok* message to the remote computer, closes the local file, and raises the *FileReceived* event.

WRITING THE CODE FOR THE GETPIC PROCEDURE

As this chapter's "Writing the Code for the *wskReceive* Winsock Control" section details, when the *wskReceive* control receives data whose header indicates the data is a picture, the *DataArrival* event will invoke the *GetPic* procedure.

The *GetPic* procedure, in turn, will retrieve the incoming data from the *wskReceive* control, write the picture file's information into a temporary file in the temporary directory, and raise the *PictureReceived* event when it finishes saving the file. The following code implements the *GetPic* procedure:

```
Private Sub GetPic(PictureSize As Long, Mode As Byte)
   Static ThisFile As Long
   Static ScratchFile As String
   Static SoFarIn As Long
   Dim SaveComplete As Boolean
   Dim DataIn() As Byte

   wskReceive.GetData DataIn, vbArray + vbByte
   If SoFarIn = 0 Then
     ScratchFile = TempFile
     ThisFile = FreeFile
     Open ScratchFile For Output As ThisFile
     Close ThisFile
     Open ScratchFile For Binary As ThisFile
   End If
   SoFarIn = LOF(ThisFile) + 1      'Set start point
   Put ThisFile, SoFarIn, DataIn()
   If LOF(ThisFile) = PictureSize Then
     SaveComplete = True
     SoFarIn = 0
   End If
   If SaveComplete Then
     tmrReceive.Enabled = False
     SaveComplete = False
     Mode = HEADERTYPE
     Close ThisFile
     wskReceive.SendData "ok"
     RaiseEvent PictureReceived(ScratchFile)
     ReceivingData = False
   End If
End Sub
```

Much as it does in the *GetFile* procedure, the *SoFarIn* variable in the *GetPic* procedure maintains information about how much of the picture file the program has already written to the disk. If *SoFarIn* is 0, the program has not yet written information to the disk, and the program must create the file on the drive to which it will write the incoming file. The *GetPic* procedure calls the *TempFile* function to create a temporary file within the system's temporary directory, opens the file for output, and then closes the file. The program code then reopens the file for binary output and begins to write the incoming data to the file.

The program code uses the *Put* method to write the *DataIn Byte* array to the file. The code then checks to determine whether the file's length equals the length the header indicates for the file. If it does, the program sets *SaveComplete* to *True*. If *SaveComplete* is *True*, the program code sends the *ok* message to the remote computer, closes the local file, and raises the *PictureReceived* event, within which it passes the name of the file that contains the downloaded picture file.

WRITING THE CODE FOR THE SENDTEXT FUNCTION

In addition to receiving incoming information, the *prjSocketsDLL* project lets you send outgoing information to the remotely connected computer. The program code for the *Send* functions is similar to the code for the *Get* procedures, except all the *Send* functions use the *wskSend* control to transmit information to the remote computer. In fact, you can think of the *Send* functions as performing the same steps as the *Get* functions, only in reverse. The following code implements the *SendText* function:

```
Function SendText(Content As String) As Boolean
   Dim Handshake As Boolean

   On Error GoTo SendFailed
   RaiseEvent SendBegin
   BufferText = ""
   If wskSend.State = sckConnected Then
      Sending = True
      wskSend.SendData DATATEXT
   Else
      RaiseEvent SockError(0, "Remote connection lost", "SendText method")
      Exit Function
   End If
   Handshake = WaitForHandshake
   If wskSend.State = sckConnected Then
      Sending = True
      wskSend.SendData CLng(Len(Content))
   Else
      RaiseEvent SockError(0, "Remote connection lost", "SendText method")
      Exit Function
   End If
   Handshake = WaitForHandshake
   If wskSend.State = sckConnected Then
      Sending = True
      wskSend.SendData Content
   Else
      RaiseEvent SockError(0, "Remote connection lost", "SendText method")
      Exit Function
   End If
   Handshake = WaitForHandshake

CompleteProcessing:
   RaiseEvent SendCompleted
   Exit Function

SendFailed:
   RaiseEvent SockError(Err.Number, Err.Description, "SendText method" & _
      vbCrLf & "      ***Connection closed***")
   Err = 0
   LockStep = CloseSockets
   Resume CompleteProcessing
End Function
```

When the *SendText* function begins its processing, the first code it executes raises the *SendBegin* event from the form. The program code then checks to be sure a valid connection exists and, if it does, calls the *wskSend* control's *SendData* method, passing the *DATATEXT* constant to the control as the header for the data. If a valid connection does not exist, the program code raises an error that indicates the lost connection. The program code then invokes the *WaitForHandshake* function, which forces the processing within the *SendText* function to stop until the remote computer informs the program that it successfully received the header information.

After the execution begins again, the program code checks to make sure the connection is still valid and then calls the *SendData* method. However, in the second invocation, the program code passes the *Content* parameter, which contains the actual text the program is to send. If the second transmission completes successfully, the program code calls the *SendCompleted* event and exits the function.

If an error occurs at any point during the function's processing, the program code calls the *SendFailed* routine, which raises the error (that is, it raises the *WinsockError* event), closes all the sockets, and exits the function.

WRITING THE CODE FOR THE SENDBINARY FUNCTION

As you have learned, the *prjSocketsDLL* project lets you send outgoing information to the remotely connected computer. In the previous section, you wrote the program code for the *SendText* function. The *SendBinary* function performs similar processing. The following code implements the *SendBinary* function:

658

```
Function SendBinary(Content As Variant)
  Dim TransferArray() As Byte
  Dim Handshake As Boolean

  On Error GoTo SendFailed
  RaiseEvent SendBegin
  MakeBA Content, TransferArray
  Sending = True
  wskSend.SendData DATABINARY
  Handshake = WaitForHandshake
  Sending = True
  wskSend.SendData UBound(TransferArray) - 1
  Handshake = WaitForHandshake
  Sending = True
  wskSend.SendData TransferArray
  Handshake = WaitForHandshake

CompleteProcessing:
  RaiseEvent SendCompleted
  Exit Function

SendFailed:
  RaiseEvent SockError(Err.Number, Err.Description, "SendBinary method" & _
      vbCrLf & "       ***Connection closed***")
  Err = 0
  LockStep = CloseSockets
  Resume CompleteProcessing
End Function
```

When the *SendBinary* function begins its processing, the first code it executes raises the *SendBegin* event. The program code then calls the *MakeBA* function to convert the data into a *Byte* array. Next, the program code calls the *wskSend* control's *SendData* method, which passes the *DATABINARY* constant to the control as the header for the data. If a valid connection does not exist, the program code will call the *SendFailed* routine. The program code then invokes the *WaitForHandshake* function, which forces the processing within the *SendBinary* function to stop until the remote computer informs the program that it successfully received the header information.

After execution resumes within the *SendBinary* function, the program code again calls the *SendData* method. However, in the second invocation, the program code passes the size of the *TransferArray Byte* array, which informs the remote computer how many bytes it will receive. The program code then invokes the *WaitForHandshake* function, which forces the processing within the *SendBinary* function to stop until the remote computer informs the program that it successfully received the array's size.

After execution resumes within the *SendBinary* function, the program code again calls the *SendData* method. In the third invocation, the program code passes the *TransferArray Byte* array itself. The program code then invokes the *WaitForHandshake* function, which forces the processing within the *SendBinary* function to stop until the remote computer informs the program that it successfully received the entire array. After the last transmission completes successfully, the program code raises the *SendCompleted* event.

If an error occurs at any point during the function's processing, the program code calls the *SendFailed* routine, which raises the error, closes all the sockets, and exits the function.

WRITING THE CODE FOR THE SENDFILE FUNCTION

As the previous sections detail, the *prjSocketsDLL* project lets you send outgoing information to the remotely connected computer. In the previous section, you wrote the program code for the *SendBinary* function. The *SendFile* function performs similar processing. The following code implements the *SendFile* function:

```
Public Function SendFile(Path As String, Filename As String) As Boolean
   Static ThisFile As Long
   Dim TransferSize As Long
   Dim Content() As Byte

   On Error GoTo SendFailed
   SendFile = True
   RaiseEvent SendBegin
   ThisFile = FreeFile
   Open Path & "\" & Filename For Binary As ThisFile
   TransferSize = LOF(ThisFile)
   On Error Resume Next
   ReDim Content(TransferSize - 1)
   If Err.Number <> 0 Then
     SendFile = False
     Close ThisFile
     GoTo CompleteProcessing
   End If
   On Error GoTo SendFailed
   Get ThisFile, 1, Content()
   Close ThisFile
   Sending = True
   wskSend.SendData DATAFILE
   Do While Sending
     DoEvents
   Loop
   Sending = True
   wskSend.SendData TransferSize
   Do While Sending
     DoEvents
   Loop
   Sending = True
   wskSend.SendData Filename
   Do While Sending
     DoEvents
   Loop
   Sending = True
   wskSend.SendData Content
   Do While Sending
     DoEvents
   Loop

CompleteProcessing:
   RaiseEvent SendCompleted
   SendFile = False
   Exit Function
```

```
SendFailed:
   RaiseEvent SockError(Err.Number, Err.Description, "SendFile method" & _
      vbCrLf & "       ***Connection closed***")
   Err = 0
   LockStep = CloseSockets
   Resume CompleteProcessing
End Function
```

When the *SendFile* function begins its processing, the first code it executes raises the *SendBegin* event from the form. The program code then opens the file it is to transfer as a binary file, and reads the file's size. After the program reads the file's size, it uses the *Get* statement to load the entire file into the *TransferArray Byte* array.

Next, the program code calls the *wskSend* control's *SendData* method, which passes the *DATAFILE* constant to the control as the header for the data. If a valid connection does not exist, the program code will call the *SendFailed* routine. The program code then uses a *Do-While* loop to wait until the remote computer informs the program that it successfully received the header information.

After the program code exits the *Do-While* loop, it again calls the *SendData* method. However, in the second invocation, the program code passes the size of the *TransferArray Byte* array, which informs the remote computer how many bytes it will receive. The program code then uses a *Do-While* loop to wait until the remote computer informs the program that it successfully received the *Byte* array's size.

After the program code exits the *Do-While* loop, it again calls the *SendData* method. In the third invocation, the program code passes the *TransferArray Byte* array itself. The program code then uses a *Do-While* loop to wait until the remote computer informs the program that it successfully received the *Byte* array's size. After the last transmission completes successfully, the program code raises the *SendCompleted* event.

If an error occurs at any point during the function's processing, the program code calls the *SendFailed* routine, which raises the error, closes all the sockets, and exits the function.

WRITING THE CODE FOR THE SENDPIC FUNCTION

As the previous sections detail, the *prjSocketsDLL* project lets you send outgoing information to the remotely connected computer. In the previous section, you wrote the program code for the *SendFile* function. The *SendPic* function performs similar processing. The following code implements the *SendPic* function:

```
Public Function SendPic(PicFileDump As String) As Boolean
   Static ThisFile As Long
   Dim TransferSize As Long
   Dim Content() As Byte

   On Error GoTo SendFailed
   RaiseEvent SendBegin
   ThisFile = FreeFile
   Open PicFileDump For Binary As ThisFile
      TransferSize = LOF(ThisFile)
      ReDim Content(TransferSize - 1)
      Get ThisFile, 1, Content()
   Close ThisFile
   Kill PicFileDump
   Sending = True
   wskSend.SendData DATAPICTURE
   Do While Sending
      DoEvents
   Loop
   Sending = True
   wskSend.SendData TransferSize
   Do While Sending
```

```
      DoEvents
   Loop
   Sending = True
   wskSend.SendData Content
   Do While Sending
      DoEvents
   Loop

CompleteProcessing:
   RaiseEvent SendCompleted
   Exit Function

SendFailed:
   RaiseEvent SockError(Err.Number, Err.Description, "SendPic method" & vbCrLf _
      & "      ***Connection closed***")
   Err = 0
   LockStep = CloseSockets
   Resume CompleteProcessing
End Function
```

When the *SendPic* function begins its processing, the first code the function executes will raise the *SendBegin* event from the form. The program code then opens the picture file it is to transfer as a binary file, and reads the picture file's size. After the program reads the picture file's size, it uses the *Get* statement to load the entire picture file into the *TransferArray Byte* array.

Next, the program code calls the *wskSend* control's *SendData* method, which passes the *DATAPICTURE* constant to the control as the header for the data. If a valid connection does not exist, the program code will call the *SendFailed* routine. The program code then uses a *Do-While* loop to wait until the remote computer informs the program that it successfully received the header information.

After the program code exits the *Do-While* loop, it again calls the *SendData* method. However, in the second invocation, the program code passes the size of the *TransferArray Byte* array, which informs the remote computer how many bytes it will receive. The program code then uses a *Do-While* loop to wait until the remote computer informs the program that it successfully received the *Byte* array's size.

After the program code exits the *Do-While* loop, it again calls the *SendData* method. In the third invocation, the program code passes the *TransferArray Byte* array itself. The program code then uses a *Do-While* loop to wait until the remote computer informs the program that it successfully received the *Byte* array's size. After the last transmission completes successfully, the program code raises the *SendCompleted* event.

If an error occurs at any point during the function's processing, the program code calls the *SendFailed* routine, which raises the error, closes all the sockets, and exits the function.

WRITING THE CODE FOR THE WSKSEND CONTROL'S EVENTS

As you have learned, the *frmWinsockFrm* form uses three *Winsock* controls to perform its processing. The *wskReceive* control receives incoming data; the *wskListen* control listens for a connect request from a remote computer. The *wskSend* control, therefore, sends the connect request to the remote computer and sends outgoing data to the remote computer. The program code includes four events for the *wskSend* control. The following code implements the *wskSend_Connect* event:

```
Private Sub wskSend_Connect()
   Waiting = False
   RaiseEvent RemoteConnected(wskSend.Remotehost)
End Sub
```

Within the *wskSend_Connect* event, the program code sets the *Waiting* variable to *False* (indicating the connection is successful) and then raises the *RemoteConnected* event.

Because the *wskSend* control only sends data, the only time it will receive data is if the remote user is sending a handshake message to the program to let the program know it received the data correctly. The following code implements the *DataArrival* event for the *wskSend* event:

```
Private Sub wskSend_DataArrival(ByVal bytesTotal As Long)
   Dim Handshake As String

   wskSend.GetData Handshake, vbString
   If Handshake = "ok" Then Sending = False
End Sub
```

The event's program code uses the *GetData* method to retrieve the incoming data from the control and then checks the data. If the data equals the *ok* message that the other controls send after a successful transmission, the program code sets the *Sending* variable to *False*—which alerts the program that the transmission is complete. Otherwise, the program code ignores any other values it receives from the *wskSend* control.

662 The *wskSend* control raises the *Error* event whenever a connection breaks, a transmission is unsuccessful, or some other communication error occurs. The following code implements the *wskSend_Error* event:

```
Private Sub wskSend_Error(ByVal Number As Integer, Description As String, _
      ByVal Scode As Long, ByVal Source As String, ByVal HelpFile As String, _
      ByVal HelpContext As Long, CancelDisplay As Boolean)
   If Number = 10037 Then
      Connected = False
   Else
      RaiseEvent SockError(Number, Description, "wskSend_Error")
      LockStep = CloseSockets
   End If
   Waiting = False
End Sub
```

If the error number equals 10037, the connection is broken, but the program will not raise an error to the client program. On the other hand, any other error number will indicate some type of transmission error, which the program code will raise within the *SockError* event.

As you learned, the *frmWinsockFrm* form uses *Timer* controls to protect against a timeout. To ensure the *Timer* controls do not invoke the *Timer* event when the program is receiving data, the program code within the *SendProgress* event resets the timer every time the *wskSend* control raises the event. The following code implements the *SendProgress* event for the *wskSend* control:

```
Private Sub wskSend_SendProgress(ByVal bytesSent As Long, _
      ByVal bytesRemaining As Long)
   tmrSend.Enabled = False   'reset timeout counter
   tmrSend.Enabled = True
End Sub
```

WRITING THE CODE FOR THE WAITFORHANDSHAKE FUNCTION

As you have learned, all the *Send* functions wait for a response from the remote computer before they continue their processing. The functions use the *WaitForHandshake* function to pause until the program receives the continuation information from the remote computer. The following code implements the *WaitForHandshake* function:

```
Private Function WaitForHandshake() As Boolean
   Do While Sending
      DoEvents
   Loop
   WaitForHandshake = True
End Function
```

As you can see, the *WaitForHandshake* function loops until the *Sending* variable is *False*. As the previous section details, the program code within the *wskSend* control's *DataArrival* event sets the *Sending* variable to *False*.

WRITING THE CODE FOR THE *frmINTERNETCHAT* FORM

Now that you have written the code for the *prjSocketsDLL* project, including all the code for the internal processing the DLL performs and the events its raises into the calling program, you can write the code for the *frmInternetChat* form. The form declares six variables that it uses throughout its processing. The following code implements the variable declarations within the *frmInternetChat* form's General–Declarations section:

```
Private Success As Boolean, DropOK As Boolean
Private PicName As String, SendFilePath As String, SendFileName As String
Private WithEvents SocketsDLL As clsSocketsDLL
```

The *Success* and *DropOK* variables are both flag variables, which indicate the program's current status. The *PicName* string will hold the filename of a picture you transmit through the program, and the *SendFilePath* and *SendFileName* variables will hold information about the path and filename of any files you transmit through the program. Finally, the *SocketsDLL* variable (which you declare with the *WithEvents* keyword) raises the events from the *prjSocketsDLL* Dynamic-Link Library (DLL) into the *frmInternetChat* form.

WRITING THE CODE FOR THE *FORM_LOAD* EVENT

As you have learned, whenever your programs load or display a form, the first program code that will execute is the program code within the *Form_Load* event. The following code implements the *Form_Load* event for the *frmInternetChat* form:

```
Private Sub Form_Load()
   Stat "Offline"
End Sub
```

Within the *Form_Load* event, the program code calls the *Stat* procedure and passes in the *Offline* string. The *Stat* procedure will display status information in the *lblStatus* control at the *frmInternetChat* form's bottom. The following code implements the *Stat* procedure:

```
Private Sub Stat(Status As String)
   lblStatus.Caption = Status
End Sub
```

WRITING THE CODE FOR THE *cmdCONNECT_CLICK* EVENT

As you learned in this chapter's "Using the *prjInternetChat* Project" section, one communicating computer must listen for a connection and the other must start the connection. To start the connection, the user must click the mouse on the *cmdConnect* button. The following code implements the *cmdConnect_Click* event:

```
Private Sub cmdConnect_Click()
   Dim Remotehost As String

   Set SocketsDLL = Nothing
   Set SocketsDLL = New clsSocketsDLL
   Remotehost = Trim$(txtHost.Text)
   If Remotehost = "" Then Exit Sub
   Stat "Connecting to " & Remotehost
   cmdListen.Enabled = False
   cmdConnect.Enabled = False
   SocketsDLL.Offset = -chkOffset.Value
   Success = SocketsDLL.Connect(Remotehost, 8888)
   Stat "Connected to " & Remotehost
```

```
    SocketsDLL.DLPath = App.Path
End Sub
```

The *cmdConnect_Click* event's program code first clears the object reference within the *SocketsDLL* control and then creates a new object reference. The program code then sets the *Remotehost* variable to the value within the *txtHost* control on the *frmInternetChat* form's Connect tab. If the user does not enter a valid host name, the program code will exit the event. If the user does enter a valid host name, the program code will change the status to reflect its connection attempt, set the *SocketsDLL* object's *Offset* property (either to 0, if the user is connecting to a remote machine, or to 10, if the user is connecting to another, local instance of the program), and invoke the *SocketsDLL* object's *Connect* method. After the connection completes, the program code changes the status bar and sets the download path to the application's current path.

WRITING THE CODE FOR THE CMDLISTEN_CLICK EVENT

664   As you learned in this chapter's "Using the *prjInternetChat* Project" section, one communicating computer must listen for a connection and the other must start the connection. To listen for a connection, the user must click the mouse on the *cmdListen* button. The following code implements the *cmdListen_Click* event:

```
Private Sub cmdListen_Click()
  Set SocketsDLL = Nothing
  Set SocketsDLL = New clsSocketsDLL
  cmdListen.Enabled = False
  cmdConnect.Enabled = False
  SocketsDLL.Offset = -chkOffset.Value
  SocketsDLL.Listen 8888
  SocketsDLL.DLPath = App.Path
  Stat "Listening for remote connection request"
End Sub
```

The *cmdListen_Click* event's program code first the clears the object reference within the *SocketsDLL* control and then creates a new object reference. The program code then listens on a port (the program uses 8888, but you can use any number, provided it is not one of the well-known port numbers on the Internet), sets the download path to the application's current path, and changes the status to reflect that the program is now listening for a connection.

WRITING THE PROGRAM CODE TO SEND TEXT, FILES, AND PICTURES

As you have learned, the *prjInternetChat* project lets you send text (from the Chat tab), files (from the File tab), and pictures (from the Picture tab) to a remote user. The code within the *CommandButton* events that makes such transmissions is all relatively similar. The Send button on each tab calls the appropriate *SocketsDLL* object's *Send* method to transmit its information. The following code implements the *cmdText_Click* event:

```
Private Sub cmdText_Click()
  Dim Success As Boolean

  Stat "Sending text"
  txtIn.Text = txtIn.Text & ">" & txtOut.Text & vbCrLf
  Scroll
  Success = SocketsDLL.SendText(txtOut.Text & vbCrLf)
  txtOut.Text = ""
  cmdText.Default = True
End Sub
```

The *cmdText_Click* event's program code first changes the status line and then sets up the outgoing text. Next, the program code calls the *Scroll* procedure, which scrolls the multi-line text box. You will write the *Scroll* procedure in the next section. After the program code scrolls the text box, it calls the *SendText* method. After the *SendText* method returns from its processing, the program code clears the *txtOut* control and returns the focus to the *cmdText* button.

When the user sends files, the program performs similar processing, except it must invoke only the *SendFile* method. To send files, the user must click the mouse on the *cmdFile* button. The following code implements the *cmdFile_Click* event:

```
Private Sub cmdFile_Click()
   Dim Success As Boolean

   Stat "Sending file: " & SendFileName
   Success = SocketsDLL.SendFile(SendFilePath, SendFileName)
End Sub
```

Just as the *cmdFile_Click* event calls the *SendFile* method of the *SocketsDLL* object, the *cmdPic_Click* event's program code calls the *SendPic* method of the *SocketsDLL* object. Before the program code calls the method, however, the program code saves a temporary copy of the file to transfer. The following code implements the *cmdPic_Click* event:

```
Private Sub cmdPic_Click()
   Dim Success As Boolean

   Stat "Sending picture"
   SavePicture picTransfer.Image, App.Path & "\vbpl.bmp"
   Success = SocketsDLL.SendPic(App.Path & "\vbpl.bmp")
End Sub
```

The program code uses Visual Basic's *SavePicture* statement to save the bitmap to a temporary file in the application path and then uses the *SendPic* method to transmit the file to the remote computer.

WRITING THE CODE FOR THE SCROLL PROCEDURE

As the previous section details, the *SendText* procedure calls the *Scroll* procedure after it adds the outgoing text to the *txtIn* control. The *Scroll* procedure moves the start point for text additions to the end of the text in the *txtIn* control. The following code implements the *Scroll* procedure:

```
Private Sub Scroll()
   txtIn.SelStart = Len(txtIn)
End Sub
```

WRITING THE SCROLLBAR EVENTS FOR THE HORIZONTAL AND VERTICAL SCROLL BARS

As you have learned, the user can use the horizontal and vertical scroll bars to change the viewing area of a picture. The scroll bars move the *picTransfer* control's position within the *picHolder* control, depending on the scroll bar's value. The user can change each scroll bar's value in one of two ways: dragging the thumb or clicking the mouse on the arrows at the scroll bar's end. The following code implements the events for the *hscPic* and *vscPic* controls:

```
Private Sub hscPic_Change()
   hscPic_Scroll
End Sub

Private Sub hscPic_Scroll()
   picTransfer.Left = -hscPic.Value
End Sub

Private Sub vscPic_Change()
   vscPic_Scroll
End Sub

Private Sub vscPic_Scroll()
   picTransfer.Top = -vscPic.Value
End Sub
```

As you can see, the program code changes the *picTransfer* control's position based on the scroll bar's value.

WRITING THE DRAG-AND-DROP EVENTS FOR THE PICTUREBOX CONTROLS

As you learned in this chapter's "Using the *prjInternetChat* Project" section, the user can drag picture files from Windows *Explorer* onto the *frmInternetChat* form and drop them onto the display area within the form. To provide such functionality to the user, the program uses two events: the *OLEDragOver* event and the *OLEDragDrop* event. As you have learned, the *frmInternetChat* form contains two *PictureBox* controls—the *picHolder* control and the *picTransfer* control the *picHolder* control contains. The following code implements the events for the *picHolder* *PictureBox* control:

```
Private Sub picHolder_OLEDragOver(Data As DataObject, Effect As Long, _
    Button As Integer, Shift As Integer, X As Single, Y As Single, _
    State As Integer)
  ParsePicDrop Data
End Sub

Private Sub picHolder_OLEDragDrop(Data As DataObject, Effect As Long, _
    Button As Integer, Shift As Integer, X As Single, Y As Single)
  picTransfer_OLEDragDrop Data, Effect, Button, Shift, X, Y
End Sub
```

When the user drags the file over the *picHolder* control, the control will raise the *OLEDragOver* event. The program code within the event will, in turn, call the *ParsePicDrop* procedure, which verifies that the file is a valid picture object. When the user drops the file onto the *picHolder* control, the control will raise the *OLEDragDrop* event. The program code within the event will then call the *OLEDragDrop* event for the *picTransfer* control, which will actually display the image.

The events for the *picTransfer* control perform similar processing, except the *picTransfer_OLEDragDrop* event will actually load and display the picture. The following code implements the *OLEDragOver* and *OLEDragDrop* events for the *picTransfer* control:

```
Private Sub picTransfer_OLEDragOver(Data As DataObject, Effect As Long, _
    Button As Integer, Shift As Integer, X As Single, Y As Single, _
    State As Integer)
  ParsePicDrop Data
End Sub

Private Sub picTransfer_OLEDragDrop(Data As DataObject, Effect As Long, _
    Button As Integer, Shift As Integer, X As Single, Y As Single)
  If DropOK = False Then _
      Exit Sub
  On Error Resume Next 'if somehow bad anyway
  PicName = Data.Files(1)
  Set picTransfer = LoadPicture(PicName)
  If Err Then
    Err = 0
    MsgBox "The data could not be loaded.", 16, "Invalid Graphics Data"
    Exit Sub
  End If
  On Error GoTo 0
  PrepPictureBox
End Sub
```

When the user drags the file over the *picTransfer* control, the control will raise the *OLEDragOver* event. The program code within the event will, in turn, call the *ParsePicDrop* procedure, which verifies that the file is a valid picture object. When the user drops the file onto the *picTransfer* control (or when the *picHolder* control invokes the *picTransfer* control's *OLEDragDrop* event), the *picTransfer* control will raise the *OLEDragDrop* event. The program code within the event will then load the picture into the *picTransfer* control.

As you will learn in the next section, the *ParsePicDrop* procedure verifies that the object the user wants to drop is a valid picture file. If it is not, the program code within the *OLEDragDrop* event will exit immediately, without performing any processing. On the other hand, if the *ParsePicDrop* procedure verifies that the picture is a valid picture file, the program code will use the *LoadPicture* method to load the picture into the *picTransfer* control. If the *LoadPicture* method fails for some reason (the file may be corrupted, for example), the event will display an error message and exit. If the program code successfully loads the picture, the event will invoke the *PrepPictureBox* procedure, which will set the *picTransfer* control's upper-left corner equal to the *picHolder* control's upper-left corner, and set up the scroll bars in the event the *picTransfer* control's picture is larger than the *picHolder* control's display area. The following code implements the *PrepPictureBox* procedure:

```
Private Sub PrepPictureBox()
  picTransfer.Move 0, 0
  If picTransfer.Width > picHolder.Width Then
    hscPic.Max = picTransfer.Width - picHolder.Width
    hscPic.SmallChange = hscPic.Max / 100
    hscPic.LargeChange = hscPic.Max / 10
    hscPic.Value = 0
    hscPic.Enabled = True
    hscPic.Visible = True
  Else
    hscPic.Visible = False
    hscPic.Enabled = False
  End If
  If picTransfer.Height > picHolder.Height Then
    vscPic.Max = picTransfer.Height - picHolder.Height
    vscPic.SmallChange = vscPic.Max / 100
    vscPic.LargeChange = vscPic.Max / 10
    vscPic.Value = 0
    vscPic.Enabled = True
    vscPic.Visible = True
  Else
    vscPic.Visible = False
    vscPic.Enabled = False
  End If
End Sub
```

667

As you can see, the program code checks the *picTransfer* control's width against the *picHolder* control's width. If the *picTransfer* control is larger, the program code enables the horizontal scroll bar. If the *picTransfer* control is smaller, the program code disables the horizontal scroll bar. The program code then performs similar processing within the height of the two controls, enabling or disabling the vertical scroll bar, as appropriate.

WRITING THE CODE FOR THE PARSEPICDROP PROCEDURE

As the previous section details, the *ParsePicDrop* procedure checks the item the user is currently dragging over the *PictureBox* controls and verifies that it is a valid picture file. The following code implements the *ParsePicDrop* procedure:

```
Private Sub ParsePicDrop(ThisItem As DataObject)
  Dim FileType As String

  On Error Resume Next
  FileType = ThisItem.Files(1)
  If Err Then
    Err = 0
    Exit Sub
  End If
  On Error Resume Next
  If Len(FileType) >= 4 Then
    FileType = LCase$(Right$(FileType, 4))
```

```
        Select Case FileType
          Case ".bmp", ".gif", ".jpg", ".ico", ".wmf"
            DropOK = True
          Case Else
            DropOK = False
        End Select
      Else
        DropOK = False
      End If
    End Sub
```

The program code first checks the *DataObject* object's *Files(1)* property, which contains the file name of the object the user is dragging. If the *DataObject* is not a file, the program code exits the procedure. If the *DataObject* is a file, the program code checks the file's extension to determine if the file is a valid file type that a *PictureBox* control can display. If it is a valid file type, the program code sets the *DropOK* variable to *True*—otherwise, the program code sets the *DropOK* variable to *False*.

WRITING THE CODE FOR THE *TXTFILE_OLEDRAGDROP* EVENT

As this chapter's "Writing the Drag-And-Drop Events for the *PictureBox* Controls" section details, to capture a user's drag-and-drop action you must place program code within the *OLEDragDrop* event. In addition to dragging picture files to the Picture tab, the user can drag files from the Windows *Explorer* to the *frmInternetChat* form's File tab. When the user drops a file on the *txtFile* control, the control will raise the *txtFile_OLEDragDrop* event. The following program code implements the *txtFile_OLEDragDrop* event:

```
Private Sub txtFile_OLEDragDrop(Data As DataObject, Effect As Long, _
    Button As Integer, Shift As Integer, X As Single, Y As Single)
  Dim FileName As String
  Dim Counter As Long

  On Error Resume Next
  FileName = Data.Files(1)
  txtFile = FileName
  If Err Then
    Err = 0
    txtFile = ""
    Exit Sub
  End If
  On Error GoTo 0
  If InStr(FileName, "\") Then
    For Counter = Len(FileName) To 1 Step -1
      If Mid$(FileName, Counter, 1) = "\" Then
        SendFilePath = Left$(FileName, Counter - 1)
        SendFileName = Right$(FileName, Len(FileName) - Counter)
        Exit For
      End If
    Next
  Else
    SendFilePath = ""
    SendFileName = FileName
  End If
End Sub
```

The program code within the *txtFile_OLEDragDrop* event first checks to be sure the item the user dropped is a valid file. If it is not a valid file, the program code will exit the event and perform no processing. If the item the user dropped is a valid file, the program code checks to determine whether the filename contains a backslash ("\")—which indicates the user dropped a file in a different path from the current path. If the filename contains a backslash, the program code parses the filename and places the path within the *SendFilePath* variable and the filename within the *SendFileName* variable. If the filename does not contain a backslash, the program code sets the *SendFilePath* variable to a *NULL* string and sets the *SendFileName* variable equal to the dropped file's filename.

WRITING THE CODE FOR THE TXTOUT_KEYPRESS EVENT

One of the *Chat* program's nicer features is that the user can send transmissions without clicking the mouse on the Send Text button—the user must only press the ENTER key. To capture the ENTER key and treat it as if the user clicked the mouse on the *cmdText* button, the program must include code within the *txtOut* control's *KeyPress* event. The following code implements the *txtOut_KeyPress* event:

```
Private Sub txtOut_KeyPress(KeyAscii As Integer)
   If KeyAscii = 13 And cmdText.Enabled Then
      KeyAscii = 0
      cmdText_Click
   End If
End Sub
```

As you can see, the program code checks to see whether the user pressed the ENTER key. If the user did and the *cmdText* button is enabled, the program will invoke the *cmdText_Click* event—sending the text within the *txtOut* control to the remote user.

WRITING THE CODE FOR THE LOCKBUTTONS PROCEDURE

When you perform transmissions, it is important to protect against the program trying to create additional transmissions before it completes the current transmission. The program code within the *frmInternetChat* form specifically protects against a user trying to send a file without first opening a valid connection. The program code calls the *LockButtons* procedure to disable the transmission buttons if a user does not have a valid connection. The following code implements the *LockButtons* procedure:

```
Private Sub LockButtons(ByVal State As Boolean)
   cmdText.Enabled = State
   cmdFile.Enabled = State
   cmdPic.Enabled = State
End Sub
```

As you can see, the program code sets the three *CommandButton* controls' *Enabled* property equal to the incoming *State* parameter.

WRITING THE EVENTS FOR THE SOCKETSDLL OBJECT

Now that you have written the program code for the *frmInternetChat* form other than the events the *SocketsDLL* object raises, you can write the event code for the events the *SocketsDLL* object raises into the form. Most of the events perform simple processing, such as changing the information in the *lblStatus* control and enabling buttons. When the program receives a file, for example, the *SocketsDLL* object will raise the *FileReceived* event and the program code within the event will display the file name and the path to which the program saved the file. The following code implements the *FileReceived* event:

```
Private Sub SocketsDLL_FileReceived(FileName As String)
   lblFileReceived.Caption = FileName
   Stat "File: " & FileName & " received saved to " & App.Path
End Sub
```

As you can see, the program code displays the filename within the *lblFileReceived* control and displays the path to which the program saved the file in the *lblStatus* control. The other events the *SocketsDLL* control raises perform similar processing. You can find the other events within the *frmInternetChat* form's program code, which the *prjInternetChat* project on the companion CD-ROM that accompanies this book contains in the *Chapter21* directory.

WRITING THE CODE TO EXIT THE PROGRAM

When you exit the *prjInternetChat* project, it is important that the program closes all open sockets. The program code within the *cmdEnd_Click* event performs the close action. The following code implements the *cmdEnd_Click* event:

```
Private Sub cmdEnd_Click()
   Set SocketsDLL = Nothing
```

```
      End
   End Sub
```

As you can see, the program code sets the *SocketsDLL* object variable to *Nothing*, which will destroy any open socket connections. The program code then exits the program. The program code within the *Form_Unload* event invokes the *cmdEnd_Click* event, as the following code shows:

```
   Private Sub Form_Unload(Cancel As Integer)
      cmdEnd_Click
   End Sub
```

ENHANCEMENTS YOU CAN MAKE TO THE PROJECTS

The *prjSocketsDLL* project is a very powerful and useful program. You can use it in many different situations—intranet transfers, direct file transfers, and more. The *prjInternetChat* program uses the *prjSocketsDLL* project effectively, but simply. Within the *prjSocketsDLL* project, you cannot enhance the DLL much because Winsock communications are relatively simple, one-to-one communications.

The *prjInternetChat* program, however, has significant room for enhancements. For example, you can change the input screen for the Chat tab so that users can enter more than a single line of text. For file transfers, you can add OLE support to the program so that the program automatically opens Microsoft *Word*®, for example, when the computer receives a *DOC* file. You can also add *ImageEdit* controls to the program, such as those you used within the *prjFileViewer* project you created in Chapter 4, "Using Multiple Forms to Load Different File Types," so that users can transmit other picture file types to remote users.

In Chapter 23, "Using the CryptoAPI to Encrypt Documents," you will learn how to encrypt information. You can add encryption support to the *prjInternetChat* program so that it encrypts all its files, pictures, and text before it transmits them to the receiving computer.

PUTTING IT ALL TOGETHER

This chapter's projects, *prjInternetChat* and *prjSocketsDLL*, introduced you to how to use the Microsoft *Winsock* control to establish direct communications with another computer over the Internet. You have also learned how to support drag-and-drop actions within your programs, how to use an ActiveX DLL to create an in-process server, and how to use the *Microsoft Tabbed Dialog* control to display multiple pages of information on a single form. In addition, you have revisited the use of custom events within your programs, the *WithEvents* keyword, and how to expose methods and properties within your classes. In Chapter 22, "Writing DCOM Objects for Networks," you will learn how to use ActiveX EXE programs and the principles of Component Object Model (COM) development to create objects that communicate across networks and are more scalable (capable of handling larger numbers of clients) than the out-of-process objects you have created in previous chapters. Before you continue with Chapter 22, however, make sure you understand the following key concepts:

✓ When you create in-process servers (programs that perform processing, but share process space with the clients that call them), you can use the ActiveX DLL project option to create the servers from within Visual Basic programs.

✓ To provide easy access to Transport Control Protocol (TCP) and User Datagram Protocol (UDP) network services, your Visual Basic programs can use the *Microsoft Winsock* control.

✓ You can raise events from any object to any other object that declares an instance of the object. Within the *prjInternetChat* and *prjSocketsDLL* projects, you raised an event from a form, to a class, to another form within a separate program entirely.

✓ You can create programs that respond to the user's mouse actions, such as dragging and dropping files. To respond to drag-and-drop events, your programs can place code within the *OLEDragDrop* and *OLEDragOver* events for the controls you want to support drag-and-drop.

✓ When you use the Windows sockets (*Winsock*) protocol to communicate with another computer over the Internet, your programs must first open a socket to that remote computer and then open a socket that holds a corresponding connection from the remote computer.

Chapter 22

Writing DCOM Objects for Networks

As you learned in Chapter 12, "Using ActiveX Automation to Create a Database Server," and in Chapter 13, "Creating a Network-Aware Client," it is easy to create out-of-process servers for Windows 95 and Windows NT with Visual Basic. As you learned in those chapters, creating an ActiveX executable (EXE) program that exposes properties and methods, installing that program to a computer, and adding a reference within the client project is all that you must do to create simple network components. The difficulty with creating network components is that you must build and deploy scalable, efficient, server-side objects. A *scalable* object is an object that works equally well when two computers are accessing the object as it will when two hundred computers are accessing the object. The *prjServer* program you created in Chapter 12, while sufficient for simple communications processing, would not work well if you had more than a few clients accessing the server. The difference between merely creating objects and creating scalable objects begins with a solid understanding of Microsoft's *Component Object Model* (COM) and *Distributed Component Object Model* (DCOM). In fact, when you create objects in Visual Basic, you simply cannot create scalable objects without completely understanding COM and DCOM.

In this chapter, you will learn the aspects of the Component Object Model (COM) and the Distributed Component Object Model (DCOM) that you must know to correctly implement scalable objects. You will learn about the interaction between a client and an in-process object and about the interaction between a client and an out-of-process object. Interactions between clients and in-process objects are not as complex as interactions between clients and out-of-process objects. However, if you intend to write scalable components, it is essential to understand what is happening behind the scenes when COM binds a client to an object. Visual Basic's developers have done an excellent job of hiding COM's details in past versions, but Visual Basic 5.0 lets you expose more COM details within your projects—providing you with more power and more flexibility in your Visual Basic objects. Visual Basic 5.0's additional power and programming flexibility lets you more closely control your COM and DCOM objects, but first you must understand more about COM and DCOM objects.

In this chapter, you will create six separate projects. The six projects consist of three project pairs, one client and one server per pair. Each pair details specific programming techniques and COM programming concerns you must consider when you write COM and DCOM components. You will work extensively with classes and the different COM characteristics all COM objects must evidence. By the time you finish this chapter, you will understand the following key concepts:

- ♦ Microsoft's Component Object Model (COM) specifies the relationships that objects in the same process should have with each other, and the communication protocols between those objects.

- ♦ Microsoft's Distributed Component Object Model (DCOM) expands on the COM specification. DCOM specifies the relationships that objects on separate computers, or operating within different processes, should have with each other, and the communication protocols between those objects.

- ♦ The fundamental concept behind both COM and DCOM is the interface. An *interface* is an agreement between a client and an object about how they will communicate with each other.

- ♦ When you define COM and DCOM objects, you will always define at least one interface.

- ♦ COM objects may fall into categories. A *category* of objects is a set of objects that all implement the same interfaces.

- ♦ A COM or DCOM object will derive all its interfaces from the base COM interface, *Iunknown*.

- Every COM or DCOM object includes three default methods that it must expose: *QueryInterface, AddRef,* and *Release.*

- You must register your COM and DCOM objects within the Windows Registry so that client programs can access the objects. If you do not register the objects, client programs will be unable to locate the object files.

- When you register a COM or DCOM object within the Windows Registry, you must reference that object's Globally Unique Identifier (GUID), which is a 128-bit (16 byte) number that uniquely identifies the object. Whenever a client program accesses a COM or DCOM object, the client program will use the GUID to reference the object within the Windows Registry.

- When you define interfaces in languages other than Visual Basic, you will use Microsoft's Interface Definition Language (IDL), which you must compile within the Microsoft Interface Definition Language compiler (the MIDL).

- Each interface that you define in a COM object will include a Universally Unique Identifier (UUID), which the operating system constructs exactly as it does a Globally Unique Identifier. When client programs access an interface the COM object exposes, the programs will actually reference the interface's UUID.

BETTER UNDERSTANDING COM

In earlier chapters, you learned how to create ActiveX components, whether the components were controls, ActiveX EXEs, or ActiveX Dynamic-Link Libraries (DLLs). As you have learned, ActiveX is a technology built around the Component Object Model's concepts. However, to write scalable DCOM components, you must now learn some COM concepts, and also some basic DCOM concepts. Before you write this chapter's projects, you must first better understand how to create COM objects in Visual Basic.

The most important concept you must learn when you consider COM is the concept of an interface. You must know what an interface is before you can do anything with COM. Conceptually, an interface is an agreement between a client and an object about how they will communicate. When you define a set of methods (that is, public functions that the object exposes), the interface becomes a communication channel between the client and the object. Within your program code, an interface is a collection of related procedures and functions. When you create objects that you build around COM and clients to communicate with the COM objects, both the clients and the objects must communicate exclusively through interfaces.

Before using interfaces was popular in large-system, object-oriented design, a client would work directly with an object's class definition. Programming directly with the object's class definition led to many problems with code versioning (that is, clients had difficulty accessing new versions of the object, and could not determine what version an object was) and code reuse. Because client code had too much "insider" information about an object's implementation details, changes to an object's code often required changes to the client's code, which made a system fragile and hard to extend. As programmers made more changes to components within the system, the likelihood that the system would fail when it tried to access an object increased significantly. Today's component-based development often requires a client and an object to reside in different binary executables, which makes reuse and versioning even more important.

COM uses a logical interface to eliminate any implementation dependencies between a client and an object. The logical interface results in systems that are less fragile and far easier to extend. An interface between two objects is actual program code; a *logical interface* is the model for the program code itself. An interface plays the mediator's role between the client and the object and is a contract that specifies the work the object must do, but it does not specify how the object should accomplish the work. In addition, an interface is a communications protocol that defines a set of methods complete with names, arguments, and return types. Just as a network cable carries important data between computers on a network without knowing the specifics of the data itself, an interface lets important information, such as data and messages, pass between the client and the object. The object's implementation may change from version to version, but the object must continue to support within its later versions every interface it supported in earlier versions. As long as an interface definition remains static, the established communication channels remain unaffected between a client and an object from version to version. Figure 22.1 shows the logical model for communication between a client and a COM object.

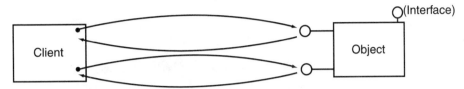

Figure 22.1 *The logical model for communication between a client and a COM object.*

COM OBJECTS IMPLEMENT INTERFACES

As the previous section details, COM objects are built around interfaces the objects expose to clients. A COM object **673** must implement at least one interface, although the object is free to implement as many interfaces as it requires. Objects can add support for new interfaces in later releases, which lets the objects evolve with demand. As long as the object continues to support every previously published interface in subsequent releases, client applications will not require modification. As a result, interfaces solve the problem of updating different versions when you use classes directly, which demonstrates one of the main reasons Microsoft created COM. A client can test for a particular behavior and *degrade gracefully* if the object does not support the functionality. When a program does not fail because it cannot perform a task, but rather performs a different or simpler task, or informs the user of the problem, programmers refer to the program as a program that degrades gracefully. On the other hand, programs that "crash," or stop working, because an object does not support a given behavior, do not degrade gracefully.

To test for a behavior, the client must query an object at run time to see whether the object supports a particular interface. COM also supports *categories*, or collections of interfaces. If an object belongs to a category, you can safely assume that the object implements all the interfaces defined for the category. Interfaces and categories help you determine an object's capabilities.

It is also possible for many different objects to implement the same interface. A single method that an interface defines can produce different behavior when a client invokes the method on implementations that different objects supply. The one-to-many relationship between an interface and various COM objects makes it possible for COM to offer polymorphic behavior—in other words, for an interface to perform different actions in different situations. As long as the client program uses interfaces to access objects, the program may switch between different object implementations with minimal impact on its code. Groups of objects that implement a specific interface or category are *plug-compatible*—because you can easily "plug" a new object in the place of an old object. COM's polymorphic nature makes COM objects highly reusable.

Note: *For more information about polymorphism, see Chapter 1, "Introduction to Visual Basic."*

Another powerful COM feature is language independence. COM clients and COM objects have the same layout and behavior at run time, regardless of which language you use to produce the component. COM's independence from any specific language lets you build systems with many different components that you or other programmers create in different languages, whether Visual Basic, C++, or Java. The language you use to create the component simply does not matter in COM. As a programmer, language independence offers you three major benefits. First, it lets you split up large systems into manageable subsystems early in the design phase. Second, it lets you implement each subsystem with a component that you can create with any COM-capable tool. Third, it lets individual teams working on each subsystem have complete control over what language the team uses to create the subsystem.

COM defines the mechanism for client–object interaction in a language-independent way. The COM standard defines the standard memory layout for COM objects and also defines the way clients invoke methods within the object. The standard COM object construction's definition lets you write objects in any language, and write the client programs that access those objects in any language. Figure 22.2 shows the standard object construction for a COM object.

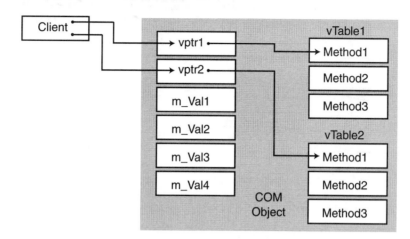

Figure 22.2 *Constructing a standard COM object.*

The object creates an array of function pointers, called a *vTable* (the "v" stands for virtual), and passes a *vTable* pointer to the client. The client sees the *vTable* as the interface and uses the *vTable* pointer it received from the client to locate a particular function pointer. When the client finds the function pointer, the client invokes the method directly. In other words, when programs access the COM object, they will always access the *vTable* and receive a *vptr* from the *vTable*. The actual method the *vptr* points to can change between program versions; so long as the client accesses the method through the interfaces that the *vTable* describes, the changes to the underlying methods are invisible to the client program. In addition, the *vTable* will reference data the object maintains—as Figure 22.2 indicates with the *m_Val1, m_Val2, m_Val3,* and *m_Val4* blocks.

When a client program accesses a COM object, it receives a pointer to an internal method within the object and uses that pointer to execute the method itself. As you have learned in previous chapters, Visual Basic cannot process pointers, and to handle a pointer that holds a function's address is beyond Visual Basic's capabilities. C and C++ can handle function pointers (memory addresses), but neither Visual Basic nor Java can handle function pointers without extra support from the compiler and a mapping layer (which maps the pointer's memory address to a type the program can handle) in the run-time engine. The compiler and the Visual Basic run-time engine work together when you create COM clients and COM objects using Visual Basic and automatically generate the mapping layer that produces the *vTable* binding.

INTRODUCING INTERFACE DEFINITION LANGUAGE

As the previous section details, COM is a definition standard that is language-independent, both when you define the COM object and when you define the client that will access the COM object. Even though COM is language-independent, there must be some official language for defining interfaces and COM classes. (COM programmers generally abbreviate COM classes as *coclasses*.) COM uses Interface Definition Language (IDL), which is similar to C, but offers object-oriented extensions that let you unambiguously define your interfaces and coclasses. C++ and Java programmers should always define the interfaces and coclasses with Interface Definition Language before they begin the actual program development for a COM-based project. When you compile the COM-based project, the compiler feeds the Interface Definition Language file to the Microsoft Interface Definition Language (MIDL) compiler, which produces a binary description file called a *type library*. For example, a typical Interface Definition Language file might define two interfaces and a coclass, as shown here:

```
[ uuid("VBPLID1")]
  interface IVBPLInterface1
   {
     HRESULT VBPLMethod1();
     HRESULT VBPLMethod2();
   }

[ uuid("VBPLID2")]
  interface IVBPLInterface2
```

```
   {
      HRESULT VBPLMethod3();
   }
[ uuid("VBPLID3")]
   coclass CVBPLClass
   {
      [default] interface IVBPLInterface1;
      interface IVBPLInterface2;
   }
```

The code within the fragment uses the *interface* keyword to define two interfaces, *IVBPLInterface1* and *IVBPLInterface2* and the *coclass* keyword to define the *CVBPLClass*. The *IVBPLInterface1* defines two methods, and the *IVBPLInterface2* defines a third method. The *CVBPLClass*, in turn, implements the two interfaces, so that the client can access the methods through the coclass and its interfaces. Unlike C++ and Java, Visual Basic does not require you to use Interface Definition Language or the MIDL compiler. The Visual Basic Interactive Development Environment (IDE) creates a type library directly from your Visual Basic source code and builds the type library information directly into your executable (EXE) or Dynamic-Link Library (DLL) binary file. If you must see the Interface Definition Language for a particular COM component, you can use the *oleview.exe* utility to "reverse engineer" a type library into Interface Definition Language text. The type library lets development tools, such as the Visual Basic compiler and the Visual J++ compiler, build the *vTable* binding at compile time.

COM uses a unique identifier called a Globally Unique Identifier (GUID). Interface Definition Language uses the keyword UUID (for Universally Unique Identifier) instead of GUID. Do not let the different terminology confuse you about the keyword's use, however—Globally Unique Identifiers and Universally Unique Identifiers are the same thing. Globally Unique Identifiers that identify coclasses are known as Class Identifiers (CLSIDs), while those that identify interfaces are known as Interface Identifiers (IIDs). Globally Unique Identifiers are long, 128-bit integers that you will most frequently use and refer to as readable, 32-digit hexadecimal numbers, as shown here:

```
[ uuid(40C3E581-F26D-11D0-B840-0000E8A1E186)]
   interface IVBPLInterface1
   {
      HRESULT VBPLMethod1();
      HRESULT VBPLMethod2();
   }
```

Interface Definition Language, type libraries, and the Windows Registry all use Globally Unique Identifiers to provide unique identification for COM entities, such as type libraries, coclasses, and interfaces. Adding Globally Unique Identifiers to the Windows Registry is an important configuration issue on any COM-enabled machine because, without the identifiers, programs are unable to access the COM components that you create. For example, the type library for every Visual Basic project you create contains the definitions for your interfaces and coclasses, including their Globally Unique Identifiers. When you register a server component or type library on a client machine, you must store the Globally Unique Identifiers for the COM object, its interfaces, and its coclasses within the Windows Registry. To ensure your objects remain consistent with each rebuild, you must set the Version Compatibility option to Binary Compatibility in the Project Properties dialog box's Component tab. If you do not set this option to Binary Compatibility, Visual Basic will assign a new set of Globally Unique Identifiers each time you rebuild your component. As a result, older client applications will try to access your COM objects with Globally Unique Identifiers that do not exist. To set the Version Compatibility option, perform the following steps:

1. Within Visual Basic, select the Project menu Project1 Properties option. Visual Basic will display the Project Properties dialog box.

2. Within the Project Properties dialog box, select the Component tab. Visual Basic will change the dialog box's display to represent your selection.

3. Within the Component tab, select the Binary Compatibility option. Figure 22.3 shows the Project Properties dialog box after you select the Binary Compatibility option within the Version Compatibility frame.

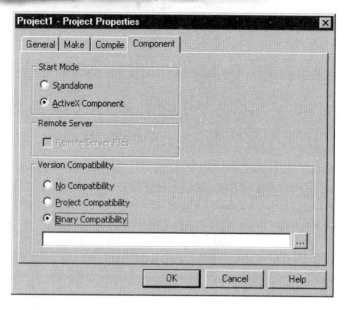

Figure 22.3 *Selecting the correct Version Compatibility option in the Project Properties dialog box.*

4. Within the Project Properties dialog box, click your mouse on OK. Visual Basic will close the Project Properties dialog box.

After you set the correct Version Compatibility option, Visual Basic will generate unique identifiers for your project, its interfaces, and its coclasses, but *only the first time you compile the project.* Each time you compile the project thereafter, Visual Basic will use the unique identifier you generated the first time you compiled it.

Visual Basic has supported *vTable* binding since Visual Basic 4.0. Visual Basic examines a type library at compile time to create *vTable* bindings. Within your Visual Basic programs, you must add type libraries into your projects from within the References dialog box. To open the References dialog box, select the Project menu References option. When you use either Visual Basic's *CreateObject* function or the *New* operator to create a COM object from a type library, Visual Basic will automatically use the default interface for the object. The Visual Basic run-time engine caches the interface pointer and stores it inside an object reference. When you invoke one of the object's methods, the Visual Basic run-time engine uses a function pointer to actually access the method, as shown in the following code:

```
Dim obj As clsVBPLClass               ' *** IVBPLInterface is [default]
Set obj = New clsVBPLClass
obj.VBPLMethod1                        ' *** obj holds IVBPLInterface pointer
obj.VBPLMethod2("Happy," "Dalmatian")
```

Visual Basic automatically creates an interface if you define a public class in an ActiveX DLL or an ActiveX EXE and, therefore, also creates a coclass. For example, if you create a class named *clsVBPLClass* with three public methods, Visual Basic will create a default interface named *_clsVBPLClass* with the same methods. Visual Basic can also hide interfaces by supplying one default interface for each coclass you create. Visual Basic automatically uses the default interface when you use the class name to reference an object. The only time your Visual Basic programs will use the class name is when the program creates an object with *CreateObject* or the *New* operator. Therefore, the use of coclasses and interfaces is transparent to Visual Basic programmers—because the run-time engine handles most of the interface work. However, you can get more out of COM if you create individual custom interfaces and implement them in one or more Visual Basic classes.

Visual Basic usually creates both a coclass and an interface for you in the type library when you create a public class. However, you can define a COM interface without defining a coclass. If you set a class's *Instancing* property to *PublicNotCreatable*, Visual Basic will create only an interface. After you create a few interfaces, you can start creating the classes that implement the interfaces. Visual Basic classes can implement an interface defined within the current project or within a project-referenced type library. To implement an interface within a project or type library, you can use the *Implements* keyword. Visual Basic 5.0's new *Implements* keyword lets you implement several interfaces in a single class, as shown here:

```
Implements IVBPLInterface1
Implements IVBPLInterface2

Sub IVBPLInterface1_VBPLMethod1()
   '*** implementation
End Sub

Sub IVBPLInterface1_VBPLMethod2()
   '*** implementation
End Sub

Sub IVBPLInterface2_VBPLMethod3()
   '*** implementation
End Sub
```

The *Implements* keyword within the previous code fragment demonstrates an important COM feature known as *interface inheritance*, which lets your programs inherit their own interfaces from many other, different interfaces within a Visual Basic class. Inheriting interfaces makes your objects more reusable—a client program can call the interface because it knows the object implements interface. In turn, that Visual Basic class might actually execute in another process, on another computer, and so on. Unfortunately, neither COM nor Visual Basic provide for another type of inheritance, *implementation inheritance*, which would let you inherit the method implementations from another class. Instead, under interface inheritance, you simply inherit the obligation to write the method implementations. Inheriting an obligation, rather than other program code, might seem strange at first. The explanation is if you inherit from an interface, the client code that uses your object can use the interface pointer, and the pointer guarantees that your object exhibits a certain behavior. Therefore, interface inheritance lets you write significantly more reusable code than implementation inheritance does—but in a different manner from implementation inheritance.

UNDERSTANDING THE *IUNKNOWN* INTERFACE

As you have learned, all COM objects must implement at least one interface. All COM interfaces must inherit from a standard interface, *IUnknown*, which means that all COM interfaces must also contain the three methods in this interface, in addition to their own methods. The *IUnknown* interface contains support for both reference counting (maintaining information about how many clients are currently accessing the object) and run-time type coercion (that is, forcing a value into a specific type). COM objects implement reference counting with two methods, *AddRef* and *Release*. These methods let objects maintain an internal count of connected clients and delete themselves from memory when no more clients are connected to the object. The third method, *QueryInterface*, lets a client move between the different interfaces an object exposes. *QueryInterface* is the cornerstone for polymorphism and updating code versions in COM. Clients can switch to a different interface to experience different behavior from an object, and they can query an object to see if the object supports a certain interface. COM's support for run-time type inspection lets clients degrade gracefully if the object does not support the client-requested interface. Figure 22.4 shows an interface's standard construction, including the three default methods all interfaces support.

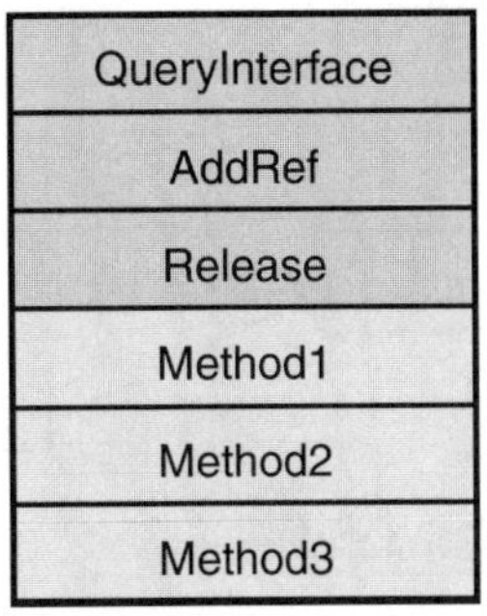

QueryInterface
AddRef
Release
Method1
Method2
Method3

Figure 22.4 The standard interface construction that COM defines.

Visual Basic programmers have used the three *IUnknown* methods for a long time—most without even knowing it. Visual Basic hides all calls to *IUnknown* within the run-time engine. Whenever a program creates or destroys an object reference, the Visual Basic run-time engine automatically calls the *AddRef* method when the program constructs the object and the *Release* method when the program destroys the object. Visual Basic also calls the *QueryInterface* method "behind the scenes"—that is, the run-time engine handles the calls to *QueryInterface* for you when you move between methods. For example, the following code fragment calls *QueryInterface* and retrieves a new interface pointer:

```
Dim ObjRef1 As IVBPLInterface1
Dim ObjRef2 As IVBPLInterface2

Set ObjRef1 = New clsVBPLClass        '*** create new object
Set ObjRef2 = ObjRef1                 '*** call QueryInterface()
ObjRef1.VBPLMethod1                    '*** invoke method
ObjRef2.VBPLMethod3
```

678

Visual Basic's automatic calls to the *AddRef* and *Release* methods are effectively automatic "garbage collection" for COM objects (that is, Visual Basic does not let destroyed COM objects simply remain in memory). Most C++ programmers are used to calling the *AddRef* and *Release* methods explicitly (that is, performing their own garbage collection), but manual garbage collection is vulnerable to reference-counting bugs that you might have a difficult time finding and resolving. Reference-counting bugs are dangerous because a bad reference count can cause a program, or even the entire operating system, to "crash." Microsoft has recently created direct COM support in the C++ compiler and frameworks, such as the *Active Template Library* (ATL), so programmers can create COM client applications without explicitly calling these methods, just as you can from within Visual Basic.

INTRODUCING *IDISPATCH*

As you have learned, when a client is capable of early binding—that is, accessing the COM object at compile time—the client will use the *vTable* to access the methods within the object. However, many development tools are incapable of binding through *vTable* interfaces at compile time. For example, *VBScript*™ is an important development tool for Web-based systems, but it cannot process a type library or create *vTable* bindings. COM provides a run time-binding protocol known as *Automation* to address less sophisticated clients (in other words, clients that cannot bind through a *vTable* interface), such as VBScript clients. Automation uses a standard COM interface called *IDispatch*. The *vTable* for an *IDispatch* interface always contains the same seven methods. The *vTable* is a single physical interface from which programs that implement object instances can create any number of logical interfaces. As long as the *vTable* bindings are consistent from one *IDispatch* interface to another, it is not necessary to generate new *vTable* bindings at compile time. Figure 22.5 shows the seven methods that comprise an *IDispatch* interface.

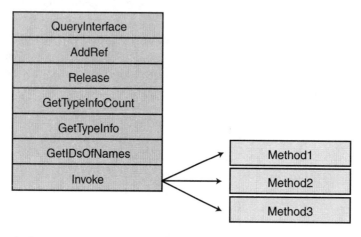

Figure 22.5 *The seven methods comprising an* **IDispatch** *interface.*

The two key *IDispatch* methods are *GetIDsOfNames* and *Invoke*. *GetIDsOfNames* lets a client get binding information at run time. The *GetIDsOfNames* function takes a string argument containing a function or property's name and returns a *DispID*, an integer value that uniquely identifies a specific method or property that the client program must then use in the call to the *Invoke* method. When a client calls *Invoke*, it must pass a large and complex set of arguments. The arguments include the *DispID*, a single array of variants containing the arguments' values, a variant for the return value, and a few other components that help identify the method call to the *Invoke* method. When a client queries for these *DispID* values at run time, the process is known as *late binding*. Using the *IDispatch* methods is inefficient (because you must obtain a method name and then invoke that method through an intermediary function), but essential for clients that cannot create *vTable* bindings at compile time.

UNDERSTANDING WHAT VISUAL BASIC DOES TO HELP PROGRAMS ACCESS COM OBJECTS

As you learned in the previous section, programs that use late binding must use the *IDispatch* set of methods to access a COM object. Most Visual Basic programmers have never heard of the *GetIDsOfNames*, *Invoke*, or *IDispatch* methods because the Visual Basic run-time engine processes these methods for you automatically. For example, Visual Basic creates a connection to the object and caches an *IDispatch* pointer when you write the following code:

```
'*** VB Calls IDispatch automatically
Dim VBPLObjRef As Object, n As Integer

Set VBPLObjRef = CreateObject("clsVBPLServer.VBPLClass")
n = VBPLObjRef.VBPLMethod("Happy", "Likes to eat")
```

Visual Basic handles the call to *VBPLMethod* by calling the *GetIDsOfNames* method and passing the string *VBPLMethod*. The *GetIDsOfNames* method, in turn, returns the *DispID* for the method. Next, Visual Basic calls *Invoke* by passing the *DispID* and all the arguments packed up as variants, and *Invoke* sends the return value back to the client as a variant. Although Visual Basic performs all the type conversion for you automatically, which makes writing Automation code easy, using *GetIDsOfNames* is not an efficient process—because you must perform two intermediate method calls to access the *VBPLMethod* method. Also, using *GetIDsOfNames* does not give your programs any type safety, which means that, if you include the wrong number or the wrong type of argument in your call to *VBPLMethod*, you will experience failure at run time, not compile time—because the Visual Basic compiler assumes any call your program makes to *IDispatch* will work.

As you learned in Chapter 1, referencing the type library for the object in your project is known as *early binding*. Referencing the type library and using the *IDispatch* interface is also early binding. A type library lets Visual Basic discover all the *DispID* values at compile time and embed them into your executable and frees your program from having to call *GetIDsOfNames* at run time. Early binding yields a significant performance improvement because it is not necessary for your program to invoke the *GetIDsOfNames* method each time it accesses a different method within a COM object. Another benefit of early binding and using a type library is that the Visual Basic compiler can check your arguments and return values to make sure you have set your types correctly. Letting the compiler check your types helps to prevent syntax errors in your compiled code. It also lets the Visual Basic IDE offer you additional information about the object and its methods while you type. On the other hand, the call to the *Invoke* method in early binding is exactly the same as it is in late binding, which means *Invoke* is not as fast as *vTable* binding. Note that you must also use the specific class name for your object variables to get early binding. If you use the *Object* type, you will always get late binding.

Dual interfaces, or *duals*, simplify binding. Duals are interfaces that let sophisticated clients use *vTable* bindings, while still offering *IDispatch* to clients that do not support *vTable* bindings. When you create COM objects in Visual Basic 5.0, the compiler will build dual interfaces for all your objects automatically. Visual Basic and C++ clients can, therefore, communicate with your objects through *vTable* binding. VBScript clients can also communicate with your objects through *IDispatch*, which lets Web-centric environments (that is, environments that you build with the intent that Internet users will be the primary object clients), such as Internet *Explorer* and *Active Server Pages* (ASP), control your Visual Basic objects as well. Figure 22.6 shows how dual interfaces work. Note that the *Method1*, *Method2*, and *Method3* methods are all part of the *vTable*, but that programs can also access the methods with calls to the *Invoke* method.

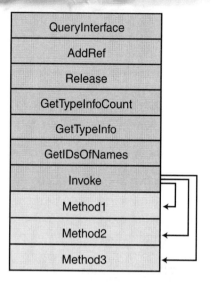

Figure 22.6 A dual interface with methods available through vTable and Invoke.

UNDERSTANDING THE BENEFITS OF THE OBJECT KEYWORD

As you learned in the previous section, any time you assign an object to a variable of *Object* type, you are using the *IDispatch* interface and late binding to communicate with the object. Using the *Object* data type is necessary in a couple situations, but you should avoid using it in all other situations because *IDispatch* is slow. There are only two good reasons to use the *Object* type: the first is to communicate with an object that implements only the *IDispatch* interface. Such *IDispatch*-only objects were common a few years ago, but most modern COM components use objects that offer a type library and *vTable* bindings to the client. If you must go through *IDispatch*, you should still use a type library (if the COM object provides one) to take advantage of early binding.

The second reason to use the *Object* type is to create a single variable, or a collection to which you assign many different kinds of objects. If you can tolerate *IDispatch*'s performance limitations, using a single *Object* variable to access a known method in many objects is an easy way to implement polymorphism within your client programs. For example, you can reference each object in a collection of objects that have no association to each other, and do not share the same interfaces, but all include a *Print* method. As you reference each object in turn, you can use the *Object* variable to invoke the *Print* method on each one—a technique that is especially helpful when you do not know at design time which objects the collection will contain.

A component that exposes coclasses to client applications is a *COM server*. As you have learned in previous chapters, and earlier in this chapter, COM defines structures for two kinds of servers, in-process servers and out-of-process servers. In-process servers reside in the client application's address space. You will use ActiveX DLL projects to implement in-process servers from Visual Basic, as you did in Chapter 21, "Using Windows Sockets for Two-Way Internet Communications." In-process servers create objects that reside in the same Win32 process as the client's program code. Out-of-process servers, or ActiveX EXEs, create their own Win32 processes. You can further divide out-of-process servers into local servers and remote servers. The distinction between local servers and remote servers tells you whether the client process and the server process run on the same computer or on different computers. The Distributed Component Object Model (DCOM) lets the client and object communicate across computer boundaries, as your programs will when the programs access remote server programs. You can create both local and remote out-of-process servers from within Visual Basic.

It is not necessary to do anything special within your Visual Basic programs to differentiate between a local server and a remote server—the underlying DCOM architecture handles most of the differences. However, you must watch out for coding techniques that do not scale well across computer boundaries—that is, techniques that get more inefficient when you move the object out-of-process. An interface design that passes data inefficiently, or incurs unnecessary round trips between the client and object, can produce satisfactory performance in either an in-process or an out-of-process component on the same computer. The same interface design will usually not perform acceptably when you use it in an out-of-process component on a different computer.

In the next section, you will learn more about DCOM principles and the factors they add to the COM principles that you have already learned. However, before you continue with the next section, make sure that you clearly understand the three binding techniques COM uses to connect a client to an object. It is particularly important to understand the performance differences between late binding and early binding. While there are many real-world scenarios where late binding does not have a significant impact on performance, large-scale components must be as efficient as possible. True *vTable* binding is always more efficient and more flexible than the two other COM communication methods that use *IDispatch*.

MOVING ON TO DCOM

Now that you have learned the basics of COM programming, it is worthwhile to learn more about DCOM programming, how it differs from COM programming, and additional issues you must consider when you write a scalable, multi-threaded DCOM server component with Visual Basic. You will also learn how to implement asynchronous method calls between a client and a remote object.

As you have learned, creating DCOM server components with Visual Basic is not particularly difficult. However, creating scalable DCOM server components with Visual Basic is more complex and requires additional programming effort. Unfortunately, an object that does not scale well is not particularly useful for professional software development.

When a client application and a COM object exist in the same process, the client can invoke a method directly through an interface pointer (or an object reference in Visual Basic). When a client creates an object from an ActiveX DLL, the client and object share the same call stack and memory addresses. When the client resides in one Win32 process and the object resides in another (which is the case whenever you work with out-of-process servers), the programming you must perform to manipulate the object becomes more complex. To correctly work with out-of-process servers, particularly remote out-of-process servers, a client must use DCOM's infrastructure to invoke a method on a remote object.

USING DCOM TO COMMUNICATE OUT-OF-PROCESS AND ACROSS COMPUTERS

As you have learned, your programs can use DCOM to communicate with out-of-process components, whether on a local machine or on a remote machine. However, you will generally use DCOM to communicate with out-of-process servers on a remote machine. DCOM lets clients and COM objects communicate out-of-process with two helper COM objects, the proxy (at the client component process) and the stub (at the server component process). These COM objects let the client and object pass the interface pointer across process boundaries. DCOM automatically inspects the type library for an object and uses the information within the library to create the proxy and stub at run time. The client communicates with the proxy (for example, uses the *vTable* to invoke a method at the proxy). The proxy, in turn, uses a *Remote Procedure Call (RPC)* channel to communicate with the stub, which communicates with the actual object itself. When information passes from the object back to the client, it follows the same process in reverse: object, stub, proxy, client. Figure 22.7 shows a logical model of proxy-stub communication between a client and an out-of-process DCOM component.

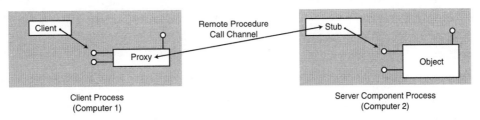

Figure 22.7 *The communication between a client and an out-of-process DCOM component.*

A proxy-and-stub pair exists for each interface pointer that the two programs (client and COM object) pass between processes. The proxy and stub assist your clients and objects by transporting method calls between processes and use an underlying protocol called the Remote Procedure Call (RPC) to communicate with each other. RPC is an industry-standard communication protocol that has reached maturity on Windows (that is, it is relatively fixed, and will maintain its communication standards for the foreseeable future), as well as many other non-Windows platforms. Microsoft

681

has layered COM and DCOM on top of RPC. The proxy and stub communicate across the RPC channel for local servers and remote servers in a way that is transparent to your Visual Basic components—in other words, your components do not know that they are communicating with a proxy or a stub instead of with an actual client or object.

The proxy and stub's best feature is that COM creates them invisibly, without program interaction or knowledge—the clients and objects will not even know that they are operating in different processes, on different machines, even in different cities. In-process and out-of-process objects appear to be the same to both the client and the object—in other words, a client cannot tell the difference between an object's interface and the proxy for the interface, nor can an object tell the difference between a client and its stub. The proxy and stub's invisibility means that when you create objects and clients, they automatically work for in-process, as well as for out-of-process, communications.

A client interacts with an object the same way, regardless of whether the object is in-process, locally out-of-process, or remotely out-of-process. You can use classes written for a DLL in an out-of-process EXE without modification. You might assume, therefore, that you can create a remote server simply by changing your project from an ActiveX DLL to an ActiveX EXE. Although such a translation will usually work, it is not necessarily the most efficient communication choice between the two out-of-process components. Many programming techniques work well in an in-process object, but do not scale when you extend the communications across process boundaries. You must consider two factors when you create remote servers: the overhead associated with a remote procedure call, and the requirements for moving large data pieces across the network.

The proxy-and-stub architecture uses a considerable amount of overhead. You can attribute much of the architecture's overhead to the fact that the operating system blocks the client's calling thread (that is, the thread stops executing) when it calls a method, and the client thread does not get control back (resume execution) until after the call returns from the object. Programmers refer to the method call and the execution return from the remote object as a *round trip*. You can imagine that the time to make a round trip to an object and back increases by an order of magnitude as you move the object out-of-process and onto another machine. Distance impacts performance significantly. Even if you could communicate between two machines 5,000 miles apart at the speed of light, a method call's time would increase by a factor of 10. The actual transmission speed, of course, is much slower than light speed. Figure 22.8 shows the impact transmission size and distance will have on round-trip communication speeds.

	With Four Bytes of Data		With Fifty Bytes of Data	
	Calls Per Second	Milliseconds Per Call	Calls Per Second	Milliseconds Per Call
In-Process	3,224,816	0.00031	3,227,973	0.00031
Local	2377	0.42	2023	0.49
Remote (Server 10' away)	376	2.7	306	3.27
Remote (Las Vegas to Baltimore)	25	4.0	22	45.48

Figure 22.8 As transmission size and distance increase, round-trip time increases when accessing a DCOM object.

UNDERSTANDING HOW TO REDUCE ROUND TRIPS

As you learned in the previous section, the impact of Remote Procedure Call round trips on your program performance is significant. When you design your interfaces, make sure that you design them to reduce round trips as much as possible. Never create multiple methods or properties when a single method can do the job just as well. For example, exposing three public properties, each of which requires a round trip, results in inefficient client code, as shown in the following code fragment:

```
objEmployee.FirstName = "Happy"
objEmployee.LastName = "Jamsa"
objEmployee.LunchTime = "Always"
```

Instead, you might provide a single method that lets the client accomplish the same task with fewer trips. For example, a *SetEmployeeInfo* method that takes the three parameters *Happy*, *Jamsa*, and *Always* lets the client push the same data to the object in a single round trip, as shown in the following code fragment:

```
objEmployee.SetEmployeeInfo("Happy", "Jamsa", "Always")
```

Moving data between the client process and the object process is known as *marshaling*. Marshaling is the proxy and stub's responsibility. Because Visual Basic accepts data types that are compatible only with the *Variant* type, your Visual Basic programs can use a COM-provided service called the *universal marshaler* to create the proxy and stub. Unfortunately, when you create the proxy and stub with the universal marshaler, you cannot customize their behavior because Visual Basic 5.0 cannot marshal user-defined types. C++ programmers can write custom marshaling code to create proxies and stubs that the programmers optimize for the data that the objects will transmit which, therefore, makes the proxies and stubs more flexible and capable of transmitting user-defined types. However, Visual Basic programmers do not have custom marshaling code capability.

683

Marshaling a lot of data in a single round trip is far better than marshaling smaller data amounts in multiple round trips, as Figure 22.8 shows. Although you should optimize round trips first, you should also be conscientious about the packets of data that you move back and forth. You must push some data from the client to the object, and you must pull other data from the object back to the client. Some data must move in both directions. To better understand the difference in movements, consider the following procedure prototypes:

```
Sub VBPLMethod1(ByVal Name As String)
Sub VBPLMethod2(ByRef Name As String)
Sub VBPLMethod3(Name As String)
```

VBPLMethod1 pushes the data from the client to the object. If you want to push only a value to the object, declare the argument as *ByVal*. *VBPLMethod2* pushes the data from the client to the object, then pulls the data from the object back to the client. *VBPLMethod3* performs the same processing as *VBPLMethod2* because Visual Basic's default passing convention is *ByRef*.

The difficult side to marshaling data is pulling data from the object back to the client in Visual Basic. COM defines parameters as either *in* parameters, *out* parameters, or both *in* and *out* parameters, but Visual Basic 5.0 does not know how to handle the *out* parameters. The only way to explicitly pull data back from the object is with a function return value. Unfortunately, you can have only a single return value for each round trip. You will usually get better results to pulling data back with *ByRef* arguments, such as the argument shown in the following code fragment:

```
Sub GetEmployeeInfo(ByRef FirstName As String, ByRef LastName As String, _
    ByRef LunchTime As String)
```

UNDERSTANDING WHY IT IS IMPORTANT TO OPTIMIZE PACKETS TO REDUCE TRAFFIC

As you learned in the previous section, "Understanding How to Reduce Round Trips," reducing round trips is an important goal when you design components that will communicate across processes, and even more important when your components communicate across networks. However, it is also important to optimize the packets you send across the network. Choose the types for your method arguments and return values wisely—smaller types result in less network traffic. For example, consider the following method declarations:

```
Sub VBPLMethod1(IntArr(1000) As Integer)
Sub VBPLMethod2(LongArr(1000) As Long)
Sub VBPLMethod3(VarArr(1000) As Variant)
Sub VBPLMethod4(Arr(1000))
```

A Visual Basic *Integer* uses two bytes, a *Long* integer uses four bytes, and a *Variant* value uses sixteen bytes. The *VBPLMethod2* method sends twice as much data across the network as *VBPLMethod1*, and *VBPLMethod3* sends eight times as much data as *VBPLMethod1*. *VBPLMethod4* is the same method as *VBPLMethod3* because the *Variant* type is Visual Basic's default data type. Sixteen bytes might not seem significant enough to make a difference when your programs transmit a single piece of data, but when your programs call methods that pass arrays back and forth to objects, such as those in the previous code fragment, the extra bytes will result in a significant impact on performance.

With the additional transmission time that variants add to your communications, it may be difficult to understand why you would ever use a *Variant* type in a remote method call. However, *Variants* provide at least one great technique for moving lots of data across the network in a single round trip. *Variants* can hold arrays, and arrays can be multidimensional. Arrays can also hold variants that hold arrays of variants that hold arrays of variants, and so on. You can define *Variant* arguments with as much complexity as you want, and the universal marshaler can do all the moving of complex data structures across the network. Again, the only significant limitation is that *Variants* cannot hold user-defined types. For now, however, you must only use types that you can assign to a *Variant*. The following code fragment shows how you can return two employee records from an object in a single round trip with a *Variant*:

```
Sub GetEmployeeInfo(ByRef arrData As Variant)
    Const ROWS = 2
    Const FIELDS = 3
    ReDim arrData(ROWS - 1, FIELDS - 1)

    arrData(0, 0) = "Happy"
    arrData(0, 1) = "Jamsa"
    arrData(0, 2) = "Always"
    arrData(1, 0) = "Max"
    arrData(1, 1) = "Jamsa"
    arrData(1, 2) = "11:00 AM"
End Sub
```

As you can see, the program code places items within the *arrData Variant*, in an array-style format. Sometimes you want many client applications to connect to a single object in a remote server. COM makes it easy for a client to create and connect to a new object, but connecting to an existing object takes a few additional steps. An existing, single-instance object is known as a *Singleton* object. Each user creates a new *Connection* object in the server, and each *Connection* object provides a method to retrieve a reference to a global object stored in a global variable—which means you then access the Singleton object through the Connection object. A Visual Basic out-of-process server can readily implement this design, as you will learn later in this chapter when you create the *prjAsyncServer2* project. Figure 22.9 shows the connection to a Singleton object through a global object reference.

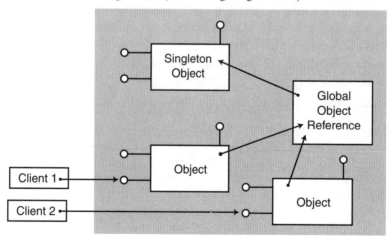

Figure 22.9 The connection to a Singleton object through a global object reference.

The code to connect to a Singleton object through a global object reference works well, as long as your server component is single-threaded. A multi-threaded component will not work the same as a single-threaded component if you use the same code you use for a single-threaded component, because every thread in your server process will own and maintain its own instance of global data. Instead, you must write your programs slightly differently to handle multi-threaded components.

To make your server component multi-threaded in a Visual Basic ActiveX EXE project, you must select the Unattended Execution property within the Project Properties dialog box. When you select the Unattended Execution option, you must also decide to give every object its own thread or to create a thread pool to limit the maximum number of threads. Visual Basic uses a round-robin algorithm (that is, Visual Basic assigns each thread in turn and starts over with the first thread after it reaches the last thread in the pool) with thread pools to assign multiple objects to a single thread when the number of objects exceeds the number of available threads. For example, if you create a pool of three threads, the component will access only the first, fourth, and seventh objects from the first thread.

Every COM object lives in an execution context called an *apartment*. Some COM processes have a single apartment, but others have multiple apartments. A COM-enabled thread lives in only one apartment. COM lets apartments be multi-threaded or single-threaded, but only C++ programmers can create components that use multi-threaded apartments—Visual Basic programmers can create only single-threaded apartments. Multi-threaded apartments can yield faster components. However, multi-threaded apartments present synchronization issues that can be complex and problematic. Programmers based Visual Basic's multi-threaded capabilities on having multiple single-threaded apartments in a single-server process.

685

Every single-threaded apartment has its own Windows message queue. (You learned about message queues in Chapter 14, "Using the Windows API to Intercept Windows Messages.") COM posts messages in an apartment's message queue to invoke methods across apartment boundaries. The single thread in each apartment retrieves the incoming messages on a First-In, First-Out (FIFO) basis. If three different clients invoke a method on an object, the object will service the methods first-come, first-serve. Although using a message queue forces the thread to process messages in order (an architecture that may not be optimal), the message queue does provide protection from synchronization problems. With a message queue, the object will never let more than a single thread access the object at a given time. There is also no chance that two threads will concurrently access an object and leave the data in an invalid state. In the context of a single-threaded apartment, every method call completes before the object begins another method call. The single-threaded apartment architecture provides a multi-threaded architecture that is slow, yet safe.

Each apartment maintains its own separate instance of global data, which means that you cannot store a single reference to a global object and expect objects in distinct apartments to recognize that reference. Visual Basic also executes *Sub Main* one time for each new apartment that the COM object creates. If your *Sub Main* procedure initializes global data, the procedure will initialize a new instance for each new apartment. In short, you cannot easily share data between objects in separate apartments. Figure 22.10 shows the single-threaded, multiple-apartment COM model.

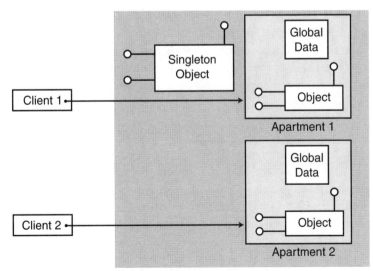

Figure 22.10 *The single-threaded, multiple-apartment COM model.*

If you use the thread-pooling option with the round-robin algorithm, sharing data gets even harder to track and understand. Groups of objects that share the same thread will share global data. The thread pool, then, creates a situation in which some objects share data, but other objects share different data, and some objects may not share any data at all.

UNDERSTANDING THE USE AND IMPORTANCE OF ASYNCHRONOUS METHOD CALLS

Any call from a client to an object is synchronous (meaning that the call does not return from the object to client until the method completes its processing) by default. A *synchronous method call* means when a client invokes a method on an object, the operating system blocks the client's execution thread until the object finishes its work and gives control back to the client. If the object takes a long time to complete its processing, the client must wait until the object is done. If a server-side object takes more than a few seconds to complete a job (and, arguably, even if the server-side object will handle many jobs simultaneously), you should use a logical *asynchronous* call to prevent the graphical user interface in the client application from losing its responsiveness.

An *asynchronous method call* means when a client invokes a method on an object, the object relinquishes control to the client immediately, and performs its work within its own execution thread. While the object performs its own processing, the client can perform its own processing at the same time. When the object finishes its processing, it will send the information back to the client—which must watch for the information while it performs its own processing. Figure 22.11 shows how your programs can use an asynchronous method call to perform processing in multiple locations simultaneously.

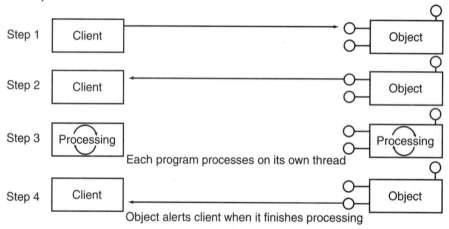

Figure 22.11 *The processing that a client and an object perform during an asynchronous method call.*

COM will support true asynchronous calls in Windows NT 5.0 but, for now, you have several choices to work from to implement asynchronous calls. Implementing an asynchronous method call requires three procedures: a method to enable a timer, a procedure with a signature the Win32 API defines for the callback function you pass within *SetTimer* when you create the timer, and a procedure to implement the asynchronous task. It is often necessary for a procedure to asynchronously call back to the client and notify the client of the procedure's completion, processing, or failure status. When you write an asynchronous procedure, you will generally use the timer to provide periodic updates on the procedure's performance.

UNDERSTANDING HOW TO IMPLEMENT ASYNCHRONOUS CALLBACKS

After you start a task running asynchronously on the server, you will need some way to notify the job's completion status to the client. The need for a callback to the client introduces the concept of *outbound interfaces*. When an object performs asynchronous callbacks, the object and client trade roles—the object acts as a client and invokes a method on the original client—now a different COM object. For such a two-way method (that is, a method that uses asynchronous callbacks) to work correctly, the original client must *also* act as a COM object. There are two ways to call from the object back to the client. The easy way to call from the object to the client is for you to use the new custom events in Visual Basic 5.0. The second, and more difficult method is for you to define a custom callback interface. Within the programs that you will create in this chapter, you will use both methods to implement asynchronous callbacks.

Using events with Visual Basic is fairly straightforward. The Visual Basic run-time engine automatically uses a few standard COM interfaces to hook up an *event sink* (a set of addresses that point to event procedures within a project) whenever you use the *WithEvents* keyword. The COM interfaces to the event sink let an object acquire an *IDispatch* pointer back to a client's event sink object. Because the object performing the callback must recognize the client program as a COM object, you can use the *WithEvents* keyword only in a class module's or a form module's declaration section. If an object defines a set of events, you can write the program code within the client programs to handle the events you want, and ignore the events you do not want to handle.

An object that raises an event must make a round trip to and from each connected client in a synchronous manner. Whenever a program connects to, and references, an event sink, the program will receive all events the object raises, whether the client provides a handler for the event or not. An object cannot be selective about which clients receive which events, nor can it give some clients priority over others. You must define a custom callback interface to completely control how your objects pass information back to the clients. Callback interfaces use true *vTable* binding, while events (and event sinks) use *IDispatch*.

To create a custom callback interface, you must define a new class within your server component project. In the new class, you will define a set of procedures without providing any implementation for those procedures. The class must only define each custom callback's interface's parameters and return values. After you create the class, you must set the class's *Instancing* property (within the Properties Window) to *PublicNotCreatable*. When you set up a class module with *PublicNotCreatable*, you define a COM-style interface, rather than a coclass. For example, you might define a simple callback interface as shown in the following code fragment:

687

```
Sub OnUpdate(PercentComplete As Integer)
  '*** no implementation
End Sub

Sub OnComplete(Successful As Boolean)
  '*** no implementation
End Sub
```

As long as both the client and the server know about the new *ICallback* interface, both processes can use the interface as a type. If you create the interface in the server, you must reference its type library in the client project. You can also create a stand-alone DLL that contains nothing except each interface's definition. Creating callback interfaces is more work, but it is well worth the trouble—particularly when you create complex production quality components. Callback interfaces are faster and more flexible than events. An advanced server design can maintain a dynamic array of callback objects, which lets you add client selectivity and prioritization to your callback notifications. Figure 22.12 shows the logical model for remote call implementation through the *ICallback* class and a *CallbackImpl* object within the client.

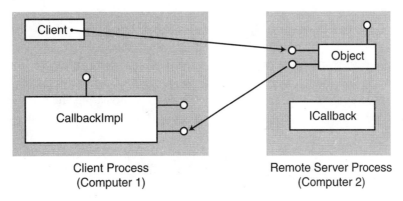

Figure 22.12 *The remote callback interface implementation from within Visual Basic.*

USING THE *prjAsyncClient1* PROJECT

Now that you better understand the underlying concepts of COM and DCOM, you are ready to begin creating this chapter's projects, which will use events and callback interfaces to implement asynchronous processing. As you have learned, you can implement asynchronous callbacks between a COM object and a client in two general ways: with events and with the callback interfaces. When you run this chapter's first program, *prjAsyncClient1.exe*, you will use events to implement asynchronous callbacks between the program and its server component, *prjAsyncServer1*.

Before you design the *prjAsyncClient1* and *prAsyncServer1* projects, you may find it helpful to run the *prjAsyncClient1.exe* program. The companion CD-ROM that accompanies this book contains the *prjAsyncClient1.exe* program within the *Chapter22* directory. As with every other program on the CD-ROM, you should run the Jamsa Press *setup.exe* program to install the *prjAsyncClient1.exe* program to your computer's hard drive before you run it. After you install the *prjAsyncClient1.exe* program to your computer's hard drive, you can run it from the Start menu. To run the program, select the Windows Start menu Run option. Windows will display the Run dialog box. Within the Run dialog box, enter *x:\vbpl\Chapter22\prjAsyncClient1.exe*, where *x* corresponds to the drive letter of the hard drive on which you installed the *prjAsyncClient1.exe* program, and click your mouse on OK. Windows will display the *prjAsyncClient1.exe* program, as shown in Figure 22.13.

688

Figure 22.13 *The **prjAsyncClient1.exe** program at startup.*

RUNNING PRJASYNCCLIENT1 FROM THE CD-ROM

As you have learned, you must first install many programs that you will use in this book to your computer's hard drive before you use them. Because the *prjAsyncClient1.exe* program uses a custom ActiveX EXE (*prjAsyncServer1*) that you must register on your computer before the program will execute, you cannot run the *prjAsyncClient1.exe* program from the CD-ROM. Additionally, you cannot run the other projects that you will create in this chapter, *prjAsyncClient2.exe* and *prjAsyncClient3.exe*, from the CD-ROM because both programs also use custom server objects.

To learn more about the Jamsa Press *setup.exe* program, see the "What's on the *Visual Basic Programmer's Library* Companion CD-ROM" section at the back of this book.

As you can see, the form the *prjAsyncClient1.exe* program displays is very simple. If you click your mouse on the Start Task button, the program will begin to make requests to the remote server object. After you click your mouse on the Start Task button, the program will periodically update the display, indicating the number of loops the remote COM object has completed. Figure 22.14 shows the *prjAsyncClient1.exe* program after the *prjAsyncServer1* component completes its processing.

Figure 22.14 *The **prjAsyncClient1.exe** program after the **prjAsyncServer1** component completes its processing.*

CREATING THE prjAsyncServer1 PROJECT

Now that you have a better idea about how you will use client and server projects to create COM objects and the client programs to access the objects, as well as the processing the *prjAsyncClient1* and *prjAsyncServer1* projects perform, you can create the projects. First, you will create the *prjAsyncServer1* project, and then you will create the *prjAsyncClient1* project. To begin the *prjAsyncServer1* project and create a blank class module, perform the following steps:

1. Within Visual Basic, select the File menu New Project option. Visual Basic will open the New Project dialog box.

2. Within the New Project dialog box, double-click your mouse on the ActiveX EXE icon. Visual Basic will close the New Project dialog box, start a new project, *Project1*, and add a class module to it, *Class1*.

3. Select the View menu Properties Window option. Visual Basic will display the Properties Window listing the *Class1* class module's properties.

4. Within the Properties Window, change the *Name* property to *DCOMObject*. Next, change the *Instancing* property to 3 - *Single Use*.

5. Select the Project menu Project1 Properties option. Visual Basic will display the Project Properties dialog box.

6. Within the Project Properties dialog box, change the *Project Name* field from *Project1* to *prjAsyncServer1*.

7. Within the Project Properties dialog box, click your mouse on the Component tab. The dialog box will display the Version Compatibility information.

8. Within the Project Properties dialog box, click your mouse on the Binary Compatibility option to select it. Click your mouse on the OK button to exit the Project Properties dialog box.

9. Within Visual Basic, select the Project menu Add Module option. Visual Basic will open the Add Module dialog box.

10. Within the Add Module dialog box, select the Module option. Next, click your mouse on the Open button. Visual Basic will open a new Code window, *Module1*.

11. Select the View menu Properties Window option. Visual Basic will display the Properties Window listing the *Module1* module's properties.

12. Within the Properties Window, change the *Module1* module's *Name* property to *mdlAsyncStart*.

13. Select the File menu Save Project As option. Visual Basic will open the Save File As dialog box and fill the *File name* field with *mdlAsyncStart*.

14. Within the Save File As dialog box, click your mouse on the Save button. Visual Basic will save the *mdlAsyncStart* module and fill the *File name* field with the *DCOMObject* class module's name.

15. Within the Save File As dialog box, click your mouse on the Save button. Visual Basic will save the *DCOMObject* class module and fill the *File name* field with the *prjAsyncServer1* project name.

16. Within the Save Project As dialog box, click your mouse on the Save button. Visual Basic will save the *prjAsyncServer1* project and close the Save Project As dialog box.

WRITING THE CODE FOR THE prjAsyncServer1 PROJECT

As you learned earlier in this chapter, when you use events to implement asynchronous callbacks, you must use the *SetTimer* Windows API function (and the *KillTimer* API function to stop timing). You must declare the API functions within the *mdlAsyncStart* module. The following code implements the declarations for the *mdlAsyncStart* module:

```
Declare Function SetTimer Lib "user32" (ByVal hWnd As Long, _
    ByVal nIDEvent As Long, ByVal uElapse As Long, _
    ByVal lpTimerProc As Long) As Long
Declare Function KillTimer Lib "user32" (ByVal hWnd As Long, _
    ByVal nIDEvent As Long) As Long
Private CurrentObject As DCOMObject
Private TimerID As Long
```

The code within the General–Declarations section defines the *SetTimer* and *KillTimer* API functions. It also declares a local instance of the *DCOMObject* class, and an identifier (similar to a window handle) for the timer the program creates with *SetTimer*.

WRITING THE CODE FOR THE GLOBALSTARTTASK PROCEDURE

As you learned in the "Using the *prjAsyncClient1* Project" section of this chapter, the user will click the mouse on the Start Task button to start the asynchronous process. The Start Task button's event code will call the *DCOMObject* class's *StartTask* method, which, in turn, calls the *GlobalStartTask* procedure. The following code implements the *GlobalStartTask* procedure:

```
Public Sub GlobalStartTask(obj As DCOMObject)
   Set CurrentObject = obj
   TimerID = SetTimer(0, 0, 50, AddressOf TimerProc)
   If TimerID = 0 Then Err.Raise vbObjectError + 1962, , _
       "No timers available"
End Sub
```

The *GlobalStartTask* procedure initializes the *CurrentObject* variable and creates a timer. The last parameter in the *SetTimer* call, *AddressOf TimerProc*, specifies that the timer should call the *TimerProc* procedure each time it fires. If the program code cannot create a new timer (because there are already too many timers open), the procedure raises an error message to the client program.

WRITING THE CODE FOR THE TIMERPROC PROCEDURE

As the previous section details, each time the timer fires, it will call the *TimerProc* procedure. Within the *TimerProc* procedure, the program code will invoke the *DCOMObject* class's *OnStartTask* method. The following code implements the *TimerProc* procedure:

```
Public Sub TimerProc(ByVal hWnd As Long, ByVal uMsg As Long, _
    ByVal idEvent As Long, ByVal lngSysTime As Long)
   KillTimer 0, TimerID
   If Not (CurrentObject Is Nothing) Then
     CurrentObject.OnStartTask
     Set CurrentObject = Nothing
   Else
     Err.Raise vbObjectError + 1, , "Something went wrong"
   End If
End Sub
```

WRITING THE CODE FOR THE DCOMOBJECT CLASS

As you have learned, when you write COM and DCOM objects that perform asynchronous processing with events, the class definitions for the objects must raise one or more events into the client program. The following code implements the General–Declarations section for the *DCOMObject* class, which declares the *DCOMObject's* events:

```
Event OnUpdate(Loops As Long)
Event OnDone(Loops As Long, Successful As Boolean)
```

The *DCOMObject* class raises the *OnUpdate* event into the client program accessing the object (which the *prjAsyncClient1* client program, for example, uses to update the display) and raises the *OnDone* event when it completes its processing.

Writing the Code for the StartTask Method

As you have learned, the *prjAsyncClient1* project calls the *DCOMObject* class's *StartTask* method when the user clicks the mouse on the Start Task button. The following code implements the *DCOMObject* class's *StartTask* method:

```
Public Sub StartTask()
   GlobalStartTask Me
End Sub
```

The *StartTask* method simply calls the *GlobalStartTask* procedure (which initializes the timer and sets up the asynchronous callbacks).

Writing the Code for the OnStartTask Method

As you learned in the "Writing the Code for the *TimerProc* Procedure" section, after you create the timer, the program will invoke the *OnStartTask* method. The following code implements the *OnStartTask* method:

```
Public Sub OnStartTask()
   RunTask
End Sub
```

The *OnStartTask* method simply calls the private (hidden) *RunTask* procedure. The following code implements the *RunTask* procedure:

```
Private Sub RunTask()
   Dim i As Long, StartTime As Long, LoopCount As Long
   For i = 1 To 10
     RaiseEvent OnUpdate(LoopCount)
     StartTime = Timer
     Do While ((Timer - StartTime) < 1)
       LoopCount = LoopCount + 1
     Loop
   Next i
   RaiseEvent OnDone(LoopCount, True)
End Sub
```

The program code within the *RunTask* procedure loops ten times. Each time through the loop, the program code raises the *OnUpdate* event to the client program. Next, the program code loops for one second, adding 1 to the loop count on each loop iteration. The program code then loops through again, until it completes ten loops. After the program code exits the *For-Next* loop, the procedure raises the *OnDone* event to the client program.

Creating the prjAsyncClient1 Project

Now that you have created the *prjAsyncServer1* project that the client will access, you can create the *prjAsyncClient1* client project. After you create the client project, you will add a reference to the server project, add controls to the form, and add the program code to perform the client processing to the project. To begin the *prjAsyncClient1* project and create a blank form, perform the following steps:

1. Within Visual Basic, select the File menu New Project option. Visual Basic will open the New Project dialog box.

2. Within the New Project dialog box, double-click your mouse on the Standard EXE icon. Visual Basic will close the New Project dialog box, start a new project, *Project1*, and add a form to it, *Form1*.

3. Select the View menu Properties Window option. Visual Basic will open the Properties Window listing the *Form1* form's properties.

4. Within the Properties Window, change the *Form1* form's property values to those Table 22.1 lists.

Object	Property	Set As
Form1	Caption	Async Communication w/ Events
Form1	Height	4140
Form1	Left	4755
Form1	Top	2430
Form1	Width	3615
Form1	Name	frmMain

Table 22.1 *The newly named* **frmMain** *form's properties.*

5. Within Visual Basic, select the Project menu Project1 Properties option. Visual Basic will display the Project1 Properties dialog box.

6. Within the Project1 Properties dialog box, type *prjAsyncClient1* within the *Project Name* field. Next, click your mouse on OK. Visual Basic will close the Project1 Properties dialog box.

7. Select the File menu Save Project As option. Visual Basic will display the Save File As dialog box and fill the *File name* field with *frmMain*.

8. Within the Save File As dialog box, click your mouse on the Save button. Visual Basic will save the *frmMain* form and fill the *File name* field with *prjAsyncClient1*.

9. Within the Save Project As dialog box, click your mouse on the Save button. Visual Basic will save the *prjAsyncClient1* project and close the Save Project As dialog box.

ADDING A REFERENCE TO THE PRJASYNCSERVER1 COMPONENT TO THE PROJECT

As you have learned, you must add a reference to each COM component that a project uses before you can use it within the project. To add a reference to the *prjAsyncServer1* component in the *prjAsyncClient1* project, perform the following steps:

1. Select the Project menu References option. Visual Basic will display the References dialog box.

2. Within the References dialog box, select the *Asynch Server Using Events* listing. Next, click your mouse on the box to the left of the listing. Visual Basic will display a check mark in the box, as shown in Figure 22.15.

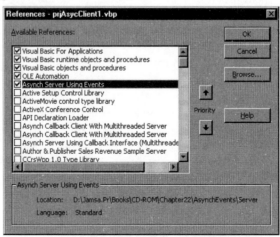

Figure 22.15 *The* **Asynch Server Using Events** *listing in the References dialog box.*

3. Within the References dialog box, click your mouse on the OK button. Visual Basic will add the *Asynch Server Using Events* COM component's type library to your project.

Adding the Controls to the frmMain Form

After you create the project, you can add the controls to the *frmMain* form. As you saw in this chapter's "Using the *prjAsyncClient1* Project" section, the *frmMain* form's display is relatively simple. In fact, the form consists of only a *CommandButton* control and a *PictureBox* control. To add the controls to the *frmMain* form, perform the following steps:

1. If Visual Basic is not displaying the *frmMain* form within an object window, double-click your mouse on the *frmMain* form listing within the Project Explorer. Visual Basic will open the *frmMain* form.

2. Within Visual Basic, select the View menu Toolbox option. Visual Basic will open the Toolbox.

3. Within the Toolbox, double-click your mouse on the CommandButton icon. Visual Basic will draw a *CommandButton* control, *Command1*, within the *frmMain* form.

4. Within the Toolbox, double-click your mouse on the PictureBox icon. Visual Basic will draw a *PictureBox* control, *Picture1*, within the *frmMain* form.

5. Within the *frmMain* form, click your mouse on the *Picture1* control to highlight it. Visual Basic will draw a small frame around the control.

6. Select the View menu Properties Window option. Visual Basic will open the Properties Window listing the *Picture1* properties.

7. Within the Properties Window, change the *Picture1* properties to the values Table 22.2 lists.

8. Repeat Steps 5, 6, and 7 to change the *Command1* properties to the values Table 22.2 lists.

Object	Property	Set As
Command1	*Caption*	*Start Task*
Command1	*Height*	375
Command1	*Left*	120
Command1	*Top*	120
Command1	*Width*	3255
Command1	*Name*	*cmdStartTask*
Picture1	*Interval*	60000
Picture1	*Height*	3015
Picture1	*Left*	120
Picture1	*Top*	600
Picture1	*Width*	3255
Picture1	*Name*	*picDisplay*

*Table 22.2 The newly named **cmdStartTask** and **picDisplay** controls' properties.*

Writing the Code for the frmMain Form

As you can probably guess from the simplicity of the output the *prjAsyncClient1* project generates, the program code within the *frmMain* form is not extensive. The most important program code section, as with any reference to a COM or DCOM component that raises events, is the declaration of the COM or DCOM object with the *WithEvents* keyword. You will declare the *frmMain* form's *lclObject* within the General–Declarations section, as shown here:

```
Private WithEvents lclObject As DCOMObject
```

As you have learned, when you declare an object with the *WithEvents* keyword, you cannot initialize the object in the same statement. In the *prjAsyncClient1* project, you will initialize the *lclObject* variable within the *Form_Load* event. The following code implements the *Form_Load* event for the *frmMain* form:

```
Private Sub Form_Load()
  Set obj = New DCOMObject
End Sub
```

WRITING THE CODE FOR THE CMDSTARTTASK_CLICK EVENT

As you have learned, the user will click the mouse on the *cmdStartTask* button to begin the *prjAsyncClient1* program's execution. The following code implements the *cmdStartTask_Click* event:

```
Private Sub cmdStartTask_Click()
  picDisplay.Cls
  lclObject.StartTask
End Sub
```

The *Cls* method clears the *picDisplay* control. The invocation of the *lclObject* object variable's *StartTask* method begins the object's asynchronous processing.

WRITING THE CODE FOR THE LCLOBJECT-RAISED EVENTS

As you learned earlier in this chapter, the *lclObject* object will raise two events into the *prjClientAsync1* project. The first event, *OnUpdate*, occurs each time the loop at the server iterates again (approximately one time each second). The following code implements the *lclObject_OnUpdate* event:

```
Private Sub lclObject_OnUpdate(Loops As Long)
  picDisplay.Print "Loops completed: " & Format(Loops, "###,##0")
End Sub
```

The program code within the event uses the *picDisplay* control's *Print* method to display information about the current number of completed loops. When the *lclObject* finishes its processing, it will raise the *OnDone* event, which simply prints summary information. The following code implements the *OnDone* event:

```
Private Sub lclObject_OnDone(Loops As Long, Successful As Boolean)
  picDisplay.Print
  If Successful Then
    picDisplay.Print "The job was successful"
  Else
    picDisplay.Print "The job was unsuccessful"
  End If
  picDisplay.Print "Total loops completed: " & Format(Loops, "###,##0")
End Sub
```

CREATING THE PRJASYNCSERVER2 PROJECT

In the "Using the *prjAsyncClient1* Project" section of this chapter, you saw the client program's display. Both the *prjAsyncClient2* and *prjAsyncClient3* projects display output similar to the *prjAsyncClient1* project. The differences are in the way the programs implement asynchronous processing. The *prjAsyncServer1* and *prjAsyncClient1* pair used events to implement asynchronous processing. The *prjAsyncServer2* and *prjAsyncClient2* pair, on the other hand, will use a callback interface to implement asynchronous processing. To begin the *prjAsyncServer2* project and to create the blank class modules, perform the following steps:

1. Within Visual Basic, select the File menu New Project option. Visual Basic will open the New Project dialog box.

2. Within the New Project dialog box, double-click your mouse on the ActiveX EXE icon. Visual Basic will close the New Project dialog box, start a new project, *Project1*, and add a class module to it, *Class1*.

3. Select the View menu Properties Window option. Visual Basic will display the Properties Window listing the *Class1* class module's properties.

4. Within the Properties Window, change the *Name* property to *DCOMObject*. Next, change the *Instancing* property to 3 - *SingleUse*.

5. Select the Project menu Add Class Module option. Visual Basic will display the Add Class Module dialog box.

6. Within the Add Class Module dialog box, double-click your mouse on the Class Module icon. Visual Basic will add a new class module, *Class1*, to the project.

7. Select the View menu Properties Window option. Visual Basic will display the Properties Window listing the *Class1* class module's properties.

8. Within the Properties Window, change the *Name* property to *ICallback*. Next, change the *Instancing* property to 2 - *PublicNotCreatable*.

9. Within Visual Basic, select the Project menu Add Module option. Visual Basic will open the Add Module dialog box.

10. Within the Add Module dialog box, select the Module option. Next, click your mouse on the Open button. Visual Basic will open a new Code window, *Module1*.

11. Select the View menu Properties Window option. Visual Basic will display the Properties Window listing the *Module1* module's properties.

12. Within the Properties Window, change the *Module1* module's *Name* property to *mdlAsyncStart*.

13. Select the Project menu Project1 Properties option. Visual Basic will display the Project Properties dialog box.

14. Within the Project Properties dialog box, change the *Project Name* field from *Project1* to *prjAsyncServer2*.

15. Within the Project Properties dialog box, click your mouse on the Component tab. The dialog box will display the Version Compatibility information.

16. Within the Project Properties dialog box, select the Binary Compatibility option. Click your mouse on the OK button to exit the Project Properties dialog box.

17. Select the File menu Save Project As option. Visual Basic will open the Save File As dialog box and fill the *File name* field with *mdlAsyncStart*.

18. Within the Save File As dialog box, click your mouse on the Save button. Visual Basic will save the *mdlAsyncStart* module and fill the *File name* field with the *ICallback* class module's name.

19. Within the Save File As dialog box, click your mouse on the Save button. Visual Basic will save the *ICallback* class module and fill the *File name* field with the *DCOMObject* class module's name.

20. Within the Save File As dialog box, click your mouse on the Save button. Visual Basic will save the *DCOMObject* class module and fill the *File name* field with the *prjAsyncServer2* project name.

21. Within the Save Project As dialog box, click your mouse on the Save button. Visual Basic will save the *prjAsyncServer2* project and close the Save Project As dialog box.

Writing the Code for the prjAsyncServer2 Project

As you have learned, the *prjAsyncServer2* project uses two classes, the *DCOMObject* class (the object itself), and the *ICallback* class (which implements the callback processing to the client). Within the *ICallback* class, you will define two procedures within the *ICallback* interface without creating implementations for those procedures. You will define the two procedures as shown within the following code:

```
Sub Update(Loops As Long)
  ' No implementation
End Sub
```

```
Sub Done(Loops As Long, Successful As Boolean)
  ' No implementation
End Sub
```

When you write the program code for the *prjAsyncClient2* project, you will provide the two callback procedures' implementations (the code that performs the actual processing).

WRITING THE CODE FOR THE MDLASYNCSTART MODULE

Just as you did within the *prjAsyncServer1* project, you must declare the *SetTimer* and *KillTimer* API functions and write the program code for the *GlobalStartTask* and *TimerProc* procedures. The code within the *mdlAsyncStart* module in the *prjAsyncServer2* project is identical to the code within the *mdlAsyncStart* module in the *prjAsyncServer1* project.

WRITING THE CODE FOR THE DCOMOBJECT CLASS

Within the *DCOMObject* class, you must define an instance of the *ICallback* class so that the class can invoke the callback procedures during its processing. The following code implements the object declaration within the *DCOMObject* class's General–Declarations section:

```
Private CallbackObject As ICallback
```

To use the callback procedures, you must initialize the *CallbackObject* variable.

WRITING THE CALLBACK REGISTRATION METHODS

As you learned in the previous section, you must initialize the *CallbackObject* variable before you can use it to implement callbacks. The *DCOMObject* class exposes the *RegisterCallBack* and *UnregisterCallBack* methods that clients will use to register the callback addresses for the declared, but not implemented, procedures within the *ICallback* interface. The following code implements the *RegisterCallBack* and *UnregisterCallBack* methods:

```
Public Sub RegisterCallBack(CB As ICallback)
  Set CallbackObject = CB
End Sub

Public Sub UnregisterCallBack()
  Set CallbackObject = Nothing
End Sub
```

The *RegisterCallBack* method accepts an object of type *ICallback* as its only parameter and sets the *CallbackObject* object variable to the *ICallback* object it receives. The *UnregisterCallBack* method sets the *CallbackObject* variable to *Nothing*.

WRITING THE STARTTASK AND ONSTARTTASK METHODS

As with the *prjAsyncServer1* project that you created earlier in this chapter, the *StartTask* method calls the *GlobalStartTask* function, which initializes and starts the timer. The following code implements the *StartTask* method:

```
Public Sub StartTask()
  GlobalStartTask Me
End Sub
```

The *OnStartTask* method simply calls the private *RunTask* function (which performs the object's actual processing). The following code implements the *OnStartTask* method:

```
Public Sub OnStartTask()
  RunTask
End Sub
```

WRITING THE CODE FOR THE RUNTASK PROCEDURE

As you have learned, the *RunTask* procedure performs the actual loop processing. The following code implements the *RunTask* procedure within the *DCOMObject* class:

```
Private Sub RunTask()
   Dim i As Long, StartTime As Long, LoopCount As Long
   For i = 1 To 10
      If (CallbackObject Is Nothing) Then Exit Sub
      CallbackObject.Update LoopCount
      StartTime = Timer
      Do While ((Timer - StartTime) < 1)
        LoopCount = LoopCount + 1
      Loop
   Next i
   CallbackObject.Done LoopCount, True
End Sub
```

The program code within the *RunTask* procedure loops ten times. Each time through the loop, the program code invokes the *CallbackObject* object's *Update* method—which actually invokes the *Update* method in the client program. Next, the program code loops for one second, adding 1 to the loop count on each loop iteration. The program code then loops through the outside loop again, until it completes ten loops. After the program code exits the *For-Next* loop, the procedure code invokes the *CallbackObject* object's *Done* method—which actually invokes the *Done* method in the client program.

CREATING THE *PRJASYNCCLIENT2* PROJECT

Now that you have created the *prjAsyncServer2* server project that the client will access, you can create the *prjAsyncClient2* client project. After you create the client project, you will add a reference to the server project, add controls to the form, and add the program code to the project to perform the client processing. To begin the *prjAsyncClient2* project and to create a blank form, perform the following steps:

1. Within Visual Basic, select the File menu New Project option. Visual Basic will open the New Project dialog box.

2. Within the New Project dialog box, double-click your mouse on the ActiveX EXE icon. Visual Basic will close the New Project dialog box, start a new project, *Project1*, and add a class module to the project, *Class1*.

3. Select the View menu Properties Window option. Visual Basic will open the Properties Window listing the *Class1* class module's properties.

4. Within the Properties Window, change the *Class1* class module's *Name* property to *CallbackImpl*.

5. Within Visual Basic, select the Project menu Add Form option. Visual Basic will display the Add Form dialog box.

6. Within the Add Form dialog box, double-click your mouse on the Form icon. Visual Basic will add a new form, *Form1*, to the project.

7. Select the View menu Properties Window option. Visual Basic will open the Properties Window listing the *Form1* form's properties.

8. Within the Properties Window, change the *Form1* form's property values to those Table 22.3 lists.

Object	Property	Set As
Form1	*Caption*	*Async Callback Interface*
Form1	*Height*	4140
Form1	*Left*	4755
Form1	*Top*	2430
Form1	*Width*	3615
Form1	*Name*	*frmMain*

*Table 22.3 The newly named **frmMain** form's properties.*

9. Within Visual Basic, select the Project menu Add Module option. Visual Basic will display the Add Module dialog box.

10. Within the Add Module dialog box, double-click your mouse on the Module icon. Visual Basic will add a new module, *Module1*, to the project.

11. Select the View menu Properties Window option. Visual Basic will open the Properties Window listing the *Module1* module's properties.

12. Within the Properties Window, change the *Module1* module's *Name* property to *mdlMain*.

13. Within Visual Basic, select the Project menu Project1 Properties option. Visual Basic will display the Project1 Properties dialog box.

14. Within the Project1 Properties dialog box, type *prjAsyncClient2* within the *Project Name* field. Next, click your mouse on OK. Visual Basic will close the Project1 Properties dialog box.

15. Select the File menu Save Project As option. Visual Basic will display the Save File As dialog box and fill the *File name* field with *CallbackImpl*.

16. Within the Save File As dialog box, click your mouse on the Save button. Visual Basic will save the *CallbackImpl* class module and fill the *File name* field with *mdlMain*.

17. Within the Save File As dialog box, click your mouse on the Save button. Visual Basic will save the *mdlMain* module and fill the *File name* field with *frmMain*.

18. Within the Save File As dialog box, click your mouse on the Save button. Visual Basic will save the *frmMain* module and fill the *File name* field with *prjAsyncClient2*.

19. Within the Save Project As dialog box, click your mouse on the Save button. Visual Basic will save the *prjAsyncClient2* project and close the Save Project As dialog box.

ADDING A REFERENCE TO THE *prjAsyncServer2* COMPONENT TO THE PROJECT

As you have learned, you must add a reference to each COM component that a project uses before you can use it within the project. To add a reference to the *prjAsyncServer2* component in the *prjAsyncClient2* project, perform the following steps:

1. Select the Project menu References option. Visual Basic will display the References dialog box.

2. Within the References dialog box, select the *Asynch Server Using Callback Interface* listing. Next, click your mouse on the box to the left of the listing. Visual Basic will display a check mark in the box.

3. Within the References dialog box, click your mouse on the OK button. Visual Basic will add the *Asynch Server Using Callback Interface* COM component's type library to your project.

ADDING THE CONTROLS TO THE *frmMain* FORM

After you create the project, you can add the controls to the *frmMain* form. As you saw in this chapter's "Using the *prjAsyncClient1* Project" section, the *frmMain* form's display is relatively simple. In fact, it consists of only a *CommandButton* control and a *PictureBox* control. To add the controls to the *frmMain* form, perform the following steps:

1. If Visual Basic is not displaying the *frmMain* form within an object window, double-click your mouse on the *frmMain* form listing within the Project Explorer. Visual Basic will open the *frmMain* form.

2. Within Visual Basic, select the View menu Toolbox option. Visual Basic will open the Toolbox.

3. Within the Toolbox, double-click your mouse on the CommandButton icon. Visual Basic will draw a *CommandButton* control, *Command1*, within the *frmMain* form.

4. Within the Toolbox, double-click your mouse on the PictureBox icon. Visual Basic will draw a *PictureBox* control, *Picture1*, within the *frmMain* form.

5. Within the *frmMain* form, click your mouse on the *Picture1* control to highlight it. Visual Basic will draw a small frame around the control.

6. Select the View menu Properties Window option. Visual Basic will open the Properties Window listing the *Picture1* properties.

7. Within the Properties Window, change the *Picture1* properties to the values Table 22.4 lists.

8. Repeat Steps 5, 6, and 7 to change the *Command1* properties to the values Table 22.4 lists.

Object	Property	Set As
Command1	*Caption*	*Start Task*
Command1	*Height*	375
Command1	*Left*	120
Command1	*Top*	120
Command1	*Width*	3255
Command1	*Name*	*cmdStartTask*
Picture1	*Interval*	60000
Picture1	*Height*	3015
Picture1	*Left*	120
Picture1	*Top*	600
Picture1	*Width*	3255
Picture1	*Name*	*picDisplay*

Table 22.4 *The newly named* **cmdStartTask** *and* **picDisplay** *controls' properties.*

WRITING THE CODE FOR THE MDLMAIN MODULE

Within the *mdlMain* module, you will write the *Sub Main* procedure. Because the *prjAsyncClient2* project is an ActiveX EXE project (remember, it must be COM-compliant, like the server, to support callback implementations), the project cannot open the form directly. Rather, the project must start within *Sub Main*, which then opens the *frmMain* form. The following code implements the *Sub Main* procedure:

```
Public Sub Main()
   frmMain.Show
End Sub
```

WRITING THE CODE FOR THE CALLBACKIMPL CLASS MODULE

As you have learned, the client program must implement the interfaces that you declared, but did not implement, within the *ICallback* class module in the *prjAsyncServer2* project. The following code implements the declarations for the *CallbackImpl* class module:

```
Implements ICallback
Public pic As Picture
```

As you learned earlier in this chapter, the *Implements* keyword tells the program that the class module implements an interface defined elsewhere. The program will use the *pic* object to display information about the program's processing.

WRITING THE ICALLBACK INTERFACE METHOD IMPLEMENTATIONS

As you have learned, when you implement callback interfaces, you will specify the interface class (in this case, *ICallback*), and then the actual method. The following code, for example, implements the *ICallback_Update* method and the *ICallback_Done* method:

```
Sub ICallBack_Update(Loops As Long)
  pic.Print "Loops completed: " & Format(Loops, "###,##0")
End Sub

Sub ICallBack_Done(Loops As Long, Successful As Boolean)
  pic.Print
  If (Successful) Then
    pic.Print "The job was successful"
  Else
    pic.Print "The job was unsuccessful"
  End If
  pic.Print "Total loops completed: " & Format(Loops, "###,##0")
End Sub
```

Both methods perform processing identical to the events of the same name in the *prjAsyncClient1* project, but they use an asynchronous callback to do the processing. The program code within the *frmMain* form sets the *pic* property value equal to the *picDisplay* control on the *frmMain* form.

WRITING THE CODE FOR THE FRMMAIN FORM

Within the *frmMain* form, you must define two objects, one to reference the *DCOMObject*, and one to reference the *ICallback* class's implementation within the *CallbackImpl* class module. The following code implements the object definitions for the *frmMain* form:

```
Private lclCallBack As CallbackImpl
Private lclObject As DCOMObject
```

WRITING THE CODE FOR THE FORM_LOAD AND FORM_UNLOAD EVENTS

When the *prjAsyncClient2* project loads the *frmMain* form, the program code within the *Form_Load* event will perform significant processing to initialize all the objects the form will use. The following code implements the *Form_Load* event within the *frmMain* form:

```
Private Sub Form_Load()
  Set lclCallBack = New CallbackImpl
  Set lclCallBack.pic = Me.picDisplay
  Set lclObject = New DCOMObject
  lclObject.RegisterCallBack lclCallBack
End Sub
```

The program code first sets the *lclCallBack* variable, and then it sets the *lclCallBack* variable's *pic* property. After it initializes the *lclCallBack* variable, the program code initializes the *lclObject* variable and calls the *RegisterCallBack* method. When the program calls the *RegisterCallBack* method, it passes the new *lclCallBack* variable into the method, which alerts the *DCOMObject* where to send its callbacks. When you unload the form, you must remove the register from callback implementation so that the operating system will eliminate the *DCOMObject* from memory. The following code implements the *frmMain* form's *Form_Unload* event:

```
Private Sub Form_Unload(Cancel As Integer)
  lclObject.UnregisterCallBack
End Sub
```

WRITING THE CODE FOR THE CMDSTARTTASK_CLICK EVENT

As you have learned, the user will click the mouse on the *cmdStartTask* button to begin the *prjAsyncClient2* program's execution. The following code implements the *cmdStartTask_Click* event:

```
Private Sub cmdStartTask_Click()
  picDisplay.Cls
  lclObject.StartTask
End Sub
```

The *Cls* method clears the *picDisplay* control. The invocation of the *lclObject* object's *StartTask* method begins the object's asynchronous processing.

CREATING THE PRJAsyncSERVER3 PROJECT

In this chapter's "Using the *prjAsyncClient1* Project" section, you saw the client program's display. Both the *prjAsyncClient2* and *prjAsyncClient3* projects display output similar to the *prjAsyncClient1* project. The differences between the programs are not visible to the user—rather, the differences are only in the way the programs implement asynchronous processing. The *prjAsyncServer1* and *prjAsyncClient1* pair used events to implement asynchronous processing. The *prjAsyncServer2* and *prjAsyncClient2* pair, on the other hand, used a callback interface to implement asynchronous processing, but the pair supported only a single server thread. The *prjAsyncServer3* and *prjAsyncClient3* pair, however, will use a callback interface to implement asynchronous processing, and will support multiple objects at the server. To begin the *prjAsyncServer3* project and to create the blank class modules, perform the following steps:

1. Within Visual Basic, select the File menu New Project option. Visual Basic will open the New Project dialog box.

2. Within the New Project dialog box, double-click your mouse on the ActiveX EXE icon. Visual Basic will close the New Project dialog box, start a new project, *Project1*, and add a class module to it, *Class1*.

3. Select the View menu Properties Window option. Visual Basic will display the Properties Window listing the *Class1* class module's properties.

4. Within the Properties Window, change the *Name* property to *DCOMObject*. Next, change the *Instancing* property to 5 - *MultiUse*.

5. Select the Project menu Add Class Module option. Visual Basic will display the Add Class Module dialog box.

6. Within the Add Class Module dialog box, double-click your mouse on the Class Module icon. Visual Basic will add a new class module, *Class1*, to the project.

7. Select the View menu Properties Window option. Visual Basic will display the Properties Window listing the *Class1* class module's properties.

8. Within the Properties Window, change the *Name* property to *ICallback*. Next, change the *Instancing* property to 2 - *PublicNotCreatable*.

9. Within Visual Basic, select the Project menu Add Module option. Visual Basic will open the Add Module dialog box.

10. Within the Add Module dialog box, select the Module option. Next, click your mouse on the Open button. Visual Basic will open a new Code window, *Module1*.

11. Select the View menu Properties Window option. Visual Basic will display the Properties Window listing the *Module1* module's properties.

12. Within the Properties Window, change the *Module1* module's *Name* property to *mdlAsyncStart*.

13. Select the Project menu Project1 Properties option. Visual Basic will display the Project Properties dialog box.

14. Within the Project Properties dialog box, change the *Project Name* field from *Project1* to *prjAsyncServer3*.

15. Within the Project Properties dialog box, click your mouse on the Unattended Execution check box to enable multi-threading. Next, click your mouse on the Thread Per Object option. When you finish, the Project Properties dialog box will look similar to Figure 22.16.

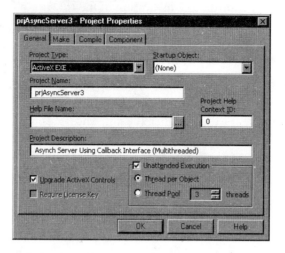

Figure 22.16 *The Project Properties dialog box after you set the component for multi-threading.*

16. Within the Project Properties dialog box, click your mouse on the Component tab. The dialog box will display the Version Compatibility information.

17. Within the Project Properties dialog box, select the Binary Compatibility option. Click your mouse on the OK button to exit the Project Properties dialog box.

18. Select the File menu Save Project As option. Visual Basic will open the Save File As dialog box and fill the *File name* field with *mdlAsyncStart*.

19. Within the Save File As dialog box, click your mouse on the Save button. Visual Basic will save the *mdlAsyncStart* module and fill the *File name* field with the *ICallback* class module's name.

20. Within the Save File As dialog box, click your mouse on the Save button. Visual Basic will save the *ICallback* class module and fill the *File name* field with the *DCOMObject* class module's name.

21. Within the Save File As dialog box, click your mouse on the Save button. Visual Basic will save the *DCOMObject* class module and fill the *File name* field with the *prjAsyncServer3* project name.

22. Within the Save Project As dialog box, click your mouse on the Save button. Visual Basic will save the *prjAsyncServer3* project and close the Save Project As dialog box.

UNDERSTANDING THE DIFFERENCE BETWEEN THE CALLBACK-USING PROJECTS

The only difference between the *prjAsyncServer2* and *prjAsyncClient2* project pair and the *prjAsyncServer3* and *prjAsyncClient3* project pair is that the *prjAsyncServer2* project uses a single-threaded COM component at the server side, and the *prjAsyncServer3* project uses a multi-threaded COM component at the server side. If you run the projects several times, you will find that the multi-threaded COM component project pair runs significantly faster than the single-threaded COM component project pair.

WRITING THE CODE FOR THE PRJASYNCSERVER3 PROJECT

As you have learned, the *prjAsyncServer3* project uses two classes, the *DCOMObject* class (the object itself), and the *ICallback* class (which implements the callback processing to the client). Within the *ICallback* class, you will define two procedures within the *ICallback* interface without creating implementations for those procedures. You will define the two procedures as shown in the following code:

```
Sub Update(Loops As Long)
    ' No implementation
End Sub

Sub Done(Loops As Long, Successful As Boolean)
    ' No implementation
End Sub
```

When you write the program code for the *prjAsyncClient3* project, you will provide the two callback procedures' implementations (the program code that performs the actual processing).

WRITING THE CODE FOR THE MDLASYNCSTART MODULE

Just as you did within the *prjAsyncServer1* project, you must declare the *SetTimer* and *KillTimer* API functions and write the program code for the *GlobalStartTask* and *TimerProc* procedures. The code within the *mdlAsyncStart* module in the *prjAsyncServer3* project is identical to the code within the *mdlAsyncStart* module in the *prjAsyncServer1* project. **703**

WRITING THE CODE FOR THE DCOMOBJECT CLASS

Just as you did within the *prjAsyncServer2* project, you must declare an instance of the *ICallback* class so that the *DCOMObject* class can invoke the callback procedures during its processing. You must also initialize the *CallbackObject* variable and expose the class's public methods. The program code within the *DCOMObject* class for the *prjAsyncServer3* project is identical to the code within the *prjAsyncServer2* project.

CREATING THE PRJASYNCCLIENT3 PROJECT

Now that you have created the *prjAsyncServer3* server project that the client will access, you can create the *prjAsyncClient3* client project. After you create the client project, you will add a reference to the server project, add controls to the form, and add the program code to the project to perform the client processing. To begin the *prjAsyncClient3* project and to create a blank form, perform the following steps:

1. Within Visual Basic, select the File menu New Project option. Visual Basic will open the New Project dialog box.

2. Within the New Project dialog box, double-click your mouse on the ActiveX EXE icon. Visual Basic will close the New Project dialog box, start a new project, *Project1*, and add a class module to the project, *Class1*.

3. Select the View menu Properties Window option. Visual Basic will open the Properties Window listing the *Class1* class module's properties.

4. Within the Properties Window, change the *Class1* class module's *Name* property to *CallbackImpl*.

5. Within Visual Basic, select the Project menu Add Form option. Visual Basic will display the Add Form dialog box.

6. Within the Add Form dialog box, double-click your mouse on the Form icon. Visual Basic will add a new form, *Form1*, to the project.

7. Select the View menu Properties Window option. Visual Basic will open the Properties Window listing the *Form1* form's properties.

8. Within the Properties Window, change the *Form1* form's property values to those Table 22.5 lists.

Object	Property	Set As
Form1	Caption	Multi-threaded Servers
Form1	Height	4140
Form1	Left	4755

Table 22.5 The newly named **frmMain** form's properties. (continued on following page)

Object	Property	Set As
Form1	Top	2430
Form1	Width	3615
Form1	Name	frmMain

Table 22.5 *The newly named **frmMain** form's properties. (continued from previous page)*

9. Within Visual Basic, select the Project menu Add Module option. Visual Basic will display the Add Module dialog box.

10. Within the Add Module dialog box, double-click your mouse on the Module icon. Visual Basic will add a new module, *Module1*, to the project.

11. Select the View menu Properties Window option. Visual Basic will open the Properties Window listing the *Module1* module's properties.

12. Within the Properties Window, change the *Module1* module's *Name* property to *mdlMain*.

13. Within Visual Basic, select the Project menu Project1 Properties option. Visual Basic will display the Project1 Properties dialog box.

14. Within the Project1 Properties dialog box, type *prjAsyncClient3* within the *Project Name* field. Next, click your mouse on OK. Visual Basic will close the Project1 Properties dialog box.

15. Select the File menu Save Project As option. Visual Basic will display the Save File As dialog box and fill the *File name* field with *CallbackImpl*.

16. Within the Save File As dialog box, click your mouse on the Save button. Visual Basic will save the *CallbackImpl* class module and fill the *File name* field with *mdlMain*.

17. Within the Save File As dialog box, click your mouse on the Save button. Visual Basic will save the *mdlMain* module and fill the *File name* field with *frmMain*.

18. Within the Save File As dialog box, click your mouse on the Save button. Visual Basic will save the *frmMain* form and fill the *File name* field with *prjAsyncClient3*.

19. Within the Save Project As dialog box, click your mouse on the Save button. Visual Basic will save the *prjAsyncClient3* project and close the Save Project As dialog box.

ADDING A REFERENCE TO THE PRJASYNCSERVER3 COMPONENT TO THE PROJECT

As you have learned, you must add a reference to each COM component that a project uses before you can use it within the project. To add a reference to the *prjAsyncServer3* component in the *prjAsyncClient3* project, perform the following steps:

1. Select the Project menu References option. Visual Basic will display the References dialog box.

2. Within the References dialog box, select the *Asynch Server Using Callback Interface (Multi-threaded)* listing. Next, click your mouse on the box to the left of the listing. Visual Basic will display a check mark in the box.

3. Within the References dialog box, click your mouse on the OK button. Visual Basic will add the *Asynch Server Using Callback Interface (Multi-threaded)* COM component's type library to your project.

ADDING THE CONTROLS TO THE FRMMAIN FORM

After you create the project, you can add the controls to the *frmMain* form. As you saw in this chapter's "Using the *prjAsyncClient1* Project" section, the *frmMain* form's display is relatively simple. In fact, it consists of only a *CommandButton* control and a *PictureBox* control. In fact, the *frmMain* form's design for the *prjAsyncClient3* project is identical to the design for the *prjAsyncClient1* and *prjAsyncClient2* projects.

WRITING THE CODE FOR THE MDLMAIN MODULE

Within the *mdlMain* module, you will write the *Sub Main* procedure. Because the *prjAsyncClient3* project is an ActiveX EXE project (remember, it must be COM-compliant, like the server, to support callback implementations), the project cannot open the form directly. Rather, the project must start within *Sub Main*, which then opens the *frmMain* form. The following code implements the *Sub Main* procedure:

```
Public Sub Main()
   frmMain.Show
End Sub
```

WRITING THE CODE FOR THE CALLBACKIMPL CLASS MODULE

As you have learned, the client program must implement the interfaces that you declared, but did not implement, within the *ICallback* class module in the *prjAsyncServer3* project. The following code implements the declarations for the *CallbackImpl* class module:

```
Implements ICallback
Public pic As Picture
```

As you learned earlier in this chapter, the *Implements* keyword tells the program that the class module implements an interface defined elsewhere. The program will use the *pic* object to display information about the program's processing.

WRITING THE ICALLBACK INTERFACE METHOD IMPLEMENTATIONS

As you have learned, when you implement callback interfaces, you will specify the interface class (in this case, *ICallback*), and then the actual method. The following code, for example, implements the *ICallback_Update* method and the *ICallback_Done* method:

```
Sub ICallBack_Update(Loops As Long)
  pic.Print "Loops completed: " & Format(Loops, "###,##0")
End Sub

Sub ICallBack_Done(Loops As Long, Successful As Boolean)
  pic.Print
  If (Successful) Then
    pic.Print "The job was successful"
  Else
    pic.Print "The job was unsuccessful"
  End If
  pic.Print "Total loops completed: " & Format(Loops, "###,##0")
End Sub
```

Both methods perform processing identical to the events of the same name in the *prjAsyncClient1* project, and the methods of the same name in the *prjAsyncClient2* project. The program code within the *frmMain* form sets the *pic* property value equal to the *picDisplay* control on the *frmMain* form.

WRITING THE CODE FOR THE FRMMAIN FORM

Within the *frmMain* form, you must define two objects, one to reference the *DCOMObject*, and one to reference the *ICallback* class's implementation within the *CallbackImpl* class module. The following code implements the object definitions for the *frmMain* form:

```
Private lclCallBack As CallbackImpl
Private lclObject As DCOMObject
```

705

WRITING THE CODE FOR THE FORM_LOAD EVENT

When the *prjAsyncClient3* project loads the *frmMain* form, the program code within the *Form_Load* event will perform significant processing to initialize all the objects the form will use. The following code implements the *Form_Load* event within the *frmMain* form:

```
Private Sub Form_Load()
   Set lclCallBack = New CallbackImpl
   Set lclCallBack.pic = Me.picDisplay
   Set lclObject = New DCOMObject
   lclObject.RegisterCallBack lclCallBack
End Sub
```

The program code first sets the *lclCallBack* variable, and then sets the *lclCallBack* variable's *pic* property. After it initializes the *lclCallBack* variable, the program code initializes the *lclObject* variable, and calls the *RegisterCallBack* method. When the program calls the *RegisterCallBack* method, it passes the new *lclCallBack* variable into the method, which alerts the *DCOMObject* where to send its callbacks. When you unload the form, you must remove the register from the callback implementation so that the operating system will eliminate the *DCOMObject* from memory. The following code implements the *frmMain* form's *Form_Unload* event:

```
Private Sub Form_Unload(Cancel As Integer)
   lclObject.UnregisterCallBack
End Sub
```

WRITING THE CODE FOR THE CMDSTARTTASK_CLICK EVENT

As you have learned, the user will click the mouse on the *cmdStartTask* button to begin the *prjAsyncClient3* program's execution. The following code implements the *cmdStartTask_Click* event:

```
Private Sub cmdStartTask_Click()
   picDisplay.Cls
   lclObject.StartTask
End Sub
```

The *Cls* method clears the *picDisplay* control. The invocation of the *lclObject* object's *StartTask* method begins the object's asynchronous processing.

ENHANCEMENTS YOU CAN MAKE TO THE PROJECTS

As you have learned, the six projects that you created within this chapter provide only the simplest of DCOM interactions. In your own projects, you should use the design principles that you have learned throughout this chapter to efficiently and effectively implement DCOM servers and clients. Using asynchronous callbacks, particularly in large, high-traffic environments, will make your components faster and more scalable, and improve performance throughout programs that use those components.

PUTTING IT ALL TOGETHER

This chapter's projects introduced you to the fundamentals (and more) of Microsoft's Component Object Model (COM) and Distributed Component Object Model (DCOM). You have moved beyond the out-of-process component creation basics and created your own components that will scale well, even in busy or traffic-heavy environments. You have learned how to define custom callback interfaces, perform asynchronous processing with events, and more. In the next chapter, Chapter 23, "Using the CryptoAPI to Encrypt Documents," you will use Microsoft's Cryptographic Application Programming Interface (CryptoAPI) to create an application that lets you encrypt and decrypt documents. Before you continue with Chapter 23, however, make sure you understand the following key concepts:

✓ Microsoft's Component Object Model (COM) specifies the relationships that objects in the same process should have with each other, and the communication protocols between those objects. You will use COM's principles when you create ActiveX EXEs, ActiveX DLLs, and ActiveX controls.

✓ Microsoft's Distributed Component Object Model (DCOM) expands on the Component Object Model (COM). DCOM specifies the relationships that objects on separate computers should have with each other, and the communication protocols between those objects. Only ActiveX EXE components support DCOM.

✓ Both COM and DCOM objects implement interfaces. An interface is an agreement between a client and an object about how they will communicate with each other. A well-constructed COM object will permit access only through its interfaces.

✓ When you define COM and DCOM objects, you will always define at least one interface, *IUnknown*, and will often define many more, each of which derives its characteristics from *IUnknown*.

✓ COM objects may fall into categories. A category of objects is a set of objects that all implement the same interfaces. You can presume that all objects that fall within the same category will share the same interfaces.

✓ Every COM or DCOM object includes three default methods that it must expose: *QueryInterface, AddRef*, and *Release*. When you define COM or DCOM objects that support non-*vTable* binding, you must also define the *GetTypeInfoCount, GetTypeInfo, GetIDsOfNames*, and *Invoke* methods within the object.

✓ You must register your COM and DCOM objects within the Windows Registry so that client programs can access the objects. If you do not register the objects, client programs will be unable to locate the object files.

✓ When you register a COM or DCOM object within the Windows Registry, you must reference that object's Globally Unique Identifier (GUID), which is a 128-bit (16 byte) number that uniquely identifies the object. Whenever a client program accesses a COM or DCOM object, the client program will use the GUID to reference the object within the Windows Registry. You will generally write GUIDs as a 32-digit hexadecimal number.

✓ When you define interfaces in languages other than Visual Basic, you will use Microsoft's Interface Definition Language (IDL). When you define interfaces in Visual Basic, the Visual Basic run-time engine handles the interface definitions on your behalf.

✓ Each interface that you define in a COM object will include a Universally Unique Identifier (UUID), which the operating system constructs exactly as it does a Globally Unique Identifier. When client programs access an interface the COM object exposes, the programs will actually reference the interface's UUID. Like GUIDs, you will generally write UUIDs as a 32-digit hexadecimal number.

Chapter 23

Using the CryptoAPI to Encrypt Documents

As companies store more and more information on computers, and as both companies and individuals transmit more digital information over the Internet and through other communication channels, such as corporate intranets and wireless transmissions, protecting that information becomes more important. To protect information from the casual observer and from the dedicated hacker, most companies and computer users turn to encryption. *Encryption* is a way to protect information. When you encrypt information, you scramble the information in a way that makes the information unreadable or unusable. The only way to read the scrambled information is to decrypt the information with a cryptographic *key*. Historically, to protect information, encryption systems used two encryption keys, one key at the sending end (to encrypt the information) and one key at the receiving end of the transmission (to decrypt the information). In historical encryption systems, both parties maintained keys in code books, with both parties having their own code book that was an exact copy of the other party's code book. In other words, to encrypt information with the historical method, one party has to, at some point, send the code book (containing the decryption keys) to the other party.

However, the mathematical processing power of computers has changed the way people use encryption. The introduction of *public-key cryptosystems* has let computer users encrypt documents and other data to send to other users, without the exchange of keys, such as the code books that encryption systems before computers used. Instead, with a public-key cryptosystem, users can post their public keys anywhere, and other users can use those public keys to encrypt documents. With public key encryption, one user can use another user's *public key* to encrypt information. Only the user who has the *private key* that corresponds to the public key can then decrypt the information. Even the user who encrypted the information cannot decrypt the information. With public-key cryptosystems, encrypting and decrypting information has become more secure and simpler for the user to accomplish. Additionally, the mathematical power of computers lets users create extremely complex keys—making the encryption harder than ever to "break"—providing greater protection for the encrypted information.

Because many computer users are using encryption, Microsoft integrated cryptographic support into the Windows NT 4.0 operating system, and also built it into the *Internet Explorer* software browser, so that Windows 95 users can manipulate encryption. Microsoft's *Cryptographic Application Programming Interface (CryptoAPI)* is a set of functions that you can use from within your Visual Basic program to provide encryption and decryption services to your program's users. In this chapter, you will use Microsoft's CryptoAPI to create a notepad-style program, *prjEncryptDecrypt*, that lets you encrypt, decrypt, save, and load text files. By the time you finish this chapter, you will understand the following key concepts:

- Within your Visual Basic projects, you can use both simple and complex methods of encryption.

- You can use two basic types of computer-based encryption: *single-key encryption* and *public-key encryption.*

- Most encryption on the Internet today is either public-key encryption or some combination of public- and single-key encryption.

- Computers mathematically manipulate transmissions with large numbers (with hundreds or even thousands of digits) to perform encryption, and then apply a related large number to the transmission to decrypt it.

- Microsoft's CryptoAPI offers a custom solution to enterprise cryptography issues, such as encrypting intranet transmissions and encrypting databases.

- A *hash* is a mathematical function you can use to generate a unique number from a file or other stream of data. A *one-way hash* is a hash that keeps the user from being able to derive the original data stream from the unique number.

- When you work with the CryptoAPI, you will work with Cryptographic Service Providers (CSP). A Cryptographic Service Provider is, essentially, the underlying cryptographic engine that your API calls will use to encrypt or decrypt a document, file, or other information. In the *prjEncryptDecrypt* project, you will work with the *Microsoft Base Cryptographic Service Provider*.

- When your programs use the CryptoAPI, your programs must get a container from the Cryptographic Service Provider (CSP), generate a key from within that container, and use the key to encrypt or decrypt the information.

- Your programs can use functions such as *CryptSignHash* and *CryptVerifySignature* to verify a *digital signature*, a unique value that verifies a file's validity. A digital signature verifies the file's origination (that is, who signed the file), and also verifies that no one modified the file after the original user signed it.

709

USING CRYPTOGRAPHY

As you have learned, the *prjEncryptDecrypt* project that you will create within this chapter uses the Microsoft CryptoAPI. As you have also learned, Microsoft provides the CryptoAPI with most modern operating systems and its *Internet Explorer* software. However, if your computer does not have the underlying support for cryptography, you will be unable to use this chapter's project. Your computer must include the following for the *prjEncryptDecrypt* program to work correctly:

1. Microsoft Windows 95, Original Equipment Manufacturer (OEM) Release 2.0 or later; or

2. Microsoft Windows NT Workstation or Server; or

3. Microsoft's *Internet Explorer* Web browser, version 3.02 or later (32-bit only)

USING THE prjENCRYPTDECRYPT PROJECT

Before you design the *prjEncryptDecrypt* project, you may find it helpful to run the program. The companion CD-ROM that accompanies this book contains the *prjEncryptDecrypt.exe* program within the *Chapter23* directory. As with every other program on the CD-ROM, you should run the Jamsa Press *setup.exe* program to install the *prjEncryptDecrypt.exe* program to your computer's hard drive before you run it. After you install the *prjEncryptDecrypt.exe* program to your computer's hard drive, you can run it from the Start menu. To run the program, select the Windows Start menu Run option. Windows will display the Run dialog box. Within the Run dialog box, enter *x:\vbp\Chapter23\prjEncryptDecrypt.exe*, where *x* corresponds to the drive letter of the hard drive on which you installed the *prjEncryptDecrypt.exe* program, and click your mouse on OK. Windows will display the *prjEncryptDecrypt.exe* program, as shown in Figure 23.1.

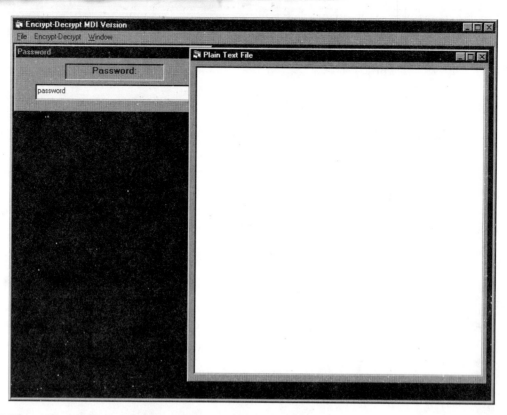

*Figure 23.1 The **prjEncryptDecrypt.exe** program's **Encrypt-Decrypt** window at startup.*

RUNNING PRJENCRYPTDECRYPT FROM THE CD-ROM

 As you have learned, you must first install many programs that you will use in this book to your computer's hard drive before you use the programs. The *prjEncryptDecrypt.exe* program, however, does not use any custom controls or references other than those that Visual Basic installs onto your system. Because the *prjEncryptDecrypt.exe* program uses no custom controls or references, you can run the program from the CD-ROM.

To run the program from the CD-ROM, perform the following steps:

1. Select the Windows Start menu Run option. Windows will display the Run dialog box.

2. Within the Run dialog box, enter *x:\Chapter23\prjEncryptDecrypt.exe*, where *x* corresponds to the drive letter of your computer's CD-ROM drive (usually D: or E:), and click your mouse on OK. Windows will run the *prjEncryptDecrypt.exe* program.

To learn more about the Jamsa Press *setup.exe* program, see the "What's on the *Visual Basic Programmer's Library* Companion CD-ROM" section at the back of this book.

Before you use the *prjEncryptDecrypt.exe* program, take a moment to familiarize yourself with the program's appearance. After you start the *prjEncryptDecrypt.exe* program, your computer will display a window that fills the entire screen (the Encrypt-Decrypt parent window). Near the top of the Encrypt-Decrypt window, you will see the File menu option. To the right of the File menu option, you will see the Encrypt-Decrypt and Window menu options. Because you have not opened a file, the program will disable these menu options. After you open a file, the program will enable some menu options and leave others disabled, depending on the type of file you open.

You can use the File menu to open both plain text and encrypted text files, and you can also save plain text and encrypted text files from within the program. After you load either a plain text file or an encrypted text file, you can use the options on the Encrypt-Decrypt menu to encrypt or decrypt the file, respectively.

UNDERSTANDING THE MESSAGE BOXES THE PROGRAM MAY DISPLAY

As you will learn later in this chapter, the CryptoAPI uses a key container (an internal structure that maintains encryption and decryption keys) to maintain information about how it should encrypt and decrypt files. When you first run the program, the program will check the system registry to determine whether you have run the program before on the current computer. If you have not previously run the program on the current computer, the program will create and then initialize the key container. If you have previously run the program on the current computer, the program will only initialize the key container (because the program created the key container on a previous instance). Figure 23.2 shows one of the two message boxes the program may display when you run it the first time.

711

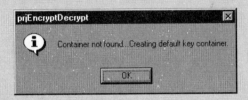

Figure 23.2 *The Creating default key container message box.*

If you have not run the *prjEncryptDecrypt.exe* program before, but another program has previously initialized the default key container, the program will alert you that it has initialized the default key container and is ready to encrypt. Figure 23.3 shows the message the *prjEncryptDecrypt.exe* program will display if another program previously initialized the default key container.

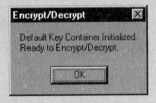

Figure 23.3 *The Default Key Container Initialized message box.*

Now that you have seen the *prjEncryptDecrypt.exe* program's layout, you can use the program to open a plain text file and encrypt the file. To open a plain text file and encrypt the file, perform the following steps:

1. Within the prjEncryptDecrypt window, select the File menu Open Plain Text option. The program will display the Open dialog box.

2. Within the Open dialog box, select the *Readme.txt* file within the *x:\vbpl\Chapter23* directory, where *x* corresponds to the drive letter of the hard drive on which you installed the *prjEncryptDecrypt.exe* program, and click your mouse on OK. The program will load the *Readme.txt* file and display it within the Plain Text File child window.

3. Within the prjEncryptDecrypt window, select the Encrypt-Decrypt menu Encrypt Text option. The *prjEncryptDecrypt.exe* program will display the newly encrypted file in the Encrypted Text child window, as shown in Figure 23.4.

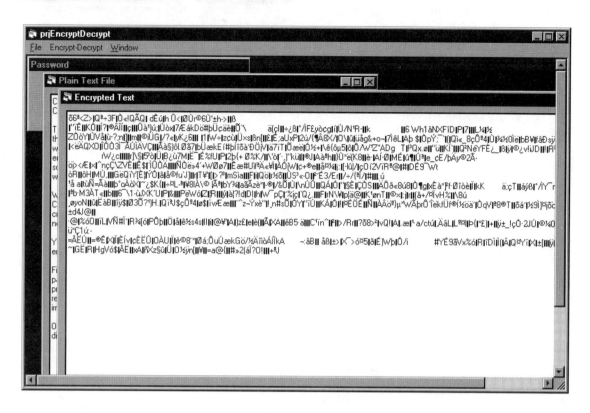

Figure 23.4 *The **prjEncryptDecrypt.exe** program after you encrypt the **Readme.txt** file.*

4. Within the prjEncryptDecrypt window, select the File menu Save Encrypted Text option. The *prjEncryptDecrypt.exe* program will display the Save As dialog box. Note that the file type of the new file to save is *etx* (for encrypted text files). Figure 23.5 shows the Save As dialog box.

Figure 23.5 *The Save As dialog box when you save encrypted text.*

5. Within the Save As dialog box, enter the file name as *readme.etx* and click your mouse on the Save button. The *prjEncryptDecrypt.exe* program will save the file and return to the prjEncryptDecrypt window.

Cryptography requires that both the encoding party (the person encrypting the document or file) and the decoding party (the person decrypting the document or file) use the correct keys (either matching keys in old-fashioned cryptography, or a public- and private-key pair in modern-day cryptography). To test that the CryptoAPI requires that the key that encrypts the document is compatible with the key that decrypts the document, you can change the text encryption key within the Password window. To change a key and test the CryptoAPI, perform the following steps:

1. Within the prjEncryptDecrypt window, select the Window menu Password option. The program will move the Password child window to the display's top.

2. Within the Password window, change the password from *password* to *Chapter23*. Next, select the Encrypt-Decrypt menu Decrypt option. The *prjEncryptDecrypt.exe* program will decrypt the previously encrypted text with the new password. As Figure 23.6 shows, the decryption will result in a file that is not the original text file.

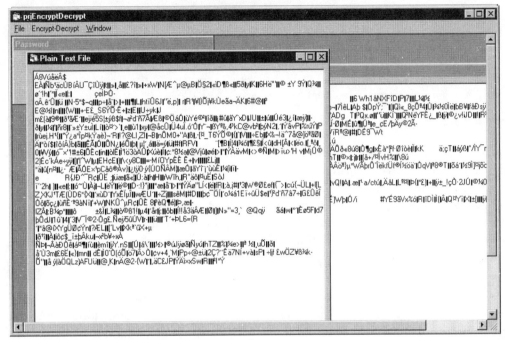

Figure 23.6 *The decryption after you change the password.*

If you change the password back to *password* and select the Encrypt-Decrypt menu Decrypt option, the program will correctly decrypt the file and display the original *readme.txt* file's text within the Plain Text File window.

BETTER UNDERSTANDING ENCRYPTION

Suppose you want to send a confidential message to your cousin over the Internet. In other words, you do not want anyone who might intercept the message to be able to read it. To protect the message you send, you will *encrypt* or *encipher* the message. You encrypt the message by changing the letters within the message in a complicated manner, rendering the message unreadable to anyone except your cousin.

You will supply your cousin with a cryptographic key that your cousin will use to unscramble the message and make it legible. In a conventional *single-key* cryptosystem, you will share the cryptographic key with your cousin *before* you use it to encrypt the message (you may send it in another e-mail, mail him a copy, and so on). For example, a simple single-key cryptosystem would shift each letter in the message forward three letters in the alphabet, with the SPACE character immediately following the letter Z. For instance, the word DOG becomes GRJ. Figure 23.7 shows a one-line document encrypted with the single-key cryptosystem.

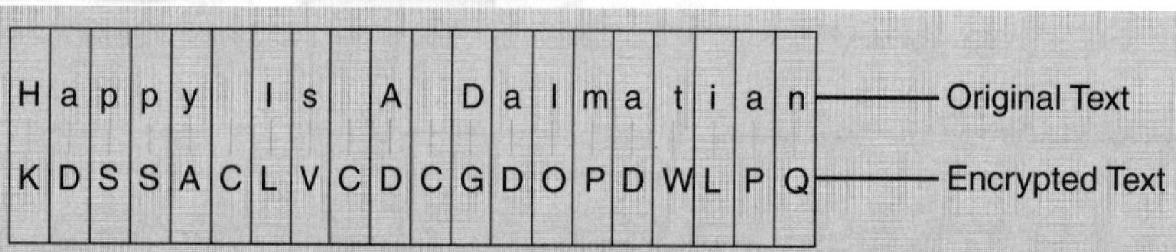

Figure 23.7 *Shifting letters to encrypt a document.*

Your cousin will get the message and shift all the letters back three letters in the alphabet to decrypt it, which will convert GRJ back to DOG. Figure 23.8 shows the key for the single-key encryption system you use to send the message to your cousin.

714

Figure 23.8 *The key for the single-key encryption system.*

CREATING THE PROJECT

Now that you have a better idea how to use the finished *prjEncryptDecrypt* project, you can begin to design it. First, you will design four empty forms—the parent form (that contains the three other forms), the password entry form, the encryption form, and the decryption form. After you design and implement the forms, you will learn more about the Windows Encryption API (Application Programming Interface). As you saw in this chapter's "Using the *prjEncryptDecrypt* Project" section, the *prjEncryptDecrypt* project includes one Multiple-Document Interface (MDI) parent form and three child forms. Additionally, you will add a module to the project to store the CryptoAPI declarations and many of the program functions and procedures that use those declarations.

CREATING THE MDI PARENT FORM

As you have learned, you will use an MDI parent form as the container for the other forms within the project. To begin the *prjEncryptDecrypt* project and design an empty MDI parent form, perform the following steps:

1. Within Visual Basic, select the File menu New Project option. Visual Basic will open the New Project dialog box.

2. Within the New Project dialog box, double-click your mouse on the Standard EXE icon. Visual Basic will close the New Project dialog box, start a new project, *Project1*, and add a form to it, *Form1*.

3. Within the new *Project1* project, select the Project menu Add MDI Form option. Visual Basic will open the Add MDI Form dialog box.

4. Within the Add MDI Form dialog box, double-click your mouse on the MDI Form icon. Visual Basic will add an MDI form, *MDIForm1*, to the new *Project1* project and display the *MDIForm1* form window.

5. Select the View menu Properties Window option. Visual Basic will open the Properties Window listing the *MDIForm1* form's properties.

6. Within the Properties Window, change the *MDIForm1* form's property values to those Table 23.1 lists.

Object	Property	Set As
MDIForm1	*Caption*	*prjEncryptDecrypt*
MDIForm1	*Height*	7905
MDIForm1	*Left*	0

Table 23.1 *The newly named **frmMDIParent** MDI form's properties. (continued on following page)*

Object	Property	Set As
MDIForm1	*Top*	0
MDIForm1	*Width*	11820
MDIForm1	*Name*	*frmMDIParent*

Table 23.1 *The newly named **frmMDIParent** MDI form's properties. (continued from previous page)*

CREATING THE FIRST CHILD FORM

As you learned in the previous section, to design a Multiple-Document Interface project, you must first add an MDI form to the project, which will act as the container for the child forms within the project. After you add the MDI form (the parent form) to the project, you can change the default *Form1* form you created with the project to be the first child form in the project. The *prjEncryptDecrypt* project uses child forms to display both encrypted and decrypted text, as well as the user's currently selected password. To change the *Form1* form's properties and set it as the first child form (which will display encrypted text), perform the following steps:

1. If Visual Basic is not displaying the *Form1* form within an object window, double-click your mouse on the Form1 icon within the Project Explorer. Visual Basic will display the *Form1* form.

2. Select the View menu Properties Window option. Visual Basic will open the Properties Window listing the *Form1* form's properties.

3. Within the Properties Window, change the *Form1* form's property values to those Table 23.2 lists.

Object	Property	Set As
Form1	*Caption*	*Encrypted Text*
Form1	*Height*	8595
Form1	*Left*	0
Form1	*Locked*	*True*
Form1	*Top*	0
Form1	*Width*	6750
Form1	*MDIChild*	*True*
Form1	*Name*	*frmEncrypted*

Table 23.2 *The newly named **frmEncrypted** child form's properties.*

CREATING THE SECOND CHILD FORM

Now that you have created the first child form, *frmEncrypted*, you can add a second child form to the project. To add a second child form (which will display plain text) to the *prjEncryptDecrypt* project, perform the following steps:

1. Within the *prjEncryptDecrypt* project, select the Project menu Add Form option. Visual Basic will display the Add Form dialog box.

2. Within the Add Form dialog box, click your mouse on the New tab and select the Form icon. Next, click your mouse on the Open button. Visual Basic will close the Add Form dialog box and add a new form, *Form1*, to the *prjEncryptDecrypt* project.

3. Select the View menu Properties Window option. Visual Basic will open the Properties Window listing the *Form1* form's properties.

4. Within the Properties Window, change the *Form1* form's property values to those Table 23.3 lists.

Object	Property	Set As
Form1	Caption	Plain Text File
Form1	Height	7845
Form1	Left	0
Form1	Top	0
Form1	Width	7290
Form1	MDIChild	True
Form1	Name	frmPlain

Table 23.3 The newly named **frmPlain** child form's properties.

CREATING THE THIRD CHILD FORM

716

Now that you have created a second child form, you can add a third child form to the project. To add a third child form (which will contain the password information for the encryption or decryption) to the *prjEncryptDecrypt* project, perform the following steps:

1. Within the *prjEncryptDecrypt* project, select the Project menu Add Form option. Visual Basic will display the Add Form dialog box.

2. Within the Add Form dialog box, click your mouse on the New tab and select the Form icon. Next, click your mouse on the Open button. Visual Basic will close the Add Form dialog box and add a new form, *Form1*, to the *prjEncryptDecrypt* project.

3. Select the View menu Properties Window option. Visual Basic will open the Properties Window listing the *Form1* form's properties.

4. Within the Properties Window, change the *Form1* form's property values to those Table 23.4 lists.

Object	Property	Set As
Form1	Caption	Password
Form1	Height	1560
Form1	Left	0
Form1	Top	0
Form1	Width	4815
Form1	MDIChild	True
Form1	Name	frmPassword

Table 23.4 The newly named **frmPassword** child form's properties.

MESSAGE AUTHENTICATION AS PART OF THE PUBLIC-KEY PROTOCOL

Public-key encryption with most computer-based cryptosystems makes extensive use of message authentication. *Message authentication* is a method that message recipients can use to verify a message's originator and validity. The sender must simply use the sender's secret key to encrypt a message, thereby signing it. The secret key creates a *digital signature* on the message that the recipient can check (or anyone else, for that matter, which is why you should only use it for signature purposes) by using the sender's public key to decrypt the digital signature.

With the process of digital signing, the message recipient can verify that the sender is indeed the message's true originator. Because only a private-key holder can create a digital signature, the digital signature guarantees the message sender's identity. Moreover, because a digital signature processes the file and creates a unique number representative of the file's contents, date, time, and so on, the digital signature, when verified, proves that no one has modified the file during or after transmission. Figure 23.9 shows how a digital signing program places a digital signature on a message, and how the message's recipient decodes the signature.

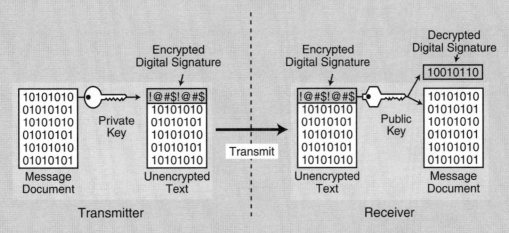

Figure 23.9 Digital signatures can accompany messages to authenticate the sender's identity.

Encrypting and decrypting large files with a public-key algorithm requires a significant amount of time. Therefore, public-key algorithms you use with files generally use digital signatures, which significantly reduces the file's transfer time because the algorithm encrypts only the signature. Figure 23.10 illustrates how a public-key algorithm creates digital signatures and uses the signatures to sign a file.

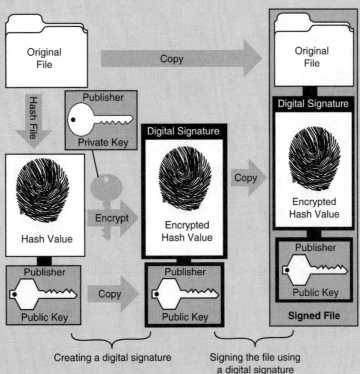

Figure 23.10 Creating and using a digital signature with a public-key algorithm.

A digital signature uses your original file's hash value (which you learned about in previous sections of this chapter), which serves as your original file's checksum or fingerprint. For example, Microsoft's *Authenticode®* (one of the Internet's most popular and commonly used digital signature technologies) hashes your file to either a 128-bit or a 160-bit value. First, the software calculates a fingerprint by hashing your file, and then the software encrypts the fingerprint with your private key. By combining the encrypted fingerprint and your public key, the software creates your digital signature. The following list outlines the steps you must follow to create a file's digital signature using your private and public keys:

1. You must note within the document that a digital signature contains the public key that your file's recipient must use to decrypt the fingerprint.

2. You first create the digital signature for a file in order to sign that file with the signature.

3. You then simply attach the digital signature to the original file.

When a message recipient receives your file, which you signed with a digital signature, the recipient can verify that the file's contents have not changed between the time you signed the file and the time the recipient received the file. Figure 23.11 illustrates how a digital signature verifies a file.

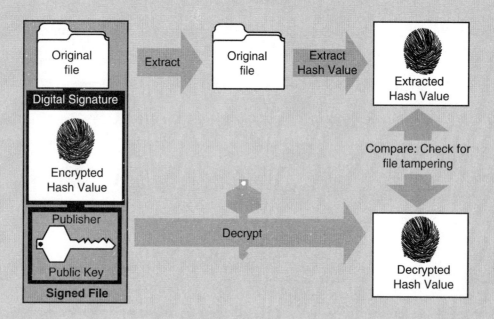

Figure 23.11 *Verifying a file with a digital signature.*

When the user receives your signed file, the user's system completes the following steps to verify the file:

1. The receiver's software unpacks the encrypted fingerprint and the public key from the digital signature.

2. The receiver's software decrypts the encrypted fingerprint using the public key.

3. The receiver's software hashes the original file to get a fingerprint, which the system compares to the value created in Step 2.

If the values in Steps 2 and 3 match, the download is successful. If the values do not match, someone has altered your file either intentionally or through a transmission error.

Unfortunately, several security issues remain unresolved (such as the truthfulness of the message signer), although *Authenticode* and other digital signature standards use *Certificate Authorities* to try and resolve them. To use *Authenticode*, you must get a digital certificate from a Certificate Authority, which is a third-party company. Certificate Authorities guarantee when a user downloads a file you sent, that you are the person who signed the file, that you are not a fictitious person, and that someone did not forge your signature. Think of a digital certificate as a notary seal on a document. When you apply for a certificate, the Certificate Authority verifies your identity and sends you your digital certificate, which contains information about your identity and a copy of your public key. The Certificate Authority's private key encrypts the certificate.

When you sign a component, *Authenticode* will append your digital signature and your digital certificate to your component. When a message recipient receives your file, which contains your digital signature and your digital certificate, the recipient can verify that no one has forged your signature. Figure 23.12 illustrates how the message recipient will verify your digital signature and digital certificate.

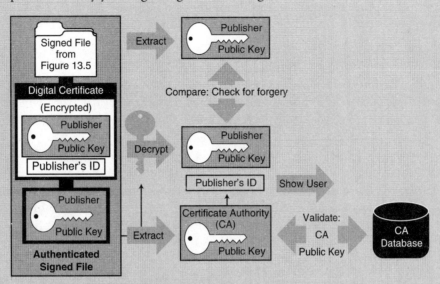

Figure 23.12 *Verifying your digital signature and certificate.*

Authenticode will verify your digital signature by comparing your public key, which your digital signature contains, against the copy your digital certificate contains. The user can review the ID information in your digital certificate to learn your identity. Users can trust your signature's authenticity because the Certificate Authority verifies your identity.

The *Authenticode* strategy depends upon two important assumptions. First, users cannot easily calculate the private key from the public key. Some experts estimate that cracking the 1024-bit digital keys *Authenticode* uses would require 90 billion MIPS (Millions of Instructions Per Second) years. In other words, one billion computers that can execute one million instructions per second would take 90 years to crack one individual's signature. However, nobody truly knows the time frame required to crack a code; many "unbreakable" codes have been broken throughout cryptography's history.

ADDING A MODULE TO THE PROJECT AND SAVING THE PROJECT

After you design the *prjEncryptDecrypt* project's blank forms, you will create a module in which to store the program code. Within the *prjEncryptDecrypt* project, the program code that you will place within the module will declare several global variables and constants, and will contain several "helper" procedures that the forms will use during their processing. To add a module to the *prjEncryptDecrypt* project, perform the following steps:

1. Within Visual Basic, select the Project menu Add Module option. Visual Basic will open the Add Module dialog box.

2. Within the Add Module dialog box, select the Module option. Next, click your mouse on the Open button. Visual Basic will open a new Code window, *Module1*.

3. Select the View menu Properties Window option. Visual Basic will open the Properties Window listing the *Module1* module's properties.

4. Within the Properties Window, change the *Module1* module's name to *mdlCryptoAPI*.

5. Select the File menu Save Project As option. Visual Basic will open the Save File As dialog box and fill the *File name* field with *mdlCryptoAPI*.

6. Within the Save File As dialog box, click your mouse on the Save button. Visual Basic will save the *mdlCryptoAPI* module and fill the *File name* field with *frmPassword*.

7. Within the Save File As dialog box, click your mouse on the Save button. Visual Basic will save the *frmPassword* form and fill the *File name* field with *frmPlain*.

8. Within the Save File As dialog box, click your mouse on the Save button. Visual Basic will save the *frmPlain* form and fill the *File name* field with *frmEncrypted*.

9. Within the Save File As dialog box, click your mouse on the Save button. Visual Basic will save the *frmEncrypted* form and fill the *File name* field with *frmMDIParent*.

10. Within the Save File As dialog box, click your mouse on the Save button. Visual Basic will save the *frmMDIParent* MDI form and fill the *File name* field with *Project1*.

11. Within the *File name* field, replace the *Project1* project name with the new *prjEncryptDecrypt* project name. Next, click your mouse on the Save button. Visual Basic will save the *prjEncryptDecrypt* project and close the Save Project As dialog box.

THE LIMITATIONS OF CONVENTIONAL SINGLE-KEY CRYPTOSYSTEMS

In conventional single-key cryptosystems, both the transmitter and the receiver use a *single key* (the same key) for both encryption and decryption. Thus, the transmitter and receiver must initially exchange a key through secure channels so that both parties have the key available before they send or receive encrypted messages over unsecure channels. Figure 23.13 shows a typical exchange using a single-key cryptosystem.

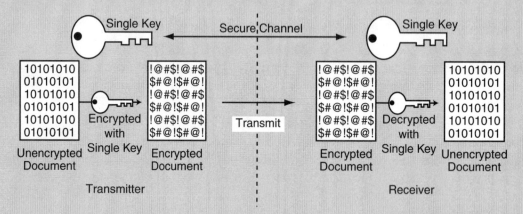

Figure 23.13 *A single-key cryptosystem exchange.*

The primary flaw when you use single-key cryptosystems on the Internet is that they require both parties to know the key before each transmission. In addition, because you will want only the recipient to have the ability to decrypt your transmissions, you must create different single keys for each individual, group, or business to which you transmit. Clearly, you will have to maintain an inconveniently large number of single keys. Also, if you use a secure channel for exchanging the key itself, you could simply transmit the data along the same secure channel (which defeats the purpose). However, most people do not have access to a secure channel, and therefore must transmit the data along an unsecure channel. Modern-day cryptographic transmissions use a new type of cryptography, called a *public-key cryptosystem,* to avoid the issues that surround single-key cryptosystems.

UNDERSTANDING THE WINDOWS ENCRYPTION API

As you learned at the beginning of this chapter, Microsoft integrated cryptographic support into its products. To provide users with the ability to manipulate encryption, the Windows NT 4.0 *Service Pack 3*, Windows 95 *OEM Service Release 2,* and Microsoft's *Internet Explorer 3.02* (and later versions) all include Microsoft's CryptoAPI. The CryptoAPI is a programming interface that you can use to add cryptographic functions to your programs. The CryptoAPI provides three basic sets of functions you will implement within your programs: *certificate functions, simplified cryptographic functions,* and *base cryptographic functions.* Figure 23.14 shows the model you will use to implement these functions.

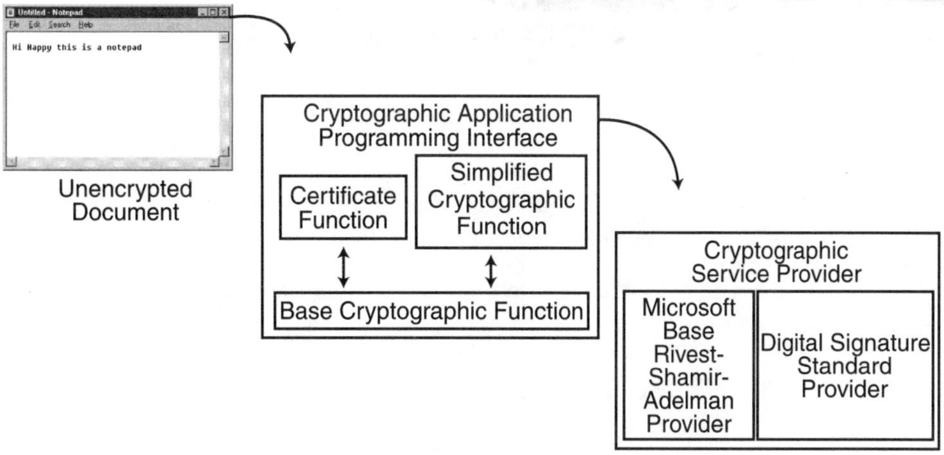

Figure 23.14 *The cryptographic model you will apply when you use Microsoft's CryptoAPI interface.*

The simplified cryptographic functions include high-level functions for creating and using keys and for encrypting and decrypting information. The certificate functions provide the means to extract, store, and verify the digital signature certificates that transmitters may enclose with documents and to enumerate the certificates previously saved to a machine. At a lower level are the base cryptographic functions, which your programs should avoid calling to prevent conflicts resulting from Cryptographic Service Providers (CSP) that you have uninstalled, another program's required use of a particular CSP, and so on.

The CryptoAPI supports multiple cryptographic providers. For example, you might use Rivest, Shamir, and Adleman (RSA) encryption with some information, and you might digitally sign other information with the Digital Signature Standard (DSS). Later sections within this chapter explain more about both RSA encryption and the DSS. Table 23.5 lists the Cryptographic Service Providers (CSP).

Cryptographic Provider Constant	Encryption	Signature
PROV_RSA_FULL	RC2, RC4	RSA
PROV_RSA_SIG	n/a	RSA
PROV_DSS	n/a	DSS
PROV_FORTEZZA	SkipJack	DSS
PROV_SSL	RSA	RSA
PROV_MS_EXCHANGE	CAST	RSA

Table 23.5 *The Cryptographic Service Providers (CSP) that the CryptoAPI supports.*

The CryptoAPI uses key databases to maintain password information. When you create an encrypted application, you must first create the necessary key databases. The best way to create an initial key database is to download all the samples from Microsoft's Developer Network, at *http://www.microsoft.com/msdn/library/devprogrs/vc++/vcsamples*. Among the samples at this site is the *InitUser.exe* program, which creates the basic key databases you need to use the CryptoAPI. Alternatively, you can initialize the key databases yourself, as the *prjEncryptDecrypt* program code does.

Using the Cryptographic API's Basic Functions

When you want to use the CryptoAPI, you must apply the basic CryptoAPI functions within your programs—which will let you perform the three basic activity types previously discussed within this chapter. The CryptoAPI's designers divided its functions into four main areas: CSPs, keys, hash objects, and signatures. Within an encryption application, you will typically call the *CryptAcquireContext* function—which will let you select or access a Cryptographic Service Provider—before any other function. You will declare the *CryptAcquireContext* function within your Visual Basic programs as shown here:

```
Declare Function CryptAcquireContext Lib "advapi32.dll" Alias _
    "CryptAcquireContextA" (phProv As Long, pszContainer As String, _
    pszProvider As String, ByVal dwProvType As Long, _
    ByVal dwFlags As Long) As Long
```

The *CryptAcquireContext* function returns a 32-bit *Long* value, which indicates to the remaining CryptoAPI functions that *CryptAcquireContext* established a working cryptography session. You may specify a particular Cryptographic Service Provider and key container through the *pszContainer* and *pszProvider* parameters.

After you obtain a handle to the successful session, you can use the functions Table 23.6 shows to perform encryption activities within your programs.

CryptoAPI Function	Description
CryptAcquireContext	Returns a handle to the key container in a Cryptographic Service Provider.
CryptCreateHash	Creates a hash object (a numeric interpretation of a value).
CryptDecrypt	Uses a decryption key to decrypt a buffer's contents.
CryptDeriveKey	Derives an encryption key from a hash object. Generally, you will hash a password or other specific string, create a hash object, and then derive the key from that object.
CryptDestroyHash	Destroys a hash object created with *CryptCreateHash*.
CryptDestroyKey	Destroys a key, whether imported (with *CryptImportKey*) or created (with *CryptDeriveKey*).
CryptEncrypt	Uses an encryption key to encrypt a buffer's contents.
CryptExportKey	Returns a key blob from a key. A *key blob* is an encrypted copy of a key that you contain within a binary, large object (or blob), and then transmit to a key's receiver. Generally, you will use a key blob to encrypt a single key and send it along with a single-key encrypted document.
CryptGenKey	Generates random keys to use with the Cryptographic Service Provider.
CryptGetHashParam	Retrieves data previously associated with a hash object.
CryptGetKeyParam	Retrieves data previously associated with a key.
CryptGetProvParam	Retrieves data previously associated with a Cryptographic Service Provider.
CryptGetUserKey	Returns the handle to a signature or previously defined key (as opposed to a key that you derive from a hash object).
CryptHashData	Hashes a data stream.
CryptImportKey	Extracts the key from a key blob.
CryptReleaseContext	Releases the handle to the key container.
CryptSetProvParam	Customizes a Cryptographic Service Provider's operations.
CryptSetProvider	Sets the default Cryptographic Service Provider.
CryptSignHash	Uses an encryption key to digitally sign a data stream. You will learn more about digital signatures in later sections of this chapter.
CryptVerifySignature	Verifies a hash object's digital signature.

Table 23.6 The **CryptoAPI** *basic functions.*

Each function applies the CryptoAPI in a manner consistent with its name. For example, to export a key is a two-step process. The first step retrieves the user's public key from the Cryptographic Service Provider using *CryptGetUserKey*. After your program has retrieved the public-key handle, you can call *CryptExportKey* to get a key blob. You can then transmit the key blob to another user, who will use the *CryptImportKey* function to retrieve the key from the key blob.

Adding the Component Controls to the Project

As you have learned, the *prjEncryptDecrypt* project has four component forms, each of which performs special processing. The *frmMDIParent* form, the *frmPlain* form, and the *frmEncrypted* form all use controls that you must add to the project as components. The project will use the *RichTextBox* control to let the user view text files, both unencrypted and encrypted. The project will also use the *Microsoft Common Dialog* control, which will display the Open File and Save As dialog boxes. To add the *RichTextBox* and *Microsoft Common Dialog* controls to the *prjEncryptDecrypt* project, perform the following steps:

1. Within Visual Basic, select the Project menu Components option. Visual Basic will open the Components dialog box.

2. Within the Components dialog box, select the *Microsoft Common Dialog Control 5.0* listing. Next, click your mouse on the box to the left of the listing. Visual Basic will display a check mark in the box.

3. Within the Components dialog box, select the *Microsoft Rich Textbox Control 5.0* listing. Next, click your mouse on the box to the left of the listing. Visual Basic will display a check mark in the box.

4. Within the Components dialog box, click your mouse on the OK button. Visual Basic will close the Components dialog box and add the controls to the *prjEncryptDecrypt* project.

Designing the frmMDIParent Form's Appearance

As you learned in the "Using the *prjEncryptDecrypt* Project" section earlier in this chapter, the *frmMDIParent* form is essentially a container for the child forms that the program will display. You will add one control to the *frmMDIParent* form—the *CommonDialog* control. In addition to the *CommonDialog* control, you will use the Menu Editor to add a menu to the *frmMDIParent* form. After you finish the *frmMDIParent* form's design, you will design the child forms for the project.

Adding the CommonDialog Control to the frmMDIParent Form

In this chapter's "Using the *prjEncryptDecrypt* Project" section, you opened several different files and file types within the *prjEncryptDecrypt* project. To display the Open File dialog box and the Save As dialog box, the *prjEncryptDecrypt* project uses the *CommonDialog* control. To add the *CommonDialog* control to the *frmMDIParent* form, perform the following steps:

1. If Visual Basic is not displaying the *frmMDIParent* form within an object window, double-click your mouse on the *frmMDIParent* form listing within the Project Explorer. Visual Basic will open the *frmMDIParent* form.

2. Within Visual Basic, select the View menu Toolbox option. Visual Basic will open the Toolbox.

3. Within the Toolbox, double-click your mouse on the CommonDialog icon. Visual Basic will draw a *CommonDialog* control, *CommonDialog1*, within the *frmMDIParent* form. Figure 23.15 shows the CommonDialog icon within the Toolbox.

Figure 23.15 *The CommonDialog icon within the Toolbox.*

4. Within the *frmMDIParent* form, click your mouse on the *CommonDialog1* control to highlight it. Visual Basic will draw a small frame around the control.

5. Select the View menu Properties Window option. Visual Basic will open the Properties Window listing the *CommonDialog1* control's properties.

6. Within the Properties Window, change the *CommonDialog1* control's properties to the values Table 23.7 lists.

Object	Property	Set As
CommonDialog1	Left	0
CommonDialog1	Top	0
CommonDialog1	Name	cdgTextFile

*Table 23.7 The newly named **cdgTextFile** control's properties.*

ADDING THE MENUS TO THE FRMMDIPARENT FORM

As you saw earlier in this chapter, the *prjEncryptDecrypt* project includes many menu items. To create the menu items for the *frmMDIParent* form, you will use the Visual Basic Menu Editor. To use the Menu Editor to create the project's menus, perform the following steps:

1. If Visual Basic is not displaying the *frmMDIParent* form within an object window, double-click your mouse on the *frmMDIParent* form listing within the Project Explorer. Visual Basic will open the *frmMDIParent* form.

2. Within Visual Basic, select the Tools menu Menu Editor option. Visual Basic will display the Menu Editor dialog box.

3. Within the *Caption* field, enter *&File*. (Remember, the ampersand symbol (&) alerts Visual Basic to accept the letter immediately following the ampersand as a keyboard shortcut for the item.) Visual Basic will display the caption in the Menu Viewer at the bottom of the Menu Editor as you type.

4. Press the TAB key to move the input cursor to the *Name* field. Enter the name as *mnuFile*.

5. Click your mouse on the Next button. Visual Basic will clear the *Caption* and *Name* fields, move the block cursor within the Menu Viewer down one line, and return the input cursor to the *Caption* field.

6. Click your mouse on the right arrow just above the Menu Viewer and to the left of the Next button. Visual Basic will display three dots on the current line in the Menu Viewer.

7. Within the *Caption* field, enter the next item's caption as *&Open Plain Text*. Visual Basic will display *&Open Plain Text*, preceded by three dots (which indicate the item is a submenu of the File menu), in the Menu Viewer as you type.

8. Press the TAB key to move the input cursor to the *Name* field. Enter the name as *mnuFileOpenPlain*.

9. Click your mouse on the Next button. Visual Basic will clear the *Caption* and *Name* fields, move the block cursor within the Menu Viewer down one line, and return the input cursor to the *Caption* field.

10. Within the *Caption* field, enter the next item's caption as *Open &Encrypted Text*. Visual Basic will display *Open &Encrypted Text*, preceded by three dots, in the Menu Viewer as you type.

11. Press the TAB key to move the input cursor to the *Name* field. Enter the name as *mnuFileOpenEncrypted*.

12. Click your mouse on the Next button. Visual Basic will clear the *Caption* and *Name* fields, move the block cursor within the Menu Viewer down one line, and return the input cursor to the *Caption* field.

13. Within the *Caption* field, enter the next item's caption as *&Save Plain Text*. Visual Basic will display *&Save Plain Text*, preceded by three dots (which indicate the item is a submenu of the File menu), in the Menu Viewer as you type.

14. Press the TAB key to move the input cursor to the *Name* field. Enter the name as *mnuFileSavePlain*.

15. Click your mouse on the Next button. Visual Basic will clear the *Caption* and *Name* fields, move the block cursor within the Menu Viewer down one line, and return the input cursor to the *Caption* field.

16. Within the *Caption* field, enter the next item's caption as *Sa&ve Encrypted Text*. Visual Basic will display *Sa&ve Encrypted Text*, preceded by three dots, in the Menu Viewer as you type.

17. Press the TAB key to move the input cursor to the *Name* field. Enter the name as *mnuFileSaveEncrypted*.

18. Click your mouse on the Next button. Visual Basic will clear the *Caption* and *Name* fields, move the block cursor within the Menu Viewer down one line, and return the input cursor to the *Caption* field.

19. Within the *Caption* field, enter the next item's caption as *E&xit*. Visual Basic will display *E&xit*, preceded by three dots, in the Menu Viewer as you type.

20. Press the TAB key to move the input cursor to the *Name* field. Enter the name as *mnuFileExit*.

21. Click your mouse on the Next button. Visual Basic will clear the *Caption* and *Name* fields, move the block cursor within the Menu Viewer down one line, and return the input cursor to the *Caption* field.

22. Click your mouse on the left arrow just above the Menu Viewer and to the left of the Next button. Visual Basic will remove the three dots on the current line in the Menu Viewer.

23. Within the *Caption* field, enter the next item's caption as *Encrypt-Decrypt*. Visual Basic will display *Encrypt-Decrypt* in the Menu Viewer as you type.

24. Press the TAB key to move the input cursor to the *Name* field. Enter the name as *mnuEncrypt*.

25. Click your mouse on the Next button. Visual Basic will clear the *Caption* and *Name* fields, move the block cursor within the Menu Viewer down one line, and return the input cursor to the *Caption* field.

26. Click your mouse on the right arrow just above the Menu Viewer and to the left of the Next button. Visual Basic will display three dots on the current line in the Menu Viewer.

27. Within the *Caption* field, enter the next item's caption as *&Encrypt Text*. Visual Basic will display *&Encrypt Text*, preceded by three dots, in the Menu Viewer as you type.

28. Press the TAB key to move the input cursor to the *Name* field. Enter the name as *mnuEncrypt_Encrypt*.

29. Click your mouse on the Next button. Visual Basic will clear the *Caption* and *Name* fields, move the block cursor within the Menu Viewer down one line, and return the input cursor to the *Caption* field.

30. Within the *Caption* field, enter the next item's caption as *Clear Plain Text*. Visual Basic will display *Clear Plain Text*, preceded by three dots, in the Menu Viewer as you type.

31. Press the TAB key to move the input cursor to the *Name* field. Enter the name as *mnuClearPlain*.

32. Click your mouse on the Next button. Visual Basic will clear the *Caption* and *Name* fields, move the block cursor within the Menu Viewer down one line, and return the input cursor to the *Caption* field.

33. Within the *Caption* field, enter the next item's caption as *&Decrypt Text*. Visual Basic will display *&Decrypt Text*, preceded by three dots, in the Menu Viewer as you type.

34. Press the TAB key to move the input cursor to the *Name* field. Enter the name as *mnuEncrypt_Decrypt*.

35. Click your mouse on the Next button. Visual Basic will clear the *Caption* and *Name* fields, move the block cursor within the Menu Viewer down one line, and return the input cursor to the *Caption* field.

36. Within the *Caption* field, enter the next item's caption as *Clear Encrypted Text*. Visual Basic will display *Clear Encrypted Text*, preceded by three dots, in the Menu Viewer as you type.

37. Press the TAB key to move the input cursor to the *Name* field. Enter the name as *mnuClearEncrypted*.

38. Click your mouse on the Next button. Visual Basic will clear the *Caption* and *Name* fields, move the block cursor within the Menu Viewer down one line, and return the input cursor to the *Caption* field.

39. Click your mouse on the left arrow just above the Menu Viewer and to the left of the Next button. Visual Basic will remove the three dots on the current line in the Menu Viewer.

40. Within the *Caption* field, enter the next item's caption as *&Window*. Visual Basic will display *&Window* in the Menu Viewer as you type.

41. Press the TAB key to move the input cursor to the *Name* field. Enter the menu's name as *mnuWindow*.

42. Click your mouse on the check box next to the *Windowlist* item. Visual Basic will place a check mark in the box.

43. Click your mouse on the Next button. Visual Basic will clear the *Caption* and *Name* fields, move the block cursor within the Menu Viewer down one line, and return the input cursor to the *Caption* field.

44. Click your mouse on the right arrow just above the Menu Viewer and to the left of the Next button. Visual Basic will display three dots on the current line in the Menu Viewer.

45. Within the *Caption* field, enter the next item's caption as *&Tile*. Visual Basic will display *&Tile*, preceded by three dots, in the Menu Viewer as you type.

46. Press the TAB key to move the input cursor to the *Name* field. Enter the menu's name as *mnuWindow_Tile*.

47. Click your mouse on the Next button. Visual Basic will clear the *Caption* and *Name* fields, move the block cursor within the Menu Viewer down one line, and return the input cursor to the *Caption* field.

48. Within the *Caption* field, enter the next item's caption as *&Cascade*. Visual Basic will display *&Cascade*, preceded by three dots, in the Menu Viewer as you type.

49. Press the TAB key to move the input cursor to the *Name* field. Enter the menu's name as *mnuWindow_Cascade*. When you finish creating the menu, the Menu Editor will look similar to Figure 23.16.

Figure 23.16 *The Menu Editor dialog box after you complete the menu design for the **frmMDIParent** form.*

Designing the frmPlain Form's Appearance

As you learned in this chapter's "Using the *prjEncryptDecrypt* Project" section, you will display non-encrypted text files within a control on the *frmPlain* form. The *RichTextBox* control that will display non-encrypted text files is the only control that you will place onto the *frmPlain* form. To add a *RichTextBox* control to the *frmPlain* form, perform the following steps:

1. If Visual Basic is not displaying the *frmPlain* form within an object window, double-click your mouse on the *frmPlain* form listing within the Project Explorer. Visual Basic will open the *frmPlain* form.

2. Within Visual Basic, select the View menu Toolbox option. Visual Basic will open the Toolbox.

3. Within the Toolbox, double-click your mouse on the RichTextBox icon. Visual Basic will draw a *RichTextBox* control, *RichTextBox1*, within the *frmPlain* form. Figure 23.17 shows the RichTextBox icon within the Toolbox.

Figure 23.17 *The RichTextBox icon within the Toolbox.*

4. Within the *frmPlain* form, click your mouse on the *RichTextBox1* control to highlight it. Visual Basic will draw a small frame around the control.

5. Select the View menu Properties Window option. Visual Basic will open the Properties Window listing the *RichTextBox1* control's properties.

6. Within the Properties Window, change the *RichTextBox1* control's properties to the values Table 23.8 lists.

Object	Property	Set As
RichTextBox1	*Height*	7215
RichTextBox1	*Left*	120
RichTextBox1	*Text*	[blank]

Table 23.8 *The newly named **rtbTextToEncrypt** control's properties. (continued on following page)*

Object	Property	Set As
RichTextBox1	Top	120
RichTextBox1	Width	6975
RichTextBox1	Name	rtbTextToEncrypt

Table 23.8 *The newly named* **rtbTextToEncrypt** *control's properties. (continued from previous page)*

DESIGNING THE frmENCRYPTED FORM'S APPEARANCE

As you learned earlier in this chapter, the *prjEncryptDecrypt* project will display non-encrypted files within the *frmPlain* form and will display encrypted files within the *frmEncrypted* form. The *frmEncrypted* form's appearance is virtually identical to the *frmPlain* form. Like the *frmPlain* form, the *frmEncrypted* form uses only the *RichTextBox* control (within which it displays encrypted text). To add a *RichTextBox* control to the *frmEncrypted* form, perform the following steps:

1. If Visual Basic is not displaying the *frmEncrypted* form within an object window, double-click your mouse on the *frmEncrypted* form listing within the Project Explorer. Visual Basic will open the *frmEncrypted* form.

2. Within Visual Basic, select the View menu Toolbox option. Visual Basic will open the Toolbox.

3. Within the Toolbox, double-click your mouse on the RichTextBox icon. Visual Basic will draw a *RichTextBox* control, *RichTextBox1*, within the *frmEncrypted* form.

4. Within the *frmEncrypted* form, click your mouse on the *RichTextBox1* control to highlight it. Visual Basic will draw a small frame around the control.

5. Select the View menu Properties Window option. Visual Basic will open the Properties Window listing the *RichTextBox1* control's properties.

6. Within the Properties Window, change the *RichTextBox1* control's properties to the values Table 23.9 lists.

Object	Property	Set As
RichTextBox1	Height	7935
RichTextBox1	Left	120
RichTextBox1	Text	[blank]
RichTextBox1	Top	120
RichTextBox1	Width	6375
RichTextBox1	Name	rtbEncryptedText

Table 23.9 *The newly named* **rtbEncryptedText** *control's properties.*

DESIGNING THE frmPASSWORD FORM

The last child form that you must design for the *prjEncryptDecrypt* project is the *frmPassword* form. The *frmPassword* form contains two controls, a *Label* control and a *TextBox* control. The program will use the password the *TextBox* control contains to encrypt and decrypt documents. To add a *Label* control and a *TextBox* control to the *frmPassword* form, perform the following steps:

1. If Visual Basic is not displaying the *frmPassword* form within an object window, double-click your mouse on the *frmPassword* form listing within the Project Explorer. Visual Basic will open the *frmPassword* form.

2. Within Visual Basic, select the View menu Toolbox option. Visual Basic will open the Toolbox.

3. Within the Toolbox, double-click your mouse on the Label icon. Visual Basic will draw a *Label* control, *Label1*, within the *frmPassword* form.

4. Within the Toolbox, double-click your mouse on the TextBox icon. Visual Basic will draw a *TextBox* control, *Text1*, within the *frmPassword* form.

5. Within the *frmPassword* form, click your mouse on the *Text1* control to highlight it. Visual Basic will draw a small frame around the control.

6. Select the View menu Properties Window option. Visual Basic will open the Properties Window listing the *Text1* control's properties.

7. Within the Properties Window, change the *Label1* and *Text1* controls' properties to the values Table 23.10 lists.

Object	Property	Set As
Label1	Alignment	2 - Center
Label1	BorderStyle	1 - Fixed Single
Label1	Caption	Password:
Label1	Font	MS Sans Serif, Bold, 10 Pt.
Label1	Height	375
Label1	Left	1200
Label1	Top	120
Label1	Width	2415
Label1	Name	lblPassword
Text1	Height	375
Text1	Left	480
Text1	Text	password
Text1	Top	600
Text1	Width	3975
Text1	Name	txtPassword

Table 23.10 *The newly named* **lblPassword** *and* **txtPassword** *controls' properties.*

When you finish designing the *frmPassword* form, it will look similar to Figure 23.18.

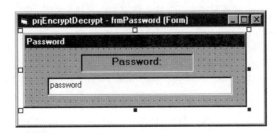

Figure 23.18 *The* **frmPassword** *form after you complete its design.*

WRITING THE PROGRAM CODE FOR THE *prjEncryptDecrypt* PROJECT

As you have seen in previous sections, the interface for the *prjEncryptDecrypt* project is relatively simple. The program uses three child forms, the *CommonDialog* control, and the *frmMDIParent* form's menu to interact with the user. The program code that implements the project is also simple, except when you work directly with the encryption and decryption processes—because encryption and decryption both require the code to perform several steps to accomplish the encryption and decryption tasks. In the following sections, you will write the program code for the *prjEncryptDecrypt* project and learn how to use several of the CryptoAPI's functions.

WRITING THE *MDL*CRYPTOAPI MODULE'S PROGRAM CODE

As with most other programs in this book that use API functions, you will declare the CryptoAPI functions within the *mdlCryptoAPI* module's General–Declarations section. You will also write program code within the module to create keys, encrypt with keys, and so on. The first section of the CryptoAPI declarations for the *prjEncryptDecrypt* project is the function declarations. The following code implements the CryptoAPI's function declarations for the *prjEncryptDecrypt* program:

```
Declare Function CryptAcquireContext Lib "advapi32.dll" Alias _
    "CryptAcquireContextA" (phProv As Long, pszContainer As String, _
    pszProvider As String, ByVal dwProvType As Long, _
    ByVal dwFlags As Long) As Long
Declare Function CryptCreateHash Lib "advapi32.dll" _
    (ByVal hProv As Long, ByVal Algid As Long, ByVal hKey As Long, _
    ByVal dwFlags As Long, phHash As Long) As Long
Declare Function CryptHashData Lib "advapi32.dll" (ByVal hHash As Long, _
    ByVal pbData As String, ByVal dwDataLen As Long, _
    ByVal dwFlags As Long) As Long
Declare Function CryptDeriveKey Lib "advapi32.dll" (ByVal hProv As Long, _
    ByVal Algid As Long, ByVal hBaseData As Long, ByVal dwFlags As Long, _
    phKey As Long) As Long
Declare Function CryptDestroyHash Lib "advapi32.dll" _
    (ByVal hHash As Long) As Long
Declare Function CryptDestroyKey Lib "advapi32.dll" _
    (ByVal hKey As Long) As Long
Declare Function CryptEncrypt Lib "advapi32.dll" (ByVal hKey As Long, _
    ByVal hHash As Long, ByVal Final As Long, ByVal dwFlags As Long, _
    ByVal pbData As String, pdwDataLen As Long, _
    ByVal dwBufLen As Long) As Long
Declare Function CryptDecrypt Lib "advapi32.dll" (ByVal hKey As Long, _
    ByVal hHash As Long, ByVal Final As Long, ByVal dwFlags As Long, _
    ByVal pbData As String, pdwDataLen As Long) As Long
Declare Function CryptReleaseContext Lib "advapi32.dll" _
    (ByVal hProv As Long, ByVal dwFlags As Long) As Long
Declare Function CryptGetProvParam Lib "advapi32.dll" _
    (ByVal hProv As Long, ByVal dwParam As Long, ByVal pbData As String, _
    pdwDataLen As Long, ByVal dwFlags As Long) As Long
Declare Function CryptGetUserKey Lib "advapi32" (ByVal hProv As Long, _
    ByVal dwKeySpec As Long, ByVal phUserKey As Long) As Long
Declare Function CryptGenKey Lib "advapi32" (ByVal hProv As Long, _
    ByVal Algid As Long, ByVal dwFlags As Long, phKey As Long) As Long
Declare Function GetLastError Lib "kernel32" () As Long
```

As you can see, the program code defines primarily CryptoAPI calls (functions that begin with *Crypt*) and the *GetLastError* function. The *GetLastError* function retrieves a numeric value from the operating system that your programs can use to respond to error messages from the operating system. In the *prjEncryptDecrypt* program, the code uses the *GetLastError* function to alert the user when a cryptographic function fails to perform the processing the program expects.

While Table 23.6 lists the basic CryptoAPI functions and explains their general use, Table 23.11 lists only the CryptoAPI functions that you will use within this program and a more specific description of each function's use.

CryptoAPI Function	Description
CryptAcquireContext	Returns a handle to the key container in a Cryptographic Service Provider (CSP). You must acquire a context (a key container) before you can use the provider to encrypt content.
CryptCreateHash	Creates a hash object. The hash object corresponds directly to the encryption key. The *prjEncryptDecrypt* program derives the hash object from the password you enter within the *frmPassword* form.
CryptDecrypt	Decrypts a buffer's contents. Within the *prjEncryptDecrypt* program, the buffer's contents correspond to the file within the *frmEncrypted* form.
CryptDeriveKey	Derives a key from a hash object. Within the *prjEncryptDecrypt* program, the correct key will correspond to the password for the file within the *frmPassword* form.
CryptDestroyHash	Destroys the hash object created with *CryptCreateHash*.
CryptDestroyKey	Destroys a key, whether imported from another provider or created within the program.
CryptEncrypt	Encrypts a buffer's contents. Within the *prjEncryptDecrypt* program, the buffer's contents correspond to the file within the *frmPlain* form.
CryptGenKey	Generates random keys to use with the Cryptographic Service Provider.
CryptGetProvParam	Retrieves data associated with a Cryptographic Service Provider. Within the *prjEncryptDecrypt* program, you will retrieve the data for the *Microsoft Base Provider 1.0* to use when it encrypts and decrypts documents.
CryptGetUserKey	Returns the handle to a signature or exchange key. Within the *prjEncryptDecrypt* program, you will check to determine whether the program has already created a key with *CryptGetUserKey*, and you will generate a new key if the user has not created the key.
CryptHashData	Hashes a data stream. After you create the hash object, you must hash data to create the correct key. Within the *prjEncryptDecrypt* program, you will hash the password you enter in the *frmPassword* form.
CryptReleaseContext	Releases the handle to the key container. Within the *prjEncryptDecrypt* program, you will release the handle when the program exits.

*Table 23.11 The **CryptoAPI** functions you will use within the **prjEncryptDecrypt** program.*

In addition to the function declarations, you will also declare constants that the cryptographic functions will use within the *mdlCryptoAPI* module's General–Declarations section. The following code implements the constant declarations for the CryptoAPI the *prjEncryptDecrypt* program uses:

```
Public Const MS_DEF_PROV = "Microsoft Base Cryptographic Provider v1.0"
Public Const PROV_RSA_FULL = 1                           'CSP Constant
Public Const ALG_CLASS_DATA_ENCRYPT = 24576              'Encrypt Algorithm
Public Const ALG_CLASS_HASH = 32768                      'Hash algorithm
Public Const ALG_TYPE_ANY = 0                            'Buffer Types
Public Const ALG_TYPE_BLOCK = 1536                       'Buffer Size
Public Const ALG_TYPE_STREAM = 2048
Public Const ALG_SID_RC2 = 2                             'RSA Type
Public Const ALG_SID_RC4 = 1                             'RSA Type
Public Const ALG_SID_MD5 = 3                             'Digital Sig. Type
Public Const CALG_MD5 = ((ALG_CLASS_HASH Or ALG_TYPE_ANY) Or ALG_SID_MD5)
Public Const CALG_RC2 = ((ALG_CLASS_DATA_ENCRYPT Or ALG_TYPE_BLOCK) _
    Or ALG_SID_RC2)
Public Const CALG_RC4 = ((ALG_CLASS_DATA_ENCRYPT Or ALG_TYPE_STREAM) _
    Or ALG_SID_RC4)
Public Const ENCRYPT_ALGORITHM = CALG_RC4                'Program algorithm
```

731

```
Public Const ENCRYPT_BLOCK_SIZE = 1
Public Const CRYPT_EXPORTABLE = 1                    ' key type
Public Const CRYPT_NEWKEYSET = 8                     ' key creation const
Public Const PP_CONTAINER = 6                        ' key container
Public Const AT_SIGNATURE = 2                        ' signature info
```

The first constant declaration specifies that the program should use the *Microsoft Base Cryptographic Provider 1.0* (which comes with *Internet Explorer 3.02* and later versions, and Windows NT 4.0) for its cryptographic provider. In addition to the *Microsoft Base Cryptographic Provider*, the CryptoAPI currently supports the Cryptographic Service Provider constants that Table 23.12 details.

Cryptographic Provider Constant	Base Cryptographic Standard
PROV_RSA_FULL	RSA
PROV_RSA_SIG	RSA
PROV_DSS	DSS
PROV_FORTEZZA	DSS
PROV_SSL	RSA
PROV_MS_EXCHANGE	RSA

Table 23.12 *The Cryptographic Service Providers that the CryptoAPI supports.*

The next constant, *PROV_RSA_FULL*, indicates the functions should use the *Rivest-Shamir-Adelman* algorithm to encrypt. The next section explains the *Rivest-Shamir-Adelman* algorithm in detail. The following 11 constants, which begin with either *ALG* or *CALG*, all specify algorithm types the functions will use when encrypting. The *ENCRYPT_ALGORITHM* constant specifies that the functions will use the *RC4* algorithm. The remaining constants specify how the encryption functions should create keys and containers.

The two public variables that the program defines maintain flag information about the state of files within the program. The following code implements the variable declarations:

```
Public EncryptedNotSaved As Boolean
Public DecryptedNotSaved As Boolean
```

The *EncryptedNotSaved* and *DecryptedNotSaved* variables hold a *True* or *False* value that the program will use to protect against the user accidentally overwriting other files.

WRITING THE CODE FOR THE INITUSER FUNCTION

As you learned in this chapter's "Using the *prjEncryptDecrypt* Project" section, the program will check each time a user runs the program to ensure that the user has a key container, a key, and other necessary encryption tools (such as a Cryptographic Service Provider compatible with the key container and key) in place to perform encryption. The program code within the *MDIForm_Load* event (which you will write later in this chapter) calls the *InitUser* function to perform such processing on its behalf. The following code implements the *InitUser* function:

```
Function InitUser() As Boolean
  Dim hProv As Long, hKey As Long, dwUserNameLen As Long
  Dim szUserName As String, sContainer As String

  InitUser = False
  dwUserNameLen = 100
  sContainer = vbNullChar
  If Not CBool(CryptAcquireContext(hProv, ByVal sContainer, _
     ByVal MS_DEF_PROV, PROV_RSA_FULL, 0)) Then
    MsgBox "Container not found...Creating default key container.", _
        vbInformation
      If Not CBool(CryptAcquireContext(hProv, ByVal sContainer, _
```

```
                ByVal MS_DEF_PROV, PROV_RSA_FULL, CRYPT_NEWKEYSET)) Then
        MsgBox "Error creating key container.", vbCritical
        Exit Function
    End If
    If Not CBool(CryptGetProvParam(ByVal hProv, PP_CONTAINER, _
        szUserName, dwUserNameLen, 0)) Then
        MsgBox "Error getting key container name.", vbInformation
        szUserName = ""
    End If
  Else
    MsgBox "Default Key Container Initialized." & Chr(10) & Chr(13) & _
        "Ready to Encrypt/Decrypt.", , "Encrypt/Decrypt"
    InitUser = True
  End If
  If Not CBool(CryptGetUserKey(ByVal hProv, AT_SIGNATURE, hKey)) Then
    If Not CBool(CryptGenKey(ByVal hProv, AT_SIGNATURE, 0, hKey)) Then
        MsgBox "Error during CryptGenKey process", vbCritical
        InitUser = False
        Exit Function
    Else
        CryptDestroyKey ByVal hKey
        InitUser = True
    End If
  Else
    MsgBox "Error during CryptGetUserKey process", vbCritical
    Exit Function
  End If
End Function
```

After the program code declares its local variables, it will call the *CryptAcquireContext* function within an *If-Then* statement. The first invocation of *CryptAcquireContext*, which passes the value 0 as the last parameter, checks to determine whether or not a default key container exists. If the default container does not exist, the program will call the *CryptAcquireContext* function again, this time with the *CRYPT_NEWKEYSET* constant as its last parameter. The second call tries to create a default container. If the second call fails, the program will display an error message and exit. If the second call succeeds (and the program creates a new default key container), the program will try to get the container name from the base services provider. If the container already exists, the program code will display a message to alert the user to the container's presence.

The *CryptGetProvParam* function tries to retrieve the key container name from the provider, which the function will place within the *szUserName* variable. If the program is unable to retrieve a key container name, it will still continue its processing because the key container's name is not particularly important, as long as the container itself exists.

The program code next calls the *CryptGetUserKey* function to retrieve a key. If *CryptGetUserKey* cannot retrieve a key, the program will display an error message to the user and exit the function. If the program successfully retrieves a key, it will use the *CryptGenKey* function to generate the key from the retrieved key information. If the *CryptGenKey* function does not generate the key, the program will display an error message and exit. If the *CryptGenKey* function generates the key, the program will delete the generated key and exit the function—because the program cannot know that the key will be the same for documents that it loads later. Rather, the program simply ensures that it can successfully generate the key.

WRITING THE CODE FOR THE CRYPTODECRYPT FUNCTION

To help you use the CryptoAPI functions within your own programs, the *prjEncryptDecrypt* program keeps most of the necessary CryptoAPI processing within the *mdlCryptoAPI* module. The *mdlCryptoAPI* module includes the *CryptoDecrypt* function, which you will use within your programs to decrypt an encrypted buffer (in the case of the *prjEncryptDecrypt* program, the file within the *frmPlain* form). The following code implements the *CryptoDecrypt* function:

```
Public Function CryptoDecrypt(InputString As String, _
    sPassword As String, ReturnString As String) As Boolean
  Dim lHExchgKey As Long, lHCryptprov As Long, lHHash As Long
  Dim lHkey As Long, lResult As Long, lPasswordCount As Long
  Dim lDecryptBufLen As Long, lDecryptPoint As Long, lPasswordPoint As Long
  Dim DecryptedText As String, sContainer As String, sProvider As String
  Dim sDecryptBuffer As String
  Dim I As Integer

  On Error GoTo DecryptError
  CryptoDecrypt = False
  sContainer = vbNullChar
  sProvider = vbNullChar
  sProvider = MS_DEF_PROV & vbNullChar
  If Not CBool(CryptAcquireContext(lHCryptprov, ByVal sContainer, _
      ByVal sProvider, PROV_RSA_FULL, 0)) Then
    MsgBox ("Error " & CStr(GetLastError) & " during CryptAcquireContext!")
    GoTo Finished
  End If
  If Not CBool(CryptCreateHash(lHCryptprov, CALG_MD5, 0, 0, lHHash)) Then
    MsgBox ("Error " & CStr(GetLastError) & " during CryptCreateHash!")
    GoTo Finished
  End If
  If Not CBool(CryptHashData(lHHash, sPassword, Len(sPassword), 0)) Then
    MsgBox ("Error " & CStr(GetLastError) & " during CryptHashData!")
    GoTo Finished
  End If
  If Not CBool(CryptDeriveKey(lHCryptprov, ENCRYPT_ALGORITHM, lHHash, _
      0, lHkey)) Then
    MsgBox ("Error " & CStr(GetLastError) & " during CryptDeriveKey!")
    GoTo Finished
  End If
  CryptDestroyHash (lHHash)
  lHHash = 0
  ReturnString = ""
  For I = 1 To Len(InputString) Step 255
    sDecryptBuffer = Mid(InputString, I, 255)
    lDecryptBufLen = Len(sDecryptBuffer)
    If Not CBool(CryptDecrypt(lHkey, 0, 1, 0, sDecryptBuffer, _
        lDecryptBufLen)) Then
      MsgBox ("Error " & CStr(GetLastError) & " during CryptDecrypt!")
      GoTo Finished
    Else
      DecryptedText = DecryptedText & sDecryptBuffer
    End If
  Next I
  ReturnString = DecryptedText
  CryptoDecrypt = True

Finished:
  If (lHkey) Then lResult = CryptDestroyKey(lHkey)
  If lHExchgKey Then CryptDestroyKey (lHExchgKey)
  If lHHash Then CryptDestroyHash (lHHash)
  If lHCryptprov Then lResult = CryptReleaseContext(lHCryptprov, 0)
  Exit Function

DecryptError:
  MsgBox ("Decrypt Error: " & Error$)
  GoTo Finished
End Function
```

In general, the program code within the function acquires a context and creates a hash to derive the decryption key from the value within the hash. Then, the program code decrypts the incoming string in blocks of 255 characters at a time. The call to *CryptAcquireContext* retrieves the default container from the system. Next, the call to *CryptCreateHash* creates a hash algorithm, which the program then uses within the *CryptHashData* function to hash the password value the *frmPassword* form contains. The following section explains hashes in detail. After the program code hashes the password, it uses *CryptDeriveKey* to create the decryption key from the newly hashed password.

The *For-Next* loop within the procedure steps through the *InputString* (which corresponds to the text within the *frmEncrypted* form's *RichTextBox* control) 255 characters at a time. Within the loop, the program calls the *CryptDecrypt* function to decrypt the buffer. The program code continues to loop until the program has decrypted every character within the *InputString* variable. After the loop exits, the function sets the *ReturnString* parameter equal to the decrypted string and sets the function to *True*. The code beyond the *Finished* label destroys the two keys and the hash, and releases the context it acquired at the function's beginning.

If the function does not successfully complete any decryption steps, the code will call the *DecryptError* subroutine, which will display a message box that alerts the user to the error, and then release the hashes, keys, and the acquired context before exiting.

735

UNDERSTANDING HASH VALUES

A *hash* function is a mathematical function that creates a unique value from the bytes that comprise a given input—a string, a file, or some other type of binary data. Moreover, a *hash* function computes the value such that you cannot derive the original information from the *hash* function. Figure 23.20 shows a model of how a program hashes a file.

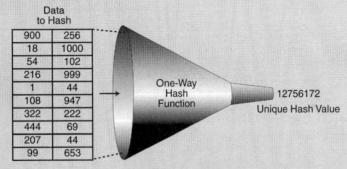

Figure 23.20 *The file passes through the **hash** function and yields a unique number.*

You can consider a hash value as a unique number that represents the incoming data stream's exact contents. Each time you pass the same stream of data (for example, a file) through the hash, the hash will always return the same hash value.

Within the *prjEncryptDecrypt* project, you will use the hash value of the password the user enters into the *frmPassword* form to derive the encryption key for the file the program is to encrypt or decrypt.

WRITING THE CODE FOR THE CRYPTOENCRYPT FUNCTION

As you learned in the previous section, the *prjEncryptDecrypt* program keeps most of the necessary CryptoAPI processing within the *mdlCryptoAPI* module to make the functions that perform the processing easier for you to reuse within your own programs. The *mdlCryptoAPI* module includes the *CryptoEncrypt* function, which you will use within your programs to encrypt a buffer—whether the buffer is a text file, a binary sequence (such as a picture), or even a short string. The following code implements the *CryptoEncrypt* function:

```
Public Function CryptoEncrypt(StringToEncrypt As String, _
    sPassword As String, ReturnString As String) As Boolean
  Dim lHHash As Long, lHkey As Long, lResult As Long
  Dim lHExchgKey As Long, lHCryptprov As Long, lCryptLength As Long
```

```
    Dim lCryptBufLen As Long
    Dim sContainer As String, InputString As String, sProvider As String
    Dim EncryptedText As String
    Dim I As Integer

    On Error GoTo EncryptError
    CryptoEncrypt = False
    sContainer = vbNullChar
    sProvider = vbNullChar
    sProvider = MS_DEF_PROV & vbNullChar
    If Not CBool(CryptAcquireContext(lHCryptprov, ByVal sContainer, _
        ByVal sProvider, PROV_RSA_FULL, 0)) Then
      MsgBox ("Error " & CStr(GetLastError) & " during CryptAcquireContext!")
      GoTo Finished
    End If
    If Not CBool(CryptCreateHash(lHCryptprov, CALG_MD5, 0, 0, lHHash)) Then
      MsgBox ("Error " & CStr(GetLastError) & " during CryptCreateHash!")
      GoTo Finished
    End If
    If Not CBool(CryptHashData(lHHash, sPassword, Len(sPassword), 0)) Then
      MsgBox ("Error " & CStr(GetLastError) & " during CryptHashData!")
      GoTo Finished
    End If
    If Not CBool(CryptDeriveKey(lHCryptprov, ENCRYPT_ALGORITHM, lHHash, _
        0, lHkey)) Then
      MsgBox ("Error " & CStr(GetLastError) & " during CryptDeriveKey!")
      GoTo Finished
    End If
    CryptDestroyHash (lHHash)
    lHHash = 0
    ReturnString = ""
    For I = 1 To Len(StringToEncrypt) Step 255
      InputString = Mid(StringToEncrypt, I, 255)
      lCryptLength = Len(InputString)
      lCryptBufLen = lCryptLength * 2
      If Not CBool(CryptEncrypt(lHkey, 0, 1, 0, InputString, lCryptLength, _
          lCryptBufLen)) Then
        MsgBox ("Error " & CStr(GetLastError) & " during CryptEncrypt!")
      Else
        EncryptedText = EncryptedText & InputString
      End If
    Next I
    ReturnString = EncryptedText
    CryptoEncrypt = True

Finished:
  If (lHkey) Then lResult = CryptDestroyKey(lHkey)
  If lHExchgKey Then CryptDestroyKey (lHExchgKey)
  If lHHash Then CryptDestroyHash (lHHash)
  If lHCryptprov Then lResult = CryptReleaseContext(lHCryptprov, 0)
  Exit Function

EncryptError:
  MsgBox "Encrypt Error: " & Error$, vbCritical
  GoTo Finished
End Function
```

In general, the program code within the function acquires a context and creates a hash to derive the decryption key from the value within the hash. Then, the program code decrypts the incoming string in blocks of 255 characters at a time. The call to *CryptAcquireContext* retrieves the default container from the system. Next, the call to *CryptCreateHash* creates a hash algorithm, which the program then uses within the *CryptHashData* function to hash the password value the *frmPassword* form contains. After the program code hashes the password, it uses *CryptDeriveKey* to create the encryption key from the newly hashed password.

The *For-Next* loop within the *CryptoEncrypt* procedure steps through the *StringToEncrypt* variable (which corresponds to the text within the *frmPlain* form's *RichTextBox* control) 255 characters at a time. Within the loop, the program calls the *CryptEncrypt* function to encrypt the buffer. The program code continues to loop until the program has encrypted every character within the *StringToEncrypt* variable. After the loop exits, the function sets the *ReturnString* parameter equal to the encrypted string and sets the function to *True*. The code beyond the *Finished* label destroys the two keys and the hash, and releases the context it acquired at the function's beginning.

If the function does not successfully complete any decryption steps, the code will call the *EncryptError* subroutine, which displays a message box that alerts the user to the error and then releases the hashes, keys, and the acquired context before exiting.

Writing the frmMDIParent Form's Program Code

As you have learned, when you work with Multiple-Document Interface (MDI) programs, the project's MDI form's *Load* event is the first program code to execute, provided your program does not use a *Sub Main* procedure. The following code implements the *MDIForm_Load* event for the *prjEncryptDecrypt* program:

```
Private Sub MDIForm_Load()
  Me.WindowState = vbMaximized
  If Not CBool(GetSetting("VBPL Encrypter", "Startup", "Initialized", _
      Default:=False)) Then
    If Not InitUser Then
      MsgBox "Unable to initialize CSP. Make sure you have one installed", _
          vbCritical
      End
    Else
      SaveSetting "VBPL Encrypter", "Startup", "Initialized", True
    End If
  End If
  frmPassword.Show
  frmPlain.Show
End Sub
```

The first *If-Then* statement uses the Visual Basic *GetSetting* function to check the *VBPL Encrypter* member's value in the registry. If the member does not exist, the program code will call the *InitUser* function—which, as you learned previously, initializes the Cryptographic Service Provider, creates a default container, and so on. If the *InitUser* function fails, the program code will display an alert message to the user and end its execution. If the *InitUser* function succeeds, the program code will set the registry value to *True* and display the *frmPassword* and *frmPlain* forms.

Writing the mnuFileOpenPlain_Click Event

As you learned in the "Using the *prjEncryptDecrypt* Project" section, users can open plain text files within the program. To open plain text files, users must select the File menu Open Plain Text option. The program will then invoke the *mnuFileOpenPlain_Click* event, which you will implement as shown here:

```
Private Sub mnuFileOpenPlain_Click()
  Dim Response As Integer

  If DecryptedNotSaved Then
    Response = MsgBox("Opening will clear unsaved plain text. " & _
        " Continue?", vbYesNo, "Open File")
    If Response = vbNo Then Exit Sub
  End If
  cdgTextFile.InitDir = CurDir$
  cdgTextFile.filename = ""
  cdgTextFile.Filter = "Text Files (*.txt)|*.txt"
```

```
    cdgTextFile.CancelError = True
    cdgTextFile.Flags = cdlOFNHideReadOnly
    On Error Resume Next
    cdgTextFile.ShowOpen
    If Err.Number <> 0 Then Exit Sub
    If Right(cdgTextFile.filename, 3) <> "txt" Then
      MsgBox "Must open text files only.", vbOKCancel
      Exit Sub
    End If
    frmPlain.rtbTextToEncrypt.LoadFile cdgTextFile.filename, rtfText
    DecryptedNotSaved = False
    frmPlain.ZOrder 0
  End Sub
```

The *If-Then* statement within the event procedure first checks the *DecryptedNotSaved* variable. If *DecryptedNotSaved* is *True*, the program code will prompt the user that continuing to open the file will result in losing all the current file's changes. If the user decides to continue, the program will display the *cdgTextFile* control's Open dialog box. After the user selects a text file, the program code loads the text file into the *frmPlain* form's *rtbTextToEncrypt* control. The program code then sets the *DecryptedNotSaved* variable to *False*, places the *frmPlain* form on top of any other forms, and exits.

WRITING THE mnuFileOpenEncrypted_Click EVENT

As you have learned, users can open previously encrypted text files within the *prjEncryptDecrypt* program. To open encrypted text files, users must select the File menu Open Encrypted Text option. The program will then invoke the *mnuFileOpenEncrypted_Click* event, which you will implement as shown here:

```
  Private Sub mnuFileOpenEncrypted_Click()
    Dim Response As Integer

    If EncryptedNotSaved Then
      Response = MsgBox("Opening will clear unsaved encrypted text. _ &
          " Continue?", vbYesNo, "Open File")
      If Response = vbNo Then Exit Sub
    End If
    cdgTextFile.InitDir = CurDir$
    cdgTextFile.filename = ""
    cdgTextFile.Filter = "Encrypted Text Files (*.etx)|*.etx"
    cdgTextFile.CancelError = True
    cdgTextFile.Flags = cdlOFNHideReadOnly
    On Error Resume Next
    cdgTextFile.ShowOpen
    If Err.Number <> 0 Then Exit Sub
    If Right(cdgTextFile.filename, 3) <> "etx" Then
      MsgBox "Must open encrypted text files only.", vbOKCancel
      Exit Sub
    End If
    frmEncrypted.rtbEncryptedText.LoadFile cdgTextFile.filename, rtfText
    frmEncrypted.rtbEncryptedText.RightMargin = _
        frmEncrypted.rtbEncryptedText.Width - 250
    EncryptedNotSaved = False
    frmEncrypted.ZOrder 0
  End Sub
```

The *If-Then* statement within the event procedure first checks the *EncryptedNotSaved* variable. If *EncryptedNotSaved* is *True*, the program code will prompt the user that continuing to open the file will result in losing all the current file's changes. If the user decides to continue, the program will display the *cdgTextFile* control's Open dialog box. After the user selects an encrypted text file, the program code loads the encrypted text file into the *frmEncrypted* form's *rtbEncryptedText* control. The program code then sets the *EncryptedNotSaved* variable to *False*, places the *frmEncrypted* form on top of any other forms, and exits.

WRITING THE MNUFILESAVEPLAINTEXT_CLICK EVENT

As you have learned, the *prjEncryptDecrypt* program will let users save plain text files that they create or edit. To save plain text files, users must select the File menu Save Plain Text option, which in turn invokes the *mnuFileSavePlainText_Click* event. The following code implements the *mnuFileSavePlainText_Click* event:

```
Private Sub mnuFileSavePlainText_Click()
  If frmPlain.rtbTextToEncrypt.Text = "" Then
    MsgBox "No text to save!", vbOKOnly
    Exit Sub
  End If
  cdgTextFile.InitDir = CurDir$
  cdgTextFile.filename = ""
  cdgTextFile.Filter = "Text Files (*.txt)|*.txt|All Files (*.*)|*.*"
  cdgTextFile.CancelError = True
  cdgTextFile.Flags = cdlOFNHideReadOnly
  On Error Resume Next
  cdgTextFile.ShowSave
  If Err.Number <> 0 Then Exit Sub
  frmPlain.rtbTextToEncrypt.SaveFile cdgTextFile.filename, rtfText
  DecryptedNotSaved = False
End Sub
```

The *mnuFileSavePlainText_Click* event first checks to ensure that there is text within the *rtbTextToEncrypt* control. If there is no text within the control, the program code will alert the user that there is no text to save, and exits the subroutine. If there is text within the control, the program code will display the *cdgTextFile* control's Save As dialog box. The program code then uses the *rtbTextToEncrypt* control's *SaveFile* method to save the file as a text file.

WRITING THE MNUFILESAVEENCRYPTED_CLICK EVENT

As the previous section details, the *prjEncryptDecrypt* program will let users save plain text files that they create or edit. The *prjEncryptDecrypt* program will also let users save encrypted files. To save encrypted text files, users must select the File menu Save Encrypted Text option, which in turn invokes the *mnuFileSaveEncryptedText_Click* event. The following code implements the *mnuFileSaveEncryptedText_Click* event:

```
Private Sub mnuFileSaveEncryptedText_Click()
  If frmEncrypted.rtbEncryptedText.Text = "" Then
    MsgBox "No text to save!", vbOKOnly
    Exit Sub
  End If
  cdgTextFile.InitDir = CurDir$
  cdgTextFile.filename = ""
  cdgTextFile.Filter = _
      "Encrypted Text Files (*.etx)|*.etx|All Files (*.*)|*.*"
  cdgTextFile.CancelError = True
  cdgTextFile.Flags = cdlOFNHideReadOnly
  On Error Resume Next
  cdgTextFile.ShowSave
  If Err.Number <> 0 Then Exit Sub
  frmEncrypted.rtbEncryptedText.SaveFile cdgTextFile.filename, rtfText
  EncryptedNotSaved = False
End Sub
```

Much as the *mnuFileSavePlainText_Click* event does, the *mnuFileSaveEncryptedText_Click* event first checks to ensure that there is text within the *rtbEncryptedText* control. If there is no text within the control, the program code will alert the user that there is no text to save, and exit the subroutine. If there is text within the control, the program code will display the *cdgTextFile* control's Save As dialog box. The program code then invokes the *rtbEncryptedText* control's *SaveFile* method to save the file as an encrypted text file.

WRITING THE MNUENCRYPT_ENCRYPT_CLICK EVENT

As you learned in this chapter's "Using the *prjEncryptDecrypt* Project" section, users can encrypt documents within the plain text form. To encrypt documents, users must select the Encrypt-Decrypt menu Encrypt option. The program, in turn, will invoke the *mnuEncrypt_Encrypt_Click* event. The following code implements the *mnuEncrypt_Encrypt_Click* event:

```
Private Sub mnuEncrypt_Encrypt_Click()
  Dim tmpString As String

  With frmPlain
    If EncryptedNotSaved Then
      Response = MsgBox("Clear unsaved encrypted text?", vbYesNo)
      If Response = vbNo Then Exit Sub
    End If
    If Len(.rtbTextToEncrypt.Text) < 1 Then
      MsgBox "No text!"
      Exit Sub
    End If
    If Len(frmPassword.txtPassword.Text) = 0 Then
      MsgBox "You must enter a password!"
      Exit Sub
    End If
    If CryptoEncrypt(.rtbTextToEncrypt.Text, frmPassword.txtPassword.Text, _
        tmpString) Then
      frmEncrypted.rtbEncryptedText.Text = ""
      frmEncrypted.rtbEncryptedText.RightMargin = _
          frmEncrypted.rtbEncryptedText.Width - 250
      frmEncrypted.rtbEncryptedText.Text = tmpString
      EncryptedNotSaved = True
      frmEncrypted.Show
      frmEncrypted.ZOrder 0
    End If
  End With
End Sub
```

The *mnuEncrypt_Encrypt_Click* event's program code first checks the *EncryptedNotSaved* variable to determine whether an unsaved encrypted text file currently exists within the *frmEncrypted* form. If an unsaved encrypted text file does exist, the program code lets the user know that continuing the current process will erase that file and lets the user choose to cancel the current process. After ensuring it can place the encrypted text within the *frmEncrypted* form, the program code checks the *rtbTextToEncrypt* control and ensures the user has loaded text to encrypt. Finally, the program code ensures that the user has entered a password.

If the program completes all three checks successfully, it calls the *CryptoEncrypt* function, which you wrote previously in this chapter. If *CryptoEncrypt* successfully encrypts the text, the program code clears the *rtbEncryptedText* control, sets the *EncryptedNotSaved* variable to *True*, and sets the *rtbEncryptedText* control's *Text* property equal to the encrypted string.

WRITING THE MNUCLEARPLAIN_CLICK EVENT

The *prjEncryptDecrypt* project lets the user clear text from the plain text window, leaving only a blank window. The ability to clear the text window is useful because it lets the user remove text without having to load a new text file over the previous text. The following code implements the *mnuClearPlain_Click* function the program will invoke when you select the Encrypt-Decrypt menu Clear Plain Text option:

```
Private Sub mnuClearPlain_Click()
  Dim Response As Integer

  If DecryptedNotSaved Then
    Response = MsgBox("Clear unsaved plain text?", vbYesNo)
```

```
      If Response = vbNo Then Exit Sub
    End If
    frmPlain.rtbTextToEncrypt.Text = ""
    DecryptedNotSaved = False
  End Sub
```

The *mnuClearPlain_Click* event first checks the *DecryptedNotSaved* variable to determine whether the *frmPlain* form contains text that the user has not saved. If the user has not saved the text, the program code will alert the user that he or she has not saved it and let the user stop the clear action. If the user has saved the text, the program code sets the text within the *rtbTextToEncrypt* control to a *NULL* string and sets the *DecryptedNotSaved* variable to *False*.

WRITING THE MNUENCRYPT_DECRYPTTEXT_CLICK EVENT

As you learned in this chapter's "Using the *prjEncryptDecrypt* Project" section, the user can decrypt documents within the Encrypted Text form. To decrypt documents, the user must select the Encrypt-Decrypt menu Decrypt option. The program, in turn, will invoke the *mnuEncrypt_DecryptText_Click* event. The following code implements the *mnuEncrypt_DecryptText_Click* event:

```
  Private Sub mnuEncrypt_DecryptText_Click()
    Dim tmpString As String

    With frmEncrypted
      If DecryptedNotSaved Then
        Response = MsgBox("Clear unsaved plain text?", vbYesNo)
        If Response = vbNo Then Exit Sub
      End If
      If Len(.rtbEncryptedText.Text) < 1 Then
        frmEncrypted.Hide
        MsgBox "No text to decrypt!"
        Exit Sub
      End If
      If Len(frmPassword.txtPassword.Text) = 0 Then
        MsgBox "You must enter a password!"
        Exit Sub
      End If
      If CryptoDecrypt(frmEncrypted.rtbEncryptedText.Text, _
          frmPassword.txtPassword.Text, tmpString) Then
        frmPlain.rtbTextToEncrypt.Text = ""
        frmPlain.rtbTextToEncrypt.Text = tmpString
        DecryptedNotSaved = True
        frmPlain.ZOrder 0
      End If
    End With
  End Sub
```

The *mnuEncrypt_DecryptText_Click* event's program code first checks the *DecryptedNotSaved* variable to determine whether an unsaved plain text file currently exists within the *frmPlain* form. If an unsaved plain text file does exist, the program code lets the user know that continuing the current process will erase that file and lets the user choose to cancel the current process. After the program code ensures that the *frmPlain* form is available for the program to write the decrypted text into, it checks the *rtbEncryptedText* control and ensures the user has loaded text to decrypt. Finally, the program code ensures that the user has entered a password.

If the program completes all three checks successfully, the program calls the *CryptoDecrypt* function, which you wrote previously in this chapter. If *CryptDecrypt* successfully decrypts the text, the program code clears the *rtbTextToEncrypt* control, sets the *DecryptedNotSaved* variable to *True*, and sets the *rtbTextToEncrypt* control's *Text* property equal to the decrypted string.

WRITING THE MNUCLEARENCRYPTED_CLICK EVENT

Much as the *prjEncryptDecrypt* program lets the user clear text from the plain text window, leaving only a blank window, the program also lets the user clear text from the encrypted text window. The ability to clear the text window is useful because it lets the user remove text without having to load a new text file over the previous text. The following code implements the *mnuClearEncrypted_Click* event the program will invoke when you select the Encrypt-Decrypt menu Clear Encrypted Text option:

```
Private Sub mnuClearEncrypted_Click()
  Dim Response As Integer

  If EncryptedNotSaved Then
    Response = MsgBox("Clear unsaved encrypted text?", vbYesNo)
    If Response = vbNo Then Exit Sub
  End If
  frmEncrypted.rtbEncryptedText.Text = ""
  EncryptedNotSaved = False
End Sub
```

The *mnuClearEncrypted_Click* event first checks the *EncryptedNotSaved* variable to determine whether the *frmEncrypted* form contains text that the user has not saved. If the user has not saved the text, the program code will alert the user that he or she has not saved it, and let the user stop the clear action. If the user has saved the text, the program code sets the text within the *rtbEncryptedText* control to a *NULL* string and sets the *EncryptedNotSaved* variable to *False*.

WRITING THE OTHER MENU EVENTS

When you designed the Window menu earlier in this chapter, you set the Window menu's *Windowlist* property to *True*—which means that the Window menu will always display a list of open child windows within the *prjEncryptDecrypt* program. You also added a Cascade and a Tile option to the menu. The Cascade and Tile options let the user organize the child windows within the *frmMDIParent* window. The Cascade option arranges child windows from the *frmMDIParent* form window's top left corner to the bottom right corner. The following code implements the *mnuWindow_Cascade_Click* event:

```
Private Sub mnuWindow_Cascade_Click()
  Me.Arrange vbCascade
End Sub
```

The *mnuWindow_Cascade_Click* event uses the *frmMDIParent* object's *Arrange* method to arrange the windows. The *vbCascade* constant is a Visual Basic-defined constant. Correspondingly, the Tile option arranges child windows, similar to floor tiles, within the parent window. The program uses the number of open child windows to determine the tiles' size. The following code implements the *mnuWindow_Tile_Click* event:

```
Private Sub mnuWindow_Tile_Click()
  Me.Arrange vbTileHorizontal
End Sub
```

The last menu event you must write for the *frmMDIParent* form is the *mnuFile_Exit_Click* event, which executes when the user selects the File menu Exit option. The following code implements the *mnuFile_Exit_Click* event:

```
Private Sub mnuFileExit_Click()
  Unload Me
End Sub
```

As you can see, the event tries to unload the parent form. As you learned in Chapter 4, "Using Multiple Forms to Load Different File Types," unloading the parent form will also unload all the child forms—and each form supports the *QueryUnload* event, within which you can place code to stop a form from unloading. The following section explains the *MDIForm_QueryUnload* event.

WRITING THE MDIFORM_QUERYUNLOAD EVENT

As you have learned in previous chapters, whenever you unload a form, your programs will invoke the *QueryUnload* event for that form. You can, in turn, place code within the event to let the user stop the unload action. The following code implements the *MDIForm_QueryUnload* event:

```
Private Sub MDIForm_QueryUnload(Cancel As Integer, UnloadMode As Integer)
   Dim Response As Integer

   If EncryptedNotSaved Then
      Response = MsgBox("Do you wish to close the program and lose " & _
           " your encrypted file?", vbYesNo)
      If Response = vbNo Then
        Cancel = True
        Exit Sub
      End If
   End If
   If DecryptedNotSaved Then
      Response = MsgBox("Do you wish to close the program and lose " & _
           " your plain text file?", vbYesNo)
      If Response = vbNo Then Cancel = True
   End If
End Sub
```

The two *If-Then* statements within the event test to determine whether or not the user has saved both the plain text and encrypted text files. If the user has not saved either file, the program code will alert the user that he or she must save a file, and let the user exit the unload process and return to the form's original state.

WRITING THE FRMENCRYPTED FORM'S PROGRAM CODE

The *frmEncrypted* form contains program code to handle three situations: when the program loads the form, when the user resizes the form, and when the user or the program unloads the form. The program code within the *Form_Load* event is relatively simple, as shown here:

```
Private Sub Form_Load()
   rtbEncryptedText.Width = Me.Width - 120
End Sub
```

The program code sets the *rtbEncryptedText* control's width to be just less than the form's width. The program code within the *Form_QueryUnload* event is correspondingly simple. The following code implements the *frmEncrypted* form's *QueryUnload* event:

```
Private Sub Form_QueryUnload(Cancel As Integer, UnloadMode As Integer)
   Dim Response As Integer

   If UnloadMode = vbFormMDIForm Then Exit Sub
   If EncryptedNotSaved Then
      Response = MsgBox("Do you wish to close the window and lose your " & _
           " encrypted file?", vbYesNo)
      If Response = vbNo Then
        Cancel = True
        Exit Sub
      End If
   End If
   EncryptedNotSaved = False
End Sub
```

The program code within the *QueryUnload* event first checks the *UnloadMode* parameter to determine if the user is actually unloading the entire program. If the user is unloading the entire program, the program code exits to let the *frmMDIParent* form's *QueryUnload* event handle the exit processing. If the user is unloading only a section of the program, the program code checks the *EncryptedNotSaved* variable. If the variable is *True*, the program code alerts the user that unloading the form will lose all the changes to their encrypted file. If the user decides to stop unloading the form, the form exits the event and returns to the *frmMDIParent* form window. If the user decides to continue, the program code sets the *EncryptedNotSaved* variable equal to *False* and lets the form unload.

WRITING THE CODE FOR THE FORM_RESIZE EVENT

The *frmEncrypted* form contains code within the *Form_Resize* event so that the user can change the *frmEncrypted* form's size. When the user changes the form's size, the form must change the *RichTextBox* control's size within the form. The following code implements the *Form_Resize* event:

```vb
Private Sub Form_Resize()
  Dim tmpHeight As Integer, tmpWidth As Integer

  If Me.WindowState = vbMinimized Then Exit Sub
  If Me.WindowState = vbMaximized Then
    tmpHeight = frmMDIParent.Height - 950
    tmpWidth = frmMDIParent.Width - 400
  Else
    If Me.Width < 1100 Then Me.Width = 1100
    If Me.Height < 1000 Then Me.Height = 1000
    If Me.Width > frmMDIParent.Width Then Me.Width = frmMDIParent.Width - 250
    If frmMDIParent.Height > 750 And frmMDIParent.Height < 7000 Then _
      If Me.Height > (frmMDIParent.Height - 750) Then Me.Width = _
          frmMDIParent.Height - 750
    tmpHeight = Me.Height - rtbEncryptedText.Top - 500
    tmpWidth = Me.Width - 250
  End If
  rtbEncryptedText.Top = 100
  rtbEncryptedText.Left = 100
  rtbEncryptedText.Width = tmpWidth
  rtbEncryptedText.Height = tmpHeight
  rtbEncryptedText.RightMargin = rtbEncryptedText.Width - 250
End Sub
```

The *Form_Resize* event will first check to see if the form is resizing because the user minimized the form. If the user minimized the form, the program code will exit the event and not perform additional processing. If the user has not minimized the *frmEncrypted* form, the user has either maximized or manually resized it. If the user has maximized the form, the program code will set the height and width for the control to the size of the *frmMDIParent* form's approximate inner window. If the user has manually resized the *frmEncrypted* form, the program code will set the height and width for the control to just less than the actual height and width to which the user resized the *frmEncrypted* form. The program code also uses a series of *If-Then* statements to ensure the user has not sized the form below a certain level (that the code specifies). Finally, the program code sets the internal *rtbEncryptedText* control's size equal to slightly less than the *frmEncrypted* form's size.

WRITING THE FRMPLAIN FORM'S PROGRAM CODE

The *frmPlain* form contains program code to handle four situations: when the program loads the form, when the user resizes the form, when the user changes the value within the *rtbTextToEncrypt* control, and when the user or the program unloads the form. The program code within the *Form_Load* event is relatively simple, as shown here:

```vb
Private Sub Form_Load()
  rtbTextToEncrypt.Width = Me.Width - 120
End Sub
```

The program code sets the *rtbTextToEncrypt* control's width to be just smaller than the form's width. The program code within the *Form_QueryUnload* event is correspondingly simple. The following code implements the *frmPlain* form's *QueryUnload* event:

```
Private Sub Form_QueryUnload(Cancel As Integer, UnloadMode As Integer)
   Dim Response As Integer

   If UnloadMode = vbFormMDIForm Then Exit Sub
   If DecryptedNotSaved Then
      Response = MsgBox("Do you wish to close the window and lose " & _
          " your plain text file?", vbYesNo)
      If Response = vbNo Then
         Cancel = True
         Exit Sub
      End If
   End If
   DecryptedNotSaved = False
End Sub
```

The program code within the *QueryUnload* event first checks the *UnloadMode* parameter to determine if the user is actually unloading the entire program. If the user is unloading the entire program, the program code exits to let the *frmMDIParent* form's *QueryUnload* event handle the exit processing. If the user is unloading only a section of the program, the program code checks the *DecryptedNotSaved* variable. If the variable is *True*, the program code alerts the user that unloading the form will lose all the changes to the encrypted file. If the user decides to stop unloading the form, the form exits the event and returns to the *frmMDIParent* form window. If the user decides to continue, the program code sets the *DecryptedNotSaved* variable equal to *False* and lets the form unload.

WRITING THE CODE FOR THE FORM_RESIZE EVENT

The *frmPlain* form contains code within the *Form_Resize* event so that the user can change the *frmPlain* form's size. When the user changes the form's size, the form must change the *RichTextBox* control's size within the form. The following code implements the *Form_Resize* event:

```
Private Sub Form_Resize()
   Dim tmpHeight As Integer, tmpWidth As Integer

   If Me.WindowState = vbMinimized Then Exit Sub
   Resizing = True
   If Me.WindowState = vbMaximized Then
      tmpHeight = frmMDIParent.Height - 950
      tmpWidth = frmMDIParent.Width - 400
   Else
      If Me.Width < 1100 Then Me.Width = 1100
      If Me.Height < 1000 Then Me.Height = 1000
      If Me.Width > frmMDIParent.Width Then Me.Width = frmMDIParent.Width - 250
      If frmMDIParent.Height > 750 And frmMDIParent.Height < 7000 Then _
         If Me.Height > (frmMDIParent.Height - 750) Then Me.Width = _
             frmMDIParent.Height - 750
      tmpHeight = Me.Height - rtbTextToEncrypt.Top - 500
      tmpWidth = Me.Width - 250
   End If
   rtbTextToEncrypt.Top = 100
   rtbTextToEncrypt.Left = 100
   rtbTextToEncrypt.Width = tmpWidth
   rtbTextToEncrypt.Height = tmpHeight
   Resizing = False
End Sub
```

The *Resize* event will first check to see if the form is resizing because the user minimized the form. If the user minimized the form, the program code will exit the event and not perform additional processing. If the user has not minimized the *frmPlain* form, the user has either maximized or manually resized it. If the user has maximized the form, the program code will set the control's height and width to the size of the *frmMDIParent* form's approximate inner window. If the user has manually resized the *frmPlain* form, the program code will set the control's height and width to just less than the actual height and width to which the user resized the *frmPlain* form. The program code also uses a series of *If-Then* statements to ensure the user has not sized the form below a certain level (that the program code specifies). Finally, the program code sets the internal *rtbTextToEncrypt* control's size equal to slightly smaller than the *frmPlain* form's size.

WRITING THE CODE FOR THE rtbTextToEncrypt_Change EVENT

The program code for the *frmPlain* form contains an additional event to those the *frmEncrypted* form contains. Because the user can change the text (either by entering new text, deleting text, or some other action) within the *rtbTextToEncrypt* control, the program code must respond to those changes. The following code implements the *rtbTextToEncrypt_Change* event:

```
Private Sub rtbTextToEncrypt_Change()
   DecryptedNotSaved = True
End Sub
```

As you can see, the event sets *DecryptedNotSaved* to *True*—which keeps the user from inadvertently overwriting edited or new text.

WRITING THE frmPassword FORM'S PROGRAM CODE

As you have learned in earlier chapters, when you load an MDI child form, the program will default to a certain size for that form. Because the *frmPassword* form should be a fixed size, you must state the form's size again within its *Load* event. The following code implements the *Form_Load* event for the *frmPassword* form:

```
Private Sub Form_Load()
   Me.Width = 4845
   Me.Height = 1590
End Sub
```

ENHANCEMENTS YOU CAN MAKE TO THE prjEncryptDecrypt PROJECT

The *prjEncryptDecrypt* project provides you with many different choices for making your own enhancements. For example, you can let the user open Rich Text files that contain bitmaps and other graphic files (rather than simply text files)—and then encrypt those graphical documents with the files.

You can also add support for digital signatures to the project. A digital signature also confirms both the file author's identity and that no one has corrupted the file during its transmission from the sender to the receiver. The CryptoAPI supports digital signatures with functions such as *CryptSignHash* and *CryptVerifySignature*.

Finally, you can take the encryption functions that you built within this project and use them within any application that requires encryption. For example, you can design a client to access a remote database through a Distributed Component Object Model (DCOM) server, such as those you created in Chapter 22, "Writing DCOM Objects for Networks." You can also build encryption support into both ends of the communication, which protects valuable information from possible theft during transmission. The applications you can build from encryption are virtually endless.

PUTTING IT ALL TOGETHER

This chapter's project, *prjEncryptDecrypt*, introduced you to the Microsoft CryptoAPI and reviewed how to manage Multiple-Document Interfaces, create menus, and handle different file types within the program's code. You also reviewed how to use the *Microsoft RichTextBox* control and the *Microsoft Common Dialog* control.

In Chapter 24, "Using the Windows Speech API to Process Voice Input," you will expand the *prjCD-ROM* project that you created in Chapter 2, "Using the Multimedia MCI Control to Create a CD-ROM Player." The new version you will build within Chapter 24 will let the user issue spoken commands to the CD-ROM player program to make it play audio CD-ROMs. Before you continue with Chapter 24, however, make sure you understand the following key concepts:

✓ You can use simple and complex encryption methods within your Visual Basic programs. Historical encryption, even the most complex, is single-key encryption—and is very simple compared to modern day encryption methods.

✓ To encrypt your programs, you can use either of the two basic types of computer-based encryption: single-key encryption and public-key encryption. Single-key encryption is generally very simple, while public-key encryption is generally very complex.

✓ Most encryption on the Internet today, as well as most other encryption that companies use within their own organizations, is either public-key encryption or some combination of public- and single-key encryption.

✓ Computers perform encryption by mathematically manipulating transmissions with large numbers, and then applying a related large number to the transmission to decrypt it. The *Rivest-Shamir-Adelman* encryption method uses large prime numbers as the basis for its processing.

✓ Microsoft's CryptoAPI offers a custom solution to enterprise cryptography issues. From within your Visual Basic programs, you can easily access the CryptoAPI and create full support for encryption and decryption within your programs.

✓ A hash is a mathematical function you can use to generate a unique number from a file or other stream of data. A one-way hash is a hash that keeps the user from being able to derive the original data stream from the unique number. When you use the *CryptGenerateHash* and *CryptHashData* functions within the CryptoAPI, you perform a one-way hashing action on the data you pass in.

✓ When you work with the CryptoAPI, you will work with Cryptographic Service Providers (CSP). In the *prjEncryptDecrypt* project, you worked with the *Microsoft Base Cryptographic Service Provider 1.0*.

✓ When your programs use the CryptoAPI, they must get a container from the CSP, generate a key from within that container, and use the key to encrypt or decrypt the information. Programs may generate a key either from a hash or from a key blob the program receives from another source.

✓ Your programs can use functions such as *CryptSignHash* and *CryptVerifySignature* to verify a digital signature, a unique value that verifies a file's validity. The *prjEncryptDecrypt* project did not use digital signatures, but you could easily add digital signature support to the project.

747

Chapter 24

Using the Windows Speech API to Process Voice Input

When personal computers first became popular in the late 1970s and early 1980s, the computer's ability to generate sound and images helped it to fascinate computer users. Although early computers had only a single speaker through which the computer could generate only the simplest sounds and music, enterprising companies soon added support for more complex sounds. Speakers, sound cards, and the computer's ability to connect to external musical devices, such as keyboards and mixing boards, quickly made the personal computer a valuable tool for musical and sound generation.

As the multimedia personal computer became more important, so did the Internet. Together with widespread access to the Internet came advances in modem and microphone technology, Internet telephony (using the Internet for phone conversations, video conferencing, and so on), and other cross-platform advancements that made recording an answering machine message, telephone conversation, and other verbal communication more common. As more people became accustomed to using a microphone and speakers with their computers, companies started to introduce *speech-recognition software*. Simply put, speech-recognition software converts the spoken word into commands the computer can understand. Most speech-recognition software centers around dictation—that is, typing dictation into a word processor, spreadsheet, or other program. However, early speech-recognition software was not very useful. For example, a sneeze, a cough, or normal background noise could easily confuse the software and result in incorrect entries into the computer. Low-quality microphones that did not clearly pick up the words the user was dictating helped contribute to the software's problems, making speech-recognition dictation a frustrating and time-consuming experience for most early users. Recent advances in software, hardware, and program logic have made speech-recognition software an important and growing market.

In this chapter's project, *prjVoiceCD*, you will use Microsoft's Speech Application Programming Interface (SAPI) to add simple commands to the *prjCD-ROM* project that you created in Chapter 2, "Using the Multimedia MCI Control to Create a CD-ROM Player." By the time you finish this chapter, you will understand the following key concepts:

♦ Microsoft's Speech Application Programming Interface (SAPI) provides an intermediate level between your applications and an underlying speech engine.

♦ The SAPI functions support two types of speech-based activity: *speech recognition* and *text-to-speech*.

♦ *Speech recognition* is the computer's ability (through software) to understand the spoken word. In this chapter's *prjVoiceCD* project, you will use speech recognition to receive command and data input from the speaker.

♦ *Text-to-speech* is the ability of a computer to convert text information into synthetic speech output. While you will not use text-to-speech in this chapter, you can easily use the provider-access concepts this chapter details to add text-to-speech support to your applications.

♦ To perform speech recognition, an application needs an audio-source object to provide speech input, an speech engine object to process the speech, and a grammar object to provide the speech engine with the lists of words or rules that determine what the engine can recognize.

♦ To use speech recognition to generate program commands, you must record into the speech-to-text conversion database the words or phrases for the engine to recognize, and you must implement a COM object within your program that receives the commands from the speech engine after the speech engine receives the commands from the audio source when the user issues the commands. You must pass the COM object's address into the speech engine when you initialize the speech engine.

♦ After your program receives the message from the engine that contains the command the engine received, you must process the command within your programs.

INSTALLING A SPEECH ENGINE

Just as with the Cryptographic Application Programming Interface (CryptoAPI) that you learned about in Chapter 23, "Using the CryptoAPI to Encrypt Documents," the Speech Application Programming Interface (SAPI) is an interface layer between your program and an underlying program, called a *Provider*, that performs services at your program's request. Like the CryptoAPI that requires Cryptographic Service Providers (CSPs), the Speech API requires Speech Service Providers (SSP), which most programmers refer to as *speech engines*. Without a Speech Service Provider, you will be unable to use the *prjVoiceCD* project.

The *prjVoiceCD* project uses Microsoft *Voice*™ and other Microsoft engines, which Microsoft distributes for free, with the Microsoft *Speech Software Development Kit* (SDK). You can download the Speech SDK from the Microsoft Web site at *http:\\research.microsoft.com\stg*, as shown in Figure 24.1.

749

*Figure 24.1 The Microsoft Speech SDK home page at **http:\\research.microsoft.com\stg**.*

Before you start to download the Speech SDK, you must make sure that you have sufficient free space on your hard drive—the compressed version of the SDK is about 12Mb. When you install the SDK, you must install it to a hard drive with 40Mb or more of free space. In addition to the engines necessary for the *prjVoiceCD* project, the Speech SDK includes the text-to-speech engine, a grammar engine, sample programs, documentation, and C/C++ header files to implement the SAPI. The Speech SDK includes over 30 example programs (most written in C/C++) that use the Speech API to perform different tasks, such as speech recognition and text-to-speech conversion.

Finally, in addition to the necessary engines, your computer must have a microphone that you can enable to receive speech commands. Most newer computers come with such a microphone. If your computer does not include a microphone, you can purchase one at a computer store for about $25.

USING THE PRJVOICECD PROJECT

Before you design the *prjVoiceCD* project, you may find it helpful to run the program. The companion CD-ROM that accompanies this book contains the *prjVoiceCD.exe* program within the *Chapter24* directory. As with every other program on the CD-ROM, you should run the Jamsa Press *setup.exe* program to install the *prjVoiceCD.exe* program to your computer's hard drive before you run it. After you install the *prjVoiceCD.exe* program to your computer's hard drive, you can run it from the Start menu. To run the program, select the Windows Start menu Run option. Windows will display the Run dialog box. Within the Run dialog box, enter *x:\vbpl\Chapter24\prjVoiceCD.exe*, where *x* corresponds to the drive letter of the hard drive on which you installed the *prjVoiceCD.exe* program, and click your mouse on OK. Windows will display the *prjVoiceCD.exe* program, as shown in Figure 24.2.

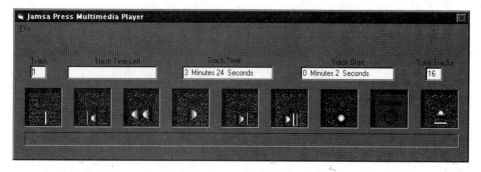

750

*Figure 24.2 The **prjVoiceCD.exe** program's window at startup.*

RUNNING PRJVOICECD FROM THE CD-ROM

Because you will use the *prjVoiceCD.exe* program to play audio CDs, it is generally a good idea to install the program to your computer's hard drive before you try to run the program. If you try to run the *prjVoiceCD.exe* program from this book's companion CD-ROM, you may encounter errors during the program's processing after you remove the companion CD-ROM from the drive and replace it with the audio CD that you want to play.

To learn more about the Jamsa Press *setup.exe* program, see the "What's on the *Visual Basic Programmer's Library* Companion CD-ROM" section at the back of this book.

Before you use the *prjVoiceCD.exe* program, take a moment to familiarize yourself with the controls on the program's display. As you have learned, the *prjVoiceCD* project will let you speak into your computer's microphone to play audio CDs from your computer's CD-ROM drive. As you learned in Chapter 2, when the program starts, you will see a medium-sized window with nine graphical buttons across the form and several text boxes above the buttons. You will use the graphical buttons to navigate and play an audio CD. From left to right, the buttons are First Track, Skip Backward, Rewind, Play, Skip Forward, Last Track, Stop/Pause, Repeat, and Eject. Labels on the text boxes above the buttons indicate that they represent the Track, Track Time Left, Track Time, Track Start, and Total Tracks. To play an audio CD that is currently in the CD-ROM drive, you can click your mouse on the Play button. Before you can issue voice commands to the program, however, you must turn on the Microsoft *Voice* engine. To turn on the Microsoft *Voice* engine, perform the following steps:

1. Select the Start menu Programs option. Windows will display the Programs menu.
2. Within the Programs menu, select the Microsoft Voice option. Windows will run Microsoft *Voice* and display the Microsoft Voice icon in the task bar. Figure 24.3 shows the Microsoft Voice icon in the task bar.

_____ *Microsoft Voice Icon*

Figure 24.3 The Microsoft Voice icon in the task bar.

Note: *If you plan to use the Microsoft **Voice** engine regularly, you can add the program to your Windows Startup program group. To add the program to your Windows Startup program group, right click your mouse on the Task bar and select the Properties option from the pop-up menu. Windows will display the Taskbar Properties dialog box. Within the Taskbar Properties dialog box, select the Add button to add the program to the Windows Startup program group.*

To use voice commands with the *prjVoiceCD.exe* program, insert a CD-ROM into the CD-ROM drive and perform the following steps:

1. Click your mouse on the Microsoft Voice icon. The Microsoft *Voice* program will display the "Microsoft Voice is Now Listening" message.

2. Into your computer's microphone, say the words "Play Compact Disk," slowly and clearly. Microsoft *Voice* will display the "Message Received" message, and the *prjVoiceCD* program will begin to play the CD-ROM in the CD-ROM drive.

3. After the CD-ROM begins playing, you can pause the CD-ROM playback. To pause the CD-ROM's playback, click your mouse on the Microsoft Voice icon. The Microsoft *Voice* program will display the "Microsoft Voice is Now Listening" message.

4. Into your computer's microphone, say the words "Pause Compact Disk," slowly and clearly. Microsoft *Voice* will display the "Message Received" message, and the *prjVoiceCD* program will pause the CD-ROM in the CD-ROM drive's playback.

5. To stop the CD-ROM's playback entirely, you can send a stop command to the program. To stop the CD-ROM's playback, say the words "Stop Compact Disk," slowly and clearly into your computer's microphone. Microsoft *Voice* will display the "Message Received" message, and the *prjVoiceCD* program will stop the CD-ROM in the CD-ROM drive's playback.

6. You can also use voice commands to move to the next song on the CD-ROM. To move to the next song, say the words "Move to Next Track," slowly and clearly into your computer's microphone. Microsoft *Voice* will display the "Message Received" message, and the *prjVoiceCD* program will move to the next track on the CD-ROM.

CREATING THE PROJECT'S FORM, MODULES, AND CLASS MODULE

Now that you have a better idea how to use the finished *prjVoiceCD* project, you can begin to design it. First, you will create an empty form that will contain all the controls the "Using the *prjVoiceCD* Project" section introduced. To begin the *prjVoiceCD* project and create a blank form, perform the following steps:

1. Within Visual Basic, select the File menu New Project option. Visual Basic will open the New Project dialog box.

2. Within the New Project dialog box, click your mouse on the Standard EXE icon. Next, click your mouse on the OK button. Visual Basic will close the dialog box and open the *Form1* form window.

3. Select the View menu Properties Window option. Visual Basic will open the Properties Window listing the *Form1* properties.

4. Within the Properties Window, change the *Form1* properties to the values Table 24.1 lists.

Object	Property	Set As
Form1	*Caption*	*Jamsa Press Multimedia Player*
Form1	*Height*	3555
Form1	*Left*	0
Form1	*StartUpPosition*	2 - *Center Screen*
Form1	*Top*	0
Form1	*Width*	11055
Form1	*Name*	*frmMMedia*

*Table 24.1 The newly named **frmMMedia** form's properties.*

5. Within Visual Basic, select the Project menu Add Class Module option. Visual Basic will display the Add Class Module dialog box.

6. Within the Add Class Module dialog box, double-click your mouse on the Class Module icon. Visual Basic will close the dialog box and add a new class module, *Class1*, to the *Project1* project.

7. Select the View menu Properties Window option. Visual Basic will open the Properties Window listing the *Class1* class module's properties.

8. Within the Properties Window, change the *Class1* class module's name to *clsSAPISink*.

9. Within Visual Basic, select the Project menu Add Module option. Visual Basic will add a new module, *Module1*, to the *Project1* project.

10. Select the View menu Properties Window option. Visual Basic will open the Properties Window listing the *Module1* module's properties.

11. Within the Properties Window, change the *Module1* module's name to *mdlSAPIDeclares*.

12. Within Visual Basic, select the Project menu Add Module option. Visual Basic will add a new module, *Module1*, to the *Project1* project.

13. Select the View menu Properties Window option. Visual Basic will open the Properties Window listing the *Module1* module's properties.

14. Within the Properties Window, change the *Module1* module's name to *mdlSpeech*.

15. Select the File menu Save Project As option. Visual Basic will display the Save File As dialog box and fill the *File name* field with *clsSAPISink*.

16. Within the Save File As dialog box, click your mouse on the Save button. Visual Basic will save the *clsSAPISink* class module and fill the *File name* field with *mdlSAPIDeclares*.

17. Within the Save File As dialog box, click your mouse on the Save button. Visual Basic will save the *mdlSAPIDeclares* module and fill the *File name* field with *mdlSpeech*.

18. Within the Save File As dialog box, click your mouse on the Save button. Visual Basic will save the *mdlSpeech* module and fill the *File name* field with the *Project1* project name.

19. Within the *File name* field, replace the *Project1* project name with the new *prjVoiceCD* project name. Next, click your mouse on the Save button. Visual Basic will save the *prjVoiceCD* project and close the Save Project As dialog box.

ADDING THE MICROSOFT PROGRESSBAR CONTROL TO THE PROJECT

As you can see from the *prjVoiceCD* project's interface in Figure 24.2, the program displays a progress bar across the bottom that indicates how far along the program is in the current track. The *Microsoft ProgressBar* control is one of the *Microsoft Windows Common Controls* that comes with Visual Basic. Before you can use the *Microsoft ProgressBar* control in the *prjVoiceCD* project, you must add it to the project as a component. After you add the *Microsoft ProgressBar* control to the *prjVoiceCD* project, Visual Basic will display the control's icon in the Toolbox. As you know, the Toolbox displays Visual Basic control icons. If you double-click your mouse on any icon in the Toolbox, Visual Basic will draw the control that the icon corresponds to within the active form. To add the *Microsoft ProgressBar* control to the *prjVoiceCD* project, perform the following steps:

1. Select the Project menu Components option. Visual Basic will open the Components dialog box.

2. Within the Components dialog box, select the *Microsoft Windows Common Controls 5.0* listing. Next, click your mouse on the box to the left of the listing. Visual Basic will display a check mark in the box.

3. Within the Components dialog box, click your mouse on OK. Visual Basic will add the *Microsoft Windows Common Controls* control components to the *prjVoiceCD* project.

ADDING THE MICROSOFT MULTIMEDIA MCI CONTROL TO THE PROJECT

As you have learned, the *prjVoiceCD* project uses the *Multimedia MCI* control to play back audio CDs. Like the *Microsoft Windows Common Controls* that you added to the project in the previous section, the *Multimedia MCI* control comes with Visual Basic. Before you can use the *Multimedia MCI* control in the *prjVoiceCD* project, you must add it to the project as a component. After you add the *Multimedia MCI* control to the *prjVoiceCD* project, Visual Basic will display the control's icon in the Toolbox. As you know, the Toolbox displays Visual Basic control icons. If you double-click your mouse on any icon in the Toolbox, Visual Basic will draw the control that the icon corresponds to within the active form. To add the *Microsoft Multimedia MCI* control to the *prjVoiceCD* project, perform the following steps:

1. Select the Project menu Components option. Visual Basic will open the Components dialog box.

2. Within the Components dialog box, select the *Microsoft Multimedia MCI Control 5.0* listing. Next, click your mouse on the box to the left of the listing. Visual Basic will display a check mark in the box.

3. Within the Components dialog box, click your mouse on OK. Visual Basic will add the *Microsoft Multimedia MCI* control component to the *prjVoiceCD* project.

ADDING CONTROLS TO THE FORM

In the *prjVoiceCD* project, you will use the *Multimedia MCI* control, the *ProgressBar* control you added to the project in the previous sections, five *TextBox* controls, five *Label* controls, nine *PictureBox* controls, and a *Timer* control. To begin, you will add each control to the *frmMMedia* form and assign properties to position each control on the form and provide a unique name for each control.

ADDING THE TIMER CONTROL TO THE FRMMMEDIA FORM

As you have learned, the *prjVoiceCD* project updates the display at regular intervals while you play an audio CD. To start the code that performs the update processing at regular intervals, you will use a *Timer* control. To add the *Timer* control to the *frmMMedia* form, perform the following steps:

1. If Visual Basic is not displaying the *frmMMedia* form within an object window, double-click your mouse on the *frmMMedia* form listing within the Project Explorer. Visual Basic will open the *frmMMedia* form.

2. Within Visual Basic, select the View menu Toolbox option. Visual Basic will open the Toolbox.

3. Within the Toolbox, double-click your mouse on the Timer icon. Visual Basic will draw a *Timer* control, *Timer1*, within the *frmMMedia* form.

4. Within the *frmMMedia* form, click your mouse on the *Timer1* control to highlight it. Visual Basic will draw a small frame around the control.

5. Select the View menu Properties Window option. Visual Basic will open the Properties Window listing the *Timer1* properties.

6. Within the Properties Window, change the *Timer1* properties to the values Table 24.2 lists.

Object	Property	Set As
Timer1	*Interval*	0
Timer1	*Left*	0
Timer1	*Top*	0

*Table 24.2 The **Timer1** control's properties.*

ADDING THE PROGRESSBAR CONTROL TO THE FRMMMEDIA FORM

As the previous section details, the *Timer1* control starts the interval processing that the program will use to update the display. The *prjVoiceCD* project uses the *ProgressBar* control to graphically display the project's progress in the current track's play. To add the *ProgressBar* control to the *prjVoiceCD* project, perform the following steps:

1. If Visual Basic is not displaying the *frmMMedia* form within an object window, double-click your mouse on the *frmMMedia* form listing within the Project Explorer. Visual Basic will open the *frmMMedia* form.

2. Within Visual Basic, select the View menu Toolbox option. Visual Basic will open the Toolbox.

3. Within the Toolbox, double-click your mouse on the ProgressBar icon. Visual Basic will draw a *ProgressBar* control, *ProgressBar1*, within the *frmMMedia* form.

4. Within the *frmMMedia* form, click your mouse on the *ProgressBar1* control to highlight it. Visual Basic will draw a small frame around the control.

5. Select the View menu Properties Window option. Visual Basic will open the Properties Window listing the *ProgressBar1* properties.

6. Within the Properties Window, change the *ProgressBar1* properties to the values Table 24.3 lists.

Object	Property	Set As
ProgressBar1	*Height*	315
ProgressBar1	*Left*	240
ProgressBar1	*Max*	100
ProgressBar1	*Min*	0
ProgressBar1	*Top*	2280
ProgressBar1	*Width*	10515

*Table 24.3 The **ProgressBar1** control's properties.*

ADDING THE MULTIMEDIA MCI CONTROL TO THE FRMMMEDIA FORM

As you learned at the beginning of this chapter, the *prjVoiceCD* project uses the *Multimedia MCI* control to play back audio CDs. Before the program can use the *Multimedia MCI* control, however, you must place the control onto to the project's form. To add the *Multimedia MCI* control to the *prjVoiceCD* project, perform the following steps:

1. If Visual Basic is not displaying the *frmMMedia* form within an object window, double-click your mouse on the *frmMMedia* form listing within the Project Explorer. Visual Basic will open the *frmMMedia* form.

2. Within Visual Basic, select the View menu Toolbox option. Visual Basic will open the Toolbox.

3. Within the Toolbox, double-click your mouse on the ProgressBar icon. Visual Basic will draw a *Multimedia MCI* control, *MMControl1*, within the *frmMMedia* form.

4. Within the *frmMMedia* form, click your mouse on the *MMControl1* control to highlight it. Visual Basic will draw a small frame around the control.

5. Select the View menu Properties Window option. Visual Basic will open the Properties Window listing the *MMControl1* properties.

6. Within the Properties Window, change the *MMControl1* properties to the values Table 24.4 lists.

Object	Property	Set As
MMControl1	*AutoEnable*	*True*
MMControl1	*Height*	540
MMControl1	*Left*	6525

*Table 24.4 The **MMControl1** control's properties. (continued on following page)*

Object	Property	Set As
MMControl1	Shareable	False
MMControl1	Top	0
MMControl1	UpdateInterval	1000
MMControl1	Width	10515

*Table 24.4 The **MMControl1** control's properties. (continued from previous page)*

ADDING PICTUREBOX CONTROLS TO THE FRMMMEDIA FORM

When you used the *prjVoiceCD* project in this chapter's "Using the *prjVoiceCD* Project" section, you used the graphical buttons on the program to manipulate the audio CD. However, for the *prjVoiceCD* project, those buttons are actually *PictureBox* controls designed to respond when a user clicks the mouse. To add the nine *PictureBox* controls that let the user control the CD's playback, perform the following steps:

1. If Visual Basic is not displaying the *frmMMedia* form within an object window, double-click your mouse on the *frmMMedia* form listing within the Project Explorer. Visual Basic will open the *frmMMedia* form.

2. Within Visual Basic, select the View menu Toolbox option. Visual Basic will open the Toolbox.

3. Within the Toolbox, double-click your mouse on the PictureBox icon. Visual Basic will draw a *PictureBox* control, *Picture1*, within the *frmMMedia* form.

4. Within the *frmMMedia* form, click your mouse on the *Picture1* control to highlight it. Visual Basic will draw a small frame around the control.

5. Select the View menu Properties Window option. Visual Basic will open the Properties Window listing the *Picture1* control's properties.

6. Within the Properties Window, click your mouse on the *Name* property and change the value from *PictureBox* to *ControlPanel*.

7. Select the Edit menu Copy option. Visual Basic will store a copy of the *ControlPanel* control in the Clipboard.

8. Select the Edit menu Paste option. Visual Basic will open a dialog box that asks, "You already have a control named '*ControlPanel*.' Do you want to create a control array?" Click your mouse on the Yes button. Visual Basic will draw a copy of the *ControlPanel* control within the *frmMMedia* form.

9. Repeat Step 8 seven more times until you have added a total of nine *PictureBox* controls to the *ControlPanel* control array.

10. Within the *frmMMedia* form, click your mouse on a *ControlPanel* control to highlight it. Visual Basic will draw a small frame around the control.

11. Within the Properties Window, change the highlighted *ControlPanel* control's properties to the values Table 24.5 lists.

12. Repeat Steps 10 and 11 until you have changed each highlighted *ControlPanel* control's properties to the values Table 24.5 lists.

Object	Property	Set As
ControlPanel(0)	Height	915
ControlPanel(0)	Left	240
ControlPanel(0)	ToolTipText	First Track
ControlPanel(0)	Top	1245
ControlPanel(0)	Width	915

*Table 24.5 The **frmMMedia** form's **ControlPanel** control array's properties. (continued on following page)*

Object	Property	Set As
ControlPanel(1)	Height	915
ControlPanel(1)	Left	1440
ControlPanel(1)	ToolTipText	Previous Track
ControlPanel(1)	Top	1245
ControlPanel(1)	Width	915
ControlPanel(2)	Height	915
ControlPanel(2)	Left	2640
ControlPanel(2)	ToolTipText	Beginning of Current Track
ControlPanel(2)	Top	1245
ControlPanel(2)	Width	915
ControlPanel(3)	Height	915
ControlPanel(3)	Left	3840
ControlPanel(3)	ToolTipText	Play
ControlPanel(3)	Top	1245
ControlPanel(3)	Width	915
ControlPanel(4)	Height	915
ControlPanel(4)	Left	5040
ControlPanel(4)	ToolTipText	Next Track
ControlPanel(4)	Top	1245
ControlPanel(4)	Width	915
ControlPanel(5)	Height	915
ControlPanel(5)	Left	6240
ControlPanel(5)	ToolTipText	Last Track
ControlPanel(5)	Top	1245
ControlPanel(5)	Width	915
ControlPanel(6)	Height	915
ControlPanel(6)	Left	7440
ControlPanel(6)	ToolTipText	Stop or Pause
ControlPanel(6)	Top	1245
ControlPanel(6)	Width	915
ControlPanel(7)	Height	915
ControlPanel(7)	Left	8640
ControlPanel(7)	ToolTipText	Repeat
ControlPanel(7)	Top	1245
ControlPanel(7)	Width	915
ControlPanel(8)	Height	915
ControlPanel(8)	Left	9840
ControlPanel(8)	ToolTipText	Eject
ControlPanel(8)	Top	1245
ControlPanel(8)	Width	915

756

Table 24.5 The **frmMMedia** form's **ControlPanel** control array's properties. (continued from previous page)

ADDING TEXTBOX CONTROLS TO THE FRMMMEDIA FORM

Now that you have the *ProgressBar* control to display the program's progress and the *PictureBox* array that you will use to let the user control the player, you will add *TextBox* controls to the *frmMMedia* form. The *TextBox* controls will display information about the CD the player is playing. To add *TextBox* controls to the *frmClient* form, perform the following steps:

1. If Visual Basic is not displaying the *frmMMedia* form within an object window, double-click your mouse on the *frmMMedia* form listing within the Project Explorer. Visual Basic will open the *frmMMedia* form.

2. Within Visual Basic, select the View menu Toolbox option. Visual Basic will open the Toolbox.

3. Within the Toolbox, double-click your mouse on the TextBox icon. Visual Basic will draw a *TextBox* control, *Text1*, within the *frmMMedia* form.

4. Repeat Step 3 four more times. Visual Basic will draw four more *TextBox* controls within the *frmMMedia* form.

5. Within the *frmMMedia* form window, click your mouse on a *TextBox* control to highlight it. Visual Basic will draw a small frame around the control.

6. Select the View menu Properties Window option. Visual Basic will open the Properties Window listing the highlighted *TextBox* control's properties.

7. Within the Properties Window, change the highlighted *TextBox* control's properties to the values Table 24.6 lists.

8. Repeat Steps 5, 6, and 7 until you have changed each *TextBox* control's properties to the values Table 24.6 lists.

Object	Property	Set As
Text1	*Height*	315
Text1	*Index*	0
Text1	*Left*	375
Text1	*Text*	[blank]
Text1	*Top*	720
Text1	*Width*	390
Text1	*Name*	*Text1*
Text2	*Height*	315
Text2	*Index*	1
Text2	*Left*	1275
Text2	*Text*	[blank]
Text2	*Top*	720
Text2	*Width*	2205
Text2	*Name*	*Text1*
Text3	*Height*	315
Text3	*Index*	2
Text3	*Left*	4080
Text3	*Text*	[blank]
Text3	*Top*	720
Text3	*Width*	2205
Text3	*Name*	*Text1*
Text4	*Height*	315
Text4	*Index*	3
Text4	*Left*	6960
Text4	*Text*	[blank]

*Table 24.6 The **TextBox** controls' properties. (continued on following page)*

Object	Property	Set As
Text4	Top	720
Text4	Width	2250
Text4	Name	Text1
Text5	Height	315
Text5	Index	4
Text5	Left	9960
Text5	Text	[blank]
Text5	Top	720
Text5	Width	390
Text5	Name	Text1

758

*Table 24.6 The **TextBox** controls' properties. (continued from previous page)*

After you finish changing each *TextBox* control's properties, you can add the labels for each text box to the *frmMMedia* form, which you will do in the next section.

ADDING THE LABEL CONTROLS TO THE FORM

As you have learned, within the *prjVoiceCD* project, you will use *Label* controls to place captions on the *TextBox* controls that display information to the user about the program's audio CD playback. Now that you have added to the form the *TextBox* controls that will display the actual information, you should add the *Label* controls to the form. To add the *Label* controls to the *frmMMedia* form, perform the following steps:

1. If Visual Basic is not displaying the *frmMMedia* form within an object window, double-click your mouse on the *frmMMedia* form listing within the Project Explorer. Visual Basic will open the *frmMMedia* form.

2. Within Visual Basic, select the View menu Toolbox option. Visual Basic will open the Toolbox.

3. Within the Toolbox, double-click your mouse on the Label icon. Visual Basic will draw a *Label* control, *Label1*, within the *frmMMedia* form.

4. Repeat Step 3 four more times to add the *Label2, Label3, Label4,* and *Label5* controls to the *frmMMedia* form.

5. Within the *frmMMedia* form, click your mouse on the *Label1* control to highlight it. Visual Basic will draw a small frame around the control.

6. Select the View menu Properties Window option. Visual Basic will open the Properties Window listing the *Label1* properties.

7. Within the Properties Window, change the *Label1* properties to the values Table 24.7 lists.

8. Repeat Steps 5, 6, and 7 to change the properties for the other *Label* controls to the values Table 24.7 lists.

Object	Property	Set As
Label1	Caption	Track
Label1	ForeColor	&H00FF0000& (Royal Blue)
Label1	Height	195
Label1	Left	375
Label1	Top	510
Label1	Width	420
Label1	Name	lblTrack
Label2	Caption	Track Time Left

*Table 24.7 The newly named **Label** controls' properties. (continued on following page)*

Object	Property	Set As
Label2	ForeColor	&H00FF0000& (Royal Blue)
Label2	Height	195
Label2	Left	1920
Label2	Top	510
Label2	Width	1125
Label2	Name	lblTimeLeft
Label3	Caption	Track Time
Label3	ForeColor	&H00FF0000& (Royal Blue)
Label3	Height	195
Label3	Left	4680
Label3	Top	510
Label3	Width	810
Label3	Name	lblTrackTime
Label4	Caption	Track Start
Label4	ForeColor	&H00FF0000& (Royal Blue)
Label4	Height	195
Label4	Left	7680
Label4	Top	510
Label4	Width	795
Label4	Name	lblTrackStart
Label5	Caption	Total Tracks
Label5	ForeColor	&H00FF0000& (Royal Blue)
Label5	Height	195
Label5	Left	9720
Label5	Top	510
Label5	Width	900
Label5	Name	lblTotalTracks

Table 24.7 *The newly named* Label *controls' properties. (continued from previous page)*

BETTER UNDERSTANDING THE SPEECH API

Speech recognition is a computer's ability to understand the spoken word for the purpose of receiving command and data input from the speaker. *Text-to-speech* is a computer's ability to convert text information into synthetic speech output. Speech recognition and text-to-speech use *engines*, which are the programs that do the actual work of recognizing speech or playing text. Most speech-recognition engines convert incoming audio data to engine-specific phonemes, which the speech engine then translates into text that an application can use. (A *phoneme* is the smallest structural unit of sound that a speech engine can use to distinguish one utterance from another in a spoken language, such as the sound "kuh" for *c* in *computer*.) A text-to-speech engine performs the same process in reverse. Vendors that specialize in speech software supply engines that you may bundle with new audio-enabled computers and sound cards (which you must purchase separately or license from the vendor).

The speech-recognition engine transcribes audio data it receives from an *audio source*, such as a microphone or a telephone line. The text-to-speech engine converts text to audio data, which audio data that engine then sends to an *audio destination*, such as a speaker, a headphone, or a telephone line. Under some circumstances, an engine may be able to transcribe audio data to or from a file.

An engine typically provides more than one mode for recognizing speech or playing text. For example, a speech-recognition engine will have a mode for each language or dialect it can recognize. Likewise, a text-to-speech engine will have a mode for each voice that plays text in a different speaking style or personality. You may optimize other modes for a particular audio sampling rate, such as 8 kilohertz (KHz) for use over a telephone line.

Speech recognition can be as simple as a predefined set of voice commands that an application can recognize. More complex speech recognition involves the use of a grammar engine, which defines a set of words and phrases that an application can recognize. A grammar engine may use rules to predict the most likely words to follow the word the user has just spoken, or it may define a context that identifies the subject of dictation and the expected language style. Both speech-recognition and text-to-speech engines may make use of a *pronunciation lexicon*, which is a database of correct pronunciations for words and phrases the application will recognize or play.

UNDERSTANDING THE SPEECH API'S COMPONENT APIS

As you have learned, you can use the Speech API to implement several different types of speech support within your applications. Microsoft divides the Speech API into two levels that you can use to implement speech in applications. The first level consists of voice commands and voice text and provides simple, somewhat limited support of speech. The second level consists of speech recognition and text-to-speech functions and lets an application fully access an engine's capabilities. Figure 24.4 shows the relationships between the high-level and low-level parts of the Speech API, the applications that use them, and the engines that they use.

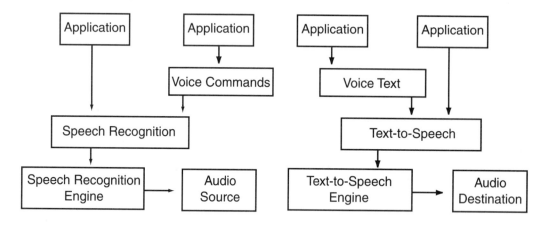

Figure 24.4 *The relationships between the Speech API, applications, and engines.*

UNDERSTANDING THE VOICE-COMMAND API

The voice-command API provides high-level speech recognition—often called *command and control*—for applications. Voice commands mimic Windows menus, which gives the user a menu of commands to speak, such as "Tell me the time" or "Open the file." A voice command can include a *list*, which contains information that changes dynamically at run time. For example, in the command "Send mail to <name>," the user could speak any word or phrase in the list called <name> as part of the command. Voice commands can also include *wildcards*, which let the user speak any words between certain key words in a phrase. For example, if an application defines a voice command of, "{wildcard} mail {wildcard} <name>", the user could say, "Send mail to Happy," "I want to mail Happy," or even "Mail, yes, I want it to go to Happy." The *prjVoiceCD* project uses the voice-command API to process incoming commands to play the CD-ROM.

An application that uses voice commands can share a speech-recognition engine and audio source—called a *voice-command site*—with other applications on the user's system. Voice commands also support OLE Automation, which you can use to implement voice-command recognition in applications you write in Visual Basic.

UNDERSTANDING THE VOICE-TEXT API

The voice-text API provides high-level text-to-speech capabilities. It is a simple way to play words and phrases over a computer speaker or a telephone line. As with voice commands, voice text can share a text-to-speech engine and an audio destination—called a *voice-text site*—with other applications on the user's system. Voice text also supports OLE Automation.

Understanding the Speech-Recognition API

The speech-recognition API provides detailed control of a speech-recognition engine for applications that require more sophisticated command and control or applications that take dictation. Depending on the engine's capabilities, an application may be able to get detailed information about a *recognition result*—that is, the word or phrase that the engine recognized—and use it to give feedback to the user or to alter the result. An application that uses speech recognition can share a speech-recognition engine and audio source with other applications on the user's computer, including applications that use voice commands.

Understanding the Text-to-Speech API

The text-to-speech API provides detailed control of a text-to-speech engine. An application can adjust the playback of spoken text by inserting text-to-speech control tags, which alter talking speed, style, pitch, and other voice qualities. An application can also get detailed information about the timing of text as the engine speaks the text, which lets the application synchronize graphic animation with the voice.

761

Understanding Speech Objects

The Speech API's definitions follow the OLE Component Object Model (COM) architecture. The speech objects that comprise voice commands, voice text, speech recognition, and text-to-speech are OLE component objects that you can either access through COM objects you create in C/C++ or through Visual Basic's OLE Automation.

The Speech API implements speech objects as C++ classes. An object essentially consists of code that has a set of member functions communicating with it (the interfaces of the object), data the calling program associates with an instance at run time, and the ability to support multiple instances of the object running at the same time. Speech objects use the OLE apartment threading model, which you learned about in Chapter 22, "Writing DCOM Objects for Networks." The OLE apartment threading model lets programs create processes containing more than one thread of execution. The apartment threading rules mean that your application must create all *notification sinks* it uses with the Speech API on the same thread that creates the audio objects and engines. A notification sink is a Visual Basic class that you will pass to the speech object that the object will call back with information about the speech object's processing.

More On the Voice Command API

As you have learned, the Voice Command API (also known as "Command and Control" speech recognition) lets the user speak a word, phrase, or sentence from a list of phrases that the computer is expecting to hear. For example, a user might be able to speak the commands, "Send mail to Happy," "Send a fax to Happy," or "Turn on the television." The number of different commands a user might speak at any time can easily number in the hundreds. With all the possibilities, the user is able to speak thousands of different commands. With command and control technology, users can talk in natural speech to their computers and do not need to train the computers to their voices, so the technology is easy to use.

Understanding Why You Might Use the Voice Command API

In general, you should use the Voice Command API within your programs only when one of the following conditions is true:

1.   Using the Voice Command API makes the program easier to use.
2.   Using the Voice Command API makes features in the program easier to access.
3.   Using the Voice Command API makes the program more fun or realistic.

If you include speech recognition in your program only because it is an attractive feature for many users, the speech recognition will likely work well for demonstrations but real users will not use the speech recognition when they use the program.

UNDERSTANDING THE VOICE-COMMAND OBJECT

The *voice-command object* manages all voice-aware programs' use of voice commands in the system. The object manages the interaction between programs and the speech-recognition engine. It also manages aspects of the interaction between the engine and the audio-input device. Before a program can use voice commands, it must create an instance of the voice-command object and register itself with the object. Your program must create a voice-command object for each audio source that the program will use. For example, if the program must recognize commands from a telephone line as well as from the computer microphone, it should create two voice-command objects.

Before a program can perform other voice-command tasks, it must register itself with the engine. By registering, the program tells the engine which site to use as the source of voice commands and passes to the voice-command object a pointer to the program's voice-command notification interface. The object calls the notification interface to notify the program about incoming voice commands. Within the *prjVoiceCD* project, the notification interface, *clsSAPISink*, captures only two events: commands that relate to the program and commands that do not. Your programs might also track when the user starts and stops speaking, whether the user speaks an unknown command, and so on.

A speech-recognition engine receives spoken audio input from the user through a voice-command site on the user's computer. A *voice-command site* consists of an audio-input device, such as a microphone or a telephone, and a speech-recognition mode. An engine typically provides several different modes for recognizing speech, each representing a different language or dialect. A program must create a separate voice-command object for each voice-command site it must use. To use a site other than the default (the computer microphone and the engine's default mode), the program must obtain the desired audio-input device's identifier and the desired mode's Globally Unique Identifier (GUID) and then pass that information to the voice-command object when the program registers itself to receive voice commands.

A program can use the *waveInGetNumDevs* and the *waveInGetDevCaps* multimedia API functions to obtain the device identifier of an audio-input device. To determine the available speech-recognition modes, a program creates a speech-recognition *enumerator*. The enumerator returns information about all modes that all engines in the user's system provides, including each mode's GUID. The voice-command object maintains a database of voice menus that programs have created. The first program to create a voice-command object causes the engine to open the database. The database remains open until the last program that is using a voice-command object releases the voice-command object. A program can use voice-menu objects to use a voice menu from the database or to add new menus to the database. It can also use a voice-menu enumerator to obtain information about each of the voice menus in the database.

WRITING THE CODE FOR THE PRJVOICECD PROJECT

Now that you have created the project's interface and learned more about the Speech API and the Voice Command API that you will use to implement voice support into the program, you can begin to design the program. You will write the code for the CD-ROM player itself first, then write the code to support the Speech API functions.

WRITING THE CODE FOR THE FRMMMEDIA FORM

After you have finished adding the controls to the *frmMMedia* form, you must write the program code that will react to the user's selections and perform the user-requested actions. The *frmMMedia* form uses several variables throughout the form to help it handle its processing. You must declare these variables within the form's General–Declarations section. The declarations for the *prjVoiceCD* project are identical to those within Chapter 2's *frmMMedia* form, except for the following additional declarations:

```
Private WithEvents SpeechObject as clsSAPISink
```

As you have learned, the *clsSAPISink* class is the notification sink for the voice-command object the program will use. The *clsSAPISink* class raises an event, so you must define an object variable to process that event. You can find the declarations in the *frmMMedia* form in the *Chapter24* directory on the companion CD-ROM that accompanies this book.

WRITING THE FORM'S STARTUP PROGRAM CODE

As you learned in Chapter 1, "Introduction to Visual Basic," when you load a form, it first invokes its *Form_Load* event, even before the computer displays the form on the screen. When you run a program that uses only one form, unless you separately declare a *Sub Main* procedure, the program's execution will begin within the form's *Load* event. The following code implements the *Form_Load* event for the *frmMMedia* form:

```
Private Sub Form_Load()
  LoadButtons
  MMControl1.Command = "Close"
  MMControl1.Visible = False
  MMControl1.Enabled = True
  MMControl1.DeviceType = "CDAudio"
  MMControl1.Shareable = False
  MMControl1.AutoEnable = False
  MMControl1.Command = "Open"
  CheckCDRom
  FirstTrack
  Set SpeechObject = New clsSAPISink
  OpenServer
  InitializeVoiceMenu
End Sub
```

The *Load* event's program code first invokes the *LoadButtons* procedure, which loads the button graphics for the form. The program code then initializes the *MMControl1* control, setting it to *CDAudio* and connecting the control to the CD-ROM drive. The program code then calls the *CheckCDRom* procedure, which initializes the program variables with information about the currently loaded CD-ROM. Next, the program code in the *Load* event calls the *FirstTrack* procedure, which sets the *Multimedia MCI* control to point to the first track on the CD-ROM.

The program code then initializes the *SpeechObject* variable and calls the *OpenServer* procedure, which opens and initializes a voice object. After you initialize a voice object, you must add a voice menu to the object so that the object can recognize commands from the user. To add a voice menu to the object, the program code calls the *InitializeVoiceMenu* procedure, which either creates the voice menu for the voice object or opens the voice menu if the program has previously created it.

WRITING THE PROCEDURES THE FORM_LOAD EVENT CALLS

As you learned in the previous section, the *Form_Load* event calls several helper procedures that the program uses to initialize the display and the connection to the audio CD. The first procedure that the *Form_Load* event calls is the *LoadButtons* procedure, which loads the graphics into the form. The *LoadButtons* procedure within the *prjVoiceCD* project is identical to the *LoadButton* procedure within Chapter 2's *frmMMedia* form. You can find the procedure in the *frmMMedia* form in the *Chapter24* directory on the companion CD-ROM that accompanies this book.

As you learned in the previous section, the *Form_Load* event also calls the *CheckCDRom* procedure. The *CheckCDRom* procedure uses the *MMControl1* control and several of its own "helper" procedures—procedures that perform simple processing and either return a single value or update the display. The *CheckCDRom* procedure within the *prjVoiceCD* project is identical to the *CheckCDRom* procedure within Chapter 2's *frmMMedia* form. You can find the procedure in the *frmMMedia* form in the *Chapter24* directory on the companion CD-ROM that accompanies this book.

The *CheckCDRom* procedure calls the *FirstTrack* procedure and the *TotalNumberTracks* procedure, which use the *Multimedia MCI* control to determine the total number of tracks the audio CD contains. The *FirstTrack* procedure within the *prjVoiceCD* project is identical to the *FirstTrack* procedure within Chapter 2's *frmMMedia* form. You can find the procedure in the *frmMMedia* form in the *Chapter24* directory on the companion CD-ROM that accompanies this book.

WRITING THE CODE FOR THE TRACK INFORMATION PROCEDURES

The *prjVoiceCD* program uses three separate procedures to get information about the current track: *getTrackLength*, *getTrackPosition*, and *getTrackNumber*. The first procedure, *getTrackLength*, uses information the *Multimedia MCI* control returns to determine the current track's length. The *getTrackLength*, *getTrackPosition*, and *getTrackNumber* procedures within the *prjVoiceCD* project are identical to the *getTrackLength*, *getTrackPosition*, and *getTrackNumber* procedures within Chapter 2's *frmMMedia* form. You can find the procedures in the *frmMMedia* form in the *Chapter24* directory on the companion CD-ROM that accompanies this book.

WRITING THE TIMER EVENT

As you have learned, Chapter 2's *prjCD-ROM* project uses a *Timer* control to periodically update information in the CD player's display. The *Timer1_Timer* event procedure within the *prjVoiceCD* project is identical to the *Timer1_Timer* event procedure within Chapter 2's *frmMMedia* form. You can find the procedure in the *frmMMedia* form in the *Chapter24* directory on the companion CD-ROM that accompanies this book.

WRITING THE EVENTS THAT RESPOND TO USER INPUT AT THE CONTROL PANEL

As you learned in this chapter's "Using the *prjVoiceCD* Project" section, to control the CD player, the user will click the mouse on the graphical buttons within the *ControlPanel* array. The *prjVoiceCD* program uses code within four separate events that belong to the *ControlPanel* array to perform its processing. The first two events, *MouseDown* and *MouseUp*, change a button's appearance when the user clicks on the button. The following code implements the *MouseDown* and *MouseUp* events:

```
Private Sub ControlPanel_MouseDown(Index As Integer, Button As Integer, _
    Shift As Integer, X As Single, Y As Single)
  ControlPanel(Index).BorderStyle = 0
End Sub

Private Sub ControlPanel_MouseUp(Index As Integer, Button As Integer, _
    Shift As Integer, X As Single, Y As Single)
  ControlPanel(Index).BorderStyle = 1
End Sub
```

The *MouseDown* event changes the user-selected button's *BorderStyle* property to no border. The *MouseUp* event, in turn, will change the style back to its original border. When the user clicks the mouse on a button, the two events in sequence will display a rapid border change on the button. The border changes give the illusion that the user has actually depressed the button momentarily when the user clicks the mouse on the button.

Although the *MouseDown* and *MouseUp* events change the button's display, the majority of the operative processing occurs within the *ControlPanel_Click* event. The *ControlPanel* array's *Click* event accepts as its sole parameter the index of the button the user has clicked. The procedure's program code then uses that index to determine what processing to perform. The following code implements the *ControlPanel_Click* event:

```
Private Sub ControlPanel_Click(Index As Integer)
  Dim I As Integer, StillTime As Long, NewTrack As Integer

  Timer1.Interval = 500
  DoEvents
  Select Case Index
    Case 0 '******* the first track button **********
      TotalNumberTracks
      FirstTrack

    Case 1 '***************** go back one track ******************
      BackTrack

    Case 2 '************** the beginning buton *******************
      MMControl1.Command = "Prev"
      getTrackPosition
      getTrackNumber
      getTrackLength
      If Not Pause Then
        MMControl1.Command = "Play"
        ControlPanel(3).Picture = LoadPicture(App.Path & "\PlayButton.bmp")
        Playing = True
      End If
    Case 3 '************** the play button *******************
      If Not Playing Then
        getRemainingTime StillTime
```

```
      MMControl1.Command = "play"
      ProgressBar1.Value = 0    'set the value of the progress bar to 0
      ControlPanel(3).Picture = LoadPicture(App.Path & "\PlayButton.bmp")
      Playing = True
      Pause = False
      getTrackPosition
      getTrackNumber
      getTrackLength
    ElseIf Playing Then
      ControlPanel(3).Picture = LoadPicture(App.Path & "\NotPlaying.bmp")
      ProgressBar1.Value = 0
      Playing = False
      If Pause Then
        Pause = Not Pause
        ControlPanel(6).Picture = LoadPicture(App.Path & "\NotPaused.bmp")
      End If
      MMControl1.Command = "Stop"
    Else
      MsgBox "Not a Valid CD-ROM in the drive."
    End If

Case 4  '***************  the next button  *********************
    If MMControl1.Track <> numTracks Then
      MMControl1.Command = "Next"
      getTrackPosition
      getTrackNumber
      getTrackLength
    End If

Case 5  '***************  the last button  *********************
    LastTrack

Case 6  '***************  the pause button  *********************
    If Not Pause Then
      MMControl1.Command = "Pause"
      ControlPanel(6).Picture = LoadPicture(App.Path & "\Paused.bmp")
      Pause = True
    Else
      MMControl1.Command = "Play"
      ControlPanel(6).Picture = LoadPicture(App.Path & "\NotPaused.bmp")
      Pause = False
    End If

Case 7  '***************  the repeat button  ********************
    RepeatButton = Not RepeatButton 'change the repeat button's state
    If RepeatButton Then
      ControlPanel(7).Picture = LoadPicture(App.Path & _
          "\RepeatButtonOn.bmp")
    Else
      ControlPanel(7).Picture = LoadPicture(App.Path & _
          "\RepeatButton.bmp")
    End If

Case 8  '***************  the eject button  ********************
    EjectButton = Not EjectButton
    If EjectButton = True Then
      FirstTrack
      MMControl1.Command = "Stop"
      Pause = True
      MMControl1.Command = "Eject"
      ControlPanel(3).Picture = LoadPicture(App.Path & "\NotPlaying.bmp")
      ProgressBar1.Value = 0
```

```
        Playing = False
        If Pause Then
          Pause = Not Pause
          ControlPanel(6).Picture = LoadPicture(App.Path & "\NotPaused.bmp")
        End If
        For I = 0 To 4
          Text1(I).Text = ""
        Next
        MMControl1.Command = "Close"
      Else
        MMControl1.DeviceType = "CDAudio"
        MMControl1.Shareable = False
        MMControl1.AutoEnable = False
        MMControl1.Command = "Open"
        MMControl1.Command = "Eject"
        FirstTrack
        TotalNumberTracks
        CheckCDRom
      End If
    End Select
  End Sub
```

The *ControlPanel_Click* event's program code uses a *Select Case* statement to determine what button the user clicked the mouse on and what action it should therefore perform. If the user clicks the mouse on the First Track button, the program calls the *First Track* procedure, which you learned about previously and which resets the playback to the first track on the CD. If the user clicks the mouse on the Back Track button, the program calls the *Back Track* procedure, which sets the playback to the previous track on the CD. You will learn more about the *Back Track* procedure in this chapter's "Writing the Code for the *Back Track* Procedure" section.

If the user clicks the mouse on the Beginning button, the program sends the *Prev* command to the *Multimedia MCI* control, which will set the current track back to its beginning and resume playback from the track's beginning point. The program will then update the display items and, if the user is currently playing the CD, start playing the CD over at the track's beginning. If the user clicks the mouse on the Play button, the program's processing will depend on whether or not the user is currently playing a CD. If the user is playing a CD, the program code will stop the CD from playing and will keep the track pointer at the current track. If the user is not playing a CD, the program code will begin to play the CD. Finally, if the user is pausing the CD, the program code will stop playing and will reset the Stop/Pause button.

If the user clicks the mouse on the Next button, the program code will send the *Next* command to the *Multimedia MCI* control, which will set the control to point to the next track. The program code will then update the display. If the user is currently playing a CD, the *Multimedia MCI* control will automatically continue playing at the next track. If the user clicks the mouse on the Last Track button, the program will call the *Last Track* procedure, which the next section explains in detail. The *Last Track* procedure uses the *Multimedia MCI* control's *Next* command to advance the CD player to the last track on the CD.

If the user clicks the mouse on the Stop/Pause button only one time, the program will either pause the CD player's playback or, if the user has already paused the CD player, will resume the playback. If the user double-clicks the mouse on the Stop/Pause button, the program will stop the CD's playback. To capture the double-click event, you must write different program code, which you will learn about later in this section. If the user clicks the mouse on the Repeat button, the program code will change the Repeat button's graphic to show that the user has selected the Repeat button. Next, the program code will set the *RepeatButton* flag variable so that the program will know to continue playing when it reaches the CD's end.

Finally, if the user clicks the mouse on the Eject button, the program code will either eject the currently loaded CD or load a new CD into the player. In either case, the program code will update the display values—disabling the display fields if the user ejects the CD or enabling the fields and putting the appropriate values into them if the user loads a new CD.

As you learned in the "Using the *prjVoiceCD* Project" section, to stop the CD player when it is playing, the user must double-click the mouse on the Stop/Pause button. To handle the processing difference between a mouse double-click and a mouse single-click, the program must capture the Stop/Pause button within the *DblClick* event. The following code implements the *ControlPanel_DblClick* event:

```
Private Sub ControlPanel_DblClick(Index As Integer)
   Select Case Index
     Case 6  '****************  the stop button  **********************
       MMControl1.Command = "Stop"
       ControlPanel(3).Picture = LoadPicture(App.Path & "\notplaying.bmp")
       ControlPanel(6).Picture = LoadPicture(App.Path & "\notpaused.bmp")
       Pause = False
       Playing = Not Playing
       ProgressBar1.Value = 0
   End Select
End Sub
```

The *DblClick* event uses a *Select Case* statement to determine on which button the user has double-clicked the mouse. If the user double-clicks the mouse on any button other than the Stop/Pause button, the event's program code performs no processing. If the user double-clicks the mouse on the Stop/Pause button, the event's program code will change the image within the button to the Stop/Pause button (from the paused image, if the program loaded it previously) and turn off the Play button. The program code will then turn off the CD player, stop the current track, and reset the *ProgressBar1* control's value to 0.

Writing the Code for the LastTrack Procedure

As you learned in the previous section, if the user clicks the mouse on the Last Track button, the *ControlPanel_Click* event's program code will call the *LastTrack* procedure. The *LastTrack* procedure resets the CD player to the last track on the CD. The *LastTrack* procedure within the *prjVoiceCD* project is identical to the *LastTrack* procedure within Chapter 2's *frmMMedia* form. You can find the procedure in the *frmMMedia* form in the *Chapter24* directory on the companion CD-ROM that accompanies this book.

Writing the Code for the BackTrack Procedure

As you learned in the "Writing the Events that Respond to User Input at the Control Panel" section, if the user clicks the mouse on the Back Track button, the *ControlPanel_Click* event's program code will call the *BackTrack* procedure. The *BackTrack* procedure will move the track counter back a single track and, if the CD player is already playing the CD, will start to play the new track. The *BackTrack* procedure within the *prjVoiceCD* project is identical to the *BackTrack* procedure within Chapter 2's *frmMMedia* form. You can find the procedure in the *frmMMedia* form in the *Chapter24* directory on the companion CD-ROM that accompanies this book.

Writing the Exit Code

Just as the first event to execute within the *prjVoiceCD* project is the *Form_Load* event, the last event to execute is the *Form_Unload* event. The *Form_Unload* procedure within the *prjVoiceCD* project is identical to the *Form_Unload* procedure within Chapter 2's *frmMMedia* form. You can find the procedure in the *frmMMedia* form in the *Chapter24* directory on the companion CD-ROM that accompanies this book.

There are two ways to exit the program: the user can either click the mouse on the Close button or select the File menu Exit option. The *mnuExit_Click* procedure within the *prjVoiceCD* project is identical to the *mnuExit_Click* procedure within Chapter 2's *frmMMedia* form. You can find the procedure in the *frmMMedia* form in the *Chapter24* directory on the companion CD-ROM that accompanies this book.

Writing the Code for the IncomingCommand Event

As you have learned, your programs must respond to incoming commands from the voice-command engine. As you will learn in the next section, the actual response to the incoming commands will occur within the *clsAPISink* class. However, the *clsAPISink* class will raise an *IncomingCommand* event to the *SpeechInput* object variable that you previously used with the *WithEvents* keyword to declare within the form's General–Declaration section. The following code implements the *SpeechInput_IncomingCommand* event:

```
Private Sub SpeechInput_IncomingCommand (Command As String)
  Select Case Command
    Case "Play Compact Disk"
      ControlPanel_Click(3)
    Case "Pause Compact Disk"
      ControlPanel_Click(6)
    Case "Stop Compact Disk"
      ControlPanel_DblClick(6)
    Case "Move to Next Track"
      ControlPanel_Click(4)
  End Case
End Sub
```

768 The incoming *Command* parameter contains the text equivalent of the user's spoken command. The *Select Case* statement within the *IncomingCommand* event invokes the *ControlPanel_Click* or *ControlPanel_DblClick* event and passes the correct index into the event so that the same event that processes user mouse actions also processes user voice input.

WRITING THE CODE FOR THE *CLSAPISINK* CLASS

As you have learned, you will place program code within the *clsAPISink* class to respond to incoming speech messages. In fact, you will declare a single event (the *IncomingCommand* event) and two functions, *CommandOther* and *CommandRecognize*, to handle the incoming message. The following code implements the event declaration for the *clsAPISink* class:

```
Event IncomingCommand(Command As String)
```

As you can see, the event declaration raises the command to the *frmMMedia* form. The two functions determine what command to raise. Whenever you write programs that accept voice commands, you must implement both functions—the OLE Automation server treats both instances differently. The first function, *CommandOther*, processes commands the OLE Automation server recognizes as not belonging to your program. The following code implements the *CommandOther* function:

```
Function CommandOther(pszCommand As String, pszApp As String, _
    pszState As String)
  If Len(pszCommand) = 0 Then
    RaiseEvent IncomingCommand ("Command unrecognized")
  Else
    RaiseEvent IncomingCommand (pszCommand & " was recognized from " & _
        pszApp & "'s " & pszState & " menu" & Chr(13) & Chr(10))
  End If
End Function
```

While the *frmMMedia* form's program code does not respond to either of the events the *CommandOther* function raises, your program code will often do so, to alert the user that the user has issued an invalid command to your program. The OLE Automation server invokes the second function, *CommandRecognize*, whenever the OLE Automation server recognizes the command belongs to the application's command set. The following code implements the *CommandRecognize* function:

```
Function CommandRecognize(pszCommand As String, dwID As Long)
   RaiseEvent IncomingCommand(pszCommand)
End Function
```

The *CommandRecognize* function will raise one of the four known voice phrases to the parent form, which will, in turn, invoke the correct method within the *ControlPanel* events.

Writing The Code for the *mdlSAPIDeclares* Module

As you have learned, you will declare variables and constants that you must use to access the Speech API within the *mdlSAPIDeclares* module. The following code implements the declarations for the *mdlSAPIDeclares* module:

```
Public Const VCMD_REGISTER As Integer = 1
Public Const VCMD_CALLBACK As Integer = 2
Public Const VCMD_MENUCREATE As Integer = 3
Public Const VCMD_AWAKE As Integer = 4
Public Const VCMD_ASLEEP As Integer = 5
Public Const VCMDMENU_ADD As Integer = 6
Public Const VCMDMENU_REMOVE As Integer = 7
Public Const VCMDMENU_LISTSET As Integer = 8
Public Const VCMDMENU_ACTIVATE As Integer = 9
Public Const VCMDMENU_DEACTIVATE As Integer = 10
Public Const ADD_CATEGORY = "General"
Public Const ADD_DESCRIPTION = "Generic Command Description"

Public objVCmd As Object, objVMenu As Object
Public FirstRegistered As Boolean
```

The constants are all values you will use when you access the *Voice* object that you create in the program. The *VCmd* object corresponds to the voice-command engine that will process voice commands. The program will use the *VMenu* object when it adds new commands to the engine's recognized command list. Finally, the *FirstRegistered* variable holds the registry value that indicates whether or not the program has already added the commands to the engine's recognized command list.

Writing the Code for the *mdlSpeech* Module

The code to register the commands with and to respond to any errors in the voice-command engine is all within the *CheckError* function. The *CheckError* function checks an incoming value against the error constants you defined within the *mdlSAPIDeclares* module, creates an error string explaining the error, and returns the error string as the function's value. The following code implements the *CheckError* function:

```
Public Function CheckError(VCMD_Cmd As Integer) As String
  Dim msg As String

  If Err.Number <> 0 Then                              'error
    Select Case VCMD_Cmd
      Case VCMD_REGISTER
        msg = "Register: "
      Case VCMD_CALLBACK
        msg = "Callback: "
      Case VCMD_MENUCREATE
        msg = "MenuCreate: "
      Case VCMD_AWAKE
        msg = "Voice Command awake: "
      Case VCMD_ASLEEP
        msg = "Voice Command asleep: "
      Case VCMDMENU_ADD
        msg = "Add command to menu: "
      Case VCMDMENU_REMOVE
        msg = "Remove command from menu: "
      Case VCMDMENU_LISTSET
        msg = "Set list of phrases: "
      Case VCMDMENU_ACTIVATE
        msg = "Activate Voice-Command menu: "
      Case VCMDMENU_DEACTIVATE
        msg = "Deactivate Voice-Command menu: "
    End Select
```

```
          CheckError = msg & "Error #" & Str(Err.Number) & " was generated by " _
             & Err.Source & Chr(13) & Chr(10) & Err.Description
       Else                                          'no error
          Select Case VCMD_Cmd
            Case VCMD_REGISTER
              msg = "Voice-Commmand registered" & Chr(13) & Chr(10)
            Case VCMD_CALLBACK
              msg = "Callback notification initiated"
            Case VCMD_MENUCREATE
              msg = "Empty command menu created"
            Case VCMD_AWAKE
              msg = "Voice Command awake"
            Case VCMD_ASLEEP
              msg = "Voice Command asleep"
            Case VCMDMENU_ADD
              msg = "Command added to menu"
            Case VCMDMENU_REMOVE
              msg = "Command removed from menu"
            Case VCMDMENU_LISTSET
              msg = "List of phrases set"
            Case VCMDMENU_ACTIVATE
              msg = "Voice-Command Menu activated"
            Case VCMDMENU_DEACTIVATE
              msg = "Voice-Command Menu deactivated"
          End Select
          CheckError = msg & Chr(13) & Chr(10)
       End If
    End Sub
```

As you can see, the program code within the function checks to determine whether the program called the function because of an error or simply for informational purposes. Whether there was an error or some other event, the function uses a *Select Case* statement to check the incoming value against the error constants list and generates a text message to return to the user.

WRITING THE CODE FOR THE OPENSERVER PROCEDURE

As you have learned, each time you access a voice or other speech-engine object, you must create an object for the program to reference. Within Visual Basic, you can use the OLE Automation engine to create a voice-engine object. You can also use custom Dynamic-Link Libraries (DLLs) that you write in C/C++ and access from within your Visual Basic programs. Within the *prjVoiceCD* project, the *frmMMedia* form's *Form_Load* event calls the *OpenServer* procedure to create the voice-engine object. The following code implements the *OpenServer* procedure:

```
Public Sub OpenServer()
  Dim Message as String

  On Error Resume Next
  Err.Clear
  Set objVCmd = Nothing
  Set objVCmd = CreateObject("Speech.VoiceCommand")
  Call objVCmd.Register("")
  Message = CheckError(VCMD_REGISTER)
  Err.Clear
  objVCmd.Callback = "prjVoiceCD.clsAPISink"
  Message = CheckError(VCMD_CALLBACK)
  Err.Clear
End Sub
```

The *OpenServer* procedure's processing first clears the *objVCmd* object variable and then creates a new *VoiceCommand* object on the *Speech* object with Visual Basic's built-in *CreateObject* command (which creates an object that the OLE Automation server manages). Next, the program code uses the *Register* method to register the new object with the operating system. The *CheckError* command verifies the program was successful registering the object and returns the value in the *Message* variable. Although the *OpenServer* procedure does not process or display the success string, within your programs you will generally want to display the information that *CheckError* returns within a status bar or other banner-type control onto which you can display informational messages.

Next, the program code uses the *Callback* method to specify the *prjVoiceCD* project's *clsAPISink* module as the recipient for commands from the *VoiceCommand* object. Again, the program code calls the *CheckError* function, but it does nothing with the return value. After the *OpenServer* procedure exits, the program is ready to receive incoming voice commands from the speech engine.

WRITING THE CODE FOR THE *INITIALIZEVOICEMENU* PROCEDURE

As you have learned, after you create a voice command object within your programs, you must also create a menu voice menu object. The *prjVoiceCD* program calls the *InitializeVoiceMenu* procedure to create the voice menu object. The *InitializeVoiceMenu* procedure, in turn, either creates the new object or loads the object from the voice-command engine's database, if the program previously created the object. The following code implements the *InitializeVoiceMenu* procedure:

771

```
Public Sub InitializeVoiceMenu()
  Dim flag As Long

  flag = vcmdmc_CREATE_NEW
  Set VMenu = Nothing
  Set VMenu = VCmd.MenuCreate("prjVoiceCD", "Test Menu", 1033, _
      "US English", flag)
  Call CheckError(VCMD_MENUCREATE)
  If Err.Number = 0 Then
    Call VMenu.Add(0, "Play Compact Disk", ADD_CATEGORY, ADD_DESCRIPTION)
    Call CheckError(VCMDMENU_ADD)
    Call VMenu.Add(1, "Pause Compact Disk", ADD_CATEGORY, ADD_DESCRIPTION)
    Call CheckError(VCMDMENU_ADD)
    Call VMenu.Add(2, "Stop Compact Disk", ADD_CATEGORY, ADD_DESCRIPTION)
    Call CheckError(VCMDMENU_ADD)
    Call VMenu.Add(3, "Move to Next Track", ADD_CATEGORY, ADD_DESCRIPTION)
    Call CheckError(VCMDMENU_ADD)
  Else
    flag = vcmdmc_OPEN_EXISTING
    Set objVMenu = objVCmd.MenuCreate("prjVoiceCD", "Test Menu", 1033, _
        "US English", flag)
  End If
  Err.Clear
End Sub
```

The *MenuCreate* command tries to create a new menu when it receives the *cmcdc_CREATE_NEW* constant. If it cannot create a new menu, the program code opens the existing menu. Otherwise, the program code uses the *VMenu* object's *Add* method to add the four program commands to the menu.

ALERTING THE SPEECH ENGINE THAT A COMMAND IS COMING

One of the nicer Microsoft *Voice* engine features is that the user can verbally alert the computer that a speech command is coming. Rather than clicking the mouse on the Microsoft Voice icon, the user can simply precede the speech command with the phrase "Computer." For example, the user can instruct the *prjVoiceCD* program to play the CD-ROM with the statement "Computer, Play Compact Disk."

ENHANCEMENTS YOU CAN MAKE TO THE prjVoiceCD PROJECT

Like many other projects that you have designed in this book, the *prjVoiceCD* project will help you write your own programs. The *prjVoiceCD* project helped you learn how to write programs that use voice commands or other speech-recognition engine or text-to-speech engine tools. You can apply the information that you have learned within this chapter to create complex voice command support within your programs, in addition to the normal mouse-and-keyboard support that your programs include. To further your knowledge of the speech-recognition and voice-command engines, you can expand the definitions the *prjVoiceCD* project uses to include all the possible commands a user might input.

PUTTING IT ALL TOGETHER

This chapter's project, *prjVoiceCD*, introduced you to working with the Speech Application Programming Interface (SAPI), particularly the Voice Command API aspect of the SAPI. You have used Visual Basic's built-in OLE Automation server to create *VoiceCommand* objects and add voice commands to your program. You have also revisited how to use the *Microsoft Multimedia MCI* control and the *Microsoft Status Bar* control. In Chapter 25, "Writing a Fax Program in Visual Basic," you will use the Microsoft Messaging Application Programming Interface (MAPI) to create a simple fax program from within Visual Basic. Before you continue with the next chapter, however, make sure you understand the following key concepts:

✓ A speech engine is a low-level program that receives input from an audio device (such as a microphone) and converts the input into text your programs can process, or that receives text input from a program and generates output to an audio device (such as a computer's speakers).

✓ The Microsoft Speech Application Programming Interface (SAPI) provides an intermediate level between your programs and an underlying speech engine.

✓ Your programs that use the SAPI functions can support two types of speech-based activity: speech recognition and text-to-speech.

✓ Speech recognition is the computer's ability (through software) to understand the spoken word. You can use speech recognition to receive command and data input from the speaker. Together with the Voice Command API, the SAPI's speech recognition capability lets your programs perform specific actions in response to verbal commands from the user.

✓ Text-to-speech is the computer's ability to convert text information into synthetic speech output. While you did not use a text-to-speech engine in this chapter, you can easily use the provider-access concepts this chapter details to add text-to-speech support to your programs. Text-to-speech programs can be powerful tools when you work with the blind, disabled individuals, in game programs, and in applications that must generate voice output.

✓ A program needs an audio-source object to provide speech input, a speech engine object to process the speech, and a grammar object to provide the speech engine object with the lists of words or rules that determine what the speech engine can recognize to perform speech recognition.

✓ To use speech recognition to generate program commands, you must record the words or phrases for the engine to recognize into the *speech-to-text conversion* database, and implement a Component Object Model (COM) object within your program that receives the commands from the speech engine when the user issues them. You must pass the COM object's address into the engine when you initialize it.

✓ After your program receives the message from the speech engine that the user has entered a speech command, you must process the command within your program. Often, you will raise events from the COM object into the client program, as you did within the *prjVoiceCD* program.

Chapter 25
Writing a Fax Program in Visual Basic

Electronics companies first introduced fax machines in the early 1980s. Early fax machines worked only with thermal paper and printed incoming faxes onto a roll. Later, companies introduced plain paper fax machines, which printed incoming faxes onto normal, copier-style paper. The fax machine quickly became an important piece of equipment in offices of all sizes. The ability to communicate information almost instantly, rather than waiting several days if you sent the information through the regular mail, or incurring overnight express shipping costs, made the fax machine a valuable, inexpensive office tool. The introduction of fax modems in the early 1990s gave desktop computers the ability to send faxes as well. For many companies, the desktop computer's ability to send faxes and e-mail, and to generate professional-quality documents quickly and easily has made the desktop computer (and its smaller cousin, the laptop computer) more important to business communications.

773

Writing fax programs for computers, however, was never easy. The conversion of a document from a binary file that the computer could read into an optical image that a fax machine could receive was a difficult process. Opening a communication channel (such as a telephone line) was also difficult. Microsoft's introduction of the Messaging Application Programming Interface (MAPI), however, has made creating programs that can fax documents much easier because it lets programmers work with a consistent set of functions that calls other programs that resolve the information into optical documents. In this chapter's project, *prjFaxProgram*, you will use the Messaging Application Programming Interface (MAPI) to write a simple fax program that can transmit faxes to any valid fax number. The program will include addressee information, the telephone number to which the program should send the fax, a "Regarding" line, a brief cover note, and space to attach Microsoft *Word*® documents or Rich Text files to the fax. By the time you finish this chapter, you will understand the following key concepts:

- The Messaging Application Programming Interface (MAPI), like the Speech Application Programming Interface (SAPI) you used in the previous chapter, is a layer between your programs and *Messaging Providers* (underlying programs) that lets you write programs with fax support without concern for the underlying Messaging Provider type.

- Microsoft divides Messaging Providers into three basic categories: *Message Store Providers*, which supply message storage, organization, and retrieval facilities for a messaging system; *Address Book Providers*, which supply message addressing and distribution list facilities to the messaging client; and *Messaging Transport Providers*, which move messages between messaging clients.

- Before you can use the MAPI functions to send faxes or other message types, you must use the *MAPILogon* API function to connect to a valid Message Store Provider.

- To send faxes, your programs will use the *MAPISendMail* API function to access a valid Messaging Transport Provider.

- Microsoft provides a subset of twelve of the most commonly used MAPI functions, which Microsoft refers to as the *Simple MAPI*. Within the *prjFaxProgram* project, you will use Simple MAPI to send a fax transmission.

INSTALLING MESSAGING SERVICES

As you will learn later in this chapter, the *prjFaxProgram* program uses the Microsoft Windows Messaging Application Programming Interface (MAPI) to send faxes. Much like the Cryptographic API and the Speech API that you learned about in previous chapters, the functions within the MAPI access low-level providers to perform their processing. The *prjFaxProgram* program will not work properly unless you have a Messaging Provider and a fax Messaging

Provider installed onto your computer. The code within the *prjFaxProgram* program presumes that Microsoft Fax is installed onto your computer. If you do not have *Microsoft Fax* installed on your computer, you must install it before you try to run the *prjFaxProgram* program. To install *Microsoft Fax*, perform the following steps:

1. Select the Windows Start menu Setting option. Within the Settings menu, select the Control Panel option. Windows will display the Control Panel window.

2. Within the Control Panel window, double-click your mouse on the Add/Remove Programs icon. Windows will display the Add/Remove Programs dialog box.

3. Within the Add/Remove Programs dialog box, click your mouse on the Windows Setup tab. The dialog box will change its display to Windows programs.

4. Within the Components list box, click your mouse on the check box next to the *Microsoft Fax* listing. Windows will place a check mark in the box.

5. Click your mouse on the OK button. Windows will install *Microsoft Fax*.

Note: *Windows may prompt you to insert your original installation disks or CD-ROM to install Microsoft Fax.*

USING THE PRJFAXPROGRAM PROJECT

Before you design the *prjFaxProgram* project, you may find it helpful to run the program. The companion CD-ROM that accompanies this book contains the *prjFaxProgram.exe* program within the *Chapter25* directory. As with every other program on the CD-ROM, you should run the Jamsa Press *setup.exe* program to install the *prjFaxProgram.exe* program to your computer's hard drive before you run it. After you install the *prjFaxProgram.exe* program to your computer's hard drive, you can run it from the Start menu. To run the program, select the Windows Start menu Run option. Windows will display the Run dialog box. Within the Run dialog box, enter *x:\vbpl\Chapter25\prjFaxProgram.exe*, where *x* corresponds to the drive letter of the hard drive on which you installed the *prjFaxProgram.exe* program, and click your mouse on OK. Windows will display the *prjFaxProgram.exe* program, as shown in Figure 25.1.

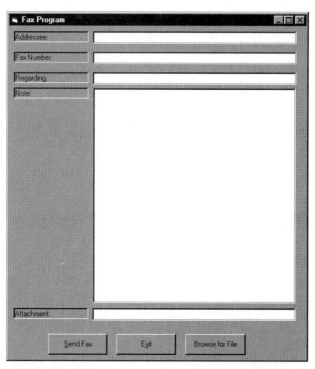

Figure 25.1 *The **prjFaxProgram.exe** program's Fax Program window at startup.*

RUNNING *prjFaxProgram* FROM THE CD-ROM

As you have learned, you must first install many programs that you will use in this book to your computer's hard drive before you use them. Because the *prjFaxProgram.exe* program does not use any custom controls that you must register on your computer before the program will execute, you can run the *prjFaxProgram.exe* program from the CD-ROM. However, before your run the *prjFaxProgram.exe* program at all, you must ensure that you install at least one Messaging Provider onto your computer. (Windows 95 and Windows NT both include the *Microsoft Fax* provider that you can install easily to your computer, if you do not have a Messaging Provider. You can install the provider from the Control Panel group's Add/Remove Programs option.) To run the *prjFaxProgram.exe* program from the CD-ROM, perform the following steps:

1. Select the Windows Start menu Run option. Windows will display the Run dialog box.

2. Within the Run dialog box, enter *x:\Chapter25\prjFaxProgram.exe*, where *x* corresponds to the drive letter of your computer's CD-ROM drive (usually D: or E:), and click your mouse on OK. Windows will run the *prjFaxProgram.exe* program.

To learn more about the Jamsa Press *setup.exe* program, see the "What's on the *Visual Basic Programmer's Library* Companion CD-ROM" section at the back of this book.

Before you use the *prjFaxProgram.exe* program, take a moment to familiarize yourself with the program's appearance. After you start the *prjFaxProgram.exe* program, your computer will display a window in the display's center (the Fax Program window). Near the top of the Fax Program window, you will see a field with the caption *Addressee*. You will enter the person's name to whom you are sending the fax within the *Addressee* field. Below the *Addressee* field, you will see the *Fax Number*, *Regarding*, and *Note* fields. You will enter the corresponding information for your fax within these fields. Below the *Note* field, you will see a field with the caption *Attachment*. In the *Attachment* field, you can attach Microsoft *Word* documents or Rich Text files to your fax. You can enter the file's pathname directly into the *Attachment* field, drag-and-drop a file into the field from Microsoft *Explorer*, or click your mouse on the Browse for File button to display the Add Attachment dialog box and load the file from that dialog box. To create and send a fax, perform the following steps:

1. Within the *Addressee* field, type the addressee's name, such as *Happy Jamsa*. Next, press the TAB key. The *prjFaxProgram.exe* program will move the insert cursor to the *Fax Number* field.

2. Within the *Fax Number* field, type the fax number. The fax number can be either seven or eight digits (for a local number), or ten to fourteen digits (for a long-distance number). You can enter the dashes within the number, but do not enter the parentheses. Next, press the TAB key. The *prjFaxProgram.exe* program will move the insert cursor to the *Regarding* field.

3. Within the *Regarding* field, type the regarding line for the fax, such as *Your New Certification*. Next, press the TAB key. The *prjFaxProgram.exe* program will move the insert cursor to the *Note* field.

4. Within the *Note* field, type a brief message for the program to display on the cover page, such as *Attached please find information about your new certification*. Next, press the TAB key. The *prjFaxProgram.exe* program will move the insert cursor to the *Attachment* field.

5. Click your mouse on the Browse for File button. The *prjFaxProgram.exe* program will display the Add Attachment dialog box. Within the *x:\vbpl\Chapter25* directory, where *x* corresponds to the drive letter of the hard drive on which you installed the *prjFaxProgram.exe* program, you will find a file entitled *FaxSample.rtf*. Double-click your mouse on the *FaxSample.rtf* file. The program will add the filename to the *Attachment* field. When you finish your entries, the *prjFaxProgram.exe* program will look similar to Figure 25.2.

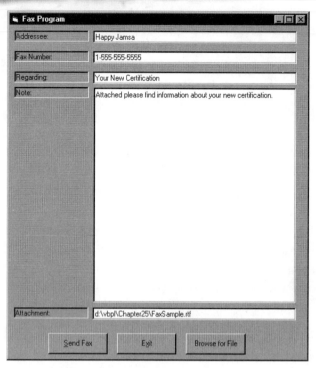

Figure 25.2 *The* **prjFaxProgram.exe** *program after you complete your entries.*

After you complete your entries, click your mouse on the Send Fax button to send the fax. The Messaging Transport Provider on your system will format the fax and either send the fax immediately or save it for later delivery, depending upon how you have configured the Messaging Transport Provider.

CREATING THE PROJECT AND ITS FORMS AND MODULES

Now that you have a better idea how to use the finished *prjFaxProgram* project, you can begin to design it. First, you will design a single empty form for the program's interface. After you design and implement the form, you will add three modules to the project that will support the program code for the MAPI functions. To begin the *prjFaxProgram* project and design the empty form, perform the following steps:

1. Within Visual Basic, select the File menu New Project option. Visual Basic will open the New Project dialog box.

2. Within the New Project dialog box, double-click your mouse on the Standard EXE icon. Visual Basic will close the New Project dialog box, start a new project, *Project1*, and add a form to it, *Form1*.

3. Select the View menu Properties Window option. Visual Basic will open the Properties Window listing the *Form1* properties.

4. Within the Properties Window, change the *Form1* property values to the values Table 25.1 lists.

Object	Property	Set As
Form1	*Caption*	*Fax Program*
Form1	*Height*	8190
Form1	*Left*	0
Form1	*Top*	0
Form1	*Width*	7335
Form1	*Name*	*frmSendFax*

Table 25.1 *The newly named* **frmSendFax** *form's properties.*

5. Within Visual Basic, select the Project menu Add Module option. Visual Basic will open the Add Module dialog box.

6. Within the Add Module dialog box, select the Module option. Next, click your mouse on the Open button. Visual Basic will open a new Code window, *Module1*.

7. Select the View menu Properties Window option. Visual Basic will open the Properties Window listing the *Module1* module's properties.

8. Within the Properties Window, change the *Module1* module's name to *mdlFaxSupport*.

9. Within Visual Basic, select the Project menu Add Module option. Visual Basic will open the Add Module dialog box.

10. Within the Add Module dialog box, select the Module option. Next, click your mouse on the Open button. Visual Basic will open a new Code window, *Module1*.

11. Select the View menu Properties Window option. Visual Basic will open the Properties Window listing the *Module1* properties.

12. Within the Properties Window, change the *Module1* module's name to *mdlMAPIDeclares*.

13. Within Visual Basic, select the Project menu Add Module option. Visual Basic will open the Add Module dialog box.

14. Within the Add Module dialog box, double-click your mouse on the Module icon. Visual Basic will open a new Code window, *Module1*.

15. Select the View menu Properties Window option. Visual Basic will open the Properties Window listing the *Module1* properties.

16. Within the Properties Window, change the *Module1* module's name to *mdlMAPIErr*.

17. Select the Property menu Project1 Properties option. Visual Basic will display the Project Properties dialog box.

18. Within the Project Properties dialog box, change the *Project Name* field's value to *prjFaxProgram*. Next, click your mouse on OK. Visual Basic will close the Project Properties dialog box.

19. Select the File menu Save Project As option. Visual Basic will open the Save File As dialog box and fill the *File name* field with *mdlMAPIErr*.

20. Within the Save File As dialog box, click your mouse on the Save button. Visual Basic will save the *mdlMAPIErr* module and fill the *File name* field with *mdlMAPIDeclares*.

21. Within the Save File As dialog box, click your mouse on the Save button. Visual Basic will save the *mdlMAPIDeclares* module and fill the *File name* field with *mdlFaxSupport*.

22. Within the Save File As dialog box, click your mouse on the Save button. Visual Basic will save the *mdlFaxSupport* module and fill the *File name* field with *frmSendFax*.

23. Within the Save File As dialog box, click your mouse on the Save button. Visual Basic will save the *frmSendFax* form and fill the *File name* field with *prjFaxProgram*.

24. Within the Save Project As dialog box, click your mouse on the Save button. Visual Basic will save the *prjFaxProgram* project and close the Save Project As dialog box.

Adding the Component Controls to the Project

As you have learned, the *prjFaxProgram* project has a single component form. The *frmSendFax* form includes controls that you must add to the project as components. The project will use the *Microsoft Rich TextBox* control to let the user add a note to the fax, and the *Microsoft Common Dialog* control to display the Open File dialog box. To add the controls to the *prjFaxProgram* project, perform the following steps:

1. Within Visual Basic, select the Project menu Components option. Visual Basic will open the Components dialog box.

2. Within the Components dialog box, select the *Microsoft Common Dialog Control 5.0* listing. Next, click your mouse on the box to the left of the listing. Visual Basic will display a check mark in the box.

3. Within the Components dialog box, select the *Microsoft Rich Textbox Control 5.0* listing.

Next, click your mouse on the box to the left of the listing. Visual Basic will display a check mark in the box.

4. Within the Components dialog box, click your mouse on the OK button. Visual Basic will close the Components dialog box and add the controls to the *prjFaxProgram* project.

ADDING THE *COMMONDIALOG* CONTROL TO THE *FRMSENDFAX* FORM

In this chapter's "Using the *prjFaxProgram* Project" section, you learned that you can attach a document to an outgoing fax. You also learned that you can use the Open File dialog box to select the file to attach. To display the Open File dialog box, the *prjFaxProgram* project uses the *CommonDialog* control. To add the *CommonDialog* control to the *frmSendFax* form, perform the following steps:

1. If Visual Basic is not displaying the *frmSendFax* form within an object window, double-click your mouse on the *frmSendFax* form listing within the Project Explorer. Visual Basic will open the *frmSendFax* form.

2. Within Visual Basic, select the View menu Toolbox option. Visual Basic will open the Toolbox.

3. Within the Toolbox, double-click your mouse on the CommonDialog icon. Visual Basic will draw a *CommonDialog* control, *CommonDialog1*, within the *frmSendFax* form.

4. Within the *frmSendFax* form, click your mouse on the *CommonDialog1* control to highlight it. Visual Basic will draw a small frame around the control.

5. Select the View menu Properties Window option. Visual Basic will open the Properties Window listing the *CommonDialog1* properties.

6. Within the Properties Window, change the *CommonDialog1* properties to those Table 25.2 lists.

Object	Property	Set As
CommonDialog1	*Left*	0
CommonDialog1	*Top*	1800
CommonDialog1	*Name*	*cdgAttachFile*

Table 25.2 *The newly named* **cdgAttachFile** *control's properties.*

ADDING THE *RICHTEXTBOX* CONTROL TO THE *FRMSENDFAX* FORM

As you learned in this chapter's "Using the *prjFaxProgram* Project" section, the user can enter notes within a *RichTextBox* control on the *frmSendFax* form. To add a *RichTextBox* control to the *frmSendFax* form, perform the following steps:

1. If Visual Basic is not displaying the *frmSendFax* form within an object window, double-click your mouse on the *frmSendFax* form listing within the Project Explorer. Visual Basic will open the *frmSendFax* form.

2. Within Visual Basic, select the View menu Toolbox option. Visual Basic will open the Toolbox.

3. Within the Toolbox, double-click your mouse on the RichTextBox icon. Visual Basic will draw a *RichTextBox* control, *RichTextBox1*, within the *frmSendFax* form.

4. Within the *frmSendFax* form, click your mouse on the *RichTextBox1* control to highlight it. Visual Basic will draw a small frame around the control.

5. Select the View menu Properties Window option. Visual Basic will open the Properties Window listing the *RichTextBox1* properties.

6. Within the Properties Window, change the *RichTextBox1* properties to the values Table 25.3 lists.

Object	Property	Set As
RichTextBox1	*Height*	5055
RichTextBox1	*Left*	2040
RichTextBox1	*TabIndex*	3

Table 25.3 *The newly named* **rtbNote** *control's properties. (continued on following page)*

Object	Property	Set As
RichTextBox1	Text	[blank]
RichTextBox1	Top	1440
RichTextBox1	Width	4935
RichTextBox1	Name	rtbNote

*Table 25.3 The newly named **rtbNote** control's properties. (continued from previous page)*

ADDING THE LABEL CONTROLS TO THE FRMSENDFAX FORM

As you learned earlier in this chapter, the *frmSendFax* form includes fields with captions to help the user design the fax he or she wants to send. To add the *Label* controls to the *frmSendFax* form, perform the following steps:

1. If Visual Basic is not displaying the *frmSendFax* form within an object window, double-click your mouse on the *frmSendFax* form listing within the Project Explorer. Visual Basic will open the *frmSendFax* form.

2. Within Visual Basic, select the View menu Toolbox option. Visual Basic will open the Toolbox.

3. Within the Toolbox, double-click your mouse on the Label icon. Visual Basic will draw a *Label* control, *Label1*, within the *frmSendFax* form.

4. Repeat Step 3 four times. Visual Basic will draw four additional *Label* controls on the *frmSendFax* form.

5. Within the *frmSendFax* form, click your mouse on a *Label* control to highlight it. Visual Basic will draw a small frame around the control.

6. Select the View menu Properties Window option. Visual Basic will open the Properties Window listing the highlighted control's properties.

7. Within the Properties Window, change the highlighted *Label* control's properties to the values Table 25.4 lists.

8. Within the Properties Window, change each remaining *Label* control's properties to the values Table 25.4 lists.

Object	Property	Set As
Label1	BorderStyle	1 - Fixed Single
Label1	Caption	Addressee:
Label1	Height	255
Label1	Left	120
Label1	Top	120
Label1	Width	1815
Label1	Name	lblAddressee
Label2	BorderStyle	1 - Fixed Single
Label2	Caption	Fax number:
Label2	Height	255
Label2	Left	120
Label2	Top	600
Label2	Width	1815
Label2	Name	lblFaxNumber
Label3	BorderStyle	1 - Fixed Single
Label3	Caption	Regarding:
Label3	Height	255

*Table 25.4 The newly named **Label** controls' properties. (continued on following page)*

779

Object	Property	Set As
Label3	Left	120
Label3	Top	1080
Label3	Width	1815
Label3	Name	lblRELine
Label4	Caption	Note:
Label4	Height	255
Label4	Left	120
Label4	Top	1440
Label4	Width	1815
Label4	Name	lblRELine
Label5	Caption	Attachment:
Label5	Height	255
Label5	Left	120
Label5	Top	120
Label5	Width	6600
Label5	Name	lblAttachment

Table 25.4 *The newly named* **Label** *controls' properties. (continued from previous page)*

ADDING THE TEXTBOX CONTROLS TO THE FRMSENDFAX FORM

As you learned earlier in this chapter, the *frmSendFax* form includes fields into which the user can enter the information for the fax the user wants to send. To add the *TextBox* controls to the *frmSendFax* form, perform the following steps:

1. If Visual Basic is not displaying the *frmSendFax* form within an object window, double-click your mouse on the form's listing within the Project Explorer. Visual Basic will open the form.

2. Within Visual Basic, select the View menu Toolbox option. Visual Basic will open the Toolbox.

3. Within the Toolbox, double-click your mouse on the TextBox icon. Visual Basic will draw a *TextBox* control, *Text1*, within the *frmSendFax* form.

4. Repeat Step 3 three times. Visual Basic will draw three additional *TextBox* controls on the *frmSendFax* form.

5. Within the *frmSendFax* form, click your mouse on a *TextBox* control to highlight it. Visual Basic will draw a small frame around the control.

6. Select the View menu Properties Window option. Visual Basic will open the Properties Window listing the highlighted control's properties.

7. Within the Properties Window, change the highlighted *TextBox* control's properties to the values Table 25.5 lists.

8. Within the Properties Window, change each remaining *TextBox* control's properties to the values Table 25.5 lists.

Object	Property	Set As
Text1	Height	285
Text1	Left	2040
Text1	TabIndex	0
Text1	Text	[blank]
Text1	Top	120
Text1	Width	4935

Table 25.5 *The newly named* **TextBox** *controls' properties. (continued on following page)*

Object	Property	Set As
Text1	Name	txtAddressee
Text2	Height	285
Text2	Left	2040
Text2	TabIndex	1
Text2	Text	[blank]
Text2	Top	600
Text2	Width	4935
Text2	Name	txtFaxNumber
Text3	Height	285
Text3	Left	2040
Text3	TabIndex	2
Text3	Text	[blank]
Text3	Top	1080
Text3	Width	4935
Text3	Name	txtRELine
Text4	Height	285
Text4	Left	2040
Text4	TabIndex	4
Text4	Text	[blank]
Text4	Top	1080
Text4	Width	4935
Text4	Name	txtAttachment

Table 25.5 *The newly named* **TextBox** *controls' properties. (continued from previous page)*

When you finish designing the *frmSendFax* form, it will look similar to Figure 25.3.

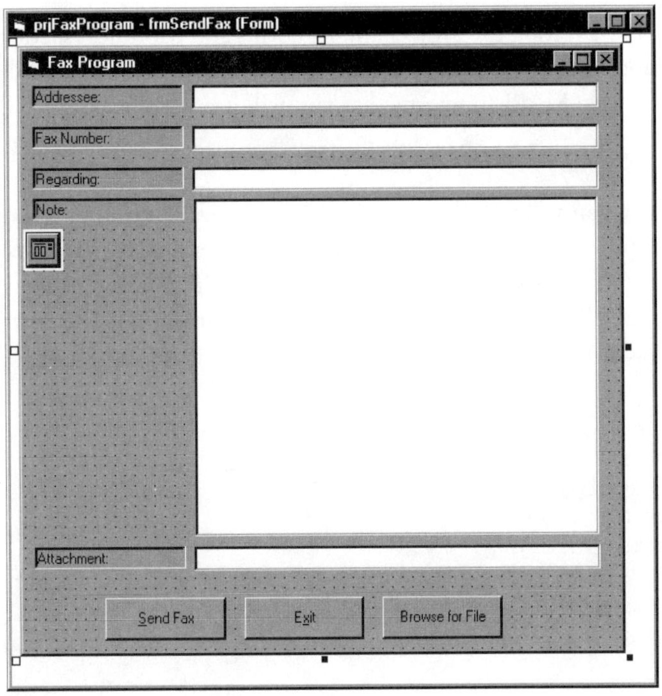

Figure 25.3 *The* **frmSendFax** *form after you complete its design.*

Understanding the Simple MAPI

The Messaging Application Program Interface (MAPI) is a set of functions that developers can use to create mail-enabled applications. The MAPI includes a subset of 12 functions called the *Simple MAPI*, which lets developers send, address, and receive messages from within Windows-based applications. With the Simple MAPI functions, you can easily add messaging power to any Visual Basic application. The Simple MAPI supports the standard interface for simple integration of Windows-based applications with mail-enabling providers. Table 25.6 details the Simple MAPI functions.

Function	Description
MAPIAddress	Addresses a mail message.
MAPIDeleteMail	Deletes a mail message.
MAPIDetails	Displays a Recipient Details dialog box.
MAPIFindNext	Returns the ID of the next (or first) specified type's mail message.
MAPIFreeBuffer	Frees memory the messaging system allocates.
MAPILogoff	Ends a session with the messaging system.
MAPILogon	Begins a session with the messaging system.
MAPIReadMail	Reads a mail message.
MAPIResolveName	Displays the Resolve Name dialog box to resolve an ambiguous or unknown recipient name.
MAPISaveMail	Saves a mail message.
MAPISendDocuments	Sends a standard mail message with documents embedded.
MAPISendMail	Sends a mail message with or without documents.

Table 25.6 *The Simple MAPI functions.*

Writing the Code for the prjFaxProgram Project

As you learned in this chapter's "Creating the Project and its Forms and Modules" section, the *prjFaxProgram* project uses three modules in addition to the *frmSendFax* form. Within the modules, you will write the program code to declare and implement the Simple MAPI functions that you will use within the *prjFaxProgram* project.

Writing the Code for the mdlMAPIDeclares Module

As the previous section details, you will write code within three separate modules to perform the MAPI processing the *prjFaxProgram* project requires. The first module, *mdlAPIDeclares*, includes the declarations for the Messaging Application Programming Interface (MAPI) the program will use. The declarations include three custom types, twelve functions, and many MAPI constants. The following code implements the custom type definitions:

```
Type MAPIMessage
   Reserved As Long
   Subject As String
   NoteText As String
   MessageType As String
   DateReceived As String
   ConversationID As String
   Flags As Long
   RecipCount As Long
   FileCount As Long
End Type
Type MAPIRecip
   Reserved As Long
```

```
    RecipClass As Long
    Name As String
    Address As String
    EIDSize As Long
    EntryID As String
End Type
Type MAPIFile
    Reserved As Long
    Flags As Long
    Position As Long
    PathName As String
    FileName As String
    FileType As Long
End Type
```

The *MAPIMessage* structure will hold all the vital information about a message packet. When you write programs that use the MAPI, you will use the *MAPIMessage* structure to pass message data from your programs to the *MAPI32.DLL* (the Dynamic-Link Library that implements the MAPI functions) and back. Table 25.7 explains the *MAPIMessage* type's members.

Member	Type	Description
Reserved	*Long*	An element Microsoft reserves for future use. You must pass 0 within this element.
Subject	*String*	The subject text. The *Subject* member's contents cannot be longer than 256 characters. If you pass an empty string, the message will not contain subject text.
NoteText	*String*	A string that contains the message text. This string can be up to about 64K in length.
MessageType	*String*	A string that indicates the message type when you use MAPI to access different mail providers.
DateReceived	*String*	A string that indicates the date and time the recipient receives the message. The string's format is YYYY/MM/DD HH:MM, for year, month, day, hour, and minute. The string reflects the time on a 24-hour clock.
ConversationID	*String*	A string that indicates the conversation thread, if any, to which the message belongs.
Flags	*Long*	A long integer value that you compose from one or more flag values. You can use the following flags within this member, which you will define later in this section: *MAPI_RECEIPT_REQUESTED*, *MAPI_SENT*, and *MAPI_UNREAD*.
RecipCount	*Long*	A value indicating to how many additional recipients the user addresses the message. If *RecipCount* is 0, the message has only one recipient.
FileCount	*Long*	A count of the number of file attachment descriptors the message includes. If *FileCount* is 0, the message has no files attached to it.

*Table 25.7 The **MAPIMessage** type's members.*

As Table 25.7 indicates, a given *MAPIMessage* can have one or more recipients. You will track message recipient information within a variable or array of type *MAPIRecip*. Table 25.8 describes the *MAPIRecip* type's members.

Member	Type	Description
Reserved	Long	A member Microsoft reserves for future use. You must pass a 0 value within this member.
RecipClass	Long	This member classifies a message's recipient. Depending on your Message Store Provider, you may be able to sort outbound messages by recipient class.
Name	String	The recipient's name, which the message will display in the message's Name area.
Address	String	Provider-specific message delivery data. The Provider will use the information within this member to address and deliver messages that it does not have in its address list.
EIDSize	Long	The *EntryID* member's size in bytes.
EntryID	String	A string that Mail Providers use to efficiently specify the recipient (generally, Mail Providers reduce the string to number sequences). Unlike the *Address* member, the *EntryID* member is unprintable.

784

Table 25.8 The **MAPIRecip** type's members.

As Table 25.7 indicates, in addition to multiple recipients, a given *MAPIMessage* object can include one or more file attachments. You will track file attachment information within a variable or array of type *MAPIFile*. Table 25.9 describes the *MAPIFile* type's members.

Member	Type	Description
Reserved	Long	A member Microsoft reserves for future use. You must pass a 0 value within this member.
Flags	Long	A long integer value that you will compose from one or more flag values. You can use the following flags within this member, which you will define later in this section: *MAPI_OLE* and *MAPI_OLE_STATIC*. If the file is an OLE object, you should set the *MAPI_OLE* flag; if the file is a static (linked) OLE object (rather than an embedded OLE object), you should also set the *MAPI_OLE_STATIC* flag.
Position	Long	Describes where the attachment will appear in the message body. Attachments replace the character at the *Position* point in the string the *MAPIMessage* object's *NoteText* member contains. You may not place two attachments within the same position, nor may you place attachments beyond the message's end.
PathName	String	The attached file's full pathname.
FileName	String	The filename for the file.
FileType	Long	This member indicates to the recipient the attached file's type. The Mail Provider sets this element and your programs cannot modify it.

Table 25.9 The **MAPIFile** type's members.

After you declare the custom types that you must use when you make MAPI function calls, you will declare the MAPI functions that comprise the Simple MAPI. Although the *prjFaxProgram* project does not use all the functions, it is worthwhile to declare them all within the *mdlMAPIDeclares* module so that you can easily reuse the functions in other projects you create. The following code implements the declarations that you will use within the *prjFaxProgram* project:

```
Declare Function MAPILogoff Lib "MAPI32.DLL" (ByVal Session As Long, _
    ByVal UIParam As Long, ByVal Flags As Long, _
    ByVal Reserved As Long) As Long
Declare Function MAPILogon Lib "MAPI32.DLL" (ByVal UIParam As Long, _
    ByVal User As String, ByVal Password As String, ByVal Flags As Long, _
    ByVal Reserved As Long, Session As Long) As Long
Declare Function MAPISendMail Lib "MAPI32.DLL" Alias "BMAPISendMail" _
    (ByVal Session As Long, ByVal UIParam As Long, Message As MapiMessage, _
    Recipient() As MapiRecip, File() As MapiFile, ByVal Flags As Long, _
    ByVal Reserved As Long) As Long
```

Within the *prjFaxProgram* program, you will use only three of the Simple MAPI functions. Your programs must invoke the *MAPILogon* function to begin a session, and will similarly invoke the *MAPILogoff* function to end a session. To actually send the fax to the recipient, the program will use the *MAPISendMail* function.

Note: *You can find the other declarations within the* **mdlMAPIDeclares.bas** *module file in the* **x:\vbpl\Chapter25** *directory, where* **x** *corresponds to the drive letter of the drive on which you installed the companion CD-ROM that accompanies this book.*

As you have learned, in addition to the custom types the MAPI function uses, you will also use several constant declarations when creating MAPI objects (such as *MAPIMessage* objects) or when calling MAPI functions. The following code implements the constant declarations for the *mdlMAPIDeclares* module:

```
Global Const SUCCESS_SUCCESS = 0              ' Function success
Global Const MAPI_USER_ABORT = 1             ' User-aborted transmission

' Error messages
Global Const MAPI_E_FAILURE = 2
Global Const MAPI_E_LOGIN_FAILURE = 3
Global Const MAPI_E_DISK_FULL = 4
Global Const MAPI_E_INSUFFICIENT_MEMORY = 5
Global Const MAPI_E_BLK_TOO_SMALL = 6
Global Const MAPI_E_TOO_MANY_SESSIONS = 8
Global Const MAPI_E_TOO_MANY_FILES = 9
Global Const MAPI_E_TOO_MANY_RECIPIENTS = 10
Global Const MAPI_E_ATTACHMENT_NOT_FOUND = 11
Global Const MAPI_E_ATTACHMENT_OPEN_FAILURE = 12
Global Const MAPI_E_ATTACHMENT_WRITE_FAILURE = 13
Global Const MAPI_E_UNKNOWN_RECIPIENT = 14
Global Const MAPI_E_BAD_RECIPTYPE = 15
Global Const MAPI_E_NO_MESSAGES = 16
Global Const MAPI_E_INVALID_MESSAGE = 17
Global Const MAPI_E_TEXT_TOO_LARGE = 18
Global Const MAPI_E_INVALID_SESSION = 19
Global Const MAPI_E_TYPE_NOT_SUPPORTED = 20
Global Const MAPI_E_AMBIGUOUS_RECIPIENT = 21
Global Const MAPI_E_MESSAGE_IN_USE = 22
Global Const MAPI_E_NETWORK_FAILURE = 23
Global Const MAPI_E_INVALID_EDITFIELDS = 24
Global Const MAPI_E_INVALID_RECIPS = 25
Global Const MAPI_E_NOT_SUPPORTED = 26
Global Const MAPI_E_NO_LIBRARY = 999
Global Const MAPI_E_INVALID_PARAMETER = 998

' Recipient constants
Global Const MAPI_ORIG = 0                    ' Originator
Global Const MAPI_TO = 1                      ' Addressee
Global Const MAPI_CC = 2                      ' carbon copies
```

```
Global Const MAPI_BCC = 3                         ' blind carbon copies

' Message classifications
Global Const MAPI_UNREAD = 1
Global Const MAPI_RECEIPT_REQUESTED = 2
Global Const MAPI_SENT = 4

Global Const MAPI_LOGON_UI = &H1                  ' Flag declarations
Global Const MAPI_NEW_SESSION = &H2
Global Const MAPI_DIALOG = &H8
Global Const MAPI_UNREAD_ONLY = &H20
Global Const MAPI_ENVELOPE_ONLY = &H40
Global Const MAPI_PEEK = &H80
Global Const MAPI_GUARANTEE_FIFO = &H100
Global Const MAPI_BODY_AS_FILE = &H200
Global Const MAPI_AB_NOMODIFY = &H400
Global Const MAPI_SUPPRESS_ATTACH = &H800
Global Const MAPI_FORCE_DOWNLOAD = &H1000

Global Const MAPI_OLE = &H1                       ' MAPI File Flag declarations
Global Const MAPI_OLE_STATIC = &H2
```

WRITING THE CODE FOR THE mdlMAPIErr MODULE

As you might guess from the module's name, you will write the program code within the *mdlMAPIErr* module to display error information to the user. The only function within the module, *MAPIErr*, receives a numeric error value from a MAPI function and converts it to a displayable string value. The following code implements the *MAPIErr* function:

```
Public Function MAPIErr(lError) As String
  Dim cRtn As String

  Select Case lError
    Case MAPI_USER_ABORT                          ' 1
      cRtn = "MAPI User Cancel"
    Case MAPI_E_FAILURE                           ' 2
      cRtn = "MAPI Failure"
    Case MAPI_E_LOGIN_FAILURE                     ' 3
      cRtn = "MAPI Login failure"
    Case MAPI_E_DISK_FULL                         ' 4
      cRtn = "MAPI Disk full"
    Case MAPI_E_INSUFFICIENT_MEMORY               ' 5
      cRtn = "MAPI Insufficient memory"
    Case MAPI_E_BLK_TOO_SMALL                     ' 6
      cRtn = "MAPI Block too small"
    Case MAPI_E_TOO_MANY_SESSIONS                 ' 8
      cRtn = "MAPI Too many sessions"
    Case MAPI_E_TOO_MANY_FILES                    ' 9
      cRtn = "MAPI too many files"
    Case MAPI_E_TOO_MANY_RECIPIENTS               ' 10
      cRtn = "MAPI Too many attachments"
    Case MAPI_E_ATTACHMENT_NOT_FOUND              ' 11
      cRtn = "MAPI Attachment not found"
    Case MAPI_E_ATTACHMENT_OPEN_FAILURE           ' 12
      cRtn = "MAPI Attachment open failure"
    Case MAPI_E_ATTACHMENT_WRITE_FAILURE          ' 13
      cRtn = "MAPI Attachment Write Failure"
    Case MAPI_E_UNKNOWN_RECIPIENT                 ' 14
      cRtn = "MAPI Unknown recipient"
    Case MAPI_E_BAD_RECIPTYPE                     ' 15
      cRtn = "MAPI Bad recipient type"
    Case MAPI_E_NO_MESSAGES                       ' 16
      cRtn = "MAPI No messages"
```

```
        Case MAPI_E_INVALID_MESSAGE              ' 17
          cRtn = "MAPI Invalid message"
        Case MAPI_E_TEXT_TOO_LARGE               ' 18
          cRtn = "MAPI Text too large"
        Case MAPI_E_INVALID_SESSION              ' 19
          cRtn = "MAPI Invalid session"
        Case MAPI_E_TYPE_NOT_SUPPORTED           ' 20
          cRtn = "MAPI Type not supported"
        Case MAPI_E_AMBIGUOUS_RECIPIENT          ' 21
          cRtn = "MAPI Ambiguous recipient"
        Case MAPI_E_MESSAGE_IN_USE               ' 22
          cRtn = "MAPI Message in use"
        Case MAPI_E_NETWORK_FAILURE              ' 23
          cRtn = "MAPI Network failure"
        Case MAPI_E_INVALID_EDITFIELDS           ' 24
          cRtn = "MAPI Invalid edit fields"
        Case MAPI_E_INVALID_RECIPS               ' 25
          cRtn = "MAPI Invalid Recipients"
        Case MAPI_E_NOT_SUPPORTED                ' 26
          cRtn = "MAPI Not supported"
        Case MAPI_E_NO_LIBRARY                   '999
          cRtn = "MAPI No Library"
        Case MAPI_E_INVALID_PARAMETER            '998
          cRtn = "MAPI Invalid parameter"
      End Select
      MAPIErr = cRtn & " [" & CStr(lError) & "]"
    End Function
```

As you can see, the program code within the function checks the error code against the error constants that you defined within the *mdlMAPIDeclares* module. When the program code finds a match, it returns a text message that explains the error to the calling procedure, which will then display the error message for the user.

WRITING THE CODE FOR THE MDLFAXSUPPORT MODULE

As you have learned, you will declare the constants and functions for the program's MAPI to use, as well as the error trapping procedure for the MAPI error values, within two separate modules. The third module, the *mdlFaxSupport* module, declares variables and includes three procedures: one procedure to start a session, one procedure to stop a session, and one procedure to perform the transmission. The following code implements the variable declarations for the *mdlFaxSupport* module:

```
Public lReturn As Long                      ' return flag
Public lSession As Long                     ' session handle
Public mpmMessage As MAPIMessage            ' message object
Public mprRecip As MAPIRecip                ' recipient object
Public mprRecips() As MAPIRecip             ' recipient collection
Public mpfFile As MAPIFile                  ' attachment object
Public mpfFiles() As MAPIFile               ' attachment collection

Public Const FaxProvider = "Microsoft Fax"
```

As you can see, the program code mostly declares variables of the custom types you defined within the *mdlMAPIDeclares* module. The program code also defines the *lReturn* variable, which the program uses to check a MAPI function call's success or failure. The *lSession* variable contains the session handle that the *MAPILogon* function returns after it successfully starts a new session. As you learned earlier in this chapter, you must connect to a provider and begin a session before you can use messaging services. The *mpmMessage* variable holds information on the message the program is to send. The *mprRecip* and *mprRecips()* variables will hold recipient information, as Table 25.8 (which explains the *MAPIRecip* type) details. The *mpfFile* and *mpfFiles()* variables will hold attachment file information, as Table 25.9 (which explains the *MAPIFile* type) details. In addition, the program code declares the *FaxProvider* constant. When you write programs for distribution, your programs should include MAPI functions beyond those the Simple MAPI uses to enumerate the avaialable providers, detect which providers are compatible with the program's desired messaging service, and select from available providers. The *prjFaxProgram*, for simplicity's sake, uses a string constant to indicate the provider.

WRITING THE CODE FOR THE *SMAPIStart* AND *SMAPIEnd* PROCEDURES

As you have learned, you should always open a MAPI session before you try to invoke any other MAPI functions. To open a MAPI session, your programs will invoke the *MAPILogon* function. The *prjFaxProgram* project "wraps" the function call within the *SMAPIStart* procedure, which verifies that the function successfully created the new session. The following code implements the *SMAPIStart* procedure:

```
Public Sub SMAPIStart(lhWnd As Long, cLogID As String)
  lReturn = MAPILogon(lhWnd, cLogID, "", _
      MAPI_LOGON_UI And MAPI_NEW_SESSION, 0, lSession)
  If lReturn <> SUCCESS_SUCCESS Then
    MsgBox MAPIErr(lReturn)
    End
  End If
End Sub
```

The *SMAPIStart* procedure accepts a window handle (which all Simple MAPI functions require) and a log-in identifier. If the *SMAPIStart* procedure receives a *NULL* string as the log-in identifier, the function will display a Log-In dialog box. If the procedure successfully logs the client into the messaging services, the program code sets the *lSession* variable to the new session's handle. If the procedure does not successfully log the client into the messaging services, the program code will display the error message that caused the log-in failure and exit the program. When using MAPI commands to send e-mail messages, for instance, it is important that your programs ensure that the user logs into the correct account so that the provider properly signs messages.

After you create a MAPI session, it is important to end the session when you finish transmitting messages. The *prjFaxProgram* uses the *SMAPIEnd* procedure to log out from a session. The following code implements the *SMAPIEnd* procedure:

```
Public Sub SMAPIEnd(lhWnd As Long)
  lReturn = MAPILogoff(lSession, lhWnd, 0, 0)
End Sub
```

As you can see, the program code within the procedure simply invokes the *MAPILogoff* function. The program code passes the *lSession* variable, together with the window handle, to the *MAPILogoff* function. The *MAPILogoff* function, in turn, will close the currently open MAPI session that the *lSession* variable references.

WRITING THE CODE FOR THE *SendSMAPIFax* PROCEDURE

As you learned earlier in this chapter, you will write three procedures within the *mdlFaxSupport* module. You have already written the first two procedures, which handle a MAPI session's creation and termination. The third procedure, *SendSMAPIFax,* transmits the file to the recipient. The following code implements the *SendSMAPIFax* procedure:

```
Public Sub SendSMAPIFax(lhWnd As Long, cFile As String, _
    cRecipient As String, cRecipientAddress As String, _
    cRELine As String, cNOTEText As String)
  Dim cName As String

  cName = Right(cFile, 9)
  mpmMessage.Subject = cRELine
  mpmMessage.NoteText = cNOTEText

  ReDim mpfFiles(0)
  mpfFiles(0).Position = Len(mpmMessage.NoteText) - 1
  mpfFiles(0).PathName = cFile
```

```
      mpfFiles(0).FileName = cName
      mpfFiles(0).FileType = 0

    ReDim mprRecips(0)
    With mprRecips(0)
      .Reserved = 0
      .RecipClass = 1
      .Name = cRecipient
      .Address = FaxProvider & "@" cRecipientAddress
      .EIDSize = 100
      .EntryID = ""
    End With
    mpmMessage.RecipCount = 1
    mpmMessage.FileCount = 1
    lReturn = MAPISendMail(lSession, lhWnd, mpmMessage, mprRecips, _
        mpfFiles, &H0, 0)
End Sub
```

The program code within the *SendSMAPIFax* procedure accepts as its incoming parameters the message recipient, the address to which to send the message, the text within the message, and the filename of the file to attach to the message. Within the procedure itself, the program code initializes the *mpmMessage* variable's members, which will contain the actual message. In addition to the *mpmMessage* variable, the program code initializes the *mpfFiles(0)* element, which will contain a reference to the attachment (if any) the user placed within the *Attachment* field on the form. Also, the program code initializes the *mprRecips(0)* element, which will contain the information about the recipient that the program will use to transmit the message itself. Note that the program code concatenates the *FaxProvider* provider constant and the "at" symbol (@) onto the address in front of the recipient's phone number. For example, a fax to 555-1212 would have the address "Microsoft Fax@5551212." The concatenation provides the MAPI with the information it requires to set the correct service and deliver the message.

The last line of code within the procedure calls the *MAPISendMail* procedure, which transmits the actual message. The program will use the available fax provider to transmit the message to the fax recipient.

UNDERSTANDING THE *MAPI* FUNCTION'S RELATIONSHIP TO *MAPI* SERVICE PROVIDERS

As you have learned, the Messaging Application Programming Interface (MAPI) serves as a layer between your programs and the actual Messaging Service Provider on the system. For example, when the *Microsoft Exchange Server* sends a message, it relies on its own internal Messaging Transport Provider to direct client requests to one or more Transport Service Providers. Windows Dynamic-Link Libraries (DLLs) serve as drivers for each Transport Service Provider. Windows DLLs also provide the interface between the Messaging API (which the *MAPI32.DLL* file defines) and the underlying messaging system or services. The MAPI defines three types of service providers:

- *Message Store Providers* supply message storage, organization, and retrieval facilities for a messaging system.

- *Address Book Providers* supply message addressing and distribution list facilities to the messaging client.

- *Messaging Transport Providers* move messages between messaging clients.

When a client application sends a message, the *MAPI32.DLL* file responds to the MAPI function call. The MAPI then routes the messages to the appropriate Message Store and Address Book Service Providers. If a user marks a particular message for sending, the message spooler (a *Microsoft Exchange*™ helper program that organizes outbound messages in delivery queues) checks the message's address to determine which Transport Provider it must use to send the message. Depending on the designated message recipient, the message spooler may call upon more than one Transport Provider.

The spooler performs other message-management functions. It directs inbound messages to a message store and handles messages that are undeliverable because no Transport Provider can carry them. The spooler also provides an important *store-and-forward* set of services. The spooler holds the message in a store if the required messaging service is currently unavailable. When the MAPI re-establishes connection to that messaging service, the spooler automatically forwards the message to its destination.

The *Microsoft Exchange* server offers more functionality than many other MAPI message stores. For instance, replicated storage services are part of the *Microsoft Exchange* server information store. The replicated storage model lets the *Microsoft Exchange* server store information within a distributed location (for example, in multiple directories on multiple hard drives on a network) without requiring users to know the actual drive or directory's location that contains the information. Figure 25.4 shows the relationship between programs, the MAPI, and the underlying Messaging Service Providers.

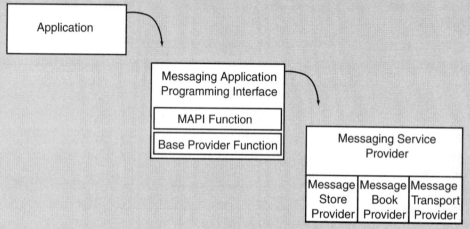

Figure 25.4 *The relationship between programs, the MAPI, and the underlying Messaging Service Providers.*

WRITING THE CODE FOR THE FRMSENDFAX FORM

As you learned in the previous section, the *SendSMAPIFax* procedure performs most of the actual fax processing within the *prjFaxProgram* program. However, the *frmSendFax* form does perform some processing of its own. The form implements drag-and-drop support for attachment files and the Attach File dialog box to help the user select the file to attach to the fax. The program code uses three variables to support the drag-and-drop process and to pass filename information to the *SendSMAPIFax* procedure. The following code implements the *frmSendFax* form's three variables:

```
Dim DropOK As Boolean
Dim SendFilePath As String, SendFileName As String
```

The *DropOK* variable will indicate whether or not a file is of a valid type for an attachment; the *SendFilePath* and *SendFileName* strings indicate the filename and fully qualified path of the file the program will send as an attachment.

WRITING THE CODE FOR THE FORM_LOAD EVENT

As you have learned in previous chapters, the first program code to execute each time the program loads a form is the program code within the form's *Form_Load* event. The following code implements the *Form_Load* event for the *frmSendFax* form:

```
Private Sub Form_Load()
  Dim cLogID As String

  cLogID = ""                           ' forces log-in dialog box
  SMAPIStart(Me.hWnd, cLogID)
End Sub
```

The program code within the *Form_Load* event calls the *SMAPIStart* procedure to create a new MAPI session. The program code passes in a *NULL* string within the *cLogID* variable. The *NULL* string instructs the MAPI provider to display a Log-In dialog box, but only if the provider requires a login. If the provider does not require a login, the program will log directly into the provider. The *Microsoft Fax* provider does not require the user to log in for the session to begin.

Writing the Code for the *cmdSendFax_Click* Event

As you learned in this chapter's "Using the *prjFaxProgram* Project" section, to send a fax, the user must click the mouse on the Send Fax button. When the user clicks the mouse on the Send Fax button, the program will invoke the button's *Click* event. The following code implements the *cmdSendFax_Click* event:

```
Private Sub cmdSendFax_Click()
  If CheckFaxValues Then
    SendSMAPIFax(Me.hWnd, txtAttachment.Text, _
        txtAddressee.Text, txtFaxNumber.Text, txtRELine.Text, _
        rtbNote.Text)
    MsgBox "Fax sent!"
  End If
End Sub
```

The *cmdSendFax_Click* event's program code first invokes the *CheckFaxValues* function, which checks the entries within the form. If the entries within the form are all valid, the program code calls the *SendSMAPIFax* procedure and passes the entries through to the function. If the entries within the form are not all valid, the procedure exits without trying to send the fax. After the *SendSMAPIFax* procedure exits, the program code displays a message box to alert the user that the program successfully sent the fax.

Writing the Code for the *CheckFaxValues* Function

As you have learned in previous chapters, it is important to test data the user enters to verify that the data is the correct type, format, and so on. Within the *prjSendFax* program, it is most important to ensure that the user entered a recipient name and a valid recipient address. The *CheckFaxValues* function checks the entries for validity. The following code implements the *CheckFaxValues* function:

```
Private Function CheckFaxValues() As Boolean
  Dim tmpString As String, i As Integer

  CheckFaxValues = False
  If Len(txtAddressee.Text) < 1 Then
    MsgBox("Must Enter Addressee Name!", vbOKOnly, "Fax Program")
    Exit Function
  End If
  If Len(txtFaxNumber.Text) < 1 Then
    MsgBox("Must Enter Fax Number!", vbOKOnly, "Fax Program")
    Exit Function
  End If
  If InStr(txtFaxNumber.Text, "(", vbTextCompare) Then
    MsgBox("Do not use parentheses in fax number!", vbOKOnly, "Fax Program")
    Exit Function
  End If
  For i = 1 To Len(txtFaxNumber.Text)
    If Asc(Mid(txtFaxNumber.Text, i, 1)) < 48 Or _
        Asc(Mid(txtFaxNumber.Text, i, 1)) > 57 Then
    Else
      tmpString = tmpString & Mid(txtFaxNumber.Text, i, 1)
    End If
  Next
```

```
      If Len(tmpString) <> 7 And Len(tmpString) <> 10 And _
          Len(tmpString) <> 11 Then
        MsgBox("Invalid fax number!", vbOKOnly, "Fax Program")
        Exit Function
      End If
      If Len(tmpString) = 10 Then _
        tmpString = "1" & tmpString
      txtAddressee.Text = tmpString
      CheckFaxValues = True
    End Function
```

As you can see, the *CheckFaxValues* function consists of five *If-Then* statements. If the user's data does not successfully meet the requirements of all five statements, the *cmdSendFax_Click* event will not execute the call to the *SendSMAPIFax* procedure. The first *If-Then* statement within the function checks the length of the *txtAddressee* field to determine whether the user entered a name within the field. If the field is empty, the program code displays a warning to the user and exits the function. The second *If-Then* statement performs similar processing on the *txtFaxNumber* field.

Next, the third *If-Then* statement checks to ensure the user did not enter parentheses in the fax number. If the user did enter parentheses, the program code displays a warning to the user and exits the function. After the program code verifies that the user did not use parentheses in the fax number, the program code uses a *For-Next* loop to step through each character the user entered as the fax number and removes any non-numeric characters from the number. After the *For-Next* loop finishes, the *tmpString* variable will contain the fax number without dashes, commas, and so on.

After the loop exits, the fourth *If-Then* statement checks the length of the *tmpString* variable. If the string's length is not 7 digits (local), 10 digits (long distance without the 1 prefix), or 11 digits (long distance with the 1 prefix), the program code displays a warning to the user and exits the function.

After verifying that the fax number is valid, the program code checks to see if it is a 10-digit number. If the number is 10 digits, the program code adds a 1 to the number's beginning.

Note: *The program code within the **prjFaxProgram** does not support international faxing or faxing within telephone-numbering systems different from the United States numbering system.*

WRITING THE CODE FOR THE CMDBROWSE_CLICK EVENT

As you learned earlier in this chapter, the user can click the mouse on the Browse for Files button on the *frmSendFax* form to use a standard, Open File-style dialog box to add an attachment to a fax. The following code implements the *cmdBrowse_Click* event:

```
    Private Sub cmdBrowse_Click()
      With cdgAttachFile
        .DialogTitle = "Add Attachment"
        .InitDir = App.Path
        .CancelError = True
        .Flags = cdlOFNHideReadOnly
        .Filter = "Word Files (*.DOC)|*.DOC|Rich Text Files(*.RTF)| *.RTF"
      End With
      On Error Resume Next
      cdgAttachFile.ShowOpen
      If Err.Number <> 0 Then Exit Sub
      txtAttachment.Text = cdgAttachFile.FileName
    End Sub
```

As you can see, the program code initializes the *cdgAttachFile* common dialog box, sets the filter to Microsoft *Word* documents or Rich Text files, and displays the dialog box. If the user selects a valid file, the program code places the filename within the *txtAttachment TextBox* control.

WRITING THE CODE FOR THE TXTATTACHMENT_OLEDRAGOVER EVENT

As you have learned, users can drag files and drop them directly onto the *txtAttachment* control. In a later section, you will write the code to process files that users drop into the control. However, it is also important to respond to the user's action before the user drops the control. When the user drags the file over the *txtAttachment* control, the control will raise the *OLEDragOver* event. The following code implements the *txtAttachment_OLEDragOver* event:

```
Private Sub txtAttachment_OLEDragOver(Data As DataObject, Effect As Long, _
    Button As Integer, Shift As Integer, x As Single, Y As Single, _
    State As Integer)
  ParseFileDrop Data
End Sub
```

The program code within the event will call the *ParsePicDrop* procedure, which verifies that the file is a valid Microsoft *Word* document or Rich Text file. The next section explains the *ParseFileDrop* procedure's processing.

WRITING THE CODE FOR THE PARSEFILEDROP PROCEDURE

The *ParseFileDrop* procedure checks the item the user is currently dragging over the *txtAttachment* control and verifies that it is a valid Microsoft *Word* document or Rich Text file. The following code implements the *ParseFileDrop* procedure:

```
Private Sub ParseFileDrop(ThisItem As DataObject)
  Dim FileType As String

  On Error Resume Next      'trap for non-file drops
  FileType = ThisItem.files(1)
  If Err Then
    Err = 0
    Exit Sub
  End If
  On Error Resume Next
  If Len(FileType) >= 4 Then            'trap for no possible extention
    FileType = LCase$(Right$(FileType, 4))
    Select Case FileType      'limit to acceptible types
      Case ".doc", ".rtf"
        DropOK = True
      Case Else
        DropOK = False
    End Select
  Else
    DropOK = False
  End If
End Sub
```

The program code first checks the *DataObject* object's *Files(1)* property, which contains the file name of the object the user is dragging. If the *DataObject* is not a file, the program code will exit the procedure. If the *DataObject* is a file, the program code will check the file's extension to determine if the file is a valid file type that the *prjFaxProgram* project will transmit. If it is a valid file type, the program code sets the *DropOK* variable to *True*—otherwise, the program code sets the *DropOK* variable to *False*.

WRITING THE CODE FOR THE TXTATTACHMENT_OLEDRAGDROP EVENT

As this chapter's "Writing the Code for the *txtAttachment_OLEDragOver* Event" section details, to capture a user's drag-and-drop action, you must place program code within the *OLEDragDrop* event. As you have learned, in addition to opening files from within the Add Attachment dialog box, the user can also drag files from the Windows *Explorer* to the *frmSendFax* form's *txtAttachment* control. When the user drops a file on the *txtAttachment* control, the control will raise the *txtFile_OLEDragDrop* event. The following program code implements the *txtFile_OLEDragDrop* event:

```
Private Sub txtAttachment_OLEDragDrop(Data As DataObject, Effect As Long, _
    Button As Integer, Shift As Integer, x As Single, Y As Single)
  Dim FileName As String
  Dim c As Long

  If Not DropOK Then
    MsgBox("DOC and RTF Files Only, Please!", vbOKOnly, "Fax Program")
    Exit Sub
  End If
  On Error Resume Next 'if not a file
  FileName = Data.files(1)
  txtAttachment.Text = FileName
  If Err Then
    Err = 0
    txtAttachment.Text = ""
    Exit Sub
  End If
  On Error GoTo 0
  If InStr(FileName, "\") Then
    For c = Len(FileName) To 1 Step -1
      If Mid$(FileName, c, 1) = "\" Then
        SendFilePath = Left$(FileName, c - 1)
        SendFileName = Right$(FileName, Len(FileName) - c)
        Exit For
      End If
    Next
  Else
    SendFilePath = ""
    SendFileName = FileName
  End If
End Sub
```

The program code within the *txtAttachment_OLEDragDrop* event first checks to be sure the item the user dropped is a valid file. If it is not a valid file, the program code will exit the event and perform no processing. If the item the user dropped is a valid file, the program code will check to determine whether the filename contains a backslash ("\")—which indicates the user dropped a file in a different path from the current path. If the filename contains a backslash, the program code will parse the filename and place the path within the *SendFilePath* variable and the filename within the *SendFileName* variable. If the filename does not contain a backslash, the program code will set the *SendFilePath* variable to a *NULL* string and set the *SendFileName* variable equal to the dropped file's filename.

WRITING THE CODE TO EXIT THE PROGRAM

When the user finishes faxing from the program, the user can exit the program. To exit the program, the user must click the mouse on the Exit button. The following code implements the *cmdExit_Click* event:

```
Private Sub cmdExit_Click()
  Unload Me
End Sub
```

As you can see, the program code within the event simply unloads the form. When the form unloads, however, the program code within the *Form_Unload* event calls the *SMAPIEnd* procedure to close the MAPI session. The following code implements the *Form_Unload* event:

```
Private Sub Form_Unload(Cancel As Integer)
  SMAPIEnd(Me.hWnd)
End Sub
```

Enhancements You Can Make to the prjFaxProgram Project

The *prjFaxProgram* project is a simple program that helps you begin to use the Messaging API (MAPI). You can use the principles you have learned in this chapter to add fax support to other programs you create or to create a fax control for your Visual Basic programs.

In addition, you can use the other MAPI functions to add more power to the program. For example, you can have the program display an address book for the user or maintain a record of outgoing faxes. Finally, you can use the Windows Telephony Application Programming Interface (TAPI) to directly manage the phone line and accept incoming faxes in addition to the outgoing faxes you created within this project.

Putting It All Together

This chapter's project, *prjFaxProgram*, introduced you to how you can use Messaging API (MAPI) functions within your programs to add messaging and fax support to your programs. In this chapter you also reviewed how to use the *CommonDialog* box and implement OLE drag-and-drop support within your program. Before you continue with your own programming of the Messaging API, however, make sure you understand the following key concepts:

✓ Like the Cryptographic Application Programming Interface (CryptoAPI) and Speech Application Programming Interface (SAPI) you used in previous chapters, the Messaging Application Programming Interface (MAPI) is a layer between your programs and Messaging Providers that lets you write programs that perform faxing and other messaging activities without concern for the underlying Messaging Provider type.

✓ Microsoft (and the Messaging API) divides Messaging Providers into three basic provider types. Different MAPI functions will access different providers. The provider types include: *Message Store Providers*, which supply message storage, organization, and retrieval facilities for a messaging system; *Address Book Providers*, which supply message addressing and distribution list facilities to the messaging client; and *Messaging Transport Providers*, which move messages between messaging clients.

✓ Your Visual Basic programs can use the MAPI functions to send messages of many types, including Internet e-mail messages, local-system e-mail messages (such as Microsoft *Mail* messages), and fax messages. Your Visual Basic programs can also use the MAPI functions to maintain information about previously sent faxes, recipients, address books, and more.

✓ Before you can use MAPI to send faxes or other message types, you must use the *MAPILogon* API function to connect to a valid Message Store Provider. When you finish working with the MAPI, you must use the *MAPILogoff* API function to close the MAPI connection.

✓ To send faxes, your programs will use the *MAPISendMail* function to access a valid Messaging Transport Provider.

✓ Microsoft's *Simple MAPI* provides a subset of twelve of the MAPI functions programmers most commonly use. Within the *prjFaxProgram* project, you used Simple MAPI to send a fax transmission.

Index

Jamsa Press Runaway Bestsellers

Rescued by C++, Third Edition

As the follow-on to the best-selling *Rescued by C++, Second Edition*, this book continues the Jamsa Press standard of step-by-step instructions and easy-to-understand examples.

The third edition also includes a CD-ROM featuring a Borland *Turbo C++ Lite*™ compiler, along with all the book's source code to help you perform easy cut-and-paste operations.

Like its previous editions, *Rescued by C++, Third Edition* assumes the reader has no prior programming experience.

$29.95 USA   ISBN: 1-884133-59-2
Available: Now!   320 pages • 8 1/2 x 10 3/8" • CD-ROM

By Kris Jamsa, Ph.D.

[T]his low cost primer...will help remove the mystique of computer software by letting a user produce a wide variety of small programs.

—James Coates, *Chicago Tribune*

ActiveX Programmer's Library

ActiveX is a new technology that lets programmers (and advanced Webmasters who understand *JavaScript*™ or *VBScript*™) bring objects to the Web. *ActiveX Programmer's Library* teaches users how to fully master ActiveX through programming examples in Visual Basic, Visual C++, *JavaScript*, *VBScript*, and Visual J++. Easy-to-understand source code lets users quickly master ActiveX while creating state-of-the-art Web sites along the way.

The book's companion CD-ROM contains source code for each object the book presents. Programmers can cut-and-paste the book's examples to their own Web sites in minutes!

$49.95 USA   ISBN: 1-884133-52-5
Available: Now!   496 pages • 8 1/2 x 10 3/8" • CD-ROM

By Suleiman "Sam" Lalani and Ramesh Chandak

There's no better way to learn software on your own than to have Kris Jamsa at your side.
—Al Harrison, Member of Advisory Board, *PC World*

Jamsa's C/C++ Programmer's Bible

Jamsa's C/C++ Programmer's Bible, a follow-on to *Jamsa's 1001 C/C++ Tips*, is the most complete reference available about the C/C++ programming language. *Jamsa's C/C++ Programmer's Bible* contains 1,500 Tips that start with basic C programming and end with the Windows Graphics Device Interface (GDI) and Windows I/O.

The book's companion CD-ROM contains the source code for over eight hundred ready-to-run programs, and a Borland *Turbo C++ Lite*™ compiler.

$49.95 USA   ISBN: 1-884133-25-8
Available: Now!   944 pages • 8 1/2 x 10 3/8" • CD-ROM

By Kris Jamsa, Ph.D. and Lars Klander

Hacker Proof is an outstanding and enlightening book; it should be required reading for every administrator. I highly recommend it!

—Elizabeth Zinkann, *SYS Admin Magazine*

Hacker Proof:
The Ultimate Guide to Network Security

Hacker Proof: The Ultimate Guide to Network Security provides a detailed examination of the security concepts network administrators, programmers, and Webmasters must know. Nonprogrammers will readily understand security threats and the steps they must perform to prevent them. Programmers will be thrilled with the detailed programming examples that demonstrate how hackers penetrate the most secure computer systems.

The book's companion CD-ROM includes software users can run to test their system security. Readers will find that *Hacker Proof*:

- Examines the common threats to any system connected to the Internet

- Provides software utilities users can run to test system vulnerability to security threats

- Explains how common tools such as CGI and HTTP leave Internet-connected systems unsecure

- Details how SSL and S-HTTP provide secure transmissions

- Provides network administrators with several tools they can use today, such as audit trails, firewalls, and encryption

$54.95 USA   ISBN: 1-884133-55-X
Available: Now!   688 pages • 7 3/8 x 9 1/4" • CD-ROM

By Lars Klander

Now Jamsa Press is making [Visual Basic] easier to use with the publication of 1001 Visual Basic Programmer's Tips.

—David Hoye, *The Arizona Republic*

1001 Visual Basic Programmer's Tips

According to Microsoft, over 3 million professional Visual Basic programmers use Visual Basic every day. *1001 Visual Basic Programmer's Tips* takes the programmer from "square one" with Visual Basic. The book teaches the "ins and outs" of the Visual Basic toolset and focuses on code, code, and more code.

Additionally, the CD-ROM contains all the supplemental files the user needs, including GIF files for image manipulation, audio files for ActiveX controls that play sound, and HTML files that provide the programs' Web interface.

$54.95 USA   ISBN: 1-884133-56-8
Available: Now!   708 pages • 8 1/2 x 10 3/8" • CD-ROM

*By Kris Jamsa, Ph.D.
and Lars Klander*

Jamsa Press . . . Providing Solutions

What's on the *Visual Basic Programmer's Library* Companion CD-ROM

The companion CD-ROM that accompanies this book includes the Visual Basic project files, forms, modules, class modules, user documents, and user controls for every program in this book. The CD-ROM also includes graphics files, text files, and all the other resource files you must have to execute the programs.

ABOUT THE SETUP.EXE PROGRAMS ON THE CD-ROM

The companion CD-ROM includes the Jamsa Press *setup.exe* program within the CD-ROM's root directory. The *setup.exe* program copies all the source files and the compiled program files on the CD-ROM to a directory you specify on your hard drive. The Jamsa Press *setup.exe* program will run automatically when you insert the CD-ROM into the CD-ROM drive.

The CD-ROM divides the programs into 25 directories, one for each chapter within the book. Each directory contains the source code and the compiled executable file within the directory. Each directory also contains a sub-directory named *Setup*, which contains the setup program necessary to install the executable to your computer. Because many of the programs within this book use custom Dynamic-Link Libraries, ActiveX controls, ActiveX documents, and ActiveX server programs, you must, in general, run each program's setup program individually to install the necessary files to your Windows system directory and to register the files within the Windows Registry. Because the CD-ROM supports so many independent installations, you must have 75 Mb of disk space free on the hard drive to which you install the book's progams. However, after you install the programs, you can easily delete the setup files, and free up most of the space the initial installation uses.

In addition to the detailed program code explanations this book contains, the source code on the CD-ROM contains extensive comments to "walk you through" each program's processing.

Because some programs in this book may require that you install additional software onto your system (such as Microsoft *Internet Explorer*®), you should read the "Using the Project" section at the beginning of each chapter before you try to run the program the chapter details.

JAMSA
P·R·E·S·S
...a computer user's best friend ®